GREAT HISTORIANS OF THE MODERN AGE

Great Historians of the Modern Age

AN INTERNATIONAL DICTIONARY

LUCIAN BOIA, Editor-in-Chief

Ellen Nore, Keith Hitchins,
and Georg G. Iggers, Associate Editors

Sponsored by the Commission on the History of Historiography of
the International Committee on the Historical Sciences

GREENWOOD PRESS
New York • Westport, Connecticut • London

Library of Congress Cataloging-in-Publication Data

Great historians of the modern age : an international dictionary /
   Lucian Boia, editor-in-chief : Ellen Nore, Keith Hitchins, and Georg
   G. Iggers, associate editors.
      p.   cm.
      "Sponsored by the Commission on the History of Historiography of
   the International Committee on the Historical Sciences."
      ISBN 0–313–27328–6 (lib. bdg. : alk. paper)
      1. Historians—Biography—Dictionaries.   I. Boia, Lucian.
   II. International Committee of Historical Sciences.   Commission of
   the History of Historiography.
   D14.G75   1991
   907'.2022—dc20   89–26009

British Library Cataloguing in Publication Data is available.

Library of Congress Catalog Card Number: 89–26009
ISBN: 0–313–27328–6

First published in 1991

Greenwood Press, 88 Post Road West, Westport, CT 06881
An imprint of Greenwood Publishing Group, Inc.

Printed in the United States of America

The paper used in this book complies with the
Permanent Paper Standard issued by the National
Information Standards Organization (Z39.48-1984).

10 9 8 7 6 5 4 3 2 1

Copyright Acknowledgment

Grateful acknowledgment is given for permission to use a revised version of A. William Salomone's
"Frederico Chabod: Portrait of a Master Historian" in *Historians of Modern Europe,* ed. Hans A.
Schmitt. © 1971 Louisiana State University Press, Baton Rouge.

Every reasonable effort has been made to trace the owners of copyright materials in this book, but
in some instances this has proven impossible. The editors and publisher will be glad to receive
information leading to more complete acknowledgments in subsequent printings of the book and in
the meantime extend their apologies for any omissions.

CONTENTS

PREFACE

This volume of *Great Historians*, devoted to historians of the nineteenth and twentieth centuries, is the fruit of ample international collaboration facilitated by the International Commission on the History of Historiography.

In this volume, we have tried to harmonize the criterion of universal value with national criteria, while at the same time illustrating certain particular domains of history. We are fully aware of the gaps left: we could not cover all national cultures, and the selection imposed by the limitations of space forced us to omit some historians who would have undoubtedly deserved entries. Besides, we observed as a rule the selection suggested by the consultants in the respective countries themselves and, out of the wish to preserve unaltered the specifics of every historiographic school, we made as few modifications as possible in the texts of the entries. We hope this explains some of the discrepancies in the volume.

Entries are arranged by countries or geographical areas and then alphabetized. The editors have provided both an index of historians and a general subject index. Cross-references are indicated by "q.v." following the name of an individual mentioned within the text who is the subject of a separate entry. English translations of books and articles in non-Western languages appear in parentheses.

In several exceptional cases we included in a certain historiography historians of a different origin, who had, however, dedicated themselves to the study of the respective history and culture (as is the case of Leo Frobenius who is included in African instead of German historiography). As a general rule, living historians are not given entries in the dictionary and historians who have died since 1987 are not represented.

We hope this work, the first of its kind, for all imperfections inherent to a pioneering work, will help provide better knowledge of world historiography with all its richness and variety.

NOTES

1. Charles-Olivier Carbonell, *Histoire et Historiens. Une mutation idéologique des historiens francais, 1865–1885* (Toulouse, 1976), pp. 71–90; Charles-Oliver Carbonell, *L'Historiographie* (Paris, 1981), p. 81.

2. For a more detailed discussion of the issue, see Lucian Boia, "Le XIXe siècle—le siècle de l'histoire?" *Analele Universitătii Bucuresti* (Istorie), (1983): 3–17.

3. Carbonell, *L'Historiographie*, p. 94.

4. John Higham, *History: Professional Scholarship in America* (New York, 1973), p. 4. Higham's book is essential for an analysis of the historian's profession at the end of the nineteenth century and in the twentieth century.

5. For "historicism," which has deep roots in German philosophy and historiography, see especially Georg G. Iggers, *The German Conception of History: The National Tradition of Historical Thought from Herder to the Present* (Middletown, Conn.: Wesleyan University Press, 1968) (new edition, 1983).

6. Of the numerous works on the current issues and tendencies of historiography, we cite only a few, more general in character: Geoffrey Barraclough, *Tendances actuelles de l'histoire* (Paris, 1980); André Burguière, ed., *Dictionnaire des sciences historiques* (Paris, 1986); Georg G. Iggers, *New Directions in European Historiography* (Middletown, Conn.: Wesleyan University Press, 1975) (new edition, 1984); Georg G. Iggers and Harold T. Parker, ed. *International Handbook of Historical Studies. Contemporary Research and Theory* (Westport, Conn.: Greenwood Press, 1979); Jacques Le Goff, ed., *La Nouvelle Histoire* (Paris, 1978).

INTRODUCTION

The nineteenth century has been called the "century of history." Does the name fit? In terms of quantity of books published, this title appears inappropriate. In France and Germany, history's share of the books produced probably stood at 15 to 20 percent in the seventeenth and eighteenth centuries but dropped to less than 10 percent in the nineteenth century.[1] Yet, these facts mirror not the absolute decrease of history in the modern era but the multiplication of other disciplines. On the other hand, in several respects, the label is accurate.[2] The idea of progress, undoubtedly a profoundly historical idea, asserted itself in the nineteenth century. History then assumed its proper role—already heralded in the eighteenth century—of explaining the progress of human civilization, of interpreting the present (and implicitly the future) through the past. Philosophy and sciences turned to a historical approach. Georg Wilhelm Friedrich Hegel (q.v.), Auguste Comte (q.v.), and Karl Marx (q.v.) articulated their philosophic systems within a historical context, while Charles Darwin's *Origin of Species* (1859) gave a definitive historical sense to the natural sciences and to life in general. In a comprehensive and profound way, the historical spirit imbued the whole thinking of that century.

The nineteenth century was equally a "century of nationalities," and the relationship between nationalism and history was by no means accidental. From the era of the French Revolution and the Napoleonic wars to the end of World War I (and continuing into the contemporary age) national movements pursued the irresistible goal of liberating peoples and of integrating them into independent national states. In search of origins and legitimacy, nation-builders turned first of all to history, sometimes distorting the past and shaping it to fit the needs of the moment. Never had history had a more prominent role, never had it had such a powerful impact on the collective mind and on politicians.

In the specialists' world, this massive dissemination of history and the historical spirit was paralleled by a process of professionalization, an effort to address the past with more scientific rigor than before by employing an increasingly precise method. Inaugurated in German universities in the eighteenth century, the professionalization of history progressed rapidly until, by 1900, it had encompassed all of Europe and America. In 1800, there were a dozen history chairs in German universities, but none in France. By 1900, there were 175 in Germany and 71 in France,[3] while the number of university professors of history in the United States rose in a single decade, 1884–1894, from 20 to 100.[4]

History also expanded both in space and in time during the nineteenth century. Jean-François Champollion (q.v.) and Heinrich Schliemann (q.v.), for example, brought to light lesser known or even extinct civilizations. Prehistory, "invented" by Jacques Boucher de Crèvecoeur de Perthes (q.v.), expanded humankind's remote past from several thousand years, as maintained by western tradition based on the Bible, to tens and hundreds of thousands of years.

The nineteenth century does not make up an entirety, however. Its first half was characterized by romantic sensibility, in the context of privileged relations between history and literature. It was the golden age of the novel and drama (Walter Scott, Victor Hugo, Alexandre Dumas). The novels of Walter Scott (1771–1832) had a tangible influence on historiography, just like the oeuvre of another great writer, the French René de Chateaubriand (q.v.). Historians vied with the writers in an attempt to "revive" the past in as dramatic and colorful a style as possible, most of them giving up the cold rationalist analysis of the eighteenth century. The Middle Ages, branded as obscurantist by rationalists, became the favorite epoch. The national spirit, the specifics of each and every culture, were then put above rationalist universalism. The French Auguste Thierry (q.v.) and Jules Michelet (q.v.), the English Thomas Babington Macaulay (q.v.) and Thomas Carlyle (q.v.) were among the most typical representatives of historiographic romanticism.

Yet writers such as François Guizot (q.v.) and Alexis de Tocqueville (q.v.) avoided the romantic outlook, thereby furthering the philosophic trend of the eighteenth century and prefiguring (especially Tocqueville) characteristically modern problems and approaches. In Germany, the home of Romanticism, historians attempted to combine this formula with a careful, critical use of written documents. Leopold von Ranke (q.v.) emerged as the most highly regarded and influential historian of the nineteenth century. For him and his disciples, history was a profession with rigorous rules and a mission, to reconstitute the past only on the basis of a minute critical analysis of the written evidence. Whereas the Romantic school favored history-as-literature, in the second half of the nineteenth century, other historians came to see their discipline as closer to a science. Professionalization, the great prestige of Ranke's method, and a scientific and cultural context increasingly dominated by natural and "exact" sciences and notions derived from evolutionary theory were responsible for the shift from novelistic to "scientific" history, which now often employed biological metaphors.

But what kind of science was history? For Auguste Comte, the founder of positivism, history became retrospective sociology, a reconstruction of the past governed by precise laws. The positivist tendency which equated history with the natural sciences as a science of society, came to full bloom in the work of the Englishman Henry Thomas Buckle (q.v.). For all its simplifications and exaggerations, positivism did suggest a possible "structuralist" approach instead of the traditional listing of facts. Yet, because it borrowed concepts and methods alien to the realm of history, most historians rejected positivism. Although some historians were influenced to some extent by the positivist philosophy, no positivist school as such could emerge in historiography. (The term *positivist* was then used and is still used in relation to a "critical" and "event-centered" historiography, which has nothing to do with the positivist philosophy and is in fact its opposite.)

Karl Marx (q.v.) and Friedrich Engels (q.v.) articulated a variant of "scientific" history—historical materialism—which influenced much of the history written after 1900. Emphasizing the decisive role of economic factors, Marxists presented the "class struggle" as the motive force of history.

Yet, most historians of the later nineteenth century favored a formula that differed from positivism and/or Marxism. According to the then prevalent "historicism,"[5] nature was separate from spirit, as natural science was from historical science. The historical sciences ("idiographic" disciplines) were seen as investigating unique, non-repetitive facts that could not be articulated into a system of laws. The "sociologizing" proposed by positivism or Marxism was therefore rejected. German philosophers, particularly Wilhelm Windelband (1848–1915) and Heinrich Rickert (1863–1938), as well as philosophical historians Johann Gustav Droysen (q.v.), Wilhelm Christian L. Dilthey (q.v.), and Alexandru D. Xenopol (q.v.), variously opposed, in principle, the application of the concepts and methods of the exact or natural sciences to history. All of them believed in a science of history, but they saw it as science with its own rules, an enterprise which aimed to single out individual facts through a critical analysis of sources, to select and interpret such evidence and, finally, to integrate it into a coherent narrative.

Understood in this way by the "critical school," the science of history reached a climax by the end of the nineteenth century. Written documents, the evidence of historical events, were systematically located, published in vast collections, and methodically analyzed. The *Introduction aux études historiques* (1898) of Charles Victor Langlois and Charles Seignobos (q.v.) perfectly illustrates the dominance of written sources and of the exclusive relationship between this sort of documentation and events. Langlois and Seignobos argued that history simply could not be made without written documents and that history would be "exhausted" when the stocks of written evidence finally gave out.

At that time, peoples with no written archives (as in Black Africa and other broad expanses of the world) were considered to be "peoples without a history." In the rest of the world the European historiographic formula gained ground. India, China, and Japan, through historians like Shigeno Yasutugu (q.v.) and Taguchi Ukichi (q.v.), assimilated the lessons of Western historiography, which eventually prevailed over their own traditions.

The "critical school" believed in a perfect, scientific, and objective history. Its conception fitted in perfectly with an age dominated by political and national interests, by state-building and international conflicts. In rejecting "retrospective sociology," historiography in fact opted for "retrospective policy," invoking the past in support of current political and national values and claims. (The German "objective" history was thus opposed to the French "objective" history, and so on.) This history, perfect in its way, underwent a crisis beginning around 1900, a profound process of reevaluation and restructuring that continues to the present. At the turn of the century, innovative personalities, such as the Germans Karl Lamprecht (q.v.) and Max Weber (q.v.), the Belgian Henri Pirenne (q.v.), and the Frenchman Henri Berr (q.v.), were already questioning the mostly political and event-centered approach. James Harvey Robinson (q.v.), in the United States, spoke of a "new history." Just as the history defended by the critical school had reflected the predominantly political and national values of the nineteenth century, this "new history" was to provide the background for an understanding of novel problems and questions of the twentieth century. Thus began the process of expanding the content of historical research. Economic and social issues, mental attitudes, the evolution of human civilization in all its many aspects took precedence in these new accountings of the past. Thus, historians, who were now expected to contribute to the understanding of complex processes, could no longer limit themselves to describing the mechanisms of political events.

Manifest since the beginning of this century and steadily gaining ascendancy has been the tendency toward a history centered on issues rather than on events, a history concerned with change and continuity in socioeconomic, political, and mental structures, a history aspiring to globalism. Partly under the direct influence of Marxism and also under the growing pressure of the realities of the time, economic and social history gained more attention in the first decades of the century. Some thinkers of the twentieth century, like Antonio Gramsci (q.v.), tried an innovatory approach to Marxism. But the Marxist outlook of history has ultimately proved to be too rigid to fit the new historiographic problems and methods. The great economic crisis of 1929–1933 stirred considerable interest in the history of economies in general and of prices in particular. At the same time, a consideration of mental structures appeared necessary, not only to "counterbalance" economic or material factors but also to articulate a complete picture of people and civilizations.

For such a many-sided history, the methodology of the critical school, centered almost exclusively on the exegesis of written sources, proved to be inadequate. In seeking out the perspectives of other disciplines, historians inevitably turned to sociology, to the economic sciences, as well as to anthropology. During the interwar period, the group around the *Annales* review, founded in 1929 by the French historians Lucien Febvre (q.v.) and Marc Bloch (q.v.), expressed the newer tendencies in their most complete form. Joined by younger colleagues, such as Fernand Braudel (q.v.), they resolutely denounced the old, event-centered history and created important landmarks on the way to a global history of civilizations and an interdisciplinary methodology.

Since World War II, people around the globe have become more aware both of the unity of humankind with its common problems and of the diversity of human cultures. National historiographic schools have come into being everywhere, integrating the generally accepted rules of the discipline with their own traditions and values.[6] There is a strong tendency, in unity and variety alike, toward a universal history and the comparative history of civilizations. The phrase "people without history" is nonsensical today, and the geographic expansion of history has been matched by an even larger expansion of historical problems. The domains of history are constantly multiplying and dividing. Whereas a few decades ago, economic, social, or cultural histories won the right to independent existences, new and newly autonomous territories are springing up today within and alongside them. Historical demography, the history of mentalities, and environmental history (or ecohistory) are only a few of the most significant and dynamic new domains. No problem seems too unusual or lacking in interest for historians today working as they are in the almost infinite realm of global history.

Consequently, methodology, which is closely related to current changes in science and technology, has experienced its own evolution. The interdisciplinary approach reaches very far, encompassing the whole range of economic, social and political sciences and unrelenting in its advance toward closer relations with the natural or the "exact" sciences. Archaeology, oral history, and other means of investigation offer information that goes much beyond the old strict limits of the archives. The oral tradition receives unprecedented attention, as disputes continue over whether or not its artifacts can be adequately represented by written language. Here, the video camera serves the historian who seeks the ultimate in accuracy. The "documentary" film emerges as a "text" in which visual and auditory evidence is assembled within a pre-conceived structure in order to make an argument about the past. Mathematics, information science, and computers have resulted in radical revamping of many methods and concepts. Now, as never before, mechanical means enable historians to gather statistical data in support of their generalizations and sometimes to enter into the realm of what-if-this-had-been-the-case-instead-of-that by testing counter-factual models. The most typical example is the "New Economic History" invented around 1960 by Robert W. Fogel.

Will this diversity of national schools, ideologies, domains, problems and methods, ranging from the still very traditional to the most sophisticated, lead to *l'éclatement* of history? We are witnessing changes in history that are in keeping with the diversity of our world, the only requisite of genuine unity being the understanding and acceptance of diversity. More than ever before, history appears as a living, permanently changing human enterprise, a continuous and forever changing dialogue between the past and the present. Is this not its very raison d'être?

Lucian Boia

REGIONAL EDITORS

CONTRIBUTORS

Walter L. Adamson, Emory University, Atlanta, Georgia

Elena Aga-Rossi, Rome, Italy

E. J. Alagoa, University of Port Harcourt, Nigeria

Margherita Repetto Alaia, Columbia University, New York

A. I. Alatortseva, National Committee of Historians of the Soviet Union

G. D. Alekseeva, National Committee of Historians of the Soviet Union, Moscow

Christian Amalvi, Bougival, France

Maurice-A. Arnould

Roger Aubert

J. R. Baines, University of Oxford, England

John Barber, King's College, Cambridge

Ligia Bârzu, University of Bucarest, Romania

A. P. Baziants, National Committee of Historians of the Soviet Union, Moscow

Tim H. Beaglehole, Victoria University, Wellington, New Zealand

Ursula Becher, Catholic University, Eichstatt, West Germany

Liuben Berov, Institute of Balkan Studies, Sofia, Bulgaria

Werner Berthold, Karl Marx University, Leipzig, East Germany

Y. L. Bessmertny, National Committee of Historians of the Soviet Union, Moscow

Ragnar Björk, Uppsala, Sweden

P. B. M. Blaas, Castricum, The Netherlands

Horst Walter Blanke

Joel Blatt, New York, New York

Pim den Boer, Utrecht, The Netherlands

Lucian Boia, University of Bucharest, Romania

J. A. Bornewasser, Nymegen, The Netherlands

Ivan Bozhilov, Institute of History, Sofia, Bulgaria

Stelian Brezeanu, Bucarest, Romania

V. I. Buganov, National Committee of Historians of the Soviet Union, Moscow

Ilse Bulhof, Rijksuniversiteit Utrecht, The Netherlands

Peter Burke, Emmanuel College, Cambridge, England

R. van Caenegem, University of Gand, Belgium

Cai Meibiao

John M. Cammett, New York, New York

Charles-Olivier Carbonell, Ceret, France

S. Y. Carp, National Committee of Historians of the Soviet Union, Moscow

R. L. Chambers

Chen Qitai

Chen Zhi-chao

Roger Chickering, University of Oregon, Eugene

Yŏng-ho Ch'oe, University of Hawaii, Honolulu

Paloma Cirujano, Madrid, Spain

Frank F. Conlon, University of Washington, Seattle

Frank J. Coppa, St. John's University, Jamaica, New York

Roland Crahay, Liege, Belgium

Ronald S. Cunsolo, Westbury, New York

M. A. Dandamayev, National Committee of Historians of the Soviet Union, Moscow

L. V. Danilova, National Committee of Historians of the Soviet Union, Moscow

Alexander De Grand, North Carolina State University, Raleigh

Charles Delvoye

Charles F. Delzell, Vanderbilt University, Nashville, Tennesse

Lajos Demény, Institute of History "Nicolae Lorga," Bucarest, Romania

Paul J. Devendittis, Hempstead, Long Island, New York

Spencer Di Scala, Sharon, Massachusetts

Dimitrije Djordjevic, University of California, Santa Barbara

L. J. Dorsman, Utrecht, The Netherlands

Richard Drake, University of Montana, Missoula

V. A. Dunayevsky, National Committee of Historians of the Soviet Union, Moscow

V. A. Dyakov, National Committee of Historians of the Soviet Union, Moscow

María Teresa Elorriaga Planes, Madrid, Spain

G. Elton, Clare College, Cambridge, England

Yu. N. Emelyanov, National Committee of Historians of the Soviet Union, Moscow

Suraiya Faroqhi, METU, Ankara, Turkey

Fritz Fellner, University of Salzburg, Austria

A. A. Formozov, National Committee of Historians of the Soviet Union, Moscow

William H. Frederick, Ohio University, Athens, Ohio

Alessandro Galante Garrone, Turin, Italy

Juan-Sisinio Pérez Garzón, Madrid, Spain

Alice Gérard, Paris, France

Paul Gerin, Liege, Belgium

Ferenc Glatz, Budapest, Hungary

Elizabeth G. Gleason, Tiburon, California

Jean Glénisson

Beate Gödde-Baumanns, Duisburg, West Germany

N. I. Golubtsova, National Committee of Historians of the Soviet Union, Moscow

J. van Goor, Rijksuniversiteit Utrecht, The Netherlands

N. A. Gorskaya, National Committee of Historians of the Soviet Union, Moscow

A. N. Goryainov, National Committee of Historians of the Soviet Union, Moscow

Conrad Grau, Berlin

E. V. Gutnova, National Committee of Historians of the Soviet Union, Moscow

Nikita L. Harwich Vallenilla, Caracas, Venezuela

Herve Hasquin

Milan Hauner, University of Wisconsin, Madison

Pieter van Hees, Utrecht, The Netherlands

Siegfried Hoyer, Karl Marx University, Leipzig, East Germany

Hu Shou-wei

Huang Lie

Georg G. Iggers, State University of New York, Buffalo, New York

Johannes Irmscher, Berlin, East Germany

Edmund E. Jacobitti, University of Illinois, Edwardsville

Hans-Peter Jaeck, Berlin, East Germany

Armin Jähne, Humboldt University, Berlin, East Germany

Richard Jenkyns, Oxford, England

B. T. Kabanov, National Committee of Historians of the Soviet Union, Moscow

A. N. Khokhlov, National Committee of Historians of the Soviet Union, Moscow

A. L. Khoroshkevich, National Committee of Historians of the Soviet Union, Moscow

R. A. Kireeva, National Committee of Historians of the Soviet Union, Moscow

V. B. Kobrin, National Committee of Historians of the Soviet Union, Moscow

Jürgen Kocka, Berlin, West Germany

Angeliki Konstantakopoulou, Fannena, Greece

D. A. Krainov, National Committee of Historians of the Soviet Union, Moscow

G. S. Kucherenko, National Committee of Historians of the Soviet Union, Moscow

Jean-Louis Kupper

L. R. Kyzlasov, National Committee of Historians of the Soviet Union, Moscow

Nanci Leonzo, Sao Paulo, Brazil

Joseph M. Levine, Syracuse University, New York

Norman Levine, University of Maryland-Baltimore County, Catonsville, Maryland

Joseph Levitt, University of Ottawa, Ontario, Canada

Sang-Woo Lim, Amherst, New York

Rudi Lindner, University of Michigan, Ann Arbor, Michigan

B. A. Litvinsky, National Committee of Historians of the Soviet Union, Moscow

Lizbeth Liubenova, Institute of History, Sofia, Bulgaria

Liu Mao-lin

M. Lordkipanidze, National Committee of Historians of the Soviet Union, Moscow

Clara M. Lovett, Washington, D.C.

Gerhard Lozek, Berlin, East Germany

S. I. Luchitskaya, National Committee of Historians of the Soviet Union, Moscow

Alan Macfarlane, Cambridge, England

Krikor H. Maksoudian, Arlington, Massachusetts

Jens Chr. Manniche, University of Aarhus, Denmark

A. H. de Oliveira Marques, New University, Lisbon, Portugal

Christo Matanov, Institute of Balkan Studies, Sofia, Bulgaria

Arpag Mekhitarian, Brussels, Belgium

E. A. Melnikova, National Committee of Historians of the Soviet Union, Moscow

Lamberto Mercuri, Rome, Italy

Edward Miller, Cambridge, England

Hans Mommsen, Ruhr-Universität Bochum, West Germany

Emilia Morelli, Rome, Italy

John A. Moses, University of Queensland, St. Lucia, Australia

F. W. Mote, Beijing, China

Bernd Mütter, Hövelhof, West Germany

V. D. Nazarov, National Committee of Historians of the Soviet Union, Moscow

V. P. Nikolayev, National Committee of Historians of the Soviet Union, Moscow

Maria Beatriz Nizza da Silva, Didade University, Sao Paulo, Brazil

Emiliana P. Noether, Storrs, Connecticut

Ellen Nore, University of Illinois, Edwardsville

C. Offringa, Utrecht, The Netherlands

K. A. Osipova, National Committee of Historians of the Soviet Union, Moscow

F. Ouellet, York University, Toronto, Canada

Harold T. Parker, Duke University, Durham, North Carolina

Louise Salley Parker, University of Alabama, Huntsville

Hebe Carmen Pelosi

William A. Percy

Eduardo Perez Ochoa

S. B. Pevzner, National Committee of Historians of the Soviet Union, Moscow

A. A. Preobrazhensky, National Committee of Historians of the Soviet Union, Moscow

Rumiana Radeva, Bulgarian Academy of Sciences, Sofia, Bulgaria

Alan J. Reinerman, Boston College, Chesnut Hill, Massachusetts

Horst Renz

Nils Johan Ringdal, Oslo, Norway

Antonio Niño Rodriguez, Madrid, Spain

Isabel de Ruschi

V. A. Rzhanitsina, National Committee of Historians of the Soviet Union, Moscow

A. William Salomone, Rochester, New York

Ilia Salomone-Smith, San Francisco, California

Masayuki Sato, Yamanashi University, Japan

Samir Saul, Montreal, Quebec, Canada

Peter Schafer, Friedrich Schiller University, Jena, East Germany

Maria Schetelich, Berlin, East Germany

Wolfgang Schieder, University of Trier, West Germany

Hans Schleier, Leipzig, East Germany

Julius Schoeps, Meerbusch, West Germany

Horst Schröder, Berlin

Reginald De Schryver

A. V. Semenova, National Committee of Historians of the Soviet Union, Moscow

I. D. Serebryakov, National Committee of Historians of the Soviet Union, Moscow

Kr. Sharova, Institute of History, Sofia, Bulgaria

V. K. Shatsillo, National Committee of Historians of the Soviet Union, Moscow

George Shaw, University of Queensland, St. Lucia, Australia

Martin Siegel, Kean College of New Jersey, Union

Peter Stadler, University of Zurich, Switzerland

Ines Stahlmann, Philipps University, Marburg, West Germany

N. V. Strelchenko, National Committee of Historians of the Soviet Union, Moscow

F. H. Stubbings, Emmanuel College, Cambridge, England

I. A. Stuchevsky, National Committee of Historians of the Soviet Union, Moscow

I. M. Suponitskaya, National Committee of Historians of the Soviet Union, Moscow

G. G. Sviridov, National Committee of Historians of the Soviet Union, Moscow

V. Tapkova-Zaimova, Institute of Balkan Studies, Sofia, Bulgaria

G. S. Tchertkova, National Committee of Historians of the Soviet Union, Moscow

Edward C. Thaden, University of Illinois at Chicago Circle, Illinois

V. A. Tishkov, National Committee of Historians of the Soviet Union, Moscow

Y. S. Tokareva, National Committee of Historians of the Soviet Union, Moscow

Jerzy Topolski, Poznan, Poland

Ronald E. Tranquilla, Saint Vincent College, La Trobe, Pennsylvania

Francesco Turvasi

E. N. Tyomkin, National Committee of Historians of the Soviet Union

Margarita Vaklinova, Institute of Archeology, Sofia, Bulgaria

M. G. Vandalkovskaya, National Committee of Historians of the Soviet Union, Moscow

Maria Veleva, University of Sofia, Bulgaria

Roberto Vivarelli, Firenze, Italy

Gerd Voigt, Berlin, East Germany

V. A. Vrevsky, National Committee of Historians of the Soviet Union, Moscow

Wang Shimin

Hans-Ulrich Wehler, University of Bielefeld, West Germany

Robert Wellens, Brussels, Belgium

Carolyn W. White, Durham, North Carolina

J. J. Woltjer, Oegstgeart, The Netherlands

Xiao Zhizhi, Wahan University, Wuchang, China

V. L. Yanin, National Committee of Historians of the Soviet Union, Moscow

Yie Gui-sheng

Yu Dan-chu

Yuan Yin-guang

Yu. N. Zakharuk, National Committee of Historians of the Soviet Union, Moscow

Zhang Chuan-xi

Johan Zwaan, Amstelveen, The Netherlands

GREAT HISTORIANS
OF THE
MODERN AGE

Great Historians: African

DIKE, Kenneth Onwuka (Awka, 1917–Enugu, 1983), Nigerian historian. Ph.D., University of London (1950); professor, principal, and vice-chancellor of the University of Ibadan (1956–1966); professor at Harvard University (1970–1979); president of the Anambra State University of Technology (1979–1983). Dike was the first Nigerian to be trained as a professional historian in the Western tradition. He became the architect of the new school of African historiography at Ibadan, which promoted the use of oral sources for the reconstruction and interpretation of the African past. He first published his views on the proper approach to African history in an article challenging the statement of the British authority, Dame Margery Perham, that Africa was "without writing and so without history." His article, "African History and Self-Government," in *West Africa* (1953), showed how such opinions were the result of prejudice and ignorance, specified the sources of African history, and stressed the relevance of the past for the contemporary struggle of African nations for independence and self-government. The African, Dike stated, "sees his past in the language he speaks today, in his music, his dance, his art, religion and institutions." He called on African statesmen and universities to set up multidisciplinary teams of researchers, since "the individual can make little impression on fields so vast" and "true political development can only take place on a basis of profound self-knowledge." Appointed supervisor of public records by the British colonial government of Nigeria in 1951, Dike published the *Report on the Preservation and Administration of Historical Records and the Establishment of a Public Record Office in Nigeria* (1954), which became the foundation stone of the National Archives of Nigeria. Dike saw Nigerian archives as being composed of two major aspects of the nation's history: the Islamic impact, and the Atlantic impact, meaning the influence of Muslim Arabs on northern Nigeria from about the tenth century, and of Western Europeans on the Atlantic coast from the fifteenth century. He concluded that "the archives of a nation are the raw material of its history and if these are not preserved, the best source for the study of that country's past will be lost."

Dike's reputation as an historian rests mainly on the book, *Trade and Politics in the Niger Delta, 1830–1885: An Introduction to the Economic History of Nigeria* (1956), a revised version of his Ph.D. dissertation. This work marked the first time oral tradition had been used in the interpretation of the written records from the British Museum and the Public Records Office to write a history on Africa from the perspective of Africans. It was a great innovation at the time and made an immediate impact on African historiography throughout Africa and the English-speaking world. In 1957 Dike followed up his earlier advocacy of multidisciplinary research by starting the Benin Study, an investigation of the ancient Benin Kingdom by a team comprising a historian, an archaeologist, an anthropologist, and an art historian. The project, described as "a new departure," was planned on the principle that "scholars working in *all* possible connected lines of research should actually work together in the field, in continual close contact with each other throughout the period of their research." Prior to this Dike had shown his ability to put his ideas into practice in enduring institutions by founding the Historical Society of Nigeria and its *Journal of the Historical Society of Nigeria*. In 1968, in collaboration with Ade Ajayi, a leading member of the Ibadan school, he published a classic study "African Historiography" in the *International Encyclopaedia of the Social Sciences*. It defined the oral basis of African historiography as well as the influences from the Muslim world and Western Europe, and it related developments in Africa to those in other parts of the world. Dike was not able to complete many of his academic plans, apparently because of his numerous national and international administrative assignments. Thus, his celebrated *Trade and Politics of the Niger Delta* (1956) was to be "merely an introduction" to the economic history of Nigeria and the events of the "crucial period," 1885–1900, which he intended as the subject of another book. Since 1963 Dike had also directed the fieldwork and had planned to produce a book on Aro history. On balance, his influence as an innovator and leader in the development of African historiography is based as much on the ideas he propagated and the institutions he built as on his personal academic research and writing.

Bibliography: J. D. Omer-Cooper, "The Contribution of the University of Ibadan to the Spread of the Study and Teaching of African History within Africa," *Journal of the Historical Society of Nigeria* 10, no.3 (1980): 23–31; H.F.C. Smith, "The Benin Study," *Journal of the Historical Society of Nigeria* 1, no.1 (1956): 60–61.

E. J. Alagoa

FROBENIUS, Leo (Berlin, 1873–Biganolo, Lake Maggiore, 1938), German historian of culture and ethnographer. Served in museums in Bremen, Basel, and Leipzig. Wrote significant papers before age twenty-five, including *Der* *westafricanische Kulturkreis* (1897; The West African Culture Circle) and *Der Ursprung der africanischen Kulturen* (1898; The origin of African Cultures). The last work was rejected by two German universities as a doctoral thesis. He later made expeditions to Africa to collect for museums and to carry out research, using painters to record aspects of African culture. He visited the Congo (1904–1906), the Western Sudan and Liberia (1907), Central Sudan (1910), Togo and Nigeria (1912), central and eastern Sudan (1912–1913), the Sahara and Eritrea (1914–1915), the Nubian Desert (1926), Southwest and Southcentral Africa (1928–1930), and the Fezzan and Libyan Desert (1932–1933). He collected a tremendous amount of oral literature and folktales and revealed to Europe the art of Ife and the Yoruba, following the British seizure of the Benin bronzes in 1897, the spectacular ruins of Great Zimbabwe, and the prehistoric rock art of Africa. He founded the Institut für Kultur Morphologie in 1925, which became the Frobenius Institut in 1945, and the Institut für Kulturgeschichte Afrikas in 1953. He taught ethnography at the University of Frankfurt (1925), became honorary professor (1934), and supervisor of the Museum of Ethnography in Frankfurt (1936). His earlier writings, which alienated him from the German academic establishment, were based on explorers' accounts and ethnographic data in museums, as was the practice of the time. But they were written in a caustic and polemical style and, more important, they offered a view of Africa opposed to that established by Georg Wilhelm F. Hegel (q.v.) to the effect that Africa was without history and not a part of the historical world. Frobenius, on the contrary, saw Africa as a major contributor to world history and culture.

In 1904 Frobenius began a new trend in anthropological research, that of direct observation in the field. His work led to the exposition of new and startling hypotheses about African culture and the nature of culture in general. He proposed, in turn, the hypothesis of culture circles in opposition to the culture complex; the Mediterranean origin of African cultures; and the theory of the submerged continent of Atlantis. These theories, together with new information and insights, poured out in numerous publications including *Und Afrika sprach* (1912; The Voice of Africa); *Atlantis, Volksmärchen und Volksdichtungen* (12 vols. 1921–1928; Atlantis, Folk Tales and Lyrics); *Atlas Africanus* (1921–1929); *Erythrä: Länder und Zeiten des heiligen Königmordens* (1930; Eritrea: Countries and Times of Holy Regicide); and *Die Kulturgeschichte Afrikas: Prolegomena zu einer historischen Gestaltlehre* (1933; The History of African Civilization. Introduction to a Doctrine of Historical Morphology). Frobenius followed "the evolutionary historical method" in the practice of "cultural morphology," whose aims were "to discover the correlations of the building of human culture as a unity, according to meaning, geographical distribution, and chronological order," using data from history, prehistory, and ethnography. He sharply differentiated his intuitive approach from the mechanistic one used by his colleagues. The intuitive observer, he pointed out, "surrenders to the inner logic of growth, evolution, and maturity, a realm which systems and experiment are powerless to unlock." By such means he sought to grasp *paideuma*, "the spiritual essence of culture in general.'' Frobenius claimed to have gained these insights through his contact with African culture. He came to the conclusion that ''it is not a question of whether human beings are better on one continent or another: they are in fact the same throughout, except for a few qualities which they imbibe as part of their cultural inheritance.'' He found that ''the despised African is closer to a daemonic or intuitive apprehension of the core of his civilization than are we intellectualized westerners, from whom the *paideuma* is hidden by an accumulation of soulless, objective facts.'' His Ethiopian Africans were more intuitive than the Hamitic, who thus ceased to be the Caucasian civilizers of other European anthropologists. Not all of Frobenius' work was commendable. His methods of acquiring artifacts were ruthless, and his research techniques unorthodox and often destructive. But his basic motivation was honorable, and his empathy with African culture impressed and influenced the founders of *Negritude*, the movement for African cultural nationalism. According to the leading exponent of the movement, Leopold Sedar Senghor, former president of Senegal, Frobenius illuminated ''all the history and prehistory of Africa . . . to their very depths.''

Bibliography: Eike Haberland, ed., *Leo Frobenius 1873–1973: An Anthology* (Bonn-Bad Godesberg, 1973); J. M. Ita, ''Frobenius in West African History,'' *Journal of African History* 13 no. 4 (1972): 673–688; Janheinz Jahn, *Leo Frobenius: The Demonic Child* (Austin, Tex., 1973); Theodor Michael, ''The Great Rediscoverer of African Civilization: On Leo Frobenius' 100th anniversary,'' *Afrika, the Review of German-African Relations* 14 no. 3 (1973): 9–15.

E. J. Alagoa

JOHNSON, (Reverend) Samuel (Hastings, 1846–Oyo, 1901), Nigerian historian. Moved from Sierra Leone to Ibadan, Nigeria (1857). Student at Abeokuta Training Institution (1863–65). Teacher at Aremo, Ibadan (1865). Promoted catechist (1875). Deacon at Ondo and then pastor of Oyo (1887). Became ''full priest'' (1888). In 1897 Johnson completed the book for which he is known and respected, *The History of the Yorubas, from the Earliest Times to the Beginning of the British Protectorate*. Johnson received his education first from David Hinderer and his wife, missionaries in Ibadan, an influence he acknowledged through dedication of his *History* to the missionary. This influence may account, in part, for the view he held that British rule of Nigeria was ordained by God. Thus, at a time when other missionary-trained Nigerians in Lagos had begun a nationalist movement against aspects of British rule, he was able to describe the 1892 attack on Ijebu as ''the dark before the dawn'' of civilization and as a salutary lesson to other Yoruba communities. And he was able to excuse the 1895 bombardment of his own Oyo as a mere administrative blunder on the part of the British authorities. His residence at Oyo in the heart of Yorubaland and his travels as a contact between its rulers and the British at Lagos were crucial in forming his view of Yoruba history. He came into contact with knowledgeable informants, some of whom he named: David Kukomi, ''patriarch of the Ibadan

Church'' who had been "a young man in the days of Abiodun"; Josiah Oni, "an intrepid trader" from the same period; and "the venerable Lagunju, the renowned Timi of Ede," acknowledged as an authority "all over the country."

Johnson's motives for writing were "purely patriotic"—to preserve knowledge of Yoruba history "as our old sires are fast dying out," and to educate the Yoruba elite, who were so knowledgeable about English, Roman, and Greek history, but ignorant of Yoruba history. He was modest as to aim and accomplishments. He had used "the better-known Royal bards" in Oyo, but thought there would be other oral sources in other parts of Yorubaland which were unknown to him. He had presented his data in such a manner as "to avoid whatever would cause needless offence" and with respect for "the cause of truth and of public benefit." His account, then, was based on "the facts as they [were] given by the bards" for the "ancient and mythological period," and "from the time of King Abiodun downwards, on eyewitnesses of the events they narrate or on those who have actually taken part in them." His objective had been "to present a reliable record of events." Modern Yoruba historians do indeed use Samuel Johnson's *History of the Yorubas* as a reliable reference work, but they criticize him for errors of interpretation. He came to believe that Yorubaland as a whole had been a unified single kingdom up to the time of Alafin Abiodun, with Oyo as the political center and Ife as spiritual head, and, therefore, that nineteenth-century problems could be solved by returning to that system, a view that was influential with the British colonial administration. Though without formal training in history, Samuel Johnson had a good sense of history. He found it difficult to knit many different events into a connected story, but could describe each episode in dramatic prose, spiced with traditional sayings of the age. In the words of Professor Ajayi, "the intellectual achievement commands our respect."

Bibliography: J. F. Ade Ajayi, "Samuel Johnson: Historian of the Yoruba," *Nigeria Magazine* 81 (1964): 141–146; O. Johnson, ed., *The History of the Yorubas, from Earliest Times to the Beginning of the British Protectorate, by the Rev. Samuel Johnson, Pastor of Oyo* (Lagos, 1921, 1937, 1956, 1957, 1960); Robin Law, "How Truly Traditional Is Our Traditional History? The Case of Samuel Johnson and His Recording of Yoruba Oral Tradition," *History in Africa* 11 (1984): 195–221; J. O. Oyemakinde, "Samuel Johnson and his *History of the Yorubas*," *The Historian* (Ibadan), 5 (1968): 166–222.

E. J. Alagoa

KAGWA, (Sir) Apolo (Uganda, 1865–Kenya, 1927), Ugandan historian. Katikkiro (prime minister) of the Kingdom of Buganda (1889–1926), knighted by the British colonial government, K.C.M.G. (Knight Commander of St. Michael and St. George) (1902). Kagwa was the first Ugandan to write the history of a major part of the country in the Luganda language through his association with Protestant missionaries. He is reported to have been encouraged to write by one of the missionaries, John Roscoe, for whom Kagwa assembled informants. Roscoe published his own book, *The Baganda*, in 1911. Kagwa acquired an early passion for writing and was motivated by a desire to record the religious and political wars of the kingdom in which he was a principal protagonist. Thus, by 1894, he had already written a small book, *Entalo za Buganda* (The Wars of Buganda), no longer extant, which recorded the events of the 1880s and 1890s leading to his appointment as Katikkiro. His major works were published later: the *Basekabaka be Buganda* (1901; The Kings of Buganda); *Ekitabo Kye Empisa za Buganda* (1905; The Book of the Manners and Customs of the Baganda); *Ekitabo Ky'Ebika bya Abaganda* (1908; The Book of the Clans of the Baganda); and *Ekitabo Kye Kika Kye Nsenene* (The Book of the Grasshopper Clan), begun in 1893 but completed between 1910 and 1912. Kagwa also wrote *Ekitabo Kye Ngero za Buganda* (1902; The Fables of the Baganda), which is not of great historical significance. He obtained the nineteenth-century calendar dates used in his books and ideas on the arrangement of data from his contacts with his missionary associates, who also got his books published in London. But the primary motivation was his own—to record the oral traditions and history of the Kingdom of Buganda, mainly of the royal court, the chiefs, and its constituent clans, during a period of rapid change.

As leader of the Protestant faction in the politics of the time, Kagwa defended its position and sometimes misrepresented the motives of opposing groups. Furthermore, his methodology did not include the citing of individual informants, but the editions of his books after 1912 did provide lists of informants. These show that he had tried to obtain information from many persons in a position to know things from direct experience. However, he appears to have left out other persons with equal or greater authority on political or religious grounds. Modern Buganda scholars have also characterized his Luganda as archaic and difficult in style. On balance, however, his historical output was sound, reliable, and authoritative, and his books have become the major source of Buganda history. Indeed, he has been termed the father of historical writing in Uganda because the later editions of his works included sections on the history of Ankole, Bunyoro, Kooki, and Toro and because he influenced historians of some of these states, such as John William Nyakatura (q.v.), the historian of Bunyoro.

Bibliography: M.S.M. Kiwanuka, "Sir Apolo Kagwa and the Pre-colonial History of Buganda," *Uganda Journal* 30, no. 2 (1966): 137–152; C. C. Wrigley, "Apolo Kagwa: Katikkiro of Buganda," *Tarikh* 1, no. 2 (1966): 14–25.

E. J. Alagoa

LEAKEY, Louis Seymour Bazett (Kabete, near Nairobi, Kenya, 1903–London, 1972), Kenyan anthropologist, ethnologist, and prehistorian of British origin. Leakey made a monumental contribution to the understanding of the prehistory of East Africa and to knowledge of the beginnings of humanity and culture. Conservator of the Nairobi Museum, creator of the Nairobi Centre of Prehistory and Palaeontology (1962), and founder of the Panafrican Congress of Prehistory and Quaternar Studies and of the Centre of Primatology in Tigoni, Leakey engaged in prodigious field, publicizing, and organizational activities.

Being a very informed person, having an uncommon imagination, and a special intellectual curiosity, he contributed to the identification of some East African Paleolithic cultures (*The Stone Age Culture of Kenya Colony*, 1931), to the recognition of the Neolithic cave-paintings from the same area, and to a better knowledge of the natural environment (physical, climatic, faunal) in which human beings evolved. He was a well-known supporter of the idea that the origins of humanity must be sought in Africa (*The Stone Age Races of Kenya*, 1935; *Olduvai Gorge*, 1951; and *Progress and Evolution of Man in Africa*, 1961). His discovery of some very important fossils (*Homo Kanamensis, Proconsul Africanus, Zinyanthropus Boisei, Kenyapithecus Wickeri, Kenyapithecus Africanus*) demonstrated: the early hominid tendency of separation (c. 12 million years ago); the great morphological diversity of the prehuman fossils; the contemporaneity of the true *Homo* line and the collateral forms (*Unveiling Man's Origins*, 1969; *Adam or Ape*, 1970, in collaboration with J. and S. Prost); and the great oldness of the first being who created culture—*Homo Habilis* (c. 1.7 to 1.8 million years), discovered at Olduvai (*Olduvai Gorge: 1951–1961*, 1965). By uncovering the cultural sequence at Olduvai, Leakey revolutionized the concept of *Homo* itself. More recent research from east of Turkana Lake and from the Omo Valley have confirmed Leakey's observations in spite of the fact that some forms which he considered as collateral (*Australopithecus* and *Erectus*) have become recognized as ancestors of *Homo sapiens sapiens*.

Bibliography: Jérôme Bechard, "Interview de Louis Leakey à Nairobi en Avril 1972," *Bulletin de la Société préhistorique française*, 76, no. 10–12 (1979): 320; Yves Coppens, "Camille Arambourg et Louis Leakey," *Bulletin de la Société préhistorique française*, 76, no. 10–12 (1979): 295–300 and the bibliography of Leakey's works, pp. 308–314; Shirley O. Coryndon, "A Bibliography of the Written Works of Louis Leakey," in G. G. C. Isaac and E. R. McCown, eds., *Human Origins: Louis Leakey and the East African Evidence, Perspectives on Human Evolution*, vol. 3 (Berkeley, Calif., 1976), pp. 542–564; Ph. V. Tobias, "Louis Seymour Bazett Leakey, 1903–1972," *Sud-African Archeaological Bulletin* 28 (1973): 37.

Ligia Bârzu

NYAKATURA, John William (Busesa, c. 1895–Hoima, 1979), Ugandan historian. Educated in Church Missionary School (1904) and Catholic Missionary School (1911), court clerk (1912), *gomborora* (subcounty) chief (1928), *saza* (county) chief (1940), chief judge of Bunyoro (1952–1953). Nyakatura's work as a historian was conditioned by the British conquest of Bunyoro, the heartland of the wider Kitara Kingdom, which had occurred by the time of his birth. He was moved by a spirit of patriotism to write as part of his effort to restore the autonomy of the provinces of Bunyoro-Kitara, which had been transferred to the neighboring Kingdom of Buganda by the British. Nyakatura served on delegations to London in 1958, 1961, and 1962 in efforts to recover the "lost counties." His major work, *Abakama ba Bunyoro-Kitara* (Kings of Bunyoro-Kitara), was begun in 1912, completed in 1938, and published in Canada in 1947. Like Sir Apolo Kagwa (q.v.) of Buganda before him, Nyakatura was encouraged in his literary efforts by colonial officials and missionaries and it was missionaries who eventually published the book. *Abakama*, written in his native Runyoro, quickly became a classic and a school textbook among the Banyoro. In the preface, Nyakatura expressed confidence in the ability of his work to resist criticism, since he had traveled widely to collect information from "many old men who were acquainted with the past." He had tried, he said, to obtain "the real truth" through the "comparison of the various sources," and he criticized books by Europeans on Bunyoro, whose authors could not name the kings of Bunyoro correctly and used other unreliable information. He expected his own book to furnish future historians with data that would enable them to produce "a better history of Kitara." He cited the names of only three informants: the ruling *omukama* (king), a prince, and a chief who gave information about the army. The *Abakama* represented "only a summary" of the data collected, and Nyakatura hoped to write another book about Bunyoro customs.

Bibliography: Godfrey N. Uzoigwe, ed., *Anatomy of an African Kingdom: A History of Bunyoro-Kitara*, a translation of J. W. Nyakatura, *Abakama ba Bunyoro-Kitara* (Kings of Bunyoro-Kitara) by Teopista Muganwa (New York, 1973).

E. J. Alagoa

PLAATJE, Solomon Tshekisho (Boshof, 1877–Kimberley, 1932), South African writer. Largely self-educated, Plaatje became official interpreter for the Kimberley Magistrate Court (1898) and secretary to the Reuters correspondent at the siege of Mafeking (1899), where he kept a diary of events. He eventually served as editor of the Setswana-English weekly *Koranta ea Batswana* (The Newpaper of the Batswana) and of the trilingual *Tsala ea Batho* (The People's Friend) of Kimberley. In 1912 he became general corresponding secretary of the new South African Native National Congress (SANNC), the forerunner of the African National Congress (ANC). He told the story of the fight of the African population of South Africa against the establishment of apartheid by the Afrikaner in his book, *Native Life in South Africa, Before and Since the European War and the Boer Rebellion* (c. 1915). Plaatje saw the Dutch-speaking Afrikaner as the enemy and expected the British government to prevent the enactment of legislation to deprive the African of basic human rights. He also hoped to convince the Afrikaner of the African's capacity to adopt the ways of Western civilization, and so persuade them to develop humane attitudes. His writing was polemical but was based on sound evidence and possessed of dignity, pathos, and eloquence. Thus, he reports that after the enactment of the Native Land Act of 1913, he toured South Africa on a bicycle to investigate its effect on the African population. He found that "awakening on Friday morning, June 20, 1913, the South African Native found himself, not actually a slave, but a pariah in the land of his birth." Although criticized by some of his colleagues as too European in his attitudes, Plaatje was a keen student of African traditions and published collections of proverbs and folktales. He also wrote a historical novel,

Mhudi: An Epic of South African Native Life a Hundred Years Ago (1930), conceived while collecting these traditions.

Bibliography: John L. Comaroff, ed., *The Boer War Diary of Sol T. Plaatje: An African at Mafeking* (Johannesburg, 1973).

E. J. Alagoa

REINDORF, (Reverend) Carl Christian (Prampram, 1834–Christiansborg, 1917), Ghanaian historian. Of Dutch ancestry, born into the Ga community near Accra. Baptized at an early age and largely self-educated after a few years of school. Served as missionary and teacher at various stations up to the time of his retirement in 1893: Damfa (1855), Abokobi (1856), Krobo (1859), Akropong in Akwapim (1860), Teshi (1864), in Mayera, and finally at Christiansborg from 1872, when he was ordained full minister. Reindorf left Basel mission from time to time to practice as trader, farmer, soldier, and doctor in the wars of the Ga against their neighbors. He completed *The History of the Gold Coast and Asante* at Christiansborg in 1889. He addressed the book to "the educated community in the Gold Coast Colony" with the "sole object" of inviting them to undertake "the study and collection of our history, and to create a basis for a future, more complete history of the Gold Coast." He acknowledged the book to be incomplete in two areas. First, his failure to treat of Fante history "from its origin," and second, the omission of European activities and their relations with the local people. The book represents a history of the coming into being of the modern nation of Ghana, beginning with the coastal peoples, and the effects of their centripetal relations with Asante, "the leading and ruling power" in the hinterland. He tried to enlist the interest of the coastal elite by collecting the names of their ancestors "who defended our country from the yoke of Asante." He urged his compatriots to complete the work he had begun, since a history written by foreigners would be "comparatively worthless." The history of the Gold Coast should be written by one "who has not only studied, but has had the privilege of initiation into the history of its inhabitants and writes with true native patriotism." His own history had been distilled from the accounts of over two hundred informants. He had also obtained written documents from missionary friends and used the published accounts of European visitors. Reindorf was a pioneer in Ghana, and his work has become an authority cited by scholars and litigants alike. Scholars criticize it for deficiencies in the interpretation of oral evidence, but acknowledge it to be invaluable, especially for Ga history.

Bibliography: Irene Odotei, "The Ga–Danme," in J. O. Hunwick, ed., *Proceedings of the Seminar on Ghanaian Historiography and Historical Research, 20th–22nd May 1976* (Legon, 1977), pp. 99–112; C. E. Reindorf, "Biography of Rev. Carl Christian Reindorf," in C. C. Reindorf, *The History of the Gold Coast and Asante, Based on Traditions and Historical Facts Comprising a Period of More Than Three Centuries from about 1500 to 1860* (Accra, 1966; reprint of Basel, 1898).

E. J. Alagoa

SAI, Akiga (Akighirga) (Shitire, c. 1898–1959), Nigerian traditional historian. First convert and associate of the Dutch Reformed Mission among the Tiv. Served as editor of a Tiv newssheet in the Gaskiya Corporation, five years as a member of the Northern Nigeria House of Assembly, and in the literature and adult education section of the Tiv Native Authority. Akiga began to accumulate knowledge about Tiv traditions from an early age, when his mother died and he became attached to his father, following him everywhere. Since his father was a blacksmith and a community leader, Akiga shared in his reputation for supernatural powers, especially as he was blind in one eye and had a deformed foot. Akiga's love for traditional lore was already established when he was given to the missionaries in 1911 at the age of about thirteen. It was this combination that resulted in his *History of Tiv*. According to Akiga: "It was while I was wandering round through every part of Tivland, preaching the Gospel of Jesus Christ, and at the same time seeing and hearing the things of Tiv, that the idea of this History took shape in my mind. So I began to ask, and to look, and to delve into everything concerning the Tiv people." He did not learn very much English and, hence, wrote in Tiv. According to Dr. Rupert East who translated about half of the original work, Akiga wrote "as freely as he would talk, in his own natural style." Akiga was explicit about his motives for writing: It was "in order that the new generation of Tiv," which was beginning to acquire "New Knowledge," "should know the things of the fathers as well as those of the present generation."

Akiga was committed to the preservation of the knowledge of Tiv traditions, but his ideas on the collection of data were practical and sensible. He was aware that not all elders were good informants: "It is the men of mature years who know best; of the very old men, one or two are wise; the ignorant are in the majority." It was necessary to question them tactfully or end up with no information at all or simply fabrications. Any suspicion that the researcher was connected with the colonial government would mean loss of confidence. Chiefs would fear loss of office, increase in taxes, or that the white man might take away the things of Tiv when he went home or forbid their continued use by the Tiv. Missionaries were not feared in this way, since "A missionary is not a white man of any consequence; he neither tries cases, nor collects taxes, nor inflicts punishments; all he does is pray." As a missionary and a Tiv, Akiga had free access to information. Yet, he exercised great care and tact, so that he was known and understood "by a large number of the Tiv tribe." As he put it: "There is no Tiv chief today who does not know me well." And he was not partial to his own Shitire clan, but recorded the traditions of every Tiv clan in equal detail. Akiga belonged to a disappearing generation, but he had the wisdom to communicate the past and what was passing to the new generation. In his own view, his conversion to Christianity gave him an advantage in doing this, since he said a man cannot tell which way the roof tilts when standing close to a house: "It is only when he steps back and stands some distance away that he gets a true view and can tell the builders how to set it right." He was sad at the prospect of so many old things disappearing, but he was not despondent: "Let us take heart," he told his Tiv readers, "the old mushroom rots, another springs up, (and) the mushroom tribe lives on." Akiga's history of the Tiv was the first in northern Nigeria written outside the Islamic tradition in the African traditional style rendered in Western script. It is unique in Africa as a successful account of the history of a large non-centralized group of the type judged by Western historians and anthropologists to be without a history.

Bibliography: Rupert East trans./ed., *Akiga's Story: The Tiv Tribe as Seen by One of Its Members* (London, 1939, 1965); B. A. Sai, " 'The Descent of the Tiv from Ibenda Hill', Annotated and Translated by Paul Bohannan," *Africa* 24 (1954): 295–310.

E. J. Alagoa

Great Historians: Arab

AL-FALAKĪ, Maḥmūd Aḥmad (al-Ḥiṣa, Egypt, 1815–1885), Egyptian astronomer (in Arabic, "falakī") and historian. A student (1833) and later a professor (1839) at the School of Engineering. Al-Falakī spent the years 1850 to 1859 in Paris specializing in astronomy. Quite apart from his purely scientific work, he put to use his technical training in studying the past. Drawing on a unique combination of the methodologies of astronomy and historical research, he wrote extensively on subjects such as the pre-Islamic calendar. He was in a position to give a practical turn to his work. After delving into cartography (1859), he became a pioneer in astro-archaeology, employing calculations in astronomy to determine the age of the pyramids (1862). In 1865 he undertook archaeological research in Alexandria on the Roman presence and subsequently prepared a nilometer following his discovery of one made in ancient times. He was minister of public works briefly in 1881, and minister of education in 1882 and 1884–1885. Al-Falakī was significant as part of a new breed of amateur historian, the scientist and/or technician, as opposed to the traditional '*ālim* (learned scholar).

Bibliography: Ismā'īl Bey Muṣṭafa and Mukhtār Bey, *Notices biographiques de S. E. Mahmoud-Pacha el Falaki* (Cairo: Imprimerie Nationale, 1886); Ahmad Sa'īd al-Dimirdāsh, *Maḥmūd Aḥmad al-Falakī* (Cairo: al-Dār al-Miṣriyya li'l-Ta'līf wa'l-Tarjama, n.d.); Jamāl al-Dīn al-Shayyāl, *al-Ta'rīkh wa'l-Mu'arrikhūn fī Miṣr fi'l-Qarn al-Tāsi' 'Ashr* (History and Historians in Nineteenth-Century Egypt), (Cairo: Maktabat al-Nahḍa al-Miṣriyya, 1958), pp. 113–120; Jurjī Zaydān, *Mashahīr al-Sharg* (Famous Men of the East), vol. 2 (Cairo: al-Hilāl, 1922), pp. 148–151; Khayr al-Dīn al-Ziriklī, *al-A'lām* (Eminent Personalities), vol. 7 (Beirut, 1980 edition), p. 164.

Samir Saul

GHURBĀL, Muḥammad Shafīq (Alexandria, 1894–Cairo, 1961), Egyptian historian and professor. Ghurbāl is considered the founder of modern Egyptian historiography, thanks to whom scholarly methods and norms were introduced in the educational system. As the quintessence of the academic historian whose whole life was devoted to no other activity than formal teaching and erudite publication, he was a novelty in Egypt. He exercised immeasurable influence on an entire generation of students, and a large part of the teaching staff in the postwar period received its training from him. Not only was Ghurbāl his country's first professional historian, but he was also the first Egyptian to be named (in 1929) to the chair of modern history at the Egyptian (now Cairo) University. He also served as adviser to the Department of Education at various times from 1940 to 1954, and engaged in numerous scholarly or cultural endeavors, such as the founding of the Egyptian Historical Society in 1947. He occasionally gave series of radio lectures on Egyptian history.

Ghurbāl was not a prolific author, and, viewing himself primarily as an educator, he once pointed to his students when asked about his publications. Nevertheless, the relative paucity of writings by a scholar of his stature should not detract from their value, for they remain the main monographs in their field. Equally important was their role as practical examples by which Ghurbāl inculcated his students with the methodology of critical historiography. His first book, entitled *The Beginning of the Egyptian Question and the Rise of Mehmet Ali*, was written in English and appeared in London in 1928. The first seven chapters formed the substance of his dissertation for the B.A. at the University of Liverpool (1919) and the last nine that for the M.A. at the University of London (1924). As the subtitle indicated, it was a study in diplomatic history based on research in the British and French archives. Never before had an Egyptian written on the modern history of his country by making systematic use of unpublished source material. Sayed Kamel had used printed sources in *La conférence de Constantinople et la question égyptienne* (1913). In that regard, Ghurbāl was a pioneer, and his book marked a date worthy of note. No less interesting was the author's approach, which set the diplomatic origins of the events in Egypt in the context of the Eastern Question, and connected the Eastern Question to the European wars involving the Napoleonic Empire. In 1944 Ghurbāl published a short work entitled *Muḥammad 'Alī al-Kabīr* (Muḥammad 'Alī the Great). It was more than a biography since the leading character appeared only after the author had meticulously prepared the stage, both in its international and its national dimensions. Ghurbāl placed this period in the Islāmic, not modern, era, and Egypt's renaissance within that of the Islamic world as a whole. Muḥammad 'Alī emerged as a reformer but, above all, as an Ottoman Muslim leader intent, at least until 1833, on strengthening the empire. Only after the peace of Quṭāhya did he turn away from it. The book illustrated one key part of Ghurbāl's outlook, namely, the central role he attributed to great individuals in the making of history. Unlike Muḥammad Ṣabrī, the other contemporary scholarly historian, who had been a student of Alphonse Aulard at the Sorbonne and a supporter of the Wafd and Sa'd Zaghlūl, Ghurbāl did not explicitly embrace nationalism. Adhering to no specific philosophy of history, his views were characterized by great restraint and detachment. The concern with "creative minorities" he developed under the influence of his mentor, Arnold Toynbee (q.v.), who had supervised his M.A. thesis. Although he was not a strict follower of Toynbee, he did adhere to his notion of "challenge and response" in the ten talks he broadcast in English in 1952 and published under the title *The Making of Egypt*. His last important work, *Ta'rīkh al-Mufāwadāt al-Miṣriyya al-Brītāniyya—al-Juz' al-Awwal* (1952; The History of the Anglo–Egyptian Negotiations—Part One), dealt with the negotiations from 1882 to 1936. As he stated in the introduction, it rested on a painstaking comparison of Egyptian and British sources, requiring further research in case of divergences. Careful scrutiny of archival material, analysis of the origins and results of events, and formulation of logical conclusions were the hallmark of his methodology and his legacy.

Bibliography: Muḥammad Anīs, "Shafīq Ghurbāl wa Madrasat al-Ta'rīkh al-Miṣrī al-Ḥadīth" (Shafīq Ghurbāl and the School of Modern Egyptian History), *al-Majallat* (The Journal), no. 58 (November 1961): 12–17; Aḥmad 'Abd al-Raḥīm Muṣṭafa, "Shafīq Ghurbāl Mu'arrikhan" (Shafīq Ghurbāl as an Historian), *al-Majallat al Ta-rīkhiyya al-Misriyya* (The Egyptian Historical Journal), 2 (1963): 255–278 (this number contains speeches made during a commemorative celebration in December 1961, pp. 7–47); Aḥmad 'Izzat 'Abd al-Karīm, "Muḥammad Shafīq Ghurbāl, Ustādh Jīl wa Ṣāḥib Madrasa" (Muḥammad Shafīq Ghurbāl, Teacher of a Generation and Founder of a School), *Al'Majallat al'Tar'īkhiyya al-Misriyya* 19 (1972): 25–31; Ahmad Khāki, "Shafīq Ghurbāl, Baḥth fī Minhajihi wa lḥkāmihi al-Ta'rīkhiyya" (Shafīq Ghurbāl, Research into His Methodology and His Historical Opinions), *al-Majallat al-Ta'rīkhiyya al-Misriyya*, pp. 33–71; Niqūlā Yūsuf, *A'lām min al-Iskandariyya* (Eminent Personalities from Alexandria), (Alexandria: Munsha'at al-Ma'ārif, 1969), pp. 295–299.

Samir Saul

AL-JABARTĪ, 'Abd al-Raḥmān (Cairo, 1753/1754–Cairo, 1825/1826), Egyptian historian and man of letters. Scion of an affluent family, al-Jabartī was raised in a cultured environment. A typical product of the traditional Azhar education, he nevertheless gave unmistakable evidence of a modern outlook on history. His emergence was all the more remarkable in that Ottoman Egypt proved particularly barren in historical writing. In his principal work, *'Ajā'ib al-Athār fi'l-Tarājim wa'l Akhbār* (Amazing Finds in Biographies and Chronicles), he stated that the study of history was neglected in his day. He himself approached the subject in the classical manner. *'Ajā'ib* was published in four volumes and covered the years 1688 to 1821. The first three volumes were written in 1805–1806, and the last was composed from 1806 to 1821. As in the medieval annals, the events were presented in chronological succession, and the matter was divided by year or month. No inner connection tied the various subjects, save their coincidence in time. Biographies abounded and occupied more space than the events. The organization of the text was disconcerting; long series of biographies or obituaries alternated with blocks of chronicles. Yet al-

Jabartī's intent and achievement went beyond those of the medieval annalist. In the preface, he declared history to be a science concerned with the condition of peoples, their customs, origins, and ultimate fate. It included the study of the lives of famous individuals. Most importantly, its purpose was to elucidate past situations and their origins. In that way, it furnished examples and teachings for the present. While 'Ajā'ib remained largely a chronicle, it demonstrated an evident groping toward causal links and underlying factors. Al-Jabartī did more than record disparate data in the form of annals. First, he sought to be accurate and critical toward his sources. Second, where he was the source as an eye witness, his observation was particularly penetrating. Finally, he reflected on his subject matter, weighed it, interpreted it, and assessed its significance. These were the features that elevated the author to the level of a historian. 'Ajā'ib was a mine of information on the period, as well as a valuable expression of an educated Egyptian's reactions to the French expedition of 1798–1801 and contact with an alien world.

On the whole, al-Jabartī proved to be impartial and open-minded, even admiring, when confronted with the innovations introduced by the French. When he was not sympathetic, he at least tried to remain fair. His attitude had been hostile in a shorter work written in 1801, entitled *Maẓhar al-Taqdīs bi-Dhahāb Dawlat al-Faransīs (Outward Celebration at the Departure of the French)*. It was an earlier effort, and its historical and historiographic value falls far short of 'Ajā'ib.

Bibliography: Muhammad Anis, "Al-Jabartī bayn Maẓhar al-Taqdīs wa 'Ajā'ib al-Athār" (Al-Jabartī Between Maẓhar al-Taqdīs and 'Ajā'ib al-Athār), *Majallat Kulliyat al-Adāb* (Journal of the Faculty of Arts), University of Cairo 18 (May 1956): 59–70; David Ayalon, "The Historian al-Jabartī and His Background," *Bulletin of the School of Oriental and African Studies* 23 (1960): 217–249; David Ayalon, "Studies in Al-Jabartī: Notes on the Transformation of Mamlūk Society in Egypt under the Ottomans," *Journal of the Economic and Social History of the Orient* 3 (1960): 275–325; Jack A. Crabbs, *The Writing of History in Nineteenth-Century Egypt: A Study in National Transformation* (American University in Cairo Press; Detroit: Wayne State University Press, 1984), pp. 43–66; Gilbert Delanoue, *Moralistes et politiques musulmans dans l'Egypte du XIXe siècle (1798–1882)* (Cairo: Institut Francais d'Archéologie Orientale, 1982), Chapter 1; P. M. Holt, "Al-Jabartī's Introduction to the History of Ottoman Egypt," *Bulletin of the School of Oriental and African Studies* 25 (1962): 38–51; Ahmad 'Izzat 'Abd al-Karīm, ed., *'Abd al-Rahmān al-Jabartī: Dirāsāt wa Buhūth* ('Abd al-Rahmān al-Jabartī: Studies and Research), (Cairo: al-Hay'a al-Miṣriyya al-'Āma li'l-Kitāb, 1976), symposium held in April 1974; Ismail K. Poonawala, "The Evolution of al-Jabaartī's Historical Thinking as Reflected in the *Muzhir* and the *'Ajā'ib,*" *Arabica*, no. 15 (1968): 270–288; Khalīl Shaybūb, *'Abd al-Rahmān al-Jabartī* (Cairo: Dār al-Ma'ārif, 1948); Richard Verdery," 'Abd al-Rahmān al-Jabartī as a Source for Muhammad 'Alī's Early Years in Egypt (1801–1821)," doctoral dissertation (Princeton University, 1967).

Samir Saul

KURD 'ALĪ, Muḥammad (Damascus, 1876–Damascus, 1953), Syrian historian and editor. Kurd 'Alī was largely self-taught and came under the influence of the reformers Muḥammad 'Abdū and Ṭāhir al-Jazā'irī. His activity as a historian partook of his general aim of promoting the cultural and intellectual awakening of the Arab nation. On the one hand, he sought to impress on the Arabs the extent of the decline they had undergone over the centuries. On the other hand, he endeavored to demonstrate the compatibility of Arab civilization and modernity. Arab civilization was not inert and had to be regenerated by developing its secular, rational, and scientific kernel. Kurd 'Alī advocated borrowing the outlook and methods of the West. He did not consider Islam to be an obstacle to reform or progress, and he vigorously contested the assertions of some Western Orientalists on that score. Kurd 'Alī founded the Arab Academy in Damascus in 1919 and twice afterward became minister of education of Syria. Through the journal *al-Muqtabas* (Quotations, or Borrowings), which he established in Cairo in 1906 and moved to Damascus in 1909, he helped educate his public about problems of contemporary civilization and the necessity for reform. In fact, he fashioned the journal into an important vehicle of the ideas of the Arab renaissance.

Kurd 'Alī's chief historical work was the massive *Khiṭaṭ al-Shām* (1925; The Districts of Syria) on which he spent twenty-five years. A distinguishing feature of this monument was the fact that it tried to combine the traditional *khiṭaṭ* form—it was the last example of the genre—with the methodology of modern scholarship, especially that of the Western orientalists. The author used Arabic, Turkish, and French sources; he also went three times to Europe to do research. However, Kurd 'Alī's modernity as a historian should not be overstressed. Although he used archival material extensively, he did not analyze it sufficiently. He was not critical enough of the sources on which he relied, and at times he seemed content to line up contradictory evidence in order to let the reader decide. In the introduction, he indicated his approach. Recent historians, he complained, had strayed to the point where they could not distinguish fact from fiction. He intended to extract the stable core from the facts and discard anything doubtful. In the section on political history, he wanted to elucidate the underlying causes of events, the sequence of their development, and the nature of the immediate and remote circumstances surrounding them. Finally, he wished to draw conclusions and elaborate general principles. History could not be bent to suit the tastes of a writer or those of his age. Inasmuch as its object was the study of the past for understanding the present and the future, it was valid only when it provided authentic information. In the first three volumes, Kurd 'Alī presented the history of Syria from the earliest times to the postwar partition in an orderly chronological pattern based on the succession of regimes. The last three volumes were divided into sections, devoted to all aspects of civilization, culture, and material life, from the arts and the economy to assorted institutions. Kurd 'Alī's other writings dealt with various facets of Islamic and Western civilization. Among them were *Gharā'ib al-Gharb* (1923; Wonders of the West), *al-Qadīm wa'l-Jadīd* (1925; The Old and the New), *Aqwāluna wa Af'āluna* (1946; Our Words and Our Deeds), and *al-Islām wa'l-Ḥaḍāra al-'Arabiyya* (1950, Islām and Arab Civilization). In all these, the author stood as a proponent of intellectual reform and cultural progress.

Bibliography: Sami Dahan, "Muḥammad Kurd ʿAlī: Notice biographique," *Mélanges Louis Massignon*, vol. 1 (Damascus: Institut Français de Damas, 1956), pp. 379–394; Sāmī al-Dahhān, *Muḥammad Kurd ʿAlī: Ḥayātuhu wa Āthāruhu* (Muḥammad Kurd ʿAlī: His Life and Influence), (Damascus, 1955); Jamāl al-Dīn al-Alūsī, *Muḥammad Kurd ʿAlī* (Baghdad: Dār al-Jumhūriyya, 1966); Joseph H. Escovitz, "Orientalists and Orientalism in the Writings of Muḥammad Kurd ʿAlī," *International Journal of Middle East Studies* 15 (1983): 95–109; Shafīq Jabirī, *Muḥāḍarat ʿan Muḥammad Kurd ʿAlī* (Lectures on Muḥammad Kurd ʿAlī), (Cairo: al-Risāla, 1957); Samir Seikaly, "Damascene Intellectual Life in the Opening Years of the 20th Century: Muḥammad Kurd ʿAlī and *Al-Muqtabas*," in Marwan R. Buheiry, ed., *Intellectual Life in the Arab East, 1890–1939* (American University of Beirut, 1981), pp. 125–153.

Samir Saul

MUBĀRAK, ʿAlī (Birinbāl, Egypt, 1824–Cairo, 1893), Egyptian engineer, historian, administrator, minister. Mubārak was an important reformer in nineteenth-century Egypt. As a high state official, his concerns ranged from renovating the system of education to undertaking public works. Although he ranked among the most prominent representatives of modern Egyptian historiography, his own bent remained largely technical-administrative and his historical approach was markedly influenced by it. From beginning to end, Mubārak's career illustrated the rise and growth of a new faction in the governing elite. Gradually replacing the traditional *ʿulamā'* corps (men of learning) bound to a religious formation, the new intelligentsia was forged to be the carrier of a secular, technical outlook. Moreover, the new culture, born of the urge to modernize the country, provided the opportunity to Egyptians of humble origins to occupy important positions in the state apparatus, hitherto monopolized by the Turkish elite. Given the ruling family's autonomist tradition vis-à-vis its Ottoman suzerains, it grasped the benefits it could derive from modernization and was not averse to promoting Egyptian elements—albeit in a capricious manner. In return, the Egyptian elements tended to remain loyal and express the historically novel phenomenon of Egyptian patriotism in terms of culture and/or material improvement, while shunning political activity. Rifaʿa Rafiʿ al-Ṭahṭāwī (q.v.) and Mubārak were the best known exemplars of this emerging breed of intellectuals-cum-public servants.

Mubārak could have stayed in the traditional educational network, from the village school (*kuttāb*) to the Azhar, and become an *ʿālim*. Instead, he entered the state system in 1836, eventually gaining admittance to the School of Engineering in 1839. From 1844 to 1850, he was part of the mission sent to Paris. On his return, he occupied various government posts in the general fields of education and public works, eventually holding the two portfolios in the Cabinet. His achievements and reforms proved to be of lasting significance. Mubārak also found the time to author very weighty works. In *Nukhbat al-Fikr fī Tadbīr Nīl Miṣr* (1880; A Selection of Thoughts on the Management of the Nile), he presented a history of Egyptian agriculture, Nile irrigation, and population. It was in fact a report drawn up at the request of the K̲h̲idīw Ismā'īl and completed in 1873. Mixing historical and specialized technical information, it concluded with proposals. Mubārak's concern with the process of social change, material betterment, and the progress of reason was apparent in *'Alam al-Dīn*, a massive book totaling 1,491 pages, divided into 125 chapters. It was written between 1868 and 1877, and published in 1882. Educational in purpose, this awkward, diffuse novel was built around the dialogues of Azharī shayk̲h̲, 'Alam al-Dīn, and an Englishman on the most diverse aspects of civilization, tradition and progress, science and technology. In Mubārak as in others, contact with the alien world of Europe provoked searching questions on the very foundations of societies, the laws governing change, and the reasons for the differences between Europe and their country. By singling out knowledge and education as the basic causes of progress, Mubārak gave an historical explanation of advances in civilization, and of the decline in the Muslim world following an era of greatness. There was nothing preordained or static about these matters. The way forward lay in reawakening the love for knowledge which Europe exemplified. As Europe borrowed constantly, so should the Muslim community. Mubārak's paramount work was the monumental *al-K̲h̲iṭaṭ al-Tawfīqiyya al-Jadīda* . . . (The New Districts of the Country in Tawfīq's Era . . .), written after 1883 and published in 1888–1889. No historian of nineteenth-century Egypt can dispense with the wealth of information contained in these 2,318 pages. *K̲h̲iṭaṭ* was an ancient historical genre, in fact, a topographical survey in which the historical material was arranged on a geographical basis. Whole volumes, or chapters, were devoted to each city or village, and the most heterogeneous information—historical, biographical, architectural, and much else—relating to that locality was assembled under the same heading. The author declared that he was continuing al-Maqrīzī's (q.v.) *K̲h̲iṭaṭ*. In that medieval format, Mubārak was able to integrate valuable new data culled from modern sources. He marshalled official documents, statistics, census records, trade reports, cadastral books, and so on, so much so that *al-K̲h̲iṭaṭ* assumed encyclopaedic dimensions. While undoubtedly present, the historical contents were presented unsystematically. Their dispersal ruled out attempts at coherent analysis or comprehensive interpretation.

Bibliography: Anouar Abdel-Malek, *Idéologie et renaissance nationale*, Chapter 6 (Paris: Anthropos, 1969); Gabriel Baer, "Alī Mubārak's *K̲h̲itat* as a Source for the History of Modern Egypt," in P. M. Holt, ed., *Political and Social Change in Modern Egypt* (London: Oxford University Press, 1968), pp. 13–27; Jack A. Crabbs, *The Writing of History in Nineteenth-Century Egypt: A Study in National Transformation* (American University in Cairo Press and Detroit: Wayne State University Press, 1984), pp. 109–119; Gilbert Delanoue, *Moralistes et politiques musulmans dans l'Egypte du XIXe siècle (1798–1882)*, Section V, Part 2 (Cairo: Institut Francais d'Archéologie Orientale, 1982); D. I. Dykstra, "A Biographical Study in Egyptian Modernization: Alī Mubārak (1823/4 –1893)," doctoral dissertation (University of Michigan, 1977); Samir Saul, "Ali Moubarak, un historien égyptien et son oeuvre," *Storia della Storiografia*, no. 5 (1984): 77–85; Biographies by Muhammad Aḥmad K̲h̲alaf Allāh (1957), Sa'īd Zāyid (1958), Muḥammad 'Abd al-Karīm (1958?), Maḥmud al-Sharqāwī and 'Abdullāh al-Mashadd (1962), and Ḥusayn Fawzī al-Najjār (1967).

Samir Saul

AL-NĀṢIRĪ AL-SALĀWĪ, Aḥmad . . . (Salā, Morocco, 1835–Salā, 1897), Moroccan historian and government official. After a solid but by no means exceptional education, al-Nāṣirī entered state service when he was about forty years of age. His employment in various administrative departments was generally modest but required him to travel widely throughout Morocco. He was thus in a position to form a comprehensive view of the country and, more practically, to obtain material for his main historical work entitled *Kitāb al-Istiqṣā' li-Akhbār Duwal al-Maghrib al-Aqṣā* (The Book of Thorough Examination on the History of the Dynasties of Morocco). Completed in 1881, it was presented to the sultan but was published only in 1894 in Cairo. It opened with introductory remarks concerning the value of the study of history. The rest of the text was divided into four parts. The first started with the life of the Prophet and continued with the four caliphs of the beginning of Islam. The author then covered the history of the Berbers—relying here on Ibn Khaldūn's (q.v.) *Kitāb al-'Ibar* (The Book of Instructive Examples)—the advent of Islam, the history of Fās, and the Idrīsī, Almoravid, and Almohad dynasties. Al-Nāṣirī did not deal with the history of pre-Islamic Morocco. In the last three parts, he gave accounts, respectively, of the Marīnid, Sa'dī, and 'Alawī dynasties. Obituary notices were included in various parts of the book. *Kitāb al-Istiqṣā'* achieved notoriety, on the one hand as the first work to be largely devoted to the history of Morocco proper, and on the other as the first to include all periods of the country's Islamic history. Previous writings had been either about the entire Maghrib or about specific periods. The author evidently read extensively and obtained official documents from highly placed men. He also used European, especially Portuguese and Spanish, publications as sources, a novel development in Moroccan historiography. Widely acclaimed, the book was considered a landmark and was used as a reference work by other historians. A reassessment took place when it was realized that the author had basically compiled in a single text extracts from older works. His reliance on al-Zayyānī (q.v.) seemed especially marked. The result was a continuous but unoriginal composition. At a time when much of the bibliographic material al-Nāṣirī employed was little known or difficult of access, *Kitāb al-Istiqṣā'* had value as a source. At present it is appreciated for the author's breadth of vision, denoting an important stage in Moroccan historiography, and for its stylistic qualities of clarity and lack of affectation. Al-Nāṣirī had other titles to his credit, for instance, in the criticism of poetry, and in subjects such as the schisms and heresies in Islam, as well as his family's genealogy.

Bibliography: Mohamed Khelifa, ''Un passage du *Kitāb al-Istiqṣā'*: Le retour du Mérinide Abou-l-Hasan de Tunis à Alger en 1349–1350,'' *Revue d'histoire et de civilisation du Maghreb* (Algiers), no. 3 (1967): 50–53; E. Levi-Provencal, *Les historiens des Chorfa*

(Paris: E. Larose, 1922), pp. 350–368; Robert Ricard, "Les ravages de l' Istiqsā'," *Hespéris* 43 (1956): 201–202.

Samir Saul

AL-RĀFI'Ī, 'Abd al-Raḥmān (Cairo, 1889–Cairo, 1966), Egyptian historian, political figure, lawyer. Al-Rāfi'ī's life and work were profoundly influenced by his early adherence to the cause of Egyptian nationalism and the struggle for independence. He became a follower of Muṣṭafa Kāmil, the founder of the Waṭanī (National) party, and from 1932 to 1946 he served as general secretary of the party. He was a member of Parliament in 1924–1925, a senator from 1939 to 1951, and a member of the Cabinet in 1949. Considerable though al-Rāfi'ī's political activities might have been, he made his mark as a historian and proved to be a prolific author. The two domains were not unrelated, for he conceived of history as a form of education in civics, a way of forming the character of the people and helping it acquire political experience. Ignorance of the nation's history, even among intellectuals, counted as a factor retarding the development of national consciousness. From 1929 to 1959, al-Rāfi'ī published a series of fourteen lengthy works recounting Egypt's past from the end of the eighteenth century to 1952. He was led to do so by his conviction, which he expressed in the first book, that continuity was a feature of Egypt's history since the people's revolts against the French expedition of 1798. The real history of nations, he stated, was that of their awakening, which remained the basis of their existence. National history was similar to a mirror reflecting their renaissance. Consequently, he viewed the history of Egypt's national movement as a cumulative succession of stages starting with Muḥammad 'Alī and reaching its zenith with Muṣṭafa Kāmil. He was alive to the danger of partisanship, as he had to be with such a program, and constantly reiterated—as, for instance, in *'Aṣr Ismā'īl* (1932; the Era of Ismā'īl)—that a historian had to weigh evidence, tell the whole truth, and adduce proof to support his analyses. In *Fī A'qāb al-Thawra al-Miṣriyya* (1947–1949; In the Wake of the Egyptian Revolution) he compared the historian to a judge of events who was duty-bound to be equitable. Although al-Rāfi'ī's interpretations were often debatable, they were not raw declarations of opinion and he made a notable effort to substantiate them with historical facts. His documentation, often archival, was abundant. Where he tended to depart from the critical outlook, it was due less to his overall patriotism than to Waṭanī party policy on specific points. For example, the party advocated national unity, even with the crown, to achieve national independence and the end of British occupation. Al-Rāfi'ī was thus relentless in his criticism of the leadership of the 'Urābī revolution of 1882 for having menaced the Khidīw. In contrast, he eulogized conciliatory leaders and highly praised Muḥammad 'Alī as the founder of the modern Egyptian state and the prime planner of its independence. It was clear that, despite his intent to write the history of the Egyptian people, al-Rāfi'ī was more interested in great individuals and their personalities. The characters of men emerged from his works as the driving force of history.

For all his shortcomings, al-Rāfiʿī must be considered one of Egypt's first thoroughly modern historians, along with Muhammad Shafīq Ghurbāl (q.v.) and Muḥammad Ṣabrī. His subjects were well circumscribed and did not begin in the remote past. His books were not compilations of disparate materials but the product of selection in connection with the issue at hand. Although he worked in the framework of the narrative, he did not shrink from the search for explanations or from interpretation and, in the process, encountered the attendant danger lurking in the path of the genuine historian, that of bias. Muṣṭafa Kāmil himself had contributed to the growth of the analytical trend through his *al-Mas'ala al-Sharqiyya* (1898; The Eastern Question). Because of its need for persuasive argumentation and its focus on a clearly defined concept, the nation, nationalism aided progress in historical methodology by favoring cogent interpretation at the expense of the eclectic amalgams of the past. Its merits and its weaknesses were also al-Rāfiʿī's.

Bibliography: There is a dearth of studies on al-Rāfiʿī. Tāriq al-Bishrī, "'Abd al-Rahmān al-Rāfiʿī, Mu'arrikhun wa Siyāsiyyun" ('Abd al-Rahmān al-Rāfiʿī, Historian and Politician), *al-Ṭalīʿa* (The Vanguard), 7, no. 12 (December 1971): 88–108; "al-Rāfiʿī wa Thawrātu Miṣr al-Thalāthu" (al-Rāfiʿī and Egypt's Three Revolutions), *al-Ṭalīʿa* (The Vanguard), no.2 (1967): 66–70; Ahmad 'Abd al-Rāhīm Muṣṭafa, "'Abd al-Rahmān al-Rāfiʿī, 1889–1966," *al-Hilāl* (The Crescent), January 1, 1967, pp. 40–47; Muḥammad Yūsuf Zāyid, "'Abd al-Rahmān al-Rāfiʿī, Mu'arrikh al-Haraka al-Qawmiyya fī Miṣr" ('Abd al-Rahmān al-Rāfiʿī, Historian of the National Movement in Egypt), *al-'Arabī* (The Arab), no. 44 (July 1962): 87–90; 'Abd al-Rahmān al-Rāfiʿī, *Mudhakkirātī, 1889–1951* (My Memoirs, 1889–1951), (Cairo, 1952).

Samir Saul

SARHANK, Ismāʿīl (? 1854–Cairo, 1924), Egyptian naval officer and instructor, historian. Sarhank was one of the technicians groomed in the second half of the nineteenth century by the growing, state-run, modernity-oriented educational system. Like Mubārak (q.v.) and al-Falakī (q.v.), he also wrote history, guided by the outlook carried over from his professional domain of specialization. Sarhank's historical work stood at the crossroads between the traditional annalistic and the modern interpretive methodology. In form, he followed the old pattern, starting with the creation and attempting a universal history of humankind. Nevertheless, he broke fresh ground in a number of ways. The subject he set out to investigate was clearly circumscribed, at least in the title of his only extant publication. He used first-hand sources extensively, aiming consciously to achieve accuracy. Finally, he did not shrink from formulating judgments or trying to seek meaning in the material at hand. Sarhank's only book was the hefty *Haqā'iq al-Akhbār 'an Duwal al-Bihār* (True Accounts about the Maritime States), inspired probably more by the author's naval career than by Alfred Thayer Mahan's (q.v.) *The Influence of Seapower upon History, 1660–1783* (1890), Volume 1, appearing in 1894, opened with the creation and proposed to give an introduction to the maritime history of the world. The author moved methodically from the Phoenicians, the Persians, the Greeks, the Macedonians, and so on, to the Muslim countries, ending with the Ottoman Empire, a chapter that took up about two-fifths of the volume. For each state, he presented the geographic background, military and commercial information, an account of its origins, rulers, and history, as well as a description of its naval power. Whereas Sarhank relied on European sources for Volume 1, his documentation was more original for Volume 2, which dealt solely with Egypt and was published in 1898. He used official records, statistics, Egyptian documents, European diplomatic correspondence, and his own personal knowledge and experience to provide valuable facts on the military history and personnel of Egypt. He also included social and economic history by adding sections on the construction of dams, railways, and factories, the sale of the Dā'ira Saniyya lands, and the establishment of the National Bank of Egypt. In those respects, he belonged squarely to Mubārak's lineage. He went further, however, because he framed the history of nineteenth-century Egypt, to which four-fifths of the volume were devoted, on a chronological instead of a topographical basis. The division was according to the reigns of Egypt's rulers, and Sarhank attempted, albeit unsystematically, explanations of historical events. His views were narrow, perhaps shaped by his professional respect for authority, but he tried to look beneath the surface of raw facts. His effort did not pass unnoticed among other historians. Volume 3 was supposed to contain the history of nearly all European states, but only a brief first part saw the light of day in 1923.

Bibliography: Little has been written on Sarhank. Jack A. Crabbs, *The Writing of History in Nineteenth-Century Egypt: A Study in National Transformation* (American University in Cairo Press; Detroit: Wayne State University Press, 1984), pp. 136–143; Jamāl al'Dīn al-Shayyāl, *al-Ta'rīkh wa'l-Mu'arrikhūn fī Miṣr fi'l-Qarn al-Tāsi' 'Ashr* (History and Historians in Nineteenth-Century Egypt), (Cairo: Maktabat al-Nahḍa al-Miṣriyya, 1958), pp. 124–139; Aḥmad Ṭarabayn, *al-Ta'rīkh wa'l-Mu'arrikhūn al-'Arab fi'l-'Aṣr al-Ḥadīth* (History and Arab Historians in Modern Times), (Damascus: Matba'at al-Inshā', 1970), pp. 85–88.

Samir Saul

AL-SHAYYĀL, Jamāl al-Dīn (Damietta, 1911–Alexandria, 1967), Egyptian historian and professor of Islamic history at the University of Alexandria (1943–1967). Al-Shayyāl was a professional historian who demonstrated the conscientious and dispassionate scholarship requisite in his position. His interests ranged over a variety of fields, such as the culture of Egypt, Islamic history, and urban history. His M.A. dissertation, accepted by the Faculty of Arts in Alexandria in 1945, dealt with the policy of translating European works implemented in Egypt in the first half of the nineteenth century. In 1950 he published *Ta'rīkh al-Tarjama fī Miṣr fī 'Ahd al-Ḥamla al-Firinsiyya* (The History of Translation in Egypt at the Time of the French Expedition), and five years later the more extensive *Ta'rīkh al-Tarjama wa'l-Ḥaraka al-Thaqāfiyya fī 'Aṣr Muḥammad 'Alī* (The History of Translation and of the Cultural Movement in the Epoch of Muḥammad 'Alī). He prepared lectures on the modern Islamic reform movement (1957) and authored a concise biography of *Rifā'a al-Ṭahṭāwī* (1958).

Turning to urban history, he wrote *Mujmal Ta'rīkh Dumyāṭ Siyāsiyyan wa Iqtiṣ-ādiyyan* (1949; Synopsis of the History of the Political and Economic History of Damietta), *Mujmal Ta'rīkh al-Iskandariyya* (1949; Synopsis of the History of Alexandria) and *Iskandariyya, Tūbughrafiyya al-Madīna wa Taṭawwuruha min Aqdam al-'Usūr ilā al-Waqt al-Ḥāḍir* (1952: Alexandria, Its Topography and Development from the Earliest Times to the Present). He composed short biographies of famous Alexandrians in *A'lām al-Iskandariyya fi'l-'Aṣr al-Islāmī* (1965; Eminent Personalities of Alexandria in the Islāmic Era). Al-Shayyāl was a firm exponent of the necessity of using primary sources for the study of the Islamic period and edited an important collection of twenty-three Fāṭimid documents on the caliphate and the ministry entitled *Majmū'at al-Wathā'iq al-Fāṭimiyya* (1958). He thus rendered a signal service to Islamic historical studies. In his two-volume *Ta'rīkh Miṣr al-Islāmiyya* (1967; History of Islamic Egypt), he stressed that history could not be confined to political and military events, but had to include the role the people played in molding society and creating the elements of civilization. Al-Shayyāl will perhaps be best remembered as a historian of Egyptian historiography; in that domain, he followed in the footsteps of Muḥammad Muṣṭafa Ziyāda. After publishing the letters of al-Maqrīzī (q.v.), he produced an important study entitled *al-Ta'rīkh wa'l-Mu'arrikhūn fī Miṣr fi'l-Qarn al-Tāsi' 'Ashr* (1958; History and Historians in Nineteenth-Century Egypt). Along with the analysis of the life and work of individual historians, he examined the separate historical genres, the conditions that influenced historical research and historical methodology. He successfully combined attention to specific questions with an awareness of larger patterns, while simultaneously placing historiography in the general context of national culture. A valuable study by al-Shayyāl came out in 1969 under the title *al-Ta'rīkh al-Islāmī wa Atharuhu fi'l-Fikr al-Ta'rīkhī al-Urrubī fī 'Aṣr al-Nahḍa* (Islamic History and Its Influence on Historical Thought in Europe During the Renaissance). He also wrote numerous articles and participated frequently in international symposia.

Bibliography: Ḥasan Ḥabashī, ''Kalimat Ta'bīn fī Dhikrati Wafāt al-Marḥūm al-Ustādh Jamāl al-Dīn al-Shayyāl'' (Speech in Commemoration of Professor Jamāl al-Dīn al-Shayyāl), *al-Majallat al-Ta'rīkhiyya al-Miṣriyya* (The Egyptian Historical Journal), 13 (1967): 3–14; Niqūlā Yūsuf, *A'lām min al-Iskandariyya* (Eminent Personalities from Alexandria), (Alexandria: Munsha'at al-Ma'ārif, 1969), pp. 300–305.

Samir Saul

AL-SHIDYĀQ, Tannūs (al-Ḥadath, Lebanon, c. 1794–Beirut?, 1861), Lebanese historian. Al-Shidyāq spent his active life in the service of the Shihāb *amīrs* (princes), while pursuing a career as a merchant and tutoring students. Al-Shidyāq's family had provided teachers and clerks to Lebanese *amīrs* of all faiths for over a century. It belonged to a socioprofessional group on which, along with the Maronite clergy, fell responsibility for intellectual activity in premodern Lebanon. It was from that milieu that several writers emerged in the mid-nineteenth century to usher in the renaissance in Arabic literature and culture.

Ṭannūs' younger brother Fāris (1804–1887) represented one such reformer. Al-Shidyāq abridged two historical works of the Maronite Archbishop al-Duwayhī—one in 1833, and another in 1845. He prepared a dictionary of Lebanese colloquial Arabic in 1833. His *Ta'rīkh Mulūk al-'Arab wa'l-Islām* (History of the Rulers of the Arabs and of Islām) was authored in 1848. The history of his family, *Ta'rīkh wa A'māl Banū al-Shidyāq* (The History and Deeds of the Scions of al-Shidyāq) was written in 1850. Al-Shidyāq's chief contribution came in the shape of a book entitled *Akhbār al-A'yān fī Jabal Lubnān* (1859; Chronicles of the Notables of Mount Lebanon). The author broke new ground in the Lebanese context by making the object of his study the history of the country as a whole rather than that of his own religious community. Previously dominated by the Maronite clergy, Lebanese historiography had been strictly confessional. Al-Shidyāq's secular approach led him to collate information in the first part of the *Akhbār* and to draft a valuable geographical, historical, and demographic intro-duction in which Lebanon was portrayed for the first time as a single unit. However, even for al-Shidyāq, the country remained in fact an abstract frame-work. In the second part, his real subject unfolded, namely, the history of twenty-five Maronite, Druze, and Muslim families of notables. Each family's genealogy was traced chronologically in a separate chapter. In the third and longest part, al-Shidyāq recounted the history of the period during which eight clans governed, a chapter being reserved for each one. His method was essentially that of the compiler, faithfully reproducing his sources without criticizing them. The *Akhbār* is still considered one of the basic compendia on the history of Lebanon.

Bibliography: Kamal S. Salibi, *Maronite Historians of Medieval Lebanon* (Beirut: American University of Beirut, 1959), pp. 161–233; Khayr al-Dīn al-Ziriklī, *al-A'lām* (Eminent Personalities), Vol. 3 (Beirut, 1980 edition), p. 231—an important modern reference work.

Samir Saul

AL-ṬAHṬĀWĪ, Rifā'a Rāfi' (Ṭahṭa, Egypt, 1801–Cairo, 1873), Egyptian teacher, editor, historian. Al-Ṭahṭāwī was one of the leading figures of the movement to reform Egypt's intellectual life and modernize its educational sys-tem. Demonstrating his commitment to progress in very diverse fields, he ex-ercised a profound influence on the cultural transformation of his country. Central to his contribution was the awakening of interest in the study of history. With al-Ṭahṭāwī, Egyptian historiography accomplished its first steps toward accep-tance as a genuine and autonomous field of learning. His reformist orientation owed much to the early friendship he established as a student at al-Azhar with Shaykh Ḥasan al-'Aṭṭār who had been a close associate of 'Abd al-Rahman al-Jabartī (q.v.). It was thanks to al-'Aṭṭār that he was chosen as chaplain to the first Egyptian students' mission to France. His stay in Paris lasted from 1826 to 1831, during which time he observed a way of life utterly foreign to his own. In 1834 he published his impressions in a work entitled *Takhlīs al-Ibrīz fī Tal-khīs Barīz* (The Purification of Gold in a Sketch on Paris). It was an account of his stay, replete with acute insights on conditions in France and the impressions they left on his mind. Like al-Jabartī, al-Ṭahṭāwī showed curiosity about the new world he encountered. His outlook was at once critical and well disposed. He admired French civilization and highly esteemed the qualities of the French people. *Takhlīs* represented an invaluable document recording contact between cultures and departure from stereotypes in Egyptian perceptions of the outside world.

Al-Ṭahṭāwī was named translator at the School of Medicine (1831) and then at the School of Artillery (1833). He was appointed director of the School of Languages (1835), an innovative center of learning where the traditional curriculum was combined with new branches of learning such as history, geography, and the natural sciences. For the first time, history was to be taught in school as a separate subject. A translation department was later adjoined to the school. From that vantage point, al-Ṭahṭāwī instilled in the minds of his students an interest in the modern world and was instrumental in the development of their critical faculties. He and his collaborators left a lasting mark on Egyptian society through their translations of European books in all fields, from law to geometry. Al-Ṭahṭāwī's own production was substantial and included works on novel subjects, such as the education of women. In 1870 he was appointed editor of *Rawḍat al-Madāris* (Garden of the Schools), a journal devoted to the introduction of a modern outlook and general enlightenment. Articles on history were numerous, often written by al-Ṭahṭāwī himself. Apart from the prominent role he accorded to the study of history, al-Ṭahṭāwī shifted the focus of attention from the Islamic past to that of Egypt. This important turn was taken in 1868 in his *Anwār Tawfīq al-Jalīl fī Akhbār Miṣr wa Tawthīq Banī Ismaʿil* (The Glow of Splendid Success in the Story of Egypt and the Strengthening of Ismaʿil's Descendants). Egypt was the framework. It became a distinct entity with a continuous history. Al-Ṭahṭāwī traced its past beyond the advent of Islam; he paid attention to Pharaonic Egypt, reflecting the advances of Egyptology. This was a great stimulus to the development of the concept of patriotism. He declared his intention of serving his country (*waṭan*) in *Manāhij al-Albāb al-Miṣriyya fī Mabāhij al-Ādāb al-ʿAṣriyya* (1869; The Course of Egyptian Hearts in the Enjoyment of the Contemporary Arts). A most eclectic book, it was conceived as a vade-mecum to contemporary civilization and a plan for the progress of Egypt. The author dealt with a wide variety of subjects, especially history and economic reforms. *Manāhij* stood at the crossroads between the medieval chronicle and modern historical writing. Although the contents were heterogeneous and the form was poorly structured, the matter was divided into subjects, rather than being strewn haphazardly in successive time frames. Moreover, al-Ṭahṭāwī did not just record; he systematically interpreted and furnished historical evidence to support his views.

Bibliography: Ahmad Ahmad Badawī, *Rifāʿa Rāfiʿ al-Ṭahṭāwī* (Cairo: Maṭbaʿat Lajnat al-Bayān alʿArabī: n.d.); Jack A. Crabbs, *The Writing of History in Nineteenth-Century Egypt: A Study in National Transformation* (American University in Cairo Press; Detroit:

Wayne State University Press, 1984), pp. 67–86; Gilbert Delanoue, *Moralistes et politiques musulmans dans l'Egypte du XIXe siècle (1798–1882)* (Cairo; Institut Français d'Archéologie Orientale, 1982), Section V, Part 1; J. Heyworth-Dunne, "Rifā'ah Badawī Rāfi' al-Ṭahṭāwī: the Egyptian Revivalist," *Bulletin of the School of Oriental and African Studies* 9 (1937–1939): 961–967, and 10 (1940–1942): 399–415; Ḥusayn Fawzī al-Najjār, *Rifa'ā al-Ṭahṭāwī* (Cairo: Dār Miṣr li'l-Ṭibā'a, 1962); *Mihrajān Rifā'a Rāfi' al-Ṭahṭāwī (Rifā'a Rāfi' al-Ṭahṭāwī Festival)* (Cairo: al-Majlis al-A'lā . . . , 1960); Ahmad Rachad, "Rifaa Rafé el Tahtaoui," *Cahiers d'histoire égyptienne*, serie 1 (1948–1949), pp. 175–185; Jamāl al-Dīn al-Shayyāl, *Rifā'a Rāfi' al-Ṭahṭāwī, 1801–1873* (Cairo: Dār al-Ma'ārif, 1958).

Samir Saul

AL-TURK, Niqūlā (Deir al-Qamar, Lebanon, 1763–Deir al-Qamar, 1828), Lebanese historian and poet. Like 'Abd al-Rahman al-Jabartī (q.v.), al-Turk wrote an account of the French expedition to Egypt. He was a poet at the court of the Druze leader, Amīr Bashīr II. Sent by his patron to Egypt in 1798 to report on French activities, al-Turk settled in Damietta until 1804. His only known work was undertaken at the request of the prince. It was entitled *Dhikr Tamalluk al-Fransawiyya al-Aqṭār al-Miṣriyya wa'l-Bilād al-Shāmiyya* (Account of the French Occupation of Egypt and Syria). Despite the acuteness of his observation, al-Turk could not be said to have produced more than a chronicle. He seldom searched for explanations beyond the surface of phenomena. His attempts to discover the causes of events were at best ephemeral. His attitude toward the French appeared as one of unqualified approval and has been thought to rest on the fact that he was a Greek Catholic (Melkite). But al-Turk was a poet prone to flourishes, much given to reciting panegyrics about rulers or important men, and the French were not the only recipients of his praise. His account has been overshadowed by that of al-Jabartī.

Bibliography: George M. Haddad, "The Historical Work of Niqūlā el-Turk 1763–1828," *Journal of the American Oriental Society* 81 (1961): pp. 247–251; Henri Pérès, "L'Institut d'Egypte et l'oeuvre de Bonaparte jugés par deux historiens arabes contemporains," *Arabica* 4 (May 1957): 113–130.

Samir Saul

ZAYDĀN, Jurjī (Beirut, 1861–Cairo, 1914), Lebanese-Egyptian historian, editor, novelist. Zaydān was one of the bevy of Syrians and Lebanese who settled in Egypt in the nineteenth century. His historical studies were part of his contribution to the awakening of an Arab national consciousness. Education and enlightenment were always primary in his view, and he never engaged in political activity. Nor did he seek political independence from the Ottoman Empire for the Arabs, fearing direct European control. Syrian and Lebanese intellectuals acted as a leaven to foster national awareness. Based on common language, culture, history, and territory, it demarcated the Arabs from other Muslims while looking beyond specific regions. Being often members of the Christian minority in a Muslim world, they were among the first to feel the need to transcend confessional divisions in society and give a secular stamp to Arab national identity. In this they encountered the ire of traditionalists, Muslim and Christian. In Zaydān's case, national outlook grew alongside, indeed arose from, a sense of individualism that led him to overcome narrow communal sentiment. He had little formal education and was largely self-taught. Although a Greek Orthodox, he was not a practicing believer. His early sympathy for Darwinism was to remain one of the basic manifestations of a rational world-view (as was his brief membership in Freemasonry). He went to Egypt in 1883 and became, for a short period, editor of the daily newspaper *al-Zamān* (Time). In 1886 he published his first book, entitled *al-Alfāẓ al-'Arabiyya wa'l-Falsafa al-Lughawiyya* (Arabic Terms and the Philosophy of Language). Therein he rejected the notion of classical norms and applied the concept of evolution to the Arabic language. He launched the periodical *al-Hilāl* (The Crescent) in 1892 and settled until the end of his life as editor and independent writer. *Al-Hilāl* was a highly successful magazine aimed at disseminating information on all aspects of modern life and culture. It was a didactic instrument of the first order and is still published today. Besides being nearly its sole writer, Zaydān was a prolific author. From 1891 to 1914 he published twenty-two historical novels (of which seventeen were set in the context of the early Muslim era). They are to be considered more as an introduction to history for the layperson than as creative endeavors. *Ta'rīkh Miṣr al-Ḥadīth* (Modern History of Egypt), appearing in 1889, was conceived as a textbook for students. Zaydān expressed his surprise that historians who wrote about Egypt had not developed a method understandable to the general public (*al-'āma*) and acceptable to the elite (*'al-khaṣa*). He was even more surprised that the country's history was not taught in schools. This, he thought, was due to the absence of a textbook. By modern history, Zaydān meant the period from the advent of Islam to his day. His methodology was not innovative since he subdivided his account according to the succession of reigns, and he relied on classical Arabic and some secondary European sources without giving references. It was to some extent forward-looking in that Zaydān concentrated on events in an orderly way, avoiding rambling digressions or accumulation of disparate information. If attempts at explanation appeared feeble, this was in keeping with the rationalist-positivist frame in which the book was cast.

Between 1901 and 1906, Zaydān published the five volumes of his magnum opus, *Ta'rīkh al-Tamaddun al-Islāmī* (History of Islamic Civilization). He stressed that the real history of the Islamic *umma* (community) was that of its civilization, and not its wars and conquests. Only Volumes 1 and 4 dealt with political history. Volumes 2, 3, and 5 presented, respectively, the wealth of the state, science and learning, and social structure and way of life. Zaydān read over one hundred Arabic and European reference works, and provided notes. Islam was approached not as a religion but as a secular culture common to all Arabs. Emphasis was placed on the period when the Arab element was dominant within Islam. He pursued this theme in a sequel published in 1908, *al-'Arab qabl al-Islām* (The Arabs before Islam). Arab civilization was detached from

Islam and taken back in time to include that of the ancients, such as the Babylonians. Islam thus became one stage in a continuous national development. His major four-volume study, *Ta'rīkh Ādāb al-Lugha al-'Arabiyya* (1910–1914; History of Arabic Literature), was really a vast intellectual history placing the various fields of learning in their historical context. Zaydān also wrote on the history of Freemasonry (1889), England (1899), Greece and Rome (1899); on geography (1891); on the lives of nineteenth–century personalities (1907), and so on. In the end, Zaydān is to be remembered, not for original or profound scholarship, but for having ably popularized a rational, factual, and analytical conception of history.

Bibliography: Anwar al-Jundī, *Jurjī Zaydān, Mun shi' al-Hilāl* (Jurjī Zaydān, Founder of al-Hilāl), (Cairo: Maktabat al-Anjlū al-Miṣriyya, n.d.); Ḥamdī Alkhayāt, *Ǧurǧī Zaidān. Leben und Werk* (Cologne, 1973); C. Desormeaux, ''L'oeuvre de Georges Zaidan,'' *Revue du monde musulman*, no. 4 (1908): 837–845; Juzīf Ḥarb, *Jurjī Zaydān, Rijāl fī Rajul* (Jurjī Zaydān, Facets of the Man), (Beirut, 1970); Muḥammad 'Abd al-Ghanī Ḥasan, *Jurjī Zaydān* (Cairo, 1970); Thomas Philipp, *Ǧurǧī Zaidān His Life and Thought* (Beirut, Orient-Institut der Deutschen Morgenlandischen Gesellschaft 1979); Louis Ware, ''Jurjī Zaidān: The Role of Popular History in the Formation of a New Arab World View,'' doctoral dissertation (Princeton University, 1973).

Samir Saul

Great Historians: Armenian

Č'AMČ'IAN, Mik'ayēl (Constantinople, 1738–Constantinople, 1823), Armenian historian. A member of the Armenian Mekhitarist order. Č'amč'ian received his education at the Mekhitarist monastery on the island of San Lazzaro in Venice. In 1762 he was ordained a priest, and from 1769 to 1775 he served as the pastor for the Armenian Catholic community of Basra, Iraq. From 1775 to 1789 he taught at the Mekhitarist monastery in Venice, and also wrote and published his three-volume *Patmut'iwn Hayoc'* (History of Armenia). Č'amč'ian spent the remaining thirty–four years of his life in Constantinople where he founded a parochial school. In 1820 he was involved in a movement that had set as its goal the unity of the Armenian Catholic and Armenian Orthodox communities. Besides his ecclesiastical duties and teaching, Č'amč'ian was a prolific writer, a grammarian, a profound theologian, and an exegetist. He is considered the first modern Armenian historian. The first volume of his book, which was published in 1784, covers the history of Armenia from the time of the creation to the year A.D. 441. The second volume, published in 1785, is about the period of Persian, Byzantine, and Arab domination and the Bagratid Kingdom, ending with the year 1080. The third volume, published in 1786, covers the events from the end of the eleventh century to the time of the author. Č'amč'ian's *History* is an encyclopedic work covering the entire breadth of the Armenian experience. It is still useful to the modern student of Armenian history, especially since he occasionally uses sources about which we do not know. Č'amč'ian generally indicates his sources and has a critical approach in evaluating their information. His philosophy of history and point of view, however, are not very progressive, and he is forever trying to show that the fathers of the Armenian Church were not in disagreement with the doctrinal formulations of the Roman Church. Although Č'amč'ian used the general historical methodology of Western scholars of his time, he was apparently little influenced by the ideas of the Enlightenment.

Bibliography: M. Chamchian, *History of Armenia, from B.C. 2247 to the year of Christ 1780*, trans. from the original Armenian by J. Avdall, 2 vols., (Calcutta, 1827); Mesrop Čanašian, *Patmut'iwn ardi hay grakanut'ean* (History of Modern Armenian Literature) Vol. 1 (Venice, 1953); Sahak Čēmčēmian, "H. Mik'ayēl Č'amč'ian ew ir Hayoc' Patmut'iwne [Fr, Mik'ayēl Č'amč'ian and his History of Armenia]," *Pazmaveb* 139, nos.3–4 (1981).

K. H. Maksoudian

MANANDIAN, Hakob H. (Akhaltskha, 1873–Erevan, 1952), Armenian historian. Received his education in the universities of Jena, Leipzig, and Strasbourg and received his Ph.D. degree from the University of Jena in 1897. In 1898 Manandian was awarded a diploma of the first order from the University of St. Petersburg as a candidate of Armenian–Persian philology. In 1909 he graduated from the University of Dorpat with a law degree. From 1900–1907 he taught at a number of schools in the Caucasus, including the Gēorgean Seminary at Vataršapat, Armenia. From 1909 to 1919 he worked at Baku as a lawyer. From 1921 to 1931 he taught at the University of Erevan; in 1939 he was elected a member of the Academy of Sciences of the USSR and in 1943 to the Academy of Sciences of the Armenian SSR. He devoted the rest of his life to research and writing. Manandian wrote more than one hundred studies in his native Armenian, Russian, and German, dedicated to various aspects of ancient and medieval periods of the history of Armenia and Transcaucasia. He focused more on economic history. He had the advantage of being a classical philologist and knowing not only Western but also several oriental languages. Trained according to the historical methodology of the German tradition, he tried to apply this tradition to a Marxist interpretation of Caucasian and Armenian history and became one of the founders of Soviet Armenian historiography. Among his major historical works are the *O torgovle i gorodakh Armenii v sviazi s mirovoi torgovlei drevnykh vremen* (1930; The Trade and Cities of Armenia in Relation to Ancient World Trade); *Feodalizme hin Hayastanum* (1939; Feudalism in Ancient Armenia), *Hayastani glxavor Čanaparhners est Pewtengeryan k'artezi* (1936; The Major Highways of Armenia according to Carta Peutingeriana); *Tigran B. ew Hrome* (1940; Tigran II and Rome) and *K'nnakan tesut'yun hay zotovrdi patmut'yan* (3 vols., 1947–1960; Critical History of the Armenian People). He also published several historical sources and made a study of the medieval Hellenizing School in Armenia. Manandian's major work was his *Critical History of the Armenian People*, which he was not able to finish. This colossal work traces the history of the Armenian people from its origins to the beginning of the fifteenth century. On the basis of original sources and modern studies, Manandian tried to reconstruct the ancient and medieval periods of Armenian history. The first volume covers the ancient period until the first century of our era. The second volume is in two parts, of which the first is devoted to the period of the Armenian Arsacid Dynasty. The second, which was to cover the period from the fifth to the eleventh centuries, was never completed. Manandian, however, had written many minor studies on various aspects of this period which were compiled and published as the second part of the second volume. The third volume is about the period of the Seljuk and Mongol rule and is probably the most vulnerable part of the entire work, since in the 1940s Manandian had no access to the latest Western scholarship on the subject. Despite the shortcomings of this work, one can see Manandian's critical approach toward the original sources.

Bibliography: L. H. Babayan and V. A. Hakobyan, *Hakob Manandyan* (Erevan, 1974) [in Armenian].

K. H. Maksoudian

Great Historians: Australian

BEAN, Charles Edwin Woodrow (Bathurst, Australia, 1879–Sydney, Australia, 1968), Australian historian. Journalist at the *Sydney Morning Herald* (1908), official war correspondent (1914), official war historian (1919). An Australian historian of great originality who created the Anzac legend from which stemmed the national belief that Australia achieved nationhood through the heroic sacrifice of the Australian and New Zealand Army Corps (ANZAC) at Gallipoli during the Dardanelles operation, 1915. Bean's ideas had their genesis in an early publication *On the Wool Track* (1910) which described the authentic Australian character as a product of the bush and the outback (the dry interior). He pictured the authentic Australian as tough, resourceful, courageous, loyal to his mates, as of exceptional endurance owing to a persistent battle against flood and drought, sardonic, and often a larrikin in his leisure time. Bean compiled *The Anzac Book* (1916) and wrote *The Story of Anzac* (2 vols., 1921, 1924) based on the theme that the heroism of the Australian infantry, made up of more townsmen than bush workers, was proof that the values of the Australian outback had molded the Australian national character. Bean's histories provided two additional themes, both touching on the unity of Australian history: First, the unity in Australian history is to be discovered in the study of the character of its peoples and their reaction to Australia's distinctive geographical environment; second, the Anzac episode is evidence of the transmission of the bush ethos of the nineteenth-century colonial era to the urban setting of twentieth-century Australia. Thus, there is a unity in Australia between its nineteenth and twentieth centuries, its colonial and its Commonwealth eras, its bush and its towns. The Anzac heroism at Gallipoli also satisfied a colonial longing for an event to prove that colonial peoples were not inferior to their mother race. Bean's glorification of Anzac created Australia's first civil religious event, the public observance of

April 25 as a day of mourning and the glorification of heroic sacrifice. In the 1920s Australians erected thousands of wayside shrines for April 25 celebrations, and the federal government built a temple of war in the federal capital, Canberra, which in size and setting has surpassed every other Australian religious building. The idea of writing Australia's history around a war event has its rival in the radical nationalist tradition which pictures Australian history as a struggle between a utopian socialism (which made Australia the world's most advanced social laboratory around 1900) and capitalism. In 1961 Bean's Anzac tradition was attacked in Alan Seymour's play *The One Day of the Year*. Public hostility toward this play persists; the Anzac tradition enjoys a favorable exposure in films and popular writing, which confirms it as a permanent feature of the Australian cultural heritage.

Bibliography: C. E. W. Bean, "The Writing of the Australian Official History of the Great War," *Journal of the Royal Australian Historical Society* 24 (1938): 85–112; K. S. Inglis, *C. E. W. Bean. Australian War Historian* (St. Lucia, 1970); K. S. Inglis, "A Sacred Place: The Making of the Australian War Memorial," *War and Society* 3, no. 2 (1985): 99–126; D. McCarthy, *Gallipoli to the Somme. The Story of C. E. W. Bean* (Sydney, 1983).

George P. Shaw

BONWICK, James (Lingfield, Surrey, England, 1817–Southwick, Sussex, England, 1906), Australian historian, pioneer archivist, and colonial schoolmaster resident in Australia 1841–1875. Bonwick wrote extensively on the origins of most Australian colonies, but is principally remembered for *The Last of the Tasmanians* (1870) and *Curious Facts of Old Colonial Days* (1870). Like most of his contemporaries he drew on oral sources. He told a gathering of the Royal Colonial Institute, London, in 1895 that he had talked directly with convicts, bush-rangers, gold-diggers, and even a member of the New South Wales Corps disbanded in 1811. The gold rushes of the 1850s greatly expanded British public interest in Australia and generated a considerable historical literature that alarmed Bonwick with its content of myth and exaggeration. To correct this distortion he set about in the 1880s establishing "a collection of records by each of the Colonies—like as Canada has so nobly made, by the hands of Mr Brymner the archivist." Bonwick recognized that the key documents on Australian colonial history were in England, returned there, and in 1887 was appointed archivist for the Official History of New South Wales. From this came the Bonwick transcripts consisting of 104,000 folios, now housed in the Mitchell Library, Sydney, and the *Historical Records of New South Wales* (8 vols., 1892–1901). These collections opened up the documents of the British Public Record Office, the principal missionary societies, and private collections in England and Ireland to Australian historians, and laid the foundation on which Ernest Scott (q.v.) and George Arnold Wood (q.v.) pioneered Australian academic history in the universities. Bonwick produced three revisionist histories of his own based on English archival investigations: *First Twenty Years of Australia. A History*

Founded on Official Documents (1882), *Australia's First Preacher: The Rev. Richard Johnson First Chaplain of NSW* (1898), and *Captain Cook in New South Wales or The Mystery of Naming Botany Bay* (1901). Bonwick's pioneering archival work was extended by F. Watson's *Historical Records of Australia* (34 vols., 1914–1926) and the Joint Copying Project which is currently placing on microfilm all documents relevant to Australia presently held in public and private collections in the United Kingdom. Another 23,000 folios of Bonwick's transcripts are in other Australian libraries.

Bibliography: *Australian Dictionary of Biography*, vol. 3 (Melbourne, 1969), pp. 190–192; James Bonwick, *The Writing of Colonial History* (Sydney, 1895); Guy Featherstone, "James Bonwick. I. Towards a Bibliography. II. The Bonwick Transcripts," *LaTrobe Library Journal* 3, no. 11 (1973): 62–70.

George P. Shaw

FITZPATRICK, Brian Charles (Warnambool, Victoria, 1905–Sydney, 1965), Australian writer and historian. Graduated from the University of Melbourne, worked as a journalist, and was awarded a university research fellowship. Despite his fellowship Fitzpatrick was never to receive a university teaching post. He produced a series of major and highly influential studies of Australian history from outside the academic establishment. These works pioneered research into the economic development of the country and bequeathed a distinctly left-wing slant to thinking about Australian development. Fitzpatrick is reputed to have been the first to apply Marxian concepts of class struggle to the whole of Australian history. Whatever is thought of the tenability of his methodology, Fitzpatrick's work represents a milestone in Australian intellectual history. His chief contributions were *British Imperialism in Australia, 1783–1883* (1939) and its sequel, *The British Empire in Australia* (1941) as well as the *Australian Commonwealth* (1936). The first two represent an attempt to unify the Australian experience within the framework of an economic interpretation. Fitzpatrick sought to show that Australian political and social history remained unintelligible unless located in the broader context of the social and economic conditions of Great Britain. He was concerned to emphasize that the economy of Australia was enmeshed into and essentially controlled by the forces and impulses of the British economy, in particular by the flow of British capital and labor (Bourke, 1974). For their time, these studies were the nearest approach to the statement of a unifying theme in Australian history. Fitzpatrick was a militant champion of social justice throughout his life. He believed that the intellectual who was involved in public affairs and prepared to inform the people could influence events. Consequently, in 1936 he founded the Australian Council for Civil Liberties and became its secretary, producing many political pamphlets.

Bibliography: Helen Bourke, "A Reading of Brian Fitzpatrick," *Labour History* no.27 (1974): 1–11; J. A. La Nauze, "The Study of Australian History," *Historical Studies* no.33 (1959): 1–11.

John A. Moses

LANG, John Dunmore (Greenoch, Scotland 1799–Sydney, Australia 1878), Australian historian. Presbyterian cleric, colonial politician, and immigration entrepreneur. Lang's *An Historical and Statistical Account of New South Wales* (2 vols., 1834, revised 1837, 1852, 1875) was the principal history of Australia available to local and British readers for most of the first century of Australian settlement. Lang turned historian to prove false the fashionable Malthusianism of his native Scotland where poverty and premature death were the accepted consequences of overbreeding. By contrast, Lang advertised Australia as an ideal location for industrious immigrants with little or no capital and was the first colonist actively to promote the immigration of the industrious poor to Australia. Such immigrants, in addition to bettering themselves, served two other purposes: First, their integrity and industry helped offset the infamy of Australia's convict origins and constituted the true foundation of a future free country; and second, their Protestant culture and their Anglo-Saxon or Celtic racial origins made Australia the ideal base from which to Christianize the Pacific. Lang wrote with a pronounced bias. He dealt favorably with persons and events that contributed to the creation of a Protestant free-settler democracy in Australia and condemned all attempts to reproduce titled classes or privileged institutions in the new settlements. Despite this bias, four of Lang's historical themes remain the subject of historical debate: first, that ex-convicts were rightfully denied civil positions in colonial life and had little influence overall on the formation of colonial society; second, that the working-class origin of most immigrants made democracy the natural form of colonial government; third, that Protestantism had a moral obligation to seek a dominant role in society; and fourth, that British interests were generally exploitative and mostly at odds with colonists' true interests. Lang's juxtaposition of evangelical religious connections and contemporary theories of political economy reflected the two intellectual movements that had a formative influence on colonial life—Utilitarianism and the evangelical revival.

Australia's intellectual traditions today still reflect the strong influence of both. Their basic incompatibility has divided Australians into two groups: those with a religious distrust of intellectual modernity and those who reject religion as anti-intellectual. Australia does not possess a modern intellectual religious tradition and remains essentially a country of nineteenth-century Utilitarian and Protestant evangelical values. Lang wrote voluminously on political and religious matters. He advocated republicanism, and to help Australians learn from the American political experience he wrote *The Coming Event; or the United Provinces of Australia* (1850) and *Freedom and Independence for the Golden Lands of Australia* (1852). He alerted Australians to the ill-consequence of excessive Irish Catholic immigration in *The Question of Questions: Or, Is This Colony to Be Transformed into a Province of Popedom*, a work that contributed significantly to the religious sectarianism still evident in Australian society.

Bibliography: D. W. A. Baker, *Days of Wrath: A Life of John Dunmore Lang* (Melbourne, 1985); George Shaw, "The Discipline of the State. Writing Australian History Since 1819," *Current Affairs Bulletin* 60, no. 4: 4–15.

George P. Shaw

MORAN, Patrick Francis (Leighlinbridge, County Carlow, Ireland, 1830–Manly, New South Wales, 1911) cardinal of the Roman Catholic Church and historian. Arrived in Australia in 1884 having been ordained a priest in Rome in 1853. After a career as professor in the Irish College in Rome, Moran returned to Ireland in 1866 to serve as secretary to his uncle, at that time the cardinal archbishop of Dublin. In 1872 Moran was consecrated bishop of Ossory (Kilkenny) and remained in that see until his appointment to Sydney in 1884. In the following year, he was made the first Australian cardinal, and he then convened the first plenary council of the Roman Church in Australia. As an historian, Moran already had a well-established record of works to his name. These all dealt with themes relating to Irish Catholicism. After his elevation to the rank of Cardinal, Moran determined to become thoroughly Australian. He conceived it as his task to write the history of Australian Roman Catholicism and to stress the Irish Catholic component in the self-perception and identity of the emergent Australian nation. As such, Moran's significance has been as a preeminently partisan Catholic historian who wrote with the historiographical assumptions peculiar to that type of scholarship, his major contribution being a *History of the Catholic Church in Australia* (1896). Moran was also vigorous in Australian political life, being a champion of labor politics as well as the federation movement prior to 1900. Furthermore, his appointment to Sydney marked the end of the control of English Benedictines over the Roman Church in Australia. As an Irishman, Cardinal Moran was distinctly better placed than his English predecessors in office to advise the faithful to think of themselves as Australians first (Inglis, 1958). In this sense Moran was an Australian national historian. It was not possible for him to separate his public activities from his scholarly output. As an Australian cardinal, Moran conceived it as Australia's destiny to become a center of Christian civilization for all the nations of Asia and the Pacific.

Bibliography: A. E. Cahill, "Cardinal Moran and the Chinese," *Manna*, no. 6 (1963): 97–107; Patrick Ford, *Cardinal Moran and the A.L.P.* (Melbourne, 1966); K. S. Inglis, "Catholic Historiography in Australia," *Historical Studies* 8 (1958): 233–253; E. M. O'Brien, "Cardinal Moran's Part in Public Affairs," *Royal Australian Historical Society* 28 (1942): 1–28.

John A. Moses

ROBERTS, Stephen Henry (Maldon, Victoria, 1901–Sydney, 1971), Australian historian and university administrator. Roberts, a graduate and research fellow at Melbourne University, undertook post-graduate studies at London and Paris in 1925–1929. He was subsequently Challis professor of modern history at the University of Sydney (1929–1947) and vice-chancellor and principal of the university (1947–1967). Roberts' *History of Australian Land Settlement 1788–1920* (1924) was the first comprehensive attempt to relate the pattern and variety of land settlement to the land legislation of all colonial and state parliaments. The book reflected Roberts' encounter with the Annales school. In *The Squatting Age in Australia 1835–1847* (1935), Roberts created a total picture of the economic, political, and social circumstances of the rise of the principal conservative force in colonial Australia. He argued that the introduction of government-regulated squatting (a license to use land for a guaranteed period without purchase) attracted "the capitalists and yeomen of England" in sufficient numbers to erode the convict milieu of colonial society and to emerge as the dominant economic and political interest by 1850. Roberts foreshadowed a further study about later conflicts between conservative rural interests and farmers and townsmen, but his dual interest in Australian and European history led him to publish *The House That Hitler Built* (1937). This work reflected Australia's keen memory of its involvement in the Great War of 1914–1918 and its abiding concern that Great Power rivalries in Europe might again disrupt its peace. Earlier, Roberts had published *The History of French Colonial Policy 1870–1925* (1929) and in 1933 the first of many editions of *History of Modern Europe*, a study of Europe and its impact on the world from an Australian's viewpoint, which became an influential matriculation text. Roberts' successor, J. M. Ward, consolidated his predecessor's interest in Australian conservatism, thereby creating a distinctive Sydney historical tradition. By contrast, the Melbourne history school concentrated on the gold rushes rather than the squatting age as formative, and cultivated the study of democracy.

John A. Moses and George P. Shaw

RUSDEN, George William (Leith, England, 1819–Melbourne, 1903), Australian historian. Educationalist, public servant, and pamphleteer. Rusden's *History of Australia* (3 vols., 1883) was the first attempt by a colonial educated Australian to write a comprehensive history of Australia that endeavored to meet the standards of contemporary English historical scholarship. Although Rusden did not write for the Australian centenary of 1888, no other historical work displaced his, making it the de facto centenary history of settlement in Australia. Being written before federation created the Commonwealth of Australia in 1901, the history had no clear national focus and reinforced the *Bulletin*'s (Australia's nationalistic weekly journal of affairs and literature) observation on the centenary of 1888 that "a hundred years have left her as they found her—a name but not a nation." Rusden wrote a separate history of each of the six colonies, injecting thematic unity into his story by uncovering a common struggle in all the colonies: first, to propagate British cultural and moral values and second, to fashion the colonial states in the mold of English institutional life. Consequently, Rusden's history of Australia was an exposition of the classic doctrine of colonization: "to found abroad a society similar to that of the mother country." Rusden emphasized the differing circumstances under which each colony was founded in order to heighten the remarkable uniformity of their struggles. His three principal themes were (1) the struggle of the penal colonies against moral turpitude and the laudable efforts of free immigrant minorities to foster public values reminiscent of rural England; (2) the struggle of all the colonies to moderate the excesses of that type of democracy natural to the lower order origins of the bulk of Australian immigrants; and (3) the struggle of colonial leaders to hold the population loyal to Britain despite meddlesome interference from London, especially by English Whig statesmen such as the third Earl Grey, which could have driven the Australian colonies in the direction of the revolutionary North American colonies. Despite this unity of colonial development, Rusden neither foreshadowed that it would culminate in a federation nor urged that it ought to, thereby heightening the suddenness with which the movement to form a Commonwealth emerged and was consummated by 1901.

To a modern reader Rusden's history is remarkable in that it makes no concession to the radical nationalist historians' belief that by the 1880s Australians were aware of their unique opportunity to avoid the social, political, and economic problems that beleaguered Britain, and were taking decisive steps toward establishing Australia as a socialist utopia. By contrast, Rusden emphasized that all Australian colonies were British in ethos, traditionalist in their institutional structure, and flush with imperial loyalty. A reprinting of the entire work in 1897, despite its length (2,090 pages), established that the history was in the mainstream of colonial thought in the later nineteenth century.

Bibliography: Stephen Shortus, "Making Sense of the Colonial Experience: George Rusden or the Bulletin," *Teaching History* 7, no. 2 (1973): 50–64; John M. Ward, "Historiography," in A. L. McLeod, ed., *The Pattern of Australian Culture* (Melbourne, 1963).

George P. Shaw

SCOTT, Ernest (Northampton, England, 1867–Melbourne, 1939), Australian historian. Professor at the University of Melbourne (1913–1931). Scott was perhaps the most influential historian of his generation since some eminent future professors of history passed through his school. These were Sir Keith Hancock, F. Alexander, Stephen Henry Roberts (q.v.), M. Clark, and N. D. Harper. Scott migrated from England to Australia in 1892 to become a journalist on the Melbourne *Herald*. He reported the great economic disasters of the 1890s as well as the rise and triumph of the movement for Australian federation. This aroused a deep interest in the birth and development of the new nation. Consequently, Scott began his career as a historian by investigating the history of European discovery by sea. Scott left journalism to become a Hansard reporter, first for the Victorian Parliament and then from 1901 to 1913 for the Commonwealth Parliament. In 1913 he was invited to apply for the chair of history at the University of Melbourne and was appointed, despite his lack of formal qualifications. Nevertheless, Scott can be regarded as the principal founder of professional history in Australia. He was a rigorous empiricist who insisted on a thorough examination of sources in the Rankean example, but he opposed theorization. Scott's reputation as an historian was achieved while he was still a Hansard reporter. His major works include *Terre Napoléon: A History of French Explorations and Projects in Australia* (London, 1910); *La Pérouse* (Sydney, 1912); *The Life of Matthew Flinders R.N.* (Sydney, 1914); *A Short History of Australia* (London, 1916); *Men and Thought in Modern History* (Melbourne, 1920); *History and Historical Problems* (London, 1925); *Australian Discoveries*, 2 vols. (London, 1929); *Cambridge History of the British Empire*, vol. 7, 4 chapters (Cambridge, 1933); *The Official History of Australia in the War of 1914–18*, vol. 2 (Sydney, 1936); and *A History of the University of Melbourne* (Melbourne, 1936).

Bibliography: *Australian Encyclopaedia* (Sydney, 1977); K. Fitzpatrick, "Ernest Scott and the Melbourne School of History," *Melbourne Historical Journal* (1968): 1–10; J. A. La Nauze, "The Study of Australian History, 1929–1959," *Historical Studies* no.33 (1959): 1–11.

John A. Moses

SHANN, Edward Owen Gilbert (Hobart, Tasmania, 1884–Adelaide, South Australia, 1935), Australian economic historian. Educated at Wesley College, Melbourne and Queens College, University of Melbourne, where he became a tutor. In 1906 Shann was acting professor of philosophy at the University of Adelaide, and in 1909–1910 he was a research student at the London School of Economics. In 1911 he was appointed lecturer in charge of history and economics at the University of Queensland. From 1913 to 1931 he held a chair in history and economics at the University of Western Australia, which from 1931 to 1935 became a chair solely for economics. In 1935 he accepted an appointment to the chair of economics at the University of Adelaide. For the years 1931–1933 Shann was economic adviser to the Bank of New South Wales as well as being one of the economists whose expertise was made use of by the Australian government during the Great Depression. Shann's publications reflect his intimate involvement in the political economy of his lifetime. The most notable works are *Cattle Chosen: The Story of the First Group Settlement in Western Australian 1829 to 1841* (1926); *The Boom of 1890–and Now* (1927); *Bond or Free? Occasional Economic Essays* (1930); *An Economic History of Australia* (1930); *The Crisis of Australian Finance, 1929–1931* (1931) (in collaboration with D. B. Copeland); *The Battle of the Plans* (1931); and *The Australian Price Structure* (1933). Shann's historiographical output is informed with a distinct point of view which was predominantly that of an Anglo-Saxon free trader, a "Manchester man." His purpose was to focus on the private activities by which British settlers had transformed a penal colony and the hunting ground of savages into a productive annex to Europe and Asia. Essentially, Shann saw the future hope for Australia in encouraging the rugged virtues of private enterprise which would provide the energies and vision to develop the resources of the Continent. By contrast, the economic activities of the state were prone to failure. For example, as a West Australian in the 1920s, Shann saw the tariff as a measure introduced to favor the interests of the city dwellers in the eastern states at the expense of the farming community.

Bibliography: *The Australian Encylopaedia* (Sydney, 1977); J. A. La Nauze, "The Study of Australian History 1929–1959," *Historical Studies,* no. 33 (1959): 1–11.

John A. Moses

TURNER, Ian (Melbourne, Australia, 1922–Melbourne, 1978), Australian historian, Communist party activist, and history lecturer at Monash University, Melbourne. Turner was foremost an apologist for the radical nationalist school of Australian historians. This school maintained that special features about Australia's historical experiences separated it radically from its European origins and justified the hope that a new kind of society might be constructed in Australia. This optimism owed much to an alleged "serious-minded meliorism" in the Melbourne intellectual tradition from which it sprang, and was essentially a thoroughly secularized form of the evangelical belief in a redeemed society which, in the case of Australia, was to take the form of a socialist utopia sometimes referred to as "the workingman's paradise". Turner's *The Australian Dream* (1968) was an anthology of Australian writings tracing the genesis of this hope. A critical question for the radical nationalists was why, given such auspicious historical roots, this socialist utopia failed to mature in Australia, especially after successes elsewhere in Russia and China. Turner's *Industrial Labour and Politics: The Dynamics of the Labour Movement in Eastern Australia 1900–1921* (1965) attempted to explain how Australia's enormous commitments to the Great War generated new and unforeseen political commitments that precipitated divisions within the socialist movement and deflected its leaders from their socialist goals. In his *Sydney's Burning* (1969), Turner explored the destruction of the truly radical leadership within the socialist movement, particularly the Industrial Workers of the World (IWW) which left it a Fabian-style movement after 1918. The radical nationalists sustained their hope for a future utopia by concentrating their historical investigation on the trade union movement and popular culture. Turner's *In Union Is Strength* (1976) summed up the history of Australian trade unions. More significant was his pioneering study of Australian popular culture, *Cinderella Dressed in Yella* (1969).

Bibliography: *Overland*, nos. 76–77 (1979), (Ian Turner Memorial Number, a double issue); J. Docker, *In a Critical Condition* (Ringwood, Australia, 1984), chs. 5–6; Ian Turner, "Australian Nationlism and Australian History," *Journal of Australian Studies*, no. 4 (1979): 1–11.

George P. Shaw

WOOD, George Arnold (Salford, England, 1865–Sydney, Australia, 1928), Australian historian. Wood, educated at Owens College, Manchester, and Balliol and Mansfield Colleges, Oxford, was appointed foundation professor of history, University of Sydney, 1891. Wood's convictions were those of a Manchester liberal whose religious nonconformist upbringing instilled in him a hatred of the injustice of English aristocratic and privileged institutions. He was also a moralist in whom a gentle agnosticism had replaced a youthful evangelical faith. Wood arrived in Sydney at an intellectually opportune moment. A small colonial intelligentsia had emerged by the late nineteenth century, a group that sought to unite the benefits of Utilitarianism with the morality, but not the religious faith, of the evangelical revival that had helped shape early colonial life. Wood brought a European, rather than an imperial, perspective to his writings on Australian history. In *The Discovery of Australia* (1922) he gave Australia a place in modern history predating its incorporation into the British Empire. He traced European awareness of Australia back to the Portuguese, linking its discovery to the "genuine scientific curiosity of the age of Roger Bacon" and thereby including Australia in the new world of the Renaissance. Later, C.M.H. Clark ingeniously developed this European perspective in his majesterial *A History of Australia* (5 vols., 1962–1981) and depicted the whole of the first century of Australian life as a rerun in an antipodean setting of the traditional struggle between three European traditions: the Protestant Reformation, the Counter-Reformation, and the Enlightenment. More influential was Wood's manuscript *Foundations of Australia* (1788–1855), which British publishers rejected, probably fearing that its failure to gratify British imperial pride would limit its sales, but extracts appeared in the *Journal of the Royal Australian Historical Society* (1922–1930). Wood argued that Australia's convict settlers were largely "innocent victims" of a vicious British system of aristocratic and agrarian exploitation, and he accused the British government of criminal neglect of the fate of the early colony. Wood credited Australia's survival to the innate good qualities of the so-called criminal convicts and to the resourcefulness of the early governors in the face of British neglect.

Wood's emphasis on the novel and the unique in Australia's origins modified George William Rusden's (q.v.) earlier description of Australia as a classical case study of a colony viewed as an extension of a mother culture. This emphasis on novelty and uniqueness was exaggerated by radical nationalist historians, including Brian Charles Fitzpatrick (q.v.), and Ian Turner (q.v.), into a claim that Australia was essentially different from Britain despite superficial likenesses. By contrast, Wood argued that the early Australian experience helped modify traditional British influences by creating a population that leaned toward nineteenth-century liberal values. In 1930 Sir Keith Hancock's *Australia* developed this idea into the classic statement that Australia was peopled by "Independent Australian-Britons" whose history was basically a struggle between parties of initiative and parties of resistance in which the edge went to the initiatives of the liberal progressives. Wood pioneered the academic study of Australian history, and his chosen topics—Australia's discovery and convict origins—remain areas of seminal debate. The Australian self-image is shaped by the questions: Did Australia originate merely as a convict settlement? Was it not part of a grander design? Did the authoritarian controls in the convict system lay the foundation of an authoritarian state? What impact has fifty years of convictism had on a country only two hundred years old? Wood's pioneering interest in Australian history was consolidated by his successor Stephen Henry Roberts (q.v.) and his pupil Max Crawford who together dominated Australian history at Sydney and Melbourne universities until, in the 1960s and 1970s at the Australian National University, C.M.H. Clark (Crawford's pupil) finally attracted an international audience to Australian history.

Bibliography: R. M. Crawford, *'A Bit of a Rebel.' The Life and Work of George Arnold Wood* (Sydney, 1975).

George P. Shaw

Great Historians: Austrian

ARNETH, Alfred Ritter von (Vienna, 1819–Vienna, 1897), Austrian historian. Arneth's career as an official (after 1868 as head of the Haus-, Hof- und Staatsarchiv) made him aware of the wealth of historical information preserved in this collection. He not only made use of it in his own publications, but was also responsible for making this collection of archival material accessible to historians. Arneth's liberal administration of the main archive of Habsburg documents made this institution a research mecca for historians for many years. Arneth himself concentrated on the history of the eighteenth century, devoting most of his work to the publication of the correspondence of Maria Theresa and her children, Maria Antoinette, Joseph II, and Leopold II. His ten volume *Geschichte Maria Theresias* (1863–1879), though abounding in personal detail and sometimes trivia, nevertheless is rich in insight into the structural changes that took place in the transformation of the Habsburg lands into a modern administration. Arneth's autobiography *aus meinem Leben* (2 Vols., 1891–1892) describing his activities as a member of the Frankfurt Reichstag of 1848 and of the Austrian Parliament, in addition to his scholarly achievements, is a valuable source for the history of Austrian liberalism.

Bibliography: Alfred Ritter von Arneth, *Aus meinem Leben*, 2 Bde (1891–1892); Paul Christoph, "Alfred v. Arneth," *Neue Österreichische Biographie. Grosse Österreicher* (Wien, 1957), S. 47–62.

Fritz Fellner

BRUNNER, Otto (Mödling, Lower Austria, 1898–Hamburg, 1982), Austrian historian. Brunner is one of the most important representatives of social history. Beginning his research activities with a study on *Die Finanzen der Stadt Wien von den Anfängen bis ins 16. Jahrhundert* (1922), Brunner soon turned to the study of the transformation of the feudal society into the modern constitutional state. His first major work, *Land und Herrschaft. Grundfragen der territorialen Verfassungsgeschichte Österreichs im Mittelalter* (1939), treated the problem of the interdependence of economic, social, and legal order in the Habsburg lands. His second major work, *Adeliges Land-leben und europäischer Geist. Leben und Werk Wolf Helmhards von Hohberg 1612–1688* (1949), illustrates the intellectual climate of Central European aristocracy and analyzes the replacement of the old feudal patrimonial order by a modern industrial social structure. Both works are remarkable for the convincing way in which they combine wide sociological perspectives with detailed factual knowledge based on intensive archival research. After the collapse of Nazi Germany, Brunner was dismissed from the chair in medieval history which he had held at the University of Vienna since 1931, and he accepted an appointment to the chair of economic history at the University of Hamburg in 1954. In his books *Neue Wege der Sozialgeschichte* (1956) and *Neue Wege der Verfassungs- und Sozialgeschichte* (1968), he presented social history as a perspective in which constitutional and economic factors are used to explain social structure. Brunner put special emphasis on using and explaining political, constitutional, and social terms and concepts in their respective historical context, a scholarly attitude that made him one of the initiators and editors of the encyclopedia *Geschichtliche Grundbegriffe* (edited since 1972 together with Werner Conze and Reinhard Koselleck). The article, "Feudalism," which he contributed to this work, illustrates in a concentrated form Brunner's way of writing social history.

   Bibliography: Erich Zöllner, "Nekrolog," *Mitteilungen des Instituts für österreichische Geschichtsforschung*, Bd. 90/1982.

Fritz Fellner

CHMEL, Joseph (Olmütz, Moravia, 1798–Vienna, 1858), Austrian historian. As director of the Haus-, Hof- und Staatsarchiv in Vienna, Chmel organized Austrian historical research. He was one of the founders of the Historische Kommission of the Austrian Academy of Sciences in Vienna in 1847, putting special emphasis on making source material on Austrian history available through extensive editorial work. He planned and originated the series *Fontes rerum Austriacarum*, himself editing the first two volumes in 1848–1850. He also founded the document collection *Monumenta Habsburgica*. In a number of small essays Chmel discussed the methods and task of historiography, assigning historical scholarship special importance in shaping patriotism by presenting the past as an element of nation-building. Chmel was not a great historian himself, publishing only one incomplete work of historiography (*Geschichte Kaiser Friedrichs IV*, 2 vols, 1840–1843), but he earned a special place in the history of Austrian historiography for his efforts in preparing the ground for future historiographical work.

Bibliography: Alphons Lhotsky, "Joseph Chmel zum hundertsten Todestag," *Anzeiger der philhist. Klasse der Österreichischen Akademie der Wissenschaften*, Jg. (1958), S. 323–347.

Fritz Fellner

DOPSCH, Alfons (Lobositz, Bohemia, 1868–Vienna, 1953), Austrian historian. Professor at the University of Vienna during 1898–1936, Dopsch was the most eminent Austrian historian in the field of medieval economic history. Trained at the Institut für österreichische Geschichtsforschung, Dopsch scorned the theoretical approach of economics and social sciences and relied instead on careful collection and analyses of original source material from which he drew his interpretations of the economic structure and reality of the early Middle Ages, opposing and discarding the accepted views. In his first book *Die ältere Sozial- und Wirtschaftsordnung der Alpenslawen* (1909) he proved, based on source material, that the then commonly accepted theory of a lower level of the Slav population of the Alpine region did not correspond to historical reality. His second major work, *Die Wirtschaftsentwicklung der Karolingerzeit* (2 vols., 1912–1913) brought a complete reevaluation of the economic situation at the time of Charles the Great based on an analysis of sources from monasteries and feudal records (Urbare). Dopsch discarded the theory of "geschlossene Hauswirtschaft" by demonstrating the continuing importance of "freie Bauern." His most important book, *Wirtschaftliche und soziale Grundlagen der europäischen Kulturentwicklung aus der Zeit von Cäsar bis auf Karl den Grossen* (2 vols., 1918–1920) turned against the then dominant view of the "Katastrophentheorie," the view that the transition of political leadership from the Romans to the Teutons had led to the destruction of ancient culture in Central Europe. Dopsch refuted this view through archaeological material as well geographical and linguistic methods and sources, and showed that, instead of a catastrophe destroying an ancient culture, the transition took place in the form of a gradual and peaceful replacement or overlaying of traditional forms by new ones. Dopsch's interpretation became the subject of a worldwide controversy centering around the opposing view of Henri Pirenne (q.v.). While Dopsch's refutation of the Katastrophentheorie became the generally accepted interpretation of early medieval history, he failed in his next book, *Naturalwirtschaft und Geldwirtschaft in der Weltgeschichte* (1930), when he tried to argue that an abstract distinction between Naturalwirtschaft und Geldwirtschaft could not be upheld by research in the concrete historical material. Otto Hintze's (q.v.) critique laid open the weakness of Dopsch's interpretation, which had overlooked the instrumental character of economic theories. In his last major work, *Herrschaft und Bauer in der deutschen Kaiserzeit* (1939), Dopsch presented his thesis of an uninterrupted continuing evolution of the European economy from the early Middle Ages to the beginning of modern times. Dopsch's position in Austrian historiography is marked by his efforts to present research in economic and social history as one of the most important fields of historiography at a time when most historians saw political history as the main field of historiography. In a sense Dopsch can be seen as the founding father of modern Austrian economic historiography.

Bibliography: "Autobiography," reprinted in Alfons Dopsch, *Beiträge zur Sozial- und Wirtschaftsgeschichte. Gesammelte Aufsätze*, 2 (Reihe, hrgb. von Erna Patzelt: Vienna, 1938); Hanna Vollrath, "Alfons Dopsch," *Deutsche Historiker*, hrgb. von H. U. Wehler, Bd. VII/1980.

Fritz Fellner

FRIEDJUNG, Heinrich (Rotschin, Moravia, 1851–Vienna, 1920), Austrian historian. Friedjung attended the courses of the Institut für Geschichtsforschung in Vienna and participated in seminars taught by Leopold von Ranke (q.v.) at the University of Berlin. After a short service as teacher in the Viennese Academy for Trade, Friedjung turned to active engagement in politics and journalism, serving in his early years with full enthusiasm the cause of pan–German nationalism. Friedjung was one of the authors of the German radical "Linzer Programm." His political and journalistic engagement formed his work as a scholar and historian. Apart from his very first book, *Kaiser Karl IV und sein Anteil am geistigen Leben seiner Zeit* (1875), all his historical writing was devoted to topics of the most recent history and centered around the problem of Austria's role and position in Central Europe and Austria's relation to Germany. His two-volume account, *Kampf um die Vorherrschaft in Deutschland 1859–1866* (1897), was a detailed description of diplomatic events and war actions in the struggle for supremacy in Germany which led to the foundation of the Second Empire under the leadership of Bismarck. In his *Österreich 1848–1860* (2 vols., 1908–1912), Friedjung narrates the political history of the Habsburg monarchy in the period of neo-absolutism from a decidedly liberal point of view. His third major work, *Zeitalter des Imperialismus* (3 vols., 1919–1920), is of great importance as one of the first accounts of the rivalry of European Great Powers between the Franco-Prussian War of 1870 and the outbreak of World War I. Friedjung restricted himself to a description of politics and international relations in the sense of diplomatic history, leaving social, economic, and cultural aspects outside his field of observation. His presentation of international relations was marred by an unabashed anti-British attitude. While working on his historical works as a free-lance scholar and writer, Friedjung remained active in his political engagement serving in an unofficial way as a propagator of an expansionist Balkan imperialism of the Austrian foreign office. This activity put him into the center of a political scandal when it turned out that he had used falsified material when attacking Serbian politicians (Friedjung-Prozess). During World War I, he took up the cause of Friedrich Naumann's Mitteleuropa idea and actively engaged in propagating a closer collaboration with the German Empire. In his scholarly historical publications, as well as in his political activities, Friedjung was a typical representative of German-Jewish liberalism in Austria.

Bibliography: Oswald Redlich, "Nekrolog," *Almanach der Akademie der Wissenschaften* (Vienna), 71 (1921); Heinrich Srbik, "Heinrich Friedjung," *Deutsches Biographisches Jahrbuch (1917–1920)* : 535–545.

Fritz Fellner

HARTMANN, Ludo Moritz (Stuttgart, 1865–Vienna, 1924), Austrian historian. Son of the German writer and participant in the 1848 Revolution, Moritz Hartmann, Ludo Moritz Hartmann grew up as a member of the Viennese Jewish-liberal bourgeoisie. A student of Theodor Mommsen (q.v.) and a graduate of the Vienna Institute für österreichische Geschichtswissenschaft, Hartmann turned first to ancient history with special emphasis on legal and administrative aspects. His first published work, *Untersuchungen zur Geschichte der byzantinischen Verwaltung in Italien* (1889), gained him the title of Privatdozent at the University of Vienna, where he taught for twenty-nine years before being appointed to a professorship. Hartmann was the first Austrian historian influenced by Marxist thinking. He regarded history as an instrument for gaining sociological insights. Together with Emil Szanto, Karl Grünberg, and Stefan Bauern, in 1893 Hartmann founded the *Zeitschrift für Sozial- und Wirtschaftsgeschichte* (since 1903: *Vierteljahresschrift für Sozial- und Wirtschaftsgeschichte*) as an instrument for research on historical phenomena in the context of economic, social, legal, and cultural components. Hartmann's *Geschichte Italiens im Mittelalter* (1897–1923) was based on a similar view of historical research. Throughout his life Hartmann engaged in adult education, which he regarded as a prerequisite for the political emancipation of the working class. *Die Weltgeschichte in gemeinverständlicher Darstellung* (1925) originated from this educational purpose of his scholarly work. Hartmann's political activities as a member of the Austrian Social Democratic party and a proponent of Austria's union with Germany led to a political prominence at the end of his life when, as first Austrian ambassador to Germany after the end of World War I, he tried to fulfill the German dream of unification inherited from 1848. Hartmann ascribed to historical research the task of presenting history "from below," describing the material and socioeconomic mass phenomena rather than a role of the individual. For Hartmann historical scholarship had to fulfill an emancipatory function.

Bibliography: Stefan Bauer, "Ludo Moritz Hartmann," *Neue Österreichische Biographie*, Bd. 3 (1925); Günther Fellner, "Ludo Moritz Hartmann," *Zeitgeschichte*, Heft 3 (1980): 83–108.

Fritz Fellner

HOERNES, Moritz (Vienna, 1852–Vienna, 1917), Austrian prehistorian. Professor at the University of Vienna. Hoernes' immense erudition was reflected in his works, which for many years were considered to be genuine archaeology textbooks—*Die Urgeschichte der Menschen* (1892); *Die Urgeschichte der Menschheit* (1895); *Der diluviale Mensch in Europa* (1903); *Kultur der Vorzeit* (3 vols., 1912). An uncommon sense of proportion and an excessive prudence saved him from hazardous ascriptions and from hypotheses ungrounded on precise facts. Trying to balance various points of view on key problems, for example, defining the origin of and the ethnic group to which certain cultures belonged (for instance, the Neolithic cultures with painted ceramics in the Carpathian–Danubian space: *Die neolithische Keramik in Osterreich. Eine Kunst- und Kulturgeschichtliche Unterschung* [1905], the first stylistic research on prehistoric European ceramics), he refrained from concluding that it belonged to certain Indo-European populations (Gustaf Kossinna [q.v.], or Hubert Schmidt [q.v.]). He also refrained from accepting the autochthonist ideas (H. Schmidt) or their evolution thanks to the oriental influences (Oscar Montelius [q.v.]). Through this attitude and his attempt to remain within the strict limits of scientific facts, Hoernes lent a particular spirit to the archaeology school in Vienna, a spirit from which his successor, O. Menghin, moved away. The same balance, the same method of work, is evident in another famous work, *Urgeschichte der bildenden Kunst in Europa*, 1898, reedited in 1915, and in 1925 published by O. Menghin. Hoernes defined art as a function of human nature (''Art is a function of human nature. Through art, our inner life finds expression. Through art, learning, pleasure and well-being are increased.'') He divided art into three ages, each one corresponding to a certain stage of socioeconomic development (*Das Dreiperioden System der Kunst* : ''These tri-partite divisions, this three-period system, corresponds in age to European prehistoric art. The era of the hunters [or the second half of the older stone age], that is, the era of primitive naturalism, the era of settled agriculture [from the beginning of the newer stone age until the end of the first iron age in middle Europe] was the time of the practice of primary geometric art. This is not new information. Not so well-known, not so generally accepted, is the nature and art of the third economic and artistic age, the era of military dominance.'' Hoernes' name is also connected with research on a Neolithic station in Bosnia, which became the eponymous station of the Butmir culture. He published his research results in collaboration with other researchers (*Die neolithische Station von Butmir bei Sarajewo in Bosnien*, I, in collaboration with W. Radimsky, 1895; II, in collaboration with Fiala, 1898), and he also initiated a local review (Sarajevo), the highly scientific *Mitteilungen aus Bosnien und Herzegovina* (1903).

Bibliography: Jan Filip, *Encyklopadisches Handbuch der Ur-und Frühgeschichte Europas* 1 (Prague, 1966), p. 491; O. Menghin, ''Moritz Hoernes,'' *Wiener Prähistorische Zeitschrift* 4 (1917): 1–23 and the bibliography; O. Menghin, ''Preface,'' *Urgeschichte der bildenden Kunst in Europas* (1925 ed.).

Ligia Bârzu

LORENZ, Ottokar (Iglau, 1832–Jena, 1904), Austrian historian. As a member of the first class in the newly founded Institut fur Österreichische Geschichtsforschung in Vienna in 1855–1856, Lorenz recommended adding Theodor von Sickel (q.v.) to the staff as a paleographer. Thus, Lorenz was instrumental in making the institute a mecca of auxiliary sciences. At twenty-nine, he became professor of history at the University of Vienna and began a career as a university teacher which lasted four decades, first at Vienna and then at the University of Jena. His main fields of research and teaching were the late Middle Ages, the eighteenth century, and problems of methodology in history. With his *Deutsche Geschichte im 13. und 14. Jahrhundert* (vol. 1, 1863, vol. 2, 1866) and his *Deutsche Geschichtsquellen im Mittelalter von der Mitte des 13, bis zum Ende des 14. Jarhunderts* (2 vols. 1886–1887, 3d ed., 1870), Lorenz gained a leading position among German historians. The collection of essays, *Drei Bücher Geschichte und Politik* (1876), describes in its title Lorenz's view of scholarship. Historical research, academic teaching, and collaboration in journals and newspapers were, for him, closely connected and mutually conditioned forms of political engagement. His scholarship was part of a career of public political activity, and his readiness to stand up for his views and to battle for his political convictions resulted in numerous conflicts with the government, with his colleagues, and even with students. Brought up in the German liberal tradition of 1848, Lorenz opposed the narrow radical nationalisms of the 1880s. In the same unrelenting way in which he fought for his political and ideological convictions, Lorenz presented his scholarly opinions. *Geschichtswissenschaft in Hauptrichtungen und Aufgaben* (2 vols., 1886–1891) provoked sharp rebuttals because of his critical discussion of main currents of contemporary scholarship. Under the influence of his friend Leopold von Ranke (q.v.), Lorenz expanded Ranke's ideas on the importance of generational groups into a concept of generational structure as a main element of periodization. His *Lehrbuch der gesamten wissenschaftlichen Genealogie* (1898) made him the founder of genealogy as an historical science. In his last work, *Kaiser Wilhelm und die Begründung des Deutschen Reiches 1866–1871* (1902), Lorenz returned to topics of contemporary history, a field he had started, by publishing several articles on current political problems in historical perspective. His essay, "Deaks Address: Entwurf und das Staatsrecht Österreichs" (1865) was part of the struggle over the reappraisal of Austro-Hungarian relations leading to the compromise of 1867. In his interpretation of history, Lorenz emphasized the role of the state and politics. In his political attitude, he moved from an outspoken Greater Austrian position to a view of history based on the idea of Kleindeutsche. His entire political and scholarly life was characterized by an eagerness to oppose established schools and dominant interpretations. While his works on political history are dated because of these strongly expressed views, Lorenz created enduring achievements by his research on genealogy and the establishment of this field as one of the auxiliary sciences of history.

Bibliography: Alfons Lhotsky, *Geschichte des Instituts für österreichische Geschichtsforschung, 1854–1954* (History of the Austrian Institute for Historical Research, 1854–1954) (1954); Heinrich von Srbik, *Geist und Geschichte vom deutschen Historismus bis zur Gegenwart* (Spirit and History from German Historicism to the Present), 2 vols. (1950–1951); Margarete Steiner, "Die Wiener Zeit des Ottokar Lorenz" (The Vienna Period of Ottokar Lorenz) Phil. Diss. (Vienna, 1954).

Fritz Fellner

PASTOR von Camperfelden, Ludwig Frh.v. (Aachen, 1854–Innsbruck, 1928), Austrian historian. Professor at the University of Innsbruck (1886), director of the Austrian Historical Institute in Rome (1901–1928), Austrian minister at the Vatican (1920–1928). Pastor was among the most prominent Catholic historians. His twenty-two volume *Geschichte der Päpste seit dem Ausgang des Mittelalters* (1886–1933) can be listed among the canon of classical works of historiography. Born to a Rhenian merchant family, Pastor was brought up as a Protestant until the death of his father when Pastor was ten years old. After his conversion to Catholicism, Pastor was greatly influenced by his history teacher, Johannes Janssen (q.v.). Moving to Austria, Pastor had close contact with Catholic historians, such as Onno Klopp and Konstantin von Hofler, who had emigrated from Germany after 1866. Although he was opposed by the liberals who controlled Austrian politics and academic life in those days, Pastor entered the University of Innsbruck. His first publication, *Die kirchlichen Reunionsbestregungen während der Regierung Karls V* (1879) clearly shows the influence of the Catholic school of historians. Researching in archives and libraries in Italy during the 1870s, Pastor collected material for a history of the Catholic Church. During those trips, he was allowed access to the Vatican collections even before these archives were opened to other historians. Using the information he had gathered in Italy, Pastor spent the rest of his life writing a history of the popes from the exile in Avignon to the end of the reign of Pope Urban VIII. Apart from two biographical studies, on Fieldmarshal Conrad von Hoetzendorf and General Viktor von Dankl (1917), which were part of Pastor's patriotic involvement in World War I, his many other publications are connected with the history of the Catholic Church. Pastor was explicitly an ultramontanist, and this attitude colored his history of the papacy and brought him into conflict with modernist circles in the Church. Nevertheless, his work will remain of lasting value for the copious sources on which his study is based. In spite of a certain apologetic attitude, Pastor never betrayed his scholarship and objectivity. He did not hesitate to criticize the policy and lives of popes such as Alexander VI and the war-loving Julius II. Pastor's *Tagebucher–Briefe–Erinnerungen*, published after his death in 1950, gives insight into his thinking, research methods, political attitudes and academic career.

Bibliography: G. Oberkofler, *Die geschichtlichen Fächer an der philosophischen Fakultät der Universität Innsbruck 1850–1945* (The History Department in the Faculty of Philosophy of the University of Innsbruck, 1850–1945) (Innsbruck, 1970); Heinrich von Srbik, "Ludwig von Pastor," in *Neue Österreichische Biographie 1815–1918*, vol. 7 (1931).

Fritz Fellner

REDLICH, Oswald (Innsbruck, 1858–Vienna, 1944), Austrian historian. Having begun his career as an archivist in Innsbruck, Redlich was appointed professor of history and auxiliary sciences at the University of Vienna in 1893, serving in this capacity until his retirement in 1929. From 1926 to 1929 he was director of the Institut für österreichische Geschichtswissenschaft. From 1919 to 1938 he was president of the Austrian Academy of Sciences in Vienna. Redlich was one of the most prominent representatives of the Vienna School of historical scholarship, in which the emphasis on auxiliary sciences and the editing of sources, especially diplomas and charters, is remarkable. Redlich was one of the leading organizers of the *Monumenta Germaniae*. Among his many works on diplomatics, the volume *Privaturkunden des Mittelalters* (1911) became a standard handbook. After 1894, Redlich directed research and publication of the *Regesta Habsburgica*, one of the best directories to diplomas of the late Middle Ages. A number of small articles dealing with problems of diplomatics and auxiliary sciences document his lifelong research in this field. In later years, Redlich turned to the early modern history of Austria, concentrating on the baroque era. *Österreichs Grossmachtbildung in der Zeit Kaiser Leopolds I* (1921) and *Das Werden einer Grossmacht. Österreich 1700 bis 1740* (1938) concentrate on political history. Redlich devoted much time to organizing research projects within the Austrian Academy of Sciences. Through his untiring efforts, the Austrian archives were preserved intact, despite political proposals to split them among the successor states after World War I.

Bibliography: Ludwig Bittner, "Oswald Redlich," *Almanach der Akademie der Wissenschaften in Wien*, 94.Jg.(1946); Heinrich von Srbik, "Oswald Redlich," in *Historische Zeitschrift*, Bd. 169 (1949).

Fritz Fellner

SICKEL, Theodor von (Aken, Elfe, 1826–Meran, 1908), Austrian historian. As member of the faculty and as director of the Institut für österreichische Geschichtsforschung from 1869 to 1891 and director of the Austrian Historical Institute in Rome from 1881 to 1901, von Sickel more than any other Austrian historian influenced the training and research organization of historical science in Austria. Having been schooled in the methods of the Ecole des chartes in Paris, Sickel transferred this approach to historical research to Vienna where, during the mid–1850s, he set up a school of training in auxiliary sciences through which, with very few exceptions, all Austrian historians had to pass. The Vienna school of historical research centered around the painstaking collection and analysis of medieval diplomas and excelled in editorial work, shunning philosophical and interpretative discussion of problems and ideas. Sickel's rather mechanical and positivist approach to historical scholarship left a permanent mark on Austrian historiography. By overrating the source value of medieval diplomas and archival source material, Sickel and his school, in a certain way, became an obstacle to further progress of historical science in Austria, while at the same time leading the Austrian institute to international recognition as a center of auxiliary sciences and organized editorial tasks.

Bibliography: Alfons Lhotsky, *Geschichte des Instituts für österreichische Geschichtsforschung, 1854–1954* (Graz, 1954); Theodor von Sickel, *Römische Erringerungen* (Vienna, 1947).

Fritz Fellner

SRBIK, Heinrich R. von (Vienna, 1878–Ehrwald, Tyrolia, 1951), Austrian historian. Grandson of Wilhelm Heinrich Grauert, a Westphalian historian who in 1850 became the first director of the Historisches Seminar at the University of Vienna, Heinrich von Srbik started his academic career as a student of Alfons Dopsch (q.v.). In 1907 he became Privatdozent for Austrian history in Vienna, in 1912 associate professor, and in 1917 full professor for modern and economic history at the University of Graz. From 1922 until 1945 Srbik taught as full professor for modern history at the University of Vienna, in 1929–1930 he served as minister of education, and from 1938 to 1945 he adhered to the German Reichstag. Because of his collaboration with Nationalsozialismus, he was deprived of his professorship at the University of Vienna in 1945; he lived in retirement in Ehrwald until his death.

In his early years Srbik devoted his research entirely to questions of economic history. *Der staatliche Exporthandel Österreichs von Leopold I bis Maria Theresia* (1907) and *Wilhelm von Schroeder. Ein Beitrag zur Geschichte der Staatswissenschaften* (1910) were important contributions to the history of the economic and administrative reorganization of the Habsburg monarchy in the period of neo-absolutism. The *Studien zur Geschichte des österreichischen Salzwesens* (1917) focused on another important aspect of Austrian economy in early modern times. The political and social upheaval following the collapse of the Central Powers at the end of World War I led to Srbik's *Die Wiener Revolution des Jahres 1848 in sozialgeschichtlicher Beleuchtung* (1919). Even before Srbik was called to the chair of modern history in Vienna, he had turned to political history, trying to combine his schooling in the methods of the Institut für österreichische Geschichtsforschung with the basic concepts of the history of ideas in his book *Wallensteins Ende. Ursache, Verlauf und Folgen der Katastrophe* (1920). Invited to contribute to the series of "Meister der Politik," edited by Erich Marcks, Srbik wrote *Metternich* (1922), which is a masterpiece of biography (as can be said of the biographical sketch, *Franz Josef I. Charakter und Regierungsgrundsätze*, published ten years later). Srbik expanded the biographical essay on Metternich into a two-volume comprehensive biography, *Metternich. Der Staatsmann und Mensch* (1925), not only showing understanding and appreciation of Metternich as a political figure, but also leading to a complete reappraisal of policies and politics in the Habsburg monarchy during the first half of the nineteenth entury. In a sometimes heated controversy with his colleague, Viktor Bibl, Srbik managed to prove the positive intentions of Metternich as a statesman, the coachman of Europe, and his achievements as an arbiter of European stability, as well as granting justice to Metternich's conservatism. (A third volume was published post-humously in 1954, summing up the scholarly controversy.) One of the main themes in his work on Metternich was Srbik's endeavor to defend Austria's role in German history against the negative interpretation given to Austrian history by the German nationalist historiography of the Heinrich von Treitschke (q.v.) brand. Srbik continued in this approach by participating actively in the political as well as historical debate on *kleindeutsche* or *grossdeutsche Geschichtsauffassung*. In a lecture given at Salzburg in 1929 and published the same year, Srbik presented his view, *Gesamtdeutsche Geschichtsauffassung*, which sought to reintegrate the history of the Habsburg Empire into the course of German history, assigning to the Austrian parts of the German Empire the special role of defending Germany's Central European position against the threat of the Ottoman Empire, at the same time advancing German culture into Eastern lands. While accepting the Bismarckian solution to the problem of German national unification, Srbik succeeded in explaining the anti-Bismarck policies of the Habsburg Empire and the small states of the so-called Drittes Deutschland as essential elements of a German historical tradition. Srbik's major work, *Deutsche Einheit. Idee und Wirklichkeit vom Heiligen Reich bis Königsgrätz* (4 vols., 1934–1942), elaborates on the basic concept of *Gesamtdeutsche Geschichtsauffassung* by describing, in the form of a history of political ideas and diplomatic dealings, the conflict between the imperial tradition of legitimacy and legality represented by the Habsburg monarchy and power politics as pursued by Bismarck's Prussia. Srbik's interpretation of German history was heavily attacked by the *kleindeutsche* school as well as by strict National Socialist historians. Nevertheless, after 1945 Srbik was accused of pan-German views and was found guilty of collaboration with National Socialism by those who judged him more by some *völkisch* concepts he had adhered to than by careful reading of his scholarly work. It must be held as an ironic twist of history that Srbik's writings (almost all of which were devoted to defending Austria's historical role against German chauvinistic interpretations), by reevaluating Austria's achievements in political culture, laid the foundation stones for the reassessment of Austrian history typical of Austrian political and historical interpretations after 1945. After retirement, Srbik turned to research in the history of historiography, a field he had entered in his university lectures in the 1930s. Shortly before his death, he published *Geist und Geschichte. Vom deutschen Humanismus bis zur Gegenwart* (2 vols., 1950/51), a history of historiography that must be rated among the best works of *deutsche Geistesgeschichte*, a history of historical writing and historical ideas showing the interdependence of historical scholarship well beyond national boundaries and nationalistic attitudes. Srbik saw himself in the tradition of the Rankean idea of history, described his position in historical scholarship as "moderate historicism," and must be listed among the great historians of the Leopold von Ranke (q.v.) school of historiography.

Bibliography: Arduino Agnelli, *Heinrich Ritter von Srbik* (Naples, 1975); Ludwig Moos, *Bildungsbürgertum, Nationalprobleme und democratisches Zeitalter. Studien zum Werk Heinrich Ritter von Srbiks* (Freiburg, 1967); Paul R. Sweet, "The Historical Writing of Heinrich von Srbik," *History and Theory* 10 (1970).

Fritz Fellner

Great Historians: Baltic

KRUUS, Hans (Tartu, 1891–Tallinn, 1976), Estonian historian. Professor at Tartu University (1934–1941), president of the Estonian Academy of Science (1946–1950), research professor at the USSR and Estonian academies of science (1955–1958 and 1958–1976, respectively). The leading Estonian historian during the interwar and post–1945 periods, Kruus studied at the Russian and Estonian universities at Tartu (Iur'ev) during and in the years immediately following World War I. He published his master's dissertation in 1924 on the first stage of the Livonian War, "Vene–Liivi sõda (1558–1561)." In this study he used both Baltic German and Russian sources as the basis for a thorough examination of the social and political crisis and the diplomatic and military events that put an end to the political power of the Teutonic Order and the bishops of the Livonian Confederation. During the 1930s, Kruus laid the foundations for modern Estonian historiography in three important books. In his doctoral dissertation of 1930 on the peasant movement of the 1840s in southern Estonia, *Talurahva käärimine Lõuna-Eestis XIX. Sajandi 40 ndail aastail* (Mit Deutschem Referat: Die Bauern-bewegung in Südestland in den 40er Jahren des 19. Jahrhunderts), he convinc-ingly demonstrated that the conversion of Estonian peasants to Orthodoxy resulted less from religious conviction or Orthodox proselytizing than it did from the economic and social conditions that existed among the peasantry in southern Estonia. Two years later, in his *Grundriss der Geschichte des estnischen Volkes*, he provided the first scholarly account of the historical forces and events that had shaped the Estonian people over the centuries. In the study he published in 1939, on the Estonian Alexander school, *Eesti Aleksandrikool*, he systematically examined the goals, organization, and tactics of the Estonian nationalist move-ment. In both *Talurahva käärimine Lõuna-Eestis* and *Eesti Aleksandrikool*, Kruus pioneered the use of quantitative data and statistical analysis in the study of

Baltic social history. In 1940 he became rector of Tartu University and deputy premier of the Estonian People's Government of Johannes Vares. After the defeat of Nazi Germany, he was minister of foreign affairs and president of the Academy of Sciences of the Estonian SSR. In 1950 Kruus fell victim to the so-called Cult of Personality. He was rehabilitated in 1955 and permitted to continue his historical research and organizational activities, first at the Institute of History of the Academy of Sciences of the USSR and then at the Institute of History of the Estonian Academy of Sciences.

During the last three decades of his life, Kruus was above all an academic administrator, coordinator of scholarly projects, publisher of general and popular accounts of Estonian history, and teacher of a new generation of Estonian historians. He continued, however, to be active as a scholar and published a number of articles on local history, folklore, and the Estonian national movement, studies that are important for the study of Estonian history. Both before and after 1940, his work as a scholar provided Estonian historians with a model of high-quality research on cultural, demographic, quantitative, and socioeconomic history.

Bibliography: Hans Kruus, *Ajaratta uutes ringides: Mälestusi 1907–1917* (The Wheel of History: Memories, 1907–1917) (Tallinn, 1979); V. Maamägi, "K 75–letiu Khansa Kruusa," in J. Kahk, ed., *Ajaloo järskudel radadel* (On Steep Paths) (Tallinn, 1966), pp. 16–28; *Studia Historica in Honorem Hans Kruus*, eds. J. Kahk and J. Vassar (Tallinn, 1971).

Edward C. Thaden

MOORA, Harri Albertovich (Ehavere, 1900–Tallinn, 1968), Estonian historian and archaeologist. Member of the Estonian Academy of Sciences. Moora's research dealt chiefly with the Iron Age in the Baltic, the ethnogenesis of its peoples, fortified settlements, the rise of a class society in the Baltic area, and its historical–cultural regions. His two-volume work, *Die Eisenzeit in Lettland bis etwa 500 n* (1929, 1938), describes the ethnic groups in the territories of Latvia and Estonia and their interrelationships as reflected in material culture forms, as well as Baltic tribes' contacts with ancient Prussians. Moora was the first to apply Marxian methodology in his analysis of all the archaeological materials on Latvia in describing the historical process on Latvian territory from the eighth millenmium B.C. to the thirteenth century against the background of the earliest history of the whole of the Baltic Area in *Pirmatanējā kopienas iekārta un agrā feodālā sabiedriba Latvijas teritorijā* (1952; The Primitive Communal System and the Early Feudal Society in the Territory of the Latvian Soviet Socialist Republic). His joint work with H. Ligi, *Khozyaistvo i obshchestvenniy stroi narodov Pribaltiki* (1969; The Economy and Social System of Baltic Peoples) is based on findings from investigations of fortified settlements. Moora's works added to a more thorough examination of ethnic processes (*Voprosi slozheniya estonskogo naroda v svete dannykh arkheologuii* (1956; Problems of Formation of the Estonian Nation in the Light of Archaeological Data). On the strength of archaeological data, he advanced the hypothesis that the ancient population of the Eastern Baltic area were proto-Europeans (Kunda culture) and not Indo-Europeans. He also substantiated the date of the Finno-Ugric peoples' resettlement into the Baltic area (extending it to the third millennium B.C.) and investigated the Finno-Ugric peoples' contacts with the Balts and Slavs.

Bibliography: *On Harri Moora's Scientific Activities. Collection of Articles* (Tallinn, 1982, in Russian, German and Estonian); "Harri Albertovich Moora," *Studia archaeologica in memoriam Harri Moora* (Tallinn, 1970) (Attached is a list of H. Moora's works.); "Shestidessyatiletye H. A. Moora" (Sixtieth Birth Anniversary of H. A. Moora), *Izvestiya Akademii Nauk Estonskoi SSR* (Bulletin of the Estonian Academy of Sciences), Social Sciences Series, 1970, no. 1.

V. A. Rzhanitsina

SAMARIN, Iurii Fedorovich (St. Petersburg, 1819–Berlin, 1876), Baltic historian. Concerned himself with Baltic history during two periods of his thirty–year active involvement in the public affairs of Russia as a government official, Slavophile thinker, peasant and municipal reformer, and Baltic polemicist and historian: first, as a government official in St. Petersburg and Riga between 1845 and 1849; and second, as an independent historical researcher and polemicist on Baltic affairs from the mid–1860s to the time of his death in 1876. Between 1868 and 1876, Samarin published his anti-Baltic-German polemics and the greater part of his historical work in six volumes entitled *Okrainy Rossii* (The Borderlands of Russia). Both the polemics and the historical studies included in these volumes were based on original source materials collected by Samarin between 1845 and 1876 on all aspects of Baltic history, especially the relations of the dominant Baltic German minority with the Russian government and with the *Undeutschen* (Estonians and Latvians). Samarin's two major works on Baltic history are his *Obshchestvennoe ustroistvo goroda Rigi* (1852; Social Order of the Town of Riga) and *Krest'ianskii vopros v Lifliandii* (1876; The Peasant Question in Livland). His study of Riga was republished in 1889 under the title of *Istoriia Rigi* (History of Riga) as Volume 7 of his *Sochineniia*. Although Samarin ostensibly wrote this work as an official report for a government commission, he skillfully developed in it his own personal views on the need to integrate Riga into a general legal-administrative order that would protect the nonprivileged majority of the inhabitants of this town from arbitrary treatment at the hands of its Baltic German ruling minority. He documents his interpretation of Riga's history with a detailed examination of the relations of this elite with the unprivileged majority of the local population as well as with the former archbishop of Riga, the Livonian Order, the Holy Roman Empire, the papacy, Poland, Sweden, and Russia. His conclusions were based on a careful study of materials in Low and High German, Latin, Polish, and Russian from the Riga archives, as well as published Baltic German and Polish sources. This was, as Latvian historian Janis Zutis (q.v.) has written, "the first scholarly *(nauchnaia)* history of Riga."

Samarin's other, and last, major historical work, *Krest'ianskii vopros v Li-*

fliandii, is a masterful, scholarly study of the emancipation of the Livonian peasants at the beginning of the nineteenth century. In analyzing the Livonian agrarian crisis at the end of the eighteenth and the beginning of the nineteenth centuries, Samarin had to depend principally on official Russian and Baltic German sources and on the memoirs and correspondence of officials and Baltic noblemen involved in the preparation of the legislation that emancipated the Estonian and Latvian serfs. In many respects, however, he understood better than most twentieth-century Baltic German, Estonian, Latvian, or Russian/Soviet agrarian historians the political and institutional context within which agrarian reform took place in the Baltic borderlands of Russia. Samarin practiced a sophisticated form of borderland social and economic history. His purpose was to demonstrate the necessity of government intervention in local Baltic affairs. He proceeded as a historian, however, on the basis of a well-documented, intelligent, and detailed discussion of the interaction of Baltic German land-owners, patricians, and pastors with Polish, Swedish, or Russian officials. He also showed how the evolution of Baltic social, political, and economic institutions affected the lives of Estonian and Latvian peasants and townsmen.

Bibliography: G. Hucke, *Jurij Fedorovich Samarin: Seine geistesgeschichtliche Bedeutung* (Munich, 1971); B. E. Nol'de, *Iurii Samarin i ego vremia* (Paris, 1926); E. C. Thaden, "Iurii Fedorovich Samarin and Baltic History," *Journal of Baltic Studies* 17 (1986).

Edward C. Thaden

TALLGREN, Arne Michel (1885–Helsinki, 1945), Finnish prehistorian and archaeologist. Professor at the University of Tartu (Estonia, 1920) and Helsinki (Finland, 1923). Tallgren was one of the greatest interwar prehistorians, a pathfinder in the effort to reconstruct Eastern and Northeastern European and Siberian ancient history, and he took a special interest in the study of the Bronze Age and the first stage of the Iron Age. An expedition to Siberia (1915), the study of several important private and/or museum collections (Zaoussailov, Tovostine), and archaeological digs helped him explain some fundamental aspects of the cultural history of the region and prove the unscientific character of certain ideas fashionable at the time, such as the notion that East European Bronze Age cultures had originated in Siberia and had been carried there by people of Finno-Ugric origin. Tallgren's most important contributions remain the critical examination and definition of cultural areas and the determination of the relative and absolute chronology of the Bronze and Iron Age in European Russia. (See *Kupfer and Bronzezeit in Nord-und Ostrussland*, I, *Die Kupfer und Bronzezeit in Nordwestrussland. Die ältere Metallzeit in Ostrussland*, 1911, and *L'époque dite d'Ananino dans la Russie Orientale durant l'ancien Age du fer*, 1919.) Historiography adopted several of his important ideas: the autonomy of the cultures in this part of Europe and their local evolution in a late Neolithic context, the importance and complexity of the cultural contacts and influences, and the role played by the North-Pontic or Scythian space and culture in constituting the Northern complexes, especially the Ananino culture. He attached great importance to the Caucasian zone as a linking point between the North-Pontic steppe and the great oriental civilizations. (See *Etudes sur le Caucase du Nord*, 1929; *Zu der Nord-kaukasischen frühen Bronzezeit*, 1931; *Caucasian Monuments: The Treasure of Kazbek, 1930*.) Although circumstances did not allow him to carry on his studies along this line of research, his opinion (*Studies of the Pontic Bronze Age*, 1937) that the most topical task for East European archaeology was to find the connections between the North shore of the Black Sea and the Near East still holds true.

Another field of research, closely connected to his definition of the cultural heritage of the Finno-Ugric peoples, was the archaeology of the Siberian and Ural-Altaic regions (*The Tasks of Ural-Altaic Archaeology*, 1918; *Bronzezeit-liches im Uralgebirge*, 1918; *Trouvailles isolées siberiennes*, 1919; *Trouvailles tombales siberiennes en 1889*, 1921; *The Prehistory of Ingria*, 1938; *The South Siberian Cemetry of Ogalkty from the Han Period, 1937*). Through this research he helped to throw light on the typical aspects of the territory between the Urals and the Sayan, and to determine the Finnic cultural provinces in Europe (*Les provinces culturelles finnoises de l'age recent du fer dans la Russie du Nord*, 1928; *Zur Osteuropäischen Archäologie: Finnisch-Ugrische, Forschungen*, 1929). He brought little-known or totally unknown facts into the scientific circuit through the first synthesis of Estonian prehistory (*Zur Archaeology Eestis I-II*, 1922–1923), in which special attention was paid to the contacts with other cultural areas (the Vistula, the Baltic sea zones, Finland), and also through his researches on the arctic zone (*The Arctic Bronze Age in Europe*, 1937). Given his general orientation, Tallgren detached himself from the descriptive school and joined the promoters of an archaeological science who saw the main task in terms of the complete reconstruction of past history. His point of view was defined in *Method of Prehistoric Archaeology* (1936) and in *Antiquity*, 11 (1937): "Archaeology should cease to be a 'natural science' founded upon the study of objects and forms and should become an economic-social, historical science. As a starting point one should take the elucidation of the economic system, of the economic and social basis of which the objects are manifestations." To all this we should add the reconstruction of ideas, the detection of cultural contacts, the study of migrations and their impact, the accurate definition of the relation, culture/ethnos. Very interesting and extremely modern was his opinion that in every culture there are characteristic elements, elements that have survived from another culture, archaisms as well as marginal aspects whose recording is compulsory. Also interesting and still valid is his idea concerning cultural mutability, expressed in the same paper: "The reconstruction of a given culture-period is a purely theoretical affair; in every stage of culture there are 'dialects', if I may use a philological metaphor, even in the earliest stage. Any reconstruction of a given culture which disregards 'dialects' may lead to serious errors." In an age when political ends were met by any means, Tallgren was utterly against using archaeology as a weapon for supporting expansion or racial ideas. He was also founder and editor-in-chief of the *Eurasia Septentrionalis Antiqua* review which was designed to promote Eastern and Northeastern European and Asiatic archaeological research.

Bibliography: Jan Filip, *Encyklopadisches Handbuch für Ur- und Frühgeschichte Europas* (Prague, 1967), pp. 1428–1429; Ella Kivikovski, "A. M. Tallgren," ESA, Supplementary Volume (Helsinki, 1953), pp. 77–122 and the bibliographical list beginning on p. 122.

Ligia Bârzu

WITTRAM, Reinhard (Bilderlingshof near Riga, 1902–Merano, 1973), Latvian historian, professor at the Herder Hochschule in Riga (1928–1939), Posen (1940–1945), Göttingen (1945–1970). Wittram was a leading authority on general European as well as Baltic and Russian history. His first two books, *Liberalismus baltischer Literaten* (Riga, 1931); and *Meinungskämpfe im baltischen Deutschtum während der Reformepoche des 19. Jahrhunderts* (Riga, 1934) examined the efforts of the Baltic German *Ständestaat* to adapt itself to changes in Russia stemming from the Great Reforms of the 1860s and 1870s. He portrayed sympathetically such leaders of Baltic German society as Hamilkar Baron Fölkersahm, Georg Baron Nolcken, Julius Eckardt, and Carl Schirren, but he also displayed an awareness of their limitations as representatives of a German landowning or intellectual elite in the context of the awakening Estonian and Latvian national movements and of reform in the Russian Empire. His awareness of the important role that both individuals, on the one hand, and general cultural, social, economic, and political forces, on the other, have played in history is even more evident in his monumental two-volume study of the reign of Peter the Great, *Peter der Grosse: Czar und Kaiser*, which he published in 1964. At Göttingen University Wittram first held the chair of Eastern European history in 1955 and then in addition, after 1959, the chair of medieval and modern European history. The wide range of his interests as a historian is suggested by such titles as *Das Nationale als europäisches Problem* (1954), *Das Interesse an der Geschichte* (1958), *Zukunft der Geschichte* (1966), *Anspruch und Fragwürdigkeit der Geschichte* (1964), and *Russia and Europe* (1973). He published the third edition of his general history of the Baltic region, *Baltische Geschichte 1180–1918: Die Ostseelande Livland, Estland, Kurland*, in 1954. It is a balanced, erudite survey that takes into account the available Estonian, Latvian, German, Russian, and Scandinavian scholarly literature up to about 1953. In this work, Wittram is especially interested in the role the Baltic Germans played in Baltic history, but he views them in terms of their interaction with Estonians, Latvians, Poles, Swedes, and Russians. Being a specialist in Russian and Baltic history, he paid particular attention to the relations of Estland, Kurland, and Livland with Russia, not only in his general Baltic history but also in more narrowly focused works such as *Drei Generationen* (1949) and the collective work *Baltische Kirchengeschichte* (1956).

Wittram contributed to the furthering of Baltic historical studies outside the

Soviet Union. He was one of the founders of the Baltische Historische Kommission in Göttingen; as its chairman over a period of twenty-two years, he presided over annual ''Baltische Historikertreffen'' in Göttingen, trained a new generation of Baltic historians, and strongly supported cooperative work with Estonian and Latvian historical researchers in exile. He also opened a dialogue with Soviet historians, especially in his thoughtful article ''Methologische und geschichtstheoretische Überlegungen zu Problemen der baltischen Geschichtsforschung,'' *Zeitschrift für Ostforschung* 20 (1971). If the initial response to Wittram's initiative was somewhat polemical, the dialogue has been continued by his former students, and in recent years Soviet Baltic historians have begun to attend Baltic conferences in Stockholm, the German Federal Republic, and North America.

Bibliography: Gert von Pistohlkors, ''Nachruf auf Professor Dr. phil. Reinhard Wittram (April 16, 1973), gehalten auf dem XXVI Baltischen Historikertreffen am 16. Juni 1973,'' *Zeitschrift für Ostforschung* 22 (1973): 698–703.

Edward C. Thaden

ZUTIS, Jānis (Kurland, 1893–Riga, 1962), Latvian historian. Docent at Voronezh University and Voronezh Pedagogical Institute (1929–1937), research scholar at the Soviet Academy of Sciences (1937–1941 and 1943–1946), professor at the Latvian State University and Academy of Sciences in Riga (1946–1962). A soldier in the Russian Army during World War I, Zutis remained in the Soviet Union and studied Russian, German, and general European medieval and early modern history at Moscow University and in connection with RANION (the Russian Association of Scientific Institutes for the Social Sciences). During the twenty-year period 1924–1944 that Zutis spent as a graduate student, docent, and researcher in Moscow, Voronezh, and Alma-Ata, he systematically examined printed and manuscript materials in Soviet archives and libraries concerning Baltic history. In 1937 he published his Candidate's dissertation on tsarist policy in the Baltic region during the first part of the eighteenth century (*Politika tsarizma v Pribaltike v pervoi polovine XVIII veka*) and more than forty articles and book reviews on various aspects of Baltic, Russian, and German history. In 1946 his doctoral dissertation, *Ostzeiskii vopros v XVIII veke* (The Baltic Question in the Eighteenth Century), was published in Riga. In this work Zutis rejected the narrowly provincial or nationalist historiography of earlier Baltic German or Latvian historians, noting quite correctly that the eighteenth-century history of the Baltic region could not be properly understood if studied in isolation from the rest of the Russian Empire. New materials discovered by Zutis in Soviet and Latvian archives enabled him to analyze in detail the nature of the economic, political, and social system on which the Baltic German legal-administrative order and Estonian and Latvian servitude were based. He did not deny that this system had much in common with the one prevailing elsewhere in the Russian Empire, but he also showed how the fiscal and administrative interests of the Russian state made unavoidable changes in the relationship of the Russian center of the empire to its Baltic periphery. At the time of Catherine II the introduction of Russian reforms in Estland and Livland even had some positive effect on peasant and urban society, but social unrest also increased. This, as Zutis noted, was a result that Catherine II and her advisers did not anticipate.

After 1945 Zutis was one of the principal architects of Marxist historiography in Latvia. Much of what he then wrote was of a pedagogical, popular, or polemical nature, but he also conducted serious scholarly research during the last decades of his life, especially on Latvian agrarian and peasant history at the beginning of the nineteenth century. Three works of capital importance which he published on this subject between 1953 and 1956 are *Latvija klaušu saimniecibus sairšanas periodā un Kauguru nemieri 1802 gadā* (Latvia in the Period of the Disintegration of the Barshchina Economy and the Kaugerhof Uprising of 1802), *Vidzemes un Kurzemes zemieku likumi XIX gadsimta sākumā (1804–1819)* (Livland and Kurland Peasant Legislation at the Beginning of the Nineteenth Century [1804–1819]), and *Vidzemes un Kurzemes zemieku brivlaišana XIX gadsimta 20. gados* (The Emancipation of the Livland and Kurland Peasants from Serfdom in the Twenties of the Nineteenth Century). These three studies, together with *Ostzeiskii vopros v XVIII veke*, laid the foundations for a flourishing school of Marxist historiography on peasant and agrarian history in the Latvian SSR.

Bibliography: K. Graudin, "Akademiku Ianu Zutisu" (To Academician Jānis Zutis Sixty-Five Years), in Latvijas PSR, Zinātņu Akadēmijas *Vēstis*, no. 10 (1958): 145–147; "Vēsturnieka Prof. Dr. Jāņa Zuša: Darbu bibliografija" (Bibliography of the Works of the Historian Prof. Dr. Janis Zutis), in Latvijas PSR, Zinatņu Akadēmijas *Vestis*, no. 10 pp. 159–72; T. Zeids, "Akadēmiķa Jāņa Zuša sešdesmit pieci dzīves gadi" (The Sixty-Fifth Birthday of Academician Janis Zutis), in Latvijas PSR, Zinatņu Akadēmijas *Vestis*, no. 10, pp. 149–157.

Edward C. Thaden

Great Historians: Belgian

BONENFANT, Paul (Jodoigne, 1899–Laon, 1965), Belgian historian. Bonenfant's scholarly training and his main activities took place at the Université libre de Bruxelles, where he was the pupil of Michel Huisman and Guillaume Des Marez. He was awarded his Ph.D. in 1921 and a special doctorate in history in 1931, and he taught there from 1930 on. His university teaching was preceded by a few years in secondary education and as the head of the archives of the Board of Municipal Assistance. As a teacher and as a scholar, he first specialized in modern history (especially the history of the eighteenth century); he later included the Middle Ages in his field of interest. Examples of his first orientation are seen in two major works: *La suppression de la Compagnie de Jésus dans les Pays-Bas autrichiens, 1773* (1925) and *Le problème du paupérisme en Belgique à la fin de l'Ancien Régime* (1934). Both of these memoirs received prizes of the Académie Royale de Belgique, and Bonenfant kept up his interest in such themes. But he became still more attracted by the Middle Ages, on which he first wrote textbooks of a general character (in collaboration with Louis Verniers) and which also captured his attention when he had to catalogue the archives of hospitals and to teach medieval history at the university. As the head of the seminar of medieval history from 1932 onward, he directed the works of as many as 129 young medievalists, more than ten of whom later became university professors. All his pupils in seminar courses acknowledged the profound influence he had on them as regards both erudition and the critical treatment of sources. Bonenfant was also a remarkable teacher in the main ancillary disciplines of history (paleography, diplomatics, historical geography) and launched several of his pupils in their careers as archivists. His personal contributions to the history of the Middle Ages were many and important. They were indeed devoted to the Low Countries, starting from the High Middle Ages (*Le duché de Lothier et le marquisat de Flandre à la fin du XIe siècle*, 1931, in the *Atlas de géographie historique de la Belgique* edited by Léon Van der Essen) and ending in the Burgundian period (*Philippe le Bon*, 1943; *Du meurtre de Montereau au traité de Troyes*, 1958). The old duchy of Brabant and the city of Brussels, however, were at the center of his work. He was also the author of excellent critical editions (*Cartulaire de l'hôpital Saint-Jean de Bruxelles*, 1953) and of textbooks of exceptional value: *Paléographie du moyen âge, avec des notions d'héraldique* (1940), *Diplomatique* (1941), and *Histoire de Belgique* (1940–1941). He was preparing a revised edition of his *Diplomatique* when he met his sudden death. He was also preparing the edition of the charters of the dukes of Brabant until the accession of Henri I (1190); this elaborate work, to which he devoted much time and which he conceived as the basis for a history of medieval Brabant, remained unfinished.

Because of his strong personality and his wide influence, Bonenfant played a major part in various Belgian institutions concerned with the organization of historical work and especially in the Commission Royale d'Histoire which has been responsible during a century and a half for the publication of the sources of the national history of Belgium. He entered the commission in 1946 and became its secretary in 1952, a post that enabled him to initiate a renewal of its activities. Among other enterprises of which he was the head were the Société Belge d'Histoire des Hôpitaux and the Commission Interuniversitaire du Microfilm, which helped to uncover the sources relating to Belgium in foreign archives. As a first-class organizer Bonenfant gave himself entirely to the many institutions on whose boards he served as well as to the young historians whom he guided with a boundless generosity of spirit.

Bibliography: Maurice-A. Arnould, "Supremum Vale," in *Hommage au Professeur Paul Bonenfant. Etudes d'histoire médiévale dédiées à sa mémoire par les anciens élèves de son Séminaire* . . . (Brussels, 1965), pp. XXIII–XXVIII, with portrait (a work that includes a list of all Bonenfant's writings: 170 books and articles and 88 reviews); Georges Despy, "Notice sur la vie et les travaux de Paul Bonenfant," *Université libre de Bruxelles. Rapport sur l'année académique 1964–1965* (1971): 244–247, which includes a supplement to the list of Bonenfant's publications; Georges Despy, "Paul Bonenfant," *Revue belge de philologie et d'histoire* 43 (1965): 1547–1557; Jean-Jacques Hoebanx, "Paul Bonenfant," *Bulletin de la Commission royale d'histoire* 150 (1984): 95–106; "Hommage au Professeur Paul Bonenfant à l'occasion du XXVe anniversaire de son enseignement à l'Université libre de Bruxelles" (Brussels, 1955), 40 pp. with portrait; Mina Martens, "L'histoire de Bruxelles dans l'oeuvre de Paul Bonenfant," *Cahiers bruxellois*, 10 (1965): 85–89; Andrée Scufflaire, "Paul Bonenfant," *Archives et Bibliothèques de Belgique* 39 (1968): 154–158.

Maurice-A. Arnould

CAPART, Jean (Brussels, 1877–Brussels, 1947), Belgian historian. Capart was the son of a well-known physician, Dr. Alphonse Capart. He is considered the pioneer of Egyptology in Belgium. His vocation for Egypt goes back as far as his youth. As there were no Egyptological studies in his country at that time, he took his degrees in law at the Free University in Brussels. Then from 1898 to 1900, through a grant, he traveled through Europe studying Egyptology in Bonn, London, and Paris. Back in Brussels, he was appointed assistant-keeper of the Egyptian Department of the Musées du Cinquantenaire, once called Musées Royaux des Arts Décoratifs et Industriels, and now Musées Royaux d'Art et d'Histoire. Later (1911) he became keeper, then (1912) secretary, and finally (1925) director of this museum. Meanwhile, from 1902 on, he was also appointed professor of Egyptology and Oriental Art at the University of Liège. In fact, he was the promoter of those new studies. Capart was often sent on mission to Egypt either to visit archaeological sites, to attend the British excavations, to which he contributed financially on behalf of the Belgian government; or to buy objects for the museum, whose Egyptian section was rather poor. Once, in 1905, he was offered a whole tomb by the Egyptian government. This was the so-called Mastaba of Neferirtenef, a priest and high official of Pharaoh Sahure, of the Fifth Dynasty. He was allowed to dig in Sakkara, dismantle the tomb entirely, and bring it to Brussels, where it is the most important monument in the museum. Before the city of Heliopolis was built by Baron Edouard Empain as a suburb of Cairo, Capart had to explore the desert in 1907, lest there should be any relics of the past. Fortunately, nothing was discovered, and the new town grew like a mushroom. He also excavated, in 1927, at Tell Heou near Nag Hammadi and found a "catacomb" of ibises, the sacred animal of the god Thot. But his real excavations started in 1937 at Elkab, the main temple of Nekhbet, goddess of upper Egypt. He worked there until the year before his death. On two occasions Capart also accompanied the royal family to Egypt. In 1923, he created the Queen Elisabeth Egyptological Foundation which became one of the most important scientific institutes of the world with its huge library, its half-yearly bulletin *Chronique d'Egypte*, and numerous publications issued during the last sixty years.

Capart delivered lectures, either in French or in English, all over the world. Among other distinctions, he was named a fellow of the Royal Academy of Belgium, and corresponding fellow of the British Academy and the French Académie des Inscriptions et Belles-Lettres. For several years, he also became advisory curator of the Art Museum of Brooklyn, New York, where he discovered a rich collection of Egyptian antiquities left by Charles Edwin Wilbour. Capart published over two hundred books and articles on ancient Egypt, for example: *Primitive Art in Egypt* (1905), *Recueil des Monuments égyptiens* (2 vols., 1902–1905), *Une Rue de Tombeaux à Saqqarah* (1907), *Abydos, le Temple de Séthi Ier* (1912), *Leçons sur l'art égyptien* (1920) and *L'art égyptien: Etudes et Histoire* (1924) with eight hundred plates in four volumes (1922–1947), *Lectures on Egyptian Art* (1928), *Documents pour servir à l'étude de l'art égyptien* (2 vols., 1927–1931), *Thebes, the Glory of a Great Past* (1926), *Memphis, à l'ombre des Pyramides* (1929), *Bulletin critique des Religions de l'Egypte* (1904–1905), and a great number of smaller books. With Sir Alan Henderson Gardiner (q.v.), he edited *Le Papyrus Léopold II* (1939) and with Georges Contenau, he wrote *Histoire de l'Orient ancien* (1939). Although most of his works are devoted to art and archaeology, nevertheless, in his explanations he always introduced much valuable historical information, which threw new light on more than one aspect of the old civilization of Egypt.

                                                                                Arpag Mekhitarian

CUMONT, Franz (Alost, 1868–Brussels, 1947), Belgian historian of religion, archaeologist, and epigraphist. Ph.D. from the University of Ghent with a thesis entitled "Alexandre d'Abonotichos. Un épisode de l'histoire du paganisme au IIe siècle de notre ère "(1887). From 1892 until 1910, Cumont was a professor of classical philology at this university. He resigned his chair when, for political and philosophical reasons, the minister of sciences and arts refused to appoint him to the course of Roman history. In 1912 he also resigned from his position as curator of the Musées du Cinquantenaire in Brussels which he had held since 1898 (*Catalogue des sculptures et inscriptions antiques—Monuments lapidaires—des Musées Royaux du Cinquantenaire*, 2d ed., 1913). His personal fortune allowed him to lead, in Rome and Paris, the life of a scholar entirely free of teaching obligations. He initiated modern Mithraic scholarship by collecting all extant archaeological monuments, inscriptions, and literary references, which he published in *Textes et monuments figurés relatifs aux mystères de Mithra* (2 vols., 1894, 1895; the conclusions of Volume 1 were reprinted separately: *Les mystères de Mithra*, 2d ed. 1902; English trans. 1903). Cumont reached the conclusion that the cult of the Iranian Mithra was altered by the Magi in Babylon and in Anatolia. But since then many scholars have thought, as R. L. Gordon (1975), that "The theory that Mithraism was simply the Western incarnation of a cult historically maintained by the Magian diaspora in Anatolia will no longer need to be taken seriously." Cumont later published with M.-A. Kugener, *Recherches sur le manichéisme* (2 vols., 1908, 1912) and with J. Bidez the collection of texts of *Les Mages hellénisés. Zoroastre, Ostanès et Hystaspe d'après la tradition grecque* (2 vols., 1938), which testified to the diversity of Magian beliefs. He carried on research in the field of ancient astrology and astral religion—*Astrology and Religion Among the Greeks and Romans* (1912); *L'Egypte des astrologues* (1937); *Catalogus Codicum Astrologorum Graecorum*, VIII, 1, *Parisini* (1929), together with contributions to many volumes of this catalogue which he initiated in 1898. He broadened the scope of his investigations to the expansion of *Les religions orientales dans le paganisme romain* (1st ed., 1906; 4th, ed., 1929; English trans. 1911). Their appeal, he explained, was due to their promise of securing holiness in this life and definite beatitude in the next. In *After Life in Roman Paganism* (1922) he examined the history of ideas prevalent in Rome concerning the fate of the soul after death. His monumental *Recherches sur le symbolisme funéraire des Romains* (1942) constitutes the most important attempt to define the philosophical and religious meaning of symbols on funerary monuments, particularly on sarcophagi. Cumont was said to be "the most brilliant exegete of the religious imagery of Roman paganism.'' *Lux perpetua*, published posthumously (1949), is a masterful and moving synthesis of his findings concerning the evolution of Roman beliefs, speculations, and practices regarding life in the hereafter.

In the first decade of the twentieth century, Cumont was a pioneer in the exploration of Anatolia and Northern Syria in search of inscriptions and archaeological monuments (*Studia Pontica*, II and III, 1906, 1910; *Etudes syriennes*, 1917). In 1922–1923 he conducted, for the Académie des Inscriptions et Belles-Lettres de Paris, the early excavations at Dura-Europos (*Fouilles de Dura-Europos 1922–1923*, 2 vols., 1926). He secured permission for Belgium to carry out excavations on the site of Apamea on the Orontes. His *Comment la Belgique fut romanisée. Essai historique* (1914) contributed to the renewal of national archaeology in Belgium.

Bibliography: R. L. Gordon, ''Franz Cumont and the doctrines of Mithraism,'' in J. R. Hinnels, ed., *Mithraic Studies* (Manchester University Press, 1975), I, pp. 215–248; Franz De Ruyt, ''Cumont, Franz,'' *Biographie nationale* (Brussels), 39, no. 1, (1976): 211–222; Franz De Ruyt, ''Notice sur Franz Cumont,'' *Académie Royale de Belgique, Annuaire 1981* 147, *Notices biographiques*: 99–114.

Charles Delvoye

DELCOURT, Marie (Ixelles, 1891–Liège, 1979), Belgian historian of ideas and religions. Delcourt was brought up in Arlon, the birthplace of her mother's family. She went to Liège University in 1911 to study the classics, continuing her studies in Paris for two years afterward. While teaching at the High School for Girls in Liège, she founded a course at the university which she entitled ''History of Humanism.'' In 1932 she was appointed assistant lecturer, becoming a full professor in 1940 and emeritus professor in 1961. All those who came into contact with her appreciated her sharp intelligence and extreme competence, her courage in overcoming a distressing physical disability, her generosity, and her campaigning spirit in favor of high ideals. She considered her instruction in the classics not as an end in itself, but as a means to approaching real human problems through texts. Her work, apart from a large number of articles and reviews, consists of about thirty books that can be listed under three headings: (1) Ancient poetry, especially the influence of Greek theater in France (1925, 1934), books on Euripides (1930), Aeschylus (1934), Plautus (1964), a remarkable translation of Euripides (1962), a book on Pericles (1939), and *Images de Grèce* (1943, reissued in 1959); (2) humanism in the sixteenth century, especially a number of studies on Erasmus and Thomas More, including the first critical edition (1936) and a French translation of *Utopia* (1966), both works being reissued together in 1983; (3) ten volumes about religion and Greek myths, including *Stérilités mystérieuses et naissances maléfiques dans l'Antiquité classique* (1939, reissued in 1981); *Oedipe ou la légende du conquérant* (1944, reissued in 1981); *L'Oracle de Delphes* (1955, reissued in 1981); *Héphaïstos ou la légende du magicien* (1957, reissued in 1981); *Hermaphrodite: mythes et rites* *de la bisexualité dans l'Antiquité classique* (1958, English translation in 1961). Here Marie Delcourt's aim was to elucidate the mental representations underlying myths and rituals. Although they have their roots in the unconscious, the word "psychoanalysis" can be used only with caution. In the first place, even though the basic idea of the emergence of the unconscious is put forward, it cannot be assimilated to Freudian schemas. Second, Marie Delcourt believes that psycho-religious facts have a history: they originate and change according to successive mentalities. Here Oedipus is not the person we refer to when we talk of the Oedipus complex. Sophocles did not suggest he was in love with his mother. Legend brought together a series of synonymous or related themes, all symbolizing the conquest of power. Then, through the centuries, people read other meanings into the story. The interpretation Sigmund Freud gave to it is no less "authentic" for being one of many; it simply belongs to a particular moment in history. Under Marie Delcourt's guidance, this is the process of discovery that can be followed whether we are studying Hephaïstos the magician, Orestes or Alcmeon, the matricides, or Hermaphroditus. These mental representations, rich in existential content, are found in the work of Marie Delcourt.

Bibliography: "Bibliographie choisie des travaux de Marie Delcourt" established by Marcelle Derwa in *Hommages à Marie Delcourt*, Brussels, coll. Latomus, vol. 114 (1970), pp. 9–19; articles written by Catherine Backes–Clement, André Green, Clémence Ramnoux, and Hervé Rousseau in *Critique*, no. 293 (October 1971): 837–896; Studies by Jules Labarbe, Roland Crahay, and Franz Bierlaire; Reminiscences by Jean Hoyoux and Alexis Curvers in *Hommage à Marie Delcourt*, Proceedings of the symposium held in Liège in 1983.

                                                                  Roland Crahay

DELEHAYE, Hippolyte (Antwerp, 1859–Brussels, 1941), Belgian bollandist. Member of the Society of Jesus since 1876, Delehaye was first professor in a high school but the *senior* of the bollandists, Father Charles De Smedt, noticed his gifts for historical research and succeeded in obtaining his transfer to the Société des Bollandistes in February, 1891. Father Delehaye emerged quickly as a first-rate scholar with the publication in 1895 of a first outline of the *Bibliotheca hagiographica graeca* (2d ed., 1909), a pioneer enterprise that became the pattern for similar repertories of Latin and oriental hagiographical texts, and with the edition, in 1912, of the Byzantine *Synaxary*, a particularly arduous work because of the complexity of the manuscript tradition. At the same time, besides numerous articles and catalogues of hagiographical manuscripts, Delehaye published regularly in the *Analecta bollandiana* critical bulletins, which are remarkable for the sharpness of his critical sense, the strength of his demonstrations, and their alert and caustic tone, stigmatizing the incompetence of the defenders of unfounded pious traditions. Hoping to divert from their prejudices those who were shocked by some of his conclusions, Father Delehaye decided to carry the debate to the level of principle and strove to apply rigorous critical methodology to the sphere of hagiography. A first outline, published as articles in the *Revue des Questions historiques* of 1903, was amplified in a book which soon became a classic: *Les légendes hagiographiques* (1905; 4th ed., 1955; Italian, English, and German translations, 1906–1907). The integrist party's attempt to put the book on the Index failed, partly thanks to the intervention of Cardinal Mercier. Other syntheses that followed, were drier and more erudite: *Les origines du culte des martyrs* (1912; 2d ed., 1933), where he attempted to show that the cult of martyrs was not a simple imitation of the cult of heroes or pagan gods but offered a typically Christian aspect; *Les Passions des martyrs et les genres littéraires* (1921); and *Sanctus. Essai sur le culte des saints dans l'antiquité* (1927), which begins with a semantic study of the words, *sanctus, martyr,* and *confessor.* At the end of his career, he summarized his main ideas in *Cinq leçons sur la méthode hagiographique* (1934).

The elaboration of his studies on the cult of the martyrs had convinced Father Delehaye of the necessity of a new edition, with a commentary, of the Hieronymian Martyrology, aiming to extract from the corrupted text the available elements. He brought this enterprise to a successful issue with the cooperation of Dom Henri Quentin (1931). Then, with the help of his fellow-brothers—he had been their president since 1912—he attempted a critical commentary on the Roman Martyrology (1941). Favored with a clear mind, going straight to the main point, and with an exceptional capacity for labor, Father Delehaye succeeded in providing hagiographical research with solid bases that remain valid today. Nevertheless, one may criticize his underestimation of oriental sources. Also, while engaging his team in general works, he stopped the progress of the *Acta Sanctorum.* The many honorific titles he received during his long career testify to the international admiration he received.

Bibliography: Roger Aubert, "Le P. Delehaye et le cardinal Mercier," *Analecta bollandiniana* 100 (1982): 743–780; "H. Delehaye," *Analecta bollandiana* 60 (1942): i–Lii (complete list of his writings); Beauduin de Gaiffier, "Delehaye," *Dictionnaire d'histoire et de géographie ecclésiastiques,* 14, col. 1490–1492; *Korespondencija Frane Bulić–Hippolyte Delehaye,* sabrao i priredio Ivan Ostojić (Split, 1984); Cunibert Mohlberg, "Il P. Ippolito Delehaye: cinquant' anni di studi agiografici," *Rendiconti della Pontificia Accademia Romana di archeologia* 49 (1942–1943): pp. 15–46; Paul Peeters, *Figures bollandiennes contemporaines* (Brussels, 1948), pp. 67–105.

Roger Aubert

GACHARD, Louis-Prosper (Paris, 1800–Brussels, 1885), Belgian archivist and historian. Details on the Parisian childhood of young Gachard are unknown. Arriving in Tournai in March 1817, where his father founded a tobacco factory, he at first worked in Casterman Printing-House until June 1819; then he joined the administration of the city, where he occupied different posts between 1819 and 1826. On July 24, 1821, Gachard was naturalized a Belgian. It was during his stay in Tournai that he began to appreciate the richness of the archives of that city. In 1822 he asked permission to examine them. His first steps, as archivist and historian, went back to this period.

Gachard drew the attention of the authorities by sending them memoranda, some of them on organizing the Archives of the Kingdom (1825). On June 21, 1826, Gachard was appointed assistant secretary in the Archives of the Kingdom. As early as September 10, 1826, he presented a report on the records of Brussels' archives. He also devoted attention to organizing the archives, including the ones located in the provinces; to looking for national archives which the Belgian government had the right to claim back from France and Austria; and to founding a historiographical commission acquainted with both history and the national archives. (This was a prefiguration of the Royal Commission of History which was founded by Leopold I on July 22, 1834.) The Revolution of 1830 and the following proclamation of independence of Belgium placed Gachard at the head of the administration of the Archives of the Kingdom (July 20, 1831). During more than half a century, he worked to inventory the documents in his keeping. He also increased the bulk of the archives by both purchasing documents and bringing back to Belgium records scattered in France, Germany, Holland, and Austria. He organized the central depository of records in Brussels as well as the already existing ones in the provinces. He founded new provincial archives in Tournai, Namur, Arlon, and Hasselt. He made long trips to Germany, Holland, Austria, Italy, and particularly Spain to catalogue foreign holdings relevant to Belgium. Gachard was equally active within different learned societies, particularly the Royal Commission of History, founded in 1834, and the Royal Academy of Belgium of which he was a correspondent member from November 15, 1837, and a full member from May 9, 1842. Gachard authored a great number of articles. He also published important texts, such as the correspondence of William the Silent (1847–1866), the correspondence of Philip II concerning the Netherlands (1848–1879), and the correspondence of Margaret of Austria, duchess of Parma, with Philip II (1857–1881). Gachard was a pioneer in the field of the history of the old institutions of the Netherlands, particularly the Estates General to which he devoted two important publications concerning the sessions of 1600 (1849) and 1632–1634 (1853–1866). A great admirer of anecdotal history, Gachard who liked to tell it in all its details according to documents, thought that any historical study based on conjecture was necessarily false. According to him, historical critique was not possible unless founded on well-established facts. With his precise and clear mind, Gachard must be considered the best representative of Belgian historiography during the first half century of Belgian independence.

Bibliography: J. Cuvelier, "Louis-Prosper-Gachard," *Biographie Nationale* 29 (1957): col. 585–608; R. Wellens, "La mission d'inspection de Gachard aux Archives de Mons et de Tournai en 1832," *Miscellanea Archivistica* 35 (1982): 5–17; R. Wellens, "Les recherches sur l'histoire des Etats généraux en Belgique au XIXe siècle," *Actes du 1er Congrès de l'Association des Cercles francophones d'Histoire et d'Archéologie de Belgique*, Congrès de Comines, 3 (1982): 403–411.

Robert Wellens

GANSHOF, François-Louis (Bruges, 1895–Brussels, 1980), Belgian medievalist. Ganshof studied both law and history in the University of Ghent, where he obtained the degrees of doctor of laws in 1921 and doctor of philosophy in 1922. He wrote his Ph.D. thesis on the *ministeriales* in medieval Germany. Henri Pirenne (q.v.) was his supervisor. In 1923, he became ordinary professor in the University of Ghent and taught there until his retirement in 1961. He carried a heavy burden of teaching in two faculties: medieval history in the Faculty of Letters and legal history in the Faculty of Law. Ganshof was a member of the (Dutch-language) Royal Academy of Sciences in Brussels and corresponding member of many others. The importance of his work was recognized, *inter alia*, by thirteen universities in three countries, who granted him an honorary degree. He lectured in many countries and was a visiting professor for longer periods in Chicago and Berkeley. His extensive scholarly production contained no less than 10 books and 197 articles, dealing essentially with the period from the eighth to the twelfth centuries. Within this span of time he steadily grew more interested in the history of the Frankish realm in general and Charlemagne in particular. His main interest was the history of law and institutions. Thus, his *Etude sur les Ministeriales en Flandre et en Lotharingie* (Brussels, 1926) tried to establish the legal and social position of that well-known class of knights of servile origin within the framework of the German constitution in the eleventh and twelfth centuries. His *Qu'est-ce que la Féodalité* (Brussels, 1944, translated into English, Portuguese, German, Spanish, and Japanese) was an attempt to analyze as precisely as possible the legal elements in feudalism, such as the nature of the fief, the rights and obligations of lord and vassal, and feudal inheritance rules. Ganshoff's "La Flandre" in *Histoire des Institutions françaises au moyen âge*, directed by F. Lot and R. Fawtier, I: *Institutions seigneuriales* (Paris, 1957), pp. 343–426 remains a classic exposition of the institutions of medieval Flanders.

Ganshof's work on Carolingian institutions resulted in a detailed analysis of the exact nature, development, and impact of the royal Frankish legislation known as the capitularies: *Wat waren de capitularia* (1955; What Were the Capitularias, translated into French and German). Ganshof was also greatly interested in agricultural history, particularly in the classic manorial period, that is, from the Carolingian age to the twelfth century—hence, his contribution, in collaboration with A. Verhulst, "Mediaeval Agrarian Society in its Prime. France, the Low Countries and Western Germany," in the *Cambridge Economic History (1966)*. His interest in more general historical themes became manifest in two books, which covered not only legal and economic but also political and cultural history. One concerned the early history of the country of Flanders: *La Flandre sous les premiers comtes* (Brussels, 1943) and the other the whole medieval period: *Le Moyen Age* (Paris, 1953), in the series *Histoire des relations internationales*, directed by Pierre Renouvin (q.v.) (English trans., New York, 1971). Ganshof was famous for his encyclopedic knowledge of all aspects of medieval life, his profound understanding of the various types of medieval source material, and the precision in his analysis of their meaning. He was wary of speculation and preferred to limit himself to describing what he could directly deduce from the most reliable texts. This approach has given several of his leading works such a finality that major changes to their principal conclusions are unlikely, even though they deal with some of the most thorny aspects of medieval history. His universal recognition as one of the leading medievalists of his time was confirmed in part by the translation of several of his works in numerous languages, European and Asiatic.

Bibliography: A complete list of all Ganshof's books (with all translations and editions) and articles will be found in R. C. van Caenegem's "In Memoriam," in *Jaarboek van de Koninklijke Academie voor Wetenschappen, Letteren en Schone Kunsten van België* (1980), pp. 231–251.

R. van Caenegem

HARSIN, Paul (Liège, 1902–Liège, 1983), Belgian historian. Professor at the University of Liège (1928–1970) where he taught both history and political economy. A member of the Conseil supérieur des finances of Belgium (1936–1940). At the University of Liège, he was taught by historian Karl Hanquet (one of Godefroid Kurth's [q.v.] disciples), by jurist Léon Graulich, who oriented him toward the history of civil law, and by Edouard Van der Smissen, a specialist in public law, public finances, and political economy. Under their influence, the young historian started doing research in these subjects which were often neglected by historians. His doctoral dissertation, "Contribution à l'histoire de la principauté de Liège au XVIIe siècle," dealt with several domains: diplomatic history, economic history, and the history of institutions. It was published in the form of articles and of a first book: *Les relations extérieures de la principauté de Liège sous Jean Louis d'Elderen et Joseph Clément de Bavière (1688–1718)* (1927). Harsin's intellectual appetite led him to Paris where, from 1925 to 1928, he attended lectures at the Ecole des chartes, Faculty of Law, studying political economy and the history of law. But it was at the Ecole pratique des hautes etudes that he found the kind of teaching he was looking for. His meeting with François Simiand (q.v.) had a decisive and deep influence on him. This master was going to guide him in one of the chief directions of his work: the study of mercantilism, banking, and economic and financial doctrines. The work that earned him the title of "élève diplômé de l'Ecole des hautes etudes de Paris" was entitled *Les doctrines économiques et financières en France du XVIe au XVIIIe siècle* (1928). It was going to be extended by other books: *Crédit public et banque d'Etat en France du XVIe au XVIIIe siècle* (1933), *John Law. Oeuvres complètes* (3 vols., 1934), *Dutot: Réflexions politiques sur les finances et le commerce. Edition intégrale publiée pour la première fois* (1935), as well as by many articles. The main orientations of his future scientific work were now apparent. The history of the principality of Liège would become his chief preoccupation. This history cannot be envisaged outside the national context in which community dissensions have called into question Henri Pirenne's (q.v.) national history, even if the initial intention of the author was to continue the work Kurth had devoted to the city of Liège in the Middle Ages. A little book, *La révolution* *liégeoise de 1789* (1954), opens the series: *Etudes critiques sur l'histoire de la principauté de Liège 1477–1795* in which successively appeared *Le règne d'Erard de la Marck 1505–1538* (1955); *La principauté de Liège à la fin du règne de Louis de Bourbon et sous celui de Jean de Hornes, 1477–1505* (1957); and *Politique extérieure et défense nationale au XVIe siècle, 1538–1610* (1959). At the same time, in many articles Harsin clarified several particular points. The whole work won him the quinquennial prize of national history for the period 1956–1960 (*Moniteur belge*, November 7, 1963). The panel of judges found the work of an "historian, accurate and precise to the smallest detail." These words indeed characterize the style and method of this tireless historian, whose main concern was to be at once thorough and comprehensive in his scientific investigation.

Particulary sensitive to H. Berr's (q.v.) and H. See's ideas, Harsin identified new fields of historical research, but at the same time he inherited principles of historical criticism developed in 1883 by the Belgian Jesuit Charles De Smedt, well known to G. Kurth (q.v.) and transmitted by K. Hanquet. In 1933 Harsin authored a manual on historical criticism: *Comment on écrit l'histoire?* (reissued and completed for the seventh time in 1964). It was more than a rewrite of Langlois and Charles Seignobos' (q.v.) work. Harsin always had a deep interest in economic policy. Part of his work deals with economic problems, and another part investigates the economic mechanisms of the past which he felt were twentieth-century problems (the periodicity of crises, deflation and devaluation, the financing of war). At the end of his academic career, Harsin was approached by his colleagues E. Labrousse and Fernand Braudel (q.v.) and he agreed to write the pages devoted to "La finance et l'Etat jusqu'au système de Law (1660–1726)" in the *Histoire économique et sociale de la France* (vol. 2, 1970). At Liège, Harsin promoted the study of demographic and social history. He received many scientific and honorary distinctions, including the Francqui Prize (1950); the *doctor honoris causa* of many universities; and the presidency of the Académie royale de Belgique. From 1965 to 1970 he was president of the International Committee of Historical Sciences.

Bibliography: *Paul Harsin. Recueil d'études* (Liège, 1970, with a biographical notice by J. Lejeune); R. Demoulin, "In memoriam le Président Paul Harsin," *Annuaire d'histoire liégeoise* (1982–1983); J. Stengers, "Hommage à Paul Harsin," *Bulletin de la classe des lettres. Académie royale de Belgique* 69 (1983): 379–381.

P. Gerin

KURTH, Godefroid (Arlon, 1847–Asse near Brussels, 1916), Belgian historian. Pupil at the Ecole normale des humanités annexée à l'Université de Liège, Kurth wrote a doctoral dissertation on *Caton l'Ancien* in 1872. That same year he became a professor at the University of Liège where he taught, among other subjects, the history of the Middle Ages. In 1906 he became headmaster of the Institut historique belge de Rome. Under the influence of the methods in use in France, and especially in Germany, Kurth organized, in 1874, a practical teaching in history. This momentous initiative—the first in Belgium—completely revolutionized the teaching of history in Belgian universities. It was the origin of immense progress. Kurth's output was enormous and if as a whole it is dated, it has not yet been superseded. In the historiography of Belgium, Kurth's work represents the transition between the romantic and university-educated historians. Kurth was a romantic in his powerful poetic inspiration but his ardent nature also created a lot of difficulty. Henri Pirenne (q.v.) said of his master that he had "l'âme d'un croisé" (the spirit of a crusader). Kurth's romantic philosophy of history inspired his whole work and, in this particular case, the book that earned him international fame, *Les origines de la civilisation moderne* (1886). This philosophy assigned in the evolution of societies an essential place to Providence: "The secret of human civilization can only be discovered through divine revelation. Whether one likes it or not, it is religious science which has the last word on the human enigma." But the founder of practical courses in history was also a great scholar who mastered perfectly the techniques of a profession where rigor and precision are necessary. His extensive philological knowledge did him inestimable service. Kurth developed his scientific activity in three main directions: (1) the history of the very beginning of the Middle Ages treated in the collected articles *Etudes franques* (1919), in *Les origines*, in his outstanding *Histoire poétique des Mérovingiens* (1893)—the most original book—and in the monograph, *Clovis* (1896); (2) the history of the diocese and the country of Liège, on which he wrote two masterpieces of analysis and synthesis: the magnificent biography, *Notger de Liège et la civilisation au Xe siècle* (1905) and the big history, *La Cité de Liège au Moyen-Age* (1909–1910). Finally, Kurth was passionately interested in toponymy—he invented the word— and he wrote about this question in a very up-to-date work, *La frontière linguistique en Belgique et dans le Nord de la France* (1896–1898). It is the greatest homage we can pay to this scholar, teeming with ideas, who with Henri Pirenne, one of his students, can be considered one of the most brilliant personalities of Belgian historiography.

Bibliography: Jules Closon, "Godefroid Kurth," *Liber memorialis. L'Université de Liège de 1867 à 1935*, no. 1 (Liège, 1936), pp. 248–302; Georges Despy, "Un article inédit de Godefroid Kurth sur le domaine de Villance au IXe siècle," *Saint–Hubert d'Ardenne. Cahiers d'histoire*, no. 3 (1979): 97–118; Léon–Ernest Halkin, "Godefroid Kurth. Documents sur les débuts de sa carrière universitaire," *Bulletin de la Société d'Art et d'Histoire du Diocèse de Liège*, no. 4 (1959): 195–231; Xavier Michaëlis, *Godefroid Kurth* (Vieux-Virton, 1961); Fernand Neuray, *Une grande figure nationale. Godefroid Kurth. Un demi siècle de vie belge* (Bruxelles-Paris, 1931); Henri Pirenne, "Notice sur Godefroid Kurth," *Annuaire de l'Académie royale des Sciences, des Lettres et des Beaux– Arts de Belgique*, no. 90 (1924): 19–261; Ernst Striefler, *Gottfried Kurth. Ein deutsch- belgisches Grenzlandschicksal* (Leipzig, 1941); Fernand Vercauteren, "Godefroid Kurth (1847–1916)," *Bulletin trimestriel de l'Association des Amis de l'Université de Liège*, no. 20, 2 (1948): 3–12.

J. L. Kupper

PIRENNE, Henri (Verviers, 1862–Uccle, 1935), Belgian historian. Pirenne studied at the University of Liège; his master was Godefroid Kurth (q.v.) who, finding his inspiration in Leopold von Ranke's (q.v.) "Seminar," initiated him in practical exercises and in the techniques of historical research. He spent two years abroad: 1883–1884 in Germany (Leipzig, Berlin), where Gustav Schmoller (q.v.) guided him in the discovery of economic history and 1884–1885 in Paris (Ecole des chartes, Ecole pratique des hautes etudes), where he was a student of the medievalist, Arthur Giry. In 1885 he was appointed professor at the University of Ghent where he taught until 1935; from March 1916 until August 1918, he was a deportee in Germany. Pirenne's work is so rich and varied that it is impossible to examine it thoroughly. Here particular attention is drawn to his scientific works which have proved most original and have stimulated debate. His *Histoire de Belgique* (7 vols., 1900–1932) assured Pirenne national glory and an exceptional reputation abroad. Belgium is not an artificial state; already in the Middle Ages there was a Belgian people characterized by a common civilization, which was both Romance and Germanic. Such is Pirenne's central thesis to which he develops a final conclusion: the Belgian state created in 1830 was an historical necessity. As soon as the first volume was published, the work became a Bible for the nationalists and for those in governmental circles who were anxious to preserve the country's unity which had been threatened by internal dissensions between the Flemish- and the French-speaking people, and to protect Belgium's independence which had been jeopardized by foreign powers. Handbooks were rewritten, and Pirenne's thesis conditioned the teaching of Belgian history for fifty years. In the last twenty-five years, his domination of Belgian historiography ended, but it remains a model of its kind, by its intelligence, erudition, literary qualities, and willingness to join in close association political history with social and economic history.

As a specialist in medieval urban history, Pirenne wrote *Histoire de la Constitution de la ville de Dinant au Moyen Age* (1889), *Les anciennes démocraties des Pays-Bas*, (1910), and *Les Villes du Moyen Age—Essai d'histoire économique et sociale* (1927). These three books, together with several articles about urban history, were republished under the title *Les villes et les institutions urbaines*, (2 vols., 1939). For Pirenne, the Western Middle Ages was characterized by the birth of cities that were the daughters of the commercial renaissance of the eleventh century. According to this conception, they were born from agglomerations founded by merchants known as free men. The medieval burghers, their organization and their professions (cloth making, metal work), the evolution of urban social structures, and the belief that a proletariat was developing excited Pirenne's curiosity. If he perfectly perceived the extraordinary urban dynamism in the Low Countries and in Italy in the thirteenth and fourteenth centuries, Pirenne nevertheless considerably underestimated the continuity of the urban phenomenon beginning in the eighth century. After World War I, Pirenne took an active part in the discussion concerning the disappearance of the Roman world and the advent of the medieval one. His positions on this subject strengthened his thesis on the revival of trade in the eleventh century because they were its corollaries. Already in his *Histoire de l'Europe des Invasions au XVIe siècle*, written while he was in captivity but not published until 1936, he had to admit that the pressure of Islam in the seventh and eighth centuries, particularly the conquest of North Africa and Spain, had provoked a break between West and East. He took up this idea again in two articles published in *La Revue belge de philologie et d'histoire* in 1922 and 1923: "Mahomet et Charlemagne" and "Un contraste économique—Mérovingiens et Carolingiens." A few months before his death Pirenne completed a book that was published posthumously, *Mahomet et Charlemagne* (1937). In short he stated, it was the Moslem invasion rather than the Germanic which caused the antique tradition to disappear, while the whole economic life in the West was destroyed between 700 and 1100 since navigation in the Mediterranean had been interrupted. If Pirenne can be reproached for undervaluing the importance of the orientation of maritime activities from the West toward the North, the role of Venice in the contacts with the East, the economic life in the cities, and especially in the countryside during this period, it nevertheless remains true that his original views have influenced research until the present day. Pirenne was the initiator of historical demography in Belgium, for example, "Les documents d'archives comme source de la démographie historique," *Actes du XIe Congrès international d'Hygiène et de Démographie*, 1903. Here he offered economic and social factors as explanatory components of history. (See, for example: "Le mouvement économique et social" in *Histoire du Moyen Age*, 8, second section in *Histoire générale* directed by Ch. G. Glotz, 1933). He revealed himself as an historian who refused specialization and for whom comparison alone made "scientific knowledge" possible ("De la méthode comparative en histoire," *Compte rendu du Ve Congrès international des sciences historiques*, 1923). Pirenne was much admired by Marc Bloch (q.v.) and Lucien Fevbre (q.v.) who saw in him a spiritual father. Although Pirenne refused the direction of the *Annales d'histoire économique et sociale* (1929), he nevertheless agreed to become a member of the editorial committee of this review for which he wrote several articles.

Bibliography: R. Demoulin, "Henri Pirenne et la naissance des Annales," in *Au berceau des Annales. Le milieu strasbourgeois: L' histoire en France au début du XXe siècle*. Actes du Colloque de Strasbourg (October 11–13, 1979), (Toulouse, 1983), pp. 271–277; F. L. Ganshof in *Biographie nationale de Belgique*, 30 (Brussels, 1958), col. 671–723; F. L. Ganshof, E. Sabbe, F. Vercauteren, and C. Verlinden, "Bibliographie des travaux historiques d'Henri Pirenne," in *Henri Pirenne. Hommages et souvenirs*, 1 (Brussels, 1938), pp. 145–164; H. Hasquin, *Historiographie et politique. Essai sur l'histoire de Belgique et la Wallonie*, 2d ed. (Charleroi, 1981); R. Hodges and D. Whitehouse, *Muhammed, Charlemagne and the origins of Europe* (London, 1983); B. Lyon, *Henri Pirenne: A Biographical and Intellectual Study* (Ghent, 1974); *La fortune historiographique des thèses de Pirenne. Actes du colloque organisé à l'occasion du cinquantenaire de la mort de l'historien belge par l'Institut des Hautes Etudes de Belgique à Bruxelles les 10 et 11 mai 1985* (Brussels, 1985).

Herve Hasquin

VAN DER ESSEN, Leo (Antwerp, 1883–Louvain, 1963), Belgian historian. Educated at the Catholic University of Louvain, Van der Essen took his Ph.D. (1905) under the direction of the famous medievalist Alfred Cauchie; his dissertation dealt with the lives of the Merovingian saints in early medieval Belgium (*Etude critique et littéraire sur les Vitae des saints mérovingiens de l'ancienne Belgique*, 1907). Subsequently, he did research in Italian archives on the Eighty Years War (1568–1648), a period of Belgium's history which proved a lasting interest for him. Upon his return to Belgium, he became lecturer (1910) and extraordinary professor (1912) at Louvain University. During World War I his professorship and scholarly work were adapted to more politically oriented activities: He entered the propaganda office of the Belgian government in France and served in the political Cabinet of Charles de Broqueville, head of the government and minister for foreign affairs. In these functions he wrote *A Short History of Belgium* (1916, 1920) and the more voluminous *The Invasion and the War in Belgium. From Liège to the Yser, with a Sketch of the Diplomatic Negotiations Preceding the Conflict* (1917; also in Dutch and French). At the Peace Conference of Versailles he acted as the historical adviser to Belgium's minister for foreign affairs, Paul Hymans. Immediately after the war, he returned to Louvain where he became full professor (1918); he was also secretary-general of his alma mater (1930–1961). In the history of the Flemish University of Louvain he was a pioneer, for he taught in the Dutch language as early as 1911. In 1939 he became a member of the new Flemish Academy of Sciences, Letters, and Arts. When he became emeritus professor (1954), he was ennobled (''Jonkheer''). Not untypically for professors of his and of later generations, Van der Essen taught, in both national languages—Dutch (Flemish) and French—on a great variety of historical subjects: Society and Institutions of the Middle Ages, Institutions of the Early Modern Times, Historical Methodology, Archive Administration, Society and Institutions of the Byzantine Empire, and General History of the Christian Missions.

Van der Essen's bibliography includes 257 items and concerns mainly four fields. First comes Belgium's history in the sixteenth and early seventeenth century. To this period he devoted two major works: *Correspondence d'Ottavio Mirto Frangipani 1596–1606* (I, 1924) and his magnum opus, but not free of some hero-worshipping, *Alexandre Farnese, prince de Parme, gouverneur-général des Pays-Bas 1545–1592* (5 vols., 1933–1937; quinquennial state prize for history), and a series of monographs among which are three chapters on political and military history during the Eighty Years' War in the fifth volume (1952) of the *Algemene Geschiedenis der Nederlanden* (General History of the Low Countries, 12 vols., 1949–1958). His second field was the history of his own university. In both fields, he published many contributions, including those in the *Bulletin* of the Royal Commission of History (Brussels); he was a member of this commission from 1922 until his death. Van der Essen also remained interested in medieval history. In addition to his dissertation, he made a vast contribution on ''Flanders in the Middle Ages from the Fourth until the Thirteenth

Century'' for the first volume (1936) of the *Geschiedenis van Vlaanderen* (History of Flanders, 6 vols. 1936–1946), and he wrote a classic on Belgium's early Christianization, *Le siècle des saints (625–739)*. *Etude sur les origines de la Belgique chrétienne* (1943, also in Dutch: *De gulden eeuw onzer christianisatie, VII-VIII eeuw*, 1943). The fourth field has close connections with Belgium's political evolution in and between the two world wars; van der Essen combined loyalty to his Belgian fatherland with support of the moderate wing of the Flemish Movement and of the cooperation of the three Low Countries as well. To this orientation we owe a series of minor, rather patriotic essays, a French and a Flemish version of his *Short History of Belgium* (1926), *Pour mieux comprendre notre histoire nationale* (1932, 1945), and *La Belgique indépendante* (1945; also in Dutch). Despite this orientation, Van der Essen remained essentially an erudite historian, not without leanings toward microhistory, having a particular interest in politico-institutional and early modern history. Like so many Belgian historians, most if not all of his publications concerned Belgian history; however, they eventually covered fifteen centuries of that history.

Bibliography: R. de Schryver, ''Leo van der Essen,'' in *Handelingen van de Koninklijke Commissie voor Geschiedenis*, 150 (1984): 81–89; Ch. Terlinden, ''Eloge funèbre de L. J. van der Essen,'' in *Bulletin de la Commission royale d'histoire*, 129 (1963): IL–LVI; J. A. van Houtte, ''In Memoriam Prof. Em. Jhr. L. van der Essen,'' in *Bijdragen voor de Geschiedenis der Nederlanden*, 18 (1963): 19–22. For Van der Essen's bibliography, see the *Bibliographie académique, Université catholique de Louvain*, IV-X.

Reginald De Schryver

Great Historians: Brazilian

ABREU, João Capistrano de (Maranguape [Ceará], 1853–Rio de Janeiro, 1927), Brazilian historian. After attending high school in Fortaleza (Ceará), Capistrano de Abreu began writing literary criticism in some local newspapers and in 1875 went to Rio de Janeiro to become a journalist. He began in the *Gazeta de Notícias* in 1879, and that same year he got a job in the National Library. In 1883 his *Descobrimento do Brasil e seu desenvolvimento no séc. XVI* (The Discovery of Brazil and Its Development in the XVIth Century) was published in Rio de Janeiro. It was a very concise work, perhaps too succinct, and each chapter contained a list of the sources used. This book had been a thesis presented to Pedro the IInd College and gave way to a new study, *O descobrimento do Brasil pelos portugueses* (The Discovery of Brazil by the Portuguese), published in 1900, and also to a chapter in the *Livro do Centenário* (Book of the Centenary), "O descobrimento do Brasil. O povoamento do solo. Evolução social" (The discovery of Brazil. The peopling of the territory. Social evolution). In 1907, for a collective volume (*Centro Industrial do Brasil. O Brasil. Suas riquezas naturais*, Vol. 1), he wrote "Breves traços da história do Brasil colônia, império e república" (Brief Sketch of the History of Colonial, Imperial and Republican Brazil), and in that same year were printed his *Capítulos de história colonial* (Chapters of Colonial History). His numerous articles in newspapers and journals were collected after his death in 1927 by the Capistrano de Abreu Society and published with the title *Ensaios e estudos* (Essays and Studies). His correspondence was edited in three volumes by José Honório Rodrigues (1954–1956), and through his letters we can see how constant a researcher he was, never entirely satisfied with what he had written.

According to Sérgio Buarque de Holanda (q.v.), "more than any other since [Francisco Adolfo de] Varnhagen (q.v.), he worked to discover, evaluate, and utilize the written testimonies of our national formation.'' But in his first years, especially in the 1870s, Capistrano de Abreu was deeply impressed by evolutionism and adhered to the doctrines of Herbert Spencer with more fervor than to Comtian positivism. When criticizing Varnhagen, he suggested a periodization for the history of Brazil. From 1500 to 1614, the settlement of the coast was the principal concern. From 1614 to 1700, the coast was settled, except for a portion of the south and the lands north of the Amazon; the internal expansion began by using the rivers. The mines dominated the period from 1700 to 1750, and the period of consolidation of the colonial system was between 1750 and 1808. Beginning in 1808, the next period marked the decomposition of the colonial system. After 1850 a new period began, and it could be described as centralizing, imperial, and industrial. But even with this neat idea of periodization he never wrote a history of Brazil—only sketches and essays. He gave the reason himself when he presented the third edition of Varnhagen's work: "It ought not be written for some time. For the present there is a need for conscientious monographs." And he pointed to some of the voids: "Nobody has yet written a history of the 'sesmarias'. There is no history of the municipalities that were first discussed by Lisboa. The history of the 'bandeirantes' is scattered in books and archives. Hardly anything is known about the history of the Jesuits, other than the period narrated by Simão de Vasconcelos, and that is almost nothing. Finally we need a history of the mining region." His main concern was geographical and demographic rather than political: He devoted slightly more than thirty pages to the Dutch Wars, a favorite topic of the older historians as of Varnhagen, while he dedicated more than a hundred pages to the settling of the "sertão." He was interested only in the colonizing expeditions. He clearly disliked studying the warlike, revolutionary, and heroic phases of the history of the extreme south.

Bibliography: Tancredo de Barros Paiva, *Bibliografia Capistraneana* (Capistranean Bibliography), reprint of the *Anais do Museu Paulista* (São Paulo, 1931); Alba Canizares Nascimento, *Capistrano de Abreu (O homem e a obra). Primeiro ensaio crítico biográfico* (Capistrano de Abreu (Man and Work). First Biographical Critical Essay, (1931); Maria Beatriz Nizza da Silva, "Histoire empirique et histoire théorique: deux chemins de l'historiographie brésilienne au XIXe siècle," in *Storia della Storiografia*, 5 (1984); J. A. Pinto do Carmo, *Bibliografia de Capistrano de Abreu* (Bibliography of Capistrano de Abreu), (1943); José Honório Rodrigues, "Capistrano de Abreu and Brazilian Historiography," in E. Bradford Burns, ed., *Perspectives on Brazilian History*, (1967); Hélio Viana, *Capistrano de Abreu. Ensaio biobibliográfico* (Capistrano de Abreu. Biobibliographical Essay), (1955).

Maria Beatriz Nizza da Silva

BELLO, José Maria de Albuquerque (Pernambuco, 1886–Rio de Janeiro, 1959), Brazilian historian. Bello became involved in politics early in life and was actively engaged until 1930, when a revolution hindered him from being instated as governor of his native state. Thereafter he devoted himself to intellectual activities, his efforts being directed mainly toward reaching an understanding of contemporary reality. His main work, *História da República 1889–1954—Síntese de Sessenta e Cinco Anos de Vida Brasileira* (A History of the Republic 1889–1954: A Synthesis of Sixty-Five Years of Brazilian Life), was produced and published by stages. The first edition appeared in 1940 and only covered the period between 1889 and 1902. The second edition, published in 1952, received the addition of nine chapters and covered the 1889–1930 period. The third and final edition (1956) was increased by a further two chapters covering the 1930–1945 period and included a "brief description" of the events that occurred between 1945 and 1954. The fourth edition (1958) received minor formal corrections. He feared to approach the more recent polemic events, for example, the suicide of President Vargas (1954), claiming the existence of "unsurmountable difficulties in clarifying their mysteries." He was particularly devoted to contemporary history and defended it with vigor, pointing out that the problems it posed were no less serious than those faced by the attempt to reconstitute the "fargone past." Several foreign books stimulated Bello in the task of interpreting Brazilian life: *America in Our Time (1896–1946)* by D. L. Dumond; *La Troisième République* (1870–1935), by Jacques Bainville; and *L'Italie Contemporaine (1871–1915)*, by Benedetto Croce (q.v.). Bello, however, adopted none of them as a model; they only contributed as guides for obtaining a vast knowledge of events in order to attain a desirable "synthesis." Readings in the philosophy and methodology of history and related sciences had little or no influence on the choice of the method he followed in preparing his book. In fact, he believed that method "should be translated particularly in a work of historical synthesis, by means of a fair balance of the parts, or, as it were, a careful distribution of the masses, logical sequence, and neatness and harmony in composition." Although based on an extremely personal notion of scientific criteria, and therefore open to contestation, *História da República 1889–1954* is still the best synthetic interpretation available on contemporary Brazilian history.

Nanci Leonzo

CALÓGERAS, João Pandiá (Rio de Janeiro, 1870–Rio de Janeiro, 1934), Brazilian historian. Calógeras began his professional life as an engineer and politician. From 1891 until his death, he collaborated extensively with journals and newspapers. His most important work was published between 1904 and 1905 under the title *As Minas do Brasil e a sua Legislação* (The Mines of Brazil and their Legislation). In its three volumes, theoretical knowledge and the experience of a professional engineer, an active politician, and a scholar of mining activities under the colonial, imperial, and republican periods are thoroughly blended. In another book, *A Política Monetária do Brasil* (1910; Brazil's Monetary Policy), he establishes a link between the monetary problems faced by the country and government policy. The first edition was published in French, after having been presented at the Third National American Conference, the major theme of which was "a detailed study of the monetary system in force in each one of the American republics, its history, the oscillations in the rate of exchange over the last twenty years, together with charts showing the influence of such oscillations on trade and industrial development.'' Calógera's work fulfilled these requirements and went so far as to offer suggestions on the measures to be taken for the ''economic redemption'' of Brazil. In 1924 he was invited to collaborate in the activities sponsored by the Brazilian Historical and Geographical Institute *in memoriam* of Emperor Peter II, on the occasion of the centennial of his birth. This collaboration originated the three volumes of *A Política Exterior do Império* (The Empire's Foreign Policy), a subject which the author investigated ''in its formative elements, in its human and mesological origins'' and ''together with the correlated factors of European history.'' The first two volumes of this work were first published in a special issue of the institute's journal. Additional editions by the National Print in Rio de Janeiro, in 1927 and 1928, made these two volumes readily available to the public. The third volume was only to appear in 1933, with the subtitle *Da Regência à Queda de Rosas* (From the Regency to the Fall of Rosas). In conformity with his ideals, he strove to uphold ''the respect for the document, an all-encompassing spirit of Americanism, and continental and social fraternity.'' *Formacão Histórica do Brasil* (The Historical Forming of Brazil) is one of his best known books, resulting from a series of lectures held at the School for Brazilian Studies, founded under the auspices of the Brazilian Historical and Geographical Institute. This book, which covers Brazil's history from the discovery up to 1929 is, however, a rather unconvincing attempt of synthesis, failing even in the intention of following the guidelines set by the historian João Capistrano de Abreu (q.v.) in *Capitulos da História Colonial* (Chapters of Colonial History), as expressed in the introduction, and petering out in a factual and chronological approach, and in inconsistent and overpatriotic conclusions.

Bibliography: Antônio Gontijo de Carvalho, *Calógeras* (São Paulo: Nacional, 1935).

Nanci Leonzo

HOLANDA, Sérgio Buarque de (São Paulo, 1902–São Paulo, 1982), Brazilian historian. Holanda studied law at the University of Rio de Janeiro (1921–1925), but he was more interested in literature than in becoming a lawyer. He published literary criticism in several newspapers and interviewed Pirandello and Blaise Cendrars for *O Jornal*. He was sent to Europe as a correspondent of this newspaper and settled in Berlin in 1929. He then had the opportunity to listen to the lectures of Friedrich Meinecke (q.v.) and to become acquainted with Max Weber's (q.v.) work. By appointment of the Brazilian Embassy in Berlin, he wrote some articles on the economic history of Brazil for the journal *Duco*. Returning to Rio de Janeiro in December 1930, he published an essay, ''Corpo e alma do Brasil'' (Body and Soul of Brazil) in 1935, in the journal *Espelho*. He prepared the book *Raízes do Brasil* (Roots of Brazil), printed in 1936, when he was an assistant to Professor Henri Hauser in the University of the Federal District. He worked for the National Institute of Books (1939–1943), and in 1941 he was invited by the Cultural Division of the State Department to be a visiting scholar in several American universities (New York, Washington, Chicago, and Wyoming). From 1944 to 1946 he was one of the directors of the National Library, and in 1944 he published with another historian, Otávio Tarquínio de Sousa (q.v.) a textbook on the history of Brazil for high school students. In 1945 his interest in the history of São Paulo began with *Monções* (Monsoons), and, while living in this city in 1946, he was nominated director of the Paulista Museum belonging to the University of São Paulo, a position he held until 1956. From 1947 to 1955 he taught Brazilian economic history in the São Paulo School of Sociology and Politics. In 1948 he organized at the University of São Paulo a seminar on the study of primary sources for the history of São Paulo in the eighteenth century. A lecture at the Historical and Geographical Institute of São Paulo was printed in 1948: *Expansão paulista em fins do século XVI e princípios do século XVII* (The Paulista Expansion at the End of the Sixteenth Century and Beginning of the Seventeenth). The second edition of *Roots of Brazil* was published that year. In 1949 he worked for Unesco and traveled to Europe. In France, in the École pratique de hautes études, he spoke about honey and wax in colonial Brazil, and his lecture was published in the *Annales* in 1950 as "Au Brésil colonial: les civilisations du miel." His long article, "Índios e mamelucos na expansão paulista" (Indians and Mestizos in the Paulista Expansion), was published in the *Anais do Museu Paulista* (vol. 13, 1948). In 1950, in the First Colloquium on Luso-Brazilian Studies, which took place in the Library of Congress in Washington, he presented a paper on rural techniques, published in the 1953 *Proceedings* by Vanderbilt University. His *Antologia de poetas brasileiros da fase colonial* (Anthology of Brazilian Poets from the Colonial Period) appeared in 1952. In 1953 he traveled with his family to Rome, where, by appointment of the Brazilian Foreign Office, he was in charge of Brazilian Studies at the University of Rome until 1954. When in Rome, he was the founder and first director of the Instituto di Studi Brasiliani. Upon his return to Brazil in 1955, he resumed his place at the Paulista Museum and at the São Paulo School of Sociology and Politics. In 1957 his book *Caminhos e fronteiras* (Paths and Frontiers) appeared, and in 1958 he wrote his thesis *Visão do Paraíso* (Vision of Paradise). He then became full professor at the University of São Paulo. He retired in 1968. During his ten years at the University Holanda organized and was first director of the Institute of Brazilian Studies, a multidisciplinary institution. He lectured in Chile in 1963 and in the United States in 1965 and 1966. In 1977 he collected several studies, old and new, in *Tentativas de mitologia* (Attempts at Mythology) and prepared an anthology of Leopold von Ranke's (q.v.) writings. From 1960 to 1977 he was the editor of the seven volumes of *História Geral da Civilização Brasileira* (General History of Brazilian Civilization), published in São Paulo with the collaboration of several Brazilian historians. Nevertheless, he wrote nearly all of the second book of Volume 3

(Monarchical Brazil) by himself. He collaborated in E. Bradford Burns' *Per-spectives on Brazilian History* (1967) with a chapter entitled "Historical Thought in Twentieth-Century Brazil."

Holanda's most successful book was *Roots of Brazil*, which underwent four-teen editions during the author's life and was translated into Italian (1954), Spanish (1955), and twice into Japanese (1971 and 1976). This work can be classified as a long historical essay in which the author proposes to explain the political and social Brazil of the 1930s through an analysis of the Portuguese colonial inheritance. The Portuguese colonization is viewed in its specificity, though in the first part the Iberian Peninsula as a whole is compared to other European countries in the century of the great discoveries. Revealing a good historiographical culture, as well as readings in anthropology, social psychology, and politics, this book is not really an historical work—not because it rejects the narrative form in favor of a more explanatory discourse, but because there is no historical subject in it. Very often it is called an "interpretation" of Brazil, the Brazil the author knew in his political and social experience. But some good sections on colonial Brazil, especially those referring to the contact between Indian and Portuguese cultures, were later developed in articles and in *Paths and Frontiers*, in which the historian describes how several aspects of the Indian material culture were adopted by the Portuguese colonists. Another issue reex-amined after twenty years of research was the difference between Spanish and Portuguese colonization in *Vision of Paradise*, the first scholarly book of this historian who began as an historical essayist. No other Brazilian historian of his generation was more open than Buarque de Holanda to the social sciences, and no other had a more acute sense of the importance of comparative history. His books are never narrowly Brazilian, though he had a great familiarity with the primary sources of the national history. In all his books the reader notes the deep knowledge of European and American historiography, as well as of the main literary sources which Buarque de Holanda used for his comparisons with Brazilian history. Because of his recent death, no book has yet been published on this learned and cosmopolitan historian.

Maria Beatriz Nizza da Silva

OLIVEIRA LIMA, Manuel de (Pernambuco, 1867– Washington D.C., 1928), Brazilian historian. Oliveira Lima's historiographic production was developed concurrently with his diplomatic activities up to 1913, in several European countries, in the United States, in Japan, and at certain South American legations. His first book, *Pernambuco: Seu Desenvolvimento Histórico* (The Historical Development of Pernambuco), published in Leipzig, in 1895, is a study of regional history perfectly inserted in a national context. It was not the author's intention to present a text supported by new documentary evidence that would permit the correction of dates and figures. His purpose, rather, was simply to draw a picture of the Brazilian political and social evolution over four centuries of history, without disregarding the "valuable contours" and putting aside its "interesting features." His "official" recognition as an historian took place in 1900, on the occasion of the contest promoted by the Association of the IV Centennial of the Discovery of Brazil, in which he won a prize for his *Memória sobre o Descobrimento do Brasil* [Memorial on the Discovery of Brazil]. After one year's residence in London (1900–1901) as second secretary to the Brazilian Legation, he concluded his book *História Diplomática do Brasil: O Reconhecimento do Império* (Diplomatic History of Brazil: The Acknowledgment of the Empire), submitted to the French publisher Garnier, and presenting the results of local research through the *Relação dos Manuscritos Portugueses e Estrangeiros de Interesse para o Brasil, Existentes no Museu Britânico de Londres* (Inventory of Portuguese and Foreign Manuscripts of Interest to Brazil, Existing in the British Museum, in London), published in Rio de Janeiro by the Brazilian Historical and Geographical Institute, in 1903. He was to make an intense use of this compilation in writing his subsequent books and for preparing his numerous lectures delivered in Brazil and abroad. The documents investigated in London, together with others retrieved in Portugal, France, the United States, and Brazil, as well as the narratives of the travellers who traversed the country, were extremely useful in writing his major work *Dom João VI no Brasil 1808–1821* (King John VI in Brazil 1808–1821), published in 1908. Most biographers of Oliveira Lima restrict themselves to pointing out in this book the rehabilitation of the personality of King John VI, often misjudged by Portuguese historians. In fact, this rehabilitation is present in the two volumes of the work, the greatest merit of which is in the attempt to reconstitute the political, economical, social, and cultural life of Brazil during the thirteen years in which the Portuguese royal family resided in Rio de Janeiro. In another book, *O Movimento da Independência* (The Independence Movement), published in 1922, he examines Brazil's political emancipation much as a drama, following the unfolding of the events in the Brazilian and Portuguese "scenes." The Portuguese, however, predominates, and almost exclusively from the political point of view. The works *Dom Pedro e Dom Miguel: A Querela da Sucessão, 1826–1828* (Dom Pedro and Dom Miguel: The Dispute over the Succession, 1826–1828) and *Dom Miguel no Trono, 1828–1833* (King Miguel on the Throne, 1828–1833), published, respectively, in 1925 (São Paulo) and 1933 (Coimbra), are a continuation of the studies taking as a starting point the year 1808, in which the Portuguese royal family arrived in Brazil.

In the year of Oliveira Lima's death appeared, also in São Paulo, *O Império Brasileiro, 1822–1889* (The Brazilian Empire, 1822–1889), in which are developed certain considerations that had initially been brought up in his lectures, for example, at the Sorbonne, in 1911, and collected in *Formation Historique de la Nationalité Brésilienne*. Besides publishing several historical, political, and literary studies in Brazilian and foreign journals and newspapers, he left a registry of his "impressions" of the countries he visited as a diplomat-historian, for example, Japan, the United States, and other countries of Spanish America. He also found time to prepare an innovative school compendium, *História da*

Civilização (Traços Gerais) (The History of Civilization [A General Outline]), divided into four parts (Antiquity and the Middle Ages, Modern Times, Contemporary Times, and the New World). Without omitting the history of the "Portuguese mother-country," it included the "conditions and events" of the historical evolution of the United States and Spanish America. His interest in Spanish America dated back to 1912, when he delivered a series of lectures in U.S. universities subsequently collected and published under the title *América Latina e América Inglesa—A Evolução Brasileira Comparada com a Hispano-Americana e com a Anglo-Americana* (Latin American and English America—Brazilian Evolution Compared to the Spanish American and Anglo-American). In 1923, during a short stay in Europe, he inaugurated the chair of Brazilian Studies at the College of Letters, University of Lisbon. His lectures held on this occasion are included in *Aspectos da História e da Cultura do Brasil* (Aspectos of Brazilian History and Culture). He chose the United States as a permanent residence and gathered a voluminous library (40,000 volumes), bequeathed in his will to the Catholic University of Washington, where he held the chair of International Law.

Bibliography: Fernando da Cruz Gouvêa, *Oliveira Lima: Uma Biografia* (Oliveira Lima—A Biography), (Recife, Instituto Arqueológico, Histórico e Geográfico Pernambucano, 1976), 3 vol.; Neusa Dias de Macedo, *Bibliografia de Manuel de Oliveira Lima* (Bibliography of Manuel de Oliveira Lima), (Recife Arquivo Público Estadual, 1968); Gilberto Freyre, *Don Quixote Gordo* (The Fat Don Quixote), (Imprensa Universitária da Universidade Federal de Pernambuco, 1968); Barbosa Lima Sobrinho, *Manuel de Oliveira Lima—Obra Seleta* (Manuel de Oliveira Lima–Selected Works) (Rio de Janeiro: INL, 1971).

Nanci Leonzo

SIMONSEN, Roberto Cochrane (Santos, 1889–Rio de Janeiro, 1948), Brazilian historian. Founder of the first School of Sociology and Politics in Brazil, located in São Paulo, which, from 1933, became an important cultural center that purported to train an elite of "personalities capable of an efficient and conscientious collaboration in conducting the life of society." At this institution, in 1936 Simonsen inaugurated the chair of national economic history, the course content of which gave origin to his book *História Econômica do Brasil 1500–1820* (The Economic History of Brazil 1500–1820). In this work which relegates "methodological concepts" and "doctrinary systematizations" to a secondary plane of interest, he investigated the "economical facts" pertinent to the history of Brazil, adding comments or, in some instances, comparing them to concurrent events in other countries. His main objective was to examine, from the point of view of "economic realities," the causes of the events, and, for this purpose, he made ample use of tables and statistics. Simonsen was not a professional historian, but this contingency in no way hindered him in conducting a pioneering and, above all, a model research on the economic history of Colonial Brazil. His entire historiographic production is intimately linked to his training as a civil engineer and to his political and business activities over more than three decades.

In *A Evoluçao Industrial do Brasil* (Brazil's Industrial Evolution), a text prepared in 1939 at the invitation of the Federal Board for Foreign Trade for the purpose of honoring a U.S. university mission visiting the country, he demonstrates a clear interest in current events, making extensive use of contemporary information and statistics for developing his analyses. The same procedure is adopted in *Aspectos da História Econômica do Café* (Aspects of the Economic History of Coffee), written in 1940. The interest in the present, with a wide knowledge of the past, is accompained by a fear for the future. It becomes, then, essential to propose solutions. A typical instance of Simonsen's doctrinaire position is the opinion submitted in August 1944 to the National Board of Industrial and Commercial Policy, under the title *A Planificaçâo da Economia Brasileira* (The Planning of Brazilian Economy). Simonsen's greatest achievement remains *História Econômica do Brasil 1500–1820*. After it was published, Brazilian historiography began to follow new paths, transcending the limits of political and administrative history to include also the economic.

Nanci Leonzo

SOUSA, Otávio Tarquínio de (Rio de Janeiro, 1889–Rio de Janeiro, 1959), Brazilian historian. Tarquínio de Sousa studied law in Rio de Janeiro until 1907, when he got his degree and entered public administration. Literary criticism and history were his hobbies. He wrote for several newspapers; in 1934 he was elected president of the Brazilian Association of Writers; and after 1939, succeeding Gilberto Freyre, he edited an historical collection called "Brazilian Documents" for an important publisher in Rio, José Olympio. Although he began his career as an historian with a book on *A mentalidade da Constituinte* (1931; The Mentality of the Constituent Assembly), he was essentially a biographer. In the 1930s, readers were used to fanciful biographies, and he was an innovator in this field, not only because he made a serious study of primary sources, but also because his scholarly erudition was well balanced by his powers as a writer. For his biography of Emperor Pedro I for the first time he did a literary search of the Archives of the Imperial House in Petropolis, near Rio de Janeiro; his three volumes are a scholarly answer to the pamphlet-like republican historiography, which since 1889 had tried to destroy the image of monarchy and especially of the first emperor. He specialized in the so-called period of the first Empire (1822–1831) and Regency (1831–1840), and his works clearly show a methodic and dynamic inquiry, passing from one politician to another in a coherent succession of personalities. His individual biographies, published from 1937 to 1953, were collected in 1957 in ten volumes with the title *História dos fundadores do Império brasileiro* (History of the Founders of the Brazilian Empire): vol. 1, *José Bonifácio*; vols. 2, 3, and 4, *The Life of Pedro the 1st*; vol. 5, *Bernardo Pereira de Vasconcelos*; vol. 6, *Evaristo da Veiga*; vol. 7, *Diogo Antônio Feijó*. With small changes, vol. 8, *Three Coups d'État*, which put together *The Mentality of the Constituent Assembly* (1931) and the book published in 1939, *History of Two Coups d'État*. Volume 9, *Facts and People*

Around a Regime, represented a new collection of articles on the period of independence, first empire, and regency, with a good chapter dedicated to a critical review of the historiography on that period. In the introduction written in 1954 for this vast *History of the Founders of the Brazilian Empire*, Tarquínio de Sousa asked himself the classical question about the role of individuals in history, discarding both Thomas Carlyle's (q.v) heroes and historical laws: "Historical facts, being unique, do not subordinate themselves to the concept of laws deducted from the repetition of phenomena in Nature. Nature and Culture, Nature and History, have their own methods, as it was shown in the works of Wilhelm Christian Dilthey (q.v.), Windelband, Rickert, Alexandre D. Xenopol (q.v.) and others, who, though disagreeing in some points of greater or smaller importance, affirmed the autonomy of historical facts and pointed to specific methods to study them." But if he opposed the idea that there are "historical laws," on the other side he refused the idea of history as merely "a vast collection of biographies." Its object is the study of the development, in time and in space, of civilizations, nations, and human groups, viewed in their political, economic, and social aspects. However, men are always present in history because each man has a personal and an historical dimension: "If great men, leaders and heroes, very often seeming to command, in reality just obey the spirit of their time, on the other hand we must agree that the ideas, the plans and the will of certain reformers in politics, in religion, in science or in art, exert an efficient action in world affairs." Inspired by Dilthey, the Brazilian historian tried to discover, based on the best primary sources, "the real nexus" by which the leaders were determined by their milieu and how they reacted to this milieu.

                                                                        Maria Beatriz Nizza da Silva

VARNHAGEN, Francisco Adolfo de (São João do Ipanema (São Paulo), 1816–Vienna, 1878), Brazilian historian. Varnhagen went to Portugal with his family in 1824, and in Lisbon he studied in the Noblemen College, the Military College, and the Marine Academy. He fought against Dom Miguel in the army commanded by Dom Pedro, ex-emperor of Brazil. His first work as an historian, *Reflexões críticas sobre o escrito do séc. XVI impresso com o título de Notícia do Brasil* (Critical Reflexions on the Sixteenth Century Work Printed with the Title Notice of Brazil), opened to him the gates of the Royal Academy of Sciences in Lisbon in 1839, as well as those of the Historical and Geographical Brazilian Institute in Rio de Janeiro. In Portugal he was on friendly terms with Alexandre Herculano (q.v.), the most outstanding Portuguese historian and the editor of the journal *O Panorama*, in which Varnhagen published the first version of his historical novel, *Crónica do descobrimento do Brasil* (Chronicle of the Discovery of Brazil). When he lived in Portugal, he pressed the institute and the Brazilian government to get copies of the manuscripts on Brazil kept in European archives and libraries, especially the Portuguese ones. For him history and geography were the most important studies in developing the spirit of nationality. In 1840 he went back to Brazil, and until 1841 he took part in the sessions of the institute, for whose journal he had already sent some biographies and some scholarly studies. He traveled to São Paulo and Santos in search of ancient manuscripts, but the poor state of municipal archives convinced him that "in the letters of the Jesuits could be found the best sources for the two first periods of the modern history of Brazil." He then collected documents with the idea of writing a general history of Brazil, and, back in Lisbon, he went on with his research in the Portuguese archives. In 1842 he was attaché to the Brazilian Embassy in Lisbon, and his career as a diplomat-historian really began. In 1846 he visited the Spanish archives (Madrid, Simancas, and Seville) in order to collect documents for the question of Brazilian boundaries. In 1847 he was appointed to the Brazilian Embassy in Madrid, and in 1850 the first and second volumes of his *Florilégio da poesia brasileira* (Florilegium of Brazilian poetry) were published in Lisbon. The third volume appeared in Madrid in 1853. In 1851 he traveled to Brazil and organized the library and the archives of the Brazilian Institute.

After returning to Madrid, Varnhagen worked hard in order to finish his *História Geral do Brasil* (General History of Brazil). The first volume was published in Rio de Janeiro in 1854, and the second one in 1857. In a letter to Emperor Pedro II, he explained the institute's indifference toward his work, saying that, while all the other historians had a very dangerous sense of nationalism, he wrote as a patriot "without hating the Portuguese or the foreigner Europe which benefits us with enlightenment." In Madrid he published an "epic–historical drama," *Amador Bueno ou a coroa do Brasil em 1641* (1858; Amador Bueno or the Crown of Brazil in 1641), and in Paris that same year he published two works on Vespucci, part of a controversy with the French geographer Armand d'Avezac–Macaya, who had reviewed his *General History of Brazil*. Both were written in French: *Vespuce et son premier voyage* and *Examen de quelques points de l'histoire géographique du Brésil*. From 1859 to 1868, he had diplomatic missions in Latin America, especially in Chile and Peru, but this period was not very productive from the historical point of view. Nevertheless in 1865 he published in Lima another book on the Florentine navigator: *Amerigo Vespucci, son caractère, ses écrits (même les moins authentiques), sa vie et ses navigations, avec une carte indiquant les routes*. Sent to Vienna, he prepared the second edition of his *General History of Brazil* (published in 1877), wrote three other books on Vespucci, one of them in Italian, and his *História das lutas com os holandeses no Brasil desde 1624 a 1654* (History of the Fights Against the Dutch in Brazil from 1624 to 1654), published in 1871. Varnhagen was indeed the first outstanding historian after the independence of Brazil, and even one of his critics, João Capistrano de Abreu (q.v), in an appendix to the third edition of the *General History of Brazil*, acknowledged his merits: "The discoveries of Varnhagen were considerable, especially for the first century of our history." He found and published in Lisbon, in 1839, Pero Lopes de Sousa's *Diário da navegação da armada que foi à terra do Brasil em 1530* (Diary of the Navigation of the Fleet Gone to the Land of Brazil in 1530), a document that clarified many obscure points. Another important task was the edition of the account of Gabriel Soares de Sousa, *Tratado descritivo do Brasil em 1587* (Descriptive Treatise on Brazil in 1587), published in Rio de Janeiro in 1851, as well as Farnão Cardim's *Narrativa epistolar* (Epistolary Narrative). As Capistrano de Abreu put it, "Varnhagen did more to make the XVIth century understood than anybody else who has written about the history of Brazil." But Varnhagen also made some discoveries about the seventeenth century, especially in the history of the Dutch War and in the history of the state of Maranhão with the edition of Maurício de Heriarte's *Descrição do Estado do Maranhão, Pará, Corupá e Rio das Amazonas* (A Description of the State of Maranhão, Pará, Corupá and the Amazon River) in Vienna in 1874. His analysis of the eighteenth century was weaker, and he wrote very little about the nineteenth century. Although he prepared in Vienna a history of independence from 1820 to 1825, he left this work unpublished. The first edition, published by the Historical and Geographical Brazilian Institute, appeared in 1917. For this work on independence, he counted on the diplomatic correspondence found in Vienna between Metternich and the Baron de Mareschal. In Brazil he had also gathered his information from contemporaries of the events. Because of the numerous materials brought to light by Varnhagen, his *General History of Brazil* is still read by professional historians.

Bibliography: Hans Horch, *Francisco Adolfo de Varnhagen. Subsídios para uma bibliografia* (Francisco Adolfo de Varnhagen. Contributions for a Bibliography) (São Paulo, 1982); Basílio de Magalhães, *Francisco Adolfo de Varnhagen (Visconde de Porto Seguro)* (Rio de Janeiro, 1928); Armando Ortega Fontes, *Bibliografia de Varnhagen* (Bibliography of Varnhagen), (Rio de Janeiro, 1928).

Maria Beatriz Nizza da Silva

Great Historians:
Bulgarian

BURMOV, Alexander Kossev (Biala Cherkva, 1911–Sofia, 1965), Bulgarian historian. Graduated in Slavonic philology and history from the University of Sofia (1939) and had a year (1940–1941) of postgraduate training in Eastern European history at the University of Vienna. Meanwhile (1932–1933) Burmov was editor of the newspaper *Worker's Literary Front*, as a result of which he spent one year in jail. In 1943–1944 he was appointed assistant professor in history at the University of Skopje. In 1946 he moved to the University of Sofia, where he was first appointed assistant professor (1946) and then professor in ordinary (1947) and head of the chair of Bulgarian and Byzantine history. In 1950 he became senior research fellow of the Institute of History of the Bulgarian Academy of Sciences and was appointed head of the Section of Sources and Bibliography of Bulgarian History. In 1962–1965 he was offered the rectorship of the Higher Pedagogical Institute of Veliko Turnovo, where he lectured in medieval history. Burmov became member of the Bulgarian Archaeological Society (1945), member of the Bulgarian Historical Society, and one of the founders of the journal *Istoriceski pregled* (Historical Review). In 1958 he was elected corresponding member of the Bulgarian Academy of Sciences. Burmov's scholarly interests embraced Bulgarian medieval history and the history of the Bulgarian national revival. His works comprising monographs and articles number some 150 titles. His major works are *Bulgarski revoliuzionen zentralen komitet, 1868–1876* (1948; The Bulgarian Revolutionary Central Committee, 1868–1876); *Istoriya na Bulgaria po vremeto no Shishmanovzi* (1947: A History of Bulgaria during the Reign of the Shismanides, 1323–1396); *Kam vaprosa za proizhoda na prabulgarite* (1948; On the Origins of the Proto-Bulgarians); *Kam istoriyata na rusko-balgaskite vrazki prez 1876* (To the History of the Russo-

Bulgarian Relations in 1876); and *Hristo Botev i negovata ceta* (Hristo Botev and His Detachment).

Bibliography: *Izbrani proizvedeniya vav tri toma* (Selected Works in Three Volumes) (Sofia, 1968–1976).

Rumiana Radeva

DIMITROV, Mikhail Dafinchkiev (Chuprene, 1881–Sofia, 1966), Bulgarian philosopher, psychologist, and historian. Concerned mainly with the revolutionary thought of the period of the Bulgarian national revival. Dimitrov studied philosophy at the universities of Sofia, Bern, and Zagreb (1903–1908) and took a degree from the University of Sofia in 1908. In 1921 he was appointed assistant in experimental psychology at the University of Sofia and *custos* of the Laboratory of Psychology. In 1941 he was appointed assistant professor at the same university, and in 1946 he was promoted to a professorship of systematic philosophy. In the same year he was elected to fellowship in the Bulgarian Academy of Sciences, and during 1947–1956 he served as secretary of its Section of Philosophy and History. In 1949 he became vice-president and held this post until 1956. His highly productive period of research in psychology did not prevent him from expanding his sphere of interest into the works and the ideology of Hristo Botev, a great Bulgarian poet, journalist, and revolutionary, the first utopian-socialist of this country, and organizer and leader of a revolutionary detachment which fell in battle in 1876. Dimitrov searched for unknown works left by Botev, examined his ideology, published a short biography of the revolutionary poet, and entered into polemics with authors who underestimated Botev's views or subjected them to wrong interpretations. In 1948 he joined a team of scholars examining documents and materials concerning Hristo Botev in the archives of Moscow, Leningrad, and Odessa. He published Botev's collected works in three volumes, supplying it with an extensive study on the ideological and political trends existing among the Bulgarian emigrants in Romania during the 1860s and 1870s. Dimitrov was one of the founders and the first director of the Botev Research Institute, which was dedicated to research on the life and works of Hristo Botev, of his contemporaries, and of the revolutionary movement during the 1880s. During the last twenty years of his life Dimitrov devoted time and energy to another great Bulgarian revolutionary and founder of the contemporary Bulgarian fiction, Liuben Karavelov. He wrote several works on Karavelov—a biography, studies on his ideology, political activities and role.

Kr. Sharova

DRINOV, Marin (Panagiurishte, 1838–Kharkov, Russia, 1906), Bulgarian historian. Assistant professor (1873) and professor (1876–1906) at the University of Kharkov. Drinov's first important work published in 1869 was entitled *Pogled varhu proizhozhdenieto na balgarskia narod i nachaloto na balgarskata istoria* (An Outline of the Origins of the Bulgarian People and the Beginnings of Bulgarian History). This study, based on a broad historical canvass and rich source material, describes the fate of the old population of the Balkan peninsula, the settlement of Slav tribes, the arrival of the Asparoukh Bulgarians, and the origins of the Bulgarian people. Some of Drinov's views have long been discarded, for example, his thesis of a complete depopulation of the Balkan lands throughout the fourth and the fifth centuries A.D., his negative attitude toward the proto-Bulgarians, and his idea that the Slav tribes settled in the Balkans should be treated as the real and only ancestors of the Bulgarian people. Nevertheless in some respects this book still has value. Also during 1869, Drinov published his second important work, *Istoricheski pregled na balgarskata zrkva ot samoto i nachalo do dnes* (A Historical Review of the Bulgarian Church Since Its Foundation). Here Drinov retraces the dissemination of Christianity in the Balkans up to the mid-ninth century, the conversion of the Bulgarian people and the origins of the Bulgarian church, the struggle for independence from Constantinople and Rome, the first Bulgarian Patriarchate and its history up to the year 1018, the restoration of the Patriarchate in 1235, the history of the archbishopric of Ohrid up to its closing down in 1767, the Bulgarian national revival, and the Church question. The history of the Bulgarian church is treated in detail and in a broad historical context. The basic value of this important work is to be found in its academic treatment, its reservedness, and its objectivity regardless of the complex and contradictory character of the problems treated.

In 1872 Drinov published one of his most significant works, *Zaseleniya balkanskogo poluostrova slavianami* (The Slav Settlement in the Balkan Peninsula). This book is a learned study of the ancient history of the Balkan peninsula, which plausibly rejects the theory of the autochthony of the Slavs. At the same time Drinov attempted to establish the thesis that the Slav tribes settled in the Balkan peninsula as early as the second and third centuries A.D., which has subsequently been proved wrong. The second part of the book is concerned with Slav–Byzantine relations and the dispersal of Slav tribes in the Balkan lands. This part was written based on abundant source material and has had a great impact on Slavonic scholarly studies. Its conclusions have been used by L. Niederle, a great authority on the ancient Slav period. Another significant book by Drinov, *Iujnye slaviane i Vizantia v x veke* (The South Slavs and Byzantium in the Tenth century), was published in 1875. With this book Drinov proved his expert knowledge not only in Bulgarian history, but also in the history of the other Balkan Slavs (Serbians and Croatians) and of Byzantium. He used diverse source material and retraced the history of the Slav peoples, the appearance of the Bogumil movement, the Bulgaro-Byzantine and Bulgaro-Russian relations (968–971), as well as the relations of Serbia and Croatia with the Byzantine Empire until the end of the tenth century. Drinov's views have had an exceptional influence on the emerging modern Bulgarian historical sciences.

Bibliography: *Izsledvaniya v chest na Marin Drinov* (Studies in Honor of Marin Drinov),(Sofia, 1960); *Sbornik za jubileya na profesora M. Drinov* (A Collection to Commemorate Prof. M. Drinov's Jubilee), (Sofia, 1900).

Ivan Bozhilov

FILOV, Bogdan (Stara Zagora, 1883–Sofia, 1945), Bulgarian archaeologist and politician. Professor at Sofia University (1914) and director of the Bulgarian Institute of Archaeology (from 1920). Founder of an important archaeological school, well known for the identification and investigation of some famous Thracian monuments, the necropole from Trebenište (*Die archaische Necropole von Trebenischte am Ochrida See*, 1927, published in collaboration with K. Schkorpil), and that from Duvanlii (*Nadgrabniti moghili pri Duvanlii vî Plovdivsko*, 1934, and *Neuentdeckte thrakische Hügelgräber von Duvanlii*, IBAI, 7, 1932–1933). His work introduced an important number of ancient sites, unknown until then. Attempting to identify the ethnic composition of the group, Filov observed important Greek components (toreutics, orfevrery, ceramics), together with the specific characteristics of the south Thracian culture. Filov published important works on the Balkan Peninsula in antiquity and in the Middle Ages, including a study of Bulgarian art: *Geschichte der altbulgarische Kunst* (1919; L'Art antique en Bulgarie). Prime minister in 1940, president of the regency in 1943, Filov was sentenced to death and executed in 1945.

Bibliography: Jan Filip, *Enzyklopädisches Handbuch zur Ur-und Frühgeschichte Europas*, I (Praga, 1966), p. 360.

Ligia Bârzu

IVANOV, Jordan (Kjustendil, 1872–Sofia, 1947), Bulgarian literary historian, historian, folklorist and ethnographer, archaeologist. Lecturer in French at Sofia University (1899–1906), a full member of the Bulgarian Academy of Sciences (from 1909), a part-time associate professor at Sofia University (1909–1917), professor in ordinary from 1925, member of the Russian Archaeological Institute in Constantinople (1912), professor in Bulgarian language and literature in the Ecole nationale des langues vivantes orientales in Paris (1920–1923, 1927–1930). Ivanov began his scientific career with research in Slavonic literatures and later switched his interest to Bulgarian history and archaeology, historical ethnography and the history of literature. His studies were characterized by close adherence to facts and their critical evaluation, as well as carefully formulated hypotheses of a general nature. His approach toward historical problems was complex; he studied them as an historian, ethnographer, archaeologist, and literary critic. Ivanov's first historical monograph, *Northern Macedonia. Historical Studies*, was published in 1906.

In the following years Ivanov directed his efforts to publishing sources. For that purpose, he visited all major archives in Bulgaria, Russia, Poland, Yugoslavia, France, Italy, Greece, England, and Spain. He opposed the mechanical presentation of literary monuments and historical sources. When publishing a text, he viewed it as a complex scientific problem and organically related it to scientific research. His desire to have a personal contact with the sources of the Bulgarian past made him undertake on-site researches, the most important of which were executed in the period 1906–1908 in Macedonia. The results of these researches were published for the first time in 1908 in his book *Bulgarian*

Ruins in Macedonia. A second extended and completed edition appeared in 1931 and a phototype edition of the second version in 1970. This notable work has two parts, the first one being Inscriptions and Notes, most of them discovered and published for the first time. They are accompanied by detailed comments that have the value of independent studies. The second part, Literary Historical Monuments, comprises about sixty old Bulgarian literary works, mainly from the Middle Ages. In 1914 Ivanov published in a separate book the original text of *Slavonic-Bulgarian History* by Paisij Hilendarsky. His studies *Saint Ivan Rilsky and His Monastery* (1917) and *The Life of Saint Ivan Rilsky* (1936) are indicative of his working method, a combination of original text publications with complex research. In 1925 Ivanov published his remarkable work *Bogomil Books and Legends*—a profound research into the history and essence of the Bogomil heresy. The book is composed of two Parts: Bogomil books and dualistic legends of Bulgarian folklore. The basic Bogomil literary monuments presented in the first part are published in their original language and are studied textually and historico-genetically. In the second part works from Bulgarian folklore—fairy tales, legends, and so on—of a dualistic nature are examined. The preface to the book represents a comprehensive study of the Bogomil heresy in Bulgaria and its distribution in the Balkans and Europe. In his scientific research Ivanov kept close to the cultural-historical and critical schools—two trends whose mutual intermingling and completion mark his whole creative work. He was famous not only for publishing Bulgarian medieval literary monuments and as a research scholar of Bulgarian medieval and modern history, but also for his studies in Old Bulgarian literature, Bulgarian folklore, medieval Bulgarian art, literary history, and so forth.

Bibliography: Jordan Ivanov, *Biobibliography*, composed by Chrăstina Gecheva (Sofia, 1974).

Christo Matanov

KATZAROV, Gavril Iliev (Koprivshtitza, 1874–Sofia, 1958), Bulgarian historian. Katzarov attended the University of Leipzig, where he majored in classical philology and history and took a Ph.D. degree in 1899. On his return to Bulgaria he was appointed assistant professor at the higher school of Sofia (1899), after which he held academic posts at the University of Sofia—associate professor (1900–1904) and professor in ordinary (1910) of oriental and classical history. In 1915 he became dean of the Faculty of History, and in 1927 he was offered the rectorship of the University of Sofia and held this post for two years. In 1929 he moved to the Archaeological Museum of Sofia where he was appointed director; subsequently (1940), he became director of the Institute of Archaeology. He was elected a fellow of the Bulgarian Literary Society (which was later expanded into the Bulgarian Academy of Sciences) (1909).

Katzarov was the first and most eminent scholar of Bulgaria who engaged in research on Thracian history and culture, as well as on the history and culture of the Balkan peoples during antiquity. He was the originator of research and of research institutions concerned with the classical antiquity of Bulgarian lands and the first to introduce ancient history to the curriculum of the University of Sofia. Katzarov was the first to place ancient history of the Balkans against the background of ancient history of the Mediterranean world, simultaneously unearthing the peculiarities of the historical development and culture of the Thracian population, as distinct from that of Greece and Rome. An increasing interest in ancient written sources concerning Thrace and Macedonia was one of the most marked characteristics of his research, and Katzarov devoted bulky studies to individual authors or problems. His first work on that subject, *The Mode of Life of the Ancient Thracians According to Classical Writers* (1913) reflected all his studies. Three years later it was expanded and published in German under the title *Beiträge zur Kulturgeschichte der Thraker* (1916). The next work, written jointly with the classical scholar D. Dechev, was entitled *Sources of the Ancient History and Geography of Thrace and Macedonia* (1915, 1949). Of particular importance are Katzarov's works on the history of Thrace and Macedonia, especially *King Philip II of Macedonia* (1922), *Peonia* (1921) and his paper "The Origins and the Heyday of the Odrissian Kingdom in Ancient Thrace" (1933). He originated a new approach to research on Thracian religion and culture, as distinct from those of classical Greece and Rome, which brought him scholarly acclaim and recognition for his pioneer work in this branch of Thracian studies. Katsarov has written many papers on Thracian deities and their monuments found in Bulgarian lands. He carried out research on inscriptions, sacred places, and written material. He gave a special attention to indigenous Thracian cults, such as Bendida and the Thracian horseman. Katzarov devoted a great number of studies on the Thracian horseman, his major work being *Die Denkmäler des Thrakischen Raitersgottes in Bulgarian* (1938). It deals with all known monuments of Ares and with all his sacred places in Bulgaria, and is the first and most serious systematization of monuments done on the basis of iconography. Katzarov's papers on Thrace and the Thracians and their religion have been published in the *Real Encyclopaedia* of Pauli-Wissowa. Katzarov is the author of the chapter on Thrace of the *Cambridge Ancient History* (1930).

Bibliography: Gavril Iliev Katzarov, *A Biobibliographical Collection* (Sofia, 1953).

MIYATEV, Krastiu (Plovdiv, 1892–Sofia, 1966), Bulgarian historian, archaeologist, and art historian. Graduated in Slavonic philology and Balkan history from the University of Vienna (1915). Miyatev took a Ph.D. in history and philosophy at the University of Berlin, where he spent two years (1922–1924) as a postgraduate student. He was *custos* of the Ethnographical Museum of Sofia (1920) and of the National Archaeological Museum (1920–1938). Miyatev was director of the Ethnographical museum during 1939–1945, and director of the

Archaeological Institute of the Bulgarian Academy of Sciences during 1951–1963. His academic career began as early as 1926 when he became assistant professor, and subsequently professor, at the Academy of Theology, where he remained until 1956. In 1945 he was elected to fellowship of the Bulgarian Academy of Sciences. Miyatev was one of the originators and leading figures of Bulgarian medieval archaeology and one of the first scholars engaged in research on Bulgarian medieval culture and art. He headed long-term archaeological excavations in the medieval Bulgarian capitals—Pliska, Veliki Preslav, and Veliko Tarnovo, covering the seventh through the fourteenth centuries. An increasing interest in architecture, painting, plastic art, artisan art, epigraphy, and ethnography was one of the most marked characteristics of this highly talented scholar. His work entitled *The Decorative Murals of the Necropolis of Sofia*, published in 1925, was the first study on early Christian monuments in Bulgaria. It is not only a comprehensive study of the characteristics of sepulchral painting during the fourth through sixth centuries A.D., but also deals with problems of the formation of style in paintings of this province of the Roman Empire, and establishes the influences of the Roman catacombs and the Greek East. His major work, *The Decorative System of Bulgarian Murals*, appeared in print in the same year. It determined the impact of Byzantium and of Byzantine painting up to the beginning of the sixteenth century and established the transition to distinct specific local peculiarities and schools common for all the Balkan religious paintings which began as early as the thirteenth century. Miyatev has produced numerous works concerned with Bulgarian art monuments.

The peculiarities of the medieval painting are the focus of Miyatev's study published in New York, *Bulgaria. Medieval Wall Painting* (1961). He was the first to prepare a generalized study on Bulgarian iconography in one of his most significant works, *Ikonite ot Balkanite* (Icons of the Balkans). It systematized and defined the characteristic features and styles of Bulgarian iconography and determined the impact of other medieval schools. Another type of research conducted by Miyatev concerned the history of Bulgarian architecture during the Middle Ages. On that subject he wrote his masterpiece, *Kraglata Zarkva v Preslav* (The Round Church in Preslav), which stands as the best Bulgarian book in the field. Miyatev also traced the relationship between early medieval architecture in Bulgaria and the well-established architecture of Byzantium: *Der Grosse Palast in Pliska und die Magnaura von Konstantinopol* (1936) and "L'Architecture de la basse Antiquité et du Moyen Age dans les Balkans" (1963). His most significant and comprehensive work, which represents an important contribution to the history of architecture, *Arhitekturata v srednovekovna Balgaria* (Architecture in Medieval Bulgaria), first appeared in Bulgarian (1965) and in 1974, in German. Miyatev's work and ideas exerted a deep influence on the further development of Bulgarian medieval archaeology. Many scholars have begun their work where his left off.

Bibliography: St. Mihailov, *Academician Krastiu Miyatev* (Sofia, 1966).

Margarita Vaklinova

MUTAFCHIEV, Peter (Bozhenzi, 1883–Sofia, 1943), Bulgarian historian, medievalist. Graduated from the University of Sofia in history and geography (1910), postgraduate student at the Univeristy of Munich (Byzantology, 1920–1922), *custos* of the National Museum in Sofia (1910–1920), assistant professor (1923), associate professor (1927); and professor in ordinary (1938) at the University of Sofia. Fellow of the Bulgarian Academy of Sciences (1937). Head of the chair of East European History, University of Sofia (1938). Mutafchiev wrote more than one hundred scholarly and journalistic works. His *Istoria na balgarskia narod* (History of the Bulgarian People), published in two volumes in 1943, covers the period from the beginnings of Bulgarian history to the 1330s (posthumously extended by Professor Iv. Duichev so as to cover all the events of the fourteenth century). It is a predominantly political history. In this outstanding work, as well as in his other writings, Mutafchiev appears as an original scholar with a very critical approach. He attempted a synthesized picture of historical events supplemented with a philosophic interpretation. In his view, the Byzantine influence was detrimental to the development of Bulgaria, and he dedicated his introductory lecture at the University of Sofia to that subject. ''The East and the West in the European Middle Ages'' appeared in print in 1925. He extended his scholarly research along these lines, concentrating on Balkan, and particularly Byzantine, history. Of particular value in the field of Byzantology is his study entitled ''Voinischki zemi i voinizi vav Vizantia prez XII–XIVv'' (Soldier's Lands and Soldiers in Byzantium During the Twelfth to Fourteenth Centuries), published in 1922, which is concerned with the problems of landownership. Studying relationships in the Balkans mostly during the Middle Ages, Mutafchiev attempted to reveal and explain the factors that had led the Bulgarian people through its ups and down, treating territorial losses as inflicted by short-sighted and selfish rulers. A few of his studies are concerned with the leadership problem, the most important being ''The Serbian Expansion in Macedonia,'' published in 1926. Worthy of mention is his study, ''Sadbinite na srednovekovnia Drastar'' (The Fate of Medieval Drastar, 1927) and his book *Bulgares et Roumains dans l'histoire des pays danubiens*, published in French in 1932. Against the background of ethnic and political relations in the lower Danubian lands during the eleventh to twelfth centuries, Mutafchiev treated the uprising of the Assen brothers and the restoration of the Bulgarian state in 1186 as a normal and natural process.

Bibliography: Peter Mutafchiev, *Izbrani Proizvedeniya* (Selected Works), edited by Prof. D. Angelov (Sofia, 1973).

V. Tapkova-Zaimova

NATHAN, Jacques Primo (Sofia, 1902–Sofia, 1974), Bulgarian economic historian. Nathan was educated in Moscow, where he graduated in economics from the Lenin International Higher School (1930). On his return to Bulgaria he took to journalism and in succession held several editorial posts during the period 1930–1939. In 1946 he became assistant professor at the University of Sofia, and in 1948 he was appointed a professor at the Karl Marx Higher Institute of Economics. From 1952 until the end of his life he held the chair of political economy at the same institute, while during 1958–1961 he held the rectorship of the institute. For two years (1949–1951) he was director of the Institute of Economics of the Bulgarian Academy of Sciences; in 1961 he was elected fellow of that academy. Nathan was one of the outstanding representatives of Marxist economic thought in Bulgaria from 1930 onwards. An increasing interest in social and economic problems was one of his most marked characteristics. His first important work, *Ikonomiceska istoriya na Bulgaria* (An Economic History of Bulgaria), was published in two volumes in 1938. Nathan elaborated on the basis of some formulations of Dimiter Blagoev and provided a new Marxist interpretation of many facts and events of Bulgarian history. Another book, *Bulgarskoto vazrajdane* (1939; The Age of the National Revival of Bulgaria), is an account of the driving forces of that period supplied with a Marxist interpretation and considered as a process beginning in the mid-eighteenth century and intensified during the second and third quarters of the nineteenth century. After the victory of the socialist revolution in Bulgaria in 1944, Nathan extended and re-edited his *Economic History of Bulgaria*, which was published again in 1958. In the same year there appeared his book, *Monopolisticheskiya kapitalism v Bulgaria* (The Monopolistic Capital in Bulgaria), written in co-authorship with L. Berov. During the 1960s Nathan published a number of works on the history of economic thought in Bulgaria: *Ikonomiceskite vuzgledi na Dimiter Blagoev* (The Economic Views of Dimiter Blagoev); *Ideologiyata na Hristo Botev* (The Ideology of Hristo Botev); *Ikonomiceskite Vazgledi na Vassil Kolarov* (The Economic Concepts of Vassil Kolarov); and *Istoriya na ikonomicheskata misal v Balgaria* (A History of Economic Thought in Bulgaria), and so on.

A special value has been placed on Nathan's book, *Marksistko-Leninskoto uchenie za obshtestveno-ikonomicheskite formazii* (The Marxist-Leninist Doctrine about the Socio-Economic Formations), which rendered Marxist theory into a form comprehensible to the layperson and supplied it with concrete examples from the economic history of Bulgaria. Nathan was editor-in-chief of the journal *Istoricheski pregled* (Historical Review) throughout the period 1945–1974. He was active in outlining the main guidelines of the development of history as a scientific discipline and in stimulating the professional careers of many Bulgarian historians belonging to the younger generation.

Liuben Berov

NIKOV, Petăr (Burgas, 1884–Sofia, 1938), Bulgarian historian. Professor in ordinary, holder of a chair in Bulgarian history at Sofia University (1936), dean of the Faculty of History and Philology; a full member of the Bulgarian Academy of Sciences (1937) and of the Bulgarian Archaeological Institute (1933), president of the Bulgarian Historical Society (1936). Nikov studied medieval and modern Greek philology and paleography with the famous Byzantologist Karl Krumbacher (q.v.) in Munich (1904–1908). He specialized at the seminar in East

European history at Vienna University with the Czech Slavist Constantin Jireček (1908–1912). He took his doctor's degree at Vienna University with the thesis, "The Principality of Vidin Till Its Annexation to Bulgaria in 1323." From 1912 until 1920 Nikov was a teacher in German and ancient Greek at the School of Commerce and the secondary school for boys in the town of Varna. In 1920 he attained the rank of an associate professor in Bulgarian history at Sofia University with the research work, *Bulgarian-Hungarian Relations, 1257–1277*. His most important lecture courses were: The Objective of the Contemporary Bulgarian Historiography, History of Byzantium, Bulgarians and Hungarians in the Middle Ages, Bulgarian Church Question, History of the Bulgarian People under the Ottoman Rule, and History of the Bulgarian People. Together with Vassil Zlatarski (q.v.) he was an editor of the magazine *Bulgarian Historical Library*. Being the first serious research scholar of the history of the Second Bulgarian kingdom, Nikov searched the archives of Munich and Vienna and found sources on the rule of Tsar Boril, documents from the collection of Cardinal Pitra, materials on the restoration of Bulgarian church independence at the time of Tsar Ivan Assen II, and introduced them in scientific circulation. He was an acknowledged authority on the history of the north-western part of Bulgaria during the Middle Ages. His studies have revealed the political activity of many rulers, including Rostislav Michailović, Jakov Svetoslav, the brothers Dărman and Kudelin, and Michail Šišman. This was the first attempt to determine the part played by the independent princes in the destiny of the Bulgarian state and to restore the political and ethnic picture of the region. Nikov studied the genealogical history of the last Bulgarian tsarist dynasty. He was the first historian to begin systematic research on Bulgarian-Tartar relations; along with it, he went into some questions on the Tartar-Koumanian and Tartar-Byzantine relation. In his studies special attention was given to the diplomatic contacts between Tsar Kaloyan and Rome and the acceptance of a union, as well as to the relations between Bulgaria and the Latin principality in Constantinople. Nikov's works are rich in interesting observations on the ethnogenetic processes in the medieval Bulgarian state.

Besides being a medievalist, Nikov was one of the first serious research scholars of the Bulgarian Renaissance period. As the first historian engaged in research on the church and the national movement of the Bulgarian people, Nikov wrote the monograph *Revival of the Bulgarian People. Church and National Struggles and Achievements* (1930). Being an outstanding representative of the critical trend, he looked for the genetic relation between the processes and phenomena, espoused objective and critical historical research, and fought against ad hoc theories.

Lizbeth Liubenova

SNEGAROV, Ivan (Ohrid, 1885–Sofia, 1971), Bulgarian historian. Snegarov was educated at the Kiev Academy of Theology from which he graduated in 1912. He took a series of teaching posts in Macedonia and Sofia. In 1933 he was appointed a professor at the Faculty of Theology of the University of Sofia, which was subsequently transformed into an Academy of Theology, and held this post until 1950. For several years (1947–1950) he was director of the Institute of History of the Bulgarian Academy of Sciences; his next post was as head of the Archives department of the same academy (1951–1959). He was elected a fellow of the Bulgarian Academy of Sciences in 1943 and was given the title "merited scholar" in 1969. His career involved three lines of historical research, his primary interest being in the field of church history. A man of wide learning, he also carried out research in the field of the cultural and political history of the Middle Ages of Bulgaria and of the Balkans, the Bulgarian national revival period, and the origination of the national liberation ideology. His major work is *A History of the Archbishopric-Patriarchy of Ohrid*, published in two volumes in 1924–1932. He also produced a number of works devoted to the history of his birthplace and to that of Thessalonika, which are concerned with the Middle Ages and the period of the national revival, the life and work of Kliment of Ohrid, and a wide range of source material, editing in Greek the "codes" of the ecclesiastical provinces of Plovdiv, Tirnovo; a biography of Neophit of Rila; the hagiographies of Nikola of Sofia, Ivan of Rila, of Ioakhim I, Patriarch of Tirnovo. Snegarov was one of the founders of the collections "Greek and Latin Sources of Bulgarian History" published regularly by the Institute of History of the Bulgarian Academy of Sciences. An outstanding scholar and expert in Old Greek and Old Bulgarian, as well as a paleographer, Snegarov treated his source material with a highly refined intellect and a critical approach. He was a fascinating narrator engaging in polemics with Yugoslavian and Greek scholars on problems connected with the national adherence of the population of Macedonia, and on ecclesiastical and other problems. Nevertheless, he was an ardent advocate of the furthering of understanding among the Balkan peoples. Snegarov co-authored the two-volume *History of Bulgaria* published by the Bulgarian Academy of Sciences. During the last two decades of his creative life, Snegarov concentrated his scholarly endeavors on contacts between the Bulgarian and Russian communities and published a number of studies devoted to this problem: *Spiritual and Cultural Links Between Bulgaria and Russia throughout the Middle Ages* (1950), and *Cultural Ties Between Bulgaria and Russia During the XVII–XVIII centuries* (1953). Another thrust of his research activities involved the consequences of Ottoman Rule in the Balkans: *The Ottoman Rule as an Impediment to the Cultural Development of the Bulgarian and the Other Balkan Peoples* (1958).

Bibliography: 100 Godini BAN (Centenary of the Bulgarian Academy of Sciences), (Sofia, 1969); V. Tapkova-Zaimova, *Etudes Balkaniques*, Sofia, 1971.

V. Tapkova-Zaimova

STRASHIMIROV, Dimiter Todorov (Varna, 1868–Sofia, 1939), Bulgarian historian, writer, and public and political figure. Strashimirov graduated from the University of Bern, Switzerland, where he took a Ph.D. in literature (1893).

On his return to Bulgaria he became a high school teacher and spent many years as teacher and high school inspector in different towns of the country. His other posts were: director of the National Theatre in Sofia and deputy director of the National Library in Sofia. He was also a member of the Bulgarian Agrarian Union. His political credo was that of a petty-bourgeois democrat, while his literary and historical views were based on the principles of the positivist cultural and historical school, whose most prominent protagonist was Hippolyte Taine (q.v.). However, Strashimirov was most strongly influenced by the historical conceptions generated by the revolutionary and democratic intelligentsia of the period of the Bulgarian national revival, for example, G. S. Rakovski, L. Karavelov, and Hr. Botev, as well as by the historians of the post-Liberation period: Z. Stoyanov and St. Zaimov. Strashimirov's first creative efforts were oriented toward poetry, literature, and literary criticism. His book, *Hristo Botev kato poet i jurnalist* (1897; Hristo Botev as a Poet and Journalist), is a sort of bridge between his literary and historical works, because he treated the poetic and publicistic works of Botev against a historical background, which provoked his studies in the history of the Bulgarian national revival. A natural consequence of this orientation of his interests was his next significant work, *Istoriya na aprilskoto vastanie* (A History of the April Uprising), published in 1907 in three volumes.

Strashimirov conducted a large-scale examination of source material—documents, memoirs, publicistics—and subjected it to a critical evaluation. This book is the first scientific study on the national revolutionary movement and enjoyed an unusually long period of scientific recognition. Strashimirov also published the *Archives of the National Revival* (1908), an original contribution based on extensive research. There followed a series of studies on Bulgarian revolutionaries like G. S. Rakovski, L. Karavelov, and Hr. Botev showing Strashimirov's interest in their biographies, ideology, and activities. Strashimirov devoted the greatest time and effort to Vassil Levski, but unfortunately he did not complete this study conceived as his most ambitious work. He published only the first volume of Levski's biography, concerned only with the sources he had carefully examined. Strashimirov was the only bourgeois scholar interested in and devoted to the problems of the national revolutionary movement and to the Bulgarian uprisings. He not only carried out extensive research and collected immense source material, but also he provided a brilliant analysis expressing his attitude of admiration. He did a great deal to raise the prestige of the heroes of the revolutionary movement, thus opposing some prevailing negative appraisals of their activities. The works of Strashimirov in the field of the Bulgarian national revival mark a significant stage in the development of the Bulgarian historical sciences.

Bibliography: M. Veleva, *Dimiter Strashimirov, A Historiographic Outline* (Sofia, 1972).

Maria Veleva

ZLATARSKI, Vassil (Veliko Tarnovo, 1866–Sofia, 1935), Bulgarian historian, archaeologist, and epigraphist. Educated in St. Petersburg (1891) and Berlin (1893–1895). Professor at the University of Sofia and holder of the chair of Bulgarian and Balkan history. A founder of the Bulgarian Historical Society (1911) and fellow of the Bulgarian Academy of Sciences (1900). Rector of the University of Sofia (1913–1914 and 1924–1925), vice-president of the Council of the Bulgarian Academy of Sciences (1926–1931), member of the Moscow Archaeological Society, fellow of the Russian Archaeological Institute in Constantinople (1899), corresponding member of the Russian Academy of Sciences in Petersburg (1909), and fellow of the Czech Academy of Arts and Sciences (1911). Zlatarski's main field of interest was medieval Bulgarian history. To that subject he dedicated his most significant and comprehensive work in four volumes entitled *Istoria na balgarskata darjava* (History of the Bulgarian State), published in the period 1918–1940. The four volumes are divided as follows: Volume 1—*Age of Hun-Bulgarian Domination, 679–852*; Volume 2—*History of the First Bulgarian Kingdom, 852–1018*; Volume 3—*Bulgaria under Byzantine Rule, 1018–1187* and *Bulgaria under the Assenids, 1187–1280*. The last volume, supplemented by Professor Ivan Duichev, was published posthumously. This impressive work was based on an exhaustive analysis of numerous Byzantine and Old Bulgarian sources. It is a comprehensive political and cultural history of the whole period. Because of his positivistic approach to history, Zlatarski lays great emphasis on the institution of the state. The periodization of his four-volume work was done on the basis of the status of the Bulgarian state. Zlatarski contributed a great deal to the development of archaeology in Bulgaria. He started archaeological excavations in the inner city of Preslav, excavated and studied the medieval town of Crven, and studied inscriptions from the Patleina Monastery. He published and interpreted many Old Bulgarian and medieval Bulgarian inscriptions. His collected works number more than two hundred books, monographs, studies, and papers. Zlatarski was known for his strong sense of social responsibility and his adherence to the ideas of the national revival period. He set himself the task of laying the foundations of a Bulgarian historical school, and accordingly, he promoted many young historians in scholarly life. He enthusiastically worked for the intellectual elevation of his own people.

Bibliography: V. Tapkova-Zaimova, ''Vassil Zlatarski et son heritage scientifique,'' *Bulletin de l'Association internationale d'etudes du Sud-Est européen* (Bucharest, 1970).

Rumiana Radeva

Great Historians: Canadian

BOURINOT, John (Sydney, Cape Breton, 1837–Ottawa, 1902), Canadian historian. Bourinot came from a family that went north after the American Revolution to continue to live under the Crown. This tradition of loyalty to the British monarchy proved to be an enormous influence in Bourinot's outlook. A very bright student, he graduated from Trinity College in Toronto in 1857. Fascinated by the workings of political institutions, he returned to Halifax to work as a short-hand reporter in the Nova Scotian legislature. In 1868 he moved to the Dominion Senate where he performed the same duties. Five years later he was named assistant clerk of the House of Commons, and in 1880 he was promoted to chief clerk. He soon established himself as Canada's leading constitutional authority, and in 1884 he brought out an impressive work on Canadian parliamentary practice. But in addition he was excited by the past and wrote a good deal about it. Indeed, some considered him the most popular historian of his day—and in 1898 he was knighted for his public services.

Bourinot's conception of Canada was that of a British country par excellence. Although he liked the United States, he believed that Congress was clearly inferior as an institution of government to Canada's Parliament. Consequently, he was certain that Canada would always resist annexation to the United States. He also thought that, since the British tradition of tolerance and the institutions that embodied it protected the French language and culture, French Canadians would be loyal to both the British monarchy and the imperial connection. The natural wealth of Canada would ensure a splendid future for both founding peoples, provided they cooperated to work in the common interest. Ironically, the great danger to the link with the Mother Country, according to Bourinot, stemmed from an instinct for liberty, natural to the British race in Canada, and the consequent endless striving for self-government which it engendered. He regarded this as an absolute, irresistible political force; Canadians would not put up with a subordinate status where vital decisions over their fate were made in London. The only way Canadian equality could be reconciled with maintaining the British tie was through some form of imperial federation, an arrangement, however, that would never spring from the deliberations of politicians. Rather, if God so willed it, the necessity for establishing such a federation would emerge as a consequence of some great crisis that would force the Mother Country and the colonies to take this historic step. As an historian, Bourinot depended on the published works of others; his special talent was to synthesize these histories in a clear and vivid style. In *Canada 1786* he re-created the grand heroic exploits of the French explorers and martyrs in the belief that they constituted a great tradition of courage and adventure and thus a splendid foundation for building a nation. Finally, in his most important work, *Canada 1760–1900*, he pictured Canada as flourishing under British rule. The Canadian Confederation in 1867 was a model for a worldwide federal system of all British countries. The optimism inherent in this work makes it clear that he believed that Canada would end up as one of the great partners in a magnificent worldwide imperial federation. As such, it is a fine example of the writing of the school of Canadian imperialist historians.

Bibliography: C. Berger, "Race and Liberty: The Historical Ideas of Sir John George Bourinot," *Canadian Historical Association Report* (1965): 87–104; Joseph Levitt, *A Vision Beyond Reach* (Ottawa, 1982); See Madge Macbeth, "A Great Canadian: Sir John Bourinot," *Dalhousie Review* 24, no. 2 (1954).

Joseph Levitt

BURT, Alfred LeRoy (Listowell, Ontario, 1888–Wellesley, Mass., 1971), essayist and English Canadian historian. Son of a merchant of German origin and an Irish mother, both Methodists, Burt grew up in the country, surrounded by people of various ethnic origins. When he was ten, the family moved to Toronto. He graduated from high school in 1906 and later enrolled in the University of Toronto's Victoria College, obtaining his B.A. in 1910. A Rhodes scholar, he studied history at Oxford and graduated in 1912. The following year he published his historical and philosophical essay, *Imperial Architects*, a text that reflects the major Canadian and British debates on the respective roles of the colony and the metropolis in a renewed British Empire. Burt saw Canada as a nation maturing under the wing of the British monarchy which would, in true egalitarian spirit, develop new ties with Britain. In 1913 he became a professor at the University of Alberta, a new institution with an enrollment of fewer than 425. During the war, he joined the active militia, and in 1918 he left Canada for England, a lieutenant in the First Canadian Tank Battalion, but the armistice was signed before he saw combat. During this transition period he participated in the organization of Khaki University under the direction of the president of his university. Its purpose was to prepare Canadian soldiers to enter British universities. In 1919 he returned to the University of Alberta, remaining there until 1930.

Burt was a liberal nationalist, hostile to imperialist currents. This outlook explains his support for the goals of the League of Nations and for the idea of a British Commonwealth based on equal partnership. His vision of Canada was expressed through his career, through both his involvement in support of the League and his writings. He saw a country composed of two nationalities, one French and one English, enriching one another, and of various regions, some of which were not understood by those in power in Ottawa. It was, he said, the case of the West, which was always dominated by political parties in Quebec and Ontario. This explains why he was so attracted to Turner's frontier thesis; his major work, *The Old Province of Quebec* (1933), rests on its theoretical and ideological premises. New France is portrayed as a North American national community, forged under an environment based on democratic values and consequently reasonably similar to other colonies on the Atlantic Coast. Thus, feudalism, absolutism, and clerical power were the artificial attributes of a new society where, in truth, the militia captain represented the triumph of popular democracy. Seen in this light, the role of the British conquest of 1760 was to stimulate, through the influence of British liberty, the movement toward the creation of a biethnic and bicultural nation, called on to join the company of the nations of the British Commonwealth. Burt's nationalism was therefore as far removed from that of abbé Lionel Groulx (q.v.) as it was from the imperialists. Two of his works, *The United States, Great Britain and British North America from the Revolution to the Establishment of the Peace after the War of 1812* (1940) and *The Evolution of the British Empire and Commonwealth from the American Revolution (1956)*, are the result of these various preoccupations. That he joined the University of Minnesota in 1930 and that in 1944 he became an American citizen is not surprising; many Canadian intellectuals acted similarly.

Bibliography: C. Berger, *The Writing of Canadian History. Aspects of English-Canadian Writing, 1900 to 1970* (Toronto: Oxford University Press, 1976), pp. 39, 43, 151, 175, 183; F. Ouellet, "L'émergence dans le Canada du XXᵉ siècle de l'histoire comme science sociale," *Transaction, Royal Society of Canada* (1982): 35–81; L. Thomas, *The Renaissance of Canadian History: A Biography of A. L. Burt* (Toronto: University of Toronto Press, 1975.).

F. Ouellet

CHAPAIS, Thomas (Saint-Denis de Kamouraska, 1858–Québec, 1946), journalist, politician, and French Canadian statesman. Chapais was born into a prominent family in the lower St. Lawrence region, which had long been involved in political life. His father, Jean-Charles, had even been one of the Fathers of Confederation. Chapais did his secondary studies at the College Ste-Anne de la Pocatière and later in 1879 obtained a law degree from Laval University. For a while he both practiced law and worked as secretary to the lieutenant-governor of Quebec. Then he became editor-in-chief of a conservative and ultramontane newspaper, *Le Courier du Canada*, a post he held for twenty years. In the course of his lengthy career Chapais occupied a variety of prestigious political positions.

In 1891 he was named a member of the Legislative Council of Quebec and was twice called on to serve in the Cabinet responsible for a minor ministry. In 1919 he was appointed to the Canadian Senate, and in 1930 he was asked to act as a Canadian delegate to the League of Nations.

Toward the end of the nineteenth century, Chapais demonstrated his interest in the history of New France in a series of articles published in the newspaper, *La Presse*, between 1897 and 1911. The research for these articles led to the publication of several books. His *Jean Talon, intendant de la Nouvelle-France (1665–1672)* was awarded the French Prix Thérouanne in 1904, and his book *Marquis de Montcalm (1712–1759)* received the French Prix Thiers in 1911. His major work, the eight-volume *Cours d'histoire du Canada*, was drawn from public lectures he gave at Laval University between 1919 and 1934. Chapais was the product of a social milieu where nationalism, conservatism, and ultra-montane clericalism—ideas becoming increasingly widespread in society as a whole—were predominant. In this milieu, it was felt that the association of French Canadians with the British Empire and Canadian Confederation would help to preserve and affirm the rights and traditions of French Canada. These ideological concerns are clearly apparent in Chapais' account of the French Canadian past, from the Conquest to Confederation. The theme of the *lutte pour la survivance* (struggle nation), so dear to François-Xavier Garneau (q.v.), also colors Chapais' retelling of how French Canadians, thanks to their ruling classes and their courage and perseverance, fought successfully to maintain their civil and political rights. Like Garneau, he praises the wisdom of the clergy and the political leaders engaged in the struggle, but he unequivocally condemns the Patriotes of 1837–1838. While he shared many of Garneau's views, Chapais' interpretation of the future prospects of French Canadians as a people in Canada and North America is more optimistic. The ideas conveyed in Chapais' work are representative of those that triumphed shortly before Quebec society became truly industrial. The fact remains, however, that even as late as the 1930s, when he published his *Cours d'histoire du Canada*, they still had a considerable impact on some segments of the French Canadian middle classes in Quebec and else-where in Canada.

Bibliography: J.-C. Bonenfant, "Retour à Thomas Chapais," *Recherches sociographiques* (1974); R. Hamel, J. Hare, and P. Wycznski, eds., *Dictionnaire pratique des auteurs québécois* (Montreal: Fides, 1976), pp. 122–125; V. Morin, "Sir Thomas Chapais, 1858–1946," *Transactions of the Royal Society of Canada* (1947): 119–125; F. Ouellet, "Historiographie canadienne et nationalisme," *Transactions of the Royal Society of Canada* (1975), pp. 25–39; F. Ouellet, "L'émergence dans le Canada du XXe siecle de l'histoire comme science sociale," *Transactions of the Royal Society of Canada* (1982): 35–81.

F. Ouellet

CREIGHTON, Donald Grant (Toronto, 1902–Brooklin, Ont., 1979), Cana-dian historian. Creighton was educated at the University of Toronto where he took courses in both English and history. In 1925 he won a scholarship to Balliol

College, Oxford, where he studied British and European history. Two years later he was appointed as a junior in the Department of History at Toronto where he spent the rest of his academic career. Creighton first made his mark with one of the classics of Canadian history, *The Commercial Empire of the St. Lawrence* (1937). Following some of the concepts of Harold Innis (q.v.), Creighton set forth one of the major explanations for the dynamics of Canadian history—the Laurentian thesis. The very nature of geography in Canada—the existence of the St. Lawrence River and its system of lakes—gave rise to an east–west trading system that would furnish the economic foundation for a separate transcontinental dominion. Moreover, it was inevitable that this economic system would be in conflict with the one to the south and that its ability to compete would depend on its connection first with France and then with Great Britain. Creighton used this thesis to explain the sweep of all of Canadian history in his monumental survey *Dominion of the North* (1944). Creighton's main political concern was to see a strong Canadian nation. Until the beginning of World War II, his main fear was that the aim of the Fathers of Confederation in creating a strong national government had been subverted by English jurists who had changed the constitution so as to give the provinces unwarranted powers. But after 1945, he became much more worried lest Canada's giant neighbor undermine its independence. As a consequence of the Cold War, Canada found itself part of the American alliance and in danger of becoming a satellite. Then, too, the massive influx of American capital and technology was leading to the pillaging of natural resources, the contamination of the environment and the "hideous evils," industrialization and urbanization. "The danger of continentalism," he warned, "economic, political, military, . . . now seem to be pressing in upon us steadily and from every side." He complained that for too long Canadian history had been dominated by the "liberal nationalists" such as Oscar Douglas Skelton (q.v.) who were obsessed with the achievement of responsible government and Dominion status. These historians had taught that the main obstacle to Canada achieving nationhood came from Great Britain. But they had overlooked the far greater danger that American imperialism represented. Indeed, without British military support and British capital, Canada would not have survived as a separate political state in North America.

One result of the impact of the war on Creighton's thought was to change his view on what constituted historical forces. There is a great deal of economic and geographic determinism in the *Empire of the St. Lawrence*, but, after the war, he turned much more to narrative history. He believed that history was an art. The main objective should be to elucidate and describe and explain the encounter between character and circumstance. "The reader," he wrote, "should be induced to accept the illusions that he is returning to the historical experience." He should not only learn about the past but experience it as a great drama. With this in mind he wrote his great two-volume biography, *John A. Macdonald* (1953 and 1955) in which the hero is at once a living person as well as an agent for the historical nation-building impulses engendered by the St. Lawrence River system. Moreover, by his enormous literary skill Creighton succeeded in re-creating the Victorian age in Canada during which Macdonald operated. During the 1960s, Creighton became even more apprehensive about American pressures on his country. Moreover, he believed that the Quebec nationalist forces were weakening Canada internally just at a time when it was in the gravest danger of becoming a colony of the greatest of modern empires. As time went on, he became more and more pessimistic, a mood that is clearly reflected in his *Canada's First Century* (1970) in which, full of sadness and despair, he sees little chance for Canada to continue to exist as an independent nation. Without question Creighton is the greatest historian yet produced in English Canada; by an extraordinary literary skill he helped to inculcate generations of readers with something of his enormous nationalist spirit.

Bibliography: C. Berger, *The Writing of Canadian History* (Toronto, 1976); R. Cook, *The Maple Leaf Forever* (Toronto, 1971), Ch. 9; Joseph Levitt, *A Vision Beyond Reach* (Ottawa, 1982).

Joseph Levitt

GARNEAU, François-Xavier (Québec, 1809–Québec, 1866), notary and French Canadian historian. Son of a poor carter, Garneau nevertheless attended J. F. Perreault's Lancaster School and, at sixteen, was taken on as a clerk in the office of the notary A. Campbell. He obtained his commission of notary in 1828. During this time he traveled in the United States, and three years later, in 1831, he went to England where D. B. Viger, a delegate of the Lower Canadian Patriots, retained him as secretary. Back in Quebec in 1833, he found employment as a bank clerk and worked intermittently as a notary until 1842 when he became translator in the Legislative Assembly. Two years later, he was appointed clerk of the city of Quebec, a position he held until his death in 1866.

In 1837, working in his spare time, Garneau began preparing his major work, his *Histoire du Canada depuis la découverte jusqu'à nos jours*, published between 1845 and 1852. While it kept its distance from the revolutionary adventure of 1837–1838 led by the Patriots, his work grew out of the nationalist ferment of the first half of the nineteenth century. Built around the idea of nation by notions of race, language, and religion, the book described how the French Canadian nation, a small Catholic people of a superior essence, was tested in the course of an interminable series of wars against the English and the Indians. But above all, his account illumines how, after the British Conquest, French Canadians struggled continuously to survive as a separate people against the pressures toward assimilation exerted by the English and the Americans. Garneau was a Gallican, and criticisms of the bishops and the Jesuits of New France with their theocratic and ultramontane designs crop up occasionally in his work. For these few remarks, made at a time when attempts were being made to forget the rebellions, to his many ultramontane contemporaries and to the successive generations of historians to this day, he appeared to be tainted with liberalism. These few anticlerical remarks, which in no way altered the fundamental character of the book, appeared so serious to an increasingly clerical society, that Garneau and those responsible for subsequent editions of his *Histoire du Canada* took pains to eliminate or at least soften them. But the fact was that Garneau's work corresponded so accurately to the expectations of the ruling classes of a conservative and clerical society that its interpretation of the French Canadian past dominated French Canadian historiography until the middle of the twentieth century. By 1944, *Histoire du Canada* had been published in nine editions, in several English translations, and was even adapted for use by elementary school children.

Bibliography: S. Gagnon, *Le Quebec et ses historiens de 1840 à 1920. La Nouvelle-France de Garneau à Groulx* (Quebec: Presses Université Laval, 1978); R. Hamel, J. Hare, and P. Wyczynski, eds., *Dictionnaire pratique des auteurs québécois* (Montreal: Fides, 1976), pp. 273–277; F. Ouellet, "Historiographie canadienne et nationalisme," *Transactions of the Royal Society of Canada* (1975): 25–39; F. Ouellet, "La formation d'une société dans la vallée du St-Laurent: d'une société sans classes à une société de classes," *Canadian Historical Review* (1981): 407–450; "François Xavier Garneau," in *French Canadian Thinkers of the Nineteenth and Twentieth Centuries* (Montreal: McGill University Press, 1966), pp. 23–40.

F. Ouellet

GROULX, Lionel (Vaudreuil, 1878–Vaudreuil, 1967), essayist, novelist, and French Canadian historian. Son of a farmer, Groulx studied classics and theology at the Sainte-Thérèse, Valleyfield, and Montreal seminaries. Ordained in 1903, he taught literature for three years at the Valleyfield Seminary before going to Rome from 1906 to 1908 to pursue doctoral studies in philosophy and theology. During this trip he spent time in Freibourg studying literature. Back in Valleyfield he resumed his professional duties, remaining there until 1915 when he was made responsible for history at the University of Montreal where he remained until 1948, teaching in the form of public lectures. His *Histoire du Canada* was to come from these lectures. From 1920 to 1928 this fervent and committed nationalist edited the periodical *Action française* and became an avid contributor in *Action nationale*. In 1946, the Institut d'histoire of the University of Montreal, the purpose of which was to train professional historians, was set up, and Groulx himself founded the Institut d'histoire de l'Amérique française to promote historical research. To broaden its influence, the following year he began the *Revue d'histoire de l'Amérique française*, which he was to direct until his death in 1967. Groulx produced a large and diverse body of work. Not counting innumerable book reviews, he can be credited with over one hundred publications, some twenty volumes, fifteen-odd pamphlets, and about seventy-five articles. This includes essays, novels, and historical writings. This committed literature reflects concerns for the present and future of an increasingly industrial and urban French Canadian people. For Groulx, the threat of extinction hung constantly over the heads of this tiny conquered people whose most enduring values developed in New France and survived a century and a half of British domination. There is no question that his pessimistic view of the present and of the future had led him to this unmatched idealization of the past. His *Histoire du Canada depuis la découverte*, published between 1950 and 1952, like the rest of his work, dwells on the tragic destiny of a people united by race, language, and religion, but conquered by a foreign race and adrift in North America. His view of New France was of a theocratic and agrarian society, led by an incomparable clergy and supported by a peasantry unique in its physical and moral health. Like François-Xavier Garneau (q.v.) and Thomas Chapais (q.v.) his interpretation of the evolution of French Canada following the British Conquest centers on the theme of *la survivance nationale*. Unlike Chapais, however, his description of this continuous struggle is marked by pessimism, for, far from having an unshakeable faith in Canadian Confederation, Groulx was drawn to the idea of an independent Quebec. Were it not for his fear of the Americans and his sensitivity to francophones living outside Quebec, Groulx would certainly have succumbed to this temptation. Groulx's influence on the evolution of Quebec is, by its breadth, unique.

Bibliography: "Lionel Groulx, prê," special issue of *L'Action nationale* (June 1968): 831–1115; R. Hamel, J. Hare, and P. Wyczynski, eds., *Dictionnaire pratique des auteurs québécois* (Montreal: Fides, 1976), pp. 321–325; F. Ouellet, "L'émergence dans le Canada du XXe siècle de l'histoire comme science sociale," *Transactions of the Royal Society of Canada* (1982): 35–81; F. Ouellet, "La formation d'une société dans la vallée du Saint-Laurent. D'une société sans classes à une société de classes," *Canadian Historical Review* (1981): 407–450; S. Trofimenkoff, *Variations on a Nationalist Theme* (Toronto: Copp Clark, 1973).

F. Ouellet

INNIS, Harold (South Norwich Township, Ontario, 1894–Toronto, 1950), economist and English Canadian historian. Son of a Baptist farmer from the Toronto region, Innis began his secondary studies in Otterville, completing them at the Woodstock Collegiate Institute. In 1913 he enrolled in McMaster University and studied there until he decided to enlist in the Canadian Army. In July of the following year he was in France with the Canadian Expeditionary Corps and was wounded during the attack on Vimy Ridge. Upon his return to Canada he quickly completed his M.A. Then, through his savings and financial support from the university, Innis began doctoral studies in economics at the University of Chicago. His thesis, published in 1923 and entitled "A History of the Canadian Pacific Railway," went further than traditional nationalist interpretations by suggesting that Canada developed as a nation in reaction to the imperatives of North American geography. Nevertheless, his choice of subject matter, as well as the way he dealt with it shows that the interest he would always have in the role of transport, technology, and communication in economic development was already apparent. Meanwhile, Innis had joined the University of Toronto as a professor.

An ardent nationalist, Innis began to see the need for a theory that explained the nation's economic development better than those developed by liberal historians. With this in mind he directed his research toward the fur trade. His staples theory grew from his own work in the archives, the reading of the work of two Americans, the economic historian, G. S. Callender, and the geographer, M. Newbigin, and discussions with his Queen's University colleague, W. A. Macintosh. His major book, *The Fur Trade in Canada* (1930), combines the idea of a Canadian economy oriented on an East–West axis because of the St. Lawrence River with the idea of a staple assured market in the metropolitan country as the driving force of the nation's economy. As Innis was primarily interested in demonstrating the uniqueness of the Canadian economy as opposed to the American, it is difficult to consider his interpretive scheme a theory. It is true that he had a tendency to view the national economy and culture as an outgrowth of European civilization—a reaction to the frontier thesis—and he raised the question of the applicability of his model to all new societies: The book he published in 1940, *Cod Fisheries. The History of an International Economy* reflects, as does his text on the paper industry, how he applied the term *staple industry*, and his last work, *Empire and Communications*, represents a broadening of his outlook. However attractive he found these theories, he was unable to examine all of the implications of his major achievement, the staple theory. As a result, in his book on the fur trade the relationship between that business and agriculture is ignored, the question of labor is barely touched on, and the issue of technological change is not explored at any length. Harold Innis' influence was enormous in Canada and abroad, but he is perhaps best known as the father of the Laurentian school of historiography. At the end of his career he was a member of several royal commissions of inquiry and was president of the Royal Society of Canada.

Bibliography: C. Berger, "Harold Innis. The Search for Limits," in C. Berger, *The Writing of Canadian History: Aspects of English Canadian Writing, 1900 to 1970* (Toronto: Oxford University Press, 1976), pp. 85–111; D. G. Creighton, *Harold Adam Innis. Portrait of a Scholar* (Toronto: University of Toronto Press, 1957); F. Ouellet, "L'émergence dans le Canada du XXe siècle de l'histoire comme science sociale," *Transactions of Royal Society of Canada* (1982): 35–81.

F. Ouellet

MORTON, William Lewis (Gladstone, Manitoba, 1908–Medicine Hat, Alberta, 1980), Canadian historian. Morton was educated in local schools, and in 1932 he entered the University of Manitoba, and won a Rhodes scholarship to study history at Oxford. In 1942 he was appointed to the University of Manitoba where he would teach for the next twenty-five years. Morton's first books expressed the bias of a Westerner who resented Eastern domination. In the *Progressive Party in Canada* (1950) he drew a sympathetic portrait of the farmers' protest movement of the 1920s. He clearly accepted the proposition that in "a federal union of free citizens and equal communities there must be . . . equality of economic opportunity and equality of political status." Seven years later he completed his greatest book, *Manitoba, A History* (1957). This work evokes the picture of a tolerant pluralistic society deeply animated by a consciousness of its identity as Western. *Manitoba* was a splendid model for the writing of regional history, a necessity in a country like Canada which spans an entire continent.

During the late 1950s, powerful economic and cultural pressures on Canada from the United States raised the question of whether Canada could retain its independence. Morton was confident that Canada would preserve its identity. For one thing Canada's separate existence was not accidental; it had come into being because it was a northern country "with a northern economy, a northern way of life and a northern destiny." Moreover, Canada was a monarchy. The crown, he believed, formed a "central part of the Canadian character and identity." The United States, held together by a social contract, embodied in a written constitution imposed a standard of uniformity on its citizens. Canada, on the other hand, united not by such a covenant but by an allegiance to the sovereign was a freer society because the individual did not have to conform to an established norm. These two ideas are major themes in his monumental survey of Canadian history, *The Kingdom of Canada* (1963). This book also reflected Morton's commitment to cultural duality; it described the clash between British Canadian and French Canadian nationalists in the late nineteenth and early twentieth centuries and the painful lesson they learn that the only mode of existence for the Canadian state is to reflect both cultures. French-English relations are also a major theme in his last great book, *The Critical Years: The Union of British North America 1957–1973* (1964), where he sums up the entire movement for confederation by writing, "The moral purpose of Confederation, the union of the provinces in a partnership of English and French was at last embodied in a territory reaching from sea to sea." Morton brought to the writing of Canadian history two important ideas: that a respect for regional identity and cultural duality could be combined with a strong central government and that Canada enjoying freedom under a monarchy had a moral significance equal to that of the United States. For this reason it had survived and would continue to survive the tremendous pressure of the United States.

Bibliography: Carl Berger, *The Writing of Canadian History* (1976); Joseph Levitt, *A Vision Beyond Reach* (Ottawa, 1982). See introductory bibliographical essay in A. B. McKillop ed., *Contexts of Canada's Past* (Toronto, 1980).

Joseph Levitt

SÉGUIN, Maurice (Horse Creek, Saskatchewan, 1918–Montreal, 1984), essayist and French Canadian historian. Séguin's family left Saskatchewan in 1921, settling in Montreal. He studied with the Jesuits of Brebeuf, enrolling in 1942 in the Faculty of Letters of the University of Montreal, where two years later he obtained his degree. Although at the time the teaching of history at the university was limited to public lectures by l'abbé Lionel Groulx (q.v.), Séguin undertook doctoral studies in history and wrote a thesis entitled "La nation canadienne et l'agriculture, 1760–1850." In 1948, having obtained his diploma, he became a professor at the University of Montreal's new Institute of History, founded two years earlier. It is here that Séguin, whose name is more closely linked than that of Guy Fregault or Michel Brunet to Montreal's neo-nationalist school, spent his entire career.

Séguin was not a prolific historian. It was only much later, succumbing to pressure from colleagues and former students, that he published the few works that give us a fairly precise idea of his thinking. In fact, his essay "L'idée d'indépendance au Québec, genèse et historique" was not published until 1967, and even then in leaflet form. It was another three years before an editor was entrusted with his Ph.D. thesis, written in 1947. Séguin's interpretation, adhered to by Groulx disciples Fregault and Brunet, kept a distance from the *lutte pour la survivance* (struggle for the survival of the people) thesis, widely accepted for over a century. This was not surprising, as unlike Groulx and his precursors, these historians had accepted industrialization and did not harbor the same fears with regard to the Americans. They spoke of the nation that came into being during the period of New France as the foundation of a perfectly normal secular society, built around the bourgeoisie. Moreover, this society, because it was French, maintained a harmonious, albeit colonial, relationship with the Mother Country. For the same reason, a similar harmony and absence of exploitation prevailed between the local bourgeoisie and other classes in colonial society. Thus, the colony had developed under ideal conditions; consequently, the British Conquest was catastrophic for this budding French Canadian nation in that it did away with the "national" bourgeoisie and condemned the nation to an anemic existence under the protection of the clergy and confined to agriculture. The British Conquest achieved this result because it had brutally transferred political and economic power into the hands of the British. For the British domination to be complete and permanent, it remained only to make the French Canadians a minority in Canada and to proletarianize them. Séguin's analysis, which had not really broken with ideas of race and which bears the influence of writings on decolonization, set the groundwork for a historiography based on the idea and the goal of the independence of Quebec. In the international political context of the past twenty-five years, it had a great influence on the rise of the now waning independence movements in Quebec.

Bibliography: J. Blain, "Maurice Séguin en la rationalisation de l'histoire nationale," preface to *La Nation canadienne et l'agriculture, 1760–1850* (Trois Rivières: Boréal Express, 1970), pp. 17–40; S. Gagnon, "Pour une conscience historique de la révolution québécoise," *Cité Libre* (1966), pp. 4–19; F. Ouellet, "La formation d'une société dans la vallée du Saint-Laurent. D'une société sans classes à une société de classes," *Canadian Historical Review* (1981): 407–450; F. Ouellet, "Les classes dominantes au Québec. Bilan historiographique," *Revue d'historie de l'amérique française* (1984): 223–243; J. P Wallot, "La recherche de la nation: Maurice Séguin," *Revue d'historie de l'Amérique française* (1985): 569–590.

F. Ouellet

SKELTON, Oscar Douglas (Orangeville, Ontario, 1878–Ottawa, 1941), Canadian historian. In 1896 Skelton entered Queen's University where he studied classics. But after leaving Queen's, his interest in current politics and economics began to grow. After graduate work at the University of Chicago in economics, he returned to Queen's in 1907 to teach. In 1913 he wrote an important outline of post-Confederation economic history and then in the next year, a history of Canadian railway building. With the coming of the war his interests became more political; in the next half a dozen years he turned out five major works, including a massive two-volume biography of Sir Wilfrid Laurier. In 1924 he accepted the invitation to leave the university to become the under secretary for external affairs, a post he filled with great distinction until his death in 1941.

In his outlook Skelton was consistently liberal. He was deeply suspicious of British imperial policy which was based on a belief in Anglo-Saxon superiority. Its aim was to expand and acquire more colonies and ultimately to transform the empire into a highly centralized organic union completely dominated by the Mother Country. This continual pressure was the greatest barrier to Canada achieving full autonomy and thus nationhood. Skelton held that imperial ties must become much looser and the empire develop into an alliance, freely entered into, of equal nations. In economic matters Skelton remained an ardent advocate of a reform-minded capitalism; he believed that the accumulation of wealth was possible only if individual initiative was given free rein. A strong supporter of free trade, he helped the Liberal government prepare the public case in support of the reciprocity agreement with the Americans in 1911. Skelton liked the United States—its free enterprise, its commitment to equal opportunities for all, its avoidance of all imperialist tendencies in its dealings with Canada. The last great theme that interested Skelton was the building of national unity between the French and English, a unity that was gravely threatened by the dangerous action of the Borden government in introducing conscription during World War I. The conscription crisis stimulated him to develop a concept of nationhood, at the very core of which was the necessity of friendship between the English and French communities. These three themes are reflected in the policies of the hero of his most important work, *Life and Letters of Sir Wilfrid Laurier (1921)*. Laurier aids immigration, fosters the building of railways, and strives for freer trade with the United States, thus encouraging the economic boom that under-pinned the emerging Canadian nation. Laurier also defends Canadian autonomy against the imperialist machinations at the time of the Boer War. More impor-tantly, Skelton made Laurier the hero of a great conscriptionist drama. Skelton's portrait of a Laurier who advocates closer economic relations with the United States, more autonomy within the empire, and tolerance between the French and English helped lay the intellectual foundations for the post–World War I program by which the Liberals managed, with the exception of the depression years, to dominate national politics between the wars.

Bibliography: C. Berger, *The Writing of Canadian History* (Toronto, 1976); Joseph Levitt, *A Vision Beyond Reach* (Ottawa, 1982); W. A. Makintosh "O. D. Skelton," in R. L. MacDougall, ed., *Canada's Past and Present: A Dialogue* (Toronto, 1965).

Joseph Levitt

WRONG, George (Grovesend Ontario, 1860–Toronto, 1948), Canadian historian. Wrong, a deeply religious person, graduated with first-class honors in moral philosophy from the University of Toronto in 1883 and shortly after was ordained in the Church of England. Instead of being given a parish, Wrong was appointed lecturer of ecclesiatical history at the Divinity School at Toronto where he remained for nine years. During this period he spent one summer in Berlin analyzing German research methods and another studying history at Oxford. In 1892 Wrong became a lecturer in history at the University of Toronto and two years later a full professor and head of the department, a post he held until his retirement in 1927. In his political outlook Wrong clung to two ideas. He wanted English Canada to understand the French better and to do more to assuage their fears of assimilation; and he remained loyal to the British connection but with a commitment to Canadian autonomy. Wrong believed that professional historians must be sure to get their facts right and must write with literary grace; an imaginative drama might give a more penetrating view of a person's character than a detailed record of his or her life. Moreover, studies of the past could illumine how well great social experiments like democracy have worked. He also believed it the historian's duty to pass moral judgments on both individuals and nations. Lastly, the study of the past helped to uncover the traditions by which a society defined its crucial values.

Although he was the first Canadian professional historian, Wrong spent little time in the archives. Much of his writing was based on secondary sources. His books are written in a literary style; they are full of heroic exploits, battles, and constitutional matters but contain little about economic development or classes. Those works on French Canada such as a *Canadian Manor and Its Seigneurs* (1908) or *The Fall of Canada; A Chapter in the History of the Seven Years War* (1914) celebrate a static rural society that retains its identity not least because the Church is such a splendid guardian of its traditions and language. *Canada and the American Revolution: The Disruption of the First British Empire (1935)* finds him blaming the British aristocracy for not accepting the American colonists as equals and thus causing a cleavage among the English-speaking peoples. Canada's experience in obtaining liberty within the British Commonwealth demonstrated how unnecessary this tragedy had been. But Wrong's most significant contributions to Canadian history were his efforts to establish professional standards. In 1896 he established the *Review of Historical Publications Relating to Canada* to evaluate books and articles in Canadian history. In 1920 the *Review* became the *Canadian Historical Review*, which functioned as the chief vehicle for history in English Canada. Wrong also led in the creation of the Champlain Society in 1905 which undertook to reprint important documents. By the 1920s it had already issued fifteen important volumes. He helped to edit a series of volumes entitled the *Chronicles of Canada;* the more than 30,000 sets that were sold did much to popularize Canadian history. Above all, he laid the foundation for a department of history at the University of Toronto that was intellectually so powerful and competent as to dominate the writing of history in Canada well into post–World War II decades.

Bibliography: C. Berger, *The Writing of Canadian History* (Toronto, 1976); Allen F. Bowker, "Truly Useful Men: Maurice Hutton, George Wrong, James Mavor and the University of Toronto, (1880–1927)," unpublished Ph.D. thesis, (University of Toronto, 1975); C. Martin, "Professor G. M. Wrong and the History of Canada," in R. Flenly, ed., *Essays in Canadian History Presented to George Mackinnon Wrong for His Eightieth Birthday* (Toronto, 1939), pp. 1–23; Joseph Levitt, *A Vision Beyond Reach* (Ottawa, 1982).

Joseph Levitt

Great Historians: Chinese

CHEN Yinque, also pronounced Yinke (Changsha, 1890–Guangzhou, 1969), Chinese historian. Chen received a classical Chinese education in his childhood and later studied at Harvard, Paris, and Berlin universities, where he majored in philology. He not only mastered various ancient East Asian, Indian, and Middle Eastern languages and was well versed in Buddhist literature, but he also read several classical and modern European languages, and absorbed the modern research methods of the Western social sciences. He became a tutor in the Institute of National Learning at Qing-hua University and later held professorships at Qing-hua, Southwest Associated University, Hong Kong University, Yenching University, and Lingnan University. He was engaged as professor of Sinology by Oxford University in 1938 (he appears in Oxford's records as Tchen Yin-koh), but he could not go there because of the war. He was concurrently head of the first department of the National Research Institute of History and Philology of the Academia Sinica; one of the directors of the Palace Museum; and a member of the board of editors of the Qing Archives. After the founding of the People's Republic of China in 1949, he was elected a standing member of the Third Chinese People's Political Consultative Conference, appointed to be the vice-director of the Central Research Institute of Culture and History, and elected academician of the Department of Philosophy and Social Sciences of the Chinese Academy of Sciences. After the war, in 1945, Chen went to England for eye treatment and to take up his post at Oxford, but his failing eyesight forced him to resign his Oxford post in January 1946 before ever having the chance to teach there. He returned to China and, even though blind, continued to teach and write copiously. His early works stressed the history of Mongolia and of Buddhism, suggesting that the materials added to *Monggu mishi* (The Secret History of Mongolia) from Senang-setsen's *Monggu yuanliu* (History of East Mongolia) are derived from the *Zhaosuo zhilun*, which in turn is derived from Indian and Tibetan tales, thus making important contributions to Mongolian historiography.

In his research on Buddhist literature, Chen made comparative analyses of India and China, the two great ancient civilizations of East Asia, proposing that some of the legends of Indian Buddhist literature informed the contents of Chinese novels, while the form of the Buddhist sutras influenced styles in Chinese literature such as *yan yi* (romances) and *tan chi* (storytelling accompanied with stringed instruments). He studied Buddhist philosophy deeply, exploring its relationship to the broader history of Chinese thought, and proposed many creative theories. His works on ancient Chinese history are highly regarded, and his major works such as *Suitang zhidu yuanyuan luelungao* (1943; Draft Essays on the Origins of Sui and Tang Institutions) and *Tangdai zhengzhishi shulunkao* (Draft Outline of Tang Political History) discuss in detail important changes from ancient times down to the Tang (618–907), suggesting that the institutions of Tang society were developed and perfected by long cumulative effects and regional diversity, not by sudden or accidental events. The political changes were reflected in the changes of the ruling strata. The ruling strata of the early Tang were mixed ones, including both Han and non-Han peoples, in which both civil and military talents existed, he argued, and the imperial house and ministers and generals were in harmony. After Empress Wu (reigned 690–705), the situation was changed gradually until Xuan Zong. As a result, the imperial examination system (civil service examinations) was set up, the *fu-bing* (militia troops) were abolished, differences between civil and military officialdom grew evident, the Han and non-Han peoples were split, and the gap between imperial house and ministers and generals appeared. Great changes came in Chinese medieval history. Chen's analysis of social strata, his description of the relationship between social strata and culture, and his periodization of Chinese ancient history open a new realm for research into Chinese history. His attempts to illuminate history through evidence in poetry was his new creation in the study of history, serving as an important source supplement to the official histories. His works using this new method include *Yan Bai shijian zhenggao* and *Liu Rushi biezhuang*. Chen has been held in high esteem by historians because of his solid basic knowledge, careful style of study, and unique learning.

Bibliography: Howard L. Boorman and Richard C. Howard, eds., *Biographical Dictionary of Republican China*, 4 vols. (New York, 1967–1971), 1:259–261; Jian Tianshu, *Chen Yinque Xiansheng biannian shiji* (The Chronological Biography of Mr. Chen Yinque), (Shanghai Ancient Books Press, 1980).

Hu Shou-wei

CHEN Yuan (Xinhui, Guangdong Province, 1880–Beijing, 1971), educator and figure in modern Chinese historiography. Professor at Beijing (1922), Yenching (1927), and Peiping Normal (1929) universities, president of Fu-Jen (1930–1952) and Beijing Normal (1952–1971) universities, director of the National

Peiping Library (1922), and the Harvard-Yenching Institute (1928–1929); academician of National Academy history (1948); and director of the Second Institute of the Academia Sinica (1954–1960). Chen made a scientific summary of traditional Chinese historiography and carried it forward in many respects. His monumental works in historical chronology, *Ershishi shuorun biao* (Tables of Lunations and Intercalary Months for the 20 Standard Histories) and *Zhongxihui shi rili* (Comparative Daily Calendar for Chinese, European, and Mohammedan History), both published in 1925, are standard references for accurate conversion of dates. In his *Shihui juli* (1928; Illustrations of Word Taboos from the Dynastic Histories), he gave a systematic analysis and summary of the practice of making imperial names taboo, and he provided rules for testing the genuineness and dates of ancient Chinese books, which are useful for solving the knotty problems in this field. In *Jiaokanxue shili* (1933; Some Explanations of Textual Criticism) he formulated four principal approaches that are still followed by Chinese scholars in textual criticism of ancient books. He is also one of the pioneers in the study of Chinese religions. In this field his works covered Christianity, Buddhism, Islam, Judaism, Zoroastrianism, and Manicheism, as well as the indigenous Chinese Taoism. In his works on the religions of China he ranges broadly through Chinese sources and is especially innovative in his use of the Taoist inscriptions and the writings of Buddhist monks, which no scholar before him had thought to use. He inquired systematically into the history of the spread of religions in China, particularly the relationship of religions with the broader sweep of Chinese culture and politics.

Chen is also noted for his historical research on the Yuan (Mongol) Dynasty (1279–1368). In an early work *Yuan xiyuren hauhua kao* (Sinification of the Western Regions Under the Yuan Dynasty, 1923), he collected fragmentary records scattered in the writings of Yuan Dynasty literati, and made a comprehensive and systematic exposition of the history of sinification of non-Chinese nationalities and foreigners in northern China under the Yuan Dynasty. His study elucidates an epochal change in the cultural intercourse of China and Chinese (Han) peoples with foreign countries. In the course of a career of more than half a century in education and in historical scholarship, he always identified closely with the destiny of his motherland and people. He devoted much attention to drawing lessons from history and attached great importance to the educational role of history. During the War of Resistance against Japan (1937–1945), when he had to stay in Beiping, then occupied by the Japanese, he finished seven monographs, including *Mingji dianguian fojiao kao* (Buddhism in Yunnan and Guizhou During the Ming Dynasty) and *Nansong chu hebei xin daojian kao* (Neo-Taoism in the Northern Provinces at the Beginning of Southern Song). In these works he extolled the national heroes of Chinese history, people who kept up the struggle against the aggression and castigated as traitors those who crossed over to the side of the aggressors. His monograph *Tongjian huzhu biaowei* (1945; The True Meaning of Hu's Annotations Revealed) is representative of his later work; it begins with a summary of the methods he used in his historical research and ends with a generalization of experience based on historical facts. Thus, he himself called it "a milestone of my learning."

Bibliography: Howard L. Boorman and Richard C. Howard, eds., *Biographical Dictionary of Republican China*, 4 vols. (New York, 1967–1971), 1: 261–264; Chen Yuan, "Wu Li," in Arthur W. Hummel, ed., *Eminent Chinese of the Ch'ing Period*. (Washington, D.C., 1943), 2: 875–877.

Chen Zhi-chao

FAN Wenlan (Shaoxing of Zhejiang, 1893–Beijing 1969), Chinese historian. Professor at Beijing University (1927–1931), Beiping Women's College of Arts and Science (1931–1934), Zhongfa University (1935) and Henan University (1936–1937); director of the Institute of History of the Academy of Marxism–Leninism (1904), vice president of the Central Academy of Yan'an and concurrently director of its Institute of History (1941–1945), president of the North University (1946–1948), vice president of Huabei University and concurrently director of the Research Department (1948–1949), research fellow and director of the Institute of Modern History of China of the Chinese Academy of Sciences (1950–1969). In his early years Fan studied philosophy (the Confucian classics), history, and literature, wrote *Qunjing gailun* (1926; General Survey of the Confucian Classics), *Zhengshi kaolue* (1931; A Brief Criticism of Dynastic Histories), and *Wen-xin dao long zhu* (1936; Notes to Liu Xie's Treatises on Literary Criticism). His first Marxist history was *Zhongguo tongshi jianbian* (A Short Course of the General History of China), edited in Yan'an in 1940–1941, in which he abandoned the interpretation of history prevalent at that time. Instead of focusing on the leaders of the ruling classes and their activities, he emphatically elucidated the activities of the masses, especially their struggles against class and national oppression, and gave a narrative of socioeconomic conditions and scientific and technological inventions, examining their application to production in various ages. The history of China, as he pointed out, had experienced the primitive commune, the slave society, and feudalism, and the feudal society (beginning from the Western Zhou in the eleventh century B.C.) must be divided into three historical epochs. Fan's suggestions, published in 1941–1942, had profound influence on the people, showing them history in a fresh, new light. Then he wrote a political history of 1840–1900, the years from the Opium War to the Boxer Rebellion, under the title of *Zhongguo jindai shi* (The Modern History of China) (vol. 1, 1946), which systematically explained the revolutionary process of the Chinese people. It showed readers a profound, completely new narrative of the aggressive nature of foreign imperialism, and the corruption of the Manchu (Qing) Dynasty (1644–1911), and thus laid a solid foundation for the study of the modern history of China.

After 1949, as he was not satisfied with the shortcomings of his *Short Course* —the use of the past to disparage the present—Fan began to revise the book under the title of *Zhongguo tangshi* (The General History of China). He only finished the first four volumes, covering China's history to the eleventh century (published 1953–1956). The new theories advanced in this book may be summed up as follows: (1) Xia (trad. 2205–1766 B.C.) was shown through archaeological evidence to have been the transition to a slave system; (2) he demonstrated that feudalism began in western Zhou (1122–770 B.C.), and redivided its stages of development; (3) he dated the formation of the Han (ethnic Chinese) nationality, with its own characteristics, to the Qin and Han period (221 B.C.–A.D. 220); (4) while paying careful attention to economic matters, he also offered extensive, original expositions of cultural developments throughout the epochs of Chinese history. Many of the articles Fan published over the years to explain his historical views were collected as *Fan Wenlan lishi lun wen xuan ji* (Collected Historical Works of Fan Wenlan). Together with Guo Moruo (q.v.) and Yuzhang he founded the Historical Society of China (1951), becoming its vice-president. Under his auspices the society edited *Zhongguo jindai shi ziliao congkan* (Series of Materials of the Modern History of China). Fan made great contributions to the foundation and development of Marxist historical study in China.

Bibliography: John D. Langlois, Jr., "Chinese Culturalism and the Yuan Analogy: Seventeenth Century Perspectives," *Harvard Journal of Asiatic Studies* 40 (1980):355–398.

Cai Meibiao

GU Jiegang (Suzhou, 1893–Beijing, 1980), Chinese historian. Head of the History Department of the Academia Sinica. Born in a scholar-gentry family, Gu received a traditional tutorial education in the Chinese classics from the age of six and later studied philosophy at Beijing University, 1913–1920. After serving as an assistant and instructor at Beijing University, 1920–1926, and editor of the Commercial Press, Shanghai, 1922–1923, he held professorships in history at Zhongshan (1927–1929), Nanjing (1929–1931), Beijing (1931–1937), Yunnan (1938–1939), Qilo (1939–1941), National Central (1941–1943), and Fudan (1943–1946?) universities. From 1949 to 1954, he taught in Shanghai and then moved to Beijing as head of the History Department of the Academia Sinica (now the Academy of Social Sciences). Later he directed projects for new recensions of the twenty-four Dynastic Histories and the *Zuzhi tongjian* of Sima Guang (1019–1086). In 1977 he was elevated to executive membership in the Academy, a post he held until his death in 1980.

Gu was a founder and organizer of modern Chinese historical scholarship. His idea of historical method is best expressed in his discussion of the "cumulative and additive" (*cengleidi zaochengdi*) process by which the ancient legends were formed: The emperors Yao, Shun, and Yu, ancient sage kings who served as metaphors for ideal monarchic rule in Chinese discourse, were not historical figures but were the creations of later ages: Yu was added in the Western Zhou (1122 B.C.? –770), while Yao and Shun first appeared only at the close of the Chunqui period (722–481 B.C.). Pseudohistorical figures also appeared in later ages by the same process: When the sage emperors Fuxi and Shennong were added to the canon, their existence was asserted to have antedated that of Shun and Yu. Thus, these historical figures appeared textually in ancient Chinese history in precisely the reverse of the chronology of their purported existence. Gu's "ancient doubting" attitude toward the classics derives from his conviction that the "methods of narratology are applicable to the study of ancient history," a conclusion he reached through his study of the plays and folk songs of his youth. "Songs and ballads change in obedience to time and place in the same manner as do narratives and plays," he asserted. His method was rooted academically in the Qing Dynasty (1644–1911) school of ancient doubters, which in turn stemmed from the Tang (918–906) and Song (960–1279) periods, but was backed with the new historical methods of Hu Shih (1891–1962), who studied experimentalism under John Dewey (1859–1952). It should also not be forgotten that the Chinese Revolution (1911–1912) freed scholars to assume a critical stance toward the Confucian canon that would have been taboo under the Qing Dynasty. This new stance was a "conversion of historical thinking" from textual criticism to historical criticism; from mere objective interpretation and evaluation of reliable historical texts that had themselves been established by a kind of textual analysis, to a sociohistorical interpretation of the texts that took due regard for the historical contexts in which they had been produced. Gu is best remembered as an author and editor of the *Gushibian* (Critiques of Ancient History, 7 vols., 1926–1941; reprinted 1982), a collection of essays on ancient Chinese history by his school of "ancient doubters," but including essays by their academic opponents, the results of a polemical debate begun in 1923.

The *Gushibian* contributed greatly to the development of Chinese historiography by taking a sharp critical scalpel to the world of ancient Chinese legend which had long been accepted as fact. However, there were limits to their "ancient doubting" and "discussing forgeries" in framing an historical image of ancient China. Particularly after the outpouring of clear results from archaeological research on the Shang (or Yin, c. 1600 B.C.–1122? B.C.) they were in time superseded by the so-called ancient-constructors, including both Marxist- and positivistic-oriented historians. Gu also earned the title of "pioneer of Chinese folklore studies." In the process of his historical criticism on the Chinese classics, he realized the importance of studies in allied disciplines in support of history, especially folkloristic knowledge. He founded the Society for Folklore Studies, the Chinese Society for Historical Geography, the Association for the Study of China's Frontier Regions, and other groups, as well as journals like the *Yanjing xuebao* (Yenching Journal), and the *Bianjiang qiukan* (Frontier Weekly), and *Wenshi zazhi* (Journal of Literature and History). Gu was a pyrrhonistic historian, who shared a critical attitude toward history with Liu Zhiji (661–721) and Zhang Qioa (1104–1162) in the history of Chinese historiography. He was the first problem-centered historian to emerge from the more than two-thousand-year tradition of discipline-centered historiography in China. Gu was an historian who put into practice the exhortation of the sculptor Auguste Rodin (1840–1917), "Do not hesitate to express what you feel, even when you find yourself in opposition to accepted ideas," in the chaotic twentieth-century China, even when he himself was buffeted by the winds of the Chinese Revolution, the Japanese invasion, the Communist Liberation, and the Cultural Revolution. Gu's autobiographical preface to *Gushibian* (1931; the Autobiography of a Chinese Historian), focussing on the formation of his learning, should stand with Johan Huizinga's (q.v.) *Mein weg tot de historie* (1947) and George McCauley Trevelyan's (q.v.) *Autobiography of An Historian* (1949) as a lucid exposition of the mind of the historian. Gu published more than seven hundred essays, books, and editions, including *Qin Han di fangshiyu rusheng* (1955, reprint 1978; Alchemists and Confucians of the Qin and Han Dynasties, *Shilin zassi* (Historical miscellany, 1963, reprinted 1977).

Bibliography: Ku Chieh–kang (Gu Jiegang), *The Autobiography of a Chinese Historian*, trans. A. W. Hummel (Leyden, 1931); J. Gray, "Historical Writing in Twentieth-Century China: Notes on Its Background and Development," in W. G. Beasley and E. G. Pulleyblank, eds., *Historians of China and Japan* (Oxford, 1961); Arthur W. Hummel, "What Chinese Historians Are Doing in Their Own History," *American Historical Review* 34, no. 4 (1929): 715–724; Ursula Richter, "Gu Jiegang: His Last Thirty Years," *The China Quarterly* 90 (1982):286–295; Laurence A. Schneider, "From Textual Criticism to Social Criticism: The Historiography of Ku Chieh-kang," *Journal of Asian Studies* 28, no. 4 (1969): 771–778; Laurence A. Schneider, *Ku Chieh–kang and China's New History* (Berkeley, Calif., 1971); Xu Guansan, *Xin shixue 90 nian* (Ninety Years of the New History), Vol. 1 (Hong Kong, 1986). Ogura Yoshihiko, *Kōnichi senka no Chūgoku chishikijin: Ko Ketsu-gō to Nihon* (A Chinese Intellectual During the War of Resistance Against the Japanese: Gu Jiegang and Japan), (Tokyo, 1987);

Masayuki Sato

GUO Moruo (Leshan, Sizhuan, 1892–Beijing, 1978), Chinese historian. Paleographer, writer, and poet, president of the Chinese Academy of Sciences (1949–1978), chairman of the All–China Federation of Literary and Art Circles (1949–1978). In his early years, Guo threw himself into the revolutionary cultural movement against imperialism and feudalism, and devoted his whole life to the revolutionary cause of the Chinese people. He made significant contributions in numerous fields. In history, he was a pioneer in the Marxist study of Chinese history. His *Zongguo gudai shehui yanjiu* (1930; Study of Ancient Chinese Society) is the first Marxist work on ancient Chinese society. It traces the development of the ancient Chinese society from the primitive commune to slave society and proves that a slave society did exist in ancient China, thus showing that the development of Chinese history is in accordance with the common law of human society as proved by Karl Marx (q.v.) and Friedrich Engels (q.v.). His study is based on the historical realities of China. In order to get first-hand data, Guo studied the archaic oracle bone and bronze inscriptions of the Shang (1766–1122 B.C.) and Chou (1122–403 B.C.) dynasties. He was not content to study the extant commentaries and textual criticism, but immersed himself deeply in paleography, adding new sources to the study of ancient history and also making a creative contribution to paleography itself. He surpassed contemporary historians and paleographers by combining the study of ancient history and paleography and also making a separate contribution to these two disciplines. His *Boci tongzuan* (1933; General Compilation of Oracle Bone Inscriptions) compiles and collates the data of the oracle bone inscriptions, thus creating a set of scientific sources.

Because of his dialectical explanation of the forms, pronunciation, and meaning of paleography, Guo considerably advanced its decipherment and precision, so that many complex inscriptions can be deciphered now. His methods of periodization, putting together fragmentary inscriptions, and completing the incomplete inscriptions overshadow the achievements of preceding scholars. His contribution to the study of the bronze inscriptions and the forms of bronzes lies in the systematic periodization of the important extant bronzes, thus producing a scientific systematization of the bronzewares and their inscriptions which had previously been completely indecipherable, and therefore unusable as historical sources. This academic result is reflected in *Liang Zhou jinwenci daxi* (1932, revised 1934; Compendium of the Bronze Inscriptions of the Zhou Dynasty). Another contribution is his periodization of ancient Chinese history. After nearly half a century of research, he finally set the transition from the Spring and Autumn Period to the Warring States Period as the demarcation between slave and feudal society in China, and he also gave a scientific explanation for this drastically changing period. His *Nulizhi shidai* (1952; The Slave Society) concentrated on this viewpoint. With regard to the history of thought of ancient China, he probed deeply into the origins of the thought of the different schools, and the relationship among them, and also commented on them. His *Qingtong shidai* (The Bronze Age) and *Shipipan shu* (1945; Ten Critiques) represent his achievements in these fields. His comments on the different schools and their doctrines are in accordance with his theories about ancient society and the periodization of ancient history, but here he explains more clearly the integration and systematic nature of his theories. *Guan Zi* was known for its obscureness, but Guo carried on a large-scale work on the basis of preceding achievements and completed *Guan Zi jichiao* (Collected Collations of Guan Zi) of more than two million words in 1956. The *Jiaguwen heji* (A Collection of the Oracle Bone Inscriptions) contains most of the oracle bone inscriptions collected at home and abroad. Most of Guo's influential historical works, like his literary works, have been translated into several languages and have sold well around the world.

Bibliography: Deng Xiaoping, *Zai Guo Moruo tongzhi zhuidaohui shang de daoci* (The Memorial Speech in the Memorial Meeting for Comrade Guo Moruo), (Beijing, 1978); David Tod Roy, *Kuo Mo-jo: The Early Years* (Cambridge, Mass.: Harvard University Press, 1971).

Huang Lie

JIAN Bozan (Hunan Province, 1898–Beijing, 1968), Chinese historian. An ethnic Uighur, professor, Mingguo University (1938–1939), Shehui University (1941–1947), Dade College (1947–1948), Yenching University (1949–1952);

professor, chairman of the History Department, vice-president, Beijing University (1952–1968); concurrently a member of the Philosophy and Social Science Division, Chinese Academy of Sciences (1949–1968). Jian is one of the founders of Marxist historiography in China. From 1926 to 1927 he took part in the First Revolutionary Civil War. Later, he devoted himself primarily to the study of Marxist theory and Chinese history, participating in the controversy over the nature of Chinese society and its social and historical problems. In 1930 he published *The Nature of China's Rural Society and the Classification of Its Stages of Historical Development, China's Rural Society in the Early Feudal Stage* and other essays, criticizing the argument that the Chinese countryside was characterized by ''a unique or Asiatic mode of production'' and demonstrating its semicolonial and semifeudal nature. In these works he also expounded his basic theory on the stages of development of Chinese society, establishing his views on ''Western Zhou (1122–770 B.C.) feudalism.'' His first significant book *Lishi zhexue jiaoding* (1938; A Course in Historical Philosophy) is the first major work by a Chinese scholar to deal with the basic principles of historical materialism in a comprehensive and systematic manner. It also summarizes and comments on some of the important problems put forward in the controversy over the nature of Chinese society and its historical and social problems. It castigates certain reactionary theories and points of view; criticizes the dogmatic tendency of indulging in idle talk only and not integrating theory with historical reality; proposes an approach integrating Marxist historical theory with China's historical reality, and thereby contributes significantly to the establishment of a new Marxist historiography in China. It further develops the author's point of view on the stages of development of Chinese society, marking off the period before the Shang Dynasty (trad. pre-seventeenth century B.C.) as a primitive clan society, the Shang Dynasty (seventeenth century–twelfth century B.C.) as a slave society, the period from the Zhou dynasty to the Opium War (twelfth century B.C.–A.D. 1840) as the age of feudal society, which is in turn divided into two stages: early feudalism (from Western Zhou to the Warring States period—c. 1122–221 B.C.) and despotic feudalism (from Qin and Han 220 B.C. –A.D 220) to the eve of the Opium War), and the period after the Opium War as a semicolonial and semifeudal society. It claims that the embryonic state of Chinese capitalism lay between the end of the Ming Dynasty and the beginning of the Qing Dynasty.

Jian's second major two-volume work, *Outline History of China* (1944–1946), is a general history dealing with the period from primitive society to the Qin and Han dynasties. It cites a broad range of historical documents and archaeological data, discussing in concrete, comprehensive fashion the developmental processes characterizing this period, and the economic and political systems, important events, major characters, and cultural achievements of the major dynasties. Together with certain related works by Guo Moruo (q.v.), Fan Wenlan (q.v.), Lu Zhenyu (q.v.) and others, it laid the foundation for China's new Marxist historiography. *Outline of Chinese History*, published in the early 1960s, of which he is editor-in-chief, is a general history dealing with the stage from primitive society to the pre-May-Fourth-Movement (1919) period. It reveals Jian's views on historiography in a comparatively comprehensive way. In the meantime, he published a number of essays criticizing the extreme leftist ideological trend, propagating the basic Marxist points of view. His major essays were gathered in *The Collected Essays of Historical Problems*. During the Cultural Revolution, he was brutally persecuted. He wrote profusely: his oeuvre of over ten monographs and some four hundred essays, have had a great impact on historical circles in China.

Zhang Chuan-xi

LIANG Qichao (Xinhui, Guangdong, 1873–Beijing, 1929), Chinese bourgeois politician, thinker, and one of the initiators and founders of Chinese bourgeois historiography. Liang took a classical Confucian education as a boy, passing the provincial examinations at age sixteen. The youngest successful candidate, he placed fifth of the hundred who passed, earning the juren degree. In the early 1890s he became a disciple of Kang Yuwei, actively participated in the 1898 reform movement, absorbed the new learning, propagated the historical outlook of evolution, criticized preliminarily the Chinese feudal "history of emperors," and introduced the Western bourgeois "history of People." After the failure of the 1898 reform movement, he took refuge in Japan, where he absorbed more foreign bourgeois historiography. He further criticized the old "feudal historiography," and wrote *Zhongguo tongshi* (A General History of China) "in order to develop patriotism." His *Zhongguoshi xulun* (1901; Discussion of Chinese History) and *Xinshixue* (1902; The New Historiography) criticize the old emperor-centered historiography as attaching excessive importance to narrating "the events of decline and prosperity of men with power." Such history is no more than a reference work for emperors and ministers; "not a work . . . written for the Nation." He also believed that "the new historiography should narrate evolutionary phenomena in order to find out truth and good examples," so as to "make the evolution of the past a guide for the evolution of the future." Later, in his *Zhongguo lijiufa* (1921–1922; Methodology of Chinese Historical Research), he pointed out further that the old feudal history like Sima Guang's *Zizhi tongjian* was "a textbook for emperors," and the new history should be "the *Zizhi tongjian* of the people," offering some proposals to implement this idea. In this work, he also introduced at great length various historical source materials and specific methods of collecting and evaluating historical materials, and advocated that historical research should reflect the spirit of "truth seeking." He also maintained that the narration of history should not be confined to individual facts, but should pay attention to the causal relations between fact and fact.

In *Zhongguo lishi yanjiufa bubian* (1926–1927; Supplement to Methodology of Chinese Historical Research), in addition to the aims of historical research and the qualifications which a historian must possess, Liang also explained briefly the importance of monographic historical studies. He showed that general history can only be properly written after completing the groundwork, in the form of a corpus of monographic studies of specialized topics. In respect to scholarly thought, his *Lun Zhongguo xueshu sixiang biangian zhi dashi* (1902; Major Trends in Chinese Scholarly Thought) is the first modern work attempting to study the history of Chinese scholarly thought using bourgeois historical theories and methods. His *Qingdai xueshu gailun* (1920, 1975; Intellectual Trends in the Qing Period [1644–1911]) and *Zhongguo jin sanbainian xueshushi* (1924; A History of Chinese Scholarship Over the Past Three Hundred Years) are both pioneering works in the study of Qing intellectual history. The first work offers a general analysis of the development of scholarly thought in the Qing Dynasty, and sums up the lessons of the intellectual experience of the Qing for the future development of scholarship. The second systematically "explains the changing trends in scholarship in the Qing, and the value of its cultural contribution," so as to "begin a more solid and greater era," on the foundation of intellectual achievements of the preceding dynasty. These three works share the following thought: The foreign learning introduced into China "will add vitality to our own learning"; if one "wants the foreign learning to become popular in his motherland," he must first be well versed in national (that is, traditional Chinese) learning; competition and discussion between different schools and opinions will benefit the progress of scholarship, while "following one academic master" and "seeking unity in thinking," will hinder this progress. In addition to his work on historical theories, historical methodology, and intellectual history, Liang wrote several valuable works dealing with ancient Chinese history, and the history of political thought, the Buddhism, the nationalities, Western learning, and sciences. His lectures on ancient Chinese thought appeared in English as *History of Chinese Political Thought* (1930). As an important part of the modern Chinese historical heritage, Liang's historical works not only continue to be used in China, but are also highly esteemed by foreign historians. Several of his works have appeared in Japanese, English, and other foreign languages, among them, *Zhongguo lishi yanjiufa*, *Qingdai xueshu gailun*, *Zhongguo jin sanbainian xueshushi*, and *Xian-Qin zhengzhi sixiangshi* (1922; History of Pre-Qin Political Thought). The famous Japanese historian Kuwabara Jitsuzō, for example, had a high regard for Liang's *Zhongguo lishi yanjiufa*. American historians credit Liang and Kang Yu-wei as laying the foundation for the revival of historical research in China.

Bibliography: Hao Chang, *Liang Ch'i-ch'ao and the Intellectual Transition in China, 1890–1907* (Cambridge, Mass.: Harvard University Press, 1971); Ding Wen-jiang and Zhao Feng-tian, *Liang Qichao nian pu changbian* (Collected Data for A Continuation of the Chronicle of Liang Qi-chao), Shanghai ren-min chu-ban-shu (Shanghai Ren-min Press, 1983); Philip Huang, *Liang Ch'i-ch'ao and Modern Chinese Liberalism* (Seattle: University of Washington Press, 1972); Arthur W. Hummel, "What Chinese Historians Are Doing in Their Own History," *American Historical Review* 34 (1929):715–724; Joseph R. Levenson, *Liang Ch'i-ch'ao and the Mind of Modern China* (Cambridge, Mass., 1953); Liang Ch'i-ch'ao, "Archaeology in China," *Smithsonian Report for 1927* (Washington, 1928):453–466; Liang Chi-chao, *Intellectual Trends in the Ching Period*, trans. Immanuel C. Y. Hsu (Cambridge, Mass., 1959); Liang Qichao, *Yinbingshi hoji juanji* (Collected Works and Essays, 24 vols.), (Shanghai, 1936); Liang Qichao, *Yinbingshi hoji wenji* (Collected Works and Essays, 16 vols.), (Shanghai, 1936).

Yu Dan-chu

LI Ji (Zhongxiang), (Hubei, 1896–Taipei, Taiwan, 1979), Chinese archaeologist. Ph.D., Harvard University (1923), researcher and head of the archaeological department of the Research Institute of History and Philology of the Academia Sinica (1929–), honorary member of the Royal Anthropological Society, Britain (1938), academician of the Academia Sinica (1948). Li was the major founder of modern archaeology in China. His first work, "The Formation of Chinese People: An Anthropological Inquiry" (1928), was his doctoral dissertation. In 1926 he became the first Chinese scholar responsible for the excavation at Xiyin Village, Xia County, Shanxi Province, and published *Prehistorical Remains at Xiyin Cun* (1927). In 1929 he led the excavation of the Yin (Shang) Dynasty (trad. 1766–1022 B.C.) ruins in Anyang, Henan Province, the largest then in China. He devoted his whole life to archaeological study of relics from the Yin Dynasty ruins, especially to the study of the pottery and bronzes. In his early years, he published *A Preliminary Discussion on the Pottery of the Shang* (1929), *Five Kinds of Bronzes from the Yin Ruins and Their Relevant Problems* (1933), and *Studies of Xiaotun Bronzes* (1948). In 1956, he published *Pottery of the Yin and Pre-Yin Period*, which, with "Corpus of Yin-Xu pottery" attached, examines systematically the colors and forms of the pottery. Later, he published *Evolution of the White Pottery of the Yin Dynasty* (1957). In 1964–1972, with the cooperation of other scholars, he made a comprehensive study of 170 pieces of bronzes from the Yin ruins, and under the general title of *Archaeologia Sinica, New Series* he published *Studies of the Bronze Gu-beaker, Studies of the Bronze Jue-cup, Studies of the Bronze Jia-vessel, Studies of the Bronze Ding-cauldron*, and *Studies of Fifty-three Ritual Bronzes*. In them, he wrote the section dealing with various forms and patterns of the bronzes. In 1977 he wrote a monograph entitled *Anyang* which was published in the United States. It summarizes the achievements of excavations on the Yin ruins, with a brief characterization of the ancient sites, tombs, and various relics discovered there. Thirty-six important essays have been collected in *Selected Essays on Archaeology by Li Ji* (1977).

Bibliography: Howard L. Boorman and Richard C. Howard, eds., *Biographical Dictionary of Republican China*, 4 vols. (New York, 1967–1971), 2:289–292; Li Chi (Li Ji), *Anyang* (Seattle, 1977); Li Chi (Li Ji), *The Formation of Chinese People: An Anthropological Inquiry* (Cambridge, Mass.: Harvard University Press, 1928); Li Chi (Li Ji), Liang Ssu-yang, and Tung Tso-pin, eds., *Ch'eng-tzu-yai: The Black Pottery Culture Site at Lung-shan-chen in Li-ch'eng-hsien, Shantung Province*, Yale University Publications in Anthropology, no. 52 (1956).

Wang Shimin

LI Jiannong (Shaoyang, Hunan, 1880–Wuhan 1963), Chinese historian. Professor at Mingde University, Hankou (1919–1922), Wuhan University (1930–

1938, 1947–1963), National Pedagogical College of Lantian, Hunan (1940–1945), and Hunan University (1946). A pioneer in the study of the history of the modern Chinese political economy. Li's first historical paper, *Wuhan geming shimoji* (1911), arguing the justness of the Revolution of 1911, exposed the incompetent, counterrevolutionary nature of the Manchu government. After advanced study in England from 1913 to 1916, Li came to believe that to reform China one must first know the contemporary conditions of the country and its history as well. This led him to study the politico-economic history of China. His *Zhuijin sanshinian zhongguo zhengzhishi* (1930; Political History of China in the Last Thirty Years) was a major work, a sound and penetrating analysis of the disputes among the feudal ruling classes and their warlords, of the political struggles and the evolution and divisions of the bourgeois parties in 1898–1928. Later, he added materials on the period 1840–1897, and revised the title to *Zhongguo jinbainian zhengzhi* (1946; The Political History of China in the Last Hundred Years). In 1956 this book was published in English by Ssu-yu Teng (Deng Si-yu, an Americanized Chinese scholar) and Jeremy Ingalls in America, and later in India. In Li's opinion, the course of history has its own continuity, as the evolution of history is much like running water, which we can turn but cannot cut off. Later changes are the results of the issues of the previous ages, and the achievements of posterity are the products of preceding years. He recognized the close relation of politics to economic and cultural developments. The decline of national strength in modern China was the result of economic backwardness, which in turn resulted from cultural, scientific, and technological stagnation. From 1921 on, Li concentrated on the study of the economic development of China. His work in this area, *Zhongguo jingjishi* (1943, revised 1957–1959; The Economic History of China) was divided into three volumes, under the titles of Drafts of the Economical Histories of the pre-Qin and Han, of the Sui and Tang, and of the Song, Yuan, and Ming dynasties. They were the first systematic monographs on historical economics to be published after the founding of the People's Republic of China. Li paid close attention to the interaction of economics and politics, but never lost sight of technology and culture, as typified in this remark: "Economic changes are the result of changes in modes of production, which result from the promotion of technology; in other words they result from the promotion of learning or culture in the society. It is the promotion of learning, rather than economic developments that is the starting point of all historical changes."

Bibliography: Li Chien-nung, *The Political History of China, 1840–1928*, trans. and ed. Ssu-yu Teng and Jeremy Ingalls (Princeton, N.J., 1956).

Xiao Zhizhi

LU Simian (Changzhou, 1884–Shanghai, 1957), Chinese historian. From 1905 on Lu engaged in historical study and teaching, becoming professor of the Senior Normal School of Shenyang (1920), instructor of the First Provincial Normal School of Jiangsu (1923), professor of the Chinese Department, and professor and director of the History Department of Guanghua University in Shanghai (1926–1952), professor of the Teachers College of Eastern China (1952–1957), and member of the Council of the History Society of Shanghai. Much of his work was based on his reading of the twenty-four official dynastic histories, which he is said to have read in their entirety over three times in fifty years, in tandem with reference to other historical writings. After reading a historical work or dynastic history, he noted parallels and made comparisons, taking copious notes in various categories. In his early days he endeavored to study the general history of China, publishing *Baihua ben guoshi* (4 vols., 1922; A Vernacular National History), which was nearly universally read by students in the 1920s, and consequently strongly influenced the study and teaching of history at that time. He published his lectures as *Zhongguo tongshi* (2 vols., 1940, 1945; Survey History of China), which was widely adopted as a university textbook. In his later years he wrote histories of the successive dynasties that have ruled China, publishing *Xian Qin shi* (1941; History of the Pre-Qin Period [to 221 B.C.]), *Qin han shi* (1947; History of Qin and Han [221 B.C.–A.D. 220]), *Liangjin nanbeichao shi* (1948; History of the Jin and the Northern and Southern Dynasties [A.D. 265–589]), and *Sui tang wudaishi* (1959; History of Sui, Tang, and the Five Dynasties [589–947]). Lu's histories of the Song, Liao, Jin and Yuan, Ming, and Qing dynasties were unfinished at his death, but he left behind his notes, which are themselves a valuable resource. All his general or dynastic histories were divided into two parts: The first part presented politics, that is, a narrative of the rise and fall of the dynasty; the second presented its institutions, decrees and regulations, and a discussion of its socioeconomic aspects, political institutions, arts and sciences, and culture. Each of his dynastic histories has its own character. As Lu himself noted, for example, *The History of the Pre-Qin Period* offers an exposition of ancient records; chronology; territories; the rise of Chinese nationalities and their western migration; institutions; and the examination and selection of the government officials. The preface of his *History of Jin and the Southern and Northern Dynasties* is noted for its exposition of falsifications and concealments in Chen Shou's *Weizhi* (History of Wei), commending the volunteers for their fight against Wei, praising Emperor Wu of the state Chen, investigating the prices, wages, and properties, and the election system. His other historical works are *Jeng zi jie ti* (1926; Explanations of the Confucian Classics and the Books of the Masters of the Various Schools), *Li xue ganggao* (1931; An Outline of Neo-confucianism), *Xianqin xueshu gailun* (1933; An Introduction to the Scholarship of Pre-Qin Times), *Shitongping* and *Zhongguo minzu shi* (1934; The History of the Chinese Nationalities), and *Lishi yanjiufa* (1945; Historical Methodology).

Bibliography: Tang Zhi-jun, "Lu Si-mian," in *The Yearbook of the Chinese Historiography* (Beijing, 1981).

Yie Gui-sheng

LU Zhenyu (Hunan Province, 1900–Beijing, 1980), Chinese historian. Professor, University of China (1933–1935), Fudan University (1940); president and professor, Delian University (1949–1950), Northeast People's University (1951–1955); professor, Central Party School of CPC (1956–1962); academician (Philosophy and Social Sciences Section), Chinese Academy of Sciences (1954–1962); adviser, Chinese Academy of Social Sciences (1979–1980). Lu was one of the founders of Marxian historical science in China. Among his distinguished works, *Shigian Jongguo shehui yanjiu* (1934; Studies on Prehistoric Chinese Society) was the first historical work in China to apply historical materialism to the study of primitive Chinese society. Using archaeological relics to construct a frame for the historical implications of ancient myths and legends, he sketched the outlines of Chinese primitive society and pointed out that the main branch of the Chinese ethnic group was a descendant of the Mongol race. He argued that there was a complete primitive society even in remote antiquity, starting from remotest times, through matriarchy to the patriach of pre-Shang times (1766 B.C.). He asserted that the ancient culture of China was created and developed successively by ancient Chinese on their own land in pre-Shang times, but that the Shang (1766 B.C.–1122 B.C.) was a slave society, followed by the feudal society of Zhou through late Qing (1122 B.C.–A.D.1840), and a semicolonial/semifeudal society that had prevailed since 1840. In *Society in the Yin and Zhou Dynasties* (1936), based on his investigation of archaeological evidence and ancient literatures, he first offered the conclusion that the Yin Dynasty was a slave society and the Zhou Dynasty was feudal. In *A Concise General History of China* (2 vols., 1941–1948) Lu further elaborated the views he set forth in these earlier works and placed them in a new context of his supplementary studies on the period after the Qin and the Han dynasties (221 B.C.–220 A.D.). He pointed out that Chinese feudal society should be classified as an initial feudal society (pre-Qin Dynasty) and an autocratic feudal society (Qin Dynasty to the Opium War). He advanced the following two points in the 1930s: (1) The construction of the initial feudal society was characterized by significant disequilibrium, and the feudal society of the "states of the marquises" began to be dominant from the spring and autumn period (772–481 B.C.); (2) The initial formation of capitalistic household handcrafts emerged in the late Ming Dynasty in the sixteenth century.

Together with Fan Wenlan (q.v.), Jian Bozan (q.v.), and others, Lu was one of the founders of research on a new general history of China. *Jongguo jengzhi sixiang shi* (1937; History of Chinese Political Thought) was a monographic study of Chinese ancient thought. Lu evaluated ancient Chinese thinkers according to their attitude toward the masses and the historical roles they played. This study marked a break with traditional research, as Lu opened a new phase in the application of Marxism to the study of the history of Chinese philosophy and thought. He also achieved outstanding success in his studies of the history of Chinese nationalities and other historic fields. He was not only a famous scholar, but also a famous revolutionist. Since 1936, as a communist he took part in the revolutionary struggles. Even under the most difficult conditions in the turbulent years of the 1960s and 1970s, he still insisted on writing and he left many manuscripts, totaling some three hundred thousand words. His books and writings have had great influence on Chinese historians for over fifty years.

Bibliography: Bai Shouyi et al., eds., *Shixue gailun* (An Outline of Historiography), (Ningxia: Ninging Renmin Chubanshe, 1983); Chen Qingquan and Su Suangbi et al., eds., *Zhongguo shixuejia pingzhuang* (Critical Biographies of Chinese Historians), (Henan: Zhongzhou juji chubanshe, 1985); Hou Wailu et al., eds., *Zhonggu sixiang tongshi* (Survey History of Chinese Thought), (Beijing: Renmin Chubanshe, 1957–1960); Liu Jie, *Zhongguo shixueshi gao* (Draft History of Chinese Historiography), (Henan: Zhongzhou Shuhuashe, 1982); Wu Ze and Yang Yixiang et al., eds., *Zhongguo lishi dacidian shixueshi juan* (The Dictionary of Chinese History, Volume on the History of Historiography), (Shanghai: Shanghai Cishu Chubanshe, 1983); Yin Da et al., eds., *Zhongguo shixue fazhan shi* (The History of the Development of the Chinese Historiography), (Henan: Zhongzhou Guji Chubanshe, 1985);

Liu Mao-lin

WANG Guowei (Haining, Zhejiang, 1877–Beijing, 1927). Chinese historian, writer, and poet. Educated in the traditional curriculum of the Confucian classics, history, and poetry, particularly the orthodox interpretations of the classics propounded by Ju Xi (1130–1200). Wang prepared for the civil service examinations, which were essentially a test of comprehensive knowledge of the classics, from 1877 to 1892. His exceptional talent and thorough training enabled him to pass the youth examinations on his first attempt, at the unusually young age of fifteen, but he never passed any of the higher level examinations, either dropping out or failing them. He worked at the newspaper *Shiwubao* (Current Affairs) in Shanghai starting in 1898. In his spare time, he entered the Tongwen xueshe (Eastern Language Institute) sponsored by Luo Zhenyu to study Japanese and English, and was influenced by the doctrines of Kant, Schopenhauer, and Nietzsche. In the spring of 1901 Luo called him to Wuchang to work as a translator and founded *Nong Bao* (Agricultural Journal). Later, Wang assumed the post of the chief of *Jiaoyu shijie zaji* (World of Education Magazine). He went to Japan to pursue advanced studies in 1902 but soon returned because of illness. During 1903–1904, he lectured at Tongzhou Shifan Xuexiao (school) in Nantong and Jiangsu Shifan Xuetang (school) in Suzhou on philosophy, ethics, and sociology, based on "the Western Learning" then being imported from Europe and America. Wang's first work, *Jingan wenji* (Essays by Jingan [a nom de plume], 1905), was a collection of essays on philosophy and literature; in 1910 he turned to poetry, publishing *Renjian cihua* (Poetic Remarks on the Human World), which has been greatly influential in literary circles. At the same time, he also studied the history of Chinese opera, ancient utensils, and ancient documents, and wrote *Xiqu kaoyuan* (On the Origins of Drama) and *Sui Tang bingfu tulu fushuo* (Illustrated Explanation of the Military Tallies of Sui and Tang). After the 1911 Revolution, he took refuge with Luo in Japan and settled in Kyoto, the center of the rapidly developing school of Japanese Sinology under the leadership of Naitō Konan (q.v.), with whom Wang frequently exchanged views. He wrote his famous *Song Yuan ciqushi* (History of Song [960–1279] and Yuan [1279–1368] Drama), a pioneering study of the history of opera in modern China. Later, he studied primarily the ancient utensils, clay seals, and wooden tablets of the Han (207 B.C.–220 A.D.) and Jin (265–420) dynasties, oracle-bone inscriptions and bronze and stone inscriptions of the Shang (1766?–1122 B.C.) and Zhou (1122–407 B.C.) dynasties, while also continuing broader research on history. His *Liushazhui jianxu* (1914; Introduction to the Desert Tablets) identifies the places where the wooden tablets of the Han and Jin were discovered, and is the first work in modern China dealing with the ancient Western frontier.

Wang returned from Japan in 1916, settling in Shanghai, where he compiled *Xueshu congbian* (1916; Survey of Scholarship) for S. A. Hardoon; meanwhile, he also taught at Canshengmingzhi University. He was the first to study the history and institutions of the Shang and Zhou using oracle-bone inscriptions, and based on them wrote *Yinshishu yitongbiao* (Chronological Tables of the Shang Dynasty), in which he worked out the chronology of the "Yinbenji" (Chronology of Shang), the "Sandai shibiao" (Historical Tables of the Three Dynasties) from Sima Qian's *Shiji* and "Gujinren biao" (Personages of Past and Present) of Ban Gu's *Han shu*, thus correcting errors in these histories. His knowledge of oracle-bone inscriptions laid the foundations for the modern study of this subject, which constitutes the principal source for Shang Dynasty history. His *Yin bucizhong suojian xiangong xianwang kao* (On the Former Dukes and Kings Who Appear in the Shang Oracle-bone Inscriptions) and the sequel study are basic contributions to the study of Shang (1766?–1122 B.C.) history. It is not only his greatest academic achievement, but also a major event in modern Chinese intellectual history. In his study of the inscriptions on oracle bones, he compared his results with *Zhouli* (The Institutions of Zhou) and concluded that "the greatest transformations in Chinese politics and culture occurred in the Yin and Zhou dynasties." In 1919, he devoted himself to study of Tang Dynasty (618–907) manuscripts unearthed at Dunhuang, in the northwest, which he exploited as sources for the history and geography, and the system of measurements of the Tang and Song (960–1279). In 1921 his important work *Guantang jilin* (The Collected Works of Guantang) in twenty volumes was published; it has been praised by scholars at home and abroad. In the summer of 1923, he was engaged as Xingzou (tutor) of the Southern Study of Pu Yi, the deposed last emperor of the Qing. In 1925 he was invited to be a tutor at the Institute of National Learning. In all his research, he attached importance to "the underground (i.e., archaeological) materials" and made full use of them to study ancient Chinese documents and history. This is "the method of dual evidence," with which historical texts and relics are checked against each other. In his remaining years, he wrote *Sanshipan kaoshi* (a biography), *Gushi xinzheng* (New Corrections for Ancient History), *Dada kao* (On the Tatars), *Liao Jin Mengu* (Mongolia in the Liao [947–1125] and Jin [1115–1234] dynasties), and many others. Lu Zhenyu (q.v.) compiled *Haining Wang Zhongque gong yishu* (The Posthumous Papers of Wang Zhongque [a nom de plume] of Haining) after Wang's death.

Bibliography: Joey Bonner, *Wang Kuo-wei, An Intellectual Biography* (Cambridge, Mass.: Harvard University Press, 1986); Chester Chen-I Wang, "Wang Kuo-wei (1877–1927): His Life and Scholarship," Ph.D. dissertation (Chicago, 1962); Benjamin Elman, "Wang Kuo-wei and Lu Hsun: The Early Years," *Monumenta Serica* 34 (1979–1980):389–401; Hermann Kogelschatz, *Wang Kuo-wei und Schopenhauer: Eine philosophische Begegnung. Wandlung des Selbenstverstännisses der chinesischin Literatur unter dem Einfluss der Klassischen deutschen Ästhetik* (Stuttgart, 1986); Wang Guowei, *Wang Guan-tang xien-sheng chuan-ji* (The Complete Works of Wang [Guowei], 16 Vols.), (Taibei: I-wen yin-shu-guan, 1974).

Yuan Yin-guang

WEI Yuan (Shaoyang, Hunan, 1794–Hangzhou, 1857), Chinese official philosopher, historian, and geographer. Son of a provincial official, Wei passed the state examination for the initial *xiucai* degree at age fifteen and continued his studies of history and philosophy, especially the heterodox theories of Ming Dynasty philosopher Wang Yangming (1472–1529). Called to the capital for study in the provincial recommendation of 1814, he passed the *juren* degree examination in 1822 and was employed by the governor of Kiangsu to edit the *Huangchao jingshi wenbian* (1826; Compendium of Qing Dynasty Essays on Statecraft). He passed the state examination for the *jinshi*, the highest degree, in 1844 and thereafter was appointed to a number of provincial posts. A leader in arguing for the application of scholarship to contemporary administrative problems, he wrote an 1825 treatise advocating ocean transport of tax rice to the capital, since the Grand Canal had become blocked with silt, and later, in the 1830s, he assisted in the reform of a regional salt monopoly. In the 1850s, he sharply criticized the prevailing pedantic textual criticism as useless learning that had confined ideas, maintaining that historical research should be connected with practical problems and that the historian should sum up historical lessons in order to correct social abuses. He recognized the seriousness of the social crisis of his day and the urgent need for reform. Thus in his compilation of *Qing jinshiwenbian*, he selected more than two thousand essays on economics, administration, and statecraft in an effort to draw attention to the practical problems of the national economy and the people's livelihood. He was roused to righteous indignation by the signing of the unequal Nanking Treaty, forced on China by the British Empire in 1842, and wrote *Shengwu ji* (Chronicle of Imperial Military Campaigns) in fourteen volumes, showing from both the military and the political viewpoint the decline of the Qing from its heyday, and pointing out expressly that the latter part of the Qianlong emperor's (reigned 1736–1796) reign was the turning point.

Wei's historical works mark a change from the tradition of "examining the history of the past only" prevailing since the Qianlong and Jiaqing periods. He wrote the *Haiguo tuzhi* (Illustrated Treatise on the Maritime Kingdoms), a geography of foreign countries, and enlarged it three times to one hundred volumes. In this work Wei drew on materials translated from Western periodicals under the direction of Lin Zexu (1785–1850, imperial commissioner at Canton); Chapter 12, dealing with Japan, was translated into English by Sir Thomas Wade. Wei suggested that it was most important to enrich the country and strengthen its military power; he also advocated that China study and learn from the West in order to resist foreign aggressors. This work was the most detailed reference book in world history and geography in the East at that time. *Hai-guo tuzhi* was very popular abroad and also influenced the Meiji reforms. Later, despite the banning, he recorded faithfully the history of the Opium War and exposed the crimes of aggressors and capitulators. In his old age, he wrote *Yuanshi xinbian* (A New History of the Yüan [1279–1368] Dynasty), intended as a critique of the official *Yuan shi* (Yuan history), which he and many of his contemporaries regarded as fundamentally flawed, and thus promoted the study of Yuan history, and of frontier historical geography. In historiography he has been described as having "the talent for writing true history." Among his other works are *Shi Guwei* (The Poetry of Guwei), *Shu Guwei* (The Works of Guwei), *Guweitang ji* (The Anthology of Guwei Studies), *Guweitang shiji* (The Collected Poems of Guwei), *Laozi benyi* (The Original Meaning of Laozi), and others.

Bibliography: Jane Kate Leonard, *Wei Yuan and China's Rediscovery of the Maritime World* (Cambridge, Mass., 1984); Li Kan, "Lun Wei Yuan," (On Wei Yuan), Lishixue, 3 (1979); Tu Lienche, "Wei Yuan," in Arthur W. Hummel, ed., *Eminent Chinese of the Ch'ing Period, 1644–1912* (Washington, D.C.: U.S. Government Printing Office, 1943), pp. 851–853; Wu Ze and Huang Liyong, *Wei Yuan Haiquo tuzhi yanjiu* (The Study of Illustrated Treatise on the Maritime Kingdoms by Wei Yuan), *Lishi yanjiu* (Historical studies), 4 (1963).

Chen Qitai

XIAO Gongquan (K. C. Hsiao, Hsiao Kung-ch'uan), (Nan'an, Jiangxi Province, 1897–Seattle, Wash., 1981), Chinese historian. Professor at various Chinese universities including Yenching University (1930–1932), Tsing Hua University (1932–1937), Sichuan University (1938–1947), and the University of Washington, Seattle, 1949–1968). Influential as classical scholar, political thinker, historian, and literary figure, Xiao was noted for his attainments in both traditional Chinese learning and Western scholarship. Reared in Sichuan Province where he was tutored at home until the age of eighteen, he prepared for university in Shanghai (1915–1918) and was admitted to Tsing Hua College (later University, then the principal institution for preparing competitively selected Chinese men for study abroad). He earned B.A. and M.A. degrees at the University of Missouri (1923–1926) and the doctorate in political philosophy at Cornell University (1926). His dissertation, *Political Pluralism: A Study in Contemporary Political Theory*, published in England in 1927, was highly praised by Harold Laski and others. Returning to China in 1927, Xiao commenced research on the history of Chinese government and political thought, a subject that occupied him for the next fifteen years, while teaching and writing in several fields. The systematic study of political thought was then a new field of intellectual endeavor in China; to it Xiao contributed the defining conceptualizations and standards as well as the most extensive analytical presentation of the development of political theory from Confucius (died 479 B.C.) to the twentieth century, in his masterwork, *Zhongguo zhengzhi sixiangshi* (A History of Chinese Political Thought) (English translation, vol.1 1979; vol. 2 forthcoming). At the University of Washington after 1949, Xiao participated in that institution's Modern China History Project, for which he conducted research (while teaching) on nineteenth- and twentieth-century Chinese social history. This led to a large and important work, *Rural China: Imperial Control in the Nineteenth Century* (1960). It is widely regarded as the definitive baseline of all subsequent social history of late imperial China. His final large work, *A Modern China and a New World: K'ang Yu-wei, Reformer and Utopian, 1858–1927* (1975), reexamines at greater length the last major figure in his *History of Chinese Political Thought*. In China between 1927 and 1949 Xiao wrote extensively for journals of political comment, identifying with no political movement but attempting to bring a modern critical spirit to bear on China's political problems. The most important of those writings were re-published in a volume entitled *Xianzheng yu minzhu* (Constitutional Government and Democracy, Shanghai, 1948). After 1949 Xiao published two retrospective volumes of his poetry and one of miscellaneous writings. His various writings, newly edited, including translations into Chinese of works written in English, is appearing in ten volumes under the title *Xiao Gongquan quanji* (The Complete Works of K. C. Hsiao, Taipei, 1982–).

Xiao belonged to the last generation of Chinese who in their youth acquired profound command of traditional Chinese learning and at the same time to the first generation of those who then were enabled to go on to acquire a similarly deep immersion in Western languages, cultures, and intellectual traditions. That combination of skills at his level of attainment was most uncommon among his contemporaries and increasingly rare thereafter. His judicious and even-minded treatment of past thinkers, his deep knowledge of political realities, and his acute analytical capacities have imparted to his historical writings great authority and continuing influence. Like many early twentieth-century Chinese intellectuals, he was acutely aware of the shortcomings of traditional Chinese society. He stressed above all China's unfortunate failure to have developed a concept of transcendent law, with consequent weaknesses in the political sphere. A man of dual culture, he nonetheless remained deeply attached to Chinese civilization. At the same time, he was somewhat pessimistic about China's future and was critical of all its modern political movements and leading figures.

Bibliography: Xiao Gongquian, *Wenxue jianwang lu*, 1972 (Autobiography, translated under the title *Critical Reflections on My Pursuit of Learning*), published serially in *Chinese Studies in History* 10, no.4 (Summer 1977 *et seq.*); Buxbaum, David C., and F. W. Mote, eds., *Transition and Permanence: A Festschrift in Honor of Dr. Hsiao Kungch'uan*, 1972 (Contains a bibliography of Xiao's writings and other materials).

F. W. Mote

Great Historians: Czechoslovakian

BRETHOLZ, Bertold (1862–1936), Bohemian historian of German tongue. Educated in Vienna where he excelled in the study of Latin paleography. In 1892 Bretholz was appointed historiographer and in 1899 chief archivist of Moravia, in which capacity he continued to publish the series of historic works and sources on the history of Moravia: *Geschichte Mährens* (1893 and 1895), and *Codex diplomaticus et epistolaris Moraviae* (15 vols. between 1836 and 1903). After Constantin Höfler (1811–1897) and Adolf Bachmann (1849–1914), Bretholz was the third significant German historian connected with Bohemia who considered "revising" František Palacký (q.v.) his lifelong task. Commissioned by the Prague Germans to write a new history of Bohemia from the German point of view, Bretholz published *Geschichte Böhmens und Mährens bis zum Aussterben der Přemysliden* (1912), in which he presented a new radical interpretation of the German colonization. Contrary to Palacký and other Czech historians, Bretholz argued that Bohemia had always been inhabited by German settlers, even prior to the arrival of the Czech tribes. This revisionist view resulted in a strong response by two leading Czech historians, Josef Šusta (q.v.) and Josef Pekař (q.v.). Between 1921 and 1925 Bretholz added three more volumes in which he pursued his extremist views on the cultural superiority of the Germans over the Czechs in such a way that a number of German historians (e.g., Karl Berger, Ernst Schwarz, Wilhelm Wostry, Adolf Zycha), writing for the *Mitteilungen des Vereins fur die Geschichte der Deutschen in Böhmen*, expressed their strong criticism. His other writings included *Lateinische Paläographie* (1906), *Neuere Geschichte Böhmens* (1920), a re-edition of the medieval *Chronica Bohemorum* by Kosmas for the *Monumenta Germaniae Historica* (1923), *Geschichte der Juden in Mähren im Mittelalter* (1934), and *Brünn: Geschichte und Kultur* (1938).

Bibliography: H. Bachmann, *Die südetendeutsche Geschichtsschreibung von Höfler bis Wostry* (Aschaffenburg, 1963–1964); F. Seibt, *Deutschland und die Tschechen* (Munich, 1974).

Milan Hauner

DOBROVSKÝ, Josef (1753–1829), founder of comparative Slavic linguistics and a major Czech scholar of the Enlightenment era. Educated for the priesthood by the Jesuit order; after its dissolution in 1773, Dobrovský became an educationalist and scholar with the support of Bohemian nobility. Goethe called him "the grandmaster of critical historical research," although his major works deal with the history of language and literature, for example, *Geschichte der böhmischen Sprache und Literatur* (1792) and *Institutiones linguae slavicae dialecti veteris* (1822). Dobrovský introduced higher standards of textual criticism, quite uncommon during his lifetime, and through his critical reviews and editions he exercised great influence on his contemporaries. In *Fragmentum pragense Evangelii s. Marci* (1778), Dobrovský seriously questioned the authenticity of the famous fragment. In his literary magazine, *Böhmische und mährische Litteratur* (1779), he subjected to scathing criticism the scholarly ineptitude of K. R. Ungar's edition of *Bohemia docta*, an encyclopedical project undertaken by B. Balbín (q.v.) a century earlier. In 1783 he questioned in several studies the historical authenticity of the most popular Bohemian saint Jan Nepomucký, whose sanctimonious cult had been one of the major accomplishments of the Catholic Church during the past decades. Dobrovský also excelled as editor of historical texts: together with F. M. Pelcl (1734–1801), the first professor of Czech language and literature at the University of Prague, he edited in 1783–1784 the oldest Czech chroniclers for the *Scriptores rerum bohemicarum* (vols. 1 and 2, 1783–1784). Dobrovský published most of his historical studies in the Proceedings of the Royal Learned Society of Bohemia: for example, "Über das Alter der böhmischen Bibelübersetzung" (1782), "Über die Einführung und Verbreitung der Buchdruckerkunst in Böhmen" (1782), "Geschichte der böhmischen Pikarden und Adamiten" (1788), "Über die ältesten Sitze der Slaven in Europa . . . " (1788), and "Beiträge zur Geschichte des Kelches in Böhmen" (1817). His most important historical studies appeared between 1803 and 1826 under the title, *Kritische Versuche, die ältere böhmische Geschichte von späteren Erdichtungen zu reinigen*; he subjected to serious criticism the authenticity of the legends surrounding the Byzantine missionaries who spread Christianity through the first Slavonic literary language in the ninth century, *Cyrill und Method, die Slaven Apostel* (1823). Among the leading personalities in Bohemia, it was Dobrovský alone, guided by his enlightened rationalism to serve nothing but the truth, who denounced singlehandedly as forgeries the recently discovered (1817 and 1818) major Czech manuscripts (Königinhofer Handschriften), while his pupils, Václav Hanka, Josef Jungmann, and František Palacký (q.v.), wanted the public to believe that the manuscripts were genuine, because of their immense propaganda value for the cause of Czech nationalism. Despite his major contribution to the revival of the Czech language and literature, all his life Dobrovský remained extremely skeptical as to the prospects of a full cultural renaissance of the Czech nation.

Bibliography: V. Brandl, *Život Josefa Dobrovského* (Brno, 1883); F. Kutnar, *Přehledné dějiny českého a slovenského dějepisectví*, vol. 1 (Prague, 1973); M. Machovec, *Josef Dobrovský* (Prague, 1964); I. Snegirev, *Iossif Dobrovsky* (Kazan, 1884).

Milan Hauner

GOLL, Jaroslav (1846–1929), founder of the positivist school in Czech historiography. Educated several generations of historians (hence, the Goll School), represented by Kamil Krofta (q.v.), Zdenek Nejedlý (q.v.), Lubor Niederle (q.v.), Bedrich Hronzný (q.v.), Josef Šusta (q.v.), Josef Pekař (q.v.), and others. After František Palacký (q.v.), he was the first Czech historian with a distinct personality and international reputation. Educated in Prague by historians V. V. Tomek, C. Höfler, and A. Gindely, and in Göttingen in the legendary history seminar of Georg Waitz (q.v.), Goll traveled widely throughout Europe. In Berlin he worked as secretary to the U.S. minister to Germany and distinguished historian George Bancroft (q.v.), often referred to as the Father of American History, who was then finishing his ten-volume *History of the United States*. Goll's reputation consisted above all in his performance as university teacher and leader of the history seminar, and less so in the quantity of his books. He wrote mostly commentaries and book reviews, and displayed a considerable talent to write and translate poetry. He started to teach at the University of Prague in 1875 and was promoted extraordinary professor five years later. In 1882, when the university was split into German and Czech sections, Goll joined the newly established Czech faculty of philosophy, of which he became dean ten years later and rector (chancellor) in 1907–1908. In 1894 Goll and a fellow historian A. Rezek founded the *Český časopis historický* (Czech Historical Journal), which aspired to rival the *Revue Historique* and the *Historische Zeitschrift*. He frequently represented Czech historians at international congresses, and for more than twenty-five years he commented in *Revue Historique* on the progress of historiography in Bohemia (see *Posledních 50 let české práce dějepisné* [Last 50 Years of Czech Historiography], edited by his pupil Josef Šusta in 1926). This did not spare him from accusations that he stood aloof from Czech politics and was cultivating history for history's own sake. Goll's first published works dwell largely on the social and religious history of the fifteenth through seventeenth centuries; of special significance are his collected articles on the Unitas Fratrum, *Quellen und Untersuchungen zur Geschichte der böhmischen Brüder* (2 vols., 1878–1882), subsequently published in the Journal of the Czech Museum (1883–1886) as *Jednota bratrská v XV. století*. In 1916 Goll prepared a separate edition entitled *Chelčický a Jednota v XV. století* (Chelčický and Unitas Fratrum in the Fifteenth Century).

The topical event for Czech historiography in the 1880s was the critical debate over the authenticity of two collections of Czech manuscript forgeries (Königinhofer Handschrift), sanctioned by the eminent historian František Palacký and worshipped by the majority of Czech patriots, in which Goll sided with the minority, arguing against the authenticity (and so did his professorial colleague T. G. Masaryk, the future president of Czechoslovakia). This stand alone made Goll more unpopular among the Czech conservative circles to whom by his temperament and persuasion he belonged. Given the range of Goll's interests, it is difficult to select one title as his most important work. His two major monographs, *Čechy a Prusy ve středověku* (1897; Bohemia and Prussia in the Middle Ages), and *Válka o země koruny české 1740–1742* (1916; The War Over the Lands of the Bohemian Crown), are little known today outside the narrow circle of specialists. Politically, Goll was a conservative who remained loyal to the idea of the Habsburg monarchy even after 1918. He did not believe in the survivability of an independent Bohemian state. In return for his loyalty, the emperor appointed him court counsellor and member of the upper house; from 1907 to 1908 Goll was tutor to the heir of the throne. Goll's fate in the newly founded Czechoslovak Republic after 1918 was very sad. His own pupils denounced him as a traitor and collaborator. Although Goll had been retired by then, his public appearances were boycotted, and he died a lonely and almost forgotten man. His shorter works, articles, and reviews, selected in two volumes, appeared posthumously in 1928–1929 as *Vybrané spisy drobné* (Selected Small Writings).

Bibliography: J. Werstadt, *Odkazy dějin a dějepisců* (Prague, 1948); K. Krofta, *Masaryk, Goll a české dějepisectví* (Prague, 1912); F. M. Bartoš, *Jaroslav Goll* (Prague, 1947); K. Kazbunda, *Stolice dějin na pražské univerzitě*, 3 vols. (Prague, 1964–1968); F. Kutnar, *Přehledné dějiny českého a slovenského dějepisectví*, vol. 2 (Prague, 1977).

Milan Hauner

HROZNÝ, Bedřich (1879–1952), Czech orientalist and founder of Hittitology. Professor of ancient oriental studies at Charles University in Prague after 1919, member of the Czech Academy of Sciences, and honorary doctor of many foreign universities. In 1915 Hrozný, who since 1905 had taught semitic languages at the University of Vienna, deciphered the cuneiform script of the Hittites, proving that theirs was an Indo-European language; he also deciphered the hieroglyphic script used by the earlier Hittites. Hrozný published his theories in *Die Sprache der Hethiter, ihr Bau und ihre Zugehörigkeit zum indogermanischen Sprachstamm* (1915); *Die Lösung des hethitischen Problems* (1915); *Hethitische Keilschrifttexte aus Bogazköi* (1919); *Code Hittite* (1922); and *Les Inscriptions hittites hiéroglyphiques* (1933–1937). His research took him to various Middle Eastern countries, India, and Crete. Although his interpretations of the origins of the proto-Indian script and languages, and of the Linear B Script on Crete, had not been widely accepted (see "Inschriften und Kultur der Proto-Inden von Mohenjo-Daro and Harappa," *Archív Orientální* 12 (1941); "Kretas und Vorgriechenlands Inschriften, Geschichte und Kultur", *Archív Orientálmí* 14 (1943); *Les Inscriptions Crétoises* (Prague, 1949). His best internationally known work is *Histoire* *de l'Asie Anterieure, de l'Inde et de la Crète* (1947), also published in Czech (1949) and English (1953).

Bibliography: V. Čihař, "Bibliographie des Travaux de Bedřich Hrozný (1902–1949)," *Archív Orientální* 17 (1949); L. Matouš, *Bedřich Hrozný: Leben und Forschungswerk eines tschechischen Orientalisten* (Prague, 1949) [also published in Czech, French, English, and Russian].

Milan Hauner

KROFTA, Kamil (1876–1945), Czech historian and diplomat. Educated in Prague under Jaroslav Goll (q.v.) and in the Viennese Institute for Study of History. Krofta's first major editorial work, *Monumenta Vaticana res gestas Bohemicas illustrantia* (2 vols., 1903–1905) was based on his research in the Vatican Archives. He also edited the protocols of the Bohemian Diet (1605–1620). Krofta's first monograph, *Majestát Rudolfa II* (1909; The Letter of Majesty by Rudolf II), like his subsequent treaties, deals with church-state relations in the sixteenth and seventeenth centuries. In 1911 Krofta published two treaties written by Petr Chelčický, the remarkable Czech religious thinker of the fifteenth century, *O boji duchovním a O trojím lidu* (About the Spiritual Struggle and About the Three Estates). One year later he was appointed extraordinary professor of Austrian history at the Czech University of Prague. After the foundation of the Czechoslovak Republic in 1918, Krofta published his short history of the peasants in Bohemia and Moravia, *Přehled dějin selského stavu v Čechách a na Moravě*. While serving as a Czechoslovak minister in Vienna (1921–1925), Krofta lectured on comparative legal history at the nearby Slovak university of Bratislava and published a number of legal studies: *Čtení o ústavních dějinách slovenských* (Reading on the Constitutional History of Slovakia), *Stará ústava česká a uherská* (1931; Old Bohemian and Hungarian Constitutions), *Konec starého Uherska* (1924; The End of Old Hungary), and *Čechové a Slováci před svým státním sjednocením* (1932; The Czechs and Hungarians Before Their Own National Unification). In 1919 Krofta began to write his contributions to *The Cambridge Medieval History*. His first chapter, "Bohemia to the Extinction of the Přemyslids," was followed by two more covering fourteenth- and fifteenth-century Bohemia and the Hussite Movement. Krofta's interests were wide ranging. In 1927 he published a monograph on the German Question in Czechoslovakia (*Němci v Čechách*) and *Stará a nová střední Evropa* (Old and New Central Europe) in 1929. Krofta also took part in the great debate about "the Meaning of Czech History." Before World War I he vehemently defended his teacher Goll and his older colleague Josef Pekař (q.v.). After the war, however, Krofta changed sides and criticized Pekař's views on the Hussite Revolution in his polemic study, *Žiška a husitská revoluce* (1936; Žiška and the Hussite Revolution, 1936). He also rejected Pekař's strong emphasis on the national idea as the principal inspiration of Czech national history. Instead, like Masaryk, he stressed the importance of the religious idea: *Náboženská otázka v našich dějinách* (1936; The Religious Question in Our History). Krofta's best known book is the popular *Malé dějiny Československa* of 1931 (The Pocket History of Czechoslovakia), translated into many languages. Krofta's trying years as a diplomat were certainly his years as Czechoslovakia's foreign minister between 1936 and 1938. Considered President Beneš' right hand prior to the Munich crisis, Krofta could not avoid imprisonment during the Nazi occupation; he died shortly after the end of the war. During the early days of the war, however, Krofta succeeded in publishing two courageous books in which he defended his strong optimism in the survival of the Czech nation: *Z dob naší první republiky* (1939; From the Era of Our First Republic), and *Nesmrtelný národ* (1940; The Immortal People).

Bibliography: J. Werstadt, ed., *O Kamilu Kroftovi, historiku a diplomatu* (Prague, 1946); F. M. Bartoš, *Kamil Krofta* (Prague, 1946); J. Gluecklich, *Kamil Krofta* (Prague, 1947).

Milan Hauner

NEJEDLÝ, Zdeněk (1878–1962), Czech historian and politician. Son of a music teacher, Nejedlý was educated at the Czech University in Prague under Jaroslav Goll (q.v.) and T. G. Masaryk, the country's future president. He ended his long career as a cultural overlord in Communist Czechoslovakia, occupying the posts of minister for education (1945–1946, 1948–1953), deputy prime minister (1953), and president of the Czechoslovak Academy of Sciences after 1952. During his lifetime he accumulated a vast number of awards and titles. A bibliography of his writings published in 1959 contains almost 400 pages and 3,808 titles. His own field of research was the history of musicology, and he was appointed the first extraordinary professor of that discipline in 1909 in Prague, after working for ten years as an archivist. His ambition drove him to occupy prominent positions as commentator, editor, and critic on virtually all aspects of Czech culture. Nejedlý's huge output embraces his manifold ideological transformations. At the beginning he was inspired by the late nineteenth-century romanticism in the tradition of František Palacký (q.v.) and Jules Michelet (q.v.). He was trained as an empiricist by the positivist methodology, influenced by Masaryk's mythologization of the Czech past, especially of the Hussite Revolution and Czech Reformation, and then embraced a variety of left-wing tendencies that ended in his holding a demonstrative Marxist-Leninist world-view. His Marxism, however, was neither genuine nor convincing; he merely adopted its label to cover his own emotional approach to history which remained that of a late romantic and populist historian. His most extensive work is the tediously voluminous chronicle on his native city, *Dějiny města Litomyšle a okolí* (vol. 1, 1903; History of the City of Litomyšl and Its Surroundings), to which he added a major seven-volume biography on his favorite Czech music composer, *Bedřich Smetana* (1924–1933), complemented by a four-volume monograph, *T. G. Masaryk* (1930–1937), and the two-volume work, *Lenin* (1937–1938). In his own field of specialization, Nejedlý published several pioneering works dealing with the history of Czech music of the Middle Ages, especially during the Hussite period: *Dějiny předhusitského zpěvu v Čechách* (1904), which was his habilitation thesis, *Počátky husitského zpěvu* (1907); and *Dějiny husitského zpěvu za válek husitských* (1913). His unabashed cult of Smetana showed frequently in his strong bias against such great national composers as Dvořák and Janáček. Apart from numerous works on Smetana, Nejedlý wrote several monographs on Czech and foreign musicians (e.g., H. Berlioz, Z. Fibich, J. B. Foerster, R. Wagner, and O. Ostrčil). Nejedlý, however, never completed his original plan of writing a comprehensive history of music; his *Všeobecné dějiny hudby* (1910; General History of Music) covers only antiquity. Nor could he fulfill his major ambition, despite all possible means put at his disposal after 1945 (including the silencing of senior historians who could challenge him), to write a multivolume major synthesis of Czech history from a Marxist point of view. Only a torso remains, *Dějiny českého národa* (2 vols., 1949 and 1955; History of the Czech Nation). In the dispute over the "Meaning of Czech History," Nejedlý contributed with *Spor o smysl českých dějin* (1914), in which his heart was with T. G. Masaryk, but his head had to bow before the formidable arguments of the leading Czech historian Josef Pekař (q.v.).

During World War I Nejedlý publicly supported the Czech writers' manifesto demanding self-determination; after 1918 he sided with the communists. In 1925 he became chairman of the Society for Cultural and Economic Relations with the USSR, traveled to many leftist and antifascist rallies in Europe, and in 1936 he went to Spain in support of the Republican cause. His collected essays from this period were published under the title *O lidovou republiku* (4 vols., 1948–1949; For the People's Republic), and *Boje o nové Rusko* (1948; Struggles for New Russia). Following the German occupation of Czechoslovakia in 1939, Nejedlý fled to Moscow where he joined exiled Czech communist leaders and taught as professor. In 1941 he was one of the organizers of the All-Slavic Congress in Moscow. He returned to Prague in 1945 with the Red Army and became the chief cultural activist of the Communist party in carrying out numerous radical measures, such as the controversial school reform. After the communist coup in 1948, to his numerous titles and posts he added the chairmanship of the newly founded Society of Czechoslovak-Soviet Friendship. Nejedlý unscrupulously used his unchallenged position of power to turn his personal preferences (e.g., composer Smetana, writer A. Jirásek, etc.) into official aims of communist cultural policy. His final interpretation of Czech history reaches its absurd apotheosis in the symbiosis between Hussitism and communism, for example, *Komunisté—dědici velkých tradic českého národa* (1946; Communists—Heirs of the Great Traditions of the Czech Nation). Nejedlý's megalomania found its direct expression in the establishment of a special institute within the Academy of Sciences whose sole purpose was to publish his collected works during his lifetime; almost fifty volumes have been published since 1948. Notwithstanding his singular talents, Nejedlý's unique career serves as a deterrent rather than an example to follow in the gallery of great historians.

Bibliography: F. Červinka, *Zdeněk Nejedlý* (Prague, 1969); V. Král, *Zdeněk Nejedlý a Gollova škola* (Prague, 1986); J. Macek, ed., *25 ans d'historiographie tchécoslovaque 1936–1960* (Prague, 1960).

Milan Hauner

NIEDERLE, Lubor (1865–1944), Czech anthropologist and archaeologist. Professor of history at Charles University in Prague after 1898. Educated in Bohemia, Germany, and France. Niederle's work is characterized by a highly synthetic view of prehistory of the Slavs, based on the study of archaeology, ethnography, and anthropology. He was co-founder of *Český lid* (1891; Czech People), which remains the principal Czech ethnographical journal and one of the chief organizers of the great ethnographic exhibition in Prague in 1895. In 1899 Niederle formulated the basic methodology for the study of archaeology, which was widely accepted abroad. His major works include: *Nástin dějin anthropologie* (1889; History of Anthropology—An Outline), *Příspěvky k anthropologii zemí českých* (1819–1894; Contributions to Anthropology in Czech Lands); *Lidstvo v době předhistorické se zvláštním zřetelem na země slovanské* (1893–1894; Mankind in the Prehistoric Age with Special Consideration for Slavic Countries); and *Manuel de l'antiquité slave* (1923–1926). His major work bears the same title as that of his great predecessor, Parel Josef Šafařík (q.v.), *Slovanské starožitnosti* (1902–1905; Slavic Antiquities), to which he added an anthropological sequel, *Život starých Slovanů* (1911–1925; The Life of Ancient Slavs). Niederle rejected the prevalent view among his contemporaries that the ancient Slavs had been primarily peaceful peoples engaged in agriculture; he equally refuted the notion that the character of the Slavs had been decisively acted on by their conquerors, the Teutons and the Tatars.

Bibliography: Jan Eisner, *Lubor Niederle* (Prague, 1948).

Milan Hauner

PALACKÝ, František (1798–1876), major Czech historian and politician. Called by his contemporaries "Leader of the Nation." Born in northern Moravia to a poor Protestant family of Bohemian Brethren. Palacký's entire education took place in Slovakia in Latin and German. After finishing his education at the renowned evangelical lyceum in Pressburg in 1818, Palacký spent some time in Vienna as a tutor before coming to Prague in 1823. By that time he already knew fourteen ancient and modern languages. His first published work was a short Czech study in aesthetics and an essay on Czech prosody, which he wrote in 1818 with his friend Pavel Josef Šafařík (q.v.). His noble patronage, his marriage to a daughter of a rich Prague lawyer and landowner, and his friendship with Šafařík and Josef Dobrovský (q.v.), proved enormously helpful. Despite the fact that Palacký was entirely self-taught as historian and never went to university, he so impressed his aristocratic patrons with the extent of his knowledge and determination to write a definitive history of Bohemia that they secured his appointment as editor of the Journal of the Czech Museum (1827) and historiographer of the Bohemian kingdom (1831), and financed his numerous trips to archives in Bohemia and abroad (especially to the Vatican in 1836–1837). He already had several critical editions of historical texts underway: *Staří letopisové čeští od r.1378 do 1527* (1829; Old Bohemian Chroniclers), published as Volume 3 in *Scriptores rerum bohemicarum*; and his first international success, *Würdigung der alten böhmischen Geschichtesschreiber* (1830), a critical analysis of Bohemian chroniclers, whom he found without exception appallingly inadequate. He also founded a new edition for the publication of Czech archival sources on the Hussite period and Reformation, *Archiv český* (6 vols., 1840–1872; Bohemian Archives); and laid the foundation for a new critical series of major Czech chronicles and other sources, *Fontes rerum bohemicarum* (8 vols., 1873–1932). In 1848 Palacký published a major topographic and genealogical work on feudal Bohemia, *Popis království českého* (Description of the Bohemian Kingdom). Palacký edited and later published his excerpts from foreign archives in *Monumenta conciliorum generalium saeculi XV.* (1857), in *Documenta Mag. Joannis Hus vitam, doctrinam, causam in Constantiensi concilio . . . illustrantia* (1869), in *Urkundliche Beiträge zur Geschichte des Hussitenkrieges*, (vol. 2, 1873), and in *Urkundliche Beiträge zur Geschichte Böhmens und seiner Nachbarländer im Zeitalter Georgs von Podiebrad* (1860). All these activities must be regarded as preparation for Palacký's major creative task, which was his magnum opus, a six-volume history of Bohemia, the first volume of which, *Geschichte von Böhmen*, appeared in 1835. In 1848 Palacký decided for political reasons to write his history first in the Czech language and to call it significantly: *Dějiny národu českého v Čechách a na Moravě* (History of the Czech Nation in Bohemia and Moravia). He completed it in the year of his death. The narrative does not go beyond the year 1526, when the Habsburg Dynasty acquired the Bohemian throne as its hereditary possession. Palacký's monumental history, with its emphasis on the Hussite Revolution as the dominant feature of European history, was the most important spiritual asset the Czech national revival movement received in its struggle with the overwhelming German challenge. It is the principle of polarity between good and evil, spanning like a red thread through his work, which Palacký used as his philosophical credo ("constant contact and conflict between the Slavs on the one hand, and Rome and the Germans on the other"). Another of Palacký's romantic aberrations (see his *Die ältesten Denkmäler der böhmischen Sprache*, 1840), was his uncritical acceptance of the major Czech "Manuscript Forgeries," "found" in 1817 and 1818, and rejected already by his teacher Josef Dobrovský. He was also driven too far by his romantic image of the alleged democratic forms of government and behavior among the early Slavs, arguing that social and legal inequalities in Central Europe were the product of German culture. This can be exemplified in the polemics against his major German rival, who was a history professor at Prague University, *Die Geschichte des Hussitenthums und Professor Constantin Höfler* (1868).

The revolutionary year of 1848 propelled Palacký to the forefront of political events. Together with Šafařík he opened the first All-Slav Congress in Prague, which was intended to serve as a counterdemonstration to the forces of pan-German nationalism gathered at the time in Frankfurt. In his famous letter to the Frankfurt deputies—which, among others, so greatly outraged Karl Marx (q.v.)—Palacký on behalf of the Czech nation deliberately opted out from the century-old territorial association of the Bohemian Kingdom with the historical German Empire. His fear was that the creation of a Greater Pan-German Reich would lead to a Prussian hegemony over Europe and to the extinction of the Czech nation. Instead, he proclaimed his loyalty to the multinational Austrian Empire which was to be reformed on the basis of federalism. He played a leading role as legislator at the constituent assembly in Kroměříž (Kremsier), but after its failure retired from active politics until 1861. Thereafter he briefly reentered politics as the leader of the Old Czech party but retired again increasingly disillusioned by Vienna. Palacký was the major advocate of Austro-Slavism ("If Austria did not exist, we would have to create it for the benefit of Europe and mankind"), projecting the future Habsburg Empire as the best safeguard for the survival of smaller nations in Central Europe, threatened simultaneously by the forces of pan-Germanism and pan-Slavism. In his most important political pamphlet, *Idea státu rakouského* (1865; The idea of the Austrian State), he redrafted his constitutional project of 1848–1849 and warned against centralism and impending dualism: "We existed before Austria, we shall exist when it is gone." When in 1867 the Austrian Germans and Hungarians proclaimed dualism, Palacký led an embittered Czech delegation in protest to Moscow. When he died in 1876, the Czech nation buried him like a king.

Bibliography: J. Charvát, ed., *Dílo F. Palackého*, 4 vols. (Prague, 1941); J. Fischer, *Myšlenka a dílo; F. Palackého*, 2 vols. (Prague, 1927); M. Jetmarová, *F. Palacký* (Prague, 1961); F. Kutnar, ed., *Tři Studie o F. Palackém* (Olomouc, 1949); V. J. Nováček, ed., *F. Palacký korespondence a zápisky* (Prague, 1898–1911); F. Palacký, *Gedenkblätter* (Prague, 1874); F. Palacký, *Zur böhmischen Geschichtsschreibung* (Prague 1871); J. Pekař, *F. Palacký* (Prague, 1912); R. G. Plaschka, *Von Palacký bis Pekar* (Graz 1955); J. Spičák, ed., *F. Palacký: Uvahy a projevy* (Prague, 1977).

PEKAŘ, Josef (1870–1937), arguably the most significant Czech historian since František Palacký (q.v.). Poor peasant's son, educated at the Czech University in Prague under Jaroslav Goll (q.v.), Pekař continued his studies in Erlangen and Berlin. Two years after the completion of his habilitation, *Dějiny Valdštejnského spiknutí 1630–1634* (1895; History of the Wallenstein Conspiracy), Pekař began to lecture at the Czech University. In the same year he took over the editorship of the *Český časopis historický* (Czech Historical Journal), which he continued to edit for the next forty years. In 1905 he was made full professor of Austrian history at the Czech University (after 1918 renamed the chair for Czechoslovak history), which he held until his death. Pekař soon showed his talent for composing a great historical synthesis, but he was perhaps even better equipped to combine political and economic themes through the medium of his cultivated prose. His tastes were distinctly conservative, molded by his Catholicism and peasant background. His preferences belonged to the world of aristocracy; he detested modern industrialization and the working class, and he feared revolutionary socialism. However, during the earlier years of his career Pekař often found himself going against the mainstream of Czech nationalism, destroying its false idols, founded on the much disputed manuscript forgeries "discovered" in 1817 and 1818. He passionately defended his nation against vilification, as in *Čechove jako apoštolové barbarství* (1897), against the renowned German historian Theodor Mommsen (q.v.), who accused the Czech nationalists of being the "apostles of barbarism," or in his polemics with Berthold Bretholz (q.v.): *Objevy Bretholzovy čili od které doby sedí Němci v naší vlasti* (1922; Bretholz's Discoveries—or Since When Do the Germans Dwell in Our Homeland). In *Nejstarší kronika česká* (1903; The Oldest Czech Chronicle), and in *Die Wenzels- und Ludmila-Legenden und die Echtheit Christians* (1906), Pekař challenged many established views on the earliest Czech legends and chronicles. In *Kniha o Kosti* (2 vols., 1909 and 1911; The Book of Kost), rated as Pekař's greatest book, he captured the complex relationship between man and land in his native region in northwestern Bohemia during and after the Thirty Years' War. Pekař's immersion in social and agrarian history resulted in the publication of *České katastry 1654–1789* (1913, 1915; Bohemian Land Registers), in which he demonstrated that the Czech lands had been the main source of income for the Habsburg Empire, especially in times of war. In his famous article "Masarykova ceská filosofie" (1912), Pekař refuted the views of his professorial colleague T. G. Masaryk on Hussitism and the Czech Reformation as mystification of the Czech past.

During World War I Pekař continued to defend the historic Czech rights in the spirit of the early Palacký within the Habsburg monarchy, since he did not believe in an independent Czech state with Slovakia. Together with Goll and Josef Šusta (q.v.) he refused to sign the 1917 Declaration of Czech Writers demanding self-determination. However, when at the end of 1918 the creation of the Czechoslovak Republic became irreversible, Pekař performed a mental somersault and warmly welcomed the new state. His political conservatism became more pronounced, as he criticized the new land reform in Czechoslovakia, which divided large aristocratic estates for the benefit of smallholders; in press articles he blamed the Bolsheviks and Jews alike for the collapse of the old order. Again he vigorously opposed the cult of Hussitism and instead put forward his revised views on baroque and the era of Catholic Counter-Reformation, which Czech nationalists regarded as the epoch of "darkness." Hence Pekař's last major work, *Žiška a jeho doba* (4 vols., 1927–1933; Žiška and His Era) and monographs like *Bílá Hora* (1921; White Mountain), *Tři kapitoly z boje o svatého Jana Napomuckého* (1921; Three Chapters from the Struggle for St. John of Nepomuk), and *Svatý Václav* (1929, 1932; St. Wenceslav). The polemics on Žiška and Hussitism overlapped with the renewed debate on "the meaning of Czech history" and its periodization. Pekař's textbook for Czech high schools, *Dějiny československé* (1921; Czechoslovak History), originally published in 1914 as *Dějiny naší říše* (History of Our Empire), became the center of controversy because of the emphasis he put on the decisive influence of Europe and of the German factor in Czech history. In his endeavor to improve Czech-German relations, Pekař underrated Hitler's Germany and fell easy prey to unscrupulous manipulators like Josef Pfitzner, a history professor from the German University in Prague and a Sudeten German activist. Although Pekař did not live to witness the tragic year of 1938, his name was misused by Nazi propaganda to foster collaboration with the Reich and to outweigh the legacy of Palacký and Masaryk. After the war communist propagandists condemned Pekař as the leading ideologist of counterrevolution. Since 1968, however, Pekař's work has enjoyed a remarkable recovery among the Czech public, and despite the official anathema, he is being reassessed as the quintessential historian since Palacký.

Bibliography: R. Holinka, *O Josefu Pekařovi* (Prague, 1937); R. Holinka, *Pekař a pekařovština v českém dějepisectví* (Brno, 1950); J. Klik, ed., *Listy úcty a přátelství* (correspondence between J. Goll and J. Pekař), (Prague, 1941); F. Kutnar, ed., *Josef Pekař: Postavy a problémy českých dějin* (Prague, 1970); J. Pachta, *J. Pekař, ideolog kontrarevoluce* (Prague, 1948); J. Pekař, *O smyslu českých dějin* (Rotterdam, 1977); *Pekařovské studie*, 2 vols., samizdat edition (Prague, 1988); J. Slavík, *Pekař contra Masaryk* (Prague, 1929).

RAPANT, Daniel (1897–1988), founder of modern Slovak historiography. Educated at the State Archival School in Prague and at the Ecole des chartes in Paris (1922–1923); received his Ph.D. in 1923. Started to work as a senior archivist in Bratislava from 1924; after 1933 he was lecturing at the Comenius University of Bratislava. Rapant made it his lifelong task to document the national revival of the Slovak nation and its struggle against magyarization. Hence, he wrote two major studies, *Vývoj rečovej otázky v Uhorsku 1740–90* (The Evolution of the Language Question in Hungary, 1740–90), and *K počiatkom maď arizácie* (Beginnings of Magyarization), both published in 1927, on this subject. He welcomed the creation of the Czechoslovak Republic in 1918. However, Rapant's views that the Czechs and Slovaks were closely related but distinct Slavic nations, each with a culture and history of its own (as he laid down in his 1930 article, "Československé dejiny: Problémy a metody,"[Czechoslovak History: Problems nad Methods]), was considered a serious challenge to the official ideology of "Czechoslovakism," postulating the existence of a single Czechoslovak nation. Rapant's major work is the thirteen-volume series, published between 1937 and 1972, *Slovenské povstanie roku 1848–1849. Dejiny a dokumenty* (Slovak Uprising 1848–1849. History and Documents). He adopted the same method of combining narrative history with documents in his subsequent publications, concerned mostly with the process of magyarization: *Slovenský prestolný prosbopis* (2 vols., 1943), *Viedenské memorandum slovenské z roku 1861* (2 vols., 1943), and *Ilegálna maď arizácia 1790–1840* (1947). Rapant did not support the racial ideology and the pro-German orientation of the clerical Slovak Republic (1939–

1945); neither was he prepared to compromise with the communist authorities after the demise of the Slovak Republic. Although professor at Comenius University in Bratislava after 1933 and its rector in 1945, Rapant was not allowed to lecture and was put onto the compulsory retirement list in 1958. His last book was *Sedliacke povstanie na východnom Slovensku roku 1831* (Peasant Uprising in Eastern Slovakia in 1831), published in 1953. In 1967 Rapant was allowed to published an important article in the review *Slovenské pohl'ady*, no. 4, discussing the place of the Slovaks in the past and the present. During the Prague Spring of 1968, Rapant emerged from obscurity to collect several overdue state awards and to become a full member of the Slovak Academy of Sciences—only to be relegated into a limbo again during the subsequent period of ''normalization.''

Bibliography: Horst Glassl, *Die slowakische Geschichtswissenschaft nach 1945* (Wiesbaden, 1971); František Kutnar, *Přehledné dějiny českého a slovenského dějepisectví*, vol. 2 (Prague, 1977).

Milan Hauner

ŠAFAŘÍK, Pavel Josef [or: ŠAFÁRIK, Pavol Jozef, in Slovak] (1795–1861), an outstanding Slovak and Czech anthropologist and historical linguist, whose *Slovanské starožitnosti* (1837; Slavic Antiquities) better known in the German version as *Slawische Altertümer* (1843), became a milestone in the historiography of early Slavs. Born in Slovakia, educated at the Evangelical Lyceum of Pressburg (Bratislava), along with his colleague František Palacký (q.v.), Šafařík gained recognition as the founder of Slavic archaeology and historic linguistics, second only to Josef Dobrovský (q.v.). Decisive for his intellectual formation was the contact with German Romanticism and the philosophy of Herder at the University of Jena (1815–1817), where he studied together with another remarkable Slovak, Ján Kollár (1793–1852). It was in Novi Sad, in what was then Lower Hungary where Šafařík was director of a Serbian college, that he wrote his first significant book which attracted wide attention, *Geschichte der slawischen Sprache und Literatur nach allen Mundarten* (1826). In 1833 Šafařík came to Prague to assume the editorship of the Journal of the Czech Museum and later the directorship of the university library. In 1845 he published the first systematic grammar of old Czech (*Počátkové staročeské mluvnice*). Such was his devotion to the Czech national revival, of which he became one of the most prominent promoters, that he refused invitations to occupy chairs of Slavic philology in Berlin, Moscow, and Breslau. It was Šafařík who opened with his moving speech the All-Slavic Congress in Prague in June 1848. Although Šafařík was a defender of the rights of education in the mother tongue as an indispensable prerequisite of every autonomous national culture, he considered his native Slovak to be merely a dialect of Czech and consequently opposed the establishment of a Slovak literary language in the 1840s.

Bibliography: V. Bechynová et al., *Korespondence P. J. Šafaříka s F. Palackým* (Prague, 1961); M. Kirschbaum, *Šafařík and His Contribution to Slavic Studies* (Cleveland, 1962); J. Novotný, *P. J. Šafařík* (Brno, 1971); K. Paul, *P. J. Šafařík* (Prague, 1961); J. Tibenský, *Pavol Jozef Šafárik* (Bratislava, 1975).

Milan Hauner

ŠUSTA, Josef (1874–1945), Czech historian. Educated at the Czech University of Prague together with Josef Pekař (q.v.) in the seminar of Jaroslav Goll (q.v.), at the Viennese Institute for the Study of History, Šusta carried out his first major research assignment in the Vatican Archives. In 1910 he succeeded Goll as professor of general history in Prague. During World War I Šusta, like Goll and Pekař, did not approve of Czech political activities undermining the Habsburg monarchy. However, after the proclamation of the Czechoslovak Republic in 1918, Šusta adhered to the new state and gained the highest academic recognition as the president of the Czech Academy of Sciences. However, he compromised himself again because of his alleged pro-Nazi activities during the German occupation (1939–1945). Unable to resolve the dilemma and too weak to defend himself, Šusta ended tragically by committing suicide in May 1945.

Šusta was a highly talented historian of prodigious capacity for work, an impressive range of interests, and a great gift for composing broader synthetic surveys in an elegant style. His penchant for social and agrarian studies of the Middle Ages resulted in his first larger monograph, *Otroctví a velkostatek v Čechách* (1899; Slavery and Country Estate in Bohemia), and a series of analytical monographs concerning the history of agriculture of his native southern Bohemia. In 1913 Šusta published his polemical study, *Nový Antipalacký* (New Anti-Palacký), in which he defended František Palacký (q.v.) against the new theory of German colonization in Bohemia during the early Middle Ages, advocated by Bertold Bretholz (q.v.). Šusta's editorial work on *Die römische Kurie und das Konzil von Trient unter Pius IV* (4 vols., 1904–1914), provided him with a major topic for his habilitation on Pope Pius IV (1900). His first synthetic presentation of modern Europe was the high school textbook, *Dějiny nového věku* (1905; History of the Modern Era), for which in 1909 he prepared a sequel, *Dějinné předpoklady moderního imperialismu* (Historical Prerequisites of Modern Imperialism). Thereafter Šusta concentrated on his intensive study of Bohemia's high Middle Ages, starting with a series of monographs entitled after the Bohemian kings, *Přemysl Otakar II* and *Václav II*, published in 1915, which culminated in the brilliant volumes, *Dvě knihy českých dějin* (1917–1919; Two Books of Bohemian History), on the last years of the Přemyslid Dynasty and the beginnings of the Luxemburg era. The two books are considered Šusta's masterpieces in the art of merging socioeconomic facts in the broad texture of political and cultural changes. Šusta continued his writing on the fourteenth-century history of the Bohemian Kingdom by contributing four new volumes (published between 1935 and 1948) to the most prestigious project of Czech historians, intended to supersede Palacký and to respond to his German critics, which was the monumental series *České dějiny* (Czech History), started under the editorship of Václav Novotný (1868–1932) in 1911. In parallel, Šusta wrote a two-volume textbook for senior high schools (1911) and started to write his modern history of Europe, *Dějiny Evropy v letech 1812–1870* (3 vols., 1922–1923), to which he added the first comprehensive diplomatic history in the Czech language, *Světová politika v letech 1871 az 1914* (6 vols., 1924–1931; World Politics). As a member of the Commission Internationale de Coopération Intelectuelle at the League of Nations, Šusta was the internationally best known Czech historian between the world wars. Like his teacher Goll, he also regularly informed foreign colleagues about the Czech historical production. In 1926 he published *Posledních padesát let české práce dějepisné* (Last Fifty Years of Czech Historiography), a collection of book reviews written by him and Goll for the *Revue Historique*, to which in 1937 he added another volume, *Posledních deset let československé práce dějepisné* (Last Ten Years of Czechoslovak Historiography). The peak of Šusta's synthetic creativity must be seen in his editorial work on the six-volume illustrated world history, *Dějiny lidstva od pravěku k novověku* (1936–1942; History of Mankind from Prehistory to the Modern Age), which remained unfinished because of the interference by German authorities during the war. Šusta's considerable literary talent found its expression in the publication of a novel, *Cizina* (1914; Foreign Land). His memoirs were published posthumously.

Bibliography: F. Kutnar, *Přehledné dějiny českého a slovenského dějepisectví*, vol. 2 (Prague, 1977); J. Šusta, *Dějepisectví* (Prague, 1946); J. Šusta, *Vzpomínky*, 2 vols. (Prague, 1947, 1963).

Milan Hauner

Great Historians: Danish

ALLEN, Carl Ferdinand (Copenhagen, 1811–Copenhagen, 1871), Danish historian. Educated in theology, professor of history at the University of Copenhagen, 1851–1871. Allen was the leading historian in the national–liberal tradition in Denmark. His first work, published in 1840, *Haandbog i Fædrelandets Historie* (Handbook in the History of the Mother Country, French trans.: Histoire de Danemark depuis le temps les plus reculés jusqu'a nos jours, 1878) met a demand for a modern complete account of the history of Denmark in accordance with the liberal attitude of the growing middle classes in their campaign against absolutism. He saw history proceeding according to a romantic model: Antiquity had been a golden age with a democratic government of free peasants; after that followed a period of decline, finally resulting in the rule of aristocracy; this was abolished with absolutism and a new era started, culminating with the introduction of democratic reforms and with democratic constitutional monarchy as the final ideal. The Handbook gained much popularity: eight editions were published up to 1881; a shortened version was used in schools; and it was used as a university textbook until about 1920. Allen maintained his view of history in his later works, of which *Det danske Sprogs Historie i Hertugdømmet Slesvig eller Sønderjylland* (2 vols., 1857–1858; History of the Danish Language in the Duchy of Schleswig or Southern Jutland) should be mentioned. This work was also meant as a support to the national struggle of Schleswig. Allen's major scientific work, however, is the unfinished *De tre nordiske Rigers Historie 1497–1536* (5 Vols., 1864–1872; History of the Three Nordic Countries, 1497–1536). Based on a large amount of documentary evidence, collected from all over Europe, it describes in detail the time before the Reformation, which Allen and his contemporaries looked on as a troubled era of transition, reminiscent of their own time. Into this he built a description of the state of society, and this was rather exceptional in the historiography of that time which was mainly event-oriented. Together with Caspar Paludan-Müller (q.v.) he was an innovator in Danish historiography with regard to the use of research principles characteristic of German historicism, especially with respect to the use of extensive contemporary source material which he endeavored to treat critically. His source critique, however, was not consistent enough for his successors, but his liberal view of the history of Denmark left a profound trace in Danish historiography.

Bibliography: Kai Hørby, "Allen, C. F.," *Dansk Biografish Leksikon* (Danish Biographical Dictionary), 3d ed., 1 (1979), pp. 121–124; Grethe Jensen, "Historikeren C. F. Allen og det danske folk" (The Historian C. F. Allen and the Danish People), *Fortid og Nutid* 31 (1984): 183–193.

Jens Chr. Manniche

ARUP, Erik (Slangerup, 1876–Copenhagen, 1951), Danish historian. Professor at the University of Copenhagen, 1916–1946. As a pupil of the innovators of Danish scientific history of the social-liberal tradition, Kristian Erslev (q.v.) and especially Julius Albert Fridericia (q.v.), Arup was an advocate of source critique as *the* method of history as an independent field of research. He favored a radical criticism of tradition, being basically skeptical of later accounts as evidence, even eyewitnesses. Instead, he emphasized the use of sources as relics (*Überreste*) and as results of connections and chains of events in the past, which the historian may draw conclusions about. He thought it was possible to separate positive facts from the sources and to coordinate and represent them in reasonable and natural causal relations. Among others he referred to the French historians Langlois and Charles Seignobos (q.v.) in support of this point of view. He was also closely attached to the Swedish historian Lauritz Weibull (q.v.). These methodological principles were combined with a positivist kind of idea of evolution or progress and a belief in universal historical laws or generalizations. His doctoral dissertation from 1907, "Studier i engelsk og tysk Handels Historie. En Undersøgelse af Kommissionshandelens Praksis og Theori i engelsk og tysk Handelsliv 1350–1850," (A Study of the Practice and Theory of Commission Trade in English and German Commercial Life 1350–1850), was a comparative analysis. Its leading idea was that the basic economic structure determined the general commercial development, which again determined the actual forms of trade and commercial law. Arup wrote a good many critical studies all of which are in some way preparatory studies to his chief work *Danmarks Historie* (2 vols., 1925–1932, vol. 3, 1955, posthumously; History of Denmark). Here Arup seeks to give an account of the general development of the Danish people and society from the fundamental conception that "the history of Danish agriculture forms the core of the history of Denmark." Decisive in his view of history was humankind's exploitation of the values of the earth and their exchange, that is, trade. It is, then, a materialistically oriented view of history but not a Marxist view. What counts is the importance of the daily work, not in confrontations (like class struggles or other clashes), but in social cooperation. Here as elsewhere he showed himself a firm supporter of the social–liberal tradition of historiography in Denmark. In his synthesis a decisive role is also given to the ideas of liberty and equality, in addition to the conception of social justice without suppression and a rational view of human nature. He was also against any form of militarism, chauvinism, and flattery of royalty. The crux of the account, however, is still the political development which he understands as a play between individuals in the light of the state of society, where the concrete interests of the persons are crucial.

In spite of the obvious ideological features in this synthesis, Arup was convinced of the possibility of reaching positive knowledge of the past, independent of time, place, and values. As a consequence, he believed in the importance of historical truth for a realistic knowledge of reality. He reappraised accepted views and emphasized other things; therefore, it is not surprising that his synthesis became very controversial. The criticism was mainly ideologically conditioned, that is to say, conservative. But colleagues also criticized it for being one–sided and subjective. The criticism discouraged Arup from continuing the work, and it remained incomplete. (The two published volumes went up to 1624, and the posthumously published material reached to about 1660.) Nevertheless—and in spite of many questionable theories and statements in the work—it became the most influential synthesis in Danish historiography for many decades, provoking and inspiring new research, and coloring the view of the past for more than one generation of historians.

Bibliography: Aksel E. Christensen, ''Arup, Erik,'' *Dansk Biografisk Leksikon* (Danish Biographical Dictionary), 3d ed., 1 (1979), pp. 303–307; Hans Kryger Larsen, *Erik Arup. En undersøgelse af Arups videnskabs-og historiesyn, 1903–1916* (A Study of Arup's View of Science and History, 1903–1916), (Odense, 1976); Jens Chr. Manniche, *Den Radikale historikertradition* (The Social-Liberal School of Historians), (Aarhus, 1981), pp. 368–386; E. Ladewig Petersen, ''Omkring Erik Arup: Struktur og graenser i moderne dansk historieforskning, c. 1885–1955'' (Around Erik Arup: Structure and Limits in Modern Danish Historical Research, c. 1885–1955), *Historisk Tidsskrift* 78 (1978): pp. 138–182:

Jens Chr. Manniche

ERSLEV, Kristian (Copenhagen, 1852–Copenhagen, 1930), Danish historian. Professor at the University of Copenhagen 1883–1916, Director of the Danish State Archives, 1916–1924. Erslev was the most outstanding and influential Danish historian of his time, an innovator and norm-setter of scientific history and of the teaching of history at the university level. His theoretical works on methodology were school-founding at least up to about 1960. Influenced by the success of the natural sciences, he was anxious to make historical studies a scientific and specialized profession. With this aim he insisted on source critique governed by strict rules. He regarded scientific history in a positivist manner as an empirical science, and systematic critical method became the password. When studying at the University of Berlin around 1880 with Nietzsche, Johann Gustav Droysen (q.v.), and Georg Waitz (q.v.), he became acquainted with the German seminar method where the sources were thoroughly discussed, and he transplanted this method to his own university. The education of historians was put into a fixed framework, and the socialization of students into well-defined professional standards of historical research became a major objective. A substantial part of the training now became a schooling in source critique. Because Erslev was an eminent teacher, he decisively influenced the following generations of historians. He outlined his conception of historical research in a long series of articles and textbooks, stressing the importance of source analysis, for instance, *Grundsætninger for historisk Kildekritik* (1892; Principles of Historical Source Critique) and *Historisk Teknik. Den historiske Undersøgelse fremstillet i sine Grundlinier* (1911; Historical Technique: An Outline of Historical Investigation, German trans., *Historische Technik*, 1928). *Historisk Teknik* was used as a university primer for more than half a century.

In the beginning of his career Erslev stressed the analysis of dependence and authenticity like his German models. He wanted to attain primary contemporary accounts. Later, however, he emphasized records, documents, and other sources that could be used as remains left over from the past. Like Droysen and Bernheim he made a distinction between accounts (*Quellen/Tradition*) and remains (*Überreste*). Originally, he saw the distinction as an absolute, material difference: Remains are positive, objective sources, while accounts have a subjective element. As time went by he realized, however, that the difference was functional and dependent on the problem posed: An account can be used as the remains of the situation in which it originated, depending on the point of view. In the essay *Historieskrivning. Grundlinier til nogle Kapitler af Historiens Theori* (1911; Historical Writing: Outlines of Some Chapters of the Theory of History), he discussed the relation and difference between scientific historical research and what he came to see as more artistic historical writing. Chronologically, Erslev's production was very varied. He tested his critical methods on subjects from very different periods. His main field, however, was the history of the Middle Ages. In addition to many articles, he wrote half a dozen monographs and syntheses, among these *Valdemarernes Storhedstid. Studier og Omrids* (1898; The Golden Age of the Valdemars [around 1200]). In this work he first analyzed some basic material conditions in the society, and the results were then used to reconstruct more comprehensive aspects of the period, such as agriculture, demography, the crown's revenue, and the development of the landowning classes. Finally, he gave a synthesizing characterization of the society on this background. It is, then, a concrete, almost paradigmatic representation of his view of historical research. Among his syntheses, Volume 2 of his *Danmarks Riges Historie* (1898– 1905; History of the Kingdom of Denmark), covering the late Middle Ages (1241–1481), should be mentioned. In his view of history he was influenced by a social-liberal view of society (John Stuart Mill). He stressed social and economic conditions and considered it the duty of the state to provide social justice in a class-divided society where evolution, to a certain extent, is characterized by clashes between the classes. As against this there is the concept of the undifferentiated "people" which implies a kind of ideal leveling of class differences which he sees as important in the course of history. In his understanding of the individual, he emphasized the rational and energetic aspect and saw great individuals as important for the development of history. In his opinion the idea of evolution and progress was fundamental to an understanding of history. In short, he was an exponent of a modern, bourgeois-progressive positivism.

   Bibliography: Aksel E. Christensen, "Erslev, Kr.," *Dansk Biografisk Leksikon* (Danish Biographical Dictionary), 3d ed., 4 (1980), pp. 242–246; Jens Chr. Manniche, *Den radikale historikertradition* (The Social-Liberal School of Historians), (Aarhus, 1981); Leo Tandrup, *Ravn* (Raven), 2 vols. (Copenhagen, 1980).

Jens Chr. Manniche

FRIDERICIA, Julius Albert (Copenhagen, 1849–Copenhagen, 1912), Danish historian. Professor at the University of Copenhagen 1899–1912. Fridericia belonged to the group of historians who were the main figures in the shift in Danish historiography from a historicist–hermeneutic orientation toward a more positivist-oriented view of history, known as the modern critical breakthrough (see also Kristian Erslev [q.v.]). This view attached great importance to systematic source critique as the crucial method of history. Fridericia's special area of research was seventeenth-century Denmark. He was a co-editor of the personal letters of King Christian IV (7 vols., 1878–1891), and his first great monograph was *Danmarks ydre politiske Historie i Tiden fra Freden i Lübeck til Freden i København 1629–1660* (2 vols., 1876–1881; The History of Denmark's Foreign Policy, 1629–1660). In this work he was still influenced by the conception of historical scholarship of the so-called Ranke-renaissance: heavy documentation, source critique, and objectivity are keywords, and the subject—foreign policy—is in accordance with the views of the German historicist tradition. But he became more and more influenced by a positivist-oriented scientific tradition in that evolutionism and concentration on the state of society and its development became the governing ideas of his research, while at the same time he maintained the source critique as the central element of historical methodology. He was very much occupied with the contemporary political struggle in Danish society, and this left its mark on his historical works, both with respect to his choice of subjects and their treatment. He supported the social-liberal democratic forces against the rightist government supported by the landed gentry. In his works he emphasized the ideas of the Declaration of Human Rights of 1789 on liberty, equality, social justice, and the duty of the state to protect the poor and weak. He saw enlightenment, education, and the struggle of ideas rooted in the material conditions of society and social classes as important forces in history; but he did not deny the role of great individuals. Fridericia lost his original faith in pure objectivity but nevertheless always tried to be fair and to approach this ideal. His main works are *Adelsvældens sidste Dage. Danmarks Historie fra Chr. IVs Død til Enevældens Indførelse 1648–1660* (1894; The Last Days of Aristocratic Government, 1648–1660), in which he described the social and political background of the establishment of absolutism in Denmark; and Volume. 4 of *Danmarks Riges Historie* (1896–1902; History of the Kingdom of Denmark) dealing with the period 1588–1699. As editor of the *Historisk Tidsskrift* (The [Danish] Historical Review), he played an important role in keeping Danish historians up to date with respect to international research.

Bibliography: Jens Chr. Manniche, *Den radikale historikertradition* (The Social-Liberal School of Historians), (Aarhus, 1981); Leo Tandrup, "Fridericia, J. A.," *Dansk Biografisk Leksikon* (Danish Biographical Dictionary), 3d ed., 4 (1980), pp. 605–608.

Jens Chr. Manniche

FRIIS, Aage (Halskov, 1870–Copenhagen, 1949), Danish historian. Professor at the University of Copenhagen, 1913–1935. Friis' research centered on subjects concerning Danish foreign policy and Danish–German relations. Among his major works are, first, *Bernstorfferne og Danmark* (2 vols., 1903–19; The Bernstorffs and Denmark), which deals with the history of the German-Danish family Bernstorff in the last half of the eighteenth century and is based on a wide collection of letters that he had unearthed and in part published. Besides, as an official historian, he worked on the history of Northern Schleswig, especially the period after the Danish–German War in 1864, and simultaneously published the documents. This work was closely connected with a political preoccupation in the Schleswig question where he was working for a Danish–German reconciliation and for the reunion of Denmark and Northern Schleswig. Methodologically, he accepted a Rankean conception of historical science without its metaphysical assumptions. His aim was understanding the past, seeing it from the inside, while he identified himself with the time and the individuals he was studying. He stressed the importance of great persons and maintained an objective scientific ideal connected with an insistence on exhaustive documentation. As a historian he was no innovator; rather, his main contribution was that of a scientific organizer and inspirer. He played an important role in Danish scientific societies and in international historical cooperation. (For instance, he was a member of the International Committee of the Historical Sciences, 1926–1947). In addition, he made an important humanitarian contribution through his help to refugees from Nazi Germany in the 1930s.

Bibliography: Erik Stig Jørgensen, "Friis, Aage," *Dansk Biografisk Leksikon* (Danish Biographical Dictionary), 3d ed., 4 (1980), pp. 649–653; Ole Lønhardt, "Aage Friss," *Nyere dansk historieforskning bd. 2* (Recent Danish Historical Research), ed. Dansk historiografisk projektgruppe (1982), pp. 5–102; Jens Chr. Manniche, *Den radikale historikertradition* (The Social-Liberal School of Historians), (Aarhus, 1981), pp. 386–393.

Jens Chr. Manniche

MÜLLER, Sophus (Copenhagen, 1846–Copenhagen, 1934). Danish prehistorian, warden of the National Museum of Copenhagen (1892–1921). Müller made fundamental contributions to the progress of prehistoric research on Denmark and Europe, mainly Northern Europe. Taking over from Christian Jurgensen Thomsen (q.v.) the concept of the Bronze Age and the divisions proposed by

J. J. A. Worsaae for this period, he delimited, on the basis of an excellent stylistic and typological analysis, some subdivisions. This fact led him to the gradual drawing up of a relative and absolute chronological system having nine stages and distinct from Oscar Montelius' (q.v.) system. The system proposed better covered the mutability of the cultural evolution and avoided the too rigid classifications: "Doubtless one does not know how to trace absolutely clear boundaries between the nine stylistic groups; adjacent groups overlap; yet each group is so strongly marked by a definite artistic taste and by its own style that its individuality is readily recognized." (*Oldtidens Kunst i Danmark: II, Bronzealderens Kunst* [L'Art de l'Age du Bronze au Danemark, 1921]. One of his main concerns was to prove continuous cultural evolution in Denmark, from the Stone Age to the Bronze Age (*Débuts et première évolution de la civilisation du bronze en Danemark*). At the same time, however, he admitted the existence of a considerable discrepancy between the Aegean–Mediterranean space and the Northern space and the impact of Mediterranean cultures, mainly the Northern Italian ones, on the Danish Bronze Age, without in any way denying the Danish originality: "Moreover, one sees in all this evolution an artistic development that is home-grown and national, which had its origin in the most advanced civilization of southern Europe and which continually received modifications from the South. In spite of these foreign influences, however, the movement was strongly independent, attained a high degree of artistic merit and produced an original style" (*Oldtidens Kunst i Danmark, II, Vor Oldtid*, 1897). Interestingly, in spite of his attachment to the idea of the originality of the Danish styles, he did not shrink from using concepts like cultural center (Kulturzentrum) and periphery (*Peripherie-peripherichen barbarischen Kulturen der Vorzeit*) in order to mark the interdependence and chronological discrepancy between the Central and Northern European cultures and the Mediterranean culture (*Urgeschichte Europas. Grundzüge einer prähistorischen Archäologie* (1905). "Von Süden aus verbreitete sich die ürsprünglich orientalische Kunst weiter durch Europa, wo sie überall im Gefolge des geschliffenen Beiles Auftritt" (Oriental art spread from the South throughout Europe, where, following the introduction of polished stone axes, it appeared everywhere). A remarkable scientific objectivity, a sense of proportion, even a certain prudence in accepting certain hardly verifiable points of view, and a serenity in judging historical phenomena are characteristic features of Sophus Müller's work, which undoubtedly account for his nondependence on the ideas spread by Gustaf Kossinna (q.v.).

Bibliography: Jan Filip, *Enxyklopäüisches Handbuch der Ur–und Frühgeschichte Europas* 2 (Prague, 1967), p. 866; H. Seger, "Sophus Müller," *Praehistorische Zeitschrift*, 24, no.3/4 (1933): 343–347.

Ligia Bârzu

PALUDAN-MÜLLER, Caspar (Kerteminde, 1805–Copenhagen, 1882), Danish historian. Professor at the University of Copenhagen 1872–1882. Educated in theology, Paludan-Müller worked for a long period in provincial grammar schools. Even though his university career started late, he was probably the most outstanding Danish historian from the 1830s onwards. His most important works deal with the period of transition from the Middle Ages to modern times, in which he saw many resemblances with his own time. *Grevens Fejde* (2 vols., 1853–1854; The Count's War [1533–1536]) was the first serious study in Danish historical research that made a critical scrutiny of the evidence and extensive use of the archives. His second major work was *De første Konger af den Oldenborgske Slægt* (1874; The First Kings of the Oldenborg Family [1448–1536]). Otherwise his main field of research was the critical–analytical inquiry. His view of history was influenced by the methodological principles of the German historical school and by Hegelian views. He was driven, he wrote, by "that sting that does not permit the true researcher to rest before, with the power of thought, he has penetrated the material and seen its inner structure." He emphasized the study of sources as fundamental to the study of history, but his source critique was not as systematic and methodical as later historians would demand. Like the German historicists, he believed that the inner nature of humankind is revealed in the course of history and that the study of history, therefore, was an important "means of education." It was the business of the historian to penetrate into the deeper inner connection of the external phenomena on the basis of an idea of universal history. Here he operated with a "gift of divination" as a methodological principle (cf. Humboldt's "intuitive faculty and connective ability"). He viewed the historical totality as an organic, coherent, continuously progressive whole, in which development takes place as a Hegelian dialectic struggle between opposites. Like Leopold von Ranke (q.v.) he demanded impartiality and justice in the judgment of historical persons and events, and he would use history to promote national self–reflection combined with a sober sense of reality. He was undoubtedly the most reflective and theoretical historian of his generation.

Bibliography: Ellen Jørgensen, "C. Paludan-Müller," *Historisk Tidsskrift*, 9.r.V(1926–1927): 349–446; Harald Ilsøe, "Paludan-Müller, Caspar," *Dansk Biografisk Leksikon* (Danish Biographical Dictionary), 3d ed., 11 (1982), pp. 138–142; Jens Chr. Manniche, *Den radikale historikertradition* (The Social-Liberal School of Historians), (Aarhus, 1981), pp. 82–88;

Jens Chr. Manniche

STEENSTRUP, Johannes (Sorø, 1844–Copenhagen, 1935), Danish historian. Professor at the University of Copenhagen, 1882–1917. Steenstrup had a many-sided production. His major work *Normannerne* (4 vols., 1876–1882, vol. 5, 1925), (The Normans, vol. 1, translated into French, 1881) is one of the earliest in-depth works on the Vikings. In addition, he did research in, for instance, legal history (he was educated in law), placenames (where his contribution counts as a pioneering work), medieval popular ballads, historical geography, and the history of historical writing. He drew inspiration from the views of history of early Romanticism. Barthold Georg Niebuhr (q.v.) was one of his idols, and, in spite of his diverse fields of interest, he saw political history as the basis of historiography in the same way as state idealists. He was a conservative both ideologically and scientifically. The tradition was important to him, and he was skeptical of the systematic source critique that became a dominant element in Danish scientific history in his time. In this field he feared the barrenness of too schematic an approach and attached great weight to the historian's ability of empathetic understanding of the past. In his view history should be pursued without passion, solely for the sake of the past, not with a contemporary purpose, but in an objective search for the truth as a moral principle. With his conservatism he was in opposition to the social-liberal tradition that was then becoming predominant in Danish historiography. This made him an influential promoter of a traditional historicist view of history, and he left his mark on this more conservative trend. Some of his works have been translated into French and English, and he regularly wrote about Danish historical writing in the *Revue Historique*.

Bibliography: Johannes Steenstrup, *Nogle omrids af min virksomhed som universitetslaerer* (Outlines of My Activities as a University Teacher), (Copenhagen, 1934); Leo Tandrup, "Steenstrup, Johannes," *Dansk Biografisk Leksikon* (Danish Biographical Dictionary), 3d ed., 3 (1980), pp. 33–38.

Jens Chr. Manniche

THOMSEN, Christian Jurgensen (Copenhagen, 1788–Copenhagen, 1865), Danish self–taught prehistorian, warden of the Museum of Northern Antiquities in Copenhagen. Thomsen arranged the collections of the Museum on the basis of a single criterion—the material of which the weapons and tools were made. By elimination, he rediscovered the system of the three ages formulated by Lucretius (*De rerum nature*, On the Nature of Things): (1) all relics associated with stone tools and weapons; (2) relics associated with bronze objects but never with iron ones; (3) relics associated with iron objects. He also laid the foundations of a new method of grouping the archaeological evidence (*Beitfaden zur nordischen Alterthumsktunde*, 1837, Danish edition, 1836). He elaborated new concepts: the Stone Age, the Bronze Age (Sophus Müller [q.v.], *Oldtidens Kunst: Danmark*, II, *Bronze alderens Kunst*, Copenhagen, 1921), and the Iron Age (Pagan Iron Age), together with sanctioning new technological and archaeological criteria for classification. He also offered solid grounds for drawing up charts of relative chronology. Thomsen's effort was not unique. Almost at the same time, the German J. Fr. Danneil came to the same conclusions. "The three ages system" proposed by Thomsen was not accepted immediately and without opposition. Sophus Müller was among those who defended Thomsen's opinion against L. Lindenschmidt, managing to impose it more easily, as more recent archaeological researches and stratigraphical observations confirmed it. Gradually, his system was extended beyond the zone and the type of antiquities for which it had been initially designed and was adopted worldwide.

Bibliography: R. Beltz, "Dreiperiodensystem," in *Reallexikon der Vorgeschichte*, II (Berlin, 1925), pp. 457–460; V. Gordon Childe, *Piecing Together the Past* (London, 1956), pp. 23–24; Jan Filip, *Encyklopädisches Handbuch der Ur-und Frühgeschichte Europas*, 2 (Prague, 1967), p. 1456.

Ligia Bârzu

Great Historians: Dutch

BAKHUIZEN VAN DEN BRINK, Reinier Cornelis (Amsterdam, 1810–Den Haag, 1865), Dutch historian and archivist. Bakhuizen studied theology, philosophy, and classics, first at the Athenaeum in Amsterdam and then at Leyden University. In 1842 he received his doctor's degree for the thesis, "Variae lectiones de historia philosophiae antiquae," in which he examined life after death in Greek thought. He had already shown his interest in the history and culture of seventeenth-century Netherlands in an essay on the political setting of several satirical poems by Joost van den Vondel. From 1843 untill 1851 he had (for personal reasons) to stay outside of the Netherlands. During this period he did research in the archives and libraries of Liège, Brussels, Bonn, Wolfenbüttel, Breslau, Prague, and Vienna, studying Greek codices and documents on the Revolt of the Netherlands. In 1851 he attained a position at the Dutch State Archives, and in 1854 he was appointed chief archivist. In this position he did much to make the rich archives accessible to scholars. When Bakhuizen started his research, the history of both the government of Philip II and the Dutch Revolt was still based mainly on narrative sources. Modern research in the archives had only just started. G. Groen van Prinsterer was editing the *Archives ou correspondance inédite de la maison d'Orange Nassau* (Leyden, 1835–1847), and in the year in which Bakhuizen left the Netherlands, the Belgian archivist L. P. Gachard was starting on his first journey to the archives in Spain. Bakhuizen's most important discovery was in Vienna; here he found the official correspondence of the governess Margaret of Parma with Philip II, which the Austrian authorities brought from Brussels to Vienna in 1794, for fear of the French revolutionary armies (and which since has been returned to the state archives at Brussels). Overwhelmed by the multitude and diversity of the newly found documents, Bakhuizen failed to write a book. His fame as a historian rests on his essays written in a vigorous style. These essays contain a curious mixture of, on the one hand, a thorough knowledge of the many sources and a penetrating criticism and, on the other hand, of sweeping generalizations and strong prejudices. His judgment on the nobility, for instance, was quite simple: The minds of the nobles were as devoid of high culture as their purses were of money. In his opinion, the burghers and not the nobles, were the driving force behind the revolt against the Spanish King Philip II. Most of his works were collected in five volumes, *Studiën en Schetsen* (Amsterdam: 's Gravenhage, 1863–1913; Studies and Sketches) of which only the first volume was edited by Bakhuizen himself.

Bibliography: G. Colmjon, *R. C. Bakhuizen van den Brink* (Rijswijk, 1950); G. J. de Vries, "R. C. Bakhuizen van den Brink als graecus," *Mededelingen der Koninklijke Nederlandse Akademie van Wetenschappen, afd. Letterkunde*, NR 44:6 (Amsterdam, 1981); G. W. Kernkamp, *Bakhuizen van den Brink* (1907), reprinted in P. A. M. Geurts and A. E. M Janssen, eds., *Geschiedschrijving in Nederland* ('s Gravenhage, 1981), 1, pp. 199–240.

J. J. Woltjer

BLOK, Petrus Johannes (Den Helder, 1855–Leyden, 1929), Dutch historian, professor at the universities of Groningen (1884–1894) and Leyden (1894–1925), where he succeeded Robert Jacobus Fruin (q.v.). During his stay in Groningen Blok showed remarkable energy. He stimulated not only local history but also started a systematic research of documents important to Dutch history. In his political history he devoted attention to social and economic facts. His remark that "many a historical fact cannot be properly understood unless we know the price of corn" became famous. In his inaugural lectures of 1884 and 1894 he tried to define history as a social science. "The history of a people is the development of its social conditions" (1884) and: "Only the history of human society as a whole is in the true sense of the word worthy of being called history" (1894). Already in 1886 he began to plan a history of the Dutch people as a social history. During twenty years Blok was very busy with his *magnum opus: Geschiedenis van het Nederlandsche volk* (8 vols., 1892–1912), the first survey of Dutch history since the eighteenth century. It was translated into English as *A History of the People of the Netherlands* (5 vols., 1898–1912), reprinted in 1970. It is still considered an indispensable account because of its wealth of data. Blok's massive survey was also translated into German between 1902 and 1918 and appeared in the series *Geschichte der europäischen Staaten* edited by Karl Lamprecht (q.v.). Blok admired Lamprecht's early studies on medieval social history but was skeptical about his psychological generalizations in the *Deutsche Geschichte*. Moreover, Blok later became irritated by Lamprecht's "historical imperialism" because he treated Dutch history as though it were an offshoot of the history of the German race. Blok's social history remained closely allied with political history and is marred by hero-worship. It is above all nationalist historiography, like most European historiography around the turn of the century. Blok, like Fruin, was a great admirer of the House of Orange, the historical symbol of national unity. He was appointed history tutor to the young Queen Wilhelmina in 1894. He (like Fruin) supported with great energy the South African Boers' struggle for freedom against the "English tyranny", longing for the survival of the *Nederlandse stam* (the Dutch-speaking stock). After finishing his main work in 1907, Blok wrote a number of serviceable biographies on great Dutch men such as William of Orange and Michael de Ruyter.

Bibliography: P. B. M. Blaas, " 'The Touchiness of a Small Nation with a Great Past': The Approach of Fruin and Blok to the Writing of the History of the Netherlands," in A. C. Duke and C. A. Tamse, eds., *Clio's Mirror: Historiography in Britain and the Netherlands* (Zutphen, 1985), pp. 133–161; E. H. Kossmann, *The Low Countries, 1780–1940* (Oxford, 1978), pp. 439–443; J. E. Kroon, *Bibliographie der werken van Petrus Johannes Blok, 1979–1925* (Amsterdam, 1925).

P. B. M. Blaas

COLENBRANDER, Herman Theodor (Drachten, Friesland, 1871–Leyden, 1945), Dutch historian. Professor at the University of Leyden for colonial history (1918–1925) and Dutch history (1925–1945). As one of the last pupils of Robert Jacobus Fruin (q. v.), Colenbrander published an important and well-documented dissertation on the Batavian period, *De Patriottentijd, hoofdzakelijk naar buitenlandse bescheiden* (3 vols., The Hague 1897–1899). In 1897 he became deputy keeper of the records and edited source material relating to the Dutch East Indian Company. In 1902 he was appointed secretary for the new State Commission of Advice for National Historical Publications at The Hague, and in 1904 he published a still important programmatic survey titled *Overzicht van de door bronnenpublicatie aan te vullen leemten der Nederlandsche geschiedkennis* (Survey of Gaps in the Knowledge of Dutch History to Be Filled by New Publications of Records). Colenbrander himself edited a very large series of volumes devoted to the political history of the revolutionary period and the first half of the nineteenth century in order to relate the history of the Old Dutch Republic to that of modern times. His *Gedenkstukken der Algemeene Geschiedenis van Nederland van 1795 tot 1840* (10 vols. in 22 parts, The Hague, 1905–1922; Sources for the General History of the Netherlands from 1795 to 1840), remains an indispensable work in spite of all its faults and misprints. As secretary of the leading Dutch monthly *De Gids* (The Guide) from 1916 to 1939, he wrote many articles about history and national and international politics. Some of these essays on history and historians are still valuable and readable because of his vivid style. He also published a large manual on Dutch colonial history, a great number of monographs about the Batavian Revolution, the so-called French period, and the first years of the Kingdom of the Netherlands. His interpretation of the Batavian Revolution—based mainly on foreign sources—is critical and unfavorable, depreciating and caricaturing the weakness of the Dutch Patriot movement. His informative monographs—being too often buttressed with extensive quotations—lack a bold conception. Although displaying an initial enthusiasm for Karl Lamprecht's (q.v.) cultural history and Henri Pirenne's (q.v.) socio-economic approach, he called in later years for a "rehabilitation of political history" (*Eerherstel der staatkundige geschiedenis*, Inaugural Lecture, 1925). As an editor of sources, Colenbrander remains a man of great significance for Dutch historiography. His last full–sized work concerns the life and times of J. P. Coen *(Jan Pietersz. Coen, Bescheiden omtrent Zijn bedrijf in Indië*, 6 vols., The Hague, 1919–1934).

Bibliography: H. T. Colenbrander, "Les rapports de la Hollande et de la France (1780–1815). Etat des travaux," *Revue d'histoire moderne et contemporaine*, 9 (1907–1908): 259–270; H. T. Colenbrander, *The Work of Dutch Historical Societies*, reprinted from the Annual Report of the American Historical Association for 1909, pp. 243–256. (Washington, D.C. 1911); B. Lyon, *Henri Pirenne* (Ghent, 1974), pp. 384–385; E. H. Kossmann, *The Low Countries 1780–1940* (Oxford, 1978), p. 741; S. Schama, *Patriots and Liberators. Revolution in the Netherlands 1780–1813* (New York, 1977), pp. 15–23.

P. B. M. Blaas

FRUIN, Robert Jacobus (Rotterdam, 1823–Leyden, 1899), Dutch historian. Professor at the Rijksuniversiteit (State University) at Leyden (1860–1894). Fruin was the first occupant of the chair for Dutch history in the Netherlands. Within the wider context of the discussions between parliamentary liberals and Calvinist monarchists on the essence of the Dutch state and civilization, Fruin provided the history of the Dutch Republic with an essentially liberal framework. Before he joined the passionate debate on the causes of the Revolt of the Netherlands, the prevailing opinion was that the Revolt and the ensuing Eighty Years' War were a war of religion, a massive defense of the true religion against an oppressive and corrupt church and a bigoted sovereign. Fruin didn't deny the decisive role of the Calvinist minority, but he subsumed the religious factor with other factors like the defense of local and territorial liberties and the rejection of foreign rule, under the concept of freedom. G. P. Gooch, in his *History and Historians in the Nineteenth Century* (2d ed., 1952), calls Fruin "a miniature Ranke [q.v.], whose fame would have been wider had he written a work of large dimensions; but it may be doubted whether it would have been so useful as the stream of monographs in which he recorded his results." Although Fruin was first and foremost a researcher, he was much more than "a miniature Ranke" who wrote only one "work of large dimensions." His meticulously researched monographs, collected in his *Verspreide geschriften* (10 vols., 1900–1905; Collected Papers) often shed new light on the main problems of the history of the Dutch Ancien Régime. His two masterworks, *Tien jaren uit den tachtigjarigen oorlog 1588–1598 (*1857–1858; Ten Years from the Eighty Years' War) and *Het Voorspel van den Tachtigjarigen Oorlog* (1859–1860; The Prelude to the Eighty Years' War)—published in the leading liberal monthly *De Gids*, and republished as a book in 1939 (reprint 1986, with an introduction by C. Offringa)—deal with two fateful episodes in the history of the Netherlands and the formation of the Dutch state and nation. Ranke—the historian of the European system of state—

wrote about the papacy, the French absolute monarchy, the rise of the English parliamentary monarchy, and the creation of the Prussian bureaucratic state. It was Fruin who put on the map of European history that unique phenomenon: the Republic of the Seven United Netherlands. Though Rankean as regards subject matter (political history) and method (the philological–historical method), Fruin—unlike his Berlin colleague—was not a conservative but a liberal who tried to reconcile a Whig interpretation of Dutch constitutional history with a profound sense of history. In his remarkable study *De drie tijdvakken der Nederlandsche geschiedenis* (1865; The Three Periods of Dutch History), Fruin views the Dutch Republic as an interim between the nascent unitary state of all the Netherlands under the House of Habsburg and the Kingdom of the (northern) Netherlands under the House of Orange. This wider-ranging study shows Fruin's ambiguous attitude toward the centuries when the United Provinces were not only a mighty economic and political power but also one of Europe's cultural centers. From his Whig point of view the Republic was a political anomaly, the offspring of a conservative revolution which for two centuries put a brake on the natural development of which the nineteenth-century unitary state with its parliamentary monarchy would be the natural outcome. However, Fruin could not overlook the greatness of this strange phenomenon among the great monarchies. After all, it was one of the cradles of Western democracy, a pioneer of commercial capitalism, and a protagonist in the adventure of European expansion overseas. Fruin judged the country's constitutional development to be of decisive importance for its history in general. Hence, his famous university lectures on the *Geschiedenis der staatsinstellingen in Nederland tot den val der Republiek* (1901; Constitutional and Institutional History of the Northern Netherlands from the Reign of Charles V until the Fall of the Republic in 1795), (edited on the basis of notes taken by some of his pupils; reprint, 1980, with an introduction by I. Schöffer).

Was Fruin a positivist? Did he believe in historical laws? The influence of a Spencerean kind of evolutionism is evident: "The state" takes on the forms which the continuously changing historical situations demand. Fruin took his stand on positivism in three orations: *De onpartijdigheid van den geschiedschrijver* (1860; the Historian's Impartiality), *Over de plaats die de geschiedenis in de kring der wetenschappen inneemt* (1878; On the Place of History Among the Sciences), and his *Afscheidsrede* (1894; Valedictory Address). In his inaugural address (1860) he compares the historian with the painter: both try to give a true picture of their subject, but neither succeeds in being truly objective. In his rectorial address (1878) he sees history approaching the status of a real science: The historian can be truly objective; his task is to look for historical laws. In his valedictory address (1894) the scientism of 1860 has made way for ideas rather similar to those expressed in 1860.

Bibliography: P. B. M. Blaas, " 'The Touchiness of a Small Nation with a Great Past': The Approach of Fruin and Blok to the Writing of the History of the Netherlands," in A. C. Duke and C. A. Tamse, eds., *Clio's Mirror: Historiography in Britain and the*

Netherlands (Zutphen, 1985), pp. 133–161; G. W. Kernkamp, *Ober Robert Fruin* (On Robert Fruin, 1910, republished in G. W. Kernkamp, *Van Menschen en Tijden*, About Men and Their Times, 1932); R. Putnam, *Annual Report of the American Historical Association* 1 (1899), pp. 515 ff.; F. Rachfahl, *Historishe Zeitschrift*, 98 (1907): pp. 507 ff.; J. W. Smit, *Fruin en de partijen tijdens de Republiek* (Fruin and the Party Strife During the Republic, 1958).

C. Offringa

GEYL, Pieter Catharinus Arie (Dordrecht, 1887–Utrecht, 1966), Dutch historian. Geyl studied Dutch language and literature from 1906 until 1911 at Leyden University and got his doctor's degree in 1913. From January 1914 until October 1919 he was London correspondent of the *Nieuwe Rotterdamsche Courant*, one of the leading Dutch newspapers. His career as an historian started in 1919 when he was appointed professor of Dutch history at University College in London. From 1936 until 1958 he was professor "in Dutch and general history after the Middle Ages" at the State University of Utrecht. Geyl's principal historical work is the unfinished (until 1798) *Geschiedenis van de Nederlandsche Stam* (1930–1959; History of the Dutch Stock). Parts of this work were translated into English *(The Revolt of the Netherlands* [1932] and *The Netherlands in the Seventeenth Century* [2 vols., 1936–1964]). In this study he summed up his "Great Netherlandish" views, in which he let the linguistic entity of the Netherlands (the Low Countries) prevail and in which he criticized the finalistic ideas of Dutch (Petrus Johannes Blok [q.v.]) and Belgian (Henri Pirenne [q.v.]) historians, who projected the contemporary frontiers of Holland and Belgium into the past as far as possible. Geyl's romantic starting point of the linguistic entity as the most important factor in forming a nationhood is contestable, but it has brought some revisions in the history of the Dutch Revolt, notably, on the cleavage in the Netherlands in the sixteenth century as being caused not by natural circumstances but by military and political decisions and the Protestantization of the Dutch Republic. Geyl's vision of the entity of the Dutch language also brought him in contact with the Flemish Movement. This lifetime involvement did not bring him to irredentism. His ideal was a "Great Netherland," but in reality he proposed a federal Belgium. His research in mostly English archives resulted in his reconsideration of the national politics of the Orange stadholders. Their dynastic ambitions were not always in close union with the interest of the Dutch Republic. According to his critics, Geyl underestimated the unifying force of the stadholders and the Orange party. His final publication on this subject is *Oranje en Stuart, 1641–1672* (1939). An English translation followed in 1969 *(Orange and Stuart, 1641–1672)*.

In World War II, in which he was a hostage of the German occupiers from October 1940 until February 1944, Geyl found a new subject in writing on historiographical problems. His first publication in this field was *Napoleon, voor en tegen in de Franse geschiedschrijving* (1946; Napoleon, For and Against, (1949). His historiographical studies on Leopold von Ranke (q.v.), Thomas

Babington Macaulay (q.v.), Thomas Carlyle (q.v.), Jules Michelet (q.v.), and on Dutch historians as Robert Jacobus Fruin (q.v.) and Jan Marius Romein (q.v.), and especially his debates with Arnold Joseph Toynbee (q.v.) brought him great fame in his own country and in the Anglo-Saxon world. With vehemence and deep conviction, but in a highly polished style, he attacked determinism and all forms of closed systems as a way of explaining the past and the course of history. The study of the past and the writing on it had to be "a discussion without end." All his life he remained a firm believer in the vitality of European culture, and his fields of interest were not limited to political and cultural history. His most important writings on historiography are to be found in *Use and Abuse of History* (1955), *Debates with Historians* (1955), and *Encounters in History* (1961). From 1961 to 1966 Geyl was a member of the editorial committee of *History and Theory*.

Bibliography: H. Rowen, "Pieter Geyl," *Encyclopedia of Social Sciences* (Biographical Supplement) V.18, pp. 232–236 (New York-London, 1979); P.van Hees, *Bibliografie van P. Geyl* (Groningen, 1972); H. W. von der Dunk, "Pieter Geyl. History as a Form of Self-Expression," in *Britain and the Netherlands*, Vol. 8, A. C. Duke and C. A. Tamse, eds. (Zutphen, 1985), pp. 185–214.

Pieter van Hees

GROEN VAN PRINSTERER, Guillaume (Voorburg, 1801–The Hague, 1876), Dutch statesman and historian. Groen studied classics and law at Leyden University and graduated in both subjects in 1823 by writing a thesis on Plato and a thesis on Justinian. To that classical education he owed his classic style and Socratic irony. Raised in a liberal environment, under the influence of J. H. Merle d'Aubigné, the chaplain of King William I at Brussels, he became a convinced adherent of orthodox Protestantism and the most prominent representative of the Dutch Réveil. In that capacity he pleaded the maintenance of the reformed confession in the Dutch Reformed Church and produced many publications on that subject. As a member of Parliament, he manifested himself as an indefatigable spokesman of the so–called antirevolutionary or Christian–historical party. Initially, he was rather conservative, but later in life he proved not averse to a democracy based on Christian foundations under the leadership of the Orange Dynasty. His thinking was influenced by authors such as J. P. F Ancillon, E. Burke, E. L. von Gerlach, François Guizot (q.v.), K. L. von Haller, H. F. R. de Lamennais, F. K. von Savigny (q.v.), and F. J. Stahl. In his best known work, *Ongeloof en Revolutie* (1847; Unbelief and Revolution), he disputed what he considered the atheistic principles of the French Revolution. As the advocate of a Christian education, he played an important part in the fight for Christian state schools. He displayed his journalistic talents in the *Nederlandsche Gedachten* (1829–1832; 1869–1876; Dutch Reflections), and the *Nederlander* (1850–1855; The Dutchman). Of his voluminous correspondence, five volumes so far have been published as part of the series *Rijks Geschiedkundige Publicatiën* (1925–   ). His bibliography *(De Vries)* comprises over 150 titles.

As an historian, he won fame by the publication of the *Archives ou correspondance inédite de la maison d'Orange–Nassau*, of which thirteen volumes were edited by Groen between 1835 and 1861. The work was completed by other scholars. He had the opportunity to work on this gigantic task because he had been appointed supervisor of the Royal House–Archive. His *Handboek der Geschiedenis van het vaderland* (1841–1846; Handbook of the History of the Fatherland), written from a Calvinistic and Orangistic view—is still reprinted regularly. In *Maurice et Barnevelt* (1875) he defended the attitude of Prince Maurice regarding the statesman Oldenbarneveld, executed in 1619, against the liberal historiography. He saw history in the light of Augustine's *De civitate Dei* as the struggle between the terrestrial and the heavenly kingdom.

Bibliography: T. de Vries, *Mr. G. Groen van Prinsterer: een bibliografie* (Utrecht, 1908); P. A. Diepenhorst, *Groen van Prinsterer* (Kampen, 1932); H. Smitskamp, *Groen van Prinsterer als historicus* (Groen van Prinsterer as a Historian), (Amsterdam, 1940); J. L. van Essen, "Guillaume Groen van Prinsterer and his conception of history," *Westminster Theological Journal* (1982): 205–249; J. Zwaan, *Groen van Prinsterer en de klassieke oudheid* (Groen van Prinsterer and Classical Antiquity), (Amsterdam, 1973), with a summary and extensive bibliography.

J. Zwaan

HUIZINGA, Johan (Groningen, 1872–De Steeg, 1945), Dutch historian. Professor in the universities of Groningen (1905) and Leyden (1915). In 1940 the Germans closed Leyden University as a retaliatory measure for the protests against the dismissal of Jewish professors. In 1942 Huizinga was taken hostage by the Germans and forbidden to return to the west of the country. He went to live in a small town in the East Netherlands and died shortly before the arrival of the Allied Forces. Huizinga, a descendant of a family that counted many Baptist clergymen and himself having an intimate knowledge of academe (his father was a professor in the medical faculty), started his studies in the literary faculty of Groningen University. Because of the slow institutional development of Dutch higher education, the student had to read a curious combination of subjects for the examination in the literary faculty. It was only in 1921, in the new Academic Statute for Dutch universities, drawn up by Huizinga, that the various subjects, including history, would become separate disciplines. In 1895 Huizinga took his degree in Dutch language and literature for which he had had to study, among other things, Gothic and Sanskrit. He went on to study in Leipzig which was a well-known center for the *Junggrammatiker*. He returned to the Netherlands as an expert philologist who was nevertheless not entirely satisfied with studying formal grammar. He had taken an ambitious subject for his M.A. thesis: the expressions for the perception of light and sound in the Indo–Germanic languages. To this end he even contacted the great psychologist Wilhelm Wundt in Leipzig. But the subject turned out to be too vast, and he finally chose a manageable subject that he himself described as an elaboration of the ideas of Sylvain Lévi about the development of the classical Indian drama.

After he took his degree (1897), Huizinga became a history teacher at a secondary school in Haarlem. Thus far he had shown little scholarly interest in history. However, trained as a linguist and an expert in Sanskrit, he had developed an early interest in ethnology (stimulated by Edward Burnett Tylor's *Primitive Culture*); he possessed a marked historical sensibility and a very sensitive eye in matters of art. He was kept informed of the ups and downs of the French symbolists by the *Mercure de France*. Rémy de Gourmont's *Le latin mystique* made a great impression on him. When in 1903 he became external lecturer in Amsterdam for classical Indian literature and Indian cultural history, he showed his versatility and the ease with which he mastered new subjects by publishing his first historical article, about the medieval history of Haarlem. The Haarlem town archives did not contain much, but Huizinga used his knowledge of the work of Karl Bücher (q.v) and Henri Pirenne (q.v.) in particular to produce with inventive comparatism, philological craft, and evocative writing an original contribution to the socioeconomic history of Holland in the Middle Ages. On the recommendation of his old teacher in Groningen, Petrus Johannes Blok (q.v.), who in the meantime had moved to Leyden, Huizinga was appointed to a post in Groningen University (1905). After Huizinga's death his large and varied oeuvre was published in a complete edition of eight volumes (4,500 pages in all), with a comprehensive register and a bibliography mentioning the many translations. A fourth part of his oeuvre concerns the Middle Ages, 10 percent the Renaissance, and 15 percent his own period. In addition, he wrote about seventeenth- and nineteenth-century Dutch cultural history, about academic history, the theory of history, and other subjects. His originality, independence of mind, and careful prose all contributed to a writing style that made the most diverse experts value his work and quote from it.

Huizinga thought two monographs his most successful work: the two studies were about nineteenth-century Dutch cultural history based on unpublished sources, oral tradition, and his own experience. One of the studies was the memorial volume for Groningen University, 1814–1914 (1914); and the other, the biography of his friend the painter Jan Veth (1927). The second work is to some extent autobiographical and describes the ideas prevailing at the turn of the century about the relationship between art and society as well as between individual and society. Huizinga's name will always be linked to his chef d'oeuvre *Herfsttij der Middeleeuwen* (1919; The Waning of the Middle Ages, 1924). Huizinga already had the idea for this book, which some consider to be the first example of the "histoire des mentalités" before World War I. In this respect his visit to the exhibition of Old Dutch art in Bruges in 1902 was important. After a few bouts of intense activity on the book, it was crowded out by other work and personal circumstances until he resumed work on it in 1915 in Leyden. The gloom of World War I together with his depression after the death of his first wife, undoubtedly were responsible for the macabre atmosphere of this work. This study of life and thought in fourteenth- and fifteenth-century France and the Netherlands was innovative in its approach to traditional literary and artistic sources and in the way it defined the issues. Subject and approach strongly resembled Jacob Burckhardt's (q.v.) chef d'oeuvre about the Renaissance (1860), but, influenced by symbolism, Huizinga's approach was more profound. Although Huizinga's treatment of the world of ideas at the Burgundy court was more profound, it was also less clear and in its composition less elegant than Burckhardt's treatment of Renaissance culture in Italy. Admired by prominent literary circles and people from the world of arts, the work had a cool reception from professional historians. Fortunately, Huizinga did not care much. For did he not prefer the prestigious cultural and political magazine *De Gids* to specialist journals? Apart from a successful biography of Erasmus (1924), and collected essays (1926 and 1929), he also published essays about the United States (1918 and 1927). Like Alexis de Tocqueville (q.v) he considered this country the pattern of modern civilization, although Huizinga stressed the cultural rather than the political aspects. Two years after Hitler's *Machtübernahme,* Huizinga's *In de schaduwen van morgen* (1935; In the Shadow of Tomorrow, A Diagnosis of the Spiritual Distemper of Our Time, 1936) made his name known to a great many people. Among his later publications his best-known are *Homo Ludens* (1938), a contribution to the theory of culture particularly appreciated by sociologists and anthropologists, and *Dutch Civilization in the Seventeenth Century* (1941). For Huizinga the theory of history remained a side-issue, less important than his practical work in history. As a newly appointed professor in 1905, Huizinga contributed to the furious theoretical debate in Germany. Although he appreciated Karl Lamprecht's (q.v.) work from the outset, he came to value it less and less. The later volumes of the *Deutsche Geschichte* were a great disappointment to him. He did not reject the use of categories and concepts but considered them mere aids to historical perception. As an antipositivist, he emphasized the need to vindicate the humanities and to reinstate them as an independent subject, the equal of the natural sciences that should be saved from the self-confident evolutionism of the sciences. Completely in line with his entire oeuvre, he described the study of history not as a science but as the "spiritual form in which a civilization renders account of its past."

Bibliography: J. Kamerbeek, Jr., "Huizinga en de beweging van tachtig," *Tijdschrift voor Geschiedenis,* 67(1954): 145–164; J. Huizinga, *Verzamelde Werken,* 9 vols. (Haarlem, 1948–1953); W. R. H. Koops, E. H. Kossmann, and G. van der Plaat, eds., *Johan Huizinga* (The Hague, 1973); W. E. Krul, "Huizinga en de taak der cultuurgeschiedenis," *Theoretische Geschiedenis* 13(1986): 149–168.

Pim den Boer

LEUR, Jacob Cornelis van (Utrecht, 1908–Java Sea, 1942), Dutch historian. Civil servant, assistant controller at Tulung Agung on Java until 1936, later employed in the section for financial and economic affairs of the Generale Secretarie, the secretariat of the governor-general of the Netherlands East Indies at Bogor. Van Leur died as a decoding officer during the battle of the Java Sea. As a nonprofessional historian, he exerted a remarkable influence on the historiography of the Dutch East Indies and on the thinking about how the history of Indonesia should be interpreted. His short life and occupation prevented the elaboration of the many ideas and theses brought forward in his relatively small oeuvre. History constituted only one of the disciplines of Indology, the training for a career with the colonial government in the Netherlands East Indies. The other elements were: Indonesian languages, law, religion, economics, and ethnology. He finished his studies at Leyden in 1934 with the defense of a doctoral dissertation "Eenige beschouwingen betreffende den ouden Aziatischen handel" (On Early Asian Trade). Among the many theses written by future civil servants and studies of Dutch colonial historians of the time, the book is a unique phenomenon. Written with the aid of published sources and secondary literature, the merit of the work should not be sought in the new material it brings to the fore. Van Leur's contribution lies first in the application of the ideas of Max Weber (q.v.) and the use of insights from economic history upon the existing body of knowledge. This method is the more rewarding because of Van Leur's wide reading in Dutch and general history and training in Indology. Central to his thesis was the history of the sea route between the Mediterranean, the Indian Ocean, and the China Sea. In large, all-encompassing steps, Van Leur perused the history of the trade between these areas, trying to establish its organization, extent, character, and impact on the areas involved. By taking the trade route as his starting point, he needed to reconsider notions taken from Western and European history and to assess their applicability to world history. The usual periodization taken from the European past did not make sense in Asian perspective. Needed was a set of categories applicable to all areas brought within the reach of one social-economic-historical system. The choice of the trading system gave Van Leur a central focus and enabled him to overcome a possible ethnocentric bias. The study of trade and connected organizations made a comparison between different societies and times possible, exposing the bias of the existing ideas on the oriental mind and attitude. The thesis was directly meant as a plea for an autonomous history of Asia and especially Indonesia. By providing the means and categories with which the history of non-European areas could be written, Van Leur hoped to free it from the monopoly of philologists. An example of the potency of the social-economic approach was his questioning of the philologists' view of the Hinduization of the Indonesian archipelago and their vagueness concerning acculturation processes connected with the coming of Islam. The thesis also aimed at a tendency among colonial historians in the 1930s to start from the European superiority and at the rather easily accepted organic explanation of Dutch expansion. By stressing the autonomous character of Indonesian history and by providing tools for independent research, Van Leur wanted Indonesians to conquer their own past. Essentially, new ideas were not touched on in his later work, which was mainly an elaboration of his first views. In Batavia Van Leur belonged to the founders of the Historical Section of the Royal Batavian Society of Arts and Sciences in 1937. The reception of his work and views in the Netherlands had only started when World War II began. After the war his major work was translated into English. His influence can still be traced in the discussion on the autonomy of Indonesian history, the problem of the impact of European trade on Asian society, the coming of Hinduism and Islam in Indonesia, and the periodization of Indonesian history.

Bibliography: *Indonesian Trade and Society: Essays in Asian Social and Economic History by J. C. van Leur* (The Hague, 1955, 1967).

J. van Goor

POSTHUMUS, Nicolaas Wilhelmus (Amsterdam, 1880–Bussum, 1960), Dutch historian. Professor in Rotterdam (1913) and Amsterdam (1921–1949). Founder of modern economic history in the Netherlands. Established several research institutes and archives. Posthumus' dissertation of 1908, "De Geschiedenis van de Leidsche Lakenindustrie, I. De Middeleeuwen" (History of the Leyden Cloth Industry, I. The Middle Ages), foreshadowed his later scientific career. It was supplemented in 1939 with a second and a third volume on the period up to and including the eighteenth century and was innovative in content and in method. He tracked the development of a branch of industry in all its aspects from the moment of the first appearance in the sources until the decline five centuries later. Posthumus connected national and local economy, prices and wages, demographical data and social structure into an integral economic history. In the process of growth and decline, in which the cloth industry developed from a putting-out system into a beginning of a manufacture, Posthumus pointed out as the most influential factors the combination of technical innovation (or stagnation) and economic factors (most of all foreign competition). With this he anticipated the postwar discussion among Dutch historians on the influence of psychological versus economic factors. His work was methodically innovating in its quantitative, statistical approach. In addition, economic theory played a role, especially in parts II and III and in a chapter on the influence of business cycles on the Leyden cloth industry.

Because of the methods used and the important position held by Leyden and the Netherlands in the early modern European economy, the work of Posthumus still has international importance. The same can be said of his *Nederlandsche Prijsgeschiedenis* (2 vols., 1946, 1964; Inquiry into the History of Prices in Holland), which was his contribution to the program of the International Scientific Committee on Price History. This price history is not only an indispensable source for European economic history, but also from the price lists in this work he inferred that the weakening of competitive abilities was an important factor in the economic decline of the Dutch Republic in the eighteenth century. In drawing this conclusion, which others later confirmed and worked out, he again pointed to the importance of external economic factors. Posthumus' oeuvre is based on and accompanied by the issuing of records like the *Bronnen tot de Geschiedenis van de Leidsche textielnijverheid* (6 vols., 1910–1922; Sources to the History of the Leyden Textile-Industry) and *Documenten betreffende de buitenlandse handelspolitiek van Nederland in de 19de eeuw* (6 vols., 1919–

1931; Documents Concerning the Foreign Trade Policy of the Netherlands in the Nineteenth Century). The importance he attached to documentation is also shown in the establishment of a great number of institutes, the most important of which are the NEHA (Dutch Economic History Archive, 1914), the IISH (International Institute for Social History, 1935), and the RIOD (State Institute for War Documentation, 1945). The importance of the NEHA is in the tracing and preservation of business archives, the publishing of sources, and the issuing of the *Economisch-Historisch Jaarboek* (Economic History Yearbook, since 1971: Economic and Social History Yearbook). The International Institute for Social History was founded when important personal and party archives were in danger of getting lost in the nazification of Germany. Preservation in Amsterdam did avert this danger and laid the foundation for further extending the institute. Originally, the institute was interested mainly in socialism and related movements, but since about 1960 there has been an active interest in the field of social history in the broadest sense. Here also a periodical was issued, the *International Review of Social History* (1930–1939, a second series since 1956). The State Institute for War Documentation was established to collect and preserve material from World War II and to support history writing on that war. On the collection of this institute is based, among other things, the multivolume official history of the Netherlands in World War II (1969–   ).

Bibliography: P. C. Jansen and W. M. Zappey, *Bibliografie van de geschriften van Nicolaas Wilhelmus Posthumus (1880–1960)* (Rotterdam, 1981).

L. J. Dorsman

ROGIER, Louis (Rotterdam, 1894–Groesbeek, near Nijmegen, 1974), Dutch historian. After having been a teacher at a secondary school for almost thirty years, and although a self-made historian, Rogier was appointed a professor at the Catholic University of Nijmegen (1947–1964). He owed his appointment, as well as his honorary degree, to the standard work *Geschiedenis van het katholicisme in Noord-Nederland in de 16e en 17e eeuw* (2 vols., 1945–1946; History of Catholicism in the Northern Netherlands in the Sixteenth and Seventeenth Centuries). Running counter to prevailing opinion and joining Pieter Geyl (q.v.), he described the decline of Catholicism in the Republic of the Seven United Provinces as the result of a political and socioeconomic process of Protestantizing; it was the Republican, comparatively tolerant variation of the princely *cuius regio illius et religio*. Only in those areas where the Counter–Reformation had been effective did Catholicism retain its predominance. Moreover, Rogier discovered in the culture of the Dutch Golden Age more elements of Catholicism than had generally been assumed. Concerning the origins of the Revolt of the Netherlands in the sixteenth century, he emphasized the *libertatis ergo*. Somewhat underestimating the influence of the Calvinistic *religionis causa*, he nevertheless attributed an important role to the abuses within the Catholic Church of the early sixteenth century. Yet again in *Eenheid en scheiding. Geschiedenis der Nederlanden 1477–1813* (Unity and Separation. History of the

Netherlands 1477–1813), published in 1952, these opinions were put into a broad profane-historical context. *Vrijheid herboren* (Reborn in Freedom), a work on the history of Catholicism in the Netherlands in the nineteenth and twentieth centuries, was published in 1953 and written in collaboration with N. de Rooy. Rewritten as *Katholieke herleving* (Catholic Renascence), this voluminous work was published in 1956 under Rogier's name only. It gave an outspoken description of the emancipation of Catholicism. The author was critical of both the national community and his own Catholic community, and—not in the least because of his expressive use of language—it met with approval as well as with opposition, right up to Vatican Circles. The only sizable work that allowed Rogier a certain reputation abroad was the volume about the Enlightenment in part IV of *The Christian Centuries. A New History of the Catholic Church* (1964) by L. J. Rogier, R. Aubert, and M. D. Knowles, eds. Here he gave a moderately positive interpretation of the Catholic Enlightenment in the German Empire.

Rogier wrote many absorbing articles and essays of a biographical kind in particular, in an idiosyncratic and somewhat solemn style. They were collected in a number of volumes during his life. He was an ecclesiastical and nationally committed historiographer who wrote in the tradition of such literary–historical predecessors—admired by him but criticized as well—as Jozef Alberdingk Thijm and Gerard Brom, both pioneers in the cultural emancipation process of the Dutch Catholics. He was an advocate of a harmonious amalgamation of Dutch citizenship and membership in the Catholic Church; this church was to be a universally accepted community in the service of all humankind. From this point of view Rogier judged the national past. In doing so he did not want to detract from a genuine quest for the historical "truth," which—in a positivistically colored conception of historiography—he imagined to be of equal import to both Protestants and Catholics. After all, knowledgeability and honesty have given his oeuvre an enduring significance.

Bibliography: J. A. Bornewasser, "Geschiedwetenschap en engagement bij L. J. Rogier (1894–1974)," *Tijdschrift voor Geschiedenis* 87 (1974): 443–459; J. A. Bornewasser, "In memoriam Prof. dr. L. J. Rogier (1894–1974)," *Bijdragen en Mededelingen betreffende de Geschiedenis der Nederlanden* 90 (1975): 71–80: J. H. Roes in *Biografisch Woordenboek van Nederland*, I (1979): 492–496.

J. A. Bornewasser

ROMEIN, Jan Marius (Rotterdam, 1893–Amsterdam, 1962), Dutch historian. Professor at the University of Amsterdam (1939–1959). While a student at Leyden University (1914–1920), where he was Johan Huizinga's (q.v.) most talented pupil, Romein lost his Mennonite faith and became an atheist and a radical socialist. He and his wife, Annie Verschoor, a distinguished writer and historian in her own right, moved in a set of brilliant young intellectuals, mostly scientists, who were ardent partisans of the October Revolution. Romein joined the Dutch Communist party and served on the staff of the communist daily *De Tribune*. In 1925 he fell a victim to a Moscow-inspired purge of the CPH

(Communist Party of Holland); he lost his job on *De Tribune* (1925) and was thrown out of the party (1927). Nonetheless, he kept his faith in the progressive nature of the Revolution. Until 1939, Romein was a free-lance publicist. He wrote comments on international affairs for the leftist weekly, *De Groene Amsterdammer*, and for the more conservative monthly, *Groot Nederland*. Romein was an ardent patriot and a convinced internationalist. He loved his country as the cradle of Erasmian humanism and civil liberties, and as a bulwark of human dignity. His oration in Amsterdam University in November 1940, "Oorsprong, voortgang en toekomst van de Nederlandse geest" (Origin, Progress and Future of the Dutch Genius), was delivered as an act of protest against the German oppressors and as an act of faith in the future of the Dutch people. In 1942 Romein was put in a concentration camp by the Germans. After he was released, he stayed hidden until the German defeat.

Whereas Huizinga re-created with artistic imagination and finesse the emotional and intellectual life of elites, the "modernist" Romein was something of an eighteenth-century "philosophe." He studied history as *histoire de civilisation*. Though a Marxist of sorts, he was much more interested in mentalities, ideas, ideologies, and art and literature as social phenomena than in the social-economic aspects of society. He demonstrated his approach in a remarkable synthesis of the history of the Low Countries: *De Lage Landen bij de zee* (1934; The Low Countries on the Sea: A History of the People of the Netherlands from Dunkirk to Delfzije). It was typical of Romein's unorthodox Marxism that he deemed it necessary to give this history of structures and mentalities a biographical dimension. In 1938–1940 he and Annie Verschoor published *Erflaters van onze beschaving: Nederlandse gestalten uit zes eeuwen* (4 vols; German trans., Ahnherren der Holländischen Kultur, 1946), thirty-six biographical essays on men and women representing Netherlands civilization from the fourteenth century to the present. In their introduction, the authors explained why it was important for Marxist historians to write history from a biographical point of view. In *De Biografie* (1946; German trans., Die Biographie, 1948), Romein dealt with the history and theory of biographical writing. Romein had learned from Huizinga to study historiography as a cultural phenomenon. In 1932, he brought out a classic work, *Geschiedenis van de Noord-Nederlansche geschiedschrijving in de Middeleeuwen, bijdrage tot de beschavingsgeschiedenis* (A History of Medieval Historiography in the Northern Netherlands: A Contribution to Cultural History). He foresaw that history would lose its cultural function, if the increasing fragmentation of historical knowledge, which had led to an anarchy of "images of the past" to "a pulverized image" (1939), could not be stopped. A new synthetic approach was urgently needed, and Romein introduced a new concept of history: theoretical history, for which the distinction between theoretical and applied physics served as a model. The theorist would have to do the thinking on fundamental problems of methodology and philosophy of history and on specific historical problems. See *Theoretische Geschiedenis* (1946; English trans., "Theoretical History," *Journal of the History of Ideas*, 9 [1948]). The craftsman would have to apply this "theory" while doing research and writing history. The guild—with Pieter Geyl (q.v.) as the leader—raised a hue and cry: they did not want to be told how to do their job. On this debate, see Romein's *In de Hof der Historie: Kleine encyclopaedie der theoretische geschiedenis* (1951; In the Garden of History: A Short Introduction to Theoretical History). To cope with the growing production of factual knowledge, Romein contrived one more device: "integrale geschiedschrijving" (integral history). Like Lucien Febvre (q.v.), Romein aimed at "total history." He differed, however, from them in that he did not plead for an interdisciplinary study of long trends. Rather, he wanted historians to study a short but decisive period in all its aspects. See *Over integrale geschiedschrijving* (1958, German trans., "Über integrale Geschichtschreibung, " *Schweizer Beiträge zur Allgemeinen Geschichte*, Bern, BD. 16).

Death prevented Romein from finishing what should have been his magnum opus, "an integral history" of European civilization to about 1900, conceived as the history of a "dialectical turnover." The descriptive part—brilliant essays on politics, social movements, sciences and humanities, arts and literature—was published posthumously: *Op het breukvlak van twee eeuwen* (2 vols., 1967; Between Past and Present: 1900 as a Turning-point), edited by Annie Romein-Verschoor. In a number of essays, several of which he republished in foreign periodicals, Romein dealt with theoretical problems, such as the conceptions of decadence (1930) and progress (1935,1950) in history, historical objectivity (1937), historical laws (1947), conservatism as an historical category (1956), and change and continuity (1963). In 1976 a selection from these essays, Jan Romein, *Historische lijnen en patronen: Een keuze uit de essays* (Historical Lines and Patterns: A Selection from the Essays), was published. Romein was deeply interested in the writing of world history. Like Max Weber (q.v.), he was fascinated by the uniqueness and expansiveness of European civilization, which he viewed as a "deviation from the common human pattern." Romein found a kindred spirit in Arnold Joseph Toynbee (q.v.), whose work he introduced to Holland in *Toynbee's studie der geschiedenis: Grondslagen ener algemene en vergelijkende beschavingsleer* (1948; Toynbee's Study of History: Principles of a General and Comparative Theory of Civilization, 1948).

Bibliography: M. C. Brands, "Jan Romein en het ordeningsprincipe: tussen dwang en vrijheid. De dialektiek van emancipatie (Jan Romein and the Principle of Ordering: Between Constraint and Freedom. The Dialectics of Emancipation)," *Theoretische Geschiedenis* 12 (1985): 485 ff.; "Jan Romein," *De Nieuwe Stem*, vol. 17 (1962), pp. 613 ff. (commemorative issue); A. F. Meeink, "Jan Romein," in A. H. Huussen, E. H. Kossmann, and H. Renner, eds., *Historici van de twintigste eeuw* (Historians of the Twentieth Century), (1981), pp. 199 ff.; Annie Romein-Verschoor, *Omzien in verwondering: Herinneringen van Annie Romein-Verschoor* (Looking Back in Wonder: Memoirs by Annie Romein-Verschoor), 2 vols. (1970, 1971); A. Tijhuis, P.A.L. Oppenheimer, and M. C. Brands, *Prof. Dr. Jan Romein: Bibliographie* (1963).

C. Offringa

Great Historians: English

ACTON, Lord (Naples, 1834–Tegernsee, 1902), English historian. John Emerich Edward Dalberg was the son of an English baronet and a German aristocrat, and was educated at a Catholic school in England and at the University of Munich, where he studied with Döllinger, whose opposition to papal infallibility he later shared. A member of Parliament and a friend of Gladstone, through whom he was raised to the peerage in 1869, Acton was also active as an editor of and contributor to a number of reviews. He was appointed Regius professor of modern history at Cambridge in 1895. Acton never wrote the books he planned (on the history of liberty, the Council of Trent, and on Döllinger). His reputation rests on his editorship of the *Cambridge Modern History* and on his penetrating, epigrammatic essays and lectures, mainly on the history of early modern Europe, which were collected into four volumes after his death: *Lectures on Modern History* (1906), *The History of Freedom, Historical Essays and Studies*, and *Lectures on the French Revolution* (both 1907). A historian of liberal principles and cosmopolitan culture, Acton is famous both for his uncompromising moral judgments ("Power tends to corrupt, absolute power corrupts absolutely"), and for his faith in impartial history ("Our scheme requires," he wrote to the contributors to the *Cambridge Modern History*, "that nothing shall reveal the country, the religion and the party to which the writers belong").

Bibliography: Herbert Butterfield, *Acton* (London, 1948); David Mathew, *Lord Acton and His Times* (London, 1968); R. L. Schuettinger, *Lord Acton, Historian of Liberty* (La Salle, 1976).

Peter Burke

BUCKLE, Henry Thomas (Lee, Kent, 1821–Damascus, 1862), British historian. Son of a rich merchant, Buckle was free to dedicate himself to historical research, with no other obligation. Powerfully influenced by the positivist philosophy of Auguste Comte (q.v.), he planned to elevate history to the dignity of a real science. He only managed to publish the first two, introductory volumes, of a vast work he had planned, *History of Civilization in England* (1857–1861). Buckle noted, to begin with, the mediocrity of a history that did nothing but accumulate facts. By his opinion, not even the most prominent historians could compare with Newton or other great scientists; history was therefore very backward as compared with the natural sciences. The purely descriptive stage of events had to be left behind, an in-depth analysis had to be undertaken of the social facts, and especially the historical regularities and laws had to be singled out. Relying on the new science of statistics, Buckle tried a somewhat sociological approach to history, insisting on the interaction between natural factors and the intellectual evolution. By method and object, history thus was nearer to the natural sciences, and separate facts acquired a meaning and unity, subject to a rigorous determinism. Unfortunately, hurrying to build the new science of history, Buckle often resorted to rash generalizations, inventing laws and determinisms based on isolated examples. The result is sometimes amazing and caricatural—for example, his explanation of Ireland's poverty through the potato cultivation or that of the Italians' and Spaniards' artistic inclinations through the frequency of earthquakes and volcanic eruptions. His work created a sensation in the world of historians and stirred lively debates. Most of them rejected his system. Isolated in his epoch, as one of the very few representatives of the historiographic positivism oriented by Comte, Buckle remains a fascinating and often interesting historian, for all his extravagance. Whereas he failed to build "a science of history," he did anticipate the decline of the event-centered history and the sociological analysis of the facts of civilization, in the sense of a quantitative history included.

Bibliography: A. W. Huth, *Life and Writings of H. T. Buckle* (1880); J. M. Robertson, *Buckle and His Critics* (1895).

Lucian Boia

BURY, John Bagnell (Monaghan, 1861–Rome, 1927), British historian. Author of a work impressive for its size and diversity, which contains books on classic history and philology, Byzantine history, and the theory and philosophy of history. Bury's major works on the history of Byzantium, a field in which he excelled, are: *A History of the Later Roman Empire from Arcadius to Irene (A.D. 395 to A.D. 800)*, 2 vols. (1889); *A History of the Eastern Roman Empire from the Fall of Irene to the Accession of Basil II (A.D. 802–867)*, (1912), and the outstanding edition of Edward Gibbon's masterpiece, *The History of the Decline and Fall of the Roman Empire*, 7 vols., (1896–1900). His works on the theory and philosophy of history are: *A History of Freedom of Thought* (1914); *The Idea of Progress* (1920); and *Selected Essays*, ed. H. Temperley (1930). "No 'Byzantine empire' ever began to exist; the Roman Empire did not come to an end until 1453." This is the opening line of the "Later Roman Empire" where Bury champions the thesis that the Roman Empire continued uninterrupted until 1453. Hence, the word "Byzantine" from the "Byzantine Empire" or "Byzantine civilization" is misleading and denies the continuity of the Roman world to the end of the Middle Ages. Likewise, the use of the terms "Eastern Roman Empire" and "Western Roman Empire" for the period after 395 is arbitrary and does not take into account the Romans' political conception of power. It is only after Charles the Great (A.D. 800) acceded to the imperial throne that two Roman empires appeared, which justifies the use of the term "Eastern Roman Empire" after the year 800. Questionable as this thesis may be, for it considers the Roman political idea exclusively and disregards the originality of the inner Byzantine structures vis-à-vis the Roman ones, his Byzantine "History" is a complex and modern ground-breaking work. An admirer of Barthold Niebuhr (q.v.) and of Leopold von Ranke (q.v.), Bury believed that erudition alone was not enough for a historian: "a systematic and minute method" in the analysis of sources was a requisite for the progress of historical sciences. Educated at the school of classic philology, Bury early advocated the autonomy of historical science which should impose its own norms. But once this status of self-reliant science was established, history must join the other human sciences because "history cannot be isolated . . . from the total complex of human knowledge; and human knowledge has no value out of relation to human life." For the same reasons history could not be a mere chronicle of political events. For Bury, as he practiced it in his own work, "the concrete history of a society is the collective history of all its various activities, all the manifestations of its intellectual, emotional and material life."

Bibliography: Norman H. Baynes, *A Bibliography of the Works of J. B. Bury* (Cambridge, 1929); J. B. Bury, *Selected Essays*, ed. Harold Temperley (Cambridge, 1930).

Stelian Brezeanu

BUTTERFIELD, (Sir) Herbert (Keighley, 1900–Sawston, 1979), British historian. Educated at Peterhouse, Cambridge, of which he was fellow (1923–55) and master (1955–1968). Regius professor of modern history at Cambridge (1963–1968). Butterfield's historical interests were unusually wide, and his books (nearly twenty altogether) range from *The Historical Novel* (1924) to *The Peace–Tactics of Napoleon* (1929), and from *The Statecraft of Machiavelli* (1940) to *Origins of Modern Science* and *George III, Lord North and the People* (both 1949). Butterfield is best known for his brief, brilliant, irreverent critique of what he called *The Whig Interpretation of History* (1931), the interpretation being defined as the tendency "to praise revolutions provided they have been successful" and "to produce a story which is the ratification if not the glorification of the present." By contrast, *The Englishman and His History* (1944) defended the Whig interpretation as "a product of the English tradition," and suggested that those who wish to drive it out, "perhaps in the misguided austerity of youth," will find the alternative worse, while *George III and the Historians* criticized Sir Lewis Namier (q.v.) and "structural analysis" and defended narrative. The history of historiography was one of Butterfield's main interests; his many contributions to the field, which was still neglected in Britain in his day, include *Man on his Past* (1955), which concentrates on Leopold von Ranke, (q.v.) and Lord Acton (q.v.) and the posthumously published *The Origins of History* (1981), which focuses on the ancient Near East. A fervent Methodist, Butterfield was much concerned with the history of the Christian religion and the Christian interpretation of history; *Christianity and History* (1949) is the best known of his many discussions of the subject. An inspiring teacher, he left his mark on a generation of Cambridge historians, from H. G. Koenigsberger to J. G. A. Pocock.

Bibliography: J. Derry, "Herbert Butterfield," in J. Cannon, ed., *The Historian at Work* (London, 1980), Ch. 11; R. W. K. Hinton, "Bibliography of Sir Herbert Butterfield's Writings," in J. H. Elliott and H. G. Koenigsberger, eds., *The Diversity of History* (London, 1970), Ch. 11.

Peter Burke

CARLYLE, Thomas (Ecclefechan in Annandale, Scotland, 1795–London, 1881), British historian. An irritable, volcanic secular prophet who denounced the materialism, utilitarianism, and cant of midnineteenth-century British society, Carlyle believed that history revealed the operations of the divine will. Educated in Scottish schools and Edinburgh University and by his voracious reading, he first supported himself by schoolmastering and private tutoring before becoming a free-lance writer in London. His forte was biography. Thinking that in each person there is a struggle between divine order and infernal chaos, he believed that the biographer must see into this spiritual struggle and vividly present it so that the reader sees it, too. Since society is the aggregate of many individual lives, history is essentially innumerable biographies, and the story of a people becomes their epic struggle to bring divine order out of chaos. "Universal History, the history of what man has accomplished in the world is at the bottom of the history of the Great Men," heroes who conquered their personal spiritual crises and then led their people to conquer theirs (*On Heroes, Hero-Worship, and the Heroic in History*, p. 1). After a brief *Life of Friedrich Schiller* (1825), which attracted little attention, Carlyle published three master works: *The French Revolution: A History*, 3 vols. (1837), *Oliver Cromwell's Letters and Speeches, with Elucidations*, 4 vols. (1845), and *History of Frederick II of Prussia, Called Frederick the Great*, 8 vols. (1858–1865), which established his reputation as one of the outstanding historians of his generation. In addition, six public lectures on *Heroes, Hero-Worship, and the Heroic in History* (1841) elaborated and illustrated his theory of history. To achieve his ideal of empathic vision into the depths of a personality involved in a major historical episode, he read widely in the available printed sources, meditated profoundly to reach a central insight, and invented stylistic innovations to awaken in the reader the excitement of being there. His *Cromwell* rehabilitated the Puritan hero by transforming him in the popular mind from an impostor and hypocrite into a practical man of action who earnestly sought to do God's Will. The battles in Carlyle's *Frederick* were studied for years in the Prussian Army staff school, and his discussions still hold up. His *French Revolution*, with its powerful portraits and scenes and its apocalyptic style that harmonizes with apocalyptic events, can still be read with profit. The Revolution was exaltation, in hope and terror. Its dominant texture was turbulence—and the search for stability and legitimate order. But in our analytic age "scientific" historians have dissected, dessicated, and homogenized the Revolution. They have killed it and then embalmed it in academic prose. If the Story is Truth, and Truth is the Story, Carlyle's dramatic tale may be more essentially true than an intellectual analysis.

Bibliography: Alfred Cobban, "Carlyle's 'French' Revolution," *History* 48 (1963): 306–316; Hevda Ben-Israel, *English Historians on the French Revolution* (Cambridge, 1968), pp. 125–127; James Anthony Froude, *Thomas Carlyle: A History of the First Forty Years of His Life, 1795–1835* (London, 1882); James Anthony Froude, *Thomas Carlyle: A History of His Life in London, 1834–1881* (New York, 1884).

Harold T. Parker

CARR, Edward Hallett (London, 1892–Cambridge, 1982), British historian. Educated at Cambridge, Carr entered the Foreign Office in 1917. A member of the British delegation to the Paris Peace Conference, he served in Riga (1925–1929) and at the League of Nations in Geneva (1930–1933). While still a diplomat, he wrote four biographies which established his reputation as an original and scholarly author: *Dostoevsky* (1931), *The Romantic Exiles* (1933), *Karl Marx: A Study in Fanaticism* (1934), and *Michael Bakunin* (1937). In 1936 he became professor of international politics at the University College of Wales. In works such as *International Relations Since the Peace Treaties* (1937), *The Twenty Years Crisis, 1919–1939* (1939), *Conditions of Peace* (1942), *Nationalism and After* (1945), and *German–Soviet Relations Between the Two World Wars* (1951), he pioneered the realistic approach to the analysis of international relations, rejecting the prevailing idealism and utopianism in academic study of the subject. His radical critique of orthodoxy was also reflected in *The Soviet Impact on the Western World* (1946) and *The New Society* (1951). As assistant editor of *The Times* from 1941 to 1946, Carr was a strong advocate of lasting cooperation with the USSR. In 1944 he decided to write the history of the Russian Revolution, and to this task he devoted most of the remaining years of his life. From 1955, working again in Cambridge, he produced fourteen volumes of *A History of Soviet Russia* (1950–1978) (two written jointly with R. W. Davies), covering the period 1917–1929, together with his final book *The Twilight of Comintern: 1930–1935* (1982). This meticulous and critical analysis of the emergence of new political and economic institutions, the changing relationship between the Communist party and Soviet society, and the origins of Stalin's revolution from above transformed the study of early Soviet history. Probably his most widely read work is *What Is History?* (1961). Rejecting traditional views of historical objectivity as illusory and attacking the empiricist approach to history, he argued for recognition of the relativity of historical knowledge and the need to set events in the context of broad historical patterns. But as throughout his work, realism was combined with a certain utopianism. For Carr, history was ultimately progressive; and an understanding of the past could provide insights into a future he viewed with optimism.

Bibliography: R. W. Davies, "Edward Hallett Carr 1892–1982," *Proceedings of the British Academy* (1983): 473–511; R. W. Davies, "From E. H. Carr's Files: Notes Towards a Second Edition of *What Is History?*," in E. H. Carr, *What Is History?*, ed. R. W. Davies (1986), pp. xvii–xlvi; Tamara Deutscher, "E. H. Carr: A Personal Memoir," *New Left Review*, no. 137 (January–February 1983): 78–86; Walter Lacqueur, *The Fate of the Revolution: Interpretations of Soviet History* (1967), Ch. 6; Kenneth W. Thompson, *Masters of International Thought* (1980), Part II, Ch. 1.

John Barber

CHILDE, V. Gordon (Sydney, 1892–Katoomba, the Blue Mountains, Australia, 1957), English pre- and protohistorian. Professor at the University of Edinburgh (1927) and at the University of London (1945), head of the Institute of Archaeology, University of London (1946–1956). An outstanding personality in European and world prehistory, Childe exercised an enormous influence on all of archaeological research because of his comprehensive vision, his capacity for synthesis, and especially his innovating spirit. In all his books, he promoted the generally accepted definition of "archaeological culture" as a set of tools, weapons, jewels, spiritual traditions, and habitat, linked together by an internal connection and joined in a well-determined way of life, in a well-determined region, each civilization or culture distinguishing itself from the others either by the typology of its constituent elements or by the statistical proportion of those elements (*Piecing Together the Past,* 1956). Childe introduced a series of concepts that remain valuable: (1) the concept of "Neolithic revolution," from his *The Dawn of European Civilization* (1925, 1927, 1939, 1947), an idea he reiterated in subsequent works: *The Most Ancient East: The Oriental Prelude to European Prehistory* (1928), *New Light on the Most Ancient East* (1934, 1935, 1952), *What Happened in History* (1942, 1943, 1946), *The Prehistory of European Society* (1958); (2) the concept of an "urban revolution": "The Urban Revolution," *The Town Planning Review* 21 (1951); and writings mentioned above. He supported the "diffusion-of-culture" thesis and the idea that European society had benefited by contact (either diffusion or migration) with the Near East: "The Orient and Europe," *AJA* 44 (1939). Contamination of European Neolithic cultures resulted, he argued, from the appearance of groups of migrant agriculturists and shepherds, while the introduction of metallurgy in the Balkan–Aegean and European space was a result of diffusion. Others argued from evidence in certain regions (the northern Balkans, the lower Danube) for autonomous development. But Childe's hypotheses in other areas have often been confirmed by modern research, for example, the role played by Troy and Northwest Anatolia in circulating forms of civilization from the East. His opinions regarding the possible homeland of the Aryans (*The Aryans: A Study of Indo-European Origins*, 1926), as well as arguments he made to combat certain unscientific or racist theses regarding their Asiatic, Central European, or North European origin, are still valid. Rejecting theories of social growth based on linear evolutionism, the notion that all human societies have evolved along parallel lines and gone through the same stages, as well as the Vienna school's historico–cultural principles, he nevertheless accepted the idea of an uninterrupted progress of humankind as dependent on constant interchange of values and innovations.

Bibliography: "Contributions to Professor V. G. Childe in Honour of His Sixtieth Birthday," *Proceedings, Prehistoric Society*, 21 (1955): 295–304, which discuss his contributions, 1915–1956; Jan Filip, *Encyklopädisches Handbuch für Ur-und Frühgeschichte Europas* (Prague, 1966), p. 226; G. R. Tigger, "If Childe Were Alive Today," *Bulletin of the Institute of Archaeology*, University of London, 19 (1982); G. R. Tigger, *V. Gordon Childe: Revolutions in Archaeology* (London, 1980).

Ligia Bârzu

COLLINGWOOD, Robin George (Cartmel Fel, Lancashire, 1889–Coniston, Lancashire, 1943), British historian and philosopher. Until he was thirteen, Collingwood was educated by his father, William G. Collingwood, a talented painter and archaeologist who was John Ruskin's secretary and biographer and became professor of fine art at Reading College. After leaving home, young Collingwood went to a preparatory school, to Rugby, and to University College, Oxford. Upon graduation in 1912, he was elected to a tutorial fellowship at Pembroke College, where he taught both philosophy and history until 1934, when he was appointed Wayne Fleete professor of metaphysical philosophy with a fellowship at Magdalen College. He gained international repute as a historian of Roman Britain, a philosopher of history, and a professional philosopher of metaphysics. In each field his views were, and still are, acute, stimulating, and controversial. Perhaps his most substantial work was as a historian of Roman Britain. At an early age, he was introduced by his father to archaeology, by digging in the ruins of a Roman fort. He continued for years his excavations into Roman remains in northern England, publishing nearly one hundred articles on his discoveries. He also wrote three larger works: *Roman Britain* (1923), a brilliant synthesis; *The Archaeology of Roman Britain* (1930), a very useful summary of archaeological knowledge to that date; and the chapters on Roman Britain in volume 1 of the Oxford History of England, *Roman Britain and the English Settlements* (1936). In addition, for the ongoing publication of every inscription surviving from Roman Britain, he contributed a sensitive, delicate, meticulous drawing of each inscription (see Collingwood and R. P. Wright, *The Roman Inscriptions of Britain*, vol. 1 [1965]). He thus participated, ably and inspirationally, in the professionalization of British archaeology, thereby rescuing it from the curiosity antiquarianism of earlier centuries. Though brilliant, his own work in archaeology and history was occasionally flawed by a tendency to push the evidence too hard, to make it yield more than it could support.

Reflecting philosophically on his practice as a working historian led Collingwood to share in the international historiographical revolt against the simplistic,
representational, correspondence theories of history that were mistakenly identified with Leopold von Ranke (q.v.). Collingwood, for example, recognized
kindred spirits in Benedetto Croce (q.v.) and Michael Oakeshott and would have
welcomed Carl Lotus Becker (q.v.). Collingwood's contribution to the revolt
was individually his own. With a subtlety not always understood or appreciated
by his critics and certainly impossible to represent here, he argued that the
historian finds out about "actions of human beings that have been done in the
past"; that action includes thought which the historian knows by reenacting it;
and that thought includes emotions, motives, acts of the will, and the like.
Collingwood's subtle elaboration in his *Autobiography* (1939) and *The Idea of
History* (1946) of this type of historical investigation added, and still adds, much
to our understanding of how a practicing historian *may* proceed. But by his
crusading, fanatical assertion that it was the only legitimate way, he dogmatically
excluded several equally valid procedures for discovering historical truth. There
are many mansions in the historian's multiverse. Collingwood's philosophy of
history was an integral part of a comprehensive metaphysical philosophy that
does not lie within the province of this article.

Bibliography: R. B. McCallum, T. M. Knox, and I. A. Richmond, "Robin George
Collingwood," *Proceedings of the British Academy* 19 (1944): 462–485; Louis O. Mink,
Mind, History and Dialectic. The Philosophy of R. G. Collingwood (Bloomington, Ind.,
1969).

Harold T. Parker

EVANS, (Sir) Arthur John (Nash Mills, Hemel Hempstead, 1851–Boar's Hill,
Oxford, 1941), English archaeologist. Evans inherited a passion for antiquities
from his father, Sir John Evans of the Dickinson paper-making firm, himself a
founder of prehistoric archaeology. At school at Harrow he excelled in classical
and modern languages, and was still a history student at Brasenose when he
published his first paper in the *Numismatic Chronicle* (n.s. 11, 1871). After
Oxford he spent a year at Göttingen and in extensive travels developed a partisan
interest in the South Slavs. His letters of this time to the *Manchester Guardian*
were republished as *Through Bosnia and Hersegovina . . .* (1876) and *Illyrian
Letters* (1878). In 1878 he married Margaret Freeman, daughter of the historian
Edward Augustus Freeman and lived for six years at Ragusa (Dubrovnik) studying local languages and antiquities and promoting freedom for South Slavs.
During the Crivoscian insurrection of 1882, he was arrested by the Austrians
and eventually expelled. In 1884 he was appointed keeper of the Ashmolean
Museum, which he transformed from an outmoded cabinet of curiosities into a
modern archaeological and art-historical museum. When Freeman died, Evans
edited and completed Volume 4 of his *History of Sicily*. Though not professedly
a historian and "hitherto content with the humbler walks of antiquity" a *Times*
reviewer held that Evans showed greater insight than Freeman himself. After

his wife's death in 1893, Evans turned his studious attention to Crete, which Schliemann and others regarded as a possible source for Mycenaean civilization. He believed it was the home of a prehistoric pictographic script which he had observed on engraved gems and Mycenaean pots. In Crete he collected many further examples, and, by 1894, published in the *Journal of Hellenic Studies* 14, an article on "Primitive pictographs and a Prae-Phoenician script . . ." With the liberation of Crete in 1899, he began a long series of excavations at Knossos (*Annual of the British School at Athens*, 8–14, 1901–1908). Besides several stages of writing, from pictographic through Linear A to the Linear B used in an archive of hundreds of clay tablets, he revealed a palatial complex spanning two millennia of an unknown Bronze Age civilization preceding and inspiring the Mycenaean. The picture was expanded by Italian, French, and British excavations elsewhere in Crete. After 1906 the inheritance of the Dickinson and Evans fortunes enabled him to devote himself without stint to exploring, preserving, and interpreting this newfound "Minoan" civilization. He devised for it a chronology of Early, Middle, and Late corresponding with the Old, Middle, and New Kingdoms of Egypt, contacts which provided a dating framework. Despite perceptive analysis, the scripts defied decipherment. The Linear A documents were published in *Scripta Minoa* I (1909), but the more numerous Linear B not until after his death (J. N. L. Myres, *Scripta Minoa* II, 1952). Evans' fuller interpretation of Knossos and the Minoan world appeared in the monumental *Palace of Minos* (4 vols. in 6, 1921–1935; index volume by Joan Evans, 1936). Evans was a fellow of the Royal Society from 1901, a founding member of the British Academy in 1902, and, during World War I, president of both the Society of Antiquaries and the British Association. He was knighted in 1911.

Bibliography: *Obituary Notices of Fellows of the Royal Society*, vol. 3 (1939–1941), pp. 941–968, by J. N. L. Myres; Joan Evans, *Time and Chance, the Story of Arthur Evans and His Forebears* (1943).

Frank H. Stubbings

FINLEY, (Sir) Moses I. (New York, 1912–Cambridge, 1986), British historian. Professor at Columbia (1933–1942) and Rutgers (1948–1952) universities and Cambridge University (Jesus College, 1955, and Darwin College, 1971). During his lifetime, Finley was considered "the best historian of the Greek societies," according to the Italian historian Arnaldo Momigliano, and he remains one of the most innovative investigators of the Greek world, especially in the socioeconomic realm. *The World of Odysseus* (1954) is the book that brought him to international recognition, making evident his original point of view on pre-archaic Greek society. Using several concepts taken from social and cultural anthropology, Finley was able to recognize in the background of the text of the *Odyssey* a society in which the *oikos* (household) has the main role and function. "The authoritarian house-hold, the oikos, was the centre around which life was organized, from which flowed not only the satisfaction of material needs including security, but ethical norms and values, duties, obligations and responsibilities and relations with the gods.'' This particular structure, as well as some other phenomena, including the gift exchange as well as their importance in the system of social and personal relations determined by it, the ambiguous status of women, the nature of the homeric royalty, the type of kinship, the importance held by some characters' heroization in the epoch's ideology and the elaboration of some real or fictive genealogies, led Finley to separate this world from the projected world of the *Iliad* and from the Greek archaic societies. This type of investigation, in which the ethnographical comparison—or at least the suggestions provoked by the ethnographical realities—are sustained by a subtle criticism of the epic text, make Finley a unique historian of the Greek "Dark Age." On the other hand, the criticism of the texts, the subtle analyses especially of some juridic sources (lows and *horoi*), allowed Finley a precise understanding of the landed property in the Greek world, mainly in classical Athens. He also defined in a very clear way the concepts of slavery and freedom and their function in Graeco-Roman society, as well as the essence of the intermediate strati between slavery and freedom—*Studies in Land and Credit in Ancient Athens, 500–200 B.C. The Horoi Inscriptions* (1952) and also the studies in *Economy and Society in Ancient Greece* (1981) and *Ancient Slavery and Modern Ideology* (1980). Finley's integrating, holistic, historical vision has endowed with a unique quality the analyses of the ways of interrelating economical, social, political, and ideological phenomena, the study of institutions, of access to power, of the systems of manipulating public opinion, and his outline of the ancient democracy—for example, his contribution on Spartan studies in *Economy and Society in Ancient Greece*, but mainly *Politics in the Ancient World* (1983) and *Democracy, Ancient and Modern* (1973). The subtle way in which he elucidates the formation of the myths and legends, their function in the Homeric society and their importance as historical sources, evident in *The World of Odysseus*, is also at the core of *Myth, Memory, History and Theory* (1965).

Finley's contribution to the progress of historiography by critical analyses of some historians of the ancient world—''Slavery and Historian,'' *Social History* 12 (1979); ''Generalization in the Writing of History'' in *The Use and Abuse of History* (1975), ''Max Weber and the Greek City-State'' in *Ancient History. Evidence and Models*, (1985)—to the defining of the historical science itself, by the more refined methods he stands for, and by clearer definition of the relations between history and related sciences or with the exact sciences, remains fundamental. With regard to this side of his activity, it is interesting to note that, although many anthropological currents and modern sociology influenced his study of ancient phenomena, Finley remained faithful to the traditional methods, mainly to the complex, multilateral, and subtle analyses of the texts, accepting the use of nonmathematical models only as a partial solution—mostly in the sense of Max Weber's (q.v.) *idealtype* (in his last work, *Ancient History. Evidence and Models*). He is rather reticent toward the mathematical models in history; Finley's lingering doubt about the value of the tradition as a historical source, in spite of the prestige brought to him by *The World of Odysseus*, is rather unusual and must be the result of a deep meditation on his own field of research. He also became quite diffident about the actual utility of the dialogue between history and anthropology for the progress of science, and about the possibility archaeology itself offers for reconstructing the whole image of a given epoch.

Bibliography: M. de Sanctis, "Moses I. Finley, Note pe una biografia intellectuale," Quaderni dei Storia 10 (1979): 3; François Hartog, "Entretien avec Moses I. Finley," in *Mythe, Mémoire, Histoire* (Paris, 1981), p. 253; Brent D. Shaw and Richard P. Saller, Introduction to *Économie et Société en Grèce ancienne* (Paris, 1984), p. 7 and the bibliography, p. 304; P. Vidal-Naquet, "Économie et société dans la Grèce Ancienne: l'oeuvre de Moses I. Finley," *Archives européennes de sociologie* 6 (1965): 111.

Ligia Bârzu

FREEMAN, Edward Augustus (Harborne, near Birmingham, England, 1823– Alicante, Spain, March 16, 1892), British historian. Educated at Trinity College, Oxford University, Freeman held a fellowship there until his marriage in 1847; he returned to Oxford in 1884 as Regius professor of modern history, a post he held until his death. He was the son of a well-to-do Birmingham family, and his independent income enabled him to devote his formidable energies to the writing of history and to prolific publication. During the decade 1860–1869, for example, "he began and wrote contemporaneously at least four major works, besides turning out nearly five hundred full-dress reviews and over three hundred shorter articles for the *Saturday Review* and other periodicals, and delivering numerous papers to learned societies" (Cronne, pp. 83–84). Within the limits of what he called Aryan culture, his range was extensive—from Homeric Greece to the federal constitution of Bismarck's German Empire—and his sense of historical continuity was strong. Although he was primarily a political historian, his first book was a *History of Architecture* (1849), he pioneered in the application of geography and topography in *The Historical Geography of Europe* (1881), and his charming historical essays on individual English towns in *English Towns and Districts* (1883) manifested a keen interest in the varied life of the people. His magnum opus was *A History of the Norman Conquest of England* (1867– 1879) in six volumes, followed in 1892 by two supplementary volumes on *The Reign of William Rufus and the Accession of Henry I* and by a brief life of *William the Conqueror* (1888). At his death he was engaged in a massive *History of Sicily* (1891–1892), which remained incomplete at three volumes. In his manual for historians, *Methods of Historical Study* (1886), and in his historical essays he said all the right things—go to the best primary sources, treat them warily, compare them carefully, and be self-conscious of your own biases. But his own work was flawed by his speed of execution, his strong partisan biases in favor of "democratic" Anglo-Saxon England and its champion Harold, and his runaway myth-making imagination, which led him to create an epic battle of Hastings that never existed except in his pages. The central thrust of his major thesis of the continuity of Anglo-Saxon institutions through the Norman Conquest has received some support from later scholarship, but every one of his detailed assertions has had to be checked for accuracy.

Bibliography: H. A. Cronne, "Edward Augustus Freeman, 1823–1892," *History*, n.s., 28 (1943): 78–92; J. H. Round, *Feudal England* (London, 1895).

Harold T. Parker

FROUDE, James Anthony (Dartington, Devon, April 23, 1818–Salcombe, Devon, October 20, 1894), British historian. Educated at Oriel College, Oxford University, Froude momentarily fell under the spell of John Henry Newman, professed Anglo-Catholicism, and accepted a fellowship at Exeter College. However, a spiritual crisis of faith forced his resignation in 1849 and led him to try free-lance writing in London. There he became a friend and disciple of Thomas Carlyle (q.v.) and turned to the writing of history. His twelve-volume *History of England from the Fall of Wolsey to the Defeat of the Armada* (1856–1870) immediately attracted marked attention, both favorable and adverse. His concept of the historian's task, as expressed in two essays, "The Science of History" (1864) and "Scientific Method Applied to History" (c. 1870), owed much to Carlyle. "Mankind are but an aggregate of individuals—History is but the record of individual action." The historian, like Shakespeare of the historical plays, should be true to nature, and the nature of human events is inherently dramatic. Froude chose for his magnum opus the period of the English Reformation, which was filled with high drama. His research into individual actions took him not only to contemporary printed chronicles and records, but also to thousands of manuscripts in the Public Record Office, the British Museum, and the archival repositories of Brussels, Simancas, Paris, and Vienna. The information, much of it new, was woven into a sustained narrative of epic structure, proportion, and pace. Its prose, at once supple and elegant, never drags, and in the great dramatic scenes, as in the executions of Thomas More, Thomas Cranmer, and Mary Queen of Scots, it reaches heights of pictorial power and truthfulness unsurpassed in the writing of any other nineteenth-century British historian. The book immediately captivated the reading public and had a sale nearly equal to the histories of Thomas Babington Macaulay (q.v.) and John Richard Green (q.v.). It was also vigorously attacked by William Stubbs (q.v.), Edward A. Freeman (q.v.), and other professional historians for its strong, distorting Protestant bias, its treatment of the break from the papacy as essentially a political decision, and its personal judgments—the portrayal of Henry VIII as a high-minded hero concerned with the safety of the commonwealth, of Mary Queen of Scots as "a bad woman," and of a vacillating Elizabeth whose lasting achievements were the work of her advisers, Burghley and Walsingham. Froude was also criticized for his carelessness in the handling of primary evidence: Apparently, he could not be counted on to copy, read, or paraphrase a source without error. His later works, the anticlerical and anti-Irish *England in Ireland in the Eighteenth Century* (1872–1874), his four-volume biography of Carlyle (1882, 1884), and the brief *Divorce of Catharine of Aragon* (1891) possessed the same virtues and defects as his masterwork. Today his books are read less as history than as enthralling literature. Publicly, he bore the attacks on him with quiet dignity, his only retort being to have inscribed on his tombstone Regius Professor of Modern History at Oxford. He had succeeded Freeman for two years, from 1892 until his death.

Bibliography: F. Smith Fossner, *Tudor History and the Historians* (New York, 1970); Frederic Harrison, "The Historical Method of J. A. Froude," *The Nineteenth Century* (1898), vol. 44, pp. 373–385; Beatrice Reynolds, "James Anthony Froude," in Herman Ausubel, *Some Modern Historians of Britain* (New York, 1951), pp. 49–65.

Harold T. Parker

GARDINER, Alan Henderson (Eltham, England, 1879–Oxford, 1963), English Egyptologist and historian. The leading twentieth-century British scholar in his field. Gardiner had inherited wealth and never held a permanent university position, but he was prominent in international Egyptology. His chief training was in Berlin, where he lived from 1902 to 1911. Thereafter, he worked in London from 1911 to 1945, and in Oxford until his death. He was primarily a philologist and grammarian, and edited a wide range of major Egyptian literary, legal, and religious texts. In the 1930s and 1940s he published many documents of the Ramessid period (c. 1300–1075 B.C.), achieving new insights into administration and taxation, as well as enhancing knowledge of land tenure and agriculture (especially in *The Wilbour Papyrus*, 4 vols., 1941–1952). His chief historical work is the semipopular *Egypt of the Pharaohs* (1961), for which he published numerous preparatory studies in the *Journal of Egyptian Archaeology* in the 1950s, and the standard edition of the Egyptian king list, *The Royal Canon of Turin* (1959). *Egypt of the Pharaohs* was the most thorough and sober Egyptian history of its time, and retains considerable value. Gardiner's philological orientation is visible is his very full exploitation of texts, of which many are cited at length. An idea of wider significance was his proposal that the Semitic, and hence the Western, alphabet was derived from an adaptation of some Egyptian hieroglyphs to write a Semitic language in Sinai in the mid-second millennium B.C. (*Journal of Egyptian Archaeology*, 3 [1916]: 1–16). This continues to be controversial, but the origin of the alphabet in Egyptian hieroglyphs is generally accepted; the Sinai script may be one of several early forms.

Bibliography: Sir Alan Gardiner, *My Working Years* (privately printed, 1962); Warren R. Dawson and E. P. Uphill, *Who Was Who in Egyptology*, 2d ed. (London, 1972), pp. 111–12; R. O. Faulkner, "Bibliography of Sir Alan Henderson Gardiner," *Journal of Egyptian Archaeology* 35 (1949): 1–12; Gardiner's papers are in the Griffith Institute, Ashmolean Museum, Oxford.

John Baines

GARDINER, Samuel Rawson (Ropley, Hampshire, 1829–Sevenoaks, 1902). British historian. Descended from Oliver Cromwell; educated at Winchester College and Christ Church, Oxford (B.A., 1851); married a daughter of Henry Irving (1856) and became a deacon in the Irvingite Church. In about 1856,

Gardiner settled into his life-work which was to study anew the course and causes of the English "Puritan" revolution, beginning with its distant origins in the reign of James I. His first publications were several articles in *Notes and Queries* and an edition of parliamentary debates for 1610 for the Camden Society (1860), which signaled his intent to write his history from a painstaking and exhaustive examination of all the original documents. In 1863 appeared two volumes entitled *A History of England from the Accession of James I to the Disgrace of Chief-Justice Coke*, the first installment of a detailed narrative that was meant to extend eventually to 1630. It was not a great success, but it was followed in due course by two additional volumes taking the story from 1616 to 1624 (1869) and then two more to 1628 (1875). Gardiner supported himself modestly by teaching at various institutions in the London area and only slowly did he gain a reputation. Between 1877 and 1882 he issued two further pairs of volumes on the reign of Charles I (1628–1642), which began to draw praise, and then he revised the whole ten to acclaim in 1883–1884 as a *A History of England from the Accession of James I to the Outbreak of the Civil War 1603–42*. Now he was rewarded with a government pension and a fellowship at All Souls College (1884). He became a founding member and frequent contributor to the *English Historical Review* (1886) and was its editor from 1891 to 1901. He continued to hold various posts in London University but turned down an offer to become Regius professor at Oxford in 1894 in order to continue his great work. His lectures were popular, and one series delivered at Oxford was published as *Cromwell's Place in History* (1896). Between 1886 and 1891, he issued three more volumes of his narrative, *A History of the Great Civil War 1642–49* (revised 1893), and between 1894 and 1901, another three, *A History of the Commonwealth and Protectorate*, interrupted by his death and completed by his student, C. H. Firth. Gardiner wrote entirely from the sources, exploiting foreign archives as well as private collections; throughout his career he continued to edit documents, a dozen volumes for the Camden Society, two for the Naval Records Society, and one for the Scottish Historical Society. He also wrote many articles, contributed frequent reviews to the *Revue Historique* and *The English Historical Review*, and composed two important monographs: one on the Gunpowder Plot (1897) and the other a biography of Cromwell (1899). He also wrote many school texts, including *Constitutional Documents of the Puritan Revolution* (1889), which long remained standard. Gardiner insisted on working within the strict limits of chronology, reading no document out of its temporal place and trying to avoid all prejudice and hindsight.

Since Roland Usher's attack in 1916, he has been consistently criticized, most recently as an example of the "Whig interpretation" of history. Nevertheless, Gardiner's history has stood the test of time perhaps better than any of his contemporaries, and it is hard to think of another English history that can match it for length, detail, and objectivity. Gardiner was not a stylist, content as Firth has said to be "the most trustworthy of nineteenth-century historians," and every student still depends on his work.

Bibliography: C. H. Firth, "Samuel Rawson Gardiner," *Dictionary of National Biography*, 2d suppl., 1901–1910 (Oxford, 1912), pp. 75–78; Erling M. Hunt, "Samuel
Rawson Gardiner," *Some Modern Historians of Britain*, eds. Herman Ausubel, J. B.
Brebner, and Erling M. Hunt (New York, 1951), pp. 99–110; W. A. Shaw, *A Bibliography of the Historical Works of Creighton, Stubbs, Gardiner and Acton* (London,
1903); Roland G. Usher, *A Critical Study of the Historical Method of Samuel Rawson
Gardiner*, Washington University Studies, III, pt. 2 (St. Louis, 1915).

Joseph M. Levine

GREEN, John Richard (Oxford, 1837–Mentone, France, 1883), British historian. Born in Oxford, Green was fascinated from youth by its surviving antiquities and the testimony they offered of the vigorous life of its people in earlier
centuries. Even as an undergraduate at Jesus College, Oxford University, he
wrote lively sketches that evoked that life. As a vicar from 1860 in an impov-
erished East End parish in London, he came to know the life of the people at
first hand. In 1862 he conceived the project of writing not another "drum and
trumpet history" of England but a history of its people. Told in 1869 that
tuberculosis left him only six months to live, he wrote in five years his classic,
nine-hundred page *A Short History of the English People* (1874). He announced
in the preface: "The aim of the following work is defined by its title; it is a
history, not of English Kings or English Conquests, but of the English People."
The aim dictated a new periodization, not by dynasties and reigns, but by epoch
and topics important to the history of the nation. The concept also governed the
selection of what was to be narrated. "I have preferred to pass lightly and briefly
over the details of foreign wars and diplomacies, the personal adventures of
kings and nobles, the pomp of courts, or the intrigues of favourites, and to dwell
at length on the incidents of that constitutional, intellectual, and social advance
in which we read the history of the nation itself." As Green knew, this concept
of social history was not new, but the sweep of his account, his powerful historical
imagination, and his rich pictorial style extinguished all competition. As a history
of the people it spoke to the people, and the book had a phenomenal sale, nearly
equal to that of Thomas Babington Macaulay's (q.v.) *History*. Nevertheless, it
was not without error. His liberal and democratic sympathies biased his account.
He adopted the prevailing emphasis on the Germanic origins of the English
constitution, and he shared the contemporary thesis that the Parliament of the
fourteenth century was virtually identical with that of the seventeenth. In later
amplifications of his theme, he published a four-volume *History of the English
People* (1880), which corrected inaccuracies of the *Short History*, and two specialized studies, *The Making of England* (1883) and *The Conquest of England*
(1883), which closed in 1066. In the last two he applied his intimate knowledge
of the English countryside (he was a great walker) to the explanation of historical
events, for example, to the routes taken by the Anglo-Saxon invaders. He thus
pioneered in the application of geography and topography to history.

Bibliography: James Bryce, *Studies in Contemporary Biography* (New York, 1903);
Alice Green, "Introduction," in *A Short History of the English People* (London, 1888);

Robert Schuyler, "John Richard Green and His *Short History*," *Political Science Quarterly*, 64 (1949): 321–354.

Harold T. Parker

GROTE, George (Beckenham, 1794–London, 1871), British historian, politician, and banker. Educated at Charterhouse, Grote entered his father's banking business at the age of sixteen. From the time of his early association with the Utilitarians, notably Jeremy Bentham and James Mill, he advocated radical causes; he was active in setting up London University and strove to free it from all connection with religion. From 1832 to 1841 he was a member of Parliament, where as a leader of the "philosophic radicals" he campaigned for the ballot. He was, in the highest sense of the word, an amateur historian. His studies of Plato and Aristotle were of considerable importance, but his greatest achievement is his *History of Greece* (1846–1856). This is marked above all by narrative clarity and independence of judgment. His praise of Athenian democracy was in conscious opposition to the toryism of William Mitford's Greek history; his open–mindedness and radical sympathies are especially evident in his sympathetic treatment of the demagogue Cleon and of Socrates' opponents, the Sophists. Unlike most British scholars, he supported F. A. Wolf's view that the Homeric epics were of multiple authorship. Despite never visiting Greece, he brought out the importance of landscape and geography in the development of a nation's history. Although he was essentially a Utilitarian, his picture of the rise and fall of Greek civilization, centered on Athens, is somewhat whiggish in character: The history ends with Alexander, and he underestimated the achievements of the Hellenistic age in science, scholarship, and the diffusion of Greek culture. His powers of analyzing tangled source material are well shown in his lucid account of the midfourth century. In its time his was the finest Greek history in any language, and though outdated by more recent archaeological and inscriptional evidence, it remains the most distinguished ever written in English.

Bibliography: M. L. Clarke, *George Grote* (1962); A. D. Momigliano, *Studies in Historiography* (1966), Ch. 3, "George Grote and the Study of Greek History"; G. C. Robertson in the *Dictionary of National Biography*, "S. V. Grote"; F. M. Turner, *The Greek Heritage in Victorian Britain* (1981).

Richard Jenkyns

HALLAM, Henry (Windsor, England, 1777–Penshurst, Kent, 1859), British historian. Educated at Eton and Christ Church, Oxford University, Hallam practiced law until a sinecure appointment in the British government and then his father's death in 1812 gave him the independent means and leisure to devote himself to the study of history. In three decades he produced three major works, each of which required ten years of preparation: *A View of the State of Europe During the Middle Ages* (1818), *The Constitutional History of England from the Accession of Henry VII to the Death of George II* (1827), and *An Introduction to the Literature of Europe During the Fifteenth, Sixteenth and Seventeenth*

Centuries (1837–1839). Each book set new and higher standards of historical scholarship in its field. Each was marked by industrious research in original printed sources and secondary authorities, judicious and balanced statement, and breadth of perspective. His first book, on the thousand years from Clovis (466–511) to the invasion of Naples by Charles VIII of France (1495), was the first extensive history of the Middle Ages in English, and it remained the standard account for his generation. After tracing, chapter by chapter, the "civil revolutions" and developing "political institutions" of France, Italy, Germany, Spain, the ecclesiastical power, and England, he concluded with a remarkable survey of "the State of Society in Europe during the Middle Ages." As early as 1818 he not only proclaimed "the new history" of the twentieth century, but he wrote it. It was the duty of the historian, he remarked, to bring the lessons of the past before the eyes of humankind. This could be done only by presenting the subject "under numerous relations." While he shared the contemporary bias against the ignorance and poverty of the early medieval centuries, he recognized and fully described the progress after the tenth century in agriculture, commerce, crafts, learning, literature, subsistence, and even farmhouse architecture. Likewise, his *Constitutional History of England* was eminently fair. A conservative Whig who believed in liberty and the balanced British constitution but opposed the parliamentary reform of 1832, he opposed the Tory history of David Hume but tried to be fair to all sides. He tried, for example, to understand Charles I, and he condemned the "excesses" of the Long Parliament after 1641. His work set a new standard of impartiality in constitutional history. Similarly, his last book was an extraordinary performance: half-century by half-century, he traced the history of European classical studies, poetry, drama, and speculative, moral, and political philosophy from Poggio Bracciolini to John Locke. During his lifetime Hallam's scholarly reputation justifiably stood very high. But now he is forgotten: his vast learning has been superseded by later research, and his grave, measured prose, which lacks the elegance of Hume and the sparkle of Thomas Babington Macaulay (q.v.), numbs the mind.

Bibliography: J. R. Hale, *The Evolution of British Historiography* (London, 1967), pp. 38–40, 197–211; T. P. Peardon, *The Transition in English Historical Writing 1760–1830* (New York, 1933), pp. 207–213, 271–276; Leslie Stephen, "Henry Hallam," *Dictionary of National Biography*, vol. 8, pp. 980–982; C. C. Weston, "Henry Hallam," in Herman Ausubel, ed. *Some Modern Historians of Britain: Essays in Honor of R. L. Schuyler* (New York, 1951), pp. 20–34.

Harold T. Parker

MACAULAY, Thomas Babington (Rothley Temple, Leicestershire, 1800– Campden Hill, Kensington, 1859), British historian. An outstanding narrative historian who thought of history as a branch of literature, Macaulay was educated at home and at Cambridge University. He practiced law for a time, but it was his brilliant literary and historical essays in the *Edinburgh Review* that won him appointment to a seat in the House of Commons. His superb oratory in support of the Reform Bill of 1832 opened preferment to public office. He served as secretary-at-war and paymaster general. As member of the Supreme Council of India he prepared the influential first draft of its penal code. He thus knew from firsthand experience the realities of legislative and party machinations, as well as the routine and maneuvers of the bureaucratic service—an admirable preparation for the type of historian he became. In 1838 he decided to write a multivolume history of England from the Revolution of 1688 to the death of George III in 1820. With tremendous energy he set to work, reading memoirs, newspapers, pamphlets, private and public archives, and traveling to locations of battles and sieges. He lived only to complete four volumes, covering the reigns of James II and William III (1685–1702). They form the substantial and eloquent fragment on which his reputation as a historian exists. His conception of the ideal history, expressed in two youthful essays, "History" (1828) and "Hallam's Constitutional History" (1828), was shaped by early reading of the great historians of Western culture from Herodotus. Thucydides, he thought, was supreme in the art of a narrative that imaginatively involved the reader in unique events as they unrolled; Tacitus excelled in the delineation of the individuality of each historical character; modern historians, such as Henry Hallam (q.v.), surpassed the ancients in their thoughtful explanation of the deeper relations among historical conditions. The ideal modern historian must fuse the imaginative, pictorial power to resurrect the living past that Walter Scott possessed with the reasoned interpretation of Hallam. He will combine the story of courts, cabinets, parliaments, and military campaigns with the history of the people, their manners and foibles, their sentiments and thoughts, and the profounder movements of their society. He will do this in a style that captivates and holds in thrall the educated reader.

To a remarkable degree, Macaulay's four-volume *History of England from the Accession of James the Second* (1848, 1855) approximated his ideal. After two chapters sketching the history of England to 1685, his celebrated cross-sectional third chapter of social history, "State of England in 1685," surpassed all previous attempts of this kind by Herodotus, David Hume, and Edward Gibbon. His ensuing political and military narrative still enthralls. Years in Parliament had ingrained in him the anxieties and habits of an orator: His eye is always on the audience, the imagined reader; every sentence as it unrolls is immediately clear, every pictorial image is immediately transparent. To be sure, there are blemishes: More ample research has modified and occasionally reversed his judgments; he was critical in the handling of evidence but not always critical enough; his personal biases (for example, anti-James II and anti-Marlborough and pro-William III) warped his narrative; he lacked insight into the deeper recesses of his historical characters; and his delight in material progress, his blatant optimism, and his patriotic pride in English material and constitutional accomplishments when midnineteenth-century England was riding high seem now so naive as to be almost inoffensive. Still, the book fascinates, especially when it is read as it is written, that is, when it is read aloud.

Bibliography: Wilbur C. Abbott, "Thomas Babington Macaulay: Historian," *Adventures in Reputation* (Cambridge, Mass., 1935), pp. 3–27; Andrew Browning, "Lord Macaulay, 1800–59," *Historical Journal* (1959): 149–160; John Clive, *Macaulay: The Shaping of the Historian* (New York, 1973); Charles Firth, *A Commentary on Macaulay's History of England* (London and Liverpool, 1938); Robert Livingston Schuyler, "Macaulay and His History—A Hundred Years After," *Political Science Quarterly* 63 (1948): 161–193.

Harold T. Parker

MAITLAND, Frederic William (London, 1850–Las Palmas, 1906), British historian. Educated at Eton and Trinity College, Cambridge, lawyer, and then Downing professor of the laws of England at Cambridge University. Maitland's historical writing was undertaken over a relatively short period of twenty-two years, during the last sixteen of which he suffered increasing ill health. Yet for many he is the greatest of British historians. As a legal writer he stands with Glanvil, Coke, and Blackstone, and as an authority within the discipline he has the stature and continuing vitality of Max Weber (q.v.), Alexis de Tocqueville (q.v.), Malthus, or Darwin within their respective sciences. His genius manifested itself in several major ways. He took as his central theme the single most important area of English history, the legal system, and within this domain he concentrated on the most difficult and important aspects: property, process, and tenure. He mapped out the world of medieval English law in an entirely new way; the map he provided is still the one we use today, with only minor details altered. He created a vision of an orderly, centralized, and sophisticated system of integrated royal power from a very early period in England. He brought central features of this unique system into sharp relief by his comparative approach. His linguistic ability and deep knowledge of continental Roman law enabled him to see the peculiar characteristics of the English legal and governmental system with an unparalleled clarity. This comparative perspective was combined with a subtle theoretical understanding. He was able to overcome the problems of combining change and continuity, enduring structures and steady growth. Maitland fused the evolutionary vision of the later nineteenth century with the newer analytic and functional traditions of the twentieth century. Thus, he showed both the origins and development of the legal and political system of England, and the interconnections of this system with social, religious, and intellectual changes. He was able to do this convincingly only because of his technical genius. Throughout his work he maintained that balance between general theory and a deep immersion in documentary sources which Marc Bloch (q.v.) was later to advocate. Indeed, Maitland could be seen as the model of everything that Bloch was to recommend in *The Historian's Craft*. Maitland mastered the extraordinarily voluminous and difficult sources of medieval law and government for the first time; he made them available through his own editions and by encouraging others, particularly through the Selden Society which he founded. Finally, his genius was expressed in his brilliant style. He makes the driest and most arcane subjects interesting through his vivacity, humor, charm, and clarity. To read his work has been likened to going on a country walk with an erudite, witty, and sympathetic guide. He explains directly and simply the new world of medieval society which he has uncovered.

The specific theories which he advanced and which altered our conception of the past are as follows: the importance of the twelfth and thirteenth centuries in laying the foundations of settled government and the common law in England; the central place of forms of action and the system of tenure in medieval society; a new analysis of Anglo–Saxon society achieved by working back from the known to the unknown; the real nature of medieval Parliaments as courts rather than political assemblies; the influence of canon law on the medieval English church. These and many current orthodoxies were first outlined by Maitland. But more importantly, he provides a wider vision. Through his energy, his intuition, and his gift of going straight to the center of problems and of deeply understanding his sources, he provided a total picture of the early roots of the first industrial nation which is still true and which still guides and overshadows us. He outlined what the problems should be, and he provided persuasive answers to many of them. He is the ancestor from whom the technical, objective, document–soaked history of the twentieth century is descended and he is still the greatest exponent of this approach. There are, of course, some revisions of emphasis to his work. For instance, his argument that England nearly accepted Roman law in the sixteenth century is an exaggeration. Or again, some argue that the world of equal citizenship and centralized national government which he rightly described for the thirteenth century was newer than he thought. Yet, in an almost unrivalled quantity of published materials, he never wrote a dull sentence and very seldom did he make a mistake. His masterly vision of a medieval England that had strong continuities with later periods, a view that stands as a bulwark against the invented revolutions of twentieth-century historians and sociologists, is enshrined in several million published words. Just to enumerate these would fill up this article. The *Dictionary of National Biography* lists twenty-four volumes that Maitland either wrote, or provided lengthy introductions for and edited. The most important of these is the nearly 1,400 pages on *The History of English Law* (1895); although published as "Pollock and Maitland," in fact all but one chapter was written by Maitland. Among his edited works the edition of *Bracton's Notebook* (3 vols., 1887) is worth singling out among many volumes. He also wrote numerous articles, most of which have been published in three volumes as *The Collected Papers of Frederic William Maitland* (1911), edited by H. A. L. Fisher.

Bibliography: H. E. Bell, *Maitland: A Critical Examination and Assessment* (1965); G. R. Elton, *F. W. Maitland* (1985); C. H. S. Fifoot, *Frederic William Maitland* (1971); S. F. C. Milsom, "F. W. Maitland," *Proceedings of the British Academy* 66 (1982): 265–81.

Alan Macfarlane

NAMIER, (Sir) Lewis Bernstein (Wola Okrzejska, 1888–London, 1960), English historian. Born Ludwik Niemirowski, the son of a Polish-Jewish landowner. Came to Britain in 1906. Studied at Balliol College, Oxford, 1908–1911, and became interested in Parliament in the eighteenth century. During World War I he started research on Europe in the nineteenth century and in the intervals worked for the Foreign Office. These two subjects remained his main preoccupations for the rest of his life. After the war he supported himself in business until he was appointed to a chair at the University of Manchester, where he remained from 1931 until his retirement in 1953. Namier made his reputation with two books, *The Structure of Politics at the Accession of George III* (1929) and *England in the Age of the American Revolution* (1930). Based on the Newcastle and Hardwicke papers in the British Museum, these books argued that in the later eighteenth century "politics still bore a local character to a remarkable degree," and that earlier interpretations which stressed the importance of the Whig and Tory parties were fundamentally mistaken. His later projects were never completed. His lectures on the role of the King, the Cabinet, and the Parliament were never made ready for publication; his biography of the eighteenth-century politician Charles Townshend and his history of Europe 1812–1918 were never written, and he did not live to see the completion of the history of Parliament from 1754 to 1790 on which he spent much of his last years. What he did produce was a flow of incisive, penetrating, and endlessly quotable essays on English and European history, most of them collected in *Avenues of History* (1952), *Personalities and Powers* (1955), and *Vanished Supremacies* (1958). Another trilogy of essays dealt with diplomatic history between the wars; *Diplomatic Prelude* (1948), *Europe in Decay* (1950), and *In the Nazi Era* (1952). However, to see Namier at his most conservative, at his most cynical, and at his most brilliant, one should turn to his wide-ranging *1848: The Revolution of the Intellectuals* (1946). Despite his belief in Zionism, he was certainly no enthusiast for national sovereignty. Nor did he care much for equality or democracy, though his nostalgia for the old regime was tempered by awareness of its weaknesses; his political position was not distant from that of Alexis de Tocqueville (q.v.) and Edmund Burke. Namier has been accused (by Sir Herbert Butterfield, q.v., among others), of taking the ideas out of political history, and of reducing it to a struggle for power in which faction and family count but principles do not. He was certainly too much an admirer of Freud and Pareto to take ideas at their face value. Although the work of his followers (the 'Namierites') fell into some disrepute in Britain in the 1960s, current work on the social history of politics owes more to his example than some of its authors might be prepared to admit.

Bibliography: J. Namier, *Lewis Namier: A Biography* (London, 1971); J. Brooke, "Namier," in *Dictionary of National Biography*; J. Cannon, "Namier," in *The Historian at Work*, ed. J. Cannon (London, 1980).

Peter Burke

NEALE, John Ernest (Liverpool, 1890–Beaconsfield, Bucks., 1975), British historian. Working his way up from a poor background, Neale came to London in 1910 with a hard–won degree of the University of Liverpool, to work under Albert Frederick Pollard (q.v.) whom he succeeded as the leading Tudor historian of his day. After a professorship at Manchester (1925–1927), he followed Pollard as Astor professor of English history at University College, London, remaining there until he retired in 1956. He was elected a fellow of the British Academy in 1949 and knighted in 1955. During his tenure he ruled the London School of History, and in his retirement he dominated the History of Parliament Trust, engaged in producing biographies of members of the English House of Commons from the fourteenth century onward. For Neale had chosen from the first to devote himself to the history of the Elizabethan Parliament and practically never stepped outside the years 1558–1603. The product of these intensive researches appeared toward the end of his career: *The Elizabethan House of Commons* (1949), and *Elizabeth I and her Parliaments* (2 vols., 1953, 1957). However, long before this he had established his fame with his biography of *Queen Elizabeth* (1934), translated into several languages and regularly reprinted. This striking commercial success clearly altered his approach to the writing of history. His excessive admiration for the queen also found expression in occasional pieces, collected as *Essays in Elizabethan History* (1958). Although he was too self-centered to be a really good teacher, his London seminar attracted students from all over the world and formed an important scholarly center. A conventional nationalist, Neale believed the English Parliament was the finest flower of human constitutional development. As a writer he cultivated effect and could deteriorate into pawkiness. In his work he overemphasized the role of the House of Commons and of alleged religious dissenters sitting there. Although all the more striking aspects of his interpretation were soon shown to rest on preconceived notions rather than scholarship, he assisted in an important deepening of the social analysis of the Elizabethan Age.

Bibliography: G. R. Elton, "Parliament in the Sixteenth Century," *Historical Journal*, no. 2 (1970): 255–278; Joel Hurstfield, "John Ernest Neale," *Proceedings of the British Academy* 63 (1977): 403–421; J. P. Kenyon, *The History Men* (1983), pp. 206–209.

G. R. Elton

PETRIE, (Sir) William Matthew Flinders (London, 1853–Jerusalem, 1942), British historian, archaeologist, and Egyptologist. One of the founders of systematic archaeology. Petrie first worked in Egypt surveying the Giza pyramids in 1880, excavating thereafter most winters until 1924. In 1926–1938 he excavated in Palestine. In 1892 he was appointed professor of Egyptology at University College, London, in a newly created and endowed department; this now houses his enormous collection of Egyptian antiquities. He published over one hundred books (many with joint authors), the majority being excavation reports, but including numerous general studies and a *History of Egypt* (6 vols., various editions, 1894–1927; vols. 4–6 by other authors). His chief contributions were in setting standards of recording and of attention to the entire archaeological record, and in establishing typological sequences for Egypt from prehistoric to Roman times. The geographical range of his work included almost all of the country. He discovered and ordered the chief periods of predynastic Egypt, from Amratian/Naqada I to Gerzean/Naqada II, as well as re-excavating the royal tombs of the first and second Egyptian dynasties at Abydos and producing a proper sequence and identification of the material culture of the time. His "Sequence Dating" of predynastic and very early dynastic finds, applied in the 1890s to material from Naqada, was an outstanding achievement in achieving a close typological seriation of prehistoric material by the use of statistical techniques, among the earliest applications of statistics in archaeology. Little in his interpretations of Egyptian history is now retained, but his integration of archaeology and prehistory with history is of fundamental importance and lasting influence.

Bibliography: W.M.F. Petrie, *Seventy Years in Archaeology* (London, 1931); Margaret S. Drower, *Flinders Petrie: a Life in Archaeology* (London, 1985); Eric P. Uphill, "A Bibliography of William Matthew Flinders Petrie," *Journal of Near Eastern Studies* 31, (1972); 356–379. Documentary material in University College London, Department of Egyptology, and Griffith Institute, Ashmolean Museum, Oxford.

John Baines

POLLARD, Albert Frederick (Ryde, I.O.W., 1869–Milford-on-Sea, 1948), British historian. In 1891 Pollard graduated with first-class honors from Jesus College, Oxford, and in 1894 he married; thereafter he lived as an historian who found relaxation solely with his family. From 1893 to 1902 he worked for the *Dictionary of National Biography*, writing some five hundred entries, and for the rest of his days his approach to history remained essentially biographical. In 1903 he obtained an unpaid professorship at University College, London, which was properly established only in 1907. Until his retirement in 1931 he remained in this position from which he dominated the London history school which he had first created, virtually singlehandedly. In the 1920s he several times tried in vain for election to Parliament as a member for his university, standing as the old–fashioned, Asquithian liberal he was. Thus, he came to employ his political and organizational gifts solely in the service of historical studies. At London, he set up the Institute of Historical Research (1921) as a center for advanced studies in England generally, and he presided for seventeen years over this highly successful creation. In 1906 he helped to found the Historical Association, which was open to everybody interested in the subject, and for six years he edited its journal, *History*. In 1920 he was elected a fellow of the British Academy. All his serious writing attended to English history in the sixteenth century: *England under Protector Somerset* (1900), *Henry VIII* (1902), *Thomas Cranmer and the English Reformation* (1904), *Factors in Modern History* (1907), *The History of England from the Accession of Edward VI to the Death of Elizabeth* (1913), and *Wolsey* (1929). The exception—*The Evolution* *of Parliament* (1920)—displayed an overconfidence in his grasp of history outside that period which the result did not justify. A formidable and relentless man, he lived by the standards of his Methodist ancestors and shaped his history to the pattern set in the nineteenth century by liberal views on progress and constitutional development. His insularity could at times become plain chauvinism. Although he knew little of manuscripts and archives, he had an excellent grasp of printed sources, including calendars of manuscripts. An exceptional memory, a penetrating intelligence, and a gift for writing powerful but controlled prose maintained his ascendancy over Tudor studies for some forty years, but the elderly roots and the narrow limits of his vision caused his work to became dated rapidly thereafter.

Bibliography: V. H. Galbraith, "Albert Frederick Pollard," *Proceedings of the British Academy* 35 (1949): 257–264; J. H. Hexter, " 'Factors in Modern History,' " *Reappraisals in History* (1961): 26–44; J. P. Kenyon, *The History Men* (1983), pp. 196–198, 202–206.

G. R. Elton

POSTAN, Michael Moissey (Tighina, 1899–Cambridge, 1981), British economic historian. Born in Russia, Postan came to England in 1919 and graduated from the London School of Economics in 1924. After research and teaching posts in London, he moved to Cambridge University in 1935 and was professor of economic history there from 1938 to 1965, exercising a decisive influence on the development of his subject both in and beyond Cambridge. His standing as a scholar was recognized by the conferment of a knighthood in 1980. His influence, grounded in his outstanding gifts as a teacher, was given much wider scope by his long editorship of *The Economic History Review* from 1934 to 1960, a journal he did much to turn into one of the most important in its field, and by his part in the international community of economic historians. (He was one of the founders and the first president of the International Economic History Association.) As a scholar one of his contributions was to provide economic history with a more precise identity, and some of his main reflections on this and allied questions are collected in *Fact and Relevance: Essays on Historical Method* (1971). His premise was that economic history indeed belongs with the social sciences, for it concentrates on those aspects of the past that are the concern of social scientists. On the other hand, among the social sciences, it has the specific characteristic that, unlike economics or sociology, for example, it does not deal with general situations reached by means of "accumulated abstraction" but with particular situations in all their complexity and comprehensible only in terms particular to that situation. Postan applied these theoretical ideas in an exceptional variety of specific investigations in which his mastery of the particular was demonstrated. Some were in modern and contemporary history, where his publications included *British War Production* (1952), and *The Economic History of Western Europe, 1945–1964* (1967); but medieval history provided his main fields of research. His earliest inquiries (begun in postgraduate study under the direction of Eileen Power) were into the history of European trade. Their results are perhaps best represented by the chapter on the trade of Northern Europe in *The Cambridge Economic History of Europe*, vol. 2 (1952) and are collected in his *Medieval Trade and Finance* (1973). Increasingly, however, Postan's main interests were focused on medieval agrarian history. His principal conclusions were again set out in a chapter in *The Cambridge Economic History of Europe* (vol. 1, 2d ed., 1966) on the rural economy and society of medieval England. Much of the detailed work underlying this statement is collected in his *Essays on Medieval Agriculture and General Problems of the Medieval Economy* (1973). These studies of trade and agriculture, in turn, led Postan to question views about the economic chronology of the Middle Ages which had been inherited from the nineteenth century and were still current when he began his work. In place of notions that assumed that these centuries witnessed unilinear progress and, in economic terms, a "continuous ascent," Postan argued for the view that they were characterized by successive ebbs and flows of economic activity, and in particular for a late medieval period of contraction following on thirteenth century expansion. In this respect, in particular, he provided a framework for much of the contemporary discussion of the medieval economy.

Bibliography: T. C. Barker, "The Beginnings of the Economic History Society," *Economic History Review*, no. 1 (1977): 1–19; M. W. Flynn and P. Mathias, "Professor Sir Michael Moissey Postan, 1899–1981," *Economic History Review*, no. 1 (1982): iv–vi; Edward Miller, "Michael Moissey Postan, 1899–1981," *Proceedings of the British Academy* (1983): 543–557.

E. Miller

STUBBS, William (Knaresborough, England, 1825–Cuddesdon, 1901), British historian. Bishop, successively, of Chester and Oxford. F. W. Maitland (q.v.) remarked of Stubbs that "no other Englishman has so completely displayed to the world the whole business of the historian from the winning of the raw material to the narrating and generalising." After receiving an excellent public school and Oxford education, Stubbs became an Anglican country parson in the village of Navestock in 1850. While diligently performing his duties to his small flock, he dedicated his leisure time to the discovery, scrutiny, and mastery of the sources of medieval English history. At first he published little, but his vast learning was known to a few discerning friends, notably Edward Augustus Freeman (q.v.) and John Richard Green (q.v.). In 1866 he was named Regius professor of modern history at Oxford University, where he remained until his elevation to the bishopric of Chester in 1884. In 1863 he began the editorship of a succession of medieval chronicles of the Rolls Series. During the next twenty-five years his consummate editing of nineteen volumes of text and his historical introductions gained him an international reputation as one of the most distinguished editors in the historical profession. In 1870 he published *Select Charters of English Constitutional History from the Earliest Times to the Reign of Edward the First*. Intended as both a reference work and a manual to be used in schools by teachers and students, this collection of sources (in medieval Latin!) and its accompanying interpretive discourse became a model for similar instructional aids.

From 1874 to 1878 Stubbs published in three volumes his narrative and generalizing masterwork, *The Constitutional History of England in Its Origin and Development* (to 1485). Its mastery and mobilization of detail to support theses congenial to the mentality of his readers made the book the historical orthodoxy of his generation. However, it soon ran into trouble. Although Stubbs preached that the historian must try to view the historical situation as his historical characters perceived it, his own reading of the sources was apparently affected by the triumph of representative government and Parliament in the nineteenth century. From Tacitus' *Germania* to the Tudors, he made representation and later the growth of Parliament the central theme of medieval constitutional history. Within two decades, however, studies of points of detail led an international band of scholars (F. W. Maitland [q.v.], J. H. Round, L. Riess, D. Pasquet, Charles Howard McIlwain [q.v.], H. G. Richardson, and G. O. Sayles, for example) to question several statements of fact and finally to accomplish a Copernican revolution in interpretation: The crown, not Parliament, was the center of medieval constitutional history. McIlwain later noted that here was an instance where historical scholars were falsifying the presentist, relativist hypothesis. While the crown's influence was declining during the nineteenth and twentieth centuries, its importance was rising in revisionist historical accounts of earlier times. Recently, on several points of detail there have been revised revisionist views in favor of Stubbs. Out of this ongoing controversy, whose parameters Stubbs had set, there is emerging a core of scholarly agreement that is "beyond the play of wind and weather" (Herbert Butterfield).

Bibliography: James Cornford, "Editor's Introduction" [to Stubbs' *Constitutional History*] (Chicago, 1979); Helen Cam, "Stubbs Seventy Years After," *Cambridge Historical Journal* 9 (1948): 129–147; F. W. Maitland, "William Stubbs, Bishop of Oxford," *English Historical Review* 63 (1901): 417–426; Geoffrey Templeman, "The History of Parliament to 1400 in the Light of Modern Research," *University of Birmingham Journal* 1 (1948): 202–231; T. F. Tout, "William Stubbs," *Dictionary of National Biography*, supplement 1 (1901–1911), pp. 444–451.

Harold T. Parker

TAWNEY, Richard Henry (Calcutta, India, 1880–London, 1962), British historian. Son of the principal of Presidency College in Calcutta, Tawney was sent to Rugby and then as a classical scholar to Balliol College, Oxford. His decisive experiences came in the ten years after his graduation in 1903. Always the Christian moralist, he lived for a time in Toynbee Hall, a social settlement house in London, became involved in the Worker Education Association, and until World War I taught tutorial classes in economic and social history to workingmen in the Manchester area and formulated a non-Marxist version of democratic Christian socialism that he urged on the Independent Labor party. After the war, he became identified with the London School of Economics, where he lectured on economic history from 1920, became a reader in 1923, and served as a professor from 1931 to 1949.

As a historian, Tawney broke with the grand literary tradition of Thomas Babington Macaulay (q.v.), James Anthony Froude (q.v.) and George Macaulay Trevelyan (q.v.). They told a story of unique events, usually a pictorial narrative of political happenings in a single country, enshrined in an eloquent, patterned style of balanced epigram and antithesis. In contrast, Tawney proceeded not by sequences of unique events but by the consideration of historical problems whose solution he developed in terms of an analytical, interrelated narrative of social, economic, ideological, and political conditions, in which his mind interplayed allusively across centuries, nations, and civilizations in an abundant prophetic prose whose rich suggestiveness still fires the imagination. He chose historical problems that had meaning for him as a reforming Christian moralist and socialist. Thus, in a decade when Edwardian England was considering agrarian reform to restore the viability of the small farmer and when Tawney's tutorial classes of workingmen needed relevant reading in economic history, he prepared for them *The Agrarian Problem in the Sixteenth Century* (1912). In it he described the changes in England's rural organization from 1485 to 1642, when the routine of subsistence farming was beginning to give way to capitalist production for the market and when the traditional open-field agriculture of the medieval village was yielding to the more profitable economy of enclosure. For him the interest of this history lay in the social attitudes of groups who were resisting capitalist encroachment, the role of the government and its law courts, and the ideas of social justice the changes spawned, ideas (he thought) were still of value for his time. Similarly, when in the twentieth century the English were asking once again whether Christian morality had anything to say about sharp business practice, Tawney published his *Religion and the Rise of Capitalism* (1926) to describe how the changing "attitude of religious thought in England towards social organization and economic issues" during and after the Reformation had created the breach between Christian ethical theory and business. From this history he resurrected the idea of social obligation. Likewise, in the 1930s the rise of fascism and Nazism stimulated him to study the relation of changing property distribution to changing political structure. Specifically, he tackled the problem of why from 1558 to 1640 political leadership in Parliament passed from the great magnates to the substantial gentry. In a stunning, controversial article, "The Rise of the Gentry" (*The Economic History Review* 2 [1941]: 1–37), he attributed the shift to the declining wealth of the magnates and the increasing substance of the gentry. "Scientific" economic historians deplored his lack of objectivity, his "misuse" of history for social purposes, his judgmental stance toward historical characters, and his inexperienced, even careless, handling of evidence. Nevertheless, his research, provocative theses, and creative genius stimulated them to investigate the problems he had opened up and to revise his provisional solutions.

Bibliography: J. H. Hexter, "Storm Over the Gentry," in *Reappaisals in History* (Evanston, Ill., 1961); J. M. Winter, "Tawney the Historian," in J. M. Winter, ed., *History and Society: Essays by R. H. Tawney* (1978), pp. 1–40.

Harold T. Parker

TOYNBEE, Arnold Joseph (London, 1889–London, 1975), British historian. After a classical education at Winchester and Balliol College Oxford, Toynbee became professor of Greek history at the University of London (1919–1924), before moving to the Royal Institute of International Affairs, where he remained for thirty-three years (1924–1956), pursuing a double career in contemporary international relations and in history, and writing more than twenty books besides the one for which he is most famous, *A Study of History* (1934–1961). This vast work, in thirteen volumes, dealt with the rise ("growth") and fall ("distintegration") of the twenty-six (or later, thirty) "civilizations" into which he divided world history. Apart from its almost incredible sweep, what is most immediately impressive about the study is its assault on ethnocentrism, from the introduction on the "Relativity of Historical Thought" to the treatment of Western civilization as one among many. Toynbee had a remarkable gift for intuitive generalization and for the creation of new concepts. Among the most important of these concepts was "Challenge-and-Response" (developed in reaction to any geographical determinism); "Withdrawal-and-Return" (a recurrent pattern in the life of a religious or political leader, from St. Paul to Lenin); and "Internal" and "External Proletariat," groups, respectively, within and beyond the borders of a particular state but opposed to its ruling class or "Dominant Minority." In the last case, the origins of Toynbee's concepts in the history of the late Roman Empire are particularly obvious; his "Heroic Ages," "Universal States," and "Universal Churches" also seem to have originated with this period in mind. There is a sense in which Toynbee was, quite consciously, the Edward Gibbon of the twentieth century, though his own brand of agnosticism was more sympathetic to religion and became increasingly so under the influence of Jung. Toynbee's study was greeted at first with a kind of awe, succeeded by a wave of criticism as the specialists discovered his many inaccuracies in their particular fields. The author was not dismayed by the criticism of such scholars as Lucien Febvre (q.v.), Pieter Geyl (q.v.), Georges Lefebvre (q.v.), William McNeill, Lewis Mumford, Oskar Spate, or Hugh Trevor-Roper (let alone the angry reaction of Jews to his description of Judaism as a "fossil"). Toynbee was open-minded to a fault, and so his reaction was to incorporate the criticisms—and even some contributions by the critics, notably Martin Wight—into the later volumes of the study, though without changing his basic framework. In any case, it might be argued that the greatest weakness of Toynbee's work lay not in any specific inaccuracy or even in the author's lack of interest in science and technology, but in his unsophisticated conceptual apparatus. He made a not uncritical use of Sir James Frazer and Oswald Spengler, but made no reference to twentieth-century sociology and anthropology, from Emile Durkheim and Max Weber (q.v.) onward. Toynbee's merits—his soaring imagination and his freedom from ethnocentrism—are seen to best advantage in two minor masterpieces, *The World and the West* (1953) and *Hellenism* (1959).

Bibliography: Pieter Geyl, *Debates with Historians* (The Hague, 1955), Chs. 5–8; Roland N. Stromberg, *Arnold J. Toynbee: Historian for an Age in Crisis* (Carbondale, Ill., 1972); *Toynbee and History*, ed. Ashley Montagu (Boston, 1956).

Peter Burke

TREVELYAN, George Macaulay (Welcome, Warwickshire, 1876–Cambridge, England, 1962), British historian. Born into an upper middle-class family, Trevelyan inherited a family tradition of writing. His father, the Liberal politician Sir George Otto Trevelyan, wrote biography and history; his great-uncle was Thomas Babington Macaulay (q.v.). Proud of these literary and Whig antecedents, he later wrote: "The best that can be said of me is that I tried to keep up to date a family tradition as to the relation of history to literature" (*An Autobiography and Other Essays*, 1949). Like his father and great-uncle, he was educated at Harrow and Trinity College, Cambridge, where he remained for ten years, having earned a fellowship for a thesis published as *England in the Age of Wycliffe* (1899). The period was important, he thought, because of the struggles for religious liberty against the power of the medieval church. In *England under the Stuarts* (1904), begun at Cambridge, Trevelyan first experimented with the Macaulayesque technique of describing the social history of the nation at a single moment, subsequently an important and successful feature of many of his works. He left Cambridge for London in 1903, the terms of his fellowship not being conducive to full-time writing and the intellectual atmosphere uncongenial to his ideas on history. Of the three Regius professors during his tenure, he respected Lord Acton, (q.v.) but not John Seeley, who had dismissed Macauley and Thomas Carlyle (q.v.) as "charlatans," nor John Bagnell Bury (q.v.), whose promotion of scientific history would, in Trevelyan's estimation, turn English historians into "Potsdam guards of learning" (*Clio, a Muse and Other Essays*, 1913). History was both an art and a science, Trevelyan believed, but he objected to scientific history because it addressed a professional audience that was separated from the ordinary, educated Englishman. History was essentially educational and poetic, worthy of a limpid style, and its proper audience was the "common reader of books." This public would make him wealthy and famous.

Trevelyan returned to Cambridge in triumph in 1927 to succeed Bury and was honored with the Order of Merit in 1930. Between his Cambridge sojourns he wrote biographies of John Bright (1913) and Lord Grey (1920), and four splendid works of nineteenth-century Italian history (1907, 1909, 1911, 1923), whose narrative descriptions of Garibaldi's Italian marches were enhanced by the author's thirty-mile walks over the appropriate sites. His *British History in the Nineteenth Century* (1922) and *A History of England* (1926) shaped the perceptions of several generations on their national history. In later years he concentrated on the foundations of England's greatness in his trilogy *England in the Reign of Queen Anne* (1931–1934). A biography of his Northumberland neighbor, *Grey of Fallodon* (1937), portrayed him in dual roles of statesman and naturalist. His last major work, *English Social History* (New York, 1942; London, 1944), "with the politics left out," was among his most popular but the least satisfactory to historians. In 1931 Trevelyan and others assumed that he was the target of Sir Herbert Butterfield's (q.v.) attack on Whig history. Although his literary style was often praised, later generations of historians were uncomfortable with an approach to history that recalled an earlier time when history was written by educated, leisured gentlemen for people very like themselves.

Bibliography: J.R.M. Butler, "Trevelyan, George Macaulay," *Dictionary of National Biography, 1961–1970*, pp. 1015–1017; G. Kitson Clark, "G. M. Trevelyan as an Historian: Charm'd Magic Casements," *Durham University Journal* 55 (1962): 1–4; Joseph M. Hernon, Jr., "The Last Whig Historian and Consensus History: George Macaulay Trevelyan," *American Historical Review* 81 (1976): 66–97; Henry R. Winkler, "George Macaulay Trevelyan," in S. William Halperin, ed., *Some Twentieth Century Historians* (Chicago, 1961).

Carolyn W. White

WOOLLEY, (Sir) Charles Leonard (London, 1880–London, 1960), British historian and archaeologist. Woolley's name is connected to the discovery of the famous royal Ur tombs (*Ur-Excavations: II: The Royal Cemetery*, 1934). Centering much of his work on Ur, Woolley helped to throw light on a past epoch formerly enveloped in myth and legend. Kings, whose divine names appeared in royal lists and who were formerly believed to be mythical characters from a time "before the Flood," proved to be real historical characters. Corroborating results of his archaeological research in Ur, Kish, and Uruk, and comparing them with the Sumerian tradition, Woolley came to several conclusions whose value has been confirmed, to a great extent, by modern research: (1) that during the early dynasties, Sumerian society possessed an urban character (*Ur of the Chaldees*, 1930); (2) that the divine royal names referred to real people; and (3) that Sumerian civilization was very ancient and had played a role as forerunner of more modern civilizations (*Ur-Excavations, II–IV, II: The Royal Cemetery*, 1934, IV; *The Early Periods*, 1956; *The Sumerians*, 1928; *Digging Up the Past*, 1930). Woolley's tendency to generalize Sumer's preeminence has been criticized for losing sight of the fact that at least Egypt, if not the Indus Valley communities as well, appeared at approximately the same time. The nature of the chronology he used, long (for Mesopotamia) and short (for Egypt), accounted, among other things, for the attitude he adopted. (4) "The Flood" probably occurred, which strengthened his stress on the informative value of tradition for any historical research: "It is never wise to reject traditions off-hand; in most cases they contain a modicum of truth even if it be only as a background for fiction." Woolley was thus a pioneer, like Wilhelm Dörpfeld (q.v.) or Carl William Blegen in the delicate field of historical critique; (5) Abraham's homeland was possibly in Ur (*Abraham*, 1935). The discovery of the Ebla archives (at Tell Mardikh) completely modified the early history of the ancient Jews, suggesting a very critical borrowing of data in the Old Testament. Woolley also maintained that Cretan art and architecture were derived from direct contact with professional architects and painters from the Asiatic mainland (*A Forgotten Kingdom*, 1953; *Alalakh. An Account of the Excavations at Tell Atchana in Hatay, 1939–1949*, 1955). His novel discoveries, daring hypotheses, and intellectual and moral qualities—lucidity, patience, reverence for scientific evidence, artistic sense, imagination, and literary talent—made of Woolley one of the best known and most widely read archaeologists of the twentieth century.

Bibliography: Jan Filip, *Encyklopädisches Handbuch der Ur-und Frühgeschichte Europas*, 2 (Prague, 1966), p. 1664; "In Memory of Sir Charles Leonard Woolley, Editorial," *Iraq* 22 (1960): i–ii; M.E.L. Mallowan, "Memories of Ur," *Iraq* 23 (1960): 1–17, with bibliography, pp. 17–19; A. Parrot, "Sir Charles Leonard Woolley," *Syria* 37 (1960): 384–386.

Ligia Bârzu

Great Historians: French

ARIÈS, Philippe (Paris, 1914–Toulouse, 1984), French historian. This "Sunday historian" as Ariès dubbed himself in the charming book of memoirs he wrote at the end of his life was one of the fathers of the New History without being a member of the establishment of *Annales*, except *in extremitate*. A historian by schooling, he failed at the examination for *agrégation* and gave up the field. He joined a society trading in tropical fruit as a documentalist and, to keep in touch with scientific life, he also worked in publishing first as a proof reader (1946) and then as a director of the collection entitled "Civilisations d'hier et d'aujourd'hui" at Plon Publishers. He started to explore unknown or almost unknown fields, as, for instance, demographic history and the history of mentalities in *L'Histoire des populations françaises et de leurs attitudes devant la vie depuis le XVIIIᵉ siècle* (1948). He discovered that birth control had appeared early in human history, and he wondered about "attitudes" on life and death, an exploration that would haunt him later. In *Le Temps de l'histoire* (1954) he expressed his admiration for Marc Bloch (q.v.) and Lucien Febvre (q.v.) after a thorough analysis of "attitude toward history" in the Middle Ages and the seventeenth century. None of his books was successful in France, including *L'enfant et la vie familiale sous l'Ancien Régime* (1960), where he proves that the child, as a specific person, is a modern invention. In the United States it was a best-seller. Henceforth, Ariès acquired some prominence: the *Annales* wrote about his book in 1963. But he did not become a celebrity until the publication of his trilogy on death, *Essais sur l'histoire de la mort en Occident du moyen âge à nos jours* (1975), which gathered together his lectures at Johns Hopkins University, a vast survey, *L'Homme devant la mort* (1977), and finally, an exquisite album, *Images de l'homme devant la mort* (1983). It was only at this point that Ariès was then received in the sanctuary of the university: in 1978, at the age of sixty-four he became supervisor at the École des Hautes Études en sciences sociales. Explorer of the collective mind, historian of the socialization of the child and of death visions, Philippe Ariès is undoubtedly a pioneer. But he is also a traditionalist in some ways. This historian who harbored a nostalgia for royalty was no believer in progress: for example, he said it was easier to die in ancient times than today when so many die alone in hospitals. This demographer preferred literary and artistic sources to statistics, unique documents to series. He liked to make extrapolations because he searched for things hardly thought of, almost undecipherable.

Bibliography: Philippe Ariès, *Un historien du dimanche* (Paris 1980).

Charles-Olivier Carbonell

BERR, Henri (Lunéville, 1863–Paris, 1954), French editor, philosopher of history, and lycée professor. Entered the École Normale Supérieure in 1881 after preparation at the Lycée Charlemagne. Though a literature major, the historian Numa Denis Fustel de Coulanges (q.v.) made the greatest impression on him while at the Normale. But after he passed the *agrégation* in 1884 Berr served as professor of rhetoric at various provincial lycées until he was called to teach French literature at the Lycée Henri IV at Paris where he remained until his retirement in 1926. During his early years as a teacher in Paris he began to publish articles in the popular press critical of the reigning positivism of the university spokesman of the early Third Republic. The animosities he created in the 1890s within these circles probably explains his inability to enter the ranks of the university faculties, even though he received his doctorate at the University of Paris in philosophy in 1899. His two ambitious theses, written under the influence of the Neo-Kantian philosopher Émile Boutroux, were entitled "Gassendi est-il un sceptique?" and "l'Avenir de la philosophie: Esquisse d'une synthèse des connaissances fondée sur l'histoire." They were published in Paris that same year.

In the wake of the scholarly meetings he attended at the Paris Exposition of 1900, the young lycée professor founded the *Revue de Synthèse Historique*, hoping to provide in its pages a forum to combat the confusing growth of specialization in historical studies and the social sciences. Berr's attack on the boundaries of the nascent academic disciplines, his energetic call for a superior form of scientific organization based on a *synthèse historique*, was ignored for the most part by the French professoriat. But in the pages of the new journal there appeared a methodological debate among the leading scholars of the time, from Émile Durkheim to Karl Lamprecht (q.v.) across the Rhine. Although young historians at the École Normale Supérieure like Lucien Febvre (q.v.) and Marc Bloch (q.v.) were inspired by Berr's leadership and joined his editorial staff, by 1911 Berr himself noted in his book *La Synthèse en histoire* that the majority of his contemporaries had failed to respond to his call for a truly integrated scientific history.

During World War I Berr joined his university colleagues and produced a remarkable number of books and articles extolling the superiority of French civilization over German "tyranny." The search for a *synthèse scientifique* continued unabated after Versailles, this time a project involving one hundred volumes written for the most part by French scholars with long introductions by Berr himself. This *Évolution de l'humanité* series seconded the efforts of the *Revue de Synthèse Historique* as the foundation for the new stages of scientific scholarship to be led by the "genius" contained within the French intellect. It should be noted that both Lucien Febvre and Marc Bloch published their most important books in this series, as did leading specialists in many disciplines of the French university until Berr's death in 1954. Berr retired from his teaching post as a lycée professor in 1925, having twice failed in his candidacy for a chair for the teaching of *synthèse historique* at the Collège de France. Instead, he devoted his full energies to work as director of the Centre International de Synthèse in Paris. These efforts were supported throughout the 1920s and 1930s by grants from French banks linked to a full-blown Fondation pour la Science and handsomely housed next to the Bibliothèque Nationale in the eighteenth-century Hôtel de Nevers. Here, a small staff persisted in disseminating the vision of a *synthèse historique*, although by 1931 the name of the journal was changed simply to *Revue de Synthèse* and the themes of the regular meetings turned increasingly to the history of science and technology. Friendship with political leaders like President Paul Doumer cleared the way for grants from the Ministry of Education. Influential professors such as Abel Rey and his old friend Lucien Febvre lent their support to what in effect can be seen as a pioneering "think tank" for scientific culture in France and Europe in the 1930s. During the German occupation Berr managed to escape arrest (he had Jewish origins) by living in obscurity in the provinces, protected to some extent by his fame as a scholar and editor. Yet in 1942 he dared to publish the autobiographical *l'Hymne à la vie*, which is a noble defense of the values of humanism and the French Enlightenment. By the time of his death in 1954 at the age of ninety-one, Berr was still director at the Centre de Synthèse at the Hôtel de Nevers, a post he had had since the end of the war, and he had completed almost three quarters of the prefaces to the hundred-volume series of the *Évolution de l'humanité*. These prefaces, along with the huge corpus of methodological writings in the *Revue de Synthèse Historique*, remain a treasure house for scholars interested in the transformation of history and the social sciences in the twentieth century.

Bibliography: S. Delorme, "Henri Berr," *Osiris* 10 (1951): 5–9; M. Siegel, "Henri Berr's *Revue de Synthèse Historique*," *History and Theory* 9, no. 3 (1970): 322–334.

Martin Siegel

BLOCH, Marc (Lyon, 1886–Les Roussilles, near Lyon, 1944), French historian. The son of the outstanding specialist in Roman history, Gustave Bloch (1848–1923), Marc Bloch was lecturer (1919), then professor of medieval history at the University of Strasbourg, and, beginning in 1936, professor of economic history at the Sorbonne. After the defeat of France in 1940 (he had joined the army as a volunteer), he continued his university activities in the "free zone" at Clermont-Ferrand and at Montpellier. After this zone was occupied in 1942, he participated in the French Resistance as a leader of the Franc-Tireur group, whose headquarters was in Lyon. Discovered by the German occupying force, he was imprisoned and tortured, and finally executed on June 16, 1944. Along with Lucien Febvre (q.v.), Bloch was a promoter of research in economic and social history. In 1929 these two historians founded the important periodical, *Annales d'histoire économique et sociale*. Influenced by sociology, especially by the work of Émile Durkheim (1858–1917), Bloch attached great importance to social groupings and structures. At the same time he was preoccupied with the need for comparative history, an idea promoted by Henri Pirenne (q.v.) at the Historical Congress at Brussels in 1923 in his account *De la méthode comparative en histoire*, an idea Bloch took over and expanded.

Interested though he was in socioeconomic history and the history of institutions, he did not neglect the history of mentalities, and he tried to establish connections among these areas of study. His first important work was *Rois et serfs, un chapitre d'histoire capétienne* (1920). Next came *Les Rois thaumaturges* (1924), an outstanding and original attempt to analyze a lesser known aspect of the medieval world-view: the belief in the healing power of monarchs and the consequences, including the political ones, of these superstitions. Later, he devoted himself to the comparative study of European agrarian history, and looking at the evolution of French rural life in a large spatial and temporal context, he published *Les Caractères originaux de l'histoire rurale française* (1931). It is a fundamental work of social and economic history; the rural evolution of France is analyzed through a comparison of French regional peculiarities. Using an original method, Bloch often starts from present realities in order to deduce the phenomena of the past, the idea being that the present is a product of history ("Le passé commande le présent"). He studies the agricultural landscape and, in accordance with its diversity, formulates conclusions about economic and social history and about various types of civilizations or world-views. Everything is viewed from the perspective of the long duration of history ("la longue durée"), a characteristic concept of the new French school of history.

Bloch's final synthesis is *La Société féodale* (2 vols., 1939–1940), a work in which his erudition, overall view, and the ingeniousness of his proofs are harmoniously combined. It is in the first place a history of medieval institutions and world-views. (Bloch was also preparing a synthesis of the medieval economy, which was to have completed the picture.) The presentation at the beginning of the first volume coordinates world-view of medieval society. Though succinct, it is one of the most brilliant chapters of twentieth-century historiography. (It foreshadows Febvre's more extensive exposition in *La Religion de Rabelais*.) The work could be criticized for its very narrow definition of feudalism, which in Bloch's view covers only Western Europe, and only from the ninth to thirteenth centuries; for him, however, feudalism which he dissociates from the "seignorial system," meant not an economic structure but an institutional organization. The work is completed to a certain extent by the chapter "The Rise of Dependent Cultivation and Seignorial Institutions," which he published in the first volume of the *Cambridge Economic History of Europe* (1941). Of his works published posthumously that promised a synthesis of economic history, noteworthy are *Esquisse d'une histoire monétaire de l'Europe* (1954) and *Seigneurie française et manoir anglais* (1960); the latter tried to define two types of rural civilization, starting from a contrast between the French and English landscape. Another book that appeared posthumously is *L'Étrange défaite* (written in 1940, published in 1946), a lucid analysis of the cause of France's defeat in 1940. Finally, the unfinished work, *Apologie pour l'histoire ou Métier d'historien* (1949), is fundamental for an understanding of his general ideas. Defining history as "a science of men in time," he insisted on the connection between past and present and committed himself to a comparative world history of issues and problems. Like Febvre, he assigned special importance to psychological factors in reconstructing historical *man*. Together with Febvre, Bloch is the founder of the French "New history" and one of the most influential historians of this century.

Bibliography: A. Burguière, "Marc Bloch," in *Dictionnaire des sciences historiques* (Paris, 1986), pp. 88–91; Hartmut Atsma and André Burguière, eds., *Marc Bloch aujourd'hui. Histoire comparée et sciences sociales* (Paris, 1990).

Lucian Boia

BOUCHER DE CRÈVECOEUR DE PERTHES, Jacques (Rethel 1788– Amiens 1868), French writer and archaeologist. Founder of the study of prehistory. A prolific author, Boucher de Perthes worked in a wide variety of genres: theater, novels, moral and philosophical essays, political economy (being one of the first supporters of free trade in France), travel books (on Turkey, Greece, Denmark, Sweden, Norway, Russia, Spain, Algeria, etc.), and memoirs (*Sous dix rois, souvenirs de 1791 à 1860*, 8 vols., 1862–1867). This modest and rather picturesque provincial scholar, who lived in the small town of Abbeville in northern France and was the animator of the local *Société d'Émulation*, was the pioneer in the field of prehistorical archaeology. The prehistoric tools he found in the 1830s in the Somme valley near Abbeville allowed him in 1836–1837 to formulate the theory that humans existed long before the "flood." His conclusions are found in *Antiquités celtiques et antédiluviennes* (3 vols., 1846–1865) and in *De l'homme antédiluvien et de ses oeuvres* (1860). Although his works were initially regarded with disbelief and even irony, they became generally accepted in time (especially after a scientific inquiry in 1859 undertaken by a commission of British experts), and they opened the way for the study of humanity's most remote past. Boucher de Perthes believed in a cyclical history of humans periodically interrupted by catastrophes.

Bibliography: Patrice Boussel, "La double vie de J. Boucher de Perthes, fonctionnaire et homme d'esprit," in Boucher de Perthes, *Petit Glossaire* (Monte-Carlo, 1961), 29 p.

Lucian Boia

BOURDEAU, Louis (Rochechouart, 1842–Billière, 1900), French historian and philosopher of history. A follower of Auguste Comte (q.v.), Bourdeau attempted to achieve in his two-volume *Théorie des Sciences. Plan de science intégrale* (1882) a general classification of human knowledge from the strict viewpoint of positive science. Bourdeau, however, was not an orthodox disciple of the founder of positivist philosophy, and he developed a personal theory with regard to the logical sequence of the various sciences and their methodological approach. As an illustration of his theoretical framework, Bourdeau began writing a series of historical studies on the evolution of the "useful arts" (*Les arts utiles*). In works such as *Les forces de l'industrie* (1884) and *Conquête du monde animal* (1885), he sought to analyze the notion of material progress in relation to human evolution. But his major contribution to historiography remains his 1888 *L'Histoire et les historiens, essai critique sur l'histoire considérée comme une science positive*, which can be considered the first and apparently the only positivist manifesto on history ever written. According to Bourdeau, history as a science cannot be conceived outside the global perspective of world evolution. Since "the human realm is defined by the use of reason," history, therefore, is "the science of the development of reason" and its object must include "the universality of facts controlled by reason." This means that "wherever human beings live, wherever they exert their reason and changes occur as a result of the labors of the human specie, there lies the stuff of which history is made." Bourdeau can then issue the following call to his fellow historians: "Check out, in each different age, the movement of population, the state of public wealth, and show the causes for their increase or their decrease; discuss the changes in tastes and habits, the advancement of sciences, the betterment of manners, the history of food, of clothing, of housing." At the same time, history, according to Bourdeau, progressively evolves in a given direction; it must be impersonal and give scant importance to individual action; it is deterministic and it obeys its own laws, which, in turn, must be identified. Bourdeau's considerations in *L'Histoire et les historiens* anticipated by more than half a century the arguments presented by the French School of the *Annales* and are still relevant for many current historiographical debates. Virtually ignored in Europe when it came out, this pioneering essay ultimately exerted considerable influence on the historical works of Latin American positivism.

Bibliography: Louis Bourdeau, *L'Histoire et les historiens, essai critique sur l'histoire considérée comme une science positive* (Paris: Alcan, 1888); Charles Olivier Carbonell, *Histoire et historiens, une mutation idéologique des historiens français, 1865–1885* (Toulouse: Privat, 1976); Charles Oliver Carbonell, "L'Histoire dite positiviste en France," *Romantisme*, nos. 21–22 (Paris, 1978): 173–186; Nikita Harwich Vallenilla, "El Positivismo Venozolano y la Modernidad," in *Actas del VI Congreso Venezolano de Historia* (Caracas: Academia Nacional de la Historia, 1989).

Nikita Harwich Vallenilla

BRAUDEL, Fernand (Luméville-en-Ornois, Meuse, 1902–Saint-Gervais, Haute-Savoie, 1985), French historian. Professor in Algeria (1924–1932), in

Paris (1932–1935), at the University of São Paulo, Brazil (1935–1937), instructor in the Fourth Section of l'École Pratique des Hautes Etudes (1937–1938); co-director, then director, of the *Annales* (1946–1985); founder (1946), then president of the Sixth Section of l'École Pratique des Hautes Etudes (1956–1972); professor at the Collège de France (1949–1972); founder and administrator of the Maison des Sciences de l'Homme (1962–1985); Member of the Institute: Académie française (1984).

Fernand Braudel is an extraordinary case. How may one account for the complexity and the richness of such an unrivalled personality, born in the Meuse and nevertheless passionately fond of the Mediterranean world? Why did this patriotic native of Lorraine write *L'Identité de la France* (1986) a long time after having put on "the seven league boots" of international capitalism? Which connection, what degree of coherence can we establish between the author of a memoir about *La Paix de Vervins* written in 1922 under the direction of the very traditional Emile Bourgeois, and the great architect of "la longue durée" (the long term) on a planetary scale? In 1937 Braudel met Lucien Febvre (q.v.) who revealed to him that "everything is history—earth, climate, geological movements" and prompted him to substitute, in a kind of Copernican revolution, the Mediterranean region for King Philip the Second's moods as the main subject of his research—in short, to prefer the empire of the Venetian merchants and the Genoese bankers to the one of the Golden Age of Spain. To understand from the maritime and terrestrial point of view the "original characters" of the Mediterranean, this physical and geological entity transcending the national, religious, and linguistic frontiers; to capture in their spatio-temporal variations the different forms of human activity which animated the Mediterranean area—the unchanging material needs, the mercantile trades, the vicissitudes of battle history—Braudel made up a global methodology on this broad geographical scale, that is he split time into three levels: a silent, almost unmoving, *mineral* history, which measures man's contacts with his natural surroundings; a *social* history which scans the life of economic groups, of peasant and urban societies, of national states; finally, a rapid, noisy, *eventful* history, which ripples the surface of things. Defended in 1947 and published in 1949 as *La Méditerranée et le monde méditerranéen à l'époque de Philippe II*, this revolutionary thesis, by its *geohistorical* conception of space and time, opened to him the doors of the Collège de France, where he followed Lucien Febvre in the chair of the history of modern civilization. In his inaugural lecture on December 1, 1950, he explained his conception of the "temps de l'histoire" ("historical time is not social time with a single and simple flow, but rather social time with a thousand speed-ups and a thousand delays") and began "among historians" the great adventure of the "longue durée" to which he devoted an article henceforth famous in the *Annales* of October-December 1958. Born of the flood-tide of the social sciences and the "structuralist" wave of the 1960s, Braudel's inaugural lecture and main "theoretical" articles were collected in 1969 in the *Écrits sur l'histoire*. This pioneer interpretation achieved its scholarly culmination in 1979 in the major trilogy: *Les structures du quotidien, Les Jeux de l'échange,* and *Le Temps du Monde.* This harmonious synthesis, sketched from 1967 in a volume of the collection *Destins du monde,* proved its author qualified to adapt his fertile intuition to the universal dimensions of *Civilisation matérielle, économie et capitalisme* from the fifteenth to the eighteenth century. As in *La Méditerranée,* but on infinitely longer distances, Braudel changes by turns into a "sprinter," a long-distance runner, and a marathon racer; as in *La Méditerranée,* but on a much more imposing scale, the architect builds a three-storied house: "at the foundation, a 'material life'— multiple, self-sufficient, routine; above this, an economic life which, in our view, has a tendency to be confused with the concurrence of a market economy; finally, the last level, capitalist activity." This division, suited to his way of thinking, never hid the complexity and the richness of the real. Braudel did not refute the Marxist duality, infrastructure/superstructure, but, instead, embraced another rigid and intangible dogma: he always perceived "several societies which coexist, not a system, but systems. Everything is to be put in the plural." At the top of such a privileged observatory, Braudel could depict as an artist the deep movements of society, this "ensemble des ensembles"; he could stage the trading ballet played by the great European cities—Venice, Genoa, Antwerp— these "économies-mondes," which dominated the Mediterranean and the North Sea, and even the "villes-mondes" like Amsterdam and London. Finally, he could discern in their stability civilizations which, far from being mortal, as Paul Valéry asserted, "kept their masses still during the monotonous passage of centuries."

To effect this prodigious total weighing of the world between the end of the Middle Ages and the beginning of the Industrial Revolution, Braudel not only invented a new perception of time, but also equipped historians with the most improved research instruments, borrowed from other social sciences: he "wanted the new history to go beyond history in order to become at once geography, sociology, economics." "History itself," he admitted, arouses me "less than the associated group of human sciences." To his detractors who reproached him for his determination to transform history into an imperialist topic, he answered that, if Lucien Febvre actually "wanted to subjugate the human sciences to history . . . he should not seek to colonize them but rather to call on them in order to see through their eyes, to borrow their language and their points of view, if only for a moment, in order to enrich our understanding. . . . History, in order to be of value, ought to be incorporated . . . into other human sciences, and, for their part, the human sciences should take into consideration the historical dimension." Henri Pirenne (q.v.), Henri Hauser, Lucien Febvre (q.v.), Marc Bloch (q.v.), and Ernest Labrousse had explored the territory of this total history before him, but he drew up the first scientific maps. With the help of a marvelous team composed of the future masters of the "Nouvelle Histoire" (G. Bollême, P. Chaunu, M. Ferro, F. Furet, P. Goubert, J. Le Goff, E. Le Roy Ladurie, Robert Mandrou (q.v.), and J. P. Vernant among others), he made his corsair fleet, which became a grand fleet flying a flag: the sixth section of the École

des Hautes Études, then la Maison des Sciences de l'Homme, the *Annales* —
ready to board the "invincible armada" of the "historicizing " history, which
he forced to surrender.

This renewing of historiography, thanks to the acquisition of the social sciences, might have produced a dry, hard, hermetic, unreadable style. But nothing
of the kind is detectable in his work. To accompany Braudel along the terrestrial
and maritime roads of the sixteenth century, that is, to pass from Philip the
Second's study at the Escorial to the Venetian merchant's shop; to read over his
shoulder the Genoese banker's correspondence with his partner from Antwerp;
roam with dusty feet about the fairs and the markets from the Atlantic to the
Urals; and finally, to knock about the world aboard galleons continues to be a
pleasure. In 1976, a Fernand Braudel Center was established at the State University of New York, Binghamton. Have foreign historians conferred such a
distinguished honor on him because he was one of the few Frenchmen in the
twentieth century to possess a cosmic vision of the past and present problems?
Or rather because he was, above all, a genuine poet, a poet who could evoke
an entire civilization from the simple aromas of the kitchen?

Bibliography: "Braudel le patron de la nouvelle Histoire," *Magazine littéraire*, 212
(November 1984); and a selection of articles published on the occasion of Braudel's
reception into the Académie Française or on his death: A. Burguière, *Le Nouvel Obser-
vateur* (December 7–14, 1985); P. Chaunu, *Le Figaro* (November 29, 1985); M. Druon,
"Discours de reception à l'Académie Française" (May 30, 1985); P. Goubert, *Le Monde*
(November 30, 1985); Claude Lévi-Strauss, *Esprit* 111 (February 1986); A. Minc, *L'Ex-
pansion* (December 20, 1985–January 9, 1986); K. Pomian, *Libération* (December 4,
1985); J. P. Hexter, "Fernand Braudel and Le Monde Braudélien," *Journal of Modern
History* 44 (1972); S. Kinser, "Analyst Paradigm? The Geo-historical Structuralism of
Fernand Braudel," *American Historical Review* 86 (1981); "Braudel dans tous ses états,"
Espaces/Temps 34|35 (1986); T. Stoianovich, *French Historical Method: The Annales
Paradigm* (Ithaca/London: Cornell University Press, 1976).

Christian Amalvi

BRÉHIER, Louis (Brest, 1868–Reims, 1951), French historian. Expert in the
history of Byzantium. Professor at the Faculté des Lettres of Clermont-Ferrand
(1899–1938). Author of a vast and varied work that stands out by its erudition
and novelty. His books are mostly devoted to Byzantium's relationships with
the Western world and to the history of the Byzantine Church and civilization.
His major works are *Le schisme oriental du XI-ème siècle* (1899); *L'Église et
l'Orient au Moyen Âge. Les Croisades* (1911); *L'Art byzantin* (1924); *L'Art
chrétien, son developpement iconographique des origines à nos jours* (1928);
and first and foremost his masterpiece *Le monde byzantin* (3 vols; 1948–1950),
(*Vie et mort de Byzance; Les institutions*; and *La civilisation byzantine*). In his
comprehensive synthesis, Bréhier approached the whole of Byzantine history
throughout its evolution, the state structures with all their peculiarities, and
Byzantine civilization in all its varied aspects. In the light of his research, he
viewed Byzantine history as "Roman in traditions, Hellenic in culture and ori-

ental in government.'' He attached great importance to its geographic environment: from this point of view, Byzantium was a bridge over two seas, "a land and sea crossroads and a connection between two worlds.''

Bibliography: Eugen Stănescu, "Byzance et son histoire dans l'oeuvre de Louis Bréhier," *Bulletin de l'Association Internationale d'études du Sud-Est européen* 6, no. 1–2, (1968): 33–47.

Stelian Brezeanu

BREUIL, Abbé Henri-Edouard-Prosper (Mortain/Manche, 1877–l'Isle Adam, Seine-et-Oise, 1961), French prehistorian of world renown. Breuil worked as a professor at the Institute de Paléontologie Humaine in Paris (1910–1960), at the Collège de France (1928–1947), and at the University of Lisbon (1942). One of the greatest researchers of the Old Stone Age, he created a totally new line of research, which provided a better understanding of the technological progress of the Old Stone Age, a more accurate relative chronology of the most ancient known time of humankind, and a contribution to reconstruction of the primitive mentality. Breuil explained the succession of cultures in the later Old Stone Age, starting from stratigraphic observation and from the guiding-fossils criterion formulated by G. de Mortillet: "Les gisements présolutréens du type d'Aurignac," *Congrès d'anthropologie de Monaco, compte rendu* (1906); "La question aurignacienne, étude critique et stratigraphique comparée," *Revue préhistorique* (1907); "L'aurignacien présolutréen. Épilogue d'une controverse," *Revue préhistorique* (1909); and "Les subdivisions du paléolithique supérieur et leur signification préhistorique," *Compte rendu* (1912, 2d ed., 1937). He established the stratigraphic location of the Aurignacian between the Mousterian and the Solutrean, as well as the subdivisions of the Aurignacian and of the Magdalenian. He also traced and defined some unknown cultures: the Clactonian ("Les industries à éclats du paléolithique ancien: Le clactonian," *Préhistoire*, 1, 29, 1932): the Levalloisian (H. Breuil, R. Lantier, *Les hommes de la pierre ancienne: Paléolothique et mésolithique;* Breuil and Lantier, "Le paléolithique ancien en Europe occidentale et sa chronologie," *Bulletin de la Société préhistorique française* 29, 1932), and the Tayacian. Breuil suggested that there was an opposition between the flake cultures and the core cultures, which succeeded one another alternatively. He also introduced new terminology, for instance, "abbevilian" instead of "chellean" or "leptolithic" as in the de Mortillet system. A view which subsequent researches disproved was Breuil's contention that migrations were responsible for the cultural changes recorded in the later Stone Age. But another series of contributions placed Breuil among the greatest experts in Old Stone Age art, as well as among the few researchers of the Old Stone Age who set as an important task the study of primitive peoples' mentality and behavior. See "Les origines de l'art," *Journal de Psychologie* 12 (1925), 23 (1926); "L'évolution de l'art pariétal dans les cavernes et abris ornés de France," XI Congrès préhistorique de France (1934); with E. Cartailhac, *La Caverne d'Altamira* (1906), republished together with H. Obermaier, *The Cave of Al-*

tamire (1935); "Una Altamira francesa. La Caverna de Lascaux en Montignac (Dordogne)," *Archivoespañol de arqueología* (1942), and *Quatre cent siècles d'art pariétal* (1952), considered to be his spiritual testament.

Among Breuil's most significant ideas were the following: (1) magic notation, a reading of the greatest part of Stone Age art as examples of sympathetic magic (. . . "likewise during the Stone Age, our painters and sculptors, thanks to beliefs in the magic of the hunt, the magic of reproduction and destruction, had discovered the social reason for exercising, developing and showing their art. They had been simultaneously artists and magicians, painting for the love of art, but also in order that desirable game would multiply, that the hunt would have a favorable result, and that harmful animals would be destroyed.");(2) the role played by the magicians, supported by the entire community, in transmitting the oral tradition and in knowing the magic value of the images created and the way in which they were rendered; (3) the unity and resemblance of mural art to furniture art, given the common traditions they reflected; (4) the social and functional character of art and other magic practices; (5) the integration of art and magic into a set of social behaviors, the handing down of tradition and of the history of the community, and ceremonies of initiation and ritual dances; and (6) the role played by the painted caves as meeting places where the spiritual life of the community was carried on. Breuil also attempted, unsuccessfully, to develop a chronology for Old Stone Age art, and he tried to discover the origin of art in the Spanish Levant. He also had interests in other categories of behavior: cannibalism, the cult of the skull, and funeral customs. See *Beyond the Bonds of History* (1949); with H. Obermaier, "Crânes paléolithiques façonnés en coupes," *L'Anthropologie* 20 (1909); "Le gisement quaternaire d'Ofnet," *L'Anthropologie* 20 (1909).

Bibliography: J. Filip, *Enzyklopädisches Handbuch der Ur- und Frühgeschichte Europas* (Prague, 1966), pp. 164–165; L. R. Nougier, "L'Abbé Henri Breuil (1877–1961)," *Travaux de l'Institut de l'Art Préhistorique* 20 (1978): 95–96; G. de Saint Martin, *Hommage à M. l'abbé Breuil* (Paris, 1957); D. de Sonneville-Bordes, *La Préhistoire moderne* (Périgueux, 1972), pp. 4, 82, 84, 125, 126.

Ligia Bârzu

CHAMPOLLION, Jean-François (Figeac, 1790–Paris, 1832), French Egyptologist. Professor at the Faculté des Lettres de Grenoble (1809–1815), curator of the Egyptian museum at the Louvre (1827), professor at the Collège de France (1831). Elected to the Académie des Inscriptions in 1831. Champollion's renown rests on his genius in unraveling the mystery of hieroglyphics, his study of the Rosetta Stone and its triple inscription (hieroglyphic, Demotic, and Greek) and his discovery, on September 14, 1822, of the key to ancient Egyptian writing and to a hitherto mysterious civilization. The works of a child-prodigy and an exceptionally gifted teenager produced a new science: Egyptology. Champollion owed his passion for oriental studies to his elder brother Jacques-Joseph Champollion-Figeac, a tradesman in Grenoble and a devotee of ancient languages, who brought him up, supervised his education, and showed him a reproduction of the Rosetta Stone when he was only eleven. His vocation was also encouraged by the prefect of Isère, the physicist Fourier, the former perpetual secretary to the Egypt Institute who was then engaged in publishing the *Description d'Égypte*, the summary of the French scientific mission's research. With Fourier's support and given his natural gifts, Champollion was admitted to the École des Langues Orientales (1807–1809), where he worked on a dictionary and grammar of Coptic. At the end of his studies, which coincided with the creation of the Faculté des Lettres of Grenoble, he was appointed a deputy professor of history (1809) and then full professor (1812). He was first dismissed in 1815 for his republican ideas and then again in 1821. Penniless, he took refuge in Paris with his brother and devoted himself entirely to deciphering hieroglyphics until the *eureka* of September 14, 1822. After twenty years of research, he disclosed the existence of alphabetic signs and, accordingly, the role of phonetic notations. In a letter to Mr. Dacier, perpetual secretary to the Académie des Inscriptions et Belles-Lettres, he recorded the results of his discovery concerning the alphabet of phonetic hieroglyphs used by the Egyptians.

In the *Précis du système hiéroglyphique des anciens Égyptiens* (1824), Champollion showed that there were three categories of signs (ideograms, phonograms, and determinatives), and he traced a hieratic paleography for one hundred signs or so. He was widely acclaimed but also harassed. The Englishman Thomas Young in particular claimed he was the first to have made the discovery. Champollion kept working hard, studying the Egyptian collection of Turin to establish a chronology of the Egypt of the Pharaohs (*Lettres à M. le duc de Blacas*, 1824), drafting the catalogue of the Egyptian museum at the Louvre he had created and directed (1827), conducting a scientific expedition to Egypt (1828–1829) with substantial results, and holding a chair of Egyptian antiquities at the Collège de France. Overworked, exhausted by academic disputes with acrimonious and second-rate scholars, he died on March 4, 1832 of galloping consumption. He left behind two masterpieces in manuscript: a *Dictionnaire hiéroglyphique* and a *Grammaire égyptienne*.

Bibliography: Charles-Olivier Carbonell, *L'autre Champollion* (Toulouse, 1984); Herminie Hartleben *Champollion, sein Leben und sein Werk* (Berlin, 1906) (French version, Paris, 1983); *Lettres de J. F. Champollion*, gathered and annotated by H. Hartleben (2 vols. Paris, 1909).

Charles-Olivier Carbonell

CHATEAUBRIAND, René, Viscount of (Saint-Malo, 1768–Paris, 1848), French writer and politician. Pair (House of Nobles) of France (1814–1830), ambassador in Berlin (1820–1821) and London (1822), minister of foreign affairs (1822–1823). Member of the French Academy (1811). Novelist, polemicist, memorialist, traveler, Chateaubriand was first of all a romantic figure. Although he was a historian only marginally, though in an original way, he had great influence on French historiography, orienting it toward the Middle Ages and away from ancient models. After he emigrated to England, in 1797 he published *Essai historique, politique et moral sur les révolutions anciennes et modernes, considérées dans leurs rapports avec la Révolution française*. It is a pessimistic work that proclaims the vanity of all revolutions, for it is human nature, alas, to be a slave. This essay pushed to the fringes of the absurd the comparison between the revolutions of the ancient world, those in England, and the revolution then running its course in France. Back in France, Chateaubriand published in 1802, with a remarkable sense of opportuneness, the five volumes of *Génie du christianisme*, a few months after the signing of an agreement between the Consulate and the Papacy. Here the author presented the beauties and virtues of Christianity in its dogmas, rites, literature, and arts. This work is an apology more than a history. It had considerable success, and many of its readers suddenly felt the urge to become historians. With the *Génie du christianisme* France discovered Romanticism: "The religious and poetic memories of ancient France were revived." And so, although the Empire did not yet exist, the Restoration was already in sight, and it would make of Chateaubriand one of its great men. From 1809 until 1841, Chateaubriand wrote his memoirs, which appeared after his death (*Mémoires d'outre-tombe*). Often admirable in style, the memoirs betray their author's gift as a chronicler—intransigent witness of his epoch— and his art as a moralist. With Chateaubriand, the historian learns that historiography is sometimes more indebted to nonhistorian than to genuine historian, to literary genius rather than to scientific rigor.

Bibliography: F. Engel-Janosi, *Four Studies in French Romantic Historical Writing* (Baltimore, 1955); P. Stadler, *Geschichtsschreibung und historisches Denken in Frankreich, 1789–1871* (Zurich, 1958); V. L. Tapié, "Chateaubriand historien" in *Livre du Centenaire*, published by M. Levaillant (Paris, 1949).

Charles-Olivier Carbonell

COMTE, Auguste (Montpellier, 1798–Paris, 1857), French philosopher. A former student of L'École Polytechnique where he taught (1822–1845) before becoming "the high priest of human kind." Comte's life and work comprise three distinct periods. The first was the period of Saint-Simonism (1817–1824). As secretary of Saint-Simon, Comte contributed to *Cathéchisme des Industriels*, in the third issue of which he published the *Système de politique positive* (1822). In this work he presented the law of the three ages: the theological age, the metaphysical age, and the positivist age, the prophet of which he became. The second period of Comte's activity was that of positivism (1826–1844). In 1826 he opened a course of positive philosophy which attracted a select audience (Humboldt, H. Carnot, Fourier, among others). His course would later be published under the title *Cours de philosophie positive* (6 vols., 1835–1842). In the first part, he demonstrated the impossibility of metaphysics; in the second part, he laid the foundations for a science of societies, sociology; and in the third part, he founded a religion. He prays for a new history which "will establish a veritable, rational filiation in a series of social events capable of permitting a reasonably systematic forecast of their subsequent succession.'' The third period, that of mysticism, finally saw Comte at the head of a "positivist church," the *Cathéchisme* of which he wrote in 1852. In an apparently contradictory manner, Comte, though not a historian, inspired two great historiographic currents: the current called positivist, on the one hand, and the school of the *Annales*, on the other. The positivist school, represented in France by *Revue Historique* and the historians of the Sorbonne (from the end of the nineteenth century to the beginning of the twentieth century), adopted his criticism of the theology of history and his will to employ nothing but observation, experiments, and reason. History thus became a "positive science." Just like Comte, the school of the *Annales* asserted the identity of history and sociology: the latter word was invented by Comte. He had no disciples among the historians: Hippolyte Taine (q.v.) and Henry Thomas Buckle (q.v.) seem to have been his only adherents. His theory of history and his historiographic methodology were systematized by an obscure philosopher of the nineteenth century (Louis Bordeau [q.v.], *L'histoire et les historiens, essai critique sur l'histoire considérée comme une science positive*, 1888). However, his influence, diffuse and indirect, was tremendous, especially in France and Brazil.

Bibliography: Ch. O. Carbonell, "L'historiographie positiviste" *Histoire et historiens*, (Toulouse, 1976). Ch. IV–3, pp. 401–408; "Les positivismes," a special of the review, *Romantisme* (Paris, 1978); L. Kolakowski, *La philosophie positiviste*, French translation (Paris, 1976).

Charles-Olivier Carbonell

DÉCHELETTE, Joseph (Roanne, 1862–Vingué, 1914), French pre- and protohistorian. Warden of the museum in Roanne. Déchelette's name is connected with the diggings in Mont Beuvray and with the discovery of the famous *oppidum* in Bibracte (*Les fouilles du Mont Beuvray de 1897–1901*, 1902; *L'Oppidum de Bibracte*, 1903), as well as with the writing of a famous textbook, *Manuel d'archéologie préhistorique celtique et gallo-romaine: I, Archéologie préhistorique (Âge de la pierre taillée, âge de la pierre polie*, I, 1908; II, *Archéologie protohistorique ou celtique*: 1. *l'âge du bronze*, 1910; *Le premier âge du fer ou époque de Hallstatt*, 1913; *Le second âge du fer ou époque de La Tène*, 1914), which was soon to become one of the required basic works for the training of any archaeologist as well as for any archaeological research. Ever prudent, he took care not to go beyond the known facts or the already demonstrated hypotheses. ("This young science has turned up many ideas. It has stirred up serious problems, formulated audacious hypotheses, sometimes far from immediate objectives. We hope that this work allows our readers to discriminate between secure facts and tentative conclusions. . . . archaeologists have understood that an indispensable preliminary activity is to describe exactly, to classify and to compare these imposing monuments, awaiting the balanced conclusions which the analytical work might someday produce, approaching only with extreme caution the domain of interpretation.'') In spite of this prudence, Déchelette was also an innovator and accepted some very debatable points of view. As to terminology, he used differentiated denominations: "Préhistoire" for the Stone Age and "protohistoire" (in a broader sense than nowadays from a temporal point of view), for the entire period from the beginning of the Bronze Age up to the Roman conquest of Gaul. He also admitted that archaeologists had to resort to various auxiliary sciences, comparative archaeology included, in order to study and make clearer the various problems raised by scientific research.

In an epoch when specialists had insufficient information on the Hallstatt and Latène ages to be able to reconstruct completely the characteristic processes for this period, Déchelette underscored the importance played by commercial interchanges with the south in the development of the communities to the north of the Alps, the lack of hiatus between the Hallstatt and Lt. I and II, the cultural similarities on the two banks of the Rhine, the expansion of the Celts during the Hallstatt period between Gaul, southern Germany and Bohemia, and the homogeneity of the Latène culture. Moreover, he even asserted that in the Bronze Age the Celts occupied northeast Gaul and southern Germany; consequently, he located the primitive homeland of the Celts in this area. Déchelette was an innovator in chronology, too, since he set against O. Tischler's chronology for the Latène period, his own system, based on typological and stylistic criteria, which subdivides the aforementioned period into three subperiods (*Manuel d'archéologie protohistorique ou celtique: II, Le second âge du fer ou époque de La Tène*, 1914). Déchelette's absolute and relative chronology for the Latène age is as highly regarded as his famous textbook, and has continued to be used in many European countries, even though a third system has been worked out on the basis of the realities in south Germany, the system of Paul Reinecke (q.v.).

Bibliography: Jan Filip, *Enzyklopädisches Handbuch der Ur-und Frühgeschichte Europas*, 1 (Prague, 1966), p. 273; Al. Grenier, "Preface," to *Manuel d'archéologie préhistorique, celtique et gallo-romaine, V. Archéologie gallo-romaine*, I (1931): 1–3; "Inauguration du Musée Joseph Déchelette à Roanne," *Bulletin de la Diana* (Montbrison), 3 (1923); Salomon Reinach, J. Déchelette, *Revue archéologique* 2 (1914): 326.

Ligia Bârzu

DIEHL, Charles (Strasbourg, 1859–Paris, 1944), French historian. member of the French Schools of Rome (1881–1883) and of Athens (1883–1885), professor at the Faculté des Lettres of Nancy and then of Paris (1899). Prominent expert in the history of Byzantium. Diehl belongs to the generation which in the late nineteenth and early twentieth centuries transformed the history of Byzantium from a hitherto unknown field into one of the most researched domains of European medieval studies. His major academic works were *Études sur l'administration byzantine dans l'exarchat de Ravenne* (1888); *L'Afrique byzantine* (1896); *Justinian et la civilisation byzantine au VI-ème siècle* (1901); and *Études byzantines* (1905). An essential part of his work includes extensive surveys and books of popularization: *Théodora, impératrice de Byzance* (1904); *Figures byzantines* (1906–1908); *Manuel d'art byzantin* (1910); *Byzance. Grandeur et décadence* (1919) and *Histoire de l'Empire byzantin* (1921). A staunch opponent of *histoire-batailles*, Diehl dealt with all aspects of Byzantine society in his work: economic and social life, institutions and art, politics and religion. In this light, he no longer viewed Byzantine history as an "immobile history"—as older generations of historians had—but as a dynamic and profoundly original one. His definition of Byzantine art as "a living art whose development follows a continuous and progressive course and which should be studied like any living organism in its evolution and successive changes" also applied to Byzantine history as a whole. The salient features of his early academic works were a minute treatment of sources and of modern relevant literature, a solid structure, and an analytic approach. His other works display his skills in depicting vast historical scenes and evince his perfect knowledge of auxiliary sources and literature. Above all, these works are written in a simple, clear, and vivid style which is the key to Diehl's tremendous success with the public at large.

Bibliography: V. Laurent, "Charles Diehl, historien de Byzance," *Revue historique du Sud-Est européen* 22 (1945): 5–23; E. Stănescu, "Charles Diehl et l'importance de son oeuvre," *Bulletin de l'Association Internationale d'Études du Sud-Est Européen*, no. 2 (1964): 12–26.

Stelian Brezeanu

DUMÉZIL, Georges (Paris, 1898–Paris, 1988), French mythologist and linguist. A former student of L'École Normale Supérieure, Dumézil taught comparative mythology at l'École Pratique des Hautes Études (1935–1948); then he occupied the chair of Indo-European Civilization, which he created, at Collège de France. He was elected a member of the French Academy in 1978. Dumézil thoroughly investigated the Indo-European heritage through myths, epics, rites, and concepts in which he tracked down and found the traces from the Ganges to the Irish Sea. He thus discovered a common and compelling ideology, the central conception of which is that of the three hierarchical functions: magic and juridical sovereignty, physical force, and fecundity. At the beginning of this research, he considered the functions of the priests, warriors, and peasants to be social (*Jupiter-Mars-Quirinus*, I–IV, 1941–1948). Consequently, these three functions were for him ideological and "classificatory" (*Idéologie tripartite des Indo-Européens*, 1958; *Mythe et épopée*, 1968–1973). Because of his method and the object of his research, he can be considered one of the fathers of structuralism. For him, comparison applies not to facts or words but to groups of gods—Vedic, Zoroastrian, Germanic, articulated according to analogous schemes, to Romance rites that correspond to Indian myths. The structure that thus came to the fore imposed for millennia on end its form on the thinking of the Indo-European peoples, except for the Greeks. Dumézil renewed or activated numerous historiographical fields, not only Indo-European mythology, but also the primitive history of Rome which seemed to him to have been created starting from mythology, and literary history, a domain in which he would demonstrate the mythological origins of a large number of epic works (*Du mythe au roman*, 1970). In medieval history, his hypothesis about a connection between the theory of the three medieval orders and the three-functional Indo-European ideology was espoused and confirmed by J. Le Goff and Georges Duby.

Bibliography: C. Scott Littleton, *The New Comparative Mythology* (Berkeley, Los Angeles; University of California Press, 1966); P. Smith and D. Sperber, "Mythologiques de Georges Dumézil," *Annales* 26, no. 3–4 (1971): 559–586.

Charles-Olivier Carbonell

DURUY, Victor (Paris, 1811–Paris, 1894), French historian. Professor at the Ecole Polytechnique (1862), Inspector General (1862), Minister of Public Education (1863–1869), Member of the Institute: Académie des Inscriptions et Belles Lettres (1873), Académie des Sciences Morales et Politiques (1879), and Académie Française (1884). This student in the École Normale Supérieure (1830), trained by Jules Michelet (q.v.), won first place in the Aggregation of history in 1833. He is listed in this dictionary for three reasons: for his scientific work, for his many popular pedagogical and didactic treatises, and above all for his ministerial action in favor of historical research (see his *Notes et Souvenirs*, 1901). His erudite output became nearly identical with his huge *Histoire des Romains* published at Hachette's in seven volumes from 1843 to 1885, in which the author's rejection of the Republic (Rome's as well as 1848's) and his justification of "Césarisme" may be read between the lines. Just as he worked on antiquity—a Latin thesis, "Tiberius," and French theses, "l'État du monde romain vers le temps de la fondation de l'Empire" (1853) and "Histoire de la Grèce ancienne" (1862)—he devoted himself at Hachette's to popular works. He composed a lecture on history and geography covering the full cycle of secondary education. Most of these classical books—about a hundred, written between 1838 and 1863—were used and republished until the end of the century. They distinguished themselves by their liberal and anticlerical attitudes. The most famous one of the series, *l'Abrégé de l'Histoire de France* (2d ed, 1851, with 275,000 copies sold between 1863 and 1880 according to Hachette's records), was violently attacked in 1853 by Louis Veuillot in the *Univers*, the organ of intransigent and ultramontanist Catholicism. In spite of or because of these attacks, Hachette republished this book until 1909. From 1861 to 1865, Victor Duruy also brought out, for the most general public, the *Histoire populaire de la France* and the *Histoire populaire contemporaine de la France* (both in four volumes). His competence in Roman history put him in touch with Napoleon the Third (who wrote the *Vie de César*), who appointed him, on June 23, 1863, minister of Public Instruction. In this key position he achieved much historical education and research: The law of 1867 requiring primary schools to teach history (the Guizot Law in 1833 had made it only optional); the decree of September 23, 1863, which mandated the teaching of contemporary history in the philosophy curriculum; and last but not least, as he cared about reviving and stimulating historical research in the university by taking his inspiration from the German model, he set up through the decree of July 31, 1868, the École Practique des Hautes Études. Its fourth section, the Sciences historiques et philologiques, in which Gaston Paris (q.v.) and Gabriel Monod (q.v.) worked from its creation, quickly became a nursery of erudite researchers coming from the old Sorbonne, the École des Chartes and the École Normale. Having failed to bequeath to posterity a work one may compare, in its speciality, to those of Gibbon or Mommsen (q.v.), Victor Duruy left to the historical community an incomparable institution, which—revived after 1945 by Lucien Febvre (q.v.), Fernand Braudel (q.v.) and Charles Morazé—became the center of the École des *Annales* and of the Nouvelle Histoire.

Bibliography: Sandra Horvath-Peterson, *Victor Duruy and French Education: Liberal Reform in the Second Empire* (Louisiana State University Press, 1984); Jean Rohr, *Victor Duruy ministre de Napoléon III: essai sur la politique de l'instruction publique au temps de l'Empire libéral* (Paris: Librairie générale de droit et de jurisprudence, 1967).

Christian Amalvi

FEBVRE, Lucien (Nancy, 1878–Saint-Amour, Jura, 1956), French historian. Professor at the universities of Dijon (1912), Strasbourg (1919) and the Collège de France (1933–1950). Febvre was among the great innovators of twentieth-century historiography. His first important work, *Phillipe II et la Franche-Comté, étude d'histoire politique, religieuse et sociale*, published in 1912, was both a regional history and an effort at "global history." In this book, besides political and diplomatic events, Febvre also treated problems concerning the economic, social, religious, and mental life of a French province in the second half of the sixteenth century. The combination of the history of material life and spiritual life was remarkable. For example, here is his analysis of the "class war" between the feudal lords and the bourgeoisie: "What separates, what sets in opposition the nobility and the bourgeois, is not only an economic clash; it is more a conflict of ideas and feelings. By reason of their manner of living, their education, their general conception of the world and of human activity, the two classes stand in bitter confrontation." Another book, *Histoire de la Franche-Comté*, also appeared in 1912. His later work covered an extraordinary variety of topics. He dealt with theoretical problems of history, the history of civilization, institutions, intellectual life and mentalities, and religious, social, economic, and cultural history. He used interdisciplinary research to link the study of history to linguistics, ethnography, folklore, demography, geography, psychology, literature, and art. Febvre opposed traditional political history and promoted thematic history, based on the significant problems of civilization concerning man: "Man is the measure of history" (L'homme, mesure de l'histoire. Sa seule mesure. Bien plus, sa raison d'être). He ridiculed the simplistic depiction of history by some historians who spoke only of "titles, names, dates, dates, titles and names." He thought history should analyze *problems* ("To pose a problem, this

is precisely the beginning and the end of all history. No problems, no history.'').
He accorded an important role to the psychological and mental factor in interpreting history; however, he believed no singular causes existed in history, and
he looked for a global explanation for historical phenomena.

Febvre's contributions concerning the relationship between history and geographic environment were especially important. These were synthesized in *La
Terre et l'évolution humaine* (1922). Rejecting deterministic theses, especially
those of Friedrich Ratzel (*Anthropogeographie*, 1882–1891) and Ellen C. Semple
(*Influences of Geographic Environment*, 1911), Febvre developed some of the
ideas expressed by the geographer P. Vidal de la Blache (1845–1918). By
applying these ideas to history, he opposed the concept of the unilateral influence
of environment and stressed that human societies could choose from among the
many possibilities offered by their environment. Geographic determinism was
replaced by geographic "possibilism." ("Des nécessités, nulle part. Des pos-
sibilités, partout.") In the second stage of his activity, Febvre concentrated on
the history of mentalities and was one of the creators of this domain of research.
In 1928 he published *Un destin: Martin Luther*, in which he described Luther's
life in the social and mental context of the period. ("This problem of relationships
between the individual and the collectivity, of personal initiative and social
necessity, is perhaps the central problem of history.") In 1942 his masterpiece,
Le problème de l'incroyance au XVIᵉ siècle: La religion de Rabelais, appeared.
Febvre depicted a striking and unexpected image of French Renaissance mentalities. He separated them from the mode of modern thought and placed them
closer to primitive mentalities. Renaissance society was portrayed as a society
lacking a scientific spirit, where fantasy and inexactitude were everywhere; it
was a peasant society that was satisfied with never knowing the exact time, a
world where everything was possible, where the real was mixed with the supernatural, "a universe inhabited by demons." This interpretation was criticized
for its unilateral character. Febvre, however, was aware of the relativity of various
points of view. He began this work with the words: "The historian is not the
one who knows, but the one who seeks." ("L'historien n'est pas celui qui sait.
Il est celui qui cherche.") He saw each epoch as a well-defined socioeconomic
and mental structure, which therefore could not accommodate elements from
other structures of other ages. Febvre's book was one of the first to promote
structuralist concepts and methods and to attempt to apply them in historical
research. He used the same approach in *Autour de l'Heptaméron* (1944), which
examined the work and thought of Queen Marguerite de Navarre (1492–1549)
within the mental context of her era. Febvre also wrote many articles. Those
with a more theoretical character appear in the volume *Combats pour l'histoire*
(1953); others are in *Au coeur religieux du XVIᵉ siècle* (1957) and *Pour une
histoire à part entière* (1962). He insisted on the need for interdisciplinary study
and group work. Together with Marc Bloch (q.v.), in 1929 he founded the
review *Annales d'histoire économique et sociale* (now: *Annales. Economies.
Sociétés. Civilisations*). This journal reflected the conception and methods of

French "new history." As the leader of the *Annales* School, Febvre exercised a decisive influence on contemporary French historiography.

Bibliography: Hans-Dieter Mann, *Lucien Febvre. La pensée vivante d'un historien* (Paris, 1971); Guy Massicotte, *L'histoire problème: la méthode de Lucien Febvre* (Quebec, 1981).

Lucian Boia

FOUCAULT, Michel (Poitiers, 1926–Paris, 1984), French philosopher and historian. Professor at the University of Clermont-Ferrand (1960–1968), at the University of Paris-Vincennes (1968–1970), and then at the Collège de France. (The chair of history of thought systems was created for him in 1970.) Foucault had a great influence on contemporary historians. He is considered a new historian, a structuralist, a Lacan of historiography, a Nietzschean spirit, and even an "accomplished historian" (Veyne, 1978). In fact, his work is complex, original, and difficult. Foucault was a new historian in his own way: He studied new fields, and total history was his method. He examined the areas of confinement, asylums, and prisons in famous works: *Folie et déraison, Histoire de la folie à l'âge classique*, 1961 (reedited collection TEL Gallimard, 1976); *Surveiller et punir, naissance de la prison* (1975). He did not live to complete his *Histoire de la sexualité* (three volumes published from 1976 to 1984). In these three works, Foucault's approach was not that of a new historian: it was neither sociological nor anthropological, and not even that of a historian of the mental universe. He was interested in power as a coherent and global system that contains the discourses, institutions, and practices of the confinement and repression he denounced. This champion of freedom, marked by the May 1968 student uprising, viewed the human world as an aggregate of powers underlying and justifying an aggregate of ideas and values specific to a certain epoch. The great confinement of the insane which begun in the seventeenth century corresponded to the philosophic triumph of reason (Descartes) and to the emergence of the ethics of work. From these new norms emerged the newly discovered abnormality of those who could not reason and work. Likewise, imprisonment was the foundation of the penal system at the end of the eighteenth century and the beginning of the nineteenth century when "a redistribution of the entire economy of coercion" took place in both Europe and the United States. Breaking with the "traditional" society, in schools, barracks, and manufacturing works power was vested in teachers, officers, and employers to "mark, train, punish and compel people to work". Hence, Foucault's structuralism was neither that of Fernand Braudel (q.v.) nor that of Lévi-Strauss.

Foucault did not analyze the slow evolution of the phenomena of the depths over a longer period nor the unvarying relations between the elements of an abstract pattern. He concentrated on breaking points, mutations, discontinuity, the passage from one system of concepts and values to another. Hence, the question: was Foucault a historian? Some argue (see *L'impossible prison*, 1980, studies collected by Michelle Perrot) that he ignored facts and people alike. After the death of God in history (Nietzsche) came the death of a man in historiography (Foucault): there were no madmen in Foucault's asylums, as there were no prisoners in his prisons. He put the diversity of the real into a web of concepts that achieved a profound clarity, although he was not necessarily certain to be right. Foucault answered criticisms even before they were made. In *Les mots et les choses* (1966) and especially in *L'archéologie du savoir* (1969), he broke with the traditional history of ideas, invalidated the concepts of tradition, evolution, and sense, rejected the division among disciplines (particularly between philosophy, law, and history), and denied the reality of a work, of a book. There were no "events in thought" but only "verbal performances" governed by an "aggregate of anonymous historical rules, always determined in time and space, which provided in a certain area . . . the conditions for the exercise of the enunciative function." To his detractors concerned over the "death of man" he stated: "We must debunk the myth of restoring the global instance of the real in its totality . . . A type of rationality, a way of thinking, a program, . . . aims to be defined and pursued, instruments to attain them, etc. . . . all this is the real, although it does not claim to be the 'reality' itself and the 'society' as a whole."

Bibliography: H. L. Dreyfus and P. Rabinow, *Michel Foucault: Beyond Structuralism and Hermeneutics* (Chicago, 1982) (French version, 1984); *L'impossible prison*, studies collected by Michelle Perrot, (Paris, 1980); P. Veyne, "Foucault révolutionne l'histoire" in *Comment on écrit l'histoire* (1978).

Charles-Olivier Carbonell

FUSTEL DE COULANGES, Numa Denis (Paris, 1830– Massy [Essonne], 1889), French historian. Professor at the Faculty of letters of Strasbourg (1860–1870). Member of the Institute: Academy of morale and political science (1875). Professor at the Sorbonne (1878–1880, 1883–1888). Director of l'Ecole Normale Supérieure (1880–1883). His contemporaries have often shown Fustel de Coulanges as anti-Michelet (q.v.). Michelet, who revived the past by a lyrical imagination in a flamboyant style was the opposite of Fustel, who promoted a scientific, positivist history—as precise in its results as the exact sciences—with a classical and moderate style. Let's examine the facts behind the accepted opinions. In *La cité antique* (1864), Fustel proposed a total interpretation of Greco-Roman antiquity based on a religious hypothesis: "[Faith] becomes established: human society is constituted. Belief changes, is modified: society passes through a series of revolutions. Faith vanishes: society takes on a new look. Such was the law of ancient times." This masterpiece of historiography shows a researcher already mastering his method and certain of his principles which, in their substance hardly changed from then on: (1) a refusal to throw the light of the present onto the past and to transpose into history contemporary prejudices—cultural, political, or religious; (2) holding the written document and the text sacred: for Fustel history was a science that was based on rigorously exploited documents; (3) a sociological conception of history: for Fustel as for Montesquieu, history could not be reduced to a set of facts, to a set of events—

political, military, diplomatic—which one could join end to end, but consisted of the science of the society as a whole, of its customs, of its beliefs.

These lines, already sketched in *La cité antique*, are expanded in his major work, *l'Histoire des institutions politiques de l'ancienne France* (6 vols, 1874–1892). His worship of the documents led him to throw down willingly the historiographic scaffolding built by the liberals to account for the origins of France. Supported by texts, Fustel proved that, contrary to the statements of François Guizot (q.v.), Augustin Thierry (q.v.), Michelet, Henri Martin, and others, Gaul was not forcibly conquered by the Germans. Instead, there was a slow and peaceful penetration of the Roman Empire by people from the East; there was no Germanization of Gallo-Roman society but a Romanization of the German tribes; finally, feudalism was not a social system imported from beyond the Rhine, but the progressive adaptation of the society of the remote Middle Ages to the slow disintegration of the Roman structures. Thus, under his pen the myth of the two antagonistic Frances breaks down, a myth that expounded in racial terms all the political and social conflicts from Clovis to 1830. Indeed, Fustel's goal in disproving this "progressivist" conception was not to enter into ideological controversy, but, on the contrary, to lift history out of the arena of partisan disputes. However, in the burning political atmosphere of the first years of the Third Republic, such a work which reinstated the religious and the sacred, the death of which had been declared by the Enlightenment; which destroyed one of the main "founder myths" of Revolution and Republic; which flaunted a quite Romanist and anti-Germanist flag, could only stir up political misunderstandings. In 1878, L. Gambetta's intervention was required to make the unwilling left agree to the creation, at the Sorbonne, of a chair of medieval history reserved to Fustel, who was suspected of monarchist and clerical views. On March 18, 1905, the young Action Française took the occasion of the historian's seventy–fifth birthday to organize the resounding "bagarre de Fustel" (Charles Maurras). Referring to his famous historiographical polemics against the Germans (especially his letter to Theodor Mommsen [q.v.] of October 27, 1870.: "l'Alsace est-elle allemande ou française?" and his article of 1871: "La politique d'envahissement: Louvois et M. de Bismarck," texts republished by Camille Julian in *Questions historiques*, in 1893), this event wrongly celebrated Fustel as a "nationaliste intégral" in advance, praising a work that dared "secouer le joug de la pensée allemande" (Paul Bourget) and assaulted the "Nouvelle Sorbonne", accused of having betrayed Fustel's message and having become an advance "bastion" of German scholarship. This misunderstanding seemed to continue, though in a minor way, about a century later, when Pierre Gaxotte declared that in France, state and university "sought to ignore Fustel." But a conference organized in January 1984 at the École Normale by specialists in all historical periods proved the enduring interest in Fustel long after his death.

Bibliography: Jean Capot de Quissac, "L'Action française à l'assaut de la Sorbonne historienne," *Au berceau des Annales: Actes du Colloque de Strasbourg* (October 1979) (Toulouse, 1983), pp. 139–191; Pierre Gaxotte, "Fustel de Coulanges, historien sous le boisseau,'' *Le Purgatoire* (Paris: Fayard, 1982), pp. 83–90; François Hartog, ''Strasbourg et l'histoire ancienne en 1919,'' *Au berceau des Annales: Actes du colloque de Strasbourg* (Octobre 1979) *publiés par C. O. Carbonell et G. Livet* (Toulouse: Presses de l'Institut d'Études Politiques de Toulouse, 1983), pp. 41–43; François Hartog, *Le XIXe siècle et l'histoire: le cas Fustel de Coulanges* (Paris: Presses universitaire de France, 1988).

Christian Amalvi

GROUSSET, René (Aubais, Gard, 1885–Paris, 1952), French historian. Professor at the École du Louvre (1928), curator of the Cernuschi Museum (1933), professor at the École des Langues Orientales (1941), curator of the Guimet Museum (1944), professor at the École de la France d'Outre-mer (1945), Member of the Académie Française (1946). Grousset's work includes three complementary historiographical levels: (1) classical history (it essentially means political, diplomatic, and military) of the Far East and of the Middle East—*Histoire de l'Asie* (1922), *Histoire de l'Extrême Orient* (1929), *Histoire des Croisades et du royaume franc de Jérusalem* (1934–1936), *l'Epopée des Croisades* (1939), *Histoire de la Chine* (1942), *Histoire de l'Arménie des origines à 1071* (1948); (2) cultural history of the civilizations of the old Far East depicting the transmission of ideas and forms along ''the Silk Route''—*Sur les traces du Bouddha* (1929), *Civilisations de l'Orient* (4 vols. 1929–1930), *Philosophies indiennes* (1931), *De la Grèce à la Chine, De l'Inde au Cambodge et à Java, De la Chine au Japon* (3 vols., 1949–1951); and (3) philosophical thought about history and changing humanity, the spirituality of which shows Grousset's descent from Bossuet—*Bilan de l'histoire* (1946) and *Figures de proue* (1949), in which he proceeds to ''examine the conscience of humanity.'' This rich work, praised by the cultured general public, may be described as popular, synthetic, and academic. Grousset never behaved like an erudite, yet he introduced orientalists' (Sylvain Lévi, Paul Pelliot, and Henri Maspero among others) research to nonspecialists, and he respected the rules of this literary type: His classic style is pleasant to read. His *Epopée des Croisades*, for instance, is as absorbing as a ''cloak-and-dagger romance'', the main springs of which are love, ambition, chivalrous heroism, fate, and treason. In his work, he mixed sparkling phrases and studied anachronisms (''history is a movie made in slow motion,'' Assyrians were ''these Hitlerites of ancient Asia''), and he respected the great men who made history and who managed the world (Alexander, Caesar, Tamerlane, Marco Polo); finally, he drew from the historical process certain moral, political, and metaphysical lessons and even universal laws about the cyclical fall of civilizations and the course of empires. This work marked an epoch: It roughly corresponded to the climax of the European colonial expansion he justified in his inaugural speech at the Académie Française (1947) by showing the French colonial empire as heir to Rome's.

Bibliography: Christian Brosio, ''René Grousset oublié,'' *Le Spectacle du monde*, no. 285 (December 1985); p. 105; *France-Asie: revue mensuelle de culture et de synthèse franco-asiatique*, 9, no. 88–89 (September–October 1953): numéro consacré à la vie et à l'oeuvre de René Grousset.

Christian Amalvi

GUIZOT, François (Nîmes, 1787–Val-Richer, 1874), French historian and statesman. Professor at the Sorbonne (1812–1815, 1820–1825, 1828–1830). Minister of the Interior (1830), of Public Instruction (1832–1836), of Foreign Affairs (1840–1848). Member of the Académie des Sciences Morales et Politiques which he revived and reorganized (1832), of the Académie des Inscriptions (1833), and the Académie Française (1836). During the Restoration Guizot was one of the leaders of the Liberal party. He was hostile both to reactionary Ultras and to democratic radicalism and, with Pierre Paul Royer-Collard, promoted the Doctrinaires, for whom he wrote the statement of principle: *Du Gouvernement représentatif et de l'état actuel de la France* in 1816. He became famous with his *Cours d'histoire moderne* (1828–1830), which he gave at the Sorbonne to an enthusiastic audience that would soon fight during the *Trois Glorieuses*. Two books were offshoots of his course: *L'Histoire de la civilisation en Europe* and *L'Histoire de la civilisation en France*, which made him the head of the philosophical trend in French historiography. Contrary to Augustin Thierry (q.v.), and the supporters of narrative history, he eliminated local color, details, and narrative to bring to the foreground the abstract, the idea, "the general and ultimate fact which comprises and sums up all the other facts." This was his definition of civilization. Two "general facts" loom large in the history of Europe and the history of France: the formation and development of nation-states (centralization and the principle of unity), on the one hand, and the liberation of the human mind (the aspiration to freedom and equality) on the other hand. Thus, for this liberal Protestant, the elevation of man—supported by the Germans, advocated by the Christian religion and the Reform—was inseparable from the construction of the modern state. We see here the doctrinaire, the man of order, the future statesman. The July Revolution and his political career seemed to have taken Guizot away from historical studies together with his friends Adolphe Thiers (q.v.) and Guillaume Barante. Later, he completed *Histoire de la Révolution d'Angleterre*, of which only two volumes had been published. But behind this apparent desertion of the historical field, prodigious activity in the realm of history continued.

Soon after 1830, Guizot laid the foundations for modern historical research. In 1834 he created the *Comité des Travaux Historiques*, sponsor of the *Collection des documents inédits*, which to this day remains a valuable source of information of over four hundred volumes. Guizot had taken an early interest in historical sources; he had published a *Collection de mémoires relatifs à l'histoire d'Angleterre* (1823) and *À l'histoire de France* (1824). But that had been a private initiative involving narrative sources, most of which had already been published. The 1834 project was fairly new: It was a state enterprise attempting to publish comprehensive primary and unexplored sources. In 1834 Guizot also set up the

Commission des Arts et Monuments and the body of inspectors of historical monuments in charge of France's archaeological and artistic patrimony. In 1846, to counter the Germans' scientific influence, he founded the École Française d'Athènes, and the following year he launched an in-depth reform of the École des Chartes. With Guizot, history turned, as Augustin Thierry put it, into "a national institution." With him, French historiography passed from the age of État Providence (Maecenas) to the age of État Patron. The 1848 Revolution put an end to his political career, and he resumed his historical work. He completed his *Histoire de la Révolution d'Angleterre* (1854–1856) of which Hippolyte Taine (q.v.) said: "Mr. Guizot now brings to narrative history the talent he displayed in the speculative history." As the historian of bourgeois revolutions in the Europe of medieval communes and in the England of the Stuarts, Guizot was considered a theorist of the class struggle and an inspirer of Karl Marx (q.v.). But his aim as a statesman was to put an end to the revolution in France just as it had been done in England by the end of the seventeenth century.

Bibliography: Ch-O. Carbonell, "Guizot homme d'État et le mouvement historiographique français," *Actes du Colloque F. Guizot* (Paris, 1976); François Guizot, *Mémoires pour servir à l'histoire de notre temps*, 9 vols. (Paris, 1858–1868); Pierre Rosanvallon, *Le moment Guizot* (Paris, 1984).

Charles-Olivier Carbonell

JAURÈS, Jean (Castres, 1859–Paris, 1914), French historian and politician. Former student at the École Normale Supérieure, Jaurès gave up teaching in 1893 for politics, journalism, and history. He was murdered by an extremist nationalist on July 31, 1914. His historical work stemmed from his philosophical training and socialist orientation. His thesis, published in 1892, was on the *Origines du socialisme allemand* and was based on the works of Luther, Kant, Fichte, and Georg Wilhelm F. Hegel (q.v.); a lecture he gave in December 1894 for the students of Paris, "Idéalisme et matérialisme dans la conception de l'histoire," heralded Jaurès' adhesion to Marxist philosophy. The previous year he had been elected a socialist deputy for the Department of Tarn. Defeated in the 1898 elections, he did not return to the university. He started to write a great history "for the workers and peasants of France." It was the *Histoire socialiste, 1789–1900*, a collective work in twelve volumes (1901–1908). He supervised its elaboration and wrote the first four volumes—*Histoire socialiste de la Révolution française* (1901–1904)—and the eleventh devoted to the *Guerre franco-allemande*. The *Histoire socialiste de la Révolution française* holds an important place in historiography, given its novel approach, on the one hand, and Jaurès' own originality, on the other. Indeed, it marks the emergence of a materialistic dialectical approach to the study and interpretation of the great revolution. Jaurès clearly followed in Marx's tracks: "The revolution indirectly prepared the way for the ascent of the proletariat. . . . But in fact it marked the political ascent of the bourgeois class." Like Karl Marx (q.v.), he maintained that economic life "was the foundation and motive force of human history." Hence, unlike all previous historians, Jaurès showed that the Revolution had taken place in a prosperous France where "the bourgeoisie became aware of its strength, wealth, rights and almost countless opportunities." Nevertheless, Jaurès' dialectical materialism was most subtle and was placed "under the triple inspiration of Marx, Michelet and Plutarch." His eloquent and lyrical style often modified the dualist vision of the class struggle to create the image of a generous and enthusiastic populism, mostly national and nationalist, rather than social and socialist. He gave prominence to great men as the heroes of a history that was not made solely by the masses. Thus, in the first years of the twentieth century, Jaurès the historian prepared and accompanied Jaurès the socialist, who, after the foundation of the newspaper *L'Humanité* (1904), drew closer to another socialist, Jules Guesde, but without giving up the hope of reconciling the collectivist trend and the personalist trend, the revolutionary ideal and reformist pragmatism into a unified socialist party.

Bibliography: J. Godechot, *Un jury pour la Révolution* (Paris, 1974); M. Rebérioux, "Jaurès historien," *La Pensée* (December 1968): 27–40. *L'Histoire socialiste de la Révolution française* was reprinted by A. Soboul, 6 vols. (Paris: Editions sociales, 1968).

Charles-Olivier Carbonell

LAMING-EMPERAIRE, Annette (?, 1917–?, 1977), French prehistorian. Head of studies at the École Pratique des Hautes Études. An outstanding personality, following the best traditions of the French prehistory school, Laming-Emperaire asserted herself both through the originality of her interpretation and intellectual independence and through her ability to revise her own opinions. Her intellectual integrity has been brilliantly described by G. Camps as a "constant concern to reformulate questions and a refusal to be tied down to a single hypothesis or to a too well constructed system," *La préhistoire* (1983). This side of her personality allows us to see more clearly why, although following Henri-Edouard-Prosper Breuil's (q.v.) ideas on the goals of prehistory ("Prehistory, like archaeology, does not aspire to be a cemetery of unconnected objects but, instead, seeks to reconstruct an entire human past," *La découverte du passé*, 1952), and on the sacred nature of Old Stone Age art ("the sacred nature of paleolithic art has been established in a manner that is without doubt definitive," A. Laming-Emperaire, *La Signification de l'art rupestre paléolithique*, 1962), she nevertheless moved away from her great professor by proposing a new methodology and a new way of interpreting the art of the Old Stone Age. Ruling out the ethnographical method only temporarily and making use of the criteria of the archaeological method, she came to several interesting conclusions: (1) Old Stone Age paintings or engravings were neither juxtapositions nor superpositions, but compositions using several recurrent themes (I. horse–reindeer–bear; II. marked human beings; III. horse–bison-aurochs; IV. horse–bison-aurochs–woman); (2) the common source of inspiration for the two groups of art monuments—the caves and the open–air dwellings; (3) the function of the latter as sanctuaries; (4) the complex character of the themes pictured there: "[The paintings] may be mythic and may recall, for example, the origin and the history of each human group in its relationships with the animal species; they may put in concrete form an ancient metaphysics and express a world system where each species, animal or human, has its place, and where the sexual division of beings assumes major importance; they can also be religious and may include some supernatural beings. They can thus be simultaneously mythical, metaphysical and religious, without distinctions between these different modes, distinctions introduced by us, and can have great meaning when they are related to the dawn of human reflection" *(La signification de l'art rupestre)*. This opinion clearly marked her move away from the prudent attitude in *L'art préhistorique* (1952), and contrasted with a more recent interpretation in *Système de pensée et organisation sociale dans l'art rupestre paléolithique, L'Homme de Cromagnon, 1868–1968* (1970), in which she proposed a new solution: Art is the clear expression of a certain social system, while the species of animals are symbols of the human communities, clearly referring to exogamous practices. Laming-Emperaire's name is also connected with research on South American prehistory (Fischer, *Weltgeschichte*, I, 1966), and with the writing of a fundamental work on the origins of the science she served, *Les Origines de l'archéologie préhistorique en France* (1964).

Bibliography: Jan Filip, *Enzyklopädische Handbuch der Ur-und Frühgeschichte Europas*, I (Prague, 1966), p. 668.

Ligia Bârzu

LAVISSE, Ernest (Le Nouvion-en-Thiérache, Aisne, 1842–Paris, 1922), French historian. Student at the École Normale Supérieure, 1862–1865. Tutor of the imperial prince, the son of Napoleon III, and secretary of the minister Victor Duruy, 1867–1869. Professor of modern history at the Sorbonne, 1888–1919. Member of the Académie Française, 1892. Director of the École Normale Supérieure, 1904–1919. The foremost academic representative of the so-called positivist school, Lavisse was, beginning in the 1890s, the undisputed master of French historiography. During the first three decades of the Third Republic, he exercised a powerful and continual influence in the political sphere and in the upper reaches of the administration concerned with public instruction, playing a decisive role in the organization of the teaching of history and hence in the formation of national feeling. He was, at the same time, "Pope and Machiavelli of the University" (D. Halévy) and the "First school teacher of France." Deeply affected by the French defeat in the war with Prussia (1870–1871), he devoted his life and his work "to the task of rehabilitation." This preoccupation was manifest in his earliest studies, which he devoted to the formation of the Prussian state with the object of understanding the reasons for the enemy's success: "Études sur l'une des origines de la monarchie prussienne ou la Marche de Brandebourg sous la dynastie ascanienne" (thesis, 1875); followed by *Études sur l'histoire de Prusse* (1879), *La Jeunesse du Grand Frédéric* (1891), and *Le Grand Frédéric avant l'Avènement* (1893). At the same time, he dedicated himself to the teaching of national history in the primary schools. With this in mind, he composed the "programs" that were followed everywhere in the centralized state, but also a series of manuals (known under the generic and nowadays legendary term of "Petit Lavisse") which were utilized from the age of seven by the majority of French pupils between 1882 and 1914. These small volumes imposed on the collective memory a vision of the past that was carefully designed to instill love of country and of the Republic while, at the same time, teaching civic virtue.

Lavisse's pedagogical role was consecrated by the *Histoire de France* in twenty-eight volumes, a veritable "monument" of French "positivist" historiography in the first third of the twentieth century. *L'Histoire de France depuis les origines jusqu'à la Révolution* (nine tomes in eighteen volumes) appeared between 1903 and 1911; then, in 1921–1922, appeared *L'Histoire de France contemporaine depuis la Révolution jusqu'à la paix de 1919* (10 vols.). Lavisse organized and coordinated the whole with the greatest care. He personally wrote tome VII (*Louis XIV*, from 1643 to 1685) of *L'Histoire de France jusqu'à la Révolution*, "a construction of impressive architecture, the product of intensive effort and reflection and of a long acquaintance with the documents; an admirable style; a vibrant sense of life" He expressed his pedagogical views in his collected articles: *Questions d'enseignement national* (1885); *Études et étudiants* (1890); and *A propos de nos écoles* (1895). In his *Vue générale de l'histoire politique de l'Europe* (1890), he presented his concept of history as a dialectic between the fatality of physical "nature" (which "determines the destinies of peoples") and "chance and liberty" (which "are opposed to natural fate and the fate born of history"). The historian's function is to trace the course of human events step by step right up to the present. The study of origins is a fascinating task, and the overall balance, accidents aside, is one of continual scientific, economic, political, and social progress—a progress toward liberty. The historian must not remain in his ivory tower. Anyone in possession of a "moral force" is duty-bound to pass it on. The historian's responsibility to the nation is, in this respect, particularly grave: "to the teaching of history falls the duty of instilling a love and understanding of the *patrie*. . . . True patriotism is at the same time a sentiment and the concept of an obligation. Now, all sentiments can be nurtured and all concepts can be taught. History must nurture the sentiment and define the concept" (*Questions d'enseignement national*, p. 208). Lavisse's patriotism is based on conscience. To love France is to love liberty and justice: "I have done my best to avoid the prejudices of patriotism, and I don't think I have exaggerated France's position in the world." But in the struggle against opposing factors of history, France is the most formidable adversary of consequential fate (*la fatalité des suites*). Ernest Lavisse, at the height of his career, composed some touching pages on his childhood and youth (*Souvenirs*, 1912).

Bibliography: P. Nora, "Lavisse, instituteur national," in *Les Lieux de mémoire*, ed. Pierre Nora, 1 (Paris: La République, 1984), pp. 246–289; P. Nora, "L'Histoire de

France de Lavisse," in *Les Lieux de mémoire*, II (La Nation, 1, Paris: 1986), pp. 317–375.

Jean Glénisson

LEFEBVRE, Georges (Lille, 1874–Boulogne-Billancourt, 1959), French historian. Born into a family of modest means in the north of France in the same year as Albert Mathiez (q.v.), but less favored than he, Lefebvre was unable to pursue classical studies. However, he did obtain his agrégation in modern history. After a lengthy period of teaching in high schools, he defended, in 1924, his thesis, "Les Paysans du Nord pendant la Révolution Française," which placed him among the master historians of the Revolution. After serving as a professor at the University of Strasbourg, 1928–1932, he accepted the chair in the history of the French Revolution at the Sorbonne in 1932. He was active in the Society for Robespierrean Studies and on the journal, *Annales historiques de la Révolution Française*. Lefebvre made important contributions to the historiography of the Revolution. A socialist of the heart, a member of the Socialist party, and an admirer of the history of the Revolution of Jean Jaurès (q.v.), the only master he recognized, Lefebvre nonetheless lacked the temperament of a polemicist, preferring a gentle approach in debate and thereby rectifying certain views of Mathiez on the "socialism" of Robespierrists. Marked not only by his birth and by his reading of Karl Marx (q.v.) and Jaurès, but also by the turbulence of his own times, Lefebvre thought of himself as a "social" historian from his very first writings (*Documents relatifs à l'histoire des subsistances dans le district de Bergues*, 1914). In his thesis on the northern peasants in the Revolution, he revealed a Revolution that was rightly of peasants, "autonomous in its origins, its methods, and above all, in its anti-capitalist tendencies." Studying the origin of these agrarian movements, he wrote *La Grande Peur de 1789* (1932) a path-breaking study in the history of mentalities. Lefebvre also made important innovations in methodology. Henri Pirenne (q.v.) praised his thesis as "a model of scientific self-denial." Promoter of statistical and quantitative history, Lefebvre also sought to define the concepts of psychological and biological history with studies of the collective mentality, revolutionary crowds, and individual states of mind. Author of a global synthesis, *La Révolution Française* (1930, re-ed., 1957), and of the brilliant *1789*, published in 1939, on the occasion of the 150th anniversary of the Revolution, he was also one of the few French historians to become interested in the history of historiography. In *Notions d'historiographie moderne* (published, 1971), he saw changed interpretations and new methods in written history as "le reflet du mouvement général de l'histoire" (the reflection of the general direction of history).

Bibliography: "Necrology," *Annales historiques de la Révolution Française* (1960); A. Soboul, "Introduction," *Études sur la Révolution Française de Georges Lefebvre* (1963).

Alice Gérard

LEROI-GOURHAN, André Georges Leándre Adolphe (Paris, 1911–Paris, 1986), French ethnologist and prehistorian, professor at Lyon University (1944), Orléans, and the Sorbonne (1956), Ethnological Institute of Paris University (1950), Collège de France (1969, professor of prehistory), co-director of the Guimet Museum (1940–1944), Musée de l'Homme and Cernuschi Museum, initiator and director of the Centre de formation aux recherches ethnologiques (1946), Centre de documentation et des récherches préhistoriques et protohistoriques (1962), transformed into the Équipe de recherches associée in 1967, member of the Académie des Inscriptions et Belles Lettres (1980), initiator and director or co-director of several important reviews, such as *Revue de géographie humaine* (1948), *Gallia Préhistoire* (director from 1962) and of the *Suppléments à Gallia Préhistoire*. His encyclopedic format, concentrated on historical fact, explains his interest in the modernization of research (*Les fouilles préhistoriques, techniques et méthodes*, 1950; *Sur les méthodes de fouilles*, 1963; *Les chasseurs de la Préhistoire*, 1955, 1983; *Fouilles de Pincevent: Essai d'analyse ethnograhique d'un habitat magdalénien*, 1973). His major objectives (the ethnographical analyses of a habitat, the organization and utilization of social spaces, as well as the initiation and development of several new directions of research— paleoethnology and paleozooanthropology) explain his scrupulous attention and his technique of examining all categories of information to obtain a general ethnographical view of the habitat and to observe its dynamics. For this he created a school of prehistoric investigations, "The Leroi-Gourhan School," or "The School of Horizontal Digging," whose ideas and methods were put into practice in Project Paranapanema (Brazil) and Proyecto Leroi-Gourhan (Paraguay). This explains the variety of his scientific writings (*Archéologie du Pacifique de Nord*, 1946; *Ethnologie et préhistoire*, 1964; and *Préhistoire de l'art Occidental*, 1965), as well as his interest in social and economic realities (ethnology, tools and machines, social structures, mentalities and beliefs) as the means of identifying the deeds of the people, their mentality, and the relations between gesture and word. He demolished traditional ideas about prehistoric religions, the relation between gesture and word, and the semiotics of rock art, and offered new models of interpretation which make yesterday's savages appear as creative and imaginative beings, even if economic, social and cultural man can only be surmised from the archaeological material. D. Lavallée (BSPF, 10–12, 1987, p. 416) expressed best Leroi-Gourhan's scientific conception in the following words: "Our greatest good fortune is to be able to thank God that we are studying man, not things."

Bibliography: Gilles Gaucher, *Andre Leroi-Gourhan, 1911–1986*, BSPF, tome 84, nos. 10–12, 1987, pp. 302–315; also the bibliography (pp. 316–323) and some commemorative papers; J. Filip, *Enzyklopädisches Handbuch zur Ur-und Frühgeschichte Europas*, II, Prague 1967, p. 701; *Les racines du monde. Entretiens avec Claude-Henri Rocquet*, Paris, 1982.

Ligia Bârzu

MANDROU, Robert (Paris, 1921–Paris, 1984), French historian. Secretary of the *Annales* (1954–1962), director of studies of Section VI of the École Pratique des Hautes Études (1957–1984), professor of modern history at the University of Paris X-Nanterre (1968–1981). The work of Robert Mandrou showed four main characteristics.(1) It renewed, thanks to *Louis XIV et son temps* (1973)— replacing in the venerable collection "Peuples et civilisations" *La prépondérance française: Louis XIV* by A. de Saint-Léger and P. Sagnac dating from 1935— an idea of history that was then archaic, the idea of the old "événementielle" history (diplomatic, political, and military). While keeping the traditional framework of the collection, Mandrou knew how to insert in his book the innovative ideas of the "École des *Annales.*" He was much more interested in "restoring the destiny of peoples forced to suffer the preponderance of Louis XIV; and more concerned about reconstituting the profound movements of social life." (Introduction). (2) His work also added to the "territoire de l'historien" a cultural history, which for a long time had been left to the specialists in art, literature, science, and ideas. Associated with Georges Duby, in 1958 he brought out the now classical *Histoire de la civilisation française* (fourth edition in 1984) and the third tome of the *Histoire de la pensée européenne: des humanistes aux hommes de science* (1973). (3) Mandrou also showed himself as a specialist in comparative history, an expert on the German world (he devoted to it his complementary thesis *Les Fugger, propriétaires fonciers en Souabe* [1969] and in 1977 obtained the establishment of the *Mission historique française* in Göttingen), and an admirer of the British liberal system. In *L'Europe absolutiste: raison et raison d'État* (1977) (first edition published in 1976 in German as *Staatsräson und Vernunft, 1549–1775*), he presented a vast survey of Europe from the classical period to the Enlightenment. But above all, (4) in the field of the "histoire des mentalités," this disciple of Lucien Febvre (q.v.) showed his ability at its best. Three pioneer books, heirs to Febvre's *Martin Luther* and *Rabelais*, gave this young discipline its charter of nobility. In 1961 the *Introduction à la France moderne* showed that "each social class, each profession, each religious group bears a characteristic vision"; it revealed "how gradually during the sixteenth and seventeenth centuries modern man was born with his new understanding of the outside world . . . and with the scientific mentality derived from it" (F. Lebrun). In 1964 his masterful analysis of *La bibliothèque bleue de Troyes*, "petit volume, mais énorme de contenu" according to P. Goubert, recorded the resounding entrance of *La culture populaire en France au XVIIᵉ siècle* as a research field. At last, in 1968 his thesis, *Magistrats et sorciers en France au XVIIᵉ siècle*, which proved according to Philippe Joutard, the author's sensitiveness to the totalitarian phenomenon in the past as in the present, revived Michelet's intuition about witchcraft, and opened a fertile historiographical working site. In 1984, death joined Philippe Ariès and Robert Mandrou, both having founded in 1967 at Plon's a pioneer collection, "Civilisations et mentalités." This collection has played a great part in making a modern and living conception of history known, first to the history community and then to the general public.

Bibliography: Philippe Joutard, *Préface à la troisième édition de la culture populaire aux XVIIè et XVIIIè siècles* (Paris: Imago, 1985); Philippe Joutard, "Robert Mandrou,"

Historiens et géographes, (July-August 1984): 1155–1157; Philippe Joutard and Jean Lecuir, *"L'itinéraire d'un historien européen du XXè siècle*,*"* in *Histoire sociale, sensibilités collectives et mentalités: Mélanges Robert Mandrou* (Paris: PUF, 1985), pp. 9–21; François Lebrun, "Hommage à Robert Mandrou," *Historiens et géographes*, (May 1984): 903–904.

Christian Amalvi

MASPÉRO, Gaston (Paris, 1846–Paris, 1916), French Egyptologist. A student of l'École Normale Supérieure; instructor at l'École Pratique des Hautes Études (1869–1874), professor at the Collège de France (1874–1880, 1886–1899), curator of the Museum of Boulaq and of Egyptian excavations and antiquities (1881–1886 and 1899–1914). Member of the Académie des Inscriptions et Belles-Lettres (1883). A precocious and self-made Egyptologist, Maspéro taught Egyptology in France and oversaw conservation and excavations in Egypt. His chief work was *Histoire ancienne des peuples de l'Orient*, the first edition of which (1875) was considerably enlarged in the three volumes that appeared from 1894 to 1899. It was the first attempt to present, starting from written and archaeological sources, a history of the peoples of Egypt and Asia Minor, no longer side-by-side but in a synchronous manner, with emphasis on their relations and their cultures. In 1880 Maspéro left for Egypt on a mission. There he founded l'Institut Français d'Archéologie Orientale. In 1881 he became director of excavations and antiquities of Egypt and curator of the Museum of Boulaq. He engaged in extensive activities: discoveries of pharaonic sarcophages at Deir-el-Bahari, the investigation of some twenty pyramids that had a reputation as "dumb" at Saqqarah, Dashour, and Meidoum, the excavation of a necropole found intact at Akhmim, the clearing out of the temple of Luxor, and the clearing of the Sphinx of Gizeh of sand. After a period in France, he resumed his work in Egypt, mainly at Karnak and Memphis. Editor of some of Jean-François Champollion's (q.v.) manuscripts and of *Mémoires* by the Egyptologist, Auguste Mariette, Gaston Maspéro illustrates the continuity of French Egyptology in the century in which it occupied first place in that field.

Bibliography: "Maspéro Gaston," in the *Grand Dictionnaire universel du XIXe siècle* by P. Larousse (1866–1879); Edouard Naville, "L'Egyptologie française pendant un siècle (1822–1922)," *Journal des Savants* (1922–1923).

Charles-Olivier Carbonell

MATHIEZ, Albert (La Bruyère, 1874–Paris, 1932), French historian. Mathiez was the first in France to devote himself to the study of the French Revolution as a professional historian trained in the mode of academic positivism. Nonetheless, his work did not appear to be any less committed, ideologically, than that of his predecessors. Born into a family of peasant origins, he was able to complete his studies as a student at the École Normale Supérieure, where he was an ardent socialist. But at that time revolutionary historiography was dominated by A. Aulard, a former professor of Italian literature who held the chair of French Revolutionary History at the Sorbonne, founded in 1886 by the Municipal Council of Paris, and it was under Aulard's direction that Mathiez completed his doctoral thesis and two monographs, *La Théophilanthropie et le culte décadaire* and *Les origines des cultes révolutionnaires*, on the religious aspects of the Revolution. These first works affirmed Mathiez' originality. Of a combative and independent temperament, extremely fond of politics, Mathiez was thus ready to reinterpret the history of the Revolution by systematically departing from Aulard's school, which, Mathiez argued, had been writing the history of the Revolution from the point of view of the antisocialist perspective of the Radical Party. His nonconformity proved costly, as he was denied the chance to succeed Aulard at the Sorbonne, despite his prestige as a scholar and his literary talent. After a career in provincial faculties (Caen, Dijon, Besançon), he taught at the Sorbonne only in the capacity of an assistant to Ph. Sagnac.

In methodology, Mathiez was no innovator. If he used Émile Durkheim's sociological approach in his theses on religious history, he quickly abandoned it, was wary of generalizations, supported the work on archival documents, and extolled the mission of republican historians to engage in civic pedagogy. His career was a twenty-year-long battle to rehabilitate the Robespierrist view of the Revolution in the face of the dominant Dantonism. The *Annales révolutionnaires*, founded in 1908, and the Society of Robespierrist Studies were the instruments of this largely symbolic struggle, in which Danton embodied parliamentary corruption, with persistent references to the present, while the uncorruptible Robespierre became the standard-bearer of a democratic and social republic opposed to compromise. The Great War (World War I) occasioned new attacks on Danton's defeatism: (*Danton et la paix*), but also innovative studies, such as *La Révolution et les etrangers,* and especially, *La vie chère et le mouvement social sous la Terreur*. In 1917 Mathiez hailed the Bolshevik Revolution as the daughter of the Jacobins' Revolution. In Lenin, he saw the successor to Robespierre. However, his adherence to the Communist party was fleeting, and Mathiez more and more assumed the role of a ''national'' historian, critical of German Marxism and Bolshevism alike, preferring to recall the tradition of French socialism during the first half of the nineteenth century. Mathiez died prematurely, without having given any genuine synthesis, three small volumes published in 1921 being works of popularization. Like Jean Jaurès (q.v.), whose *Histoire Socialiste* he re-issued in 1922, Mathiez wanted to explain the Revolution by conflicts among and within the various classes. Nevertheless, he wrote a history that was, above all, political, dominated by the role of parties and factions and by the intrigues and passions of their leaders. But he revitalized this history by his appreciation for psychological nuance and concrete economic situations. *La Vie chère sous la Terreur* was, in this respect, a pioneering monograph. As a man of action, a writer, and a remarkably stimulating professor, Mathiez knew how to appeal to a vast public for whom he remained, as L. Febvre remarked, ''the passionate historian of a burning history.''

Bibliography: Georges Lefebvre, *Etudes sur la Révolution Française* (1963); Necrology in *Annales historiques de la Révolution Française* (1932).

Alice Gérard

MICHELET, Jules (Paris, 1798–Hyères, 1874), French historian. Lecturer at the École Normale Supérieure (1827–1838), assistant to François Guizot (q.v.) at the Sorbonne (1834–1835), professor at the Collège de France (chair of history and morals, 1838–1851), head of the historical section of the record office (1830–1852). Dismissed after the coup d'état of December 2, Michelet could barely make a living from writing. His first works were those of a philosopher and a teacher of history. In 1827 he translated *Scienza nuova* by Giambattista Vico under the title *Principes de la philosophie de l'histoire* and published a *Précis d'histoire moderne* for students in colleges in order to present, he said, "to children a row of images and to grown-ups a string of ideas." The idea as an image and the fact as a symbol is the method he would later use in the *Histoire de France*. Michelet's major work, the *Histoire de France*, was written in two periods: from 1833 to 1844, the first six volumes cover the origins to the Middle Ages, and from 1855 to 1867, eleven volumes cover modern times. Meanwhile, Michelet wrote a *Histoire de la Révolution française* (1847–1853). It was in 1830, in the enthusiasm of the July Revolution, that he visualized France as "a soul and a person" and history as "an integral resurrection of the past" (*Préface* of 1833). In fact, he covered everything: the soil, the people, the leaders, the events, the institutions, and the beliefs. While the first volume, devoted to the races that had fought for the possession of Gaul, owed much to Augustin Thierry, (q.v.), the following volumes gave a measure of Michelet's profound originality: a superb *Tableau de France*, where geology poetically matches the collective psychology of provinces served as an introduction to the Middle Ages, sympathetically presented in a succession of pictures, portraits, reflections, and erudite notes.

The year 1843 marked a turning-point. Michelet and Edgar Quinet (q.v.) published together their course at the Collège de France on *Les Jésuites*, a violent attack on the Roman Catholic Church. Then, Michelet started to write a *Histoire de la Révolution* in a patriotic vein, "an epic poem with the people as the hero." He saw the revolution from the perspective of the people. Caused by the misery of the people (*plebs*), the Revolution was basically French because it was mainly the work of the people (*populus*)—"an epoch of one mind, a sacred epoch when the entire nation, regardless of parties and of the opposition of classes advanced under a fraternal banner," because it achieved the unity of the nation and endowed France with the mission of bringing Freedom to the world. There, in Paris, in the Bastille Square, history reached a climax, as "the war of people against nature, of the spirit against matter, of freedom against fate," as Michelet had written a few years before in an impassioned essay (*Introduction à l'histoire universelle*, 1831). With the *Histoire de la Révolution* completed and the 1848 Revolution suppressed, Michelet resumed the *Histoire de France* which he had interrupted with the end of the reign of Louis XI. His outlook changed; he gives a sombre picture of the Middle Ages: it is a "strange and monstruous state of things"; it is in Michelet's own words "my enemy." A few years before Jacob Burckhardt (q.v.), he viewed the Renaissance in a global way as a special moment in civilization, as the dawn of modern times, and Columbus, Copernicus, and Luther as the three prophets of reason. In the ensuing volumes, where the Ancien Régime and the kings are severely judged, his passion distorted his interpretation of the documents, and the historian gave way to the polemicist. Undoubtedly, this change can be explained by his family misfortunes and the hardships he encountered at the end of his life. A romantic poet, Michelet made his work his life. "This book is my life, the only event of my life" (*Préface* of 1869 to the *Histoire de France*). His was a poetical method, even when he made use of primary sources. An archivist, when he went over his records, he heard "these papers which are not papers but lives of men, provinces, people who had all lived and spoken." As a writer, his style was utterly symbolic; he played on analogies, multiplied the vitalist metaphors, continually used anthropomorphic images: "The Bastille was not taken, she surrendered. Her guilty conscience troubled her, rendered her insane." Michelet's romantic style reveals a romantic philosophy of history. His vitalism and anthropomorphism evince, respectively, an optimistic progressivism and a unity of being. There are no causes in Michelet's work but identities. Jeanne d'Arc is the People and the Revolution; her nature is equal to theirs. Hence, history is a sort of relay in which heroic figures embody the avatars of the nation. In his nonhistorical works, which were most successful, Michelet gave free rein to his compassionate and romantic genius, which made of him another Victor Hugo. His poems on nature, *l'Oiseau* (1856), *l'Insecte* (1857), *la Mer* (1861), and *la Femme* (1859), are a mixture of silly things and effusions, pantheism and scientism, anticlericalism and love for the little people. *La Bible de l'Humanité* (1864), more than his *Histoire du XIXe siècle* (1872–1875) which he left unfinished, appears as the crowning of an immense work which, like Balzac's work, "we approach in search of reinvigoration and elation" (A. Thibaudet). Gabriel Monod (q.v.), who was his student and apparently a very different historian from Michelet, stated: "Michelet left behind masterpieces to be admired, not models to be imitated." Today, the New History sees in him a pioneer of the history of the collective mind, of the psychohistory of the depths, and also an instance of the inevitable historiographical subjectivism. Michelet is thus very much in fashion.

Bibliography: Michelet, *Oeuvres complètes*, the first critical edition, supervised by Paul Viallaneix, is in press, Vol.1 (Paris: Flammarion, 1971). R. Barthes, *Michelet* (Paris, 1954) (2d ed., 1975); J. Michelet, *Journal*, 2 vols. (Paris, 1959–1961); *Michelet cent ans après*, (Grenoble, 1975); G. Monod, *La vie et la pensée de Jules Michelet* (Paris, 1923), 2 vols.; P. Viallaneix, *La Voie royale. Essai sur L'idée de peuple dans l'oeuvre de Michelet* (Paris, 1971).

Charles-Olivier Carbonell

MIGNET, Auguste (Aix-en-Provence, 1796–Paris, 1884), French historian. A self-made historian who sided with the left before 1830, an academic conservative after 1830, Mignet illustrated, throughout a long career, the successive functions of the bourgeois historian in the nineteenth century. Born into a lower middle-class family, Mignet was a brilliant student of law and made a start in the liberal battle, along with his friend, Adolphe Thiers (q.v.), by means of journalism and history. He was laureate at the Academy of Nîmes and later, at the Academy of Inscriptions and Belles-Lettres in Paris; his prize essay on the feudal system expounded his theory of historical "laws." He came to Paris in 1821, and there he became known for his articles in the *Courrier français* and through his courses at the Athénée, a sort of "free university." But it was the *Histoire de la Révolution Française*, written in two years, while Mignet was in full battle against the Ultras of the Restoration, that, in 1824, brought him national and, soon, international fame. These two classically composed, hastily written volumes were successful because, for the first time, they gave a rational and clear explanation of the revolutionary phenomenon. Inspired not only by Montesquieu (q.v.), but also by J. de Maistre, Mignet applied a determinist and finalistic diagram to the event, seeming thus to justify, not only 1789, as Mme de Staël had done, but also the violence and the Reign of Terror: "Trois années de dictature de salut public, si elles ont été perdues pour la liberté, ne l'ont pas été pour la Révolution." (Three years of dictatorship in the name of public safety— if they had been a loss for the cause of liberty, they were not a loss for the cause of the Revolution.) This observation shocked a number of readers, liberals included.

Mignet was most original in his analyses of social history, however schematic they may have been. The class struggle (between the aristocracy and the commoners, but also, within the commoners, between the bourgeoisie and the "populace") was, for him, a revolutionary mechanism, the necessity of which he demonstrated and the movement of which he unraveled. In this respect, Friedrich Engels (q.v.) and G. Plekhanov considered Mignet a forerunner of dialectical materialism. This interpretation immediately launched a theoretical quarrel, for or against "fatalism," the philosophy of history whose focus was also political. In fact, Mignet contributed substantially through this book and through his articles in the *National* to preparing people to see the Revolution of 1830 as a "necessary" complement of 1789. Translated into some twenty languages, the work served as a global guide to revolution, both theoretical and practical, during the nineteenth century. After 1830, Mignet left the political scene to Adolphe Thiers (q.v.) and François Guizot (q.v.) and dedicated himself to being an official historian concerned with the organization of historical work. He sought to make history a "national institution," a guarantor of progress. The Academy of Moral and Political Sciences, of which Mignet was perpetual secretary from 1837 to 1884, must have been the laboratory for this philosophical history, influenced as it was by the eclecticism of Victor Cousin, whose ideas appear in Mignet's still-famous *Notices* and necrological *Éloges*. Mignet was director of the Diplomatic Archives and a founding member of the Historical Committees of the Ministry of Public Instruction. His "Introduction" to *Négociations relatives à la Succession d'Espagne* (1840) brilliantly established diplomatic history as a field of study in France. With his *Antonio Pérez et Philippe II* (1844), Mignet

renounced his ambition to synthesize in favor of a series of postitivist monographs.

Bibliography: Yvonne Kniebiehler, *Naissance des sciences humaines: Mignet et l'histoire philosophique au XIXème siecle* (Flammarion, 1973).

Alice Gérard

MONOD, Gabriel (Le Havre, 1844–Paris, 1912), French historian. From 1869
to 1905, professor at the École Pratique des Hautes Études and head of the fourth
section (history and philology). Lecturer at the École Normale Supérieure (1880–
1904). Professor at the Collège de France (chair of general history and historical
method) from 1905 to 1911. Member of the Académie des Sciences Morales et
Politiques from 1897. Monod did not write much. His major works include
studies on medieval sources, *Études critiques sur les sources de l'histoire mér-
ovingienne* (1872–1885), and *De l'histoire carolingienne* (1898), a textbook on
bibliography, *Bibliographie de l'histoire de France* (1888) and two historiographical studies *Les maîtres de l'histoire. Renan, Taine, Michelet* (1894) and
Jules Michelet. Étude sur sa vie et ses oeuvres (1905). Monod gave impetus to
the historical movement in France. He more than anyone else was the promoter
of the methodical, critical, and positive school, sometimes inadequately called
positivist. In 1866 Gaston Paris (q.v.) and Paul Meyer, two linguists, asked the
twenty-two-year-old Monod to join them at the *Revue critique d'histoire et de
littérature* they edited, which attacked the rhetorical and credulous historians
who then dominated the Sorbonne and the academies. In 1869 Victor Duruy
(q.v.) invited him to come to the École Pratique des Hautes Etudes, which he
had just created, to help him introduce German-type seminars into French higher
learning. In 1876 Monod founded the *Revue historique* which he turned into a
forum of the new history, following the German model. It gave pride of place
to the critique of texts as method, political history, and the "chronicle of states"
as domains, and the erudite monograph, or the thesis firmly rooted in the sources
as genre. In the article that opened the first issue of the review—"Le progrès
des études historiques en France depuis le XVIe siècle"—the true manifesto of
the "positivist" school, Monod stated his willingness to combine the erudite
tradition, that of the *maurist* and *chartist* tradition, with the literary tradition,
so that soon after their defeat, French historians might answer the German
challenge and take their revenge. He had his own opinions. As a liberal Protestant, he turned the *Revue historique* into a weapon to combat clericalism and
ultramontanism. As a moderate republican, he stood up for Dreyfus and violently
attacked the nationalists. A contradictory man, he admired Germany, the University of Göttingen, where he had been a student of Georg Waitz (q.v.) and
Richard Wagner, whom he regularly visited in Bayreuth, but as a son of Alsace
and a devoted patriot, he wanted more than anything else to regain the lost
provinces. An erudite philologist, he worshipped Jules Michelet (q.v.), his old
master, and at the end of his life rejected the historical micrography promoted
by his students. Supervisor of the thesis of Lucien Febvre (q.v.), he supported

Henri Berr's (q.v.) attempts at renewal in *Revue de synthèse historique*, thus demonstrating a rare open-mindedness.

Bibliography: Ch-O.Carbonell, *Histoire et historiens, une mutation idéologique des historiens français, 1865–1885* (Toulouse, 1976); E. d'Eichtal, *Quelques âmes d'élite* (Paris, 1919); G. Monod, *Portraits et souvenirs* (Paris, 1897).

Charles-Olivier Carbonell

MORTILLET, Gabriel de (Meylan, Isère, 1821–Saint-Germain-en-Laye, 1898), French prehistorian. Warden of the museum in Saint Germain, professor at the Ecole d'Anthropologie (1878), editor-in-chief of the review *Materiaux pour l'histoire de l'homme* (1864) and of *L'Homme*. De Mortillet contributed to the the progress of prehistorical research, especially on the Old Stone Age. Under the influence of Christian Jurgensen Thomsen's (q.v.) "three ages system" and Jean-Baptiste Lamarck's "transformism," he worked out a series of new concepts as well as a sketch for a relative chronology of the Old Stone Age which was to be used up to the midtwentieth century, not only in Western Europe but throughout the continent, as well as in Asia and Africa. As early as 1869 Mortillet foreshadowed in *Essai d'une classification des cavernes et des stations sous abri*, the principles of the typological method, which did not achieve theoretical expression until 1903, that is, he established the chronology by taking into account certain types of fossils ("guiding fossils"), the complexes designated by them, and the cultures whose names they expressed which are to be found up to the present. To this principle he added stratigraphical observation (on the basis of data available in France and Switzerland). The divisions proposed in 1869 were revised and reworked in 1883 in *La Préhistorique, Antiquité de l'homme, Paléoethnologie ou archéologie préhistorique*, a work through which he extended the principles of his method to other epochs and introduced for the first time in the history of science the concept of "prehistory". DeMortillet's role as a forerunner of prehistorical research was completed by his opinion that a set of "guiding-fossils" could be used not only to define a certain archaeological culture, but also to define a people known only from the written records of history, an idea that was to be developed by Gustaf Kossinna (q.v.) and Gordon Vincent Childe (q.v.). De Mortillet was reproached for his too strict dependence on the natural sciences and the linear evolutionism which dominated the period and for considering human culture as a continuation of organic evolution, thus imposing the categories of natural history on human history. Nevertheless, he succeeded in imposing a system of universal values which was based on archaeological criteria, thereby contrasting with other divisions that had been proposed before him, grounded on geological sequences or on the evolution of fauna.

Bibliography: G.V. Childe, *Piecing Together the Past* (London, 1956), pp. 25–27; Jan Filip, *Enzyklopädisches Handbuch der Ur-Und Frühgeschichte Europas*, II (Prague, 1967), p. 856; Laming-Emperaire, *Origines de l'archélogie préhistorique en France* (Paris, 1964).

Ligia Bârzu

PARIS, Gaston (Avenay, Marne, 1839–Cannes, 1903), French historian. Professor at the Collège de France (1872–1903), president of Section IV of the Ecole Pratique des Hautes Études (1886–1895), Member of the Institute: Académie des Inscriptions et Belles Lettres (1876), and Académie Française (1896). Paying homage to his father, Paulin Paris (1800–1881), a teacher in the Collège de France, when he succeeded him in 1872 as professor of the history of French literature in the Middle Ages, Gaston Paris stressed the distinctiveness of his own generation—Paul Meyer's (1840–1917) and Gabriel Monod's—from his father's romantic one: "We attach less importance to appreciating the Middle Ages than to knowing and understanding them" (*Revue internationale de l'enseignement*, March 15, 1882). To know the Middle Ages and to understand them as an expert and an erudite, not as a dabbler or an aesthete, Paris schooled himself in the German "séminaire" (trained by Friedrich Diez in Bonn and then by Ernst Curtius in Göttingen). From 1858 to 1861, he underwent his novitiate at the École des Chartes, trained by, among others, Louis Quicherat, and in 1865, he finally completed his doctoral thesis, "Légende poétique de Charlemagne," proving that literary texts are irreplaceable historical documents. The Academy des Inscriptions conferred on his thesis the Gobert Prize in 1866, when he was twenty-seven years old. Paris's massive work—which fills about thirty columns in the general catalogue of the Bibliothèque Nationale—encompassed two large areas: comparative mythology and the literary history of the Middle Ages. It depended on a strict mastering of Romance philology and showed Gaston Paris's will to disseminate in French universities the scientific method and state of mind which were guiding the German "seminaire" and to replace rhetoric by criticism in the study of philology and history. The same requirements of erudition prompted him to create high-level research centers that greatly contributed to arousing slumbering or indifferent academics, and that opened a road to Gabriel Monod's *Revue Historique*: *La Revue critique d'histoire et de littérature*, founded in 1866 with Paul Meyer; in 1872, still with Paul Meyer, the review *Romania*; and in 1875, the *Société des anciens textes français*. He appeared for thirty years as an international "chief" of a learned history reinvigorated by the iron–bound method of philology. In a symbolic way, when Henri Berr (q.v.) stood as candidate in 1903 for a professorship in the Collège de France, he attempted to win over Gaston Paris, "one of the powerful animators of the new Sorbonne" (Siegel, 1983), to his plans for "historical synthesis." Gaston Paris and his friends, Paul Meyer and Gabriel Monod, did not by chance belong to the first Dreyfusard "intellectual" cell. All of them considered that "the religion of philosophy . . . is not only mistress of Science but also of morality and virtue" (G. Monod quoted by Madeleine Rebérioux).

Bibliography: *Correspondance de Frédéric Mistral avec Paul Meyer et Gaston Paris recueillie et annotée par Jean Boutière; introduction d' Hedwige Boutière* (Paris: Didier, 1978), Publications de la Sorbonne, série documents, Vol. 28; Martin Siegel, "Henri Berr et la Revue de synthèse historique," in *Au berceau des Annales: actes du colloque de Strasbourg (octobre 1979)*, published by Ch-O Carbonell and G. Livet (Toulouse:

Presses de l'Institut d'Études Politiques de Toulouse, 1983), pp. 205–218; Madeleine Rebérioux, "Histoire, historiens et dreyfusisme," *Revue historique* (April–June 1976): 407–432.

Christian Amalvi

PARROT, André (Désandans, 1901–Paris, 1980), French archaeologist and historian. Professor at L'École du Louvre and at the Protestant Theology Faculty of Paris, Warden of the Louvre Museum (1968), editor-in-chief of *Syria* review, of *Revue d'art oriental et d'archéologie*, and of *Revue d'Assyriologie* (1954). One of the greatest authorities of contemporary historiography, a researcher of the prehistory and history of the Near East, especially Mesopotamia. Parrot's name is connected with the discovery of a famous Sumerian town, Mari (*Mari, une ville perdue . . .*, 1945, re–issued, 1948) and with the series of reports on the diggings in Mari published in *Syria* during 1935–1975. His interests in the Syrian-Mesopotamian zone materialized either in specialized papers (A. Parrot, *Tello. Vingt campagnes de fouilles 1877–1933*, 1948; *Archéologie Mésopotamienne. Les étapes*, 1946) or in works for the cultured public (A. Parrot, *Découverte des mondes ensevelis*, 1954, as well as the great syntheses "L'Univers des formes," *Sumer*, 1960, and *Assur*, 1961). Parrot's personality was defined by three qualities: his ability to subordinate detail to some general, guiding ideas, his understanding of efforts made by the archaeologist as part of a collective endeavor to reconstruct an historical age, and the absolute necessity of relating archaeological fact to information originating in other kinds of sources, mainly epigraphic. (From this point of view his reports on the diggings in Mari and Larsa can be considered genuine models worth following.) Ernest Will completes the picture by mentioning that Parrot demanded that all archaeologists breathe life into the fragments dug up: "For him the archaeologist was a historian, an indispensable man for certain periods and civilizations whose mission could be none other than to restore a page of history." This point of view was brilliantly illustrated in *Mari* (1948): "Whatever the case may be with Mari, there are new pages of ancient history to be inserted among the chapters already written, often surprising additions but with much to teach. This capital of the Middle Euphrates region, established on one of the most important communication links of Eastern antiquity, the route from the Indies by way of the Persian Gulf, the route from Asia Minor to the Mediterranean along the river, a transition point between two distinct regions running along the edge of a desert, [Mari] caravan stop and city of warehouses, was also the center of a strong government whose friendship was sought and whose wrath was feared." On the basis of certain texts and elements of mural decorations, he suggested a close connection between Mari and the Cretan world, regarding the town as a place of initiation into court life: "The palace offers the most convincing testimony to complete success. One of the tablets gives the impression that [the palace] was considered abroad as one of the wonders of the world at that time." Given his interest in biblical archaeology ("Déluge et Arche de Noé," *Cahiers d'Archéologie biblique*, No. 1, "La

Tour de Babel,'' *Cahiers d'Archéologie biblique*, No. 2, ''Ninive et L'Ancien Testament,'' *Cahiers d'Archéologie biblique*, No.3), Parrot proposed with some documentary support the possible function of the town as a stopping place for Abraham on his way from Ur to Haran (*Mari*, p. 209). His literary talent, together with his interest in uncovering new sites, account for the great popularity of Parrot's scientific work.

Bibliography: Ernest Will, ''André Parrot,'' *Syria*, 58 (1981): 1; the partial list of works in *Mari, Capitale fabuleuse* (Paris, 1974), pp. 194–206.

Ligia Bârzu

QUINET, Edgar (Bourg, 1803–Paris, 1875), French historian, philosopher, poet, and politician. Professor of foreign literatures at the Faculty of Lyon (1838–1842); holder of the chair of the literature of southern Europe at the Collège de France (1842–1846 and 1848–1851). Quinet was twice dismissed for his subversive ideas—for anti-catholicism in 1846 and for republicanism in 1852. Quinet was a philosopher of history who made a name for himself in 1825 when he translated the *Idées sur la philosophie de l'histoire* by Johann Herder, and when one of his last works, *La Création* (1870) poetically combines Darwin's evolutionism and historical scientism. He was also a historian of religions: He brought the *Vie de Jésus* by Strauss to public attention when he wrote an essay on it in 1838; earlier, after returning from a stay at the University of Heidelberg, he had written a book on *L'Origine des dieux*. Poet and historian, he produced extensive epic poems—*Ahasvérus* (1833), *Napoléon* (1836), and *Prométhée* (1838)—and devoted his thesis to *L'épopée indienne*.

A revolutionary historian of 1848, Quinet took part in the revolution of 1848, arms in hand, and advocated the great revolutionary principles of that year: democracy and the republic—which turned him into an outlaw from 1852 to 1870—the fundamental civil liberties and the people's right to be their own masters. He supported the Greek and Romanian independence movements, and his *Révolutions d'Italie* was the Bible of Italian patriots. Likewise, his outstanding historical works are devoted to revolutions. In *Révolutions d'Italie*, the first part of which was published, quite appropriately, in 1848, Quinet was searching for ''the soul of Italy'' in all its revolutions—political and social, literary and religious. It was the Italian people he wanted to know on their soil and in their monuments, from ancient times to Mazzini: a people in whom he saw a symbol of spiritual and social progress and an example for all oppressed peoples. A thoroughly researched historical work, the *Révolutions d'Italie* is also a prophetic work that would ordinarily have advanced the Risorgimento movement. Instead, *La Révolution* (1865) caused an uproar in revolutionary circles. Quinet bluntly began with the affirmation that ''the French Revolution should not be extolled'' and concludes with the statement: ''I showed the mistakes of the revolutionaries.'' In between he highly praised the principles of 1789, but he was hard on Robespierre and the Terror. Rejecting the determinist thesis, he took the view that the Terror could have been avoided and just as Alexis de Tocqueville (q.v.)

and contrary to Louis Blanc or Blanqui, he declared that "in the Terror, the new people suddenly turned into reactionaries." He drew a parallel between two ways in history, that of civic equality—Rome, the absolute monarchy, Catholicism, the Jacobins, Napoleon's Empire—and that of freedom illustrated in the past by Athens, the Reform, and the Girondins and in the future—or at least he thought so—by the Protestant Republic. A cosmopolitan, a European influenced by Germany and fascinated by southern Europe, Quinet was in fact a moralist, an intransigent "cleric," a thinker whose influence, mostly indirect, on the political staff of the Third Republic was considerable.

Bibliography: A. Galante Garrone, *E. Quinet, La Rivoluzione* (Turin, 1933); Mme E. Quinet, *E. Quinet, avant et depuis l'exil* (Paris, 1889); A Valès, *Edgar Quinet, sa vie, son oeuvre* (Carriére-sous-Poissy, 1936).

Charles-Olivier Carbonell

RENAN, Ernest (Tréguier, 1823–Paris, 1892), French historian, philologist, and philosopher. Holder of the chair of Hebrew, Chaldean, and Syriac languages at the Collège de France (1862–1864 and 1870–1890). Member of the Académie des Inscriptions (1856) and of the Académie Française (1879). Renan lost his faith and gave up the priesthood in 1845 and turned toward philosophy and philology. He brilliantly passed the aggregation in philosophy in 1848, and in 1852 he wrote his doctoral thesis, "Averroès et l'averroïsme." Influenced by his friend, the chemist Marcellin Berthelot, in 1848 he started to write *L'avenir de la science*, which was not published until 1890. Renan wanted to reconcile German science with French freedom and to replace religion with science—as he believed science alone could unravel the mystery of man—and to place humankind under the rule of scholars. Then he devoted himself to the study of Semitic languages. In 1847 the Académie des Inscriptions honored his paper on the *Histoire générale des langues sémitiques*, a paper that he extended and published in 1855. He classified oriental manuscripts in Rome (1849–1850), and he completed an inventory of Syriac manuscripts at the Bibliothèque Nationale, where he worked from 1851 to 1864. He was entrusted with an archaeological mission to Phoenicia (1860–1861) and went to Palestine. His scientific reputation brought him to the Académie des Inscriptions, and he contributed to well-known periodicals, the *Journal des Débats* and the *Revue des Deux-Mondes*. The *Vie de Jésus* turned him into a celebrated historian (1863). In this widely acclaimed book, Renan made use of the works of German christologists, but he did it in his own way. As a rationalist, he left out the fantastic, mysterious, and miraculous elements and from a hitherto sacred biography, that of our Savior Jesus Christ, he made a lay biography, that of a man called Jesus of Nazareth. As a philologist, he treated his sources cautiously, often expressing his doubts by adding "I believe," "it seems," "in my opinion." As an artist, he gave a sweet but rather dull description of Palestine, daily life, and women in love. The book caused an uproar: The Catholic clergy accused him of desecration, and the critics blamed him for too great an admiration for the man Jesus. The *Vie de Jésus* is the first volume of the seven that make up the *Histoire des origines du christianisme* which he finished in 1882. The last volumes, more erudite than poetical, did not raise such an outcry. Renan's last historical work was *Histoire du peuple d'Israël* (1887–1893).

A progressive and idealist conception gives unity to these works: The Hebrew people, chosen by the single God, were as important as the Greek people and were called on to free humankind from fear of and belief in myths and nature, but it was Christianity, in which the two trends merged that gave men a new conception of the universal order. Like all French historians, Renan was shocked by the Commune and military defeat, and he reacted in a contradictory way: by a fierce nationalism that made him write *Réforme intellectuelle et morale* (1871) for the regeneration of his homeland and then by a mild skepticism about human beings that appeared in the *Drames philosophiques* which he wrote at the end of his life.

Bibliography: *Cahiers Ernest Renan*, published from 1971 by the Société d'études renaniennes (Édit. Nizet, Paris); René Dussaud, *L'oeuvre scientifique d'Ernest Renan* (Paris, 1951); Keith Gore, *L'idée de progrés dans la pensée de Renan* (Paris, 1970); Henriette Psichari, *Renan d'après lui-même* (Paris, 1937); *Ernest Renan*, catalogue, Bibliothèque Nationale (Paris, 1974).

Charles-Olivier Carbonell

RENOUVIN, Pierre (Paris, 1893–Paris, 1974), French historian. Professor at the Sorbonne (1933) and its dean (1955–1958). President of the Fondation Nationale des Sciences Politiques. Elected to the Académie des Sciences Morales et Politiques in 1946. Touched by the Great War in his own person (his left arm was amputated in 1917) and in his spirit, this brilliant scholar was admitted to the *agrégation* when he was not yet twenty. He focused on the history of World War I early in his life. In 1920 he was the head of the War History Library at the Sorbonne, where he gave a course on the Great War in 1922. In 1925, he published *Les Formes du gouvernement de guerre* and in 1925 *Les Origines immédiates de la guerre*, a trenchant work in the heated historiographical debates of that time characterized by constant use of sources and a serene tone. It is still the traditional diplomatic history of the chancelleries. Three works would gradually break with this approach and replace diplomatic history by the history of international relations: *La crise européenne et la Grande Guerre (1904–1918)*, vol. 19 of the collection *Peuples et civilisations* (Paris, 1934; 4th ed., 1962), *La question d'Extrême-Orient, 1840–1940* (Paris, 1946) and finally, the great *Histoire des relations internationales* (8 vols., Paris, 1953–1958), supervised by Renouvin for which he wrote tomes five to eight. "The geographic conditions, the demographic movements, the economic and financial interests, the traits of the collective mind, the great sentimental trends, these are the underlying forces which provided the framework for the relations among human groups." This is how Renouvin summed up his theory of deep-seated forces at work among them. As innovative as this theory might be, it was still a traditional interpretation.

Indeed, for Renouvin the state always came first: "It is the action of States which is in the center of international relations" but the role of individuals was crucial. Under Renouvin's influence a "new history" emerged which was not the New History of Fernand Braudel (q.v.), but a history of foreign policies open to economic analysis, social history, cultural history, and geopolitics. The *Introduction à l'histoire des relations internationales* which he published in 1964 with his student J. B. Duroselle was the final testament of this master who was ignored by the *media* and the public at large but whose influence has been considerable in the French and European historiography.

Bibliography: Jean-Baptiste Duroselle, "De l'histoire diplomatique à l'histoire des relations internationales," *Mélanges Renouvin* (Paris, 1966); Jean-Baptiste Duroselle, "Pierre Renouvin," *Revue d'histoire moderne et contemporaine* (1975).

Charles-Olivier Carbonell

SEIGNOBOS, Charles (Lamastre, Ardèche, 1854–Ploubozlanec, Côtes-du-Nord, 1942), French historian. Student at the École Normale Supérieure, 1874–1877. Seignobos' university career, which began in 1879, was crowned with the post of professor of modern and contemporary political history at the Sorbonne in 1925. He devoted himself first to the history of the Middle Ages ("Le régime féodal en Bourgogne jusqu'en 1360," thesis, 1882), but soon turned to the study of the contemporary world and began to gain a reputation among the cultivated public with *L'Histoire politique de l'Europe contemporaine* (1897). His scientific work developed thereafter in the shadow of Ernest Lavisse (q.v.) whose favorite disciple he became. Under Lavisse's direction he composed tomes VI, VII, and VIII of *L'Histoire de France contemporaine*, published in 1921–1922, dealing with the period 1848–1914. In 1933 *L'Histoire sincère de la nation française*, first issued in English (The History of the French People, New York, 1932), was a major success and constituted the popular acceptance of his work as a historian. Like Lavisse, he was also a pedagogue, the author of an impressive number of manuals for use in the secondary schools. However, his name remains associated above all with a small volume written in collaboration with Charles-Victor Langlois (1863–1929) in 1898: *L'Introduction aux études historiques*. This was the simple publication of a course at the Sorbonne whose only objective was to propose to beginning historians a methodology "already secure in certain respects, still incomplete on some points of capital importance." Because it was in line with the perspectives previously explored by positivist thought and because it was written skillfully and was full of authoritative formulas, that essay, which might appear to confuse history with method based on three centuries of humanist erudition, Benedictine and Germanic, became, so to speak, the official bible of French history students. This explains why beginning in 1929, it was a favorite target for Lucien Febvre (q.v.) and the historians of the *Annales* School who undertook to discredit, in the eyes of the younger generation, "history à la Seignobos" which they accused of being blind and sterile and limited to political events. Seignobos, who had completed his theoretical views in 1901 (*La méthode* *historique appliquée aux sciences sociales*), never abandoned his initial concepts: "History is most decidedly a science."

Bibliography: "Bibliographie des oeuvres de M. Charles Seignobos," in Charles Seignobos, *Études de politique et d'histoire* (Paris, 1934), pp. xix–xxvii.

Jean Glénisson

SIMIAND, François (Gières, 1873–Saint-Raphaël, 1935), French sociologist, economist, and historian. A former student of the École Normale Supérieure, agrégé in philosophy, professor with the École Pratique des Hautes Études, then with the Conservatoire National des Arts et Métiers, and finally (1932–1935) with the Collège de France, where he taught the history of labor. A disciple of Émile Durkheim and a socialist campaigner, Simiand participated in setting up the *Année sociologique* in 1898 and, at the beginning of the century, edited the "Bibliothèque socialiste." His works directed French historians toward a new history. First, there was his famous polemic with Charles Seignobos (q.v.), triggered in 1903 by an article he published in the young *Revue de Synthèse historique*: "Méthode historique et science sociale." Denouncing the positivist idols—political, individual, and chronological—Simiand asserted that there was no science of the unique, there was only a science of the repeatable, of regularity. Afterward, he wrote his thesis ("Le Salaire des ouvriers des mines de charbon en France," 1904), and his major book *Le Salaire, l'évolution sociale et la monnaie* (1932). These models of analysis integrated the methods of the sociologist, the economist, and the historian alike. He discovered the cycles of expansion (phase A) and recession (phase B); priority emphasis on the monetary phenomena; and a general theory of economic and social evolution which he described as follows: "a social monetarism with inciting fluctuation." His influence in France was considerable: The *Annales* group (founded in 1929) acknowledged him as one of their own, and Ernest Labrousse recognized "the essential ties" between the two of them.

Bibliography: M. Lazard, *François Simiand, l'homme et l'oeuvre* (Paris, 1936), and the debate that opposed M. Levy-Leboyer; "L'héritage de F. Simiand," *Revue historique* 1 (1970): 77–120); J. Bouvier: "Fou F. Simiand?" *Annales E. S. C.* 5 (1973): 1173–1192.

Charles-Olivier Carbonell

TAINE, Hippolyte (Vouziers, 1828–Paris, 1893), French historian. One year after he left the École Normale Supérieure (1851), Taine gave up teaching to live off his writing. In 1864, however, he became a professor of the history of art and of aesthetics at the École des Beaux-Arts in Paris. He was elected at the Académie Française in 1878. A philosopher by training, he gained fame in 1857 with his work *Études sur les philosophes français du XIXe siècle*, a virulent attack on the eclectic philosophy of Victor Cousin and the idealism of university circles. His book *De l'intelligence* (1870) synthesized the theories he had applied in this works on literary history and the history of art. Taine used the same method in both fields. In his *Histoire de la littérature anglaise* (1856–1863) and in his *Philosophie de l'art* (1882), where he gathered a number of articles on the art of Greece, Italy, and the Netherlands, Taine advocated an absolute determinism: "All the sentiments, all the ideas . . . have their causes and their laws: the assimilation of historical and psychological researches to chemical and physiological researches is my aim". Seeing art and literature as the natural functions of this "superior animal" which is man, Taine considered the great writers and artists to be people governed by a "faculté maîtresse" (a predominant characteristic) which the historian was obliged to discover. For instance, he wrote an *Essai* (1855) on Livy, who had the gift of oratory. But this "faculté maîtresse" was also conditioned by "la race" (inherited personality), "le milieu" (soil, climate and social system), and "le moment" (historical situation). In the *Origines de la France contemporaine* (6 vols., 1876–1894), Taine applied his method to a large historical subject, "l'Ancien Régime, la Révolution and l'Empire." It is a masterpiece of naturalist historiography. "A historian," he wrote, "must be allowed to work as a naturalist: I viewed my subject as the metamorphosis of an insect"—and a monument of ill-will severely questioned by Adolphe Aulard (*Taine historien de la Révolution Française*, 1907) and by Albert Mathiez (q.v.) ("Taine historien," *Revue d'histoire moderne et contemporaine*, 1906–1907, pp. 257–284). Taine's approach is psychological when he deals with the populace and the leaders; he paints a robot-portrait of the Jacobin, a man with a fixation, haunted by abstractions. For Taine, the Revolution embodied the "classical spirit," disregarding the concrete for the essential and the universal. This psychopathic tendency accounted for the Terror which Taine depicted in ghastly details with the horrified complacency of the witness of the communard crisis. The *Origines de la France contemporaine* is a most pessimistic work about the "human beast" set free in periods of anarchy. It is also an indictment in which the author cleverly chooses and combines facts in a somewhat biased way. Finally and most importantly, it is a weapon in the arsenal of counterrevolutionaries. Taine's influence was considerable, as it underlay the works of reactionary historians and today inspires those who seek to escape Marxist Scripture.

Bibliography: A. Chevillon, *Taine. Formation de sa pensée* (Paris, 1932); A. Cresson, *H. Taine, sa vie, son oeuvre* (Paris, 1951); François Leger, *La jeunesse d'Hippolyte Taine* (Paris, 1980); H. Taine, *Vie et correspondance*, 4 vols. (Paris, 1902–1904).

Charles-Olivier Carbonell

THIERRY, Augustin (Blois, 1795–Paris, 1856), French historian. Former student of the École Normale Supérieure, secretary of Saint-Simon (1814–1817) with whom he published treatises on the regeneration of man, and, after breaking off with Saint-Simon, journalist at *Censeur européen* (1817–1820), then at *Courrier français* (1820–1821). Dismissed for his liberal ideas, Thierry devoted himself to historical studies until the end of his life, although he became blind in

1826. He was elected to the Académie des Inscriptions et Belles-Lettres in 1830. Under the title *Dix ans d'études historiques* (1834), Thierry collected his articles in *Censeur européen* and under the title *Lettres sur l'histoire de France* (1827) his articles from *Courrier français* to which he added fifteen new letters. These two works are in a way the manifesto of the French romantic school, whose solitary champion until then had been René Chateaubriand (q.v.). Thierry virulently attacked the "classic" historians such as Paul Velly and Louis Pierre Anquetil. He demanded that a history of the lower classes also be written—"commoners have their history just as the nobility"—as well as a history of the provinces before their often brutal incorporation into the kingdom of France. Suggesting new fields for study, Thierry also propounded new methods: a return to sources, to old chronicles, and to the scholars of the seventeenth and eighteenth centuries, and the use of local color to give a vivid picture of history and to show the exoticism and often the barbarousness of bygone times. Behind all this lies a theory of history: Conquest is the major event, for it results in the coexistence of the races and the continuation of their conflicts. The *Conquête de l'Angleterre par les Normands* (1825) popularized this theory which Thierry applied to Great Britain, but French readers were well aware that it also applied to France, since the Franks sought a role similar to the Normans as a master race. This work, which was a best-seller, marked the birth of the narrative school in France within the romantic historiographic movement. This "epic of the vanquished" is in fact a long dramatic story written with simplicity and emotion.

Thierry was soon criticized for blindly relying on his sources—the *Roman de Rou* in particular—and for the simplicity of his theory, but such attacks did not prevent him from writing the *Récits des temps mérovingiens* (1833–1840), undoubtedly the most read book of history by generations of French students for over a century. "The sense of discipline of the Romans vies with the violent and barbarous instincts of the Franks" in Merovingian times. Thierry did not give a poetical account of this dramatic and even horrible conflict, as Jules Michelet (q.v.) did, but he rewrote the story in *Histoire des Francs* by Gregory of Tours in a slightly romantic manner. A protégé of François Guizot (q.v.), he was influenced by him and modified his method. In 1836 the Comité des Travaux Historiques (Committee on Historical Works) put him in charge of the publication of *Documents inédits sur l'histoire du Tiers État* (4 vols., 1850–1870). In 1850 he published his *Essai sur le Tiers État* in which he abandoned narrative history for the philosophy of history and set forth the theory—abandoned today—of an opposition, in the "communal revolution," between the southern consular regime and the regime of sworn-in commune specific to northern France. Thierry is an important French historian not so much because of his works as because of the impetus he gave to the French historiographic movement at the dawn of the romantic age.

Bibliography: L. Gossman, *Augustin Thierry and Liberal Historiography* (Middletown, Conn.: Wesleyan University Press, 1976); C. Jullian, "Augustin Thierry et le mouvement historique sous la Restauration,'' *Revue de Synthèse Historique* 12 (1906); R. N. Smith-son, *Augustin Thierry, Social and Political Consciousness in the Evolution of a Historical Method* (Geneva: Librairie Droz, 1973); F. Valentin, *Augustin Thierry* (Paris, 1895).

Charles-Olivier Carbonell

THIERS, Adolphe (Marseille, 1797–Paris, 1877), French historian and states-man. Thiers' work was narrowly tied to his political stance. His two great studies, *Histoire de la Révolution française* and *Histoire du Consulat et de l'Empire*, were written during times when, as the opposition, he was out of power. Thus, these works had a considerable impact and contributed substantially to the pop-ularity and prestige of a future founder of the Republic. Born to a family of modest means, Thiers studied law at Aix-en-Provence, with Auguste Mignet (q.v.), who was later his most faithful friend and whom he joined in Paris after 1821, in order to take part together in the liberal struggle through journalism (articles in the newspaper, *Constitutionnel*) and the editing of *Histoire de la Révolution*, a reply to counterrevolutionary authors of the time, such as Jacques de Lacretelle. Thiers began as an amateur historian. Then, after the publication of Mignet's *Histoire de la Révolution Française* (1824), he became more me-thodical and developmental, publishing ten volumes on the Revolution in 1827 (2d ed., 1828), which immediately attained considerable success. Thiers' *Rév-olution*, more narrative and less pedantic than Mignet's, was equally marked with the seal of "necessity," with revolutionary "excesses" attributed to "cir-cumstances" and to the resistance of aristocrats. It became the *Vulgate* of liberal thought, as well as a reference for revolutionaries of all sorts. Thiers achieved success, not by presenting previously unpublished evidence, but rather by his captivating tone and lively political realism. By no means a philosopher, in spite of the accusation of "fatalism," Thiers was a convinced disciple of Charles Talleyrand, and, like his mentor, he adopted "reason of state" as his principle of judgment. Like Mignet, he did not hesitate to make the Convention legitimate and the Terror necessary, in the name of effective government, even by a dic-tatorship. As a partisan of constitutional monarchy, liberal, yet distrustful of democracy, Thiers gave the Revolution an image in keeping with the interests of the bourgeoisie, battling the Ultra rearguard of the Restoration. An actor in the forefront of the bourgeois revolution of 1830, a journalist of the *National*, and a minister and president of the Council several times under the July Mon-archy, Thiers returned to historical studies after 1840, the time of his disgrace. He resumed his 1827 project and wrote the *Histoire du Consulat et de l'Empire*, a work that was more elaborate than the preceding one and that brought him renown and fortune, as Napoleon's "national historian." Alexis de Tocqueville (q.v.) was one of the rare critics who noted that "après Thiers, l'histoire de l'Empire restait à écrire." (After Thiers, the history of the Empire remains to be written.) Although it relied on many printed sources and on extensive oral inquires and exhibited the author's deep interest in military and financial matters, Thiers' work has some scholarly defects that are very evident today. Yet, his writings were great "best-sellers" in the nineteenth century. He placed his talent for clear, animated narration in the service of the imperial legend, of which he was, between 1830 and 1848, one of the principal architects. The first volumes justified the Consulate and the Empire up to 1807 and pictured Napoleon as a providential leader who saved the civil accomplishments of the French Revolution. Writing of Napoleon's later career, Thiers judged the imperial despot very severely: "Qui aurait prévu que le sage de 1800 deviendrait le fou de 1812?" (Who could have foreseen that the sage of 1800 would become the madman of 1812?) However, Thiers rehabilitated the Napoleon of 1815, who became, he argued, a sincere pacifist and a constitutionalist. By means of his pen, Thiers the historian was thus an originator of two great myths: the idea of a unitary Revolution and the legend of Napoleon the Great, which appeared in the collective mentality of nineteenth-century France.

Bibliography: P. Guiral, *Thiers* (Fayard, 1986).

Alice Gérard

TOCQUEVILLE, Alexis de (Paris, 1805–Cannes, 1859), French political theoretician, historian, and political figure. Son of Count Hervé de Tocqueville, a prefect in the period of the Restoration. After studying law, Tocqueville became a magistrate at the Versailles tribunal (1827–1832). In 1831–1832 he undertook a journey to the United States, which was essential in the crystallization of his political conceptions. In 1841 he was elected a member of the French Academy. A member of the French Parliament beginning in 1839 and minister of foreign affairs for a few months in 1849, he withdrew from public life in 1851. An aristocrat in an epoch defined more and more by its bourgeois values and its egalitarian tendencies, Tocqueville tried to grasp the sense of historical evolution by detaching himself from the spirit of the Ancien Régime while maintaining a distance from the society in which he lived. The result was a profoundly original opus, the deep philosophical and political meditations of an independent spirit, one almost isolated in its own times. Influenced to a certain extent by Montesquieu (by the importance he gave to the study of laws and institutions) as well as by his contemporary François Guizot (q.v.), (his philosophical treatment of history, his interest in the evolution of civilization), Tocqueville went further than they, giving up narration completely and concentrating on deep analyses of particular problems, of particular historical and political structures. The United States became a research laboratory for Tocqueville. The result was a book that enjoyed great success, *De la démocratie en Amérique* (2 vols., 1835–1840), an outstanding analysis of the formation of the American nation and of the American political system. America, however, was not an end in itself but a point of departure for understanding the entire historical process. Tocqueville thought that the essence of history (of a providential nature) was the progressive development of equality. Democracy—meaning an increasingly pronounced equality of social conditions—represented the objective direction, which could not be resisted, of human evolution. The essential problem remained, however, the relationship between democracy and liberty—the key, in fact, to his entire philosophical, political, and historical system. Democracy could be associated with liberty, but at the same time it could give rise to totalitarian or tyrannical systems incomparably more dangerous than the absolutism of the past, systems whose appearance was facilitated by the growing uniformity of society and the disappearance of the "intermediary powers." Starting from the past, Tocqueville pondered the future and evidenced a rare farsightedness: The problem facing mankind was to find those means that would allow the survival and the extension of freedom under the conditions of increasing equality.

In 1856 Tocqueville published *L'Ancien Régime et la Révolution*, the first volume (which was to be the only one) of a projected study of the French Revolution. Other historians saw in the Revolution a break between the old and new societies. Tocqueville insisted, on the contrary, on historical continuity. He considered the Revolution a logical result of the old regime; it merely accelerated and completed an ongoing evolution. Through its bureaucratic administration, the monarchic regime had already superceded feudalism and had thus prepared the ground for subsequent historical transformations: the affirmation of equality and increasingly centralized political rule. It was an original interpretation, presented with great depth and rigorousness. Tocqueville had the merit of combining social and political aspects to formulate an analysis that transcended the actual event and rose to the level of a true philosophy of history. He successfully combined erudition and a spirit of synthesis with a sober and precise style. Few historians have remained as up to date as he; far from becoming outdated, his work still offers material for study and reflection.

Bibliography: S. Drescher, *Dilemmas of Democracy. Tocqueville and Modernization* (University of Pittsburgh Press, 1968); A. Jardin, *Alexis de Tocqueville, 1805–1859.* (Paris, 1984); Michael Hereth, *Alexis de Tocqueville. Die Gefährdung der Freiheit in der Democratie* (Kohlhammer, 1979); J. Lively, *The Social and Political Thought of Alexis de Tocqueville.* (Oxford, 1962); M. Zetterbaum, *Tocqueville and the Problem of Democracy.* (Stanford, Calif., 1967).

Lucian Boia

Great Historians: German

BELOCH, Karl Julius (Petschendorf [now in Poland], 1854–Rome, 1929), German historian of the ancient world. Suffering from bronchitis, Beloch went to Italy early in life and attended the University of Parma in 1872. After a short stay in Rome, he continued his studies in 1873 in Heidelberg, attending lectures by A. Köchly, O. Ribbeck, and K. Fischer and taking a doctor's degree in 1875 on the subject of the Greek colonies in Campania. In 1877 his habilitation was in Rome, where he became professor of ancient history and was involved in establishing a modern system for higher education in Italy. In 1893 he stood unsuccessfully for the Caprivi election as a candidate of the Fortschrittspartei (Progress party) in Kreis in the district of Stralsund-Rügen. From the autumn of 1912 to the summer of 1913, he was a professor in Leipzig and then served as a professor in Rome again. Dismissed from university service during World War I, he was reinstated as ordinarius for ancient history in 1924. In 1891 he founded the *Studi di Storia antica*, and in 1900 he began the *Biblioteca de Geografia Storica*. His students included Gaetano de Sanctis (q.v.), E. Brecchia, and L. Pareti. Beloch represented an almost hypercritical, rationalistic, and at the same time modernistic, conception of history. In his *Die Bevölkerung der griechisch-römischen Welt* (Leipzig, 1886), he used statistical research methods in a new way and downgraded the significance of slavery in ancient societies both quantitatively and qualitatively. In his major work, *Griechische Geschichte*, (4 vols., Strasbourg, 1893–1904), he placed Athens and Sparta in the general picture of history, paying special attention to social-economic relations as well as to economic history and on a theoretical basis ascribed a determining role in the historical process to the people, rather than to prominent individuals. He favored separating ancient history and classical philology. He was liberal-minded and an opponent of Bismarck and the German Junker state, but he was no friend either of the Weimar Republic.

                                                                    Armin Jähne

CONZE, Werner (Neuhaus, Elbe, 1910–Heidelberg, 1986), German historian. Professor of modern history at the universities of Posen (1944–1945), Münster (1952–1957), and Heidelberg (1957–1979). Conze founded social history in modern German historiography. His program was to end the separation between purely political history focused only on the state and history focused solely on society. For him social history was allied with both historiography and sociology. His early books—*Hirschenhof, Die Geschichte einer deutschen Sprachinsel in Livland* (1934), and *Agrarverfassung und Bevölkerung in Litauen und Weissrussland* (1940)—related political events to demographic and statistical methods. Conze believed that this was the only way one could historically measure the complex mixture of nationalities found in East Central Europe. The formation of a national society—not that of a nation-state—was also the most important problem for Conze in his later studies on nationalism. He saw the context in which "modern nations (begin) to form themselves and to become isolated from one another" in the emergence of a "social movement." (See *Sozialgeschichte 1800–1850* ; 1976.) He pointed out again and again that "the national movement in its roots was also a social movement . . . and vice versa" (*Nation und Gesellschaft. Zwei Grundbegriffe der Geschichte im revolutionaren Zeitalter*, 1963). His book *Polnische Nation und deutsche Politik im ersten Weltkrieg* (1958), as well as his *Die deutsche Nation. Ergebnis der Geschichte* (1963), supports the fruitfulness of this method. With his study *Vom 'Pöbel' zum 'Proletariat'. Sozialgeschichtliche Voraussetzungen für den Sozialismus in Deutschland* (1954), he gave powerful impulses to modern research into the history of the workers and of the workers' movement in Germany. For Conze this research was the starting point for linking social history with the history of concepts (Begriffsgeschichte), as exemplified in his lexicon, *Geschichtliche Grundbegriffe. Lexikon zur politisch-sozialen Sprache in Deutschland* (5 vols. to date, 1972–1984). Conze viewed the change in historical concepts around 1800 as an indicator of the revolutionary transition to the industrial era. As an historian of his times, Conze gave important impulses to party history, an area in which he, too, early linked questions of political history with those of sociology. From the time of his 1954 study, *Die Krise des Parteienstaates in Deutschland 1929– 1933*, he set new standards for German contemporary history through his investigations into the end of the Weimar Republic. In the interdisciplinary *Arbeitskreis für moderne Sozialgeschichte*, which he founded in 1957 and led until his death, his conceptions of social history are being developed further.

                                                                    Wolfgang Schieder

DELBRÜCK, Hans (Bergen, 1848–Berlin, 1929), German historian and publicist. After his study of history, Delbrück was educator of princes in the house of the German crown prince (1874–1879); after 1885 he was a professor at Berlin university. He was also a free–Conservative deputy in the Prussian "Land" Parliament and the Reichstag (1882–1885, 1884–1890). He attained great influence as the year-long editor of the *Preussische Jahrbücher* (1883–1890) together with Heinrich von Treitschke (q.v.); from 1890 until 1919 he was the sole responsible editor. He was shaped by the Borussian school of historiography and acted as the co-author of many a historical legend. At the same time he did not shy away from persistently criticizing and publicly refuting those legends which he recognized as false. In foreign policy, he pursued pro-imperialist, yet moderate, objectives, but domestically, he advocated social reforms. After 1918 he belonged in the company of those few historians who supported the Weimar Republic and fought against the so-called myth of the stab in the back concerning the causes for the defeat. With the biography *Das Leben des Feldmarschalls Grafen Neithart v. Gneisenau* (2 vols., 1882), he turned mainly to military history. The studies, *Friedrich, Napoleon, Moltke, Ältere und neuere Strategie* (1892), resulted in a sensational dispute on strategies. Later controversies related to ancient military history. His four-volume *Geschichte der Kriegskunst im Rahmen der politischen Geschichte* (1900–1920), which beyond its title was also linked with the description of economic and social questions, became his standard work. His work, *Ludendorffs Selbstporträt* (1922), was an assessment of his adventurous strategy in World War I. His *Weltgeschichte* (5 vols., 1923–1928) concentrated primarily on countries and personalities, diplomacy, and wars, and is of secondary importance compared with his other works.

Bibliography: Arden Buchholz, *Hans Delbrück. The German Military Establishment* (Iowa City, 1985); Karl Christ, "Hans Delbrück," *Von Gibbon zu Rostovtzeff* (Darmstadt, 1972), pp. 159–200; Gordon A. Craig, "Delbrück: The Military Historian," *Makers of Modern Strategy*, ed. E. M. Earle (Princeton, N.J., 1963); Hans Schleier, "Hans Delbrück," *Gestalten der Bismarckzeit*, ed. 6. Seeber (Berlin, 1978), pp. 378–403.

Hans Schleier

DILTHEY, Wilhelm Christian Ludwig (Biebrich a. R., 1833–Seis b. Basen, 1911), German philosopher and historian of ideas. Professor at the universities of Basel (1866–1868), Kiel (1868–1871), Breslau (1871–1882), and Berlin (1882–1905). After brief theological studies, Dilthey transferred his interests to philosophy. He studied in Berlin with Friedrich Adolf Trendlenburg (history of philosophy) and Leopold von Ranke (q.v.). He wrote his dissertation on Schleiermacher (1864). Dilthey is most widely known for his innovative work on the theory of history and the human sciences generally. In his influential *Einführung in die Geisteswissenschaften* (1883), he argued for understanding (*Verstehen*) as the appropriate method for the systematic study of man, his world, and history. Since human beings are goal oriented, he reasoned, an understanding of man, his actions and his products, involves, first, an understanding by means of reexperiencing (*Nachempfinden*) of the motives that prompt people engaged in practical life to their actions, and writers, artists, and thinkers to their various cultural products, such as works of art and rituals. Second, the understanding of man involves, in studying individuals, social groups, and cultural products, the discernment of psychological and cultural structures or patterns (*Zusammenhänge*). In his *Idea of History* (1946), Robin George Collingwood (q.v.) introduced Dilthey's concept of *Verstehen* (reexperiencing) in the Anglo-Saxon world, using, however, only the aspect of reexperiencing motives. Dilthey contrasted his conception of *Verstehen* with *Erklären*, the method used in the natural sciences, of causal reasoning and explaining by natural laws. Just as the study of external nature had in the course of its development become divided among several natural sciences, so the study of man had become differentiated in separate studies: psychology, anthropology, political economy, history, law, philology, philosophy, literature, and the arts. For these disciplines Dilthey coined the word *Geisteswissenschaften*.

Soon after the publication of his *Einführung*, he faced a problem he could not solve. In the human sciences man studied not external nature, but himself. Man could study himself by studying methodically and systematically the actions the human being had performed and the cultural products the human mind had produced in the course of history. In the sense of being methodical, the human sciences could be scientific, but could they also be called scientific in the sense of being objective? Could man's mind in its effort to understand itself and the human world it had created transcend its own time and culture? Could it obtain an objective view? Could a subject ever know itself objectively? In order to answer this vexing question, the central problem of his later philosophy, Dilthey conducted an investigation into the possibilities, but most of all the limits, of human reason. He termed this enterprise a *Kritik der historischen Vernunft*, and it caused him to write several highly original essays. (1) In "Erlebnis und Dictung" (1877), he ascribed to religious thinkers, artists, and philosophers the function of transforming their private experiences into universally valid symbols, and he explored the links that connect creative individuals with their age and culture. (2) In "Ideen über eine beschreibende und zergliederende Psychologie" (1894), he distinguished a humanistic descriptive psychology for the study of personality structure (i.e., the psychic structure that an individual "self" acquires through experience) and for the study of personality development (a history structured over time) from traditional somatically oriented psychology using the casual approach of the natural sciences. (3). In "Der Aufbau der geschichtlichen Welt in den Geisteswissenschaften" (1910), he transformed his *Verstehen* approach to a hermeneutic approach. The products in which man articulated his experience of life (written texts and inscriptions, but also landscapes, buildings, and social structures, in addition to actions and history) had to be interpreted like texts. In order to ward off arbitrary interpretations in the study of the human world, Dilthey proposed rules taken from hermeneutics (the study of the meaning of texts). He acknowledged that in contrast to the knowledge gained in the natural sciences, the interpretations arrived at in the human sciences could never be final: The interpreter is always caught in the "hermeneutic circle": New experiences lead to new interpretations; new interpretations lead to new experiences, and so on. (4) In "Die Typen der Weltanschauung und ihre Ausbildung in den metaphysischen Systemen" (1911), he formulated his doctrine of world-views (*Weltanschauungslehre*): In the course of history humankind has interpreted life in various ways, each of which has its validity. These interpretations cannot be systematized into one system or reduced to one truth. Because of this essay Edmund Husserl stigmatized Dilthey as a historical relativist. Martin Heidegger, on the other hand, acknowledged in *Sein und Zeit* (1927) the impact Dilthey had on his thought. Since the 1960s on, Dilthey has been a major influence on historically minded philosophers, such as Jürgen Habermas and Hans-George Gadamer.

Bibliography: Ilse N. Bulhof, *Wilhelm Dilthey: A Hermeneutic Approach to the Study of History and Culture* (The Hague, 1980); *Dilthey Jarbuch für philosophie und Geschichte der Geistewissenschaften* (founded in 1983); Rudolf A. Makkreel, *Dilthey: Philosopher of the Human Studies* (Princeton, N.J., 1975); Ernst Wolfgang, ed., *Dilthey und die Philosophie der Gegenwart* (Orth: Freiburg und Müchen, 1985).

Ilse N. Bulhof

DÖRPFELD, Wilhelm (Barmen, Rhenish Prussia, 1853–Berlin, 1940), German architect and protohistorian, H. Schliemann's collaborator and continuator at Troy (1890), and fellow researcher at the Mykenian research stations in Continental Greece (Orchomenos, 1880, and Tirynth, 1884–1886). Considered to be "Schliemann's greatest discovery," Dörpfeld initiated scientific archaeological diggings, applying systematically, and for the first time the stratigraphic method. The most spectacular result recorded was the accurate definition of Troy's relative and absolute chronology (the nine superposed settlements) achieved by confronting stratigraphic observations with architectonic detail and typological study, as well as by comparing it, carefully so as to record every detail of plane, with other settlements synchronous with those on Hissarlik hillock. Ruling out Schliemann's old hypothesis, according to which Priam's Troy was on the level of Troy II, Dörpfeld proved the fortified town's existence long before the contacts with the Mykenian world, the series of catastrophes that mark the passage from one age to another (*Troya and Ilion*, 2 vols., 1902) and brought arguments, valid until the University of Cincinnati expedition resumed the diggings, in favor of the opinion that Troy VI was the same as Priam and Homer's Troy: "The builders constructed on Level VI a strong fortress out of a series of concentric terraces. This fortification was the hearth of Priam, the Troy of Homer." We can therefore say that Dörpfeld is the second discoverer of Troy, given his fieldwork in order to produce, preserve, and study the results of the diggings. But we should bear in mind the fact that, although he made this effort to order the evidence from Troy and therefore set right Schliemann's opinion, he never questioned the value of Schliemann's intuition concerning the localization and identification of the famous fortified town. The second area in which Dörpfeld concentrated his interest was the Northwest of Peloponnesus

and the Ionian Islands where he tried to discover the homelands of some of the
Homeric heroes, especially of Ulysses. Coming back to Olympia, he detected
the prehistoric levels which preceded by more than a millennium the constructions
connected with the pan-Hellenic complex there (*Alt Olympia*, 1935). Finally the
negative results of the investigations in Ithaca and the discovery of the tumular
tombs in the Nidhri Plain (Levkas) convinced him that Ulysses' real homeland
was that small island (*Briefe über Leukast Ithaka*, I-VI, 1905–1912).

Bibliography: Jan Filip, *Encyklopädischees Handbuch der Ur–und Frühgeschichte
Europas* I (Prague, 1966), p. 302.

Ligia Bârzu

DROYSEN, Johann Gustav (Treptow, Pomerania, 1808–Berlin, 1884), German historian and theorist of historiography. Along with Heinrich von Sybel
(q.v.) Droysen was one of the founders of the Prusso-kleindeutsche conception
of history. After studying, he became a teacher in Berlin (1831), a professor of
classical philology (1835), and later, a professor of history at the universities of
Kiel, Schleswig-Holstein (1840), Jena, Thuringia (1851), and finally Berlin
(1859). As the son of an army chaplain, the War of Liberation against Napoleonic
power made a lasting impression on him, creating his ardent attachment to
Prussia. In his *Geschichte Alexanders des Grossen* (1833) and *Geschichte des
Hellenismus* (2 vols., 1836–1843) he told the history of Macedonia and Greece
as a model for Prussia and Germany. Droysen believed in Prussia's vocation to
lead Germany, and he was one of the leading publicists in the movement for
German unification. (His newspaper articles were collected as *Politische Schriften*, 1933; his famous *Vorlesungen über die Freiheitskriege* was published in
two volumes in 1846.) During his Kiel professorship, he took an interest in the
Schleswig-Holstein question. With his *Die Herzogthümer Schleswig-Holstein
und das Königreich Dänemark seit dem Jahre 1806* (1850; English transl., 1850),
which formed German opinion, he supported the rights of the duchies. In 1848
he became a member of the Frankfurt *Paulskirche* Parliament and secretary of
the Committee for the Constitution. (See his *Aktenstücke und Aufsezchnungen
. . .* , 1924.) In 1849, after the Prussian Frederick William IV had refused the
imperial crown, he retired in disappointment and took no further active part in
politics. But his private letters (*Briefwechsel*, 2 vols., 1929) contained much
political comment, and he did not hesitate both to stylize the life of Yorck von
Wartenburg (3 vols., 1851–1852) into a paradigm of national patriotism and to
publish the *Geschichte der preussischen Politik* (14 vols., 1855–1886). The
Geschichte der preussischen is based mainly on archival sources, going up to
only 1756 and remaining unfinished like his *Geschichte des Hellenismus*. But
whereas the former work has to be considered the result of a misconception
(Droysen imputed a continuity to Prussian politics from the fifteenth to the
nineteenth centuries that is inconsistent with historical facts), the latter is one
of the most excellent pieces of historiography ever written. Here, for the first
time, the peculiarity of the Hellenistic epoch was elucidated, with Hellenism

conceived as a distinctive East-West culture, as the amalgamation of Western and Eastern culture civilizations.

Droysen is still remembered not because of his historiographical works or his political participation, but rather, because of his theoretical contribution. He repeatedly lectured on historical theory, first in 1857 and all together seventeen times. He himself published only a *Grundriss der Historik* (1868, 1882; English transl., 1893); his complete manuscripts on *Historik* have been published posthumously (1937; Hubner, ed., 1977; Leyh, ed., 1977). Droysen first related systematically the theoretical elements of the *historical encyclopedia* and *historical methodology*, which before then had been treated separately or only superficially related. At the same time, he integrated the four ideal-typical orientations of theoretical self-reflection on history as a discipline: the humanistic-rhetorical, the auxiliary-encyclopedic, the historicophilosophical, and the epistemological or historicological traditions. This was done with a synthesizing power that remains unsurpassed to this day in the field of historical theory. In contrast to the Enlightenment's historiography or even to early historicism, the "encyclopedia" was no longer merely a survey and a summary of the state of research. It was also an explicit reference for historical interpretation, which translated historical knowledge into a program of research and thereby generated new research. Thus, the "encyclopedic" tradition was now related to methodology in such a way that the concept of method that had hitherto been confined to the auxiliary-scientific part of historical research changed qualitatively to become the canon of historical research. Research, which was explicit methodological rules, was directed through the "encyclopedia" to the realm of the historically researchable. In doing so, this realm was organized by guidelines through which the "transactions" (*Geschäfte*) of the past become meaningful history. Through the explication of such guidelines, Droysen's *Historik* exercised the function of the philosophy of history without endangering the empirical character of historical knowledge and the openness of research. For him, it was not possible to endanger research, for he still explained historical research epistomologically and found the beginnings of his philosophy of history in the epistemological foundations of historical studies.

In contrast to subsequent works on historiography, in which the humanistic-rhetorical tradition of thought was largely lost, and with it the reflection about historical writing as a problem in theory, Droysen succeeded (with his *Topik*) in fully integrating this type of historics—albeit with a qualitative change necessitated by the increasingly scientific treatment of history. In his *Historik*, Droysen developed the theory of historical understanding that was continued by Wilhelm Christian L. Dilthey (q.v.) and Heinrich Rickert ("Our method is, having researched, to understand"). This self-reliant historical perception matured in dispute with West European positivism, which claimed to raise historical studies to the rank of a science by subjugating them to the determinants of natural law. Moreover, Droysen expounded his views contrary to Leopold von Ranke's (q.v.) critical school, especially to the idea of objective facts as asserted by

Ranke. Ingeniously, Droysen distinguished between "die sogenannten Tatsachen in ihrer einstigen Wirklichkeit" (the so-called fact in its earlier reality) and those fragments of them that have not yet perished and are still present. In the meantime, Droysen's ethical optimism, based on idealistic philosophy, has become suspect. However, in his opinion, the idea of history was "the increasingly restless humanity, the progressive creation" that realized itself in the "sittlichen Gemeinsamkeitch" (moral communities). Ethics was the law of history, "the moral world order, the dominion and formation of moral might." In this view, a deep confidence in the strength of moral intentions is alive—intentions have to be proved true not only in state and nation, but also in all "moral communities." Unquestionably, the categories of "nation" and "state" are Droysen's most important categories. During his historical development, his once liberal positions altered: They accepted all *realpolitische* changes, though by critical distance. Like Heinrich von Treitschke (q.v.), Droysen finally even vindicated the *starken Machtstaat*, thus justifying imperialism, militarism, and the oppression of political opposition. In this respect, Droysen surely is not to be regarded as a paradigm for modern historiography. Yet the resourcefulness of his *Historik* has neither been exhausted nor surpassed.

Bibliography: Gunter Birtsch, *Die Nation als sittliche Idee. Der Nationalstaatsbegriff in Geschichtsschreibung und politischer Gedankenwelt Johann Gustav Droysens* (Cologne, 1964); Benedetto Bravo, *Philologie Histoire, Philosophie de l'Histoire, Etude sur J. G. Droysen, Historien de l'Antiquite* (Breslau, 1968); Otto Hintze, "Johann Gustav Droysen" (1904), in Hintze, *Gesammelte Abhandlunge*, vol. 2 (Göttingen, 1982), pp. 453–499; Wolfgang Hock, *Liberales Denken im Zeitalter der Paulskirche, Droysen und die Frankfurter Mitte* (Münster, 1957); Jörn Rüsen, *Begriffene Geschichte. Genesis und Begrundung der Geschichtstheorie J. G. Droysens* (Paderborn, 1969); Jörn Rüsen, "Johann Gustav Droysen," in Hans-Ulrich Wehler, ed., *Deutsche Historiker*, vol. 2 (Göttingen, 1971), pp. 7–23.

Horst Walter Blanke

EBERT, Max (Stendal, 1879–Berlin, 1929), German prehistorian. Professor at the University of Königsberg (1921, 1923–1927), at Herder Institute in Riga (1922–1923), and at the University of Berlin (1927–1929). Ebert centered his research on Northeastern and Eastern Europe, being particularly interested in the history and archaeology of the Goths as well as in their new North-Pontic homeland (*Sudrussland im Altertum*, 1921), suggesting the origin, in the same zone, on the basis of a middle Latène sketch, of a type of fossil considered to be a genuine "guiding fossil" of the early culture of the oriental Germans—*Fibel mit Umgeschlagenem Fuss*. Study of antiquities in a series of Baltic provinces (Kurland, Livland, Estland) resulted in *Baltische Studien zur Archäologie und Geschichte* (1914). With Max Ebert a new stage in European pre- and protohistory began. The narrow vision centered mainly on Europe, which had been preferred before him, was replaced by a new spirit, an internationalist one, manifest in the two periodicals initiated by Ebert: *Vorgeschichtliches Jahrbuch* and *Vorgeschichtliches Forschungen*. His lifelong work remains *Reallexikon der*

Vorgeschicht, edited in fourteen volumes during 1921–1929. It reflects not only his great power of work, but also a bright mind open to whatever meant discovery or scientific contribution, regardless of the continent to which they referred.

Bibliography: Jan Filip, *Encyklopädisches Handbuch der Ur-und Fhürgeschichte Europas*, 1 (Pargue, 1966), p. 318; H. Seger, "Max Ebert," *Nachrichtenblatt für deutsche Vorzeit* 5 (Heft 12, 1929): 177–179.

Ligia Bârzu

ENGELS, Friedrich (Barmen, 1820–London, 1895), German philosopher, sociologist, economist, historian, theorist, functionary, and adviser to the international working-class movement. Commercial apprenticeship and business activities (from 1842 with interruptions until 1869 in Manchester), private scholar, and publicist (in London since 1870), Engels was above all a self-taught scholar in philosophy, political economy, history, the military sciences, philological, and natural-science disciplines. Like Karl Marx (q.v.) yet independently of him, he developed from an adherent of Georg Wilhem F. Hegel (q.v.), the "Young Hegelians," Feuerbach and bourgeois democratism, into a dialectical materialist and scientific communist. After 1844 he had a close friendship and companionship with Marx, and he displayed an active political and military involvement in the 1848–1849 Revolution by means of the programe of the Communist League. His most important works were: *Die Lage der arbeitenden Klasse in England* (1845); *Der deutsche Bauernkrieg* (1850); *Herrn Eugen Dührings Umwälzung der Wissenschaft (Anti–Dühring)* (1876–1878); *Die Entwicklung des Sozialismus von der Utopie zur Wissenschaft* (1880); *Der Ursprung der Familie des Privateigentums und des Staates* (1884); *Ludwig Feuerbach und der Ausgang der klassischen deutschen Philosophie* (1888); jointly with Marx: *Die Heilige Familie* (1845), *Die deutsche Ideologie* (1845–1847), *Manifest der Kommunistischen Partei* (1848), and *Revolution und Konterrevolution in Deutschland* (1851–1852). In close connection with the struggle for democracy and socialism, the endeavors to combine Marxism and the working-class movement, a great number of theoretical and historiographical works appeared. Apart from the works jointly written with Marx, the following deserve special attention in terms of theory of history: "Antidühring," "Ludwig Feuerbach," and the "Altersbriefe" on historical materialism, its application to research and representation of history. Turning against the vulgarizations of historical materialism, Engels attempted to conceive and apply it as as a method for thorough investigations into history. Contrary to positivist views, he stressed the difference between the character and the mode of action of the laws in nature and society and the active role of the superstructure and social consciousness. In this sense he applied historical materialism to the entire development of world history, starting from man's evolution and primitive society up to the emergence and development of class societies, to the history of the working-class movement and the history of sciences.

While Marx concerned himself primarily with French history, Engels dealt mainly with German history under the aspects of world history and class struggles. Criticisms by reactionaries had always been linked to the emphasis on progressive forces and facets in German history. He regarded the German working class as the instrument overcoming the "German misery," perceiving this term especially as the temporary backwardness of Germany vis-à-vis France and England. He saw in the German working class "the heir of German classical philosophy" and all progressive traditions of German history.

Bibliography: Horst Bartel/Walter Schmidt, "Friedrich Engels zu einigen Grundproblemen der Geschichte des deutschen Volkes im 19. Jahrhundert," *Jahrbuch der Geschichte*, vol. 6 (1972): 147–190; Werner Berthold, "Zu den Altersbriefen von Friedrich Engels," *Storia delle Storiografia. Rivista internazionale*, 6 (1984): 113–117; William Otto Henderson, *The Life of Friedrich Engels*, 2 vols. (London, 1976); Gustav Mayer, *Friedrich Engels. Eine Biographie*. Den Haag 1934 (Köln, 1975); E. M. Sukov a.o., *Engels i problemy istorii* (Engels and the Problems of History) (Moscow, 1970).

Werner Berthold

GERVINUS, Georg Gottfried (Darmstadt, 1805–Heidelberg, 1871), German historian and literary historian. First employed as a commercial clerk, before he began his studies in 1825. Disciple of Friedrich Schlosser (q.v.). Habilitation in Heidelberg, 1830. Professor in Göttingen, 1835. Here, after protesting against the breach of the Constitution as one of the so-called Göttingen Seven, expelled from Göttingen. After 1844 honorary professor in Heidelberg. From 1847 to July 1848 Gervinus ran the *Deutsche Zeitung*, organ of the South German moderate Liberals. The Frankfurt Parliament's lack of activities in the 1848 Revolution prompted him to resign his membership. He was one of the few who turned in 1848 from the moderate to the left wing of liberalism. In the period of reaction he favored continuing the revolution and the national unification of Germany with the establishment of a Republic. For his *Einleitung in die Geschichte des 19. Jahrhunderts* (1853) he was put on trial. As an opponent of Prussianism and of Bismarck's foundation of the Reich, he died completely lonely. His publications are devoted to history and historiography, the history of literature, music, culture, and politics. His major historical work, the incomplete *Geschichte des 19. Jahrhunderts seit den Wiener Verträgen* (8 vols., 1855–1866) sympathetically depicted national and revolutionary movements in Europe and South America and condemned reactionary feudal forces. With his *Geschichte der poetischen Nationalliteratur der Deutschen* (5 vols., 1835–1842) he had already founded the modern German literary historiography. In his *Grundriss der Historik* (1837) he pleaded for cooperation between research, theoretical, historical questions, and an aesthetically effective presentation of history in the creative process of the historian. In addition, he gained a great reputation for the cultivation and propagation of the works of Shakespeare and Handel in Germany and translated several of Handel's oratorios from English into German.

Bibliography: Gangolf Hübinger, *G. G. Gervinus. Historisches Urteil und politische Kritik* (Göttingen, 1984); *G. G. Gervinus Leben. Von ihm selbst* (Leipzig, 1893); Jörn Rüsen, "Der Historiker als Parteimann des Schicksals," *Objektivität und Parteilichkeit*

(Munich, 1977), pp. 77–124; Gerhard Schilfert/Hans Schleier, "G. G. Gervinus als Historiker," *Studien über die deutsche Geschichtswissenschaft*, ed. J. Streisand, vol. 1 (Berlin, 1963), pp. 148–169.

Hans Schleier

GRAETZ, Heinrich (Xions, Posen, 1817–Munich, 1891), Jewish historian and biblical scholar. Lecturer at the Jewish-Theological Seminary in Breslau (1853) and titular professor (Honorarprofessor) at Breslau University (1869). Graetz's best known work is the eleven-volume *Geschichte der Juden von den ältesten Zeiten bis auf die Gegenwart* (1853–1875), which was influenced by the ideas of George Wilhelm F. Hegel (q.v.), Humboldt, and Leopold von Ranke (q.v.). This work, which follows Barthold Georg Niebuhr's (q.v.) philological-critical method, views and portrays the overall history of the Jews as a unity for the first time. Graetz was reproached for faulty methods and lack of objectivity. His historical interpretation of Jewish history as intellectual and passionate ("do research and roam on foot, think and tolerate, learn and suffer"), as expressed for the first time in the philosophical essay "Die Konstruktion der jedischen Geschichte" (1846), was especially subject to criticism. In his monthly journal *Jeschurun*, S. R. Hirsch described Volume 4, which discussed the Talmudic epoch, as "a superficial fantasy." Abraham Geiger deplored Graetz' work as "stories, but no history" (*Judische Zeitschrift fur Wissenschaft und Leben*, IV, 146 ff). Heinrich von Treitschke's (q.v.) attack on Graetz' publication "Ein Wort über unser Judentum" (*Preussische Jahrbücher*, 1879) started a controversy in which both Jewish and non-Jewish authors took part. Although almost everyone deplored Treitschke's anti-Semitic stance, many—among them Hermann Cohen and Harry Breslau—did not take Graetz' side. One of those who supported Graetz was Ludwig Philippson, who cited the merit of his work in Jewish history. Graetz edited the *Monatschrift für Geschichte und Wissenschaft des Judentums (MGWJ)* and published hundreds of historical and critical essays. His translations included *Ecclesiastes (Kohelet)*, in 1870; and *The Song of Solomon (Schir haschirim)* in 1871. He wrote critical commentaries to the *Psalms* (1882–1883), to the *Proverbs of Solomon* (1884), and to *Job* and *Esther*. One of his most important critical analyses is *Emendationen (Emandationesin plerosque Sacrae Scripturae Veteris Testamenti libros*, Breslau, 1892–1894). Graetz sympathized with Jewish nationalism, although he refused to participate in the Chibbat Zionist movement. He was a committee member of the Alliance Israélite Universelle and did much to help the education of orphans in Palestine. In 1872 he visited Palestine and later published a report about the "Chalukka," the protests launched by the Palestinian community.

Bibliography: S. Baron, *History and Jewish Historians* (1964), pp. 269–275; G. Deutsch, *Heinrich Graetz a Centenary* (1917); G. Herlitz, in *YLBI* 9 (1964): 76–83; R. Michael, in *YLBI* 9 (1964): 91–121; 13 (1968): 34–56. *Encyclopaedia Judaica*, vol. 7, pp. 845–850; J. Meisl, *Heinrich Graetz . . . zu seinem 100. Geburtstag* (1917).

Julius Schoeps

GRIEWANK, Karl (Bützow, 1900–Jena, 1953), German historian. Griewank graduated in Rostock in 1922, and was a leading member of the Notgemeinschaft der deutschen Wissenschaft beginning in 1926. As a member of the Bekennende Kirche he maintained a critical and distant stance on fascism. Only after the Nazi defeat did he receive a professorship in Berlin. In 1947, he was appointed professor of medieval and modern history at the University of Jena, where as teacher and scholar he made an important contribution to the development of antifascist democratic historiography in the German Democratic Republic. During the period in Jena, he reached the highpoint of his intellectual activity, which was acknowledged through his appointment to the Department of History of the Academy of Sciences in Berlin (1951), the Scientific Advisory Board for the Museum of German History, Berlin (1952), and as secretary for the Historical Commission of the Bavarian Academy of Sciences, Munich (1951). From 1947 on he was editor of the *Deutsche Literaturzeitung*. His chief works are: *Brief wechsel der Königin Luise mit ihrem Gemahl Friedrich Wilhelm III. 1793–1810* (1929); *Die französische Revolution 1789–1799* (1948); *Deutsche Studenten und Universitäten in der Revolution von 1848* (1949); *Der Wiener Kongress und die europäische Restauration 1814–15* (1954; 1st ed., 1942); and *Der neuzeitliche Revolutions begriff* (1955, with a bibliography of his writings). Griewank's scholarly rank revealed itself in his humanistic, democratic orientation, which remained free of nationalistic narrowness. His command of historical material was based on a broad knowledge of sources. Though marked by intellectual history influences, his conception of history did not ignore social questions.

Bibliography: "Zum Andenken an Karl Griewank," *Zeitschrift für Geschichtswissenschaft*, no. 6 (1953): 997–999; "Nekrolog Karl Griewank," *Historische Zeitschrift* 177 (1954): 665–667.

Peter Schafer

HARNACK, Adolf von (Dorpat, 1851–Heidelberg, 1930), German Church historian. The son of a professor of theology, Harnack obtained the doctorate with a dissertation on Church history in 1874. His academic career led him to Giessen, Marburg, and, in 1888, to Berlin where, both in the epoch of Emperor William II and in the Weimar period, he exerted influence as a "rational Republican" far beyond his own subject as a science organizer and science politician. Apart from his professorship, he held the office of director-general of the Prussian State Library (from 1905 to 1921) and the function of founder president of the Kaiser-Wilhelm-Gesellschaft (which was essentially oriented toward natural science) for the promotion of sciences (from 1910 onward); he exercised both functions with great effect. In addition, he was co-founder (1903) and (until 1911) chairman of the evangelical-social congress. Theologically, Harnack belonged to Protestant liberalism in its manifestation as cultural Protestantism. Repeatedly, he came into conflict with the Prussian Church authorities, and, as a result, he was never elected or appointed to ecclesiastical posts. His views were put forth in his lectures on *Das Wesen des Christentums* (1900), translated into fifteen languages. With his critical-historical method, his *Lehrbuch der Dogmengeschichte* (3 vols., 1885–1890) dealt with the development of Church dogma, "a work of the Greek mind on the soil of the Gospel," through the second half of the third century. *Das apostolische Glaubensbekenntnis* (1892, 27 editions in all), which emerged against the political background of the Church, portrayed the current figure of the Apostles' Creed as the baptismal symbol of the South Gallic Church of the fifth century. *Die Mission und die Ausbreitung des Christentums in den ersten drei Jahrhunderten* (1902) showed the internal and external conditions under which Christianity developed into a world religion within a historically short period. Harnack's Berlin Academic Treatise and papers were published under the title *Kleine Schriften zur Alten Kirche* (1980, with a foreword by v. Jürgen Dummer). In 1900 the jubilee year, Harnack presented the three-volume *Geschichte der Königlich Preussischen Akademie der Wissenschaften zu Berlin*. One of Harnack's most important science-organizational achievements was to provide substantiation for the Early Fathers' Commission of the Berlin Academy in an attempt to prepare source materials for the development of the Christian religion, starting from the Palestinian beginnings to the Catholic Church of the Reich, to be published in a critical edition. In his two–volume *Geschichte der altchristlichen Literatur* (1893–1904), he presented the materials passed on to him for his editorial activities (manuscripts, early editions, and former translations). The series, *Die griechischen christlichen Schriftsteller der ersten drei Jahrhunderte*, was established for these editions, while for preparatory studies and the edition of supplementary materials, notably oriental sources, the *Texte und Untersuchungen zur Geschicht der altchristlichen Literatur* was published. From 1881 to 1910 Harnack was co-editor of *Theologische Literaturzeitung*.

Bibliography: Johannes Irmscher, *Adolf Harnack und der Fortschritt in der Altertumswissenschaft* (Berlin, 1981); Friedrich Smend, *Adolf von Harnack. Verzeichnis seiner Schriften* (Berlin, 1927); Agnes v. Zahn-Harnack, *A. v. Harnack* (Berlin [West], 1951).

Johannes Irmscher

HEEREN, Arnold Hermann Ludwig (Arbergen near Bremen, 1760–Göttingen, 1842), German historian. Like many other scholars of his time, Heeren was the son of a Protestant vicar. But rather than the religious conviction of his family, the urban atmosphere of Bremen and its merchants' economic interests had the most influence on him. In the tradition of his father, he first studied theology but soon changed his mind, and, influenced by the historian Ludwig Spittler and the philologist Wilhelm Heyne, he devoted himself to an academic career. In 1787 he became a professor of philosophy at the University of Göttingen and in 1799 a professor of history, as successor of Spittler. Beginning his career, he had difficulties finding his position among scholars as famous as Heyne on one side and the historians, Johann Gatterer, August Ludwig von Schlözer, and Spittler, on the other side. This was not only the result of a special constellation at the University of Göttingen. The problem was more complex.

Heeren worked in a transitory epoch of historical science. Others—like Gatterer and Schlözer—had made their contribution to the development of historical science in the German Enlightenment. What was Heeren's part in this scientific development? Was he able to create new ideas, to find new directions? His first eminent work was published in 1793–1796: *Ideen über die Politik, den Verkehr und den Handel der vornehmsten Völker der Welt*. It was translated into English (1833), French (1800), and Dutch (1824–1827) and had several editions. In many respects this was a work of the German Enlightenment, and in main parts it followed the scientific rules which other historians like Schlözer had introduced in historical research and historiography. It was important for Heeren to be in communication with the public. He wrote not for scholars, but for a cultured people; indeed, his literary style was appreciated by many readers, and his success as a writer was remarkable. The structure of his work resembled universal history, and he preferred a systematic view, like the historians of the Enlightenment. Like them he was interested in general human activities and did not reduce history to the actions of great politicians. But political history was his most important subject of research. "I was most attracted by this part of the universal history, which is the most important of our age: the political and economic one." In analyzing economic and political factors, he sought to penetrate the historical context and to understand it more precisely. The result of this approach was his work *Geschichte des europäischen Staatensystems und seiner Kolonien* (1809). It is remarkable that he was not interested in national history, but primarily in the external connections between the European states. To guarantee peace between them, a balance was necessary, and this was possible—that was Heeren's conviction—through colonies and the free trade system.

Even though his historical judgment was concerned with political categories, the political consequences of historical knowledge did not interest Heeren. He wanted to inform and teach the reader what was worth knowing. But he hesitated to discuss problems or topics of contemporary history. He preferred subjects of ancient times and studies of exotic countries like India—and it may be that he wished to avoid giving precise answers to controversial questions of his time. Critics reproached him for his caution. His inability to understand and interpret the new romantic ideas was another point of criticism. Soon, he was no longer able to meet the demands of the new and dominant historical school. Even though he always stressed critical method, his work, because of its structure as a more general survey, could not be empirically exact. But Heeren's destiny was to be involved in the transformation of historical science without having the creative imagination to find new directions of thought.

Ursula A. J. Becher

HEGEL, Georg Wilhelm Friedrich (Stuttgart, 1770–Berlin, 1831), German philosopher. Hegel studied theology at Tübingen (1788–1793) and obtained a tutorship at Berne and Frankfurt am Main (1793–1801). He was a private lecturer and then professor at Jena (1801–1806), editor at Bamberg (1807), teacher at

Nuremberg (1808–1816), and full professor with chair at Heidelberg (1816–1818) and at Berlin (1818–1831). His most important works are: *Phänomenologie des Geistes* (1807), *Wissenschaft der Logik* (1812–1816), *Grundlagen der Philosophie des Rechts* (1820–1821), and *Vorlesungen über die Philosophie der Weltgeschichte* (read in 1822–1830, published in 1837). Complete edition: *Werke*, 20 vols. (Stuttgart, 1927–1940); *Werke*, 20 vols. (Frankfurt am Main 1969–1971). In continuation of the world-historic concepts of progress ranging from Fontenelle, Condorcet, Iselin, Johann Herder to the other historians and philosophers of history of the Enlightenment, Hegel, in making use of the experience of revolution, reform, and restoration, outlined a comprehensive view of world history on the basis of a consistent objective idealism and with the use of a dialectical scheme of concepts that was teleologically aimed at bringing about the bourgeois-capitalist society with its constitutional monarchy. His concept of world history excluded stateless peoples and comprised only "world-historical peoples." This world-historical concept, embodying "reason" and the "world spirit" for a certain period, like the "Volksgeist" (spirit of peoples), meant increasingly gaining self-consciousness and freedom, which was regarded as progress. However, it was decisive that this process could only be put into effect in the history of humankind, by human actions. In addition, the notions of reason, freedom, and progress expressed fundamental demands of progressive citizenry. Hegel divided world history into four great epochs, or worlds: (1) The Oriental world, (2) the Greek world, (3) the Roman world, and (4) the German world. The Lutheran Reformation was of central importance to him, as were the Great French Revolution and especially Napoleon, who was viewed as the enforcer. From him, Hegel expected the impetus for implementing the bourgeois society by way of reforms. But after Napoleon's defeat, Hegel oriented himself toward Prussia where such reforms had already been carried out. Napoleon had a decisive influence on the formation of Hegel's view on the role of "world historical individuals." These were used by the *Weltgeist* in an attempt to achieve its purpose in the world-historical peoples concerned ("stratagem of reason"). His *Philosophie der Weltgeschichte* was both a challenge and a warning example for the professional science of history. Notably for Marxist history, it presented the dialectical method and a great number of insights into the historical process which were of great importance.

Bibliography: Werner Berthold, "Zur Stellung Hegels in der Geschichte der Geschichtswissenschaft," *Wissenschaftliche Zeitschrift der Karl-Marx-Universität Leipzig*, Gesellschafts-und Sprachwissenschaftliche Reihe, no. 6 (1982): 509–512; Georg Biedermann, "Zum Ursprung der Hegelschen Geschichtsauffassung und Methode," *Jahrbuch für Geschichte* 19 (1979): 217–250; Joachim Ritter, *Hegel und die französische Revolution* (Cologne, 1957); Ernst Schulin, *Die weltgeschichtliche Erfassung des Orients bei Hegel und Ranke* (Göttingen, 1958); Joachim Streisand, *Kritische Studien zum Erbe der deutschen Klassik. Fichte–W. v. Humboldt–Hegel* (Berlin, 1971).

Werner Berthold

HINTZE, Otto (Pyritz, Hinterpommern [now Poland], 1861–Berlin, 1940), German historian. Professor at the University of Berlin (1899–1922); married

(1912) to the historian Hedwig Hintze (born Guggenheimer). An outstanding administrative and social historian with particular interest in the early modern period. First a specialist of Prussian history, Hintze later broadened his scope of interest and produced model studies in comparative history of a universal range. A student of Johann Gustav Droysen (q.v.) and an assistant to Gustav Schmoller (q.v.), he combined his solid training as a historian in the Prussian-German tradition with access to historical sociology and economics as presented by the German historical school. He was one of the editors of the multivolume *Acta Borussica*, a collection of documents pertaining to the administrative history of absolutist Prussia. Here he developed his approach, which combined administrative, constitutional, social, and economic history, though with a particular stress on the modernizing role of the government. Two monographs emerged: *Die Preussische Seidenindustrie im 18. Jahrhundert und ihre Begründung durch Friedrich den Grossen* (1892); *Einleitende Darstellung der Behördenorganisation und allgemeinen Verwaltung in Preussen beim Regierungsamt Friedrichs II* (1901). Major articles, which covered several centuries and increasingly included international comparisons, established him as a leading historian of modern European state formation ("innere Staatsbildung"): "Die Entstehung der modern Staatsministerien" (1908), "Der Commissarius und seine Bedeutung in der allgemeinen Verwaltungsgeschichte" (1910). In "Der Beamtenstand" (1911) he wrote a classic analysis of the rise of the bureaucracy and civil servants, again moving beyond the Prussian–German example, which he, however, continued to regard as paradigmatic. At the five hundredth anniversary of the Hohenzollern Dynasty, he was selected to write "Die Hohenzollern und ihr Werk" (1915), which was not only an official Festschrift to honor royal greatness, but also a broad and intensively researched synthesis of Prussian history, still useful today. In the famous "Lamprecht Streit" of the 1890s, a fundamental controversy among German historians about the relative importance of social structures, "collectivities" and generalizations in history, Hintze took a productive middle position, advocating systematic comparison and a combination of both hermeneutic and analytical approaches ("Über individualistische und kollektivistische Geschichtsauffassung," 1897). Hintze had started to move beyond historicism. A moderate liberal-conservative, he was convinced of the strength and the virtue of the monarchical-bureaucratic Prussian-German system, which he regarded as fully appropriate to the special geographical condition and statist traditions of Prussia/Germany.

World War I, the defeat of Germany, and the revolution of 1918–1919 represented a watershed in Hintze's life and work. Both his political beliefs and his basic assumptions guiding his scholarly work were shaken, but Hintze succeeded in developing a productive response. His later work was less centered around "the state" than his earlier writings. Social structures and processes, societies, and economies were increasingly regarded as topics in their own right. Hintze became more interested in societal forces of change. He was one of the few German historians of prominence who did not reject systematic approaches but instead advocated the development of "concrete abstractions" and historical typologies. He reviewed Max Weber (q.v.) and Werner Sombart ("Der moderne Kapitalismus als historisches Individuum," 1929). Prussia ceased to be his major interest and reference point for comparison. He extended his scope of study back into the pre–absolutist periods and beyond Europe (including Japan). In 1929–1931 appeared three lengthy articles, masterful works of synthesis: "Wesen und Verbreitung des Feudalismus"; "Typologie der ständischen Verfassungen des Abendlandes"; "Weltgeschichtliche Bedingungen der Repräsentativverfassungen." Hintze was prominent but isolated, particularly after the National Socialists took over. He did not develop a "school." But his work exerted strong influence on historians like Gerhard Oestreich, Dietrich Gerhard, Hans Rosenberg, and Felix Gilbert. Without necessarily accepting his earlier statist orientation, many West German historians of the 1960s, 1970s, and 1980s have seen him as a model for the writing of comparative social history in a broad and nonspecialized sense.

Bibliography: Most of Hintze's major articles are in Otto Hintze, *Gesammelte Abhandlungen*, G. Oestreich, ed., 3 vols. (Göttingen, 1962–1967), including good introductions by the editor and a bibliography of Hintze's publications in vol. 1, pp. 563–579; O. Büsch and M. Erbe, eds., *Otto Hintze und die moderne Geschichtswissenschaft* (Berlin, 1983); D. Gerhard, "Otto Hintze: His Work and His Significance in Historiography,": *Central European History*, 3 (1970): 17–48; Felix Gilbert, ed., *The Historical Essays of Otto Hintze* (New York, 1975); J. Kocka, "Otto Hintze," in H. –U. Wehler, ed., *Deutsche Historiker* (Göttingen, 1973), pp. 275–298; B. Oestreich, "Hedwig und Otto Hintze. Eine biographische Skizze," *Geschichte und Gesellschaft*, 11 (1985): S. 397–419; W. M. Simon, "Power and Responsibility. Otto Hintze's Place in German Historiography," in L. Krieger and F. Stern, eds., *The Responsibility of Power: Historical Essays in Honour of Hajo Holborn* (New York, 1967), pp. 199–219.

Jürgen Kocka

HOETZSCH, Otto (Leipzig, 1876–Berlin, 1946), German historian. In 1902 in Berlin Hoetzsch joined the circle around Theodor Schiemann, where he became familiar with his main theme, Russian history. After 1913 he was professor at the University of Berlin until 1935 when he was dismissed at the instigation of the fascist ministry of propaganda. In 1945–1946, seriously ill, he resumed his teaching and research activities at the same place. Before 1914 he had traveled ten times to Russia, and later, until 1934, he visited the Soviet Union eight times where he was well acquainted with many persons from science and politics. From 1920 to 1929, he belonged to the German-national faction of the German Reichstag and played an important role in the discussion of German foreign policy. In 1928 he organized a "Russian Week for Historians" in Berlin. As author and editor he published: *Russland. Eine Einführung auf Grund seiner Geschichte von 1904 bis 1912* (1913, 1917); *Die internationalen Beziehungen im Zeitalter des Imperialismus. Dokumente aus den Archiven der Zarischen und der Provisorischen Regierung* (16 vols., 1931–1943); *Grundzüge der Geschichte Russlands* (1949, posthum.). Hoetzsch was an historian of political history who was also open to economic and sociohistorical considerations. The central notion of his historical thought was the state. He used the comparability of social and political institutions in West and East European history as the basis from which to derive the political affiliation of Russia to the Pan–European union of states and cultures, thus divorcing the Soviet Union from the historico–political notion of "Asia" without, however, consistently applying this proposition to the foundations of his research.

Bibliography: Fritz Epstein, "Otto Hoetzsch," *Neue Deutsche Biographie* 9 (1972): 371–372; Gerd Voigt, *Otto Hoetzsch 1876–1946. Wissenschaft und Politik im Leben eines deutschen Historikers* (Berlin, 1978).

Gerd Voigt

JANSSEN, Johannes (Xanten, Lower Rhine, 1829–Frankfurt am Main, 1891), German historian. Catholic theologian and priest (1860), son of a wicker-worker. Having taken his doctor's degree in Bonn in 1853 and having qualified as a university lecturer in Münster in 1854, Janssen was until his death professor of history for Catholic pupils at the Gymnasium in Frankfurt. Impeded in his academic career in Prussia by his Catholic denomination, he nevertheless rejected chairs at Catholic universities abroad (Washington, 1883; Rome, 1883, 1890). After the *Kulturkampf*, the conflict between the state and the Catholic Church, Janssen was the most influential historian of Catholic Germany. Johann Friedrich Böhmer, historian of the Middle Ages and librarian in Frankfurt, persuaded Janssen to the old Reich, which had perished in 1806, and to the *grossdeutsch* idea in its Catholic-Habsburg sense. Nevertheless, Janssen at first adopted a positive attitude toward Bismarck's founding of the Second Empire of 1871. But the *Kulturkampf* changed his opinion completely. After 1857, at Böhmer's suggestion, he studied the German late Middle Ages which at that time was considered a period of religious and national decay. In the first instance, these studies led to the two-volume source-edition, *Frankfurts Reichskorrespondenz* (1863–1873). From 1876 on, his *Geschichte des deutschen Volkes seit dem Ausgang de Mittelalters* appeared in eight volumes. It was supposed to end with the dissolution of the old Reich, but it only got as far as the Thirty Years' War. The last two volumes were published after Janssen's death by a pupil of his, the historian of the papacy, Ludwig von Pastor (q.v.) (1854–1928). Janssen deliberately planned his major work as a counterpart to Leopold von Ranke's (q.v.) *Deutsche Geschichte im Zeitalter der Reformation* (6 vols., 1839–1847), which was written from the Protestant point of view and focused on political history.

According to his own statement, Janssen was not primarily interested "in the so-called affairs of state and governmental operations, campaigns and battles, but in the German people in its changing states and fortunes." Thus, he created the first comprehensive and academic cultural history of the fifteenth and sixteenth centuries in Germany and became a precursor of modern social history. Janssen's religious-denominational intentions corresponded to his presentation of the fifteenth century as a flourishing age in all spheres of life which was then crushed by the Reformation—especially by the doctrine of the meritlessness of good deeds and its political exploitation by the princes. In his work, Ranke stated the opposite. Hence, a historical-genetic explanation of the Reformation was not achieved. When Janssen's work was published at the climax of the *Kulturkampf*—in Berlin alone more copies were sold than in the whole of Austria—it met with violent criticism from Protestant as well as liberal quarters. He defended himself in two replies, *An meine Kritiker* (1882) and *Zweites Wort an meine Kritiker* (1883). Janssen did by no means meet with complete rejection from the non-Catholic side (e.g., Jacob Burckhardt [q.v.] and Nietzsche). He believed in an objective historical truth that was to be found in the sources. Thus, he quoted from them extensively, but without critically checking their respective relativity and their expressiveness, and without discussing the criteria for his selection in principle. Notwithstanding his intensive study of sources, he could thus arrive at a concept of history as the fulfillment of a divine doctrine of salvation in the Catholic sense. This position was irreconcilable with the academic concept of historicism, which at that time was firmly established at the leading universities—and especially with its *kleindeutsch*-Prussian (i.e., Germany without Austria) version. So the Catholic historians who worked their way up at German universities after the *Kulturkampf* had to tackle Janssen critically, for example, not only Heinrich Finke but also Pastor. Most of all, those Catholic historians extended the source material basic for the analysis and evaluation of the age of the pre-Reformation. Janssen experienced a certain revival, not only among Catholic scholars, when after World War I the possibility of absolute unconditionality and objectivity of historical science was increasingly doubted. The broad mass of the Catholic *Bildungsbürgertum*, the educated middle classes, had accepted his interpretation of Reformation history since the period of the *Kulturkampf*. Volumes 1–6 of his *Geschichte des deutschen Volkes* appeared from 1913 to 1924 in their seventeenth to twentieth editions, revised by Pastor. In academic Catholicism, only Joseph Lortz' (1887–1975) work *Die Reformation in Deutschland* (1939–1940) effected a more balanced interpretation of the age of the pre-Reformation and the Reformation. In a wide Catholic public, only the experience of National Socialism and the Second Vatican Council had the same effect. It is to Janssen's merit, apart from giving new impulses to social history, that he critically questioned the one-sided Protestant view of the pre-Reformation and Reformation. Moreover, he raised the question of the relationship between modern historical science and Catholic belief for the general public. But he was not able to present a solution on the basis of general agreement. None has been offered to date.

Bibliography: Wilhelm Baum, "Johannes Janssen (1829–1891). Persönlichkeit, Leben und Werke," Diss. Ms. (Innsbruck, 1971); Hubert Jedin, "Johannes Janssen," *Neue Deutsche Biographie*, 10 (1974): 343 f.; Bernd Mütter, *Die Geschichtswissenschaft in Münster zwischen Aufklärung und Historismus* (Münster, 1980).

Bernd Mütter

KAUTSKY, Karl (Prague, 1854–Amsterdam, 1938), German socialist theorist and publicist. Student of history, philosophy, and law at Vienna University, 1874–1879. The initial phase of Kautsky's literary activity bore the strong imprint of Darwinism, which fascinated him by its materialist world outlook. In the early 1880s he became a Marxist. In 1883 he founded the journal, *Neue Zeit*, which under his direction became the most important theoretical periodical of the German and international workers' movement. Kautsky emerged as leading theorist of the Second International Workers' Association (Second International) in 1889. He essentially helped popularize Marxism, particularly its conception of history. His historical interest was devoted mainly to the emergence of Christianity, the German peasants' war, the French Revolution of 1789–1794, the history of the workers' movement as well as to historico-philosophical questions. Among his major historical publications are *Die Klassengegensätze von 1789* (1889), *Ethik und materialistische Geschichtsauffassung* (1906), *Der Ursprung des Christentums* (1908), *Die materialistische Geschichtsauffassung* (2 vols., 1927), and *Krieg und Demokratie. Eine historische Untersuchung und Darstellung ihrer Wechselwirkung in der Neuzeit* (1932). After World War I Kautsky advocated the social-reformistic concept of the so-called third road between capitalism and socialism, at first in the USPD (Unabhängige Sozialdemokratische Partei Deutschlands), which he founded in 1917, and then again, from 1922 in the German Socialist party.

Bibliography: Werner Blumenberg, *Karls Kautskys literarisches Werk. Eine bibliographische Ubersicht* (s'Gravenhage, 1968); Werner Holzheuer, *Karl Kautskys Werk als Weltanschauung* (München, 1972); Karl Kautsky, *Erinnerungen und Erürterungen* (Den Haag, 1960).

Gerhard Lozek

KEHR, Eckart (Brandenburg an der Havel, 1902–Washington, D.C., 1933), German historian. Kehr studied history, philosophy, economics, and sociology at the University of Berlin, chiefly with Friedrich Meinecke (q.v.), Ernst Troeltsch (q.v.) Adolf von Harnack (q.v.), Smend, and Spranger. In 1927 he received his doctorate with a dissertation, written under Meinecke's direction and based on a broad set of sources, on "The Building of the German Battle Fleet and Party Politics (1894–1901)," exposing the internal political, social, and ideological presuppositions of German imperialism. The study appeared as a book in 1930 (reprint in 1965; in English, 1975). The reactions to it were in part emphatically positive and in part equally negative. It is still one of the best monographs about imperial Germany. In the six years preceding 1933, Kehr wrote over a dozen brilliant essays dealing with important problems of Prussian-German social and constitutional history in the nineteenth and the early twentieth centuries. He also wrote the manuscript of a book, "Economics and Politics in the Time of Prussian Reform," which was lost, as well as drafts of further projects and lectures he gave beginning in 1929 at the "Hochschule für Politik" in Berlin. After 1931 he worked on a four-volume edition of documents about Prussian fiscal policy from 1806 to 1815. With a Rockefeller grant he traveled to the United States in early 1933 in order to prepare a comparative international study of the policies concerning loans before 1820. At the age of thirty, he died there suddenly of a congenital heart ailment.

In the German historical profession of the Weimar Republic, Kehr was considered an outsider because of his controversial themes, his methodological-theoretical approach, and his political position. But he differed from older liberal or Social-Democratic outsiders such as Gustav Mayer, Veit Valentin, Arthur Rosenberg, and others who were denied a university career in remaining close to the university milieu. He never lost touch with important scholarly institutions, and his writings were reviewed regularly. In addition, he enjoyed the protection of his extremely important uncle, the medieval historian Paul Fridolin Kehr, who at the time played a key role in university decisions. Kehr therefore continued to be hopeful that he would have a university career. Kehr was politically on the left without being a member of a party. In England he would have been considered a typical "radical." He recognized the National Socialist danger early but preached to deaf ears. His efforts to newly analyze German history in the period since the "dual revolution" at the end of the eighteenth century led him to a socioeconomic explanation of politics under the dominant perspective of the "primacy of domestic politics." With his unorthodox interpretation of Max Weber (q.v.) and Karl Marx (q.v.), he came astonishingly close to his goal of determining as precisely as possible the influence and function of social and economic interests. In part, however, he was prevented from a more precise judgment in keeping with reality by his polemical tendency, the enormous speed with which he worked in view of his heart ailment, and his conscious one-sidedness. With his intense striving for rational, scientific insight and political education, he passionately pursued the problem of the connection between economy, society, and political domination which he considered fundamental.

Having been ignored and forgotten in Germany for nearly twenty years, Kehr has had a uniquely delayed influence in the Federal Republic of Germany since about 1965, both because of his emphatic separation from the main current of German historiography and because of his insights and conceptions which have been very fertile for the critical history of modern German society and politics. Historiographically, the effect of this rediscovery was connected with the advance of West German social history, politically with the reform movement at the end of the 1960s and the early 1970s. Kehr's effect on numerous historians and social scientists, who have been attracted as much by his penetrating interpretations as by the stimulating partisanship of his sharp judgments, remains undeniable. Kehr can be viewed as one of the few nonconformists of modern German historical science who decades after their deaths still elicit emphatic support or rejection.

Bibliography: Hans-Ulrich Wehler, ed., *Deutsche Historiker* (Göttingen, 1971); Hans-Ulrich Wehler, " 'Einleitung' to Eckart Kehr," *Der Primat der Innenpolitik* (Berlin,

1965); Hans-Ulrich Wehler, *Historische Sozialwissenschaft und Geschichtsschreibung* (Göttingen, 1980).

Hans-Ulrich Wehler

KOSSINNA, Gustaf (Tilsit, 1859–Berlin, 1931), German pre- and protohistorian. Professor at the University of Berlin (1902). One of the European prehistorians of great authority who enjoyed a large audience, Kossinna was interested mainly in the ancient history of the Germans, in problems of Indo–European research, and, to a lesser extent, in European prehistory. He initiated a new line of research in German and European prehistory, which appealed to many national schools of archaeology. Kossinna's contribution can be summarized as follows: (1) he founded the German school of prehistory; (2) influenced by some parallel sciences (ethnology) or the natural sciences (biology), he initiated a new method of archaeological research (*Siedlungsarchäologische Methode. Die Herkunft der Germanen. Zur Methode der Siedlungsarchäologie*, 1912); (3) although deeply attached to the Scandinavian archaeologists' work, he moved away from them (Oscar Montelius [q.v.] and Sophus Müller [q.v.], as well as from other prehistorians (V. Gordon Childe [q.v.]), since he asserted the originality and autonomy of prehistoric Europe as against the Orient, combatting the *Ex Oriente lux* thesis; (4) he promoted pre- and protohistoric research by editing a review of European reputation, *Mannus–Zeitschrift für Vorgeschichte*, and a collection, *Mannus–Bibliothek–Bücherei* ; (5) using his method, he tried to determine the primitive homeland (Urheimat) of the Indo-Europeans (Indo-Germans in his terminology), and to establish the precise moment of the German tribes' dispersion and the archaeological facts overlapping with this phenomenon ("Die Vorgeschichtliche Ausbreitung der Germanen in Deutschland," *Zeitschrift, des Vereins für Volkskunde* 6 (1896); "Die Indogermanische Frage. Archäologisch Beantwortet," *Zeitschrift für Ethnologie* (1902); *Die deutsche Vorgeschichte, eine hervorrangend nationale Wissenschaft* (1914, 1921, 1926, 1927, 1936 eds.); and several other monographs). He also attempted to detect other Indo-European groups (the Illyrians, the Thracians), as well as the borderline between the Urfinnen and the Urindogermanen. Kossinna's line of research was widely adopted outside of Germany. Nevertheless, Kossinna may be reproached for (1) introducing an excessively nationalistic, even chauvinistic, spirit into prehistory, which accounted for the raising of his thesis to the level of state doctrine after 1933; (2) for his rigid thesis concerning the relation between the race/ethnos, language/cultural area; (3) for his totally unscientific assertions regarding the northern homeland of the Indo-Europeans and the ethnic unity of certain cultures. Yet, Kossinna's method survives these tendentious orientations and forced applications as a way of determining the nuclear areas of certain cultures. His ideas about the progress in space of the carriers of a culture, his accurate definition of cultural development at the very moment of a certain group's breaking up, and his hypotheses on the direction of the migrations remain valid.

Bibliography: V. Gordon Childe, *The Aryans* (London, 1926), pp. 169–170; V. Gordon Childe, *Piecing Together the Past* (London, 1956), p. 28; Jan Filip, *Encyklopädisches Handbuch der Ur-und Frühgeschichte Europas* 1 (Prague, 1966), pp. 626–627; H. Hahne, ed., "25 Jahre Siedlungsarchäologie," *Mannus-Bibliothek Nr.22* (Leipzig, 1925), pp. i–vi; Martin Jahn, "Gustaf Kossinna," *Nachrichtenblatt für deutsche Vorzeit* 7, no. 12 (1931); 225–226.

Ligia Bârzu

KRUMBACHER, Karl (Kürnach/Bavaria, 1856–Munich, 1909), German historian. Father of modern Byzantine studies as a self-reliant discipline in historical research and higher learning. Member of the Royal Academy of Bavaria. Krumbacher was a remarkable organizer, a professor and scholar who worked to free Byzantine studies from the classic history and philology and establish it as an autonomous discipline. In 1892 he founded the first relevant scientific publication *Byzantinische Zeitschrift* which from the very beginning was an essential tool in the development of Byzantine studies. In his capacity as professor at the University of Munich (1892–1909), he created the first world chair of Byzantine studies (1896) and the first seminar of Byzantine and neo-Greek philology (1897). His seminar turned into the most important international training center for young specialists in Byzantine history. It had an overwhelming impact on the assertion of the discipline in higher learning and research in Europe. His work *Geschichte der byzantinischen Literatur* (1891), with a second edition twice as big as the first in 1897, is Krumbacher's scientific will and testament. The first step on an untrodden path, it is a pioneering work, and one hundred years after its publication, it remains the foundation of any research in this field. Unlike most of the historians of his generation, he advocates the profound originality of Byzantine history, which emerged in the Roman world in the fourth century, in politics and religion, art and culture, language and literature. Educated in the rigid atmosphere of the German school of history, Krumbacher is renowned for his minute investigation and accurate method.

Bibliography: Fr. Dölger, "Karl Krumbacher," in *Chalikes*, ed. H.-G. Beck (München, 1958), pp. 121–135.

Stelian Brezeanu

LAMPRECHT, Karl (Jessen 1856–Leipzig 1915), German historian. Professor at the universities of Bonn (1885), Marburg (1890), and Leipzig (1891). Lamprecht's historical achievements have remained largely obscured amidst the controversies associated with his name. Under the patronage of Gustav Mevissen, Lamprecht established the *Gesellschaft für rheinische Geschichtskunde* in the early 1880s and became one of the modern pioneers of interdisciplinary regional history in Germany. His own study of the economics of the Mosel and middle Rhine valleys, *Deutsches Wirtschaftsleben im Mittelalter*, appeared in three volumes in the middle of the same decade and anticipated the quantitative and statistical methods of later economic history. Lamprecht's interest in promoting regional history was lifelong, and during his tenure in Leipzig he was instrumental in establishing the Commission for Saxon History and, at the University of Leipzig, the *Institut für Landesgeschichte und Siedlungskunde*.

In the 1890s, Lamprecht became embroiled in the most bitter debate the German historical profession has ever witnessed. In the early volumes of his monumental *Deutsche Geschichte*, which began to appear in 1890, the historian attempted to work out a morphological framework for German history, in order to synthesize, in a manner analogous to the methods of the natural sciences, the economic, political, moral, and artistic dimensions of the German experience in successive historical periods, each characterized by a dominant tendency that Lamprecht called its "diapason." In these early volumes, he implied that the transition from one period to the next was governed by changes in the economy and by property relations. This proposition, like Lamprecht's devotion to analogies from the natural sciences, was ideologically repugnant to the political historians who dominated the academic discipline in Wilhelmine Germany. The debate that ensued between them and Lamprecht revealed the philosophical inconsistencies in Lamprecht's thinking, as well as the extraordinary carelessness of much of his research. In the later volumes of the *Deutsche Geschichte*, which appeared after the turn of the century, Lamprecht expunged all traces of historical materialism and instead emphasized the historical morphology of collective psychic forces. By then, however, it was too late, for the historian had been utterly defeated in his confrontation with his enemies. His later attempts to apply his framework to the study of world history went entirely ignored in the German academic community. In recent years Lamprecht's reputation has been salvaged a little, for despite the admitted weaknesses of his approach, the genre he called *Kulturgeschichte* did attempt to expand the scope of historical study far beyond the politics of the nation-state. The "total history" he aspired to write was to encompass the broader realms of society and culture, as well as civilizations around the globe.

Bibliography: Bernhard vom Brocke, "Karl Lamprecht," *Neue Deutsche Biographie* 13 (1982): 467–472; Ursula Lewald, "Karl Lamprecht und die Rheinische Geschichtsforschung," *Rheinische Vierteljahrsblätter* (1956): 279–303; Luise Schorn-Schütte, *Karl Lamprecht: Kulturgeschichtsschreibung zwischen Wissenschaft und Politik* (Göttingen, 1984).

Roger Chickering

LEPSIUS, Richard (Naumburg, 1810–Berlin, 1884), German Egyptologist. Son of a Prussian district administrator, Lepsius at the universities of Leipzig, Göttingen, and Berlin gained the historical, classical, and linguistic foundations on which he pursued his studies in Egyptology, sponsored primarily by Karl Josias von Bunsen in Paris, Italy, and London. His publications, which among other things corroborated the decipherment of the hieroglyphs by Jean Francois Champollion (q.v.), brought him the associate professorship in Berlin and the leadership of the expedition sent by King Frederic Wilhelm IV to Egypt and Ethiopia on the recommendation of Alexander von Humboldt. The expedition ended in 1845 and produced many important results. Some twelve hundred ancient monuments, among them three sacrificial altars from graves of the ancient empire, were brought back as donations of the Viceroy Muhammad Ali and made the Egyptian Museum in Berlin one of the richest of its kind. The archaeological and epigraphic results of the expedition were reflected in the twelve–volume work, *Denkmäler aus Ägypten und Äthiopien* (1849–1859), which today remains a standard work of Egyptology, the concern of which was popularized by Lepsius' *Briefe aus Ägypten, Aethiopien und der Halbinseldes Sinai* (1852). In 1846 Lepsius received a full professorship, and in 1849 he published his pioneering work, *Chronologie der Ägypter*; in 1855 he became associate director and in 1865 director of the Egyptian Museum, which he built up in line with historical aspects. He was instrumental in reorganizing the archaeological institute in Rome and contributed to restructuring the Prussian State Institution (1871) into an Institute of the Reich (1874). His linguistic studies, important for the development of African studies, culminated in the *Nubische Grammatik* (1880). He helped prepare the way for Meroe studies.

Bibliography: Georg Ebers, *Richard Lepsius. Ein Lebensbild* (1885; reprint Osnabrück, 1969); Fritz Hintze and Gerhard Rühlmann, "Karl Richard Lepsius—Begründer der deutschsprachigen Ägyptologie," *Das Altertum* 30 (1984).

Johannes Irmscher

MARX, Karl (Trier, 1818–London, 1883), German philosopher and economist, theorist, and political organizer of the international working–class movement. Marx, son of a lawyer, studied in Bonn and Berlin. He took his doctor's degree at Jena on ancient Greek philosophy. Politically, he developed from a radical democrat to a communist, from a philosophical and ideological left–wing Hegelian to a materialist. In 1842–1843 he was editor of the *Rheinische Zeitung für Politik, Handel und Gewerbe*. In 1848–1849 he was the chief editor of the *Neue Rheinische Zeitung*. In French exile (1844), he began preliminary work on the critique of the bourgeois economy. At the same time, related to an intended critique on policy ("Kritik der Politik"), he conducted studies on the "History of the Convention." Together with Friedrich Engels (q.v.), Marx wrote the *Manifest der Kommunistischen Partei* (1848) for the Communist League. After the revolution of 1848–1849 Marx emigrated to England. In London, after four years of work, his most important economic work *Das Kapital* (vol. 1, 1867) appeared. In 1867 he was elected a member of the newly established International Workers' Association. He exerted a sustained influence on the emergence and programs of the national workers' parties.

Marx's most important historiographic works (*Die Klassenkämpfe in Frankreich*, 1850; *Der Achtzehnte Brumaire des Louis Bonaparte*, 1852; and *Der Bürgerkrieg in Frankreich*, 1871) were written as political and militant programmatical works. Their aim was to analyze the situation created by the events of 1848–1849 and 1870–1871 in the interest of the revolutionary socialist/communist movement rather than to give only a depiction *sine ira et studio*. Like all other contemporary historians, Marx based his explanations and interpretations on insufficient sources and materials as well as on historically limited knowledge.

As a political thinker and actor, he raised socially relevant questions, new to the science of history, questions which he undertook to resolve with scientifically painstaking care. Marx's *Achtzehnte Brumaire des Louis Bonaparte* may claim to be an attempt to solve the historical problem: How was it possible that the Bonapartist coup of December 1751 was successful? Thus, it has a methodologically exemplary effect. The methodological principles of the dialectic-materialistic conception of history worked out by Marx and Engels earlier in the *Deutsche Ideologie* (1845–1846) found its adequate historiographic application. Marx and Engels considered history to be an irreversible process of historical formation of socioeconomic, political, and ideological relations ("formations" or "forms") which, created by antagonistic human activities, determine by themselves human thinking and action as objectively given indispensable conditions. To recognize the determination of political action by the ruling economic, social, and state relations was the subject of Marx's analysis in the *Klassenkämpfe in Frankreich*. In the historical narration of *Achtzehnte Brumaire*, Marx described the actions and counteractions of classes, parties, and persons of French society between February 1848 and December 1851. Proceeding from an intense analysis into "relations" and "circumstances," he demonstrated how the room for maneuver was progressively narrowed down for the "subjects" of historical dialectics: for Louis Napoleon the coup d'état became a real possibility, whereas the success of the coup appeared to result from the class struggles of the Second Republic.

The conception of class struggle is crucial to the Marxian approach to the history of humankind since the dissolution of primitive society. The existence of social classes, according to Marx, was based on historical forms of production. Class relations and class struggles were therefore always the mediating links between economic analysis and political historiography. Marx viewed the relationship between class and individual, social interest (need) and individual motive as the very problem of research to be solved always anew at the concrete historical subject. Exact analyses have shown that Marx did not simply "derive" his historiographic interpretations and explanations from the categories of his social and historical theory (basis–superstructure, social formation, productive forces–production relations, state, ideology). Marx, in the historiographical passages of his economic works (e.g., in Chapter 24 of *Kapital*: the so-called "original accumulation"), outlined the genesis (or dissolution) of economic relations. In many of his works there are historiographic excursions, with studies of the processes of ideological formation and scientific progress. Throughout his life Marx strove to confirm, to correct, as well as to extend his teachings by studying historical reality.

Bibliography: *Formationstheorie und Geschichte. Studien zur Historischen Untersuchung von Gesellschaftsformationen im Werk von Marx, Engels und Lenin*, eds. Ernst Engelberg and Wolfgang Küttler (Berlin, 1978); Heinz Heitzer and Wolfgang Küttler, *Eine Revolution im Geschichtsdenken. Marx, Engels, Lenin und die Geschicht wissenschaft* (Berlin, 1983); Hans-Peter Jaeck, *Die französische Revolution von 1789 im*

Frühwerk von Karl Marx (Berlin, 1979); *Das geschichtswissenschaftliche Erbe von Karl Marx*, ed. Wolfgang Küttler (Berlin, 1983); Leonard Krieger, "Marx and Engels as Historian," *Journal of the History of Ideas* 14 (1953): 381–403; *Marks-istorik* (Marx as a Historian) (Moscow, 1968).

Hans-Peter Jaeck

MAYER, Gustav (Prenzlau, 1871–London, 1948), German historian. After studying political economy and taking his doctor's degree (1890–1893), Mayer worked as editor and foreign correspondent of *Frankfurter Zeitung* (1896–1906), and then became a private scholar. He came into contact with leading personalities of the European working-class movement and began doing research into its German development. His great number of studies, among them *J. B. v. Schweitzer und die deutsche Sozialdemokratie* (1909) were based on many unknown sources. Another salient subject for him was *Die Trennung der proletarischen von der bürgerlichen Demokratie in Deutschland* (1911). Originally, the reactionary Berlin professors prevented his habilitation (1917) and his university career; nevertheless, against their will, he was appointed to a professorship in 1922 by the Weimar government. Because of the great amount of source material he discovered, he was a pioneer in many questions concerning the history of the working-class movement. The rediscovery of unpublished works resulted in the edition of *Ferdinand Lassalle. Nachgelassene Briefe und Schriften* (6 vols., 1921–1925). Many biographical rediscoveries on the young Friedrich Engels (q.v.) were attributable to him. His two-volume biography, *Friedrich Engels* (1920–1934), remains a standard work today. In it he also acknowledged the importance of Karl Marx' (q.v.) and Engels' "Deutsche Ideologie," which had fallen into oblivion. In search of sources, he worked together with the Marx-Engels Institute in Moscow, since he was always anxious to do justice in his historical judgment to all factions of the working-class movement. Politically left-liberal, he was close to the Social Democrats. His works were characterized by social-reformist ideals, with all their limitations. Dismissed by the Nazis in 1933, this scholar of Jewish descent was forced to emigrate in 1934. Since he lived in London or Oxford, it was difficult for him to raise funds and support for his research activities. Using exclusively local sources, he wrote *The Political History of the English Labour Movement from 1857–1872. Documents and Commentaries*, which, however, remained unpublished.

Bibliography: Gustav Mayer, *Erinnerungen* (Zurich, 1949); Hans Schleier, "Zu Gustav Mayers Wirken und Geschichtsauffassung," *Evolution und Revolution in der Weltgeschichte. Ernst Engelberg zum 65. Geburtstag*, vol. 1 (Berlin, 1976), pp. 301–326; Hans–Ulrich Wehler, "Gustav Mayer," in H. U. Wehler, ed., *Deutsche Historiker*, vol. 2 (Göttingen, 1971), pp. 120–132.

Hans Schleier

MEHRING, Franz (Schlawe, 1846–Berlin, 1919), German Marxist historian, literary scientist, and publicist. Studied classical philology at Vienna and Berlin universities (1866–1870). As political friend of Johann Jacoby and Guido Weiss,

Mehring began his journalistic career as a contributor to different liberal democratic press organs, among them the *Frankfurter Zeitung* (1874–1875) and the Berlin *Volks-Zeitung* (1886–1890). Following the ideas of Ferdinand Lassalle, Mehring at first held a reformist view of socialism based on a democratic-emancipatory idea of the role of the workers' movement. The paper, ''Herr von Treitschke der Sozialistentödter und die Endziele des Liberalismus'' (1875), a critical analysis of the ideas of the conservative Prussian historian Heinrich von Treitschke (q.v.), was characteristic of his position. In the second half of the 1870s, Mehring temporarily turned away from the workers' movement. The brochure, *Die deutsche Sozialdemokratie, ihre Geschichte, ihre Lehre*, published in 1877, testified to that. The struggle (1878–1890) against Bismarck's Socialists Act, directed against the Social Democrats, linked him again more closely with the social democratic movement. This development finally led to the transition to Marxist positions and his joining the Social Democratic Party (1891). As editor and co-publisher of the weekly *Neue Zeit* and other social democratic organs, Mehring wrote his most important historical works in the following three decades. In 1893 his first history, *Die Lessing-Legende*, appeared (with the supplement, *Uber den historischen Materialismus*). In a sharp polemic with the established historiography, Mehring dealt with the historical genesis of the Prussian state up to the end of the eighteenth century. He not only divested the Prussian King Friedrich II of all false glory, but at the same time also integrated the early phase of classical German literature into the bourgeois struggle for emancipation, thus creating essential criteria for a Marxist historiography and literary criticism. Mehring was one of the first historians to make the development of a workers' movement a subject of comprehensive studies. Among his most important works are the four-volume *Geschichte der Deutschen Sozialdemokratie* (1897) as well as the biography, *Karl Marx—Geschichte seines Lebens* (1918). Both publications were pioneer works of Marxist historiography. The 1897 work were contained the first attempt at overall description of the political German workers' movement from its beginning up to the Erfurt Party Congress of Social Democracy in 1891; the 1918 work constitutes the first comprehensive biography of the founder of scientific socialism. As far as Mehring's other works are concerned, his introduction to and annotations on the literary bequest of Karl Marx (q.v.), Friedrich Engels (q.v.), and Ferdinand Lassalle (1902), *Eine Geschichte der Kriegskunst* (1908) as well as the *Deutsche Geschichte vom Ausgang des Mittelalters* (1910), deserve special emphasis. Mehring's historiographic maxim was: ''Every historical figure finds his historical right only in his historical environment.'' On the eve of World War I, Mehring was among the leading representatives of the left-wing of Social Democracy. In September 1914 he opposed the granting of war credits. Because of his antiwar struggle, he was detained in 1916 for some months. He was a co-founder of the revolutionary Spartacus group (1916) and of the Communist party of Germany (KPD, 1918).

Bibliography: Thomas Höhle, *Franz Mehring, 1869–1891* (Berlin, 1956); Hans Koch, *Franz Mehrings Beitrag zur Entwicklung der marxistischen Literaturtheorie* (Berlin,

1959); Walter Kumpmann, *Franz Mehring als Vertreter des historischen Materialismus* (Wiesbaden, 1966); Josef Schleifstein, *Franz Mehring, 1891–1919* (Berlin 1959).

Gerhard Lozek

MEINECKE, Friedrich (Salzwedel, 1862–Berlin, 1954), German historian. Disciple of Johann Gustav Droysen (q.v.), Heinrich von Sybel (q.v.), and Heinrich von Treitschke (q.v.). Archivist in Berlin (1887), professor in Strasbourg (1901), Freiburg (1906), and Berlin (1918); editor of the *Historische Zeitschrift* (1896–1935); chairman of the Historical Commission of the Reich (1928–1935); rector of the Free University in West Berlin (1948). Meinecke was the founder of an elitist history of ideas with which he intended to overcome the one-sidedness of conventional political historiography. A pronounced political adaptability to changing realities was a basic feature of his long life. In the creative period before 1914, Meinecke turned from a conservative into a moderate liberal closely connected with Friedrich Naumann. In 1907 his first important work in the history of ideas, *Weltbürgertum und Nationalstaat. Studien zur Genesis des deutschen Nationalstaates*, appeared. Rejecting the ideas of cosmopolitanism, he tried to draw connecting lines between the German classical age and the romantic movement, the conservative counterreaction to the 1848 Revolution and the national state created by Bismarck. In this state he saw implemented the unity of power and spirit. At the same time, he alleged the superiority of the German spirit over other ways of thinking. That is why, at the initial stage of World War I, he advocated chauvinistic positions. In the interest of the preservation of the Wilhelmian Empire, he later pleaded for limited reforms in the interior and a negotiated peace (Verhandlungsfrieden) outwardly. After 1918 Meinecke was among the few German historians who fully accepted the parliamentary form of government of the Weimar Republic. This was reflected in his second, probably most significant, work in terms of history of ideas, *Die Idee der Staatsräson in der neueren Geschichte* (1924). Rendering reason of state the central category of modern thought on the state, he now postulated the dualism of spirit and power, thus deviating from his former views. As he upgraded cosmopolitan ideas, Meinecke simultaneously advocated an equation of German and Western ways of thinking.

Meinecke's attitude toward the fascist régime after 1933 wavered between rejection, resignation, and partial approval, above all of its foreign policy. Retired in 1932, he withdrew from all scientific-political functions by 1935. He mainly devoted himself to laying the philosophical and methodological foundations of his conception of history. In 1936 he published his major work, *Entstehung des Historismus*. Meinecke understood by historicism not just a scientific method pure and simple, but a world outlook the core of which was formed by the individual principle and the individualizing method based on it. Immediately after the end of the war, he wrote the brochure, *Die deutsche Katastrophe*, which became his most widespread publication. He was anxious to preserve the putatively positive traditions of the Prussian–German state and to tie them to the ideology of the Occident. In terms of historiography, he endorsed a synthesis of Leopold von Ranke (q.v.) and Jacob Burckhardt (q.v.). Again he made a point of urging a reconciliation between the German way of thinking, resulting from historicism, and the Western way of thinking more strongly bearing the imprint of natural right. Meinecke exerted a durable, strong influence on historiography, helped by numerous followers.

Bibliography: *Friedrich Meinecke heute*, hrsg. v. Michael Erbe (Berlin [West], 1981), with comprehensive bibliography; Walter Hofer, *Geschichtsschreibung und Weltanschauung. Gedanken zum Werke F. Meineckes* (München, 1950); Gerhard Lozek, "Friedrich Meinecke," *Studien über die deutsche Geschichtswissenschaft*, Bd. II, hrsq.v. Joachim Streisand (Berlin, 1965); R. W. Sterling, *Ethics in a World of Power* (Princeton, 1958).

Gerhard Lozek

MEYER, Eduard (Hamburg, 1855–Berlin, 1930), German historian. Professor of ancient history in Leipzig (1884), Breslau (1885), Halle (1889), and Berlin (1902–1923). Meyer's bibliography comprises more than five hundred titles out of the most diverse fields of ancient history. His authority is founded on his *Geschichte des Altertums*, first published in five volumes between 1884 and 1902 (new ed., 1984). It dealt with the beginnings of the ancient East and Greece until 350 B.C., and it only touched on Roman history in passing. An enormous increase in factual knowledge made available by the new specialized historical sciences made possible for the first time an integrated view of ancient history. On the other hand, in the last period of his life, later scientific findings necessitated a repeated revision of Meyer's work. In connection with this main work, Meyer wrote some other important books, such as the *Geschichte des alten Ägyptens* (1887), the first synopsis of Egyptian history, and the *Ägyptische Chronologie* (1904). Meyer also applied himself to Roman history, publishing *Caesars Monarchie und das Principat des Pompeius* in 1918. This work was obviously formed by Meyer's political conservatism. He was an engaged supporter of the monarchy and a public supporter of annexation from the beginning of World War I. Some of his belligerent wartime essays were collected in *Weltgeschichte und Weltkrieg* (1916). His antidemocratic conviction was repeatedly expressed in historical works dealing with the phenomenon of universal monarchy: *Geschichte des Altertums; Alexander der Grosse und die absolute Monarchie* (1910); and *Kaiser Augustus* (1903). Meyer's conservatism also informed his essays on economic history: *Die wirtschaftliche Entwicklung des Altertums* (1895) and *Die Sklaverei im Altertum* (1898), which can only be understood in the context of their vehement rejection of newer ideas in the field of national economy and economic theory. His modernizing interpretation of the ancient economy ("The flowering of antiquity corresponds to that of modern times; it is in all respects a modern time") was to be a guidepost for German studies of the ancient world until the middle of the twentieth century. His arguments in *Zur Theorie und Methodik der Geschichte* (1902) were equally in accordance with a conventional notion of history and rejected all theories of a regulated and gradual historical progress as well as any orientation of historical study toward fields other than politics and the state. Typical was his definition: "History is not a systematic science. . . . The object of history always is the investigation and presentation of individual processes which we can best identify as individual summarizations." Nevertheless, the general context of his work was always conditioned by his awareness of himself as a universal historian. Beginning with his doctoral thesis, "Set-Typhon. Eine religionsgeschichtliche Studie" (1875), he was also interested in religious history and treated such questions in monographs throughout his life: *Die Entstehung des Judentums* (1896); *Die Israeliten und ihre Nachbarstämme* (1906); *Ursprung und Geschichte der Mormonen* (1912), up to his final large work in three volumes, *Ursprung und Anfänge des Christentums* (1912–1923).

Bibliography: Karl Christ, "Eduard Meyer," *Von Gibbon zu Rostovtzeff* (Darmstadt, 1979), pp. 286–333; Hans Marohl, "Eduard Meyer," *Bibliographie* (Stuttgart, 1941).

Ines Stahlmann

MOMMSEN, Theodor (Garding, Schleswig-Holstein, 1818–Berlin, 1903), German historian and jurist. Professor of law at the universities of Leipzig (1848–1851), Zurich (1852), and Breslau (1854). In 1858 the Prussian Royal Academy of Sciences in Berlin appointed Mommsen editor-in-chief of the *Corpus Inscriptionum Latinarum*. In 1861 he became professor of Roman history at the University of Berlin. Mommsen's overall interpretation of Roman history has not been equaled since his own time and earned him the description "il grande maestro" from his Italian contemporaries. The very beginning of his academic work already shows his numerous interests and talents. He took his doctoral degree in 1843 with a work on the history of law and saw himself throughout his life primarily as a student of law. His next substantial publication was a collection of epigraphic sources: *Inscriptiones Regnis Neapolitani Latinae* (1852). Nevertheless, he acquired greater publicity with his *Römische Geschichte* (I–III, 1854–1856, V, 1885; the fourth volume has never been published). The fact that Mommsen was awarded the first Nobel Prize for literature for this work in 1902 points to a characteristic aspect of his historical writings: Although they were based on intensive research in original sources, they were highly conditioned by the strong desire to present the historical facts artistically ("it was necessary to bring the old masters down from the level of fantasy where they had appeared to the masses and to bring them into the real world where one hates and loves") and by a very conscious "moral-political effort," on which he put more emphasis than on the "inherited values." For Mommsen, the historian had an obvious "duty to instruct readers as to their future attitude toward the State."

The national unity of Germany was the political ideal for which Mommsen struggled, not only with his interpretation of Roman history, the first phase of which he saw as an important Italian unifying process. To reach this aim of national unity he took an active part in the Revolution of 1848, in which he also worked as a politically committed journalist. Because of his involvement in this progressive movement, the "Achtundvierziger" was dismissed in 1851 from his professorial chair in Leipzig. From 1863 to 1866 he was deputy for the German Progressive party, from 1873 to 1879 he was deputy for the National Liberals in the Prussian Chamber of Deputies, and from 1881 to 1884 he represented the Liberal Secession in the Deutsche Reichstag. With his *Roman History*, Mommsen became famous far beyond the circle of historians of the ancient world; in the narrower academic field he acted above all as the effective initiator of major systematic projects of basic research. Apart from the above-mentioned *Corpus Inscriptionum Latinarum*, he initiated the work on *Corpus nummorum*, founded the *Archiv für Papyrusforschung*, promoted research on the Limes Germanicus and the *Thesaurus Linguae Latinae*, and for many years was head of the *Auctores Antiquissimi* section of the *Monumenta Germaniae Historica*. In addition to opening up new sources for research, he interpreted the ancient documents in numerous philological, legal, epigraphical, numismatical, and historical studies. (They are collected in his *Gesammelte Schriften*, I–VIII, 1905–1913. Abt.1: *Juristische Schriften*. Abt.2: *Historische Schriften*. Abt.3: *Philologische Schriften*. Abt.4: *Epigraphische und numismatische Schriften*.) He also acquired lasting recognition as a model publisher of original texts and as their critical commentator. His editions of *Juris anteiustiniani Fragmenta* (1861), of *Res gestae divi Augusti* (1865; 2nd ed., 1883), of *Digesta Iustiniani Augusti* (I–II, 1866–1870), and of the *Codex Theodosianus* (1905) remain fundamental. Besides his preoccupation with legal sources, Mommsen carried on his work as jurist with his important work, *Römisches Staatsrecht* (I–III, 1871–1888). He aimed to show an abstract system of constitutional law, which he created by adopting a synchronic perspective. This abstraction was to be valid for the different epochs of Roman history. As a result of his desire to systematize, Mommsen claimed the same degree of relevance for the structure-forming institutions of Roman constitutional law—magistracy, citizenship, and senate—throughout the whole period of development of the constitution. The early monarchy and the Principate were in this way interpreted as different forms of the magistracy. Mommsen realized that his concept was open to attack, but it has remained indispensable as a comprehensive view as well as for many detailed legal questions. The same is true for his *Römisches Strafrecht* (1899). Mommsen's typical way of historical interpretation by relating legal and historical perspectives stabilized the already predominating legalistic German approach to Roman history, which neglected the economic and social basis. His treatment of numerous detailed problems, as well as his major works, provoked substantial discussions, which are still going on: whether it is his abstract sketch of Roman constitutional law or his *Römische Geschichte*, which is full of subjective interpretations or, more particularly, his idealistic view of Caesar. The effect of his work on German historical research was firmly based on the authority created by his enormous competence. His influence as scientific coordinator of projects, which still continues, cannot be overestimated. Even if more recent discoveries have altered some of Mommsen's findings, he remains a master of almost all aspects of Roman historical studies. Although he promoted specialization through the major research projects which he himself initiated, he nevertheless viewed this tendency in a skeptical way: "The best of us perceive that we have moved from being scientists to being mere technicians."

Bibliography: Karl Christ, "Theodor Mommsen," *Ders., Von Gibbon bis Rostvzeff* (Darmstadt, 1972), pp. 84–118; Alfred Heuss, *Theodor Mommsen und das 19. Jahrhundert.* (Kiel, 1956); Lothar Wickert, *Theodor Mommsen. Eine Biographie*, I-IV (Frankfurt am main, 1959–1980); Albert Wucher, *Theodor Mommsen. Geschichtsschreibung und Politik* (Göttingen, 2nd ed., 1968).

Ines Stahlmann

NIEBUHR, Barthold Georg (Copenhagen, 1776–Bonn, 1831), German historian. Niebuhr, the son of an engineer and explorer, studied history and law at the then Danish University of Kiel, worked for some time as the private secretary of the Danish minister of finance, and completed his education in Edinburgh. After 1800 he was employed in the Danish public service; in 1804 he became director of the National Bank. In 1806 Baron von Stein, the Prussian chief minister, won him over for Prussia, where Niebuhr, linked with the Reformist party, became privy state councillor and head of the section for state debts and banking. Because of differences with Chancellor Hardenberg, he resigned from state administration, and in 1810 he became state historiographer and was elected member of the Academy, where he did great service to the reorganization of the society of scholars. At the same time he began lecturing at the newly founded Berlin University which provided the basis for his *Römische Geschichte* (1811–1812). By that he established the historical-critical method, a fertile orientation toward the early history of Rome combining descriptions of late Roman literature mixed with legends and myths together with the ethnographic analogy relating to Niebuhr's associations with his youth and the familiar rural communities in Holstein. The national upheaval of 1813 again challenged Niebuhr as a financial expert and publisher who, in the pamphlet *Preussens Recht gegen den sächsischen Hof* (1814), corroborated the Prussian legend of the national mission of Prussia. In 1816 Niebuhr went to Rome as Prussian ambassador to the Vatican. This stay gave him opportunity for detailed studies in ancient history (special studies for the third volume of his *Römische Geschichte* published in 1832; discovery and assessment of manuscripts, among other things, of Rhetor Fronto and of the jurist Gaius, fragments of Sallust, Cicero, Livius, support for the inscriptions of the Berlin Academy). After his return in 1823, he was appointed a member of the Prussian State Council, guided by the principle that the historian had also to be a practical statesman. However, he did not assume any public post but taught at the newly founded University of Bonn. It was here that he initiated the *Corpus scriptorum historiae Byzantinae*, briefly called the Bonn Corpus for its place of publication. Niebuhr, as characterized by an appropriate contemporary formulation, is the scholar among the statesmen and the statesman among the scholars. His *Kleine historischen und philologischen Schriften* was published in two volumes (1823–1843); his revealing correspondence has been collected since 1926.

Bibliography: Karl Christ, "Barthold Georg Niebuhr," *Von Gibbon zu Rostovtzeff. Leben und Werk führender Althistoriker der Neuzeit* (Darmstadt, 1979), pp. 26–49; Johannes Irmscher, "Zum 200. Geburtstag Barthold Georg Niebuhrs," in Elisabeth Charlotte Welskopf, *Probleme der Sklaverei als Privateigentumsverhältnis in der Antike* (Berlin, 1977), pp. 45 ff.; Seppo Rytkönen, *Barthold Georg Niebuhr als Politiker und Historiker* (Helsinki, 1968).

Johannes Irmscher

RANKE, Leopold von (Wiehe, Kursachsen, 1795–Berlin, 1886), German historian. Taught at the University of Berlin from 1825 until his retirement in 1871. Ranke was the son of a lawyer, but the descendant of a long line of Lutheran clergymen. Ranke has repeatedly been called the father of historical science who with Barthold Georg Niebuhr introduced critical methods into historical research. This identification rests in part on the methodological appendix to his first major work, *The Histories of the Germanic and Latin Nations* (1824) and on its famous Preface in which he called for a scientific history based exclusively on the critical examination of primary sources, especially of memoirs, diaries, letters, reports from embassies, and original narratives of eyewitnesses. The task of the historian, he wrote, is to reconstruct the past, free of any moral judgments, *"wie es eigentlich gewesen."* Critical methods, however, long preceded Ranke. Ranke's contribution consisted more in the professionalization of historical studies, that is, in the rigorous application of critical methods to historical writing, than in a methodological innovation. Ranke viewed history as a special discipline, requiring careful preparation and training. He was in a position at the University of Berlin in his seminars to train a large number of leading historians in his approach, historians who then occupied major chairs of history in Germany and to some extent even abroad. Ranke's fame, however, transcended his role as a teacher of scholars. He was without question one of the great narrative historians of the nineteenth century. He succeeded, where his predecessors in eighteenth-century Germany, for example, Schlözer and Gatterer, had failed: in combining the critical examination of the texts with a sweeping narrative that synthesized the data into a comprehensive story.

Several misapprehensions have arisen about Ranke which need to be corrected. Ranke was not the hard-nosed, fact-oriented specialist whom the American founders of the profession admired. He was at all times concerned with the broad context of modern European history, and although he rejected the introduction of explicit theories into historical writing, he operated with implicit philosophic assumptions. These assumptions at times contained serious contradictions. Thus, he insisted that he was not a philosopher and yet was convinced that there were great God-inspired "moral energies" at work. While he insisted on strict method in establishing the facts, he was also convinced that the great lines of development in history emerged intuitively from the immersion of the historian into the documents without any special methodology. States constituted "ideas of God," each unique and individual, incapable of being explained in terms of external factors. Within modern history he portrayed the interplay of the great modern states in the balance of power. Although he does not ignore literature and culture, he sees them as subordinate to the power political aspects of the state and has little understanding for social and economic factors. He calls for strict impartiality but inserts his conservative political bias into his historical account. He proclaims that "all epochs are equally immediate to God," yet throughout his writings traces the progress of a conservative, Protestant social and political order and denies the non-European peoples the dignity of a historical development of their own. He stands out among nineteenth-century historians by his broad European approach which contrasts with the narrow nationalism of many of his colleagues. His main theme in a host of histories of the papacy, Germany in the Age of the Reformation, and France and England in the early modern period is the emergence of this conservative social order as it is embodied in the modern European state system. He did not succeed in completing his final work, a history of the world, or rather of the Western world, from Near Eastern antiquity. Ranke's influence should not be overstressed. From the perspective of today he appears less as the "father of historical science"—even his disciples went in very different directions—than as a writer who must be seen in the political, social, and, last but not least, religious context of his formative years in early nineteenth-century Germany.

Bibliography: C. Hinrichs, *Ranke und die Geschichtstheologie der Rankezeit* (Göttingen, 1954); Georg G. Iggers and Konrad Von Moltke, eds., *Leopold von Ranke. The Theory and Practice of History* (Indianapolis, 1973); Leonard Krieger, *Ranke. The Meaning of History* (Chicago, 1977); Theodore Von Laue, *Ranke. The Formative Year* (Princeton, n.g., 1950); Friedrich Meinecke, *Die Entstehung des Historismus* (Berlin, 1936); Ernst Schulin, *Die weltgeschichtliche Erfassung des Orients bei Hegel und Ranke* (Göttingen, 1958); Rudolf Vierhaus, *Ranke und die soziale Welt* (Münster, 1957).

Georg G. Iggers

REINECKE, Paul (1872–1959), German pre- and protohistorian. Chief curator at the Museum in Munich. One of the most outstanding personalities of twentieth–century European prehistory, Reinecke carried on an immense activity for over five decades. Taking up a vast study, from prehistory to the Middle Ages, he bequeathed an immense work whose scientific value is still intact. Reinecke was a genuine master of significant detail, and his scientific contribution, which materialized not in bulky books but in studies of great erudition, can be considered a model of archaeological research. Many of his studies have been collected in two volumes: *Kleine Schriften zur Vor- und Frühgeschichtlichen Topographie Bayern* (1962) and *Mainzer Aufsätze zur Chronologie der Bronze und Eisenzeit* (1965). Although he was interested in numerous problems, from Neolithic art ("Ein spätneolitisches Marmoridol aus Sardinien," *Germania* 25, 1941) and other aspects of Neolithic archaeology ("Zur Kenntnis der frühneolithischen Zeit in Deutschland," *Mainzer Zeitschrift*, 1908) to Roman provincial archaeology and history ("Burgi des spätromischen Limes der Provinz Raetien," *Deutsche Gaue*, 1912; "Beiträge zur Geschichte Raetiens in der römischen Kaiserzeit," *Zeitschrift der Hist. Ver. fur Schwaben u. Neuburg*, 1913; "Die Porta principalis destra in Regensburg," *Germania*, 1958), including the age of migrations and medieval archaeology ("Slavische Schläfenringe in Dalmatien," *Zeitschrift für Ethnologie*, 1896; "Studien über Denkmäler des frühen Mittelalter," *Mitteilungen der Anthropologischer Gesellschaft in Vienna, 1899*; "Slavisch oder Karolingisch," *Prähistoristorische Zeitschrift*, 1928), Paul Reinecke is remembered mainly for his studies of and interest in restricted categories of objects, for instance, the helmet and the fibula, and for some systems of chronology for the three stages of the age of metal: bronze, Hallstatt, Latène. Deliberate analysis of funeral rites and ritual, of sets of characteristic objects and their typology, enabled him to delimit the differences as compared to the Northwest German and Scandinavian zones for which the system of Oscar Montelius (q.v.) and Sophus Müller (q.v.) could be used. For the southern region of Germany he proposed his own variants, irrespective of age, on the quadripartite principle (A–D) in a series of studies based on restrained sets of deposits or discoveries of a funeral character ("Zur Chronologie der jüngeren Bronzezeit und der älteren Abschnitte der Hallstattzeit in Süd- und Norddeutschland," *Korrespondenzblatt der deutsche Gesellschaft für Anthrop, enth u. Urgeschichte*, 1900; "Grabfunde der frühen Bronzezeit aus Rheinhessen," *Korrespondenzblatt d. Westd. Zeitschrift*, 1901; and others). The presentation was very rigorous and based strictly on facts. Very seldom did he venture to write longer studies. Reinecke does not seem to have been influenced by any of the trends that dominated European archaeological research at the time. Neither the excesses of Gustaf Kossinna's (q.v.) school nor the tendencies of the cultural-historical school interested or exerted any influence on him.

Bibliography: K. Bohner and F. Wagner, "Introduction," *P. Reinecke, Mainzer Aufsätze zur Chronologie der Bronze und Eisenzeit* (Bonn, 1965), including a bibliography of Reinecke's work, 1896–1964, pp. 145–156; Jan Filip, *Encyklopädisches Handbuch der Ur- und Frühgeschichte* 2 (Prague, 1967), p. 1133; Friedrich Wagner, "Paul Reinecke zum 70 Gebrustage," *Nachrichtenblatt fur Deutsche Vorzeit*, Heft 5–6 (1942): 127–129.

Ligia Bârzu

RITTER, Gerhard (Bad Sooden, 1888–Freiburg, 1967), German historian. Professor at the University of Hamburg (1924) and at the University of Freiburg (1925). In his first period, the epoch of the Weimer Republic, Ritter concentrated on late medieval and Reformation history. Four books appeared during this first period, the most important of which was his *Luther, Gestalt Und Symbol* (1925). Written as a response to the German collapse of 1918, his work on Luther revealed both his German nationalism and his political conservatism. He defended the unique qualities of the German spirit, of which Luther was a symbol, indicating that Germany should not be influenced by the materialist and liberal West. Ritter's second period began with the crisis of the Weimer Republic and the advent of Hitlerism, when he responded to Germany's political catastrophe by changing his area of specialization and by moving from medieval-Reformation to modern German history, from cultural-religious history to political biography. In 1931 his *Stein* appeared and in 1936 his *Friedrich Der Grosse*. In both works, Ritter emerged as a defender of the Prussian Bismarckian tradition, a posture he was to retain for the remainder of his life. Ritter drew a distinction between the Machtpolitik of Bismarck and the romantic Bonapartism of Naziism. Whereas in the Frederician-Bismarckian tradition politics controlled military policy and moderation prevailed over unrestrained expansionism, in Naziism it was militarism that controlled politics and racial imperialism that conquered moderation. Another book from this second period was his *Machtstaat und Utopie* (1940), a philosophical speculation on the nature of power. In this book, Ritter compared the utopian humanism of Thomas More to the political realism of Machiavelli, claiming that because of Germany's geographic position, situated between Gaul and Slav, the country had no choice but to be political realist in the Machiavellian tradition. Combining devotion to the Lutheran faith with his advocacy of Machtpolitik, Ritter adhered to the Lutheran notion of a radical divorce between the divine and the historical.

The third period of Ritter's career began with the fall of Hitler when, like the German nation in general, Ritter began to speculate on the causes for the triumph of National Socialism. In this period of national self-introspection, Ritter had two overriding purposes: (1) to protect the Prussian-Bismarckian tradition; (2) to see the origins of National Socialism not in aristocratic conservatism, but in mass democracy. Ritter's desire to defend the nineteenth-century traditions of German idealism inspired what was to be the most productive period of his career, the span from 1945 until 1967, which covered the fifty-seventh to the seventy-ninth years of his own life. Among the many works of this period was his *Carl Goerdeler und Die Deutsche Widerstandsbewegung* (1956), which was an attempt to cleanse the German conscience and prove that a resistance to Hitlerism had existed. *Das Deutsche Probleme* (1962) was an attempt, like Friedrich Meinecke's (q.v.) *Das Deutsche Katastrophe*, to reevaluate the German past, but Ritter found the responsibility for twentieth-century totalitarianism in the Rousseauist democratic heritage, and not in the Prussian conservative tradition. His greatest work, the four-volume *Staatskunst und Kriegshandwerk*, of which the first volume appeared in 1954, was written to absolve the Bismarckian tradition of responsibility for both World War I and World War II. Ritter became the main opponent of Fritz Fischer, who traced German Bonapartism back to Ludendorf and Hindenburg, accusing Fischer of creating a second war guilt mentality. In terms of historiographic principles, Ritter perpetuated the Rankean school. After he abandoned the field of late medieval and German Reformation cultural history, he was an advocate of political history, focusing on the role of heroic personalities, and firmly upholding the priority, against the innovations of Eckart Kehr (q.v.), of foreign policy considerations over internal-domestic considerations in the shaping of national destiny.

Bibliography: Andreas Dorpalen, "Gerhard Ritter," *Deutscher Historiker*, 1 (Göttingen, 1971): S. 86–99; Norman Levine, "Gerhard Ritter's Weltanschauung," *The Review of Politics*, no.2 (1968): 209–227; William H. Maehl "Gerhard Ritter," in Hans A. Schmitt, ed., *Historians of Modern Europe* (Baton Rouge, 1971), pp. 151–205; Peter Schumann, "Gerhard Ritter und die deutsche Geschichtswissenschaft nach dem Zweiten Weltkrieg," *Rudolf Vierhaus zum 60. Geburtstag* (Göttingen, 1982); Klaus Schwabe, *Gerhard Ritter: Ein Politischer Historiker in seinen Briefe* (Boppard, 1984), S. 1–170.

Norman Levine

ROSENBERG, Hans (Hannover, 1904–Freiburg, 1988), German-American historian. As a student of Friedrich Meinecke (q.v.) at Berlin, Rosenberg started as an intellectual historian with philosophical inclinations. His dissertation (1925) and other works dealt with the nineteenth-century liberal, Rudolf Haym. Under the traumatic experience of the crisis of Weimar Germany, he turned to the history of social structures, political power relations, economic processes, and collective mentalities. From this resulted his pioneering study on the world economic crisis, 1857–1859. In 1932 Rosenberg received his habilitation at the University of Cologne. Because of his Jewish origins and his strong commitment to liberal-democratic values, Rosenberg had to leave Germany together with his wife, for England in 1933 and went to the United States in 1935. After 1938 he taught at Brooklyn College (today City University of New York) and after 1958 at the University of California at Berkeley. In 1949 and 1950 he served as a guest professor at the Free University of Berlin. In 1977 the Rosenbergs returned to Germany. He became an honorary professor at Freiburg University and received an honorary doctorate from Bielefeld University.

Rosenberg's research aimed at a "comprehensive social history of the preindustrial Prussio-German ruling elites from the late medieval period to the twentieth century." Like other emigré scholars, Rosenberg compared German with Western developments in order to identify factors that may, in the long run, have contributed to the "German divergence from the West" in the nineteenth and twentieth centuries. Rosenberg was critical of traditional political history. He aimed at a "history of society," including economic, social, political, and cultural change. He stressed structures and processes. He applied concepts and theories from the neighboring social sciences to his painstaking empirical research. While he never finished his history of the Prussio-German Junkers, he published seminal articles on this topic (e.g., "The Rise of the Junkers in Brandenburg-Prussia, 1410–1653," *American Historical Review* 49 [1943–1944]: 1–22, 228–242; "Die Demokratisierung der Rittergutsbesitzerklasse" in *Festgabe für Hans Herzfeld* [Berlin 1958], pp. 459–486). His book *Bureaucracy, Aristocracy and Autocracy. The Prussian Experience 1660–1815* (1958) was a critical assessment of the Prussian upper classes. It became a classic. His early article, "Political and Social Consequences of the Great Depression of 1873–

1896'' (*Economic History Review* 13 [1943]: 58–73), was enlarged into an influential and experimental book: *Gross Depression und Bismarck-Zeit* (1967), in which he used Nicolai Kondratieff and Joseph Schumpeter's notion of "long waves" to reinterpret Central European economic, social, and political history from the 1860s to the 1890s. Some of Rosenberg's articles were published in *Politische Denkströmungen im deutschen Vormärz* (1972) and in *Machteliten und Wirtschaftskonjunkturen* (1978). The 1978 work includes his autobiographical retrospective "Rückblick auf ein Historikerleben zwischen zwei Kulturen." Rosenberg became the most important "founding father" of modern social history in the Federal Republic of Germany.

Bibliography: Gerhard A. Ritter, "Hans Rosenberg 1904–1988," *Geschichte und Gesellschaft* 15 (1989); Hans-Ulrich Wehler, ed., *Sozialgeschichte Heute. Festschrift für Hans Rosenberg zum 70. Geburtstag* (Göttingen 1974), pp. 9–21; Heinrich August Winkler, "Hans Rosenberg 1904–1988," *Historische Zeitschrift*, 248 (1989).

ROTHFELS, Hans (Kassel, 1891–Tübingen, 1976), German historian. Professor at the universities of Königsberg (1926–1933), Chicago 1949, and Tübingen 1951). Stemming from a half-assimilated German–Jewish family, Rothfels converted to Protestantism in 1911, being a student of Friedrich Meinecke (q.v.). After a serious riding accident as an army officer in 1915, he started his professional career with a dissertation, "Carl von Clausewitz. Politik und Krieg" (Berlin, 1920), which was followed in 1924 by *Bismarcks englische Bündnispolitik*. Both publications signified his main historical interest which consisted in combining Meinecke's concept of the history of ideas with the notion of "Realpolitik" and German "Machtstaatsgedanke" as represented in the writings of the national-liberal historian Hermann Oncken. Adhering to the so-called front generation, Rothfels took a critical stance toward an unlimited justification of the reign of Emperor William II and tended to contrast William's more or less dilettantish world policy with Bismarck's uncontested statesmanship. Influenced by the writings of the Oswald Spengler and Moeller van den Bruck, Rothfels interpreted the social policies of Bismarck not only within the context of Prussian socialism, but also as an outcome of the necessities of Prussia's raison d'état and the primacy of foreign policy. His source collection, *Otto von Bismarck. Deutscher Staat*, tended to depict Bismarck as representative of the German " Staatsgedanke" whose principal political values differed fundamentally from the Western tradition. He emphasized that even after its foundation, the empire represented the prenationalistic Prussian tradition. In contrast to the well-established national-liberal picture of Bismarck's alleged "Realpolitik," Rothfels maintained that Bismarck's policy was directed against the dominant trends of the nineteenth century, especially against bourgeois nationalism. In conjunction with this, Bismarck never lost the ethical foundations of responsible rulership and was anything but a pragmatist of power politics.

During the Königsberg years, Rothfels developed the concept of the "autonome Ostseite des Reiches'' (the autonomous Eastern orientation of the empire), claiming that Bismarck fought against the destructive and revolutionary forces of his century and anticipated by that the future of a collection of the various Central East European peoples under German cultural preponderance and military protection. Rothfels' attempt to connect Bismarck's Prussiandom with the federal Reich idea stood within the context of neoconservative dreams of establishing a transnational central European cooperation, as was proposed by Giselher Wrising's program for "Zwischeneuropa." This concept rejected Western political centralism and claimed to fulfill a bridging function between Western capitalism and Eastern native socialism. Rothfels regarded the frontier province of East Prussia as genuine ground for rejuvenating the German people. His neoconservative leanings, however, never suppressed his predominantly historicist approach and his image of the historian as trustee of historical tradition. He perceived himself basically as a political historian, and he never hesitated to enter the field of political debate, although he did not identify himself with any political party. Obviously, he was one of the leading opponents of the peace treaty of Versailles, and he did not display much loyalty to the Weimar Republic whose foundations appeared to him as transplanted from the West to the fundamentally different German state tradition. Hence, he was deeply embittered when attacked by Nazi agencies after January 1933 for his Jewish origins. He failed to secure his professorship at Königsberg and was later also deprived of the promised membership within the Berlin Philosophical Faculty. He left Germany at the last possible moment in the fall of 1939, going first to England and later to the United States. Among the few emigré historians who returned to Germany after World War II, Rothfels engaged in the fight against the notion of a German collective guilt by his study *The German Opposition to Hitler* (Chicago, 1948). His pioneering study on the national-conservative resistance broke the Allied taboo in this field and proved to be the starting point of the West German research, although with a strong conservative bias. During the postwar years Rothfels adapted his principal views to a completely new political environment, but while supporting the chancellor democracy of the 1950s and 1960s, he did not change his former views significantly. His main importance lay in the fact that, through his energy and personal radiation, research on the Third Reich was professionalized and in the long run also brought to the first reluctant history departments. As editor of the *Vierteljahreshefte für Zeitgeschichte* (1953 ff.) he exerted an irreplaceable influence on the development of the historical field in West Germany. His expectation that World War II would result in the extinction of the nation-state tradition, at least in Europe, proved to be wrong.

   Bibliography: Werner Conze, "Hans Rothfels," *Historische Zeitschrift*, 237 (1983): 311–360; Hans Mommsen, "Hans Rothfels," in H. -U. Wehler, ed., *Deutsche Historiker*, 9 (Göttingen, 1982), S. 127–147.

                                                             Hans Mommsen

RUBEN, Walter (Hamburg, 1899–Berlin, 1982), German Indologist and historian. Student of Indology and classical philosophy in Bonn and Berlin; Ph.D. thesis, 1924, doctorate, 1927, both on Indian philosophy. After emigration from Germany, professor of Indology at Ankara University (1935–1948), then at Santiago de Chile (1948–1949). In 1950, returning to Germany (the German Democratic Republic), head of the Indian Institute, Humboldt University, Berlin. Member of the German Academy of Science, 1955, Director of the Institute of Oriental Studies of this academy, 1963. Ruben's methodological approach to the study of ancient India had a great impact on modern Indology. In his early works on Indian philosophy and the epics he followed the comparative method, relating Indian phenomena to those of other ancient countries. Stimulated by a research tour to India, during which he studied pre-Aryan tribal culture (1935–1936), Ruben was the first Sanskritist to stress the impact of tribal traditions on the so-called Sanskrit culture of ancient India and to make this impact a subject of studies (*Eisenschmiede und Dämonen in Indien*, 1939). After World War II, Ruben's main concern was the interpretation of Indian history along Marxist lines: definition of the mode of production prevailing in ancient India, periodization of Indian history according to stages in socioeconomic development and so on (*Die gesellschaftliche Entwicklung im alten Indien*, vols. 1 6, 1967–1973). Discussing the "Asiatic mode of production," Ruben coined the term Ancient Oriental Class Society which is now generally accepted in German Marxist historiography as a term for a type of early class society not dominated by slavery. Ruben's last works were dedicated to the methodological aspects of writing a cultural history of ancient India and aimed to show the interaction of the socioeconomic and cultural-ideological spheres (*Kulturgeschichte Indiens*, 1978). His understanding of Indology as a complex science contributed to the emergence of the concept of Indology now current in most countries of the world.

Bibliography: Joachim Herrmann, "Laudatio fur W. Ruben," *Indiens Rolle in der Kulturgeschichte* (Berlin, 1980), pp. 5–9; Horst Krüger, "W. Ruben zum 70 Gebrustag," *Neue Indien Kunde* (Berlin, 1972), pp. 5–11.

Maria Schetelich

SAVIGNY, Friedrich Karl von (Frankfurt, 1779–Berlin, 1861), German historian. Co-founder and leading representative of the school of historical law which was founded as a scientific and political countermovement to the French Revolution in Germany. With his works on legal history, legal scholarship, and legislative politics, mainly his *Geschichte des Römischen Rechts im Mittelalter* (6 vols., 1815–1831), *Recht des Besitzes* (1803), *System des heutigen römischen Rechts* (8 vols., (1840–1849), and *Vom Berufe unserer Zeit für Gesetzgebung und Rechtswissenschaft* (1814), he influenced the process by which legal history became an autonomous discipline and provided the basic sociopolitical and theoretical foundations for private civic law in Germany and Europe. Like all phenomena, institutions, and views at the end of the eighteenth and in the first half of the nineteenth centuries, Savigny's work reflects the basic contradiction between feudalism and the bourgeois social movement which dominated that historical epoch. In the interest of a gradual transformation and adjustment of the prevailing property relations to the processes of production and reproduction which increasingly prevailed in Prussia/Germany, Savigny maintained his mystically abstractly based theory of the "more objective" descendence of law from the "Spirit of the folk"—in opposition to the progressive dominance of the Code Civile which followed natural law and was a result of the French Revolution. He then raised "the organic development of law," which he viewed in conjunction with the theoretical and practical elaboration of the Roman system of private law, free of state legislation, as the realm in which actual history takes place as the basis and the criterion of social development in general and of national history in particular.

Bibliography: Karl Marx, "Das philosophische Manifest der historischen Rechtsschule," *Marx-Engels Gesamt-Ausgabe (MEGA)*, vol. 1, no.1 (Berlin/GDR, 1975), pp. 191–198; Horst Schröder, *Friedrich Karl von Savigny—Geschichte und Rechtsdenken beim übergang vom Feudalismus zum Kapitalismus in Deutschland* (Frankfurt am Main, Bern, New York, 1984); Roderich Stintzing and Ernst Landsberg, *Geschichte der Deutschen Rechtswissenschaft* (München and Berlin, 1910), vol. 3, 2 Text, pp. 186–253; Adolf Stoll, *Friedrich Karl von Savigny—Ministerzeit und letzte Lebensjahre* (Berlin, 1939); Adolf Stoll, *Friedrich Karl von Savigny—Professorenjahre in Berlin* (Berlin, 1929).

Horst Schröder

SCHLIEMANN, Heinrich (Neu-Buckow, Mecklenburg-Schwerin, 1822–Naples, 1890), self-taught German prehistorian. "A dilettante of genius, an animated amateur always ready to make a sacrifice" (Ion Andriesescu, q.v.). Despite his lack of method, Schliemann helped to throw light on the origins of European civilization. His field researches in Orchomenos (1880: *Bericht über meine Ausgrabüngen in boöt, Orchomenos*, 1881), Tiryns (1884–1885: *Tïryns*, 1885), and Mykene (1876–1877: *Mykene*, 1878) made him realize the great originality and antiquity of the vestiges brought to light, vestiges that he assigned to an independent civilization, the "Mykenian civilization", Schliemann was therefore the first to use this term in an archaeological sense. With this, Schliemann opened a new chapter, unknown until then in European history and underlined the role played by continental Greece in the Bronze Age, as a cradle of an original civilization and as a linking point between the Near East and the rest of Europe. Even if some of Schliemann's localizations proved to be inaccurate, we cannot deny the importance of his activity. His second memorable discovery was Troy, localized through details found in the *Iliad* on Hissarlik hillock in the Northwestern part of Asia Minor. Again, it was his uncommon intelligence, his intuition doubled by a remarkable power of work, perseverance, and infectious enthusiasm that helped Schliemann trace a multimillenary settlement whose identification still preoccupies the scientific world. A significant detail here is that

Schliemann accepted a first-rate collaborator like Wilhelm Dörpfeld (q.v.), and especially that he willingly gave up his first hypotheses, among which was the assimilation of Troy II to Priam and Homer's Troy (*Trojanischen Altertümer*, 1874; *Atlas der trojanishen Altertümer*, 1874; *Ilios*, 1881). It is notable that, although some people question the validity of Schliemann's identification of Troy-Hissarlik and look somewhere else for the fortified town under whose walls the Greeks and the Trojans fought, Schliemann's opinion met with great success and even convinced historians like R. Virchow, Dörpfeld, Hubert Laurahutte Schmidt (q.v.), A. Goetze (the last ones being Dörpfeld's collaborators) and C. Blegen, head of research in 1938.

Bibliography: W. Dörpfeld, *Troja und Ilion*, 1 (Athens, 1902), pp. 1–26; M. Ebert, *Realexikon der Vorgeschichte*, 13 (1929), pp. 442–448; Jan Filip, *Encyklopädisches Handbuch der Ur- und Frühgeschichte Europas* 2 (Prague, 1967), p. 124; H. Schliemann, *Bericht über die Ausgrabungen in Troia am Jahre 1890* (Leipzig, 1891); H. Schliemann, *Selbsbiographie*, herausgegeben von Sophia Schliemann (Wiesbaden, 1955); Carl Schuchardt, *Schleimann's Ausgrabungen in Troja in Lichte der heutigen Wissenschaft* (Leipzig, 1890; English translation, *Schliemann's Discoveries of the Ancient World* (New York, 1979).

Ligia Bârzu

SCHLOSSER, Friedrich Christoph (Jever, East Frisia, 1776–Heidelberg, 1861), German historian. Head of the so-called Heidelberg school and representative of the "subjective" conception of history. Born and raised in the Oldenburg countryside, Schlosser studied theology at the University of Göttingen (1794), whereupon, after 1797, he had several jobs as private tutor, chaplain, and schoolmaster in Jever, Altona (near Hamburg), and Frankfurt. At the Frankfurt *Gymnasium* his main task was to teach universal history (1811), as he also did at the newly founded Frankfurt *Lyceum* (1812). In 1817 he accepted an invitation to Heidelberg as professor of history where he remained until his death. Schlosser first gained fame with his *Geschichte der bilderstürmenden Kaiser des oströmischen Reiches* (1812) and his works on universal history, that is, the *Weltgeschichte in zusammenhängender Erzählung* (1816–1824) and the *Universalhistorische Übersicht der Geschichteder alten Welt und ihrer Kultur* (6 vols., 1826–1834). Without doubt his main work is the *Geschichte des 18. Jarhunderts und des 19. bis zum Sturz des französischen Kaiserreichs mit besonderer Rücksicht auf geistige Bildung* (7 vols., 1836–1849; English transl. in 8 vols., 1843–1852). Besides those works he published several articles and booklets, among them a study on Dante (1855, 2d ed., 1860); many book reviews were scattered in the volumes of the *Heidelberger Jahrbücher*. He was also editor of the *Archiv für Geschicte und Literatur* (1830–1835). Although his works were written in the age of romanticism and historicism, Schlosser was an historian of the Enlightenment par excellence. The harsh judgments running through his historiographical works as leitmotifs are gathered from Kant's system of ethics. Schlosser did not plead for a specific political system, but he worked on the moral improvement of humankind; he preached individual, rather than political, morality. Therewith the old theological moral code was only presented in a new form. For there is only one moral code, that is the way of living of a "wahren und rechtschaffenden Mannes," namely, that of the decent German citizen living in a provincial town at the end of the eighteenth century. Rarely has any historian accomplished his program as thoroughly as Schlosser. Truly his "subjective" historiography has been confronted with Leopold von Ranke's (q.v.) "objectivism." Indeed, modern critical researchers did not take him seriously during his lifetime. But the great public did not mind these flaws: Schlosser was perhaps the most popular historian in Germany during four decades. Georg Gottfried Gervinus (q.v.), K. Hagen, and L. Häusser were his most important students.

Bibliography: Ottokar Lorenz, "Die philosophische Geschichtschreibung (Friedrich Christoph Schlosser)," *Die Geschichtswissenschaft in Hauptrichtungen und Aufgaben kritisch erörtert* (Berlin, 1886), pp. 1–89.

Horst Walter Blanke

SCHMIDT, Hubert (Laurahütte, 1864–Steglitz, 1933), German prehistorian. Professor at the University of Berlin (1907), one of the founders of the German modern prehistory school, known as the discoverer of two renowned Neolithic cultural complexes with world-famous painted ceramics—Cucuteni (Romania) and Anaw (Turkestan) and also as the author of two monographic studies of these two complexes, that is, *Exploration in Turkestan, Expedition of 1904; Prehistoric Civilizations of Anaw: Origins, Growth and Influence of Environment*, Vols. I-II (1908), and *Cucuteni in Oberen Moldau, Rumanien* (1932). The value of Schmidt's field research was enhanced by his interest in the environment, to which he paid special attention, as well as by his stylist's gifts displayed in the study of ceramics. In this latter case, even if some of the stratigraphic remarks did not prove to be true, as in Cucuteni, even if some categories were wrongly catalogued (as, for instance, the so-called Mynian ceramics of Cucuteni), even if the opinion concerning the origins of Cucuteni culture and its diffusion as the natural result of scientific progress is debatable, his monograph on the Cucuteni station is unparalleled in archaeological literature and places Schmidt among the greatest stylists of the world. The same stylist's gifts are to be noticed on the occasion of the publication of the Heinrich Schliemann (q.v.) collection (*Heinrich Schliemanns Sammlung trojanisches Altertümer*, 1902) as well as in his share of the monograph owing to Wilhelm Dörpfeld (q.v.), on the final results of the diggings in Troy. Closer to the Scandinavian school (Oscar Montelius [q.v.], Sophus Müller [q.v.]) rather than to the national German school which was to be formed around Gustaf Kossinna (q.v.). Schmidt attached great importance to the oriental influence on Europe and the East Mediterranean region as a linking point between the East and Europe: "In eastern Mediterranean circles, in fact, it was already possible in so early a time to build a bridge between Europe and the Orient" (*Vorgeschichte Europas, I. Stein und Bronzezeit*, 1924). He also differs from the same archaeologist's thesis concerning the relation of race/culture/language: "From all of our understanding, there remains only one unanswered question: which languages have these tribally characterized human groups spoken?'' and later on: ''The names of the peoples of Europe from the Bronze Age remain completely unknown to us, that is to say, they [the names] are hidden in the darkness of prehistory because these people cannot speak to us of their own names for themselves and for others.'' In exchange, he was greatly influenced by some parallel branches of science, such as ethnology, from which he took the culture circle concept which he adapted to the prehistoric realities (*Vorgeschichte Europas*), and he was open to the innovations coming from the natural sciences. Schmidt was the first prehistorian to study the phenomenon of a human community's adaptation to the environment. Finally, we should also note Schmidt's effort to work out a more accurate terminology meant to suggest the individual's gradual estrangement from the animal condition and his coming closer to the dawn of civilization, a terminology that Schmidt made use of in *Vorgeschichte Europas: Urgeschichte* (Stone Age) *Vorgeschichte* (later Stone Age and Bronze Age), and *Frühgeschichte* (Iron Age).

Bibliography: Jan Filip, *Encyklopädisches Handbuch für Ur- und Frühgeschicte Europas*, 2 (Prague, 1967), p. 1234; H. Seger, ''Hubert Schmidt,'' *Praehistorische Zeitschrift* 23 (1932): 375–377.

Ligia Bârzu

SCHMOLLER, Gustav (von) (Heilbronn, 1838–Harzburg, 1917), German economist and historian. Professor at the universities of Halle (1864), Strassburg (1872), and Berlin (1882). It was long said of Schmoller that he was a great economist in the eyes of historians and a great historian in the eyes of economists. In truth his scholarship kept him in a state of tension with the practitioners of both disciplines in imperial Germany, but his reputation as a historian has undergone a resurgence in recent years. Schmoller was convinced that economic activity, founded in collective enterprise, constituted the basis of human civilization, but he resisted the claim made by classical political economists, as well as their heirs in the late nineteenth century, that the economic context of the human condition could be understood abstractly by means of theory or deductive reasoning. Instead, he insisted, comprehending the full complexity of this context demanded careful attention to its historical development and to the diverse ways it had been shaped by political forces and cultural norms. Only after empirical research into the historical development of diverse national economic systems might tentative theoretical synthesis become possible. Schmoller's own historical research focused primarily on two areas. During his years in Halle, he composed a series of monographs on the state's formative influence on the economy of Brandenburg-Prussia in the sixteenth, seventeenth, and eighteenth centuries; he also wrote seminal articles on the evolution of that state's administrative apparatus. During his years in Strassburg, Schmoller turned to this city's history and produced several important studies on the manner in which policy and economic development intersected in the struggle of the guilds for municipal power. Upon his return to Berlin, Schmoller continued to promote the study of economic history broadly conceived, both as editor of the monumental *Acta Borussica* and as the moving force in the *Verein für die Geschichte der Mark Brandenburg*. Schmoller was the leading representative of the historical school of national economy in imperial Germany, but his interest in the history of economic institutions and domestic public policy earned him the suspicion of many of the country's leading academic historians, for whom the state's power, foreign policy, and international relations constituted the proper subject matter of the historical discipline. That young German scholars nonetheless produced first-rate works of economic, social, and cultural history during the imperial epoch was due in no small part to Schmoller's influence and encouragement.

Bibliography: Paula Relyea Anderson, "Gustav von Schmoller (1838–1917)," in S. William Halperin, ed., *Essays in Modern European Historiography* (Chicago and London, 1970), pp. 289–317; Carl Brinkmann, *Gustav Schmoller und die Volkswirtschaftslehre* (Stuttgart, 1937); Fritz Hartung, "Gustav von Schmoller und die preussische Geschichtsschreibung," *Schmoller's Jahrbuch*, no.2 (1938): 277–302; Otto Hintze, "Gustav von Schmoller," *Deutsches Biographisches Jahrbuch* (1917–1920): 124–34; Forthcoming dissertation by Manfred Schön of the University of Düsseldorf.

Roger Chickering

SCHNABEL, Franz (Mannheim, 1887–München, 1966), German historian. Professor at the Technical University of Karlsruhe (1922) and at the University of München (1947). President of the Historische Kommission bei der Bayerischen Akademie der Wissenschaften (1951–1959). Among middle-class German historians Schnabel, a liberal Catholic, was one of the few to approve the first German Republic. In 1936 the National Socialists forced him to leave his chair and to stop research. After the end of the Nazi regime, he first directed the reconstruction of the schools and educational system in the land of Baden, and then he took over the chair for modern and contemporary history at Munich, teaching there as an admired and celebrated scholar until the age of seventy-five. He believed in the double and difficult task for historians of being "political educator and at the same time historical thinker." A great master in the art of delineating large-scale historical problems in a vivid style, he attracted a large audience not only at the university, where about a thousand students of all faculties used to listen to his lectures, but also in many public conferences and broadcasts. Neither typically a star nor typically an academic manager, this grand seigneur of historical sciences in the early Federal Republic of Germany impressed simply by the impact of his personality. His special approach to history, studying the coherence and interactions of consciousness and facts, was already evident in his first books, *Der Zusammenschluss des politischen Katholizismus in Deutschland im Jahre 1848* (1910) and *Geschichte der Ministerverantwortlichkeit in Baden* (1922). From his educational philosophy resulted the very successful textbook, *Grundriss der Geschichte für die Oberstufe höherer Lehranstalten-Neueste Zeit* and a popular version for a wide public (1923 ff.).

In 1931 he published *Freiherr vom Stein*, which started a controversy with Gerhard Ritter (q.v.), and *Deutschlands geschicht liche Quellen und Darstellungen in der Neuzeit. 1. Teil: Das Zeitalter der Reformation, 1500–1550*, an annotated bibliography of generally appreciated originality. However, he refrained from continuing it in order to concentrate all energies on his principal work, *Deutsche Geschichte im Neunzehnten Jahrhundert*, certain of inducing a new kind of historiography: "I am conscious that with this work I was trying to find a way that is alien to German historiography as it has been heretofore. I have taken care to seek and to present the internal interconnections in all areas of life. . . . I concerned myself with many problems and circumstances that one does not find in our history books, and I have also rejected much that people in our profession have thoughtlessly included. This is so because it is not only my responsibility to portray past eras and cultures, but also to understand the present through its past and to grasp life through its development." Four volumes appeared between 1929 and 1937: *Die Grundlagen, Monarchie und Volkssouveränität, Erfahrungswissenschaften und Technik*, and *Die religiösen Kräfte*. The publication of the fifth volume, already set for the press, dealing with the national idea and movement, was blocked by National Socialist censorship. It has finally been decided that there will be no posthumous publication. The work stops before 1848. The originality of all four volumes, repeatedly reissued since 1947, may be attributed to Schnabel's ability to draw the coherence and interactions of ideas, consciousness, structures and personalities in various areas of human life. In addition, he did pioneer work in the third and forth volume by his common treatment of arts and sciences as "Erfahrungswissenschaften" (experiential sciences) and by his inclusion of subjects like technology and religious forces. A collection of his most important essays, *Abhandlungen und Vorträge 1914–1965*, was edited in 1970 by a team of his former disciples. His papers have been deposited in the Bayerische Staatsbibliothek München, but permission is needed to consult them.

Bibliography: Lothar Gall, "Franz Schnabel 1887–1966," *Die grossen Deutschen unserer Epoche* (hrg. v. L. Gall, Berlin, 1985), pp. 143–155; Karl-Egon Lönne, "Franz Schnabel," *Deutsche Historiker*, hrg. v. H. -U. Wehler, Bd. IX (1982): 81–101; Heinrich Lutz, "Einleitung," *Franz Schnabel, Abhandlungen und Vorträge* (1970): X–XXIV; Friedrich Hermann Schubert, "Franz Schnabel und die Geschichtswissenschaft des 20. Jahrhunderts," *Historische Zeitschrift*, 205 (1967): 323–357.

Beate Gödde-Baumanns

SCHUCHHARD, Carl von (Hannover, 1859–Berlin, 1943), German prehistorian. Warden of Kestner museum in Hannover; for a long period of time the incontestable mentor of the German school of archaeology, a real patriarch. A prominent personality outside Germany as well, given the fame he gained by editing a synthesis on European pre- and protohistory (*Alteuropa in seiner Kultur und Stilenentwicklung*, 1919, sometimes re-edited under a slightly modified title, *Alteuropa, Eine Vorgeschichte Unseres Erdteiles*, 1926 and 1935, or *Alteuropa-*

Kulturen-Rassen-Völker, 1941) and another on German prehistory (*Vorgeschichte von Deutschland* (1928; re-edited in 1934, 1935, 1939, 1943). Based on his general orientation, Schuchhard can be considered an exponent of autochthonist conceptions on a European or national scale. Therefore, he can be called an a priori opponent of the theses spread by the supporters of the *ex Oriente lux* theory. Although less aggressive and even less engaged in archaeological–ethno–linguistic controversies, Schuchhard agreed to the fundamental idea concerning the overlapping of race/culture/language and tried to distinguish between the antiquities ascribed to various ethnic groups. For instance, he took the late Lausitz culture as material evidence for the existence of the Semnons. He drew a very interesting distinction between the Slavs' culture and the culture of the German tribes, grasping their characteristic features.

Bibliography: Jan Filip, *Encyklopädisches Handbuch der Ur- und Vorgeschichte Europas* 2 (Prague, 1967), pp. 1248–1249.

Ligia Bârzu

STREISAND, Joachim (Berlin, 1920–Berlin, 1980), German historian. As the son of a Jewish bookseller, Streisand had to give up his study of philosophy and history (1938–1942), was forced into military service, and interned, but escaped further prosecution by illegal residence. After 1945, he was employed in public education and as a lecturer in Berlin. He completed postgraduate study and habilitation in history at different institutions; after 1963 he was professor at Humboldt-University Berlin. From 1968 until his sudden death, he was president of the Historiker Gesellschaft (Society of Historians) of the German Democratic Republic. His important works are: *Deutschland von 1789 bis 1815* (1959); *Geschichtliches Denken von der deutschen Frühaufklärung bis zur Klassik* (1964); editor of the *Studien über die deutsche Geschichtswissenschaft* (2 vols., 1963–1965); *Kritische Studien zum Erbe der deutschen Klassik* (1971); *Deutsche Geschichte in einem Band. Ein Überblick* (1974); and *Kultur in der DDR* (1981). He became a Marxist after 1945. In the 1950s he played a leading role in the construction of the Museum of German History in Berlin and in the foundation of the *Zeitschrift für Geschichtswissenschaft*. After 1962 he was secretary and later head of the collective of authors preparing the college textbook on German history. In addition, he wrote a great number of studies on German history from the eighteenth to the twentieth century. He played a particularly meritorious role in establishing the history of the science of history as a separate discipline in research and university teaching. His own activities were also aimed at the theory and methodology of history, the development of sociology and social sciences in Marxist and non-Marxist fields, and the coordination of different sciences. Many of his studies reflect his great interest in literature, music, and culture at large.

Bibliography: Hans Schleier, ''Joachim Streisand,'' *Wegbereiter der DDR-Geschichtswissenschaft* (Berlin, 1986).

Hans Schleier

SYBEL, Heinrich von (Düsseldorf,1817–Marburg, 1895), German historian. Professor in Bonn (1844), Marburg (1845), Munich (1856), and Bonn (1861); from 1875 on director of the Prussian archives in Berlin. As a disciple of Leopold von Ranke (q.v.) Sybel always remained committed to Ranke as to historical methods, but politically he opened up new ways. Representative of the interests of the moderate–liberal bourgeoisie, he propagated the unification of Germany as a nation-state under Prussian leadership and advocated these aims even as a deputy (between 1848 and 1880). He belonged to the leading representatives of the Prussian German school of historiography. In his speech ''Über den Stand der neueren deutschen Geschichtsschreibung'' (1856), he stood up openly for the political function of historiography and outlined the historiographic-ideological guidelines of the Prussian school. In the Prussian constitutional conflict still Bismarck's opponent, from 1864 onward, he supported Bismarck's policies almost unconditionally. Especially in his late works, he propagated the Prussianization of Germany. One of his first publications (*Der heilige Rock zu Trier*, 1844) was already intended to criticize certain tendencies of the Catholic Church, and later, in the 1870s, he was a supporter of Bismarck's cultural struggle by resorting to historiographic means. He also advocated the oppression of the German working-class movement by Bismarck's law against socialists. His first works were devoted to medieval subjects, among other things, *Geschichte des ersten Kreuzzuges* (1841) and *Die Entstehung des deutschen Königtums* (1844). Beginning in 1859, he conducted a long-lasting dispute with the Austrian historian Julius Ficker on the justification of the Italian policy pursued by the medieval German emperors. After 1848–1849 he turned to the study of modern history. His major work *Geschichte der Revolutionszeit von 1789 to 1800* (5 vols., 1853–1879) was written under the impact of the 1848–1849 Revolution; he advocated the inevitability of bourgeois forms of government and economy, but wanted to replace revolutions by reforms from above. Vast records from the archives of different European countries were used to connect French revolutionary events to the European foreign policy of that age. By contrast, his *Die Begründung des Deutschen Reiches durch Wilhelm I* (7vols., 1889–1894, incomplete) was, despite numerous sources, an apologetic vindication of Bismarck's policies, and Sybel even criticized the policy of the liberals between 1848 and 1871 which he himself had defended earlier. In later years he increasingly followed an individualizing, theory-averting interpretation of history based on the history of policy and persons.

Sybel was, at the same time, an organizer of science on a large scale. As a university teacher he attracted a great number of students, and he managed to get them employed in important institutions inside and outside Prussia. The improved organization of historical seminars at universities, which he prompted from 1856 onward became exemplary. The *Historische Zeitschrift*, which he founded in 1859 and edited until his death, developed into one of the leading organs of German historical science as its Secretary and (after Ranke's death 1886) as its Chairman. He was co-founder of the Historical Commission in

Munich 1858); he determined far-reaching research projects. As the director of the Prussian State Archives, he was in charge of the comprehensive modernization of its organization and initiated large-scale editions of source materials, among other things the *Publikationen aus den Preussischen Staatsarchiven* (1878 ff.) and *Acta Borussica* (1888 ff.), also glorifying Prussia's policy. The foundation of the Historical Institute in Rome (1888) was also attributable to his influence.

Bibliography: Volker Dotterweich, *H.v. Sybel. Geschichtswissenschaft in politischer Absicht (1817–1861)* (Göttingen, 1978); Folkert Haferkorn, *Soziale Vorstellungen H.v. Sybels* (Stuttgart, 1976); Hans Schleier, *Sybel und Treitschke* (Berlin, 1965); Hellmut Seier, *Die Staatsidee H.v. Sybels in den Wandlungen der Reichsgründerzeit 1862/71* (Lückeck/Hamburg, 1961).

Hans Schleier

TREITSCHKE, Heinrich von (Dresden, 1834–Berlin, 1896), German historian. Taught at the universities of Leipzig, Freiburg, Heidelberg, and Kiel; called in 1873 to the chair at the University of Berlin previously held by Leopold von Ranke. (q.v.). Treitschke was perhaps the most widely read professional historian in late nineteenth-century Germany and the one with the greatest influence on German public opinion. Yet, in an age that stressed rigorous methods of research, he worked not only relatively independently of these scholarly standards but also openly admitted that he was no scholar. He had had little seminar training and himself trained no students in seminars. He saw his foremost task as that of a political activist, as the preceptor of the nation, and throughout his career he offered courses in politics as well as history, two disciplines which, for him, were closely interwoven. He traveled the road of many German liberals from the parliamentary and civil libertarian ideals of 1848 to the social conservatism and aggressive nationalism of the period after 1871. His work can be divided into two periods. The first, beginning with his habilitation thesis of 1858, on the "Science of Society," consists of his broad essays on politics, in which he compared patterns of centralism, federalism, and local self-government in a variety of Western European societies and the United States. His aim was to create a liberal united Germany under Prussian leadership. He admired the British system but rejected the classical liberal separation of state and society. Critical of Ranke's narrative approach to history, he proceeded analytically. Despite his admiration of Prussia, he criticized its failure to reform and advocated a constitutional monarchy with a strong parliament and provisions for due process of law. After 1858 Treitschke was closely associated with the *Preussische Jahrbücher*, which pursued these aims. During the incipient stages of the constitutional conflict in Prussia, he sided with the liberals against Bismarck but, like many liberals, swung over to Bismarck after the Danish War and supported the constitution that Bismarck introduced, which seriously limited the authority of Parliament.

The *German History in the Nineteenth Century,* of which by the time of his death he had completed five volumes leading up to 1848, marks the second important stage of his work. This is narrative rather than analytical history, with an emphasis on the role of important personalities and less attention to institutions and societal factors. Centered on politics, it nevertheless contains a good deal of information on literature, science, and manners. The five volumes as they proceed became increasingly, stridently anti-democratic, opposed not only to socialism but also to social reform, anti-Semitic and Anglophobic. Treitschke became an ardent proponent of an expansive German foreign policy aimed at breaking Great Britain's naval and colonial leadership. The new Right enthusiastically received these ideas in the Wilhelminian period which saw in him the prophet of Germany's mission at home and abroad.

Bibliography: Walter Bussmann, *Sein Welt- und Geschichtsbild* (Göttingen, 1952); Andreas Dorpalen, *Heinrich von Treitschke* (New Haven, Conn., 1957); Hans Schleier, *Sybel und Treitschke* (Berlin/GDR, 1965).

Georg G. Iggers

TROELTSCH, Ernst (Augsburg, 1865–Berlin, 1923), German historian. Professor of theology at the universities of Bonn (1892) and Heidelberg (1894), and professor of philosophy at the University of Berlin (1915). Troeltsch's literary works are of an entirely historical nature, despite the fact that, as a theologian, he had to support systematic theology and speculative ideas. His characteristic philosophy is based on a historical approach and the theory that thoughts and concepts are only formed in real-life circumstances and that they cannot be represented in abstract ways, far removed from reality. Troeltsch's name has, above all, a lasting association with the application of the following ideas: (1) The so-called modern age begins, not with the Reformation in the sixteenth century, but with the Enlightenment in the eighteenth century; the reason for this is that medieval elements are still to be found in Luther's world of thought. (2) One must distinguish, accordingly, between an "old' and a "new" form of Protestantism. (3) The Anglo–Saxon Baptists and the sect-movements, therefore, have a lasting impact on the creation of attitudes in the modern world and society, that is to say, on their genuine subjectivity. (4) Troeltsch transferred sociological methodology into the sphere of ecclesiastical history and the history of ideas. In so doing, he helped to remove the metaphysical and theological way of regarding history, which had long since been shattered, and replaced it with a more reliable, empirical way of looking at things. He especially remained aware of the fact that a certain amount of evaluation and a subjective and personal approach always belong to an empirical view of the world. This cannot be avoided. (5) Troeltsch gave people a greater awareness of the problematical nature of historicism and worked on overcoming it. This proclaimed goal arose from the knowledge that "mere empiricists never attain unity and coherence, just as little as philosophers, who work purely on the principles of formal logic, never come to terms with the real world."

Troeltsch's literary works branched out in many directions and touched on numerous themes. His first work, *Vernunft und Offenbarung bei Johann Gerhard und Melanchthon* (1891), deserves special mention. He focused on proof that medieval elements had been accepted into the Protestant faith. These elements reduced the contemporary effect of Protestantism and were inappropriate to its nature. It was only, he argued, with a departure from any form of supra-naturalism that adequate contact with reality could be guaranteed and consequently lead to a modern form of history. *Die Absolutheit des Christentums und die Religionsgeschichte* (1902) is of particular significance, because Christianity was examined from a historical point of view rather than in completely relative terms. Troeltsch did not claim that Christianity was absolutely right because statements about religions could only be the result of a historically inherent comparison. This approach was used in *Protestantisches Christentum und Kirche in der Neuzeit* (1906). *Die Soziallehren der christlichen Kirchen und Gruppen* (1912), above all, secured Troeltsch permanent fame. He worked on this book in close academic contact with Max Weber (q.v.); in it was clearly presented the process of the emergence of religious communities, taking Christianity as an example. This main work was a social history, which stretched from the nineteenth century right back to the beginnings of Christianity. The content of *Augustin, die christliche Antike und das Mittelalter* (1915) demonstrated that Troeltsch not only regarded the medieval mind with a critical eye, but also knew how to respect it in a positive way. Throughout his life, he considered the problem of how the historical representation of reality remained dependent on the evaluative subjectivity used by the historian. This problem was treated fundamentally in *Der Historismus und seine Probleme* (1922). It can be considered as the other main work.

Troeltsch's life-span coincided almost exactly with that of the German Empire. In 1871, as a five-year-old child, he was drawn into the high-spirited celebrations, which marked the beginning of the empire, and he outlived this political creation by only five years. Troeltsch can, therefore, be regarded as being a significant representative of that era, and his academic work can be considered as being an expressive embodiment of the imperial spirit. It was no accident that Troeltsch became a staunch advocate of democracy as soon as the inner limits of the system had become evident in 1918. The aforementioned task of finding a balance between the empirical attitude and that of subjective evaluation remains a lasting problem, which will never be solved conclusively. Because this problem received extensive consideration in Troeltsch's works, his name could be said to be synonymous with a realistic figure of history and with the theory that history is an important tool for understanding within a society. Where absolute values are lacking, careful historical investigation becomes the means of orientation in life.

Bibliography: K. E. Apfelbacher, *Frömmigkeit und Wissenschaft* (Munich, 1978), p. 17ff.; U. Bussmann, "Fremdsprachige Veröffentlichungen Ernst Troeltschs," *Mitteilungen der Ernst-Troeltsch-Gesellschaft I and II* (Augsburg, 1982–), pp. 26–34, 89–94; F. W. Graf and H. Ruddies, *Ernst Troeltsch Bibliographie* (Tübingen, 1982).

Horst Renz

VALENTIN, Veit (Frankfurt am Main, 1885–Washington, D.C., 1947), German historian. After the study of history (1903–1906), Valentin was concerned with research on the history of the 1848 German revolution, which became the focus of his studies, among others *Frankfurt a. M. und die Revolution von 1848/49* (1908). He was a private lecturer at the University of Freiburg, 1910, and extraordinary professor, 1916. In 1917, he was forced to retreat from his right to hold lectures. Shifting from conservative to liberal positions, during World War I he came into conflict with the pan-Germans, who compelled him to leave the university. As a left-liberal and pacifist among historians, he was one of the few proponents of the Weimar Republic. As a maverick historian, in 1920 he found employment in the Archives of the Reich and a secondary occupation at the Berlin Trade College. Among his numerous historical and historico-political writings of the 1920s, the *Geschichte des Völkerbundgedankens in Deutschland* (1920), a study on the Frankfurter Paulskirche of 1848–1849 (1919), and *Das Hambacher Nationalfest* (1932) best characterized his objectives. After years of preparatory work, the *Geschichte der deutschen Revolution von 1848/49* (2 vols., 1930–1931) became his standard work, with the democratic movement described sympathetically and in great detail in the various German lands. Dismissed by the Nazis in 1933, he emigrated first to Great Britain and then in 1939, to the United States, without, however, finding permanent university employment. His individualizing, event- and personality-related interpretation of history became especially apparent in his *Weltgeschichte* (1939) and *The German People* (1946). In exile he wrote *Bismarcks Reichsgründung im Urteil der englischen Diplomaten* (1937), as well as voluminous studies on Bismarck–Bleichröder–Rothschild and on German emigrants of the 1848 Revolution in the United States, which he himself was unable to complete.

Bibliography: Richard H. Bauer, "Veit Valentin," in S.W. Halperin, ed., *Some 20th Century Historians* (Chicago, 1961), pp. 103–141; Elisabeth Fehrenbach. "Veit Valentin," *Deutsche Historiker*, vol. 1 (Göttingen, 1971), pp. 69–85; Will Schaber, *Perspektiven und Profile. Aus Schriften Veit Valentins* (Frankfurt am Main, 1965), pp. 7–46; Hans Schleier, "Veit Valentin," *Die bürgerliche deutsche Geschichtsschreibung der Weimarer Republik* (Berlin, 1975), pp. 346–398.

Hans Schleier

WAITZ, Georg (Flensburg, 1813–Berlin, 1886), German medievalist and constitutional historian. The son of a merchant, Waitz began to study law at Kiel in 1832 and one year later went to Berlin University where he came under the influence of Karl von Savigny (q.v.), Karl Lachmann (Germanist), and Leopold von Ranke (q.v.), with Waitz being his leading disciple. After his dissertation (1836) as staff member he assisted in publishing the *Monumenta Germaniae Historica* (MGH) by Georg Heinrich Pertz in Hannover. Both separately and in the *Archiv für ältere deutsche Geschichtskunde* he published the results of extensive travels by order of the MGH, with discoveries of manuscripts on the activities of the Gothic missionary, Ulfilas. In 1842 he was appointed to the chair of history at the University of Kiel; in the same year he married Clara, the daughter of the philosopher Wilhelm Schelling. A program on the millennial of the Contract of Verdun (1843) stimulated him to his lifework, the *Deutsche Verfassungsgeschichte*, the first two volumes of which appeared in 1844–1847; volume 3 (1860) through volume 8 (1878) followed after longer periods (reprint of the third edition, 1953–1955). In Kiel he also edited the collection of documents of the Schleswig–Holstein–Lauenburg Society for Patriotic History (vols. 1/2, 1839–1858) and wrote *Schleswig-Holsteinische Geschichte* (1851–1852) in three books; he also assumed the editing of the *Nordalbingische Studien*.

Politically oriented toward the liberal bourgeoisie, in 1837, Waitz, with other historians, protested the removal from office of the ''Göttingen Sieben,'' and in 1846 he sat in the Schleswig-Holstein diet as the speaker of his university against the attempts by the Danish king to enforce the inheritable rule of his House over Schleswig and Lauenburg. Rebuked by the Royal Danish House, in 1847 he was prompted to receive the call to a professorship at Göttingen. In the spring of 1848 he was initially a member of the caretaker government of Schleswig-Holstein, and then of the National Parliament at Frankfurt (the ''Casino'' faction), pursuing a policy of establishing a federal German state under an emperor. On May 20, 1849, he resigned his seat in the Paulskirche, and began his lectures at Göttingen and the edition of further medieval chronicles. His historical exercises on the critique of medieval sources had educated quite a number of later professors at German universities and attracted foreign historians. In 1859 the Bavarian Academy appointed him to the newly founded historical commission; after 1862 by order of this commission he edited the *Forschungen zur deutschen Geschichte* (until 1886). He became intensely engaged in the revival of the Schleswig-Holstein question in 1863. After the occupation of Hannover by Prussian troops (1866), he apparently gave up for a short period; yet he later identified himself fully with the Prussian-German unification. After several futile attempts, it was possible in 1875, prompted by Ranke, to get him a professorship in Berlin. He also became the manager of the newly established central directorate for MGH, supporting further the ''scriptores'' series also edited by Waitz. He took over the edition of the documentary book and the Hanseatic editions for the *Hansische Geschichtsverein* founded in 1871. His Germanistic interests were reflected in his commemorative address on the one hundredth birthday of Jakob Grimm (1861) and in the edition of two volumes of letters of Caroline Schelling, the wife of his father-in-law.

Bibliography: Hubert Maximilian Ermisch, ''Georg Waitz und sein Leben,'' *Jahrbuch der schleswigholsteinischen Universitätsgesellschaft 1927* (1928); L. S. Hermann Hagenah, ''Georg Waitz als Politiker,'' ibid, *1930* (1931); Ernst Steindorff, *Bibliographische Übersicht über Georg Waitz Werke, Abhandlungen, Ausgaben, kleine kritische und publicistische Arbeiten* (1886).

Siegfried Hoyer

WEBER, Max, (Erfurt, 1864–München, 1920), German sociologist, historian, economist, philosopher, and political theorist. Weber studied at the universities of Heidelberg, Strassburg, and Berlin, and became professor of economics (*Nationalökonomie*) first at the University of Freiburg in 1894 and then at Heidelberg in 1897. Having suffered a nervous breakdown in 1898, he resumed his academic activities as a coeditor of the *Archiv für Sozialwissenschaft und Sozialpolitik* in 1904, living as a private scholar in Heidelberg until he accepted a chair at the University of Vienna in 1918 and later at München in 1919. Throughout his academic career, his scholarly activity was closely interwoven with the political developments of the day (*Gesammelte Politische Schriften* [GPS], 1980[1921]; *Zur Politik im Weltkrieg. Schriften und Reden 1914–1918*, in *Max Weber Gesamtausgabe* [MWG], 1984; *Zur Neuordnung Deutschlands. Schriften und Reden 1918–1920*, in *MWG*, 1988).

Although Weber is best known as one of the major expounders of modern sociology, he is also considered a historian of exceptional originality. He began his career as a legal and agrarian historian of the ancient and medieval periods. His doctoral dissertation, a history of medieval commercial law, later became the basis for his lifelong interest in the development of modern capitalism (*Zur Geschichte der Handelsgesellschaft im Mittelalter* 1889, reprinted in *Gesammelte Aufsätze zur Sozial-und Wirtschaftsgeschichte* [GASW], 1924). His habilitation treated Roman agrarian and social history (*Die Römische Agrargeschichte in ihrer Bedeutung für das Staats-und Privatrecht*, 1891, new edition in *MWG*, 1986). His two other studies of the social history of antiquity are regarded as classic examples of "structural history" in that they showed how economic changes influenced religion, how innovations in tactics brought about transformations in social stratification, and how the distribution of political power impeded the growth of capitalism (*Die sozialen Gründe des Untergangs der antiken Kultur*, 1896; *Agrarverhältnisse im Altertum*, 1897, both reprinted in *GASW*, 1924). At first a student of the prominent Roman historian of the day, Theodor Mommsen (q.v.), he turned his attention from Roman studies to Prussian agrarian questions, to which he applied an analysis of power politics, and plunged himself into social polemics (*GASW*, 1924; *Gesammelte Aufsätze zur Soziologie und Sozialpolitik* [GASS], 1924; *Die Lage der Landarbeiter im ostelbischen Deutschland 1892*, in *MWG*, 1984). The second phase of Weber's academic production began with his widely known treatise, *Die protestantische Ethik und der "Geist" des Kapitalismus* (1904–1905, reprinted in *Gesammelte Aufsätze zur Religionssoziologie* [GAR], 1920), which recaptured the importance of Calvinistic asceticism in the modern business ethic.

Weber regarded every world-view and institution as having a "developmental history," the record of its structural changes and transformations. He also envisaged a "universal history" in which he attempted a synthetic portrayal of given historical and cultural eras, developing his innovative methodology of comparative historical research on world religious institutions. In a series of his experimental studies in the economic ethics of world religions, consisting of Confucianism and Taoism, Hinduism and Buddhism, and ancient Judaism, he confirmed the originality of the Puritan contribution to the modern capitalist spirit

(*Die Wirtschaftsethik der Weltreligionen*, 1915–1918, reprinted in *GAR*, 1921). Weber came to reject the prevalent historical methodology of the German historicist tradition, by which he himself had been strongly influenced. Instead, he adopted the methodology of "Kulturwissenschaft," affirming the particularity and autonomy of the human sciences. He also developed a series of abstract means of "ideal types" as an analytical heuristic device for sociological and historical investigations (*Gesammelte Aufsätze zur Wissenschaftslehre* [GAW], 1968 [1922]). In fact, the diversity and fragmentation of the Weberian corpus defy systematic interpretation. Many sociological subdisciplines have thrived in the fertile soil of Weber's seminal, yet disparate, writings (*Wirtschaft und Gesellschaft* [WG], 1976 [1921]). Consequently, reading Weber's works taken in isolation from the entire context has yielded both fruitful and yet sometimes impoverishing results in these natural specializations. A latent unity in all the apparent disunity, however, can be found by considering Weber's own ambition to create a "universal-developmental history" of world civilizations. He ultimately aspired to produce a comprehensive theory concerning the developmental articulations of change as well as of the general historical relationship between economic and social institutions. In this endeavor, he insisted that his sociology presumed to be nothing more than a hermeneutical instrument for the contextualization of historical knowledge. In his words, "sociology seeks to formulate type concepts and generalized uniformities of empirical process, whereas history strives for the causal analyses and explanation of individual actions, structures, and personalities that have cultural significance" (*WG*, 1976). In the final analysis, the categorization of Max Weber as a historian depends on the relevance of a distinction between traditional historiography and the "universal-historical" systematization of historical sociology. Like Karl Marx (q.v.), Weber was keenly aware of the implications of the development of modern Western capitalism, and his secular theory of capitalism is regarded as the most comprehensive general theory of the origins of capitalism yet available (*Wirtschaftsgeschichte. Abriss der universalen Sozial-und Wirtschaftsgeschichte*, 1958 [1924]). However, Weber did not share Marx's teleological view of history concerning the plight of the capitalist system ("Der Sozialismus," in *GASS*, 1924). If he was unwilling to sing capitalism's swan song, however, neither was he prepared to sing its praises. He held little hope for escaping the future "iron cage" of the bureaucratic rationalization that was being increasingly enforced as the capitalist system developed. This irrational result of the process of rationalization is the tragic irony of human history. But he struggled against his own pessimism by pursuing knowledge of history and society in the strategic hope of maintaining an ethic of personal responsibility in a "disenchanted" world. Upon these philosophical convictions Max Weber devoted his life's labor (*Wissenschaft als Beruf*, 1919, reprinted in *GAW*, 1968; "*Politik als Beruf*," 1919, reprinted in *GPS*, 1980). In terms of theory and methodology, Weber's profound influence on modern historical study can hardly be overestimated. The Weberian corpus as a rich quarry of historical scholarship remains to be fully exploited.

Bibliography: Jürgen Kocka, ed., *Max Weber. Der Historiker* (Göttingen, 1986); Wolfgang Mommsen, "Max Weber," *Deutsche Historiker*, Band III (Göttingen, 1972): 65–90; Pietro Rossi, *Vom Historismus zur historischen Sozialwissenschaft* (Frankfurt, 1987); Guenther Roth and Wolfgang Schluchter, *Max Weber's Vision of History* (Berkeley, Calif., 1979); Arnold Zingerie, *Max Webers historische Soziologie* (Darmstadt, 1981).

Sang-Woo Lim

WINTER, Eduard (Grottau, 1896–Berlin, 1982), German historian. A man of Bohemian descent, educated in Innsbruck, Winter taught at the German University of Prague until 1945. After 1947, he had a full professorship of East European history at the Martin-Luther University Halle–Wittenberg, or Humboldt University in Berlin. In 1955 he became a full member of the Academy of Sciences of the German Democratic Republic in Berlin. His rich, substantive, and far-ranging research covered primarily the intellectual history of Europe, the role of the Catholic Church, and the history of German-Slavic reciprocity. Among his works are: *Der Josefinismus und seine Geschichte* (1943, 1962); a book on Bernard Bolzano (1932–1982); *Russland und das Papsttum* (3 vols., 1960–1972); a trilogy on German-Slavic relations in the eighteenth and nineteenth centuries (1953, 1954, 1955); as well as publication on early humanism (1964); early Enlightenment (1966), and early liberalism (1968)—all deserve special mention. Important also were his editions of source materials, published partly in collaboration with Soviet scholars, on German-Russian relations in the eighteenth century: D. G. Messerschmidt (5 vols., 1962–1977), L. Euler (3 vols., 1959–1976), and A. L. von Schlözer (1961). As an inspiring scholar, esteemed teacher, and meritorious organizer of collective historical activities, he promoted the development of history in the fields with which he dealt, especially during the most creative decade of his activities in the German Democratic Republic.

Bibliography: *Wegbereiter der deutsch-slawischen Wechselseitigkeit* (1983), complete bibliography; Eduard Winter, *Mein Leben im Dienste des Völkerverständnisses* (1981); *Zeitschrift für Geschichtswissenschaft*, 6 (1961), 6 (1966), 9 (1971), 9 (1976), 9 (1981), 7 (1982).

Conrad Grau

Great Historians: Greek

AMANTOS, Konstantinos (Chios, 1874–Athens, 1960), Greek historian. Amantos came from a peasant family. He received primary and secondary education in his hometown and served as a teacher (1893–1897). He started his university studies in Athens in 1898. In 1899 he went to Germany (universities of Berlin and Munich) where he took courses with Wilamovitz, Diels, Krumbacher (q.v.), and others. In 1903 he obtained his doctorate ("Die Suffixe der neugriechischen Ortsnamen. Beitrag zur neugriechischen Ortsnamenforschung"). He taught for some years in secondary education (Chios, 1904–1911, Cyprus, 1911, Cairo, Egypt, 1912–1914). From 1914 to 1924 he was appointed a redactor and later a director of the center founded by Venizelos's government for the Redaction of a Historical Dictionary of the Greek Language. In 1925 he was elected professor of Byzantine history at the University of Athens, and the following year a member of the Academy of Athens. He gave courses until 1939 when he retired as required by law. From January until April 1945 he served as prime minister and minister of education (N. Plastiras's government). During this short period he introduced the law recognizing the spoken Greek language as the official one. As a result, he faced such a furious opposition by some reactionary circles of Greek society that the governments that followed withdrew it. He founded the reviews *Chiaka Chronika* (1911–1926) and *Aegaeon* (1935–1936). He was director of the review *Hellenika* (1928–1939) in collaboration with Socratis Kougeas (q.v.). Amantos's scientific interests cover a number of fields: they extend from linguistics, particularly onomatology (see *Linguistic Studies*, Athens, 1964), philology, and history to geography and the study of the rural environment. Through these themes historical knowledge was linked in a creative way with the present. The unbroken continuity of the Greek nation, the identity of modern Greek culture, the Slavic question, the educational question, the depopulation of the villages, the geographical discontinuity of Greece, the destruction of forests, and the necessity for renewed cultivation were some of the questions which interested him. One can detect a kind of ruralism in a book written in collaboration with Konstantinos Karavidas and Nikolaos Anagnostopoulos titled *The Density of Our Rural Population and the Means to Its Realization* (Athens, 1927). Besides Byzantine history, he also studied ancient and especially modern Greek history (see studies about Rhegas Phaeraios, Korais, Al. Mavrokordatos as well as the volume containing several articles titled Brief Studies, Athens, 1940). The unbroken continuity of Greek history was one of the fundamental ideas in the same way as Konstantinas Paparrigopoulos (q.v.) established it. Initially, Amantos wrote about local history. In this group of studies Chios has a predominant place. Amantos's duties as a professor led him to write a synthetic work about Byzantium, *Introduction to Byzantine History*, Athens, 1931–1933; 2d ed., 1950). On the other hand, the political and military situation of the midwar period made him face the respective questions of the past: Balkan neighbors and populations in Asia Minor are some of these points. See *Greeks in Asia Minor During the Middle Age* (Athens, 1919); *Relations Between Greeks and Turks from the Eleventh Century until 1821* (Athens, 1955); *Contribution to the History and Ethnology of Macedonia* (Athens, 1920); *The Northern Neighbors of Greece, Bulgarians-Albanian-Yugoslavs* (Athens, 1923); *Macedonian Hellenism During the Last Middle Age Period and the First Period of Turkish Domination until the Eighteenth Century* (Thessalonica, 1952). Generally, in Amantos's work one can discern some themes that reveal new aspects of Byzantine history (Byzantine everyday life, state organization, economy, and philanthropy) as well as his interest in finding several factors contributing to historical evolution (geography, economy, rural policy, etc.), something that makes his problematic rich. During the postwar period, however, it was not easy for progressive historians such as Amantos and Kougeas to maintain their prior midwar period stance concerning the new national questions and the social, political, and ideological situation in Greece. Their political and ideological positions came to be identified with those of the dominant political forces. As a solution to the social, economic, educational, and ideological problems confronted by the Greek state, Amantos proposed the Greek-Christian spirit in *Historical Relation Among Greeks, Serbians, and Bulgarians* (Athens, 1949).

Bibliography: *Nea Estía* November 15, 1961, pp. 998–1002 and 1472–1497, several articles; I. Notaris, *K. Amantos as a Teacher of the Nation* (Athens, 1961); Gr. Spanos, *Amantos and Chios* (Athens, 1975); N. Tomadakis, "K. Amantos" *Athena* 63 (1959) 3–14 (in Greek); D. V. Vayacacos, "Constantin I. Amantos (1879–1960)," *Onoma* 8 (1958–1959): 481–487; D. Zakythinos, "K. Amantos," *Epeterís Etaireías Byzantinon Spoudon* 29, 1959, pp. 449–56 (in Greek).

Angeliki Konstantakopoulou

KAROLIDIS, Paul (Enderlik, Turkey 1849–Athens, 1930), Greek historian. Karolidis studied at Constantinople (Nation's High School), Smyrna Evangelical

School), and the University of Athens. He obtained his doctorate at the University of Tübingen in 1872. He was professor of Lycaeum in Athens until 1886, after which he taught as a university lecturer. He was elected professor in Konstantinos Paparrigopoulos' (q.v.) chair of History of the Greek Nation (1893). From 1908 until 1912 he was a representative of the Aïdini region in the Turkish Parliament (see *Speeches and Memoranda Delivered in the Ottoman Parliament*, Athens, 1913). After three years in Germany (1912–1915), he was offered a post at the University of Athens. Because of political reasons he was dismissed by the Venizelos government (1918–1920). He retired in 1922. His deep royal convictions (see "The Greek Royalty as a National Idea." Speech Delivered . . . , Athens, 1916) as well as his disgust at Venizelos did not prevent him from actively supporting Venizelos's return to the political scene in December 1923, as Venizelos was at that moment the only guarantee of the king's stay. Initially, Karolidis produced some linguistic studies about the idioms spoken in Asia Minor (See *Kappadokika*, 1874). During his professorship he showed a greater interest in studies about wider historical subjects (see *Introduction to Nineteenth Century History,* Athens, 1892–1893, 3 vols.; *Introduction to the Universal or World History*, Athens, 1894, which later numbered the first of a ten-volume work titled *Universal or World History*, Athens, 1926). Karolidis continued writing history on the unbroken continuity of the Greek nation, namely Paparrigopoulos's thesis. Karolidis revised Paparrigopoulos's *History of the Greek Nation*, brought it up to date, and reprinted it twice (1902–1903, 4th ed., 5 vols. and 1922–1925, 5th ed., 6 vols.). Karolidis's historical conception may be summed up as follows: (1) concerning his theory, an extreme idealism is evident: providence dominates the historical process even during the period before Christianity; (2) concerning his methodology one can discern a somewhat positivist tendency, particularly regarding his choice and criticism of historical documents. His idealistic points of view, probably with more facts unknown to us concerning professional and personal contacts, made him an opponent of Spyridon Lambros (q.v.). As the German historical school of this period was very familiar to him, he translated some voluminous works by Fr. Herzberg.

Bibliography: S. Kougeas, "P. Karolidis," *Nea Estía* 8, no. 89 (September 1, 1930): 935–937 (in Greek); Sp. Lambros, *Karolidis' Lack of Knowledge* (Athens, 1892); E. P. Photiadis, "P. Karolidis," *Elleniká* 4 (1931): 291–300 (in Greek).

Angeliki Konstantakopoulou

KORDATOS, Yanis (Zagorá Piliou, 1891–Athens, 1961), Greek historian. Kordatos' father was a landowner and merchant. He studied at the Greek-German Lyceum of Smyrna, where Demetrios Glinos, a Hegelian scholar, was teaching, and at the Greek-French Lyceum of Constantinople. The events he lived through in Volos during the period 1909–1910 (farmers' mobilizations, labor strikes, the "atheist incident" of Volos, etc.) left a lasting impression on him and caused him to turn to the study of the most avant-garde works of his time, such as the *Social Question* (1907) by Y. Skliros. He studied law at the University of Athens.

During his studies he founded, together with others, the "student society." After
he got his degree (1917) he did not practice the profession of lawyer. He worked
as a journalist and systematically applied himself to the writing of historical
studies. He was one of the founding members of the Socialist Labour party of
Greece (1918) which from 1920 was called the Communist SLP. He was charged
with the management of the *Rizospastis*, the journalistic organ of the above-
mentioned party, as well as the secretariat of the party (1921–1924). In October
1924, because he disagreed with the position of the Communist party of Greece
regarding the support to the demand for autonomy of Macedonia, he retired from
active political life. After that time he did not participate in any left-wing opposition group. During the 1940s he was among those communists who were
persecuted and imprisoned. His son was murdered for political reasons.

Kordatos was editor of the series "Ancient Greek Poets and Writers" which
was published by the publishing house Zacharopoulos (1938–1941). In his voluminous oeuvre the first systematic attempt is made to investigate Greek history
on the basis of the theory of historical materialism. His first book, *The Social
Significance of the Greek Revolution of 1821* (1924), constituted a landmark in
Greek historiography, and, as was to be expected, it raised a storm of protests
from the clergy and other intelligentsia and representatives of the ruling classes
in Greece. This book essentially upset the perception of the historical unity of
the Greek nation and its uninterrupted continuity. In other words, Kordatos
refuted the schema which Konstantinos Paparrigopoulos (q.v.) had postulated
since the middle of the previous century and which was the prevailing historical
perception. In this manner he also showed the crumbling ideological foundations
on which the policy of the "Great Idea" was built, right after the catastrophe
of Asia Minor (1922). With the introduction which was added to the fourth
edition of the *Social Significance* (1945) concerning the "roots of modern Greek
nationality and the formation of the modern Greek nation," Greek history was
outlined in a radically different manner and the historically defined character of
the Greek nation was emphasized. Thus, based on the definition of the nation
advanced by Joseph Stalin, the origins of modern Greek nationality were sought
not in antiquity, but in the fourteenth century, when the first signs of the existence
of merchant capital could be observed. But Kordatos' historical perception and
its specific application to Greek history was criticized for other reasons by the
leadership of the CPG and by Marxist historians. The criticism of this group
was centered mainly on the character of the bourgeoisie and the role it played
during the Greek revolution of 1821. This issue became a more burning one
from the 1930s onward, when a change can be observed in the CPG's policies,
for it simultaneously touched on the question pertaining to the character of the
social revolution as it was envisioned by the Greek communists of the mid-war
period. Specifically, Kordatos' position that the 1821 Revolution was a bourgeois
democratic one and that, consequently, the communists should proceed toward
a popular democratic revolution is substantiated by the position advanced by G.
Zevgos which was based on the position already prevailing in the Communist

Internationale (1931) that the bourgeoisie did not play, nor would it ever do so, any progressive role. ["The revolution in Greece should have to be bourgeois democratic.]" In spite of the vehemence of this intra-Marxist dialogue, Kordatos recognized some points of partiality in his work; therefore, he took this into account in subsequent editions. The contrary circumstances did not prevent him from a voluminous output on an admirable variety of subjects. For example, we may mention *Modern Greek Political History* (1925); *History of the Greek Labor Movement*, (2 vols., 1931–1932); *New Preface to Homer* (1940); *History of Our Language Question* (1943); *Ancient Comedy and Tragedy* (1954) (this work received a negative critique from P. Lekatsas); and *Ambelakia and the Myth Concerning Its Cooperative* (1955). Kordatos wrote theoretical and historical articles in many magazines and translated the *Communist Manifesto* of Marx and Engels (1927). Kordatos' overall conception of Greek history constitutes in essence a revolutionary act in the field of historical studies in Greece. Of course, his works were often not fully substantiated, and the data were sometimes applied mechanistically to the theory of stages regarding historical process, which during the mid-war period prevailed among communist circles. He also tended to over-emphasize the economic factor. Nonetheless, beyond doubt, Kordatos' oeuvre has constituted a serious counterweight to prevailing historical ideas, and it has opened new perspectives for a fruitful investigation of historical problems.

Bibliography: Ph. Iliou, "The Ideological Use of History. A Comment on the Debate Between Kordatos and Zevgos," *Anti* 46 (1976): 31–34; D. Mexis, *The Historian Y. Kordatos and His Work* (Athens, 1975); Y. Notari, *The Macedonian Question as Seen by "Yanis" Kordatos* (Athens, 1985); P. Noutsos, "Y. Kordatos' Theory of History," *The Origins of Greek Marxism. An Introduction* (Ioannina, 1987), pp. 35–37.

Angeliki Konstantakopoulou

KOUGEAS, Socratis (Doloi Laconias, 1877–Athens, 1966), Greek historian. Kougeas studied (1894–1899) and obtained his doctorate (*De novo Xiphilino Codice Iberitica 812*, 1901) at the Faculty of Letters of the University of Athens. Having won a scholarship he was able to continue his studies abroad. He worked under the guidance of several eminent university scholars such as Fr. Blass, C. Robert, Wilcken, and Herzberg in Halle; Otto Crusius and Karl Krumbacher (q.v.) in Munich; Adolph von Harnack (q.v.) and Wilamovitz in Berlin; Charles Diehl (q.v.) and Jacob in Paris (1904–1909). After returning to Athens (1910), he worked for some years in secondary education until his appointment as a secretary of the state archives in 1916. In 1918 he was elected professor of general history and later of ancient history at the University of Athens. He kept this position until 1947 except for a short period when he was dismissed for political reasons in 1920–1922. He was director of the Manuscripts Department of the National Library in 1926–1966, a member of the Academy of Athens (1930), and a member of the Archeological Institute of Berlin from 1929 on as well as of the International Committee of Historical Sciences. He was named honorary doctor of the University of Tübingen and of the University of Thessalonika and honorary professor of the Panteios High School. In cooperation with Konstantinos Amantos (q.v.), he edited the review *Helleniká* (1928–1939). Retaining the historical tradition inaugurated by Konstantinos Paparrigopoulos (q.v.) and Spyridon Lambros (q.v.) with a somewhat renewed thematic, and having obtained during his postgraduate studies a stern methodology for criticizing the sources (manuscripts and epigraphical texts), he was able to study, from a philological and historical perspective, ancient, medieval, and modern Greek history. An illuminating example of this positivist combination of history and philology is provided by his study entitled *Arethas of Caesareia and His Works. Contribution to the History of the First Renaissance of Classical Letters During the Byzantine Period* (Athens, 1913), reprinted with an English preface by Ph. Demetracopoulos (1985). Arethas's biography and in general the matter of classical tradition in ninth-century Byzantium and the earlier period known as the Dark Ages was studied for the first time. In addition to the subjects concerning Byzantine history and culture, he tried, based on epigraphical material to clarify the institution of ancient Greek corporations among several city-states at a moment when the contemporary European states, after the World War I shock, were in search of a relative association (see *The Idea of the League of Nations According to Ancient Greeks*, Athens, 1928, granted in 1921). The material on the Greek state and the foreign archives enabled him to study historical questions and personalities in modern Greek history (i.e., the 1770 revolution, Koraïs, Kapodistrias, the I. Stavros's Archive) as well as great figures in European history associated with Greek history and cultural life (i.e. Goethe, Karl B. Hase, Barthold Georg Niebuhr [q.v.], Friedrich von Savigny [q.v.] and others). He also contributed a great deal to local history and particularly to that of his home town (see "Herkunft und Bedeutung von neugriechischen Niklianoi und Psamegioi," *Glota* 1 [1909]: 86–104). His political and scientific ideas were the target of criticism by colleagues as well as other people (E. Pantelakis, 1915; M. Volonakis, 1917–1918; K. Logothetis, 1924; Y. Vlahoyannis, 1935–1937).

Bibliography: Honorary volume of the review *Hellenika* 15 (1957) with a catalogue of his works, *Nea Estia* 80 (1916):1439–1450, several articles, D. Zakythinos, "S. Kougeas," *Praktiká tns Akademías Athenon* 48 (1973): 211–225 (in Greek).

Angeliki Konstantakopoulou

LAMBROS, Spyridon (Corfu, 1851–Athens, 1919), Greek historian. In his youth Lambros used to write poems and other literature. Subsequently, however, he turned to the study of history. He studied at the Faculty of Letters of the University of Athens (1867–1871) and at the University of Berlin (1872 and 1875), at Leipzig, where he maintained his thesis (1873), Paris, London, and Vienna. He followed lectures by Theodor Mommsen (q.v.), Ernst Curtius, Johann Gustav Droysen (q.v.), et al. In 1878 he taught at the University of Athens as lecturer in history and paleography, a subject included in the university curriculum for the first time. In 1887 he was elected professor of general history and held the chair until 1917. Beginning in 1895 he was head of the National Society that had been formed to help solve national issues. He was president of the league of Greek athletic and gymnastic clubs (1897–1906), and in 1908 he was appointed chairman of the Supervisory Council of secondary education. In 1913 he participated in the committee sent to Italy by the Greek government to settle the Epirote issue. In a critical historical point in time the king appointed him prime minister and minister of education (September 1916–April 1917). When the Thessaloniki movement led by Venizelos prevailed, he was brought to trial, his estate was confiscated, and he was exiled to Skopelos (1917–1919). He left a voluminous oeuvre, both published and unpublished. From 1904 to 1917 he published the magazine *Neos Ellinomnimon* (13 vols.) which contained exclusively his own studies. The publication of the magazine continued after his death. In total twenty-one volumes were published (see register of the *Neos Ellinomnimon*, 1930). For Lambros, as for Konstantinos Paparrigopoulos (q.v.), his duty as a historian was ''simultaneously scientific and national.'' That is why, next to his scientific activities, the effort to popularize and transmit this historical knowledge to a wider audience by lectures, publications, and so on, and his simultaneous involvement in public and social life (participation in conferences, associations, societies in Greece and abroad) can be considered his most important fields of action. In his work (480 published and 280 unpublished books and articles) a variety of issues of medieval and modern Greek history are examined, as well as questions pertaining to the Greek communities of Europe. As representative of these works, we might mention *Athens Toward the End of the Twelfth Century* (1878). Smaller essays were collected in the volumes: *Historical Essays* (1884), *Discourses and Articles* (1902), and *Miscellaneous Pages* (1905). His translations also enrich Greek historical bibliography. Apart from the historical works of Viktor Grigorovius, Ernst Curtius, Gustave Schlumberger, Pietro Bertolini, William Miller, and others, he also translated books that contributed to the methodological and theoretical education of Greek historians. Influenced by the European positivist historians, Lambros chose works to be translated into Greek: for example, the *Introduction aux études historiques* by Charles Victor Langlois and Charles Seignobos (q.v.) (1902) and the *Handbook of Greek and Latin Paleography* by Edward Maunde Thompson (1903). In other words, with the translations of the above works, as well as with articles concerning the west European positivist historians (Leopold von Ranke [q.v.] in *Estia* 1886, Curtius in *Discourses and Articles* 1902, etc.), he may be considered as the historian who made the most serious effort to introduce in Greece theoretical and methodological principles as enunciated by the positivist historical school. It should not be considered irrelevant to this perception of his that he alone among the Greek historians occupied himself systematically with modern Greek historiography.

Lambros perceived the science of history as being closely linked with philology. That is why he made relentless efforts to bring to light medieval and modern Greek texts that could be found in the archives of monasteries, European cities, and Greek libraries. It was not by chance that his attention was directed to the material of these two historical periods. He believed that study of medieval and modern Greek history would restore the origins of national unity, and arguments would be found in favor of the national claims. Apart from philology, archaeology, ethnology (Völkerpsychologie), and geography too can contribute to gaining knowledge of the past, as can the progress of technology. Under no circumstances does the latter reveal the national soul. The concept of a national soul occupies an important place in Lambros' work, with the meaning it acquired through the studies of the German idealist philosophers (Herder) and positivist psychologists (Wund). For him it does not refer simply to the nation, and not much less to the state either, but to the race (*genos*). Thus, the "movements of the national soul" as a historical theme fit in with the unfulfilled national Greek claims of his time (Macedonia, "Great Idea," etc.). As a whole, therefore, these elements sketch a manifest positivist perception that simultaneously comprises some idealistic elements.

Bibliography: G. Charitakis, "Catalogue of Sp. P. Lambros's Publications," *Neos Ellinomnimon* 14 (1917): 145–95; *Kritika Psulla* 2, no. 9 (May 1973): 133–92, several articles on Lambros; A. Skias, "Sp. Lambros," *Neos Ellinomnimon* 14 (1917): 115–39; A. Skias, *Sp. Lambros's Unpublished Works*, Athens, 1921.

Angeliki Konstantakopoulou

PAPARRIGOPOULOS, Konstantinos (Constantinople, 1815–Athens, 1891), Greek historian. Paparrigopoulos' father, a merchant and banker, was a native of Vytina in the Peloponnese and had settled in Constantinople. When the Greek Revolution broke out in 1821, he was killed by the Turks along with other members of the family. His wife, together with their ten children, left Constantinople for Odessa where they remained until 1830. There Paparrigopoulos studied at the Lycée Richelieu on a scholarship granted by Tsar Alexander I. After the establishment of the free Greek state, the family settled in what was then the Greek capital, Nafplion. Until 1834, when he was assigned as an employee to the Ministry of Justice during the ministry of K. Schinas, he did not systematically study at the gymnasium. With the implementation of the law on autochtonous and heterochtonous citizens, Paparrigopoulos and his three brothers were discharged as heterochtonous citizens from the government jobs they held (May 1845). Through the goodwill of Prime Minister Kolettis, he was soon rehabilitated professionally. The next year he was appointed professor of history at the sole gymnasium of Athens (March 1846). He obtained a doctorate from the University of Munich in January 1850 in absentia on the basis of historical works he had written in the meantime. This degree opened the door to a university career. In 1850 he was appointed lecturer at the faculty of law of the University of Athens and a year later assistant professor at the Faculty of Letters. From 1856 until his death he taught as a full professor, but his activities were not restricted to teaching at the university. He published magazines (*Pandora*, 1850) and newspapers (*Spectateur de l'Orient*, 1853–1857, and *Hellin*, 1858–1860).

He was a member of many associations and committees and a founding member of the Association for the Propagation of Greek Letters (1869). Later, the government asked him to get in touch with the Ecumenical Patriarchate concerning the settlement of ecclesiastical issues that had arisen after the annexation of Thessaly to the Greek state (1882). Paparrigopoulos also undertook to come to an understanding with the German cartographer H. Kiepert who had already drawn a map of the Balkans, so that the ensuing publication would not contain any incorrect ethnographical data (1878). For him the teaching and study of history was not simply a scientific occupation. Rather, history was "the Gospel of the present and the future of the fatherland." That is why the themes of his historical studies never strayed far from national issues.

Paparrigopoulos' activities as a writer began with the publication of the essay "On the Settlement of Slavic Tribes in the Peloponnese" (1843), which was not the only study on this subject published that year. The works by Jacob Philipp Fallmerayer and mainly his visit to Athens (1842) presented Greek scholars with the occasion to write more studies aimed at refuting the theory of the German historian. According to Fallmerayer, the nearly depopulated Greek area was penetrated gradually from the sixth century onwards by Slavic tribes. As a result of this event, together with the movement of Albanian tribes to the same area in a later period, the ethnological composition of the population was altered to such a degree that by the middle of the nineteenth century it was impossible to consider the inhabitants of the Greek state as Greeks. In his 1843 study Paparrigopoulos sought to refute this theory which undermined the ideological foundations of the newly established Greek state. His debut as a writer broadly outlined the path he would follow in his subsequent studies. The unity of Greek history from antiquity to the modern era and the mission of the Greek state in the propagation of civilization throughout the Eastern world are the basic points of his entire work. But in order for the unity of the Greek nation to become evident, it was necessary to rehabilitate and establish Byzantine history as the connecting link between antiquity and the modern era. That is why Paparrigopoulos in his writings repeatedly referred to Fallmerayer's thesis on the Slavic issue. The Greek state, that is, the social forces that were now emerging, needed strong ideological elements that could be drawn not only from the ancient but also primarily from the Byzantine past.

Paparrigopoulos was not the first to conceive the unity of Greek history as a historiographical demand. Initially, European and Greek historians—among them Zinkeisen and Zambelios—refuted Fallmerayer's theory, and conceived and established this "historico-legal" system. Paparrigopoulos also wrote the *Handbook of General History* (2 vols.; 1849–1852); *History of the Greek Nation from the Ancient Years until Today* (1853); and the basic work for which he gained the title of "national historiographer," *History of the Greek Nation*, circulated in issues from 1860 to 1874 (5 vols.). A sixth volume with an epilogue and indexes was circulated in 1877. A summary of this last work was translated into French and published with the financial support of the Greek Parliament

(1878). A host of historical essays accompanied the publication of this work. It was not without obstacles that Paparrigopoulos' views on the unity of Greek history became the prevailing perception. A group of scholars, mainly professors of the university, obstinately emphasized the importance of the ancient Greek over that of Byzantium, thereby continuing the west European tradition of the eighteenth-century Enlightenment. However, that historical perception did not seem to correspond to the modern national viewpoint, especially political demands. Most importantly, it did not provide ideological cover for the "Great Idea" as far as the historical past was concerned. Paparrigopoulos' historical perception can in general be ranged under the tendency of nineteenth century historicism.

Among the European historians Paparrigopoulos admired Thomas Babington Macaulay (q.v.) and François Guizot (q.v.). For him divine Providence constituted a key concept in the explanation of the historical past. In other words, there is a question here of the "histoire-tableau." Methodologically, there are prescientific elements in his work, because he was given to writing a synthetic history that met a primary ideological, political, and national demand. In the long course of his career he clashed over basic historical questions with Konstantinos Sathas (q.v.), Paul Karolidis (q.v.), and Spyridon Lambros (q.v.).

Bibliography: K. Th. Dimaras, *K. Paparrigopoulos* (Athens, 1986) (in Greek); G. Veloudis, "Jacob Philipp Fallmerayer und die Entstehung des neugriechischen Historismus," *Südostforschungen* 29 (1970): 43–90.

Angeliki Konstantakopoulou

SATHAS, Konstantinos (Athens, 1842–Paris, 1914), Greek historical researcher. Sathas began university studies at the Faculty of Medicine of the University of Athens, but he discontinued them and, under the guidance of the numismatist Pavlos Lambros, father of historian Spyridon Lambros (q.v.), he applied himself to the collection and publication of texts pertaining to medieval and modern Greek history. The discovery and publication of a manuscript with the text of the *Unpublished Chronicle of Galaxidi* (1865) at the beginning of his involvement with historical research augured a steady course in that direction. The collection of texts dating from the years of Venetian rule with the title *Unedited Greek Documents* (2 vols., 1867), the work *Modern Greek Philology* (1868), a collection of biographies, most of them already known, of Greek scholars from the time of the Turkish occupation (1453–1821), together with the supplement *History of the Modern Greek Language Question* (1870), and finally the work *Greece under Turkish Rule* (1869), made him widely known. With the financial support of the Greek state, he was repeatedly sent to various European libraries in order to collect and publish relevant material from the archives (1870–1888). These investigations resulted, among other things, in the works *Medieval Library* (7 vols., Venice, 1872–1894), *Cretan Theater* (Venice, 1878), and *Unedited Documents Relating to History from the Greek Era to the Middle Ages published under the Greek Chamber of Deputies*, 9 vols., Paris,

1880–1890. In spite of the fact that he was autodidactic, he managed to bring to light an enormous amount of archival records pertaining to medieval and modern Greek history throughout the second half of the nineteenth century, that is, during a period when historians were being called on to substantiate, using mostly medieval sources, the unity of Greek history. However, it is because, among other reasons, he worked as an isolated scholar outside academic institutions, that he organized the material which he brought to light on the basis of a different set of problems and often in a way difficult to follow. Thus, to the famous Slavic question that the German historian Jacob Fallmerayer raised, he gave a paradoxical answer, emphasizing exclusively the intermingling of the Greek population with the Albanian intruders (*Documents*, I, 1880). That is why it has been aptly claimed that Fallmerayer Slavicized Greece, whereas Sathas Albanianized it. As for the question of the unity and continuity of the ancient, medieval, and modern Greek civilization, which constituted yet another vital problem for the ideological consolidation of the modern Greek state, there too Sathas advanced an equally unfounded and peculiar point of view. According to his views, the ancient Greek religion was preserved until the period of the Crusades and the fall of Byzantium: *La Tradition Hellénique et la Légende de Phidias de Praxitèle et de la Fille d'Hippocrate au Moyen Age* (Paris, 1883) and *Documents* (VII, 1888). He was criticized by N. Politis (*Bulletin of the Historical and Ethnological Society* 1, 1883, pp. 71–101).

These peculiar views, together with his omissions and methodological errors, brought Sathas into conflict with several historians, especially his contemporaries Spyridon Lambros (q.v.), N. Politis, A. Dimitrakopoulos, Kremos, and I. Pantazidis. It is within this framework that we also have to understand his avowed conflict with Konstantinos Paparrigopoulos (q.v.). Nevertheless, in spite of Sathas' eccentric historical perception, he also possessed a certain creative originality. The fact that he turned toward the study of texts and subjects which until then were unknown and did not belong to official historiography gave an impulse to the historical studies of the second half of the nineteenth century. Examples are *Digenis Akritas* which he published together with Em. Legrand (1875), and subjects such as the presence of Greek troops in the West (Stradioti, *Estia*, 1885) or "the social situation, commerce, shipping" as traced through the reports of the Venetian consuls (*Economic Review*, 1878–1879).

Bibliography: K. Th. Dimaras, *To Vima* (newspaper) (October 3, 1969); (June 5, 12, 19, 1970); (February 1, 1974, in Greek); D. Pikramenou, "On K. N. Sathas's Activities (1858–1861)," *O Eranistis* 8, no. 48 (1970), 260–273, also listing bibliography.

Angeliki Konstantakopoulou

Great Historians:
Hungarian

DOMANOVSZKY, Sándor (Nagyszeben/Sibiu, 1877–Budapest, 1955), Hungarian historian. A professor with the University in Budapest (1909), where starting in 1954 he headed the chair of history of the Magyar culture. A group of young experts grew up around Domanovszky, dedicating their activity to the investigation of the agrarian history of Hungary, especially of the lords' households in the sixteenth-eighteenth centuries. Those experts' works were published, edited by Domanovszky in the fifteen volumes of the collection *Tanulmányok a magyar mezögazdaság történetéhez*, which appeared between 1932 and 1943. Between 1913 and 1943 Domanovszky headed the *Századok* review. He initiated the elaboration and edited the five-volume history of the Hungarian culture and civilization: *Magyar müvelödéstörténet*. Through careful preparation and based on extensive documentary material, Domanovszky approached the issues relating to the narrative sources of fourteenth- and fifteenth-century Hungary (A Dubnici Křónika in *Századok* 1899; "A Budai Krónika," in *Századok*, 1902; *Kézai Simon mester krónikája. Forrástanulmány*, 1906; *Die Chronik Simonis von Kéza*, in *Ungarische Rundschau*, 1912; *Die Interpolationen der Viener Ungarischen Bilderchronik*, in *Ungarische Rundschau*, 1912; "Anonymus és a II. Géza-korabeli Gesta," in *Századok*, 1933) participating in the preparation of the critical edition of Magyar narrative sources, *Scriptores rerum Hungaricarum*, edited by Imre Szentpétery. Domanovszky presented the conclusions of his investigations relating to the formation of the class of nobility in Hungary in the paper "La formation de la class nobiliare en Hongrie," delivered at the International Congress of 1933 in Warsaw. Another domain of investigation in which Domanovszky distinguished himself was economic history, especially the history of home and foreign trade and the lords' great households. Among those studies are the syntheses: "Zur Geschichte der Gutsherrschaft in Ungarn," in *Wirtschaft und Kultur. Festschrift zum 70 Geburtstag von Alfons Dopsch* (1938); *Die historische Entwicklung Ungarns, mit Rüchsicht auf seine Wirtschaftgeschichte* (1913), "A harmincadvám eredete," in *Ertekezések a Történeti Tudományok Köréböl* (1916); *A mázsaszekér*, in *Fejérpataky-Emlékkönyv* (1917); and *A szepesi városok árúmegállító joga* (1922). Domanovszky also published books and syntheses of Hungary's history in German, French, Italian, and Finnish).

Bibliography: Sándor Domanovszky, *Gazdaság és társadalom a középkorban*, ed. Glatz Ferenc (Budapest, 1979).

Lajos Demény

FEJÉRPATAKY, László (Eperjes/Presov, 1857–Budapest, 1923), the most outstanding representative of studies on Magyar medieval diplomacy at the end of the nineteenth century and the beginning of the twentieth century. After studying the critique of sources at the Institute of History in Vienna, Fejérpataky was first the director of the Széchényi National Library and then professor at the University in Budapest, where he taught medieval diplomacy and sphragistics, was vice-president of the Society of Hungarian History, and later was curator and curator-general of the Hungarian National Museum (Magyar Nemzeti Múzeum). Fejérpataky conducted systematic investigations in the archives of Vienna, Rome, Insbruck, Munich, and Dalmatia in connection with papers and documents on Hungary. In the Hungarian historiography Fejérpataky laid the foundations for the investigation and critical editing of medieval sources, published a number of studies on medieval diplomacy, such as *A pannonhalmi apátság alapító oklevele* (1878); "Kálmán király oklevelei," in *Akadémiai Értekezések a Történeti Tudományok köréböl* (1892, with the documents reproduced in facsimile); *Oklevelk II. István korából* (1895); *A királyi kancellária az Árpádok korában* (1885); "Taplóczai Bertalan oklevélformulái a XIV. századból," in *Magyar Könyvszemle* (1886), and *III. Béla király oklevelei* (1900). As part of the vast activity of editing the diplomas, he began editing of the documents from the period of Sigismund of Luxembourg; they were not published until 1951, under Elemér Mályusz. Fejérpataky also started the editing in facsimile of the painted heraldic diplomas, the first of which emanated from the Hungarian royal chancellory under the rule of Sigismund of Luxembourg (*Monumenta Hungariae Heraldica*, Vols. 1–2, 1901–1902). In 1892 Fejérpataky produced a facsimile edition of Anonymus' work (*Gesta Hungarorum*) and published the earliest urban accounts of the Kingdom of Hungary (*Magyarországi városok régi számadáskönyvei*, 1885). Also noteworthy are Fejérpataky's basic study on the accounts of the papal tithe collectors of Hungary in the thirteenth and fourteenth centuries ("Pápai adószedök Magyarországon a XIII. és XIV. században" in *Századok*, 1887) and the study on Magyar chronicle writing during the Arpadian Dynasty ("Irodalmunk az Arpádok korában," in *Figyelö*, 1888).

Bibliography: Csánky Dezsö, "Fejérpataky László," in *Századok* (1922); Áldásy Antal, "Fejérpataky László," in *Magyar Tudományos Akadémia. Emlékbeszédek* (Budapest, 1924).

Lajos Demény

HAJNAL, István (Nagykikinda, 1892–Budapest, 1956), Hungarian historian. Professor at the University of Budapest (1930), where he taught modern world history and the auxiliary disciplines of history (Latin paleography, diplomacy, and so on). Hajnal helped promote the renewal of Hungarian historical thinking. He was also a fecund partisan of interdisciplinary research, a pioneer of investigations into comparative history of Latin writing in Europe, a man who gave new foundations to paleography. He was the first Hungarian historian to thoroughly investigate the development of technique and its influence on society. In the field of historical thinking, his studies on the relationship between historical science and sociology were original for his day. He also published monographs on Hungary's political history in the seventeenth and nineteenth centuries, especially with reference to the foreign policy of the 1848–1849 Hungarian government headed by Lajos Batthyány and to the activity of the Hungarian emigration directed by Louis Kossuth after 1849. He also edited sources.

Hajnal wrote some important works in international languages: "Le rôle social de l'écriture et l'évolution européenne" in *Revue de l'Institute de Sociology Solvay* (Brussels, 1934); *Vergleichende Schriftproben zur Entwicklung und Verbreitung der Schrift im 12–13. Jahrhundert* (1943); and *L'enseignement de l'écriture aux universités médiévales* (1954).

Bibliography: Glatz Ferenc, "Hajnal István történetírása," *Valóság*, no. 3 (1988); Wellmann Imre, "Hajnal István," in *Századok* (1956); Irinyi Károly, "Hajnal István szociologiai történelemszemlélete," in *A Debreceni Kossuth Lajos Tudományegyetem Évkönyve* (1962); Jakó Zsigmond, *Les débutes de l'écriture dans les couches laïques de la société féodale en Transylvanie* (Considerations sur l'études de la paleographie sur de nouvelles bases), in *Nouvelles études d'Histoire présentées au X$_c$ Congres des Sciences Historiques. Rome, 1955* (Bucharest, 1955).

Lajos Demény

HÓMAN, Bálint (Budapest, 1885–Vác, 1953), Hungarian historian. After he graduated from the University of Budapest in philology and got his diploma of doctor of philosophy, Hóman became director of the Library of the University of Budapest in 1915; director of the Széchényi National Library in 1922; director general of the Magyar National Museum in 1923; between 1925 and 1931, a lecturer on the medieval history of Hungary at the University of Budapest; and until 1942 a minister of cults and education in various governments, supporting the German political orientation. Hóman wrote a number of monographs on Hungarian towns of the early Middle Ages (*A magyar városok az Árpádok korában*, 1908); on the evolution of coinage and money circulation in Hungary between 1000 and 1325 (*Magyar pénztörténet 1000–1325*, 1916); on financial and economic policies during the reign of King Charles Robert (*A magyar királyság penzügyei és gazdaság politikája Károly Róbert korában*, 1921); on the development of historical literature in Hungary in the eleventh through thirteenth centuries (*A Szent László-kori Gesta Hungarorum és a XII-XIII századi leszármazói*, 1925); on the interpretation and study of sources (*A forráskutátás* *és forráskritika története*, 1925) and other monographs. He wrote and published with Gyula Szekfü (q.v.) the amplest synthesis on the Hungarian history issued in the interwar period: *Magyar történet*, vols. 1–4 (1935–1936). The part concerning the history of the Hungarians until 1458 of this synthesis was written by Hóman. Likewise, between 1935 and 1937, Bálint Hóman, Gyula Szekfü, and Károly Kerény also supervised the publication of a world history synthesis (*Egyetemes történet*) in four volumes.

Lajos Demény

HORVÁTH, Mihály (? 1809–? 1878), Hungarian historian. Horváth was born in a small town in southern Hungary, the son of the local surgeon. After taking his vows in 1832, he became a parish priest in the economically undeveloped villages of eastern Hungary. He later became acquainted with and involved in the aims and goals of the reform movement. In his application for membership in the Hungarian Academy of Sciences in 1835, he prepared a history of trade and commerce in medieval Hungary. He was elected a member of the academy in 1839. In 1844 he was appointed a history teacher to the Theresianum in Vienna where young nobles from throughout the monarchy took part in "elite" training. It was there that he wrote the first textbooks on contemporary Hungarian history: *A magyarok Története Európába költözésuktöl mostanáig* (The History of the Hungarians from their Arrival in Europe to the Present) (Budapest, 1841) and *A magyarok története a bölcsészettanuló ifjúság számára* (1847; The History of the Hungarians for Young Students of the Arts). Horváth's historiographical tenets were directly influenced by W. Wachsmuth. He clarified and expanded on Wachsmuth's basic principle: namely, historians must deal not just with the ruling circles, but also with the life of the people and their habits and values. Likewise, his interest in Alexis de Tocqueville (q.v.) led him to write the history of the development of democracy in Hungary. The basic premise of his 1841 book was the inevitable and necessary movement of society toward equality in Hungary. He looked forward to the material and intellectual development of the lower classes and to their greater public awareness of politics. In this book, he was also the first to write in depth on the Hungarian peasant uprising of 1514, stressing the legitimacy of the peasants' bitterness and how the nobility had deprived them of their "natural rights and freedoms" in restricting their freedom of movement. According to the "norms" of romantic historiography, it was virtually an indictment of the nobility. Horváth was active in politics at the time of the 1848 War of Independence. The first independent parliamentary government (April 1848) made him bishop of Csanád. He was also spokesman for clergymen supporting the revolution. At the time of the radicalization of the revolution, he remained loyal to the head of state, Lajos Kossuth, who was calling for the deposition of the Habsburgs. Horváth became the radical government's minister for religious and public instruction and, in one of his writings, he too called for the overthrow of the Habsburgs. After the failure of the revolution, he was forced to emigrate (1849–1866). It was in this period that he wrote his greatest historiographical works. Though published outside Hungary, they were written in Hungarian. He lived in Paris and Brussels where he worked as a tutor. Later, at the time of the Austro-Hungarian Compromise of 1867, he was granted an amnesty. In 1867 he became vice-president (later president) of the newly established Historical Society and was celebrated by the nation as "historian laureate."

While in exile Horváth wrote the first large-scale synthesis of Hungarian history, *Magyarország történelme* (2 vols., 1860–1863; History of Hungary). He also wrote two massive works on contemporary history: *Huszonöt év Magyarország történetéböl 1823-töl 1848-ig* (2 vols., 1867; Twenty–five Years of Hungarian History: 1823–1848), and *Magyarország függetlenségi harcának története 1848 és 1849–ben* (3 vols., 1865; Hungary's War for Independence, 1848–1849). These last two works have remained to this day valuable references on the history of the Hungarian reform period as well as the most outstanding works of contemporary historiography in Hungarian. In his works, political history was central, although rural politics played as much a part as the actual government. Horváth devoted special attention to the society as a whole, and his social histories on the behavior of the nobility and the artisans are still valuable. He made extremely accurate and detailed character sketches of his heroes. Horváth combined all of this with clear construction and a very readable literary Hungarian prose style. It was at this time that Hungarian literary language broke away from Latin and German literary forms, and Mihály Horváth became the creator of Hungarian "historical prose." His works could be found on the bookshelves of the cultured middle class for over half a century.

Ferenc Glatz

KARÁCSONYI, János (Gyula, 1858–Nagyvárad/Oradea, 1929), Hungarian historian. After he completed his theological studies in Budapest, Karácsonyi worked for a while with the University of Budapest; then he became a canon and, after 1923 the bishop of Oradea. For decades he studied the diplomas issued by the royal chancellory, drawing up and publishing a register of fake diplomas and diplomas with a wrong date or without any date up to 1400 (*A hamis, hibáskeletü és keltezetlen oklevelek jegyzéke 1400-ig*, 1902). He thereby provided an instrument without which no expert in the epoch could work. His numerous studies of diplomacy, genealogy, and critique of sources are very exacting and thorough. Karácsonyi also wrote monographs of the life and work of St. Gerard (*Szent Gellért élete és müvei*, 1887), of the golden bulla (*Az arangybulla*, 1899), of King St. Stephen (*Szent István király élete*, 1904), and a number of works on the history of the Catholic Church in Hungary and its relations with the Catholic Church in Western Europe. He produced an extensive, three-volume monograph of the Békés comitatus (*Békés vármegye története*, 1896), including profuse information on local history. His synthesis of tribes and kin with the Hungarians (*Magyar nemzetségek a XIV. század közepéig*, vols. 1–3, 1900–1901), remains the main source of information in this respect. Together with S.

Boróvszky, he put out a critical edition of the famous register of Oradea, *Az idörendbe szedett váradi tüzespróba-lajstrom* (Budapest, 1903), which he extended with explanations and a rich scientific apparatus.

Bibliography: Csánki Dezsö, "Karácsonyi János," in *Századok*, nos. 1–3 (1929).

Lajos Demény

MARCZALI, Henrik (Marcali, 1856–Budapest, 1940), Hungarian historian. Author of syntheses, of fundamental monographs and numerous studies devoted to eighteenth-century political, economic, social, and cultural history, founder and editor of the first (twelve-volume) synthesis of world history in Hungarian historiography: *Nagy Képes Világtörténet*, published between 1898 and 1905. After graduating from Budapest University, Marczali continued his studies in Vienna, Paris, and Berlin. In 1895 he became a professor in Budapest, and in 1893 a corresponding member of the Hungarian Academy of Sciences. After the fall of the Republic of Councils, Marczali was fired for his advanced views. An expert with a wide horizon, conversant with both European and Hungarian history, Marczali produced works of great erudition. In his first major work he focused on the influence of geographic environment on Hungarian history. Together with David Angyal and Sándor Mike he produced the two-volume synthesis of the sources of Hungarian history (*A magyar történet kútföinek kézikönyve*, 1901), and he wrote volumes 1, 2, and 7 of the big synthesis of history of Hungary (*Magyar nemzet története*, 1895–1898). Marczali's works provide especially rich information on the history of the eighteenth century. He produced bulky monographs on the rule of Joseph II (*Magyarország története II. József korában*, vols. 1–3, 1881–1888), Maria Theresa, and the 1790–1791 Diet (*Az 1790–1791 országgyülés*, vols. 1–2, 1907). He also published a synthesis of Hungarian constitutional history in German (*Ungarische Verfassungsrecht*, 1911) and another one in English about eighteenth-century Hungary, printed at the University of Cambridge (*Hungary in Eighteenth Century*, 1910).

Bibliography: István Hajnal, "Marczali Henrik," in *Századok* nos. 4–6 (1940), Emma Lederer, "Marczali Henrik helye a magyar polgári történettudományban," in *Századok* (1962).

Lajos Demény

PÁRDUCZ, Mihály (Biserica Alba near Baziass, 1908–Budapest, 1974), Hungarian pre- and protohistorian. Professor at the University of Szeged (1946). Known for his numerous contributions to the study of the material culture of the allogeneous groups of people that settled in the middle Danube area or between the Danube and the Tisza. Párducz's scientific work can be subdivided into three areas: (1) Works that throw light on the presence of the Scythians in this region, the main characteristics of their antiquities, and how they integrated into the Hallstatt culture and environment. This interest resulted in a bulky monograph, *Le cimetière hallstattien de Szentes-Vekerzug* 1 (1952), 2 (1954), 3 (1955), and in a series of micromonographs, for example, "The Scythian Age Cemetery at

Tápiōszele," *Acta Archaeologica* 18 (1966), as well as in synthetic studies. Grounding his observations on details of ritual (the relation between inhumation and cremation) and on the nature of the objects used, especially the ceramics, Párducz spoke about the Sythian Age rather than of Scythian culture, and he attempted to define the nature of the relations between natives and migrants. (2) A second, more definitive, series of works, which centered on the study of the Sarmatian antiquities in Hungary. In this area he wrote several studies and a large monograph, *Denkmäler der Sarmatenzeit Ungarns* (1941–1950), characterized by the scientific objectivity peculiar to his entire work. (3) A study of archaeological evidence and ethnic problems of the Hunnic Age: "Archäologische Beiträge zur Geschichte der Hunnenzeit in Ungarn," *Acta Archaeologica* 11 (1959); *Die enthnische Probleme der Hunnenzeit in Ungarn* (1963), to which could be added a series of shorter studies. This part of his work was also characteristically respectful of truth and science.

Bibliography: Jan Filip, *Encyklopädisches Handbuch der Ur- und Frühgeschichte Europas* 2 (Prague, 1967), p. 999; József Korek, "Mihály Párducz," *Archaeologiai Értesitō* 2 (Szám, 1974): 304–305.

Ligia Bârzu

PAULER, Gyula (Zágráb/Zagreb, 1841–Badacsónytomaj, 1903), Hungarian historian. After completing his studies at the University in Budapest, in 1874 Pauler was appointed chief archivist at the Hungarian National Archive, which he reorganized based on the Western model, becoming its director. At first, he wrote primarily works of philosophy of history, especially regarding the positivist school and its most prominent representative Auguste Comte (q.v.): "A pozitivizmus hatásáról a történetírásra," in *Századok* (1871); "Comte Agost és a történelem," in *Századok* (1873). Together with Sándor Szilágyi (q.v.), Pauler edited the collection of sources regarding the Hungarians' dismounting (*A magyar honfoglalás kútföi*, 1900), a work to which he contributed heavily, using sources unknown until that time. His chief work was a basic monograph on Hungary's history under the Arpadian kings (*A magyar nemzet története az Árpádházi királyok korában*, vols. 1–2, 1893). Pauler wrote a bulky work about the anti-Habsburg conspiracy of the 1770s led by Ferenc Wesselényi, Palatine of Hungary (*Wesselényi Ferenc nádor és társainak összeesküvése*, vols. 1–2, 1876), and a study on Hungary's history to the foundation of the kingdom (*A Magyar nemzet története Szent Istvánig*, 1900). He also participated in the editing of the collection regarding the Austro-Hungarian monarchy in documents and pictures and wrote a monograph on the Hungarian kings of the Habsburg Dynasty (*A Habsburg királyok története 1526–1825*). Pauler's book on the occupation of Bosnia was entitled *Wie und wann kam Bosnien an Ungarn* (1894).

Bibliography: Károlyi Árpád, "Pauler Gyula emlékezete," in *Magyar Tudományos Akadémia. Emlékbeszédek* (Budapest, 1913); Thallóczi Lajos, "Pauler Gyula emlékezete," *Századok* (1911).

Lajos Demény

SZABÓ, István (Debrecen, 1898–Debrecen, 1969), Hungarian historian. After obtaining doctoral degrees in political science (1923) and juridical science (1927) at the University of Szeged and in letters (1928) at the University of Debrecen, István Szabó first taught at Debrecen. Between 1928 and 1943 he was a scientific adviser with the Hungarian National Archive in Budapest, after which he became professor at Debrecen University and director of the Institute of History, remaining until 1959. Szabó was the most prominent twentieth-century representative of research into Hungary's agrarian history and peasantry questions. In the agrarian history he combined research with thorough investigations into the formation and evolution of rural settlements and their structure, and with surveys of historical demography. His surveys and monographs, relying on vast documentary material, gathered meticulously during his activity with the Archive, produced a realistic picture of the social structures, of the everyday life, of the mind and relations between the enfeoffed peasantry and the landlords, with a detailed presentation of the feudal duties. Farming techniques, the soil exploitation system, the organization of the peasant households and of the lords' households, the specific share of the various branches of agriculture, and the workforce are among the many aspects investigated by Szabó. His chief works are *A debreceni tanyarendszer kialakulása* (1929); *Ugocsa vármegye* (1937); *Tanulmányok a magyar parasztság történetéből* (1940); *A magyarság életrajza* (1941); *Ungarische Volk, Geschichte und Wandlungen* (1944); *A jobbágy birtoklása az örökös jobbágyság korában* (1947); *Bács, Bodrog és Csongrád megye dézsmalajstromai 1522-ből* (1954); "Magyarország népessége az 1330—a és az 1526—as évek között," in *Magyarország történeti demográfiája* (1963); "A predium. Vizsgálódások a korai magyar gazdaság—és településtörténelem köréből," in *Agrártörténeti Szemle* (1963); *A középkori magyar falu* (1966); *A magyar mezőgazdaság története a XIV. századtól az 1530—as évekig* (1975).

Bibliography: István Sinrovics, "Szabó István 1898–1969," in *Levéltári Közlemények* no. 1 (1969).

Lajos Demény

SZEKFÜ, Gyula (Székesfehérvár, 1883–Budapest, 1955), Hungarian historian. The most prominent figure in Hungarian historiography between the two world wars. After completing his university studies, Szekfü worked with the Hungarian National Museum in 1904, between 1909 and 1913 with the Hungarian National Archives, and then at Haus-, Hof- und Staatsarchiv in Vienna. In 1916 he began teaching modern history at the University in Budapest. He had been educated under the influence of the German school of history, represented by Leopold von Ranke (q.v.), and was especially influenced by Friedrich Meinecke (q.v.). Szekfü's orientation since the beginning of his career as a historian was toward analyzing historical phenomena in their whole complexity. He studied and presented the major events and representative personalities of the Hungarian history in their international context and from a European perspective. Szekfü showed continual interest in social and cultural history, also publishing special surveys on the characteristic features of the social structure under the Magyars in the Middle Ages, the history of the state and of the law, and the correlation between the state and the nation in Hungarian history. Some of his works generated powerful controversies among the Hungarian intelligentsia and were sometimes received with overwhelming negativity because they reversed the traditionalist outlook. Nonetheless, through the precision with which he supplied his information, the keen critical spirit in his analysis of sources and data, and his European perspective, Szekfü was the most outstanding representative of the critical renewal and the reconsideration of history of the Magyars in the first half of the twentieth century. He was a severe critic of the romantic trend in historiography. Possessed of a capability for synthesis, matched by a clear and elevated style, he produced one of the best syntheses of Hungary's history since 1458 as well as the modern epoch (vols. 3–5 of *Magyar történet*, 1937–1938, 2d ed.). Other works include *Adatok Szamosközy István történeti munkáinak bírálatához* (1904); "Szerviensek és familiarisok," in *Akadémiai Értekezések a Történettudomány Köréböl* (1912; the German version in *Ungarische Rundschau*, no. 3, 1913); *A számüzött Rákóczi* (1913); *A magyar állam életrajza* (1918); *Iratok a magyar államnyelv kérdésének történetéböl* (1926); *Bethlen Gábor* (1929); *Három nemzedék és ami következik* (1934), *Állam és nemzet* (1942); and *Forradolom után* (1947).

Bibliography: *Emlékkönyv Szekfü Gyula a történetíró . . . 60. születésnapjára* (Budapest, 1943); Mérei Gyula, " Szekfü Gyula történetszemléletének birálatához," in *Századok* (1960); Mérei Gyula, "Szekfü Gyula történetírásának kérdései," in *Társadalmi Szemle*, no. 7 (1954); Révész Imre, "Szekfü Gyula," in *Akadémiai Értesítö* (1955); Zoványi Jenö, *Szekfü és társai történetírása* (Budapest, 1938); József Szigeti, *A magyar szellemtörténet birálatához* (Budapest, 1964); Németh László, *Szekfü Gyula* (Budapest, 1940); Pethö Sándor, *Szekfü Gyula történetírása* (Budapest, 1933).

Lajos Demény

SZENTPÉTERY, Imre (Középpalojta, 1878–Budapest, 1950), Hungarian historian. The most outstanding researcher of the early Hungarian Middle Ages. Szentpétery completed his higher studies at the University of Budapest, and after study travels in France and Germany he was appointed to the University of Debrecen and then at the University of Budapest, where since 1923 he had been professor of auxiliary sciences or history (chronology, diplomacy, heraldic, and especially Latin paleography), being the founder of a school in this domain. Between 1937 and 1938 Szentpétery directed the two-volume critical edition of the Hungarian narrative sources of the eleventh to thirteenth centuries, under the title *Scriptores rerum Hungaricarum tempore ducum regumque stirpis Arpadianae gestarum*. With his comprehensive and multilateral research, Szentpétery laid new foundations for the critical study of the diplomas and papers issued by the chancellory of the Arpadian kings. He studied those sources in the context of the institutions that created them. Thus, his studies were published on the Royal Chancellory, the Royal Council, along with a string of studies of heraldic, chronology, paleography, and diplomacy, many of them also published in foreign reviews of specialty. After a number of studies devoted to the critical analysis of royal acts of donation or of other kind, in 1923 Szentpétery started the editing of his second fundamental work, namely, the critical regesta of the diplomas issued by the Hungarian kings of the Arpadian Dynasty (*Regesta regum stirpis Arpadianae critico-diplomatica*, vols. 1–2, 1923–1943), publishing those regesta until the year 1272. (The collection was continued by Iván Borsa, who between 1961 and 1987 edited parts III and IV of the second volume, making use of the work Szentpétery left unpublished.) Szentpétery's prestigious publication included the information and regesta of 4,410 royal diplomas issued between 1001 and 1301. Without his elaboration of working instruments in the domains of diplomacy, chronology, and Latin paleography, no medievalist could work on the history of a given period and region.

Bibliography: Ember Győző, ''Szentpétery Imre,'' in *Akadémiai Értesítő* (1950); *Szentpétery-Emlékkönyv* (Budapest, 1938; with the complete list of the works published by Szentpétery to that date drawn up by Iván Janits).

Lajos Demény

SZILÁGYI, Sándor (1827–1899), Hungarian historian. Member of the Hungarian Academy of Sciences, director of the University Library in Budapest. From 1875 to his death in 1899 Szilágyi was the editor of the major review of Hungarian history: *Századok*; he was also the founder of the periodical that published the sources, *Történelmi Tár* (in which he himself published a large number of sources regarding Transylvania's history in the sixteenth and seventeenth centuries) and of the publication *Magyar Történelmi Életrajzok*. Szilágyi's works and publications remain an extremely rich source of information. He edited the resolutions and acts of the Transylvanian Diets between 1540 and 1699 in twenty-one volumes under the title *Monumenta Comitialia Regni Transilvaniae* (1875–1898), extending them with ample expositions of political history. He published other sources, such as *Actes et documents pour servire à l'histoire de George Rákóczi Prince de Transylvanie avec les Francqis et les Suedois dans la Guerre de Trente ans* (1874); *Okmánytár II. Rákóczi György diplomácziai összeköttetéseihez* (1874); *A két Rákóczy György családi levelezése* (1875); *Levelek és okíratok I. Rákóczy György keleti összeköttetései történetéhez* (1883); and *Transylvania et bellum boreo-orientale* (1890–1891). Of the lavishly documented works of interpretation, most noteworthy are *Erdélyország története* (vols. 1–2, 1866); *Báthory Gábor fejedelem története* (1867); *A Rákócziak kora Erdélyben* (1868); *Bethlen Gábor és a svéd diplomácia* (1882); *II. Rákóczy György* (1891); and *I. Rákóczy György* (1893). By the end of the century, Szilágyi was also the chief editor of the ten-volume synthesis of Hungarian history, *A Magyar nemzet története*, published between 1895 and 1898. The political history of sixteenth- and seventeenth-century Transylvania and its diplomatic relations with the various European countries are well documented in Szilágyi's works.

Bibliography: Károlyi Árpád, *Szilágyi Sándor emlékezete* (Budapest, 1900); Vértes Miklós, Szilágyi Sándor, in *A Könyvtáros*, no. 8 (1956); Fraknói Vilmos, "Emlékbeszéd Szilágyi Sándor rendes tag felett," in *A Magyar Tudományos Akadémia. Emlékbeszédek* (with an annex comprising the huge list of Sándor Szilágyi's published works, drawn up by Lajos Dézsi) (Budapest, (1902).

Lajos Demény

Great Historians: Indian

CHAUDHURI, Sashi Bhusan (Agartala, Tripura, 1905–Calcutta, 1983), Indian historian. Sashi Bhusan Chaudhuri made a significant contribution to modern Indian historiography through his published research on popular discontent in India during East India Company rule. Educated at Comilla, Scottish Church College, Calcutta, and Dacca University (1927), he taught at M. C. College, Sylhet, Dacca University, and Presidency College, Calcutta. Between 1958 and 1960 he was editor, *Gazetteers of India*. Thereafter he was appointed professor and head of the History Department at Burdwan University, becoming vice chancellor in 1971 until his retirement in 1973. As a pupil of Romesh Chandra Majumdar (q.v.), Chaudhuri began research in early Indian history. His *Ethnic Settlements in Ancient India* appeared in 1955. In his teaching and research, however, he turned to modern Indian history, and it was in this field that he made his most substantial contributions through the study of popular political discontent. His *Civil Disturbances During the British Rule in India, 1765–1857* (1955) and *Civil Rebellion in the Indian Mutiny, 1857–59* (1957) both highlighted the extent and significance of popular uprisings in the subcontinent. His work stood in contrast to conventional historical interpretations which emphasized the period of East India Company rule in India as a time of relative quiescence. Similarly, with respect to the turmoil of 1857–1858, Chaudhuri offered evidence of popular anti–British activities and challenged those historians who emphasized the limited character of participation and the essentially military mutinous nature of the uprisings. This emphasis on civil disturbances placed Chaudhuri at direct odds with his mentor, Ramesh Chandra Majumdar. In 1965 Chaudhuri published *Theories of the Indian Mutiny, 1857–59: A Study of the Views of an Eminent Historian*, which presented his critique of Majumdar's *The Sepoy Mutiny and the Revolt of 1857*, rev. ed. (Calcutta: Firma K. L. Mukhopadhyay, 1963). After his retirement, Chaudhuri published *English Historical Writings on the Indian Mutiny*. From his service in the Gazetteers office, he also published a history of the Indian gazetteers which provides a useful survey of a major source for Indian social and economic conditions. In a sense, Chaudhuri's work was a pioneering exploration of what would be later termed a "history from below."

Bibliography: Ranajit Sen, "Dr. S. B. Chaudhuri," *Quarterly Review of Historical Studies*, 23 (1983–1984): 56–60.

Frank F. Conlon

DUTT, Romesh Chunder (Calcutta, 1848–Baroda, 1909), Indian civil servant and economic historian. Romesh Chunder Dutt was an exemplary product of what has been called the Bengal Renaissance. As a young man he followed his family's traditions of education, literary prowess, and government service, ultimately journeying to England in 1868 to appear for (and pass) the Indian Civil Service examination. He was also called to the bar. He returned to India in 1871 and entered his career in the Indian Civil Service as an assistant magistrate in a rural Bengal district. He rose to become a magistrate and collector in 1881 and a commissioner in 1894. In spite of these promotions, Dutt frequently felt and resented the effects of British racial attitudes. His observations and practical experience in Indian administration led him far from his earlier confidence that the British conquest of his native Bengal had been a positive historical event in that it "removed Bengal from the moral atmosphere of Asia to that of Europe" (R. C. Dutt, *Three Years in Europe, 1868 to 1871, with an Account of a Second Visit to Europe in 1886*, 3d ed. [Calcutta, 1890]). In 1897 he resigned from the Civil Service and again voyaged to England, where he lectured on Indian history in the University College, London. He began research on the economic history of British rule in India and became active in the moderate wing of Indian nationalism, serving as president of the Indian National Congress in 1899. Although during his Indian Civil Service career he had written four historical novels in Bengali, Dutt now turned his literary skills to historical publication, opening in 1900 with a polemical critique of Britain's agrarian policies in India, *Open Letters to Lord Curzon on Famines and Land Assessments in India* (London, 1900). He expanded his horizons during the next few years, publishing a two-volume study of the economic history of British India. Based on parliamentary papers, official reports, and statistics, this work constituted the first systematic effort at Indian economic history in a time when that subdiscipline was little developed. He emphasized the impact of enhanced revenue demands on agriculture and of commercial and tariff policies on Indian manufacturers.

Recent economic historians have faulted Dutt for some of his interpretations concerning the negative impact of British policies on India's economy. Nevertheless, it appears that in early twentieth-century India Dutt's volumes were the most influential, widely read, and quoted critique of colonialism. As such, Dutt not only helped to shape the political thinking of innumerable Indian nationalists, but also encouraged them to become more history-minded. In 1904 Dutt took up appointment in the government of the princely state of Baroda and had just assumed the prime ministership when he died in 1909. Apart from his brief period as a lecturer in London, he was never a professional teacher of history. Nonetheless, through his writings he gave Indian history prominence in the minds of several generations of Indian nationalism.

Bibliography: Rabindra Chandra Datta, *Romesh Chunder Dutt* (New Delhi: Publications Division, Ministry of Information and Broadcasting, 1968; Nilmani Mukherjee, "Romesh Chunder Dutt (1848–1909)," *Quarterly Review of Historical Studies* 3 (1963–1964): 183–188; Pauline Rule, *The Pursuit of Progress: A Study of the Intellectual Development of Romesh Chunder Dutt, 1848–1888* (Calcutta: Editions Indian, 1977).

Frank F. Conlon

HABIB, Mohammad (Lucknow, 1894–Aligarh, 1971), Indian historian. Habib was a significant contributor to the study of medieval Indian history. He attended the college at the M.A.O. Collegiate School, Aligarh, and obtained a B.A. degree from Allahabad University in 1916. He then proceeded to England, where he completed studies at New College, Oxford, and also succeeded in gaining admittance to the bar. He was called back to India by the Muslim political leader Mohammad Ali and Motilal Nehru to teach at the new "national college," the Jamia Millia, Aligarh. In 1922 Habib joined Aligarh Muslim University and was appointed to the rank of professor of history less than a year later. He served at Aligarh for the rest of his career in many capacities, including head of the History and Political Science departments, as well as dean of the Faculty of Arts. He retired in 1958 and was thereafter awarded a doctor of letters degree by Aligarh University. He was a member of the United Provinces Legislative Council, 1927–1930 and surfaced in Indian politics again in 1967, when he was the candidate for vice-president of India for the opposition parties. Professor Habib's work was characterized by a willingness to adopt unconventional interpretations of the subject. In his study of Mahmud of Ghazni, he concluded that the sultan's invasions of India were motivated less by religious fervor than by a desire for economic gain. This conclusion profoundly shocked many Muslim intellectuals for whom the other explanation was both familiar and satisfying. Habib also took a lead in criticizing the British historian of medieval India, Sir Henry Elliot, arguing that Elliot had contributed directly to a sense of communalism by misrepresenting Hindus to Muslims and Muslims to Hindus. It was Habib's conviction that "the history of India as Indians have understood it, is the history of her religious and cultural movements." In that connection he was deeply interested in medieval traditions of Islamic mysticism, although he had an intellectual commitment to Marxism. He was the first Indian historian to make systematic use of sufi (mystical) literature for developing a social and cultural history of the medieval period. Although not a prolific author, his influence on the modern interpretation of medieval India was vital, particularly in the setting of Aligarh Muslim University where he shaped and led a distinguished department, which attained greatness as a center of medieval Indian studies. His instruction and encouragement of others in medieval history may have reduced his publication productivity, but contributed to the development of a rigorous modern historiography of medieval and Mughal India.

Bibliography: Important works by Mohammad Habib: *Delhi Sultanate:* Volume 5 of Comprehensive History of India (New Delhi: People's Publishing House, 1970), editor with K. A. Nizami; *Hazrat Amir Khusrau of Delhi* (Bombay: Taraporevala, 1927); "Introduction" to revised vol. 2 of H. M. Elliot and J. Dowson, *A History of India as Told by Its Own Historians* (Aligarh: Cosmopolitan, 1952); *Political Theory of the Delhi Sultanate*, with A. U. Salim Khan (Allahabad: Kitab Mahal, 1961); *Politics and Society During the Early Medieval Period* (New Delhi: People's Publishing House, 1974); *Sultan Mahmud of Ghazni* (Delhi: S. Chand, 1967; orig., 1951). Work concerning Mohammad Habib: K. A. Nizami, "Introduction", pp. v–xvii, in *Politics and Society During the Early Medieval Period: Collected Works of Professor Mohammad Habib*, vol. 1 (New Delhi: People's Publishing House, 1974).

Frank F. Conlon

KHAN, Sir Shafa'at Ahmad (Moradabad, U.P., 1893–Delhi, 1947), Indian historian and politician. Shafa'at Ahmad Khan played a significant role in the spread within India of the European model of historiography, which emphasized close scrutiny and analysis of documentation, and in the process he made significant contributions to the history of early modern India. Following his secondary education in India, he studied in England at Cambridge and subsequently was awarded a doctor of letters degree by Dublin University in 1918. He served as senior lecturer in history for the London County Council, 1917–1919, before returning to India where, after one year as reader in economics at the University of Madras, he was appointed professor and head of the Department of History of Allahabad University, a post he held from 1921 through 1940. He took up diplomatic responsibilities as India's high commissioner to South Africa during 1941–1945, and in 1946 he served briefly as a minister in the interim government of India. Earlier in his career he had been a member of the Legislative Council, United Provinces, 1924–1930, and an active advocate of Muslim political and social grievances, serving as a Muslim delegate to the Round Table Conferences, 1930–1932. In 1930 he was knighted by the British government, an honor which he subsequently resigned in 1946. Although well known as a proponent of Muslim separatism, in his later years he joined the Indian National Congress and opposed the demand for Pakistan. In 1946 he was assaulted by a Muslim extremist and ultimately died from the effects of the attack.

Shafa'at Ahmad Khan was deeply committed to the historical method of close analysis of documents. His historical study of the seventeenth-century English East India trade emphasized the development and impact of mercantilist theories on the English government's relations with the East India Company. He subsequently produced a major survey of English documentation on the same period. Although his political activities and public services lessened further opportunities for research, he remained a staunch advocate of objective, scientific historiography throughout his professional career. Beginning in 1920, he founded and edited the *Journal of Indian History*, relinquishing this post in 1924. He was president of the All India Modern History Congress at Poona in 1935, which laid the foundations for the new Indian History Congress two years later, of which he was a founding member and leader. He is credited with the conception of the *Comprehensive History of India* volumes sponsored by the Indian History Congress. These significant institutional contributions played a major role in the growth and influence of the historical profession in India.

Bibliography: Important works of S. A. Khan: *The East India Trade in the XVIIth Century in Its Political and Economic Aspects* (New Delhi: S. Chand, 1975, orig. pub. in 1923); *Sources for the History of British India in the Seventeenth Century* (London: Oxford University Press, 1926). Works concerning S. A. Khan: Naresh K. Jain, *Muslims in India:* A Biographical Dictionary, vol. 2 (New Delhi: Manohar, 1983), pp. 9–11; Bisheshwar Prasad, "Sir Shafaat Ahmad Khan," pp. 146–157, in S. P. Sen, ed., *Historian and Historiography in Modern India* (Calcutta: Institute of Historical Studies, 1973); "Shafa'at Ahmad Khan," *Journal of Indian History*, 25 (1947): 211–212.

Frank F. Conlon

KOSAMBI, Damodar Dharmanand (Kosben, Goa, 1907–Poona, 1966), Indian mathematician and historian. Kosambi was an eminent Indian mathematician whose personal intellectual interests led him into research on Indological subjects, such as the Sanskrit poetry of Bhartrihari and the *Subhasitaratnakosa* as well as the pre- and protohistory of the subcontinent. Wandering the Deccan plateau Kosambi collected microliths and discovered and analyzed megaliths, seeking to reconstruct the earliest history of human occupation in that region. Although he pursued history as an avocation, while sustaining research and theoretical insights in mathematics, Kosambi contributed nearly one hundred scholarly articles or essays on facets of ancient Indian history and culture. His application of statistical techniques to analysis of coin hoards proved a significant contribution to the developing field of Indian numismatics. Kosambi also developed an interpretation of historiography inspired in part by his own observations of the mosaic of Indian life and culture and in part by his reading of Marx and other materialist interpreters of history. He first presented this synthesis in *An Introduction to the Study of Indian History* (Bombay, 1956) and further developed these ideas in *Culture and Civilisation of Ancient India in Historical Outline* (London, 1965). Professional historians regarded both works as stimulating though unconventional.

Kosambi observed that "if history means only the succession of outstanding megalomaniac names and imposing battles, Indian history would be difficult to write. If however it is more important to know whether a given people had the plough or not than to know the name of their king, then India has a history. . . . History is the presentation in chronological order of successive changes in the means and relations of production" (*The Culture & Civilization of Ancient India In Historical Outline*, p. 10). Although he never held a professional academic appointment in history, Kosambi's works were influential in the field as they offered a critical and stimulating means toward rethinking the history of traditional India.

Bibliography: Important works by D. D. Kosambi: *The Culture & Civilization of Ancient India in Historical Outline* (London: Routledge & Kegan Paul, 1965) [published in United States under the title *Ancient India: A History of Its Culture and Civilization* (New York: Pantheon Books, 1965)]. Works about D. D. Kosambi: Dwijendra Narayan Jha, "D. D. Kosambi," pp. 121–132, in S. P. Sen, ed., *Historians and Historiography in Modern India* (Calcutta: Institute of Historical Research, 1973); Professor D. D. Kosambi Commemoration Committee, *Science and Human Progress* (Bombay: Popular Prakashan, 1974); *Exasperating Essays* (Poona: People's Book House, 1957); *Introduction to the Study of Indian History* (Bombay: Popular, 1956); *Myth & Reality: Studies in the Formation of Indian Culture* (Bombay: Popular, 1962).

Frank F. Conlon

KRISHNASWAMI AIYANGAR, Sakkottai (Sakkottai [Tamilnadu], 1871–Madras, 1947), Indian historian. Aiyangar played a prominent role in the modern development of historical studies of South India. His education was initially in the sciences at Central College, Bangalore, and he taught mathematics in schools before taking up the study of history, completing an M.A. degree in 1899. He joined Central College as a lecturer in history the following year, and in 1904 he became a professor of English. In 1914 the University of Madras created a new chair in Indian history and archaeology to which Krishnaswami Aiyangar was appointed. He held this professorship until 1929. In 1919 he lectured at Calcutta University on the contributions of South India to Indian civilization and received an honorary doctorate. In his career at Madras, Aiyangar produced a series of significant works that explicated the important developments of South Indian culture and history. His work, *Some Contributions of South India to Indian Culture* (1923), emphasized the South's traditions of ritual and devotionalism (*bhakti*) as well as the distinctive administrative forms of that region. His research on Tamil literature helped to establish the conventional chronology of South Indian history, and his contributions to the dynastic histories of the Pallavas and Cholas remain useful even today. His *South India and Her Muhammadan Invaders* (1921) analyzed South India from the decline of the Cholas to the rise of the Vijayanagar Empire. In 1930 he delivered the Sir William Meyer Lectures on the development of Hindu Administrative Institutions in South India.

Aiyangar also made a substantial professional contribution as an editor of scholarly journals. He was a founder of the Mythic Society of Bangalore and served as editor of its *Quarterly Journal*; later he served as joint editor of *Indian Antiquary*, and in 1924 he entered into long-term service as editor of the *Journal of Indian History*. During his tenure of over twenty-two years, he frequently took responsibility for the publication's financial burdens as well as its editorial content. Just before his death, he transferred the *Journal* to Travancore University (later the University of Kerala). He was active in the Indian History Congress and was its general president in 1940. That same year the Bombay Branch of the Royal Asiatic Society awarded him the Campbell Gold Medal in recognition of his lifetime contributions to the study of Indian history and civilization.

Bibliography: Other important works by S. K. Aiyangar: *Evolution of Hindu Administrative Institutions in South India* (Madras: University of Madras, 1931); *Sources of Vijayangar History* (Madras: University of Madras, 1919). Works concerning S. K. Aiyangar: G. S. Dikshit, "S. Krishnaswami Aiyangar," pp. 60–68, in S. P. Sen. ed., *Historians and Historiography in Modern India* (Calcutta: Institute of Historical Studies, 1973); *Dr. S. Krishnaswami Aiyangar Commemoration Volume* (Madras: S.K.A. Commemoration Committee, 1936).

Frank F. Conlon

MAJUMDAR, Romesh Chandra (Khandarpada, Bengal, India [now Bangladesh], 1888–Calcutta, 1980), Indian historian. Romesh Chandra Majumdar was probably modern India's most prolific and influential practitioner of the historian's craft. His college studies commenced at Brajamohan College, Barisal, continued at Ripon College, and concluded at Presidency College, Calcutta. At Calcutta University, he completed an M.A. degree in 1911, won the Premchand Roychand Studentship in 1912 for a thesis on the "AndhraKushana Age," and in 1918 published his Ph.D. dissertation, *Corporate Life in Ancient India*. He first taught at the Dacca Teachers' Training College, but joined the University of Calcutta Post-Graduate History Department in 1913. In 1921 he was appointed professor of history at Dacca University, becoming vice chancellor in 1937 and retiring in 1942. He later held visiting positions at Benares Hindu University, Nagpur University, University of Pennsylvania, and University of Chicago. He was active in the All India Oriental Conference, Asiatic Society of Bengal, and played a leading role in the Bharatiya Vidya Bhavan. He established his early reputation in the exploration of ancient Indian history and institutions and Indian influences in Southeast Asia. Subsequently, he participated in the University of Dacca's collaborative *History of Bengal* and, after independence, was named the general editor of the Bharatiya Vidya Bhavan's *The History and Culture of the Indian People*. Although each volume included contributions from many scholars, Majumdar himself produced many of the chapters on a wide range of topics.

In the later years of his career, Majumdar increasingly turned his attention to the history of modern India, producing a series of somewhat controversial studies on nineteenth-century Bengal, the Indian Mutiny of 1857, and a history of the freedom movement. Majumdar was an outspoken advocate of the view that an objective historian could measure his work only by reference to truth, expressed without fear or favor. He felt his historical perspectives to be rooted in objective readings of facts; yet in his later career from those readings he developed some controversial interpretations that contrasted significantly with conventional Indian historiographical views. One aspect of interpretation noted by many critics was the degree to which communalism and ethnic tensions between Hindu and Muslim religious communities were emphasized as long-term phenomena of Indian life and culture. With respect to 1857, Majumdar emphasized the parochial and reactionary elements over any hint of a birth of nationalist purpose. His emphasis on truth and objectivity did not always allow for the possibility of alternative truths, giving some of his later work a certain emotional quality. In recognizing this aspect, it must nonetheless be conceded that Majumdar was one of modern India's most influential historians whose breadth of study and prolific publication yielded a major body of significant works.

Bibliography: Important works by R. C. Majumdar: *Ancient Indian Colonies in the Far East*, 2 vols. (Lahore: Punjab Sanskrit Book Depot, 1927); *Corporate Life in Ancient India* (Calcutta, 1919); *Glimpses of Bengal in the Nineteenth Century* (Calcutta: Firma K. L. Mukhopadhyay, 1960); *Historiography in Modern India* (Bombay: Asia, 1970); *The History and Culture of the Indian People* (editor and author), 11 vols. (Bombay: Bharatiya Vidya Bhavan, 1951–1977); *History of Bengal, Vol. 1 (Hindu Period)* (Dacca: Dacca University, 1943); *History of the Freedom Movement in India*, 3 vols. (Calcutta: Firma K. L. Mukhopadhyay, 1961–1962); *The Sepoy Mutiny and the Revolt of 1857*, rev. ed. (Calcutta: Firma K. L. Mukhopadhyay, 1963). Works concerning R. C. Majumdar: Tarasankar Banerjee, "Ramesh Chandra Majumdar: The Historian of Indian Nationalism," *Journal of Indian History*, 59 (1981):347–360; H. B. Sarkar, "R. C. Majumdar and His Work on South and South-East Asia: A Panoramic Review (1888–1980)," *Journal of Indian History*, 60 (1982):306–329; Himansu Bhusan Sarkar, *R. C. Majumdar Felicitation Volume* (Calcutta: Firma K. L. Mukhopadhyay, 1970).

Frank F. Conlon

NILAKANTA SASTRI, Kallidaikurichi Aiyah Aiyar (Kallidaikuruchi, Tirunelveli Dt., Madras [Tamilnadu], 1892–Madras, 1975), Indian historian. Nilakanta Sastri was perhaps the most productive and influential recent Indian historian whose research emphasized the history and culture of far southern India. Sastri assumed his first teaching position following completion of his M.A., when he became a lecturer in Hindu College, Tirunelveli (Tinnevely), (1913–1918), followed by a year as professor at Benaras Hindu University (1919–1920), and then service as principal of Sree Meenakshi College, Chidambaram, to 1928. From 1929 until retirement in 1947, Sastri was successor to Sakkattai Krishnaswami Aiyangar (q.v.) as professor of Indian history and archaeology at the University of Madras. He held a professorship in Indology at the University of Mysore (1952–1956) before returning to Madras to head the Unesco Institute of Traditional Cultures of South East Asia (1957–1971). Sastri's first book was *The Pandyan Kingdom* (London, 1929), which presaged his long-term commitment and contributions to the history of the far South. Much of his work over the next two decades involved the patient working out of a plausible and documented chronology of South Indian history, emphasizing political developments. In his publications Sastri set patterns and priorities for historical research on the far South which remained dominant until very recently. He published *Foreign Notices of South India* in 1939, and two years later he took up questions of *Historical Method in Relation to Problems of South Indian History* (1941), which he later revised and enlarged to relate to Indian history generally in 1956.

Following his retirement from Madras in 1947, he published several further studies on South India as well as South Indian relations with Southeast Asia, and in 1955 he produced a landmark survey of South India's history from prehistoric times to the fall of Vijayanagar in the sixteenth century. In southern India, particularly Tamilnadu, interpretation of regional history could not be entirely divorced from public controversies arising from the sociocultural and political platforms of the Dravidian and non-Brahman movements regarding Aryan-northern influences. Within this context, throughout his career, Nilakanta Sastri emphasized the special circumstances of the far South and its history, yet stated in his *History of South India* that "History begins in South of India as in the North with the advent of the Aryans" (p. 68).

Not all of Sastri's twenty-five books were on South India. He edited the *Age of the Nandas and Mauryas* (1952) and *A Comprehensive History of India, Vol. 2: The Mauryas and Satavahanas* (1957), as well as three general surveys of India's history. While new interpretations of the nature of state and economy have called into question some of Nilakanta Sastri's views on southern India's past, his contributions represent the most extensive and influential work on that region by any modern historian.

Bibliography: Other important works of K. A. Nilakanta Sastri: *The Colas*, rev. ed. (Madras: University of Madras, 1955, orig. pub. in 2 vols., 1935–1937); *A History of South India from Prehistoric Times to the Fall of Vijayanagar*, 4th ed. (Madras: Oxford University Press, 1976; orig. pub. 1955); *Studies in Cola History and Administration* (Madras: University of Madras, 1932); (w/ N. Venkataramanayya), *Further Sources of Vijayanagar History* (Madras: University of Madras, 1946). Works concerning K. A. Nilakanta Sastri: S. Ganesan et al., eds., *Professor K. A. Nilakanta Sastri Felicitation Volume* (Madras, Committee, 1971); G. Subbiah, "K. A. Nilakanta Sastri (1892–1975)," *Journal of Indian History* 60 (1982):331–346.

Frank F. Conlon

PANIKKAR, Sardar Kavalam Madhava (Kavalam, Kerala, 1895–Mysore, 1963), Indian diplomat and historian. Much of Panikkar's career lay not in the study of history, but in the making of it as a journalist, government servant, and diplomat. Following his education in Madras and Oxford, he took up an appointment at Aligarh Muslim University (1919), but left teaching for journalism and service for various Indian princely states. After 1947 Panikkar played a pivotal role as India's ambassador to the People's Republic of China. Panikkar's historical training manifested itself in *Indian States and the Government of India* (1932), based on his Calcutta University Readership Lectures. While he initially wrote on early India as in his *Sri Harsha of Kanauj* (1922), he later turned to the history of his native Kerala's encounter with colonialism, *Malabar and the Portuguese*, and *Malabar and the Dutch* (1931), which saw reincarnation as *A History of Kerala, 1498–1801* (1960). His period in state service in Kashmir and Patiala led, perhaps not coincidentally, to a historical biography of *Gulab Singh* (1930), followed by *The Indian Prince in Council—A Record of the Chancellorship of His Highness the Maharaja of Patiala* [on the Chamber of

Princes] (1936). Just prior to his appointment to Bikaner's service, Panikkar published *His Highness the Maharaja of Bikaner: A Biography* (1937). His diplomatic career in the era of Jawaharlal Nehru's nonalignment policy further stimulated Panikkar's earlier interest in the issues surrounding European colonialism in Asia. Panikkar's belief in an ideal of Asian solidarity was evident in what would be his most popular and influential work, *Asia and Western Dominance* (1953), which offered a critical analysis of European colonial expansion and domination in what he termed the Gama epoch of Asian history, 1498 to 1945. Some Western reviewers criticized the work for its open skepticism of the positive contributions of Western colonialism in Asia and an underlying hostility to Christian missionaries. It was precisely this quality—that of looking at the history of colonialism from an Asian point of view—that defined Panikkar's achievement and his influence.

Apart from his careful early work on the Indian states, Panikkar's importance as a historian rested more on his ability to consolidate and articulate a new postcolonial view of Asian and Indian history than in any detailed monograph grounded in archival research. His history was a history for a new era of a new India in a new Asia. His *A Survey of Indian History* (1947 and twelve reprints to 1962) provided a literate narrative of India's national past written clearly from an Indian perspective. Panikkar's interest in reorienting Indian historiography may be seen in *India and the Indian Ocean—An Essay on the Influence of Sea Power on Indian History* (1945) which emphasized independent India's need to grow as a maritime power. In *Geographical Factors in Indian History* (1955) he emphasized the possibilities of subcontinental political unity, while *The Determining Periods of Indian History* (1963) stressed that that unity ultimately rested on a continuity and integration of the Hindu community.

Bibliography: Tarasankar Banerjee, *Sardar K. M. Panikkar: The Profile of a Historian* (Calcutta: Ratna Prakashan, 1977); K. K. N. Kurup, ''Sardar K. M. Panikkar (1895–1963),'' *Journal of Indian History*, 60 (1982):347–363; K. M. Panikkar, *An Autobiography* (Madras: Oxford University Press, 1977).

Frank F. Conlon

PISSURLENCAR, Pandurang Sakharam Shenvi (Pissurlem, Goa, 1894–Panaji, Goa, 1969), Indian historian and archivist. Pissurlencar was an important promoter of modern historical studies on the Portuguese in India. Educated in Marathi and Portuguese schools, in 1916 he entered the Escola Normal for a teacher training course. Beginning in 1916 he held appointments as primary school teacher of mathematics and Portuguese. Although without formal historical training, Pissurlencar developed a scholarly interest in Indian history and wrote two Portuguese-language textbooks based on secondary materials on ancient India (1922, 1925). Jadunath Sarkar (q.v.) is said to have urged Pissurlencar to study Portuguese India where he could make a real contribution. Pissurlencar began publishing articles in local journals based on documentation found in the Goa Archives. In 1931 he was appointed head of the General and Historical

Archives of Portuguese India, which he held until retirement in 1961. Finding the archives to be deteriorating and poorly organized, he devoted much of his career to rectifying these conditions. He published a handbook to the Goa Archives, *Rotiero dos Arquivos da India Portuguesa* (1955), which made the collection's rich historical content accessible to scholars. Following the end of Portuguese rule in Goa (1969), Pissurlencar made a substantial contribution to continued development of historical research on Portuguese India through donation of his library and manuscript collection to a newly established Centre of Historical Research. He was made the Centre's director and appointed an honorary professor of history of Bombay University. In addition to making the documentary record of Portuguese India available for research, Pissurlencar published source materials and wrote useful historical narratives. His *Regimentos das Fortalezas da India* (Ordinances for the Fortresses of India) (1951) provides data on the Portuguese ports and enclaves and Portuguese administrative and commercial policies around the Arabian Sea from Mozambique to Ceylon. In *Agentes da Diplomacia Portuguesa na India* (1952; Agents of Portuguese Diplomacy in India), he opened vistas on Portuguese relations with Indian powers as well as throwing unique light on the considerable dependence of the Portuguese Indian state on Indian agents and representatives. He next published *Assentos do Conselho do Estado* (1953–1957) (Proceedings of the Council of State) covering the period 1618–1750. He also produced a series of studies on the relations of the Portuguese and the Marathas.

Pissurlencar was officially recognized for his many contributions to archival and historical activity in the awarding of a knighthood (*chevalier*) by the Portuguese government in 1952. He received gold medals from the Asiatic Societies of Bengal and Bombay in 1948 and 1953, respectively, and was awarded an honorary D. Litt. degree by the University of Lisbon in 1956. Pissurlencar played a crucial role in the modern historiography of Portuguese India. Apart from his own contributions as a historian, his organization and preservation of the historical archives at Goa saved a major repository for future research scholars. However, because his education had been in Marathi and Portuguese, his writings appeared almost entirely in those languages. Consequently, his work has not enjoyed as wide a scholarly audience in India as those historians who have published work in English.

Bibliography: Important works by P.S.S. Pissurlencar: *Agentes de Diplomacia Portuguesa na India* (Portuguese Diplomatic Agents in India), (Bastora: Tipografia Rangel, 1952); *Portuguese-Mahratta Relations*, translated from the Marathi by T. V. Parvate (Bombay: Maharashtra State Board for Literature & Culture, 1983). Work concerning P.S.S. Pissurlencar: B. S. Shastry, "P.S.S. Pissurlencar," pp. 385–395, in S. P. Sen, ed., *Historians and Historiography in Modern India* (Calcutta: Institute of Historical Studies, 1973); *Regimentos das Fortalezas da India* (Ordinances for the Fortresses of India (1951).

Frank F. Conlon

RAJWADE, Vishwanath Kashinath (Poona (Pune), 1864–Dhulia (Dhule), Maharashtra, 1926), Indian historian. Rajwade was a major contributor to the growth and development of historical studies in the western Indian region of Maharashtra, primarily in the field of Maratha history. Born and raised in modest circumstances, Rajwade attended Wilson and Elphinstone Colleges in Bombay before completing his studies at Deccan College, Poona, finally receiving his B.A. degree in 1890. He taught in Poona for several years. By 1893, having lost his wife and children to illness, he resolved to take up a life of scholarly exploration, collecting and later editing and publishing old documents of the Maratha period. He also edited periodicals and wrote pieces for various news-papers and journals. Beginning in 1898, he began publishing his "Collection of Maratha History" (*Marathyancya Itihasaci Sadhane*), which continued to appear until the twenty-second volume in 1921. This series contained copies of a wide variety of Marathi language historical documents which Rajwade had uncovered. He wandered through western India seeking historical family papers from the era of Maratha rule, collecting originals in a few cases and making copies in most. It has been reported that because his knowledge of Persian was limited, he did not collect many documents available in that language. The accuracy of his copies also has been the subject of critical comment.

An ardent nationalist, Rajwade strongly advocated the exclusive use of Indian languages by Indians. In his own case all of his publications were exclusively in the Marathi language, in which his own writing was particularly direct and sharp. According to N. R. Phatak (1972), "Rajwade's intellect was penetrating and his insight subtle, his capacity to work and tenacity were tremendous." His nationalism led him to avoid requests for official patronage from the British government. This meant that most of Rajwade's work was carried out on a hand-to-mouth basis with restricted resources. Seeking to provide alternatives to gov-ernmental patronage for historical scholarship, he launched what would become the premier institution for the study of Maratha history—the Bharatiya Itihasa Samshodak Mandala at Poona, although he soon left the organization and settled at Dhulia to pursue an independent research career. The subject of Maratha history was not without contemporary political and social significance. In an era of burgeoning anti-Brahmanism, Rajwade's caste identity and his interpretations of the relationship of Shivaji and Samarth Ramdas would inevitably be the objects of criticism. His views on some aspects of Maharashtrian history as expressed in his introductions and monographs were sometimes idiosyncratic. While some of Rajwade's conclusions may be open to debate, his work as a collector and a compiler of Maharashtra's historical documentary legacy constitutes an enduring contribution to the modern study of history.

Bibliography: Important works by V. K. Rajwade (all in Marathi): *Marathyancya Itihasaci Sadhane*, 22 vols. (Wai, Kolhapur, Pune, Mumbai, Dhule, various publishers, 1898–1921); *Shrisamartha Ramadasa* (Satara: Vinayak Shankar Vaidya, Sh. 1848, i.e., A.D. 1926). Works concerning V. K. Rajwade: G. H. Khare, "Vishwanath Kashinath Rajwade," pp. 200–206, in S. P. Sen, ed., *Historians and Historiography in Modern India* (Calcutta: Institute of Historical Studies, 1973); N. R. Phatak, "Research and Writing of History in Maharashtra," pp. 148–156, in J. P. De Souza and C. M. Kulkarni, eds., *Historiography in Indian Languages* (Delhi: Oriental Publishers, 1972); Vi. Ka. Rajvade, "Rajvadyance Atmakathan," (Rajwade's Autobiography), pp. 1–22, in Ra. Pra. Kanitkar, ed., *Rajvade Darshan* (Marathi, A Vision of Rajwade), (Pune: Modern Book Depot Prakashan, 1965).

Frank F. Conlon

SARDESAI, Govind Sakharam (Hasol, Ratnagiri Dt., Maharashtra, 1865–Kamshet, Maharashtra, 1959), Indian historian. Sardesai, a leading historian of Maharashtra and the Marathas, was educated in rural schools of Ratnagiri District of the erstwhile Bombay Presidency, passed the matriculation examination in 1884, and entered the elite Elphinstone College, Bombay, from where he passed the B.A. examination of Bombay University in 1888. The following year he joined the service of the princely state of Baroda, first as a reader to the Maharaja, and later as an administrator of accounts. As a member of the Maharaja's entourage, he visited Europe on four occasions. At the instance of Maharaja Sayajirao, Sardesai translated Machiavelli's *The Prince* and Seeley's *Expansion of England* into Marathi. Subsequently, Sardesai was placed in charge of tutoring the princes of Baroda and began writing a Marathi narrative of the history of the lineage and of the Marathas generally. The first two volumes, *Masalmani Riyasat*, were published in 1898. He then began what would be an eight-volume work, *Marathi Riyasat* (1902–1922). These dense volumes contain lengthy extracts of contemporary documents. As such, this work was the only detailed history of the Marathas from Shahaji through to the dissolution of the princely state of Satara. Sardesai followed these works with two volumes, *British Riyasat* (1923–39), covering the emergence of British domination in the subcontinent to 1858. The *Riyasat* volumes are vast collections of documents made available in modern Marathi print, presented without extensive analysis of reliability of source and sometimes without evaluation of events or actors. Sardesai was a longtime friend of another major Indian historian, Jadunath Sarkar (q.v.), who arranged for him to deliver a series of lectures in English on the history of the Marathas. These lectures were published as *Main Currents of Maratha History* in 1926 and brought Sardesai to a wider public audience.

A few years later Sardesai was appointed to edit a series of volumes of documents selected from the Peshwa Daftar, a surviving collection of manuscript documents from the time of Maratha rule. These were put into modern Marathi script in a forty-five volume set, followed by a collection of *Poona Residency Correspondence* edited in collaboration with his colleague Sarkar. Sardesai published *The New History of the Marathas*, a three-volume narrative devoted almost exclusively to political history. Sardesai perceived a need to communicate to a wider audience beyond Maharashtra, fearing that the preference of Maharashtrians for writing in Marathi was cutting the region's history off from the interests of other Indian scholars who did not know that language. He observed that "the Marathas have long been misjudged by their rivals and adversaries and painted in the blackest colours both during and after the period of their downfall." The resulting narrative reflects Sardesai's long-term historiographical orientation. The *New History* was a history of politics and public affairs with little attention to social or economic developments. Nevertheless, as such it represented an important and accessible synthesis of Maratha history for those readers who do not read Marathi.

Bibliography: Important works of G. S. Sardesai: *Hindusthanaca Arvacin Itihasa: Marathi Riyasat* (History of Modern India: Maratha Rule), 13 vols. (Bombay: various publishers, 1902–1944); *Hindusthanaca Arvacin Itihasa: Musalmani Riyasat* (History of Modern India: Muslim Rule), 4 vols. (Baroda and Bombay: various publishers, 1898–1932); *Main Currents of Maratha History* (rev. & enl., Bombay: Phoenix Publications, 1958; orig. pub., 1926); *New History of the Marathas*, 3 vols. (Bombay: Phoenix Publications, 1946–1948); Editor, *Selections from the Peshwa Dafter*, 45 vols. (Bombay: Government Central Press, 1929–1933); Editor, w/ Jadunath Sarkar, *English Records of Maratha History: Poona Residency Correspondence* (Bombay: Government Central Press, 1936–1958). Works concerning G. S. Sardesai: Sir Jadunath Sarkar, "Govind Sakharam Sardesai," pp. 291–304 in S. R. Tikekar, ed., *Sardesai Commemoration Volume* (Bombay: Keshav Bhikaji Dhawale, 1938); S. R. Tikekar, *On Historiography: A Study of Methods of Historical Research and Narration of J. N. Sarkar, G. S. Sardesai and P. K. Gode* (Bombay: Popular, 1964).

Frank F. Conlon

SARKAR, (Sir) Jadunath (Karachmaria, Rajshahi district, Bengal, 1870–Calcutta, 1958), Indian historian. Sir Jadunath Sarkar was one of India's leading historians specializing on the Mughal period. Educated in Rajshahi and Calcutta, he entered Presidency College, Calcutta, completing his B.A. in 1891 with double honors in English and history, and in 1892 he passed the M.A. examination in English literature. While teaching English literature at Calcutta colleges, Sarkar pursued and won the Premchand Roychand Scholarship (1897), and the following year he entered the Provincial Educational Service. He served as professor of English at Presidency College, Calcutta and Patna, where he shifted to the History Department, serving there until 1917. After one year at Benaras Hindu University, he joined the Indian Educational Service and was at Ravenshaw College, Cuttack, from 1919 to 1923 when he returned to Patna, where he retired in 1926. He was then appointed vice chancellor of Calcutta University until 1928. In 1929 he was knighted. Other recognition of his work included appointment as honorary fellow of the Royal Asiatic Society of Great Britain and Ireland, Asiatic Society of Bengal, and Honorary Life Member of the American Historical Association. This recognition was the byproduct of Sarkar's monumental contributions to the study of Mughal India. His prize thesis, *The India of Aurangzib, Its Topography, Statistics and Roads*, was published in 1901. Thereafter he wrote a five-volume history of the reign of the Mughal Emperor Aurangzib. In the same period he produced *Shivaji and His Times*, a study of Mughal administration and a translation of a life of the Bengali saint, Chaitanya. In conjunction with Govind S. Sardesai, he edited volumes of the Poona Residency Correspondence, while taking up a four-volume study of the

Fall of the Mughal Empire. He wrote a total of eighteen books, edited and/or translated thirteen other volumes, and wrote innumerable articles and essays.

Sarkar's reputation lay not in the sheer bulk of his productivity, but in his sustained use of a method of research that required collection and analysis of all relevant medieval chronicles, diaries, court newsletters, and so on. Sarkar collected hundreds of documents, and subjected them to intense textual criticism. Because he publicly doubted the veracity of some of these medieval sources, he found them, particularly in the case of certain Maratha documents, to be sources of controversy. His unwillingness to exempt the Maratha hero Shivaji from criticism led to strong antipathy toward Sarkar by many Maharashtrians. On the other hand, probably his closest friend and academic colleague was a leading Maratha historian, Govind S. Sardesai. While Sarkar emphasized the careful and exhaustive analysis of original medieval documentation, his presentation of historical materials did not simply reproduce the Mughal chroniclers. He urged that an accurate understanding of the large-scale forces operating in the subcontinent in Mughal times and of the failures of both Mughals and Marathas would better serve the needs of modern Indians than a thoughtless patriotic broadside.

Bibliography: Selected important works by Sir Jadunath Sarkar: *Fall of the Mughal Empire*, 4 vols. (Calcutta. M. C. Sarkar & Sons, 1932–1950); *History of Aurangzib*, 5 vols. (Calcutta: M. C. Sarkar & Sons, 1912–1924); *House of Shivaji* (Calcutta: M. C. Sarkar & Sons, 1940); *Maasir-i-Alamgiri: A History of the Emperor Aurangzib-Alamgir of Saqi Mustaid Khan* (Calcutta: Asiatic Society, 1947); *The India of Aurangzib—Topography, Statistics and Roads* (Calcutta: Bose Brothers, 1901); *Shivaji and His Times* (Calcutta: M. C. Sarkar & Sons, 1919); *Short History of Aurangzib* (Calcutta: M. C. Sarkar & Sons, 1930); Editor, *History of Bengal, Volume II* (Dacca: Dacca University, 1948). Works about Sir Jadunath Sarkar: Hari Ram Gupta, ed., *Life and Letters of Sir Jadunath Sarkar* (Hoshiarpur: Panjab University, 1958) (vol. 1 of Sir Jadunath Sarkar Commemoration Volume); Kirin Pawar, *Sir Jadunath Sarkar: A Profile in Historiography* (New Delhi: Books & Books, 1985); A. L. Srivastava, "Sir Jadunath Sarkar," in S. P. Sen, ed., *Historians and Historiography in Modern India* (Calcutta: Institute of Historical Studies, 1973), pp. 132–145.

Frank F. Conlon

SEN, Surendra Nath (Mahilara, Dt. Barisal, Bengal [now Bangladesh], 1890– Calcutta, 1962), Indian historian. Sen's professional career as historian provides a remarkable picture of broad intellectual interests and careful scholarship in a wide variety of subjects and periods. He began his higher education in Brajmohan College, Barisal, passing the First Arts examination of Calcutta University, but was forced by poverty to interrupt his studies with work as a primary school teacher in rural Bengal. He completed his B.A. at Dacca College in 1913 and his M.A. in 1915. He was appointed professor of history, Robertson College, Jabalpur, in 1916–1917 and then joined the new Post-Graduate History Department of Calcutta University in 1917 as lecturer. He won the Premchand Roychand scholarship and completed a thesis on Maratha administration, in recognition of which he received the Ph.D. in 1927. In 1925 he went to Oxford for the B. Litt.

degree. Upon returning to Calcutta, he was appointed in 1931 to the new Asutosh Professorship of Medieval and Modern Indian History. In 1939 he joined the government of India as keeper of imperial records, a position which at independence became director of the National Archives of India. In 1949 he was appointed professor of history at Delhi University, and from 1950 to 1953 he served as vice chancellor. During 1957–1958 he was visiting professor of Indian history at the University of Wisconsin. In 1958 Oxford University conferred the degree of D. Litt *honoris causa* in recognition of his contributions.

Sen's initial historical research at Calcutta into the history of the Marathas represented something of a breakthrough from the prevalent pattern of interest and research on ancient India. He made careful study of Marathi, Persian, and Portuguese. His works included a translation of the *Sabhasad Bakhar, Siva Chhatrapati* (1920), and a compilation, *Foreign Biographies of Shivaji* (1927). Unlike many contemporaries, Sen showed an interest in institutional history, and in his *Administrative System of the Marathas* (1923) he revealed the Maratha rule to have been a complex and effective one contrary to portrayals by British historians. During his period at Oxford, he also wrote the *Military System of the Marathas* (1928). Thereafter Sen's work on Maratha topics was limited to a series of papers brought together in essay collections, *Studies in Indian History* (1930) and *Early Career of Kanhoji Angria and Other Papers* (1941). He was among the founders of, and an active participant in, the Indian History Congress, serving as general president of its 1944 Madras session. He was an organizer of the History Congress' *Comprehensive History of India* project, although the press of work and health prevented him from completing his assigned volume in the series. After his appointment as keeper of imperial records, he served *ex officio* as secretary to the Indian Historical Records Commission. While at the Archives, Sen edited two works—a compilation of eighteenth- and nineteenth-century Bengali documents and a collection of accounts of European travelers to India. His final historical work was *Eighteen Fifty-seven* (1957) which had been commissioned by the government of India. Although he had to complete the task in less than two years and faced a subject fraught with enormous documentation and emotional patriotic significance, Sen consistently put forward a dispassionate analysis, neither blindly accepting that the 1857 movement had been a "national war of independence," save possibly in two regions, nor pronouncing it to be purely a military mutiny. The work reflected the dominant theme of Sen's career—dedication to an ideal of objective historiography in all research. In his own work as a scholar and teacher, as an organizer and as an archivist, he set a high standard of energy and objectivity for all who would study the history of the subcontinent, while leaving behind studies that remain standard works more than a half century later.

Bibliography: Anil Chandra Banerjee, "Dr. Surendra Nath Sen," pp. 352–358 in S. P. Sen, ed., *Historians and Historiography in Modern India* (Calcutta: Institute of Historical Studies, 1973); Nilmani Mukherjee, "Late Dr. Surendra Nath Sen," *Quarterly Review of Historical Studies*, 1 (1962–1963):54.

Frank F. Conlon

SINHA, Narendra Krishna (Chatarpur, Rajshahi dt., Bengal, 1903–Calcutta, 1974), Indian historian. Sinha was a distinguished pioneer in the study of the economic history of Bengal. He entered Rajshahi College where he passed the First Arts examination in the first division with "distinction" in history. He then entered Presidency College in Calcutta and graduated in 1924 with First Class History honors. In 1926 he completed a master of arts degree in History at Calcutta University before commencing research on the history of the Sikh ruler, Ranjit Singh. This work won for him the Premchand Roychand Studentship in 1931, and the Ph.D. degree was awarded in 1936. His *Ranjit Singh* (1933) and *Rise of the Sikh Power* (1936) were both skilled examples of what might be called conventional political history. Thereafter he turned to the study of Bengal's social and economic structure in the eighteenth century. Each of his three volumes on the subject varied in style and content. The first (1956) was a densely documented survey of the decline of Bengali trade and manufacturing in the eighteenth century. Sinha also discovered and began to report on the world of the Indian traders. In his second volume (1962) he reassessed the agrarian system in Bengal at the end of the Mughal age and the opening of East India Company rule (or misrule). Finally, in Volume three (1970) Sinha returned to the familiar world of Calcutta trade and commerce, leaving the later history of agrarian life to others.

In his research Sinha was deeply committed to the significance of the act of dealing with primary documents, and he played a major role in the Indian Historical Records Commission in locating and preserving significant materials. He edited a volume published in the Fort William–India House Correspondence series as well as an important source of economic and social data, the *Midnapore Salt Papers (1781–1807)* (1954). Sinha's approach to economic history was not directly influenced by modern econometric models or by ideological priorities. His viewpoint was pragmatic, and shortly before his death Professor Sinha described his methodology as "home made." He thought that "one need not necessarily seek the security of methodological shelter or advance along ideological tram–lines. There must not be any devaluation of common sense." True to his dictum, Narendra Krishna Sinha laid the foundation for all future research on the economic history of modern Bengal and left a legacy of stimulating interpretations toward the rethinking of the history of eighteenth-century India.

Bibliography: Important works by N. K. Sinha: *The Economic History of Bengal, from Plassey to the Permanent Settlement*, 3 vols. (Calcutta: Firma K. L. Mukhopadhyay (1956–1970); Editor, *History of Bengal, 1757–1905* (Calcutta: University of Calcutta, 1967). Works concerning N. K. Sinha: Tarasankar Banerjee, "Narendra Krishna Sinha: The Scholar Extraordinary (1903–1974)," *Journal of Indian History*, 60 (1982): 375–390; Ashin Das Gupta, "On Narendra Krishna Sinha, The Historian," *Bengal Past and Present* 95 (January–June, 1976): unpaginated, [pp. i–vii].

Frank F. Conlon

Great Historians: Irish

LECKY, William Edward Hartpole (Newton Park, County Dublin, 1838–London, 1903), Irish historian and essayist. Born into a prosperous and well-connected Irish family, Lecky belonged to the long line of gentlemen scholars and men of letters that had distinguished British historiography during the eighteenth and nineteenth centuries. Educated at Trinity College, Dublin, he was encouraged by his undergraduate reading of Henry Thomas Buckle's (q.v.) *History of Civilization in England* always to tackle the large subject. His first book, *The Rise and Influence of Rationalism in Europe* (1865), published when he was twenty-seven years old, traced the history of "the mental tendency" in Western culture since the Middle Ages to apply reason to natural and social phenomena, with the consequent decline of magic, witchcraft, a sense of the miraculous, and religious persecution and an increasing secularization of politics. His second book, *History of European Morals from Augustus to Charlemagne* (1869), studied the rise of those Christian perspectives and ideals whose decline he had recorded in the first volume. Discursive, diffuse, often based on evidence too slender to support the assertions, the narrative in the two works still flows easily like a broad river, the observations are sensible if shallow, and the total effect was pleasing to the rationalistic educated public of his day. The two books won Lecky instant literary success and admission to the most select London literary circles. However, his lasting fame as a historian rests on his eight-volume *History of England During the Eighteenth Century* (1878–1890) on which he spent nineteen years. Based on wide research in the primary printed and manuscript sources, he came closer than any other historian of his generation to resolving the central problem of the New History: how in the history of a national society to make a synthesis of social forces and then to make it move. In his own words his aim was "to disengage from the great mass of facts those which relate to the permanent forces of the nation, or which indicate some of the more enduring features of national life. The growth or decline of the monarchy, the aristocracy, and the democracy, of the Church and of Dissent, of the agricultural, the manufacturing and the commercial interests; the increasing power of Parliament and of the press; the history of political ideas, of art, manners, and of belief; the changes that have taken place in the social and economical condition of the people; the influences that have modified national character; the relations of the mother country to its dependencies . . . form the main subjects of this book.'' (vol. 1, v–vi) Although his anxiety to refute "the calumnies" of James Anthony Froude (q.v.) with respect to the Irish people led him to devote a disproportionate amount of space to Ireland, his fascinating interwoven history of British politics and society is still worth reading for its substance and method.

   Bibliography: James J. Auchmuty, *Lecky: A Biographical and Critical Study* (Dublin and London, 1945); Charles F. Mullett, "W. E. H. Lecky (1938–1903)," in Herman Ausubel, J. Bartlet Brebner, and Erling M. Hunt, eds., *Some Modern Historians of Britain* (New York, 1951), pp. 128–149.

Harold T. Parker

Great Historians: Italian

ALBERTINI, Luigi (Ancona, 1871–Rome, 1941), Italian historian. Owner/ director of the *Corriere della Sera* of Milan from 1900 to 1925 and senator of the realm from 1915 to 1929. Albertini also briefly served as editor of a liberalist economic journal, *Credito e Cooperazione*, from 1895 to 1896, and served as Italy's chief delegate to the Washington Naval Disarmament Conference in 1921. His first work was a slim volume entitled *La questione delle otto ore di lavoro* (The Eight Hour Question) (1894) stemming from his experience with Salvatore Cognetti de Martiis and Luigi Einaudi (q.v.) in the Laboratorio di Economia Politica. In this work, a young Albertini supported the classic nineteenth-century liberal belief in the stabilizing goodness and common sense of the middle classes and in liberalism as a method of government based on liberty and legitimate authority. Sensitive to the condition of the working classes, he nevertheless insisted that only sound social legislation from the governing class could alleviate the plight of the laboring poor. The seeds of a consistent ideology of conservative liberalism were planted here and grew steadily when Albertini joined Milan's *Corriere della Sera* in 1896 and soon made it Italy's greatest and most influential daily newspaper until his ouster by Benito Mussolini in 1925. In self-imposed exile within Italy, he opposed the fascist regime in memorable Senate speeches, later published as *In difesa della libertà* (1947; In Defense of Liberty). Albertini left the Senate in 1929 and in bitter retirement wrote his major historical works. He was watched and hounded by the fascist authorities and suffered physical and moral debilitation after 1938.

Albertini died in 1941, before completing, and perhaps revising, his monumental memoirs, *Venti anni di vita politica* (5 vols., 1950–1953; Twenty Years of Political Life). These important volumes cover a period from 1898 to 1918 and were meant to be ''an outpouring of a liberal faith and a lesson for the

future,'' a paean to ''the principle of liberty,'' which Albertini never lived to
see revived. This represents history as moral exhortation and, at its most profound, history as polemic. At this level, *Venti anni di vita politica* is a relentless
sustained indictment of Giovanni Giolitti and Giolittism, the betrayal of the
liberal state of the Risorgimento to those forces subversive of it—clericalism
and socialism. While Albertini failed to reach his projected goal and his memoirs
stop at 1918, rather than 1925, he used every opportunity to draw a straight line
from Giolitti to Mussolini. The work is characterized by meticulous and scrupulous documentation, but on domestic policy this translated into a vindication
of the political line of Albertini's editorials and the policy of his own newspaper.
The history of a newspaper becomes the history of an epoch in Italy and in
Europe, a magnum opus that falls somewhere between history and memoirs.
But this does not detract from a work that is an extremely valuable historical
source, reconstructing and illuminating a crucial and turbulent period through
the prism of the mind of one of its greatest figures. A chapter in the memoirs
planned on the crisis of July 1914 blossomed into the publication that firmly
established Albertini's reputation as historian, *Le origini della guerra del 1914*
(1943), translated and published in English as *The Origins of the War of 1914*
(3 vols., 1952–1957). Remarkably objective, though clearly imputing responsibility for the outbreak of war in 1914 to the Central Powers, and especially
Germany, minutely detailed, this is the definitive military-diplomatic history of
the origins of the Great War. Albertini, and his friend and collaborator, Luciano
Magrini, interviewed the primary players and actors from the various governments, and also examined the relevant archival sources from the Congress of
Berlin in 1878 to war in 1914. The objective integrity of the study is enhanced
by the fact that it was written prior to World War II and is not colored by the
harsher anti-German revisionism of the post–World War II period. Also published
posthumously, Albertini's correspondence, *Epistolario, 1911–1926*, 4 vols. (ed.
Ottavio Bariè) (1968), is itself a rich font of historical information.

Bibliography: Alberto Albertini, *Vita di Luigi Albertini* [Life of Luigi Albertini] (Milan,
1945); Ottavio Bariè, *Luigi Albertini* (Turin, 1972); Paul J. Devendittis, ''Luigi Albertini:
Conservative Liberalism in Thought and Practice,'' *European Studies Review*, no. 1
(1976): 139–147; Giovanni Spadolini, ''Un ventennio di vita politica,'' in *Il mondo di
Giolitti* (The World of Giolitti), (Florence, 1969), pp. 48–70.

                                                                    Paul J. Devendittis

AMARI, Michele Benedetto Gaetano (Palermo, 1806–Florence, 1889), Sicilian historian, statesman, and patriot. Imbibing liberal, democratic, and atheistic
sympathies from his grandfather and other family members, the youthful Amari,
who took ''his last communion at age twelve'' and studied metaphysics at the
university at thirteen without believing in it, although having become a clerk in
the Bourbon bureaucracy at fourteen, enrolled in the Carbonari and supported
the revolutionaries of 1820. In the meantime Amari continued to work in the
Bourbon service while preparing for the day of revolution by physical condi-

tioning, hunting, devouring history, and reading French and English authors: Voltaire, Rousseau, Shakespeare, most of the English poets, and above all Scott, in whose fantasies his imagination and veneration of the past fired romanticism in contrast to the rationalism of Hume and Gibbon. His book, *Un Periodo delle storie Siciliane del XIII secolo* (1839), ostensibly on the Sicilian Vespers, contained oblique criticisms of the Bourbon regime, and Amari narrowly escaped arrest in 1842. He made his home in Paris, earning a tenuous living by writing, and met such great literary figures as Augustin Thierry (q.v.) and Jules Michelet (q.v.). Though consorting with Italian political exiles, he also read French translations of Muslim works on Sicily, which inspired him to learn Arabic when he was already approaching forty. As the gradual ascent of Cavour in Italy confounded his democratic hopes, he turned increasingly to Arabic studies which began to bear fruit in translations, commentaries, and monographs. When his *Observations of the Public Law of Sicily* urging the restoration of the liberal constitution of 1812 won acclaim, he went to Palermo from which the Bourbons had been evicted. After being appointed to the War Committee and a chair in law at the university, he was also elected a deputy from Palermo to the Provisional Assembly, which named him minister of finance (in the Stabile Cabinet). After its collapse, he went as emissary to Paris and London to beg help for the faltering revolution. Failing to get any, he retired in 1849 to fight on the island, which Bourbon troops had meanwhile regained. Back in Paris Amari resumed his pursuit of the history of Sicily under the Arabs, supporting himself exiguously by cataloguing Arabic manuscripts in the Bibliothèque Nationale, where he became conservator. After the uprisings of 1859, Amari received chairs of Arabic first at Pisa and then at Florence. After Garibaldi liberated Sicily, he received a government post there where, although proudly Sicilian, he enthusiastically endorsed union with the kingdom ruled by Victor Emmanuel. After having served as minister of education in two cabinets, he went back to his chair at Florence, dying, having gained many honors and respect for his erudition from friends around the world.

From Amari's first essay in 1832 on *Marmion* by Sir Walter Scott, his productivity remained prolific in the area of literary criticism as well as history until his death almost fifty years later and it spanned geographic as well as linguistic boundaries. *An Episode of Thirteenth Century Sicilian History* (1839), reissued in an expanded form as *La Guerra del Vespro* (The war of the Vespers), went through nine editions. The last edition, thoroughly documented especially as to overtaxation by this historian, himself a minister of finance, appeared in Milan in 1886 and was translated by the earl of Ellesmere (3 vols., London, 1850) as *The War of the Sicilian Vespers*. One of the most learned productions of the Risorgimento, it laid the blame for the bloody Easter rising of 1282 on the oppressive government of the Angevin French with their haughty airs and heavy taxes in such a way that contemporaries could not fail to note the parallels with the corrupt despotism of the reigning Neapolitan Bourbons. In medieval as in nineteenth-century Sicily, the French king and nobles were thus the oppressors of an Italian population which, as Amari claimed, were prone to sudden passionate outbreaks and bloody massacres in the name of long-suffered injustices. He described this with the understanding of a romantic nationalist. Thus, Amari's pen prepared the way for swords, Garibaldi and Victor Emmanuel. Verdi's *Sicilian Vespers* (1855), composed to a French libretto and boldly premiering at the Paris Opera, echoed perhaps for the ears of Napoleon III, Amari's lament about the oppressiveness of French monarchical regimes in Italy. However sympathetic to the Sicilians, Amari, foremost an Italian patriot, always eschewed separatism for the island. Amari's *Quelques Observations sur le droit public de la Sicile* (Paris, 1848), on the other hand, offered a positive solution to the crisis described in the *War of the Sicilian Vespers*, namely, the resuscitation of the constitution of 1812 in the Kingdom of the Two Sicilies. In this way Amari prefigured Cavour's liberalization of the Savoyard constitution in the 1850s. Thus, no scholar, not even Gioberti (q.v.) with his impractical vision of an Italy united under the pope, contributed more to the unification of Italy. Benedetto Croce (q.v.) did not disagree as to the excellence and influence of Amari's scholarship. More original and influential on future scholarship than his work on the Vespers and the constitution were Amari's pioneering Arabic studies: *Biblioteca arabo-sicula* (1857) and, more importantly, *La Storia dei Musulmani di Sicilia* (3 vols., Florence, 1854–1872, with a second edition issued just before his death). In this work he took into account two and a half centuries of Muslim rule on the island and explained the entire process through which Islam spread from Arabia to Sicily and the Muslim encounters with Byzantines and Franks in the Mediterranean world, the survival of Arabic culture and its effect on the kingdom of the Normans and the Hohenstaufens, and, finally, the forcible removal of the Sicilian Muslims to Lucera and indirectly the effect of this culture on the personality of Frederick II and his conflict with the papacy. He used numismatics, archaeology, and philology with great competence. He remained a fatalist, however: "The destiny of humanity runs like the mountain streams to the sea." With this monumental opus Amari established himself as the foremost Italian orientalist of his age, and it remains the principal source of information on the Muslims in Sicily. The Italian pioneer of scientific historical research on the Arabs, Amari rivalled Ernest Renan (q.v.), Sir Richard Burton, Louis Massignon, Edward William Lane, and Antoine-Isaac Silvestre Sacy.

   Bibliography: R. Romeo, "Michele Amari," *Dizionario Biografico Degli Italiani* (DBI) (1960–Present), pp. 637–654. Many unedited works, including autobiographical as well as historical and political, are in the *Fondo Amari* in the National Library at Palermo. The bibliography of his published and unpublished works takes up two large printed pages of the DBI.

William A. Percy

AQUARONE, Alberto (Barcelona, 1930–Rome, 1985), Italian historian. Professor at the universities of Pisa (1963–1974) and Rome (1974–1985). After studies in law and early research in legal history, Aquarone turned to modern history, focusing on legal institutions and the organization of political systems. He approached historical problems from a comparative and interdisciplinary perspective, successfully combining administrative, political, and economic history. Growing up in Trieste, with its Austro-Hungarian heritage, Aquarone transcended narrowly drawn national and professional boundaries in his intellectual life. His work ranged through a great variety of topics and settings, from the American and French constitutions to the organization of the Italian fascist state. The unifying thread of his oevre was Aquarone's conception of history as a search for the "connection between human conduct (viewed not only in terms of individual and collective actions, but also thought, ideas, and emotions) and a complex series of powerful and impersonal forces, such as the geographic, economic, social, institutional preconditions" between human "rationality and irrationality." Hence, he became interested in those historical periods in which such connections between structural factors and human conduct were most striking—periods of crisis and transition such as the turn of the last century and in the postrevolutionary periods, when a new order had to be built on the ruins of the old.

Aquarone's approach is already apparent in his earlier work. His *Due costituzioni settecentesche. Note sulla Convenzione di Filadelfia e sulla Assemblea Nazionale Francese* (Two Constitutional Conventions of the Eighteenth Century. Notes on the Philadelphia Convention and the French National Assembly), published in 1959, was the first comparative study of the two conventions, analyzing the process by which two revolutions organized themselves in political systems. In 1961, together with G. Negri and C. Scelba, he edited an exhaustive documentary collection in two volumes on the formation of the United States (*La formazione degli Stati Uniti. Documenti*), which included the first Italian translation of James Madison's records of the Philadelphia convention. The same year he published a book on a completely different subject: *Grandi cittá e aree metropolitane in Italia. Problemi amministrativi e prospettive di riforma* (Large Cities and Metropolitan Areas in Italy. Administrative Problems and Possibilities of Reform). In this important and original study Aquarone used a sociological methodology for a comparative analysis of the great urban development of the postwar period of the three largest Italian cities.

Aquarone's research in Italian history addressed mainly two periods: the fascist regime and the age of Giolitti, who, in the first years of the twentieth century, presided over Italy's transition from an essentially agricultural to an industrial society. His most celebrated work, *L'organizzazione dello stato totalitario* (The Organization of a Totalitarian State), appeared in 1965; together with R. De Felice's first volume of Mussolini's biography, it helped to prompt a scholarly reexamination of fascism. Aquarone's book reconstructed, on the basis of unpublished archivial documentation, the gradual transformation of the fascist movement into a "regime" through legislation and formal organization of power. This work also contributed to the debate over the distinct nature of Italian fascism, curtailed as it was by the monarchy and the Catholic Church. Aquarone first subjected the age of Giolitti to theoretical analysis in his essay, "Alla ricerca dell'Italia liberale" (In Search of Liberal Italy), part of a collection of essays by the same title published in 1972. He described the period as the "age which bridged, on the one hand, the final abandonment of what may be termed the era of risorgimento and, on the other, the laying of the foundation of modern Italy." The work was followed, in 1981, by the publication of *L'Italia giolittiana. Le premesse politiche ed economiche* (Giolitti's Italy. Political and Economic Bases), the first volume of his exhaustive research into the period. Unfortunately, he did not live to finish the second volume. Related to his research on the Giolitti period, Aquarone wrote a series of essays on Italian colonialism. These essays addressed the problems of colonial administration, of the economic exploitation of overseas territories, and of the accompanying nationalistic ideology. Aquarone's interest in late nineteenth-century colonialism also led him to an examination of the origins of American imperialism (*Le origini dell'imperialismo americano*, 1973). Aquarone's contributions to European and American historical scholarship, and especially his originality of outlook in different historical fields, have secured him an important place in contemporary historiography.

Bibliography: L. De Courten, *Storia Contemporanea*, no. 5–6 (1985); C. Ghisalberti, "Ricordo di Alberto Aquarone" (Remembering Alberto Aquarone), *Clio*, no. 4 (1985): 503–524; "L'organizzazione dello stato totalitario," debate with participants, R. Romeo, F. Gaeta, R. De Felice, P. Ungari, and C. Pavone, in *Il Cannocchiale*, no. 3 (1966): 85–104.

Elena Aga-Rossi

BALBO, Cesare (Turin, 1789–Turin, 1853), Italian writer, historian, and statesman. Balbo played a key role in the formulation of the moderate and Neo-Guelph program in the Risorgimento and served as the first prime minister of constitutional Piedmont. Born of a noble Piedmontese family, he was educated by his father Prospero in exile in Barcelona, Bologna, and later in Florence. He was initially a student of mathematics, but the turbulent political developments of his day turned his interest increasingly toward history. In 1808 his father obtained a post for him in the imperial system and he traveled to Florence, Rome, Paris, and Illyria as an auditor of the Council of State. In 1814 following the Restoration, Cesare entered the Piedmontese Army, but when his father obtained the post of ambassador to Spain in 1816, he ventured to Madrid with him, remaining there until 1818. In the Iberian Peninsula he appreciated the ardent Catholicism of its people which aroused the national resistance to French oppression, and this stimulated his career as a historian as he wrote an account of the Spanish uprising against the French from 1808 to 1814. The resulting *Studii sulla guerra d' indipendenza di Spagna e di Portogallo* was published in 1847. Although he was inspired by Spanish Catholicism, his three years in Spain also reinforced his liberal and constitutional beliefs and convinced him of the errors of absolute and arbitrary government. Balbo's reformism was considered too gradualist by some of the younger officers in the army which he rejoined in 1819, and too radical by the government in Turin. Although he took no part in the revolutionary events of 1821, of which he disapproved, he was suspected of sympathizing with the revolutionaries, and an angry Charles-Félix, King of Sardinia, forced him into confinement and exile. When he was finally allowed to return home, he was denied public office so that Balbo dedicated himself to historical and literary works to express his moderate position.

In 1830 Balbo produced his *Storia d'Italia sotto i Barbari*, followed by his *Pensieri ed Esempi* which remained unpublished until 1854. Then in 1837–1838 he worked on his *Vita di Dante* which appeared in two volumes in 1839 wherein, among other things, he traced the origins of the ills that beset the Italian nation. His *Meditazione storiche* appeared in 1842. In these works Balbo pointed to the gradual progress of civilization and society in a Christian atmosphere, combatting at once the ideas of the retrogrades and the Saint Simonians. Balbo insisted that the papacy, with its temporal power which assured the independence of the Church, was essential to the mission of Italy, which had once served as head and guide for all of Christiandom. Central to Balbo's historical vision was his conviction of the preeminent role of Christianity in the development of civilization and human liberty. He was thus profoundly influenced by, and in substantial agreement with, much of Vincenzo Gioberti's (q.v.) work, although he showed far greater political realism in his writing than did the Piedmontese priest. Balbo's historico-political works derive both their strength and weakness from his theocratic conception of the evolution of civilization. The publication of Gioberti's *Primato* in 1843 electrified Balbo and inspired him to publish his *Delle Speranze d'Italia* (1844), dedicated to Gioberti. This was followed by his *Sommario della storia d'Italia* and the *Lettere politiche* published between 1844 and the revolutionary outburst of 1848. The *Speranze*, the most popular and influential of Balbo's books, urged the dynastic Savoyard state to achieve Italian unity, convinced that "porro unum necessarium." The popularity of the *Speranze* helped make Balbo the acknowledged leader of the moderate party, to whom Charles-Albert, King of Sardinia, turned during the turbulent days of 1848. Balbo was subsequently appointed prime minister of the first constitutional government in Piedmont (March 1848–July 1848), seeking to implement the British parliamentary and gradualist system, which he had long admired. The times were not propitious for his experiment, and he was forced to resign. Balbo remained a simple deputy, defending his liberal conservative principles and the temporal power of the papacy. From the Chamber he opposed Piedmont's anti-ecclesiastical legislation, refusing to support the Siccardi Laws of 1850 and the institution of civil matrimony in 1852. In his last years Balbo returned to writing, producing his *Meditazioni storiche* and *L'Idea della civilta cristiana*.

Bibliography: E. Passerin D'Entreves, "Balbo, Cesare," *Dizionario biografico degli Italiani*, vol. 5, (1899) 395–405; E. Ricotti, *Della vita e degli scritti del conte Cesare Balbo. Rimembranze* (Florence: 1856); Luigi Salvatorelli, *Il pensiero politico italiano da 1700 al 1870* (rev. ed., Turin: Einaudi, 1949); G. B. Scaglia, *Cesare Balbo. Il Risorgimento nella Prospettiva Storica del "Progresso Cristiano"* (Rome, 1975); Nino Valeri,

"Cesare Balbo," in Cesare Balbo, *Pagine scelte* (Milan: Istituto editoriale cisalpino, 1960).

Frank J. Coppa

BATTAGLIA, Roberto (Rome, 1913–Ostia, 1963), Italian historian. A graduate of the University of Rome, Battaglia first published studies (1942–1943) on the history of baroque art in Rome. During the Italian-Ethiopian war of 1935–1936 he was an army officer in Africa; he was called back into military service in 1940. When Italy surrendered in September 1943, he became a partisan fighter in the "Giustizia e Liberta" formations of the Action party in Umbria, the Marches, and Rome. After Rome was liberated in June 1944, he was parachuted into the upper Garfagnana region of the Apennines, where he helped organize the "Lunense" partisan division, of which he became political commissar. In 1946 he published a beautifully written diary of this experience, *Un uomo, un partigiano* (A Man, a Partisan). At war's end he was elected to the communal council of Carrara and was later an official in the Ministry of Postwar Assistance. When the Action party dissolved, he joined the Italian Communist party in 1946, accepting various political and cultural assignments. He later confessed that he "never could understand just what the Action Party had stood for." As a member of the National Secretariat of the Syndicate for the Middle Schools, he sought to incorporate into the curriculum a better understanding of the Resistance.

In 1952 Battaglia brought to fruition his *Storia della Resistenza italiana* (History of the Italian Resistance), which received the Viareggio Prize in 1953 and enjoyed wide distribution and translations. In 1962 he completed a manuscript for the revised third edition. It appeared posthumously in 1964 and included an enlarged bibliography broken down by regions. Meanwhile, in 1955, aided by Giuseppe Garritano, he brought out an abridged version of the work. Battaglia's pioneering study was quite readable and had the merit of discussing the movement as a whole and of describing the parallel development of the Committees of National Liberation in the South as well as in the German-held area in the north. Battaglia also clarified the different forms of guerrilla warfare in the countryside and cities. He pointed out that in Italy the armed Resistance of 1943–1945 arose later than elsewhere in Europe but attained a greater level of organization and development. Moreover, it began as a political rather than a military movement, its origins dating back to the advent of fascism. Battaglia stressed (and probably exaggerated) the popular nature and "unity" of the Italian Resistance; he perceived the "second Risorgimento" as differing from the original one in this regard. The book had its flaws. The author's communist slant led to frequent misinterpretations of Allied policies, and his economic explanation for the coup d'état of July 25, 1943, seems simplistic. Some portions of the book reflect the author's former Action party perspective—for example, his critique of the government of Premier Ivanoe Bonomi (1944–1945). Thus, the book tends to be syncretic. A series of articles written for the communist weekly, *Vie nuove*, were reworked (1960) into the book, *La seconda guerra mondiale* (The Second World

War). In 1958, he published *La prima guerra d'Africa* (The First War in Africa), a brilliant study of the 1896 conflict with Ethiopia. He made use not only of Italian sources (memoirs of combatants, parliamentary papers, and official correspondence), but also of Ethiopian imperial chronicles. Somewhat surprisingly, the Marxist author did not see Francesco Crispi's war as resulting from economic causes. He attributed it instead to the inflammatory rhetoric of certain writers in the democratic tradition of the Risorgimento. The book was also noteworthy for its stress on the resistance conducted by Abyssinian tribes. While working on a history of the Italian Communist party, Battaglia died unexpectedly. Ernesto Ragionieri (q.v.) has collected Battaglia's miscellaneous writings and commentaries in a volume entitled *Risorgimento e Resistenza* (1964).

Bibliography: Carlo Francovich, "R. B.," *Il ponte* 19, no. 2 (1963): 159–162; G. P. Nitti, "Roberto Battaglia," in *Dizionario biografico degli Italiani* (Rome, 1965), vol. 7, pp. 218–219; Ernesto Ragionieri, "Ritratto di R. B.," *Studi storici* 4 (1963): 197–206.

Charles F. Delzell

BIANCHI, Nicomede (Reggio Emilia, 1818–Turin, 1886), Italian historian, politician, and archivist. Trained as a physician, Bianchi became involved in politics during the 1848 Revolution at Modena, acquiring that enthusiasm for moderate liberalism, Italian unification, and the House of Savoy which thereafter became his guiding principles. The conservative revival in late 1848 forced him to flee to Piedmont, where he was appointed to the chair of modern history at the University of Nice. There he wrote his first historical work, *I ducati estensi dall'anno 1815 all'anno 1850* (1852; The Estensi Duchies from the Year 1815 to the Year 1850). Like most of his work, it is less a work of objective scholarship than a polemic, in favor of the Risorgimento, the moderates, and Piedmontese leadership of the national cause, and against both the conservative rulers and the radicals. Nonetheless, its account of economic and cultural conditions was balanced and is still useful. Still less attempt at impartiality was made in his *Vicende del mazzinianesimo politico e religioso* (1854; The Fortunes of Political and Religious Mazzinianism) and *Storia della politica austriaca rispetto ai sovrani e ai governi italiani dall'anno 1791 al maggio 1857* (1857; History of Austrian Policy Toward the Italian Sovereigns and Governments from 1791 to May 1857), both written to exalt the leadership of the House of Savoy by denouncing its enemies on the left and the right. An admirer and protege of Cavour, after Cavour's death Bianchi wrote *Il conte Camillo di Cavour* (1863; Count Camillo di Cavour), the first serious biography of that figure. It was intended to refute the criticism instigated by Cavour's enemies and to establish his key role in Italian unification. Consequently, Cavour's faults and errors are ignored, the importance of Napoleon III is downplayed, and Cavour is depicted as acting in perfect accord with Garibaldi during the events of 1860.

In 1865 Bianchi's most important work began to appear, *Storia documentata della diplomazia europea in Italia dall'anno 1814 all'anno 1861* (1865–1871;

Documented History of European Diplomacy in Italy from 1814 to 1861). He had begun this project as early as 1856, encouraged by Cavour, who opened the archives of Piedmont and the other Italian states to him. This rich mass of documentary material allowed Bianchi to present the first detailed account of the diplomacy of the Risorgimento. The defects of the work have often been pointed out. His bias in favor of the national cause, Piedmont, and the moderates, and against Austria, the radicals, and the other Italian states, led Bianchi not merely to distorted interpretations of the course of events, but to deliberately misleading editing of the documentary sources. Nonetheless, it is a work of great importance. It marks the real beginning of the historical study of the diplomacy of the Risorgimento, and is a work on which all later studies of that field have ultimately rested. It remains an essential work today, both for its panoramic survey of the topic and for the richness of its documentation. The success of this study led to Bianchi's appointment first to direct the State Archive in Turin in 1870 and then as superintendent of the Piedmontese Archives in 1874. His last major work was his *Storia della Monarchia Piedmontese dal 1773 al 1861* (1877–1885). The work is marred by the author's usual bias, but, once again, is of value for the richness of its documentation and its role as the starting point for future work on the subject. In sum, although Bianchi's deeply held political convictions all too often distorted his scholarship, his work has had a major impact on the historiography of the Risorgimento. No scholar in that field can ignore it.

Bibliography: G. Sforza, "Uno storico del Risorgimento italiano, Nicomede Bianchi," *Rassegna storica del Risorgimento* (1917), pp. 213–266.

Alan J. Reinerman

BLANCH, Luigi (Lucera, 1784–Naples, 1872), Italian historian and soldier. After serving as an officer in the Neapolitan Army under both the Bourbons (1801–1806, 1815–1820) and Murat (1808–1815), Blanch welcomed the 1820 Revolution at Naples and served the revolutionary government on various diplomatic missions. His writings of this period, all unpublished until long after his death, reveal him as a moderate liberal in the tradition of the Enlightenment. He believed that a constitutional monarchy would be the ideal government, but Italy was not yet ready for it. In the meantime, he advocated an enlightened absolutism as the best way to meet Italy's needs. Nor did he consider Italian unification practical within the foreseeable future, though desirable in the abstract. Holding such ideas, he could have no sympathy with the Carbonari or with later radicals such as Mazzini. He remained interested in military affairs, on which he published his study *Della scienza militare considerata nei sui rapporti con le altri* (On Military Science considered in relation with the Others) in 1834. This was an attempt, on which Blanch had long meditated, to write a study of war as an expression of society, intimately related to its political, economic, and social conditions. Whether for lack of time or perhaps of the necessary analytical power, Blanch did not produce the vast military history he had planned. Rather, he wrote only a brief study in which his dominant thesis, though often asserted, was never proved. He explained his concept of history in various articles of the 1840s published in the Neapolitan journal *Museo di scienza e letteratura*. In "Guerra sociale" (1844; Social War) and "Polibio considerato come storico" (1845; Polybius Considered as an Historian), he argued that the study of history was necessary in order to understand and solve the problems of society, for with the immutability of human nature the same problems would recur throughout history. Consequently, he stated that the historian's approach must be logical and analytical, rather than artistic, so that he would be able to explain the problems of the past and apply the understanding thus gained to those same problems when they recur, albeit in different form, in modern society. Blanch returned to political life during the 1848 Revolution, writing in favor of a moderate consitution modeled on the French Charter of 1830, and denouncing the radicals' demand for a more democratic government and for war with Austria. Disillusioned by the radical turning of the revolutionary movement, after 1848 he became increasingly conservative, defending the Bourbon regime against the criticism of Gladstone and arguing that even the most conservative of constitutional governments would probably fail at Naples, where an enlightened despotism along the lines of that of Murat would be most suitable. After unification, he retreated into silence until his death in 1872.

Bibliography: Luigi Blanch, *Scritti Storici*, ed. Benedetto Croce (Bari, 1945).

Alan J. Reinerman

BORTOLOTTI, Franca Pieroni (Florence, 1925–Florence, 1985), Italian historian of feminism and pacifism. She was professor of History of Political Parties and Movements at the University of Siena and may be regarded as the author of groundbreaking works in the field of women's history in Italy and indeed a founder of that branch of research in Italian scholarship. She defended her dissertation on Guizot in 1950 at the University of Florence. Her advisor was Gaetano Salvemini (q.v.), following the death of her previous sponsor, the Europeanist and historian of ideas, Rodolfo Morandi (q.v.). Franca's family had been militant Communists since the day of the founding of the Italian party in 1921, and Franca herself was a part of the network of the Resistance in Florence from 1943–1945. A dedicated militant in her youth, she was an active member of the Italian Communist Party to her last days. The intellectual fervor at the University of Florence during the 1950s, and the scholarly and moral leadership of Delio Cantimori (q.v.), her sponsor, led Bortolotti to concentrate on the study of "disenfranchised groups." Thus studies on women workers of the Tobacco State Monopoly in Florence covered the work lives and political activity of generations of women, from their early unionization at the end of the nineteenth century through their resistance to Fascism. During her research on women, and until the early 1970s, she often met with skepticism from other historians, including her close associates. Franca Pieroni Bortolotti's crucial role as an historian was her unearthing of Anna Maria Mozzoni (1837–1920), the radical

Mazzinian pro-feminist who recognized that the status of women was at the very heart of the building of unified Italy as a liberal state. Bortolotti's first volume, *Alle origini del movimento femminile in Italia (1848–1892)* (Torino: Einaudi, 1963) is Mozzoni's political biography from her early years in liberal circles in Lombardy (still under Hapsburg domination), through her unceasing struggle against the narrow boundaries assigned to women by the new Italian state. Anna Maria Mozzoni's basic tenet was that liberalism and democracy in Italy had to be measured against the capacity of the state to promote the civil and social condition of women, to fully integrate them as citizens and contributors to the material and moral growth of the nation. Eventually her egalitarian beliefs, which Bortolotti traced to the influences of early nineteenth-century Enlightenment, drew the feminist to foster the organization of "leagues" of women workers, which gradually merged after 1892 into the newly founded Partito dei Lavoratori Italiani, later Partito Socialista, which listed Mozzoni among its founders. Bortolotti rediscovered and edited a collection of Mozzoni's major writings, *Anna Maria Mozzoni. La liberazione della donna* (Milano: Mazzotta, 1975).

When organized socialism came to the forefront of Italian politics, Anna Kuliscioff became Mozzoni's interlocutor on emancipation and the links between the "woman's question" and socialism. Their interaction sharpened on the issue of protective legislation for working women, which Kuliscioff promoted and Mozzoni opposed. The debate between Mozzoni and Kuliscioff, and Mozzoni's disillusionment with Socialist Party conservatism towards women, as shown by Socialist handling of women's suffrage, provide the pattern for the reconstruction of the women's emancipation movement in Italy around the turn of the century in Bortolotti's other major work, *Socialismo e questions femminile (1892–1922)* (Milano: Mazzotta 1974). This was followed by *Femminismo e partiti politici in Italia (1919–1926)* (Roma: Editori Riuniti 1978) in which Bortolotti's choice of chronological boundaries witnesses her increasing attention to the problem of periodization of Italian women's history. Periodization and the related issue of defining the women's movement as a political movement on its own, but also constantly in relationship with parties and political institutions, were at the core of most of Bortolotti's work from the late 1960s to the end. These efforts produced a vast body of research and writing. Although she did not extend beyond the onset of Fascism in Italy, she participated on a local research project on women from 1922 to the postwar in Emilia-Romagna, working on the years 1943–1945. Following Mozzoni, Bortolotti made the "women's issue" the vantage point from which to judge the quality and potential for democratic expansion or decline in a society. To her Italy was a case in point, given the dramatic quality of its last hundred years.

The research on the women's movement in the late 19th century and its close link with socialism at its origins led Bortolotti to pioneer another field of research. In her eyes the mobilization of labouring and middle class women in the late nineteenth century appeared to combine three goals: feminism, pacifism, and Europe's political reunification. Her research uncovered the existence of a popular peace movement symbolized by the International Association of Women, founded in Bern by Maria Goegg in 1868 in affiliation with the Ligue de la Paix et de la Liberte. An entirely forgotten chapter concerning the history of early peace movements in Europe came to light, as well as the historical figures of active pacifists, such as Maria Goegg and Eresto Teodoro Moneta, the Italian Nobel Laureate for Peace in 1907. As outlined in her introduction to a collection of essays published posthumously in the volume *La donna, la pace, L'Europa, L'Associazione Internazionale delle Donne dalle origini alla prima querra mondiale* (Milano: Mazzotta, 1985), Bortolotti showed the persistence in nineteenth-century Europe of currents of national patriotism which did not turn into aggressive nationalism, and linked the ideal of social equality between sexes and the ideal of democratic and peaceful progress of nations. Along this line of research Bortolotti contributed biographies of men and women to the *Biographical Dictionary of Modern Peace Leaders* (Harold Josephson, ed. Westport, Conn.: Greenwood Press, 1985).

In sketching a rich network of women, thinking and mobilizing, active women of different social statuses and persuasions, radical, conservative and reactionary, their press, their writing, their organizing, the support they won and the rejections they suffered, the shape they themselves gave to their role in society, the way they related to politics and institutions—Bortolotti drew an astonishing picture of the presence of women in the Italian political and social scenery. The immense wealth of primary sources that Bortolotti uncovered provides references for historians to come. While many of those sources are still largely untapped, just as many of her historical questions still await further investigation, Franca Pieroni Bortolotti has already inspired a younger generation of scholars, mostly women, who are working to include the essential category of gender in the historical scholarship of modern Italy. In recognition of the pioneering quality of Bortolotti's work, a panel at the 102nd Annual Meeting of the American Historical Association (December 27–30, 1987) was dedicated to her life and work.

Bibliography: F. Pieroni Bortolotti, "Rassenga di storia del femminismo", *L'Italia unita. Problemi e interpretazioni storiografiche*, ed. R. Rainero (Milano: Marzorati, 1981); F. Pieroni Bortolotti, "A Survey of Italian Research on the History of Feminism," *The Journal of Italian History*, 3, 1978; for a general evaluation of Bortolotti's work, see Annarita Buttafuoco's introduction to her edition of Bortolotti's unpublished writings: Franca Pieroni Bortolotti, *Sul movimento politico delle donne. Scritti inediti* (Roma: Utopia, 1987).

Margherita Repetto Alaia

BOTTA, Carlo (San Giorgio Canavese, 1766–Paris, 1837), Italian historian, physician, and Risorgimento figure. Botta was a man of contrasts and contradictions, first embracing and then criticizing the French Revolution. Conservative in his approach to literature and a defender of the Italian classical tradition, he waged war on the romantic writers of the age and condemned Gallic influences that "polluted" the Italian language. He had a passionate love for Italy but became a French citizen after 1814. Nor could he decide the form of government he favored for the peninsula. At one point he called for a federal republic on the Roman model, the next favoring a reformist regime of the eighteenth-century variety with a restricted popular representation. Trained as a physician, he achieved fame as an historian. Botta received his degree in medicine at the University of Turin but soon became involved in political matters. Following the outbreak of the French Revolution he was incarcerated in his native Piedmont (1794–1795) for spreading radical ideas. Upon his release he went into exile, returning to his homeland in 1795 as a surgeon in the French Army of the Alps. After the Restoration in Italy, he chose to remain in France. In 1809 his *Storia della guerra d'indipendenza degli Stati Uniti d'America* was published in Paris. The theme of the work is the love of liberty which characterized American society from the founding of the colonies to their rebellion against the Mother Country. The hero of his study is George Washington, who is polemically contrasted with Napoleon, just as the American Revolution is contrasted with the French. While Botta used a variety of primary sources, he included dialogues which he arbitrarily assigned to characters to clarify and support his contentions. This was in keeping with his view that history was a humanistic study to instruct and entertain rather than simply reconstruct the past record. The same attitude permeates his *Storia d'Italia dal 1789 al 1814* (Paris, 1824) which remains the author's most important historical work. Here he exalted the Italian reformist movement of the eighteenth century and saw the French intrusion interrupting this earlier pacific reformism. He also showed himself critical of the intellectual arrogance and utopianism of those who did not respect the Italian past and wished to reconstruct the political and social structure anew.

In 1832 Botta published his last historical work, *Storia d'Italia continuata da quella del Guicciardini sino al 1789*. The preface of this work is particularly interesting because of his discussion of historical methodology in general, and his own in particular. Here Botta grouped historians as the "patriotic," whose aim was not simply the truth but to arouse love of one's country, the "moral," those whose major objective was to turn the readers toward the good and against that which was bad, and finally the "naturalists" or "positivists," those who described atrocious as well as beneficent developments in the same detached manner, and justified those who triumphed simply because they won. Without reservation, Botta placed himself in the second category and looked to Tacitus as a model, indicating that he could never assume the role of a narrator without considering moral judgments. In his opinion, a writer who did not exalt virtue and condemn vice was not worthy of the name historian. In this regard Botta's historiography looked backward rather than to the "scientific" history of the nineteenth and twentieth centuries.

Bibliography: G. Talamo, "Botta, Carlo," *Dizionario Biografico degli Italiani*, vol. 13, pp. 364–371.

Frank J. Coppa

CANTIMORI, Delio (Russi near Ravenna, 1904–Florence, 1966), Italian historian. Cantimori's studies at the Scuola Normale Superiore and the University of Pisa were completed in 1929, and included work under G. Gentile, G. Saitta, and a grounding in *Germanistik*. A stint as instructor in secondary schools was followed by years of research in the libraries and archives of several countries, especially Switzerland, and the gathering of material on the thought and writings of sixteenth-century Italian religious dissenters. Over one hundred reviews, preparatory essays, and articles preceded the publication of his first book, *Per la storia degli eretici italiani del sec. XVI in Europa* (Contributions Toward the History of Italian Heretics of the Sixteenth Century in Europe) (Rome, 1937), a collection of texts with a contribution by Elisabeth Feist. To the same year belong numerous entries in the *Enciclopedia Italiana*, many on heretics. A docent of church history in 1936, he became professor of history in 1939, teaching first at the University of Messina and subsequently at the Scuola Normale Superiore in Pisa (which now houses his library), the University of Pisa, and from 1951 until his death at the University of Florence.

Cantimori was one of the most outstanding historians in Italy after World War II. His masterpiece remains a standard work for the study of sixteenth-century religious history: *Eretici italiani del Cinquecento. Ricerche storiche* (1939; Italian Heretics of the Sixteenth Century. Historical Investigations), translated by Werner Kaegi as *Italienische Häretiker der Spätrenaissance* 1949). Cantimori's views on the significance of radical thinkers critical of all organized churches, or heretics in this specific sense, have been seminal for subsequent works on the intellectual history of the Reformation period. Breaking with hagiographic depictions of these men as martyrs on the one hand or mavericks on the other, Cantimori saw the heretics he discussed as intellectually rooted in Italian humanism and champions of the ideals of toleration, religious freedom, the dignity of the individual as thinker, and the removal of the state from matters of doctrine and dogma, all developing out of Italian culture of the Renaissance. Examining their religious thought, their ethics and philosophy, Cantimori, in the final analysis, presents the heretics persecuted by the Inquisition in Italy and by Protestants elsewhere as the precursors of modern liberal thought. In his opinion their major achievement, despite their diversity, was to spread their ideas throughout Europe and to sow seeds that would mature later, most notably in seventeenth-century biblical criticism and Unitarianism, and possibly in Deism. This view of nonconformists as carriers of ideals of *humanitas* links his *Eretici* with his next book, *Utopisti e riformatori italiani, 1794–1847. Ricerche storiche* (1943; Italian Utopian and Reform Thinkers, 1794–1847. Historical Investigations). His interest in the Enlightenment led to a specific focus on democratic and utopian advocates of egalitarianism, Italian Jacobins, and social revolutionaries like Filippo Buonarroti. In this connection he noted that "the cultural history of states is not fashioned only from official documents . . . and memoirs of the victors and rulers, but also out of the written and published records of aspirations, passions, programs, hopes, attempts that failed . . . they are no less real because historiographical conformism condemned them to long silence'' (*Studi di Storia*, p. 635). Changing his political allegiance to the Italian Communist party during the later stages of World War II, and remaining its member until 1956, Cantimori turned his attention to Marxism, translating the first volume of *Das Kapital* (Rome, 1951–1952). Although the topics of his university courses and seminars testify to a continuing interest in varieties of socialist thought, his main field of inquiry and research remained the sixteenth century. In second place came his abiding concern for historical methodology, as can be seen in the collection *Storici e storia. Metodo, caratteristiche e significato del lavoro storiografico* (1971; Historians and History. Methods, Character and Significance of Historiographical Work).

A personal view of Cantimori's profession as historian emerges from his letters to Francesco Rossi, editor of the periodical *Itinerari*, written during the last years of his life and published together as *Conversando di storia* (1967; Discussions on History). Perhaps the best evidence of the breadth and openness he brought to his work can be found in his essays gathered in *Studi di Storia* (1959; Studies in History) which show the wide range of his historical inquiries in early modern and modern history and methodology. Another valuable collection of essays on the sixteenth century appeared posthumously as *Umanesimo e religione nel Rinascimento* (1975; Humanism and Religion During the Renaissance). His last book, *Prospettive di storia ereticale italiana del Cinquecento* (1960; Perspectives on the History of Sixteenth-Century Italian Heresy), condenses the results of years of research into a slim but seminal volume. He envisioned a broad approach in which the history of beliefs, piety, and heterodoxy would be interwoven with such themes as Nicodemism, the development of pacifism, and irenic ideas. Ultimately, he envisioned a synthesis of religious and political history. His essay ''Le idee religiose del Cinquecento'' (Religious Ideas of the Sixteenth Century), *Storia della letteratura italiana*, vol. 5 (Milan, 1967), pp. 7–87, adumbrates the approach he might have taken. Cantimori was a complex thinker and stylist of great subtlety. His personal political and intellectual itinerary can serve as a commentary on modern Italian thought, as extant literature on it shows. As a historian he was significant not because of theoretical innovations, but because of the exemplary practice of his craft. Mistrusting general principles as points of departure for historical work, he was committed to the careful structuring of arguments on the basis of meticulously examined texts, holding that one's political, philosophical, or religious convictions should never be allowed to imprison the mind or determine the scrupulous use of evidence. Because of these convictions he was able to appreciate the work of historians very different from himself, to maintain a wide network of professional contacts, and to influence his students. Cantimori chose to exalt and, to a certain extent, identify himself with what he believed to have been the noblest values of the Italian Renaissance thinkers: toleration and freedom of inquiry and choice for the individual.

Bibliography: B. V. Bandini, ed., *Storia e Storiografia. Studi su Delio Cantimori* (Rome, 1979); Marino Berengo, "La ricerca storica di Delio Cantimori," *Rivista Storica Italiana* 79 (1967): 902–943; Eric Cochrane and John Tedeschi, "Delio Cantimori: Historian (1904–1966)," *Journal of Modern History* 39 (1967): 438–445; Giovanni Miccoli, *Delio Cantimori* (Turin, 1970): includes a bibliography of Cantimori's writings and a list of his university courses and seminars; entry in *Dizionario Biografico degli Italiani*, vol. 18 (Rome, 1975), pp. 283–290.

Elisabeth G. Gleason

CANTÚ, Cesare (Brivio, 1804–Milan, 1895), Italian historian, romantic novelist, and patriot. A prolific writer, Cantú wrote popular works noted for their moralizing and their contribution to the civic formation of Italians rather than for their scholarship. Profoundly Catholic, at the Barnabite college of San Alessandro in Milan he fell under the sway of romantic and Neo-Guelph thought. In 1821 he obtained a position teaching literature at the *ginnasio* of Sondrio where he remained until he transferred to Como in 1827; in 1832 he returned to the *ginnasio* San Alessandro of Milan as a professor. These were the years of his historical and literary formation. In 1828 he published his novella *L'Algiso* which focused on the struggle of the Lombard communes against Frederick I and the positive role of the Church in reawakening the Italian spirit. Patriotic themes as well as an appreciation for the unifying role of the Church also pervade his historical study *La Storia della città e diocesi di Como* (Como, 1828–1829). In Milan Cantú began a study of the province of Lombardy which led to the volume *Sulla storia lombarda del Secolo XVII* (Milan, 1832). This was followed by the article "Parini e il suo secolo" published in the *Indicatore* of 1833. Both works contain the author's basic conviction that the Lombard communes had developed a high civilization that was compromised first by Spanish misgovernment and later by Napoleonic and Hapsburg centralization. His increasing criticism of Austrian policies led to his imprisonment from November 1833 to October 1834.

Well received was Cantú's historical masterpiece, the monumental *Storia universale* published in thirty-five volumes from 1838 to 1846, which assured the author a steady income. The first eighteen volumes examine the political history of humanity from the creation to Cantú's time; documents and notes were placed in the next sixteen volumes, which also included a compendium of legislation, a chronology, and consideration of such subjects as the art of war, archaeology, geography, literature, philosophy, religion, biography, and other diverse matters. The thirty-fifth volume included tables and indices. Written in a vivid style with the aim of indoctrinating as well as educating, the work was flawed more by error of interpretation than of fact. Generally, the closer Cantú got to his period, the less balanced and objective his treatment. Still, the *Storia* was a notable contribution, the best read and most consulted historical work for Italians for over half a century. After the creation of the Italian Kingdom, Cantú served in the Chamber of Deputies from 1860 to 1861 and again from 1865 to

1867. Following this political period he returned to his historical studies, aided by his appointment as superintendent of the State Archives of Lombardy in 1873. In these years he produced his last major historical work, *Della indipendenza d'Italia Cronistoria* which was published in Turin from 1872 to 1877. Tinged by Catholic and communal views, Cantú in his history of the unification showed himself to be critical of those who wielded power such as Napoleon and Cavour while sympathetic to those who were defeated such as Garibaldi, Carlo Cattaneo, and even Pius IX and Franz-Josef. The man who proclaimed himself the last of the romantics in 1893 remained to the end a polemicist as much as a historian.

Bibliography: M. Berengo, "Cantú, Cesare," *Dizionario Biografico degli Italiani*, vol. 18, pp. 336–344.

Frank J. Coppa

CATTANEO, Carlo (Milan, 1801–Castagnola di Lugano, Switzerland, 1869), Italian historian. Educated at the Liceo Sant' Alessandro in Milan and then at the private school of philosophy and jurisprudence founded by Gian Domenico Romagnosi (q.v.), Cattaneo finished his formal studies at the Faculty of Law of the University of Pavia. Having neither independent means nor a real interest in the practice of law, he supported himself by teaching in secondary school and by writing for scholarly periodicals such as Romagnosi's *Annali Universali di statistica*. Through his association with other contributors to *Annali*, Cattaneo in the 1830s developed an interest in political economy and more specifically in the relationship between political institutions, legal systems, and economics. This relationship became the central theme of his own scholarly investigations and writings, as well as of the periodical *Il Politecnico* which he founded in 1839. A voracious reader and a tireless researcher, Cattaneo published articles on many topics, from the social and economic conditions of the peasantry in the Po Valley and in Ireland (the native land of his wife Anna Pyne Woodcock) to the economics of slavery in the southern United States and of protectionism in the Habsburg Empire and in the German states. A friend of Richard Cobden and other English free traders, Cattaneo contributed to the international debate on the influential tract by the German philosopher Friedrich List, *Das nationale System der politischen Oekonomie* (1841).

Cattaneo made several distinctive contributions to the writing of history in nineteenth-century Italy. One contribution was as editor of the monograph series he entitled "I documenti della guerra santa." From his home near Lugano in the early 1850s, he collected and solicited contributions from participants in the Revolution of 1848, particularly those who had fought in the war in northern Italy. Moderate liberals, Mazzinians, and independent republicans alike wrote memoirs of the revolution, and sent copies of correspondence, broadsides, newspapers, and other memorabilia to be included in the series. Despite occasional problems with Swiss censors and chronic financial woes, three volumes of documents were published between 1850 and 1855 under the title *Archivio triennale delle cose d'Italia*. To this day it remains a fundamental primary source for the history of Italy's Risorgimento. *Archivio* included Cattaneo's own polemic but thorough account of the revolution, *Dell'insurrezione di Milano nel 1848 e della successiva guerra* (1849).

Cattaneo's other major contribution was his exploration in historical perspective of the basic character of Italian civilization. Like his teacher, Romagnosi, Cattaneo believed that all human civilizations were the expression of universal laws but also that the development of each one reflected the impact of geography and other external circumstances. The influence of Romagnosi's historical thought is evident in Cattaneo's first historically oriented work, *Notizie naturali e civili su la Lombardia* published in 1844 on the occasion of the Sixth Congress of Italian Scientists. A report on the physical and social conditions of Lombardy, *Notizie* was not a historical work, but it presented contemporary information in historical perspective, calling attention to the impact of human events and environmental and economic conditions on the development of Lombard civilization. To this methodology Cattaneo returned in a seminal essay published in the October-December 1858 issue of *Il Crepuscolo*, "La città considerata come principio ideale delle istorie italiane." Responding to Mazzini, the theorist of a republican "Third Rome," but also to the proponents of a centralized state under constitutional monarchy, Cattaneo argued that the distinguishing feature of Italian civilization was the autonomy and influence of its urban centers both large and small. To propose that the Italian state could be organized, like the French or the Spanish, around a capital to which other historic cities would be subordinate was to misunderstand the most characteristic features of Italian civilization. These were its strongly urban flavor, its cultural and economic diversity, and its decentralized political power. On this historical analysis, Cattaneo rested not only his opposition to the unitary state but also his faith in an Italian democracy "on which people could keep their hands" and in the long-term possibility of an Italian federation within a United States of Europe.

Bibliography: Luigi Ambrosoli, *La formazione di Carlo Cattaneo* (Milan: Ricciardi, 1959); Giuseppe Armani, "Cattaneo e Garibaldi," *Il Ponte*, 38, nos. 11–12 (1982): 1164–1179; Giuseppe Armani, "Gli scritti su Carlo Cattaneo," *Bollettino della Domus mazziniana*, 28 (1982): 123–212; Clara M. Lovett, *Carlo Cattaneo and the Politics of the Resorgimento* (The Hague: Njihoff, 1972).

Clara M. Lovett

CHABOD, Federico (Val d'Aosta, 1901–Rome, 1960), Italian historian. Chabod was an historian's historian, one of the most brilliant and sensitive historical minds of the twentieth century. Although Chabod ultimately succeeded in dominating the pull between the time of his subjects and the time of his reconstruction, his major works also reveal his own historical moment. His maturity coincided with the period of Italian fascism, which he sketched in *L' Italie contemporaine* (1950; A *History of Italian Fascism*, translated by Muriel Grindrod, 1963). Against the recollections of Gioacchino Volpe that, in the early 1930s, Chabod was "proffered" and most reluctantly accepted the "party card," there stands the testimony of Walter Maturi that "everyone knew" where Chabod's "sympathies . . . lay," despite the fact that he was "prudentissimo." Perhaps Chabod sought to preserve his authenticity within and yet against them. He did not avoid participation. In 1924–1925, he studied with the "notoriously" antifascist Gaetano Salvemini (q.v.), and in 1926 he actively aided Salvemini's escape to freedom. That same year Chabod went to Berlin to study with Friedrich Meinecke (q.v.). During the 1930s, Chabod opposed fascist "Italianization" of his native Val d'Aosta and from 1944 to 1946 helped save it from French annexation. During World War II, Chabod actively fought Nazism-fascism as he joined the Action party and became a leader of the resistance movement in northern Italy. In each case, Chabod acted for something "concrete." In neither life nor in historiography would Chabod commit himself to abstract principles, theories, or systems of ideas. He gave a special place to *valori* (values). What linked Chabod the man and Chabod the historian was a subtle motivating humanism. Chabod's attitude was divided and may be said to have been "Machiavellian" in intellectual passion and "Guicciardinian" in psychological inclination. For his essays on *his* two major figures of Renaissance Italy, see *Scritti su Machiavelli* (1964) and, on Guicciardini, *Scritti sul Rinascimento* (1967). In Chabod's masterpiece, the *Storia della politica estera italiana dal 1870 al 1896: Le premesse* (1951), Cavour is offstage. The purely Machiavellian character of Cavour's action prevailed in the making of a national state. But in less creative and constructive guise, that "action" could shatter the "Guicciardinian" balance that Chabod regarded as a kind of "ideal type." Chabod had experienced such a shattering vicariously in the crisis of the Renaissance, and as a witness of the twentieth-century Italian and European crisis. In both crises, Chabod had discovered a metamorphosis of values that had led to the victory of egotistical and vitalistic urges over the ideal balance. Thus, Chabod sympathized with Charles V's efforts to maintain the unity of the empire and with the post-Cavourian liberalism of the moderate elite in Italy. Even while World War II was still raging, during the winter of despair 1943–1944 Chabod lectured at the University of Milan on the "idea of Europe" which had now overtaken the old "idea of nation." A United States of Europe was the last hope, and, for Chabod, Europe had become a faith. See *L'idea di nazione* (1961) and *L'idea d'Europa* (1961).

From 1946 until his death, Chabod plunged into his rich historiographical activity, the many-sided labors of his teaching at the University of Rome, the directorship of the Croce Institute in Naples, the editorship of the *Rivista storica italiana*, and in 1955 the presidency of the International Committee of Historical Sciences. In Chabod's historiographical production, there were four dominant but related themes—Machiavelli and the Renaissance, Italy and Europe during the age of Charles V, the Reformation as a crisis of the Italian conscience, and post-Risorgimento Italy in the crisis of modern Europe. For Chabod, history is part of life recaptured and understood, not just a survey of the past as if it were once and for all fixed. For Chabod, writing history entailed confronting problems, the historian's and history's. Once Chabod grappled with an historical problem, he never really let go, thereby creating an interplay of theme and variations. To compound critical difficulties, it is not easy to categorize Chabod's works as major and minor. His brief entries in the *Enciclopedia Italiana* under "Machiavelli," "Guicciardini," "Calvin," "Boulainvilliers," "Borghesia," "Illuminismo," and a few others are truly great, perhaps in a sense in which his fantastically rich *Storia di Milano: L'epoca di Carlo V* (1961) is not great. Along with his *Storia: le premesse*, the lesser known long essay, *Per la storia religiosa dello Stato di Milano* (1938), is also a masterpiece. For Chabod, "historical reality" *in sè e per sè* (in and for itself) was evidently short of Leopold von Ranke's (q.v.) *wie es eigentlich gewesen* but also beyond Machiavelli's *la verità effettuale della cosa*. Chabod seems to have assumed that concentration through the monograph on a particular historical problem of "universal" significance with the study conducted on the basis of original research and reinterpretation of sources was the ideal structure within which to search for historical truth in the twentieth century. He emphasized a vigorous methodology, which at a certain point gives way to the "art" of historiography. After method serves its function, style makes its claims felt. In Chabod's works, his historical sense, instinct, and scent are his style, and style is the man. For Chabod, no less decisive than facts among the forces of history is consciousness. Neither Renaissance Italy, nor the empire of Charles V, nor liberal Italy before fascism had to succumb to the forces that were bent on their destruction. What men do with facts, how they are affected by them, at what point and how they translate them into ideas, beliefs, faiths, myths, and motives for "free" historic action ultimately proves more important than the inert "force of things." Men need not be prisoners of geography, circumstances, tradition, or of history itself. Chabod developed his own uniqueness with reference to his great contemporaries, Benedetto Croce (q.v.), Gaetano Salvemini (q.v.), Friedrich Meinecke (q.v.), and the French *Annales* School. If Chabod "started" with Ranke, he ended under the renewed attraction of Jacob Burckhardt (q.v.), but it was Burckhardt the seer of the contemporary crisis of values rather than the historian of the Renaissance.

Chabod's *Storia della politica estera italiana: le premesse* (1951) made historiographical history. In his reconstruction of the post-Risorgimento, facts and ideas, society and consciousness, politics and culture, biography and historiography constitute the counterpoints of an intricate and subtle treatment of a grandiose theme. As Italy had joined the community of European states, both the universalistic idea of Rome and the idea of Europe had been shattered. Under Bismarck Europe had become a fiction and national power the reality. Chabod's principal theme is the stupendous problem of how Cavour's successors, the liberal-moderate ruling classes of post–1870 Italy, placated, if they did not resolve, the conflicts engendered at home and abroad by the Italian national revolution, and how they achieved Italy's survival. The major task of these classes and their political leaders, as Chabod sees it, appears to have been a search for a delicate balance between the ideals of liberty that had inspired the Risorgimento and the realities of power. Chabod's *Storia* is documentation and evocation, historical reconstruction and spiritual reflection, fact and idea, wrought through the discipline of rigorous method, and finely fused through the uniqueness of style.

A. William Salomone

[*Ed. note*: Illness and death precluded Professor Salomone's completion of this work. This essay was synopsized by Joel Blatt using Salomone's own words from his "Federico Chabod: Portrait of a Master Historian," in *Historians of Modern Europe*, ed. Hans A. Schmitt (Baton Rouge: Louisiana State University Press, 1971), pp. 255–290. See that essay for elaboration of themes and bibliography.]

COLLETTA, Pietro (Naples, 1775–Florence, 1831), Italian historian, patriot, and military man. Started his military career in 1796 in the Neapolitan Army under the Bourbons. In 1799 Colletta supported the French-inspired Republic of Naples and at its fall was imprisoned by the king. When the French reconquered southern Italy, he served Joseph Bonaparte and Murat in important military and administrative positions and fought in the Napoleonic campaigns of 1814 and 1815. Given a minor post by the Bourbons at their restoration to the Neapolitan throne in 1815, he began writing his eyewitness account of the last campaign fought by the Napoleonic troops in Italy, *Memoria militare sulla campagna d'Italia dell'anno 1815* (A Military Memoir on the Italian Campaign in 1815), published posthumously. Reinstated to his army rank in 1817, Colletta was appointed commander of the Salerno garrison, but in 1820 he joined the revolutionists and was briefly minister of war in the new government in 1821. Once the revolt was suppressed, Colletta was arrested and exiled to Brünn in Moravia. In 1823 he got permission to go to Florence, where he spent the rest of his life. In Florence he became a friend of Gino Capponi, member of the Viesseux circle and a contributor to the *Antologia*. During the last years of his life, Colletta wrote the *Storia del reame di Napoli dal 1734 al 1825* (History of the Kingdom of Naples from 1734 to 1825), the work for which he is best remembered. The *Storia* condemned both the despotic Bourbon monarchy and Jacobinism.

For Colletta, the best form of government was a strong constitutional monarchy that would advance and defend progressive reforms against the twin threats of revolution and reaction. The *Storia* expressed the sentiments of a man of action, imbued with the ideas of the Enlightenment. Using Tacitus as his model, Colletta condemned the misrule in Naples by the Bourbons and a do-nothing nobility. Published posthumously by Capponi in 1832, the *Storia* was reissued two years later, and again in 1846 and 1861. The 1861 edition was obviously timed to coincide with Garibaldi's expedition of a thousand against the Bourbon Kingdom. A French translation appeared in 1835 and two British versions in 1858 and 1860. As an historical work, the *Storia* was open to criticism. As a political document, it made an important contribution to the literature of the Risorgimento and was widely read during the nineteenth century. By exposing the shortcomings, petty despotism, cruelty, and unenlightened government of the Bourbons,

Colletta provided powerful arguments to their enemies and helped to undermine support for them not only in Italy, but also abroad.

Bibliography: P. Colletta, *History of the Kingdom of Naples, 1734–1825*, trans. S. Horner [With a supplementary chapter 1825–1856], 2 vols. (Edinburgh, 1858); P. Colletta, *Storia del Reame di Napoli*, with introduction and notes by Nino Cortese, 3 vols. (Naples, 1953–1957); Nino Cortese, "La vita di Pietro Colletta," *Rassegna storica del Risorgimento*, no. 4 (1920): 657–675; Benedetto Croce, *Storia della storiografia italiana nel secolo decimonono* (Bari, 1921), 1, pp. 84–89; A. Scirocco, "Pietro Colletta," *Dizionario biografico degli italiani*, vol. 27 (Rome, 1982), pp. 27–34.

Emiliana Pasca Noether

CROCE, Benedetto (Pescasseroli, 1866–Naples, 1952), Italian philosopher, historian, and political figure. Croce was twentieth-century Italy's foremost thinker, and he left his influence on nearly every political, literary, philosophical, and artistic movement in the country. Even today in Italy, one must come to grips with Croce's controversial interpretations before discussing almost any subject in Italian history or culture. Croce's life appears to have involved various and often contradictory phases but can generally be seen as one long effort to lead a spiritual renewal of Italy (and the West in general) against naturalism, materialism, positivism, and any doctrine that took initiative and responsibility in history away from the individual. These ideas appear as the central focus of his "Philosophy of Spirit" and are the driving force in his journal *La Critica* (1903–1944) and its successor *Quaderni della critica* (1944–1952).

Croce entered Italian political/cultural life in the 1890s and to understand his enormous impact, one must understand the Italy Croce entered. Italy was barely a generation old in 1890 and was ruled by a tiny elite that was intent on preserving constitutional government (and its own position) and doing so on an extremely limited franchise. There were unique reasons for this. Originally, Italy had been united without popular support; the rulers were afraid to allow popular sovereignty because the masses were controlled by forces hostile to the new national government—if not to the existence of the new state itself. Little effort was made, therefore, to involve the masses in the nation; they remained alienated and in the hands of hostile forces. In the 1890s, these forces were, on the one hand, the Church (the "Black International") and the socialists (the "Red International"). In the late 1890s violence from below and repression from above made it clear that the masses could no longer be ignored. It fell to the liberal Prime Minister Giovanni Giolitti to try to woo the masses from their violent leaders and the elite from their illusions, to lead the population into the state and, at the same time, to reform and preserve the liberal constitutional system. He received little help. Culturally, questions were raised about the success of the Risorgimento, about Italy's purpose as a nation, about whether the bourgeoisie who had made the state had used up its political capital, and about whether or not forces on the far right or left might not be better suited to leading Italy. Italy stood at a crossroads when Croce entered the scene. Croce had little to say about Giolitti's efforts and, in fact, associated himself with Giolitti's most ardent enemies. Italy needed a spiritual rebirth. At first, Croce supported the far left Sorelian wing of the Italian Socialist party (PSI) against the moderate social democratic ideas of the PSI's titular head, Filippo Turati. Croce championed the idea that the proletariat could renew Italy spiritually, but only if the PSI adopted Sorel's ideas. Eventually, but clearly by 1911, Croce became disenchanted with the PSI. Although the Sorelian-Mussolinian wing was now on the ascendant, Croce despaired of it ever doing anything to give Italy a spiritual rebirth. He began to see the emerging nationalist forces as those most likely to renew Italy. Croce moved farther and farther to the right, praising Heinrich von Treitschke (q.v.), German *Machtpolitik*, and the idea of the ethical state that would supply Italians with a morality more suited to a great state than anarchic liberal individualism or democratic socialism. During World War I, Croce continued to defend German thought and condemned the "decadent" thought of the *entente* and, after the war, he advocated extreme right-wing ideas and wrote in the reactionary journal *Politica*. Croce became minister of education in Giolitti's last government (1920–1921) and instituted changes compatible with his philosophy. When Mussolini took over the state and appeared to be capable of renewing Italy, Croce gave him his support. Then, in 1925, he broke with the fascist state and became, for many, an inspiration for resistance to fascism. In 1928 he wrote the *Storia d'Italia (1870–1915)* (History of Italy, 1870–1915), which praised Giolitti as the best of Italy's liberal ministers, implying that Italy had not needed rescuing by Mussolini. Because of his opposition to the fascists, Croce was consulted by the Allies in 1943 and served as a minister without portfolio in the Badoglio government. After the war, Croce was associated with Italy's Liberal party, and favored the abdication of Victor Emmanuel III and retention of the monarchy. He espoused a conservative solution to Italy's postwar problems and was gradually pushed aside by those to his left.

Croce's "philosophy of spirit" underwent many transformations but several exceptional ideas recur in his thought. (1) Immanence is favored over transcendence, and all philosophies of history are vigorously opposed. (2) Dialectic of distinct forces is stressed against Hegelian *Aufhebung*. History does not move forward because of conflict between opposites but because of the play of merely "distinct" forces. This is an extremely fruitful and important part of the philosophy of spirit. (3) Life is a constant dialectic between "amoral political forces" and the world's various ethical forces. (The term *ethical* is neutral.) This led Croce to his celebrated idea of ethical/political history: A state or a culture is not created by a constitution and other formal organizations. It must have some kind of ethical principles that hold it together, and these are to be studied as methods for controlling, educating, and shaping a people. (4) There are no absolutes in history. The individual constantly remakes his or her ethics and there are no checks or limits on power in this respect. (5) History is the story of liberty. This is not a political but a metaphysical idea—namely, that people are absolutely free to set themselves any ethic, law, or limit they like.

(6) Life is in constant flux, and any attempt to establish political, ethical, or religious limits is naive. (7) Hostility to all abstract ideas and a constant polemic against any attempt to capture life in some metaphysical formula pervades Croce's thought. See *Estetica come scienza dell'espressione e linguistica generale* (1902; Aesthetics as Science of Expression and General Linguistics); *Logica come scienza del concetto puro* (1909; Logic); *Filosofia della pratica. Economia ed etica* (1909; Philosophy of the Practical: Economic and Ethical); *Teoria e storia della storiographia* (1917; History and Theory of Historiography); *Storia d'Italia (1870–1915)* (1928; History of Italy); *Storia d'Europa nel secolo decimonono* (1933; History of Europe in the Nineteenth Century); *La storia come pensiero e come azione* (1938; History as Thought and Action); *Filosofia, poesia, storia* (1951; Philosophy, Poetry, [and] History).

Bibliography: Carlo Antoni, *Commento a Croce* (Bari, 1955); A. Robert Caponigri, *History and Liberty: The Historical Writings of Benedetto Croce* (London, 1955); Edmund E. Jacobitti, *Revolutionary Humanism and Historicism in Modern Italy* (New Haven, Conn., 1981); Fausto Nicolini, *Benedetto Croce* (Bari, 1962).

Edmund E. Jacobitti

CUOCO, Vincenzo (Campomarano, 1770–Naples, 1823), Italian historian, educational theorist, and political activist. Educated at Naples, Cuoco became, with Mario Pagano, Domenico Cirillo, Vincenzo Galiani, and others, a follower of a certain revolutionary interpretation of the Neapolitan philosopher, Giambattista Vico. These thinkers saw in Vico's praise for common sense, his denial of the existence of heroic figures like Homer, and other leveling ideas, a link with revolutionary republicanism. Cuoco, therefore, became a participant and an official in the ill-fated Neapolitan Revolution of 1799. This revolution, trying to emulate events in France, established the short-lived Parthenopean Republic— named after one of the Sirens that lured Ulysses to his death. The revolution lacked popular support and, although Cuoco knew this and warned the other leaders, he was not heeded. When Cardinal Ruffo's forces retook Naples and carried out a bloody massacre, Cuoco managed to escape to France, where in 1800 he set out an account of the revolution (*Saggio Storico sulla revoluzione napoletanan del 1799*; Essay on the Neapolitan Revolution of 1799). A shrewder second edition (1806) established two ideas that are usually associated with Cuoco. The first was the idea of "passive revolution": the revolution had failed because it had been passive and had not established itself in the minds of the people. The second was the doctrine of the "two peoples"; according to this idea, two peoples inhabited southern Italy, the conscious and the unconscious— those who were educated (usually abroad) in revolutionary ideas and those who were indoctrinated by the Church. These two peoples were separated by "two languages and two hundred years"; a revolution could succeed only if the unconscious could be "educated."

After the French retook Italy, Cuoco returned with them to Italy, first to Milan. He served first as editor of *Redattore Cisalpino*, the official organ of the Cisalpine

Republic. Later he became editor of *Giornale Italiano*, also in Milan. In these papers he wrote primarily on educational matters, developing his ideas on the relationship between political revolution and education. Probably in 1803, he began work on a "novel" entitled *Platone in Italia* (Plato in Italy), an allegorical work that discussed Italian political problems under the guise of ancient problems. In 1809 he returned to Naples and became an official in the government of Murat. Again, he was especially interested in education and in 1809 delivered to Murat his *Rapporto al re Murat e progetto di decreto per l'organizzaione della pubblica istruzione* (Report to King Murat on the Decree for the Organization of Public Instruction). This report and the other writings on education present an anti-metaphysical, concrete, and practical kind of education as the most desirable. With the restoration in 1815, Cuoco managed by subterfuge to keep his position; but eventually the strain affected his mind. He died following complications developing from a broken leg. Today, he is remembered chiefly for the doctrine of the "passive revolution," which was taken up by Antonio Gramsci (q.v.) as a vital component in his idea of hegemony. See *Saggio storico sulla rivoluzione napoletana del 1799 seguito dal rapporto al cittadino Carnot di Francesco Lomonaco*, ed. F. Nicolini (Bari: Laterza, 1913); and *Scritti varii*, eds. F. Nicolini and N. Cortese (Bari: Laterza, 1924).

Bibliography: Edmund E. Jacobitti, *Revolutionary Humanism and Historicism in Modern Italy* (New Haven, Conn.: Yale University Press, 1981); G. Oldrini, *La cultura filosofica napoletana dell'ottocento* (Bari, 1973).

Edmund E. Jacobitti

DE RUGGIERO, Guido (Naples, 1888–Rome, 1948), Italian philosopher and historian of philosophy. Taught at the universities of Messina and Rome, until dismissed from his post in 1942 for political activity against fascism. In 1912 De Ruggiero's *La filosofia contemporanea* (Contemporary Philosophy) brought him scholarly recognition. This book was the first of many that were to make him one of Italy's leading philosophers during the twentieth century. Welcomed in the Neapolitan circle around Benedetto Croce (q.v.) and Giovanni Gentile, he collaborated with Giuseppe Prezzolini's Florentine periodical, *La Voce*, and began to write his lifework, the monumental ten-volume history of philosophy from the Greeks through Georg Wilhelm F. Hegel (q.v.) This activity was interrupted by World War I during which De Ruggiero fought in the Italian Army. After the war, he spent some months in England and in 1921 published two very different works, which represented the scholarly and public facets of his writing: *Il pensiero politico meridionale nei secoli XVIII e XIX* (Eighteenth- and Nineteenth-Century Political Thought in Southern Italy) and *L'Impero brittanico dopo la guerra. Studio politico* (The British Empire After the War. A Political Study). At this time he was also contributing interpretive articles on Italian affairs to various newspapers. During these years he refined his personal philosophy. More than abstract principles, it was a moral, ethical system of daily life.

In 1924 and 1925, as liberal Italy waged a losing rear-guard action against fascism, De Ruggiero contributed to *Rinascita liberale* (Liberal Revival), a journal that defended liberal monarchical Italy against the growing encroachments of fascism. As fascism exerted increasing control over all aspects of life, Italians faced hard choices. In 1924 De Ruggiero wrote his *Storia del liberalismo europeo* (1925; History of European Liberalism). It was not only a history of liberalism, but also a vindication of its enduring cultural and ethical values, and an analysis of its crisis in the twentieth century. To write such a book, to warn that "without freedom, religious faith degenerates into . . . servile submission; science congeals into dogma; art shrivels into imitation; the production of economic wealth declines; and the life of human society sinks to the level of animal society" was a public declaration of political faith, if not of war. Acclaimed in Italy and abroad, the book appeared in numerous editions in many languages, and during the years of dictatorship it was read and cherished by all Italians who hoped for and believed in freedom. Throughout the 1930s De Ruggiero remained aloof from the regime, "an exile at home." Only among trusted friends did he express his aversion to the Black Shirts. By the early 1940s Italians were becoming increasingly restive and what had been a passive opposition became active. In 1941 the publisher Laterza of Bari reissued De Ruggiero's history of European liberalism. In the same year, De Ruggiero became politically *engagé*, participating in the founding of the clandestine Action party. Removed from his teaching post, he was imprisoned in June 1943. Liberated at the fall of fascism a month later, he became minister of public education in the first Ivanoe Bonomi Cabinet. Subsequently, he joined the Republican party. During the remaining years of his life De Ruggiero worked for the rebirth not only of Italy, but also of Europe. His articles in *La nuova Europa* (The New Europe), subsequently collected and published under the title *Il ritorno alla ragione* (Return to Reason), condemned the irrationality of fascism and called for a return to reason and morality in public life. Whatever the role of liberalism today, De Ruggiero's history of European liberalism remains a classic study of liberalism as a political system based on freedom where individual rights are protected by law. His newspaper articles elaborated and applied its principles to the problems and issues of his time.

Bibliography: G. De Ruggiero, *Existentialism*, ed. R. Heppenstall, trans. E. M. Cocks (London, 1946); G. De Ruggiero, *The History of European Liberalism*, trans. R. G. Collingwood (London-New York, 1927); G. De Ruggiero, *Il ritorno alla ragione* (Bari, 1946); G. De Ruggiero, *Modern Philosophy*, trans. A. H. Hannay and R. G. Collingwood (Westport, Conn., 1969 [1921]); G. De Ruggiero, *Moral Philosophy*, trans. R. G. Collingwood (London-New York, 1921); G. De Ruggiero, *Scritti politici, 1912–1926* [Political essays], ed. Renzo De Felice, N.p. [1963]; Eugenio Garin, "Guido De Ruggiero," *Belfagor*, no. 6 (1958): 722–728; G. De Ruggiero, *Storia della filosofia*, 10 vols. (Laterza, 1912–1947); Luigi Salvatorelli, "Guido De Ruggiero politico," *Belfagor*, no. 6 (1949): 670–678.

Emiliana Pasca Noether

EINAUDI, Luigi (Carrù, Cuneo, 1874–Rome, 1961), Italian economist and publicist, directly involved in politics after World War II. Professor at the University of Torino (1902), member of the Senate (1919), member of the government (1947), and president of the Italian Republic (1948–1955). Though not a professional historian (trained as an economist, his academic discipline was public finance), Einaudi cultivated historical studies all his life, and he was in fact one of the founders in Italy of modern economic history and of the history of economic thought. His first historical works were *Le entrate pubbliche dello Stato sabaudo nei bilanci e nei conti dei tesorieri durante la guerra di successione spagnola* (1907) and *La finanza sabauda all'aprirsi del secolo XVIII e durante la guerra di successione spagnola* (1908). Based on very thorough archival research, these works were part of a general project to investigate the social and economic life of Piedmont from the end of the seventeenth century to the French Revolution. Einaudi's part (other contributors were Giuseppe Prato and Salvatore Pugliese) examined the whole financial machine of the Piedmontese state in the difficult years 1698–1713. The technical analysis of the budget, however, was not an end in itself; what Einaudi aimed at and brilliantly succeeded in doing was to show how strictly connected economic mechanisms are to the human beings among whom they operate. Einaudi's picture therefore pointed out how the Piedmontese subjects reacted to the financial measures imposed by the demands of the state and what specific repercussions the war events had on the entire social fabric of Piedmont. Then as well as later Einaudi's economic history was in fact a social history.

This lesson was once again fully illustrated by Einaudi, some years later, in *La condotta economica e gli effetti sociali della guerra italiana*, published in 1933 as a volume of the well-known series on the social history of World War I promoted by the Carnegie Foundation. In this work Einaudi provided not just a picture of the war economy in Italy, but a convincing interpretation of the reasons why in Italy the war effort had such devastating effects on the whole society to the point of producing the collapse of the liberal state and opening the door to fascism. At this time Einaudi had already brought his attention to the conditions that make possible in a modern country the life of liberal institutions. His contention was that, based as they are on a certain desire for independence, which at least some of the citizens feel, some economic freedom is a basic requirement for the existence of these institutions. Along this line, Einaudi engaged in a most interesting discussion with Benedetto Croce (q.v). about the relationship between free trade and liberalism. The main texts of this discussion, which went on from 1929 to 1948, were later collected in B. Croce and L. Einaudi, *Liberismo e liberalismo* (1957). In the meantime the fascist authorities had forced Einaudi in 1935 to stop publishing the journal he had been editing since the beginning of the century, *La Riforma Sociale*. This gave Einaudi the occasion to start a new journal of scholarly character, specifically dedicated to economic history and the history of economic thought, *Rivista di Storia Economica* (1936–1943). Part of the many essays on these topics published by

Einaudi in this journal and elsewhere were later collected in *Saggi bibliografici e storici intorno alle dottrine economiche* (1957). Both for cultural as well as political reasons, which kept economic and social history at the fringe of Italian historical studies in the first half of this century, the importance of Einaudi's historical work was not generally recognized until after the end of World War II. Nevertheless, his works are still necessary points of reference not just for the documentation on which they are based, but also for their intellectual strength and for their capacity to grasp and render most vividly a whole historical picture.

Bibliography: *Bibliografia degli scritti di Luigi Einaudi, a cura di Luigi Firpo* (Torino, 1971); R. Faucci, *Luigi Einaudi* (Torino, 1986); R. Vivarelli, "Liberismo, protezionismo, fascismo. Per la storia e il significato di un trascurato giudizio di Luigi Einaudi sulle origini del fascismo," in R. Vivarelli, *Il fallimento del liberalismo. Studi sulle origini del fascismo* (Bologna, 1981), pp. 163–344.

Roberto Vivarelli

FARINI, Luigi Carlo (Russi, 1812–Quarto, 1866), Italian historian, physician, and politician. While a medical student at Bologna, Farini became involved in the 1831 Revolution, and he remained active in the Liberal movement thereafter. He helped draw up the "Proclamation of Rimini" of 1845, a key statement of the moderate liberal position. He welcomed the reforms of Pope Pius IX, served in the first liberal ministry of the Papal State as secretary general of the Ministry of the Interior, and was appointed by Pellegrino Rossi to head the Department of Public Health in 1848. After the assassination of Rossi, in whom he had placed his hopes for a successful moderate liberal government for the Papal State, Farini was deprived of his office by the radicals and fled to Piedmont, which thereafter became his home. Up to this point, his numerous publications had dealt only with medical science, but in reaction to the events of 1848, he turned his attention to history and wrote his most important historical work, *Storia dello Stato Romano dal 1815 al 1850* (1850–1853; history of the Roman State from 1815 to 1850). A classic expression of the moderate liberal interpretation of the Risorgimento, it was equally critical of the retrograde and arbitrary papal regime and of the radicals who plotted against it. Although it sparked a bitter polemic with the radicals, the book was a great success, and established Farini as one of the leading historians among the moderates. He followed it in 1854 with Storia d'Italia dal 1814 ai nostri giorni (1854–1859; History of Italy from 1814 to Our Days). This book expanded his moderate liberal interpretation of the Risorgimento to cover the entire peninsula and stressed, as his previous work had not done, the key role that Piedmont had to play in the liberation of Italy. Hereafter he was increasingly involved in politics, serving in the Piedmontese Parliament from 1849 to 1865 as an important supporter and adviser of Camillo Cavour, who upon joining the government had turned over to Farini the direction of his paper, *Risorgimento*. After the outbreak of war and revolution in central Italy in 1859, Cavour sent him to Modena as his commissioner; with great skill Farini was able to engineer the annexation of all Emilia to Italy in

1860. He encountered greater difficulties when he was sent late in 1860 to manage the annexation of southern Italy to the united kingdom. In 1862 he was himself asked to form a ministry, but his failing health forced him to resign within a few months, and he went into retirement until his death in 1866.

Bibliography. Luigi Rava, ed., *Epistolario di L. C. Farini* (Bologna, 1911–1935); Piero Zama, *Luigi Carlo Farini nel Risorgimento italiano* (Faenza, 1962).

Alan J. Reinerman

FERRARI, Giuseppe (Milan, 1811–Rome, 1876), Italian historian. The younger son of a physician, Ferrari was educated at the Liceo Sant'Alessandro in Milan and at the University of Pavia, where he earned a law degree in 1832. Like his friends Carlo Cattaneo (q.v.) and Cesare Cantù (q.v.), he also frequented the home of the eminent jurist and philosopher Gian Domenico Romagnosi (q.v.), whose devoted disciple he became. Through Romagnosi's influence, Ferrari left the practice of law to pursue a major study of the life and works of the seventeenth-century Neapolitan philosopher Giambattista Vico. After Romagnosi's death, Ferrari edited his mentor's unfinished manuscripts and published his intellectual biography. Like other Milanese intellectuals of his generation, in the late 1830s Ferrari came under police surveillance for possible involvement in antigovernment activities. In 1838 he decided to leave the stifling atmosphere of his native city for a sojourn in Paris, the hub of many political and social experiments of his day. Ferrari's work on Vico, published in a French edition by Eveillard, gave him access to several intellectual circles and salons in the French capital and to the stars on the faculty of the prestigious Collège de France, especially Claude Fauriel, Jules Michelet (q.v.) and Edgar Quinet (q.v.). So dazzled was he by their ideas and oratorical brilliance that he decided to settle in France permanently and to pursue an academic career.

Having taken the required competitive examinations in the fall of 1841, Ferrari was awarded a lectureship at the University of Strasbourg. There he became the center of a stormy controversy between conservative Catholics, on one hand, and advocates of a secular curriculum and of religious minorities on the other. The outbreak of revolution in Paris in February 1848 and the appointment of the radical Hippolyte Carnot as minister of public education saved Ferrari from dismissal, but he was soon replaced by a more highly qualified lecturer. Reluctantly, he accepted a teaching assignment at the Lycèe in the small town of Bourges, where he remained from January to June 1849, when he was accused by local police of having led a demonstration against the government of Louis Napoleon Bonaparte. He fled to Brussels but was able to return to Paris early in 1850, when the charges against him were dropped. Thereafter, although watched by the Bonapartist police, he was able to resume his intellectual pursuits in peace. In the 1850s he wrote the works that made his reputation as a philosopher of history: *Filosofia della rivoluzione* (1851), *La federazione republicana* (1851), and *Histoire des révolutions d'Italie* (1858). *Filosofia della rivoluzione* was an analysis of the French Revolution of 1789–1793, the key event in modern history that had opened up the possibility of a secular culture and of economic and social justice. However, the promise of the Great Revolution had not been fulfilled, and intellectuals had a duty to continue the struggle. *La federazione republicana* was Ferrari's contribution to the political and intellectual debates on the failure of the 1848 Revolution in Italy. He argued that the failure of revolution proved the fallacies of Mazzini's brand of nationalist propaganda and action. The Mazzinian theory of national unity, Ferrari argued, was not applicable to Italy, whose history had been shaped by two universal and federal institutions, the papacy and the empire. Moreover, the Mazzinian program largely ignored social and economic divisions in Italian society in the name of an abstract political unity. Only a program that built on Italy's federal traditions offering the prospect of social justice could generate the popular enthusiasm needed to break the power of the Church and of Austria in Italian affairs. In his four-volume *Histoire des révolutions*, Ferrari reconstructed thousands of episodes in Italian history in support of the thesis stated briefly and polemically in *La federazione republicana*.

Despite his academic and political misfortunes, Ferrari was comfortable with his life in Paris and found it difficult to leave in 1859–1860. But the lure of politics in the new state proved irresistible. Elected to the new Italian Parliament in 1860 from a rural district in northwest Lombardy, he served until his death, with the exception of only one brief interval in 1866–1867. Even while active and visible as a member of the democratic minority in the Chamber of Deputies, Ferrari continued his studies in the philosophy of history. The herculean labors of collecting and organizing historical data for the *Histoire des révolutions* led him to think that alternative methodologies were possible and desirable. Like his contemporaries Justin Dromel and Gustav Ruemelin, Ferrari thought that a *science of history* could be developed to transcend the limitations both of anecdotal evidence and of descriptive treatment of such evidence. By a rather tortuous intellectual path that included a reinterpretation of his youthful interest in Vico, Ferrari arrived at his last works, *Teoria dei periodi politici* (1874) and *L'aritmetica della storia* (1875). *Teoria* is one of the most interesting, albeit little known, examples of attempts to explain historical change through generational theory. Ferrari formulated the hypothesis that change occurred through the actions of four successive generations: innovators or precursors, revolutionaries, reactionaries, and, finally, a "resolutive generation." This last generation encompassed and integrated the achievements of the preceding ones, giving birth to a new phase of civilization; then, in turn, it was challenged by innovators, and the cycle repeated itself. In his last essay, Ferrari attempted to go beyond generational theory to the formulation of actual mathematical laws by which to analyze recurring patterns or cycles in history.

Bibliography: Silvia Rota Ghibaudi, *Giuseppe Ferrari. L'evoluzione del suo pensiero, 1838–1860* (Florence: Olschki, 1969); Clara M. Lovett, *Giuseppe Ferrari and the Italian Revolution* (Chapel Hill: University of North Carolina Press, 1979); Giuseppe Monsagrati, "A proposito di una recente biografia di Giuseppe Ferrari; vecchie tesi e nuove ipotesi," *Rassegna storica del Risorgimento* 76, no. 3 (1980): 259–296.

Clara M. Lovett

FERRERO, Guglielmo (Portici, 1871–Geneva, 1942), historian, psychologist, and sociologist. Ferrero studied at Pisa and Turin, where he collaborated with Cesare Lombroso on *La donna delinquente* (The Delinquent Woman). Alone he produced *I simboli* (1893) and *L'Europa giovane* (1897; Young Europe). A radical, he published a novel dealing with the corruption of the 1890s. While still young he became an editor of *Secolo*, a publication from Milan, and he involved himself in political journalism. He turned increasingly from sociology to history, publishing *Grandezza et decadenza di Roma* (5 vols., 1902–1907); *Greatness and Decline of Rome* (Eng. trans. 1909) treating Roman history from the Gracchi to the death of Augustus. His emphasis was not on the conflict between republicans and imperialists as in the nineteenth-century historians Theodor Mommsen (q.v.) and Victor Duruy (q.v.), but instead on changing manners and morals corrupted by increasing luxury and the expenditures associated with an imperialist economy. He compared the tensions he saw in Roman society arising from the growth of a new mercantile aristocracy with those of prewar capitalistic Europe. The work was a great success in America, which, like Rome had been, was a rich republic with greater power but with more elected officials than bureaucrats. Better received by the literate public than by specialists, this work made Ferrero world famous by the outbreak of World War I. In that war, being a socialist he proposed that Italy intervene on the side of the Allies because they supported democracy.

After the war Ferrero published *La ruine de la civilisation antique* (Paris, 1921; Ital. trans., Milan, 1926) and *Roma antica* with C. Barbagallo (3 vols., 1921–1922). He also published a tetrology of historical romances, *La Terza Roma (The Third Rome)*, between 1926 and 1930. Having fled Mussolini in 1930, he became professor at Geneva, where he taught contemporary history from the French Revolution to the present. He published *Aventure: Bonaparte en Italie (1796–1797)* (Paris, 1936), *Reconstruction: Talleyrand à Vienne (1814–1815)* (Paris, 1940), and *Pouvoir* (New York, 1942). In these antifascist works this hero of the exile stigmatized Napoleon as bringing fear and disorder into a world liberated by Talleyrand's principle of legitimacy. One of his most prescient works, translated as *The Women of the Caesars* (New York, 1911), shows how much more liberated and dominating good and bad Roman women were than their Greek sisters. "Among ancient societies the Roman was probably that in which, at least among the better classes, women enjoyed the greatest social liberty and the greatest legal and economic autonomy. There she most nearly approached that condition of moral and civil equality with man which makes her his comrade, and not his slave—that equality in which modern civilization sees one of the supreme ends of moral progress."

Bibliography: C. Barbagallo, *L'opera storica di G. F. e i suoi critici* (Milan, 1911); Benedetto Croce, *Storia della storiografia italiana nel secolo XIX*, 3d ed.; L. Salvatorelli, *G. Ferrero storico di Roma* (1947).

William A. Percy

GAETA, Franco (Venice, 1926–Rome, 1984), Italian historian. Having graduated from the University of Padua in 1950, Gaeta completed preparations with a study grant at the Crocean Institute of Historical Studies, Naples, directed by Federico Chabod (q.v.). Gaeta was known as an original thinker, an exhaustive researcher who distinguished himself in several fields. Among the university positions he held was a chair in both medieval and modern history at the University of Aquila, and later one in modern history at the University of Rome. The Venetian scholar participated in numerous conferences; he collaborated in collections of essays and professional journals on a wide spectrum of history. Gaeta attracted early attention with his *Lorenzo Valla. Filologia e storia dell'Umanesimo italiano* (Naples, 1955). He utilized the Viconian thesis concerning the intimate connections between language and historical development as a reflection of a people's advance toward self-consciousness. This approach was sustained by his editing of *Niccolo Machiavelli, Lettere* (Milan, 1961), and the Florentine thinker's *Istorie fiorentine* (Milan, 1962). New ground was broken with the publication between 1958 and 1967 of four volumes on aspects of papal diplomacy during the Reformation and Counter-Reformation, with emphasis on the institution of the Nuncio office in Venice. Gaeta's interest in contemporary history is illustrated by his general account, "La seconda guerra mondiale e i nuovi problemi del mondo (1939–1960)," *Storia universale*, ed Corrado Barbagallo (Turin, 1930–), vol. 4, part 4 (1964), and by *Democrazie e totalitarismi dalla prima alla seconda guerra mondiale* (Bologna, 1982). In *La crisi del fine secola e l'età giolittiana* (Turin, 1982), Gaeta argued that Giovanni Giolitti's rule had been essentially positive and a potentially decisive watershed in modern Italian history.

Undoubtedly, Gaeta's major contribution was his study and interpretation of modern Italian nationalism. The anthology, *La stampa nazionalista* (Bologna, 1965), was included in the series, *Il periodo fascista: stampa e opinione pubblica*, directed by Renzo de Felice. It represented a documentary examination of nationalist polemics on the critical issues confronting Italy from the organization of the Italian Nationalist Association in December 1910 to its fusion with the National Fascist party in March 1923. Within a month there appeared *Nazionalismo italiano* (Naples, 1965), in which Gaeta attempted to understand the phenomenon by separating the political stance of the movement from the historical background. Gaeta saw nationalism as the emergent ideology of the Italian bourgeoisie, whose conservative-reactionary outlook emanated from the *destra liberale* of the Risorgimento–Unification Era. He also exposed and delineated the contradictions. Nationalism spoke of continuing the Risorgimento and, indeed, completing it by bolstering the authority of the state, promoting national unity, cementing social solidarity, and giving Italy its rightful place in a world of competitive states. At the same time it championed the replacement of the liberal parliamentary regime by a political order that was in clear opposition not only to the Italian Risorgimento but also to the course of European history since the Enlightenment and the French Revolution of 1789.

Ronald S. Cunsolo

GHISALBERTI, Alberto M. (Milan, 1894–Rome, 1986), Italian historian. Professor at the universities of Palermo (1936), Perugia (1939), and Rome (1941) where he was also *preside* of the Faculty of Letters. He had fought in World War I and had been awarded the Silver Medal for military valor. He received degrees *honoris causa* from the French universities of Aix-en-Provence, Toulouse, and Paris-Sorbonne. Parallel with his university career, he became actively interested in the organization of specialized studies first as secretary general (1935) and then as president (1951) of the Istituto per la Storia del Risorgimento Italiano. He gave the Instituto an international character particularly by participating in the biennial Congresses of eminent historians from outside Italy and, no less important, in encouraging the establishment of "centers of study" of the Risorgimento in important cities of the world. Ghisalberti's professional work was almost totally dedicated to the history of the Risorgimento era, which he conceived as the Italian aspect of the great European national-cultural movements from the mideighteenth century to the outbreak of the Great War of 1914. His ideas and interpretations concerning this Italian function of the history of modern Europe are to be found in his *Albori del Risorgimento* (1931; The Dawn of the Risorgimento) and *Introduzione alla storia del Risorgimento* (1942; Introduction to the History of the Risorgimento). His research spanned various fields, as his numerous writings attest, but were concentrated chiefly on Rome during the nineteenth century. He also explored themes of ideological-social history in such works as *La partecipazione popolare al Risorgimento* (1945); *Il movimento nazionale dal 1831 alla vigilia della prima guerra d'indipendenza* and *La Seconda restaurazione 1849–1852* (1959); and, finally, in his *Liberalismo moderato nel Risorgimento* (1961). His studies of such diverse personalities of the Risorgimento era as Felice Orsini, Giuseppe Mazzini, Giuseppe Montanelli, and Massimo d'Azeglio, published between 1955 and 1972, reveal a sensitive subtlety of biographical treatment that is one of the truly exceptional historiographical characteristics of A. M. Ghisalberti. The fine homage paid him on his seventy-fifth birthday with the presentation to him of a four-volume *Bibliografia dell'età del Risorgimento* (Rome, 1971–1974) was a worthy testimonial of the admiration and gratitude of his disciples and friends.

Emilia Morelli

GIOBERTI, Vincenzo (Turin, 1801–Paris, 1852), Italian theologian, philosopher, priest, and writer. Political figure who played a key role in the elaboration of the Neo-Guelph program in Italy and an important part in the Risorgimento. In 1838 Gioberti published his first work, the *Teorica del sovrannaturale*, followed by *L'Introduzione allo studio della filosofia* (1840). He was convinced that without a philosophical concept of the nature of being or an ontology, one could not construct a political program, a religious system, or even a morality. He did so in these works stressing that God is the only being (Ens), while all else is mere existence. From his formula "the Ens creates existence" he derived another, "religion creates morality and human civilization." Since he believed that Christianity was the sole religion that preserved in its integrity and entirety the divine revelation, Gioberti found within Catholicism the entire civilization of humanity, and in the history of Catholicism, the history of humankind. In light of the fact that the Church had its center in Italy, where its head resided, the history of Italy was tied to that of Catholicism, and therefore to that of civilization itself. From this flowed Italy's civilizing mission and its conciliation of tradition and progress. These ideas were to reemerge in his political writings and political program which called for a confederation of Italian states under the presidency of the Pope and the military force of the Kingdom of Sardinia. This was the message of his *Del primato morale e civile degli Italiani* (1843), which depicted the Church as the axis for human life in general and specifically marked as essential for the restoration of Italian supremacy. Gioberti insisted that the peninsula could be revived under a confederation of Italian princes under the Pontiff whose moral regime would be upheld by the military might of Piedmont. In his words he did not describe Italy's present situation but the ideal, which might be realized. Liberty was a necessary ingredient in Gioberti's scheme, which led him to oppose the Jesuits, whom he depicted as the enemy of the freedom and the national aspirations he cherished.

President of the Chamber of Deputies after his triumphant return to Piedmont in 1847, he later served as prime minister from December 1848 to February 1849. Pio Nono's refusal to declare war on Austria during the revolutionary upheaval of 1848 shattered the Neo-Guelph program and disillusioned Gioberti, altering his attitude. His new view was outlined in his *Nel Rinnovamento civile d'Italia* (1851) wherein he looked to Piedmont rather than the papacy to assume the initiative in unification and called for a national union in place of the confederation he had earlier proposed. His suggestion that the end of temporal power would revitalize religion, as well as the pantheistic ontologism of his philosophy, contributed to his work being placed on the Index. On the other hand, it provided a program for Camillo di Cavour and Piedmont to pursue, leading to the proclamation of the Kingdom of Italy in 1861.

Bibliography: A. Anzilotti, *Gioberti* (Florence: Vallecchi, 1931); Giovanni Giammona, *La problematica filosofica e pedagogica di Vincenzo Gioberti* (Catania: Edigrof, 1973); August Guzzo, ed., *Scritti scelti* (Turin: UTET, 1966); A. Omodeo, *Vincenzo Gioberti e la sua evoluzione politica* (Turin: Einaudi, 1941).

Frank J. Coppa

GRAMSCI, Antonio (Ales, Sardinia, 1891–Rome, 1937), Italian political and cultural theorist, philosopher, communist leader, journalist. Gramsci and Benedetto Croce (q.v.) are the two most important Italian political thinkers of the twentieth century, and, along with George Lukács, Gramsci was one of the two most influential and consequential independent Marxist theorists of his era. Born into a Sardinian family of modest means, Gramsci won a scholarship to the University of Turin in 1911, specialized ultimately in linguistics and philosophy, but also participated in the broader cultural politics of the city, which became especially inflamed after Italy's 1911 entry into war with Libya. His early political interest centered primarily on the "Southern Question," and he lent enthusiastic support to the movement led by Gaetano Salvemini (q.v.) to bring the Italian South into closer economic and political alignment with the more industrial and prosperous North. He appears to have had some early interest in Futurism, and he wrote substantially about theater (especially Pirandello) in his early journalism (1915–1918). He rejected Italian socialism in the form he found it (dominated by the positivism and, in political terms, the reformism of Filippo Turati), and even when he joined the PSI (Italian Socialist party) in 1914, he played a very independent role in its organization. He was severely critical of it during the "Red Years" of 1919–1920, and participated in the party split that resulted in the formation of the PCI (Italian Communist party) at Livorno, in January 1921. One of his main activities after leaving the university in 1914 was in journalism. He wrote on every conceivable cultural and political topic for both the socialist and mainstream-liberal press, and he founded two reviews of his own, the short-lived *La Città Futura* and *L'Ordine Nuovo*—respectively, the "future city" and the "new order." His other principal activity was in political organizing, first in Turin where he theorized and helped organize the "factory council" system of the Red Years, destroyed in the general strike of September 1920, and then as the Italian Communist representative to the Comintern (1922–1923) and as the party's general secretary (1924–1926). His politics were an original mix of idealist and Leninist themes. The idealistic strain came from Antonio Labriola (q.v.) and Giovanni Gentile as well as Croce. The Leninist strain creatively developed within the Italian context, emphasized democratic organization of the working class from below and guided without imposing political education of all "subaltern" classes and broad-based "subaltern" alliances, particularly of workers and peasants (the latter an original Gramscian conception inspired by and derived from Salvemini's (q.v.) social thought and Lenin's revolutionary praxis).

Returning from his Comintern stint in Russia via Vienna in 1923, and then on to Italy in 1924 as an elected parliamentary deputy (which theoretically granted him freedom of political activity), Gramsci worked tenaciously against fascism, but eventually became one of its most internationally celebrated victims. Ironically, however, his imprisonment by the fascist regime in late 1926 until his death in 1937 gave him an opportunity for sustained historical and theoretical expression which he very likely would not otherwise have had. His *Quaderni del Carcere* (*Prison Notebooks*), written between 1929 and 1935 and published after the war, take up approximately twenty-four hundred pages of text in the 1975 critical edition, and discuss an astonishingly wide range of subjects from Dante's *Divine Comedy* to Japanese Shinto. In addition, he wrote about nine hundred pages of *Lettere dal Carcere* (*Prison Letters*), which open up his personal feelings, his relationships with others, his love of folklore, and his memories of Sardinian life, among many other matters. These are commonly and rightly regarded in Italy as a major literary document. The *Notebooks* permit no such quick summary, but their principal themes include the following. First, Gramsci self-consciously dedicated himself to the study of the role of intellectuals in politics, both as defenders (sometimes unconscious) of an incumbent system and as its underminers. This theme led him into a detailed historical estimation of the role of intellectuals in the Risorgimento, and more recently, in sustaining fascism. On fascism, Gramsci believed, for example, that Croce, by living in Italy and participating in the cultural life of Italy under fascism, actually served the regime as a "hegemonic" support despite his publicly stated but superficial (because unaware of itself as gesture) opposition. The theme also led him into a detailed analysis of prominent intellectuals in earlier Italian history (above all Niccolo Machiavelli, Vincenzo Cuoco [q.v.], and Giuseppe Mazzini) as well as in modern European history generally, and into a sociological typologizing of intellectuals into the now celebrated categories of "traditional" (ostensibly independent of class) and "organic" (consciously class-based). Second, Gramsci moved from an analysis of intellectuals to the broader question of "hegemony," the process by which political forces attempt to shape and develop cultural traditions to lend "consent" to their goals and policies. In this multifaceted theory, Gramsci attempted to account for such matters as how average people (the "man-in-the-mass") could have "contradictory consciousnesses" (i.e., complex blends of inherited and generally accepted "common sense" with half-conscious utopian strivings); and how political movements could organize themselves to maximize their consensual support.

Gramsci believed that the leftist Action party, led by Mazzini, while democratic in spirit, was insufficiently "Jacobin," that is, self-conscious about the concrete task of mass organization within civil society, that is, of "hegemony," especially in building connections between the country and the city. Cavour's moderates, on the other hand, while much more politically astute, lacked both the capacity for and the interest in such organization. In Italian history, Gramsci reluctantly concluded, "the Jacobin force has always been lacking." Italy had paid the price for this in the post-Risorgimento era, where the insufficient development of a mass-based ("national-popular") political culture bore primary responsibility for its culmination in the fascist "passive revolution." Yet it should be remembered that the *Notebooks*, for all their intellectual reach and penetration, are not a finished theoretical and historical statement or even a continuous narrative (let alone a schematic argument as the present article may lead one to think), but an open-ended set of reflections often occasioned by specific books and articles. It is for his fertile imagination and intellectual range rather than for his systematizing or organizing powers that Gramsci as thinker is so important and so worthy of study.

Bibliography: English readers will find much of Gramsci's writing available in *Selections from the Prison Notebooks*, eds. Q. Hoare and G. Nowell-Smith (New York, 1971); *Letters from Prison*, ed. L. Lawner (New York, 1973); *History, Philosophy, and Culture in the Young Gramsci*, eds. P. Cavalcanti and P. Piccone (St. Louis, 1975); *Selections from Political Writings, 1910–1920*, and *Selections from Political Writings, 1921–1926*, both ed. Q. Hoare (New York, 1977 and 1978); and *Selections from Cultural Writings*, eds. D. Forgacs and G. Nowell-Smith (Cambridge Mass., 1985). But serious students will need to consult the *Quaderni del Carcere*, ed. V. Gerratana, 4 vols. (Turin, 1975) and the *Lettere dal Carcere*, eds. S. Caprioglio and E. Fubini (Turin, 1965). Important secondary works include: Walter L. Adamson, *Hegemony and Revolution* (Berkeley, Calif., 1980); John Cammett, *Antonio Gramsci and the Origins of Italian Communism* (Stanford, Calif., 1967); Martin Clark, *Antonio Gramsci and the Revolution That Failed* (New Haven, Conn., 1977); Alastair Davidson, *Antonio Gramsci: Towards an Intellectual Biography* (London, 1977); Joseph V. Femia, *Gramsci's Political Thought* (Oxford, 1981); Jackson Lears, "The Concept of Cultural Hegemony: Problems and Possibilities," *American Historical Review* 90, 3 (June 1985): 567–593; Franco Lo Piparo, *Lingua, intellettuali, egemonia in Gramsci* (Bari, 1979). On Gramsci's historical thought, see also: Aldo Garosci, "Totalitarismo e storicismo nel pensiero di Gramsci" in *Pensiero politico e storiografia moderna* (Pisa: Nistri-Lischi, 1954), pp. 193–257; Giuseppe Galasso, *Croce, Gramsci e altri storici* (Milan: Il Saggiatore, 1978), pp. 116–265; and Massimo L. Salvadori, *Gramsci e il problema storico della democrazia* (Torino: Einaudi, 1973), particularly pp. 207–363.

Walter L. Adamson

JEMOLO, Arturo Carlo (Rome, 1891–Rome, 1981). Italian historian, professor at the universities of Bologna and Rome. He is one of the most characteristic personalities in Italian historiography of this century in his role as a scholar of canon and ecclesiastical law. He is the best disciple of Francesco Ruffini, the historian of the Count of Cavour's concept of religious freedom. Particular in Jemolo is the coexistence of two profound and sincere sentiments: the Catholic, a religiosity ingrained with an austere Jansenism, and the liberal, inherited from the Risorgimento.

As a historian, he can be considered the last great representative of liberal Catholicism. Among his many writings, two works are especially notable. *Il Giansenismo in Italia prima della Rivoluzione* (Jansenism in Italy Before the Revolution) (1928) opens with a broad-ranging introduction on seventeenth- and eighteenth-century French Jansenism. With a wealth of new research, Jemolo then portrays the physiognomy of Italian Jansenism, examining its origins, its theological structure, its doctrines of ancient mold, defining it as "the last wave of the Middle Ages lapping the shores of the eighteenth century."

In its most original aspect, this book, already anticipated by other short studies since 1914, is a clear confutation of the thesis of the historian Ettore Rota, who had provided a different image of the Italian Jansenists, portraying them as *déguisés* innovators, republicans with Jacobin tendencies, revolutionary precursors of Risorgimento patriots, champions of liberty and democracy. Jemolo's sharp judgment of this interpretation was perhaps overly severe; in fact, he himself later attenuated his view, recognizing that towards the end of the eighteenth century Italian Jansenism especially in Pavia and Liguria did accept some Enlightenment and democratic ideas. But his admonition on historical methodology, the need for attention to the entire development of any religious movement from its origins, remains exemplary.

Jemolo's other great work, *Chiesa e Stato in Italia negli ultimi cento anni*

(Church and State in Italy in the last Hundred Years) (1948), published when Italian historians seemed often to favor political, economic, and social themes, is a great history which goes well beyond its premise—to reconstruct the relationship between two institutions, State and Church—and develops into a sophisticated analysis of Italian spirituality between the nineteenth and twentieth centuries.

In these two works as in many other pages on the history of the last centuries, Jemolo was always a severe critic of Jacobin excesses as he was of truculent and vulgar anticlericalism. He respected and admired the inflexibility of the consistently secular thought of a philosopher like Benedetto Croce (q.v.) or a historian like Adolfo Omodeo (q.v.). He loved to rebuild the most humble and hidden aspects of the life of past generations. He appreciated historians who did not yield to the temptation to transfer to the past the thoughts and aspirations of their own time and who did not give "sharp judgments" inspired by a vision of things "characteristic of those who do not understand or distinguish varying colors, but only black and white." He was, like the Jansenists he loved, a pessimist; but he confided that believers in God and believers in values like liberty and the dignity of man could always unite in order to emerge from the dark into the light of reason.

Bibliography: As yet, there does not exist a broad and solid work on Jemolo as a historian. His book *Anni di prova*, Vicenza, 1969, is partially autobiographical and can be usefully consulted.

Alessandro Galante Garrone
(Trans. Spencer Di Scala)

LABRIOLA, Antonio (Cassino, 1843–Rome, 1904), Italian philosopher. In 1861 Labriola went to study philosophy at the University of Naples, the center of Italian Hegelianism. Since the 1840s, Italian Hegelianism—with its idea of an "ethical state" linking individual to individual and province to province in a single culture with a single ethic—had been the ideology of radical Italian nationalists. From the outset, the young and reputedly very brilliant Labriola was steeped in Hegelian philosophy. From Georg Wilhelm F. Hegel (q.v.) and later from Karl Marx (q.v.), Labriola learned not only to admire the ethical state, but also to scorn positivism, naturalism, and other static explanations of the world. Labriola studied at Naples until 1874, when he secured a position teaching philosophy at the University of Rome. In the years at Naples and for many years after his move to Rome, Labriola advocated a political/cultural program that ran counter to the bourgeois government's cautious and transformist policies. The government sought to maintain secular, liberal, and constitutional government without input from a presumably untrustworthy population. Where the government was frightened of the masses, especially in the religious south, Labriola advocated the widening involvement, education, and indoctrination of the masses and the implementation of the Hegelian idea of the ethical, as opposed to the liberal, neutral state. As this policy was implicitly and explicitly unpalatable to the moderates in power, Labriola moved farther and farther to the political left and toward radical socialism. In 1887 he abandoned gradualist tendencies, spoke of a complete rupture with the government, and announced that socialism and bourgeois government were separated by irreconcilable differences.

Labriola wrote little; most of his ideas were conveyed in lectures and letters. Hence, it is difficult to characterize his ideas, although one can discern a considerable intellectual debt to Bertrando Spaventa. When Labriola finally became a revolutionary, he became part of and helped to establish a "tradition" of socialism that saw Marxism as a "self-sufficient" way of life, a *weltanschauung*. In Italy, this idea was associated with the complex ideas of Bertrando Spaventa, Antonio Labriola, Benedetto Croce (q.v.), Rodolfo Mondolfo, Antonio Gramsci (q.v.), and Antonio Banfi. Establishing the existence of—let alone characterizing—such a tradition of Marxists and non-Marxists, revolutionaries, idealists, and so on is risky, however. Generally, Labriola (and this tradition) ignore economics, metaphysics, abstract materialism, "systems," and especially—and above all—positivist, orthodox, Kautskian Marxism. Labriola instead advocated a concrete, antimetaphysical, and flexible revolutionary program divorced from preconceptions and committed to the "philosophy of *praxis*." Indeed, he may be the first in Italy to have used those words. When the Italian Socialist party was founded in 1892 and the positivist moderate, Filippo Turati, became its titular head, Labriola would have nothing to do with it. Ironically, it was Labriola who, at the turn of the century, brought Benedetto Croce into the struggle with Turati and other positivist socialists; and it was Croce who—after attacking the positivists—issued a most devastating critique of Marxism as a philosophy of history and a *Weltanschauung*. To Croce, it mattered little whether people were determined by material or ideal forces or how removed, mediated, or indirect those forces were. Determinism was determinism, and calling it *praxis* or some other euphemism could not disguise it. Likewise, a philosophy of life was a philosophy of life, and if Marxism was such a philosophy, its central thesis was simply that, in the study of society, people should pay attention to economics—along with other factors. After the encounter with Croce, Labriola continued his struggle with Turati, but his brand of Marxism went into serious decline, and, after his death, his ideas were intermingled with, if not replaced by, Crocean-Sorelian Marxism. See *Opere*, ed. Luigi Dal Pane, 3 vols. (Milan, 1959–1962); *Essays on the Materialist Conception of History*, trans. Charles H. Kerr (Chicago, 1903); *Socialism and Philosophy*, trans. E. Unterman (Chicago, 1918); Giuseppe Berti, "123 lettere inedite di Antonio Labriola a Bertrando Spaventa," *Rinascita* 10, no. 1 (January 1954): 65–87; Berti, "Lettere inedite di Antonio Labriola: alcune lettere a Ruggero Bonghi," in *Rinascita* 11, no. 3 (March 1954): 217–228; Labriola, "Lettere napoletane," *Cronache Meridionali*, August 4, 1954, pp. 558–584; Labriola, *Lettere a Benedetto Croce (1885–1904)* (Naples, 1975).

Bibliography: Benedetto Croce, "Antonio Labriola, Ricordi," *Scritti varii di filosofia e politica*, ed. B. Croce (Bari, 1906), pp. 498–504; Benedetto Croce, "Come naque e come morì il marxismo teorico in Italia (1895–1900)," in *Materialismo storico e economia marxistica* (Bari, 1968), pp. 253–294; Luigi Dal Pane, *Antonio Labriola nella politica e nella cultura italiana* (Turin, 1975); Eugenio Garin, "Introduzione" to Antonio Labriola, *La Concezione materialistica della storia* (Bari, 1965); Valentino Gerratana, "Introduzione" to *Scritti politici* (1886–1904) of Labriola (Bari, 1970); Paul Piccone, "Labriola and the Roots of Eurocommunism," *Berkeley Journal of Sociology* 32 (1977–1978): 3–44.

Edmund E. Jacobitti

LEVI DELLA VIDA, Giorgio (Venice, 1886–Rome, 1967), Italian historian. From 1914 to 1956, with a long interruption, Levi Della Vida was a professor of Arabic, of Semitic philology, and of Islam at the Oriental Institute of Naples and at the universities of Turin and Rome. From 1931 to 1939 he was a scientific collaborator in the Vatican Library. In April 1938 he was invited by the Foundation Michonis to give three lectures at the Collège de France. The lectures were published under the title *Les Semites et leur role dans l'histoire religieuse* (Paris, 1938). In 1931 he refused to take an oath of allegiance to fascism, was deprived of his teaching position, and went to America. From 1939 to 1945 and from 1946 to 1948, he taught at the University of Pennsylvania. As a highly reputed scientist, he was a member of several foreign academies and earned an *ad honorem* doctorate at the universities of Algiers and of Paris. Although he was an expert of the classic Greco-Roman world, Levi Della Vida dealt specifically with Semitic civilizations, Arabs and Hebrews. His first two works, *Storia e Religione dell'Oriente Semitico* (1924; History and the Religion of Semitic East) and *Gli Arabi nella Storia* [The Arabs in History] (*Enciclopedia Italiana*, Vol. 3, 1929, pp. 820–839), are particularly significant for his historical method. According to F. Gabrieli, he brought to perfection "the harmony between philology and history which has never been realized in his great predecessors" (Gabrieli, 1975, p. 66). Levi Della Vida conceived philology and literary criticism (in this field he accepted J. Wellhausen's historical criticism), not as an end in themselves, but as a means of history. He was concerned with the objectivity of history: "Historical science, when it is honestly professed, does not put itself at any party's disposal" (*Storia e Religione nell'Oriente semitico*, p. 87). In this way, the task of history consists in "a laborious and disinterested effort to deliver our past from the mists which envelop it" and, at the same time, "to make our present better known and understood." Levi Della Vida took a position against both a positivistic and idealistic conception of history. He considered as a determinant "the work of individual personalities who are the only elements of historical events which our mind perceives directly." To the historicism of Benedetto Croce (q.v.), he opposed a "moral dualism" and, consequently, he refused the conception that the moral and religious sense is overcome and absorbed by philosophy. "Man is a believing animal as much as he is a logical animal, and his rational activity never succeeds in overcoming his need to possess a concrete and categorical certainty through an act of irrational faith" (*Aneddoti e svaghi arabi e non arabi*, Milan, 1959, p. 340).

In 1932 Levi Della Vida applied the same method to the history of Israel in his work, *Storia e religione degli Ebrei fino al ritorno dall'esilio babilonese* (History and Religion of the Hebrews until the Return from the Babylonian Exile), (*Enciclopedia Italiana*, Vol. 13, 1932, pp. 331–344). In this work, he applied biblical criticism with perfection. He distinguished between a theological and historical conception of the religion of Israel and, indirectly, of Christianity. He noticed that the historical method "is not against religion, but simply outside of religion." According to his conception that history is made by men, he recognized the important role played by the prophets, with their moral and religious ideal, in the history of Israel. The moral and religious component Levi Della Vida found in history, and his competence in biblical criticism, explain the admiration and sympathy he had for the protagonists of the modernistic movement in the Catholic Church: "The strength of the modernist movement is not in the value of its philosophical system, but in the riches of the religious sentiment of those who started it and of those who follow it." (See *Fantasmi ritrovati*, Venezia, 1966, and *Aneddoti e svaghi arabi e non arabi*, p. 331 ff). According to his principle that history lets us better know and better evaluate our present, Levi Della Vida, himself a Jew, gave the following judgment of the Anti-Semitism of his time. "I consider myself simply a free believer (or misbeliever) of Jewish origin; and, if I would attach any importance to this 'ethnic' circumstance, I would promote racialism, don't you think so? I protest against Anti-Semitism in the name of the principles (which are universal patrimony) of tolerance, of freedom, of historical understanding. I, too, have joined the Italy-Israel Association, but I would also have joined an association for the friendship of Italy and Ghana or one for the friendship of Italy and Egypt." And he does not hesitate to point out a deeper root and a more universal reason of that historical phenomenon: "I do not think that the Anti-Jewish component of the recent image of the swastica is very important. More important is the rebirth of the totalitarian spirit, under any label it adopts—that horrible monster which shall rise again from its ashes until the dissention between 'capitalistic democracies' and 'people democracies' is settled.—When and how, I do not know" (Letter to F. Nicolini, January 17, 1960).

Bibliography: F. Gabrieli, *La storigrafia arabo-islamica in Italia* (Naples, 1975); F. Gabrieli, S. Moscati, A. Schiaffini, and L. Salvatorelli, *Giorgio Levi Della Vida* (Rome, 1968); S. Moscati, *Ricordo di Giorgio Levi Della Vida* (Rome, 1968); Fulvio Tessitore, "Giorgio Levi Della Vida nella storiografia italiana tra Otto e Novecento," in *Levi Della Vida Giorgio, Arabi ed Ebrei nella storia* (Naples, 1984), pp. 11–48.

Francesco Turvasi

MATURI, Walter (Naples, 1902–Rome, 1961), Italian historian of Naples, the Risorgimento, and historiography. A student of Michelangelo Schipa at the University of Naples, Maturi taught in lycées in Benevento and Turin prior to becoming professor of the history of the Risorgimento at the University of Pisa in 1939. In 1948 he moved to the University of Turin. He was a painstaking teacher who identified himself generally with Benedetto Croce's (q.v.) liberal, ethico-political school of historiography. He was also influenced by Adolfo Omodeo and Giustino Fortunato, and he admired Friedrich Meinecke's (q.v.) conception of modern history as a conflict between power politics (Kratos) and morality (Ethos). Maturi was one of the most discerning critics of modern Italian historical literature; his preferred form of exposition was the historiographical essay. From 1930 to 1932 he was an editor of the new *Enciclopedia Italiana* and a graduate student at Gioacchino Volpe's (q.v.) School of Modern and Contemporary History in Rome, where his close friends were Federico Chabod (q.v.) and Carlo Morandi. His first major publication (1929) was in diplomatic history, *Il concordato del 1818 tra la Santa Sede e le Due Sicilie* (The Concordat of 1818 Between the Holy See and the Two Sicilies). Other studies in this field (appearing in the *Rivista storica italiana*, 1938–1939) dealt with the Congress of Vienna and the restoration of the Bourbons in Naples, and with Neapolitan foreign policy from 1815 to 1820. These interests, combined with those regarding the rise of political and religious ideologies, led Maturi to publish in 1944 his masterpiece, a lively biography of Ferdinand I's reactionary minister, the Prince of Canosa (*Il principe di Canosa*). He skillfully and tolerantly shed light on the intransigent Catholic world of the Restoration era, symbolized by the quixotic figure of Canosa who struggled against the new liberal ideas. A model of ethico-political history, the biography deals not only with the Prince's public but also his private life.

Meanwhile, Maturi's vision expanded from early nineteenth-century Neapolitan history to the broader problems of Italian unification. In a very original article on the meaning of the concept of Risorgimento, published in 1936 in the *Enciclopedia Italiana*, Vol. 29, pp. 434–439, he asserted the ethico-political character of this complex social and historical process, taking issue with the Savoyard myth that credited unification to the House of Savoy. The article greatly displeased De Vecchi di Val Cismon, the minister of education, but remains an important point of departure for the study of the Risorgimento. Maturi's perceptive essay, "Partiti politici e correnti di pensiero nel Risorgimento" (Political Parties and Currents of Thought in the Risorgimento), appeared in 1951 in Ettore Rota, ed., *Questioni di storia del Risorgimento e dell'unità d'Italia*. His increasingly European view was also revealed in the 1953 bibliographical essay, "Metternich," in E. Rota, ed., *Questioni di Storia contemporanea*. In the 1950s Maturi helped plan the *Documenti diplomatici italiani: Prima Serie, 1861–1870* and himself edited the first two volumes covering 1861–1862. In 1950 he contributed an exhaustive bibliographical essay on modern and contemporary history to a festschrift honoring Benedetto Croce, *Cinquant'anni di vita intellettuale italiana, 1896–1946* (Fifty Years of Italian Intellectual Life). Maturi's projected history of Italy in the Napoleonic era remained unfinished when he died unexpectedly in 1961. A devoted group of students gathered his informative lecture notes from previous years and published them as *Interpretazioni del Risorgimento* (Turin, 1961). Ernesto Sestan wrote the preface to it, while Rosario Romeo (whose positive interpretation of Cavour and the liberals in the Risorgimento was generally in harmony with Maturi's judgments) updated the bibliography. The volume brims with analyses of the publications of specialists (mostly Italian) on the Risorgimento. *Miscellanea Walter Maturi* (Turin, 1966) is a posthumous festschrift in his honor.

Bibliography: Narciso Nada, "Bibliografia degli scritti di W.M.," *Rivista storica italiana* 73 (1961): 230–253, and 74 (1962): 361–368; Rosario Romeo et al, "Walter Maturi . . . ," *Rassegna storica del Risorgimento* 48 (1961): 553–610; Massimo L. Salvadori, "Walter Maturi," *Nuova rivista storica* 51 (1967): 405–460; Ernesto Sestan, "Walter Maturi," *Rivista storica italiana* 73 (1961): 209–229; Franco Venturi, *Historiens du XXe siècle: Jaurès, Salvemini, Namier, Maturi, Tarle* (Geneva, 1966), pp. 101–106.

Charles F. Delzell

MERLINO, Francesco Saverio (Naples, 1856–Rome, 1930), political activist, lawyer, and historian. Trained as a lawyer, Merlino became an anarchist when he defended anarchist revolutionaries Carlo Caffiero and Errico Malatesta after an attempted 1877 overthrow of the Italian government. Merlino also defended Gaetano Bresci, King Humbert I's assassin. Among the most intelligent of Italian anarchist intellectuals, Merlino became the primary figure in the Neapolitan movement, which he reorganized in 1881. In 1883 the police accused him of organizing a criminal association. Tried and condemned in Rome the following year, Merlino fled into French exile. From France, he traveled widely throughout Europe and the United States and contributed to many reviews. When Italy underwent a series of revolts in 1894, some anarchist-inspired, Merlino returned to his native country hoping to participate in a successful revolution. The actions failed, after which he clandestinely went to Naples. There the police arrested him and obliged him to serve his 1884 sentence. He left prison in 1896. The same period witnessed Merlino's gradual withdrawal from the anarchist movement. He began revising Marxist theory contemporaneously with but independently of Eduard Bernstein, publishing *Pro e contro il socialismo* (1897), *L'Utopia collettivista e la crisi del "socialismo scientifico"* (1898), and numerous articles in his review, *Rivista critica del socialismo*. He joined the Italian Socialist party and in 1901 attacked party leader Filippo Turati's reformism. By assigning the party's revolutionary role directly to the workers, Merlino anticipated the revolutionary syndicalism of thinkers such as Antonio Labriola (q.v.).

Merlino left active political life shortly thereafter to devote himself to the law. With fascism's rise, however, he took a stand against the dictatorship by publishing two critical works. Merlino published his major historical book in French exile, *L'Italie telle qu'elle est* (Paris, 1890). In order to describe "Italy as it really is," Merlino vowed to get below the surface of events. He therefore traced the process by which the bourgeoisie united Italy politically and "divided it into two enemy nations." Since Merlino defines the major purpose of unification as the exploitation of the South, he discerns no substantial difference between the monarchists and republicans who contested the shape postunification Italy should assume. In fact, after 1876 the left adopted the repressive techniques and exploitive policies of its predecessors. For Merlino, the Risorgimento thus established the domination of the southern Italian peasant by the northern bourgeoisie. This development produced the triumph of industry over agriculture and of capital over land. Merlino's book represents one of the earliest and clearest expositions of this thesis, commonly found in later historiography. In addition to its general thesis, the author's determination to produce a ''detailed and documented'' work accounts for its strength. Critics have considered the slight role which industry and the workers' movement play in Merlino's book a limitation; both in their infancy in 1890s Italy, they generated political movements that seized center stage. In fact, despite its strengths, *L'Italie telle qu'elle est*, a product of Merlino's anarchist phase, places the peasant at the center of the historical and revolutionary process.

Bibliography: Pier Carlo Masini, ''Scritti di Francesco Saverio Merlino,'' *Movimento operaio* 2, no. 13 (October-November, 1950): 404–413; Pier Carlo Masini, *Storia degli anarchici italiani*, 2 vols. (Milan, 1969 and 1981); Emilio Papa, *Per una biografia intelletuale di Francesco Saverio Merlino* (Milan, 1982).

Spencer M. Di Scala

MORANDI, Rodolfo (Milan, 1902–Milan, 1955), Italian historian. This influential socialist intellectual and economic historian set the tone and policies which the Italian Socialist party followed from World War II to the late 1950s. A premier example of the antifascist generation that matured under Mussolini's dictatorship, Morandi established a clandestine group while still a student at the University of Milan. In connection with his philosophical studies, he traveled to Germany to study Georg Wilhelm F. Hegel (q.v.) and Kant. Later, he headed the socialist clandestine network in Italy. Because of these activities, the regime imprisoned him in 1937, but he went free upon Mussolini's fall in 1943. Morandi fled to Switzerland but soon returned to Italy, organizing the military resistance around Milan and Turin. Obsessed by his vision of a third world war between the forces of capitalism and socialism, Morandi dropped his previous criticism of communism and successfully advocated the Popular Democratic Front alliance between Italian socialists and communists. He also reorganized the Socialist party on the communist model, imposing strict discipline on the previously loose socialist organization. These policies provoked serious splits among the socialists and profoundly influenced postwar Italian history. Morandi became famous upon publication in 1931 of his chief historical work, *Storia della grande industria in Italia*. Critics of the time recognized him as a historian of the highest caliber. Consequently, he became primarily interested in industrial policy and economic planning as they related to the coming of socialism. From 1946 until the left's exclusion from the government in 1947, Morandi served as minister of industry. A first-class book, Morandi's *Storia* analyzes the history, policies, and social impact of Italian heavy industry from its beginnings to 1931. The first book to attempt such an analysis down to modern times, the book also aroused immediate interest because of the Great Depression. Morandi sought both to provide a solid industrial history and to determine how industrial history influenced political events, particularly the rise of fascism.

Morandi interpreted Italy as suspended in a preindustrial phase while other nations progressed. In addition, he already discerned a difference between areas of the north, where the domestic system prevailed, and the south, where government protection gave the impression of industrial development. Morandi also argued that the free trade policies of the postunification governments exacerbated the economic situation. Not until governments adopted protectionist tariffs in 1878 and 1887 did they favor development of industrial development, which, however, did not take off until 1898. For Morandi, industry had a negative role during the first four decades of unification. In a memorable chapter, he darkly describes the harsh working conditions in the factories and the backward mentality of the industrialists. Between 1898 and 1913, modern industry became rooted in Italy, but the long lag behind other countries disarticulated this development from the nation's civil progress. Conditions produced by World War I and its own retarded development thrust Italian industry into a monopolistic phase imposed by finance capitalism. Protected by fascism, these finance capital monopolies repressed the workers and established powerful trusts dominating production and profit in key areas such as artificial fibers, chemicals, steel, and electricity. Morandi's *Storia della grand industria* continues to influence the interpretations of historians, while the work's caliber has caused commentators to regret fascist police destruction of his research notes for a history of Italian agriculture.

Bibliography: Aldo Agosti, *Rodolfo Morandi. Il pensiero e l'azione politica* (Bari, 1972); *Opere di Rodolfo Morandi* (Turin, 1961).

Spencer M. Di Scala

MOSCA, Gaetano (Palermo, 1858–Rome, 1941), Italian political theorist and politician. Following temporary junior academic appointments at the universities of Palermo (1885) and Rome (1888)—during which time he also edited the journal of the Chamber of Deputies—Mosca found regular teaching work at the University of Turin (1896). He taught constitutional and administrative law as well as the history of political theories. While at the University of Turin he became actively engaged in politics, first in 1908 as a deputy in Parliament and then, in 1919, as a senator. From 1914 to 1916 he served as undersecretary for colonial affairs. In 1923 he began teaching at the University of Rome, and he retired ten years later. Mosca early exhibited an original mind, and in 1884 the young scholar published a book that had taken shape during his student days at the University of Palermo while he was under the intellectual influence of Hippolyte Taine (q.v.), *Teorica dei governi e governo parlamentare*. This book sketched ideas that received a much fuller treatment twelve years later, after Mosca's understanding of politics had been deepened by his experience as editor of the Chamber's journal, in *Elementi di scienza politica*. Mosca began by observing that all systems of government are run by the dominant few, what he called the political class. He offered this observation as the major premise in his argument against the democratic and socialist theories that had evolved from Rousseau to Marx. As a minor premise, Mosca reminded his readers of the principal invalidating flaws in democratic and socialist rhetoric, that all power and wealth rightly belonged to the people. His conclusion was inescapable: Democracy and socialism rested on a wholly fictitious theory of human nature and on a radically utopian interpretation of history. The people on the one hand and the proletariat on the other do not exist, Mosca proclaimed. Only individuals exist, the few who rule and the many who are ruled. Oligarchy, not the general will or dialectical materialism, drives history. Mosca hated and feared the Marxists most of all. To him they were "new wolves," characterized by a degree of ferocity not previously seen in history, and he predicted that once in power they would behave in a far more predatory manner than previous elites had. Against the dangerous illusions and obsessive class hatreds of Marxism, Mosca counseled an evolutionary course for Italy. He did so despite his harsh criticisms of the parliamentary regime—a system of negative selection, he called it—that had failed to fulfill the promise of the Risorgimento. Feeble though Parliament admittedly was in his view, society would benefit more from the reform and improvement of existing elites than from their sudden overthrow at the hands of the hate-filled Marxist revolutionaries who populated his nightmares.

Mosca's conservative liberalism had nothing in common with the positive content of fascism, but the fascists used the elitist critique of parliamentary institutions as a battering ram against the old order. Repelled by this misappropriation of his ideas, Mosca revised subsequent editions of *Teorica* and *Elementi* to reflect his concern over fascism's abrupt and severe alteration of Parliament. In his 1925 farewell speech to the Senate, he dramatically condemned the antiparliamentary actions of Mussolini's regime. Mosca neither wrote works of history nor fully utilized historical materials in his theoretical writings. Nevertheless, in *Teorica* and *Elementi* he proposed an interpretation of history that added rigor and tone to the philosophy of anti-Marxist historians in Italy where Marxism was destined to become a dominant force in historical writing.

Bibliography: Ettore A. Albertoni, ed., *Studies on the Political Thought of Gaetano Mosca: The Theory of the Ruling Class and Its Development Abroad* (Milan: Giuffre, 1982); Mario Delle Piane, *Gaetano Mosca. Classe politica e liberalismo* (Naples: Edizioni Scientifiche Italiane, 1952); James H. Meisel, *The Myth of the Ruling Class: Gaetano Mosca and the Elite* (Ann Arbor: University of Michigan Press, 1958); James H. Meisel, ed., *Pareto and Mosca* (Englewood Cliffs, N.J.: Prentice-Hall, 1965).

Richard Drake

OMODEO, Adolfo (Palermo, 1889–Naples, 1946). Italian historian and professor at the universities of Catania and Naples. He was among the first lay scholars at the beginning of the century to study and teach the history of the Church and Christianity, which were at that time neglected in Italy. A student of Giovanni Gentile's, to whose philosophy he initially adhered (breaking away from it later to embrace Benedetto Croce's (q.v.) thought, he quickly revealed a powerful vocation for the strong and concrete substance of history. From his first youthful work on *Gesiè le origini del Cristianesimo* (Jesus and the Origins of Christianity), to the excellent *Paolu di Tarso* (Paul of Tarsus, Peoples' Apostle) and to *The Johannine Mystique* (The Mysticism of John) he affirmed himself along with Luigi Salvatorelli (q.v.) as one of the greatest Italian historians of religion. Unlike Salvatorelli, who emphasized institutions, the Church apparatus, mass religiosity, and the social climate, Omodeo concentrated on heroic individualism, intellectual and moral physiognomy, and unmistakable pathos.

Omodeo's interest in the religious aspect of reality never flagged. But his country's modern misadventures—participation in World War I, and Fascism (which he, like Croce, opposed)—transformed this scholar of ancient religions into a great historian of the modern era.

In *L'età del Risorgimento* (The Age of the Risorgimento) and *Momenti della vita di guerra* (Aspects of Life during the War), he opposed violence, aggressive nationalism, and the tyrannical suppression of liberty to the ideals of liberty, human gentleness, and the European spirit inherited from the best nineteenth-century liberal and democratic Italian leaders. From this polemical tension was born a radical revision of the Risorgimento.

In this field, his masterpiece, which, unfortunately, remains unfinished, is *L'opera politica del Conte di Cavour* (The Political Opus of the Count of Cavour). This work definitively places the great Piedmontese statesman within his human and political context and limits—a Cavour tested by the lazy backwardness of the Savoyard state, reactionary forces, especially the rabid clericalism of the Jesuits, and the enormous international difficulties, all of which are confronted with genial ardor—a Cavour animated above all by a burning faith in liberal civilization which with the England of the period reached one of its highest levels. One of his most original themes of interpretation (besides the fine historical judgments on the participation of Piedmont in the Crimean War) is his insight into the dialectical and complementary relationship between Cavour and Mazzini, the other great architect of Italian unity. Without Mazzini's apostolate (and, one must add, the armed hand of Garibaldi), Cavour could not have accomplished the miracle of 1859–61, Italian national unity. It was a discordant harmony, a reciprocal integration of tasks.

Also greatly effective are Omodeo's studies of the Italian Restoration, Charles Albert, and Vincenzo Gioberti (q.v.)—his burning polemics against the court historians who did not share his moral disdain for the fascist regime.

With the spread of fascism in the 1930s and the transformation of Fascism into Hitlerian Nazism, Omodeo shifted his view from the Risorgimento to Europe. This enlargement of his horizon produced another important work, also unfinished but teeming with important insights, *La cultura francese nell'età della Restourazione* (French Culture During the Restoration), a culture radiating from France onto the rest of Europe.

With the passing of the years and the inexorable coming of the second world war, Omodeo, as politician and historian, exalted the heroic significance of every struggle anywhere in the world for the conquest or reconquest of liberty. To the static Crocean formula of "the religion of liberty," he counterposed the dynamic formula of "liberating liberty." The fundamental characteristic of Omodeo's historical work was the attraction which religions and movements in the process of being born exercised upon him. His fascination with whether they concerned historical "dawns": the origins of Christianity, the Risorgimento, or French liberalism of the Restoration era, was perhaps his most characteristic historiographical feature. He dreamed of ending his work with the history of another of these historical springtimes, the fifth century of Athens, to peer into and, in his words, to "examine the Age of Pericles and the tragedy of the Peloponnesian war till the death of Socrates." But death caught him exhausted by work, shortly after his country's liberation.

Bibliography: A. Garosci, "Adolfo Omodeo," in *Rivista storica italiana*, 77, 1965, pp. 173–98, 639–86; 1966, pp. 140–83. This is the most exhaustive essay written on Omodeo. See also the excellent study by Giacomo Marzi, *Adolfo Omodeo. La Storiografia della Restaurazione francese* (Rome: Edozimi dell' Atenco, 1982).

Alessandro Galante Garrone
Trans. Spencer Di Scala

ORIANI, Alfredo (Faenza, 1852–Casola Valsenio, 1909), Italian novelist, playwright, and historian. After taking a degree in jurisprudence at the University of Rome, Oriani abandoned all thoughts of a law career and, under the pseudonym Ottone di Banzole, wrote an autobiographical novel, *Memorie inutili* (1876). This and the other Oriani novels that followed over the next six years portrayed the author's anguished response to his times. His passionate convictions about the moral bankruptcy of his age soon led him to write topical essays about contemporary problems. *Matrimonio e divorzio* (1886), in which he vigorously defended the family as the fundamental nucleus of the nation, was typical of his conservative preachments. Later in the decade Oriani began to compose historical works that were inspired by Hegelian dialectical theories about liberty as the end and governing principle of history. First in *Fino a Dogali* (1889) and then, more systematically, in the nine hundred-page long *Lotta politica in Italia: origini della lotta attuale, 476–1887*, Oriani put forward his interpretation of Italy's magnificent but tragic history. The moral intensity of these books was their distinguishing characteristic. He used *Fino a Dogali*, a reference to Italy's humiliating 1887 defeat in Africa, as a vehicle for prophecy regarding Italy's inevitable mission on that continent after an absence of nearly two thousand years. The similarly hortatory *Lotta politica* surveyed Italian history from the fall of the Western Roman Empire to the post-Risorgimento period. Oriani concluded that, because Italy had been made by schemes and compromises, not by revolution, all the work of true unification remained to be done. Only heroic action could bring his ideal Italy into existence.

Oriani the historian challenged the historical canons of his day. At a time when Leopold von Ranke's (q.v.) ideas on archival research were transforming the historical profession into the essentially monographic industry it has become, Oriani bitterly declared that a superstitious reverence for documentation threatened to kill history as a form of meaningful intellectual activity. The spirit counted more than the fact; a person's heroic attainment of his or her full spiritual growth, the transcendent theme of the ages, would not likely be susceptible to the kind of documentation presently in vogue. Professional historians either ignored or pilloried Oriani's work, and *La lotta*—which he had published at his own expense—was a spectacular disaster for him. With charges of plagiarism ringing in his ears, Oriani was advised to resume writing fiction. By then his health and finances had been permanently undermined. He continued to write novels, plays, and essays, but failure dogged him until the end. *Rivolta ideale* (1908), Oriani's last major work, won him a *succès d'estime* on the extreme right, for in this book he defended the state as the only antidote for democratic anarchy. The Nationalists in particular found much to admire in Oriani's dreams of Italian glory in Africa, and his premature death gave them cause to think of him as a martyr in the crusade for imperialism. After World War I Oriani's work attracted a cult following in fascist circles. In 1924 the fascist government declared his home, Il Cardello, a national monument, and Mussolini himself took responsibility for the national edition of his works, which ran to thirty volumes (1923–1933). With the defeat of fascism in World War II, his name fell into disrepute. The recent efforts of some historians notwithstanding, knowledge of Oriani's career remains confined to a small body of specialists, and his historical speculations are of interest mainly for the light they shed on how his fascist admirers chose to think about Italy's past.

Bibliography: Luisa Mangoni, "Alfredo Oriani e la cultura politica del suo tempo," *Studi storici*, 25 (1984), pp. 169–180; John Thayer, *Italy and the Great War* (Madison: University of Wisconsin Press, 1964).

Richard Drake

PIERI, Piero (Sondrio, 1893–Turin, 1979), the most illustrious Italian military historian of the twentieth century. During 1912–1915 Pieri attended the prestigious Scuola Normale Superiore di Pisa, where in his final terms he was a student of Gaetano Salvemini (q.v.) at whose suggestion and under whose supervision he wrote and presented his brilliant *tesi di laurea* (doctoral thesis) on "Milan from March to August 1848." In 1914–1915 like his master Salvemini and many other liberal nationalists and democratic members of the intelligentsia, Pieri was an ardent interventionist who saw an Italian struggle against Austria as "the last war of the Risorgimento." With the outbreak of the Italian war in May 1915, Pieri enlisted and soon became an officer of the celebrated Alpine Corps. He was twice decorated with the "Medal of Valor." At the end of the war and then through almost three years of social, political, and ideological dissension in Italy (1920–1922), which ended with the fascist "March on Rome" in October 1922,

Pieri remained close to his old master Salvemini not only professionally but also in political-ideological orientation. He contributed to Salvemini's weekly review, *L'Unità* (a title later adopted by the official organ of the Italian Communist party), even at the risk of compromising his academic career through the resentment of the patently emerging ultranationalist and fascist "victors" of the internal national struggle. Even after the full victory and consolidation of the fascist regime in 1925, Pieri signed an open protest against the arbitrary arrest of Salvemini by the fascist police. In 1929 Pieri joined Gino Luzzatto and Corrado Barbagallo as an editor of the *Nuova Rivista Storica*. Almost incredibly, during the fascist period Pieri astutely managed to hide or disguise his deep antifascist sentiments. It was quite ironic then that in February 1945 he and his entire family were arrested and imprisoned by the special "black police" of the shadowy "Social Republic of Salo," headed by the ghostly surviving Duce of a vanished fascism.

After World War II, Pieri and his assistant, Carlo Peschedda, edited the volume containing the collection of Salvemini's writings on the Risorgimento in the Feltrinelli edition of the *Opera Omnia*. Pieri's academic career was at first varied but eventually took him to his first important post at the University of Naples (1922–1935) and then, until his retirement in 1963 and as Emeritus, until his death in 1979, to the University of Turin. During the two decades 1935–1955 he wrote numerous articles, monographs, and biographies of Italian military leaders, theorists of the art of war, and strategists (among them Machiavelli, Montecuccoli, Eugene of Savoy, Giuseppe Palmieri, Pisacane, and Martelli). He contributed to the *Enciclopedia Italiana*. In 1929 and 1934 he was awarded the Ministerial Prize of the Accademia dei Lincei. Among his most substantive and emblematic works are: *Il Rinascimento e la crisi militare italiana* (1934; 1952; The Renaissance and the Italian Military Crisis); *Storia militare del Risorgimento. Guerre e insurrezioni* (1962; Military History of the Risorgimento. Wars and Insurrections); and *L'Italia nella Prima Guerra Mondiale* (1965; Italy in the First World War). In the *Military Crisis of the Renaissance* one can capture the quintessence of Pieri's innovative method and treatment of the history of the "art of war" before the bloody dawn of the nuclear age. That first volume is both emblematic and paradigmatic when compared to his later works. One must, of course, make necessary adjustments of perspective on the "cosmic" differences between the era of the Renaissance, the Risorgimento, and the lacerating time of the Great War 1914–1918. Pieri's complex variations of Karl von Clausewitz's theory of war as the "continuation of politics by other means" is essentially "anti-Machiavellian." War is seen, beyond the precipitating elements of a military clash, as a function of the organic "national" situation. Such a situation includes economic-social factors, first of all, and institutional and political balances, psychological, and military preparations for the duration and nature of a forseeable conflict, the realities and potentialities of human, material and spiritual resources, and, not least, the cohesion of a society and the strength of its commitment to defend itself, to fight, to conquer, to win, or to die for a common cause. Wars are won not by soldiers alone but by the solidarity of the entire community of citizens and their leaders, cemented long before the first hostile encounter occurs, before the first shot is fired.

For Pieri, in the Renaissance Italy lost her *libertà* to the Northern "Barbarians" not only because it was divided *externally* but also, in crucial cases (for instance, Florence and Tuscany, the Papal States, the Kingdom of Naples) because the *stati* were divided *within* themselves. In the Risorgimento, wars and insurrections became uncoordinated efforts at national independence, political-institutional change, and social liberation. The variety and simultaneity of the combatants' objectives, together with the general passivity of the larger masses of the people, at the same time prevented a "full" victory of a "free Italy" and, at least for the democratic wing of the national movement, led to the irreparable sacrifice of acceptance of the "half" victory of a not completely united nation under Liberal-Piedmontese hegemony. Finally, in the Great War a courageous and self-sacrificing people, just barely arrived at the self-consciousness of being members of a half-century-old united nation, of a common fatherland, was deprived of its reward and fulfillment in the postwar period (1919–1922) by the promiscuously combined dissension and moral activism of the pseudorevolutionists of extreme right and left and their persistent nihilistic cries about a "great betrayal" and a "mutilated victory" perpetrated, so they ranted, by the old liberal, democratic, and socialist ruling classes of the Giolittian era. Such acute analyses, singularly illuminating insights, and wisdom of judgment as his works contain on the subtle relations between war and "politics," as well as "peace" and conflict during epochal moments of crisis in modern Italian and Western history, have earned Piero Pieri an eminent place as a noble citizen in the classic European republic of historical intelligence.

Bibliography: There is not yet a full-fledged bio-critical study on Piero Pieri. The editor of this entry, A. William Salomone, utilized some personal correspondence to fill in some wide gaps in the data publicly available. For the larger Italian historiographical context of Pieri's work, see A. William Salomone, "Italy" in Georg G. Iggers and H. T. Parker, eds., *International Handbook of Historical Studies: Contemporary Research and Theory* (Westport, Conn., 1980), pp. 233–251 passim.

Lamberto Mercuri

PISACANE, Carlo (Naples, 1818–Sanza, Salerno, 1857), Revolutionary ideologue, activist, and military historian of the Risorgimento. Of a noble South Italian family, Pisacane rose to a high place in the officers' engineering corps of the Bourbon Army. In 1847 he left his post and fled to join Italian refugee patriots in Marseilles, London, and Paris. Soon he enlisted in the Foreign Legion in Algeria where he participated in the French repression of the Algerian independence movement. As soon as he heard of the revolutionary uprisings that had broken out in Milan in March 1848, he returned to participate with the Lombard patriots (among them the great leader, Carlo Cattaneo [q.v.], in the conclusive stages of the revolt. In the course of the clashes Pisacane was severely wounded. In the spring of 1849 he rushed to join Garibaldi, Mazzini, and other leaders to become a member of a special commission attached to the War Ministry of the recently proclaimed Roman Republic. Before long Pisacane became the organizing and propulsive force of the special commission, and almost immediately he was raised to the rank of chief of the General Staff in charge of the defense of the Eternal City against inter-Italian reactionary forces and foreign (chiefly French) troops.

Pisacane documents his disagreements with Garibaldi concerning the conduct of the war and comments on the protagonists of the tragic experience of the Roman Republic in his work, *Guerra combattuta in Italia negli anni 1848–1849* (1851; On the War Fought in Italy 1848–1849). After the fall of the Roman Republic, Pisacane's exile took him to Genoa, Lausanne, London, and finally Lugano. There he met again with Cattaneo and with French socialists. These new French contacts apparently precipitated a crisis in Pisacane's "Mazzinian" political faith and led him to seek different solutions to his revolutionary theories such as the sponsoring of insurrectionary-mass revolutionary movements. This profound change of revolutionary strategy is documented in the collection of his historical-political essays on Italy, published posthumously in 1858–1860, *Saggi storici e politici sull'Italia*, 4 vols. By 1855 there occurred a rapprochement with Mazzini in the hopeful view of a popular initiative in the reprise of the revolutionary movement, undoubtedly in contrast to the political-diplomatic and soon hegemonic strategy that had been adopted by Count Cavour in Piedmont. Pisacane planned and, in due time, informed Mazzini himself that he intended to engage in an expedition aiming at the liberation of the South. Pisacane persisted with his plan despite grave dissension in the Neopolitan committee. On June 24, 1857, he penned and left in the keeping of his English friend, Jessie White Mario, his populist revolutionary and political testament, *Testamento politico*. In it he renewed expression of his faith in the final triumph of a libertarian socialism and in the secure conquest of Italian independence and freedom to be achieved by a populist revolutionary movement. Despite Pisacane's exhortations and gallant example in battle against the Bourbon troops which had been quickly dispatched to Sapri, the expedition ended in a general massacre of the rebels. Wounded, Pisacane refused to be taken prisoner and committed suicide in the field. Despite the unavoidable romanticizing to which Pisacane's figure lends itself (as in Luigi Mercantini's famous poem, *La spigolatrice di Sapri*, which was translated into many languages), in Pisacane there is without a doubt a truly genuine exemplar of the revolutinary hero-patriot. He was not only a leader-participant, but also a keen critical historian of some of the most crucial political and military events of the Risorgimento.

Bibliography: Carlo Pisacane, *Saggio su la Rivoluzione*, ed. Giaime Pintor (2 ed., Turin: Einaudi, 1944; Leopoldo Cassese, *La spedizione di Sapri* (Bari: Laterza, 1969); Nello Rosselli, *Carlo Pisacane nel Risorgimento italiano* (Turin: Bocca, 1932); Luciano Russi, *Pisacane e la rivoluzione fallita del 1848–49* (Milan: Jaca Book, 1972).

Lamberto Mercuri

RAGIONIERI, Ernesto (Sesto Fiorentino, 1926–Florence, 1975), Italian historian. For more than forty years, Ragionieri was connected with the University of Florence, first as a student and then as a professor. His ties to his family, and to Sesto and Florence, continued as important influences on both his emotional and intellectual life. Gaetano Salvemini (q.v.), Delio Cantimori (q.v.), and Carlo Morandi were perhaps most important in Ragionieri's early professional development (cf. his "Carlo Morandi," *Belfagor* 300 [1975]: 669–706). He particularly admired their ability to sustain intensely felt political values and ideals while maintaining the highest professional standards in their work as historians. Although a dedicated communist from his student days until his untimely death, Ragionieri continued to insist on the importance of "scientific reflection" in the historian's craft.

Ragionieri's earliest work was devoted to the history of ideas, especially in historiography. His first book, *La polemica sulla Weltgeschichte* (1951), was in this area. Afterward, the focus of Ragionieri's studies changed, but, as will be seen, his interest in German history and culture remained central to his work. The early 1960s were concentrated on two separate but for him deeply related problems: (1) the history of the Italian labor movement before World War I and (2) the origin and nature of the united Italian state. The first fruit of this period was his *Un comune socialista, Sesto Fiorentino* (1953). This work, which immediately attracted wide recognition, was important because it successfully combined the two themes mentioned above. Moreover, it encouraged the development of a new and richer genre of local history. Though not published in its entirety until 1967, Ragionieri's *Politica e amministrazione nella storia dell'Italia unita* was an outgrowth of his work on Sesto and emphasized the history of local socialist administrations in Italy as well as the impact on them of the central government, particularly through the prefects.

In other works of this period, *Socialdemocrazia tedesca e socialisti italiani, 1875–1895* (1961) and *Il marxismo e l'Internazionale* (1968), Ragionieri made significant contributions to the history of Marxist theory in its impact on the Italian and German labor movements of the nineteenth century. Especially noteworthy were his studies of Franz Mehring (q.v.), the "Nestor" of German social democracy, and his discovery of a series of articles by Antonio Labriola (q.v.) on Francesco Crispi's reactionary period. In all this work, Ragionieri's view of the Risorgimento became ever clearer and generally was close to that of Antonio Gramsci (q.v.). As he wrote in 1962, the Risorgimento and its historical consequences must be viewed in a generally positive way. However, he also felt it necessary to point out the many "disparate and contradictory elements" which it contained. The last ten years of Ragionieri's life were dedicated mostly to the history of the Italian Communist party (PCI) and the Comintern and to the editing and publication of Palmiro Togliatti's *Opere*, a labor that can be called monumental. In addition to a series of essays on key moments in Togliatti's life (*Palmiro Togliatti* [1973]), Ragionieri lived to edit the first three volumes of the *Opere*, more than three thousand pages covering 1917 through 1935 and including

674 pages of "Introduction," which was published separately after Ragionieri's death as *Palmiro Togliatti: Per una biografia politica e intellettuale* (1976). Another important collection of Ragionieri's essays on the Comintern and the PCI was published posthumously under the title of *La Terza Internazionale e il Partito comunista italiano* (1978). Ragionieri's final work, completed and prepared for publication by a group of students and friends, was his massive contribution to Luigi Einaudi's (q.v.) *History of Italy* ("la storia politica e sociale," *Storia d'Italia* 4 Tome 3 [1976]: *Dall' Unita ad oggi*, pp. 1667–2483). Although he died at the age of forty-nine, Ragionieri produced more than seven hundred publications. His impact on the Italian historical profession was not limited to his writing. He himself considered his "work as a teacher as an integral part of my activity as an historian and Communist intellectual." From 1957 to 1975, he directed at least seventy-seven doctoral theses at the University of Florence, and many of his students later became productive and influential historians.

Bibliography: *Bibliografia degli scritti di Ernesto Ragionieri* (Florence: Instituto Ernesto Ragionieri, 1980); Enzo Collotti, "Il lavoro dello storico," *Italia contemporanea*, 120 (1975): 3–18; Giuseppe Galasso, "L'itinerario storiografico di Ernesto Ragionieri," *Nuova Antologia* 112 (1977): 211–219; Eugenio Garin, "Ernesto Ragionieri," *Belfagor* 33 (1978): 297–320.

John M. Cammett

ROMAGNOSI, Gian Domenico (Salsomaggiore, 1761–Milan, 1835), Italian essayist and historian. Trained as a notary and lawyer, Romagnosi worked in Piacenza and Trento before being appointed to a chair of jurisprudence at the University of Parma in 1802 and then at the prestigious University of Pavia in 1807. He became very active in political and constitutional issues during the French occupation of northern Italy and especially during the Napoleonic Kingdom of Italy. Having taken Milanese citizenship in 1813, however, he was able to stay on in Milan and to establish a private school after the return of the Austrian administration. He also continued his association with the secret lodge Gioseffina whose members were dedicated to a restoration of constitutional government. A work of his on this topic, *Della costituzione di una monarchia nazionale rappresentativa* (On the Constitution of a Representative National Monarchy) was published anonymously in Lugano, Switzerland, in 1815. Romagnosi did not join the networks of Carbonari that flourished in Milan in the early 1820s, but he did become implicated in the conspiracy trial against his disciple and collaborator Silvio Pellico. Although acquitted of conspiracy charges, after December 1821 he was forced to close his school. Disabled by a stroke, he spent the remainder of his life housebound and dependent on financial assistance from friends and former students.

Romagnosi wrote for the leading magazines of his generation, among them *Biblioteca italiana*, *Annali di statistica*, and *Antologia*. His scholarly works reflected a central concern with the application of philosophy to the art of government. A well-governed state, he thought, was the ideal vehicle for the advancement of civilization. He viewed applied philosophy (*filosofia civile*) both as an outgrowth of and an improvement on natural philosophy. Among his historical works, *Genesi del diritto penale* (1791; Genesis of Penal Law) and *Assunto primo della scienza del diritto naturale* (1820; First Principle of a Science of Natural Law) formulated the concept that natural law as well as human laws take on different form and meaning in accordance with times, places, and types of civilizations within which they develop. These works prepared the ground for Romagnosi's crowning achievement as a historian, his work *Dell'indole e dei fattori dell'incivilimento* (1832; On the Nature and Factors of the Process of Civilization) which critiqued the universal "laws of progress" formulated by French and Anglo-American eighteenth-century philosophers. Romagnosi argued that such laws could only be interpreted and understood if proper attention was paid to local traditions and specific cultural, geographical, and other factors that shaped civilizations. Toward the end of his life he returned to his earlier interest in law and public administration and wrote drafts of political and constitutional works that were completed by his disciples and published posthumously: *Della vita degli stati* (1845; On the Life of States), *Diritto naturale politico* (Political Natural Law), and *La scienza delle costituzioni* (1847; The Sciences of Constitutions). His work as a philosopher, jurist, and historian had a profound impact on those Lombard intellectuals who became active in the movement for economic development and political reform in the 1840s, especially Carlo Cattaneo (q.v.), Cesare Cantù (q.v.), and Giuseppe Ferrari (q.v.).

Bibliography: Robertino Ghiringhelli, "G. D. Romagnosi e gli Annali universali di statistica," *Risorgimento* 32, no. 3 (1980): 221–280; Bruno Di Sabantonio, "Illuminismo e storicismo in G. D. Romagnose," *Risorgimento* 33, no. 1 (1981): 1–22; Enrico Sestan, *Opere di G. D. Romagnose, C. Cattaneo e G. Ferrari* (Florence: Ricciardi, 1957).

Clara M. Lovett

ROSSELLI, Nello (Sabatino) (Florence, 1900–Bagnoles de l'Orne, France, 1937), Italian historian. Rosselli was born to Giuseppe Emanuele Rosselli and Amelia Pincherle into a Jewish family deeply involved in Risorgimento activity. Advised by Gaetano Salvemini (q.v.), Rosselli turned his dissertation into his first important book, *Mazzini e Bakunin: Dodici anni di movimento operaio in Italia* (1927; Mazzini and Bakunin: Twelve Years of the Worker's Movement in Italy, 1860–1872). Rosselli had anticipated the longer work in two significant articles of 1924, both focusing on the early histories of workers and socialist organization in Italy and both published after his death in a collection of essays, *Saggi sul Risorgimento e altri scritti* (1946; Essays on the Risorgimento and Other Writings).

As Rosselli became involved in historical research, the rise of fascism to power in October 1922 impinged on his personal and intellectual life. He was an active antifascist, founding, in 1925, a courageous underground publication, *Non Mollare* (Don't Give In). Thus, the problems of Italy's public life and of his historical research fused. When his book appeared in 1927, Rosselli was interested in elucidating the basic problem of the relationship between the Italian popular masses and the Italian state. Mazzini, he argued, had been aware of the need to solve the social question with the cooperation of the masses, but he had failed and this failure resulted in the fragility of the Italian liberal state. In spite of arrests and confinement in 1927 and 1929, Rosselli joined the Scuola di Storia Moderna e Contemporanea directed by Gioacchino Volpe (q.v.) from 1927 to 1930, and was asked to research relations between England and the Italian preunification states from 1815 to 1861. In 1953 this research (completed in 1936) was published as *Inghilterra e regno di Sardegna dal 1815 al 1847* (England and the Kingdom of Sardinia, 1815–1847). As a reaction to the official historiography of the regime, which regarded the fascist state as having achieved the integration of the masses, a goal that had eluded the Liberal state, Rosselli deepened his exploration of the Risorgimento, focusing on Carlo Pisacane (q.v.) in *Carlo Pisacane nel Risorgimento italiano* (1932; Carlo Pisacane and Italian Unification) and broke new ground again. According to Rosselli, Pisacane had concluded that social revolution was essential to political revolution and independence from foreign domination. Rosselli disagreed, viewing Pisacane's lack of success as proof that social revolution required prior achievement of basic political freedom. During the last years of his life, Rosselli developed two paths of research. One investigated federalist thought in the Risorgimento. The other would have resulted in a major history of Italy from 1815 to fascist times, a history focused on fundamental questions about the nature of the unification and of the state and society born from that process. The work remained uncompleted. On June 9, 1937, while visiting his exiled brother Carlo in France, both men fell victim to an ambush perpetrated by members of a French right-wing group as part of a plot orchestrated by the Italian fascist government.

Bibliography: Zeffiro Ciuffolette, "Nello Rosselli: A Historian Under Fascism," *Journal of Italian Historical Studies* 1, no. 2 (Autumn 1978): 287–314; *Giustizia e Liberta nella lotta antifascista e nella storia d'Italia: Attualita dei fratelli Rosselli a quaranta anni dal loro sacrificio* [Proceedings of an international conference held in Florence, June 10–12, 1977] (Florence, 1978); Gaetano Salvemini, *Carlo and Nello Rosselli: A Memoir* (London, 1937).

Margherita Repetto Alaia and Joel Blatt

SALVATORELLI, Luigi (Marsciano, Perugia, 1886–Rome, 1974), Italian historian and journalist. Upon graduation from the University of Rome in 1907, Salvatorelli turned to journalism and historical studies. In 1915 he was appointed professor of Church history at the University of Naples but was called away for military service. Offered the co-directorship of *La Stampa* in Turin in 1920, he decided to switch his career to journalism. Because he was a radical democrat, the fascist dictatorship forced him to resign in 1925. He turned once more to historical writing. After the overthrow of the dictatorship, he returned to part-time journalism, editing the republican Action party's periodical, *La Nuova Europa* (1944–46), in which he advocated a postwar federation of Europe.

Salvatorelli's enormous scholarly output can be divided into three major categories: the history of Christianity and relations between Church and state; the history of international politics since the Napoleonic era; and the history of Italy in virtually all its aspects but especially the periods of the Risorgimento and fascism. Seldom was his research compartmentalized; there was constant overlapping of interests and interpenetration of moral judgments. He conceived history to be an "ethico-political" process in which religion was often an essential aspect. In addition to writing a number of popular biographies of Saint Francis of Assisi, Saint Benedict, and Constantine the Great in the late 1920s, Salvatorelli published in English and Italian (1929) a scholarly essay, *From Locke to Reitzenstein: The Historical Investigation of the Origins of Christianity*. Another major study, *Storia della letteratura latina cristiana dalle origini alla metà del VI secolo* (History of Christian Latin Literature from Its Origins until the Mid-Sixth-Century), came out in 1936. Salvatorelli was determined, in his own words, "to remain a rationalist in an era of spreading irrationalism." His critical attitude toward the Church as an authoritarian institution can be seen in *Chiesa e Stato dalla rivoluzione francese ad oggi* (1955; Church and State Since the French Revolution); *La politica della Santa Sede dopo la guerra* (1937; Postwar Policies of the Holy See); and *Pio XI e la sua eredità* (1939; Pius XI and His Legacy). Broader works of history were *L'Italia medievale dalle invasioni barbariche agli inizi del secolo XI* (1937; Medieval Italy from the Barbarian Invasions to the Start of the Eleventh Century) and *L'Italia comunale dal secolo XI alla metà del secolo XIV* (1940; Italy in the Age of the Communes from the Eleventh to Mid-fourteenth Centuries). His *Concise History of Italy from Prehistoric Times to Our Own Day* (1940) became a familiar text, as did *Storia del Novecento* (History of the Twentieth Century) in 1957 and *Storia d'Europa* (History of Europe) in 1961. In international history, one thinks of his hostile *Leggenda e realtà di Napoleone* (Napoleon in Legend and in Reality) and *Politica internazionale dal 1871 ad oggi* (International Politics from 1871 to the Present), published, respectively, in 1944 and 1976.

It was during the fascist regime that Salvatorelli's ideas regarding the Risorgimento matured, stimulated by the research of Francesco Ruffini and Adolfo Omodeo [q.v.] on Cavour and Mazzini, and of Cesare Spellanzon on the federalist group. Salvatorelli's major contribution in this field was *Il pensiero politico italiano dal 1700 al 1870* (Italian Political Thought, 1700–1870). First published in 1935 and then in an enlarged edition of 1940, it stressed the continuing impact of the eighteenth-century Enlightenment. In 1945 a polemical work, *Casa Savoia nella storia d'Italia* (The House of Savoy in Italian History), criticized "court historians" who sought to magnify unduly the role of the Savoyards in shaping Italian history. More enduring was his insightful *Pensiero e azione del Risorgimento* (The Risorgimento: Thought and Action), written in 1943 when the dictatorship was coming to an end. In *La Rivoluzione Europea 1848–1849* (1950), he underscored democratic nationalism as the common theme. With respect to fascism, Salvatorelli's *Nazionalfascismo* (1923) was an illuminating analysis of the radical new movement which he interpreted as "the class struggle of the petty bourgeoisie wedged in between capitalism and the proletariat." Most valuable of all was his massive, pioneering study, written with another antifascist journalist Giovanni Mira, *Storia d'Italia nel periodo fascista* (History of Italy in the Fascist Era), which first appeared in 1952 and was subsequently revised in 1964. Written before the archives were opened, it was based on published sources and provided a mine of information. In his later years Salvatorelli was elected to the Accademia Nazionale dei Lincei and to the International Council of the Historical Sciences.

Bibliography: Articles by Norberto Bobbio, Alessandro Galante Garrone, Giovanni Spadolini, and Leo Valiani in *Nuova Antologia* 115, no. 2134 (1980); Charles F. Delzell, "Introduction" to Luigi Salvatorelli, *The Risorgimento: Thought and Action* (New York, 1970); "Omaggio a Luigi Salvatorelli," *Rivista storica italiana* 78 (1966): 469–543; Armando Saitta, "Luigi Salvatorelli," *Critica storica* 14 (1977): 91–148.

Charles F. Delzell

SALVEMINI, Gaetano (Molfetta, Bari, 1873–Capo di Sorrento, 1957), Italian historian. Professor at the universities of Messina, Pisa, Florence, and Harvard University. Coming from a poor family of the Puglie, Salvemini felt an early profound disdain for the revolting and unjust fate of the people of southern Italy. At Florence he became enthused with the emerging socialism of the period and the care of the Marxist doctrine, whose essential human message took hold of his fiery and generous spirit. At the same time, he strengthened himself in the discipline of history under the guide of masters such as Pasquale Villari (q.v.) and Cesare Paoli. From this linking of excellent historical method and political passion emerged in 1899 one of his best works, *Magnati e popolani in Firenze dal 1280 as 1295* (Magnates and Common People in Florence from 1280 to 1295). In this work, the social struggle between magnates and common people replaced the political struggle between papacy and empire, Guelphs and Ghibellines. The common people were not "proletarians" but, if anything, precursors of the modern bourgeoisie: an emerging class that fought against those who controlled economic power. The socialist principle of the class struggle furnished the young historian with this interpretive tool, but despite some perhaps too rigid schematicisms, that work became famous both for its innovative charge and for the fascination of its style and very clear writing. The Marxist stamp of Salvemini's first writings was quickly attenuated, so as practically to disappear. Furthermore, he ended by withdrawing from the study of the Middle Ages, spurred by an impassioned participation in the politics of his time.

The fin-de-siècle crisis—1898–1899—witnessed a grave reactionary movement supported by the monarchy. The young Salvemini had just "discovered" the writings of the great democratic Lombard Carlo Cattaneo (q.v.), one of the leaders of the Milanese Revolution of 1848. Under the pseudonym *Rerum Scriptor* he then published *I partiti politici milanesi nel secato XIX* (1899; The Italian Political Parties in the Nineteenth Century), a small book that revealed a new historiographical vision of the struggle among the parties. The inspiring influence of Cattaneo (to whom Salvemini later dedicated a number of pithy pages) gradually became even more incisive and profound than Karl Marx's (q.v.). Socialist ideals, however, were not renounced, and the class struggle as the yeast of history was never renounced by historian and politician Salvemini.

An ardent socialist militant during the first decade of the century, he expressed his fierce commitment in two excellent books (1905). *La Rivoluzione francese* (The French Revolution) answered the secret intent to counterpose the reformist socialism to the confused revolutionism of socialists such as Enrico Ferri. In the footsteps of French historiography, from Alexis de Tocqueville (q.v.) to Aulard, he demonstrated with great lucidity how on one hand the slow preparation, over centuries, and on the other, the precipitation of events through the blindness and errors of the French monarchy and the aristocrats led to the grand and terrible results of the Revolution. The book thus aimed at warning the Italian ruling class not to block essential democratic reforms. Even the little book on Mazzini deserves to be remembered as an answer both to socialist incomprehensions and to the idolatry of the Mazzinians. Above all it illustrated, despite the weaknesses of Mazzini's doctrines, the value of continuous preaching as a means of awakening combative energies, and his divinatory ideas (which have been revived in this century) on the necessity of a new Europe founded on the harmonious collaboration of free peoples and nationalities.

The tragedy of the Messina earthquake of 1908, in which Salvemini lost his wife and five children, seemed to destroy him. But soon he again consecrated himself to the political struggle (against Giovanni Giolitti or the degenerations of the Socialist party), to his studies, and to teaching. The Libyan War, World War I, and then the struggle against fascism saw him in the front lines. Forced into exile in 1925, he worked to make the free world understand the disgracefulness of Mussolini's dictatorship, and he defended his oppressed country's cause. In the meantime he continued his work as a scholar and teacher. His recently published Harvard University lecture notes illustrate how he made young Americans understand the history of his country, even reaching fresh conclusions. During his exile he published studies in the diplomatic history of Italian fascism, using the same method with which in his own country he had written about the history of Italian foreign policy from 1871 to 1914.

Bibliography: Michele Cantarella, *Bibliografia Salveminiana, 1892–1984* (Rome: Bonacci Editore, 1986); A. Galante Garrone, *Salvemini e Mazzini* (Florence, 1981): E. Sestan, ed., *Atti del convegno su Gaetano Salvemini, Firenze, 8–10 November 1975* (Milan, 1977); E. Sestan, ed., "Salvemini storico," *Gaetano Salvemini* (Bari, 1959); Massimo L. Salvadori, *Gaetano Salvemini* (Turin, 1963).

Alessandro Galante Garrone

SANCTIS, Gaetano de (Rome, 1870–Rome, 1957), Italian historian. De Sanctis received his doctorate at Rome in 1892, having studied with E. De Ruggiero (q.v.), F. Halbherr, E. Piccolomini, L. Pegorini, and G. Beloch, of whom he became the favorite disciple. In 1900 at age thirty he became full professor at Turin where he taught until called to Rome in 1929 to succeed Beloch. He founded a school of historians that began the Italian digs on Crete and pioneered those in Cyrenaica. He explored all fields of classical antiquity: history, archaeology, philology, epigraphy, and numismatics. His greatest work, *Storia dei Romani*, 4 vols. (Turin, 1907–1923), went as far as the middle of the second century A.D. In it he confronted the great difficulties of the beginnings of Italian history from the rise of Rome and explained the expansion institutionally. A good Catholic, De Sanctis became president of the *Enciclopedia Italiana* after World War II, succeeding Giovanni Gentile, the fascist philosopher. Too important to be avoided even during the fascist period, he was one of the twelve who refused to take the oath of loyalty to Mussolini in 1932. His outstanding epigraphy appeared in *Iscrizioni*.

Bibliography: B. Croce, *Storia della storiografia italiana nel secoto decimonono*, 2 vols. (3 ed. rev.; Bari-LaTerza, 1947), II, 245–249; Arnaldo Momigliano, "G. de Sanctis," *Rivista Storica Italiana*, 69 (1957): 177–195.

William A. Percy

TASCA, Angelo (Moretta, 1892–Paris, 1960), Italian historian and politician. With Antonio Gramsci (q.v.), Tasca founded the revolutionary journal *Ordine nuovo* in 1919. In 1921 he broke with the Italian Socialist party to join the newly created Partito Comunista d'Italia. Tasca was one of the most prominent leaders of the party after 1926. In 1928 he was sent as representative of the Communist party to the Third International in Moscow, where he repeatedly clashed with Stalin. He was expelled from the party on Stalin's orders in 1929. In 1934 Tasca rejoined the Italian Socialist party and began to contribute a regular column on foreign policy for the French Socialist party paper, *Le Populaire*. During the late 1930s Tasca became increasingly anticommunist and led the faction of the Italian Socialist party which opposed Unity of Action with the communists. After the fall of France in June 1940, Tasca, who had become a French citizen in 1936 and directed Italian-language broadcasts for the French radio, opted for collaboration with the pro-Axis Vichy regime. Disillusionment with Vichy followed rapidly, however, and Tasca began to work for the Belgian Resistance. After 1945 he withdrew from an active political career amidst much misunderstanding over his wartime role. Tasca's reputation as a historian stands on his classic *Rise of Italian Fascism*, first published in France in 1938 as *La naissance du fascisme* and republished in an amplified and fully documented Italian edition in 1950 as *La nascita e l'avvento del fascismo*. This book was based on Tasca's extensive collection of documents and newspapers and remains the finest study of the seizure of power by the fascists. His most perceptive pages dealt with the social origins of the fascist movement, especially the rise of agrarian fascism in the Po Valley in 1920 and 1921. Tasca offered a thorough critique of the revolutionary left, whose errors contributed to defeat at the hands of the fascists. Finally, he traced a democratic and nonstatist alternative for European socialism.

Tasca devoted two notable studies to the French Communist Party: *Physiologie du Parti communiste francais* (1948), which offered a political and structural analysis of French communism and its militants; and *Les Communistes francais pendant la drôle de guerre* (1951) in which Tasca used the documents collected while at Vichy to reveal the extent to which the French Communist party encouraged a defeatist attitude in France during the initial stage of the war. Tasca also wrote one of the first studies of Soviet foreign policy during the years of the Hiter-Stalin pact (*Deux ans d'alliance germano-soviétique* [1949]. Perhaps Tasca's greatest contribution as a historian of the working class was through his vast collection of newspapers, documents, and letters which he left to the Istituto Giangiacomo Feltrinelli in Milan on his death in 1960. These materials provide a unique source for scholars interested in the history of the Italian Communist and Socialist parties from 1919 to 1940. They served in part as the basis for Tasca's own reconstruction of the early years of the Italian Communist party which he published in six long articles in the weekly *Il mondo* in 1953 (now gathered and reprinted as *I primi dieci anni del PCI* [Bari: Laterza, 1971]).

Bibliography: Giuseppe Berti, ed., *I primi dieci anni del PCI. Annali dell'Istituto Giangiacomo Feltrinelli 1966* (Milan: Feltrinelli, 1966); Giuseppe Berti, ed., *Problemi del movimento operaio: Scritti critici e storici inediti di Angelo Tasca. Annali dell'Istituto Giangiacomo Feltrinelli 1968* (Milan: Feltrinelli, 1969); A. De Grand, *In Stalin's Shadow: Angelo Tasca and the Crisis of the Left in Italy and France, 1919–1945* (De Kalb, Ill.: Northern Illinois University Press, 1986); A. Riosa, *Angelo Tasca socialista* (Venice: Marsilio Editori, 1979).

Alexander De Grand

VALERI, Nino (Padua, 1897–Rome, 1978), Italian historian. After serving in World War I as an observation officer in the Air Force, Valeri studied under Giorgio Falco at the University of Turin. Teaching first in the middle schools, he became a professor of medieval and modern history at the University of Catania in 1942. In 1946 he moved to Milan's Bocconi University and thence to the University of Trieste. In 1954 he joined the Faculty of Teacher Training at the University of Rome, and in 1961 he accepted the chair of modern history in its Faculty of Letters. Adhering more or less to Benedetto Croce's (q.v.) ethico-political school of historiography, he sought to understand rather than to condemn the past. For Valeri, conditions were more important than individuals in shaping history. His first important scholarly books were the volumes *L'eredità di Gian Galeazzo Visconti* (1938; The Heritage of Gian Galeazzo Visconti); *La vita di Facino Cane* (1940; The Life of Facino Cane); and *L'Italia nell'età dei principati, 1343–1516* (1949; Italy in the Era of the Principalities). In the last-named work he took up successively the highlights of various Italian states: Naples under Robert of Anjou; Rome at the time of Cola di Rienzo; Milan under Giovanni Visconti; Florence at the time of the War of the Eight Saints; and Milan under Gian Galeazzo Visconti. The author contended that the equilibrium in the Italian state system of the 1300s was the result not of plans of gifted individuals but of bitter experience in the sterile conflicts for hegemony, struggles that were punctuated by ephemeral moments of truce. Subsequently, his interests shifted to the eighteenth century; in 1937 he published a psychological study of *Pietro Verri*, whom he perceived as a truly liberal reformer. Still later, he turned to the post-Risorgimento era, giving special attention to the era of Giolitti and the advent of fascism. It is in this field that his work is most memorable. *La lotta politica in Italia dall' unità al 1925: Idee e documenti* (1945; The Political Struggle in Italy from Unification to 1925: Ideas and Documents) was an anthology that focused on major controversies and came to be widely used in Italian universities. In 1956 he published *Da Giolitti a Mussolini* (From Giolitti to Mussolini), covering the years from the crisis of liberalism in 1915 to the general ruin of the old political world at war's end and the emergence in the early 1920s of a new kind of "revolutionary" liberalism espoused by the Turin journalist, Piero Gobetti. He also brought out a reprint (1948) of Gobetti's short-lived periodical, *Rivoluzione Liberale*.

In 1971 Valeri published a serene biography, *Giolitti*, in the series "La vita sociale della nuova Italia" which he directed for Unione Typigrafico-Editore Torinese of Turin. Among this book's numerous merits is its long bibliographical essay. Valeri portrayed Giolitti as the dominant figure in Italy at the turn of the century, a politician who enabled the parliamentary monarchy to renew itself in a period of socioeconomic progress and in a climate, albeit imperfect, of liberty. Giolitti, an empiricist, probably did not then have clearly in mind the great reforms he would enact a decade or so later. In 1915 Giolitti, the neutralist, was overwhelmed by the conservatives and revolutionary interventionists. After the Great War he understood the need to strengthen Parliament and to broaden its powers with respect to making war; yet he was also willing to form an electoral alliance with Benito Mussolini and to allow him to come to power in 1922. It was only when Mussolini imposed the dictatorship in the winter of 1924–25 that Giolitti grasped fascism's true nature. Although Valeri admired Giolitti, he stopped short of rating him a great statesman; he saw him instead as a kind of "anti-hero" who adjusted pragmatically to changing circumstances. Valeri was also fascinated by the flamboyant Gabriele D'Annunzio. In 1963 he wrote *D'Annunzio davanti al fascismo* (D'Annunzio in the Face of Fascism), in which he analyzed the poet-condottiere's ambivalent attitude toward fascism between the Fiume expedition of 1919 and his retirement on Lake Garda. Valeri also served as general editor for UTET of its multivolume *Storia d'Italia*. His swansong (1972) was a collection of historiographical essays, *Tradizione liberale e Fascismo* (The Liberal Tradition and Fascism), which evaluated various publications of the 1960s.

Bibliography: Ettore Passerin d'Entrèves, "Nino Valeri (1897–1978)," *Rivista storica italiana* 92 (1980): 427–431; Cesare Luigi Musatti, Giulio Cervani, and Stelio Zeppi, *Ricordo di Nino Valeri* (Rome, 1978); Rosario Romeo, "Nino Valeri," *Rassegna storica del Risorgimento* 65 (1978): 356–358.

Charles F. Delzell

VILLARI, Pasquale (Naples, 1827–Florence, 1917), Italian historian and politician. Professor at the University of Pisa (1859–1865) and at the Royal Istituto di studi superiori of Florence (1865–1913). Villari served in the Chamber of Deputies from 1870 to 1876 and then again from 1880 to 1882 before becoming a senator in 1884. Villari held several high government posts in the field of education, and in 1891 prime minister Di Rudinì appointed him minister of public instruction. From 1896 to 1903 he presided over the Dante Alighieri Society. Villari passed his Neapolitan childhood in an atmosphere dense with Risorgimento patriotism. Another patriot, Francesco De Sanctis, became Villari's intellectual mentor, and both men participated in the failed Revolution of 1848 against the Bourbons. Arrested on May 15 of that year and shortly afterward banished from the kingdom, he found refuge in Florence. Villari spent much of the next decade in the Florentine archives, performing the research that simultaneously resulted in the completion of his training as a historian and in his first two books, *Introduzione alla storia d'Italia dal cominciamento delle Repubbliche del Medioevo alla riforma del Savonarola* (1849) and *L'origine e il progresso della filosofia della storia* (1859). Although these early works easily stood on their own merits—they exhibited impressive archival research and lively historical writing—only with his next work, *Storia di Gerolamo Savonarola e dei suoi tempi* (2 vols., 1859–1861) did Villari establish himself as one of Italy's foremost historians. He followed the enormous success of *Savonarola* with the three-volume *Niccolò Machiavelli e i suoi tempi* (2 vols., 1877–1882). Villari then published a major historical work about once a decade for the rest of his long life: *I primi due secoli della storia di Firenze*, begun in 1866, appeared in 1893–1894; *Le invasioni barbariche in Italia* in 1901; and *L'Italia da Carlo Magno ad Arrigo VII* in 1910.

Villari thrilled to the positivist advances in what that generation believed to be the "historical sciences," but for him positivism possessed interest primarily for its innovative research techniques. He could only conceive the historical process itself in the idealistic and even spiritual terms of Giambattista Vico. As for the historians among his own contemporaries, Villari always remained closer to Leopold von Ranke (q.v.), who believed that history was both an art and a science, than to Henry Thomas Buckle (q.v.) who proposed to convert history into an exact science by basing it on statistics. Historians should avail themselves of the analytical tools provided by scientists, Villari thought, but he took a stand with Vico in resisting the intellectual imperialism of science in historiography: human imperfections and ambiguities would always mock the efforts of science-intoxicated historians to write about the past as though it were fully comprehensible in rational terms alone. "Religion begins where reason ends and where reason can reach there is no room for religion," Villari wrote, but he contended that both faith and reason were equally necessary for the individual's intellectual being. Villari envisaged his own work both as a truthful analysis of the central paradox in Italian history—the country's magnificent cultural achievements coupled with its paralyzing political failure—and as a moral prescription for its manifold shortcomings in the present which, he believed, had arisen from the moral defects of the Renaissance. For him Machiavelli and Savonarola represented the two sides of Italy's spiritual nature during the seminal Renaissance period, and while the extraordinarily limpid and acute analytical talents of the patriotic Florentine chancellor deserved commendation, there was something fatally wrong with a culture that could produce so palpable an attack on virtue as *The Mandragola*. It was the moral earnestness of the Dominican monk that elicited his highest praise as a historian and his emulation in public life. It was not, then, simply chance that led Villari to the lifelong contemplation of Savonarola as a subject for historical research. A large Savonarolian element colored his own character, which expressed itself in such classic jeremiads as "Di chi la colpa?" (1866), *Lettere meridionali* (1875), and "Dove andiamo?" (1893). Numerous other occasional pieces by Villari were republished in *Saggi e scritti* (various editions from 1884 to 1914). This giant among the historians of his day, whose books still bear rereading, successfully combined two careers: as a moral essayist on contemporary Italy and as a researcher in the Italian historical archives. With consummate skill and an immense moral authority, Villari passed back and forth between these occupations serene in the faith of Thucydides that the lessons of the past give the historian unique and privileged insights into the present nature of things.

Bibliography: Marialuisa Cicalese, *Note per un profilo di Pasquale Villari* (Rome: Istituto storico italiano per l'età moderna e contemporanea, 1979); Francesco de Aloysio, "Il vichismo di Pasquale Villari: un itinerario nelle regioni dello storicismo," *Nuova Rivista Storica* 62, nos. 1–2, pp. 29–81.

Richard Drake

VOLPE, Gioacchino (Paganica, Aquila, 1876–Sant'Acrangelo di Romagna, 1971), Italian historian. Outstanding representative during the first half of the century of the conservative nationalist school. Volpe studied at the Scuola normale of Pisa and in Berlin and held the chair of modern history at the University of Rome from 1924 to 1940. He was also director of the Scuola di Storia Moderna e Contemporanea. He joined the fascist movement in 1920 and became its semiofficial historian with *L'Italia in cammino*, written in 1927 in answer to Benedetto Croce's (q.v.) *Storia d'Italia*, and with his *Storia del movimento fascista* (1939). During the fascist years he was deeply involved in a number of significant cultural projects of the regime as a founder of the Istituto Fascista di Cultura, a member of the Accademia d'Italia, and director of the *Rivista Storica Italiana* and the Istituto di Studi di Politica Internazionale. But Volpe remained more within the monarchical and nationalist tradition than that of fascism and in 1943 supported the royal decision to dismiss Mussolini. As a major organizer of culture during the fascist era, Volpe had great influence on several generations of Italian historians of all political persuasions from Nello Rosselli (q.v.), Federico Chabod (q.v.), and Carlo Morandi to younger historians like Rosario Romeo and Renzo De Felice, who appreciated his attention to social history while often disagreeing with his politics.

Volpe's major historical writings are divided between Italian medieval and modern history. His most significant works on medieval history are *Studi sulle istituzioni comunali a Pisa* (1902), *Movimenti religiosi e sette ereticali nella societa medievale italiana* (1912–1913), *Medio evo italiano* (1922), and *Il medioevo* (1927). In these books and articles Volpe paid special attention to the interaction of economic, religious, legal, and political history as he traced the rise of the city-state out of the fusion of Roman and Lombard culture and the gradual creation of a new civilization around the Italian communes. The formation of a national and statist tradition which was already implied in Volpe's work on the High Middle Ages became the central theme of his writing on modern Italy. His early interest in social and economic history was balanced by a strong nationalist perspective, which took a more political direction during World War I. Like many conservative intellectuals who came of age during the troubled decade of the 1890s, Volpe was struck by the fragility of the state that emerged from the Risorgimento. His judgment was harsh on those men, especially the great liberal prime minister, Giovanni Giolitti, and on movements, like Italian socialism, which seemed to weaken the cohesiveness of the Italian state. Although Volpe did not abandon the social and economic realism that allowed his work to rise above its narrow political perspective, the measure of historical truth and justice became the national state. In this optic, fascism became the triumph of national will. This essentially political judgment was tempered after the fall of fascism in Volpe's last major work, *Italia moderna 1815–1915* (1943–1952). Some of the negative judgments on the post-Risorgimento, the Giolittian era, and the role of socialism in national life were softened and a more balanced picture emerged.

Bibliography: Innocenzo Cervelli, *Gioacchino Volpe* (Naples: Guida, 1977); Convegno di Studi su Gioacchino Volpe, *Atti del convegno di studi su Gioacchino Volpe nel centenario della nascita, Ottobre 1876* (Rome: G. Volpe, 1977); Edward R. Tannenbaum, "Gioacchino Volpe," in Hans Schmitt, ed., *Historians of Modern Europe* (Baton Rouge: Louisiana State University Press, 1971); Gabriele Turi, "Il problema Volpe," *Studi storici* 19 (January-March 1978): 175–186.

Alexander De Grand

Great Historians: Japanese

ASAKAWA Kan'ichi (Fukushima, 1873–Vermont, 1948), Japanese historian. Professor at Yale University. After graduating from Tôkyô Senmon Gakkô (now Waseda University) in 1892 and Dartmouth College, 1899, Asakawa took the Ph.D. from Yale University in 1902 and lectured at Yale on Japanese and medieval European history from 1907 to 1942. After publishing his doctoral thesis, *The Early Institutional Life of Japan: A Study in the Taika Reform of 645* A.D. (1903), he turned his attention to the fact, as he saw it at the time, that Japan was the only country besides Western Europe to experience an era of true feudalism. He began a series of comparative studies of feudal institutions in Japan and Western Europe, publishing numerous articles later collected as *Land and Society in Medieval Japan* (1965) and his monumental *The Documents of Iriki* (1929; repr. 1955), his greatest contribution to the world of historical scholarship. This work, based on historical documents from a single rural locality over the "longue durée," the feudal estate—later village—of Iriki, from 1135 to 1870, accounted for the essential qualities of feudalism in Japan, which he located in world history by comparisons with feudalism in Western Europe. He concluded that, in Europe, the feudal contract between lord and vassal, characterized by its strong mutuality, attained its highest development in France, and in England extended the relationship between king and nation to become the foundation of political freedom. In contrast, in Japan the system of imperial bureaucracy, which had originated in China and whose importation he had studied in *Early Institutional Life*, prevented the development of a strongly mutual feudal contract. All chance of such a contract was finally stifled by the autocratic system established by Toyotomi Hideyoshi (1536–1598) and the Tokugawa shogunate (1603–1868). In Europe, the idea of freedom, justice, and duty fostered in feudalism gave rise to modern society, but in Japan the contribution of feudalism issued not from the feudal contract, but from the idea of absolute loyalty of the warrior to his lord, and the relative economic equality of the peasant. Asakawa's scholarship has been a major stimulus to the development of English-language historical studies on Japan, helping to establish a strong tradition of institutional historical studies. He also gave serious attention to contemporary issues and trends, publishing *The Russo-Japanese Conflict* (1904), and *Nihon no kaki* (1909; A Time of Crisis for Japan), in which he tried to warn Japan of the dangers in the course it was pursuing.

Bibliography: Kan'ichi Asakawa, *The Documents of Iriki, Illustrative of the Development of the Feudal Institutions of Japan* (New Haven, Conn., 1929; repr., Tokyo, 1955); Kan'ichi Asakawa, *The Early Institutional Life of Japan, a Study in the Reform of 645* A.D. (Tokyo, 1903; 2d ed., New York, 1963); Kan'ichi Asakawa, *Land and Society in Medieval Japan*, ed., Committee for the Publication of Dr. K. Asakawa's Works (Tokyo, 1965); Abe Yoshio, *Saigo no Nihonjin: Asakawa Kan'ichi no shôgai* (The Last Japanese: The Life of Asakawa Kan'ichi) (1983) John W. Hall, "Kan'ichi Asakawa: Comparative Historian," in *Land and Society in Medieval Japan* (Tokyo, 1965), pp. 3–21; John W. Hall and Abe Yoshio, "Asakawa Kan'ichi to iu hito o shitte imasu ka?" (Do You Know a Man Called Asakawa Kan'ichi?), in *Chûô kôron* (Central review, December 1981):182–195.

Masayuki Sato

FUKUZAWA Yukichi (Osaka, 1835–Tokyo, 1901), Japanese historian. Propagator of Western culture and educator. Born in a poor, low-ranking warrior family of the Nakatsu domain (now Oita Prefecture). After studying Confucianism, Chinese classics, and histories, Fukuzawa studied Western arts and sciences through the Dutch language (the only Western language officially allowed in Japan at the time) at Nagasaki and Osaka during 1854–1858. In 1858 he founded a school of the Dutch language at Edo (now Tokyo). In 1859, after encountering Western merchants in the newly opened port of Yokohama, he realized the importance of English and started to study that language, by means of which he continued to study the Western arts and sciences. In 1860–63 he visited the United States and the European countries three times as a member of Japanese missions, adding to his stock of information on Western cultures. In 1868 he renamed his school Keio Gijuku (now Keio University), where he devoted the remainder of his life to writing and educating. In his scholarship Fukuzawa argued the line of modernizing Japan through Westernization, at a time when Japan had just ended more than two hundred years of relative isolation from the West; he was a major figure provoking the alteration of the traditional Japanese way of thinking that had been based largely on Confucian ethics.

Fukuzawa's main work as a historian and as a scholar as well was *Bunmeiron no gairyaku* (1875; An Outline of a Theory of Civilization), in which he discussed the nature of civilization, the history of the development of civilization in Japan and in the West, and the national independence of Japan, based partly on such European stage theories of history as those of Henry Thomas Buckle (q.v.) and François Guizot (q.v.). In that work, he was most emphatic about the necessity of knowing the history of civilization, putting stress on "intellect" and the notion that civilization is "the progress of the knowledge and virtue of the general public," which evolves through the three stages of savage, half-civilized, and civilized. To attain national independence, Fukuzawa argued that since Japan was then in the half-civilized stage, it had to advance to the level of the Western cultures, the "civilized" stage. This highly valued "intellect" necessarily constituted a criticism of the traditional idea of history as a moralistic mirror: a didactic history, a history of heroes and great men, a nation's times of peace and war, rise and fall, and a history of the true relations of sovereign and subjects. (See Tokugawa Mitsukuni, Rai Sanyô.) He urged, instead, the need for historical research on "national traits of the general public," that is, a history with the development of the society and culture as its subject, an idea expressed in the passage: "[Histories of Japan written up to this day] are not the history of Japan, but merely the history of Japanese political powers. [This lack of true history] results from the carelessness of [Japanese] scholars, and is a very crucial matter from a national point of view." It comes down to the fact that Fukuzawa the scholar introduced Western culture, or more precisely, the history of the Western mentality to the Japanese people for the purpose of building a modern Japan, and mapped out the future course of Japan through the Western historical experience, extricating Japanese from the Confucian world order. (See Hayashi Tatsuo.) Fukuzawa's method of introducing Western culture and thought, common among Japanese scholars of his day, was largely through translation of Western works into Japanese. This often required him to create new Japanese terms appropriate to the original concept: Japanese acceptance of Western culture proceeded on the foundation of its own traditional learning, even though Western ideas suffered a certain transformation in the process of translation. Yet it was only this process of translation and transformation that made it possible for Japan to develop its own scholarship. The existence of a Japanese tradition of learning constituted a characteristic feature of Japanese modernization, in comparison with the processes of modernization in the other countries. It also constituted the driving force of Japanese independence behind the scenes and kept Japan from becoming a cultural (and linguistic) colony of the West. Through his experience at an early age, Fukuzawa found the hindrance to Japanese modernization in "the feudalistic pedigree system" (the traditional Japanese social system of one's life being fixed only by his birth and lineage). To replace this system, he proposed ideas of independence, freedom, and equality based on Western individualism. This was later compiled as *Gakumon no susume* (1872–1876; An Encouragement of Learning), a best-seller in the Meiji period (1868–1912), in which he discussed the idea of learning in an open society. *Seiyô jijyô* (3 vols., 1866–1870; Conditions in the West) introduced the political and cultural system of the West. His work was widely read in his own time, serving as an intellectual asset for all Japanese, and it is still influential among Japanese historians and intellectuals. (See Taguchi Ukichi, Takekoshi Yosaburô, Tsuda Sôkichi and Hani Gorô.)

Bibliography: *Fukuzawa Yukichi Zenshû* (Complete Works of Fukuzawa Yukichi), 22 vols. (1958–1971); *The Autobiography of Fukuzawa Yukichi*, trans. Eiichi Kiyooka (1966); *Eine autobiographische Lebensschilderung*, trans. Hidenao Arai (1971); *An Encouragement of Learning*, trans. David A. Dilworth and Umeyo Hirano (1969); *An Outline of a Theory of Civilization*, trans. David A. Dilworth and G. Cameron Hurst III (1973); Carmen Blacker, *The Japanese Enlightenment: A Study of the Writings of Fukuzawa Yukichi* (1964); Albert M. Craig, "Fukuzawa Yukichi no rekishi ishiki to bunmei kaika" (Historical Consciousness of Fukuzawa Yukichi and the Enlightenment), *Fukuzawa Yukichi nenkan* (Yearbooks of Fukuzawa Yukichi), vol. 12 (1985), pp. 243–250.

Masayuki Sato

HANI Gorô (Gunma, 1901–Kanagawa, 1983), Japanese historian. Son of a wealthy provincial merchant, Hani studied philosophy at the University of Heidelberg (1922–1924) and history at Tokyo Imperial University (1924–1927). After graduating from Imperial University, he taught at Jiyû Gakuen (school) and Nihon University. He started his career as a historian with a translation of Benedetto Croce's (q.v.) *Teoria e storia della storiografia* in 1926. Inclined to an interest in the methodology of history, both by his training and by his work in translating Croce, and caught up in an intellectual tide of proletarianism sweeping Japan's left in the mid- and late 1920s, he found his future course in proletarian history, publishing a collection of essays in 1929 as *Tenkanki no rekishi gaku* (History in a Changing World), and immediately after World War II, *Rekishi gaku hihan josetsu* (1946; Introduction to a Critique of History). In 1932–1933, Hani, together with Hattori Shisô (q.v.), assisted the pioneering Marxist historian Noro Eitarô (q.v.) with the series *Nihon shihon shugi hattatsu shi kôza* (Studies in the History of the Development of Capitalism in Japan), to which he himself was an important contributor on the historical aspects of the Meiji Restoration of 1868. This work formed the basis for his idea of what he called "the people's view of history." He returned to the Meiji Restoration again after the war, arguing in *Meiji ishin* (1946; The Meiji Restoration) that the Restoration was a severe setback, but in this setback he tried to find the sprouts of a new creativity. After being released from a brief imprisonment in 1933, under the 1925 Peace Preservation Law, for his Marxist political views, he published several intellectual-biographical studies. *Makiaberi kunshu ron* (1936; The Prince of Machiavelli, 1936), *Hakuseki-Yukichi* (1937; Arai Hakuseki and Fukuzawa Yukichi), *Mikeruangero* (1939; Michelangelo), and *Kurôche* (1939; Croce) incited the youth of Japan in the oppressive atmosphere of the late 1930s. He was briefly imprisoned once more in 1945, just before the end of World War II. Released after the war, Hani was elected to the House of Councillors (upper house of the national Diet), where he worked for the founding of the National Diet Library. After the war, he was more active as a critic than as a historian. His *Toshi no ronri* (1968; The Logic of the City) arguing the necessity of an alliance of municipalities, on the model of the free cities of Renaissance Italy, had a wide influence on the student movement of the late 1960s and the 1970s. Throughout his career he was a Marxist historian, but one who transcended formulaic applications of Marxism to examine history with his own vision and insight.

Bibliography: *Hani Gorô reikishi ron chosaku shû* (Collected Historical Works of Hani Gorô), 4 vols. (1967); Haga Noboru, *Hihan kindai Nihon shigaku shisô shi* (Critics in the History of Modern Japanese Historical Thought), (1974); Winston Kahn, "Hani Gorô: A Radical Democrat's Critique of Japanese Society," *Japan Interpreter*, 11 no. 2 (1976):186–202.

Masayuki Sato

HATTORI Shisô (Shimane, 1901–Tokyo, 1956), Japanese historian. Professor of Hôsei University. Son of the chief priest of a Buddhist temple. Hattori studied sociology at Tokyo Imperial (now Tokyo) University. After graduating from the university in 1925, he continued his research at the Sangyô Rôdô Chôsajo (Institute for Research on Industrial Labor), Rôdô Nômintô Shokikyoku (Secretariat of the Labor-Farmer Party), Chûô Kôron Publishing Company, and Puroretaria Kagaku Kenkyûjo (Institute for Proletarian Science). He worked at Kaô Sekken (The Kaô Soap Company, Ltd.) during 1938–1945. In 1946 he established the Kamakura Academia (Kamakura Academy) with his colleagues. In 1952 he was appointed professor of Hôsei University, serving there until his death. He began his career as a historian in 1928 with *Meiji ishin shi* (History of the Meiji Restoration), in which, using comparisons with the English and French revolutions, he insisted that the Meiji Restoration of 1868 was not a bourgeois revolution, but both the last form of feudalistic rule and the rise of autocracy, as a transitional form of the state to bourgeois rule. This work pioneered the study of the Restoration from a materialistic point of view. Together with Noro Eitarô (q.v.) and Hani Gorô (q.v.) he contributed to the series *Nihon shihonshugi hattatsushi kôza* (7 vols., 1932–1933; studies in the History of the Development of Capitalism in Japan).

In 1933 Hattori concentrated his concern on how the Meiji Restoration enabled Japan to maintain national independence, while India and China, under assault from the West in the midnineteenth century, were unable to do so. As an answer he proposed, in "Meiji ishin no kakumei oyobi han kakumei" (1933; Revolution and Counter-revolution in the Meiji Restoration), "Ishinshi hôhôjô no shomondai" (1933; Methodological Problems in the History of the Restoration), and "Gen man'yu no rekishiteki jôken" (1934; Historical Conditions of "die eigentliche Manufakturperiode") his theory that the Japanese economy had already reached the stage of Karl Marx's (q.v.) "die eigentliche Manufakturperiode" as the interior background, which made it possible for Japan to develop capitalism after the Restoration and accordingly produced a state strong enough to resist external pressures. Hattori's theory provoked a controversy with Tsuchiya Takao, professor of Tokyo University. This controversy, known as the "Manufacture Debate" on Japan's stage of development, grew into a larger debate, the so-called debate on Japanese capitalism (see Noro Eitarô). In the late 1930s, a time of systematic suppression of radicals, he abandoned writing, working at the Kaô

Soap Company, Ltd. After World War II, he vigorously resumed his scholarly endeavors, publishing works on the Freedom and People's Rights Movement of 1874–1884, the emperor system of Japan, and the thought of the Buddhist evangelist Shinran (1173–1262). He also published historical narratives and essays including *Kurofune zengo* (1933; The Time of the Black Ships), *Meiji no seijika tachi*, 2 vols. (1950–1954; Statesmen of the Meiji period), and so on.

Bibliography: *Hattori shisô zenshû* (Complete Works of Hattori Shisô, 24 vols., 1970–1976); *Hattori Shisô chosaku shû* (Works of Hattori Shisô, 7 vols., 1955); Hattori Shisô, "Absolutism and historiographical interpretation," *Japan Interpreter* 13, no. 1 (1980): 15–35; Hugh Borton, "Modern Japanese Economic Historians," in W. G. Beasley and E. G. Pulleyblank, eds., *Historians of China and Japan* (1961), pp. 288–306; Fujii Shôichi, "Hattori Shisô," in Nagahara Keiji and Kano Masanao, eds., *Nihon no rekishika* (Historians of Japan) (1976), pp. 265–274; Germaine A. Hoston, *Marxism and the Crisis of Development in Prewar Japan* (1987).

Masayuki Sato

HAYASHI Tatsuo (Tokyo, 1896–Kanagawa, 1984), Japanese scholar of European intellectual history. Professor of Meiji University. Hayashi studied aesthetics and art history at Kyoto university during 1919–1922. He was professor of Tôyô University (1924–1935), editor of the journal *Shisô* (Ideas) (1927–1928, 1929–1945), chief editor of *Sekai dai hyakka jiten* (Heibonsha's World Encyclopedia, 32 Vols., 1955–1960, 1951–1958), and professor of Meiji University (1956–1963). Hayashi was a historian who indicated what the study of Europe should be for Japanese: The modernization of Japan from the Meiji Restoration of 1868 onward was essentially a process of Westernization. Japan devoted phenomenal amounts of its national energy to learning from Western culture and science. For several decades after the Meiji Restoration, Japanese scholars of Western culture selected and introduced Western things they thought helpful in the making of modern Japan, mainly from Britain, France, and Germany. (See Fukuzawa Yukichi.) After World War I, Japanese students of the West began to grasp European culture and history on its own terms, that is, as a cultural unity. Japan accumulated a great deal of knowledge about the West, without the West realizing it, through study by Japanese scholars who had never been to the West and who were unable to speak Western languages, but could read Western languages, including Greek and Latin, at will. This is the same attitude as early modern Japanese Sinologists toward Chinese culture. (See Ogyu Sorai.)

Among these, Hayashi was the most eminent historian. His most prominent work as a historian was his pentalogy on the Renaissance: "Bungei fukkô" (1928; Renaissance) on the Humanism movement; "Hatsumei to hakken no jidai" (1927; Age of Invention and Discovery), a study of the influence of utopian literature; "Runessansu no idai to taihai" (1955; Greatness and Decadence in the Renaissance), a discussion of the political and social aspects of the Renaissance; "Runessansu no botai" (1956; Womb of the Renaissance), a study of the economic foundations of the Renaissance. This series was complete in "Seishinshi—hitotsu no hôhô josetsu" (1969; Intellectual History: A Discourse on Method), Hayashi proposed an "archaeology of mentalité," which, like archaeology as a necessary part of history, was intended to grasp the prototype of the Western mentality through detailed analysis of culture and society in history, based on his methodological assumption that historical study resolves itself into the elucidation of prototypes of mentalities. His study of Europe extended from floriculture to political journalism, from Greek tragedy to Marxism, from the translation of Wilhelm Bousset's *Jesus* (1906) to that of Jean Henri Fabre's *Souvenirs entomologiques* (10 vols., 1879–1907), as well as European history and culture. His other works are *Rusô* (1936; Jean Jacques Rousseau), *Shisô no unmei* (1939; Fate of Thought), *Rekishi no kurekata* (1946; The Waning of History), *Shakaishi teki shisôshi* (1949; Socio-historical History of Thought, with Miki Kiyoshi et al.), *Kyôsanshugiteki ningen* (1951; Communistic Man), *Hangoteki seishin* (1954; Ironic Spirit), and *Shisô no doramaturugii* (1974; Dramaturgy of Thought, a Dialogue with Kuno Osamu). His great work after World War II was the compilation of *Heibonsha's World Encyclopedia*, which represents the postwar Japanese culture. Hayashi, a pacifist and a liberal all his life, said, "I am a historian, but do not like to make a deal with history" (1939).

Bibliography: *Hayashi Tatsuo chosaku shû* (Works of Hayashi Tatsuo), 6 vols., (1971–1972); "Tokushû: Hayashi Tatsuo to gendai nihon no shisô" (Special number: Hayashi Tatsuo and the modern Japanese thought), *Gendai shisô* (Modern Ideas), 12–9 (1984); "Tsuitô: Hayashi Tatsuo" (Memorial addresses for Hayashi Tatsuo), *Gekkan hyakka* (Monthly encyclopedia), 262 (1984).

Masayuki Sato

ISHIMODA Shô (Hokkaidô, 1912–Tokyo, 1986), Japanese historian. Professor at Hôsei University. Ishimoda first studied philosophy, and then history, at Tokyo Imperial University, graduating in 1938. He held the chair in Japanese political history at Hôsei University during 1948–1981. Devoting himself to the study of ancient and medieval Japanese history, he published *Chûsei teki sekai no keisei* (1946; The Rise of the Medieval World), which follows the major currents of Japanese history from ancient times to the Middle Ages, using historical documents over the "longue durée" of the tenth to the sixteenth century to trace the history of a single feudal manor, the Kuroda no shô (Kuroda manor), in Iga Province (now NW Mie Prefecture), a major part of the fiscal operation of the great Buddhist temple Tôdaiji in Nara. Ishimoda summarized his conception of this work when he wrote, "the history of the manor was for me, first of all, a place where people lived, confronted difficulties, and made history." He was an apostle of the materialistic view of history, and his account stressed both Todaiji's administration of the estate, oppressing the people as temple serfs, and the weakness of the people, who had to suffer under this governance. This work was widely read among historians and students as a protest against the imperialistic view of Japanese history and influenced postwar Japanese historical scholarship to make a fresh start in examining the Japanese past. Ishimoda soon followed with two collections of essays, *Rekishi to minzoku no hakken: reki-*

shigaku no kadai to hôhô (1952; Discovering History and the People: Subject and Method in Historical Scholarship), and *Zoku rekishi to minzoku no hakken: Ningen-teikô-gakufû* (1953; Discovering History and the People, Continued: People; Resistance; Academic Fashion), characterized, as the titles show, by his idea that history should deal with the problems posed by life in the everyday world.

Ishimoda's later work is represented by *Nihon no kodai kokka* (1971); The Ancient Japanese State) in which he tried to examine the history of the ancient Japanese state as a dialectic between the internal forces of Japanese politics and the challenges presented by the tense international situation created by the unification of China (the Sui and Tang Empires) and the unification of Korea (Silla). He argued that the great institutional reforms of the seventh century (the Taika Reform, A.D. 646, and the succeeding half-century of reform) which created the ancient "imperial" state, were largely a defensive response to the perceived international threat. This view is now standard in Japanese scholarship, and has transformed the study of institution-building in the ancient state. His other works include *Kodai makki seiji shi josetsu* (1956; Introduction to [Japanese] Political History of the Late Ancient Period); *Chûsei no hô to kokka* (1960; Law and the State in Medieval [Japan]); *Nihon kodai kokka ron* (2 vols., 1973; A Theory of the Ancient Japanese State); *Sengo rekishigaku no shisô* (1977; Historical Thought in Postwar [Japan]); and *Nihonshi gaisetsu* (2 vols., 1980; An Outline of Japanese History).

Bibliography: A full bibliography of Ishimoda's works is included in the journal *Hôgaku shirin* (Hôsei University Review of Law and Political Sciences), 84, no. 1 (1986): 95–109; *Rekishi hyôron* 346 (August 1986): 81–82, gives a brief chronology of Ishimoda's career; Doi Masaoki, "Ishimoda Shô to seiyô kodai-shi kenkyû" (Ishimoda Shô and the Study of Ancient Western History), in *Rekishi hyôron* 436 (August 1986): 12–22; Hara Hidesaburô, "Ishimoda shigaku to kodai-shi kenkyû" (Ishimoda's Historianship and the Study of Ancient History), in *Rekishi hyôron* 436 (August 1986): 2–12. Matsushima Eiichi, "Ishimoda Shô shi no omomi" (The Dignity of Prof. Ishimoda Shô), in *Tosho shinbun* (Tosho Newspaper, February 8, 1986); Nagahara Keiji, "Ishimoda shô shi o itamu" (Mourning Prof. Ishimoda Shô), in *Asahi shinbun* (Asahi newspaper, January 21, 1986); Umeda Kinji, "*Rekishi to minzoku no hakken* no kandô" (On Being Moved by [Ishimoda's] *History and the Discovery of the Volk*), in *Rekishi hyôron* 436 (August 1986): 23–31.

Masayuki Sato

NAITÔ Konan (Akita, 1866–Kyoto, 1934), Japanese historian. Professor of Chinese History at Kyoto Imperial University. Born Naitô Torajirô, son of a Confucian scholar, Naitô took introductory lessons in the Chinese classics from his father in early childhood. Graduating from the Akita Normal School in 1885, he went to Tokyo and was active in Chinese issues as a journalist. In 1907 he was offered the newly established chair of Chinese history at Kyoto Imperial University, becoming a professor there in 1909, and was named to the Imperial Academy in 1926. He was the first scholar of Chinese history to abandon the traditional Confucian moralistic approach to Sinology, founding modern methodologies, and laying the foundations of Kyoto's strong modern tradition in Chinese studies. Based on his belief, rather fresh and objective for its time, that East Asian culture was a universal entity separate from the particular nations that produced it, he gave careful attention to determining the nature of East Asian culture, that is, to defining Chinese culture, which he saw as the nucleus, and Japanese culture, which he saw as an extension of it. His attitude toward cultures of the past was characterized by an approach to ideas and constructs not as timeless entities, complete and monolithic, but as modes of thought that were in flux in their own time. This attitude is apparent in his entire oeuvre, from his maiden effort, *Kinsei bungaku shi ron* (1871; On the History of [Ideas in] Early-Modern [Japanese] Literature). Naitô's China studies were grounded primarily in the textual criticism methodologies of the Qing period (1644–1911), but with due regard for the rapidly developing European Sinological tradition and including numerous critical textual studies of the Chinese classics, and positivistic studies of Chinese history. He covered most periods of Chinese history in a tetralogy, published posthumously: *Shina jôko shi* (1944; Ancient Chinese History); *Shina chûko no bunka* (1947; Medieval Chinese Culture); *Shina kinsei shi* (1944; Early-Modern Chinese History); and *Shinchôsh: tsûron* (1944; Introduction to the History of the Qing Dynasty).

Naitô's magnum opus, the fruit of a lifetime of Sinological studies, *Shina shigaku shi* (History of Chinese Historiography), also published posthumously, in 1949, discussed the development of Chinese historiography from the origin of the post of historian in the archaic Chinese state through developments in nineteenth-century Chinese historiography. He focused here on the central organizing concepts in the development of Chinese historiography, giving high praise for their creative contributions as historians and historiographers to Sima Qian (135?–93? B.C.), Liu Zhiji (661–721), Zheng Qiao (1104–1162), and Zhang Xuecheng (1738–1801). Naitô was the first scholar to recognize Zhang's importance as a historical theorist of unique significance. Naitô also published works on Japanese history, including *Nihon bunka shi kenkyû* (1924; Studies in Japanese Cultural History) and *Sentetsu no gakumon* (1946; Scholarship of Former Sages).

Bibliography: *Naitô Konan zenshû* (Complete Works) 14 vols. (1961–1976); Aoe Shunjirô, *Ryû no seiza: Naitô Konan no Ajia teki shôgai* (Constellation of the Dragon: The Asiatic Life of Naitô Konan) (1966); Joshua Fogel, *Politics and Sinology: The Case of Naitô Konan, 1866–1934* (1984); Miyakawa Hisayuki, "An Outline of the Naitô Hypothesis and Its Effects on Japanese Studies of China," *Far Eastern Quarterly*, 14, 4 (1955): 533–552; Ogawa Tamaki, "Naitô Konan no gakumon to sono shôgai" (The Life and Scholarship of Naitô Konan), in *Nihon no meicho 41, Naitô Konan* (Masterpieces of Japan, 41: Naitô Konan, 1971); Yue-him Tam, "An Intellectual's Response to Western Intrusion: Naitô Konan's View of Republican China," in Akira Iriye, ed., *The Chinese and the Japanese: Essays in Political and Cultural Interactions* (Princeton, N.J., 1980): 161–183.

Masayuki Sato

NAKADA Kaoru (Kofu, 1877–Tokyo, 1967), Japanese historian. Professor of legal history at Tokyo University. After graduating from the law faculty of Tokyo Imperial (now Tokyo) University in 1900, Nakada continued his studies in the graduate school and became an associate professor there in 1902. On returning from study abroad in Germany and France during 1908–1911, he was appointed full professor in 1911 and served until his retirement in 1937. He is known as the founder of the modern tradition of Japanese legal history. He was particularly interested in the study of the medieval manor and, subsequently, in the rural community and rights of common in the medieval and early modern periods. His work is distinguished by his comparative method, always comparing Japanese legal history with that of Europe to illuminate the points at issue. His career as a legal historian began with the publication of a series of essays: "Nihon shôen no keitô" (1906; The Origins of the Japanese Manor), in which he sought models for the Japanese manor in Tang China (618–907), and "Ôchô jidai no shôen ni kansuru kenkyû" (1906; Study of Manor in the late Heian Period), in which he elucidated the system of the medieval law of *jus in rem*. Throughout these works he refers to the European medieval manor, stating "the character of the Japanese manor bears a striking resemblance to that of Frankish period Europe in Immunität." From the 1920s, his interest shifted to the early modern legal history: He published "Tokugawa jidai no mura no jinkaku" (1920; Juridical Character of the Tokugawa-period [1600–1868] Village), "Meiji shonen ni okeru mura no jinkaku" (1927; Juridical Character of the Early Meiji Period [1868–1912] Village), and "Meiji shonen no iriai ken" (1928; The Rights of Common in the Early Meiji Period), in all of which he tried to demonstrate that "the traditional Japanese village is a juridical person, similar to the German Genossenschaft." He was more interested in the resemblance of Japanese legal history to that of the European, than in subtle distinctions resulting in differences between the social contexts. Most of his major works were published as *Hôseishi ronshû* (Collected Essays on Legal History, 1926–64) in four volumes.

Bibliography: Nakada Kaoru, *Tokugawa jidai no bungaku to shihô* (Literature and Private Law in the Tokugawa Period) (1923, rep. 1984), with explanation by Ishii Ryôsuke; Nakada Kaoru, *Nihon hôseishi kôgi* (Lecture on Japanese Legal History) (1983); Ishii Ryôsuke, "Nakada sensei no gyôseki ni tuite" (On the Works of Master Nakada), in Nakada Kaoru, *Hôseishi ronshû*, vol. 4 (rev. ed., 1971), pp. 317–327; Ishii Shirô, "Nakada Kaoru" in Nagahara Keiji and Kano Masanao, eds., *Nihon no rekishika* (Japanese Historians) (1976), pp. 116–125.

Masayuki Sato

NORO Eitarô (Hokkaido, 1900–Tokyo, 1934), Japanese historian. Marxist economist. After studying at Keio University, Noro continued his research on Japanese capitalism after 1926 at the Sangyô Rôdô Chôsajo (Institute for Research on Industrial Labor) and the Puroretaria Kagaku Kenkyûjo (Institute for Proletarian Science). His first work as a historian was published as "Nihon shihon shugi zenshi" (1927; Prehistory of Japanese Capitalism), in which he surveyed

Japan's history from ancient times to the Meiji Restoration (1868), reviewing processes of development and change from a Marxist, historical materialist viewpoint. The same year he published "Nihon shihon shugi hattatsu shi" (History of the Development of Japanese Capitalism), in which he argued that the Meiji Restoration was a bourgeois revolution, revealing the characteristics of the development of Japanese capitalism, and the fundamental contradictions in the survival of both absolutist state authority and feudalistic exploitation in the peasant village. These two studies, originally published as part of a major project by the leading socialist scholars in Japan, *Shakai mondai kôza* (1926–1927; Lectures on social issues, 13 vols.), were later combined with his other essays on Japanese capitalism and published as *Nihon shihon shugi hattatsu shi* (1930), the first genuinely historical-materialist book on the history of Japanese capitalism. Noro played a leading role in editing the influential and controversial *Nihon shihon shugi hattatsu shi kôza* (7 vols., 1932–1933; Lectures on the History of the Development of Japanese Capitalism), in which the "Lecture Faction" (*Kôza-ha*) set forth its view—that of the 1932 Comintern as well—in the Japanese Marxist ideological controversy over the nature of the Meiji Restoration and the stage of development in Japanese capitalism (see Hani Gorô [q.v.]), a view contrasting with the Labor-Farmer Faction (*Rônô-ha*). Noro was also active as a leading theoretician of the Japan Communist party in the early 1930s but was arrested in 1934, and died in police detention. His work has continued to have great theoretical influence on academic historians of Japan since World War II.

Bibliography: *Noro Eitarô chosaku shû* (Collected Works), 3 vols. (1949); *Noro Eitarô zenshû* (Complete Works), 2 vols. (1965); Noro Eitarô. *Shohan Nihon shihon shugi hattatsu shi* (The First Edition of the "History of the Development of Japanese Capitalism,"[with explanatory note and chronology]), 2 vols., (1983); Germaine A. Hoston, *Marxism and the Crisis of Development in Prewar Japan* (1987); Kitayama Shigeru, "Nihon kindai shigaku no hatten" (Development of Modern Japanese Historical Scholarship), in *Iwanami kôza Nihon rekishi* (Iwanami Lectures on Japanese History) 22 (1972): 105–163; Kuno Osamu and Tsurumi Shunsuke, *Gendai Nihon no shisô* (Contemporary Japanese Thought) (1956).

Masayuki Sato

RAI San'yô (Osaka, 1780–Kyoto, 1832), Japanese historian. Son of a Confucian scholar, Rai grew up in Aki Province (now Hiroshima Prefecture). In 1797 he went to Edo to study at the official shogunal Confucian academy, the Shôheikô, founded by Hayashi Razan, and returned to Aki the next year. Moving to Kyoto in 1811, he founded a private academy and spent the rest of his life as a historian, writer, and poet. He is best remembered as author of the *Nihon gaishi* (1827; Unofficial History of Japan), the most widely read and influential work of history in nineteenth-century Japan. It became a touchstone of the political activists in midcentury who sought the overthrow of the Tokugawa shogunate and a restoration of direct imperial government. These goals were accomplished in 1868 as the Meiji Restoration, which is often seen as the starting point of Japan's modernization. Rai's historical philosophy that, "When things reach an extreme

they are bound to change, and when things change they are bound to succeed,''
combined with his focus on the imperial institution, and his advocacy of a
restoration of imperial rule, enjoyed great popularity among the rising generation
who promoted the Meiji Restoration (1868) and had a profound influence on
them. It has been called ''a bridge to the final and dissident stage of [imperial]
loyalism in the Tokugawa period. . . . , [defined by] a regret that the political
power that had once belonged to the emperor had passed into the hands of the
military families.'' *Nihon gaishi* is a history of Japan from the tenth to the
eighteenth century, a history of the rise and fall of national military hegemons
from the Genji and Heike families that took secular power in the early medieval
period, to the founding and flourishing of the Tokugawa shogunate, the national
warrior administration under which Rai himself lived. *Nihon gaishi* is written
in a Japanese version of classical Chinese, modeled on the style of Si-ma Qian's
Shi-ji (C. 92.–89 B.C.; Records of the Grand Historian) and informed by the
ethical interpretations of the Zhu Xi school of Neo-Confucianism. Although in
many places historically inaccurate, Rai captivated his readers with his concise
and lucid narration and his florid literary style. His personal judgments about
historical events, inserted parenthetically throughout, inspired his readers to
imperial loyalism. He also published *Nihon seiki* (1845; Political Account of
Japan), a history from the legendary founder of the empire, Emperor Jinmu, to
Emperor Goyôzei (reigned 1586–1611). He also wrote poetry and essays in
classical Chinese on a wide range of subjects from Japanese history.

Bibliography: W. G. Beasley and Carmen Blacker, ''Japanese Historical Writing in
the Tokugawa Period (1603–1868),'' in Beasley and E. G. Pulleyblank, eds., *Historians
of China and Japan* (1961), pp. 245–263; Nakamura Shin'ichirô, *Rai San'yô to sono
jidai* (Rai San'yô and His Times) (1971); *Rai San'yô zensho* (Complete Works), 8 vols.
(1983); Burton Watson, ''Historian and Master of Chinese Verse: *Rai San'yô*, '' in Japan
Culture Institute, ed., *Great Historical Figures of Japan* (1978), pp. 221–242.

Masayuki Sato

SHIGENO Yasutsugu (Satsuma Province [now Kagoshima Prefecture], 1827–
Tokyo, 1910), Japanese historian. Professor at the Imperial University (now the
University of Tokyo). Son of a rural samurai, Shigeno attended the Satsuma
domain academy, the Zôshikan, and then went to Edo in 1848 to study at the
shogunal Confucian academy, the Shôheikô, founded by Hayashi Razan. His
studies there of *kôshôgaku*, a form of textual criticism, were to determine his
later characteristics as a historian. In 1864 he returned to teach at the Zôshikan,
and while there he compiled his *Kôchô seikan* (1865; General Mirror of the
Imperial Dynasty), on orders of the daimyo. In 1868 a movement led by a
combination of Satsuma and three other domains overthrew the Tokugawa shogunate, an event known as the Meiji Restoration. Bringing an end to 260 years
of Tokugawa rule and 700 years of warrior governance, the Meiji government,
centered on the emperor, started the active, purposeful modernization of Japan.
Many of the most active leaders of the Restoration were rural samurai from

Satsuma and Chôshû (now Yamaguchi Prefecture), and they largely controlled the new government. In 1871 Shigeno went to Tokyo, and in 1875 he entered the Shûshi Kyokyu (Historical Bureau), where he served as vice-director. When the bureau was absorbed by Imperial University (now the University of Tokyo) in 1888, he became a professor there.

Shigeno was a founder of modern Japanese historical scholarship: After the Restoration, the government established the Historical Bureau directly under the Council of State, intending it to complete the compilation of the *Dai Nihon shi* (History of Great Japan, 1657–1906) begun by Tokugawa Mitsukuni in 1657, a project in which Shigeno participated as de facto director. He rejected the Confucianistic idea of moralistic interpretation of history as an organizing principle but placed high value on the traditional scholastic method of textual criticism (*kôshôgaku*), reinforced by modern European methods of positivist historiography. G. G. Zerffi's *The Science of History* (1879), which resulted from a request Shigeno presented through Suematsu Kenchô, was the first influence in the transmission of modern European methods to Japan. Shigeno was among the first Japanese who tried to establish modern Japanese historical scholarship on the basis of both Chinese and European ideas of history, an effort that is clear from his "Kokushi hensan no hôhô o ronzu" (1880; On Methodology in the Compilation of Japanese History). Besides founding and directing numerous major historical compilation projects, several of which continue to this day, he published many monographs on historical method and Japanese history, and co-authored *Kokushigan* (1890; Survey History of Japan) with two of his Imperial University colleagues. He was nicknamed Doctor of Denial because of his use of positivistic methods to demonstrate the apocryphal nature of some purportedly historical figures and events.

Bibliography: *Shigeno Hakase shigaku ronbun shû* (Collected Historical Papers of Dr. Shigeno), ed. Ôkubo Toshiaki, 3 vols. (1938–1939); Iwai Tadakuma, "Shigeno Yasutsugu," in Nagahara Keiji and Kano Masanao, eds., *Nihon no rekishika* (Historians of Japan) (1976), pp. 3–10; Numata, Jiro, "Shigeno Yasutsugu and the Modern Tokyo Tradition of Historical Writing," in W. G. Beasley and E. G. Pulleyblank, eds., *Historians of China and Japan* (1961), pp. 264–287; Ôkubo Toshiaki, "Shimazu-ke hensan *Kôchô seikan* to Meiji shoki no shûshi jigyô" (The *Kôchô seikan* Compiled by the Shimazu Clan, and the Historiographical Enterprise of the Early Meiji Period), in *Shigaku zasshi* (Journal of History), 50, no. 12 (1939): 1419–1463; Ozawa Eiichi, *Kindai Nihon shigaku shi no kenkyû: Meiji hen* (Studies in the History of Modern Japanese Historiography: The Meiji Period, 1968).

Masayuki Sato

SHIRATORI Kurakichi (Chiba, 1865–Kanagawa, 1942), Japanese scholar of Asian history. Professor at Tokyo Imperial University. Shiratori was educated at the Imperial University (later Tokyo Imperial; now University of Tokyo), 1887–1890, where he learned the modern German method of history from Ludwig Reiss, a student of Leopold von Ranke (q.v.). On graduation he served as professor at Gakushûin (now Gakushûin University) and then studied in Europe,

1901–1903, returning to Japan to become professor of oriental history at Tokyo Imperial University (1904–1925). He was a member of the Imperial Academy during 1919–1942. Shiratori was a founder in Japan of historical studies of Asia based on modern methodologies and devoted himself to terminating the long, strong tradition of Confucian ideas and methods of historiography. Believing that "History is a science of combinations, [seeking] to find the invisible relations among historical events and to combine them," he directed his interest to peoples on the periphery of ancient China, especially in Korea, Manchuria, Central Asia, and Southwest Asia, and concentrated on illuminating their historical interactions. His methodology was to employ folkloric, historical, geographic, and particularly linguistic techniques to examine critically historical documents in a wide range of languages to identify the true situations of the peoples and nations under study. Particularly adept at the linguistic analysis of Chinese historical documents, he used these techniques to elucidate the study of the non-Chinese peoples of Asia. Some of these studies were compiled as *Seiiki shi kenkyû* (2 vols., 1941–1944; Studies on Central Asia), which includes studies on the ethnic filiation of the peoples of ancient Central Asia, their geographic distribution, spheres of activity, and migration routes, as well as how these changed over time; and historical-geographic analyses of place names, locations of fortified towns, and trade routes. His nearly two hundred studies on these topics were compiled in *Shiratori Kurakichi zenshû* (10 vols., 1969–1971; Complete works).

Shiratori also produced critical studies of the founder myths of China and works on ancient Japanese history and the filiation of the Japanese language, published as *Nihongo on keitô* (1950; Filiation of the Japanese Language); *Shindaishi no shin kenkyû* (1954; New Studies on the Age of the Gods), and published numerous studies translated into English, German, and French, as well as Chinese. He also led the effort, sponsored by the South Manchurian Railway, in establishing the Railway's Research Department. This effort produced numerous studies of virtually every aspect of Manchurian history, ethnography, and economy. Shiratori was one of the founders of the Mitsubishi-sponsored Tôyo Bunko (Oriental Archive), which as a result of Shiratori's efforts remains one of the world's most important collections of historical materials on Asia.

Bibliography: Ishida Mikinosuke, "Shiratori Kurakichi Sensei shôden" (Short Biography), in *Shiratori Kurakichi zenshû* 10 (1971): 519–540; Oyama Masaaki, "Shiratori Kurakichi," in Nagahara Keiji and Kano Masanao, eds., *Nihon no rekishika* (Historians of Japan) (1976), pp. 78–85; Stefan Tanaka, "Shina: Japan's Representation of China, 1894–1926," Ph.D. thesis (University of Chicago, 1986); Tsuda Sôkichi, "Shiratori Hakase shôden" (Short Biography), in *Tsuda Sôkichi zenshû* (Complete Works of Tsuda Sôkichi), 24 (1965), pp. 107–161; John Young, *The Research Activities of the South Manchurian Railway Company, 1907–1945: A History and Bibliography* (1961); "Zadankai: Sengaku o kataru—Shiratori Kurakichi hakase" (Symposium: Recalling Dr. Shiratori Kurakichi), in *Tôhôgaku* 44 (1972):152–182.

Masayuki Sato

TAGUCHI Ukichi (Edo [now Tokyo], 1855–Tokyo, 1905), Japanese historian and economist. Son of a low-ranking samurai. Taguchi's family was riven by the Meiji Restoration of 1868. After studying history and economics as a research student of the Ministry to Finance in 1874, he worked in the Ministry until 1878. In 1879 he founded the *Tôkyô keizai zasshi* (Tokyo Journal of Economics) modeled on *The Economist* of London, and the historical journal *Shikai* (The Sea of History) in 1891, while contributing to the development of historical studies as publisher of many historical masterpieces, such as Hanawa Hokiichi's *Gunsho ruijû* (Classified Collection of Japanese Classics and Sources), and *Kokushi taikei* (1897–1901; Collection of National Histories), major compilations on Japanese history that remain standard today. Taguchi was the first Japanese historian to introduce economic causation to the explanation of Japanese history, and is best remembered as author of the *Nihon kaika shôshi* (6 vols., 1877–1882; A Short History of Japan's Enlightenment). By a history of enlightenment he meant a history that emphasized historical causality rather than mere chronological narration and historical portraits of great men; in it he covers political, economic, social, and religious aspects of Japanese history from ancient times to the end of the Tokugawa shogunate in 1868. In this work he regards as the driving force of history a human nature that seeks to "cling to life and escape death," a nature that left such marks as the doctrine of the immortality of the soul, worshipping the departed souls of ancestors, the spread of Buddhism, feudalistic ethics, and so on, in Japanese history. The other informing idea of this work, that "the development of the people's consciousness keeps pace with the development of money and property," shows his economic vision in the interpretation of history, taking as central the relationship between the development of culture and the development of production, which accordingly brought about a social-historic view of history. In his *Jiyû bôeki Nihon keizai ron* (1878; Free Trade: On the Japanese Economy), he developed his economic ideas about history, treating the Meiji Restoration of 1868 as a change from a feudal society to "the new society"; from a system of "enforced allocation" to "free and natural allocation" of occupation and social role, which he concluded was a natural consequence of the resolution of economic and historical laws. After 1891 he adopted a style of historical presentation that he called "girdling": describing the aspects of an entire age through individual historical figures. Thus, he published many historical biographies. He was also active in politics and business, and remained a laissez-faire economist all his life.

Bibliography: *Teiken Taguchi Ukichi zenshû* (Complete Works of Master Teiken, Taguchi Ukichi), 8 vols. (1927–1929); *Nihon kaika shôshi* (A Short History of Japan's Enlightenment), ed. Kaji Ryûichi (1964; repr. 1980); Hugh Borton, "Modern Japanese Economic Historians," in W. G. Beasley and E. G. Pulleyblank, eds., *Historians of China and Japan* (1961), pp. 288–306; Ozawa Eiichi, *Kindai Nihon shigaku shi no kenkyû: Meiji hen* (Studies in the History of Modern Japanese Historiography: The Meiji Period) (1968).

Masayuki Sato

TAKEKOSHI Yosaburô (Musashi Province [now Saitama Prefecture], 1865– Tokyo, 1950), Japanese historian, statesman. Also known by the *nom de plume* of Sansa. After graduating from Keiô Gijuku (now Keio University), Takekoshi became a journalist, writing for Tokutomi Sohô's (q.v.) *Kokumin shinbun*; later receiving the patronage of Saionji Kinmochi, then the education minister, he became editor-in-chief of Saionji's journal, *Sekai no Nihon* (Japan in the World). He also became a counselor to the Ministry of Education, was elected to the Diet in 1902 as a member of the Seiyûkai party, and was appointed to the House of Peers in 1923 and to the Privy Council in 1940. He retired from politics on the eve of the Pacific War. He started his career as a historian with his *Shin Nihon shi* (1891–1892; History of the New Japan), a history of the Meiji Restoration of 1868 in which he interpreted the Restoration as being caused not by reverence and loyalty to the emperor, but by the collapse of the feudal society of its own weight, and the new vital power released by that collapse. He developed the idea afresh in his *Nisen gohyaku nen shi* (1896; 2,500-year History [of Japan]), laying stress on the economic aspects of Japanese history. He was the first modern Japanese historian to acknowledge any positive contribution of the Tokugawa (1603–1868) feudal regime, which he saw as establishing the foundations of a people able to stand by themselves, raising the idea that "the world belongs not to a single person, but to all people," arguing that Japanese history had produced many men like John Hampden (English statesman, 1594–1643) among its lower samurai and village headmen. His conclusion that the energies stored up during the Tokugawa period made possible the continuation of Japan after the Restoration remains a seminal contribution. His idea of history took full form in his *Nihon keizai shi* (8 vols., 1919; Economic History of Japan), his magnum opus, which is still a highly regarded work. Taking the position that "the first cause in history consists in the economic motives of mankind," and that it was the economic motives of humankind that, in the course of time, made institutions, enacted laws, suppressed rebellions, and invaded foreign countries, he wrote his economic history of Japan as an integral part of world history. This insightful work was later published in English as *The Economic Aspects of the History of the Civilization of Japan* (3 vols., 1930). He published many other works on Japanese history, including English editions of his *Japanese Rule in Formosa* (1907) and *The Story of Wakô: Japanese Pioneers in the Southern Regions* (1940).

Bibliography: Peter Duus, "Whig History, Japanese Style: The Min'yûsha Historians and the Meiji Restoration," *Journal of Asian Studies*, 33, no.3 (1974):415–436; Iwai Tadakuma, "Nihon kindai shigaku no keisei" (The Rise of Modern Japanese Historical Scholarship), in *Iwanami kôza Nihon rekishi* (Iwanami Lectures on Japanese History), 22 (1963):59–103; Kuwabara Takeo, *Rekishi no shisô* (Historical Thought) (1965); Nishida Takeshi, " 'Heimin shugi' kara 'Jiyû teikoku shugi' e: Takekoshi Sansa no seiji shisô" (From 'Populism' to 'Liberal Imperialism': Takekoshi Sansa's Political Thought), in *The Annals of the Japanese Political Science Association* (1982): 75–105; Ozawa Eiichi, *Kindai Nihon shigakushi no kenkyû: Meiji hen* (Studies in the History of Modern Japanese Historiography: The Meiji Period) (1968).

                                                                                  Masayuki Sato

TOKUTOMI Sohô (Higo Province [modern Kumamoto Prefecture], 1863–Atami, 1957), Japanese historian and journalist. Born Tokutomi Iichirô, son of a country samurai, Tokutomi studied at the Kumamoto Yôgakkô (Kumamoto School of Western Studies) and Dôshisha (now Dôshisha University) in Kyoto, from which he resigned in 1880, a few weeks before he was to graduate. Returning home, he studied and taught in Kumamoto for six years, publishing *Shôrai no Nihon* (1886; Japan in the Future), in which he argued for "democratic progressivism," political and social reforms after the model of Western democracy. This work established his status in the world of journalism, and he accordingly left for Tokyo. There he founded a publishing house, Min'yûsha (The Society of Friends of the People), started a journal, *Kokumin no tomo* (Friend of the Nation) in 1887, and launched a newspaper *Kokumin shinbun* (The Nation Newspaper) in 1890. In the early 1890s he began to see his views as too romantic, particularly in the aftermath of the Triple Intervention of 1895, in which Germany, France, and Russia forced the retrocession of Liaotung. He moved from liberalism to imperialistic nationalism, publishing *Dai Nihon bochô ron* (On the Expansion of Great Japan). In 1911 he was rewarded for his work as a progovernment publicist and adviser by appointment to the House of Peers, where he served until 1945. His apparent inconsistency, turning from liberalism to nationalism, kept intellectuals at a distance; his journal was discontinued in 1898, and his newspaper was twice put to the torch by mobs angered by his support for the government. He closed his newspaper in 1929 to devote himself entirely to writing, but kept his interest in state affairs, remained close to the governments in power, and was a leading figure in press circles until the end of World War II. He was purged from public life by the Occupation after the war.

As a historian, Tokutomi won immortality through numerous biographies of Japanese historical figures, and his magnum opus, *Kinsei Nihon kokumin shi* (A History of the Japanese Nation in Early-Modern Times, 1918–1962), in 100 Volumes. Tokutomi was a journalist of the past: His idea of history was best expressed in his saying that, "history is the newspaper of yesterday; the newspaper is the history of tomorrow." He began his career as historian with his biography of Yoshida Shôin (1893), one of the most prominent political and intellectual figures in the prelude to the Meiji Restoration of 1868. In this work Tokutomi defined the Restoration as a revolution and argued that Shôin was a "revolutionary precursor." Tokutomi had not yet turned away from liberalism, and his reading of Shôin reflected his desire for a second Restoration, which would replace the oligarchic clan government and aristocracy that had resulted from the Meiji Restoration. But after his turn to nationalism, in the revised edition of *Yoshida Shôin* (1908), he substituted the term "reformation" for "revolution," and further published numerous hagiographical biographies of the leaders and high officials of the Restoration. At the age of fifty-six, Tokutomi commenced what was to be his lifework, *Kinsei Nihon kokuminshi*, in which he aimed to write of the reign of the Emperor Meiji (reigned 1868–1912), showing it as an era in which Japan was unified around the central figure of the emperor and when Japan's power became apparent to the world. He started his account in the late sixteenth century, when Japan was reunified after a century of civil war by Oda Nobunaga (1534–1582) and Toyotomi Hideyoshi (1536–1598). The earlier volumes of this work were originally published serially, chapter by chapter, in the *Kokumin shinbun*, the later volumes in the *Ôsaka Mainichi shinbun* and *Tôkyô Nichinichi shinbun*, and only subsequently as books. Tokutomi completed *Kinsei Nihon kokumin shi* in 1952, when he was in his ninetieth year. He collected primary sources widely for his history, which was essentially narrative rather than analytical and tended to focus heavily on great men as movers of history. Yet the books were intended for a mass audience; they were immensely popular and served to give great numbers of Japanese a detailed familiarity with early-modern Japanese history.

Bibliography: Tokutomi Sohô, *Sohô jiden* (Autobiography) (1935); Peter Duus, "Whig History, Japanese Style: The Min'yûsha Historians and the Meiji Restoration," *Journal of Asian Studies*, 33, no. 3 (1974): 415–436; John D. Pierson, *Tokutomi Sohô, 1863–1957: A Journalist for Modern Japan* (1980); Kenneth B. Pyle, *The New Generation in Meiji Japan* (1969); Sugii Mutsurô, *Tokutomi Sohô no kenkyû* (1978).

Masayuki Sato

TSUDA Sôkichi (Gifu, 1873–Tokyo, 1961), Japanese historian. Professor at Waseda University. After graduating from Tôkyô Senmon Gakkô (now Waseda University) in 1891, Tsuda served as a middle school teacher, until he was recruited in 1907 by Shiratori Kurakichi (q.v.) to join the newly formed Research Department of the South Manchuria Railway. He taught at Waseda from 1918 to 1940, becoming professor in 1919. He wrote that "History is a process of human mentalities and daily life," and all his work was based on this conception. His was an independent mind, not identified with any particular scholarly faction; he was a historian who pursued his interpretations of Japanese history through the rational judgment that was his personal credo. In *Jindai shi no atarashii kenkyû* (New Studies of the Age of the Gods, 1913), and *Kojiki oyobi Nihon shoki no kenkyû* (Studies on the *Kojiki* and *Nihon shoki*, 1919), he made a critical examination of Japan's two oldest extant historical works, the *Kojiki* (Record of Ancient Matters; see Ô no Yasumaro in Boia, ed., *Great Historians from Antiquity to 1800*), and *Nihon shoki* (Chronicle of Japan; see Prince Toneri in ibid.). He separated those stories fabricated by the compilers to legitimate imperial rule from accounts that he deemed factual; at the same time he revealed the mentality of the ancient Japanese by interpreting the fabricated accounts as expressions of that mentality. In the process, Tsuda established the historical utility of these ancient texts and the limits of their value, providing valuable underpinnings to all subsequent studies of ancient Japanese history. His *Bungaku ni arawaretaru waga kokumin shisô no kenkyû* (4 vols., 1916–1921; Studies on the Mentality of Our People as Expressed in Literature) is a history of Japanese thought from the sixth through the nineteenth centuries, examining Japanese literature to focus on changes in the national mentality. Holding that in Japan literature offered the clearest expression of the people's daily life and values, morals, religion, and conceptions of the individual and the world, he extracted from literature a history of the social, political, and economic life of the people. These studies, particularly his studies of ancient Japanese history, offered a compelling alternative to the nationalistic interpretations that both underlay the official imperial ideology of prewar Japan and informed much of its orthodox scholarship. Many of the advances that have been made in postwar understanding of ancient Japanese history by scholars like Ishimoda Shô (q.v.) rest squarely on Tsuda's work. Tsuda also made valuable contributions to the study of the Chinese classics and ancient Chinese thought in such studies as *Saden no shisôshi teki kenkyû* (1935; Intellectual-historical Studies of the *Zuo-zhuan*), and *Jukyô no kenkyû* (1950–1956; Studies in Confucianism).

Bibliography: *Tsuda Sôkichi zenshû* (Complete Works), 33 vols. (1963–1965); Ienaga Saburô, *Tsuda Sôkichi no shisôshi teki kenkyû* (Studies of Tsuda Sôkichi from the Viewpoint of the History of Ideas) (1972); Kadowaki Teiji, "Tsuda Sôkichi," in Nagahara Keiji and Kano Masanao, eds., *Nihon no rekishika* (Historians of Japan), (1976), pp. 165–174; Ômuro Mikio, *Adiantum shô: Tsuda Sôkichi no sei to jôchô* (Eulogy on Adiantum: The Life and Spirit of Tsuda Sôkichi), (1983); Ueda Masaaki, ed., *Hito to shisô: Tsuda Sôkichi* (Men and Ideas: Tsuda Sôkichi, 1974).

Masayuki Sato

TSUJI Zennosuke (Hyôgo, 1877–Tokyo, 1955), Japanese historian. Professor at Tokyo University. After studying history at Tokyo Imperial (now Tokyo University) during 1896–1900, Tsuji received the doctorate in literature for his study on the history of Japanese Buddhism in 1901 and joined the Historiographical Institute at Tokyo Imperial University in 1902. Beginning in 1911 he taught history at the university, became a full professor in 1923, and was concurrently director of the Historiographical Institute from 1928. Tsuji was the first historian to cast an objective light on the history of Buddhism in Japan: Influenced by his father who was a devotee of the Shinshû sect of Buddhism, Tsuji took an interest in the historical aspects of Buddhism in Japan and, after graduating from the university, devoted himself to that field. Sectarian and doctrinal Buddhist history predominated at that time, but Tsuji's attitude toward the history of Japanese Buddhism was decidedly academic and positive, standing aloof from any sectarian interest. He is best remembered as the author of *Nihon bukkyô shi* (10 vols., 1944–1955; History of Buddhism in Japan), in which he treats Buddhism, from its introduction to Japan in the first half of the sixth century to the early Meiji period (1868–1912), as an indispensable constituent element of culture in Japanese history: He "observe(d) the influence of Buddhism on Japanese culture, illuminate(d) the relationship between Buddhism and Japanese society, mentality and politics, and also explicate(d) how Buddhism integrated itself to Japanese culture." The traits Tsuji identified as characteristic of Japanese Buddhism were its transformation into a state religion; its function as a protector of the state; and its essentially secular, nonspeculative nature.

As characteristic of Japanese Buddhism, he pointed out its scale as an enterprise of national importance and its realistic and practical nature without indulging in vain speculations. He also demonstrated through use of historical sources, that Buddhism united with indigenous Japanese forms of worship of the souls of departed ancestors, and showed how it merged with Japanese national life, through an examination of thought, literature, language, printing, education, medicine, music, economy, social works, and development of local and popular culture. His contribution to the study of Japanese Buddhism lies in his demonstration that "Buddhism has been thoroughly digested in the Japanese mental and material life for the fourteen hundred years and has formed an essential part of Japanese and their lives: Japanese have been unconsciously living a life imbued with Buddhistic culture." Tsuji could be characterized as a social historian of Japanese Buddhism. He also published many works and historical compilations including *Nihon bukkyô no kenkyû* (2 vols., 1944–1945; Studies on the History of Buddhism in Japan) and *Meiji ishin shinbutsu bunri shiryô* (5 vols., 1931; The Collection of Historical Materials on the Separation of Shintoism and Buddhism in the Meiji Restoration, ed. with S. Murakami and J. Washio). Besides his studies on the history of Buddhism, he published *Nihon bunka shi* (11 vols., 1948–1953; A Cultural History of Japan) and *Tanuma jidai* (1915; The Tanuma Era). *The Tanuma Era* (1760–1786) is one of his few historical narratives, arguing that the age of Tanuma Okitsugu, chief shogunal minister from 1772 to 1786, was an era of bright, progressive activity, foreshadowing the Meiji Restoration of 1868. In contrast to the common opinion of the period as a dark age, his interpretation, combined with his social-historic viewpoint, still captivates Japanese historians. *Kaigai kôtsû shiwa* (1917; Historical Essays on [Japanese] Foreign Relations) is noteworthy for Tsuji's view that Japanese culture has developed under the impetus of stimuli from foreign countries, and in correlation with the degree and intensity of foreign relations. He also organized many projects of the historical compilations in Japan, as the first director of the Historiographical Institute (see Shigeno Yasutsugu).

Bibliography: Tsuji Zennosuke, *Nihon bukkyô shi* (History of Buddhism in Japan), 10 vols. (1944–1955); Sakamoto Tarô, "Honkai komon zen rijichô Tsuji Zennosuke no kôkyo wo itamu" (Mourning the Death of Tsuji Zennosuke, an Adviser to and the Ex-Chairman [of the Historical Society]), *Shigaku zasshi* 64–11 (1955): 80–84; Fujitani Toshio, "Bukkyôshika to siteno Tsuji zennosuke no ichi" (The Place of Tsuji Zennosuke as a Historian of Buddhism), *Rekishi hyôron* 75 (1956): 86–91; Matsushima Eiichi, "Tsuji Zennosuke," in Nagahara Keiji and Kano Masanao eds., *Nihon no rekishika* (Japanese Historians) (1976): 185–194.

Masayuki Sato

UCHIDA Ginzô (Tokyo, 1872–Kyoto, 1919), Japanese historian. Professor of Kyoto University. After graduating from Tôkyô Senmon Gakkô (now Waseda University) in 1889, Uchida studied Japanese history at Imperial (later Tokyo Imperial, now Tokyo) University during 1893–1896. He taught economic history at the Tôkyô Senmon Gakkô and Imperial University. During 1903–1906 he studied in England, France, and Germany. On returning from his studies abroad, he was appointed to a newly founded chair in history at Kyoto Imperial University and stayed there until his death in 1919. Uchida laid the academic foundations of Japanese economic history, insisting that the historian should stand aloof from historical study based on the scholastic method of textual criticism and bibliographical study (Kôshôgaku; see Shigeno Yasutsugu). He started his career as a historian with "Keizai shi no seishitsu oyobi han'i ni tsukite" (1898; On the Nature and Scope of Economic History) in which he stressed the reciprocal relations among economic phenomena and the entire social context, a theory he published in his *Nihon kinsei shi* (1903; Early Modern Japanese History), taking a broad view of the Tokugawa period in the international environment to elucidate affirmatively the social and cultural aspects of the period. Though much influenced by the theories of economic development of the German historical school of economics during his study in Europe, he maintained a relativistic rather than a nomothetic viewpoint of history, in which he contrasts with his contemporary, Fukuda Tokuzô (1874–1930), in his *Die Gesellschaftliche und Wirtschaftliche Entwicklung in Japan* (1900). He studied intensively the system of state allotment of farmland in ancient Japan and landownership in early modern Japan, not as mere economic history but as social and cultural history. These studies were compiled as *Nihon keizai shi no kenkyû* (2 vols., 1921; Studies on Japanese Economic History).

Uchida also produced pioneer works on the study of historiographical perspective (which he himself called historical theory): He put emphasis on the inevitability of "selecting historical facts" in historical studies, stating that "the historian, taking his stance on ground distinct from that of the text critique historians, should select and collect historical facts on his own initiative," to indicate the limitations of the historiography of the textual critics. Methodologically, he proposed his own conception of a historical framework, analyzed into five categories: ethnohistory, national history, social-group history, clan history, and individual history, in "Rekishi no riron oyobi rekishi no tetsugaku" (1900; The Theory of History and the Philosophy of History). He assumed a critical attitude toward the main-current historical scholarship guided by the Kôshôgaku principle, and he founded the modern Kyoto tradition of historical scholarship with Hara Katsurô, Miura Hiroyuki, and Naitô Konan (q.v.). His scholarship was later developed by Nishida Naojirô for cultural history and by Honjô Eijirô for economic history.

Bibliography: *Uchida Ginzô ikô zsenshû* (Complete Posthumous Works of Uchida Ginzô), 5 vols. (1921); Uchida Ginzô, *Kinsei no nihon: Nihon kinsei shi* (Early Modern Japan: Early Modern Japanese History) ed. Miyazaki Michio (1975); Hugh Borton, "Modern Japanese Economic Historians," in W. G. Beasley and E. G. Pulleyblank, eds., *Historians of China and Japan* (1961), pp. 288–306; Honjô Eijirô, "Uchida Ginzô sensei" (Master Ginzô Uchida), in *Honjô Eijirô chosakushû* (Collected Works of Honjô Eijirô), 10 vols. (1971–1973), 10, pp. 238–247.

Masayuki Sato

WATSUJI Tetsurô (Hyôgo, 1889–Tokyo, 1960), Japanese historian and philosopher. Professor at Tokyo Imperial University (later University of Tokyo). Son of a physician, Watsuji studied philosophy at Tokyo Imperial University. After graduating in 1912, he taught ethics at Kyoto Imperial University (1925–1934) and at Tokyo Imperial University (1934–1949). Watsuji started his career as a philosopher, publishing *Niiche kenkyû* (1913; Studies on Nietzsche) and *Zeeren Kirukegôru* (1915; Sören Kierkegaard), in which he studied the formation of the modern sense of self. In a series of essays collected as *Gûzô saikô* (1918; Resurrecting Idols), he held that that process inevitably clashed with traditional authority and ideas, at the sacrifice of "meaninglessly vandalized traditions and idols." In this work he sought "the eternally present life that exists in the midst of the ancient," a concern that led him to an interest in ancient Buddhist images and the composition of his widely read *Koji junrei* (1919; Pilgrimage to Ancient Buddhist Temples). It was this pilgrimage that guided his attention to the history of Japanese culture and to the writing of his first work of historical scholarship, *Nihon kodai bunka* (1920; Ancient Japanese Culture), in which he examined Japanese culture before the introduction of Buddhism in the early sixth century, which would reveal "the image of the true Japanese culture, uninfluenced by [alien] Buddhist culture." Increasingly, Watsuji's scholarly concerns turned from philosophy to history, publishing *Bunka to bunka shi to rekishi shôsetsu* (1916; Culture, Cultural History, and the Historical Novel), a translation of Karl Lamprecht (q.v.), *Moderne Geschichtswissenschaft (1919; Rampurehito: kindai rekishigaku)*, and *Nihon seishin shi kenkyû* (1926; Studies in the History of the Japanese Spirit).

In an era when concern for a uniquely Japanese spirit (*Nihon seishin*), informed by a national ethics (*kokumin rinri*), increasingly dominated public discussion of both political and intellectual issues, Watsuji brought intellectual rigor to the increasingly nationalistic debate. Yet as he, too, saw "the core of ethical value in the Japanese tradition and the reason for its superiority to other traditions in the Way of Reverence for the [Japanese] Emperor" (Bellah, p. 579), he functioned as one of the intellectual leaders of prewar Japanese nationalism. In his *Ningen no gaku to shite no rinri gaku* (1934; Ethics as the Study of Man), he argued for ethics as the study of laws of human relations. This idea offered the basis for a best-seller, which appeared as *Fûdo: ningen gaku teki kôsatsu* (1935; Climate: An Anthropological Contemplation, 1935, translated as *A Climate*, 1960), in which he studied the topographical interrelationship of human beings and nature. Taking Asia, the Near East, and Europe as monsoon, desert, and pasture areas, respectively, he concluded that the basis of human existence lay in human relationships with the social community, as well as with the natural environment.

Following World War II, the year after he retired from Tokyo University in 1949, Watsuji published his *Sakoku: Nihon no higeki* (1950; Closing the Country: The Tragedy of Japan), in which he argued that—as Japan's defeat in the war showed—the principal weakness of the Japanese people was their "lack of the scientific spirit," deriving from a disrespect for rational thought and inference. This, he held, resulted from the isolation of Japan from the mainstream of the development of empiricism and modern science, because of the closing of the country from the early seventeenth century to the midnineteenth. Because academic historians were interested almost exclusively in glorifying the "hothouse" culture of Japan in the age of seclusion, they had failed to concentrate on the defective result. He argued that in the act of "closing the country" in the age of Europe's great expansion, an age that brought a new world in both religion and the spirit of rationality, as well as geographically, Japan had chosen a passive, retrogressive path, the path to what he called "the tragedy of Japan." In his last years Watsuji published other works on Japanese cultural history, including *Nihon rinri shisô shi* (1953; History of Japanese Ethical Thought) and *Katsura rikyû* (1955, 1958; Katsura Imperial Villa). He is generally seen not only as a conservative ethical philosopher and scholar of ethics, but also as a distinguished cultural historian with an original viewpoint.

Bibliography: *Watsuji Tetsurô zenshû* (Complete Works of Watsuji Tetsurô), 20 vols. (1961–1963); Watsuji Tetsurô, *A Climate* (1960); Watsuji, Tetsurô, "The Significance of Ethics as the Study of Man," trans. David A. Dilworth, in *Monumenta Nipponica* 26, 3–4 (1971); Robert N. Bellah, "Japan's Cultural Identity: Some Reflections on the Work of Watsuji Tetsurô," *Journal of Asian Studies*, 24, 4 (1965); William R. LaFleur, "Buddhist Emptiness in the Ethics and Aesthetics of Watsuji Tetsurô," *Religious Studies* 14 (1978).

Masayuki Sato

YANAGITA Kunio (Hyôgo, 1875–Tokyo, 1962), Japanese folklorist and historian. Graduating from Tokyo Imperial University in 1900, Yanagita worked as a government bureaucrat during 1900–1919. Retiring as chief secretary to the House of Peers in 1919, he devoted all his efforts to the study of folklore. He was adviser to the Privy Council in 1946. Yanagita pioneered in the field of social history, as well as founding the discipline of folklore studies in Japan. In opposition to the political-historical approach that dominated Japanese historical studies at the time, he proposed to approach history through a folkloric focus on social history and the history of daily life, and he devoted his own life to elucidating the social life and mentalities of Japan of past times, traveling widely throughout Japan to collect materials from the oral tradition. In effect, his folklore studies were part of historical scholarship and as such were a forerunner of today's social history movement in Japan. He focused on the history and daily life of the masses, whom he took to be the central actors in history. He coined the term *jômin* (common people; menu people) and took writing the "history of the *jômin*" as his central task. A distinctive, and for its time original—even radical—feature of his method was to depart from the established methods of historical research that relied exclusively on written, documentary sources, and to make full use of unwritten materials: legend, folktales, manners, and customs. He articulated his method in *Kyôdo seikatsu no kenkyû hô* (1935; Research

Methods for the Study of Community Daily Life) and "Kokushi to minzoku-gaku" ([Japanese] National History and Folklore Studies), in *Iwanami kôza Nihon rekishi* (1935; Iwanami Lectures in Japanese History, 17). Yanagita published over one hundred books, including *Meiji Taishô shi: sesô hen* (1931; A History of the Meiji-Taishô Periods [1868–1926]: Aspects of Daily Life), a modern history of Japan through an examination of the sensibilities of daily life; *Momen izen no koto* (1939; How It Was Before Cotton Cloth), examining changes in the diet, clothing, and shelter characterizing Japanese life, as viewed through the feelings of people who used them; and *Senzo no hanashi* (1946; About Our Ancestors), a study of the worship of the souls of departed ancestors that is at the heart of Japanese religious life.

In his later years, Yanagita participated in the debate in Japan over the origins of the Japanese people, proposing his own theory of an origin in the South Pacific (as opposed to northeast Asia) which stressed rice cultivation, in *Kaijô no michi* (1961; A Road on the Sea). He was also an active research entrepreneur and organizer, publishing academic journals, and in 1935 he founded the Nihon Minzoku Gakkai (Folklore Society of Japan). Few scholarly figures in Japan have inspired such a devoted academic following: His students and followers continue to apply his methods today, while the study of his works is a separate subdiscipline itself, pursued in the quarterly *Yanagita Kunio kenkyû* (Yanagita Kunio Studies). Most of his oeuvre is contained in *Yanagita Kunio zenshû* (1962–1964; Complete Works, 1st ser., 31 vols.; 2d ser., 5 vols.).

Bibliography: Yanagita Kunio, *About Our Ancestors: The Japanese Family System*, trans. Fanny Hagin Mayer and Yasuyo Ishiwara (1970); Yanagita Kunio, *The Legend of Tôno*, trans. Ronald A. Morse (1975); Yanagita Kunio, comp. and ed., *Japanese Manners and Customs in the Meiji Era*, trans. and adapted by Charles Terry (1957); Josef Kreiner, "Notes on Yanagita Scholarship—By way of General Survey," *Proceedings of the Association Commemorating the Centenary of Yanagita Kunio's Birth* (1976): 149–152; Fanny Hagin Mayer, "The Yanagita Kunio Approach to Japanese Folklore Studies," *Transactions of the Asiatic Society of Japan*, 3d ser., 13 (1976); Ronald A. Morse, "The Logic of Yanagita Folklore Studies," *Proceedings . . . Yanagita Kunio's Birth*, pp. 153–154; Ronald A. Morse, "The Search for Japan's National Character and Distinctiveness: Yanagita Kunio (1875–1962) and the Folklore Movement" (Ph.D. diss. 1975); Nakai Nobuhiko, *Rekishi gakuteki hôhô no kijun* (The Standards for a Historical Method) (1973); Takayanagi Shun'ichi, "Yanagita Kunio: Review Survey," *Monumenta Nipponica* 29, no.3 (1974): 329–335; Wakamori Tarô, *Yanagita Kunio to rekishigaku* (Yanagita Kunio and the Study of History) (1975); *Yanagita Kunio kenkyû shiryôshû* (Collected Studies on Yanagita Kunio), 11 vols. (1986).

Masayuki Sato

Great Historians: Korean

CH'OE Nam-sŏn (Seoul, 1890–Seoul, 1957), Korean historian. Ch'oe Nam-sŏn is also known by his literary name, Yuktang. He was precocious as a child; when he was only eighteen years old in 1908, he started Korea's modern literary movement by writing free verses in the journal he published. The following year, he organized Chosŏn Kwangmunhoe, a publishing house, to publish valuable historical materials. He is also well known for drafting the Declaration of Korea's Independence in the great March First Movement of 1919. But he is better known for his extensive historical writings. He devoted much of his historical scholarship to the studies of Tan'gun, the legendary founder of ancient Korea, to challenge Japanese scholars who tried to represent Korean history in a negative image. When certain Japanese scholars characterized the Korean civilization as a mere reflection of China, Ch'oe Nam-sŏn wrote "Pulham munhwa ron" (Discourse on the Pulham Civilization) in 1925, "Tan'gun ron" (Discourse on Tan'gun) in 1926, and "Salman-gyo tapki" (Study of Shamanism) in 1917, among others. In these studies, he traced the existence of a primitive civilization in ancient Korea before the introduction of the Chinese influence on the Korean peninsula. Through his meticulous analysis of etymologies, folklores, and ethnography as well as historical records of Northeast Asia, Ch'oe Nam-sŏn argued that the proto-Korean civilization, which he called the Pulham civilization, was founded on the concept of "*Park*," meaning light or sun-worshipping, and that Tan'gun referred to a religious head of shamanism, rather than a historical figure, among the primitive peoples in Northeast Asia centering around Korea. In addition, he wrote many popular histories, such as *Chosŏn yŏksa kanghwa* (1930; A Survey of Korean History), *Kosat'ong* (1943; A Cultural History), *Kungmin Chosŏn Yŏksa* (1945; People's Korean History), and *Kuknan Kŭkpok ŭi yŏksa* (1953; History of Overcoming National Crises), for the purpose of enlightening the public so that they would become more aware of their national heritage.

Bibliography: Cho Yong-man, *Yuktang Ch'oe Nam-sŏn* (Seoul, 1964); Hong Il-sik, *Yuktang yŏn'gu* (Study of Yuktang) (Seoul, 1959); Yi Ki-baek, "Minjok chuŭi sahak ŭi munje (Problems in the Historiography of the Nationalist Historians)," *Minjok kwa yŏksa* (People and History) (Seoul, 1971).

Yŏng-ho Ch'oe

PAEK Nam-un (Koch'ang, 1895–P'yŏngyang ?), Korean historian. Having graduated from Tokyo Commercial College, Paek Nam-un taught at Yŏnhŭi Christian College in Seoul until 1945. He then moved to North Korea, where he became the minister of education in 1948, the president of the Academy of Sciences in 1956, and the chairman of the Supreme People's Assembly in 1961. His fame as a historian started with the publication of *Chōsen shakai keizai shi* (1933; Social economic History of Korea) and *Chōsen hōken shakai keizai shi* (1937; Feudalistic Social and Economic History of Korea), both written in Japanese. With the publication of these two monumental works, Paek Nam-un became the first Korean to have systematically applied the Marxist interpretation to Korean history. Paek originally intended to write a multivolume Marxist history of Korea, but was able to complete only these two volumes up to the end of Koryŏ in 1392. As a Marxist historian, he rejected the notion that Korea had followed a unique historical course against the global historical principle. Instead, he insisted that Korean history "has progressed more or less along the same developmental stages as many other peoples have followed in accordance with the unitary historical law that governs the world history" (*Chōsen shakai keizai shi*). Such an interpretation enabled him to repudiate the claims made by Japanese scholars, such as Fukuda Tokuzō, that Korea had historically remained backward, lagging behind Japan and other countries. Paek Nam-un then applied the Marxian scheme of historical development to Korean history by treating ancient Korea before the Three Kingdoms as the primitive communal stage, the Three Kingdoms period (1st century B.C. to A.D. 935) as the slave society, and the Koryŏ (918–1392) and the Yi (1392–1910) dynasties as the feudal society. Such periodization was a pioneering attempt, which had been widely accepted by Korean and Japanese historians until the rise of a new generation of historians in Korea after 1950.

Yŏng-ho Ch'oe

SIN Ch'ae-ho (Ch'ŏngju, 1880–Lushun, 1936), Korean historian. Sin Ch'ae-ho is also known by his literary name, Tanje. Having received the Confucian education in his youth, he at first became a journalist and then went on to become a nationalist historian and revolutionary. His early historical view was influenced by Charles Darwin and Herbert Spencer as he read their ideas through the writings of Liang Ch'i-ch'ao and Yen Fu of China. In his first important historical work, *Toksa sillon* (1908; New Discourse in Reading History), Sin Ch'ae-ho attempted a new interpretation of Korea's ancient history from a nationalistic standpoint. When Japan annexed Korea in 1910, he moved to China to fight for Korea's independence. While carrying out his nationalist struggle, he visited numerous historical sites of ancient Korea in Manchuria and made extensive use of library resources in Beijing and elsewhere in China. Based on these research efforts, Sin Ch'ae-ho wrote a number of important studies, mostly on ancient Korean history. In 1924 and 1925 he published seven studies, which were later reprinted in the book entitled *Chosŏn-sa yŏn'gu ch'o* (A Draft Study of Korean History). One of the studies included in this work is "Chosŏn yŏksa sang ilch'ŏnnyŏllae cheil taesakŏn" (The Greatest Incidents in the Past One Thousand Years in Korean History), in which he argued that the defeat of the rebellion of Monk Myoch'ŏng in 1135 signified an important watershed in Korean history as it marked the decline of Korea's native spirit and tradition and the triumph of China-centered Confucianism, represented by Kim Pu-sik, who later wrote *Samguk sagi* (History of Three Kingdoms) according to the Confucian world-view. In 1931 he published *Chosŏn sanggo-sa* (Ancient History of Korea), in whose introduction he outlined his view of history: "What is history? [History] is a record of the condition of mental activities of the struggle between 'ego' and 'non-ego' in human society as it expands from chronological sequence to spatial dimension." Obsessed by the humiliation and indignities that his country had suffered at the hands of alien powers, Sin Ch'ae-ho often used history as an instrument to arouse patriotism and nationalism among his countrymen by discovering and emphasizing the so-called pure Korean tradition, untainted by foreign influence. In the end he joined the anarchist movement in 1926 and was imprisoned by the Japanese authorities in 1929 at Lushun Prison where he died in 1936.

Bibliography: Kajimura Hideki, "Sin Ch'ae-ho no rekishigaku" (Historical Studies of Sin Ch'ae-ho), *Shisō* (March 1969); Michael Robinson, "National Identity and the Thought of Sin Ch'ae-ho," *Journal of Korean Studies* 5 (1984); Sin Il-ch'ŏl, *Sin Ch'ae-ho ŭi yŏksa sasang yŏn'gu* (A Study of Historical Thought of Sin Ch'ae-ho) (Seoul, 1981); Yi Man-yŏl, "Tanje sahak ui paegyŏng kwa kujo" (Background and Structure of Historical Studies of Sin Ch'ae-ho), *Han'guk Kŭndae yŏksahak ŭi ihae* (Understanding Korea's Modern Historiography) (Seoul, 1981).

Yŏng-ho Ch'oe

YI Pyŏng-do (Yongin, 1896– ?), Korean historian. Yi Pyŏng-do received the Korean classical education in his early years and graduated from Waseda University in Tokyo in 1919, where he studied under Yoshida Tōgo and Tsuda Sōkichi. He taught at Seoul National University from 1945 until 1962 when he became professor emeritus. He was the first Korean to have received training in the modern historiographical method. Whereas the nationalist historians, such as Sin Ch'ae-ho (q.v.) and Ch'oe Nam-sŏn (q.v.), studied Korean history to serve their nationalistic purposes, Yi Pyŏng-do emphasized the objective approach to history. In his celebrated *Han'guk-sa taegwan* (1963, 4th rev. ed.;

Grand Survey of Korean history), he wrote: "It is wrong to treat history from a subjective viewpoint without regard to objectivity or from prejudicial historical perspective." He also stressed a critical approach in the treatment of historical sources, as well as history itself. Yi Pyŏng-do was a prolific scholar, and some of his early studies were written and published in Japanese until the formation of Chindan Hakhoe (the Chindan Academic Society) in 1933, which began the publication of *Chindan hakpo* (the Chindan academic journal) under Yi Pyŏng-do's editorship. Many of his studies dealt with the ancient history of Korea, some of which have been reprinted in one volume under the title of *Han'guk kodaesa yŏn'gu* (1976; Studies on Korea's Ancient History). In "Kija Chosŏn ŭi chŏngch'e wa sowi Kija p'algyojo e taehan s.ı koch'al" (New Study on the True Identity of Kija Chosŏn and the So-called Eight Commandments of Kija), Yi Pyŏng-do refutes the long-held notion that Kija of ancient Korea was a refuge from China and asserts that the so-called Kija Chosŏn was in fact ruled by a Korean tribe headed by the Han clan. His studies on the commentaries of Han China in Korea (108 B.C.–A.D. 313) throw new light on the nature and geographical boundaries of Chinese colonies in early Korea. *Koryŏ sidae ŭi yŏn'gu* (1947, rev. 1980; Study of the Koryŏ Period) is another seminal study in which he traces and analyzes how the popular belief in geomancy affected the history of Koryŏ (918–1392). Through these and other studies, Yi Pyŏng-do has made significant contributions to an understanding of Korean history. As his country's first practitioner of modern historical methodology and as one of the most important teachers for the younger generation of historians, Yi Pyŏng-do has elevated the historical scholarship in Korea to a higher level of maturity.

Bibliography: Yi Pyŏng-do, "Na ŭi hoegorok (My memoir)," in *Sŏnggijip* (Collection of Miscellaneous Writings) (Seoul, 1983).

Yŏng-ho Ch'oe

Great Historians: New Zealand

BEAGLEHOLE, John Cawte (Wellington, 1901–Wellington, 1971), New Zealand historian. Beaglehole grew up in New Zealand at a time when intellectual and cultural interests were strongly focused on Britain. After graduating and lecturing briefly at Victoria University College in Wellington, he traveled to London on a scholarship to pursue postgraduate research. He believed that his future as a writer and historian lay in Britain. London captivated him and was always to do so, but when in 1929 he completed his Ph.D. thesis (on British colonial policy in the mid-nineteenth century) jobs were not there to be had, and with reluctance, he returned to New Zealand to a period of temporary jobs and unemployment before being appointed to the staff of Victoria College where he remained until his retirement in 1966. A radical, influenced by contact with H. J. Laski and R. H. Tawney, he found little to celebrate in New Zealand in the depression years, and his personal experience at the time was to make him a passionate defender of civil liberties. His critical view of New Zealand society, however, was slowly transmuted into an abiding scholarly preoccupation with the formation of new societies, with the influence of inherited characteristics, of the environment, and with the constitutional and cultural achievement of nationhood. He wrote prolifically on many aspects of New Zealand. *New Zealand: A Short History* appeared in 1936, and *The University of New Zealand: An Historical Study*, the following year. Comment on the arts, painting, music, typography, and architecture reflected the breadth of his interests. The Labour Government, elected in 1935, gave hope to those who believed New Zealand had within it the capacity to become a nation, and Beaglehole's involvement with planning the celebrations for New Zealand's centenary in 1940 was a key experience in his emergence as a New Zealand scholar. He gave an account of the process in a lecture given in 1954, "The New Zealand Scholar," a lecture that also revealed his knowledge of colonial America, especially New England, one of his great interests as a teacher.

In 1934 Beaglehole published *The Exploration of the Pacific* and unwittingly embarked on his greatest work as an historian. In 1940 there followed *The Discovery of New Zealand*. By then he had plans for an edition of the journals of Captain James Cook as a preliminary to a life of Cook, but work could only begin when war ended and travel and access to records were again possible. The first volume of *The Journals of Captain James Cook on His Voyages of Discovery: The Voyage of the Endeavour 1768–1771*, published by the Cambridge University Press for the Hakluyt Society, appeared in 1955; *The Voyage of the Resolution and Adventure 1772–1775* followed in 1961; and the final volume, *The Voyage of the Resolution and Discovery 1776–1780*, in 1967. *The Endeavour Journal of Joseph Banks 1768–1771* was published in 1963. To his role as editor Beaglehole brought great strengths; a scholar increasingly at home in the Pacific while steeped in the literature of eighteenth century Britain, he drew on the expert advice of a wide range of scholars in fields as diverse as oceanography and art history, and his annotation of the Journals stands as a model of clarity and judgment. The introductory sections reveal a master of prose—Cook's first arrival at Tahiti is described in a particularly memorable passage—as well as Beaglehole's growing fascination with character, above all with the character of Cook himself. Editing the journals, which Beaglehole had seen as a preliminary to the life of Cook, in the event took over twenty years, and the biography was in draft but not completely revised at the time of his death. It appeared in 1974. Beaglehole's major work on Cook and exploration began as a digression from his developing interest in his own country, and he always expected to return to writing New Zealand history. Yet in some ways it was a clearer expression of his historical skills. A skeptic when it came to philosophies of history, he liked Marc Bloch's (q.v.) phrase, "the historian's craft," and while he recognized the forces shaping human society, his fascination was in a way a romantic one with how individuals acted within their time and circumstance. His approach at its most characteristic is seen in his essay "The Death of Captain Cook," first published in 1964. Steeped in the records, brooding on the physical setting— be it London, Matavai Bay in Tahiti, or Ship Cove in New Zealand—he sought through the historical imagination to re-create the past as a part of our own experience.

T. H. Beaglehole

CONDLIFFE, John Bell (Melbourne, 1891–San Francisco, 1981), New Zealand historian and economist. Professor at the universities of Canterbury, 1920–1926; secretary of the Institute of Pacific Relations, Honolulu, 1927–1931; Secretariat of the League of Nations, 1931–1937; professor at the London School of Economics, 1937–1939, University of California (Berkeley), 1939–1958. Condliffe was one of the first generation of New Zealand scholars to receive a modern training in scholarship. After service in the New Zealand Army in France (where he was wounded), he studied at Cambridge University, partly under J. M. Keynes, as a research student. In 1923 he published the first useful short history of New Zealand since W. P. Reeves' *Long White Cloud*. Condliffe's was more up to date but less interesting. In 1927 he left New Zealand to live in Honolulu, where he edited two large surveys, *Problems of the Pacific*, in 1928 and 1929. These were essentially conference papers and colloquies from conferences of the American Institute of Pacific Relations. In 1930 he published his most important book on New Zealand, *New Zealand in the Making*, which is still one of the best surveys of the economic and, in some ways, social history of the country. It is based on extensive research, especially in official statistics. The chapter, "The Economic Status of the Maoris," was strongly influenced by the assistance of his friends, Sir Apirana Ngata and Te Rangihiroa (Dr. Peter Buck), as well as Felix Keesing, the anthropologist. In 1957 Condliffe made a prolonged visit to New Zealand, and published *The Welfare State in New Zealand* and a second edition of some chapters of *New Zealand in the Making* in 1959. Though packed with information, these books were not as impressive as the first edition. After thirty years abroad, he had lost touch with the research of younger New Zealand scholars. Condliffe was a voluminous writer. In 1971 he published a biography of his old friend, *Te Rangi Hiroa*. Though an improvement on anything else written about the leaders of the "Young Maori party," it was not a well-constructed narrative. He also published notable works on world trade.

McLINTOCK, Alexander Hare (Gore, 1903–Dunedin, 1968), New Zealand historian. Assistant lecturer in history (1940–1946) and English (1950–1951) at the University of Otago; parliamentary historian (1952–1967). McLintock was a leading historian of that generation which trained in imperial history and then turned to study its own society. His first book, *The Establishment of Constitutional Government in Newfoundland, 1783–1832: A Study in Retarded Colonisation* (1941), allowed him to study the last bastion of British mercantalism and to trace the emergence of representative government (which he called constitutional government). McLintock was influenced by Thomas Babington Macaulay's (q.v.) faith in liberty; Thomas Carlyle's (q.v.) belief in heroic leaders; and the new science of geography (although he was no determinist). His major theme, however, was the movement toward representative government. On his return from Britain to New Zealand in 1940, his interest in imperial history waned. The history of New Zealand was not taught in the country's universities; McLintock was one of a small band of professional historians who brought about a shift in focus. In 1946 he agreed to write a general history of his native province and to act as editor for a series of seventeen local histories to commemorate the Centennial. With speed he wrote a long—some would say excessively long— history of his province, *The History of Otago: The Origins and Growth of a Wakefield Class Settlement* (1949). McLintock neglected some issues, such as urbanization and business, but partially made up for it with *The Post of Otago* (1951). Yet both books, like his first, were most concerned with the "great principles of local government, not least among the democratic glories of our British Commonwealth.'' The local histories which he edited, bringing them up to his own professional standards as best he could, completed an extraordinary project (and helped make local history the most popular genre of the postwar decade).

In 1952 McClintock was appointed Parliament's historian, and he immediately began work on *Crown Colony Government in New Zealand* (1958). Although criticized for being too partial to the white colonists, it was a detailed account of the campaign for self-government. Like his other works, this book revealed his sensitivity to geography and the interplay of institutional, legal, and social developments with the intellectual currents of the time. More than in his earlier works, he allowed himself to adopt Olympian poses and quite ignored the new methods of Sir Lewis Berstein Namier (q.v.). He next attempted, without computers, to analyze all the roll-call votes in Parliament's history and he turned (probably in relief) to create *A Descriptive Atlas of New Zealand* (1959) and a three-volume *Encyclopaedia of New Zealand* (1966). He brought together an impressive reference work which, while organized topically, was infused with McLintock's vision of the nation's past. The volumes were especially strong on natural history, geography, and history. He had also enjoyed a distinguished career as an amateur engraver, exhibiting in London and Paris, but he destroyed all he could, his notes and papers too, then wrote his own obituary, and died in 1968 of cancer.

REEVES, William Pember (Lyttelton, 1857–London, 1932), New Zealand historian. Minister of education and labour, 1891–1896; agent-general and high commissioner for New Zealand in London, 1896–1908; director of the London School of Economics, 1908–1919. Reeves was not a trained historian but a journalist and lawyer, yet he wrote several outstanding volumes of history. These were based on voluminous reading rather than ''research,'' as well as on his personal experience of colonial and political life. In 1898 he published a small book, *The Story of New Zealand*, and an expanded version of it, *The Long White Cloud*, a translation of the Maori name for New Zealand, *Aotearoa*. This was an outstanding example of the genre, the ''short history'' of a country. It was beautifully written, in modern prose, and gave an intelligent and coherent interpretation of the country's history which was scarcely challenged before the 1950s, when it was still in print. New Zealanders saw their past largely in his terms. Reeves was probably the main authority on the radical legislation passed in the Australasian colonies at that time. He interpreted it in terms of his own Fabian socialist views. In 1902 he published a two-volume survey of this legislation, *State Experiments in Australia and New Zealand*, which discussed land taxes, the women's vote, labor laws, old age pensions, and other topics. As a comparative study it has not been superseded. Reeves also published several volumes of verse, which was not as impressive as his history.

Bibliography: Keith Sinclair, *William Pember Reeves. New Zealand Fabian* (Oxford, 1965).

Great Historians: Norwegian

KEYSER, Rudolf (Oslo, 1803–Oslo, 1864), Norwegian historian. Professor (1837) at the University of Christiania (Oslo). Although Keyser was not the first professional lecturer and researcher of history in Norway, he established history as an academic discipline. Together with his student and friend, Peter Andreas Munch (q.v.), he founded the Norwegian historical school, which rested heavily on the Germans, Barthold Georg Niebuhr (q.v.) and Leopold von Ranke (q.v.), but also on early archaeological and linguistic research, especially the works of Rasmus Rask and Jacob Grimm. Keyser is most widely known for his now abandoned theory about an original immigration to Scandinavia by "Dancs" from the north, that is, through Finland and southwards along the coast. This theory was first presented in his thesis, *Om Nordmaendenes Herkomst og Folkeslaegtskab* (On the Descent and Kinship of the Norwegians) from 1839. The theory was based on archaeological findings along the coast in combination with linguistic studies. Its main importance today is methodological, since his study represents the first "scientific" study of history ever undertaken in Norway. According to this theory, southern Sweden and Denmark were already populated by "Goths," while Norway and northern Sweden were uninhabited as the immigrants proceeded southward. The tight cultural connection between the "Danes" and the "Goths" caused the development of one common Scandinavian culture over the years, but the social differences between the different areas remained, so that Norway and northern Sweden retained a democratic structure, while the southern areas, where an original conquest had taken place, became fundamentally aristocratic.

Keyser was the first historian to regard Norwegian history as a causal process dominated by social and political structural phenomena. Most of Keyser's individual theories and explanations have, of course, been replaced. But he is still recognized as the first theoretician within Norwegian historiography. The pointing out of historical differences between Denmark and Norway became the leading issue in Keyser's work and created some of the background for the notion of a separate Norwegian historical school. Keyser spent much time arguing that the classical Norse literature was purely Norwegian, not Icelandic or Scandinavian. He also maintained that the Norse language was Norwegian, while Danish and Swedish represented younger, degenerated linguistic stages. Many of his arguments are presented in his book, *Om Nordmaendenes Videnskabelighed og Literatur i Middelalderen* (1866; On the Erudition and Literature of the Norwegians During the Middle Ages). These theories did little to make Keyser recognized in Denmark. One major theme runs throughout his work: Historical "development" represents decline and degeneration, and the Norwegian decline started the very moment political power was concentrated in the hands of the first Norwegian king. Ever since, Norwegian history has been the history of the centralization of power and the loss of political participation.

Bibliography: Per Sveaas Andersen, *Rudolf Keyser, Embetsmann og historiker* (Rudolf Keyser, High Official and Historian), (Oslo, 1961); John Sannes, *Patrioter, intelligens og skandinaver* (Patriots, Intelligence and Scandinavianism), (Oslo, 1958); Jaacob Worm-Muller, "Synet på Norges historie" (The View of Norwegian History), *Norsk historisk Videnskap i femtiar* (Kristiania, 1920).

Nils Johan Ringdal

KOHT, Halvdan (Tromsø, 1873–Oslo, 1965), Norwegian historian and politician. Professor at the University of Oslo (1910). Foreign minister in a Social Democratic government (1935–1941). For half a century Koht dominated Norwegian historiography. As an historian he was a generalist and extremely productive (Bibliography, vol. 1, 1964; vol. 2, 1974). His works include early modern American history (*Genesis of American Independence*, 1910), medieval and modern German history, biographies of Ibsen (*The Life of Ibsen*, 1931) and Bismarck, as well as Norwegian diplomatic history (*Die Stellung Norwegens und Schwedens im Deutsch-Danishen Konflikt*, 1908), and political and social history from medieval times to World War II. As a politician, Koht has been an object of public hatred, as his personal pacifism often is used to explain Norway's lack of resistance to the German invasion. He gave his personal views on this matter in his book, *Norway Neutral and Invaded* (1941). Koht was programmatically positive toward Marxism and was politically affiliated with the socialist movement all his life. Philosophically, however, he was not a Marxist. He was influenced more by Karl Lamprecht (q.v.) than by any Marxist lecturer through his studies in Germany, and he himself claimed that he was initiated to Marxism through the American scholar, Edwin R. Seligman. In addition, the influence of the national democratic ideas of the Norwegian historian, Ernst Sars (q.v.), is obvious throughout his work. Koht was the first historian to introduce the notion of class struggle as an explanatory force in the study of Norwegian history, best and most systematically done in his most famous and widely read *Norsk bondereising*, 1926 (*Les luttes des paysans en Norvege*, Paris, 1929). This work clearly demonstrated the synthesis of left-democratism and Marxism which characterized his work as well as the Social Democratic party whose ideology he strongly influenced. Many of Koht's best studies were not published separately, however, but were included in his numerous anthologies, for instance, *Innhogg og utsyn i norsk historie* (1921; Insights and Surveys of Norwegian History); *Essais sur l'etude de l'histoire du sentiment national* (1952); and *Driving Forces in History* (1964). The general principles of his notion of the classes and the state were also very obvious, though less elegantly carried out in the two volumes he wrote for the Cambridge Medieval History, vols. 6 and 8, *The Scandinavian Kingdoms Until the End of the 13th Century* (1929) and *The Scandinavian Kingdoms During the 14th and 15th Centuries* (1936).

Koht was in no way the first Norwegian historian to utilize a comparative perspective, but he was the first to stress that Norwegian history is part of and fundamentally follows the same developmental stages as other European nations. Methodologically, he was not a nationalist, but ideologically, he obviously was. According to Koht, Norwegian history, just as any national history, was a cyclic evolution where one class after another struggled for national predominance. Shortly after its rise, however, any victorious class tended to defy the nation: The aristocracy fought its way to national power throughout the early Middle Ages. But as its wealth grew, its egotism led its members into Scandinavistic politics and national betrayal. According to Koht, Norway as a nation was almost nonexistent in the period of the fifteenth and sixteenth centuries, as no class took responsibility. The merchants and industrial capitalists repeated this historical law by deserting the nation as soon as they had acquired national power. The lower classes tended to be more responsible, that is, better nationalists, according to Koht. The period from 1814 (independence) to 1884 (introduction of parliamentary system) was the period when the peasant class took up its national heritage, socially, culturally, and politically. By 1884 there was only one underclass left: the industrial workers, who had not yet grown into national maturity. In Koht's philosophical consideration, Norwegian history came to an end as the Social Democrats came into office in 1935, and he himself became foreign minister.

Bibliography: Halvdan Koht, *Aus den Lehrjahren eines Historikers* (Stuttgart, 1953); Halvdan Koht, *Education of An Historian* (New York, 1957); Halvdan Koht, *Historiker i laere* (Oslo, 1951); Ottar Dahl, *Historisk materialisme, Historieoppfatningen hos Edvard Bull og Halvdan Koht* (Historical Materialism: The View of History of Edvard Bull and Halvdan Koht), (Oslo, 1952); Sigmund Skard, *Mennesket Halvdan Koht* (Halvdan Koht the Man), (Oslo, 1982).

Nils Johan Ringdal

MUNCH, Peter Andreas (Oslo, 1810–Rome, 1863), Norwegian historian. Professor (1841) at the University of Christiania (Oslo). Together with his friend and teacher, Rudolf Keyser (q.v.), Munch established history as an academic discipline in Norway and founded the Norwegian version of the German historical school. While of the two Keyser was the controversial theoretician, Munch was the one who worked and published extensively. Together they did a lot to lay the foundation for and inspire Norwegian nineteenth-century nationalism. As he was a pioneer within the fields of geography, archaeology, Nordic linguistics, and literature, anyone studying Scandinavian medieval issues cannot overlook Munch's work. His study from 1840, *Norse Mythology*, is widely read and has become an international classic. His most outstanding work is his grand historical contribution, *Det norske folks historie* (7 vols., 1852–1859; The History of the Norwegian People), the first academic presentation of Norwegian history from the immigration until the reformation. The first four volumes were translated into German, and, in parts, into English: *Die nordisch-germanischen Volker, ihre altesten Heimath-Sitze, Wanderzuge und Zustande* (1853); *Das heroische Zeitalter der nordisch-germanischen Volker und die Wikinger-Zuge* (1854); and *The Norwegian Invasion of Scotland in 1263* (1862). The first four volumes are still of much use to the scholar working with medieval history, as many sources are presented with a critical insight of surprisingly high standard. Munch did more to explain and modify the general arguments of the Norwegian historical school, that is, Keyser's theories, than to create his own. On some individual issues he argues differently, however: the Norwegian local chieftains in the centuries before the civil wars in the twelfth century—Keyser's "leaders of the people"—are regarded by Munch as aristocrats, independent both in relation to the king and to the "people." While the truly Protestant Keyser had stressed how the intrigues from the Catholic clergy during the civil wars had damaged the king as well as the people, Munch regards the aristocracy as a whole, economically and politically.

Bibliography: John Sannes, *Patrioter, intelligens og skandinaver* (Patriots, Intelligence, and Scandinavianism), (Oslo, 1958); Jacob Worm-Muller, "Synet på Norges historie," (The View of Norwegian History), *Norsk historisk Videnskap i femti år* (Kristiania, 1920).

Nils Johan Ringdal

SARS, Ernst (Kinn, Western Norway, 1835–Oslo, 1917), Norwegian historian. Professor (1874) at the University of Christiania (Oslo), honorary professor at the University of Copenhagen (1879). Sars was the founder of the left-national tradition in Norwegian historiography, the only true evolutionist historian in Norway, inspired by French and British evolutionism and by historians like Numa Denis Fustel de Coulanges (q.v.) and Francois Guizot (q.v.). Sars was a political ideologist in the struggle for the parliamentary system and was celebrated as a national hero after the secession from Sweden in 1905. No other historian has been as widely read and as influential in Norway. His pamphlet, *Historisk Indledning til Grundloven* (1882; Historical Introduction to the Constitution), had a particularly sharp polemical style, which explains its central role during the political struggles of the 1880s. The same theories are developed on a broader, more academic, scale in his main work, *Udsight over den norske historie* (4 vols., 1877–1891; View of Norwegian History). While Rudolf Keyser (q.v.) had seen Norwegian history as a continuous depravation of the national spirit and power, Sars succeeded in establishing history as a process of uneven development fundamentally characterized by *growth*. The strength and the unique qualities of historical life in one period will cause weakness and insipidity in the next.

Although they basically belonged to the same Germanic culture, Denmark and Sweden's political development came earlier than Norway's. As Norwegian society developed, however, it became exceedingly stronger. In Sars' terms, the Viking expansion was seen as the last Germanic tribal migration. As the most northerly of the Germanic tribes surmounted its backwardness, Norwegians became the most active and advanced among all. Thus, the Vikings came to influence historical development in general, that is, *world history*. State building occurred later in Norway than in any other Germanic cultural area. For that reason also the Norwegian medieval kingdom became stronger and more successful than the neighboring states. A vital medieval state-building required the integration of the aristocracy into the state. But as Norwegian chieftains had been independent for so long, the struggle between them and the kings was bound to become harder than anywhere else. Thus, royal power had to obtain an absolute victory or suffer a total loss. While Sweden and Denmark developed kingdoms of "middle strength," the aristocracy experienced a total defeat in Norway and became forever cut off from politics. This is Sars' explanation of how flourishing Norway of the twelfth and thirteenth centuries became backward Norway of the Middle Ages. Yet, the stagnation caused by Norway's lack of vital aristocracy in early modern history led to progress on another level. The lack of aristocratic power had preserved the peasantry in a position of relative freedom, which enabled Norway's early democratic development in the nineteenth century. Thus, Ernst Sars furnished the democratic movement among peasants and intellectuals with an ideology which argued that democracy was an historical inevitability.

Bibliography: Ottar Dahl, *Norsk historieforskning i det 19. og 20. århundre* (Norwegian Historical Writing in the Nineteenth and Twentieth Centuries), (Oslo, 1959); Trygve Raeder, *Ernst Sars. Mannen og verket* (Ernst Sars, the Man and His Work), (Oslo, 1935); Nils Johan Ringdal, "Ernst Sars og den komparative metode" (Ernst Sars and the Comparative Method), *Tidsskrift for samfunsforskning* 23 (1982): 31–47.

Nils Johan Ringdal

Great Historians: Polish

ASKENAZY, Szymon (Zawichost, 1865–Warsaw, 1935), Polish historian. Askenazy came from a Jewish family that had lived in Poland for centuries. He was most influenced by Max Lehmann of Göttingen University (under whose supervision he wrote his doctoral dissertation, "Die letzte polnische Königswahl," 1894) as well as by French historians, mainly Albert Sorel. Active at Lvov University from 1893, he was appointed professor in 1907; in the same year he was elected member of the Polish Academy of Learning. In 1920–1923 he was the first Polish delegate to the League of Nations; he resigned when Roman Dmowski, whose strongly nationalist policy he opposed, became minister for foreign affairs. He was not admitted to lecture in Warsaw University but held a professorship *honoris causa*. He was a liberal, opposed to all extreme ideologies. He was opposed to factographic historiography but at the same time was not interested in discovering regularities in human history. In the conceptualization of history he ascribed the principal role to great political ideas, which allow an integrated approach to events. Like Sorel, about whom he wrote that he "had been a great historian in the triple sense of the word: scholarly, civic, and literary," he believed that a historian has a civic duty that makes him active politically and also makes him reach his readers by the aesthetic form of his works. His outstanding works, oriented antipositivistically, marked by great literary values, were a conscious voice in the great political debate on the misfortunes of Poland. He was sharply criticized by Marceli Handelsman (q.v.) for hagiographic undertones in his works. When concerned with the eighteenth century, he referred to the interpretation of Tadeusz Korzon (q.v.), who demonstrated that the Polish nation and state began to revive at that time. His *Przymierze polsko-pruskie* (1897–1900; The Polish-Prussian Alliance) was aimed at the claims of the Cracow school that the break with Prussia had adverse effects for Poland. Askenazy strove to demonstrate that the tentative alliance with Prussia was realistic, but its chances were frustrated by an unfavourable coincidence of events.

In his later works Askenazy became concerned with the nineteenth century and primarily rehabilitated the Napoleonic period in Poland, in which he differed from Korzon, who gave the pride of place to Kościuszko. Askenazy pointed to the importance of the Polish Legions and the Duchy of Warsaw. He worked on that subject together with his disciples. His study *Ksiażę Józef Poniatowski, 1763–1813* (1905; Prince Józef Poniatowski, 1763–1813) was a pioneer work in the use of the sources. He extolled the prince, linked to Napoleon, as a national hero and a personification of military virtues, and thus signally contributed to the formation of the Napoleonic legend in Poland. Next, he published a two-volume monograph on Walery Łukasiński (*Łukasiński*, 1908), co-organizer of the National Patriotic Society, representative of the independence movement of the liberal gentry, and prisoner of the tsarist authorities. That monograph was in fact a synthesis of the political history of the Kingdom of Poland. The summing up of Askenazy's studies of the Napoleonic period from the point of view of the Polish cause is to be found in his three-volume work *Napoleon a Polska* (Napoleon and Poland, publication started in 1913, with the full text appearing in 1918–1919), where he pointed to the convergence of the Polish and the French reason of state and Napoleon's positive role for Poland. In all, Askenazy's production was very large (more than 250 works). He was the most important Polish historian of politics at the turn of the eighteenth and the early nineteenth centuries.

Bibliography: Józef Dutkiewicz, *Szymon Askenazy i jego szkoła* (Szymon Askenazy and His School), (Warsaw, 1958); Andrzej Zahorski, "Szymon Askenaz i jego dzieło (Szymon Askenazy and His Work)," in S. Askenazy, ed., *Ksiaże Józef Poniatowski, 1763–1813*, introduced by Andrzej Zahorski, with an afterword by Stanisław Herbst (Warsaw, 1974), pp. 5–34.

Jerzy Topolski

BAŁABAN, Majer (Lvov, 1877–Warsaw, 1942?), Polish historian. Of Jewish origin, Bałaban was the most eminent student of the history of Polish Jews. He wrote his doctoral thesis (1904) under the supervision of Ludwik Finkel at Lvov University ("Żydzi lwowscy na przełomie XVI i XVII wieku" [1906; Lvov Jews at the Turn of the Sixteenth Century], which started his research of many years that yielded numerous books on the history of Jews in Poland and on the bibliography of that history. Being at the same time a teacher of the Mosaic religion, he strove to make its study more modern. In 1927 he was appointed professor of the Polish Free University to lecture on the history of the Jews. In 1928 he obtained *venia legendi* (habilitation) in Warsaw University where he held lectures and seminars, creating a center of lively interest in the history of the Jews. He was one of the organizers and the director of the Institute of Judaistic Sciences in Warsaw (1930–1905). Following a strongly supported motion of

Marceli Handelsman (q.v.) he was given the title of professor, but no chair of the history of the Jews was formed. His plans to publish a bibliography of the history of the Jews (vol. 1, *Bibliografía historii Żydów w Polsce i w krajach ościennych za lata 1900–1930*—Bibliography of the History of the Jews in Poland and in the Neighboring Countries for 1900–1930, published in 1939) were frustrated by the war. Confined to the Warsaw ghetto he died there at the end of 1942 or early in 1943. His works, of great scholarly value were published in Polish, Hebrew, German, Yiddish, and Russian, and cover a wide range of subjects, from economic history to the history of mentality, and show the peculiarities and problems of the situation of the Jews and their place in the history of Poland. His major works, next to that on Lvov Jews, include *Dzieje Żydów w Krakowie i Kazimierzu do 1868 roku* (1912, 1931–1936; History of the Jews in Cracow and Kazimierz up to 1868), *Dzieje Żydów w Galicji i Rzeczypospolitej Krakowskiej 1782–1868* (1935; History of the Jews in Galicia and the Republic of Cracow 1782–1868), *Żydzi w Austrii za Cesarza Franciszka Józefa I 1848–1908* (1909; The Jews in Austria under the Emperor Franz Joseph 1848–1908), *Die Judenstadt von Lublin* (1919), and *Zabytki historyczne Żydów w Polsce* (1929; Historical Monuments of the Jews in Poland). To these must be added numerous valuable minor studies on the language of the Polish Jews, Jewish printing shops, Jewish schools, Hugo Grotius' interest in a trial for a ritual murder in Poland, the participation of the Jews in the Legions and in the army of the Duchy of Warsaw, mysticism and messianic movements among Polish Jews, and so on. His research was synthesized in *Jidn in Pojln* (1930; Jews in Poland). Bałaban's interest in the Frankist movement in Poland in the eighteenth century manifested itself in a number of studies and a three-volume work on Frank and Frankism, which appeared in Hebrew in Tel-Aviv in 1934–1935. On his sixtieth birthday, a special book was published in 1937, which stated that Bałaban's work "gives testimony to the historical truth and provides objective conditions for the evaluation of the role [of the Jews] in the life of Poland."

Bibliography: I. M. Biderman, *Mayer Balaban Historian of Polish Jewry* (New York, 1976); Krystyna Pieradzka, "Majer Bałaban (1877–1943)," *Kwartalnik Historyczny* (1939–1945): 414–415; Michał Szulkin, "Prof. Majer Bałaban (w stulecie urodzin)" (Professor Majer Bałaban—on the Hundredth Anniversary of His Birth), *Biuletyn Żydowskiego Instytutu Historycznego*, no. 1/101 (1977): 3–16.

Jerzy Topolski

BOBRZYŃSKI, Michał (Cracow, 1849–Łopuchówek, near Poznań, 1935), Polish historian. The most eminent representative of the so-called Cracow school of history (see Walerian Kalinka [q.v.], Stanisław Smolka [q.v.]). He took his Ph.D. for his thesis, "O ustawodawstwie nieszawskim Kazimierza Jagiellończka" (1873; Casimir Jagellonian's Nieszawa Legislation) and continued his studies under Rudolf Sohm in Strasburg. He obtained his *venia legendi* (habilitation) in the history of German law. Beginning in 1877, he was a professor at Jagellonian University in Cracow, and he combined his academic career with an outstanding political career. He was also director of the archives of municipal and provincial documents in Cracow, and elected a member of the Academy of Learning in 1878. Connected with the group of Cracow conservatives, he favored positivist "organic work" (and not national uprising), seeing in it the best road to the recovery of independence. From 1885 on, he held many high political posts. He was in charge of the school system in Galicia (southern Poland) and succeeded in raising the educational standards. In 1908 he became the lieutenant of Galicia and performed that function for five years, viewing favorably the independence movement which was then being organized in that province. He foresaw changes in the international situation (including the conflict between Austria and Germany on the one side and Russia on the other) and believed that the movement had its chances. He thought that he would succeed in singling out Galicia and combine it with the then Russian-held Kingdom of Poland into a single political entity. In his historical works he strove to demythologize the history of Poland. In his opinion a strong state conscious of its political goals would secure the favorable development of the nation, while in the past in Poland the myth of freedom ended in anarchy. It was in that anarchy that he saw the principal cause of the fall of the Polish state in the late eighteenth century. Bobrzyński was convinced that history is marked by certain regularities concerning which the historian should formulate hypotheses which he must later verify. "The value of the historian and his work," he wrote, "is determined mainly by how he avails himself of the results of the social and political sciences and how he mutually can contribute to their further development." He claimed that next to its scholarly functions, history has certain social tasks which consist in making one's nation realize "its character, conditions of existence and resources, its special strivings and aspirations, so as to bring out those scholarly principles which in its life and development play a greater role than they do in the development of other nations" (*W imię prawdy dziejowej. Rzecz o zadaniu historii i dziesiejszym jej stanowisku* [1879; In the Name of Historical Truth. On the Task of History and Its Present Position, 1879]). That set of opinions, to which he remained faithful all his life, had been shaped in his youth. When he was only thirty years old, he published his best known work, which until recently was used as a handbook of Polish history, namely, *Dzieje Polski w zarysie* (2 vols., 1879; An Outline of the History of Poland). He was sharply criticized for it by the numerous advocates of the traditional national hagiography.

Bobrzyński rendered great services to the study of Polish political and legal institutions. He originated the publication of the imposing series *Starodawnego Prawa Polskiego Pomniki* (Monuments of Old Polish Law), of which he edited vols. 3, 5, 6, and 7 (1874–1985). He published legal and political treatises of M. Taszycki, S. Zaborowski, P. Włodkowic, and J. Ostroróg, studied the status of King Casimir the Great; and jointly with Stanisław Smolka (q.v.) prepared a biography of J. Długosz (1893). Bobrzyński also wrote on the position of peasants in old Poland. His paper *O dawnym prawie polskim: jego nauce i umiejetnym badaniu* (1874; Old Polish Law, Its Teaching and Competent Study) holds a special place. When Poland regained independence, he concerned himself with current history; his *Wskrzeszenie państwa polskiego* (2 vols., 1920–1925; The Restoration of the Polish State) covered the period 1914–1923. S. Estreicher wrote that Bobrzyński held liberal opinions tinged with authoritarianism and elitism but opposed to chauvinism. In historical research he made it a point to avoid all dogmatism. His works are marked by precision of thought and realism of judgment.

Bibliography: Wojciech M. Bartel, "Michał Bobrzyński 1849–1935," in C. Bobińska and J. Wyrozumski, eds. *Spór o krakowska szkołe historyczna* (The Controversy over the Cracow School of Historiography), (Cracow, 1972), pp. 145–189; S. Estreicher, *Michał Bobrzyński* (Warsaw, 1936); Waldemar Łazuga, *Michał Bobrzyński. Myśl historyczna a działalność polityczna* (Michał Bobrzyński. Historical Thought and Political Activity), (Warsaw, 1982); Marian Henryk Serejski and Andrzej Feliks Grabski, "Introduction," to Michał Bobrzyński, *Dziełe Polski w zarysłie* (An Outline of the History of Poland), (Warsaw, 1974), pp. 5–34; Andrzej Skrzypek, "Michał Bobrzyński jako organizator nauki i wydawca źródeł" (Michał Bobrzyński as the Organizer of Science and Editor of Sources), *Kwartalnik Historyczny* (1978), no. 3, pp. 643–653; Stanisław Zakrzewski, *Michał Bobrzyński, Próba charakterystyki* (Michał Bobrzyński. A Tentative Characteristic), (Lvov, 1935).

Jerzy Topolski

HALECKI, Oskar (Vienna, 1891–White Plains near New York, 1973), Polish historian. Docent in Jagellonian University in Cracow in 1916–1918; in 1918–1939 Halecki held the chair of the history of Eastern Europe at Warsaw University. He was a member of the Polish Academy of Learning. The outbreak of World War II found him in Switzerland, from where he went to France to organize the Polish University in exile in Paris. After the defeat of France in 1940 he left for the United States, where he organized the Polish Scientific Institute in New York, of which he was director (1942–1953) and president (1953–1962). In 1944–1961 he headed the department of the history of Eastern Europe at Fordham University in New York. After his retirement he lectured in many universities in the United States and in Europe. Highly valued by Pope Pius XII (to whom he dedicated a separate study), he was awarded the papal Order of St. Gregory the Great.

Halecki's scholarly interests focused on Polish modern history, the history of Lithuania, and the history of the Byzantine Empire. He conducted his research from the point of view of great historical processes; in particular he strove to bring out the principal moments in the history of Europe and to point to the role of the Eastern issue, which in his opinion was a menace to European civilization. In that connection he emphasized the historical mission of the Church of Rome. He called Central Eastern Europe (i.e., the countries between Germany, the Balkans, and Russia) the borderlands of Western civilization. In 1915 Halecki wrote his doctoral dissertation on the history of the Reformation in Poland ("Zgoda sandomierska 1570, jej geneza i znaczenie w dziejach reformacji polskie za Zygmunta Augusta"—The Sandomierz Agreement of 1570, Its Origin and

Importance in the History of the Reformation in Poland under Sigismundus Augustus), and then concerned himself with the union between Poland and Lithuania. In 1918–1920 he published his fundamental *Dzieje Unii Jagiellońskiej* (History of the Jagellonian Union), in which he defended the Jagellonian conception of pre-partition Poland (as opposed to the Piast conception). He accordingly assessed the union very positively and emphasized Poland's contribution to the development of culture and religion in the eastern territories connected with the Polish state. His works on the history of Lithuania include *O początkach parlamentaryzmu litewskiego* (1916; The Beginnings of Lithuanian Parliamentarism), *O początkach szlachty i heraldyki na Litwie* (1916; The Beginnings of Nobility and Heraldry in Lithuania), and *O zabytkach języka polskiego na Litwie w wiekach średnich* (1917; Monuments of the Polish Language in Medieval Lithuania). He also has to his credit a study of the relations between Poland and Hungary in the Middle Ages (*O genezie i znaczeniu rządów andegaweńskich w Polsce*—The Origin and Importance of the Angevin Rule in Poland, published in 1921), in which he strove realistically to assess their significance. He was one of the pioneers of Byzantine studies in Poland, which he combined with the study of the history of the Church union (*Un empereur de Byzance à Rome. Vingt ans de travail pour l'union des Eglises et pour la défense de l'Empire de l'Orient 1355–1377*, 1930). He concluded his research on the Byzantine problem with *From Florence to Rome 1439–1596* (1958).

Halecki summed up his reflections on European history in *The Limits and Divisions of European History* (1950). In the history of Europe he singled out three large periods: the Mediterranean period (until the fall of the Roman Empire, and more fully until the restoration of the empire by Otto I in 962), the European period (whose end is indicated by such facts as the abdication of Charles V in 1555, the religious peace in Augsburg in 1555, the Confederation of Warsaw in 1573, the defeat of the Spanish Armada in 1588, and the Edict of Nantes in 1598), and the Atlantic period, marked by increased European influence and a change in its political structure owing to the idea of the sovereignty of states. That role of the continent ended in the twentieth century, when Europe ceased to be the center of universal history (*The Millennium of Europe*, 1963). Halecki also wrote synthetic works on the history of Poland (1933, 1945, 1960), including his study *Poland (East Central Europe under the Communists*, 1957).

Bibliography: Janusz Pajewski, "Oskar Halecki (26 V 1891–17 IX 1973)," *Kwartalnik Historyczny*, no. 4 (1975): 915–916; Gothold Rhode, "Drei polnische historiker—drei Persönlichkeiten der Zeitgeschichte. Zum Tode von Marian Kukile, Oskar Halecki und Stanisław Kot," *Jahrbücher für Geschichte Osteuropas* N. F., Bd XXIV, H. 4 (1976): 537–546; Piotr Wandycz, "O dwóch historykach" (Two Historians [M. Kukiel and O. Halecki]) *Zeszyty Historyczne*, no. 32 (1975): 61–65.

Jerzy Topolski

HANDELSMAN, Marceli (Warsaw, 1882–Dora-Nordhausen, concentration camp in Germany, 1945), Polish historian. In 1915–1939 professor in Warsaw

University, founder of his own school of history, one of the most popular Polish historians between the world wars. Handelsman combined profound knowledge and methodological experience with broad vistas and dislike of factographical historiography. All his studies, both in medieval history and in the history of the eighteenth and nineteenth centuries, were undertaken with a view to analyzing a more general idea. In medieval history he looked for the essence of the feudal system (*Z metodyki badań feudalizmu*—1917; The Methodology of the Study of Feudalism; *Féodalité et féodalisation dans l'Europe occidentale*, 1923), and intended to study the Merovingian state and society (*Le soi-disant precepte de 614*, 1926). Concerning both the Middle Ages and later eras, he was interested mainly in the development of nations (*Le rôle de la nationalité dans l'histoire du Moyen-Age*, 1930, *Rozwój narodowości nowoczesnej*—1924; The Development of Modern Nationalities). He wrote that the task of research should be "to link the development of Poland with the contemporaneous development of great Western European nations and to bring out the impact of Polish life upon the lives of the neighbouring nations in Central Eastern, and Southern Europe." He defined his method as sociopsychological and opposed to biographical. But he was gradually inclined to the biographical, that is, he ascribed the decisive role in history to eminent personalities. That was manifested in his comprehensive unfinished monograph *Adam Czartoryski* (4 vols., 1948–1950). He won greatest renown for his *Historyka* (Historics, 1921, 1928, so named after Joachim Lelewel's (q.v.) work of the same title). It was a unique work in the Polish historiography of the interwar period. In this work Handelsman strove to transfer to Poland the antipositivist ideas, which stressed the creative role of the historian in research. For Handelsman mental phenomena were the principal motive power of historical development, and for him historical reality was also mental in character. History studies individual phenomena, at most looking for genetic connections, without being concerned with general causality.

Bibliography: Aleksander Gieysztor, "Afterword" to M. Handelsman, *Sredniowiecze polskie i powszechne* (Polish and Universal Middle Ages), (Warsaw, 1966), pp. 350–371; Tadeusz Łepkowski, "Introduction" to M. Handelsman, *Rozwój narodowości nowoczesnej* (The Development of Modern Nationalities), (Warsaw, 1973), pp. 5–18; Tadeusz Manteuffel, *Handelsman Marceli*, in *Polski Słownik Biograficzny* (The Polish Biographical Dictionary), vol. 9/2, no. 41 (1961): 268–271; Jerzy Topolski, *Handelsman Marceli*, in *Filozofia w Polsce, Słownik Pisarzy* (Philosophy in Poland. Dictionary of Authors), (Wrocław, 1971), pp. 100–101.

Jerzy Topolski

KALINKA, Walerian (Bolechowice near Cracow, 1826–Lvov, 1886), Polish historian. Ideological founder of the so-called Cracow school (see Michał Bobrzyński [q.v.] and Stanisław Smolka [q.v.].) In his youth Kalinka held democratic and anticlerical opinions, but he soon adopted an opposite political and ideological standpoint and sought to interpret the history of Poland in that spirit. This change in viewpoint was largely attributable to his desire to be part of the aristocracy. He obtained the post of secretary to W. Zamoyski, in 1861 he became a custodian in the Polish Library in Paris, and he was also an active member of the Bureau of Hotel Lambert (the conservative group of Polish émigrés led by A. Czartoryski). But he soon shifted directions again and was ordained a priest in 1870. During the January Insurrection in 1863, although he was in charge of Czartoryski's political correspondence, he was opposed to the uprising. He concluded that it would be more effective to paint a less romantic picture of the past and thus shape the attitude of the Polish people. In *Ostatnie lata panowania Stanisława Augusta* (2 vols., 1868; The Last Years of the Reign of Stanislaus Augustus), he proposed that the Poles themselves were guilty of the partitions of their country, which were a "deserved penance." He blamed neither the magnates nor the king, but rather the defects of the Polish nation; he failed to notice the efforts made in the period of reforms. In his historical writing he followed the fundamental principles of the modern historical method (as understood in the nineteenth century), being in that respect a pioneer in Polish historiography. As a priest he published the first monograph of the Four-year Diet, which adopted the constitution of May 3, 1791, based on much more comprehensive sources than his previous work (*Sejm czteroletni*—1880–1886; The Four-year Diet). He defended the realistic attitude of the king and criticized the patriotic party for breaking away from Russia. He also criticized republicanism and democratism and blamed them for anarchism. Kalinka's work was unanimously accepted as an outstanding scholarly achievement. He was also active politically, representing the interests of the Church of Rome, and he took part in numerous charitable undertakings. In all he wrote twelve volumes, published in 1891–1892.

Bibliography: Stefan Kieniewicz, "Kalinka Walerian," in *Polski Słownik Biograficzny* (The Polish Biographical Dictionary), 11/3, no. 50 (1935) pp. 449–452.

Jerzy Topolski

KONOPCZYŃSKI, Władysław (Warsaw, 1880–Młynik near Ojców, 1952), Polish historian. Professor in the Jagellonian University in Cracow, member of the Polish Academy of Learning. Influenced by Tadeusz Korzon (q.v.) and Szymon Askenazy (q.v.). Konopczyński wrote his doctoral dissertation under Askenazy's supervision and Askenazy also inspired him to a laborious study of archives in Poland and abroad. Konopczyński's research was focused on the history of Poland in the eighteenth century. He later availed himself of the results of his archival search conducted for many years, which made it possible for him greatly to extend the source base for the study of the times in which he was interested. He was one of the most esteemed historians in the period between the world wars. He was influenced by antipositivist ideas, mainly Wilhelm Dilthey (q.v.) and Karl Lamprecht (q.v.). He stressed the role of free will and was opposed to deterministic interpretations. History, as he saw it, was to be "the history of aspirations and actions," set in social structure and in "the spirit of the times." He criticized historical materialism, which, however, he did not know and did not understand; rather his dislike was politically oriented, because he did not deny the role of the economic factor. His theoretical views and the clearly marked political tendency in the nationalist spirit of Roman Dmowski (for which he was criticized by Michał Bobrzyński, q.v.) accounted for a disproportion between the scope of, and the novel approach to, factographical reconstructions in his works and their inner coherence and in-depth explanations. Too greatly concerned with the search for the ideological motives of human actions, he did not consider the point of view of social history. For all the advances made in research and the questioning of his many too arbitrary opinions, Konopczyński's works concerned with the eighteenth century have retained their current value. Of special importance are *Geneza i ustanowienie Rady Nieustającej* (1917; The Origin and the Establishment of the Permanent Council), *Fryderyk Wielki a Polska* (1947; Frederick the Great and Poland), *Sejm grodzieński* (1907; The Grodno Diet), *Polska w dobie wojny siedmioletniej* (2 vols., 1901–1911; Poland at the Time of the Seven Years' War), *Stanisław Konarski* (1926), *Kazimierz Pułaski* (1931), and *Konfederacja barska* (2 vols., 1936–1938; The Bar Confederacy). His study of the first partition of Poland remains in manuscript form, and only volume 1 of his *Polscy pisarze polityczni XVIII wieku* (Polish Political Writers in the Eighteenth Century) saw publication in 1966. The publication of his methodological work was barred by censorship in 1949.

Konopczyński also edited historical sources, in particular the diaries of the Diet (for the years 1746, 1748, 1750, 1754, 1758), and founded and edited the Polish Biographical Dictionary. He was also the author of a synthetic history of Poland (2 vols., 1936; *Dzieje Polski nowożytnej*—History of Modern Poland). He expressed certain ideas of the Cracow school of history (see Michał Bobrzyński, Walerian Kalinka [q.v.], Staninsław Smolka [q.v.]), but was less radical in their formulation. He criticized the nobility, which he largely blamed for the loss of independence, but he did not go as far as Bobrzyński did in his criticism of the old freedom.

Bibliography: Władysłław Czapliński, *Władysław Konopczyński jakim go znałem* (Władysław Konopczyński as I Knew Him), in *Portrety uczonych polskich* (Ten Portraits of Polish Scholars and Scientists), selected by Andrzej Biernacki (Cracow, 1974), pp. 243–250; Emanuel Rostworowski, *Konopczyński Władysław* in *Polski Słownik Biograficzny* (The Polish Biographical Dictionary), vol. 13/4, no. 59, (1968): 556–561; Emanuel Rostworowski, *Władysław Konopczyński jako historyk* (Władsłław Konopczyński as a Historian), in Celina Bobińska and Jerzy Wyrozumski, eds., *Spór o historyczną szkołę krakowska* (The Controversy over the Cracow School of History), (Cracow, 1972), pp. 209–235.

Jerzy Topolski

KORZON, Tadeusz (Minsk in Byelorussia, 1839–Warsaw, 1918), Polish historian. An outstanding representative of the so-called Warsaw school, which adapted some elements of positivism and also embraced Leopold von Ranke's (q.v.) slogan "wie es eigentlich gewesen," interpreted as the striving for objectivism in historical research. The slogan was difficult to put into effect without the instrument of theory, whose role was understood by Joachim Lelewel, but which was seriously used only by Jan Rutkowski (q.v.). Hence, in practice the axis of conceptualization in the study of the past by members of the Warsaw school (including Korzon) consisted in pointing to the positive moments in the history of pre-partition Poland, in particular to the economic development and reforms during the reign of Stanislaus Augustus Poniatowski (1764–1795). The Warsaw school differed in that respect from the Cracow school (see Michał Bobrzyński, [q.v.], Walerian Kalinka [q.v.], Stanisław Smolka [q.v.]), which stressed the weakness of the Polish state and saw in it the principal cause of the partitions (and not the aggressive policy of Poland's neighbors). Korzon brought out the differences between the two interpretations in his paper read at the second General Congress of Polish Historians, in Lvov in 1890, ("O błędach historiografii maszej w budowaniu dziejów Polski"—The Errors of Our Historiography in the Construction of the History of Poland). There he blamed the Cracow school for subjectivism and making use of historical writing for political purposes.

It can be said generally that Korzon's work was an incessant discussion with various conceptions and approaches: with radical positivism (like that of Henry Thomas Buckle [q.v.]), with the various historians from the Cracow school, with conceptions that either idealized pre-partition Poland or painted it in excessively dark colors. Korzon's principal work, which made him an authority in Poland, was *Wewnętrzne dzieje Polski za Stanisław Augusta 1765–1794* (The Home History of Poland Under Stanislaus Augustus, 1765–1794; vols. 1–4 1882–1886, 2d ed., vols. 1–6, 1897–1902). The study, based on vast examination of sources and a long list of research questions, showed for the first time the demographic and economic development of Poland in that period, the state of public administration and the army, and the social and political structure of the country. It thus pointed to the roots of the vitality of the Polish nation after the partitions, inherent in the second half of the eighteenth century. Korzon condemned the magnates but saw many positive values in the lower nobility. He saw the negative elements in the past of Poland mainly in the low level of the political culture of those who influenced the government. The revival came only in the times of Stanislaus Augustus Poniatowski. In Korzon's opinion, the fall was the greatest in the period of the first partition of Poland. Korzon overly condemned King Stanislaw Augustus just as he overly idealized Tadeusz Kościuzko (*Kościuszko, Biografia z dokumentów wysnuta*—1894; Kościuszko, A Biography Based on Documents). In the last-named work and in his monograph dedicated to King Jan Sobieski (*Dola i niedola Jana Sobieskiego*—1898; The Fortunes and Misfortunes of Jan Sobieski), Korzon departed from interpreting historical change by the actions of the people in favor of the decisive role of outstanding personalities. That is to say, he passed from a collectivist to a heroistic conception. When the Polish Academy of Learning (of which he was a member) planned the publication of a Polish encyclopaedia, Korzon was asked to write a small book on Polish military history. He ended up writing a three-volume work *Dzieje wojen i wojskowości w Polsce* (1912; A History of Wars and Military Art in Poland), which became an important inspiration for the development of military history in Poland. He also wrote *Historia handlu w zarysie* (1914; An Outline of the History of Trade) and school handbooks. He enjoyed great moral authority in the country. Although he held no seminars and did not accept university chairs that were offered to him, some historians (in particular Szymon Askenazy [q.v.]) considered themselves his disciples.

Bibliography: Władysław Konopczyński, *Korzon Tadeusz*, in Polski Słownik Biograficzny (The Polish Biographical Dictionary), vol. 14/4, no. 61 (1969), pp. 178–181; Marian Henryk Serejski and Andrzej Feliks Grabski, *Tadeusz Korzon a idea odrodzenia narodowego w dobie stanisławowskiej* (Tadeusz Korzon and the Idea of National Revival Under Stanislaus Augustus), in Tadeusz Korzon, *Odrodzenie w upadku, Wybór pism historycznych* (Revival in the Fall, Selected Historical Writings), edited and introduced by M. H. Serejski and A. F. Grabski (Warsaw, 1975), pp. 5–37.

Jerzy Topolski

KOSTRZEWSKI, Jozef (Weglewo, 1885–Poznan, 1969), Polish pre- and protohistorian. Professor at the University of Poznan after 1919 and considered to be the founder of the Polish archaeological school. Kostrzewski edited several important reviews, for example, *Prżeglad Archeologiczný* (Archaeology Review). He was particularly interested in the problems of Great Poland's prehistory, on which he wrote a great synthesis, *Wielkopolskaw' Cżasach Przedhistorycznych* (1914, 1923, 1955, German ed., 1943; Great Poland in Prehistoric Times). He also wrote a series of studies on the famous settlement, Lausitz in Biskupin, for example, *Un village fortifié sur un marais du premier âge du fer, découvert à Biskupin, Grande Pologne* (1936). Eventually, he extended his investigations to other provinces, for instance, Pomerania (*The Prehistory of Polish Pomerania*, 1936). Kostrzewski did much to clarify the cultural evolution in Poland during the Bronze and Iron Ages and to determine the areas of diffusion of certain cultures. He proposed a relative and an absolute chronology, thus connecting the system of Oscar Montelius (q.v.) to the realities of Poland. Three large problems arrested Kostrzewski's attention. First, he focused on the ethnic unity of the Lusacian culture carrier. Rejecting all other solutions, which assigned this culture to various ethnic groups—Tracian according to Hubert Laurahutte Schmidt (q.v.), Illyrian, Germanic or Celtic according to Gustaf Kossinna (q.v.)—Kostrzewski assigned the Lusacian culture to the proto-Slavs.

Kostrzewski constantly returned to this idea, either in special papers—*Praslowian szczyzna* (1946; The Proto-Slavs' Country), *Kultura luzycky na Pomorzu* (1958; The Lusacian Culture in Pomerania) or in syntheses, such as *Kultura prapolska* (1947–1949; Prepolish Culture, with a French edition, *Les Origines de la Civilisation polonaise*, Paris, 1949). According to Kostrzewski, Poland had been inhabited by discernibly Slavic peoples at least since the second millennium B.C. His hypothesis has not been universally accepted. A second major concern of his research involved the pre- and protohistoric migrations on Poland's territory (Celts and Germans) and the nature of the contacts between the local communities and the newcomers. Kostrzewski hypothesized a situation of long-term German-Slavonic relations and mutual influences (*Germanie Przedhisto-ryezni w Polsce* (1946; Prehistoric Germans in Poland). Finally, he attempted to determine the material culture of the different Germanic tribes settled in the Southeastern region of the Baltic Sea, on the Oder and the Vistula during the first to fourth centuries A.D. (*Die Ostgermanische Kultur der Spätlatenezeit*, 1918). Thus, he stood opposed to the vision of Kossinna's school.

Bibliography: Jan Filip, *Encyklopädisches Handbuch der Ur- und Frühgeschichte Europas* I (Prague, 1966), p. 631; W. Hensel, "35 lat naukowej działalnosce Jozefa Kostrzewskiego," *Slavia Antigua* I (Poznan, 1948), pp. 3–37, with a list of papers appearing during 1945–1947, pp. 38–41; K. Jazdzewski, "Józef Kostrzewski, Pracei materily Muzeum w Łodzi," *Seria Arch.* 17 (1970): 5–13; Zofia Kurnatowska, "Józef Kostrzewski against the Background of His Time," *Przegládt Arch.*, 33 (1985): 5–18; *Wiadomosciach Archeologicznych*, 16, pp. 9–34, contains a complete bibliography.

Ligia Bârzu

KUTRZEBA, Stanisław (Cracow, 1876–Cracow, 1946), Polish historian. One of the founders of the modern history of law and politico-legal institutions in Poland. Professor in, and rector of, the Jagellonian University in Cracow, president of the Polish Academy of Learning. Kutrzeba broke with the idea that historiography should be a vehicle of a conservative political program oriented toward promoting a strong state, which was the tradition of the so-called Cracow school of history (see Michał Bobrzyński [q.v.]). His ideas were closer to those of Gabriel Monod (q.v.) and contemporaneous French historiography. He was an active journalist but did not associate himself with any political group. He strove to be as useful as possible to the Polish state revived after World War I, but he always defended the freedom of science and university self-management. He worked as an expert at the Polish Bureau for the Peace Congress in Paris (1919). After World War II he took part in the negotiations in Moscow on the formation of the Provisional Polish Government of National Unity. He combined an all-round knowledge of sources with broadness of research horizons. His *Historia ustroju Polski w zarysie* (4 vols., 1905–1917; A History of the Polish Political System in Outline) has largely retained its value to this day. It was the first study of its kind in Polish historiography. The same applies to his *Dawne Polskie prawo sadowe* (2 vols., 1921; The Old Polish Court Law), and *Historia źródeł dawnego prawa polskiego* (2 vols., 1925–1926; A History of the Sources to the Old Polish Law), not to mention other monographs. He eventually presented his own conception of the development of the politico-legal institutions in Poland, as seen against the broad social and economic background. He also published numerous original studies in social and economic history. Among them are *Finanse Krakowa w wiekach średnich* (1899; The Finances of Cracow in the Middle Ages), *Handel Krakowa w wiekach Średnich na tle stosunków handlowych Polski* (1902; The Commerce of the City of Cracow in the Middle Ages in the Light of Polish Commercial Relations), and *Taryfy celne i polityka* *celna w Polsce od XIII do XV wieku* (1902; Custom Tariffs and Customs Policy in Poland in the Thirteenth to Fifteenth Centuries).

Kutrzeba rendered enormous services in the publication of sources on the pre-partition history of Poland, including the model edition of *Regesta thelonei aquatici Vladislaviensis secule XVI* (1915, jointly with F. Duda), *Akta unii Polski z Litwa* (1932; Documents of the Union of Poland and Lithuania, jointly with W. Semkowicz), *Polskie ùstawy i artykuły wojskowe od XV do XVIII wieku* (1932; Polish Military Laws from the Fifteenth to the Eighteenth Century, 1932), *Polskie ustawy wiejskie XV-XVIII wieku* (1938; Polish Rural Laws from the Fifteenth to the Eighteenth Century, jointly with A. Mańkowski).

Bibliography: Bogusław Leśnodorski, "Vivimus ut doceamus," in *Alma Mater w podziemiu* (The University in the Underground), (Cracow, 1964), pp. 233–278; "Stanisław Kutrzeba," *Państwo i Prawo* no. 3 (1946): 78–83; Adam Vetulani, "Kutrzeba Stanisław," *Polski Słownik Biograficzny* (The Polish Biographical Dictionary), vol.16/2, no. 69 (1971), 314–318.

Jerzy Topolski

LELEWEL, Joachim (Warsaw, 1786–Paris, 1861), the most eminent Polish historian in the nineteenth century. One of the founders of professional European historiography and a pioneer in the search for the theoretical basis for the conceptualization of historical narration. Lelewel combined the rationalism of the Enlightenment with romantic ideas and the striving for a scientific methodology of history. He wrote many works in that field (including *Nauki dajace poznać źródła historyczne* [1822; Disciplines Which Inform Us About Historical Sources], four of which appeared in 1862 under the collective title *Historyka* (Science of History). He completely broke off with the providential and personalistic treatment of history. Lelewel propounded the idea of interpretative history that refers to an analysis of social and economic life as well as to the knowledge of human nature. Among the mechanisms that explain historical change, he gave the pride of place to "collective" forces. He was a forerunner of the idea that history should integratively cover all the manifestations of life and human activity, as well as the need to link national history to universal history. From that point of view he not only marked an immense progress as compared with Adam Naruszewicz's work, but also charted the paths for the development of Polish historiography in the future. He went far ahead of the standard research methods of his times. He began lecturing in Vilna University in 1815 but was given the chair of history only in 1821, when he won the competition with his study, *O historii, jej rozgałęzieniu i naukach związek z nia majacych* (On History, Its Ramifications and Related Disciplines). His lectures on universal history, the history of historiography, and the methodology of history enjoyed enormous popularity.

Removed from the university for his independence activities, Lelewel settled in Warsaw in 1824 and dedicated himself to research work, without neglecting his political activity. After the outbreak of the Insurrection of 1830, he was elected president of the Patriotic Society. He joined the insurgent national government but raised many reservations as to its small social and political radicalism. His idea was that the Polish uprising should be treated as a component part of European movements for social and political liberation. After the fall of the uprising, he was active as an émigré (France, Belgium) and inspired the formulation of programs for the restoration of independence on the basis of republican ideas. From 1847 on he cooperated with Karl Marx (q.v.) and Friedrich Engels (q.v.) who valued him highly. His historical works were ideologically connected with his political activity. In lieu of the monarchical conception of the history of Poland, he suggested a republican and democratic conception and looked in the history of Poland for the actions of the masses.

The years 1855–1864 saw the appearance of twenty volumes of Lelewel's works on the history of Poland, *Polska, dzieje i rzeczy jej* (Poland, Its History, and Things Polish). His major works include *Dzieje starożytne* (1818; Ancient History), *Panowanie Stanisław Augusta* (1818; The Reign of Stanislaus Augustus), and *Historyczna paralela Hiszpanii z Polska w w. XVI, XVII, XVIII* (1831; The Historical Parallel Between Spain and Poland in the Sixteenth to Eighteenth Centuries). In that work he demonstrated in a masterly manner the possibilities inherent in the comparative method. His conception of history as a struggle between peasants and nobility can best be seen in his synthetic work *Uwagi nad dziejami Polski i ludu jej* (Comments on the History of Poland and Its People; French edition, 1844, Polish edition, 1855). He also wrote popular works (e.g., *Dzieje Polski potocznym sposobem opowiedziane* [1829; The History of Poland Narrated in an Ordinary Manner]). He was concerned with all historical epochs, from ancient history to his own times (e.g., *Polska odradzająca sie* [1836; Renascent Poland], with Polish history and universal history alike. He was also active in bibliography, historical geography, and numismatics. He suggested a new approach to bibliography (*Bibliograficznych ksiag dwoje* (1823, 1826; Two Books of Bibliography). He wrote on geographical studies in antiquity and on the history of geography and discoveries. He was one of the founders of modern numismatics (*Numismatique du Moyen-Age* [1835]; *Etudes numismatiques et archéologiques* [1841]. The same largely applies to cartography, which owes to Lelewel its pioneer work *Géographie du Moyen-Age* (1852–1857). Lelewel belongs to the group of his contemporaries that include Leopold von Ranke (q.v.), Augustin Thierry (q.v.), Jules Michelet (q.v.), Thomas Carlyle (q.v.), François Guizot (q.v.), and F. Palacký (q.v.). He shared with them the idea that historiography is an instrument of both acquiring knowledge of the world and shaping the world.

Bibliography: Nina Assorodobraj, *Kształtowanie się założeń teoretycznych historiografii Joachima Lelewela* (The Formation of the Theoretical Assumptions of Joachim Lelewel's Historiography), (Warsaw, 1957); Stefan Kieniewicz, *Lelewel*, in *Polski Słownik Biograficzny* (The Polish Biographical Dictionary), vol. 17/1, no. 72 (1972): 21–25; Stefan Kieniewicz, *Samotnik brukselski* (The Lonely Man in Brussels), (Warsaw, 1964); Marian Henryk Serejski, *Koncepoja historii powszechnej Lelewela* (Lelewel's

Conception of Universal History), (Warsaw, 1964); Jerzy Topolski, *Joachim Lelewel—prekursor historii gospodarczej i nowoczesmego modelu badań historycznych w Polsce* (Joachim Lelewel—The Forerunner of Economic History and Modern Historical Research in Poland), in J. Topolski, ed., *Prawda i model w historiografii* (Truth and Model in Historiography), (Łódź, 1982), pp. 89–114.

Jerzy Topolski

ŁOWMIAŃSKI, Henryk (Daugudzie in Lithuania, 1898–Poznań, 1984), Polish historian. Professor at the universities of Vilna (1932–1939) and Poznań (1945–1968). One of the outstanding historians in Polish historiography. A pioneer of the theoretical explanatory trend in the model of historical research. To achieve that and to construct historical narratives Łowmiański followed, in both general reflection and research practice, the idea of integrated (as to the interpretation of the subject matter of historical research and the methods of studying it) reconstruction of the past and the idea of making such a reconstruction as coherent as possible by conceptualization based on a theory. In that respect his attainments can be compared only with those of Joachim Lelewel, considering the differences in the advancement of historiography. For Łowmiański, integrated research was based on an analysis of the past from the point of view of society and the various forms of its life. That was accompanied by the point of view of the nation and the state in those periods when their role was of historical importance. This approach to historical data brought Łowmiański close to the theory of historical materialism which, after 1945, he used in his research in a masterly manner by applying theoretical concretization (and not merely the factographic, which consisted in seeking examples that would support theoretical theses adopted in advance).

Łowmiański was interested mainly in the ancient and medieval history of Baltic and Slavonic societies and states. In that respect he won renown as an expert on an international scale. Research based on a broad comparative background, rigorous criticism of sources, compilation of data obtained from written, archaeological, and linguistic sources, and adoption of theoretical conceptions brought excellent results, particularly *Studia nad początkami społeczeństwa i państwa litewskiego* (1931–1932; Studies in the Origins of the Lithuanian society and State), *Podstawy gospodarcze formowania się państw słowiańskich* (1953; The Economic Foundation of the Formation of Slavonic States), *Zagadnienie roli Normanów w genezie państw słowiańskich* (1957; The Problem of the Role of the Normans in the Origin of Slavonic States), and to his principal work, *Poczatki Polski* (6 vols., 1964–1985; The Origins of Poland), which has as its part *Religia Słowian i jej upadek* (1979; The Religion of the Slavs and Its Fall). His integrated and comparative approach made it possible for him to examine the various theses, which could emerge "as long as interest in political history was dominant and as long as the process of history was treated as a result of the initiatives of individuals and dynasties, and mass scale processes were neglected." This applied, for example, to the role of the Normans in Kiev Russia and the Slavization of the Polish territories. According to Łowmiański, the role of the sources "manifests itself fully only when one treats the past as an integrated process, takes into account and carefully examines all spheres of life, and not merely some of its aspects." Łowmiański himself was guided by those rules in his research on the history of the Grand Duchy of Lithuania, the Teutonic Knights, and other problems.

Bibliography: Zbigniew Wielgosz, *Łowmiański Henryk*, in *Wielkopolski Słownik Biograficzny* (The Biographical Dictionary of Wielkopolska), (Poznań, 1981), pp. 435–436.

Jerzy Topolski

PAWIŃSKI, Adolf (Zgierz, 1840–Grodzisk near Warsaw, 1896), Polish historian. Professor at Warsaw University (1868–1975), director of the Central Archives of Old Documents (1875–1896). Obtained his methodical training mainly in Germany (seminars of Leopold von Ranke [q.v.], P. Jaffé, and especially Georg Waitz [q.v.]), but theoretically and philosophically was oriented toward positivism, although he criticized the radical approach (as that of Henry Thomas Buckle [q.v.]). In his opinion historical research should be neutral and scientifically objective. "It is a sin against science," he wrote, "to contribute passing currents of today's opinions to the sphere of facts that form the picture of the historical life of a given nation." But he did not always succeed in putting that idea into practice, as is evident in his tendentiously anti-German study, *Polabskie Slavjanie* (1871; The Slavs of the Polaby Region). But his other works and publications of sources have retained their importance in the history of law, political history, and economic history. A special mention is due to his pioneer work, *Rządy sejmikowe w Polsce 1572–1795* (1888; Rule by Provincial Diets in Poland, 1572–1795), which forms part of the five-volume publication, *Dzieje ziemi kujawskiej oraz akta historyczne do nich służące* (History of the Kujawy Region and the Historical Documents for Them). *Rządy* shows the role of that important old Polish institution of political self-government by the nobility, although it does not bring out the negative aspects of the provincial diets, which were in agreement with the spirit of the so-called Warsaw school of history that viewed the pre-partition history of Poland optimistically. Pawiński's still greater undertaking consisted in initiating the historical sources, the greatest of its kind in Polish historiography in the nineteenth century (*Źródła dziejowe z XVI wieku*— Historical Sources from the Sixteenth Century, 20 vols. of which appeared in Pawiński's lifetime). In Volume 13 Pawiński published *Skarbowość w Polsce i jej dzieje za Stefana Batorego* (1881; The Fiscal System in Poland and Its History under Stefan Bator), which is valued to this day. In this work he concentrates on the weakness of the old Polish fiscal system, in which he saw the causes of the later deformations of the Polish political system. Pawiński was also very active in the popularization of science. He supervised the translation of the ten-volume version of Thomas Babington Macaulay's (q.v.) *History of England*. His series *Polska XVI wieku pod względem geograficzno-statystycznym* (5 vols.)

is still used today as an important source of statistical research on sixteenth-century Poland.

Bibliography: Juliusz Bardach, "Pawiński Adolf," in *Polski Słownik Biograficzny* (The Polish Biographical Dictionary), vol. 25/2, no. 105 (1980): 407–412; Henryk Olszewski, "Adolf Pawiński i jego dzieło" (Adolf Pawiński and His Work), in A. Pawiński, *Rządy sejmikowe w Polsce* (Rule by Provincial Diets in Poland), edited and introduced by H. Olszewski (Warsaw, 1978), pp. 5–40.

Jerzy Topolski

POTKAŃSKI, Karol (Prędocinek near Radom, 1861–Cracow, 1907), Polish historian. One of the most interesting personalities in Polish historiography, an outstanding innovator in historical research, marked by broad scientific interests (including natural science) and by numerous contacts with the artistic world, connoisseur of literature and art. Potkański was on friendly terms with Henryk Sienkiewiez, Stanislaw Ignacy Witkiewicz, Sr., Stanislaw Ignacy Witkiewicz, Jr., Jacek Malczewski (who painted his portraits) and others. While he came from the gentry he cut himself off from the conservatism and loyalism of his contemporaries from the Cracow school of history and was inclined to support the ideology of the peasant movement and—despite the fact that he was a positivist in his interpretation of the world and in historical research—the independence movement which referred to Romanticism. Unconventional in his way of life, he treated research work as a calling and not as an ordinary profession; he did not care about academic degrees and university titles. In 1900 he was persuaded to pass the doctoral examinations on the strength of one of his already numerous works, as a result of which he was appointed professor at Jagellonian University in Cracow in 1901 and elected member of the Polish Academy of Learning. Despite an advancing illness he was very active in all fields of his historical interests to the end of his life.

In his works Potkański combined his profound knowledge of research techniques of a medievalist with the catalogue of research problems enlarged by his knowledge of sociology, geography, ethnology, linguistics, psychology, and law. For him psychology was a *sui generis* link between social and natural phenomena, which made it possible to take into account the peculiarities of the social world. He disclaimed Bucklean determinism but stressed the dependence of human history on the natural environment. But he interpreted that dependence rather possibilistically, as the various factors, largely economic, which manifest themselves in human actions. In many works, especially those dealing with the settlement of the various territories, which are in the field of socioeconomic history and are valuable to this day, he tried to demonstrate the interdependence of the natural environment, social organization, and the settling of territories. In each field he combined precision of proofs with the intention of charting new paths. In *Zagrodowa szlachta i włodycze rycerstwo w województwie krakowskim w XV i XVI wieku* (1888; Petty Gentry and Yeoman-like Knights in the Cracow Province in the Fifteenth and Sixteenth Centuries), he was the first to point to the role of the economic factor in the origin of the petty gentry. In his many works on the history of settlements, he used the retrogressive and the comparative method to reconstruct dynamically the history of the peasant class, thus modernizing research in that field—for example, *Studia nad pierwotnym osadnictwem w Polsce* (Studies in Primary Settlements in Poland) and *Studia osadnicze* (1922; Studies in Settlements), concerned primarily with settlements in the Radom forest, the Kurpie forest, and the Podhale region. The same applied to his genealogical and other studies. His research work can be divided into three fields: (1) studies in old Slavs (e.g., *Lachowie i Lechici*, 1897), (2) studies in the early socioeconomic history of the Polish state (e.g., *Kraków przed Piastami*—1899; Cracow Before the Piast Dynasty; *Opaetwo na łęczyckim grodzie*—1903; The Abbey in Łęczyca Stronghold Town; *Geneza organizacji rodowej*—1905; The Origin of the Stronghold Town Organization), (3) studies in the sociopolitical history of fourteenth-century Poland (*Studia and XIV wiekiem*—1899, 1900, 1901, 1905, 1906; Studies Concerned with the Fourteenth Century). All of Potkański's works have retained their value.

Bibliography: Henryk Baryez, *Wizerunek uczonego z epoki Młodej Polski* (A Portrait of a Scholar from the Modernist Epoch) in H. Barycz, *Na przełomie dwóch stuleci* (At the Turn of the Nineteenth Century), (Wrocław-Warszawa-Kraków-Gdańsk, 1977), pp. 68–168; Franciszek Bujak, *Zycie i działalnosc Karola Potkańskiego, 1861–1907* (The Life and Work of Karol Potkański, 1861–1907), in *Pisma pośmiertne Karola Potkańskiego* (Posthumous Works of Karol Potkański), vol. 1. (Cracow, 1922), pp. 1–90; Andrzej Polański, *Wyjaánianie historyczne w pracach Karola Potkańskiego* (Historical Explanation in the Works of Karol Potkański), manuscript of the dissertation written under the supervision of Jerzy Topolski in the Poznań University Institute of History.

Jerzy Topolski

RUTKOWSKI, Jan (Warsaw, 1886–Poznań, 1949), Polish historian Rutkowski obtained his Ph.D. in Lvov in 1909 for his *Skarbowość polska za Aleksandra Jagiellończyka* (The Polish Fiscal System under Aleksander the Jagellonian). In 1910–1911 he studied at the École Pratique des Hautes Études in Paris, where he wrote his novel work *Étude sur la répartition et l'organisation de la propriété foncière en Bretagne au XVIIe siècle* (1912), on the strength of which he obtained *venia legendi* (habilitation) in Lvov. In that work, based on an exhaustive study of sources, he traced the degree of decomposition of the traditional structures of feudal property under the impact of economic organization based on money and the market. He was in close contact with H. Sée and was valued highly by Lucien Febvre (q.v.) and Marc Bloch (q.v.). From 1919 on, with a break during World War II when he stayed in Warsaw, he was professor in Poznań University in charge of the chair of economic history. He was the founder of modern economic history. Jointly with F. Bujak in 1931 he organized the *Roczniki Dziejów Społecznych i Gospodarczych* (Annals of Social and Economic History), which joined the ranks of *The Economic History Review* (1927) and *Annales d'Histoire Économique et Sociale* (1928). He was the author of the first synthetic economic history of Poland (1923, 1946, 1947–1950), the best to this day. Its

French translation, *Histoire économique de la Pologne avant les partages* (1927), is still the only one of its kind in a Western language.

Rutkowski's principal works were concerned with the agrarian history of the early modern period. They marked successive stages of a research program intended to explain the profound socioeconomic change in Poland in the sixteenth to the eighteenth century (in particular the transition from the economy based on money rent to the system of the manorial serf economy) and to demonstrate the essence and the functioning of the feudal period. That program was closely linked to his criticism of earlier studies in economic history and of the factography that dominated historiography. Rutkowski urged historians to a conscious and methodologically correct effort to obtain theoretical foundations of their research and to concentrate on explaining the fundamental problems of history. He also proclaimed the slogan of neutralizing the direct influence of extrascientific factors on research (objectivism and demystification). In his study of economic history he postulated the use of sources that give facts and the elimination of arbitrary formulations by statistical rigor. He put those ideas into effect and published *Studia nad położeniem włościan w Polsce w XVIII wieku* (1914; Studies in the Situation of Peasants in Poland in the Eighteenth Century) in which he reconstructed the peasant population. Other works in the same category included *Przebudowa wsi w Polsce po wojnach z połowy XVII wieku* (1917; The Restructuring of the Rural Areas in Poland after the Wars in the Midseventeenth Century), which analyzed the role of the devastations for the agrarian system (despite the fact that strong motives for a change were inherent in the mechanisms of the distribution of incomes), and *Poddaństwo włościan w XVIII wieku w Polsce i w niektórych innych krajach Europy* (1921; The Serfdom of Peasants in the Eighteenth Century in Poland and in Some Other European Countries). In that work, which is a case of historiography reaching for theoretical explanations, Rutkowski analyzed the connections between the economic (particularly agrarian) system of Poland and the disaster of the partitions. The financial and military weakness of the Polish state was due not to that system, but to a set of political and ideological factors. Rutkowski's research was to be crowned by *Badania nad podziałem dochodów w Polsce w czasach nowożytnych* (Studies in the Distribution of Incomes in Poland in Modern Times), which was planned for a number of volumes. Volume 1 appeared in 1938; the material for Volume 2 was lost during World War II, as was a manuscript of his book on dualism in the economic development of Europe in the sixteenth century. His studies on the distribution of incomes combined his reflections on the theory of the feudal system (his book was the first consciously constructed model of that system with reference to the countries to the east of the Elbe in modern times), the construction of syntheses in economic history (he conceived the study of the distribution of income among the social classes and groups as the axis of his synthesis), and the vast statistical studies showing the real distribution of income from Polish agriculture in the sixteenth century between the peasants and the landowners. Rutkowski's conception of the distribution of incomes in the perspective of a historical synthesis is the most outstanding theoretical conception in Polish historiography in the first half of the twentieth century and one of the few, as to its scope, in world historiography. Rutkowski must be classed as a forerunner of the most ambitious modern trends in historiography. In his theoretical reflection he was influenced by historical materialism but was opposed to its one-sided interpretations.

Bibliography: Witold Kula, "Introduction," to Jan Rutkowski, *Studia z dziejów wsi polskiej XVI-XVIII wieku* (Studies in the History of the Polish Rural Areas in the Sixteenth to the Eighteenth Century), (Warsaw, 1956), pp. 6–61; Władysław Rusiński, "Jan Rutkowski. Wspomnienie pośmiertne" (Jan Rutkowski A Reminiscence), *Roczniki Dziejów Społecznych i Gospodarczych*, vol. 11 (1949), pp. 2–21; Jerzy Topolski, "Jan Rutkowski and His Conception of Historical Synthesis," *Storia della Storiografia*, no. 2 (1983), 44–60; Jerzy Topolski, "Le programme théorique de J. Rutkowski et sa réalisation," *Studia Historiae Oeconomicae* 16 (1983); 29–51; Jerzy Topolski, *O nowy model historii. Jan Rutkowski (1886–1949)* (Toward a New Model of History. Jan Rutkowski, 1886–1949), (Warsaw, 1985).

Jerzy Topolski

SEREJSKI, Marian Henryk (Warsaw, 1897–Warsaw, 1975), Polish historian. In 1929–1939 Serejski lectured at Warsaw University and from 1938 as a docent. In 1946–1965 he was professor at Łódź University and from 1953 concurrently head of the research center for the history of historiography in the Polish Academy of Sciences Institute of History. At first (under Marceli Handelsman [q.v.]) he was interested in the Dark Ages (*Idea Imperium Romanum w Galii Merowińskiej* —1925; The Idea of the Roman Empire in Merovingian Gaul, and *Idea jedności karolińskiej, Studium nad geneza, wspólnoty europejskiej w średniowieczu* — 1937; The Idea of Carolingian Unity. A Study in the Origin of the European Community in the Dark Ages, 1937). These works were marked by an analysis of the development of ideas from the point of view of social history. This in turn formed a transition to a new field of research, which nevertheless remained within the history of ideas, namely, the history of historiography. It was in that sphere that he had his greatest achievements as the founder of the modern history of historiography in Poland. His concern with that field of research was announced by his programmatic paper read at the Seventh General Congress of Polish Historians in Wrocław in 1948, namely, "Problematyka historii historiografii z punktu widzenia jej uwarunkowania społecznego" (Problems of the History of Historiography from the Point of View of its Social Conditionings). "The fundamental task of the historian of historiography," he said, "is to find the relationships between the development of historical thought and life, i.e., the system of social relations, the culture of a given epoch, political events, etc." These methodological directives were combined with the striving for a comparative treatment of the ideas covered by the study and the treatment of national history in connection with universal history. His intention was to write a synthetic history of Polish historiography from the eighteenth to the end of the nineteenth century, based on numerous studies in the history of Polish and

European historiography. Its first outline, *Zarys historii historiografii polskiej* (An Outline of the History of Polish Historiography), 2 vols., appeared in 1954–1956.

Among Serejski's special studies perhaps his best is *Europa a rozbiory Polski. Studium historiograficzne* (1970; Europe and the Partitions of Poland. A Study in Historiography), in which he traced the changing reactions of European historiography to the fall of Poland in the late eighteenth century, and to several works dedicated to Joachim Lelewel (q.v.): The works on Lelewel have a pioneering value. See *Joachim Lelewel. Z dziejów postepowej myśli historycznej w Polsce* (1953; Joachim Lelewel. A Contribution to the History of Progressive Historical Thought in Poland), *Koncepcja historii powszechnej Joachima Lelewela* (1958; Joachim Lelewel's Conception of Universal History), and *Joachim Lelewel 1786–1861, Sa vie et son oeuvre* (1961). Serejski initiated the publication of Lelewel's works and became editor-in-chief of the series and editor of some volumes. He also analyzed the approach of Polish historiography to the problems of the nation and the state in *Naród i Państwo w polskiej myśli historycznej* (1973; The Nation and the State in Polish Historical Thought), in which he stated that the distinct feature of Polish historiography, as compared with historiography in other countries, was manifested in the dilemma: the nation versus the state.

Bibliography: Andrzej Feliks Grabski, "Marian Henryk Serejski (3 V 1897 – 23 X 1975)," *Kwartalnik Historyezny*, no. 2 (1976): 497–504.

Jerzy Topolski

SMOLEŃSKI, Władysław (Grabienice Małe, district Przasnysz, 1851–Warsaw, 1926), Polish historian. Representative of the so-called Warsaw school of historiography (see Tadeusz Korzon, [q.v.], Adolf Pawiński [q.v.]), elected member of the Polish Academy of Learning in 1918, professor at Warsaw University from 1919. Like Korzon, Smoleński concentrated on the eighteenth century, pointing to the revolution in the second half of that century, which, however, resulted in his underestimation of the importance of the earlier periods (*Przewrót umysłowy w Polsce w wieku XVIII*—1891; The Intellectual Revolution in Poland in the Eighteenth Century). Influenced by positivism, he preached the need to study the history of civilization and not the traditionally interpreted political history. In his opinion historiography should be free from proclaiming extrascholarly programs and from dependence on religious ideology. Like other representatives of such a program, he failed to put his ideas into practice. Smoleński's historical writings, while based on ample sources and full of new content, were nevertheless a voice in the discussion of the history of Poland. For Smoleński, the main mechanisms of historical development, again in agreement with the positivist standpoint, are inherent in the intellectual development of human beings, and historical syntheses have as their axis not the state (as was the case of the Cracow school) but the nation. Smoleński was being attacked by Church circles for his anticlericalism. He saw the sources of the national revival in the second half of the eighteenth century not in the magnates and the nobility (except for the petty gentry, which he evaluated positively), but in the burghers, to whom he dedicated a number of studies (e.g., *Mieszczaństwo warszawskie w końcu XVIII wieku*, 1917; Warsaw Burghers in the Late Eighteenth Century). Historiography served him in his struggle against backwardness, the national betrayal of the magnates, the policy of reconciliation with the partition powers, and the theological view of the world. Like other representatives of the Warsaw school he strongly emphasized Poland's connections with Western civilization and its civilizational mission in the East. These opinions intensified as Smoleński turned toward conservatism. He particularly emphasized the role of religious factors (the Roman Catholic reaction) in the fall of the Polish state in the late eighteenth century. He evaluated very highly the effect of the reforms carried out under Stanislaus Augustus, and, unlike Korzon, he positively assessed the monarchic character of those reforms and the role of the king (*Kuźnica Kołłatajowska*— 1885; The Kołłataj Group and *Ostatni rok Sejmu Wielkiego*—1896; The Last Year of the Long Diet). The totality of his opinions on the history of Poland appears in his *Dzieje narodu polskiegi* (1897–1898; A History of the Polish Nation), vols. 1–2. He also wrote on the history of historiography (*Szkoły historyczne w Polsce*—1886; Historical Schools in Poland).

Bibliography: Celina Bobińska, "Władysław Smoleński," in W. Smoleński, *Wybór pism* (Selected Writings), selected and introduced by C. Bobińska (Warsaw, 1954), pp. xlii–lxix; Andrzej Feliks Grabski, "Poglady Władysława Smoleńskiego na dzieje Polski" (Władysław Smoleński's Views of the History of Poland), in A. F. Grabski, *Perspektywy przeszłośei* (Perspectives of the Past), (Lublin, 1983), pp. 414–443; Andrzej Wierzbicki, "Czarnowidztwo czy apologia? W poszukiwaniu prawdy historycznej" (Pessimism or Apology? The Search for Historical Truth), in Władysław Smoleński, *Przewrót umysłowy w Polsce XVIII wieku* (The Intellectual Revolution in Poland in the Eighteenth Century), edited and introduced by Andrzej Wierzbicki (Warsaw, 1979), pp. 5–22.

Jerzy Topolski

SMOLKA, Stanisław (Lvov, 1854–Nowoszyca in Polesie, 1924), Polish historian. Organizer of the first historical seminar in Poland and of the school of medieval research in the Jagellonian University in Cracow, where he was a professor. One of the outstanding representatives of the Cracow school (see Michal Bobrzyński [q.v.], Walerian Kalinka [q.v.]), one of Kalinka's successors who laid special stress on the adoption in Polish historiography of new methods of criticism of historical sources developed in European historiography. Elected member of the Polish Academy of Learning in 1881, secretary general of that academy, rector of Jagellonian University. For considerations of health, Smolka spent the last twenty-five years of his life in isolation. (He abandoned his university chair.) He was strongly influenced by his stay at the University of Göttingen (1871–1874), in particular by the seminar of Georg Waitz (q.v.), which shaped his personality as a historian of the Middle Ages. That inspired his first study, *Henryk Brodaty, ustep z dziejów epoki piastowskiej* (1872; Henry the Bearded, a Chapter in the History of the Piast Period), and his principal comprehensive work, *Mieszko Stary i jego wiek* (1881; Mieszko the Old and His

Times), which have retained their scholarly value to this day. In 1877, confident in the developing historical method, Smolka wrote that "the sharp eye of historical criticism will always, sooner or later, discover such deviation which is an offense against the scientific method." A positivist in the sphere of methods, he was opposed to all deterministic interpretations and to the search for laws in history. For this reason he criticized Michał Bobrzyński (q.v.) in his study *O pojęciu, zadaniu i stanowisku historii* (1879; On the Concept, Tasks and Position of History), and he was also convinced about the peculiarities of historiography as compared with the natural sciences. He saw the motive power of history in human actions, but not in the personalistic spirit. He was mainly interested in society, which he emphasized in *Mieszko Stary*. He originally believed that the causes of the later fall of the Polish state could be traced back to the Middle Ages, but he soon revised that view and pointed to elements of development in the usually negatively assessed period of the split of medieval Poland into provinces. Under the influence of K. Szajnocha, representative of traditional historiography treated in the literary manner, Smolka used to add rhetorical elements which did not suit his sober scholarly prose. His *Mieszko Stary* is in fact an outline of social, economic, and cultural history in twelfth-century Poland. Smolka collected his various studies in medieval history in *Szkice historyczne* (2 vols., 1882, 1883; Historical Essays), in which he revised many then prevailing opinions. He gradually turned his interests toward the Jagellonian epoch, to which he dedicated his equally valuable works (*Kiejstut i Jagiełło*—1889; Kiejstut and Jagello, and *Najdawniejsze pomniki dziejopisarstwa litewskiego*—1890; The Oldest Monuments of Lithuanian Historiography). He also published a comprehensive work on the political and economic conceptions of F. K. Drucki-Lubecki, who pursued a policy of close cooperation with Russia in the Kingdom of Poland (*Polityka Lubeckiego przed powstaniem listopadowym*—2 vols., 1907; Lubecki's Policy Before the Uprising of 1830) and 4 vols. of Lubecki's correspondence 1909).

Bibliography: Henryk Barycz, *Stanisław Smolka w zyciu i nauce* (Stanisław Smolka—Man and Scholar), (Cracow, 1975); Aleksander Gieysztor, "Stanisław Smolka jako mediewista" (Stanisław Smolka as a Medievalist), in Celina Bobińska and Jerzy Wyrozumski, eds. *Spór o historyczna szkołe krakowska* (The Controversy over the Cracow School of History), (Cracow, 1972), pp. 95–118.

Jerzy Topolski

WOJCIECHOWSKI, Tadeusz (Cracow, 1838–Lvov, 1919), one of the most eminent Polish historians in the nineteenth century. Contributed greatly to the modernization of Polish medieval research. Wojciechowski's success was due to the combination of positivist inspirations with the mastery of source criticism, fine historical imagination, and talent. His principal works have retained their conceptual value to this day. His mentality resembled that of Karol Potkański (q.v.). At first he worked in the Jagellonian Library in Cracow. He did not obtain his university chair until 1883 at the University of Lvov. The delay was due to the originality of his opinions. He was on friendly terms with outstanding sociologist Ludwik Gumplowicz, with whom he shared an interest in new trends in science and philosophy. Wojciechowski saw the principal object and subject of history in man in the sense of "nation, society," that is, the individual in collective, social activity. He stated that the historian should explain human actions by reconstructing the goals of those actions. One has to single out the actions of those who "do not only what others do, but also something more." He maintained that this was not to say that in society there was an abyss between the masses and the genius. What applied to society also applied to "those collective bodies which we call nations." Wojciechowski stressed the role of class struggle (for power) within society, although he did not use such terminology. For all his references to positivism, he did not accept the conception of self-realizing progress in history, but rather used the term *development*. He pointed to the fact that history has no "ready prescriptions for direct use," but as the science of the past gives one indispensable orientation in actions (*Co to jest historia i po co sie jej uczymy* —1883; What Is History and Why We Learn It).

Each of Wojciechowski's works brought some novel interpretation. His *Chrobacja. Rozbiór starzytności słowiańskich* (1873; Chrobacja. An Analysis of Slavonic Antiquities) is probably the most original Polish medieval study in the nineteenth century. His thesis on the archaic character of patronymic names was recently adopted and developed by Henryk Łowmiański (q.v.), the best Polish medieval scholar in the twentieth century. Wojciechowski was the first to point to the value of toponomastic data, and he outlined the method of using them. He was a pioneer of the retrogressive method. In 1904 he published his novel work *Szkice historyczne jedenastego wieku* (Historical Essays Pertaining to the Eleventh Century). In one of those essays he pointed to the political character of the conflict between King Boleslaus II and Bishop Stanisłaus. He discredited the legend that made the bishop a martyr for faith, which provoked violent protests from conservative circles, including many historians. He was attacked by Stanislaus Smolka (q.v.), who postulated that the study of the case of Bishop Stanislaus be dropped for lack of reliable sources (whereas Wojciechowski stressed the importance of hypotheses based on an integrated vision of the period). Wojciechowski's conceptions were marked by a rejection of deeply rooted myths and legends and by a considerable amount of anticlericalism. Despite the resistance of many historians, his ideas found acceptance among a large part of the Polish intelligentsia in the early twentieth century.

Bibliography: Henryk Barycz, "Tadeusz Wojciechowski, Odnowiciel polskiej mediewistyki" (Tadeusz Wojciechowski, Renovator of Polish Medieval Studies), in H. Barycz, *Wśród gawędziarzy, pamiętnikarzy i uczonych galicyjskich* (Galician Story-tellers, Memoirs Writers and Scholars), vol. 2 (Cracow, 1963), pp. 147–176; Aleksander Gieysztor, "Introduction" to T. Wojciechowski, *Szkice historyczne XI wieku* (Historical Essays Pertaining to the Eleventh Century), edited and introduced by A. Gieysztor (Warsaw, 1970), pp. 1–36.

Jerzy Topolski

Great Historians:
Portuguese

ARAÚJO, Alexandre Herculano de Carvalho e (Lisbon, 1810–Val-de-Lobo, 1877), Portuguese historian, known simply as Alexandre Herculano. From 1820 to 1831 Araújo studied in the Oratorian College and in the Commerce School and attended a course in diplomatics. As a liberal, he was pursued by the absolutists and went into exile in England and in France, where he dedicated himself to historical research. In 1832 he joined the liberal army commanded by Dom Pedro (ex-emperor of Brazil) and took part in several military actions against the absolutist forces commanded by Dom Miguel, Dom Pedro's brother. With the liberal victory he returned to his country, and in 1837 he edited *O Panorama*, a weekly journal, where he published historical novels and scholarly studies. In 1839 he was appointed director of the Royal Libraries Necessidades and Ajuda. In 1840, elected a Deputy, he presented to the Assembly a plan for popular education. His main work as an historian (he was also a poet and a novelist), *História de Portugal* (History of Portugal), was published between 1846 and 1853, in four volumes. From 1851 to 1853 he attacked the new government through two newspapers, *O País* and *O Português*. From 1853 to 1854 he traveled in Portugal collecting documents for his *Portugaliae Monumenta Historica*, promoted by the Royal Academy of Sciences. The three volumes of *Da origem e estabelecimento da Inquisição em Portugal* (On the Origin and Establishment of the Inquisition in Portugal) were published in 1854, 1855, and 1859. In 1860 he took part in the writing of the Portuguese Civil Code, supporting civil marriage. In 1867 he left Lisbon and retired to his farm in Val-de-Lobos, where he died in 1877.

Herculano thought that it was impossible to write history without an accurate study of primary sources, and he was genuinely horrified by hasty generalizations and syntheses built with insufficient or inadequate data. Until monographs were sufficiently numerous and until paleontology, ethnography, numismatics, and epigraphy were able to make their contributions to history, any attempt at synthesis would be premature and even dangerous because it would divert the mind and slow down the real progress of historical studies. He criticized Vico and Herder; he fought against the philosophies of history such as those of Johann Gottlieb Fichte, Friederich Schelling, and Georg Wilhelm Hegel (q.v.), who had tried to put the facts into patterns that were the fruit of their imagination. For Herculano, philosophy of history would be possible only when general laws had changed history into a real science. The most urgent task was to save the documents kept in ecclesiastical archives throughout Portugal, which were almost lost to posterity because of insects and mold. But if Herculano was a scholarly historian with an interest in collecting and criticizing documents in the German way, he was also influenced by the social and political ideas of the French historians. He never forgot that he was a liberal. He thought that the history of individuals should give way to the "history of society," that is to say, "the history of the great moral individual called people or nation." In the introduction to the *History of Portugal*, Herculano makes explicit what he understands by the complex idea of nation, saying that human societies differ among themselves because of some factors that guarantee their individual existence: race, territory, and language. Each nation has its character, and the real task for the historian is to study this character and see if the social and political institutions of his time are suited to it. He believed that his country had to create a link between its ancient freedom before absolutism and its new freedom, without any utopias or counterfeited institutions. He did not intend to revive the medieval institutions, but, after studying them, he found in them almost all the principles of freedom people thought had been discovered in the nineteenth century. Because these principles had existed in the past, they were more real, more solid, than if they had been discovered only by the progress of social sciences. When Herculano wrote his *History of the Inquisition*, he confessed that his intention was a political one, but at the same time he affirmed that his book had been written with the greatest scruples and that all the atrocities described in his narrative were also described in the sources. Belonging to the romantic and learned period of the historiography of the nineteenth century, Herculano conceived history as a political weapon and as a science. He despised political history and wanted to write a social history in spite of the literary aspects of his narrative. But in his historical novels, like *O Bobo* (The Jester), he could choose his representative heroes and display all his powers as a writer.

Bibliography: Fortunato de Almeida, *Alexandre Herculano historiador* (Alexandre Herculano Historian), (Coimbra, 1910); Joaquim Barradas de Carvalho, *As ideias políticas e socia is de Alexandre Herculano* (Alexandre Herculano's Political and Social Ideas), (Lisbon, 1949); Carlos Portugal Ribeiro, *Alexandre Herculano. A sua vida e a sua obra* (Alexandre Herculano. His Life and His Work), (Lisbon, 1933–1934), 2 vols.; António José Saraiva, *Herculano e o liberalismo em Portugal* (Herculano and Liberalism in Portugal), (Lisbon, 1977); António Sérgio, *Alexandre Herculano. Sobre história e his-*

toriografia (Alexandre Herculano. On History and Historiography), (Lisbon, 1942); António de Serpa Pimentel, *Alexandre Herculano e seu tempo. Estudo crítico* (Alexandre Herculano and His Time. A Critical Study), (Lisbon, 1881); Agostinho da Silva, *Alexandre Herculano* (Lisbon, 1942); (several authors), *Herculano e a sua obra* (Herculano and His Work), (Oporto, 1978).

Maria Beatriz Nizza da Silva

AZEVEDO, João Lúcio de (Sintra, 1855–Lisbon, 1933), Portuguese historian. After attending the Commerce School in Lisbon, Azevedo immigrated to Brazil when he was eighteen years old. He settled in Belém, in the northern Province of Pará, and got a job in a bookshop. As a self-taught man he became interested in local history, and his first articles were published in Pará in 1893: *Estudos de História Paraense* (Studies on the History of Pará). It is a scholarly work, in which the author wanted "to establish the truth of some events," based on primary sources, and it opened the gates of the Brazilian Historical and Geographical Institute to him. He returned to Portugal in 1900 and soon after his arrival published in Lisbon *Os jesuitas no Grão-Pará. Suas missões e a colonização. Bosquejo histórico com vários documentos inéditos* (1901; The Jesuits in Great-Pará. Their Missions and the Colonization. An Historical Sketch with Several Unpublished Documents). Other works followed: *O Marquês de Pombal e a sua época* (1909; The Marquis of Pombal and His Time), where the author intended to eliminate the controversy about this character, either too highly praised or too severely detracted in Portuguese historiography; *A evolução do Sebastianismo* (1918; The Evolution of Sebastianism) in which he analyzed the belief that King Sebastian of Portugal would return from the battlefield in North Africa; *História dos cristãos novos portugueses* (1922; History of Portuguese New Christians); *História de António Vieira* (1918–1921; History of António Vieira); *Épocas de Portugal económico* (1929; Ages of Economic Portugal); and *Novas Epanáforas. Estudos de História e Literatura* (1933; New Epanaphora. Studies on History and Literature).

Lúcio de Azevedo was, as can be seen by the subjects of his books, a Luso-Brazilian historian, deeply interested in the history of colonial Brazil because of the years spent in that country and his friendship with Brazilian historians such as Capistrano de Abreu (q.v.). He took part in the Congress of the History of America in 1922 in Rio de Janeiro, with a communication on the politics of Pombal toward Brazil, later published in *New Epanaphora*. As an editor, in 1915 he presented some unknown texts written by António Vieira, a Jesuit famous for resisting efforts to enslave Indians, and in 1916, nineteen letters of this same Jesuit. Later, in 1925–1928, he organized the critical edition of Vieira's letters. Lúcio de Azevedo's work presents a good example of the dynamics of historical research and writing. All his books are connected, each one leading the way to another. In *The Jesuits in Great-Pará* he underscored the point that the history of that northern region of Brazil could not be written without the history of the Jesuits, because its central fact was the fight between them and the lay population on account of the Indians. In the biography of António Vieira, the subject of the Indians' freedom is stressed and presented as the cause of conflict between Jesuits and colonists. The chapter on "cryptojudaism" certainly led him to write the *History of Portuguese New Christians*. Although he accepted Alexandre Herculano Araújo's (q.v.) *On the Origin and Establishment of the Inquisition in Portugal* as perfect from the factual point of view, he thought that Herculano was too much of a polemicist and that the history of the Inquisition and of the new Christians should be written in a more neutral style. Azevedo intended to penetrate the spirit of that age and its ideas. He refused to see those subjects with the ideas of his own time: "Only in that way can we understand the moral, religious and political phenomena and the men's behavior." He had no intention of judging or of taking sides and he was not as certain as other historians about the loss of men and money caused by the expulsion of the Jews and the establishment of the Inquisition. "These are intricate problems, about which it is easier to express oneself by sentiment than decide according to reason."

Maria Beatriz Nizza da Silva

BARROS, Henrique da Gama (Lisbon, 1833–Lisbon, 1925), Portuguese historian. Of bourgeois origins, Barros took a law degree at the University of Coimbra. He became a civil servant in the central and local administration: administrator of the Sintra Municipality, secretary-general of the Lisbon district government, twice governor of Lisbon, member of the Supreme Administrative Court, member and president of the Court of Exchequer. He also took some interest in politics, being appointed a peer in 1906. His work as an historian started late in his life. Until 1885 he only published a useful analytical index of current legislation (*Repertorio Administrativo* [. . .], 1860). Nonetheless, he prepared a great general history of the Portuguese administration from its beginnings to the nineteenth century, and for it he collected extensive materials both in the archives and in the existing literature. The first volume of this opus was published in 1885 under the title of *História da Administração Pública em Portugal nos séculos XII a XV*, and the critics unanimously welcomed it as a major contribution. Gama Barros succeeded in publishing three other bulky volumes, in 1896, 1914, and 1922, all devoted to the Middle Ages only. Its original plan was changed into a general political, administrative, and economic history of Portugal in the Middle Ages. A disciple of Theodor Mommsen (q.v.), Numa Denis Fustel de Coulanges (q.v.), and Alexandre Herculano Araújo (q.v.), he was especially interested in institutions, which he analyzed with enormous detail and precision. His type of history was a positive and learned description of the past. Although neglecting broad interpretations and comprehensive syntheses, he tried to put together historical data often ignored by his contemporaries, such as population, techniques, mentalities, landownership, trade and industry, and daily life. He was also one of the first in Portugal to use systematically and critically archival sources as a basis for his conclusions.

Bibliography: António Ferrão, "Gama Barros e a sua obra," *Boletim da Segunda Classe da Academia das Ciências de Lisboa* 19 (1935); Torquato de Sousa Soares, "Introdução" and "Observações" to the second edition of Gama Barros' *História da Administração Pública em Portugal nos séculos XII a XV*, vol. 1 (Lisbon, 1945); *Revista Portuguesa de História* 4 (Coimbra, 1949), devoted to Gama Barros.

A. H. de Oliveira Marques

CORTESÃO, Jaime (Ançã, near Coimbra, 1884–Lisbon, 1960), Portuguese historian. Although he studied medicine in Lisbon, Cortesão preferred to be a high school teacher of history and literature, to write in literary journals, and to give a course on "National History" in what in 1912 was called the People's University, an idea he fought for. He took part in World War I as a doctor, and in 1919 he was the director of the National Library. In 1921 he was elected to the Academy of Sciences, and in 1922 he took part in a cultural mission to Brazil, during the visit of the Portuguese president to that country for the Centenary of Brazilian Independence. An adherent of the Spanish Republic, he lived in that country from 1931 to 1932, doing historical research in the Archives in Seville and teaching there about the Atlantic discoveries. In 1939 he escaped to France, but, upon returning to Portugal in 1940, he was sent to prison for his political ideas. Nevertheless, he received permission to travel to Brazil.

Cortesão's years of exile were, from the historical point of view, a very productive period because until 1957 he had the opportunity of researching in the best Brazilian Archives for the study of Luso-Brazilian history. This was already his main subject when living in Europe: In 1922 he published in Lisbon *A expedição de Pedro Álvares Cabral e o descobrimento do Brasil* (The Expedition of Pedro Álvares Cabral and the Discovery of Brazil); in 1926 he presented a paper in Rome, in the Twenty-second International Congress of Americanists, "Le Traité de Tordesilhas et la découverte de l'Amérique"; from 1931 to 1934 he wrote several chapters on colonial Brazil for the *História de Portugal* (History of Portugal) edited by Damião Peres (q.v.). During his first years in Rio de Janeiro he was the critical editor of two important documents: *A carta de Pero Vaz de Caminha* (Pero Vaz de Caminha's Letter) and *Diálogos das Grandezas do Brasil* (Dialogues on the Greatnesses of Brazil) by Ambrósio Fernandes Brandão, both in 1943. In 1944 he was in charge of the organization of the maps belonging to the Ministry of Foreign Affairs, and in 1945 he began his lectures in Rio Branco Institute, created by this ministry for the preparation of diplomats. His subject was the history of political cartography of Brazil. As a result of this research, in 1944 he published *Cabral e as origens do Brasil (Ensaio de topografia histórica dos primeiros passos de Pedro Álvares Cabral no litoral brasileiro)* (Cabral and the Origins of Brazil. An Essay on Historical Topography of the First Steps of Pedro Álvares Cabral on the Coast of Brazil). In 1947 he began his research on Alexandre de Gusmão and the Madrid Treaties, looking for documents not only in Brazilian Archives but also in Portugal. The work, in five volumes, was published in 1950, and the next year he began the edition of manuscripts of the De Angellis Collection in the National Library, where he also worked as a researcher. Five volumes were published between 1951 and 1960. In 1952 he was invited to organize the important historical exhibition in São Paulo to commemorate the fourth centenary of this town, which would take place in 1954. He traveled to Europe to collect documents, and as a result of this task three books were published: *A fundação de S. Paulo, capital geográfica do Brasil* (The Foundation of S. Paulo, Brazil's Geographical Capital) in 1955; *Pauliceae Lusitana Monumenta Historica* in 1956–1960; and *Raposo Tavares e a formação territorial do Brasil* (Raposo Tavares and the Territorial Formation of Brazil) in 1958. After returning to Portugal in 1957 he published the first volume of *Os descobrimentos portugueses* (Portuguese Discoveries) in 1960, as well as *A política de sigilo nos descobrimentos* (The Seal Policy in the Discoveries). Jaime Cortesão was indeed a Luso-Brazilian historian if we make an exception: *Os factores democráticos na formação de Portugal* (The Democratic Factors in the Formation of Portugal), written as an introduction to the *História do regime republicano em Portugal*, edited by Luís de Montalvor (Lisbon, 1930). As an historian he stressed the importance of geography and what was then called geopolicy. Brother of a cartographer, Armando Cortesão, he always wrote about space and time and always integrated history and geography. Not only did he discover old maps, later collected and published by the Brazilian Ministry of Foreign Affairs after his death, but he also made his own maps because he needed these didactic instruments for his course on the history of Brazilian cartography. Cortesão tried to demonstrate that the Portuguese expansion and colonization was in several ways different from the Spanish settlements in South America and that this difference derived from the national character of each people. Very often in his articles published in newspapers in Rio de Janeiro and São Paulo, he spoke in terms of "ideal types," comparing Portuguese and Spaniards. On the other hand, he pointed to the cultural melting pot resulting from the Portuguese colonization in Brazil, suggesting that the colonists did not impose their culture and adopted the native one in many aspects.

Bibliography: Isa Adonias, *Jaime Cortesão e seus mapas* (Jaime Cortesão and His Maps), (Rio de Janeiro, 1984); Óscar Lopes, ed., *Jaime Cortesão* (Lisbon, n.d.); Ricardo Saraiva, *Jaime Cortesão. Subsídios para a sua biografia* (Jaime Cortesão. A Contribution for His Biography), (Lisbon, 1953); special number of the journal *Prelo*, Lisbon (December 1984), dedicated to Jaime Cortesão with articles by Joel Serrão, Jorge Borge de Macedo, José Manuel Garcia, Maria Beatriz Nizza da Silva, and others.

Maria Beatriz Nizza da Silva

FREIRE, Anselmo Braamcamp (Lisbon, 1849–Lisbon, 1921), Portuguese historian. Freire was a member of the new liberal aristocracy of wealthy bourgeois origin. He succeeded as a peer to his uncle, the politician Anselmo José Braamcamp. Although politics did not interest him much, he was nonetheless elected president of the Sintra City Council and later, becoming a Republican, president of the Lisbon City Council (1908), member of the first Republican Parliament

(1911), and president of its upper chamber, the Senate (1911). As an historian he studied above all Portuguese genealogy and heraldry, which he definitely proposed as scientific branches of history, based on archival and other sources. He wrote several books and articles on those subjects: *Brasões da Sala de Cintra* (3 vols., 1899–1905; 1921–1930; 1973), *Critica e Historia* (Lisbon, 1910), *Armaria Portugueza* (Lisbon, 1908), *Gil Vicente, Trovador, Mestre da Balança* (Lisbon, 1917). One of his major contributions for history was his direction and subsidizing of *Archivo Historico Portuguez* (11 vols., 1903–1921), a review devoted to positivist history with a systematic and extensive publication of sources. There he included many other important articles on the fifteenth and sixteenth centuries.

Bibliography: Luis de Bivar Guerra, "Introduction," to *Brasões da Sala de Cintra*, 3d ed., Vol. 1 (Lisbon, 1973); José Miranda do Vale, *Anselmo Braamcamp Freire (1849– 1921). Sua Actividade Política* (Lisbon, 1953).

A. H. de Oliveira Marques

MARTINS, Joaquim Pedro de Oliveira (Lisbon, 1845–Lisbon, 1894), Portuguese historian. In 1856 Oliveira Martins began his studies in the Academy of Fine Arts, and the next year he went to the Central Lyceum in Lisbon, but his father's death interrupted his studies, and he got a job as a clerk in an office. His historical novel, *Febo Moniz*, was published in 1867. He wrote for several newspapers between 1869 and 1870, when he traveled to Spain, as a mines administrator. In that country he wrote *A teoria do socialismo. Evolução política e económica das sociedades da Europa* (The Theory of Socialism. Political and Economic Evolution of Societies in Europe), published in Lisbon in 1872. Upon return to Portugal in 1873, he worked in the construction of a railway in northern Portugal and published *Portugal e o socialismo. Exame constitucional da sociedade portuguesa e a sua reorganização pelo socialismo* (Portugal and Socialism. Constitutional Analysis of Portuguese Society and Its Reorganization Through Socialism). In 1874 his work *O helenismo e a civilização cristã* (Helenism and Christian Civilization) was printed. He presented himself in the elections of 1879 as a member of the Socialist party, and that same year he edited a "Library of Social Science," where he published his *História da civilização ibérica* (History of Iberian Civilization) and his *História de Portugal* (History of Portugal). In 1880 he was the president of the Commercial Geography Society in Oporto. During the 1880s he published several books: *As raças humanas e a civilização primitiva* (Human Races and Primitive Civilization) in 1881; *Sistema dos mitos religiosos* (System of Religious Myths) in 1882; *Quadro das instituições primitivas* (Tableau of Primitive Institutions) in 1883; *Tábuas de cronologia e geografia histórica* (Tables of Chronology and Historical Geography) in 1884; *História da República romana* (History of the Roman Republic) in 1885, to name only a few. This activity as a writer did not prevent him from leading a very active political life, and in 1886 he was elected deputy. Leaving Oporto, he settled in Lisbon in 1888. In 1891 he published *Os filhos* *de D. João I* (The Sons of John the 1st), followed the next year by the *Vida de Nun' Álvares* (Life of Nun'Álvares). He accepted the Ministry of the Treasury in a very difficult moment for public finances but resigned soon after, traveling to London.

Oliveira Martins' last years were dedicated to writing and traveling in Spain. In 1879, when his *History of Portugal* appeared, Oliveira Martins distinguished two aspects of history: One of them describes the system of institutions and of collective ideas; the other presents the real sketch of manners and characters, the painting of places and details that form the scenery of the historical theater. Both are essential, but in his *History of Iberian Civilization* the historian emphasized the first aspect, writing as a scientist. Meanwhile, in his *History of Portugal* he tried to make men real, writing with something he called "historical intuition" and looking for a literary style. With the passing of years Oliveira Martins became more and more attached to the idea of history as an art. In 1891, when he published *The Sons of John the 1st*, he wrote that "the art of writing history was undergoing a change" and that, since history always implies a "revival" of the past, "the artistic or synthetic procedure will always be the more adequate." Despising scholarly analysis and critical controversies, he thus took pleasure in his mission as an artist and tried "to create works to please the learned and the unlearned." He even went so far as to point to Plutarch as a model, because Plutarch put psychological analysis and biography in the heart of study and observation of past ages. For Oliveira Martins there was no historical material when there were no prominent characters. The task of the historian was "to explain, to define and to guess what was hidden in the souls of those rude men of other ages."

Bibliography: F. Castelar, *A História de Portugal de Oliveira Martins* (The History of Portugal by Oliveira Martins), (Porto, 1884); Albino Forjaz de Sampaio, *Oliveira Martins. A sua vida e a sua obra* (Oliveira Martins. His Life and His Work), (Lisbon, 1926); Georges Le Gentil, *Oliveira Martins. Algumas fontes da sua obra* (Oliveira Martins. Some Sources of His Work), (Lisbon, 1935); Óscar Lopes, *Oliveira Martins e as contradições da geração de 70* (Oliveira Martins and the Contradictions of the Generation of the 70's), (Oporto, 1946); Manuel Mendes, *Oliveira Martins. O homem e a vida* (Oliveira Martins. The Man and His Life), (Lisbon, 1947); Queirós Veloso, *No centenário do nascimento de Oliveira Martins o historiador* (In the Centenary of the Birth of Oliveira Martins the Historian), (Lisbon, 1945).

Maria Beatriz Nizza da Silva

PERES, Damião (Lisbon, 1889–Porto, 1976), Portuguese historian. Peres took a degree at the former Lisbon High School of Arts (Curso Superior de Letras) and later became a professor of History at the universities of Porto and Coimbra. He also taught in several secondary schools. He published a vast and varied work on several periods of Portuguese history, covering the Middle Ages (*D. João I*, 1917; *Como nasceu Portugal*, 1938; edition of Medieval chronicles), the seventeenth century (*A Diplomacia Portuguesa e a sucessão de Espanha*, 1931), and especially the Discovery period (*O Império Português na hora da*

Restauração, 1940; *História dos Descobrimentos Portugueses*, 1943–1946; and *O Descobrimento do Brasil por Pedro Álvares Cabral*, 1949). In the field of numismatics he also played an important part as director of the Lisbon Mint Museum and publishing several books and articles on Portuguese coins and monetary history (*História Monetária de D. João III*, 1957; *História dos Moedeiros de Lisboa* [. . .], 2 vols., 1964–1965). He edited Portugal's most important general history (*História de Portugal*, 8 vols. and one Suppl., 1928– 1938 and 1954), where he wrote several reliable chapters. His was a learned and highly objective history, always based on archival sources and therefore still useful to modern researchers.

Bibliography: Torquato de Sousa Soares, "Prof. Doutor Damião Peres," *Revista Portuguesa de História* 10 (Coimbra, 1962), pp. V–XII.

A. H. de Oliveira Marques

RAU, Virgínia (Lisbon, 1907–Lisbon, 1973), Portuguese historian. Rau obtained a Ph.D. in history at the University of Lisbon, where she taught for many years in the School of Arts (Faculdade de Letras). She worked on several areas and epochs, including prehistory (several articles, published in 1945–1953), the Middle Ages (*Subsídios para o Estudo das Feiras Medievais Portuguesas*, 1943; *Sesmarias Medievais Portuguesas*, 1946), the seventeenth century (*D. Catarina, Rainha de Inglaterra*, 1941), and the Discovery period (*O "Livro de Rezão" de António Coelho Guerreiro*, 1956; *Os Manuscritos do Arquivo da Casa Cadaval respeitantes ao Brasil*, in collaboration with Maria Fernanda Gomes da Silva, 2 vols, 1956–1958; *O Açúcar na Madeira nos fins do século XV*, in collaboration with Jorge Borges de Macedo, 1962). Well known outside of Portugal, she became a specialist in economic history, writing several monographs on the subject (*A Casa dos Contos*, 1951; *A Exploração e o Comércio do Sal de Setúbal*, 1951) and working extensively on the economic and political relations between Portugal and other countries (numerous articles, some of them collected in books: *Estudos de História Económica*, 1961; *Estudos de História*, 1968; *Estudos sobre História Económica e Social do Antigo Regime*, posthumous work, 1984). She knew well both national and foreign archives and was one of the first Portuguese scholars to develop studies on economic history at university levels and to call the attention of her students to such matters. Her vast and important work is now being collected and systematically published in books.

Bibliography: José Manuel Garcia, "Virgínia Rau—a Vida e a Obra," introduction to his edition of Virginia Rau, *Feiras Medievais Portuguesas* (Lisboa, 1982), pp. 8–29.

A. H. de Oliveira Marques

RIBEIRO, João Pedro (Porto, 1758 - Porto, 1839), Portuguese historian. Ribeiro was of lower urban origins; he was ordained a priest and later became a canon in the chapters of Porto, Viseu, and Faro cathedrals. He also studied canon law at the University of Coimbra, where he received a Ph.D. and taught diplomatics for several years. He then went to Lisbon, where he became a civil servant and taught the same subjects at the royal Torre do Tombo archives. He was the founder in Portugal of scientific diplomatics and paleography and wrote several books and articles about them: *Observações Historicas e Criticas* [. . .] (1798); *Dissertações Chronologicas e Criticas* [. . .] (5 vols., 1810–1836); *Reflecções Historicas* (2 vols, 1835–1836). He also published learned essays especially on the Middle Ages, all systematically followed by confirming documents: *Memorias para a Historia das Inquirições dos primeiros Reinados de Portugal* (1815); *Memorias para a Historia das Confirmações Regias nestes Reinos* (1816); and *Memorias Authenticas para a Historia do Real Archivo* (1819). His work was of paramount importance for the coming Portuguese historians, making possible Alexandre Herculano Araújo's (q.v.) modern historiography in the 1840s and 1850s. Besides diplomatics and palaeography, he introduced other so-called auxiliary sciences, such as chronology and sigillography in Portugal.

Bibliography: Rui Abreu Torres, "Ribeiro, João Pedro," *Dicconário de História de Portugal*, directed by Joel Serrão, vol. 3 (Lisboa, 1968), pp. 643–644; Pedro de Azevedo, "Linhas gerais da História da Diplomática em Portugal," *O Instituto* 74, no. 3 (1927): 226–242; Inocêncio Francisco da Silva, *Diccionario Bibliographico Portuguez*, vols. 4 and 10 (Lisboa, 1860–1883).

A. H. de Oliveira Marques

SANTARÉM (2nd Viscount of), Manuel Francisco Mesquita de Macedo Leitão e Carvalhosa (Lisbon, 1791–Paris, 1856), Portuguese historian. A member of the upper aristocracy, Santarém followed the royal family to Brazil (1808) when Napoleon's armies invaded and conquered Portugal. In Brazil he became interested in historical studies. A diplomat and a politician, he represented Portugal in France and in Denmark and was appointed secretary of state for home affairs (1827), navy and overseas affairs (1827), and finally foreign affairs under Miguel I (1828–1833). When the liberal army drove away Miguel's absolutist rule, the viscount of Santarém left Portugal for Paris (1834), where he died. In France he wrote most of his books, devoted to the history of Portuguese overseas expansion and the history of Portugal's foreign relations: *Memoria sobre a prioridade dos Descobrimentos Portuguezes na Costa da Africa Occidental* (1841); *Quadro Elementar das Relações Politicas de Portugal com as diversas potencias do Mundo* (10 vols., 1842–1853); *Corpo Diplomatico Portuguez* (1846); *Essai sur l'histoire des progrès de la Géographie après les grandes découvertes du XVe Siècle* (3 vols., 1849–1852), preceded and followed by an important historical *Atlas* (3 vols., 1841–1849). He was extremely critical in presenting facts and making conclusions, as a result of which his works are still valuable and useful. He ignored or discredited all sorts of legends and misconceptions, especially about the history of overseas expansion, which he tried to base on scientific grounds.

Bibliography: António Baião, *O Visconde de Santarém, Guarda-Mor da Torre do Tombo* (Lisboa, 1909); M. A. Ferreira de Almeida, *O Visconde de Santarém. Apontamentos para a sua Biographia* (Lisboa, 1903); several articles in encyclopedias and the

Dicionário de História de Portugal, directed by Joel Serrão, vol. 2 (Lisboa, 1968); Jordão de Freitas, *O 2° Visconde de Santarém e os seus Atlas Geographicos* (Lisboa, 1909).

A. H. de Oliveira Marques

Great Historians: Romanian

ANDRIESEŞCU, Ion (Jassy, 1888–Bucharest, 1944), Romanian prehistorian. Professor at the University of Bucharest (1923), warden of the National Museum of Antiquities (1927–1933). Andrieseşcu founded the Romanian school of prehistory and guided all activity in this field of research during the whole interwar period as a professor, editor-in-chief of *Dacia*, and also as editor-in-chief of the review founded on his initiative, *The Review of Prehistory and National Antiquities*. Broad-minded and open to the movement of ideas in his time, he was not fettered by any of its theses, being totally antidogmatic. "What always spoils science," he wrote, "is dogmatism." He contributed to knowledge of ancient Romanian history (*Contributie la Dacia înainte de Romani* [1912; A Contribution to Dacia before the Coming of the Romans]), to studies on the Bronze Age, the first written by a Romanian historian (*Asupra epocii de bronz în România* [1912; On the Bronze Age in Romania]; and "Nouvelles contributions sur l'âge du bronze en Roumanie," *Dacia* 2 [1925]), and to research on the later Stone Age in the South-Carpathian zone ("Les fouilles de Sultana," *Dacia* 1 [1925]). Under the impact of Gustaf Kossinna's (q.v.) school, he attempted to determine the geographical diffusion and the material culture attributed to the Tracians and the Geto-Dacians ("Les fouilles de Piscul Crăsani,"[1923]; *Asupra răspîndirii nordvestice a tracilor* [On the Northwestern Diffusion of the Tracians], 1931; "Consideratii asupra tezaurulut de la Vâlci Trân, lîngă Plevna [Considerations on the Treasure of Vâlci Trân, near Plevna]," 1925), and he thus opened a new line of research which is still pursued. He asserted, on archaeological grounds, the unity of the cultural development of the entire Carpathian-Pontic-Danubian space, therefore rejecting the ideas spread by Gordon Vincent Childe (q.v.), Paul Reinecke (q.v.), and others, who on no scientific grounds, separated Transylvania's evolution from that of the rest of Romanian territory and who made use of a special terminology ("the Hungarian Bronze") to designate the Bronze Age cultures in this zone. Emphasizing the role played by the Carpathians as a linking point and not as a borderline ("the marvellous Carpathian-Danubian bronze culture is far from being 'Hungarian', from confining itself therefore to the present territory of our neighbours' political crown. The Carpathians, now less than ever, are neither a weir nor a line separating one country from another"), as well as the unity of the Romanian space, he qualified the "Hungarian Bronze" notion as political and unscientific (*Curs de preistorie generală şi a Europei sudestice* [1937, 1938; A Course on General and South-Eastern European Prehistory]). Finally, Andrieşescu intuited and demonstrated in *De la preistorie la Evul Mediu* (1924; From Prehistory to the Middle Ages), the importance of archaeological research for the reconstruction of Romanian history from the Roman Dacia to the foundation of the first feudal states.

Bibliography: Jan Filip, *Encyklopëdisches Handbuch der Ur- und Frühgeschichte Europas* I (Prague, 1966), p. 31; Th. Sauciuc-Săveanu, "Le Professeur Ion Andrieşescu," *Dacia* 9–10 (1941–1946), Bucharest (1945), pp. 7–9.

Ligia Bârzu

BĂLCESCU, Nicolae (Bucharest, 1819–Palermo, 1852), Romanian historian and political figure. A participant in the revolutionary movement of 1840 in Wallachia, jailed between 1840 and 1843, founder of the secret society Frăţia (Brotherhood) in 1843, Bălcescu lived in Paris between 1846 and 1848, where he gathered historical material but was also politically active. He was one of the leaders of the 1848 Revolution in Wallachia, an exponent of the most radical of its demands. After the defeat of the revolution, he lived in exile, first in France, and then, seriously ill, in Italy. He may be considered the most important Romanian historian of his generation. Together with the philologist and historian August Treboniu Laurian (1810–1881), he founded the periodical *Magazin istoric pentru Dacia* (1845–1847; Historical Magazine for Dacia), in which the two historians printed, along with a series of studies, the Wallachian chronicles, which had remained unpublished until then. These were also published separately under the title *Cronicarii Ţării Româneşti* (2 vols., 1846–1847; Chroniclers of Wallachia). He wrote studies on the history of institutions, the army, and especially, social history: *Despre starea socială a muncitorilor plugari în principatele romane în deosebite timpuri* (1846; On the Social Condition of the Ploughmen in the Romanian Principalities in Different Periods); *Question économique des Principautés Danubiennes* (1850). In his analysis of the process of transforming the peasantry into serfs in medieval times, he reached the conclusion that the peasants had to be freed and allotted land. His most extensive work is *Istoria românilor sub Mihai Vodă Viteazul* (History of the Romanians under Prince Michael the Brave) (unfinished, published in part in 1861 and in its entirety in 1878). In presenting the first unification of the three Romanian states (Wallachia, Transylvania, and Moldavia) brought about by Michael the Brave in

1600, Bălcescu was giving expression to the national ideals of his times, which were marked by the struggle to create a unified state; for that reason the work has enjoyed great popularity and influence in Romanian culture. On the other hand, by criticizing the social policy of the ruler, he implicitly affirmed the need for certain radical social reforms, especially for the benefit of the peasantry. For Bălcescu, history and militant politics were two facets of the same activity, the purpose of which was to serve the progress of his country.

Bibliography: Dan Berindei, *Nicolae Bălcescu* (Bucharest, 1966, in English); Valeria Stan, *Nicolae Bălcescu* (Bucharest, 1977, in English).

Lucian Boia

BOGDAN, Ioan (Braşov, 1864–Bucharest, 1919), Romanian historian and philologist. University studies at Iaşi; then between 1887 and 1890 specialization in Slavonic languages and literature at Vienna, St. Petersburg, Moscow, Kiev, Cracow. Professor of Slavic studies at the University of Bucharest between 1891 and 1919. According to Petre P. Panaitescu (q.v.), Bogdan was "the true founder of Slavic historical studies" in Romania. (These studies had been started, but without a precise method, by Bogdan Petriceicu Hasdeu [q.v.]). He founded Slavo-Romanian philology as a distinct area of research by defining its contents and methods. He distinguished himself by his editing and rigorous interpretation of the ancient sources, which were written in Slavonic, of Romanian history, especially the first annals and chronicles: *Vechile cronice moldoveneşti pînă la Ureche* (1891; Ancient Moldavian Chronicles up to Ureche); and *Cronici inedite atingătoare de istoria românilor* (1895; Unpublished Chronicles Which Touch on Romanian History). Among his important critical editions of documents, *Documentele lui Ştefan cel Mare* (2 vols., 1913; The Documents of Stephen the Great) deserves special mention. As an editor of sources, Bogdan has remained unsurpassed in Romanian historiography and has become a model for others. He also wrote studies on social history and on Romanian medieval institutions as well as on the relations between the Romanians and various Slavic nations. In his methodical approach, Bogdan may be compared to his contemporary Dimitrie Onciul (q.v.), with whom he set the foundation of the "critical school" of Romanian historiography; he surpassed Onciul, however, through his wider understanding of history, and through his preoccupation with socioeconomic and cultural problems. In *Istoriografia română şi problemele ei actuale* (1905; Romanian Historiography and Its Current Problems), he elaborated on a program of global research of the past, which included the study of social, economic, and demographic structures, the history of institutions, of cultural life, and so on. He thus emerges as a pioneer in the "new history," not only in Romania, but also in the context of universal historiography.

Bibliography: Paul E. Michelson, "The Birth of Critical Historiography in Romania: The Contributions of Ioan Bogdan, Dimitrie Onciul, and Constantin Giurescu," *Analele Universităţii Bucureşti* (Annals of the University of Bucharest), History (1983): 59–76.

Lucian Boia

BRĂTIANU, Gheorghe I. (Ruginoasa, 1898–Sighetul Marmaţiei, 1953), Romanian historian and political figure. Studied at Iaşi and Paris. Professor of world history at the universities of Iaşi (1923–1940) and Bucharest (1940–1947) and director of the Institute for World History at Bucharest (1940–1947). The son of the famous liberal political figure, Ion I. C. Brătianu, he was an active member of the National Liberal party, and from 1930 to 1938 he led a breakaway faction of this party. He was arrested in 1950 and died in prison. Trained as a medievalist, Brătianu dealt with a wide range of subjects and was preoccupied with both world history and Romanian history from medieval times to modern times. He was a follower and successor of Nicolae Iorga (q.v.), interested, as was Iorga, in comparative history, in historical analogies and parallelisms, and in the problem of the integration of Romania's national history into world history. Influenced at the same time by new historiographic trends, he showed a special interest in socioeconomic history in the spirit of the *Annales* school, with which he maintained close ties (especially with Marc Bloch [q.v.]). He began with a study of medieval Italian commerce in the Black Sea basin (*Recherches sur le commerce génois dans la Mer Noire au XIIIᵉ siècle*, 1929), and various problems of Byzantine history: *Privilèges et franchises municipales dans l'empire byzantin*, 1936; *Etudes byzantines d'histoire économique et sociale* (1938). Also noteworthy are his contributions to the problem of the transition from antiquity to medieval times. He amended Henri Pirenne's (q.v.) thesis by arguing that a break had taken place many centuries earlier between the urban, industrial, and commercial character of the Mediterranean East on the one hand and the rural bases of the western economy on the other. Brătianu, with international collaboration, was preparing an original synthesis of European medieval history (*Une Nouvelle histoire de l'Europe au Moyen Âge*), which put far greater emphasis than had been done up to that time on the eastern part of the continent; the work was not completed as a result of the outbreak of World War II. He devoted a long time to studying the history of the Black Sea Basin and of the civilizations that followed and penetrated one another in that area. The work appeared posthumously in 1969, under the title *La Mer Noire. Des origines à la conquête ottomane*. He also wrote a book about French foreign policy in the time of Napoleon III: *Napoléon III et les nationalités*. He was preoccupied with the different ways peace was organized in the course of world history. In the field of Romanian history, he wrote on the problem of the continuity of the Romanian people and opposed immigration theories: *Une énigme et un miracle historique: le peuple roumain* (1937); on the unified character of the history of the Romanian people: *Origines et formation de l'unité roumaine* (1943); and on the formation of the Romanian states in the Middle Ages, showing himself to be a precursor in the endeavor to reappraise historical tradition: *Tradiţia istorică despre întemeierea statelor româneşti* (1945; The Historical Tradition Concerning the Foundation of the Romanian States). He researched the ''assemblies of the Estates General'' in the Romanian lands, using a comparative approach to European history: *Sfatul domnesc şi adunarea ţărilor în principatele române* (posthumous edition, 1977; The Prince's Council and the Assembly of the "Estates General" in the Romanian Principalities). He wrote a monograph on Bessarabia (*La Bassarabie*, 1943). On modern Romanian history he published the work *Acţiunea politică şi militară a României în 1919, în lumina corespondenţei diplomatice a lui Ion I. C. Brătianu* (1939; Romania's Political and Military Actions in 1919, in Light of Ion I. C. Brătianu's Diplomatic Correspondence). A victim of the communist dictatorship, Brătianu was not able to accomplish his oeuvre; even so, it remains one of the most representative of the Romanian historiography.

Bibliography: Lucian Boia, "Gheorghe I. Brătianu (1898–1953)," *Studii şi articole de istorie* (Historical Studies and Articles), 27–28 (1978); 169–173; Valeriu Râpeanu, "Gheorghe I. Brătianu," in *Cultură şi istorie* (Culture and History) (Bucharest, 1981); E. Turdeanu, "L'Oeuvre de G. I. Brătianu," *Revue des études roumaines* 7–8 (1961): 137–152; *Confluente istoriografice românesti si europene. Gheorghe I. Brătianu* (1988; Romanian and European Historiographical Confluences. G. I. B.), editor, Victor Spinei; Lucian Boia, "Tradition historiographique roumaine et 'nouvelle histoire': l'oeuvre de G. I. Brătianu," *Ibid.*, pp. 3–12.

Lucian Boia

DAICOVICIU, Constantin (Căvăran, 1898–Cluj, 1973), Romanian historian. University studies in Cluj and brushup at the Romanian School in Rome, between 1925 and 1927. Assistant professor (1928), reader (1932), and professor (1938–1968) in archaeology and ancient history of Romania at the University of Cluj, of which he was the rector between 1957 and 1968. Daicoviciu also held important political functions. Archaeologist and historian of the ancient world, he dedicated most of his activity to the investigation of the Dacian strongholds in the Orăştiei Mountains (in Transylvania), the zone where Dacia's capital Sarmizegethusa lay. The diggings which he directed contributed knowledge about pre-Roman Dacia and about the period of Roman rule in Dacia, and the formation of the Romanian people through the Daco-Roman synthesis. His master book is *La Transylvanie dans l'antiquité* (1945), followed by various works about Dacian strongholds and a number of articles referring to Romania's ancient history, gathered in the volume *Dacica* (1969). He was also a remarkable organizer of archaeological research and the founder of a school that made important contributions to molding new generations of archaeologists.

Bibliography: *In memoriam Constantini Daicovicii* (Cluj, 1974).

Lucian Boia

ELIADE, Mircea (Bucharest, 1907–Chicago, 1986), Romanian historian of religions and writer. Studies at Bucharest University, completed in India between 1928 and 1932. His Indian experience was decisive for his literary career (the novel *Maitreyi*, 1933) as well as for his scientific career. Eliade's doctoral paper, dealing with Yoga *(Essai sur les origines de la mystique indienne)*, was published in French in 1936. He taught at the University in Bucharest, starting in 1933, and then, during World War II he worked in diplomacy, as cultural attaché in London and Lisbon. After 1946 he taught in Paris and other West European cities, and in 1956 he settled in the United States as professor of the history of religions at the University of Chicago. Along with Georges Dumézil (q.v.), Eliade is the most outstanding contemporary analyst of myth and of religious phenomena. An encyclopaedic and intuitive spirit, he felt attracted to and was influenced at the beginning by the somewhat similar personality of Bogdan Petriceicu Hasdeu (q.v.), whose work he brought out in 1937 in a critical, annotated edition. Eliade's whole oeuvre is oriented to the profound, hidden zones of the spirit, without a barrier between literary fiction and the "scientific" realm. Eliade aspired after a global understanding of human spirituality, in the investigation of which he started from the dimensions of the "sacred" through a universal study of the myths, religious ideas, and beliefs. According to him, myths reflect the primordial, essential structures of a community, thus offering fundamental means of historical and cultural analysis. Of a very vast oeuvre, the following represent only a few titles: *Traité d'histoire des religions* (1949); *Le mythe de l'éternel retour* (1949); *Myth and Reality* (1963); *De Zalmoxis à Gengis-Khan* (1970); *Australian Religions* (1973); *Histoire des croyances et des idées religieuses*, 3 vols. (1976–1983).

Bibliography: Thomas J. J. Altizer, *Mircea Eliade and the Dialectic of the Sacred* (Philadelphia, 1963); *Cahiers de l'Herne Mircea Eliade* (Paris, 1978); *Imagination and Meaning. The Scholarly and Literary Worlds of Mircea Eliade*, ed. Norman J. Girardot and MacLinscott Ricketts (New York, 1982); John A. Saliba, "Homo religiosus," in *Mircea Eliade* (Leyden, 1976).

Lucian Boia

GIURESCU, Constantin (Chiojd, 1875–Bucharest, 1918), Romanian historian. University studies at Bucharest, under the direction of Dimitrie Onciul (q.v.), later becoming a faithful practitioner of the critical method promoted by Onciul. Continued his studies at Vienna between 1903 and 1906. From 1912 on Giurescu was lecturer in Romanian history at the University of Bucharest. He made important contributions to the study of the Romanian chronicles by publishing several critical editions and a series of original interpretations of these documents: *Contribuţiuni la studiul cronicilor muntene* (1906; Contributions to the Study of the Wallachian Chronicles); and *Contribuţiuni la studiul cronicilor moldovene* (1907; Contributions to the Study of the Moldavian Chronicles). Through his subtle analysis of Romanian-Ottoman relations in medieval times, he reached new conclusions about the nature of these relations: *Capitulaţiile Moldovei cu Poarta Otomană* (1908; Capitulations of Moldavia to the Ottoman Porte). He studied the period of Austrian domination in Oltenia (1718–1739) on the basis of documents from the Vienna archives, which he gathered in *Material pentru istoria Olteniei supt austrieci* (3 vols., 1913–1944; Material for the History of Oltenia Under the Austrians). In the last period of his career he devoted himself to the problems of the social history of the Romanian states in medieval times and published studies distinguished by the excellence of the information they contained and by their logic and able presentation: *Vechimea rumâniei în Ţara*

Româneasca şi legătura lui Mihai Viteazul (1915; The Antiquity of Serfdom in Wallachia and the Convention of Michael the Brave); *Despre rumâni* (1916; About Serfs); *Despre boieri* (1920; About Boyars). He proved, among other things, the existence of a dependent peasantry before the foundation of the Romanian states in the fourteenth century (contrary to current opinions that binding the peasants to the land was legislated in Wallachia only in 1595).

Bibliography: Paul E. Michelson, "The Birth of Critical Historiography in Romania: The Contributions of Ioan Bogdan, Dimitrie Onciul, and Constantin Giurescu," *Analele Universităţii Bucureşti* (Annals of the University of Bucharest), (1983): 59–76.

Lucian Boia

GIURESCU, Constantin C. (Focşani, 1901–Bucharest, 1977), Romanian historian. Son of Constantin Giurescu (q.v.) Professor of Romanian history at the University of Bucharest, 1926–1948 and 1963–1975. In his many specialized works and syntheses, Giurescu dealt with almost all aspects of Romanian history; he was especially interested in political and institutional history. His method is noteworthy for its thorough establishing of facts, based on vast documentary material. His basic work, which enjoyed wide appreciation, is *Istoria românilor* (5 vols., 1935–1946; History of the Romanians), (up to the year 1821); a new edition (together with Dinu Giurescu), unfinished, was begun in 1974; and a synthesis appeared in one volume in 1943 and, together with Dinu Giurescu, in 1971 and 1975. Other works include *Contribuţiuni la studiul marilor dregătorii în secolele XIV–XV* (1926; Contributions to the Study of the High Political Offices in the Fourteenth and Fifteenth Centuries); *Viaţa şi opera lui Cuza Vodă* (1966; The Life and Works of Prince Cuza); *Istoria Bucureştilor* (1967) (English edition: *History of Bucharest*, 1976); *Tîrguri sau oraşe şi cetăţi moldovene din secolul al X-lea pîna la mijlocul secolului at XVI–lea* (1967; Moldavian Market Towns or Cities and Fortified Towns of the Tenth to the Midsixteenth Centuries); *Transylvania in the History of the Romanian People* (1968); *The Making of the Romanian Unitary State* (1971); *The Making of the Romanian People and Language* (1972); *Contribuţiuni la studiul originilor şi dezvoltării burgheziei române pînă la 1848* (1972; Contributions to the Study of the Origins and Development of the Romanian Bourgeoisie up to 1848); *Contributions to the History of Romanian Science and Technique* (1974); *Probleme controversate ale istoriografiei româneşti* (1977; Controversial Problems in Romanian Historiography); *A History of the Romanian Forest* (1980).

Bibliography: Paul E. Michelson, "The Master of Synthesis: Constantin C. Giurescu and the Coming of Age of Romanian Historiography, 1919–1947," in *Romania Between East and West: Historical Essays in Memory of Constantin C. Giurescu* (New York and Boulder, Colo., 1982); Al. Zub, "Constantin C. Giurescu und der Ursprung seiner Synthese des rumänischen Geschichte," *Südost-Forschungen* (Munich) 38 (1979): 191–206.

Lucian Boia

HASDEU, Bogdan Petriceicu (Cristineşti, Bessarabia, 1838–Cîmpina, 1907), Romanian historian, philologist, linguist, and writer. Not having completed his studies in law at Kharkov, Hasdeu moved to Moldavia in 1857 and then to Bucharest in 1863. He was professor of comparative philology at the University of Bucharest (1874–1900) and director of the State Archives (1876–1899). He was a polyglot, a remarkable Slavicist, the editor of Romanian and foreign sources: *Arhiva istorică a României* (4 vols., 1864–1867; Historical Archive of Romania). Of his early historical works, *Ioan Vodă cel Cumplit (1572–1574)* (1865; Prince John the Terrible [1572–1574]), a monograph on the Moldavian ruler, enjoyed great success. Hasdeu contributed substantially to extending the field of history and its methods of research by promoting interdisciplinary studies and especially by using linguistics along with other sciences: anthropology, biology, folklore, political economy. This approach appears in his unfinished work, *Istoria critică a românilor* (2 vols., 1873–1875; Critical History of the Romanians), in which he tried to reconstruct, giving an overall view, the civilization that existed on Romanian territory from antiquity to the fourteenth century. In an original manner he stressed the evolution of the relationship of society with the environment. He assigned special importance to the Dacian substratum of the Romanian people and through subtle deductions tried to determine the Dacian elements in the Romanian language, something that had not been considered until then. He tried to construct a personal system of philosophy of history by combining material, spiritual, and deistic elements and suggesting that an equilibrium existed between the objective laws of nature, Providence, and free will. In the second part of his career, he devoted himself especially to linguistics, which, however, he studied in close connection with history; he tried through etymology to bring light to the obscure periods of early Romanian history. The most important result of these efforts is the *Etymologicum Magnum Romaniae* (3 vols., 1886–1893), an etymological dictionary of the Romanian language, conceived on a huge scale, of which Hasdeu completed only letter A and a part of letter B. He launched the theory of the value of the circulation of words by defining the profile of a language not through the number of words of different origins it possesses, but through the frequency with which these words are used (which makes Romanian, regardless of its brute number of words, a Romance language and English a Germanic language). Hasdeu's work combines hazardous, often fanciful, hypotheses with productive, innovative ideas. The result is a synthesis of the romantic spirit with positive research.

Bibliography: Lucian Boia, "Littérature et histoire dans l'oeuvre de B. P. Hasdeu," *Synthesis* (Bucharest), 6 (1979): 85–92.

Lucian Boia

IORGA, Nicolae (Botoşani, 1871–Strejnic, near Ploieşti, 1940), Romanian historian, writer, journalist, and political figure. The bulk and variety of Iorga's writings are unique in world literature: almost fourteen hundred books and pamphlets, nearly twenty thousand articles on history, literature, and politics. University studies at Iaşi, additional studies in Paris during 1890–1893 at the Ecole pratique des hautes études as a student of Gabriel Monod (q.v.) and Ch. Bémont. Iorga received a diploma from this school on the basis of his thesis "Philippe de Mézières, 1337–1405, et la croisade au XIVe siècle" (1896); he was granted a doctorate at Leipzig with his thesis "Thomas III, marquis de Saluces," (1893). He was professor of world history at the University of Bucharest (1894–1940). In the political sphere Iorga was an animating force of national life, of the struggle for a united Romanian state, a struggle that ended with the creation of Greater Romania in 1918. He ran the newspaper *Neamul românesc* (1906–1940; The Romanian People); he created the Nationalist Democratic party in 1910; he was president of parliament in 1919 and prime minister in 1931–1932. Because of his struggles against the Romanian fascist organization, the Iron Guard, and his opposition to Nazi expansionist tendencies, he was killed by Iron Guardists on November 27, 1940. Iorga understood history as an organic process; he was a proponent of the unity of world history, in the center of which he placed nations, which he considered "necessary and permanent creations." He did not accept the division of history, for "there exists only one development, and all aspects of life are encompassed within it." He thought that to write history requires intuition, poetic talent even. It was impossible otherwise to make the past come to life. His theoretical works are contained in *Generalităţi cu privire la studiile istorice* (General Comments on Historical Studies), published in 1911, 1933, 1944. He studied all aspects of Romanian history, publishing some thirty thousand documents, especially in the collection *Studii şi documente cu privire la istoria românilor* (31 vols., 1901–1916; Studies and Documents Concerning the History of the Romanian People), and countless monographs and syntheses: *Istoria literaturii române în secolul al XVIII-lea* (1901; History of Romanian Literature in the Eighteenth Century); *Istoria bisericii române* (2 vols., 1908–1909; History of the Romanian Church), *Istoria armatei române* (2 vols., 1910–1919; History of the Romanian Army); *Istoria comerţului românesc* (1915; History of Romanian Commerce), *Istoria românilor din Ardeal şi Ungaria* (1915; History of the Romanians of Transylvania and Hungary; French edition: *Histoire des Roumains de Transylvanie et de Hongrie*, (1915–1916); *Istoria românilor prin călători* (4 vols., 1920–1922; History of the Romanians Through the Eyes of Travelers); *Războiul pentru independenţa României* (1927; The War for the Independence of Romania); *Istoria lui Mihai Viteazul* (2 vols., 1935; The History of Michael the Brave); *La place des Roumains dans l'histoire universelle* (3 vols., 1935–1936); *Istoria Bucureştilor* (1939; The History of Bucharest).

Among Iorga's general works on national history the following are the most important: *Geschichte des rumänischen Volkes*, (2 vols., 1905); *Histoire des Roumains et de leur civilisation* (1920) (English edition: *A History of Romania: Land, People, Civilization*, 1925); *Istoria românilor*, (10 vols., 1936–1939), (French edition: *Histoire des Roumains et de la romanité orientale*, 1937–1945). He made important contributions to the study of the Byzantine Empire, in whose civilization he saw a viable synthesis, which continued to exist even after the fall of Constantinople: (*The Byzantine Empire*, 1907; *Histoire de la vie byzantine*, 3 vols., 1934; *Byzance après Byzance*, 1935; and to the study of the history of the Ottoman Empire, which he considered to a certain extent the continuation of the Byzantine Empire (*Geschichte des Osmanischen Reiches*, 5 vols., 1908–1913). He published works on the history of the Crusades: *Notes et extraits pour servir à l'histoire des croisades au XVᵉ siècle* (6 vols., 1899–1916); *Brève histoire des croisades* (1924); on the history of relations between East and West: *Relations entre l'Orient et l'Occident au moyen-âge* (1923); on the history of the Balkan nations: *Histoire des Etats balcaniques jusqu'à 1924* (1925); on the history of France, *Histoire du peuple français*, Romanian edition in 1919, French edition in 1945; on the history of Italy as well as other European nations. He became interested in American history and culture after traveling to the United States in 1930: *America şi românii din America* (1930; America and the Romanian Americans). He wrote several general works on world history, culminating with *Essai de synthèse de l'histoire de l'humanité* (4 vols., 1926–1928), in which he tried to give a totally integrated presentation of world history as opposed to separate accounts of the various nations and civilizations. Wishing to emphasize the "absolute unity of human life at any point in space or time," he set about preparing a large work, *Istoriologia umană* (Human Historiology), centered on "historical similarities, parallelisms and repetitions." His tragic death prevented the completion of this project. Iorga's work, astonishing in its erudition, variety, and creative imagination, is the most important Romanian contribution to world historiography.

Bibliography: *Nicolas Iorga. L'homme et l'oeuvre*, recueil édité par D. M. Pippidi (Bucharest, 1972); Bianca Valota Cavallotti, *Nicola Iorga* (Naples, 1977); Barbu Theodorescu, *Nicolae Iorga. Biobibliografie* (Bucharest, 1976).

Lucian Boia

KOGĂLNICEANU, Mihail (Iaşi, 1817–Paris, 1891), Romanian historian and political figure. A member of a noble family, Kogălniceanu studied at Lunéville (1834–1835), and then at Berlin (1835–1838), where he attended lectures by Leopold von Ranke (q.v.) and Friedrich C. Savigny (q.v.). At Berlin in 1837 he published three works, one on the Romanian language and literature (*Romänische oder Wallachische Sprache und Literatur*), another on the gypsies (*Esquisse sur l'histoire, les moeurs et la langue des Cigains*), and a third, his principal work (*Histoire de la Valachie, de la Moldavie et des Valaques transdanubiens*). This work, conceived in a profoundly national Romanian spirit, set out to familiarize outsiders with Romanian history. After returning to Moldavia, he edited *Arhiva românească* (1841–1845; Romanian Archive), the first historical periodical to appear in Romania. Then between 1845 and 1852 he published in three volumes *Letopiseţele Ţării Moldovei* (The Chronicles of Moldavia), the first edition of the Moldavian chronicles, which until then had been preserved in manuscripts (new edition, 1872–1874). He also published in French, *Fragments tirés des Chroniques moldaves et valaques pour servir à l'histoire de*

Pierre le Grand, Charles XII, Stanislas Leszczynski, Démètre Cantemir et Constantin Brancovan (1845). In his opening address to the course in national history held at the Michael Academy in Iaşi in 1843–1844, he formulated a program of militant national history, which would underscore the unity of the Romanian people. In the second half of his life, Kogălniceanu dedicated himself almost exclusively to political activities. He played an important role in the 1848 Revolution and, in 1859, in the unification of Wallachia and Moldavia, a union that gave birth to the Romanian state. He was prime minister in the years 1863–1865; together with Prince Cuza, he was responsible for a series of reforms, which became the basis of the modern Romanian state. He was foreign minister during the war of independence (1877–1878).

Bibliography: Nicolae Ciachir and Constantin Buşe, *Mihail Kogălniceanu* (Bucharest [in English], 1967); Al. Zub, *Mihail Kogălniceanu, Biobibliografie* (Biobibliography), (Bucharest, 1971); Al. Zub, *Mihail Kogălniceanu istoric* (Mihail Kogălniceanu Historian), (Iaşi, 1974); Al. Zub, *Mihail Kogălniceanu, un fondateur de la Roumanie moderne* (Bucharest, 1978).

Lucian Boia

LUPAŞ, Ioan (Sălişte, 1880–Bucharest, 1967), Romanian historian. Lupaş began his career in Transylvania, which was then still under Austro-Hungarian rule, as a professor at the Orthodox seminary in Sibiu (1906–1909) and as the archpriest of Sălişte (1909–1919). After the union of Transylvania with Romania (1918), he became professor of Romanian history at the University of Cluj (1919–1946); there he also organized and headed the Institute of Romanian National History (1920–1945). Lupaş studied the most diverse aspects of Transylvanian history from the Middle Ages to modern times: *Mitropolitul Andrei Şaguna* (1909; Metropolitan Bishop Andrei Şaguna); *Istoria bisericească a românilor ardeleni* (1918; Church History of the Transylvanian Romanians); *Cronicari şi istorici români din Transilvania* (1933; Romanian Chroniclers and Historians of Transylvania); *Răscoala ţăranilor din Transilvania la anul 1784* (1934; The Peasant Uprising in Transylvania in 1784); *Voievodatul Transilvaniei în secolele XII–XIII* (1936–1937; The Principality of Transylvania in the Twelfth and Thirteenth Centuries). His main contributions concerned the organization of Transylvanian institutions in the Middle Ages, Church history, cultural history, and the Romanian national movement. Lupaş insisted on the complete integration of Transylvanian history into Romanian history and, in general, on the unity of the Romanian people throughout their evolution, as he traced the manner in which the Romanian nation and the united Romanian state was formed: *Istoria unirii românilor* (1937; History of the Unification of Romania). According to his demonstration, Greater Romania, the unification of which was completed in 1918, is based on a geographical, ethnic, linguistic, religious, and cultural unity, on the entire common history of the Romanians. In Lupaş's view, historical evolution centers in the first place around the national factor. He also published in German a series of studies on Romanian history: *Zur Geschichte der Rumänen*.

Aufsätze und Vorträge (1943). Lupaş was the uncontested head of the Cluj school of history between the two world wars.

Bibliography: *Omagiu lui Ioan Lupaş la împlinirea vîrstei de 60 de ani* (In Honor of Ioan Lupaş at the Age of 60), (Bucharest, 1943).

Lucian Boia

NESTOR, Ion (Focşani, 1905–Bucharest, 1974), Romanian pre- and protohistorian. Professor at the University of Bucharest (1945–1973) and warden of the National Museum of Antiquities (1947–1951), Nestor was one of the most prominent personalities of Romanian historiography, contributing to the reorientation of Romanian archaeological research and to the creation of a national school for the first millennium and medieval archaeology. A man of great intellect, he introduced a modern, European vision into Romanian archaeology. Gifted with rare intuition and an acute sense of scientific rigor, he wrote the third great synthesis on Romanian prehistory and protohistory, following Ion Andriesescu (q.v.) and Vasile Parvan (q.v.): *Der Stand der Vorgeschichts Forschung in Rumänien* (1933). He differed from his predecessors in the vastness of the problems he dealt with (from the Old Stone Age to the Roman epoch), in his consistent use of modern concepts, in the balance of his interpretation, and especially in the sharp criticism of incorrect interpretations concerning the various cultural aspects in the Carpathian-Pontic-Danubian region. His intellectual qualities were brilliantly demonstrated in the chapters he wrote for the first volume of *History of Romania* and by his contribution to the volume, *Storia del popolo romeno* (1971; History of the Romanian People), and to *Istoria societătii primitive* (1970; History of Primitive Society).

Bibliography: M. Babeş, "Ion Nestor," *Acta archaeologica Carpathica* (1975): 257–258; Jan Filip, *Encyklopädisches Handbuch der Ur- und Frühgeschichte Europas* 2 (Prague, 1967), p. 893; G. Stefan, "Ion Nestor, (1905–1974)," *Dacia*, N. S. 19 (1975): 5–7, with a list of works (M. Babeş), pp. 7–9.

Ligia Bârzu

ODOBESCU, Alexandru (Bucharest, 1834–Bucharest, 1895), Romanian archaeologist and protohistorian. Professor at the University of Bucharest (1874). Odobescu occupies a leading place in Romanian historiography as a man of encyclopaedic training, as the first professor of archaeology at a Romanian university, as a researcher who strove to raise his work to the level of real science, and finally as author of numerous studies on his speciality. Although he accepted the notion that archaeology has a historical character ("Walking side by side with history, archaeology itself throws light on history, explains it, lends color and emotion to it, revives it and completes it"), he did not transcend J. Winckelmann's (1717–1768) thesis, according to which archaeology was a history of art: "the place that [archaeology] deserves, as a science completing history, is similar to that 'the good' and especially 'the beautiful' hold near the truth" or "as a history of the fine arts of ancient times." Odobescu's name is connected with a series of studies that culminated in his outstanding paper on the treasure of Pietroasa, published in Paris, partly posthumously, *Le trésor de Petrossa. Historique-Description. Études sur l'orfévrerie antique* (1889–1900; critical edition, Bucharest, 1976, in Alexandru Odobescu, *Works*, IV). Although some of his conclusions have been refuted, most of his hypotheses have retained their validity.

Bibliography: M. Babeş, "Odobescu şi tezaurul de la Pietroasa (Odobescu and the Treasure of Pietroasa)," in *Alexandru Odobescu, Opere IV, Tezaurul de la Pietroasa* (Works IV, The Treasure of Pietroasa), (Bucharest, 1976), pp. 5–34, with a list of papers by Odobescu on the treasure of Pietroasa, pp.34–40; D. Tudor, "Alexandru I. Odobescu arheolog (Alexandru I. Odobescu, Archaeologist)," in *Istoria archeologiei* (History of Archaeology), (Bucharest, 1961), pp. 7–46, with a bibliography, pp. 47–51.

Ligia Bârzu

ONCIUL, Dimitrie (Straja, Bucovina, 1856–Bucharest, 1923), Romanian historian. Studied at the University of Cernăuţi (Chernovtsy) and then specialized at Vienna during 1879–1881. Professor at the Lyceum and the Normal School in Cernăuţi, then from 1896 until his death, professor of Romanian history at the University of Bucharest. Director of the State Archives (1900–1923). Disciple of the Austrian historian, Ottokar Lorenz (q.v.), and influenced by the German and Austrian schools of history, he contributed substantially to the introduction in Romanian historiography of a new method of critical and rigorous research. His seminar became the nucleus of a school of history with precise rules of investigation, in opposition to the romanticism of the preceding period. A very scrupulous historian, in large measure dedicated to education and to the organization of historical studies, he has left behind a rather limited work, most of it written in his youth. His studies are distinguished by solid documentation and logical argumentation. Onciul made important contributions with original viewpoints to two important problems of Romanian history: first, the origins and continuity of the Romanian people, where he maintained in *Teoria lui Rösler* (1885: Rösler's Theory), a study that began where Alexandru D. Xenopol's (q.v.) work of the same name left off, the theory of "admigration": that the formation of the Romanian people occurred equally north and south of the Danube, and that there were permanent human contacts between these zones; second, the foundation of the Romanian states in medieval times: various studies, later gathered in the volume *Originile Principatelor române* (1899; Origins of the Romanian Principalities). A typical exponent of the critical school and an essentially political historian who based his work on the analysis of written sources, Onciul showed little understanding of socioeconomic history or the history of civilization; that is why his attempts at synthesis—*Din istoria României* (1908; From the History of Romania)—are not convincing.

Bibliography: Teodor Bălan, *Dimitrie Onciul* (Cernăuţi, 1938); Paul E. Michelson, "The Birth of Critical Historiography in Romania: The Contributions of Ioan Bogdan,

Dimitrie Onciul, and Constantin Giurescu,'' *Analele Universităţii Bucureşti* (Annals of the University of Bucharest),(1983): 59–76.

Lucian Boia

OŢETEA, Andrei (Sibiel, 1894–Paris, 1977), Romanian historian. University studies in Paris. Lecturer (1927), then professor (1934) at the University in Iaşi, and between 1947 and 1964 professor at the University of Bucharest and director (1956–1970) of the N. Iorga Institute of History. In Paris Oţetea delivered a doctoral thesis on Guicciardini: *François Guichardin. Sa vie publique et sa pensée politique*, 1926. He also wrote on the Oriental question (*Contribution à la Question d'Orient*, 1930), as well as a synthesis on the Renaissance: *Renaşterea şi Reforma* (1941; The Renaissance and the Reform), in which he offered a markedly social-economic interpretation of that phenomenon. After World War II he concentrated on Romanian history in the modern era as viewed from a European perspective. *Tudor Vladimirescu şi mişcarea eteristă în ţările române* (1945; Tudor Vladimirescu and the Hetairist Movement in the Romanian Principalities) is a minute presentation of the relations between the 1821 Romanian Revolution and the Greeks' liberation movement. Interested in the "passage from feudalism to capitalism" in Romanian society, Oţetea sustained the phenomenon of the "second serfdom," integrating the Romanian countries' social history into a wide East European area. Characteristic of his work are the analyses of socioeconomic factors and the investigation of the national-universal relation. He edited the synthesis *Istoria poporului român* (1970; The History of the Romanian People), of which an American edition was also put out in 1974.

Bibliography: Andrei Oţetea, *Scrieri istorice alese* (Selected Historical Writings), edited and introductory survey by Florin Constantiniu and Şerban Papacostea (Cluj, 1980).

Lucian Boia

PANAITESCU, Petre P. (Iaşi, 1900–Bucharest, 1967), Romanian historian. Lecturer (1927–1932) and professor (1932–1941) of Slavic history at the University of Bucharest. Between 1954 and 1965, a researcher at the N. Iorga Historical Institute in Bucharest. Panaitescu was a remarkable Slavicist and continued the research begun by Ioan Bogdan (q.v.); among other things he studied old Romanian culture and Romanian-Slavic cultural relations, especially those between Romanian and Polish culture: *Nicolas Spathar Milescu (1636–1708)*, (1925); *Influenţa polonă în opera şi personalitatea cronicarilor Grigore Ureche şi Miron Costin* (1925; Polish Influence in the Works and Personalities of the Chroniclers Grigore Ureche and Miron Costin); *Emigraţia polonă şi revoluţia română de la 1848* (1929; Polish Emigration and the Romanian Revolution of 1848); *Călători poloni în ţările române* (1930; Polish Travelers in the Romanian Lands). His articles and monographs devoted to the Romanian Middle Ages and, to a certain extent, to the modern age, show him to be an erudite and original historian who possessed the power of both analysis and synthesis, and who was concerned with the evolution of ideas and of world-views as well as with socioeconomic and institutional structures. He insisted on the important role played by economic and social factors in interpreting history as a whole. Two monographs are devoted to the history of Wallachia during the rules of Mircea the Old (1386–1418) and Michael the Brave (1593–1601): *Mihai Viteazul* (1936; Michael the Brave); *Mircea cel Batrîn* (1944; Mircea the Old). Other works include *Interpretări românești, studii de istorie economică și socială* (1947; Romanian Interpretations, Studies in Social and Economic History); *Viața feudală în Țara Românească și Moldova* (1958; Feudal Life in Wallachia and Moldavia), in collaboration; *Dimitrie Cantemir. Viața și opera* (1958; Dimitrie Cantemir. Life and Works); *Obștea țaranească în Țara Românească și Moldova* (1964; The Peasant Community in Wallachia and Moldavia); *Inceputurile și biruința scrisului în limba română* (1965; The Beginning and Triumph of Writing in the Romanian Language); *Introducere la istoria culturii românești* (1969; Introduction to the History of Romanian Culture), German edition: *Einführung in die Geschichte des rumänischen Kultur* (1977). He was also a remarkable editor of medieval chronicles and documents.

Bibliography: Ștefan Gorovei, "Petre P. Panaitescu—coordonate ale unei evoluții" (Petre P. Panaitescu—the Coordinates of an Evolution), in *Anuarul Institutului de istorie și arheologie A. D. Xenopol* (Yearbook of the A. D. Xenopol Institute of History and Archeology), (Iași, 1982), pp. 499–523.

Lucian Boia

PÂRVAN, Vasile (Perchiu, 1882–Bucharest, 1927), Romanian historian. After studies at the University of Bucharest and an initial activity devoted to the Romanian Middle Ages in general (under the influence of Dimitrie Onciul, q.v.) Pârvan specialized in ancient history at the German universities of Jena, Berlin, and Breslau between 1904 and 1909. His doctoral thesis was entitled "Die Nationalität der Kaufleute im römischen Kaiserreiche" (1909). From 1909 on, he was professor of ancient history and epigraphy at the University of Bucharest. At first he concerned himself with the general history of the Roman Empire and published a monograph on Marcus Aurelius, *M. Aurelius Verus Caesar și L. Aurelius Commodus* (M. Aurelius Verus Caesar and L. Aurelius Commodus), in 1909, the same year his doctoral thesis was published. Then he turned to the history of Roman Dacia and brought important contributions to the problem of the Romanization of the Dacians: *Contribuții epigrafice la istoria creștinismului daco-roman* (1911; Epigraphical Contributions to the History of Daco-Roman Christianity); *Inceputurile vieții romane la gurile Dunării* (1923; The Beginnings of Roman Life at the Mouth of the Danube). As an archaeologist he carried out digs in the Dobrogea, at the Romano-Byzantine citadel Ulmetum (between 1911 and 1914) and especially at the Greek citadel Histria; the excavation begun here in 1914 and conducted by him until his death constitutes one of the most beautiful achievements of Romanian archaeology. After World War I Pârvan enlarged the extent of his excavations into the Danube Plain and concentrated his efforts on the reconstruction of the Geto-Dacian civilization (from about 1000 B.C. to the

Roman conquest of A.D. 106). The result was the monumental monograph *Getica. O protoistorie a Daciei* (1926; Getica. A Protohistory of Dacia). Relying on very extensive material, part of which he himself discovered in the course of his archaeological excavations, Pârvan created a total synthesis of the material and spiritual culture, and of the history of the Geto-Dacians. At the same time he insisted on the gradual "Westernization" of Dacia, such that in A.D. 106 the region was ready to assimilate Latin culture and language. These problems are also covered in the work published in English in 1928, *Dacia. An Outline of the Early Civilizations of the Carpatho-Danubian Countries*. Pârvan was a historian of ideas who tried, starting from raw archaeological material, to reconstruct a civilization in its totality, especially the spiritual life of an epoch. He also wrote works on the theory of history: *Idei şi forme istorice* (1920; Historical Ideas and Forms), and *Memoriale* (1923; Memorials), where he placed the accent on spiritual factors and on the cultural significance of historical facts. Pârvan remains above all the true founder of the Romanian school of archaeology, which has generally developed along the lines he drew out.

Bibliography: Al. Zub, *Les dilemmes d'un historien: Vasile Pârvan (1882–1927)* (Bucharest, 1985).

Lucian Boia

ŞINCAI, Gheorghe (Rîciu, 1754–Şinca, 1816), Romanian historian from Transylvania. Şincai can be considered the most important historian of the Transylvanian School, a cultural and national movement of Transylvanian Romanians under Habsburg rule. His works, like those of Samuil Micu (1745–1806) and Petru Maior (1760–1821), who were erudite and militant at the same time, illustrate the effort of the Transylvanian School to find in the study of history and philology arguments for defending the political rights of the Romanians. Following his studies at the De Propaganda Fide school in Rome (1774–1779) and at Vienna (1779–1782), Sincai became director of the Romanian Greek-Catholic schools in Transylvania; he succeeded in raising the number of these schools to 300. He got into conflict with church authorities, however, and lost his post. Between 1804 and 1808 he worked at the printing office of the University of Buda; his final years were difficult. In spite of a difficult, even dramatic life, the remarkably erudite Şincai was able to write his extensive work, *Hronica românilor şi a mai multor neamuri* (Chronicle of the Romanians and Other Peoples). In his lifetime, however, he was unable to publish more than a fragment of it, in 1808–1809; the first complete edition was not published until 1853–1854, in three volumes. The work is based on a huge amount of material, most of it unpublished, gathered in the course of an entire lifetime. It is a complete, extremely detailed, and unified history of the Romanian people from the beginning of the Daco-Roman wars (A.D. 86) to the year 1739. Conceived in a profoundly national spirit, the work underscores the pure Latin origin, continuity, and unity of the Romanian people, and their struggle for independence. It remained the principal overview of Romanian history until Alexandru Xenopol

(q.v.) published his work at the end of the nineteenth century. Together with
S. Micu, Şincai published *Elementa linguae Daco-Romanae sive Valachicae*
(1780), a Romanian grammar, that demonstrates the Latinist tendencies of the
Transylvanian School.

Bibliography: Mircea Tomuş, *Gheorghe Şincai. Viaţa şi opera* (Gheorghe Şincai. Life
and Works), (Bucharest, 1965).

Lucian Boia

XENOPOL, Alexandru D. (Iaşi, 1847–Bucharest, 1920), Romanian historian.
After studying philosophy and law in Germany at the universities of Berlin and
Giessen (1867–1871), Xenopol worked first as a public prosecutor and then as
an attorney-at-law for the court in Iaşi. In 1883 he became a professor of Romanian history at the University of Iaşi. He distinguished himself at a very young
age with his articles on the philosophy of history, which were published in
Convorbiri literare (Literary Conversations), a periodical published by Junimea
(The Youth), the most important cultural society in Romania at that time. (Later,
he would dissociate himself from it.) Of these early works, the most important
is "Istoriile civilizaţiunii" (1869; Histories of Civilization), an analysis of the
works of François Guizot (q.v.), W. E. H. Lecky (q.v.), J. W. Draper (q.v.),
and especially Henry Thomas Buckle (q.v.). Influenced by positivist philosophy,
Xenopol conceived of history as a social science governed by laws, but he
criticized Buckle's extreme view, which likened history to the natural sciences.
Xenopol thought that the laws of history were, in the first place, psychological
and that "the basis of scientific history is the psychology of nations." The work
of his later years concentrates on both Romanian history and theoretical problems
of history. His works are distinguished for their spirit of synthesis and for their
logic and clarity. His first extensive historical work was *Războaiele dintre ruşi
şi turci şi înrîurirea lor asupra ţărilor române* (2 vols., 1880; The Wars Between
the Russians and the Turks and Their Influence on the Romanian Lands), followed
by *Teoria lui Rösler. Studii asupra stăruinţii românilor în Dacia Traiană* (1884;
Rösler's Theory. Studies on the Continuity of the Romanians in Trajan Dacia),
(and in French: *Une énigme historique. Les Roumains au Moyen-Âge*, 1885),
which argues for the continuity of the Romanians north of the Danube. His major
work is *Istoria românilor din Dacia Traiană* (6 vols., 1888–1893; The History
of the Romanians in Trajan Dacia), (and an abridged French edition: *Histoire
des Roumains de la Dacie Trajane*, 2 vols., 1896), the first modern synthesis
of Romanian history (until 1859) which makes good use of all the documentary
material published up to that time. Alongside political history, which predominated, he included special chapters on social and economic life, institutions and
law, administration, culture, and so on. Other historical works on the Romanians
include *Domnia lui Cuza Vodă* (2 vols., 1903; The Reign of Prince Cuza) (which
continues *Istoria românilor* through the period 1859–1866, when modern Romania was formed); *Istoria partidelor politice în România* (1910–1911; The
History of the Political Parties in Romania). In the field of philosophy of history,

Xenopol published *Les Principes fondamentaux de l'histoire* (Paris, 1899), a revised version of which was completed and published in 1908 under the title *La Théorie de l'histoire*. Moving away from positivist philosophy, he thought two branches of science existed: the sciences of coexistence and the sciences of succession. The second branch, which includes history, covers events that are never repeated in an identical manner. For this reason, history could never be subject to laws. "Coexistence gives birth to laws, succession to series," he asserted, judging that individual, unrepeatable historical events should be organized in series (chains of occurrences, which connect historical events in cause and effect relationships). As to the causes of historical evolution, he believed that there existed, along with certain constant factors such as race and physical environment, an indefinite evolutionary force and, alongside it, certain auxiliary forces: the intellectual sphere, survival instinct, individuality, and chance. Outstanding is Xenopol's effort to prove that history is a science, moreover, that it has its own characteristics and methods of investigation, that the laws and methods of natural science cannot be applied to it mechanically, as certain positivists (Buckle, in particular) tried to do. In this respect his approach is similar to that taken by his German contemporaries W. Windelband and H. Rickert.

Bibliography: Al. Zub, *L'historiographie roumaine à l'age de synthèse: A. D. Xenopol* (Bucharest, 1983).

Lucian Boia

Great Historians: Russian and Soviet

ARTSIKHOVSKY, Artemy Vladimirovich (St. Petersburg, 1902—Moscow, 1978), Soviet historian and archaeologist. Graduated from Moscow University in 1925. In 1929 Artsikhovsky completed his postgraduate studies at the Research Institute of Archaeology and Art Studies of the Russian Association of Social Science Research Institutions, defending his candidate's thesis *Kurgany vyatichei* (The Barrows of the Vyatichi), published in Moscow in 1930. He was a researcher for the Museum of History in Moscow (1925–1938); an associate with Moscow University (1927–1931) and with the Institute of the History of Material Culture of the USSR Academy of Sciences (Institute of Archaeology) (1931–1960); from 1937, professor of the chair of archaeology at Moscow University's Department of History, head of the chair (1939–1978); editor-in-chief of the journal *Sovetskaya arkheologiya* (Soviet Archaeology) (1956–1978); and corresponding Member of the USSR Academy of Sciences (1960). His principal works fall into three cycles. Of greatest significance for the study of Barrow antiquities of the Eastern Slavs (above all, the Vyatichi) are the chronological classificatory systems of antiquities for reconstructing the social characteristics of the tribal and territorial communities in the ninth through twelfth centuries. The university lecture courses *Vedeniye v arkheologiyu* (1940, 1941, and 1947; Introduction to Archaeology) and *Osnovy arkheologii* (1954 and 1955; Fundamentals of Archeology) provided an insight into the law-governed development patterns of human society. The first of these lecture courses summarized for the first time in the practical teaching of archaeology the antiquities of the USSR, Western Europe, and the Near East from the Paleolithic era to the seventeenth century. The second course was a more detailed exposition of the principal archaeological facts covering the same period and confined to Soviet territory.

The archaeology and history of medieval Novgorod was the third main theme in Artsikhovsky's scholarly work. In 1929 he launched a Novgorod archaeological expedition which, since 1932, has been conducting regular archaeological excavations of this hub of ancient Russia's political and cultural life. The expedition's major discovery was the birchbark scrolls, of which 669 have been found to date. Their abundance demonstrated for the first time the high literary level in medieval Novgorod. No less importantly, they permitted the urban estates to be personified, giving archaeology a new impetus and drawing it closer to traditional historical research in terms of goals and programs. Studies in auxiliary historical disciplines also occupied a prominent place in Artsikhovsky's work— (cf. his *Drevnerusskiye miniatury kak istoricheskiy istochnik* (1944; Old Russian Miniatures as a Historical Source).

Bibliography: "A. V. Artsikhovsky," *Materialy k biobibliografii uchyonykh SSSR, seriya istoriya* (Biographical Bibliography on Soviet Scholars, History series), issue 12 (Moscow, 1973).

V. L. Yanin

BAKHRUSHIN, Sergei Vladimirovich (Moscow, 1882–Moscow, 1950), Soviet historian, specialist on Russian feudal history. Bakhrushin graduated from the Department of History and Philology at Moscow University (1900–1904). He became assistant professor in 1908, and from 1917 (with short intervals) until his death he was professor at Moscow University. From 1937 until his death in 1950 he was an associate with the Institute of History of the USSR Academy of Sciences. He traveled the long road from being an adherent of economic materialism to becoming a convinced Marxist. In the twenty years from 1920 to 1940, he launched a number of promising historiographic trends, the most important of which were a study of the initial stage of capitalist genesis, the emergence of commercial capital, and the formation of the all-Russian market. His investigations resulted in the posthumously published monograph, *Ocherki po istorii remesla, torgovli i gorodov Russkogo tsentralizovannogo gosudarstva XVI-XVII vv* (1952; Essays on the History of Crafts, Commerce and Towns of the Centralized Russian State in the Sixteenth and Seventeenth Centuries). This work presented a sweeping panorama of the main socioeconomic processes that occurred in Russia in the late Middle Ages and early New Times. He also wrote a number of works on the social structure of Kievan Rus and the early class formations in Siberia, Central Asia, and the Volga area, and he contributed substantially to the study of the socioeconomic foundations of state centralization and its specific mechanism. His books on the opening of Siberia and the history of non-Russian peoples in feudal Russia, as well as his documentary publications, retain their significance to this day. He participated in preparing school and college textbooks and labored energetically to popularize knowledge of history.

Bibliography: A. A. Zimin, "Tvorchesky put Sergeya Vladimirovicha Bakhrushina" (Sergei Bakhrushin's Creative Work), *Nauchnye doklady vysshei shkoly, Istoricheskiye nauki*, no. 2 (Moscow, 1961); *Problemy sotsialnoekonomicheskoi istorii feodalnoi Rossii* (Problems of the Socioeconomic History of Feudal Russia), (Moscow, 1984).

L. V. Danilova

BARTHOLD, Vassily Vladimirovich (St. Petersburg, 1869–Leningrad, 1930), Russian orientalist. Barthold was graduated from the Department of Oriental Languages of St. Petersburg University (1887–1891) where he specialized in the Arabic, Persian, Turkish, and Tatar languages. From 1896 throughout his lifetime he lectured at St. Petersburg (Leningrad) University. He set himself the task of examining Central Asian history "within the framework of the historical development patterns as applied to Europe." His fundamental two-volume monograph, *Turkestan v epokhu mongolskogo nashestviya* (1898–1900; Turkestan During the Mongol Invasion), brought him a doctorate in oriental history. This work probed deeply into the sources, historical geography, and destinies of Central Asian peoples in the time span from the Arab conquest to the Mongol invasion, that is, from the sixth and seventh to the twelfth centuries. In 1928 Barthold's "epoch-making work" (to quote E. D. Rose) was translated, with supplements, into English as *Turkestan Down to the Mongol Invasion* (subsequent printings 1958, 1968). In 1910 Barthold was elected corresponding member and, in 1913, full member of the Russian Academy of Sciences. Following the October Revolution of 1917, he was director of the Institute of Turkic Studies, headed the country's leading oriental studies institution, the Collegium of Orientalists, and the Central Asian Department in the Academy of Material Culture, acting as its deputy chairman. His vast legacy contains eight hundred-odd works, including *Svedeniya ob Aralskom more i nizovyakh Amu-Daryi s dreveneishkh vremen do XVII veka* (1902; Information on the Aral Sea and the Lower Reaches of the Amu Darya from the Earliest Times to the Seventeenth Century), *Istoriko-geografichesky obzor Irana* (1903; Historical and Geographical Description of Iran), *K istorii izucheniya Vostoka v Evrope i v Rossii* (1911, 1912; On the History of Oriental Studies in Europe and Russia), *Islam* (1918), *Kultura musulmanstva* (1918; Moslem Culture), *Musulmansky mir* (1922; The Moslem World), *Iran. Istorichesky obzor* (1926; Iran. Historical Overview), and *Istoriya kulturnoi zhizni Turkestana* (1927; A History of Turkestan Culture). His works differ from those of others in their profound analysis and comprehensive source studies, with emphasis placed on political, cultural, and economic aspects. The class struggle and popular movements and their place in history received much coverage. His basic premise was that "one and the same laws of historical evolution apply to both Europe and Asia" (1899).

Bibliography: V. V. Barthold, *Four Studies on the History of Central Asia*, vol. 1 (Leiden, 1956); 1962, vol. 2 (Leiden, 1958); V. V. Barthold, *La découverte de l'Asie. Histoire de l'orientalisme en Europe et en Russie* (Paris, 1937); V. V. Barthold, *Sochineniya* (Works), vols. 1–9 (Moscow, 1963–1977); V. V. Barthold, *12 Vorlesungen über die Geschichte der Türken Mittelasiens* (Berlin, 1935); N. M. Akramov, *Vydayushchiisya russkii vostokoved V. V. Barthold. Naucho-biografichesky ocherk* (V. V. Barthold, Outstanding Russian Orientalist. Biographical Essay), (Dushanbe, 1963); B. V. Lunin, *V. V. Barthold* (Tashkent, 1970).

B. A. Litvinsky

BICHURIN, Nikita Yakovlevich (Kazan Province, 1777–St. Petersburg, 1852), a prominent Russian orientologist-sinologist. Bichurin's real name was Pichurinski and he took the monk's name of Iakinf and pseudonym of Bichurin. Having completed his schooling at the Theological Academy of Kazan in 1799, Bichurin became an instructor in grammar and rhetoric there. He took the monastic vows in 1800, was promoted to Archimandrite, and was appointed father superior of Ascension Monastery near Irkutsk and rector of the local seminary in 1802. He was appointed head of the Russian Orthodox Mission to Beijing in 1807. During his thirteen-year stay in the capital city of China, Bichurin translated into Russian a multivolume work on China's ancient and medieval history (*Zi-zhi tung-jian-gaug-mu*), a geographical description of the Qing Empire (*Da qing yi-tung-zhi*), and various writings on Mongolia, Tibet, and East Turkestan. Upon returning to St. Petersburg in 1822, he was charged with negligence of his missionary duties, stripped of his rank, demoted to monk, and exiled for life to Valaam Monastery on Lake Ladoga. After three years he was allowed to move to the Alexandro Nevskaya Lavra in St. Petersburg and was assigned to the Asiatic Department of the Foreign Ministry to translate diplomatic correspondence from Beijing. Concurrently, he devoted his time to research and publishing. In 1828–1829 he published six books, five of which had a wealth of historical information from Chinese sources: *Opisaniye Tibeta v nyneshnem ego sostoyanii* (Description of Tibet in Its Present Condition); *Zapiski o Mongolii* (Notes on Mongolia); *Opisaniye Chjungarii i Vostochnogo Turkestana v drevnem i nyneshnem sostoyanii* (Description of Dzungaria and Eastern Turkestan in Ancient Times and Today); *Istoriya pervikh chetirekh khanoviz doma Chinguizova* (The Life Story of Four Descendants of Genghiz Khan), and *Opisaniye Pekina* (Description of Beijing). In 1830 he commenced work on two new books: (*Istoriya Tibeta i Khukhunora s 2282 goda do R.Kh. i po 1227 po R.Kh.* (1833; History of Tibet and Huhunor from 2282 B.C. to A.D. 1227), and *Historicheskoye obozreniye oiratov, ili kalmikov, s XV stoletiya do nastoyashchego vremeni* (1834; Historical Review of Oirats or Kalmyks from the Fifteenth Century to the Present). He supplied facts from the latter book for Pushkin's "Pugachev Story." Bichurin helped open the first school in Russia to teach the Chinese language (Kyakhta, May 1835). His two books on modern China—*Kitai, ego zhiteli, nravi, obychai, prosveshcheniye* (1840; China, Its Inhabitants, Manners, Customs and Education), and *Statisticheskoye opisaniye kitaiskoi imperii* (1942; A Statistical Description of the Chinese Empire), were based on the information he drew from his translation into Russian (1835–1837, Kyakhta) of the "Code of Laws of the Great Oing Dynasty" (*Da Qing hui-diang*). The last fundamental publication of this outstanding and tireless student of the Orient was *Sobraniye* *svedenii o narodakh, obitavshikh v Srednei Azii v drevniye vremena* (1851; Collection of Data on the Peoples That Inhabited Central Asia in Ancient Times).

Bichurin is often called "a free-thinker in cassock" as attested by his translation in verse of Voltaire's "Henriade," which was never published. He was the first in Russia and world science to argue that Chinese culture was original and distinctive in contrast to the then predominant doctrine in Western Europe that the Chinese and their civilization were of Egyptian and Babylonian origin. His works based on concrete historical material contributed importantly to the spread of accurate scientific information about the peoples of China, Mongolia, and other Asiatic peoples, not only in Russia, but also in Western Europe where they were well known and highly valued. His posthumous publications include the following: *Sobraniye svedenii o narodakh, obitavshikh v Srednei Azii v drevniye vremena* (vols. 1–2, Moscow, Leningrad, 1850–1953; Collection of Data on the Peoples that Inhabited Central Asia in Ancient Times); and *Sobraniye svedenii po istoricheskoi geographii Vostochnoi i Srednei Azii* (1960; Collection of Data on the Historical Geography of East and Central Asia).

Bibliography: L. I. Chuguevski, "N. Y. Bichurin's Heritage: New Facts about His Manuscripts," *Narody Azii i Afriki* (Asia and Africa Today), no. 3, (1966); A. N. Khokhlov, "N. Y. Bichurin and His Works on Mongolia and China," *Problemy istorii* (Problems of History), no. 1 (1978): 55–72; *N. Y. Bichurin i ego vklad v russkoye vostokovedeniye (k 200-letiyu so dnya rozhdeniya), Materialy konferentsii* (N. Y. Bichurin and His Contribution to Russian Oriental Studies (For the Bicentenary of His Birth), Proceedings of the Jubilee Conference, Parts 1–2 (Moscow, 1977); P. E. Skachkov, *Ocherki istorii russkogo kitayevedeniya* (Essays on the History of Russian Sinology), (Moscow, 1977).

A. N. Khokhlov

CHEREPNIN, Lev Vladimirovich (Ryazan, 1905–Moscow, 1977), Soviet historian, academician who specialized in the history of the Soviet Union, East and Southeast Europe during feudalism, historiography, source studies, and auxiliary disciplines. Upon finishing his education at Moscow University in 1922, Cherepnin did postgraduate studies at the Institute of History of the Russian Association of Research Institutions. He lectured in Moscow at the History and Archives Institute (1942–1949), at the university (1944–1960), and at the Institute of International Relations (1946–1952). In 1946 he joined the Institute of History of the USSR Academy of Sciences, where later he headed the sector of Russian feudal history (from 1951 until his death). In 1958 he was elected member and in 1970 vice-president of the International Commission on the History of Representative and Parliamentary Bodies. The International Association of Slavonic Studies made him a member in 1965. He was awarded the 1957 Lomonosov Prize, the 1972 State Prize of the Moldavian Republic, and the USSR State Prize posthumously in 1981. He was the author of hundreds of scientific articles. His works on the formation of the Russian centralized state in the fourteenth and fifteenth centuries and its development as an estate-represented monarchy in the sixteenth and seventeenth centuries are: *Russkiye feodalnuye arkhivy XIV-XV* *vekov* (Parts I-II, 1948, 1951; Russian Feudal Archives of the Fourteenth and Fifteenth Centuries), *Obrazovaniye Russkogo tsentralizovannogo gosudarstva v XIV-XV vekakh* (1978; Formation of the Russian Centralized State in the Fourteenth and Fifteenth Centuries).

Cherepnin investigated the genesis of feudal relations in Kievan Rus, formulated a conception of the shaping and consolidation of state and private feudal landownership, studied the history of forms of feudal dependence of various categories of peasants, and specific features of the state and estate structure in Russian lands from the tenth to the thirteenth centuries. He was the author of a series of works dealing with the theoretical and methodological problems of the feudal formation in Russia (*Voprosy metodologii istoricheskogo issledovaniya. Teoreticheskiye problemy istorii feodalizma* (1981; Methodological Problems of Historical Research. Theoretical Issues of the History of Feudalism). Cherepnin formulated a number of principles of the comparative-historical study of feudal societies, using the countries of Europe to illustrate his point. He elaborated theoretical and applied problems of source studies, historiography, and auxiliary historical disciplines: *Russkaya metrologiya* (1944; Russian Metrology); *Russkaya khronologiya* (1944; Russian Chronology); *Russkaya paleografiya* (1956; Russian Paleography), *Novgorodskiye berestyanye gramoty kak istoricheskiy istochnik* (1969; The Novgorodian Birch-Bark Scrolls as a Historical Source), and others.

Bibliography: *Lev Vladimirovich Cherepnin (1905–1977). Materialy k biobibliografii uchenykh SSSR* (Lev Vladimirovich Cherepnin [1905–1977]. Biobibliographical Materials of Soviet Scholars), The History Series, Issue 14 (Moscow, 1983).

V. D. Nazarov

DERZHAVIN, Nikolai Sevastyanovich (Preslav Village near Berdyansk, 1877–Leningrad, 1953), Soviet historian and philologist. After graduation *cum laude* from a gymnasium in Simferopol (1896) and the Institute of Languages and Literature in Nezhinsk (1900), Derzhavin taught the Russian language and literature in Tiflis and Batumi, was associate professor and professor of Petrograd (Leningrad) University in 1912–1917; and defended his thesis for a master's degree in 1917. It was a two-volume study entitled *Bolgarskiye kolonii v Rossii* (1914–1915; Bulgarian Colonies in Russia) summing up his graduate research project into the language, customs, and everyday life of South Russian Bulgars and marked with an interdisciplinary approach to the subject. After the October Revolution of 1917, he took an active part in the development of Soviet science and culture. He was rector of Leningrad University (1922–1925); head of the chair of Slavic languages of the same university (until 1930); and in charge of the Institute of Western and Eastern literatures and Languages under the auspices of Leningrad University (1922–1933). During this period he was concerned mostly with investigation of languages and methods of teaching philological disciplines as an active supporter of Nikolai Iakovlevich Marr's "new linguistic doctrine." According to Marr, languages such as Old Georgian and Old Armenian were related to the Semitic languages, Arabic and Hebrew. Stalin criticized this theory (*Guide Larousse* VI:310). He also published a series of papers on problems of higher education, *Vysshaya shkola i revolutsiya* (1923; Higher Education and the Revolution). From 1931 he was a member of the USSR Academy of Sciences, director of the Academy's Institute of Slavonic Studies in Leningrad, and head of a chair at the Institute of History and Languages of Leningrad. In planning the activities of the new Institute of Slavonic Studies he did much to define the theoretical principles of Soviet research in this field based on Marxist methodology and history (*Nashi zadachi v oblasti slavyanovedeniya* (1931; Our Tasks in Slavonic Studies). In the 1930s he concentrated on research into the history of Bulgarian literature and the early history of Slavs, specifically Slav ethnogenesis (*Ob etnogenese drevneishikh narodov Dneprovsko-Dunayskogo basseina* (1939; On Ethnogenesis of the Ancient Peoples of the Dnieper-Danube Basin); a series of his works also dealt with the history and contemporary progress of Slavonic studies.

During the war years 1941–1945 Derzhavin removed to Moscow. He was head of the chair of Slavic languages of Moscow University and an active member of the Antifascist Committee of Soviet Scientists and of the Pan-Slavic Committee; a member of the Presidium of the USSR Academy of Sciences (1942) and of the Academy of Pedagogical Sciences (1944); head of the chairs of Slavic languages and Slavic literatures of Leningrad University (the early 1950s) and in charge of the Leningrad group of the USSR Academy of Sciences' Institute of Slavonic Studies (1950). In the 1940s and early 1950s he authored and published his major works on the early history of the Slavs: *Slavianye v drevnosti* (1945; Slavs in Ancient Times), and *Proiskhozhdeniye russkogo naroda—velikorusskogo, ukrainskogo, belorusskogo* (1944; The Origins of the Russian People: Great Russians, Ukrainians and Byelorussians); on Russian-Bulgarian ties: *Plemennye i kulturnye svyazi bolgarskogo i russkogo narodov* (1944; The Tribal and Cultural Ties of the Bulgarian and Russian Peoples); and on the antifascist struggle of Slavic nations: a series of publicistic articles. His four-volume work, *Istoriya Bolgarii* (1945–1948; A History of Bulgaria), summed up his research into Bulgarian history and culture and was much acclaimed as the first thorough investigation of the subject by a Soviet scholar.

Bibliography: A. N. Goryainov, "On the Training of Specialists in Slavonic Studies at Leningrad University (in the 1920s)," in *Istoriographicheskiye issledovaniya po slavyanovedeniyu i balkanistike* (Historiographic Research in Slavonic and Balkan Studies), (Moscow, 1984), pp. 261–283; K. I. Logachev, "Soviet Slavonic Studies up to Mid-Thirties," *Sovetskoye Slavyanovedeniye* (Soviet Slavonic Studies), no. 5 (1978): 91–103; *Nikolai Sevastyanovich Derzhavin* (Leningrad, 1949), 72 pp.; "Nikolai Sevastyanovich Derzhavin," *Kratkiye soobshcheniya Instituta slavyanovedeniya* (Brief reports of the Institute of Slavonic Studies), (1953), issue 2, pp. 84–95.

A. N. Goryainov

DJAVAKHISHVILI, Ivan Alexandrovich (Tbilisi, 1876–Tbilisi, 1940), Soviet historian of Georgia. Member of the Georgian Academy of Sciences (1939);

specialist on Georgian ancient and medieval history. Djavakhishvili's works laid a solid foundation for the development of new Georgian historiography. His range of scientific interests included problems of ethnogenesis and the economic, social, socio-legal, and political aspects of Georgia's history. As a student of Georgia's economic history he was actually a trailblazer. In his dissertation for a master's degree ("The State System of Ancient Georgia and Armenia," 1906), he was the first to point to a class society in these two countries. He compiled a special paper on the history of Georgia's social and political movement in the nineteenth century (*The Political and Social Movement in Georgia in the 19th Century*, 1906). His other major works (Georgian-language editions) are the following: *A History of the Georgian People*, vols. 1–4, 1908–1949; *A History of Georgian Law*, vols. 1–2, 1930–1934. They treat the pivotal problems of Georgia's ancient and medieval history in close relationship with the history of contiguous countries. He also studied general problems of ethnogenesis of the Caucasian peoples (*Introduction to a History of the Georgian People*, 1937) and contributed significantly to studies of Georgian historical sources and auxiliary historical disciplines (*Historical Tasks, Sources and Methods in the Past and Today*, vols. 1–4, 1916–1926; Ancient Georgian Historical Literature, 1916; *Georgian Numismatics and Metrology*, 1925; *Georgian Palaeography, Georgian Diplomacy*, 1926). He discovered and published a manuscript of the *Chronicles Karthlis Tshovreba* and *Ahali Karthlis Tshovreba* (Georgia's Modern History) and a series of other valuable historical sources and literary monuments. His works are also of great use and interest for students of the history of Armenia, the North Caucasian peoples, their languages and cultures, and of Persia.

Bibliography: *A Jubilee Collection Dedicated to Academician I. A. Djavakhishvili's Centenary* (Tbilisi, 1976, in Georgian); A. Surguladse, *Ivané Djavakhishvili (1876–1940)* (Tbilisi, 1976); *Transactions of the Joint Scientific Session of the Georgian Academy of Sciences and the State University of Tbilisi Dedicated to Academician I. A. Djavakhishvili's Centenary* (Tbilisi, 1976).

V. A. Rzhanitsina

DUBNOW, Simon (Mstislawl, 1860–Riga, 1941), Jewish historian and author. Self-taught, resident between 1880 and 1906—at times an illegal resident—in St. Petersburg, Mstislawl, Vilna, and Odessa, where he was influenced by Achad Haam. Dubnow was a lecturer on Jewish history at the Institute for Jewish Studies in St. Petersburg (1908), one of the founders and leaders of the Jewish Historical-Ethnographical Society, and editor of the newspaper *Jewrelskala Starina* (1908–1918). After the Bolshevik Revolution, he became professor at the Jewish adult education college (1919–1921), which was supported by the government, but since he did not support the Revolution, he left Russia. He resided in Berlin (1922–1933) until Hitler came into power and then fled to Riga. There he continued his work until the Germans took over the city. On December 8, 1941, he was murdered by a Gestapo officer, a former student of his. Dubnow began his literary career in 1880 with an essay on the history of the Jewish intellect in *Russkiy Yevrey*. From 1882 on, he worked for the newspaper *Voshod*, in which he published historical essays on the Sabbatian and Frankist movements. He also wrote about the origin, nature, and history of Hassidism, and took an interest in the religious struggles of Russian Jewry at the turn of the century. At the beginning of the 1890s, Dubnow attempted to encourage a general interest in the problems of writing Russian-Jewish history. He also developed the idea of a Russian-Jewish Society (1891) and collected Russian-Jewish documents. His publications on the history of the Jews in Eastern Europe included "Akten des jüd. Reichstags oder der Vierlander Synode" *(Yevr, Starina*, 1912) and "Pinkas Hamedina" (*Das Protokollbuch des litauischen waad von 1623–1761*, Berlin, 1924). At first, Dubnow was influenced by Heinrich Graetz. His work "Was ist jüdische Geschichte?" (*Voshod*, 1893), which was published in English in 1903 under the title "Jewish History, an Essay in the Philosophy of History," interpreted the history of the Jews as a history of Jewish intellect. Dubnow was later preoccupied with sociohistorical, economic, and legal problems, as well as with aspects of Jewish daily life, as shown in his *Die Weltgeschichte des jüdischen Volkes* (10 vols., 1925–1929), which came out in several languages.

As a critic and journalist, Dubnow adopted the view of "absolute rationalism and cosmopolitanism" at the beginning of the 1880s. He resisted rabbinicism in favor of Jewish religious reforms; and during the 1880s and 1890s, he declared his belief in evolution and nationalism. As shown in certain essays ("Briefe über das alte und neue Judentum," *Voshod*, 1897–1902), Dubnow interpreted the Jews as a cultural-historical group that had achieved unity because of their earlier independent development as a society, even though they had lost some of the attributes of a group. (See "Das Selbstbewusstsein einer Nation ist das wichtigste Kriterium ihrer Existenz".) He supported national and cultural autonomy, hoping a solution could be found for the Jewish problem in the Diaspora. Dubnow followed the example of Theodor Herzl, in rejecting assimilation. These ideas greatly influenced the intellectual and domestic politics of the Jews in Eastern Europe.

Bibliography: S. W. Baron, *History and Jewish Historians* (1964), index; B. Z. Dinaburg-Dinur in *Zion* 1 (1936), 95–128; J. Fraenkel, *Dubnow, Herzl and Ahad Haam* (1963); J. Meisl in *Socino-Blatter*, 1 (1925–1926); J. Meisl in *Festschrift zum siebzigsten Geburtstag* (1930), 266–295; A. S. Steinberg, ed., *Simon Dubnow, the Man and His Work* (1963), pp. 225–251, 254–255 (autobiography).

Julius Schoeps

GILFERDING, Aleksander Fyodorovich (Warsaw, 1831–Kargopol, 1872), Russian historian and linguist. Upon graduating from the university in Moscow in 1852 and after receiving his master's degree for the paper "Ob otnoshenii yazyka slavyanskogo k yazykam rodstvennym" (On the Relationship of the Slavonic and Kindred Languages) a year later, Gilferding engaged in research and was elected corresponding member of the St. Petersburg Academy of Sciences in 1856. For the next four years he served as the Russian consul in Bosnia, and then in the Asiatic Department of the Foreign Affairs Ministry and in the Committee for the Kingdom of Poland where he actively participated in legislative activities. In 1870 he became chairman of the Ethnographic Department of the Russian Geographic Society and spent the following two years traveling to the Olonets Province (northern regions of Russia) to verify the findings of folklorist P. Rybnikov. There he recorded over three hundred *bylinas* (epic songs), which were published posthumously in 1873 (*Onezhskiye byliny, zapisannye Aleksandrom Fyodorovichem Gilferdingom letom 1871 g* (Bylinas from Lake Onega Region Collected by Gilferding in the Summer of 1871). The book was republished many times and served long as a study source of the Russian north, its language, lifeways, and folk art.

As a liberal from his student years, Gilferding maintained close ties with the Slavophiles and, at their request, passed secret documents of the Russian government to A. Herzen. In addition to his philological research, he was also involved in the history of Western and Southern Slavs. He was the first to make a detailed study of the history of the Baltic Slavs, focusing on their social system. He also gathered interesting factual material pertaining to Slav-German relations in the Middle Ages (*Istoriya baltiiskikh slavyan* (1854–1855; The History of the Baltic Slavs), *Borba slavyan s nemtsami na Baltiiskom Pomorie v srednie veka* (1862; The Slavs' Struggle Against the Germans in the Baltic Maritime Province in the Middle Ages). Other major contributions to historical science were his *Pisma ob istorii serbov i bolgar* (1854–1855; Letters on the History of the Serbs and Bulgarians) and *Bosniya, Gertsegovina i Staraya Serbiya* (1859; Bosnia, Herzegovina and Old Serbia) which was based on historical documents the author had found himself and on personal observations. He published *Ocherk istorii Chekhii* (1862; Essay on the History of Bohemia) and *Gus: ego otnosheniye k pravoslavnoi tserkvi* (1871; Jan Hus: His Attitude to the Orthodox Church), and wrote a number of articles on the Polish question. Some of his articles, including "Drevneishiy period istorii slavyan" (1868; The Earliest Period in the History of Slavs), dealt with common Slavonic problems. His career was greatly influenced by Slavophilic ideas and by his own idealist world-view. His writings, on the other hand, based on a vast body of historical material, testify to his conscientiousness as a scholar.

Bibliography: K. H. Bestuzhev-Ryumin, "Aleksander Fyodorovich Gilferding," *Russkaya starina* (Russian History), no. 10 (1880): 431–433; L. P. Lapteva, "Gilferding," *Slavyanovedeniye v dorevolutsionnoi Rossii i biobibliografichesky slovar* (Slavonic Studies in Pre-Revolutionary Russia: A Bio-Bibliographical Dictionary), (Moscow, 1979), pp. 121–125; A. N. Pypin, "Aleksander Fyodorovich Gilferding," *Vestnik Evropy* (The European Herald), Book 8 (1872): 902–907; I. V. Yagich, *Istoriya slavyanskoi filologii* (History of Slavonic Philology), (St. Petersburg, 1910), pp. 769–774.

A. N. Goryainov

GORDLEVSKY, Vladimir Alexandrovich (Sveaborg, 1876–Moscow, 1956), Russian authority on Turkish studies. Gordlevsky received degrees from the

Special Classes of the Lazarev Institute of Oriental Languages (Moscow, 1895–1899) and from the Department of History and Philology of Moscow University (1899–1904). After a three-year tour (1904–1907) of Turkey, Syria, and France to prepare for a professorship and to perfect his knowledge of Turkish and Arabic, he attended lectures at the Collège de France and the Ecole Pratique des Hautes Etudes in Paris. From 1907 to 1950 he lectured at various institutions of higher learning, mainly at the Lazarev Institute, otherwise known as the Moscow Institute of Oriental Studies, and beginning in 1919 he combined his teaching activities with academic pursuits on the staff of various institutions in Moscow, and from 1938 to 1956, at the Institute of Oriental Studies under the USSR Academy of Sciences. He received a tenured professorship in 1925 and was elected corresponding member of the USSR Academy of Sciences in 1929. The year before that, he became honorary member of the Historical Society in Istanbul (Turkey). In 1934 he was made doctor of philology on the strength of his academic achievements, and in 1946, full member of the USSR Academy of Sciences. He began publishing in 1900 and had to his credit a total of 263 research papers (seven co-authored), 106 reviews, and 22 translations. He edited sixteen fundamental works and his own four-volume collected works, published posthumously.

Gordlevsky was concerned primarily with Turkish studies, a domain in which he exhibited wide-ranging interests as a historian, ethnographer, Islamicist, linguist, literary scholar, and folklore specialist. His research method was distinguished by meticulous study of archival documents combined with extensive fieldwork. Caution and conscientiousness made him introduce the term *silhouettes* in publications in which he was not fully satisfied with his conclusions. He was adept in writing miniature essays. His articles of several pages, such as "The Derebeys," "Mevlevi," "Godless Dervishes," "Double Believers," "The Juruks," "On the Moslem-Judaic Sect of Denme," "What Is 'Barefooted Wolf'?," "Was the Turkish Sultan a Caliph?," are original in presentation and distinctive in their profound and apt characterizations. Gordlevsky's heritage includes a fundamental work on the history of the Seljuk state in Asia Minor, a study of the social and economic life of this huge Middle East region from the eleventh through the thirteenth centuries. He contributed greatly to the development of a number of branches in Turkish studies, including the Turkish dialect of the Karaimes. Gordlevsky trained several generations of specialists.

Bibliography: N. A. Baskakov, "V. A. Gordlevsky—filolog-istorik" (V. A. Gordlevsky: Philologist and Historian), in *Akademiku V. A. Gordlevskomy k ego, 75-letiyu* (To Academician Gordlevsky on his 75th Birth Anniversary), (Moscow, 1953), pp. 10–22; A. P. Baziyants, *Vladimir Aleksandrovich Gordlevsky* (Moscow, 1979), 80 pp; E. Y. Bertels, "V. A. Gordlevsky," in *Akademiku V. A. Gordlevskomy k ego 75-letiyu* (To Academician Gordlevsky on His 75th Birth Anniversary), (Moscow, 1953), pp. 5–9; I. Y. Krachkovsky, "V. A. Gordlevsky," in *Trudy Moskovskogo instituta vostokovedeniya* (Transactions of the Moscow Institute of Oriental Studies), no. 4 (Moscow, 1947), pp. 3–6.

A. P. Baziants

GORODTSOV, Vassily Alexeevich (Bubrovichi, Ryazan Province, 1860–Moscow, 1945), Russian-Soviet archaeologist. After finishing military school, Gorodtsov served as an officer and retired in 1906. He showed an interest in archaeology from his early years. He investigated the archaeological remains in the dunes of the Oka River (a Neolithic site in the vicinity of Shumash and Dubrovichi, villages in Ryazan Province, 1889). His academic, pedagogical, and public activities were associated with the Russian Historical Museum (1903–1929), Popular University (1915–1918), First Moscow State University (1920–1930), and the Chernyshevsky Institute of Philosophy, Literature, and History. Simultaneously, he was employed at the Russian Association of Social Science Research Institutions (1920–1930) and at the Institute of History of Material Culture of the USSR Academy of Sciences (1930–1945). His works number some two hundred, devoted to various problems of archaeology, from Paleolithic times to the Middle Ages. Particularly noteworthy are his fundamental monographs: *Pervobytnaya Arkheologia* (1903; Prehistoric Archaeology); *Bytovaya Arkheologiya* (1910; Mobiliary Archaeology), and *Arkheologiya* (Archaeology), Volume 1: *Kamenny Vek* (1923; The Stone Age). He worked out his own classification of the evolution of human society. Drawing on geological findings and data from other sciences, he singled out two cycles: the period of human emergence and the period when humans established themselves and formed society. He referred to the first period as Pliocene, while the appearance of the first implements of labor he associated with the second period. He pointed to the existence of simultaneous Paleolithic cultures and correctly evaluated and interpreted Moustierian burials. He was the first to discover Paleolithic dwellings (Timonovka Paleolithic site, 1934), and one of the first to excavate Neolithic and Bronze Age sites in the European part of the Soviet Union. He published his findings in his definitive study *Kultury Bronzovogo veka v Sredney Rossii* (1914; Bronze Age Cultures in Central Russia). He established the existence of a whole series of Bronze Age cultures such as the Volosovo, Panfilovo, Fatianovo, Pit-Grave, Catacomb, Timber Grave, and Cimmerian. He greatly contributed to the study of the Scythian and Sarmatian cultures, Dyakovo culture, Finnish artifacts, the archaeology and history of the Slavs, the Russian Middle Ages, the steppe nomads (Pechenegs, Torks, Polovtsi) and other peoples that formerly inhabited the territory of the Soviet Union.

Gorodtsov's greatest contribution to archaeology was his typological method (*Tipologichesky metod v arkheologii* (1927; Typological Method in Archaeology). Also noteworthy are his works (*Rukovodstvo dlya arkheologicheskikh raskopok* (1914; Manual on Archaeological Excavations) and *Russkaya Doistoricheskaya Keramika* (1901; Russian Prehistoric Ceramics). His articles on numismatics, epigraphy, and art history are well known among specialists. He was responsible for a galaxy of renowned Soviet archaeologists known as the Gorodtsov School. He supervised and contributed to the huge project of systematizing the stocks and opening exhibitions of the State Historical Museum. His fruitful academic, educational, and public work earned him the Order of Lenin.

Bibliography: A. Y. Bryusov, "V. A. Gorodtsov. K stoletiyu so dnya rozhdeniya" (V. A. Gorodtsov. For the Centenary of His Birth), *Transactions of the State Historical Museum* 37 (1960): 7–11; M. V. Friche, *V. A. Gorodtsov, K 40-letiyu ego nauchno-issledovatelskoi i nauchno-poznavatelnoi deyatelnosti* (V. A. Gorodtsov. On the Occasion of the Fortieth Anniversary of His Academic and Teaching Careers), *Transactions of the Department of Archaeology of the Institute of Archaeology and Art Studies* 4 (1928): 5–8; Y. V. Gotye, "V. A. Gorodtsov. Po povodu 35-letiya nauchnoi deyatelnosti" (V. A. Gorodtsov. On the Occasion of the Thirty-Fifth Anniversary of His Academic Career), *Golos minuvshego* (The Voice of the Past), no. 3 (1923): 160–166; D. A. Krainov, "K 125-letiyu so dnya rozhdeniya V. A. Gorodtsova" (For the 125th Birth Anniversary of V. A. Gorodtsov), *Sovetskaya arkheologiya* no. 4 (1985): 265–268; Y. I. Krupnov, "O zhizni i deyatelnosti V. A. Gorodtsova" (On the Life and Work of V. A. Gorodtsov), *Sovetskaya Arkheologiya* (Soviet Archaeology), 25 (1956): 5–12; B. A. Rybakov, "Vassily Alexeevich Gorodtsov. 1860–1945. Obituary," *Proceedings of the Academy of Sciences*, History and Philosophy Series 2, no. 1 (1945): 47–49.

D. A. Krainov

GOTIE, Yuri Vladimirovich (Moscow, 1873–Moscow, 1943), Russian historian, archaeologist, authority on source studies. From 1891 to 1895 Gotie studied in the Department of History and Philology of Moscow University under Vassili Osipovich Klyuchevsky (q.v.). In 1903 he became assistant professor, in 1915 extraordinary professor, and in 1917 professor of the chair of Russian history at Moscow University. Simultaneously, he taught in other higher educational establishments. As of late 1939 he was professor in the Department of History at the university. From 1922 until 1930 he headed the Department of Russian History at the university. From 1922 until 1930 he headed the Department of Russian History at the History Museum. The year 1922 saw him elected corresponding member of the USSR Academy of Sciences and 1939, academician. His works were devoted to seventeenth and eighteenth-century Russia. Klyuchevsky gave a high mark to his university research "Oborona granits Moskovskogo gosudarstva" (Defense of the Muscovite State's Boundaries). In 1906 Gotie received a master's degree for "Zamoskovny krai v XVII v. Opyt issledovaniya po istorii ekonomicheskogo byta Moskovskoi Rusi" (1906; 2d ed. 1937; Moscow Province in the Seventeenth Century. An Essay on the Economic History of the Moscow State). After analyzing cadasters and census books, he defined the boundaries of the Great Russian center in the seventeenth century, and described the country's devastation by the Swedish-Polish invaders and its later rehabilitation. He came to the conclusion that the estate system expanded because of large-scale land grants and intensified serf bondage. His fundamental study, *Istoriya oblastnogo upravleniya ot Petra I do Ekateriny II* (vols. 1–2, 1913–1914; History of Regional Management from Peter I to Catherine II), demonstrated the genesis of central and provincial administration and concentrated on the regional administration reform of 1727. The second volume gives a detailed description of supervisory bodies, extraordinary and temporary regional institutions, and their extinction in connection with the pending 1775 reform.

In *Ocherki po istorii materialnoi kultury Vostochnoi Evropy do osnovaniya pervogo Russkogo gosudarstva* (vols. 1–2, 1925–1930; Essays on the History of Material Culture of Eastern Europe Prior to the Emergence of the First Russian State), drawing on extensive archaeological and historical material, Gotie reconstructed the earliest period of Russian history: It was the first attempt to combine material and historical sources. As a foremost authority on the history of the Southern Slavs he published a special lecture course which he brought up to the beginning of World War I, *Istoriya yuzhnykh slavyan* (1916; History of the Southern Slavs). Noteworthy among the great number of documentary collections he edited are *Pamyatniki obornony Smolenska 1609–1611 gg* (1912; Memorials of the 1609–1611 Smolensk Defense) and *Angliiskiye puteshestven-niki v Moskovskom gosudarstve v XVI veke* (1937; English Travelers in the Muscovite State in the Sixteenth Century). From 1909 to 1917, Gotie contributed regular surveys of Russian historical writings to *Revue Historique*. He authored chapters and sections for the textbook *Istoriya SSSR. S drevneishikh vremen to kontsa XVIII v.* (Vol. 1, 1939; History of the USSR. From the Earliest Times to the Late Eighteenth Century).

Bibliography: N. M. Asafova, *Yu. V. Gotie, Materialy k bibliografii trudov uchenykh SSSR. Seria istorii*, vyp. I (Materials on the Bibliography of Soviet Scholars), History Series, Issue I (Moscow, 1941); V. I. Picheta, "Academik Yu. V. Gotie" (Academician Yu. V. Gotie), *Istoricheskiye zapiski* 15 (1945): 301–314.

Yu. N. Emelyanov

GRANOVSKY, Timofei Nikolaevich (Orel, 1813–Moscow, 1855), Russian historian, medievalist, and public figure. After graduation from the Department of Law at the University of St. Petersburg in 1835, Granovsky went to Germany to continue his education at Berlin University under Leopold von Ranke (q.v.), Friedrich C. Savigny (q.v.), and Gerhard Ritter (q.v.) and studied Georg Wilhelm Hegel's (q.v.) philosophy (1837–1839). From 1839 throughout his life he remained professor of world history at Moscow University, where he pioneered studies of the West European Middle Ages. He gained wide popularity and significantly influenced public opinion in Russian with his three public lecture courses: from 1843 to 1844, on the history of the Middle Ages; in 1845 and 1846, on the comparative history of England and France, and in 1851, on four profiles (Tamerlane, Alexander the Great, Louis IX, and Francis Bacon). He published his master's thesis "Wollin, Jomsburg and Vineta" in 1845, his doctorate "Abbot Suger" in 1849, his survey *Istoricheskaya literatura vo Frantsii i Germanii v 1847* (Historical Literature of France and Germany in 1847) in 1847–1848, reviews *Chteniya Niebura o drevnei istorii* (Niebuhr's Lectures on Ancient History) in 1853–1856, and *Pesni Eddy o Nibelungakh* (Nibelungenlieb in Poetic Edda) in 1851. In the 1850s he began work on a textbook on world history part of which was published.

Granovsky's writings are a testament to his far-flung historical interests and copious knowledge. His world-view was partially influenced by the French historians Augustin Thierry (q.v.), Jules Michelet (q.v.), and Francois Guizot (q.v.), and to a far greater degree by Hegelian philosophy and the German historical school of Barthold Georg Niebuhr (q.v.), Ranke, and Savigny. He perceived progress in the advance of ideas and education, and in the "moral perfecting of people." By closely connecting the past to the present, he acknowledged the historian's moral right to judge prominent men of the past. His admiration for the cultural development of the West made him one of the most consistent "Westerners" of the 1840s and 1850s. His lectures and works reflected his progressive and anti-serfdom views, albeit limited by his liberal ideology. While showing compassion for the popular masses, he disapproved of "extreme measures" such as revolutionary acts of the people. He gave careful scrutiny to constitutional forms of government, and he denounced monarchical despotism and the Catholic Church. His foremost interest was in transitional periods such as the downfall of the Roman Empire and the formation of royal power, the antifeudal struggle of the medieval urban communes, the seventeenth-century English Revolution, and the French Revolution. His political sympathies were with the Girondists rather than the Jacobins. Herzen and Chernyshevsky had high praise for his academic and public activities. He was a strong influence on Russian historical thought.

Bibliography: M. A. Alpatov, "Trudy T. N. Granovskogo" (Granovsky's Works), *Ocherki istorii istoricheskoi nauki v SSSR* (Essays on Soviet Historiography), (Moscow, 1955), vol. 1; S. A. Asinovskaya, *Iz istorii peredovykh idei v russkoi medievistike (T. N. Granovsky)* (From the History of Progressive Ideas in the Russian Medieval Studies. T. N. Granovksy), (Moscow, 1955); A. I. Danilov, "T. N. Granovsky i nekotorye voprosy sotsialnoi istorii rannego srednevekovya" (Granovsky and Certain Problems of Early Mediaeval Social History), *Uchenye zapiski Tomskogo universiteta* (Transactions of Tomsk University), no. 16 (1951); L. E. Kertman, "Evolutsiya istoricheskikh vzglyadov T. N. Granovskogo" (Evolution of Granovsky's Historical Views), *Naukovi zapiski Kievskogo derzhavnogo universiteta* (Transactions of Kiev State University), 6, no. 1 (1947); E. A. Kosminsky, "Zhizn i deyatelnost T. N. Granovskogo" (The Life and Work of T. N. Granovsky), *Vestnik MGU* (Herald of Moscow University), no. 4 (1956); *T. N. Granovsky, Bibliografiya (1828–1967)* (T. N. Granovsky. Bibliography. 1828–1967), (Moscow, 1969); T. N. Granovsky, *Sbornik statei* (Collected Articles), (Moscow, 1970); C. Vetrinsky (V. E. Cheshikhin), *T. N. Granovsky i ego vremya* (T. N. Granovsky and His Time), (St. Petersburg, 1905).

B. T. Kabanov

GREKOV, Boris Dmitrievich (Mirgorod, 1882–Moscow, 1953), Soviet historian and public figure. Having enrolled in Warsaw University in 1901, Grekov continued his studies at the Department of History and Philology of Moscow University (1905–1907). He attended seminars headed by D. M. Petrushevsky, K. Lyubavsky, and A. S. Lappo-Danilevsky. His master's thesis, "Novgorodsky dom sv. Sofii. Opyt izucheniya organizatsii i vnutrennikh otnoshenii krupnoi tserkovnoi votchiny" (Part I, 1914; The Novgorod House of St. Sophia. A Practical Study of the Structure and Internal Relations of a Large Church Estate), brought him a master's degree in 1910; in 1914 he became professor at St. Petersburg University while lecturing at other educational establishments. He spent 1921 working at Petrograd University; from 1924 to the mid–1930s he was an associate with the Central State Archives, the State Academy of the History of Material Culture, and the Leningrad branch of the Institute of History. From 1937 through 1953 he headed the Institute of History of the USSR Academy of Sciences, and in 1944 he simultaneously was director of the Institute of the History of Material Culture, for three years. The next four years he headed the Institute of Slavonic Studies. Elected corresponding member of the USSR Academy of Sciences in 1934, the following year he was made academician. In 1939 the USSR Academy of Architecture made him a member, and in 1947 he received membership in the Polish and Bulgarian Science Academies, and was chosen an honorary member of the Byelorussian Academy and doctor of philosophy of Prague University. He served as academician-secretary of the Division of History and Philosophy of the USSR Academy for eight years, beginning in 1946. Grekov was active in state and public life.

Grekov's work covered the history of the people of the USSR and of the Southern and Western Slavs from the sixth through the twentieth centuries. He was the first to characterize the Old Russian society as a feudal society, on the basis of interpreting feudalism as a socioeconomic formation (*Feodalnye otnosheniya v Kievskom gosudarstve* [1935; Feudal Relations in the Kievan State]); the third and subsequent editions bore the title *Kievskaya Rus* (3d ed., 1939; Kievan Rus). The history of the peasantry was central to all his works (*Krestyane na Rusi s drevneishikh vremen do serediny XVII v.* [1946, 2d ed., vols. 1–2, 1952–1954; Russian Peasantry from Ancient Times to the Mid Seventeenth Century]). He dated the beginning of Russian statehood in the form of Slavonic tribal unions from the sixth to the eighth centuries, when analogous processes took place not only among the Western and Southern Slavs but also among the Eastern Slavs. His research into *Russakaya Pravda* (The Code of Laws) produced a handsome publication in two volumes, *Pravda Russkaya* (vol. 1, 1940; texts, vol. 2, 1947; The Russian Code of Laws). Having studied *Russkaya Pravda* in the contexts of other earlier Slavonic written monuments, Grekov published his findings on Croatian legal regulations (*Vinodolsky statut ob obshchestvennom i politicheskom stroe Vinodola* (1948; The Statute of Vinodol on Its Social and Political Order); *Politsa. Opyt izucheniya obshchestvennykh otnoshenii v Politse XV-XVII vv* (1951; Polica. An Essay on Social Relations in Polica from the Fifteenth Through the Seventeenth Centuries) and on Polish law (*Polskaya pravda. Opyt izucheniya obshchestvennogo i politicheskogo stroya Polshi XIII v. po polskoi pravde ("Kniga prava")* (Vol. 1, 1957; The Polish Code of Laws. An Essay on Social and Political Order in Thirteenth-Century Poland According to the Polish Code of Law [Book of Laws]), *Izbr. trudy* (Selected Works). This comprehensive investigation of Slavonic legal documents brought to light common patterns of class society's development in the Slavonic countries and its local variants. He contributed to Soviet historiography with studies of Lenin's works, analyses of M. V. Lomonosov's, V. C. Vassilevsky's and S. A. Zhebelev's writings, and with articles assessing the progress of Soviet historiography. The Mongol invasion and the Golden Horde were discussed in the book *Zolotaya Orda i ee padeniye* (1950; The Golden Horde and Its Downfall) (written together with A. Y. Yakubovsky). The Decembrists and eighteenth-century sociopolitical history were all subjects that interested him; he authored college textbooks and popular science publications, edited numerous documentary publications, including several on the history of autonomous republics (Tatar and Mordovian) and Union Republics (Uzbek, Tajik, Turkmen), and was editor-in-chief of the *Istoricheskiye zapiski* (Historical Notes) journals (1937–1953).

Bibliography: V. I. Picheta, "Boris Dmitrievich Grekov," in *Materialy k biografii uchenykh SSSR* (Materials on Biographies of Soviet Scholars), History Series, Issue 2 (Moscow-Leningrad, 1947); V. I. Shunkov, "Boris Dmitrievich Grekov (1882–1953)," in B. D. Grekov, *Izbrannye trudy* (Selected Works), vol. 1 (Moscow, 1957).

N. A. Gorskaya

GRUSHEVSKY, Mikhail Sergeyevich (Khelm, 1866–Kislovodsk, 1934), Ukrainian historian. Majored in history and philology at the University of Kiev and wrote his master's thesis *Barskoye starostvo* (1894; The Bar Starostvo). Joined the chair of world history at the University of Lvov to lecture on the history of the Ukraine. Grushevsky was elected chairman of the Historico-Philological Section of the Shevchenko Scientific Society (1897). He was among the founders of the National-Democratic party of Galicia (1899). Having returned to Russia in 1908, he settled in Kiev where he was active in setting up the Society of Ukrainian Progressivists, a political organization close to the Constitutional-Democratic party. During World War I, he advocated the Ukraine's secession from the Russian Empire to become a German protectorate. In 1914 he was arrested and exiled to live in Simbirsk and later Kazan. After the 1917 February Revolution, he joined the Ukrainian Socialist-Revolutionaries party and headed the counterrevolutionary Central Rada which opposed Soviet rule. In early 1919 he emigrated to Austria and established in Vienna the Ukrainian Institute of Sociology which was to become the ideological center of the Ukrainian nationalist movement. With the end of civil war in Russia, he abandoned his anti-Soviet activities, denouncing them in his appeals to the government of the Ukrainian Republic. He was granted permission to return to continue research. In 1924 he was elected academician of the Ukrainian Academy of Sciences, and in 1929 academician of the USSR Academy of Sciences. He headed the Ukrainian History Sector of the Division of History of the Academy of Sciences and was editor-in-chief of the *Ukraina* journal. In 1930 he removed to Moscow.

Grushevsky authored a great many works on Ukrainian history in which he drew widely on written, archaeological, and ethnographic sources. He was particularly attentive to the history of the Ukrainian peasantry and merchants. The national exclusiveness of the Ukrainian people and the classless nature of Ukrainian society were his central ideas. His major works include *Istoriya Ukraini-Rusi* (vols. 1–10, 13 books, 1898–1936; History of the Ukraine and Russia, in Ukrainian) and *Istoriya ukrainskoi literatury* (Vols. 1–5, 1923–1927; History of Ukrainian Literature, in Ukrainian). He presented a panorama of Ukrainian history from the fourth to the mid-seventeenth centuries. His *Illustrirovannaya istoriya ukrainskogo naroda* (1913; Illustrated History of the Ukrainian People) covered the period to the early twentieth century. He considered Kievan Rus to be a Ukrainian state; he denounced the Ukraine's unification with Russia and Bogdan Khmelnitsky's political activities, and praised those of I. Vygonsky and I. Mazepa. He tended to overrate the effect of the Ukraine's cultural and political ties with its Western neighbors on the destinies of its people.

Bibliography: M. M. Lipovchenko, *Na sluzhbe antinatsionalnoi politiki* (Serving Anti-National Policies), (Moscow, 1973, in Ukrainian); *Materiyali do bibliografii drukovanikh prats akad. Grushevskogo za 1905–1928. Yubileiny zbornik na poshanu akad. Mikhaila Sergievicha Greshevskogo* (Materials for the Bibliography of Academician Grushevsky's Works, 1905–1928. A Jubilee Collection) (in Ukrainian), vol. 3 (Kiev, 1929); *Ocherki istorii istoricheskoi nauki v SSSR* (Essays on the History of the Soviet Historical Science), vols. 3–4 (Moscow, 1963–1966).

A. A. Preobrazhensky

GUBER, Alexander Andreyevich (Kamenka Village, Kiev Province, 1902–Moscow, 1971), Soviet orientalist, specialist on Southeast Asian history. Outstanding promoter of scientific research, corresponding member of the USSR Academy of Sciences (1953), academician (1966). After graduating from the Moscow Institute of Oriental Studies in 1925, Guber worked at the Central Statistical Board (1925–1927), the Institute of History of the USSR Academy of Sciences (1938–1945; 1957–1968), the Institute of Pacific Studies (1945–1950), the Institute of Oriental Studies of the USSR Academy of Sciences, as deputy director and director (1950–1956), and the Institute of World History of the USSR Academy (1968–1971); he lectured at the Oriental Working Peoples' Communist University (1927–1937), at Moscow University (1937–1971); and he was editor-in-chief of the journal *Novaya i noveishaya istoriya* (Modern and Contemporary History) (1956–1962). He was one of the initiators of Soviet historical studies of Southeast Asia, mainly of Indonesia, the Philippines, and Vietnam (*Indonesia. Sotsialno-economicheskiye ocherki* (Moscow-Leningrad, 1932; Indonesia. Socioeconomic Essays); *Filippiny* (Moscow, 1937; The Philippines); *José Rizal* (Moscow, 1937); *Filippinskaya respublika 1898 g. i amerikansky imperialism* (Moscow, 1948; The 1898 Republic of the Philippines and U.S. Imperialism); and *Novaya istoriya stran zarubezhnogo Vostoka* (Moscow, 1961; Modern History of Eastern Countries). He elaborated certain major problems of the historical development of Eastern countries, including the emergence of the colonial Indonesian social structure, and was the first to define the class nature and motive forces of the Philippine revolution. He authored works on the general problems of the colonial peoples' national liberation movement, on the history of international relations, and on oriental studies, and taught lecture courses on the history of oriental countries.

Bibliography: P. N. Demichev, B. N. Ponomarev, M. V. Keldysh, et al., "Akademik A. A. Guber" (Academician A. A. Guber), *Vestnik AS SSSR* (Moscow, 1971), no. 8; O. S. Larionova, "Bibliografiya osnovnykh trudov akademika A. A. Gubera" (Bibliography of Main Works by Academician A. A. Guber), *Kolonializm i natsionalno-osvoboditelnoye dvizheniye v stranakh Yugo-Vostochnoi Azii* (Colonialism and the National Liberation Movement in the Countries of Southeast Asia), (Moscow, 1972), pp. 294–310; B. A. Udler, "Vydayushchiysya issledovatel i organizator nauchnogo tvorchestva. K 70-letiyu so dnya rozhdeniya akademika A. A. Gubera" (An Outstanding Scholar and Science Promoter. The Seventieth Birth Anniversary of Academician A. A. Guber), *Novaya i noveishaya istoriya* (Moscow, 1972), no. 4, pp. 211–212.

V. A. Vrevsky

JANASHIA, Simon Nikolaevich (1900–1947), Georgian Soviet historian. Author of a scientific periodization of the ancient and medieval history of Georgia. Analyzing the evidence of linguistics, numismatics, archaeological material, and the written sources in different languages, Janashia studied the problem of formation of the state in Georgia ("The Origin of Social Classes and the State Among Georgian Tribes," 1932), and questions of the origin and genetic relations of the Georgian tribes with the peoples of the Caucasus and the Ancient East. He substantiated the thesis on the local, Caucasian origin of the Georgian ethnos, the ethnic affinity of the Georgian tribes with the ancient peoples of the Near East and other peoples of the Caucasus ("Tubal-Tabal, Tibaren, Iber," 1937; "The Ancient National Tradition on the Original Habitat of the Georgian Tribes in the Light of the History of the Near East," 1940). He also dated the emergence of the ancient Georgian states. Janashia made a substantial contribution to the study of the origin and development of feudal relations in Georgia; he substantiated the thesis on the development of feudalism on the basis of the disintegration of the communal system and the turning of free commoners into serfs; and he shed light on the basic internal and external factors leading to the spread of Christian ideology and to the declaration of Christianity as the state religion early in the fourth century. The tenth to the twelfth centuries hold a special place in the history of medieval Georgia, for that was the period when feudal Georgia attained the acme of its power and culture. Janashia identified the principal antecedents of the historical process of reunification of Georgian lands and the creation of a united Georgian feudal monarchy ("The Feudal Revolution in Georgia," 1935; "Georgia on the Road to Early Feudalization," 1937, "A History of Georgia from Ancient Times to the Turn of the 13th Century," 1943). Janashia was a prominent public figure and a major organizer of science and scholarship; he was president of the Academy of Sciences of the Georgian SSR, director of the Institute of History, head of the History Department of Tbilisi State University, director of archaeological excavations in Mtskheta, the ancient capital of Georgia, and one of the first interpreters of the rich materials shedding light on many important questions of the history of classical Georgia.

For his contribution to science and scholarship and the training of scientific personnel Janashia was twice awarded the State Prize of the Soviet Union (1942 and 1947). His numerous works on political, social, and ethnic history, on problems of historical geography, and the history of medieval Georgian culture are being published in six volumes; volumes 1–4 were published in 1949–1968.

M. Lordkipanidze

KARAMZIN, Nikolai Mikhailovich (Mikhailovka Village, Samara Province, 1766–St. Petersburg, 1826), foremost Russian nobleman, historian, writer, and journalist. Karamzin was educated at a Moscow private school and took the Grand Tour in 1789–1790. He was a witness to the early stage of the French Revolution and hailed it as the beginning of a new age. The next stages of the Revolution, however, produced a distinctly negative assessment and left an imprint on his conception of history. In 1803, Tsar Alexander I appointed him official historiographer of the Russian Empire. His *Pisma russkogo puteshest-vennika* (1790s; Letters of a Russian Traveler); *Zapiska o drevnei i novoi Rossii* (1811; Notes on Old and New Russia); and his articles and novels contain a full exposition of his historical views. His chief work, *Istoriya gosudarstva rossi-iskogo* (History of the Russian State), was published in twelve volumes beginning in 1803. It was the first complete history of Russia from the earliest times to the seventeenth century. Karamzin's historical conception was an intricate combination of enlightened ideas and feudal ideology. He disregarded the popular masses believing they had no role to play in history, and considered "the great ones" to be the mainspring of historical progress. He also imparted great significance to the psychological background of historical events. Although a supporter of autocratic rule, he sharply criticized despotic abuse of power, especially during Ivan the Terrible's reign. His ideal was an "enlightened monarchy" based on "primordial laws." He saw serfdom as an inalienable part of Russian life. In his writings he emphasized Russia's uniqueness and its distinct historical development. He pointed out, however, that many stages of Russian history coincided with those of the West European countries (the appanage period, the formation process of the Russian centralized state). His historical views rested on rationalist ideas of social development, faith in the ultimate triumph of progress, reason, and enlightenment. History, in his opinion, was an important means of education and, to some extent, an example to follow in practical activities. In his writings he drew on a vast amount of sources. He was the first to use the earliest chronicles, legal deeds, memoirs, and other materials that found their way into his *Istoriya gosudarstva rossiiskogo*. They do, in fact, constitute its most valuable section.

Bibliography: N. Y. Eidelman, *Posledniy letopisets* (The Last Chronicler), (Moscow, 1983); *Istoriografiya istorii SSSR* (Historiography of USSR History), (Moscow, 1961); L. G. Kislyagina, *Formirovaniye obshchestvenno-politicheskikh vzglyadov N. M. Karamzina* (1785–1803) (Shaping of Karamzin's Socio-Political Views. 1785–1803), (Moscow, 1971).

A. V. Semenova

KAREYEV, Nikolai Ivanovich (Moscow, 1850–Leningrad, 1931), Russian historian. Founder of the "Russian school" in the historiography of the French Revolution. Graduated from Moscow University in 1873 where he studied under V. I. Guerie. Professor at the University of Warsaw (1879–1884) and St. Petersburg University (from 1885); corresponding member of the Russian Academy of Sciences (1910); and honorary member of the USSR Academy of Sciences (1929). His views on history are expounded in the following works: *Osnovnye problemy filosofii istorii* (1897; Basic Problems of the Philosophy of History), *Istoriko-filosofskiye i sotsiologicheskiye etyudy* (1899; Historico-Philosophical and Sociological Sketches); *Teoriya istoricheskogo znaniya* (1913; Theory of Historical Knowledge); Historiology, 1915; *Sushchnost istoricheskogo protsesa i rol lichnosti v istorii* (1914; The Essence of the Historical Process and the Individual's Role in History).

Departing from Auguste Comte's (q.v.) division of sciences into specific and abstract, Kareyev classified them as "phenomenological" (which include history) and "nomological." In his view, the philosophy of history is designed to develop ideals according to which actual history should be judged; it must provide orientation and stimuli for the successful accomplishment of the tasks of human existence. Proceeding from this subjective-teleological concept, he attached great importance to the role of individuals who create ideals that integrate into social consciousness and, in his opinion, motivate social activity. Besides historical-philosophical and sociological investigations, Kareyev did special research into historiography and world history, paying much attention not only to political and spiritual, but also to economic, aspects of historical developments. The results were summed up in the following works: *Ocherk istorii reformatsionnogo dvizheniya i katolicheskoi reaktsii v Polshe* (1866; An Essay on the History of the Reformist Movement and Catholic Reaction in Poland); *"Padeniye Polshi" v istoricheskoy literature* (1888; "Poland's Fall" in Historical Literature); *Polskiye rehormy XVIII v.* (1890; Polish Reforms in the Eighteenth Century); and *Istoriya Zapadnoi Evropy v novoye vremya* (1892–1917; Contemporary History of Western Europe). His master's dissertation (Krestyane i krestyanskiy vopros vo Frantsii v poslednei chetverti XVIII v. (1879; Peasants and the Peasant Problem in France in the Last Quarter of the Eighteenth Century), an uncommon piece of research based on a vast amount of archive and printed sources, demonstrated the antifeudal nature of the peasant movement during the Revolution. Together with certain other of his works (*Parizhskiye sektsii vremen frantsuzskoi revolyutsii Revolutsionnye komiteti Parizhskikh sektsii* (1913; The Revolutionary Committees of the Paris Sections), *Beglye zametki po ekonomicheskoi istorii Frantsii v epokhu revolyutsii* (1913–1915; Brief Notes on French Economic History in the Revolutionary Epoch), and *Istoriki frantsuzskoi revolyutsii* (1924; Historians of the French Revolution), his dissertation drew scholarly attention to the agrarian problem and the role of the "lower classes" in the French Revolution and contributed to further progress in its socioeconomic interpretation. His works gave birth to the tradition developed by Ivan Vassilievich Luchitsky (q.v.), Maksim M. Kovalevsky (q.v.), J. Jaurès, A. Mathiez, Georges Lefelvre (q.v.), Evgeny V. Tarle (q.v.), Y. Zaher, Nikolai M. Lukin (q.v.), A. Soboul, and V. Dalin, among others.

Bibliography: V. M. Dalin, *Istoriki Frantsii XIX-XX vekov* (French Historians of the Nineteenth-Twentieth Centuries), (Moscow, 1981); L. V. Gnatyuk, "N. I. Kareev's Sociological Concept," in *Aktualnye problemy istorii filosofii narodov SSSR* (Vital Problems of the History of Soviet Peoples' Philosophy), (Moscow, 1972), pp. 497–516; A. N. Nechukhrin, "N. I. Kareev on the Classification of Social Sciences," in *Problemy vseobshchei istorii i istoriografii* (Problems of World History and Historiography), (Tomsk, 1979), pp. 181–194; B. G. Veber, *Istoriograficheskiye problemy* (Historiographic Problems), (Moscow, 1974); V. P. Zolotarev, "Class Struggle in N. I. Kareyev's Concept," in *Voprosi otechestvennoi i vseobshchei istorii v trudakh russkikh istorikov XIX-nachala XX veka* (National and World History in the Works of Russian Historians of the Nineteenth-Early Twentieth Centuries), (Voronezh, 1983), pp. 77–85.

S. Y. Carp

KHVOSTOV, Vladimir Mikhailovich (Kazan, 1905–Moscow, 1972), Soviet historian. Specialist in modern history and international relations; member of the USSR Academy of Sciences since 1964 (corresponding member since 1953). Khvostov's career as teacher and researcher began in Kazan in 1925. In 1934–1941 he was assistant professor and then professor of Moscow University. Later, he worked at the Central Committee of the Communist party of the Soviet Union (1944–1945 and 1957–1959) and was director of the Higher Diplomatic Academy of the USSR Ministry of Foreign Affairs (1945); head of the chair of international relations of the Academy of Social Sciences under the CPSU Central Committee (1946–1954); and department chief and member of the Collegium of the USSR Ministry of Foreign Affairs. As expert and adviser he was included in Soviet delegations to many international conferences and U.N. General Assembly sessions. Khvostov was director of the USSR Academy of Sciences' Institute of History (1959–1967); president of the USSR Academy of Pedagogical Sciences (1967–1971); and academician-secretary of the USSR Academy of Sciences' Division of History. He was also a member of the German Democratic Republic Academy of Sciences (1967) and the Serbian Academy of Sciences and Arts (1965) and twice winner of the USSR State Prize (1942 and 1946). As a historian, Khvostov wrote prolifically on the history of German imperialism, Italy, Great Britain, the German Democratic Republic, and other countries, in addition to many books on Soviet history. As researcher he was mostly interested in the history of international relations, and in Russia's and the Soviet Union's foreign policies. His outstanding works in this field include the following: *Istoriya diplomatii* (History of Diplomacy), 2 vols., 1957 (2d revised and enlarged edition, 1963); *40 let borbi za mir* (1957; Forty Years of Struggle for Peace); *Problemi istoriyi vneshnei politiki SSSR i mezhdunarodnikh otnosheniyi* (1976; Historical Problems of Soviet Foreign Policy and International Relations); *Izbrannye trudy* (1976; Selected Works); and *Problemi istorii vneshnei politiki Rossii i mezhdunarodnikh otnosheniy* (1977; Historical Problems of Russia's Foreign Policy and International Relations at the Turn of the Nineteenth Century), *Izbrannye trudy*.

Bibliography: *Istoriya i istoriki* (History and Historians), 1971, (Moscow, 1973), pp. 377–386 (enclosed is a list of V. M. Khvostov's publications in 1965–1972); A. Z. Manfred and Y. A. Polyakov, "Outstanding Soviet Historian Vladimir Mikhailovich Khvostov (June 1905–March 9, 1972)," *Istoriya SSSR* (History of the USSR), no. 4 (1972); P. N. Pospelov, S. D. Skazkin, and I. D. Ostoya-Ovsyanyi, "Academician Vladimir Mikhailovich Khvostov," *Novaya i noveishaya istoriya* (Modern and Contemporary History), no. 5 (1970): 235–241; L. V. M. Stern, "Chwostow zum Gedenken," *Zeitschrift für Geschichtswissenschaft*, no. 6 (Berlin, 1972): S. 743–744; *Voprosi istoriyi vneshnei politiki SSSR i mezhdunarodnikh otnosheniyi. Sbornik statei pamyati akademika Vladimira Mikhailovicha Khvostova* (Historical Problems of Soviet Foreign Policies and International Relations. Collection of Articles in Memory of Academician Vladimir Mikhailovich Khvostov), (Moscow, 1976); "Wladimir Michailowitch Chwostow," *Spiegel*, no. 13 (1972).

N. V. Strelchenko

KLYUCHEVSKY, Vassili Osipovich (Voskresenskoye Village, Penza Uezd, 1841–Moscow, 1911), Russian historian. Klyuchevsky was the son of a clergyman. From 1851 to 1860 he studied in Penza in the parish theological school, then in the Uezd theological school, and later in a seminary. In 1861 he entered the Department of History and Philology of Moscow University. During his student years he was greatly influenced by F. I. Buslayev, S. V. Eshevsky, S. M. Solovyev (q.v.), and A. P. Shchapov. Upon graduation in 1865, he was chosen to remain at the university to prepare for a professorship. His candidate thesis "Skazaniya inostrantsev o Moskovskom gosudarstve" (Foreign Accounts of Muscovy) could be characterized as a source study. Although written in the traditions of the historical-juridical school, it exhibited the author's interest in economic problems. His master's thesis, "Drevnerusskiye zhitiya svyatykh kak istoricheskiy istochnik" (1781; Old Russian Saints' Lives as a Historical Source), a fundamental source study, required a detailed investigation of some five thousand descriptions of lives, their classification and clarification of origin. In 1882 he defended his doctorate, "Boyarskaya Duma drevney Rusi" (The Boyar Duma in Old Rus), in which he demonstrated that the history of a government institution belonged to social history rather than to the history of law. In 1867 he began to lecture on Russian and world history in specialized educational establishments. In 1879 he replaced his teacher, S. M. Solovyev, at Moscow University, where he worked first as assistant professor, and, beginning in 1882 for thirty years, as professor. He was also university dean and prorector. In 1889 he was elected corresponding member of the Academy of Sciences, and in 1900 academician of the Belle Lettres Division. He belonged to the Moscow Archaeological Society, the Society of Lovers of Russian Literature, and the Society of History and Russian Antiquities, and contributed to the journals *Russkaya mysl* (Russian Thought), *Pravosslavnoye obozreniye* (Review of the Russian Orthodoxy), *Drevnyaya i novaya Rossiya* (The Old and New Russia), and others.

Klyuchevsky extended considerably the range of historical research, making intensive studies of problems of economic history, the economic and legal aspects of peasant servitude in Russia, and the financial history of Muscovy. He was the first to establish a correlation between sixteenth- and nineteenth-century monetary units and to introduce the concept of "social classes" in Russian historiography. He investigated the role of autocracy in Russian history and delved deeply into the history of Russian culture. Klyuchevsky created a general concept of Russian history that was most fully expressed in his famous *Kurs russkoi istorii* (A Course of Russian History). As distinct from Solovyev who sought to avoid dividing or dismembering Russian history into periods, he emphasized periodization, simultaneously departing from the traditional eighteenth- and nineteenth-century division according to reigns. He based his periodization on multiple factors—geographical, economic, social, and political. His *Course* ran to many editions both in this country and abroad.

Bibliography: E. G. Chumachenko, *V. O. Klyuchevsky-istochnikoved* (Klyuchevsky and Source Studies), (Moscow, 1970); R. A. Kireyeva, *Klyuchevsky kak istorik russkoi istoricheskoi nauki* (Klyuchevsky as a Russian Historiographer), (Moscow, 1966); M. V. Nechkina, *Vassily Osipovich Klyuchevsky. Istoriya zhizni i tvorchestva* (Klyuchevsky: His Life and Work), (Moscow, 1974).

R. A. Kireeva

KONRAD, Nikolai Iosifovich (Riga, 1891–Moscow, 1970), Russian orientalist, historian, and philologist. Educated at St. Petersburg University, the Department of Oriental studies; majored in Chinese and Japanese (1912). Konrad visited Japan following his graduation (1912) and stayed there from 1914 to 1917 to study the language, literature, and philosophy, as well as Chinese philosophy at Tokyo University. From 1920 to 1922 he headed the University of Oryol, and from 1922 to 1939 he held the chair of Japanese philology, set up on his initiative. Simultaneously, from 1931 to the end of his life, he was on the staff of the Institute of Oriental Studies, USSR Academy of Sciences. He received a professorship in 1926 and his doctor's degree in philology in 1934, the same year he was elected corresponding member of the USSR Academy of Sciences and in 1958 a full member. Konrad initiated academic Japanese studies in the Soviet Union and is responsible for a number of standard Russian translations of Japanese classics such as *Isemonogotari* (1921) and *Kojoki* (1921). He readied for publication an anthology of Russian translations from Japanese and critical essays: *Yaponskaya literatura v obraztsakh i ocherkakh* (1927; Japanese Literature: Selected Pieces and Essays). Konrad also wrote on modern and contemporary literature and art in Japan. He made an appreciable contribution to Soviet Sinology and published his own translation of two ancient Chinese treatises on the art of war: *Sun-tzu* (1950) and *Wu-tzu* (1958), together with an essay on each. In 1923, he published *Yaponia. Narod i gosudarstvo* (Japan: The People and State) followed by a lifelong study of Japan's socioeconomic system. He closely scrutinized political, economic, and ideological processes and phenomena and critically analyzed historical and cultural documents, thus re-creating in his works true historical settings, lifeways, and common folk activities.

In his last studies Konrad sought to outline the general course of history in ancient times and in the Middle Ages. That is, during the slave-owning and feudal stages, on the basis of historical material of the East (primarily China and Japan) and of the West (mainly Western Europe), Konrad maintained that the Renaissance should be viewed not as a local but as a worldwide phenomenon, characteristic of all major cultural nations: *Zapad i vostok* (1966; East and West). He was noted for his comprehensive approach to the history of each country under study, considering it not in isolation but in close connection with other countries. Many of his works have been translated into foreign languages. He is highly appreciated in Japan. The academic edition of his selected works in three volumes on history, literature, and drama was published posthumously in the Soviet Union in 1974–1976, as were his *Ocherki yaponskoi literatury* (1973; Essays on Japanese Literature), and *Yaponskaya literature (ot Kojiki to Tokutomi)* (1974; Japanese Literature from Kojiki to Tokutomi).

Bibliography: *Istoriko-filologicheskiye issledovaniya. Sbornik statei k semidesyatiletiyu akademika N.I. Konrada* (Historico-Philological Studies. Collected Articles for the Seventieth Birth Anniversary of Academician Konrad), (Moscow: Nauka Publishers, 1967); *Istoriko-filologicheskoye issledovaniye. Sbornik statei pamyati akademika N.I. Konrada* (Historico-philological Study. Collected Articles in Memory of Academician Konrad), (Moscow: Nauka Publishers, 1974).

G. G. Sviridov

KOSMINSKY, Evgeni Alekseevich (Warsaw, 1886–Moscow, 1959), Russian Soviet historian and medievalist. Following graduation from Moscow University in 1910, Kosminsky was professor at his alma mater (1915–1952); chairman of medieval West European history (1934–1949, excluding 1941–1943); researcher of the USSR Academy of Sciences' Institute of History (1936–1959); head of the medieval history division (1947–1952) and of the Byzantine Empire history division (1952–1959) of this institute; corresponding member (1939) and full member (1945) of the USSR Academy of Sciences; merited scientist of the USSR (1947) and honorary doctor of Oxford University (1956). Kosminsky was mostly a student of the economic and social history of medieval England; he was also interested in historiography, the history of the Byzantine Empire, and the English Revolution of the 1640s–1660s. He had 270 publications. His major works are the following: *Angliiskaya derevnya v XIII veke* (1935; The English Village in the Thirteenth Century), and *Issledovaniya po agrarnoi istorii Anglii XIII v.* (1947; Studies in the Agrarian History of England in the Thirteenth Century) and a series of articles on the social history of England in the fourteenth and fifteenth centuries. ("The Evolution of Feudal Rent in England from the Eleventh to Fifteenth Century," *Past and Present*, no. 7 (1955); "Peut-on considérer XIVᵉ et XVᵉ siécles comme l'époque de la décadance de l'économie européenne," in *Studi in onore di Armando Sapori*, 1957).

Kosminsky's original concept of the landed hereditary estate as a social organization to exploit the peasantry, and archive sources helped him prove that F. Simbom's and Paul G. Vinogradov's (q.v.) classical estate theories, as well as F. W. Maitland's (q.v.) and his school's critique, were wrong. Statistical analysis of the sources revealed a great variety of estate structures and rent relations in England as early as the thirteenth century, and a high level of commodity-money relations and its contradictory effect on the agrarian system. He established that, contrary to the opinion of P. G. Vinogradov, D. M. Petruschevski, and many others, the estate (manor) was affected by an everyday, limited, but acute peasant struggle against the feudal lords. He was the first to raise the problems of wage labor under feudalism and of different economic interests of big and small feudal lords. Thus, using the historical material pertinent to England, he posed a number of important general problems relevant to the social, economic and, partly, political history of West European feudalism as a whole, which explains the noticeable impact which many of his inferences made on Western and, particularly, English medieval history studies. His books on historiography include *Istoriographiya srednikh vekov* (1963; Historiography of the Middle Ages), and numerous articles on this subject in *Problemy angliiskogo feodalizma i istoriografii srednikh vekov* (1963; Problems of English Feudalism and Medieval Historiography), which gave a thorough, objective analysis of historical thinking and science in the past and the present, including medieval history studies in the Soviet Union. His approach to historiographic investigations proved very fruitful for Soviet scholars in this field. Kosminsky contributed significantly to the revival of Byzantine studies in the Soviet Union based on new methodological principles.

Bibliography: M. A. Barg, "E. A. Kosminsky as England's Agrarian History Student," *Sredniye veka*, Issue 37 (Moscow, 1973), pp. 273–277; "E. A. Kosminsky's Scientific and Social Activities (For His Seventieth Birth Anniversary)," *Sredniye veka* (The Middle Ages), Issue 8 (Moscow, 1956), pp. 5–15; E. V. Gutnova, "Evgeny Alekeevich Kosminski," *Problemy iostorii* (Problems of History), no. 9 (1972); E. V. Gutnova and N. A. Sidorova, "E. A. Kosminsky's Scientific Works and Activities," in *Problemy angliiskogo feodalizma i istoriografii srednikh vekov* (Problems of English Feudalism and Medieval Historiography), (Moscow, 1963), pp. 3–34; M. Postan, "Academician E. A. Kosminsky," *Past and Present*, no. 16 (1959): 95; Z. V. Udaltsova, "E. A. Kosminsky's Role in the Development of Soviet Byzantine Studies," *Sredniye veka* (The Middle Ages), Issue 37 (Moscow, 1973), pp. 278–283.

E. V. Gutnova

KOVALEVSKY, Maksim Makcimovich (Kharkov, 1851–Petrograd, 1916), Russian historian, sociologist, ethnographer, lawyer, and public figure. Received his education at the University of Kharkov. Upon graduation in 1872, Kovalevsky traveled to Berlin, Vienna, Paris, and London to perfect his knowledge. In 1878–1887 he was professor of public law and comparative law history at Moscow University, Department of Law. In 1887 he was removed from teaching because of his liberal political views. He lived abroad from 1888 through 1908, lecturing in European and U.S. universities; he was one of the initiators of the International Institute of Sociology (Paris, 1894) and the Russian Higher School of Social Sciences (Paris, 1901). On his return to Russia in 1905 he continued teaching. In 1906 he founded a noninfluential Constitutional Monarchy party of Democratic Reforms with its own paper *Strana* (1906–1907). He was elected deputy to the First State Duma in 1906 and to the State Council in 1907, and member of the Russian Academy of Sciences in 1914. His early works on the social and political history of England of the late Middle Ages, *Obshchestvennyi stroi Anglii v kontse srednikh vekov* (1880; England's Social System in the Late Middle Ages) traced the effect of economic development on government institutions. Of particular interest were his works on the community. In his *Obshchinnoye zemlevladeniye, prichiny, khod i posledstviya ego razlozheniya* (1879; Communal Ownership of Land, Its Causes, Progress, and After-Effects of Decay), which is a comparative historical study of the community in different countries, he argued both with the Russian Narodniks and West European scholars (Numa Denis Fustel de Coulanges, [q.v.]) who advocated the perpetuity of private ownership of land.

As an ethnographer Kovalevsky is known for his studies of the tribal relations and common law among Caucasian peoples based on the findings of three expeditions in which he took part. He proved the historical role of an extended family, or a patriarchal family community as a form of tribal disintegration. Karl Marx (q.v.) and Friedrich Engels (q.v.) highly appreciated these and previous works by Kovalevsky on the community. His monograph *Proiskhozhdeniye sovremennoi demokratii* (vols. 1–4, 1895–1897; The Origin of Modern Democracy) was the major historiographic treatise in prerevolutionary Russia on the prerequisites and the early period of the French Revolution. His work *Ot priamogo harodopravstva k predstavitelnomu i ot patriarkhal noi monarkhii k parlamentarizmu* (vols. 1–3, 1906; From Direct to Representative Popular Rule and from Patriarchal Monarchy to Parliament) treated the history of state systems and political doctrines from the democracy of Athens to Rousseau. Kovalevsky also authored a three-volume work *Ekonomichesky rost Evropy do vozniknoveniya kapitalisticheskogo khoziaistva* (1898–1903; The Economic Growth of Europe Before the Rise of the Capitalist Economy), (enlarged German edition: *Die Ökonomische Entwicklung Europas bis zum Beginn der Kapitalistischen Wirtschaftsform*, Berlin, 1901–1914, Bd. 1–7).

Kovalevsky viewed population growth as the major factor in economic changes. Several of his works deal with sociology, which he considered to be a general theory of social development. He was a positivist, an evolutionist, and a supporter of Auguste Comte's (q.v.) and Herbert Spencer's ideas. He was influenced by Marx and Engels whom he knew personally, and Spencer as well. He espoused the idea of gradual improvement of social institutions in contrast to Marxism. In his early works he explained social evolution as the result of socioeconomic processes; later, he switched over to a multifactoral approach, attributing an important role in history to psychology and biology.

Bibliography: Y. N. Emelyanov, "M. M. Kovalevski. Bibliographicheski ocherk, bibliographiya sochineni i trudov o Kovalevskom" (M. M. Kovalevsky. Biographical Essay and a Bibliography of Articles and Works about Him), *Istoriya i istoriki. Istoricheskiy ezhegodnik* (History and Historians. Historical Yearbook), (1980, Moscow, 1984), pp. 298–337; B. A. Kaloev, *M. M. Kovalevski i ego issledovaniya gorskikh narodov Kavkaza* (Kovalevsky and His Studies of the Caucasian Mountain Peoples), (Moscow, 1979); *M. M. Kovalevski. Ucheniyi, gosudarstvennyi i obshchestvenniyi deyatel i grazhdanin. Sbornik statei* (M. M. Kovalevsky the Scholar, Statesman, Public Figure and Citizen. Collection of Articles), (Petrograd, 1917); B. G. Safronov, *M. M. Kovalevski kak sotsiolog* (Kovalevski the Sociologist), (Moscow, 1960).

I. M. Suponitskaya

KRACHKOVSKY, Ignatii Yulianovich (Vilno, 1883–Leningrad, 1951), Soviet Arabist. A graduate of the Department of Oriental Languages of St. Petersburg University (1905), Krachkovsky became assistant professor (1910), and then professor at Petrograd University (1918), head of the chair of Arab philology of the university's Eastern Department (1944–1950), associate with the Asiatic Museum (1916), and head of the Arab Study of the Institute of Oriental Studies of the USSR Academy of Sciences (1930). He was a member of the USSR Academy of Sciences (1921), the Arab Academy (Damascus), the Iranian Academy of Sciences, the Polish Academy of Sciences, the German Society for Oriental Studies, the Royal Asiatic Society of Great Britain and Ireland and others, a member of the Russian (All-Union) Geographical Society (1909, vice-president, 1937–1945), and a member of the Russian Archaeological Society (1908–1923) and of the Russian Palestinian Society (1915). He specialized in the history of Arab culture of the sixth through twentieth centuries and source studies (*Izbr. soch.*, vols. 1–6, Moscow-Leningrad, 1955–1960; Selected Works). Using literary sources, he traced the ideological shifts in the ninth-century Caliphate (see his numerous articles, *Izbr. soch.*, vols. 2, 6). In making public an Arabic document dated 717–719 found on Mount Moog in the upper reaches of Zeravshan ("Drevneishii arabskii dokument iz Srednei Asii"—The Earliest Arabic Document from Central Asia, *Izbr. soch.*, vol. 1), he proposed a fresh approach to the spread of Islam in Central Asia, the organization of Arab administration there, relations between the local nobility and conquerors, the position of the maula, and so on. His studies of Arabic culture in Spain (*Arabskaya kultura v Ispanii* (1937; Arabic Culture in Spain), "Arabskaya poeziya v Ispanii" (Arab Poetry in Spain), *Izbr. soch.*, vol. 2, revealed the major cultural centers, the correlation of local and Arabic languages, specific features of cultural life, and Arab scientific and cultural penetration of Western Europe. In furtherance of Russia's oriental research traditions (Kh. Fren, V. Rozen, Vassily V. Barthold, [q.v.], P. Kokovtsev), he worked out a plan of publications of Arab sources on the history of Soviet peoples (1932), edited *Puteshestviye Ibn Fadlana na Volgu* (1939; Ibn Fadhlan's Travels Along the Volga), and *Materialy po istorii turkmen i Turkmenii* (1939; Materials on the History of the Turkmens and Turkmenia).

Krachkovsky launched studies of modern Arabic literature in the second half of the nineteenth and twentieth centuries, noting the predominance of general

Arabic traditions in Syrian and Lebanese literatures and of local traditions in Egyptian literature (*Izbr. soch.*, vol. 3). His fundamental survey, *Istoriya arabskoi geograficheskoi literatury* (History of Arabic Geographical Literature) (*Izbr. soch.*, vol. 4), analyzes the development of that branch of science from pre-Islamic times to the nineteenth century and the Arabic influence on Persian and Turkish geography. He dealt with the history of Arabic studies in *Istoriya russkoi arabistiki* (A History of Russian Arabic Studies), in *Polveka ispanskoi arabistiki* (Half a Century of the Spanish Arabic Studies) and in a number of articles devoted to certain scholars (*Izbr. soch.*, vol. 5).

Bibliography: V. I. Belyaev and I. N. Vinnikov, "Pamyati akad. Krachkovskogo" (In Memory of Academician Krachkovsky), *Palestinsky sbornik* 1, no. 63 (1954): 91–105; H. H. Giesecke, "I. J. Krackovskij (1883–1951)," *ZDMC* (1955): 6–17; Th. Menzel, "Über die Werke des russischen Arabisten I. Krackovskij," *Archiv orientalni*, no. 1 (1930): 54–86; I. N. Vinnikov, " Dopolneniya k bibliografii trudov akad. I. Y. Krachkovskogo" (Supplements to Academician Krachkovsky's Bibliography) *Palestinsky sbornik* 1, no. 63 (1954): 125–129; I. N. Vinnikov, *I. Y. Krachkovsky* (Leningrad, 1949); A. Y. Yakubovsky, "I. Y. Krachkovsky kak istorik" (Krachkovsky the Historian), *Izvestiya Akademii Nauk (IAN)*, Seriya istorii i filosofii (Bulletin of the Academy of Sciences. History and Philosophy Series), no. 1 (1945): 40–46.

S. B. Pevzner

LAMANSKI, Vladimir Ivanovich (St. Petersburg, 1833–St. Petersburg, 1914), Russian historian, linguist, and ethnographer. A graduate of the University of St. Petersburg (1854), Department of History and Philology; assistant professor (1865) and professor (1871), Department of Slavic Languages, University of St. Petersburg (until 1888); professor of the General Staff Academy (until 1900). Lamanski's master's dissertation (1859) was "O slavyanakh v Maloi Azii, Afrike i Ispanii" (On Slavs in Asia Minor, Africa and Spain). He received his Ph.D. (1871) for a paper entitled "Ob istoricheskom izuchenii greko-slavyanskogo mira v Evrope" (On Historical Studies of the Graeco-Slavic World in Europe). In 1900 he was elected a member of the Russian Academy of Sciences; he was also chairman of the Division of Ethnography of the Russian Geographical Society and an active member of the Slavic Committee of St. Petersburg. As a researcher he dealt with practically all Slavic-related disciplines, but mostly with their historical aspects. His principal historical concept was based on contrasting the "Graeco-Slavic, Eastern-Christian world" to the "Roman-German, Catholic-Protestant world." In his critique of the prejudiced and falsified history of the Slavic peoples in Western European, especially German, historiography, he judged the historical development of the West and its civilization from no less biased pan-Slavic positions. Nonetheless, his numerous works on the history and culture of the Slavs are based on a wealth of factual material and are still of certain value.

Bibliography: P. D. Draganov, "The Bibliography of V. I. Lamanski's Works of Science and Fiction and Materials for His Biography," in *Novyi sbornik statei po slavyanovedeniyu, sostavlennyi i izdannyi uchenikami V. I. Lamanskogo* (A New Collection of Articles on Slavic Studies Compiled and Published by V. I. Lamanski's Disciples), (St. Petersburg, 1905); L. P. Lapteva, "Lamanski Vladimir Ivanovich," in *Slavyanovedeniye v dorevolyutsionnoi Rossii. Bibliographicheskiy slovar* (Slavic Studies in Russia Before the Revolution. Bibliographical Dictionary), (Moscow, 1979); I. A. Linnichenko, "Patriarkh russkogo slavyanovedeniya" (The Patriarch of Russian Slavic Studies), *Goloss Minuvshego* (The Voice from the Past), no. 2 (1916).

V. A. Dyakov

LUCHITSKY, Ivan Vassilievich (Kamenets-Podolsky, 1845–Poltava, 1918), Russian historian. Specialist on the Middle Ages and modern history. Luchitsky received his education at the Department of History and Philology of the University of Kiev (1868), and he then studied at the Ecole des chartes and the Ecole pratique des recherches historiques and worked in foreign archives (1872–1874). He was professor at the University of Kiev (1877–1918), and lecturer at the Higher Women Courses and Lesgaft Courses in Petrograd (1918). He was elected corresponding member of the Russian Academy of Sciences in 1908. In his first writings, *Gugenotskaya aristokratiya na yuge Frantsii v 1572 g.* (1869; The Huguenot Aristocracy in Southern France in 1572), his master's thesis "Feodalnaya aristokratiya i kalvinisty vo Frantsii" (1871; The French Feudal Aristocracy and the Calvinists), and his doctorate "Katolicheskaya liga i Kalvinisty vo Frantsii" (1877; The Catholic League and the Calvinists in France), he advanced an innovative conception of the religious wars, exposing their sociopolitical and class nature by demonstrating that the religious mantle of the Huguenot wars concealed clashing class groups. The greater part of his work is devoted to the history of the community ("Syabry i syabrinnoe zemlevladeniye v Malorossii" (The Syabry and Syabry Land Tenure in the Ukraine), *Severny vestnik* (1889, no.1, The North Herald), "Begetrii. Ocherk iz istorii ispanskikh uchrezdenii" (The Behetrias. Essay on the History of Spanish Institutions), *Universitetskiye izvestiya* (1882, no. 1; The University Bulletin), and "Pozemelnaya obshchina v Pirineyakh" (The Land Community in the Pyrenees), *Otechestvennye zapiski* (1883, nos. 9–10; Russian Notes). This cycle, based on materials from various countries, showed the multiformity of the community, traced its evolution, and set out to prove that it was a law-governed developmental stage.

Luchitsky is best known for his works on French agrarian history and was the first to apply statistical research methods to the study of hitherto neglected archival documents. In his books *Krestyanskoye zemlevladeniye vo Frantsii nakanune revolutsii* (1900; Peasant Land Tenure in France on the Eve of the Revolution); *Sostoyaniye zemledelcheskikh klassov vo Frantsii nakanune revolutsii i agrarnaya reforma 1789–1793 gg.* (1900; The Conditions of the Landtilling Classes in France on the Eve of the Revolution and Agrarian Reforms of 1789–1783), he identified specific features of peasant land tenure on the eve of the French Revolution. He also initiated Spanish and Scandinavian studies in Russia: "Krestyane i krestyansky vopros v Danii 16 i 18 v." (Peasants and the Peasant

Question in Denmark of the Sixteenth and Eighteenth Centuries), *Severny vestnik* (1889, no. 12; The North Herald); "Obshchestvenny stroi Shvetsii i razvitiye ee konstitutsii" (The Swedish Social Structure and Constitutional Development), *Istoricheskoye obozreniye* (1892, vol. 5; Historical Review); "Napoleon i Ispaniya" (Napoleon and Spain), *Otechestvennaya voina i russkoye obshchestvo 1812 g.* (1911, vol. 2; The Patriotic War and Russian Society in 1812). He founded a school of historical studies engaged mainly in agrarian history. Among his pupils were the prominent historians V. K. Piskorsky, D. M. Petrushevsky, and Eugeny V. Tarle (q.v.).

Bibliography: A. Se, "Chem ekonomicheskaya i sotsialnaya istoriya Frantsii 18 v. obyazana trudam I.V. Luchitskogo" (The Indebtedness of French Economic and Social History of the Eighteenth Century to Luchitsky), *Nauchno-istorichesky zhurnal* (A Journal of History), no. 14 (1914): 22–29; P. F. Laptin, "Problemy obshchiny v trudakh I. B. Luchitskogo" (Community Problems in Luchitsky's Works), *Sredniye veka* (The Middle Ages), Issue 23 (Moscow, 1963): 216–226; Ph. Sagnac, "La propriété foncière et les paysans en France au VXIII s. d'après les travaux de M. J. Lutchisky," *Revue d'histoire moderne et contemporaine* (Paris, 1901): 151–171; "Spisok pechatnykh trudov I. V. Luchitskogo" (A List of Luchitsky's Works), *Istoriya i istoriki* (History and Historians), (Moscow, 1985); B. G. Veber, "Proiskhozhdeniye religioznykh voin v osveshchenii I. V. Luchitskogo" (The Origin of Religious Wars in the Views of Luchitsky), *Frantsuzsky ezhegodnik* (The French Yearbook), (Moscow, 1958), pp. 514–559.

S. I. Luchitskaya

LUKIN, Nikolai Mikhailovich (Kuskovo Village, Moscow Province, 1885–?1940), Soviet historian. Graduated from Moscow University in 1909; trained under Robert Yuryevich Vipper (q.v.); was involved in the revolutionary movement; joined the Communist party in 1904; became associate professor at the University of Moscow in 1916. During this period Lukin continued underground Bolshevik activities as a contributor to the newspapers *Nash Put*, *Social Democrat*, and *Pravda* and he was the author of booklets on burning political issues. In October 1918 he received a professorship at Moscow University; in 1921 he was appointed dean of the Department of Social Sciences. He was also on the teaching staff of the Academy of the General Staff of the Workers' and Peasants' Red Army, the Moscow Institute of History, Philosophy, and Literature, and the Communist University. He was a founding father of the Socialist (later Communist) Academy, the Red Professoriate Institute, and the Institute of History of the Russian Association of Social Science Research Institutions. His other appointments and functions were as follows: member of the USSR Academy of Sciences (from 1929); contributor to and editor of *Bolshaya sovetskaya entsiklopediya* (The Larger Soviet Encyclopaedia) and member of its chief editorial board (1927); a founder of the Society of Marxist Historians (1925); editor-in-chief of the journal *Istorik-marksist* (Marxist Historian) (1933–1938); director of the Communist Academy's Institute of History (1932–1936); and first director of the USSR Academy of Sciences' Institute of History (1936–1937). In 1923 he published *Noveyshaya istoriya Zapadnoi Evropy* (Contemporary History of

Western Europe), the first Marxian manual on the subject. He led a team of authors who drafted a new history textbook for schools (1935–1936) and universities (1938). His attention centered on the new history of Western Europe (mostly France and Germany). His book *Maximilien Robespierre* (1919) and his articles on the Convent's food policy and the Jacobins' policy toward farm hands, as well as his article entitled "Lenin and the Problem of the Jacobinian Dictatorship," played an important role in developing the Marxist concept of the French Revolution. The history of the 1871 Paris Commune was another avenue of research. His book *Parizhskaya kommuna 1971 g.* (1921; The Paris Commune of 1871) touches on the major historical aspects of the world's first proletarian state.

In the early 1920s Lukin was one of the first Soviet scholars to turn to the history of Germany during imperialism. In 1925 he published his *Ocherki po noveishei istorii Germanii* (1890–1914; Essays on the Modern History of Germany). He was also concerned with methodology and periodization as editor of the multivolume *Vsemirnaya istoriya* (World History) compiled by a team of historians in the latter part of the 1930s. His works were published in three volumes in the Soviet Union in 1960–1963.

Bibliography: V. A. Dunayevski and A. V. Tsfasman, "The Centenary of Academician Nikolai Lukin," *Vestnik AN SSSR* (Bulletin of the USSR Academy of Sciences), no. 7 (1985); *Evropa v novoye i noveisheye vremya. Sbornik statei pamyate akademika N. M. Lukina* (Europe in Modern Times. A Collection of Articles in Memory of Academician Lukin), (1966); I. S. Galikin, *N. M. Lukin—revolutsioner, ucheny* (N. M. Lukin the Revolutionary and Scholar), (1984); V. A. Gavrilichev, "N. M. Lukin and His Role in Soviet Historiography of the Great French Revolution," *Frantsuzsky ezhegodnik* (French Yearbook), (1965).

V. A. Dunayevski

MANFRED, Albert Zakharovich (St. Petersburg, 1906–Moscow, 1976), Soviet historian. Specialized in the history of the New Times, mainly French history. Manfred's interests concentrated on the French Revolution and the Napoleonic period, the history of international relations, and the international working-class movement. His first important work was published in 1929. Beginning in 1930, he lectured at the higher educational establishments of Yaroslavl and, later, Ivanovo. He moved to Moscow in 1940 to become lecturer at the Moscow Regional Teachers' College (1940–1949), at the History Department of Moscow University (1945–1948), at the Institute of International Relations (1946–1949), and at the Institute of Foreign Languages (1956–1961). In 1945 he became an associate with the Institute of History of the USSR Academy of Sciences (in 1968 with the Institute of World History of the USSR AS); in 1966 he became head of the sector of the history of West European countries. He dealt with wide-ranging issues and published over two hundred works, including *Vneshnyaya politika Frantsii 1871–1891* (1952; French Foreign Policy in 1871–1891); *Ocherki istorii Frantsii XVIII–XX vv.* (1961; Essays on the History of Eighteenth to

Twentieth-Century France); *Traditsii druzhby i sotrudnichestva. Iz istorii russko-frantsuzskikh i sovetsko-frantsuzskikh svyazei* (1967; Traditions of Friendship and Cooperation. From the History of Russian-French and Soviet-French Ties); *Napoleon Bonaparte*, 1971; *Obrazovaniye russko-frantszuskogo soyuza* (1975; Formation of the Russian-French Alliance); *Tri portreta epokhi Velikoi frantsuzckoi revolutsii* (1978; Three Pen-Portraits of the Great French Revolution Epoch).

Manfred's writings are distinguished by their profound content and scintillating style. Even those on highly specialized subjects found a wide readership and often were printed in big editions. His best known books include *Marat* (1962) and *Frantsuzskaya burzhuaznaya revolutsia knotsa XVIII v. (1789–1794)* (1950; The French Bourgeois Revolution of the Late Eighteenth Century (1789–1794). It was revised, considerably enlarged, and published under the title *Velikaya frantsuzckaya burzhuaznaya revolutsiya XVIII v. 1789–1794* (1983; The Great French Bourgeois Revolution of the Eighteenth Century, 1789–1794). Manfred was a member of several editorial boards and made major contributions to numerous collective efforts: *Parizhskaya kommuna 1871 g.* (vols. 1–2, 1961; The 1871 Paris Commune); *Kratkaya vsemirnaya istoriya* (vols. 1–2, 1966; An Outline of World History); *Istoriya Frantsii* (vols. 1–3, 1972–1973; History of France), and many others. He labored energetically on documentary publications, dealing mostly with the French Revolution. An accomplished organizer and manager, Manfred was among the founding fathers of the French History Group at the Institute of History of the USSR Academy of Sciences, which he headed from 1962 to 1976. He also launched the *French Yearbook (Frantsuzski ezhegodnik)* and was its editor-in-chief from 1962 until his death in 1976. Manfred was elected doctor honoris causa of Clermont-Ferrand University (France), co-chairman of the International Commission of Historians of the Eighteenth-Century French Revolution, member of the USSR-France Society's presidium, and member of the National Committee of Soviet Historians.

Bibliography: *Bibliografiya trudov A. Z. Manfreda i Literatura ob A. Z. Manfrede* (Bibliography of Works by Manfred and About Him), compiled by S. N. Gurvich and M. I. Kovalskaya, in *Istoria i istoriki. 1975* (Moscow, 1973), pp. 352–365; V. Dalin, "Albert Manfred," *Annales Historiques de la Révolution Francaise*, no.1 (1978); V. M. Dalin, "Master istoricheskogo portreta" (Master of Historical Pen-Portraits), in V. M. Dalin, *Istoriki Frantsii 19–20 vekov* (French Historians of the Nineteenth and Twentieth Centuries), (Moscow, 1981), pp. 302–315; V. M. Dalin and S. V. Obolenskaya, "A. Z. Manfred (1906–1976)," in *Istoriya i istoriki. 1975* (History and Historians. 1975), (Moscow, 1978); *Dopolneniye k bibliografii trudov A. Z. Manfreda i k literature o nem* (Additional Materials to Bibliography of Works by Manfred and About Him), compiled by S. N. Gurvich and V. A. Pogosyan, in *Istoria i istoriki. 1976* (Moscow, 1979), pp. 395–397; "Pamyati A. Z. Manfreda" (in Memory of A. Z. Manfred), in *Frantsuzsky ezhegodnik* (Moscow, 1978), pp. 5–30; E. A. Zhekova, "Manfred zabelezhitelen predstavitel na sovetskata istoricheska nauka" (Manfred as an Outstanding Representative of the Soviet Historical Science), in A. Z. Manfred, *Napoleon Bonaparte* (Sofia, 1978).

G. S. Tchertkova

NECHKINA, Militsa Vassilyevna (Nezhin, 1901–Moscow, 1985), Soviet historian. Academician of the USSR Academy of Sciences (1958), full member of the Academy of Pedagogical Sciences of the Russian Federation (1947), State Prize-Winner. Upon graduation from Kazan University in 1921, Nechkina began teaching, first at Kazan University, later in Moscow in a school for workers at the Oriental Working Peoples' Communist University, and at Moscow University and the Academy of Social Sciences under the Soviet Communist party's Central Committee. In 1924 she took up part-time work at the Institute of History of the Russian Association of Research Institutions and at the Red Professoriate Institute where she participated in Mikhail Nikolaevich Pokrovsky's (q.v.) seminar. In 1935 she received her doctorate degree and a professorship at the Institute of History of the USSR Academy of Sciences and later at the academy's Institute of USSR History. She was a scholar of wide-ranging interests, focusing on the nineteenth-century Russian revolutionary movement, historiography, certain general problems of the USSR, history, and its methodology. Her research methods were based on a creative assimilation of Marxist-Leninist theory and methodology, a profound knowledge of Lenin's conceptions, and a comprehensive and detailed analysis of historical sources. She wrote the monographs *Obshchestvo soyedinennykh slavyan* (1927; United Slavs Society), *Griboedov i dekabristy* (1947; Griboedov and the Decembrists), *Vosstaniye 14 dekabrya 1825 g.* (1956; The December 14th Uprising of 1825), *Dvizheniye dekabristov* (1955; The Decembrists' Movement), and *Vassily Osipovich Klychevsky. Istoriya zhizni i tvorchestva* (1974; Klyuchevsky. His Life and Work). Among other activities she supervised and contributed to the documentary publications *Vosstaniye dekabristov* (The Decembrists' Uprising), facsimile editions of the Free Russian Printshop publications—*Kolokol* (The Bell), *Polyarnaya zvezda* (The Polar Star), *Golosa iz Rossii* (Voices from Russia), and others. Many collectively written works, handbooks, and college and school textbooks on the history of the USSR were brought out under her editing.

Nechkina made a major contribution to the study of the Decembrist movement; she defined its place in the Russian and world historical process. She also delved into the nobility's revolutionary sentiments; researched the revolutionary movement of the 1860s in connection with the first revolutionary situation in Russia; studied Herzen's, Ogarev's, and Chernyshevsky's theoretical writings and practical revolutionary work; and examined the program, tactics, and organizational structure of the Zemlya i Volya (Land and Freedom Society) in the 1860s. The results of her personal efforts and of the scientific collective she headed were summarized in the collections *Revolutionnaya situatsiya v Rossii 1859–1861 gg.* (Issues 1–8, 1960–1979; The 1859–1861 Revolutionary Situation in Russia) and a collective monograph of the same title. Historiographic problems figured prominently in her work. She was a competent organizer and represented Soviet science abroad on many occasions. She was decorated with three Orders of Lenin, the Friendship of Peoples Order, and other government awards.

Bibliography: L. B. Cherepnin, "Akademik Militsa Vassilievna Nechkina (tvorchesky put)" (Academician Nechkina. Her Creative Work), in *Problemy istorii obshchestvennogo dvizheniya i istoriografii* (Problems of the History of Social Movements and Historiography), (Moscow, 1971).

M. G. Vandalkovskaya

NEUSSYKHIN, Alexandr Iosifovich (Moscow, 1898–Moscow, 1969), Soviet authority on medieval history. A Ph. D. in history since 1946. Neussykhin's major field of specialization was the social and economic history of the early Middle Ages in Western Europe and German medieval history. He showed an interest in Marxism while in the Gymnasium. A graduate of Moscow University (1921), he wrote his thesis ("The Social System of Ancient Germans") for a master's degree in 1929. His teaching career began in 1927. In 1934 he was awarded a full professorship; he was a lecturer on medieval history at the Moscow Institute of Philosophy, History and Literature (1934–1941), at the University of Tomsk (1941–1942), and at Moscow University (1943–1959). Beginning in 1936, he was a senior researcher at the Institute of History of the USSR Academy of Sciences. In 1946 he wrote his doctor's thesis, "Property and Freedom as Dealt with in Barbarian Codes of Law. Essays on the Evolution of Barbarian Society in Western Europe in the Fifth to Eighth Centuries" (published as a book entitled *Problemy evropeiskogo feodalizma* [Problems of European Feudalism] in 1974). Neussykhin focused his attention on the transition period from antiquity to the Middle Ages, with special insights into the social nature of ancient German society, the ways and forms of emergence of early class societies in the German kingdoms in the sixth to eighth centuries, the evolution of property rights, the social status and community organization of the Germans, and the genesis of feudal relations in the German village in the eighth through twelfth centuries. His research methods are characterized by an overall study of large complexes of the similar sources, analysis of the content and evolution of key social concepts of the society under study, reconstruction of individual "economic biographies," and a typological analysis of social processes.

The major results of Neussykhin's research work include: development of the concept of the prefeudal period as a transitory stage from primitive society to early feudalism among German peoples (outlined and formulated in an article entitled "Prefeudal Period as a Transitory Stage from the Tribal System to Early Feudalism," *Problemy Istorii* (no. 1, 1967; Problems of History); refutation of the theory of the mark that denied changes in the free German community in the period between primitive society and the Middle Ages and a definition of the basic stages and modifications in its development (a chapter by Neussykhin in the book *Istoriya krestyanstva v Evrope. Epokha feodalizma* [vol. 1, 1985; A History of Peasants in Europe. Feudal Epoch]); establishment of an interrelationship in the evolution of communal and family forms; and description of how free Germans were involved in feudal dependence and how social inequality turned into class inequality (his book *Vozniknoveniye zavisimogo krestyanstva kak klassa rannefeodalnogo obshchestva v Zapadnoy Evrope VI–VII vv.* (1956; The Rise of Dependent Peasants as a Class in the Early Feudal Society in Western

Europe in the Sixth to Eighth Centuries. The newness of the scholar's conclusions and research methods, as well as his mastery as a tutor, paved the way for the emergence in the 1940s–1960s of the Neussykhin School in Soviet medieval studies, to be joined by most of the leading students of the European early Middle Ages.

Bibliography: Y. L. Bessmertny, "Certain Features of A. I. Neussykhin the Researcher," *Problemi evropeiskogo feodalizma* (Problems of European Feudalism), (Moscow, 1974), pp. 20–34; a list of A. I. Neussykhin's works, in ibid., pp. 521–529;. A. I. Danilov, "A. I. Neussykhin, Student of Mediaeval History, Scholar and Teacher," *Sredniye veka* (The Middle Ages), Issue 32 (1969): 5–12; L. T. Milskaya, "A. I. Neussykhin the Scholar, Tutor and Man," in A. I. Neussykhin, *Problemi evropeiskogo feodalizma* (Problems of European Feudalism), (Moscow, 1974), pp. 7–19.

Y. L. Bessmertny

OKLADNIKOV, Aleksei Pavlovich (Konstantinovka Village, Irkutsk Province, 1908–Moscow, 1982), Soviet archaeologist and historian. Graduated from the Irkutsk Pedagogical Institute in 1934. Headed the Department of Ethnography at the Irkutsk Local Lore Institute in 1928–1934. Led the Angara archaeological expedition of the Museum in 1932–1934. Having concluded his postgraduate studies at the Academy of the History of Material Culture in Leningrad in 1938, Okladnikov became a candidate of sciences (history) the same year and a doctor of sciences (history) in 1947. He was senior research worker (1938–1952); head of the Leningrad Department of the Institute of the History of Material Culture of the USSR Academy of Sciences (1949–1952); head of the institute's Paleolithic Sector (1952–1961); deputy director of the Economics Institute of the Siberian branch of the USSR Academy of Sciences (1961–1966); and head of the Humanities Department of the Siberian branch (1961–1966). He was also head of the Department of World History and professor at Novosibirsk State University (1962–1981); a corresponding member of the USSR Academy of Sciences (1964); a full member (1968), and director (1966–1981) of the Institute of History, Philology, and Philosophy of the Siberian branch of the USSR Academy of Sciences, which he founded.

Okladnikov published more than 450 papers, including 50 monographs, many of which have been published abroad. He wrote highly important studies about the evolution of early Anthropoids, their settlement on the Asiatic continent, the migration of Paleosiberian tribes to America and the formation of its earliest population, primitive beliefs and the development of the early human's non-material culture, the origins of art, the ethnogenesis of the peoples of Siberia and the Far East, prehistoric archaeology and the history of Central Asia, problems in the ethnography, mythology, and folklore of the peoples of the world, and the history of science. He headed major expeditions that studied sites in the wastes of the Asiatic mainland and the coastlines and islands of the Arctic and Pacific Oceans. Okladnikov discovered quite a few major archaeological cultures and sites (the Neanderthal burial in the Teshik-tash cave in Uzbekistan, the Jebel cave site in Turkmenistan, the Lower Paleolithic Ulalinka site in the Altai Mountains, the Buret's site on the Angara River, famous for its earliest sculptures, and so on).

Bibliography: *Aleksei Pavlovich Okladnikov. Akademiya nauk SSSR. Materialy k bibliographii uchyonykh SSSR, seriya istoriya* (Aleksei Pavlovich Okladnikov. The USSR Academy of Sciences, Biographical Bibliography on Soviet Scholars, History Series), Issue 13 (Moscow, 1981), prefaced by R. S. Vasilyevsky; *Annotirovannaya bibliographiya nauchnykh trudov akademika A. P. Okladnikova* (1968–1973) (Annotated Bibliography of Academician A. P. Okladnikov's Works [1968–1973]), (Ulan-Ude 1974); V. Larichev, *Sorok let sredi sibirskikh drevnostei. Materialy k biografii akademika A. P. Okladnikova. Annotirovannaya bibliografiya (1926–1967)* (Forty Years of Research into Siberian Antiquities. Materials for Academician A. P. Okladnikov's Biography. An Annotated Bibliography [1926–1967]), (Novosibirsk 1970).

L. R. Kyzlasov

OLDENBURG, Sergei Fyodorovich (Nerchinsk District, Chita Province, 1863–Leningrad, 1934), Russian and Soviet orientalist. Oldenburg graduated from the Department of Oriental Languages of St. Petersburg University in 1885. He concentrated on the history of India, ancient Indian literature and art, with special emphasis on Buddhism, its art, ideology, and philosophy. He received his master's degree in 1895, became professor in 1897, was elected extraordinary academician of the Russian Academy of Sciences in 1903, and full member in 1908. He was permanent secretary and acting vice-president of the Russian Academy of Sciences—the USSR Academy of Sciences (1904–1929). From 1916 through 1934 he was director of the Asiatic Museum, which, on his initiative, became the Institute of Oriental Studies of the USSR Academy of Sciences (1930). Oldenburg made a weighty contribution to the study of Buddhism and Buddhist art of Central Asian peoples; he launched the widely known "Bibliotheca Buddhica" series, organized several large-scale expeditions to Central Asia in search of ancient written and artistic monuments, heading two of them, to Turfan (1909) and to Dunhuang (1914–1915). Together with his colleagues, he unearthed unique ancient Indian written and cultural monuments relating to Buddhism, dating back to the mid-first millennium A.D., including texts written in what is called the Buddhist Sanskrit and in the Tokharian and Saka languages. In the early twentieth century the Central Asian variant of ancient Indian writing and the three above-mentioned languages were a *terra incognita* for European orientalists, awaiting exploration through concerted efforts by the world's foremost authorities in the field. This ushered in a new field of knowledge: Central Asian philology. Oldenburg published a series of Sanskrit and Sak texts in *Zapiski vostochnoi komissii Rossiiskogo arkheologicheskogo obshchestva* (Transactions of the Russian Archaeological Society's Oriental Commission). For a long time he shared the conception of progressive historical evolution. In the 1920s he wholeheartedly adopted the historical materialism of Karl Marx (q.v.), Friedrich Engels (q.v.), and Lenin. His many articles, totaling over five hundred, deal with the topical problems of the history of Indian and Central Asian cultures and give a sweeping panorama of his chief scientific conclusions.

Bibliography: *Sergeyu Fyodorovichu Oldenburgu. K pyatidesyatiletiyu nauchno-obshchestvennoi deyatelnosti 1882–1932* (To Sergei Fyodorovich Oldenburg. On the Fiftieth Jubilee of His Scientific and Social Activity, 1882–1932), (Leningrad, 1934); *Vestnik Akademii Nauk SSR*, no.9 (1934): 108–127.

E. N. Tyomkin

PANKRATOVA, Anna Mikhailovna (Odessa, 1897–Moscow, 1957), Soviet historian, educator, and science promoter. Academician of the USSR Academy of Sciences (1953), political and public figure, corresponding member of the German and Roumanian Academies, honorary member of the Hungarian Academy, Bureau member of the International Committee on Historical Sciences, head of the National Committee of Historians of the Soviet Union, chairman of the Association for the United Nations in the USSR. Pankratova graduated from Odessa (Novorossiisky) University, with a degree in history in 1917. In 1925 she completed studies at the Red Professoriate Institute. She joined the Communist party in 1919. She had some two hundred works to her credit dealing with the history of the USSR, the Russian working-class and labor movement in Europe, and the 1905–1907 revolution. She was editor-in-chief and co-author of a school textbook on the history of the USSR. Her participation in the collective effort *Istoriya diplomatii* (History of Diplomacy) brought her the USSR State Prize.

Pankratova made a major contribution to source studies, the methodology of research into the history of the proletariat and industrial enterprises. Using the Marxist-Leninist theory and methodology as a reference point, she studied the history of the protoproletariat in Russia, the alienation process of the producer from the means of production, the emergence and growth of the working class within the disintegrating feudal formation, the appearance of the capitalist structure in the second half of the eighteenth century, the conditions and size of the Russian proletariat, the proletariat's vanguard role in the 1905–1907 revolution, the decisive role of the working class in the overthrow of tsarism, and the triumph of the 1917 socialist revolution in building the USSR's socialist foundations. Pankratova's works had a tangible influence on Soviet historiography of the working class and its revolutionary struggle. She was on the editorial boards of the journals *Istorik-Marxist* (Marxist Historian) and *Borba klassov* (The Class Struggle), and was editor-in-chief of the collected articles *Istoriya proletariata v SSSR* (History of the Proletariat in the USSR) issued in 1930–1935 and of the *Voprosy istorii* (Problems of History) journal, published in 1953–1957. Her main works include *Fabzavkomy v Germanskoi revolutsii* (Moscow, 1924; Factory Committees During the German Revolution), *Fabzavkomy i profsoyuzy v revolutsii 1917 goda* (Moscow, Leningrad, 1927; Factory Committees and Trade Unions in the 1917 Revolution), *Formirovaniye proletariata v Rossii (17–18 vv.)* (Moscow, 1963; Formation of the Proletariat in Russia in the Seventeenth and Eighteenth Centuries), and *Rabochii klass Rossii. Izbrannye trudy* (Moscow, 1983; The Russian Working Class. Selected Works).

Bibliography: *Bolshaya sovetskaya entsiklopedia* (The Larger Soviet Encyclopaedia), 3d ed., vol. 19 (Moscow, 1975); *Iz istorii rabochego klassai revolutsionnogo dvizheniya* (From the History of the Working Class and the Revolutionary Movement), (Moscow, 1958); *Sovetskaya istoricheskaya entsiklopediya* (The Soviet Encyclopaedia of History), vol. 10 (Moscow, 1967).

G. D. Alekseeva

PASHUTO, Vladimir Terentyevich (Leningrad, 1918–Moscow, 1983), Soviet historian. Pashuto graduated from the Department of History of Leningrad University in 1914, defended his candidate's thesis in 1949, *Ocherki po istorii Galitsko-Volynskoi Rusi* (1950; Essays on the History of Galich-Volhyn Rus), and received a doctorate in 1959, "Obrazovaniye Litovskogo gosudarstva" (1959; Formation of the Lithuanian State). He was elected corresponding member of the USSR Academy of Sciences in 1976. He was vice-president of the International Commission on the Estate and Representative Organizations, and member of the Bialystok Scientific Society. From 1945 on he was associated with the Institute of History (since 1969 the Institute of the History of the USSR) of the USSR Academy of Sciences, where he headed the sector of history of the earliest states on the USSR territory (1969–1977) and the department of precapitalist formations (from 1977). He also lectured at the Moscow History and Archives and Pedagogical Institutes.

Pashuto's interests embraced the emergence and development of class societies and the feudal state in the Slavonic and East Baltic countries. One of his writings took up the social structure and legal regulations of the Prussians, the Slavonic population on the Isle of Korčula, the formation of the feudal state in Lithuania and Rus. (Corresponding chapters are in *Drevnerusskoye gosudarstvo i ego mezhdunarodnoye znacheniye* [1965; The Old Russian State and its International Significance]. This research led to the conception of synchronous stages in the history of East European peoples and to the wide use of the comparative-typological method in the study of state formation and feudal structures (A. P. Novoseltsev, V. T. Pashuto, and L. V. Cherepnin, *Puti razvitiya feodalizma* [1972; Ways of Feudal Development]). He contributed significantly to the study of Old Russian diplomacy and foreign policy. See *Vneshnyaya politika Drevnei Rusi* (1968; Foreign Policy of the Old Rus), "Opyt periodizatsii istorii russkoi diplomatii" (An Essay on Periodization of the History of Russian Diplomacy), *Drevneishiye gosudarstva na territorii SSSR* (1984; The Earliest States on the Territory of the USSR, pp. 6–25). He laid special emphasis on Russia's traditional links with the European countries. Two of his books are devoted to the Russian people's struggle against foreign invaders (*Geroicheskaya borba russkogo naroda za nezavisimost v 12–14 vv.* ([1956; The Heroic Struggle of the Russian People for Independence Between the Twelfth and Fourteenth Centuries]), and *Alexander Nevsky* (1974, 1975). His interests pivoted on historiography and, in particular, critical scrutiny of the *Ostforschung* theoretical foundation and their use in historical writings: *Revanshisty-psevdoistoriki Rossii* (1971; The Revanchists as Pseudo-Historians of Russia). He launched the serial publication of historical sources *Drevneishiye istochniki po istorii narodov SSSR* (The Earliest Sources on the History of Peoples of the USSR) which covered all kinds of written monuments: narrations of classical antiquity and the Middle Ages, legal, epigraphic, and cartographic works of Europe and the Arab East. For his scientific and public activities he was decorated with government medals and orders.

Bibliography: A. P. Novoseltsev, "Tvorchesky put V. T. Pashuto" (Pashuto's Creative Work), *Istoria SSSR* (History of the USSR), no. 4 (1984): 80–91; "Spisok pechatnykh trudov V. T. Pashuto" (A List of Pashuto's Published Works), *Arkheografichesky ezhegodnik za 1983 god* (Archaeographical Yearbook, 1983), (Moscow, 1985), pp. 295–304.

E. A. Melnikova

PICHETA, Vladimir Ivanovich (Poltava, 1878–Moscow, 1947), Soviet historian. Graduate of Moscow University (1901), Department of History and Philology; assistant professor of Moscow University and lecturer at the Higher Women's Courses in Moscow (1906–1921); professor at Minsk and Moscow universities (1921–1947); member of the Byelorussian Academy of Sciences (1928); corresponding member (1939) and member of the USSR Academy of Sciences (1947). Picheta focused on the history of Eastern and Western Slavs in the feudal period, mostly the history of Russia, Belorussiya, and Lithuania as related to Polish history—for example, *Agrarnaya reforma Sigizmunda-Avgusta v Litovsko-Russkom gosudarstve* (vols. 1–2, 1917, 2d ed., 1958; Sigizmund-August's Agrarian Reform in the Lithuanian-Russian State); and *Belorrusiya i Litva XV–XVI v.v. Issledovaniya po istorii sotsialno-ekonomicheskogo, politicheskogo i kulturnogo razvitiya* (1961; Byelorussia and Lithuania in the Fifteenth and Sixteenth Centuries: Studies in the History of Social, Economic, Political, and Cultural Development). He was an outstanding organizer of Slavonic studies in the Soviet Union and a brilliant teacher. (Many of his students would become eminent scholars of Slavic history.) He headed the Department of Southern and Western Slavs at Moscow University (from 1939); he was chief of the Slavonic studies section at the Institute of History of the USSR Academy of Sciences; and a founding father of the USSR Academy of Sciences, Institute of Slavonic Studies (1946–1947).

Bibliography: E. Y. Dukor, *Vladimir Ivanovich Picheta. Bibliographicheskii ukazatel* (V. I. Picheta. A Bibliographical Index), (Minsk, 1978); *Slavyane v epokhu feodalizma. K stoletiyu akademika V. I. Pichety* (Slavs in the Epoch of Feudalism. For Academician V. I. Picheta's Centenary), (Moscow, 1978).

V. A. Dyakov

POKROVSKY, Mikhail Nikolaevich (Moscow, 1868–Moscow, 1932), Soviet historian, public figure, and statesman. Joined the Bolshevik party in 1905;

elected to the USSR Academy in 1929. In 1891, upon completing his education at Moscow University, Department of History and Philology, Pokrovsky was chosen to prepare for a professorship. He was active in the Russian social movement and participated in the 1905–1907 Revolution and the great 1917 Revolution. He was the first chairman of the Moscow Soviet of Workers' and Soldiers' Deputies, from October 1917 to March 1918, and was deputy people's commissar of education of the Russian Soviet Federated Socialist Republic from May 1918 until he died. He conducted a vast amount of educational and organizational work in the domain of history and public education. He was a member of the International Committee of Historical Sciences and participated in international congresses. He authored a great number of works on Russian history, especially the history of the revolutionary movement, foreign policy, and historiography. His was a long and hard road to Marxist-Leninist methodology in history. Early in his scientific career he was greatly influenced by Vassili O. Klyuchevsky (q.v.), Paul G. Vinogradov (q.v.), and legal Marxism. His adoption of economic materialism was the first step away from an idealistic interpretation of history. He proposed a progressive thesis on the unity of the historical process in Russia and the West. The evolution of his views was reflected in his recognition of the historic significance of the class struggle and the necessity of its culmination in a social revolution. In his generalizing work, *Russkaya istoriya s drevneishikh vremen* (1910–1914; History of Russia from the Earliest Times), he analyzed Russia's past according to the teaching on socioeconomic formations and severely criticized bourgeois conceptions concerning the nonagricultural character of Old Rus, the absence of feudalism in Russia, and the formation of the Russian centralized state resulting from "the princes' unification policy." He disproved the theory that the state held all Russian estates in bondage. His first efforts, however, bore the negative aspects of his conception: an oversimplified approach and abstract sociologizing, and an exaggeration of commercial capital's role in the historical process. The post-October period of Pokrovsky's activity showed maturity and greater emphasis on modern developments. He wrote the first popular exposition of Russian and Soviet history, *Russkaya istoriya v samom szhatom ocherke* (1920; Concise Russian History), which ran into ten enlarged editions edited by the author. He concentrated on Lenin's theory of the socialist revolution, on the 1917 October Revolution and its history: *Oktyabryskaya revolutsiya* (1929; The October Revolution. Collection of Articles), and on the nineteenth-century Russian revolutionary movement.

Pokrovsky's works testified to a cardinal shift in his views on fundamental historical problems (the periodization of the Russian revolutionary movement, the essence of Russian revolutionary democracy and Narodism, the nature and motive forces of the first Russian bourgeois-democratic revolution, and the correlation between spontaneous and consciously guided elements in a revolution). He regarded studies of imperialism as a central task of history. His own interpretation of this formation was profoundly erroneous. His gradual mastering of Lenin's theory of imperialism led him to a correct evaluation of Russia's imperialist nature in the pre-October 1917 period, which was reflected in his works on Russia's foreign policy: *Imperialisticheskaya voina* (1928; The Imperialist War). To the very last he perfected his outlook on history and progressed in his views to approach the Leninist concept of the historical process. He made a great contribution to the emergence of Soviet historical science.

Bibliography: *Ocherki istorii istoricheskoi nauki v SSSR* (Essays on the History of Soviet Historical Science), vols. 3–4 (Moscow, 1962–1966); O. D. Sokolov, *M. N. Pokrovsky i sovetskaya istoricheskaya nauka* (Pokrovsky and Soviet Historical Science), (Moscow, 1970).

A. I. Alatortseva

PORSHNEV, Boris Fyodorovich (St. Petersburg, 1905–Moscow, 1972), Soviet historian and sociologist. Porshnev graduated from Moscow University in 1925 and in 1929 completed a postgraduate course at the Institute of History of the Russian Association of Social Science Scientific Institutions, where he studied under Vyacheslav P. Volgin (q.v.). He held doctorates in history and philosophy, was honorary doctor of Clermont-Ferrand University (France), and a member of the Italian Institute of Sociology. His scientific and teaching career began in 1929 in Rostov-on-Don; later he removed to Moscow. In 1943 he became senior researcher with the Institute of History (from 1968, the Institute of World History) of the USSR Academy of Sciences and Professor at Moscow University. Porshnev published about two hundred works, many of which were translated into foreign languages. His scholarly interests were concentrated on the history of popular movements in seventeenth-century France. His major work, *Narodnye vosstaniya vo Frantsii pered Frondoi. 1623–1648* (1948; Popular Uprisings in France Prior to the Fronda, 1623–1648), paved the way to fundamental new research in this field. No less significant are his achievements in the study of eighteenth-century French Utopian communism (*Meslier*, 1964) which he regarded as a reflection of popular aspirations, a most important part of the national culture, and an ideological source of Marxism. Both books and his other writings focus on the decisive role in history of the popular masses and the class struggle. In his *Ocherki politicheskoi ekonomii feodalizma* (1956; Essays on the Political Economy of Feudalism) and *Feodalizm i narodnye massy* (1966; Feudalism and the Popular Masses) he offered a theoretical generalization of the problems of feudalism, capitalist genesis, and the transition from feudalism to capitalism. Problems of the social, political, and military history of the European nations, the international relations system, and Russia's place in it were discussed in two monographs, *Frantsiya, Angliiskaya revolutsiya i evropeiskaya politika v seredine XVII v.* (1970; France, the English Revolution and European Politics in the midseventeenth Century), and *Tridtsatiletniaya voina i vstupleniye v nee Shvetsii i Moskovskogo gosudarstva* (1976; The Thirty-Years War and Sweden and Muscovy's Entry into It).

Social psychology was another field that drew Porshnev's attention. His book *Sotsialnaya psikhologiya* (1966; Social Psychology) and collected articles *Isto-*

riya i psikhologiya (1971; History and Psychology) which he edited won him popularity both in the Soviet Union and abroad. He also worked in borderline fields and in disciplines that combined the social and natural sciences. He authored fundamental research on ethnography, anthropology, and biology. Marked attention was shown to published materials on the "abominable snowman," which he edited, and to his posthumously published *O nachale chelovecheskoi istorii* (1974; On the Origins of Human History), which he considered his lifetime work. He regarded human labor, purpose-oriented and conscious speech-regulated labor, to be a specific feature of humans, based on three indispensable and self-sustained factors—labor implements, speech, and the social character of labor. He stated they were interconnected and mutually dependent and, therefore, emerged simultaneously. He concentrated on the notion of the "instinctive labor" of protohumans and demonstrated how it evolved into the social being's conscious activity.

Bibliography: "Boris Fyodorovich Porshnev," *Voprosy istorii* (Problems of History), no. 1 (1973); V. A. Dunayevsky and G. S. Kucherenko, *Zapadnoevropeisky utopicheskiy sotsializm v rabotakh sovetskikh istorikov* (West European Utopian Socialism in Soviet Historical Writings), (1981); Kh. N. Momdjan, S. A. Tokarev, and L. I. Antsyferova, "Introduction," to B. F. Porshnev, *O nachale chelovecheskoi istorii (Problemy paleopsikhologii)* (On the Origins of Human History: Problems of Palaeopsychology), (1974); "Spisok trudov B. F. Porshneva" (Bibliography of B. Porshnev's Works), *Istoriya i istoriki* (History and Historians), (1966, 1973).

G. S. Kucherenko

SHAKHMATOV, Aleksei Aleksandrovich (Narva, 1864–Petrograd, 1920), Russian scholar, linguist, and textual critic. An authority on Russian chronicles and cultural history. In 1887 Shakhmatov graduated from the Department of History and Philology at Moscow University. While a student he wrote a fundamental study, *Issledovaniye o yazyke novgorodskikh gramot XIII-XIV vv.* (1866; Studies of the Language of Thirteenth and Fourteenth-Century Novgorodian Deeds), the first in a series on the history of the Russian language and historical dialectology. In 1890 he became assistant professor at Moscow University, following which he worked in the Saratov *Zemstvo* for three years. He took this opportunity to study peasant life, land tenure reforms, and speech. In this space he completed his thesis "Issledovaniya v oblasti russkoi fonetiki" (Studies in Russian Phonetics) which brought him a doctorate in 1894. He was elected adjunct professor of the Academy of Sciences and moved to St. Petersburg the same year. Later he became extraordinary (1897) and ordinary (1898) academician of the St. Petersburg Academy, full member of the Serbian Academy of Philosophical Sciences (1904), corresponding member of Cracow (1908) and Berlin (1910) universities, professor at St. Petersburg University (1910), and chairman of the Division of the Russian Language and Literature of the Academy which, under his guidance, became the philological center of Russia. He resumed publication of the *Polnoye sobraniye russkikh letopisei* (Complete Russian Chronicles), supervised the printing of a monumental series of Church Slavonic and

Old Russian texts, and helped compile dictionaries and the *Entsiklopediya slav-yanskoi filologii* (Encyclopaedia of Slavonic Philology). He figured prominently in the reform of Russian orthography.

Shakhmatov's many studies of the Russian chronicles constituted an epoch and brought about a revolution in research methods. As distinct from his predecessors who regarded the chronicles as a collection of diverse materials, Shakhmatov saw them as finished works. He was the first to carry out a comprehensive systematized investigation of all chronicle materials from ancient times to the seventeenth century. He discovered a pattern of Russian chronicle-writing and formulated the principles of his textual comparison method. He foretold the existence of certain chronicles, after boldy experimenting with reconstructions of eleventh and twelfth-century written monuments, and later they were unearthed. He had a tremendous influence on his contemporaries and succeeding historians using his methods.

Bibliography: V. I. Buganov, *Otechestvennaya istoriografiya russkogo letopisaniya* (Russian and Soviet Historiography of the Russian Chronicles), (Moscow, 1975); L. L. Muravyeva, *Letopisaniye Severo-Vostochnoi Rusi kontsa XII–nachala XI veka* (Chronicles of the Late Thirteenth and Early Fourteenth Centuries in Northeastern Russia), (Moscow, 1983); *Ocherki istorii istoricheskoi nauki v SSSR* (Essays on Historiography in the USSR), (Moscow, 1963), vol. 3; M. N. Tikhomirov, "Shto novogo vnes A. A. Shakhmatov v izucheniye drevne-russkich letopisei" (The New Elements Shakhmatov Introduced into the Study of Ancient Russian Chronicles), in M N. Tikhomirov, *Russkoye letopisaniye* (Russian Chronicles), (Moscow, 1979).

R. A. Kireeva

SHCHERBATSKY, Fyodor Ippolitovich (Kalisz, Poland, 1866–Borovoye, 1942), Russian Indologist specializing in the culture and history of ancient and medieval India. On being graduated from the Department of History and Philology at St. Petersburg University with a degree in Sanskrit, Indian history, and literature, Shcherbatsky continued his education in Austria and Germany. From 1901 to 1930, he lectured at St. Petersburg (Leningrad) University. (He was elected corresponding member of the USSR Academy of Sciences in 1910 and Full Member of the Academy in 1918.) He made a trip to India in 1910 in connection with his studies. His research centered on source studies, on historico-philosophical problems, and on collecting and publishing manuscripts pertaining to the history of Buddhism. His major works include *Buddistskaya Logika* (Buddhist Logic), 2 vols., English edition, 1930–1932; publications of sources (texts and translations) in the series "Bibliotheka Buddhica"; "Kistorii materialisma v Indii" (On the History of Materialism in India), in *Vostochnye Zapiski* (vol. 1, 1927; Eastern Notes), "Nauchnye dostizheniya drevnei Indii" (1923; Scientific Achievements in Ancient India), *Report on the Activities of the Russian Academy of Sciences* (1924); and the Russian translation of *Arthashastra* by Kautilya made with his participation and under his editorship (1959). His theory was based on the premise that a study of ancient Indian thinking reveals its correspondence to the universal laws of thinking, which is evident not only from its philosophy but also from mathematics, physics, and other natural sciences. His work remains an important contribution to the overcoming of Eurocentrism. His ideas enjoy tremendous international prestige and have been further elaborated in the works of other Soviet Indologists. He was elected honorary member of several orientalist societies abroad.

Bibliography: *Indiyskaya kultura i buddizm. Sbornik statei k stoletiyu so dnya rozhdeniya Akademika F. I. Shcherbatskogo* (Indian Culture and Buddhism. Collection of Articles for Academician F. I. Shcherbatsky's 100th Birth Anniversary), (Moscow, 1972); *Izbrannye Trudy Russkikh Indologov-Philologov* (Selected Works of Russian Indologist-Philologists), (Moscow, 1962), pp. 340–342; V. I. Kalyanov, "Akademik F. I. Shcherbatsky," (Academician F. I. Shcherbatsky), *Izvestia Academii nauk, Otdeleniye yazyka i literatury* (Proceedings of the USSR Academy of Sciences, Language and Literature Department) 5, no. 3 (1946): 245–252.

I. D. Serebryakov

SKAZKIN, Sergei Danilovich (Novocherkassk, 1890–Moscow, 1973), Soviet medievalist. Full member of the USSR Academy of Sciences (1958) and of the USSR Academy of Pedagogical Sciences (1947). Skazkin was awarded the title of Hero of Socialist Labor in 1970. Upon completing his studies at Moscow University's Department of History and Philology in 1915, he joined its staff in 1920, receiving a professorship from the Department of History in 1935 and the chair of medieval history in 1949. He was appointed head of the section of medieval history at the Institute of History (renamed Institute of World History in 1968) of the USSR Academy of Sciences (1962) and served as editor-in-chief of the yearbook *Sredniye Veka* (Middle Ages) beginning in 1959. His scholarly interests were wide ranging and diverse. In his over fifty-year academic and teaching career, he not only established his own research school, but he also blazed new trails in Soviet medieval studies. His pivotal themes were agrarian history, the nature of feudal land tenure, special features of the French and Spanish agrarian systems, the history of West European peasantry, the various paths taken by feudal relations, and the conditions underlying their genesis.

Skazkin devoted much attention to the study of what he called "the second edition of serfdom" in Central and Eastern Europe. According to his theory, agriculture developed in two ways in the late Middle Ages (the sixteenth to eighteenth centuries): the disintegration of feudal relations and the emergence of capitalism in most countries of Western Europe, and the consolidation of the corvée system in areas west of the Elbe (*Genezis kapitalizma v promyshlennosti i selskom khozyaistve* (1965; The Genesis of Capitalism in Industry and Agriculture). His extensive research into medieval history was consummated in his definitive monograph *Ocherki po istorii Zapadno-evropeiskogo krestyanstva v sredniye veka* (1968; Outline History of West European Peasantry in the Middle Ages). The book is based on a course of lectures read by the author to students and postgraduates at the Department of History at Moscow University. He was also concerned with the history of the feudal state and was the first Soviet scholar to study the multiple forms absolutism took in various European countries, while emphasizing that it was invariably the gentry that provided the social foundation for absolute monarchies. Skazkin was greatly interested in medieval cultures and ideologies, and he is credited with works on the history of the Renaissance and Humanism, heretical movements, and so on. See *Izbrannye trudy po istorii* (1973; Selected Historical Writings); and *Iz istorii sotsialno-politicheskoi i dukhovnoi zhizni Zapadnoi Yevropy v sredniye veka* (1981; From the History of Sociopolitical and Spiritual Life in the Medieval Western Europe). In his earlier research he was likewise concerned with modern history of the eighteenth and nineteenth centuries, in particular with agrarian relations in prerevolutionary France and the history of diplomacy. In his monograph *Konets Avstro-Russko-Germanskogo Soyuza* (1928; The End of the Austro-Russo-German Alliance), he drew on previously unpublished records. Together with Evgeni A. Kosminsky (q.v.) he was the first editor and one of the authors of the university course on medieval history. Skazkin has made a sizable contribution to the Marxist interpretation of medieval history. He was one of the most well-loved professors at Moscow University and educated many future scholars, particulary medievalists.

Bibliography: Y. V. Gutnova, *Sergei Danilovich Skazkin*, in the series, *Biobibliografiya Sovetskikh uchenykh* (Biographical Bibliography on Soviet Scholars), (Moscow, 1967); Y. V. Gutnova and A. N. Chistozvonov, "Akademic S. D. Skazkin i problemy medievistiki" (Academician S. D. Skazkin and Problems of Medieval Studies), in *Yevropa v sredniye veka: ekonomika, politika, kultura* (Europe in the Middle Ages: Economics, Politics, Culture), (Moscow, 1972); Y. V. Gutnova, V. M. Dalin, et al., "Akademic S. D. Skazkin" (Academician S. D. Skazkin), in *Voprosy Istorii* (Problems of History), no. 4 (1966).

V. K. Shatsillo

SOLOVYEV, Sergei Mikhailovich (Moscow, 1820–Moscow, 1879), Russian historian. Academician (1872). Born into a clergyman's family, Solovyev, received his education at Moscow University (1838–1842), was influenced by Timofei N. Granovsky, and works by François Guizot (q.v.), Augustin Thierry (q.v.), and M. Evers, and Georg Wilhelm F. Hegel's (q.v.) philosophy. In 1845 he started to read a course on Russian history at Moscow University. He defended his master's thesis, "Ob otnoshenii Novgoroda k velikim knyazyam" (On Novgorod's Attitude to the Grand Princes) and, in 1847, his doctorate "Istoriya otnoshenii mezhdu russkimi knyzyami Ryurikova doma" (History of Relationships of the Russian Princes of the House of Ryurik). He held a professorship at Moscow University beginning in 1847, was the dean of the university's Department of History and Philology from 1864 through 1870, and university rector in 1881–1877. During the last years of his life he chaired the Moscow Society of Russian History and Antiquities and was director of the Armory. He had numerous works to his credit, including *Istoriya Rossii s drevneishikh vremen* (29 vols., 1851–1879; History of Russia from the Earliest Times), fundamental monographs *Imperator Aleksandr I. Politika. Diplomatiya* (1877; The Emperor Alexander I. Policy. Diplomacy), and *Publichnye chteniya o Petre Velikom* (1872; Public Lectures on Peter the Great). As a liberal who negatively assessed serfdom and the despotic power of tsarist autocracy, he feared peasant movements and had little in common with revolutionaries. His *Istoriya Rossii* most fully reflects his historical conception, which was opposed to subjectivist views of the historical process expressed by Nikolai M. Karamzin (q.v.) in his *Istoriya gosudarstva Rossiiskogo* (History of the Russian State). He regarded social history as the onward development of an integral whole taken within the context of its inner interrelationships and interaction of varied factors, among which he gave predominance to the state.

Being a follower of the state school of historical thought, Solovyov saw historical development as changes of state forms. He recognized that serfdom and the state based on it were law-governed phenomena, but he refused to see the class struggle as an historical regularity. For many, this position revealed his methodological and class-oriented narrowmindedness. A proponent of comparative-historical methods, he discerned in Russian history both common traits of European development and specifically Russian features. Solovyev's studies of Russian history brought a vast amount of archival documents to scholarly attention. His was a substantial contribution to the study of certain periods. He associated the earlier history of Russia with the processes occurring within the country (urban development, colonization of contiguous territories), he rejected the conquest periodization of ancient history and the identification of the ''Norman'' and ''Mongolian'' periods, and he considered the transition from clan to state relations to be of the utmost importance. For the first time in Russian historiography, he connected the state's centralization with the struggle to cast off the Mongol yoke. He saw the emergence of serfdom as the result of Russia's specific natural conditions and the states' requirements, while playing down its class nature. He regarded the Great Upheaval as a reaction of antistate forces to the centralization process and the seventeenth- and eighteenth-century peasant wars as the natural course of history. His interests focused on the reforms of Peter the Great, and he was the first to demonstrate their objectively law-governed nature. His works greatly influenced Russian historical thought and have retained their significance to this day.

Bibliography: L. V. Cherepnin, ''Solovyev kak istorik'' (Solovyev as a Historian), in S. M. Solovyev, *Istoriya Rossii s drevneishikh vremen*, Book 1 (Moscow, 1959); V. E. Illeritsky, *Sergei Mikhailovich Solovyev*, (Moscow, 1980); *Ocherki istorii istoricheskoi nauki v SSSR* (Essays on Historiography in the USSR), (Moscow, 1950), vol. 2; *S. M. Solovyev. Personalny ukazatel literatury (1838–1981)* (S. M. Solovyev. Personal Bibliography (1838–1981), (Moscow, 1984).

M. G. Vandalkovskaya

SPITSIN, Alexander Andreyevich (Yaransk, Vyatka Province, 1858–Leningrad, 1931), Russian archaeologist and historian. On graduating from the University of St. Petersburg in 1832, Spitsin taught at a classical school in Vyatka and studied local history. He investigated some Iron Age fortified settlements in the Kama area, proving their links with Ananyino-type burials: *Arkheologi-*

cheskiye razyskaniya o drevnikh obitatelyakh Vyatskoy gubernii (1893; Archaeological Studies of the Early Settlers of Vyatka Province). In 1892 he was invited to serve on the Imperial Archaeological Committee in St. Petersburg where he worked until it became the Academy of the History of Material Culture. As a member of that academy (1919–1931), he worked on a vast project of systematizing archaeological finds—both incoming from all over the country and those accumulated in Russian museums in the previous two hundred years. The materials he studied ranged chronologically from the Paleolithic *Russky paleolit* (1915; The Russian Paleolithic), to the late Middle Ages. They came from a vast territory stretching from Poland to Eastern Siberia and from the Kola Peninsula to Transcaucasia. This work was reflected in the committee's annual reports, province-by-province overviews of Russian antiquities (1895–1899), and more than three hundred books and papers by Spitsin.

Spitsin identified the Bronze Age Fatyanovo culture, *Mednyi vek v Verkhnem Povolzhye* (1903; The Copper Age in the Upper Volga Region), and the Dyakovo culture, *Gorodishcha dyakova tipa* (1903; Settlements of the Dyakovo Type). He also studied Lithuanian: *Lyutsinskiy mogilnik* (1893; The Liucin Burial Ground); Finnish: *Drevnosti basseina rek Oki i Kamy* (1901; The Antiquities of the Oka and the Kama Basins), 1901; *Drevnosti Kamskoi chudi po kollektsii Teploukhovykh* (1902; The Antiquities of the Kama Chud from the Teploukhovs' Collection); and Slavic monuments: *Kurgany Peterburgskoi gubernii v raskopkakh L. K. Ivanovskogo* (1896; The Burial Mounds of Petersburg Province Excavated by L. K. Ivanovsky). By mapping the types of ornaments from Central Russian burial mounds, he showed the correspondence between the groups thus specified and the distribution of the Old Russian tribes described in the chronicles, *Rasseleniye drevnerusskikh plemyon po arkheologicheskim dannym* (1899; The Distribution of Old Russian Tribes from Archaeological Data). He also published the manuals *Arkheologicheskiye razvedki* (1908; Archaeological Surveys), *Arkheologicheskiye raskopki* (1910; Archaeological Excavations), and *Kurs russkoi istoricheskoi geografii* (1917; A Course of Russian Historical Geography). Spitsin lectured at the University of St. Petersburg (Leningrad) and left extremely rich archives, which Soviet archaeologists still use today.

Bibliography: B. A. Latynin and T. S. Passek, "K stoletiyu so dnya rozhdeniya A. A. Spitsina" (For the the 100th Birth Anniversary of A. A. Spitsin). *Sovetskaya arkheologiya*, no. 3 (1958): 3–6; "Spisok uchyonykh trudov A. A. Spitsina" (List of Scholarly Works by A. A. Spitsin), *Sovetskaya Arkheologiya*, 10 (1948: 12–20).

A. A. Formozov

STRUVE, Vassily Vassilievich (St. Petersburg, 1889–Leningrad, 1965), Russian and Soviet orientalist. Struve received his education at St. Petersburg University, Department of History and Philology, where he majored in Egyptian history of the ancient, Graeco-Roman and Byzantine-Arabic periods. His teacher was B. A. Turayev (q.v.). Struve was chosen to remain at the University for research and teaching. He spent the 1914 summer semester at the University of

Berlin attending courses of prominent Egyptologists, Erman, Edouard Meyer (q.v.), and Meller. In 1919 he took up Akkadian, Hebrew, Aramaic, and other Semitic languages while continuing his studies of Egypt. It was during the 1930s that he delved into the historical problems of ancient Middle East countries, especially of socio-economic relations. In 1933–1934 he concluded that the Orient had also lived through slavery. His other activities were the following: head of the Egyptian Department of State Hermitage (1914–1933), professor at Petrograd (Leningrad) University (1916–1965), member of the USSR Academy of Sciences (1935), director of the Leningrad Institute of Oriental Studies of the USSR Academy of Sciences (1941–1950), and head of its Ancient East Department (1958–1965). Over four hundred works were printed under his name. The main ones include "Peterburgskiye sfinksy" (Sphinxes of St. Petersburg), *Zapiski klassicheskogo otdeleniya Rossiiskogo arkheologicheskogo obshchestva* (VII, 1912; Transactions of the Classical Antiquity Department of the Russian Archaeological Society); *Proiskhozhdeniye alfavita* (1923; Origins of the Alphabet); "Mathematischer Papyrus des Staatlichen Museum der schönen Künste in Moskau," *Quellen und Studien zur Geschichte der Mathematik*, hrsg. O. Nengebauer, I. Stenzel und O. Toeplitz. Abt. A, Bd. 1, 1980; *Istoriya drevnego Vostoka* (1941; History of the Ancient Orient); *Gosudarstvo Lagash. Borba za rasshireniye grazhdanskogo prava v Lagashe XXV-XXIV vv do n.e.* (1961; The State of Lagash. Struggle for Broader Civil Rights in Lagash in the 25th–24th Centuries B.C.); *Etyudy po istorii Severnogo Prichernomorya, Kavkaza i Srednei Azii* (1968; Essays on the History of the Northern Pontic Area, the Caucasus and Central Asia); and *Onomastika rannedinasticheskogo Lagasha* (1984; Onomastics of Lagash of the Early Dynasties).

Bibliography: *Drevnii Egipet i drevnyayu Afrika. Sbornik statei, posvyashchenny pamyati akademika V. V. Struve* (Ancient Egypt and Ancient Africa. A Collection of Articles Commemorating Academician V. V. Struve), (Moscow, 1967), pp. 5–7; *Drevnii mir. Akademiku V. V. Struve. Sbornik statei* (The Ancient World. To Academician V. V. Struve. A Collection of Articles), (Moscow, 1962), pp. 9–22.

M. A. Dandamayev

TARLE, Evgeny Viktorovich (Kiev, 1874–Moscow, 1955), Russian and Soviet historian, educated at Kiev University, under Ivan Vassilievich Luchitsky (q.v.). Tarle was assistant professor at St. Petersburg University (1903–1917) and professor at Dorpat (Yuriev) University (1913–1918); in 1917 he took a professorship at Petrograd University. Following the October 1917 Revolution he worked at the Central Archives, the Academy of Sciences, the Institute of History at Leningrad University, the Leningrad Branch of the Russian Association of Social Science Research Institutions, Leningrad and Moscow universities, and the Institute of International Relations at the USSR Ministry of Foreign Affairs. The USSR Academy of Sciences made him an academician in 1927. He attended international congresses of historians held in Brussels (1923) and Oslo (1928), the World Congress of Culture Workers in Wroclaw (1948), and participated in the Soviet Peace Committee. Among many other activities he was a member of the Society of the History of the French Revolution and a member of other French learned societies, received honorary doctorates from the universities of Brno, Oslo, Prague, Paris, and Algiers, was elected to the Norwegian Academy and the Academy of Political and Social Sciences of Philadelphia, and was corresponding member of the British Academy for the Promotion of Historical, Philosophical, and Philological Studies.

Tarle wrote extensively on West European modern history, especially France, as well as on Russian history, using Soviet, French, British, German, and Dutch archives. His interests centered on socioeconomic problems, the working-class movement and the history of social thought, international relations, and Russia's foreign policy. His best known monographs are: *Obshchestvennye vozzreniya Tomasa Mora v svyazi s ekonomicheskim sostoyaniem Anglii ego vremeni* (1901; Social Views of Thomas More in Relation to the British Economy of His Time); *Rabochii klass vo Frantsii v epokhu revolutsii* (Parts 1–2, 1909–1911; The French Working Class During the Revolution); *Rabochii klass vo Frantsii v pervye vremena machinnogo proizvodstva* (1928; The French Working Class During the Emergence of Machine Production); *Zherminal i prerial* (1937; Germinal and Prairial); *Kontinentalnaya blokada* (1913; The Continental System); *Talleyrand* (1934); *Napoleon* (1936); *Nashestviye Napoleona na Rossiyu. 1812 god.* (1938; Napoleon's Invasion of Russia. The Year 1812); and *Krymskaya voina* (vols. 1–2, 1941–1942; The Crimean War). Many of his works were published abroad. His works were published in twelve volumes in the USSR (1957–1962) and supplemented by *Iz literaturnogo naslediya akademika E. V. Tarle* (1981; From Academician Tarle's Literary Heritage).

Bibliography: E. I. Chapkevich, *Evgeny Viktorovich Tarle* (1977); V. I. Durnovtsev, "Novoye o Tarle" (More Information on Tarle), *Frantsuzsky ezhegodnik* (French Yearbook), (1976); A. S. Erusalimsky, "Evgeny Viktorovich Tarle," in E. V. Tarle, *Sochineniya* (Works), vol. 1; A. Z. Manfred, *"Akademik Evgeny Viktorovich Tarle"* (Academician Evgeny Viktorovich Tarle), *Vestnik Akademii Nauk SSSR* (Herald of the USSR Academy of Sciences), no. 3 (1976); V. I. Rutenburg, "Tarle—ucheny i obshchestvenniy deyatel" (Tarle the Scholar and Public Figure), *Problemy istorii mezhdunarodnykh otnoshenii* (Problems of the History of International Relations), (1972).

V. A. Dunayevsky

TIKHOMIROV, Mikhail Nikolaevich (Moscow, 1893–Moscow, 1965), Soviet historian. From 1902 through 1911 Tikhomirov took training at the Petersburg School of Commerce. In 1913 he enrolled in the Department of History and Philology of Moscow University from which he graduated in 1917. He studied under M. M. Bogoslovsky and Sergei V. N. Bakhrushin (q.v.). From 1919 through 1923 he was assistant lecturer at Samara University; later, he moved to Moscow where he taught in a secondary school and worked for the Society for the Study of Moscow Region and the Manuscript section of the State Museum of History. In 1934 he became assistant professor and in 1939 professor at Moscow University. In the same year Tikhomirov defended his doctorate,

"Issledovaniye o Russkoi Pravde. Proiskhozhdeniye tekstov" (Studies of the Russkaya Pravda. Text Origins). The year 1946 saw him elected corresponding member and 1953, academician of the USSR Academy of Sciences. His research included the history of the peoples of the USSR and the Slavonic countries of Central Europe from ancient times to the twentieth century. His cycle on socio-economic history comprises histories of Old Russian towns, including Moscow. They contain detailed descriptions of the advance of urban crafts, their differentiation, urban political and cultural life, and the class struggle. Tikhomirov was also interested in the Russian Middle Ages. He forwarded a thesis about the existence in Russia of merchants' and craftsmen's guilds similar to those of the Middle Ages in Western and Central Europe.

Tikhomirov's books and articles on the class struggle in feudal Russia form a special group (*Krestyanskiye i gorodskiye vosstaniya na Rusi XI-XIII vv.* (1955; Peasant and Urban Revolts in Russia in the Eleventh to Thirteenth Centuries); *Pskovskoye vosstaniye 1650 g.* (1935; The 1650 Pskov Uprising); and others. Some of his works concentrate on the national liberation struggle against foreign invaders. He also published a series of works on the history of Russian culture, on the origins of Slavonic writing and Novgorodian birch-bark scrolls, on Andrey Rublev, on the library of Ivan the Terrible, on the founding of Moscow University, and so forth. He authored many works on the historical sources on friendship between the Russian, Ukrainian, and Byelorussian peoples, and other Slavonic nations, and on their cultural interlinkage. He also wrote on source studies and other auxiliary historical disciplines, and contributed to the description and publication of Russian chronicles, especially in the "Complete Russian Chronicles" series resumed, on his initiative, in 1949. His interests centered on historical geography, *Rossiya v XVI stoletii* (1962; Russia in the Sixteenth Century), archaeography, and historiography. Textbooks on source studies and the history of the USSR also came from his pen. He compiled and edited numerous documentary publications and founded *Arkheograficheskiy ezhegodnik* (Archaeographic Yearbook).

Bibliography: *M. N. Tikhomirov (Materialy k biobibliografii uchenykh SSSR)* (M. N. Tikhomirov. Biobibliographical Materials of Soviet Scholars), (Moscow, 1963); I. P. Staroverova, *Rukopisnoye naslediye M. N. Tikhomirova v Arkhive AN SSSR. Nauchnoye opisaniye* (M. N. Tikhomirov's Manuscripts in the Archives of the USSR), (Moscow, 1974); "Zhizn i deyatelnost M. N. Tikhomirova. Bibliografiya" (M. N. Tikhomirov's Life and Work. Bibliography), in *Novoye o proshlom nashei strany* (New Data on Our Country's Past), (Moscow, 1967).

V. I. Buganov

TURAYEV, Boris Alexandrovich (St. Petersburg, 1868–Petrograd, 1920), Russian scholar, founder of the National schools of Ethiopian studies, Egyptology, and ancient history of the Orient. Turayev produced some two hundred books, articles, reviews, and other publications and was responsible for four hundred encyclopedia entries. Famous for his inordinate erudition and his far-flung interests, he was fluent in many ancient languages and engaged in Ethiopian studies, Egyptology, Coptic studies, Semitic studies, Assyriology, and Hittitology. His works bear the mark of his talent as historian, philologist, archaeologist, and art scholar. His major work is the two-volume *Istoriya drevnego Vostoka* (1935; Ancient History of the Orient), 1935, which drew on a vast body of specialist literature and sources in many languages and is noted for its profound source analysis. This fundamental lifetime study is a review of the Middle East, but its wealth of factual material, excellent philological background, immense chronological span (from ancient times to the Middle Ages), inclusion of outlying Eastern civilizations within the general historical course, and its original creative style made the book a must for many generations of Russian and Soviet orientalists. Turayev's monograph, *Egipetskaya literatura* (Egyptian Literature), was for a long time the best of its kind. His world outlook was that of a consistent idealist. Studying the ancient religions of the Middle East, he searched for points of similarity with Christian teachings. He laid stress on Russia's geographical proximity to the Middle East, where the first civilizations appeared. Consequently, he held that Russian scholars were duty bound to study this area in detail.

An ardent patriot, Turayev remained in Russia after the Great October Socialist revolution and to his life's end worked fruitfully in revolutionary Petrograd. The strictly scientific principles of his research method and his rejection of pan-Babylonianism, racism, and modernism were of great benefit in advancing Soviet studies of the ancient Orient. He combined his academic activities with teaching and popularizing scientific knowledge. He taught at St. Petersburg University for more than twenty years, delivered lectures, published popular science books and articles, and edited the series "Cultural and Historical Monuments of the Ancient Orient." According to Academician Vassily Vassielievich Struve (q.v.), Turayev was "a most distinguished representative of Russian science prior to the Revolution."

Bibliography: Y. A. Belyaev, *B. A. Turayev: 1868–1920 (K 25-letiyu so dnya smerti)* (B. A. Turayev: 1868–1920 [On the Twenty-Fifth Anniversary of His Death]), BM (1945); *Drevny Vostok. Pamyati akademika Turyayeva* (Ancient Orient. In Memory of Academician Turayev) (Moscow, 1980); M. A. Korostovtsev, "Academik B. A. Turayev. O stile raboty uchenogo" (Academician B. A. Turayev. On the Scholar's Style of Work), *Vestnik drevnei istorii* (Ancient History Herald), no. 2 (Moscow, 1974).

I. A. Stuchevsky

USPENSKY, Fyodor Ivanovich (Kostroma, 1845–Leningrad, 1928), Russian Byzantinist. Academician (1900); assistant professor (1874–1879), and professor (1879–1894) at the Novorossiisk University in Odessa. Uspensky founded the Russian Archaeological Institute in Constantinople in 1894 and remained its director through 1914. He headed its expeditions to Bulgaria, Syria, Palestine, and Asia Minor, and was editor of the institute's *Transactions*. From 1915 to 1928 he edited *Vizantiisky vremennik* (Byzantine Journal) and during 1922–1927 he was professor at Leningrad University. He authored some two hundred works, the most important of which is the three-volume *Istoriya Vizantiiskoi imperii* (History of the Byzantine Empire), based on vast source materials and covering the history of Byzantium and contiguous regions from the fifth through fifteenth centuries. The monograph deals with Byzantine-Slavic relations, peasant land tenure and the rural community, and the impact of the Slavic social order on the Byzantine socioeconomic system. It was the first work to postulate the protracted existence of the rural community and its effect on socioeconomic relations within the empire. Following the 1917 Revolution he headed a number of commissions: on the study of Russo-Byzantine relationships, on publication of Charles Du Cange's *Glossarium ad scriptores mediae et infimae graecitatis*, and on the study of Constantine Porphyrogenitus. It was then that he pioneered investigations of sources related to the history of the Trebizond Empire (*Ocherki po istorii Trapezundskoi imperii* [1929; Essays on the History of the Trebizond Empire]). In 1927, together with B. N. Beneshevich, he published collected documents from John the Precursor's Monastery at Trebizond. He also examined the history of Byzantine culture (*Ocherki po istorii vizantiiskoi obrazovannosti* (1891; Essays on the History of Byzantine Learning).

Bibliography: S. N. Kapterev, *Uspenskiana* (I. Khronologichesky ukazatel trudov. II. Literatura o F. I. Uspenskom) (I. Chronological Index of Uspensky's Works. II. Works About F. I. Uspensky), *Vizantiisky vremennik* (Byzantine Journal), vol. 1, 26 (1947); Z. V. Udaltsova "K voprosu ob otsenke trudov akademika F. I. Uspenskogo" (On the Evaluation of Academician F. I. Uspensky's Works), *Voprosy istorii* (Problems of History), no. 6 (1949) ; Z.V. Udaltsova, "Vizantinovedeniye" (Byzantine Studies), *Ocherki istorii istoricheskoi nauki v SSSR* (Essays on the History of Historical Science in the USSR), vol. 2 (Moscow, 1960), pp. 508–524, vol. 3 (Moscow, 1963), pp. 514–526, vol. 4 (Moscow, 1956), pp. 615–621.

K. A. Osipova

UVAROV, Aleksei Sergeyevich (St. Petersburg, 1825–Moscow, 1884), Russian archaeologist and art historian. Educated at the universities of St. Petersburg, Berlin, and Heidelberg. In 1848 Uvarov studied ancient cities (Chersonese, Neapolis, Olbia) in the northern Black Sea region, *Issledovaniye o drevnostyakh Yuzhnoi Rossii i beregov Chornogo morya* (vols. 1, 2, 1851; Study of the Antiquities of Southern Russia and the Black Sea Coast). In 1851–1854 he excavated 7,757 old Russian burial mounds in Vladimir Province, which he attributed to the Finnish tribe called Mere. Despite this error and other inaccuracies in documenting the excavation process, the book *Meryane i ikh byt po kurgannym raskopkam* (1872; The Meres and Their Everyday Life from the Data of Mound Excavations) was of great significance at that time owing to the orientation, new at the time, toward reconstructing the everyday life of ancient peoples from archaeological finds, including most ordinary ones. In 1877 Uvarov discovered Karacharovo on the Oka River—one of the first Paleolithic sites on Russian territory. In 1881 he published the two-volume overview, *Arkheologiya Rossii. Kamennyi period* (The Archaeology of Russia. The Stone Age). He also studied the history of Christian art, *Khristianskaya simvolika* (vol. 1, 1908; Christian Symbolism). Uvarov was one of the founders of the Archaeological Society at St. Petersburg (1846), and founder (1864) and president of the Moscow Archaeological Society; he initiated several archaeological congresses and chaired the first six (1869, Moscow; 1871, St. Petersburg; 1874, Kiev; 1877, Kazan; 1881, Tiflis; 1884, Odessa). He was one of the founders (in 1872–1883) and the first head of the Russian Museum of History in Moscow, to which he donated his rich collection of antiquities, icons, manuscripts, and so forth. Building up museum exhibits and convening scholars at congresses, Uvarov succeeded in bridging the gaps dividing the various fields of archaeology: the archaeology of prehistoric society, studied mostly by natural historians; the archaeology of antiquity, traditionally associated with art history; and medieval archaeology. This promoted the establishment of archaeology in Russia as a unified scientific discipline providing a historical perspective.

Bibliography: A. A. Formozov, *Nachalo izucheniya kamennogo veka v Rossii* (The Early Studies of the Stone Age in Russia), (Moscow, 1983), pp. 84–104; A. S. Uvarov, *Sbornik materialov dlya biografii i statyi po tvorcheskim voprosam* (Collection of Biographical Materials and His Articles on Problems of Creativity), (Moscow, 1910), pp. 3–172.

A. A. Formozov

VASSILIEV, Vassily Pavlovich (Nizhnii Novgorod, 1818–St. Petersburg, 1900), Russian Sinologist. Upon completing his studies at Nizhnii Novgorod Gymnasium in 1834, Vassiliev enrolled in the Oriental Department of the History and Philology Faculty of Kazan University, from which he graduated in 1837. In 1839 he received his master's degree for his "Obosnovaniya buddiiskoi filosofii" (Substantiations of the Buddhist Philosophy) and was sent to Beijing to study the Tibetan language. There he spent the next ten years of his life as a secular member (a student) of the Russian Orthodox clerical mission. Between 1850 and 1855 he was professor in the Chinese and Manchurian Languages Department at Kazan University, lecturing in history and literature, and from 1855 until his death in 1900 he was with the Oriental Department of St. Petersburg University. In 1886 he was elected to the Russian Academy of Sciences, following which he revisited China, in 1890, traveling to the town of Kuldja. His main works are: *Istoriya i drevnosti vostochnoi chasti Srednei Azii ot X do XIII vv. s prilozheniyem perevodov kitaiskikh izvestii o kidanyakh, chzhurzhenyakh i mongolotatarakh* (1857; History and Antiquities of the Eastern Part of Central Asia from the Tenth to the Thirteenth Centuries Supplemented with Translations of Chinese Sources on the Khitais, Chzurchzenians, and Mongol-Tartars), *Svedeniya o manchzhurakh vo vremena dinastii Yuan i Min* (1863; The Manchus During the Yuan and Ming Dynasties), a series of articles on Russo-Chinese relations, Chinese historical geography, epigraphics, numismatics and archaeology, translations of Chinese writings (*Ninggut Jilue* and others, 1857), works on the history of religion: *Buddizm, ego dogmaty, istoriya i literatura* (Parts 1–

3, 1857, 1869; Buddhism, Its Dogmata, History and Literature), *Religii Vostoka: konfutsianstvo, buddizm, daosism* (1873; Religions of the East: Confucianism, Buddhism, Taoism), lecture courses, *Materialy po istorii kitaiskoi literatury* (Materials on the History of Chinese Literature), and *Ocherk istorii kitaiskoi literatury* (1880; Essays on the History of Chinese Literature).

Vassiliev's numerous works on wide-ranging historical problems exhibited a thoughtful approach to Chinese sources, especially to those on the history of China's foreign links. An adherent of the autochthonous emergence of the Chinese civilization, he assigned great importance to the cultural influence of its neighbors. He overestimated the role of the state in surmounting social-class contradictions. Being opposed to the then prevalent theory of Asian nations' "racial inferiority," he disapproved of the Western colonial policy, especially the British. The bulk of his writings and translations remain in manuscript form.

Bibliography: Z. I. Gorbacheva, N. A. Petrov, G. F. Smykalov, and B. I. Pankratov, "Russky kitayeved V.P. Vassiliev (1818–1900)" (V. P. Vassiliev, the Russian Sinologist, 1818–1900), *Ocherki po istorii russkogo vostokovedeniya* (Essays on the History of Oriental Studies in Russia), (Moscow, 1956), pp. 232–340; A. N. Khokhlov, "V. P. Vassiliev v Nizhnem Novgorode i Kazani" (V. P. Vassiliev in Nizhnii Novgorod and Kazan), *Istoriya i Kultura Kitaya* (Sbornik pamyati akad. V. P. Vassilieva) (Chinese History and Culture. In Memory of Academician Vassiliev), (Moscow, 1974), pp. 28–70; P. E. Skachkov, *Ocherki po istorii russkogo kitayevedeniya* (Essays on the History of Sinology in Russia), (Moscow, 1977).

A. N. Khokhlov

VESELOVSKY, Stepan Borisovich (Moscow, 1876–Moscow, 1952), Soviet historian, foremost authority on the Russian Middle Ages. Veselovsky received his education at the Department of Law, Moscow University (1896–1902). His first election was to the Moscow Society of History and Russian Antiquities in 1907. During the prerevolutionary period he became a member of twelve scientific societies. The year 1908 marked the beginning of his prolonged and fruitful work in the Archaeographic Commission of the Academy of Sciences. He was chief inspector and a member of the Central Archive of the RSFSR Collegium (1919–1920), a full member of the Institute of History of the Russian Association of Social Science Research Institutions, (1923–1929), and a senior research associate with the Institute of History of the USSR Academy of Sciences as of 1936. He lectured at Moscow University and other higher educational establishments. In 1929 the USSR Academy of Sciences elected him a corresponding member, and in 1946 academician. That same year the Order of Lenin was conferred on him. His scholarly interests embraced Russian history of the fourteenth to seventeenth centuries. In 1915 and 1916, respectively, he published the first and second volumes of his fundamental work, *"Soshnoye pismo"*. *Issledovaniye po istorii kadastra i pryamogo oblozheniya Moskovskogo gosudarstva* ("Soshnoye pismo." Studies on the History of Cadastre and Direct Taxation in the Moscow State) based on a vast body of factual material. In his writings published in the 1920s and 1940s he revised a great many views on feudal land tenure, the origins and evolution of legal and tax immunity, the correlations of patrimonial estates, estates granted for military service and the peasant community, and the political struggle during the reigns of Ivan the Third and Ivan the Terrible. His most important works of the period are a fundamental monograph, *Feodalnoye zemlevladeniye v Severo-Vostochnoi Rusi* (vol. 1, 1947; Feudal Land Tenure in Northeastern Russia, and two posthumously published books, *Issledovaniya po istorii klassa sluzhilykh zemlevladeltsev* (Studies on the History of the Class of Landowners in Military Service) and *Issledovaniya po istorii oprichniny* (1969; Studies on the History of Oprichmina). He also prepared for publication voluminous documents on Russian history of the fourteenth to seventeenth centuries. His *Trudy po istochnikovedeniyu i istorii Rossii perioda feodalisma* (1978; Works on Source Studies and the History of Russia of the Feudal Period), were of great importance.

Bibliography: L. V. Cherepnin, "Akademik Veselovsky Stepan Borisovich (Tvorchesky put") (Academician Veselovsky and His Work), in *Istoriya i genealogiya. S. B. Veselovsky i problemy genealogicheskikh issledovanii* (History and Genealogy. S. B. Veselovsky and Problems of Genealogical Research) (Moscow, 1977); *Ocherki istorii istoricheskoi nauki v SSSR* (Essays on Soviet Historiography) (Moscow, 1966), vol. 4 (Moscow, 1985), vol. 5.

L. V. Danilova

VINOGRADOFF, Paul Gavrilovich (Kostroma, Russia, 1854–Paris, 1925), Anglo-Russian historian. Vinogradoff's brilliant career owed much to his father, a history teacher at the gymnasium of Kostroma before becoming director of several schools in Moscow in 1855. As a student at the University of Moscow, Vinogradoff made rapid progress in his chosen fields of history (particularly medieval economic and social history) and philosophy. At graduation his thesis, "Landed Property Under the Merovingians," won him a year's scholarship to study at the University of Berlin in the seminars of Theodor Mommsen (q.v.), noted for his "scientific history," and of Heinrich Brunner, a specialist in Germanic law. His seminar paper for Mommsen on "Emancipation and the German *Volkrechten*" was published in the *Forschungen zur Deutschen Geschichte* (1876). After returning to lecture at the University of Moscow and the Women's University, he traveled to Italy to research his master's thesis, "The Origins of Feudal Relations in Lombardy." Later published in the *Journal of the Russian Ministry of Education* (1880), it broke new ground in comparative institutional history. Against the theory that Lombard feudalism had arisen amid conditions characteristic of Frankish society, he showed that in fact it had originated in a state of affairs resembling that of the late Roman Empire. For his doctoral dissertation he turned to England, whose archives contained, as he discovered, a treasure of virtually untapped manuscript sources in medieval history and law. Having retained his faculty status at the University of Moscow, he was awarded for his dissertation, "Villainage in England," not only a Ph.D. in 1884, but upon publication in 1887, a full professorship. From undergraduate days he had been a liberal in politics, and in 1901, finding it impossible to obey the autocratic orders of the tsarist government to report radical students in his classes, he emigrated to England. There he was awarded the Corpus Chair of Jurisprudence at Oxford University (1903), and after the Bolshevik Revolution he became a British citizen. At Oxford he introduced the Continental seminar method for advanced study in history and continued his prolific and markedly original publications.

Vinogradoff's *Villainage in England* is considered his best work. The subject, as he explained, was one to which he could relate, for it had not been long (1861) since Russia had had a system of serfdom. Using his method of proceeding from the known legal customs of the eleventh century backward into the lesser known practices of earlier times, he concluded that the English peasants were originally free and that the communal structure of rural England was "more ancient than the manorial order" and was "more deeply laid." Building on that conclusion, *The Growth of the English Manor* (1904) traces the evolution of the manor from its Celtic beginnings through the Roman and Anglo-Saxon centuries into the feudal age initiated by the Norman Conquest. Application of the comparative method enabled him to identify the manor as *the* typical institution of medieval civilization, corresponding to the *civitas* in classical antiquity. Using comparison to distinguish uniqueness, his *English Society in the Eleventh Century* (1908) argued that the Norman Conquest blended Anglo-Saxon, Danish, and Norman-French institutions into a society unlike any Continental counterparts.

Bibliography: C. K. Allen, "Sir Paul Gavrilovitch Vinogradoff (1854–1925)," *Dictionary of National Biography*, 1922–1930, pp. 871–874; H. A. L. Fisher, "Memoir," *The Collected Papers of Paul Vinogradov* (Oxford, 1928), vol. 1, pp. 4–74, William S. Holdsworth, *The Historians of Anglo-American Law* (New York, 1928), pp. 84–91; William S. Holdsworth, "Professor Sir Paul Vinogradoff, 1854–1925," *Proceedings of the British Academy* (1924–1925): 486–501; F. M. Powicke, "Sir Paul Vinogradoff," *Modern Historians and the Study of History: Essays and Papers* (London, 1955), pp. 9–18.

Louise Salley Parker

VIPPER, Robert Yuryevich (Moscow, 1859–Moscow, 1954), Russian and Soviet historian. Member of the USSR Academy of Sciences (1943). After graduation from Moscow University, Vipper spent some seventy years teaching history at high schools in Moscow and Odessa and at the universities of Moscow and Riga. A talanted lecturer and instructor, he became famous as a public speaker and a popularizer of history. He authored a large series of history books for secondary schools. He was a democrat, a patriot, and an atheist who admired the Age of Enlightenment and who always had a large following among progressive-minded students. Many of them were to become outstanding Marxist historians, such as academicians Vyacheslav P. Volgin (q.v.), Nikolai M. Lukin (q.v.), Sergei D. Skazkin (q.v.), and N. M. Druzhinin. His adherence to the ideas of the Enlightenment was manifested in his atheistic works on the history of early Christianity: *Vozniknoveniye khristianskoi literatury* (1946; The Rise of

Christian Literature); *Rim i ranneye khristianstvo* (1954; Rome and Early Christianity). His democratic principles were reflected in his lectures on the history of antiquity, wherein he always sympathized with Athens and Rome: *Istoriya Gretsii v klassicheskuyu epokhu v IX-IV vv. do n.e.* (1916; Greek History in the Classic Epoch from the Ninth to Fourth Centuries B.C.); *Otcherki istorii rimskoi imperii* (1908; Essays on the History of the Roman Empire). In his work as teacher, enlightener, and popularizer, he drew on his vast research studies in history.

Vipper's legacy numbers over three hundred works, in which he emphasized socioeconomic aspects, the problems of classes and class struggle, and democracy. His specific interests were as follows: (1) the history of antiquity; (2) the sixteenth century in Western and Eastern Europe, *Vliyaniye Kalvina i kalvinizma na politicheskiye ucheniya i dvizheniya XVI veka* (1984; The Influence of Calvin and His Teachings on the Political Doctrines and Movements of the Sixteenth Century) and *Ivan Grozny* (1922; Ivan the Terrible); (3) social movements and doctrines in the West in the sixteenth to nineteenth centuries, *Obshchestvennye ucheniya i istoricheskiye teorii XVIII i XIV vv. v sviazi s obshchestvennym dvizheniem na zapade* (1900; The Social Doctrines and Historical Theories of the Eighteenth and Nineteenth Centuries in Connection with the Social Movement in the West); and (4) serfdom in Livonia. He was the first Russian historiographer to portray the economic, social, political, and cultural histories of peoples and countries as an integral worldwide historical process through a synchronized description of events in different countries with the accent on their interrelationship and interdependence, reproducing a sweeping panorama of developments in Eastern and Western Europe in the sixteenth century.

Bibliography: N. I. Colubtsova, "Academician Robert Yuryevich Vipper, 110th Birth Anniversary," *Nauka i religiya* (Science and Religion), no. 7 (Moscow, 1969); A. P. Danilova, "R. Y. Vipper as authority on the history of antiquity," *Vestnik drevnei istorii* (Herald of Ancient History), no. 1 (Moscow, 1984); K. K. Lussis, "R. Y. Vipper: Towards a Materialistic Comprehension of History," *Izvestiya AN Latviiskoi SSR* (Bulletin of the Latvian Academy of Sciences), no. 3 (Moscow, 1976); V. P. Volgin, "Vipper, Robert Yuryevich," *Bolshaya Sovetskaya Entsiklopediya* (Larger Soviet Encyclopaedia), vol. 11 (Moscow, 1930).

N. I. Golubtsova

VLADIMIRTSOV, Boris Yakovlevich (Kaluga, 1884– Leningrad Region, 1931), Russian-Soviet orientalist. Vladimirtsov attended the School of Living Oriental Languages at the Sorbonne and the Collège de France from 1905 to 1906. In 1909 he graduated from the Department of Oriental Languages at St. Petersburg University (named Petrograd University from 1917 to 1924 and the present Leningrad University). There he made his career as assistant professor (1918) and professor (1921). He was one of the founders of the Leningrad Institute of Living Oriental Languages and a staff member of the Asiatic Museum attached to the Institute of Oriental Studies of the USSR Academy of Sciences (1915–1931). He was elected corresponding member of the USSR Academy of Sciences (1923) and full member (1929). In 1924 he was elected to the Mongolian Academic Committee and included in the USSR Academy of Sciences' Commission on Mongolia in 1926. Vladimirtsov was a foremost authority on Mongolia, having made close studies of its history, ethnography, literature, and languages. He went on several expeditions there. His first printed work, *Turetsky narodets Khotony* (Khotons, a Turkish Ethnic Group), written together with A. N. Samoilovich, came out in 1916. He published a total of about seventy writings. His historical studies retain their importance to this day. The more noteworthy are *Buddizm v Tibete i Mongolii* (1919; Buddhism in Tibet and Mongolia); *Chingiz Khan* (1922; Genghis Khan), published in England in 1930 and in Turkey in 1950; and *Obshchestvenny stroi Mongolov. Mongolsky kochevoi feodalizm* (1934; Mongols' Social System. Nomad Feudalism), also published in France: *Le régime social des Mongols, le féodalisme nomade* (Paris, 1948).

Vladimirtsov was the first to hypothesize "stages" in the development of social relations among nomads previously considered incapable of advancing beyond the clan system. From the vantage point of historical materialism, he defined twelfth-century Mongolian society as being feudal. According to contemporary Soviet scholars, he overstressed the degree of feudalization of Mongolian society in the twelfth and thirteenth centuries and unjustifiably tried to make the "seignorial-vassalic" relations of Western Europe fit the East. His was a sizable contribution to linguistics, *Sravnitelnaya grammatika mongolskogo pismennogo yazyka i Kalkhasskogo narechiya* (1929; Comparative Grammar of the Mongolian Written Language and the Khalkha Dialect), and to philology and literary history, *Mongolsky sbornik rasskazov iz pañcatantra* (1921; Mongolian Collection of Stories from Pañcatantra); *Mongolooiratsky geroichesky epos* (1923; Mongolian-Oirat Heroic Epic); and *Obraztsy mongolskoi narodnoi slovesnosti* (1926; Selected Pieces from Mongolian Folklore). He authored a great many historico-philological and ethnographic articles and notes in which his vast scientific erudition was matched with his investigative talent and outstanding literary gift. He trained numbers of specialists on Mongolia, among them scholars from Buryatia, Kalmykia, and also Mongolia.

Bibliography: V. M. Alexeyev, "Pamyati akademika B. Y. Vladimirtsova" (In Memory of Academician B. Y. Vladimirtsov), *Vestnik Akademii nauk* (Bulletin of the USSR Academy of Sciences), no. 8 (1931); *Filologiya i istoriya mongolskikh narodov* (Philology and History of Mongolian Peoples), (Moscow, 1958), with bibliography of B. Y. Vladimirtsov's works and articles by N. P. Shastina and G. N. Rumyantsev; S. F. Oldenburg, "B. Y. Vladimirtsov," in *Izvestiya Akademii nauk. Otdeleniye obshchestvennykh nauk* (Proceedings of the USSR Academy of Sciences. Section of Social Sciences), no. 8 (1932); A. Y. Yakubovsky, "Iz istorii izucheniya Mongolov perioda XI-XIII vekov" (From the History of Studying Eleventh-Thirteenth Century Mongols), in *Ocherki po istorii russkogo vostokovedeniya* (Essays on the History of Russian Oriental Studies), V. I (Moscow, 1953).

V. P. Nikolayev

VOLGIN, Vyacheslav Petrovich (Kharkov, 1879–Moscow, 1962), Soviet historian. Academician (1930). Volgin graduated from Moscow University, in the class of Robert Yuryevich Vipper (q.v.). He began his teaching career in 1914 and was one of the founders of the Socialist (later renamed Communist) Academy of the Institute of the Red Professoriate and of the Social Sciences Faculty at Moscow University. He initiated the Research Institute of History in 1922 under the auspices of Moscow University. Later it was incorporated into the Russian Association of Social Science Research Institutions. From 1921 to 1925 he was rector of Moscow University, and from 1925 to 1930 dean of the University's Department of History and Philology. He attended international congresses of historians in Oslo (1928) and in Warsaw (1933) and served on the International Historical Committee. His other functions included president of the Library Commission at the USSR Academy of Sciences, academician-secretary of the Academy's Division of History and Philosophy, chairman of the Council on the academy's branches, vice-president of the USSR Academy of Sciences, and deputy chairman of the academy's Publishing Council. He was a founder of the academy's *Vestnik* (Bulletin) and the journal *Izvestiya Akademii Nauk SSSR* (Proceedings of the USSR Academy of Sciences). He edited the journal *Voprosy istorii* (Problems of History), *Frantsuzskiye yezhegodniki* (French yearbooks), and the series *Literaturnye pamyatniki* (Literary Monuments). His achievements won him the Lenin Prize. His first academic publications date back to 1906, and in 1908 he wrote *Zhan Melie i ego "Zaveshchaniye"* (Jean Meslier and his "Le Testament") which came out in 1918.

The history of socialist ideas was the main theme of Volgin's research. His major works were *Ocherki po istorii sotcialisma* (1923; Essays on the History of Socialism), and *Istoriya sotialisticheskikh idei* (1928, 1931; History of Socialist Ideas), which established this subject as a separate branch of Soviet historical studies. Volgin created an integral theory of the development of socialist ideas in pre-Marxian times which became a pivotal theory for the history of socialist thought as a separate discipline in historical science. He substantiated the division of the doctrines current in those days into socialist-utopian and communist-utopian and distinguished between such notions as utopian socialism and egalitarianism. The last-named notions and his approach toward the principle of "common property" as a criterion for referring a certain doctrine either to pre-Marxian communism or socialism were of great importance for fully understanding the evolution of socialist thought. Of particular interest are his works on socialist thought in France: *Sotsialnye i politicheskiye idei vo Frantsii pered revolyutsiyei (1748–1789)* (1940; Social and Political Ideas in France on the Eve of the Revolution: 1748–1789) and *Razvitiye obshchestvennoi mysli vo Frantsii v XVIII veke* (1958; The Evolution of Social Thought in France in the Eighteenth Century). They revealed the role of pre-Marxian socialism as an essential part of society's intellectual life. The "Precursors of Scientific Socialism" series, published on Volgin's initiative, enjoyed widespread popularity. His collected works in five volumes came out in 1975–1979. Many of his works have been translated into English, French, German, Polish, Chinese, and other languages.

Bibliography: V. A. Dunayevsky and G. S. Kucherenko, *Zapadno-yevropeisky utopichesky socialism v rabotakh sovetskikh istorikov* (West-European Utopian Socialism in the Works of Soviet Historians), (Moscow, 1981); *Istoriya sotsialisticheskikh ucheniy* (History of Socialist Teachings), collection of articles published in honor of Academician Volgin, (Moscow, 1964); "K 80-letiyu akademika Volgina" (For the Eightieth Birth Anniversary of Academician Volgin), in *Voprosy Istorii* (Problems of History), no. 9 (1959); "K 90-letiyu so dnya rozhdeniya akademika V. P. Volgina" (For the Ninetieth Birth Anniversary of Academician Volgin), in *Novyaya i noveishaya istoriya*, no. 6 (1969); "Vospominaniya o V. P. Volgine" (Reminiscences about V. P. Volgin) in *Frantsuzsky yezhegodnik, 1969* (French Yearbook, 1969), (Moscow, 1970); A. Z. Manfred, "K 80-letiyu Akademika V. P. Volgina" (For the Eightieth Birth Anniversary of Academician Volgin), in *Novaya i Noveishaya istoriya* (Modern and Contemporary History), no. 4 (1959); *Vyacheslav Petrovich Volgin* (Moscow, 1954); "Iz istorii sotsialno-politicheskikh idei" (From the History of Sociopolitical Ideas), in the collection of articles published to mark the seventy-fifth birthday of Academician Vyacheslav Petrovich Volgin (Moscow, 1975).

Y. S. Tokareva

YABLONSKIS, Konstantinas Ionovich (Jelgava, 1892–Vilnius, 1960), Soviet Lithuanian historian. Member of the Lithuanian Academy of Sciences; specialized in the feudal period of Lithuanian history, specifically the legal and economic status of peasants in the sixteenth century and the class struggle. His major works include *XVI amžiaus belaisviai kaimynai Lietuvoje* (1930; Bondmenkaimynai in Lithuania in the Sixteenth Century); and *Lietuvos valstiečui kova prieš feodalu priespauda iki valaku reformos, Lietuvos istorijos instituto darbai.* (vol. 7, 1957; The Struggle of Lithuanian Peasants Against the Feudal Yoke Before the Land Reform). Yablonskis was a foremost authority on historical sources and archaeography. He compiled and published the following documentary collections: *XVI amziaus Lietuvos inventoriai* (1934; Lithuania's Inventories of the Sixteenth Century); *Lietuviski zodziai senosios Lietuvos rasziniu kaloje* (Part 1, 1941; Lithuanian Words in Business Correspondence in Old Lithuania); *Lietuvos valstiečiu, ir miestelenu, ginčai su dvaru valdytojais. I d, XVI–XVII a.; II d, XVIII a.* (1959, 1961; Litigation of Lithuanian Peasants and Inhabitants of Small Settlements with Estate Managers, Part I, sixteenth-seventeenth centuries; Part II, eighteenth century); also a posthumous edition of the collection *Lietuvos inventoriai XVII a.* (Lithuania's Inventories of the Seventeenth Century) compiled jointly with M. Jučas, 1962; and a series of other publications. Yablonskis wrote a number of essays about Lithuanian intellectuals of the sixteenth and seventeenth centuries, including M. Daukshe, A. Kulvetis, M. Pyatkyavicus, and M. Mazividase.

Bibliography: *Ocherki istoriyi istoricheskoi nauki v SSSR* (Essays on the Records of Historical Science in the USSR), vol. 7 (Moscow, 1968); K. I. Yablonskis, *Arkheogra-*

phicheskiyi ezhegodnik za 1961 god (1961 Archaeographical Yearbook), (Moscow, 1962), pp. 476–478 (a list of Yablonskis' works); Y. M. Yurginis, *Arkheologuicheskoye nasledstvo Konstantina Yabloniskisa* (Konstantin Yablonskis' Archaeographical Heritage), *Istochnikovedcheskie problemi istorii narodov Pribaltiki* (The Study of Sources Problems of the History of Baltic Peoples), (Riga, 1970), pp. 145–151.

V. A. Rzhanitsina

YEFIMENKO, Pyotr Petrovich (Kharkov, 1884–Leningrad, 1969), Soviet archaeologist. Head of the Soviet school of Paleolithic studies. Educated at the University of St. Petersburg. In 1919 Yefimenko associated with the archaeological departments of a number of Leningrad's museums and the State Institute of the History of Material Culture. His first archaeological excavations were on the rivers Oskol and Donets (1900–1902). He participated in the famous excavations of a Paleolithic site at Mezin in 1909. The excavations provided the basis for a description, the first in Russian archaeological literature, of flint tools of the Paleolithic era: *Kremnyovye izdeliya paleoliticheskoi stoyanki v s. Mezine Chernigovskoi gub.* (1912; Flint Tools of the Paleolithic Site in the Village of Mezin, Chernigov Province). From 1923 through 1936, he headed expeditions studying Paleolithic sites on the Don River (Kostenki, Borshevo). He worked out a new method for studying Paleolithic settlements. Jointly with his student-followers, he periodized Paleolithic sites in the European USSR. Of special significance is his monograph *Pervobytnoye obshchestvo* (1934; Primitive Society). *Dorodovoye obshchestvo* (Pre-clan Society) was the first attempt at a Marxist interpretation of the Paleolithic on the basis of a vast body of factual material. The monograph *Kostenki I* (1958) sums up many years of research at the unique Paleolithic site. Yefimenko's wide-ranging interests included the study and interpretation of sites of the Neolithic, *Stoyanki kamennogo veka v okrestnostyakh g. Izyuma* (1926; Stone Age Sites near the Town of Izyum); the Bronze Age, *Abashevskaya kultura v Povolzhye* (1961; The Abashevo Culture in the Volga Area), with co-authors; the early Middle Ages, *Ryazanskiye mogilniki* (1926; The Burial Grounds of Ryazan) (the latter work offered a method for a historical analysis of mass burial grounds and a chronological division of its burials); and old Russian, *Drevnerusskiye poseleniya na Donu* (1948; Old Russian Settlements on the Don) with co-authors. In 1945 he became a member of the Ukrainian Academy of Sciences. As director of the Institute of Archaeology of the Ukrainian Academy of Sciences (1946–1954), he spared neither time nor effort to promote archaeology in the Ukraine. He was associate professor and later professor at Leningrad University (1924–1939).

Bibliography: "Pamyati P. P. Yefimenko" (In Memory of P. P. Yefimenko), *Kratkiye soobshcheniya Instituta arkheologii Akademii nauk SSSR* (Brief Communications of the Institute of Archaeology of the USSR Academy of Sciences), Issue 131 (1972): 3–4; A. N. Rogachov, "P. P. Yefimenko i voprosy sotsiologii pervobytnogo obshchestva (Kratkiy ocherk)" (P. P. Yefimenko and Problems in the Sociology of Primitive Society: A Brief Outline), *Kratkiye Soobscheniya Instituta arkheologii Akademii nauk SSSR* (Brief Communications of the Institute of Archaeology of the USSR Academy of Sciences),

Issue 131 (1972), pp. 5–10; P. N. Tretyakov, "Pyotr Petrovich Yefimenko," *Sovetskaya arkheologiya*, no. 1 (1970): 310–312.

Yu. N. Zakharuk

ZHUKOV, Evgeni Mikhailovich (Warsaw, 1907–Moscow, 1980), Soviet historian, specialist on the methodology of history, oriental studies, and international relations. A graduate of the Leningrad Institute of Oriental Studies, Zhukov completed his courses for a master's degree at the USSR Academy of Sciences' Institute of Oriental Studies in Leningrad. Later, he taught at the Leningrad Institute of Oriental Studies and Leningrad University. In 1940 he wrote his doctor's thesis, "Istoriya yaponskogo militarizma" (History of Japanese Militarism), and in 1944 he received a professorship in oriental history. He was director of the USSR Academy of Sciences' Institute of Pacific Studies in Moscow (1943–1950), head of the chair at the Academy of Social Sciences under the CPSU Central Committee (1946–1976), and director of the USSR Academy of Sciences' Institute of World History (1968–1980). In 1958 he was elected a member of the USSR Academy of Sciences. His subsequent functions were as follows: academician-secretary of the History Division of the USSR Academy of Sciences (1958–1971 and 1975–1980); chairman of the National Committee of Soviet Historians (1973–1980); and president of the International Committee of Historical Sciences (1972–1975). His book *Istoriya Yaponii* (1940; History of Japan) dealt with a number of aspects of Japanese history, including analyses of changing social setups, the Meiji Revolution, and the emergence of liberal-democratic movements. Zhukov made a contribution to the theory and history of colonialism and the national liberation struggles in Asia and Africa, their phases and place in the worldwide historical process. He was editor-in-chief of a thirteen-volume work, *Vsemirnaya istoriya* (1956–1973; World History), a Marxist-Leninist study of human society from ancient times to our days, and a sixteen volume work, *Sovetskaya istoricheskaya entsiklopediya* (Soviet Historical Encyclopaedia), spanning historical knowledge accumulated by Soviet historiography. Zhukov's book *Ocherki metodologii istoriyi* (1980; Essays on the Methodology of History) sums up his long research into the subject and method of historical science, laws of the worldwide historical process (correlation of social and historical laws, socioeconomic formations, social revolutions, and periodization of history), the researcher's laboratory (historical facts and historical sources, historian's language) and the correlation of the past and present.

Bibliography: V. A. Tishkov, "Pamyati Evgeniya Mikhailovicha Zhukova" (In Memory of Evgeni Mikhailovich Zhukov), *Narodi Asii i Afriki* (Asia and Africa Today), no. 6 (1980): 237–240.

V. A. Tishkov

ZIMIN, Aleksandr Aleksandrovich (Moscow, 1920–Moscow, 1980), Soviet historian, authority on medieval Russian history. From 1938 through 1942 Zimin studied at Moscow University and then at the Central Asian University. Following his postgraduate studies, he joined the Institute of History of the USSR Academy of Sciences where he worked until 1947. He then lectured at the Moscow State History and Archives Institute, where he became professor in 1971 and continued there through 1973. Russian social and political history during the formation of a centralized state in the fifteenth and sixteenth centuries was his chief subject. In his book series, *Reformy Ivana Groznogo* (Reforms of Ivan the Terrible), *Oprichnina Ivana Groznogo* (The Oprichnina of Ivan the Terrible), and *Rossiya na poroge novogo vremeni* (1960, 1964, and 1972; Russia on the Threshold of New Times), he gave an in-depth analysis of the social phenomena in the Russia of that period, opposing the traditional view of *oprichnina* as an anti-boyar measure. He also studied humanitarian tendencies in fifteenth and sixteenth century Russian social thought, *I. S. Peresvetov i ego sovremenniki* (1958; Ivan Peresvetov and His Contemporaries), and other works. Investigation of the Boyar Duma composition, the Imperial Court, palace institutions, the executive magistracy, and landed aristocracy took up much of his work. He drew widely on genealogical materials. He made a substantial contribution to studies of Russia's ancient history *(Kholopy na Rusi s drevneishikh vremen do kontsa XV veka)* (1973; Russian Serfs from Ancient Times to the Late Fifteenth Century). He gave a unique interpretation to certain of the articles of *Russkaya pravda* (The Code of Laws). A number of articles dealt with the conditions of peasants in the sixteenth and seventeenth centuries and their class struggle. He did much to advance source studies, textual research of Russian chronicles, stories and tales, publicist writings, and legal acts. He was active in documentary publication and historiographic investigation.

Bibliography: S. M. Kashtanov, "Aleksandr Aleksandrovich Zimin—issledovatel i pedagog" (Alexander Zimin—the Scholar and the Teacher), *Istoriya SSSR*, no. 6 (1980): 152–157; V. B. Kobrin, "Aleksandr Aleksandrovich Zimin. Uchenyi. Chelovek" (Alexander Zimin, The Scholar and the Man), *Istoricheskiye zapiski* 105 (Moscow, 1980): 294–309; "Spisok pechatnykh trudov A. A. Zimina" (A List of Zimin's Published Works), *Arkheographichesky ezhegodnik za 1980 g.* (Archaeographic Yearbook, 1980), pp. 274–284.

V. B. Kobrin and A. L. Khoroshkevich

Great Historians: Southeast Asian

ABDUL HADI bin Haji Hassan (Melaka, 1900–Melaka, 1937), Malay historian. Abdul Hadi was educated in local Malay schools and at seventeen years of age moved from the school at Kampung Batang Tiga to the Malay College in Melaka, where he took a special interest in the study of Malay literature and history. He was known by his classmates as a bookworm and received the nickname "Tawarikh" (history) as a reflection of his passion for that subject. Abdul Hadi's career as a teacher and writer was short, but he made a deep impression on students and colleagues, and is remembered as an important figure in the Malay intellectual life of the day. His most intense period of work occurred between 1922 and 1929, when he taught at the Sultan Idris Malay Teachers' Training College at Tanjung Malim. There he founded the Melaka Malay Teachers' Union (1923) and acquired a reputation among students for his energetic teaching style and his efforts to ensure that students not only committed their study materials to memory, but also acquired a genuine interest in and devotion to the Malay past. In 1925 he wrote the enormously influential three-volume text *Sejarah Alam Melayu* (History of the Malay World), which was later expanded to five volumes by his best known pupil, Buyong Adil. This work moved far beyond the Anglicized "Malay" histories of Richard Winstedt and others used at the Malay College in Melaka and a number of other elite schools, histories that generally applied non-Malay values and adopted the rather narrow perspectives of state histories rather than anything broader. By contrast, Abdul Hadi saw the Malay world not as a collection of sultanates or states but as a much larger entity of peoples sharing language, culture, and race over an archipelagic expanse. While there was no room for obvious anti-British sentiment in the *Sejarah Alam Melayu*, its implicit pride in Malay culture and accomplishments, and its relegation of the British to a more ancillary role in events than they had in conventional colonial histories, prompted later readers to call it the first national Malay history. As such, the *Sejarah Alam Melayu* inspired generations of young teachers-in-training, who in turn used its lessons in their own teaching. In 1929 Abdul Hadi accepted the challenging post of commissioner of Malay schools in Kelantan, a position which he intended to use to revitalize Malay studies, blending traditional materials and modern methods. But in 1933 his health failed and he was forced to retire, cutting short his pioneering attempt to rethink and revive Malay history in terms both Malay and modern.

Bibliography: Abdul Hadi bin Haji Hasan, *Sejarah Alam Melayu*, vols. 1–3 (Singapore: Education Department, 1925–1930); Khoo Kay Kim, "Local Historians and the Writing of Malaysian History in the Twentieth Century," in Anthony Reid and David Marr, eds., *Perceptions of the Past in Southeast Asia* (Singapore: Heinemann, 1979), pp. 299–311.

William H. Frederick

ABDULLAH bin Abdul Kadir, Munshi (Melaka, 1797–Jeddah, 1854), Malay language teacher, interpreter, and chronicler. Abdullah's father, a prosperous Arab-Tamil businessman who married first an upcountry Malay and then a Malay-Indian woman, was a good linguist and sufficiently learned to become the teacher of Europeans such as William Marsden as well as a manuscript collector for Dutch East India Company officials. He forced habits of study on his son at an early age; at eleven Abdullah was teaching Malay to Hindustani soldiers to make pocket money while he attended school. In 1819 Abdullah moved to Singapore, where he was in demand by government officials, missionaries, and businessmen to give Malay language lessons and act as representative and interpreter in important matters. Most of the important Europeans of the day had reason to be grateful for his services, though few of them acknowledged their debt; Thomas S. Raffles, for example, does not mention his name. In 1837 Abdullah participated in an expedition to the east coast states of Kelantan and Pahang, acting as interpreter for a group sent by Singaporean merchants interested in developing trade there. Later he wrote about his experiences in the *Kisah Pelayaran Abdullah* (Story of Abdullah's Voyage). This work is full of description and social commentary, especially on the life and behavior of rural Malays, much of which is of interest to historians of the period. (Abdullah's son Munshi Mohamed Ibrahim [q.v.] made a similar trip in 1870 and wrote a comparable account.) Abdullah's major work, however, is the famed *Hikayat Abdullah* (Autobiography of Abdullah), published in 1847. In this description of the founding and early days of the British settlement in Singapore, Abdullah departed radically from traditional Malay historical writing. He wrote in the first person and strove to depict people and events in a realistic light, that is, as they appeared to him or as contemporary oral and written sources verified. His judgments of others were shrewd, perhaps especially those of British figures he knew, such as Raffles, John Nicol Farquhar, and John Crawfurd. He had a deep appreciation of what changes brought by the British might mean for traditional Malay society. "The old order perishes," he wrote, "a new world comes into being, and all around us is change."

Abdullah, who was religious and deeply tied to traditional ways, was torn between his admiration for British civilization and his dedication to what he perceived as an older and superior morality. He neither parroted the opinions of the British nor sided blindly with the sultans and tradition, though in the end he clearly felt he might be out of place in the changing present, to say nothing of the future. Nevertheless, he unflinchingly advised fellow Malays that "progress"—whatever that might be—could not be stemmed and that they must meet the future. Abdullah's memory was excellent, and his powers of description were precise, so that the *Hikayat* remains an extremely valuable historical source for Malay society in the early nineteenth century. But the author did not, in fact, possess much knowledge or understanding of the history of the Malay states, a limitation of some importance to later readers. Abdullah's talents as an essayist and biographer are perhaps most evident in the *Hikayat*, but he also made his mark as a writer with a strong, original style. All his works, including a recension of the *Sejarah Melayu* (Malay Annals) and his own final *Kisah Pelayaran Abdullah ke Negeri Jeddah* (1854; My Voyage to Jeddah), were written in an admirably modern Malay. The *Hikayat* was for years a standard item in government examinations in the Malay language, and it inspired several generations of Malays with both ideas and the way in which they could be expressed. Without doubt, as some nationalist critics have remarked, he went a little too far in his admiration of British ways; yet he never considered himself anything else but a Malay, and he occupies an honorable place in Malay intellectual history, which he both made and recorded.

Bibliography: Abdullah bin Abdul Kadir, *The Hikayat Abdullah*, trans. A. H. Hill (Kuala Lumpur: Oxford University Press, 1970).

William H. Frederick

AGONCILLO, Teodoro A. (Lemery, Batangas, 1912–Manila, 1984), Filipino writer and historian. Educated at the University of the Philippines in the mid–1930s, Agoncillo joined the faculty of that institution in 1958, teaching both history and Tagalog language and literature, and serving as chairman of his department from 1963 to 1969. He was a member of many academic associations and societies in the Philippines and the United States; from 1967 until his death he acted as consultant to the National Library; and he was a member of the National Historical Commission. Agoncillo wrote more than a dozen books and many articles on the Philippine past, establishing himself as a major voice in the development of the contemporary historiography of his country. He possessed a colorful, expressive writing style that gave his books a lively quality and was particularly well suited to one of the forms Agoncillo favored, the one-volume survey history. Either alone or in collaboration with another author, in the 1960s and 1970s he published four different treatments of the grand sweep of Philippine history, several of which went through numerous editions and were popular with the general public, for whom they were intended. In works such as *A Short*

History of the Philippines (1969), *A Short History of the Filipino People* (with Oscar Alfonso, 1960), and *History of the Filipino People* (with Millagros Guerrero, 4th ed. 1974), he attempted to break the mold of Philippine history as it was commonly taught to schoolchildren and explained in their texts. For example, he abandoned the approach that placed heavy emphasis on the years of Spanish colonization, saying that before 1872 the written sources tell very little about what Filipinos—as distinct from Spaniards, the colonial government, and the Church—thought and did; therefore there was no reason to delve deeply into them. He noted, too, that it was illogical for Filipino histories to recount Magellan's "discovery" of the Philippines, since, of course, Filipinos knew perfectly well where the islands were and who inhabited them. In adopting this point of view, Agoncillo brought popular Filipino historiography to a new nationalist stage, one that did not merely view matters from the obverse of the colonial perspective but from a new position altogether, and that applied a number of concepts from the social sciences and Marxist historiography as analytical tools. While not universally accepted, even by Agoncillo's Filipino colleagues, the concept represented an important challenge to indigenous as well as foreign historians of the Philippines.

Agoncillo's special field of interest was the Philippine Revolution. Particularly through his monumental two-volume study, *Revolt of the Masses: The Story of Bonifacio and the Katipunan* (1956) and *Malolos: The Crisis of the Republic* (1960), based on exhaustive research using archival records and oral sources in addition to much of the surviving published material, he laid out a demanding social interpretation based on class analysis. In Agoncillo's view, the revolution had its genuine beginnings in the masses but was later betrayed by Filipino intellectuals and the "middle class," who feared revolution and supported only reform, and who ultimately collaborated with the Americans in a recolonization of their nation. This view was not an entirely novel one, but no writer had stated it as clearly and in as scholarly a manner as Agoncillo. Critics replied that no hard evidence was offered to support Agoncillo's description of classes in late nineteenth-century Philippine society, and that just because the revolutionary armies were made up of peasants the conclusion could not be drawn that the revolution was one of and by the masses. Agoncillo's interpretation became the focus of a heated debate, or rather a series of debates, and although it is perhaps true that in very general terms his view has become commonplace among prominent Philippinists, especially in the United States, the arguments continue down to the present. By opening up some of the most sensitive topics in Philippine history to new and bristling interpretation (he also wrote several works on the Japanese occupation, among them his final study *The Burden of Proof: The Vargas-Laurel Collaboration Case* [1984]), Agoncillo performed a service of lasting value.

Bibliography: Teodoro Agoncillo, *Filipino Nationalism, 1872–1970* (Quezon City: R. P. Garcia, 1974); Teodoro Agoncillo, *A Short History of the Philippines* (New York: New American Library, 1969).

William H. Frederick

ALI, Mohammed (Madiun, 1912–Jakarta, 1974), Indonesian teacher, historian, and archivist. Educated in Dutch-run colonial schools to roughly the Teacher's Training School level, he taught primary school from 1933 until the revolutionary period (1945–1949), when he spent brief periods teaching secondary school and working for the Ministry of Religion. Later he moved to the Ministry of Education and Culture, teaching first in a high school and then at a teacher's training institute. During this period he also studied history at the University of Indonesia, where he was apparently influenced by the Swiss scholar A. van Arx. From 1957 to 1970 he served as head of the National Archives and taught courses in national history at both the University of Indonesia and Pajajaran University. Mohammed Ali's views on the nature of Indonesia's past were nationalist and, more vaguely, socialist; they were also controversial and debated heatedly in their day. His outlook was generally grim, and he was far more apprehensive about the past than, say, the political leader Achmed Sukarno. Most of Indonesian history, he implied strongly, consisted of unrelieved and aimless warfare, remnants of which were very much in evidence in the mid-twentieth century. In his best known and most original work, *Perjuangan feodal* (1954; The Feudal Struggle), Mohammed Ali portrayed traditional leaders and the elites around them as "feudal" figures ruling in feudal fashion, sending the masses to war and manipulating social division for their own purposes. He suggested that the entirety of Indonesian history could be seen as a struggle against feudalism, and in such a scheme the coming of the Dutch in the late sixteenth century changed nothing of significance. Indeed, there were three feudalizations of Indonesia—Hindu, Moslem, and Dutch—which served to reinforce each other rather than alter the situation. Herein lay the source of, among other characteristics, the "submissive mentality" of the Indonesian people, especially the peasantry. These ideas represented an obvious effort to escape the strictures of the old Dutch colonial historiography and were therefore in a sense nationalist. There was also a populist ring to the accompanying admonition that the history of "the people" had been forgotten in all this feudal history, a circumstance that needed to be rectified.

The picture Mohammed Ali painted of Indonesian society did not win favor among more optimistic nationalist thinkers, and it was some years before other scholars took up the task of devising methods with which to highlight nonelite Indonesian history. Spurred perhaps by the needs of his students, especially those eager to become school teachers, Mohammed Ali devoted much attention to the problem of writing a full-blown national history. Between 1953 and 1955 he published a comprehensive secondary school text in eighteen sections of sixty pages each, but he did not reveal his authorship until 1960. It was reprinted three times, the last in 1969. In the early 1960s he proposed a periodization scheme in which Indonesia's past was divided into three unequal eras: (1) international freedom, 146–1910; (2) international dominance, 1910–1945; and (3) international responsibility, 1945–present. This placed the story of Indonesian peoples' past in a global context. Since it was really not possible to speak of national unity until, at best, the early twentieth century, he designated the subperiod 1511–1910 as one of local struggles for independence, with the following subperiod comprising national struggles. However much he tried to free himself and his country's history from an essentially colonial intellectual framework, Mohammed Ali ironically remained captive to many of its paradigms. By the late 1960s his work was being rapidly replaced by a new generation of Indonesian historians, less concerned with the colonialism-versus-nationalism struggle and intent on arriving at new formulations through which a distinctly Indonesian history could be brought to life.

Bibliography: Mohammed Ali, *Perdjuangan feodal* (Bandung: Ganaco, 1954); Mohammed Ali, *Sedjarah dalam revolusi dan revolusi dalam sedjarah* (Jakarta: Bhratara, 1965); H. A. J. Klooster, *Indonesiërs Schrijven Hun Geschiedenis* (Dordrecht: FORIS, 1985).

William H. Frederick

ALI HAJI ibni Raja Ahmad, Raja (Selangor, c. 1809–c. 1870), Buginese ruler of Riau, religious scholar, and historian. For Ali Haji history was something of a family industry. His father, Raja Ahmad, was probably the first to conceive the idea of an epic history of the Buginese people in the Malay world, and wrote the *Syair Perang Johor* (The Story of the Johor War). Ali Haji finished his father's work and composed many others; at least two of his daughters and one son were responsible for related historical and literary pieces. At the age of twenty Ali Haji was well-traveled, having gone to Batavia (Jakarta) and Mecca with his father. At thirty he was joint regent of Lingga for Sultan Mahmud, who was deposed in 1857. A valued administrator and respected community leader, he nevertheless devoted much time to scholarship, which was of high quality. Ali Haji's first published work was the *Syair Sultan Abdul Muluh* (The Story of Sultan Abdul Muluh), which appeared in 1847. He composed a number of other short histories in subsequent years, among them the *Silsilah Melayu dan Bugis* (The History of the Malay and Buginese Peoples). This became the foundation for his masterwork, the *Tuhfat al-Nafis* (The Precious Gift), which was completed in the late 1860s. It carried the story of the Buginese begun by his father up until 1864 and remains one of the historical monuments of the Malay world. The perspective of the *Tuhfat al-Nafis* is, understandably enough, a Buginese one, and its principal theme is the justification and legitimization of Buginese rule in Malay society. But it is also concerned with preserving Malay traditions and the Islamic community. Like much court writing of the time, especially that with a historical bent, Ali Haji's work sought to instruct the rulers in proper behavior and decision making; the chief goal was harmony in the state and in society at large. He wrote, "Disharmony within a state arises when a man seeks to follow his own desires rather than the laws of Allah. A historical record is therefore intended to be a lesson for the present, a means of perpetuating the memories of rulers, both good and bad, as a guide for future generations." Probably his views reflected those of many educated contemporaries. In the *Tuhfat al-Nafis* and other works, the importance of human responsibility in history is emphasized. Events are not simply matters of *takdir* (fate), and Ali Haji refuses to lean on fate as an explanation; he searches instead for human failings, especially ignorance and failure to follow God's law, and he shows how they affect the historical outcome.

Ali Haji's work is of special interest today because of the extraordinary care he is known to have taken in collecting and recording facts. He used many sources in the court libraries of Riau, Siak, and Kalimantan, and in private collections. He made a practice of identifying sources, which was almost unheard of in traditional writing. He also utilized personal recollection and the memories of others about comparatively recent events and personages, which represented an additional change in the older historiography. Perhaps these innovations were suggested to Ali Haji by the special circumstances in which he wrote: he could see, with the expansion of Western power in the Malay archipelago, that the old ways of life were threatened and might soon come to an end. Would it not require extraordinary methods at least to preserve this traditional past, if not carry it forward? Thus, the *Tuhfat al-Nafis* was intended as not only a hopeful guide for the next generation but also, as Ali Haji himself noted sorrowfully, as a "testament to the history of a great kingdom that is now no more."

Bibliography: Barbara Watson Andaya and Virginia Matheson (trans. and annot.), *Tuhfat al-Nafis* (Kuala Lumpur: Oxford, 1982); Virginia Matheson, "The *Tuhfat al-Nafis*: Structure and Sources," *Bijdragen tot Taal-, Land- en Volkenkunde* 128, no. 3 (1971): 379–390.

William H. Frederick

COSTA, Horacio de la (1916–1977), Filipino historian. De la Costa, a Jesuit priest, received his doctorate in history from Harvard University in 1951. In the following year he returned as dean of arts and sciences to the Ateneo de Manila, where he remained except for periods of service as the first Filipino provincial of the Jesuits in the Philippines and as assistant to the Father General of the Society of Jesus in Rome. He published five books and a number of articles on the history of the Philippines, was a member of the National Historical Institute, and received the Republic Heritage Award for distinguished historical writing in 1965. De la Costa was highly regarded as a professional historian, the first and most prominent member of a postwar generation of Filipinos schooled in prestigious Western universities, exposed to the latest historiographical ideas and methods, and in touch with fellow historians around the world. In the 1960s, many regarded him as the finest modern historian the Philippines had produced, and his opinions were much in demand by foreigners as well as his own countrymen. The work for which he is perhaps best known among fellow historians, *The Jesuits in the Philippines, 1581–1768* (1961), is a refinement of his doctoral dissertation. It represents a continuation of the long tradition of the friar chronicle in the Philippines, but it raised this genre to the level of modern historical writing by virtue of its exacting use of archival materials, its meticulous citations, and its awareness of the historiographical pitfalls found in earlier histories by ecclesiastics. It also surpassed previous works in its insistence on contributing to a wide, "national" view of its subject.

Under different circumstances, de la Costa would perhaps have become a nationalist historian comparable in outlook and fervor to many contemporaries elsewhere in Southeast Asia, but his Jesuit background and the essentially conservative graduate education (and, perhaps, personality) brought him to occupy instead a very modest position which many might find difficult to identify as nationalistic at all. Indeed, de la Costa abhorred what he regarded as the exaggerated claims of nationalist historians regarding, for example, the level of civilization of precolonial Filipino life; his own view was that early Filipino culture was primitive and that on the whole Spain and the Catholic Church had had an invaluable civilizing effect. While he sympathized with the goal of independence in the Philippine Revolution, he could not entirely hide his distaste for the immoderate, even radical proponents of freedom from Spanish or American rule; he saw too clearly how complex such issues were, and steered vigorously away from easy answers or extreme positions. Rather than condemning American rule altogether, for example, he tended to emphasize that, whatever else might have been unsatisfactory, American education was an important benefit to Filipinos. In one form or another views of this sort were found in de la Costa's *The Trial of Rizal* (1961) and *Readings in Philippine History* (1965). The caution—some would say forced balance—of this "gentle nationalism" has not, on the whole, carried through into subsequent Filipino and Western historical writing on the Philippines, which has so often been characterized by extreme national pride or anticolonial feeling. It is also true that the historiographical agenda has changed since the 1960s and now, with good justification, has turned attention to local, peasant, oral, and other histories. Still, de la Costa's scrupulous attention to detail, his refusal to adopt simplistic conclusions, and his respect for original sources remain a sound legacy on which Filipino historians of all shades of opinion may draw.

Bibliography: Horacio de la Costa, *The Background of Nationalism and Other Essays* (Manila: Solidaridad, 1965); Horacio de la Costa, *The Jesuits in the Philippines* (Cambridge, Mass.: Harvard University Press, 1961).

William H. Frederick

DAMRONG RAJANUBHAB, Prince (1862–1943), Thai statesman, bureaucrat, and historian. A son of the Thai ruler known in the West as Mongkut or Rama IV (reigned 1851–1868), Damrong studied classics at a palace school and from the age of seven took English lessons from a tutor hired by his elder half-brother, King Chulalongkorn (reigned 1868–1910). At fifteen he graduated from the Military Pages School and, from that point, except for two brief periods of learning as a Buddhist monk, was largely self-taught. His first major administrative appointment was as director of the new Education Department in 1887. After a brief assignment as royal ambassador to Europe, he presided over the Ministry of Interior from 1892 until his dismissal in 1915. Especially in the latter post he exhibited an unfailing interest in modernization and improvement, often along Western lines but always cognizant of Thai realities and tradition. Thus, his early interest in historical subjects found a more practical application than might otherwise have been the case: Knowing the past was important not only to the present but also to the business of shaping the future. On retirement from administration, Prince Damrong headed the National Library and the National Museum, both of which he worked hard to develop into outstanding collections. Earlier (1904) he had helped found the Siam Society. The notion of learning from records of the past was not, of course, strange to Thai society of that or any earlier day. But Damrong, influenced to a considerable degree by Leopold von Ranke (q.v.) and the "scientific method," adopted a rather new perspective on the Thai past and sought to alter the methods and outlook of the traditional *tamnan* and *phongsawadan* genres of Thai historiography. He aimed to collate and summarize the full range of indigenous written sources and, taking a rigorous "rationalist" approach, make them yield a more modern sort of history emphasizing chronological development, "progress," hard evidence rather than myth, and national identity or a sense of the nation-state. Prince Damrong wrote over one thousand different works, divided for the most part into three categories. Perhaps the most valuable were the new, and usually annotated, editions of older works or compilations of new, general histories. In 1901 he published his edition of Chaophraya Thipakorawong's (q.v.) chronicle of the first Chakri reign (*Phraratchaphongsawadan krung rattanakosin: ratachakan 1*); his edition of Thipakorawong's Royal Autograph Chronicle (of Ayuthia) (*Phraratchaphongsawadan chabap phraratchahatlekha*) appeared in 1912, with extensive commentary in a corrected 1914 edition. Two years later he published his chronicle of the second Chakri reign, based on Thipakorawong's work, and during the 1920s he began a history of the fifth reign, that of his brother, but never completed it. Prince Damrong was also convinced of the importance of personal history and published hundreds of biographies of Thai figures. Finally, he wrote a large number of short works of a topical or thematic nature, many of which, like the biographies, were turned out quickly for publication as cremation volumes, distributed in memory of the deceased.

   Prince Damrong bridged traditional and modern styles of Thai historiography. He attempted to apply scientific methods of organization and investigation to his work, deliberately wrote for a broad audience by taking a storyteller's approach and avoiding Sanskrit and Pali vocabulary, and attempted to synthesize past historians' work to accommodate modern sensibilities. At the same time, he remained to some degree tied to the traditional focus on kings, courts, and prominent leaders, and his periodization retained much of the style of the old chronicles. Like many traditional historians, Damrong wrote essentially to instruct those who wielded power, and avoided extensive analysis and interpretation. His work became an important window through which Westerners could view the Thai past with some comprehension, but more importantly it was the basis on which a new generation of Thai historians, no longer concerned with the difficult first rejection of myth and tradition as explanation, could begin their studies.

Bibliography: Kennon Breazeale, "Transition in Historical Writing; The Works of Prince Damrong Rachanuphap," *Journal of the Siam Society*, 59, no. 2 (1971): 25–49; Charnvit Kasetsiri, "Thai Historiography from Ancient Times to the Modern Period," in Anthony Reid and David Marr, eds., *Perceptions of the Past in Southeast Asia* (Singapore: Heinemann, 1979), pp. 156–167; Damrong Rajanubhab, "Our Wars with the Burmese," *Journal of the Burma Research Society*, 38 (1955): 121–196, 40 (1957): 135–240, 40 (1958): 241–347; Damrong Rajanubhab, "The Story of the Records of Siamese History," *The Siam Society, Fiftieth Anniversary Publication* 1 (Bangkok: The Siam Society, 1954), pp. 79–98.

William H. Frederick

DE LOS REYES y Florentino, Isabelo (Vigan, Ilocos Sur, 1864–Manila, 1938) Filipino lawyer, journalist, politician, and popular historian. Growing up in a well-to-do family, de los Reyes was educated by a tutor and friars. At sixteen he enrolled in a Manila college and later studied law and paleography at the University of Santo Tomás. He exhibited both passion and talent for writing. After several failures in business, in 1889 he founded the first vernacular Filipino newspaper, *El Ilocano*, which was not a commercial success, and later worked as a journalist and free-lance writer. He was jailed by the Spanish and then offered a position in the Madrid government. He took up the pen against Spanish rule and in the early American years began a political career that culminated in three terms in the Philippine Senate. He was both a follower of socialist ideas and a founder of the Aglipayan (Philippine Independent) Church. He spent much time and effort researching and writing historical works, most of which appeared in serialized form in newspapers before being published as pamphlets or books. The best examples are *Las Islas Visayas en la Epoca de la Conquista* (1887), *Prehistoria de Filipinas* (1889), and *Historia de Ilocos* (2 vols., 1890), the first local history written by a Filipino. His goal was to "establish a past"—and an identity—for the Filipino people, and he is a founding father of nationalist historiography in the Philippines.

For the most part, however, de los Reyes' methods were considered weak even by those contemporaries who sympathized with his aims. Indeed, he based most of his work on Spanish materials, which he treated uncritically, and he seems frequently to have written without any firm sources at all. His work on Ilocano folklore and customs (1889), however, based more directly on observation and original investigation, was considered of interest, and his *Sensacional Memoria sobre la Revolucion Filipina* (1897), written inside Bilibid Prison where de los Reyes learned first hand the story of the Katipunan from revolutionary members, became a curious contribution to revolutionary history in the Philippines. For de los Reyes, nationalism in history was still vague and the "scientific" methods of historical investigation still unclear. However, he was able to reach a large audience and is considered an important member of the so-called

Propaganda Movement, whose greatest exponent was José Protacio Rizal Mercado y Alonzo Realonda (q.v.).

Bibliography: Isabelo de los Reyes y Florentino, *Historia de Ilocos*, 2 vols., 2d ed. (Manila: La Opinion, 1890); Isabelo de los Reyes y Florentino, *Las Islas Visayas en la Epoca de la Conquista*, 2d ed. (Manila: de Chofré, 1889); Isabelo de los Reyes y Florentino, *Prehistoria de Filipinas* (Manila: Esteban Balbás, 1889); John N. Schumacher, "The 'Propagandists' Reconstruction of the Philippine Past," in Anthony Reid and David Marr, eds., *Perceptions of the Past in Southeast Asia* (Singapore: Heinemann, 1979), pp. 264–280; Gregorio F. Zaide, *Great Filipinos in History* (Manila: Verde Bookstore, 1970).

William H. Frederick

HTIN AUNG, Maung (1909–1979?), Burmese educator and historian. Htin Aung graduated from the University of Rangoon in 1928 and went on to acquire a number of higher degrees in the United Kingdom, including a Ph.D. at Trinity College, Dublin. He was admitted to the bar in 1932. He became the first Burmese to be appointed to senior rank at the University of Rangoon, where he was professor of English from 1936 to 1946 and served as rector from 1946 to 1958. He held a variety of distinguished positions, including chairmanship of the Burma Historical Commission and the Burmese ambassadorship to Sri Lanka, and received honorary degrees from several universities, including Johns Hopkins (1951). After 1962 he was visiting professor at Columbia and Wake Forest Universities.

Htin Aung wrote a number of historical works, most of them seeking in one way or another to right the interpretational balance which he believed had been upset by British historical studies of Burma. In *The Stricken Peacock: Anglo-Burmese Relations 1752–1948* (1965), he attempted to show a rather different view of the topic than was available from British sources, which tended to portray the Burmese in highly negative terms. *Burmese Monk's Tales* (1966) utilized unusual sources to show a rather different side of daily life in nineteenth-century Burma and how it was disrupted by the British. His *Burmese History Before 1287: A Defense of the Chronicles* (1970) criticized the work of, among others, Gordon Luce and Pe Maung Tin (q.v.) on the *Royal Glass Palace Chronicle* and other Burmese historical materials, claiming for them both greater accuracy and a higher degree of usefulness than Western scholarship generally allowed. *A History of Burma* (1967) presented a comprehensive survey of the Burmese past, based more heavily than any previous such work on Burmese rather than Western materials; it remains the best study of its kind, though its conclusions have by no means gone uncontested. Htin Aung, who was not trained as a historian and who was not in the strict sense a professional scholar in that field, has been heavily criticized for a seeming disregard for accepted Western historical methods, careless handling of facts, and heavy-handed chauvinism. In *A History of Burma*, for example, his portrayal of the Burmese kingship, especially during the nineteenth century, was so sympathetic that he appeared to many specialist readers to be dealing in fantasy rather than history, particularly since the citations to support this viewpoint were either not up to modern historiographical standards or were lacking altogether. Yet Htin Aung's effort to reframe and compose a linear Burmese history understandable in modern, Western terms is typical of similar activities by nationalist writers elsewhere in postwar Southeast Asia and certainly contains thematic suggestions that deserve more detailed examination. Whether Burmese historians will soon take up the task is in question, for ironically Htin Aung appears to have chosen foreigners rather than his own countrymen as his principal audience, and his work presents us with the rather odd example of a nationalist history comparatively little known at home.

Bibliography: Htin Aung, *Burmese History Before 1287, A Defense of the Chronicles* (Oxford: Asoke Society, 1970); Htin Aung, *Epistles Written on the Eve of the Anglo-Burmese War* (The Hague: M. Nijhoff, 1968); Htin Aung, *A History of Burma* (New York: Columbia University Press, 1967).

William H. Frederick

JIT PHUMISAK (Samsamai Sisutphan) (1930–1966), Thai musician, poet, essayist, and historian. The son of a provincial government officer, Jit Phumisak as a child moved frequently with his family but graduated from a Bangkok high school and later studied at the prestigious Chulalongkorn University. There he discovered politics and the study of history, and constructed an attractive writing style that derived some of its power from a sophisticated understanding of classical Thai language. Because Jit's writings were anti-imperialist, Marxist, and socially challenging, he soon ran afoul of the conservative Sarit government and was jailed from 1957 to 1964. His reputation grew while in prison, as he had songs and essays smuggled out and distributed; on his release he joined the guerrilla opposition and two years later was shot and killed by government forces.

Jit Phumisak's most influential work is the article "Chomna Khong Sakdinathai Nai Patchuban" (The Real Face of Thai Feudalism Today), originally published in 1957 and reprinted in monograph form (with an abbreviated title) several times since. This analysis of the development of Thai society from the thirteenth century to 1932, with both implicit and explicit indications of its contemporary relevance, is not strictly speaking Marxist but it is founded on the idea that Thai society is divided into distinct classes. Jit identified these classes as the oppressors—the *sakdina* or feudals—and the oppressed—the *phrai* and *that*, or peasants and slaves—and argued that in the struggle between the two the *sakdina* were victorious because of their control over the land and therefore over the key to economic power. He described how Thai society had passed from a kind of "pre-*sakdina* " stage during the Sukothai period in the thirteenth and fourteenth centuries, to full-blown feudalism during the early Ayuthia period beginning in the mid fourteenth century, to the changed but structurally linked Bangkok period after the late eighteenth century. Jit's description of how the *sakdina* class used history reveals a good deal about his own view. "The subject of history," he wrote, "is the subject of man's social struggle for later generations. The studying of history is the heart of studying social development, a major key which opens to right actions. The *sakdina* realize this fact, [and] therefore they have controlled the study of history in their hands, and used this subject for their own class's benefit.'' ''The Real Face of Thai Feudalism Today,'' however, was as much an example of linguistic virtuosity as social history, for in the course of the long essay Jit transformed the Old Thai word *sakdina* into a modern Thai equivalent of the English ''feudalism,'' and gave it a rich new political resonance reaching far beyond that term. From the historiographical point of view Jit's work is significant because it opened up large areas of debate on the nature of Thai history, especially in such sensitive areas as Buddhism (the subject of an early essay on materialism) and the development of social classes. In his wake came critical works, some Marxist and some non- and even anti-Marxist, that quarreled, for example, over the characterization of *sakdina* and its significance; the more conservative and perhaps ''standard'' view is that the *sakdina* system cannot be equated with Western feudalism, that Thai social classes do not exist in quite the same way they are theorized about in the Western context, and that the foundation of real power in Thai society is not land at all but human labor, controlled by intricate systems of human relationships. Such questions will for some time remain at the heart of Thai efforts to understand their own history, and are also likely to be the points at which Thai and foreign scholarship will most easily—and most noisily—meet.

Bibliography: Jit Phumisak, *Thai Radical Discourse. ''The Real Face of Thai Feudalism Today''* trans., annot., and intro. by Craig J. Reynolds (Ithaca, N.Y.: Cornell University Southeast Asia Program, 1987); Charnvit Kasetsiri, ''Thai Historiography from Ancient Times to the Modern Period,'' in Anthony Reid and David Marr, eds., *Perceptions of the Past in Southeast Asia* (Singapore: Heinemann, 1979), pp. 156–170; Craig J. Reynolds and Hong Lysa, ''Marxism in Thai Historical Studies,'' *Journal of Asian Studies* 43, 1 (November 1983): 77–104.

William H. Frederick

KALAW, Teodoro Manguiat (Lipa, Batangas, 1884–Manila, 1940), Filipino statesman, journalist, and historian. Born to a wealthy family, Kalaw was groomed for an intellectual life and completed his education at the Liceo de Manila and the Escuela de Derecho, where he finished his law studies and taught for several years after his graduation in 1905. While still a law student, he was also a reporter for *El Renacimiento Filipino*, of which he became the last editor; the paper was closed in 1908 as a result of a libel suit over Kalaw's article concerning U.S. Secretary of Interior Dean C. Worcester. In 1909 he became the youngest member of the Philippine Assembly and went on to serve the government in a number of ways. He was twice director of the National Library (1916–1917 and 1929–1939), and received many awards and honorary memberships on both sides of the Pacific. Kalaw wrote extensively in Spanish, Tagalog, and English on a wide variety of subjects, but his most durable works concerned the Philippine Revolution. His *Epistolario Rizalino* (5 vols., 1930–1937) remains a basic source of Rizaliana, and another work, *La Revolución*

Filipina na con Otros Documentos de la Época (2 vols., 1931), is a basic, though not complete, collection of the writings of Mabini. Kalaw's biographical treatments of prominent figures of the revolution such as Mabini and del Pilar, while in some respects outdated by subsequent research and marred by nationalist romanticism, nevertheless continue to be useful. His legal training enabled him to produce meaningful works on the Malolos Constitution (1910) and the constitutional ideas of the revolution in general (1914). His popular survey of the Philippine revolution, *La Revolución Filipina*, which first appeared in Spanish and English in the mid–1920s and was reprinted as late as 1969, has by this time lost both its currency of scholarship and much of its flavor, but it was probably the best treatment of the revolution by a Filipino written in the period before World War II. Kalaw does not fall readily into a particular school or stream of Philippine historiography, but it may be sufficient to portray him as a transitional figure, between the so-called propagandists on the one hand and contemporary professional historians such as Horacio de la Costa (q.v.) and Teodoro Agoncillo (q.v.) on the other, a powerful writer who was able to contribute to the gradually coalescing national history more soundly and more colorfully than many of his predecessors.

Bibliography: Teodoro Kalaw, *Aide de Camp to Freedom* (Manila: T. Kalaw Society, 1965); Theodoro Kalaw, *The Philippine Revolution* (Manila: J. B. Vargas Foundation, 1969); Teodoro Agoncillo, "Philippine Historiography in the Age of Kalaw," *Solidarity* (Manila), 5 (1984): 3–16; Gregorio F. Zaide, *Great Filipinos in History* (Manila: Verde Bookstore, 1970).

William H. Frederick

MOHAMED IBRAHIM, Munshi (Melaka, c.1840–1904), Malay court recorder and emissary, historical writer. The son of the well-known language teacher and chronicler Abdullah bin Abdul Kadir Munshi (q.v.), Ibrahim Munshi was educated at the English missionary school run by B. P. Keasberry in Singapore. He was schoolmaster at the Telok Belanga Malay School in the 1860s and then went into the employ of Abu Bakar, maharaja (and later sultan) of Johor, whose classmate Ibrahim had been. (The title *munshi*, also held by his father, indicates his position as a teacher of language and literature, mostly to Europeans.) In the years 1871–1872 Abu Bakar sent Ibrahim on a series of five voyages to Malaya's east coast, about which he wrote two books of accounts; the second of these was lost, but the first (covering all the voyages but one) has survived as the *Kesah Pelayaran Mohamed Ibrahim Munshi* (The Story of the Voyages of Mohamed Ibrahim Munshi) (1872, with an addition in 1874; first printed in 1919). In 1878 Ibrahim accompanied his patron to Europe and wrote the short *Pemimpin Johor* (A Guide to Johor). Not long afterward he was appointed state secretary of Johor, a position in which he served with sufficient distinction to be awarded the highest honors of the court. Whereas his father was torn between the worlds of Malay tradition and colonial "modernity," Ibrahim betrayed no such confusion. His *Voyages* show him to be proud of his

Malay identity—one might almost say "nationalist"—yet at the same time admiring of the modern, Western outlook on the world. He remained steadfastly loyal to his maharaja, yet never questioned the superiority of the British. He was very critical of the "backward" behavior of upcountry Malays and extolled the virtues of cooking with butter rather than Malay fermented fishpaste, but he sought only to be more truly Malay by championing change and modernization in his own society and culture. The material contained in *Voyages* reflects much careful research using written and oral sources, political analysis, and insightful characterizations of Malay leaders and British mores. In addition, Ibrahim is clear about expressing his own ideas and judgments as opposed to received opinion. All of this represents not a sudden departure from traditional Malay historiography (Ibrahim's father had already pioneered many of these alterations), but a further step—and one of considerable value to contemporary scholars—in the development of the modern Malay historiography that is still gradually taking shape.

Bibliography: Amin Sweeney and Nigel Phillips (trans. and intro.), *The Voyages of Mohamed Ibrahim Munshi* (Kuala Lumpur: Oxford University Press, 1975).

William H. Frederick

MONYWE HSAYADAW (1766–1834), Burmese monk, Pali scholar, epigrapher, and chronicler. The Monywe Hsayadaw and the Thawkapin Hsayadaw were principal consulting editors appointed in 1829 by King Bagyidaw (reigned 1819–1838) to compile a new official historical chronicle of the realm. The chronicle took its name, the *Hmannan Mahayazawindawgyi* (The Great Royal Glass Palace Chronicle), from the project's headquarters. Though only the earliest portions of this important work have been translated into English, it remains by far the best known and—for better or worse—among Westerners probably the most influential piece of precolonial Burmese historical writing. Like other histories of its type, the *Hmannan Mahayazawindawgyi* was concerned with the duties of kings, the nature of the state, and the proper relationship of these to religion. It was also a deliberate revision or "purification" of the work of U Kala, who several generations earlier had compiled a standard chronicle in which many dates and other details were by the early nineteenth century thought to be in error. Over a period of four years, a staff of chroniclers combed not only the royal histories but also local and monastic records, literature, and extensive commentaries on inscriptions, searching for new information as well as evidence for needed corrections. The editors believed that their version substantially improved on the accuracy of U Kala's chronicle, though it is now clear that they utilized many of the same incorrect readings and incorrect copies of inscriptions made use of by U Kala. The Monywe Hsayadaw was aware of some of these difficulties and took the unusual step of warning readers that discrepancies existed but that greater accuracy was not possible without further checking. Although frequently treated in Western accounts as merely a compilation of legend and fancy, the *Hmannan Mahayazawindawgyi* displays such qualities largely in the early sections, which discuss the origins of the Burmese and their state. The later portions offer a rather different account of the past which is factual and much concerned with the accuracy of dates, though centered on the activities of the court and silent on criticisms or topics to which the ruler might have been expected to be sensitive. The *Hmannan Mahayazawindawgyi* carries the story of the Burmese kingdom to 1821; in 1867 King Mindon (reigned 1853–1878) ordered a new committee to bring the work up to 1854, and in 1905 the story was further expanded to cover the entire Konbaung Dynasty, which had ended its rule in 1885.

The Monywe Hsayadaw also authored at least one additional chronicle on which he worked for many years, now generally identified as the *Mahayazawingyaw*. Still unpublished and incompletely known, it concerns among other things pre-Ava literature, the rise of the first Konbaung ruler, and the history of the author's home village and its most prominent inhabitants.

Bibliography: U Tet Htoot, "The Nature of the Burmese Chronicles," and Tin Ohn, "Modern Historical Writing in Burmese, 1724–1942," both in D. G. E. Hall, ed., *Historians of Southeast Asia* (London: Oxford University Press, 1961), pp. 50–62 and 85–93; partial English translation of the *Hmannan Mahayazawindawgyi : The Glass Palace Chronicle of the Kings of Burma*, Pe Maung Tin and Gordon H. Luce, trans. (London: Oxford University Press, 1923 [reprint, New York: AMS Press, 1976]).

William H. Frederick

NONG, Oknha Vongsa Sarapech (c. 177?–c. 184?/186?), Khmer (Cambodian) court official and chronicler. Very little is known about this figure; even his precise identity is in doubt, since several individuals with the same name and similar titles apparently wrote at roughly the same time. Nong is believed to have composed the so-called *Nong Chronicle* (c. 1818), which covers the period 1414–1800. It follows closely the pattern of traditional Khmer and Thai royal historiography—that is, it constitutes a palace-centered view of events—and attempts to reconstruct Khmer history between the fourteenth and eighteenth century, using Thai sources as a base, since adequate original Khmer materials did not apparently exist. What may be referred to as the Nong genre is the lineage of historical works continuing with this chronology and often copying much of the *Nong Chronicle*, for example, Prince Nupparot's *Brah raj bansavatar khattiya maharaj* (1878; The Royal Chronicle of the Great Ksatriya Kings). This tradition is distinguished from that associated with the twentieth-century palace official Khmer Thiounn (q.v.).

Bibliography: Mak Phoeun, "L'Introduction de la Chroniques Royale du Cambodge du Lettré Nong," *Bulletin de l'Ecole Française d'Extrême-Orient*, 67 (1980): 135–145— French translation: "Chronique Royale du Cambodge," Francis Garnier, trans. *Journal Asiatique*, 18 (1871): 336–385, 20 (1872): 112–144—modern Thai translation in *Phongsawadan Khamen* I (1914); Michael Vickery, "Cambodia After Angkor, the Chronicular Evidence for the Fourteenth to Sixteenth Centuries," Ph.D. diss. (Yale University, 1977); Michael Vickery, "The Composition and Transmission of the Ayudhya and Cambodian

Chronicles,'' in Anthony Reid and David Marr, eds., *Perceptions of the Past in Southeast Asia* (Singapore: Heinemann, 1979), pp. 130–154.

William H. Frederick

NOTOSUSANTO, Nugroho (Lembang, Central Java, 1931–Jakarta, 1985), Indonesian military officer, civil servant, novelist, educator, and historian. The eldest son of a professor of law at Gadjah Mada University, Nugroho Notosusanto attended schools in Malang, Jakarta, and Yogyakarta; studied at the University of London in the early 1960s; and in 1977 received his doctorate in history from the University of Indonesia with a dissertation entitled ''The Peta Army During the Japanese Occupation.'' As a teenager he had been a freedom fighter during the Indonesian Revolution (1945–1949) and made his literary debut with a collection of short stories about his experiences entitled *Hujan Kepagian* (1958; Rain in the Morning). He enjoyed a promising reputation as a writer but chose to pursue history as his principal career, studying and teaching at the University of Indonesia, where he also filled several administrative positions, and at the Indonesian Army's National Defense Institute. In 1964 he became head of the Center for Armed Forces History. He served as rector of the University of Indonesia from 1982 and, concurrently, as minister of education from 1984 until his death. He wrote nearly thirty academic books and pamphlets, four works of fiction, and a large number of articles.

Nugroho's ideas about history and his influence on historical writing in modern Indonesia are controversial among Indonesian and Western scholars. Although he hoped to move beyond the rather simple nationalism of predecessors such as Muhammad Yamin (q.v.), he may be classified as a nationalist historian. He generally viewed history as a science, containing a single identifiable truth, and though frequently at the center of debate on historical issues he was not entirely comfortable with the idea of history as a public art. He seems to have felt that Indonesia's ''national interest'' demanded a unitary and unarguable picture of its past, especially where such events as the revolution and the momentous upheaval of 1965 were concerned. He was an unabashed modernist, deeply influenced by reading in Western historical theory, and he had little patience with indigenous, precolonial historical writing. His career as a historian coincides with the rise of the Indonesian military's New Order, and he was often accused, particularly by opponents of that government, of acting as its apologist. His works on the military history of the revolution, on *The Coup Attempt of the September 30 Movement in Indonesia* (1968), on the origins of the Indonesian state ideology known as the Pancasila, and a number of other topics all took strong positions supporting—some even said defining—the ''official'' view. Nugroho's work on the six-volume *Sejarah Nasional Indonesia* [National History of Indonesia] (1975) was widely criticized as being academically weak, and his defense of his doctoral dissertation became the focus of considerable academic turmoil. The reputation of being something less than an independent scholar was only strengthened by his tenure as rector of his alma mater and as minister of education, in which roles he took positions widely identified as being not only progovernment but also government-serving. It may be that political issues can never be sufficiently separated from Nugroho's life and work to allow a more even-handed evaluation of his historical writings, but there is some reason to caution against dismissing them altogether. Nugroho lies at the center of the development of the post-1965 "standard" version of Indonesian political history, which does not represent an entirely new line of interpretation but a continuation of ideas already very much in force. As this is the history which, in one form or another, millions of Indonesian children read each school year, it bears scrutiny, not only for the shape of its account but also for the nature of its historiographical assumptions. Nugroho's influence in creating a powerful literal and figurative school of military history in Indonesia must also be taken into account. Furthermore, some of Nugroho's intrepretations, may be worthy of a second, calmer look, among them the idea that the Peta Army created during the Japanese occupation (1942–1945) was not—strictly speaking—the forerunner of the modern Indonesian Army, and that there were perhaps a number of sources of inspiration for the Pancasila other than Sukarno's imagination (*Proses Perumusan Pancasila Dasar Negara* [1981; The Origins of the Pancasila]).

Bibliography: Nugroho Notosusanto, *The Peta Army During the Japanese Occupation of Indonesia* (Tokyo: Waseda University Institute of Social Studies, 1976); Nugroho Notosusanto, *Proses Perumusan Pancasila Dasar Negara* (Jakarta: Balai Pustaka, 1981); Nugroho Notosusanto and Ismail Saleh, *The Coup Attempt of the September 30 Movement in Indonesia* (Jakarta: Pembimbing Masa, 1968); H. A. J. Klooster, *Indonesiërs Schrijven Hun Geschiedenis* (Dordrecht: FORIS, 1985).

William H. Frederick

PANE, Sanusi (Muara Sipongi, Tapanuli, 1905–1968), Indonesian teacher, journalist, and writer. The son of the aristocrat and writer Sutan Pangarubaan Pane, Sanusi Pane received a European-style education in colonial schools in Sumatra and Java. He graduated from a government-run Teachers' College in 1925 and later taught at that level until 1934, when he was forced to resign because of his membership in a political party. Subsequently, he taught at private, Indonesian-run Perguruan Rakyat schools in Bandung and Jakarta. Like his brother Armijn Pane, he took an early interest in writing and the world of literature; in the mid–1920s he directed the newspaper *Kebangunan* with Muhammad Yamin (q.v.), in the early 1930s he was responsible for the periodical *Timbul*, and later in that decade he took a position with Balai Pustaka, the government publishing house. During the Japanese occupation (1942–1945), he was head of the Office of Cultural Affairs and continued to be associated with this department during the Indonesian Revolution. In 1948 he was seriously injured in an automobile accident and produced very little afterward.

Sanusi Pane's works range widely over drama, poetry, and essays, often on historical themes, and were written in Dutch as well as Indonesian. Not unlike the *pujangga* or court poets of eighteenth- and nineteenth-century Java, he spent much effort reinterpreting and even translating classic stories. His drama about fourteenth-century Java, *Sandhyakala ning Majapahit* (1933; A Story of Maja-pahit), and his rendition of the eleventh-century Javanese poet Mpu Kanwa's *Ardjuna Wiwaha* (1940; The Marriage of Arjuna), are perhaps the best examples. He produced several historical works, however, of which the four-volume *Sedjarah Indonesia* [History of Indonesia] (1943–1945) was easily the most influ-ential; it was reprinted many times and served as a school textbook and standard national history for nearly three decades. Sanusi's text is not the product of original research, its factual material being drawn from earlier studies, most of them by Dutch scholars. What Sanusi wanted to present was not only a patriotic, pro-Indonesian view of the past, but one that was wide-angled and written in a style the public could understand. The interpretation found in the *Sedjarah Indonesia* is anti-Dutch and Indonesian nationalist in character, though the na-tionalism is muted, owing at least in part to the wishes of the Japanese occupation government's Department of Information, which sponsored it. Discussion of the heroes who struggled against Dutch rule is not placed in a direct, modern na-tionalist context, and the national movement of the 1920s and 1930s receives little mention, a circumstance that Sanusi regretted and rectified in a postwar edition. Whatever its shortcomings, in comparison with other historical works of the occupation Sanusi's manages to maintain a dignified approach by focusing its attention largely on antiquities (particularly the expansion and power of Ma-japahit) and, without the shrillness seen in other works, the nineteenth-century wars between Indonesiäns and the Dutch (particularly the Diponegoro War and the Padris War). The *Sedjarah Indonesia* is significant chiefly because it rep-resents the first modern Indonesian effort to view and draw lessons from the entire breadth of the Indonesian past. In a volume published in 1952 under the title *Indonesia Sepandjang Masa* [Indonesia Through the Ages], Sanusi took the opportunity to improve on some of the general themes neglected in the *Sedjarah Indonesia* and to say more about the purpose and significance of his torical writing. He considered "objective" history an impossibility; only God knew everything and was able to understand it objectively. He also argued that there was no intrinsic reason to assume that the Old Javanese poets or political leaders were inferior to contemporary writers and politicians, implying that he had doubts about an always-progressing, linear view of history. Finally, Sanusi understood the value of histories written by nonspecialists and maintained that, although specialization in historical studies was invaluable, the modern Indo-nesian historian's task was to bring together existing knowledge into a compre-hensible whole, a true national history. The goal has proved elusive. Not until 1975 did a *Sejarah Nasional* (National History), in six volumes and authored by a group of specialists, supersede Sanusi's contribution, and it did not receive wide support as the standard work it was intended to be. Most historians in Indonesia would agree that a satisfactory single-volume, popular national history remains to be written.

Bibliography: Sanusi Pane, *Sedjarah Indonesia*, 4 vols. (Jakarta: Balai Pustaka, 1945); H. A. J. Klooster, *Indonesiërs Schrijven hun Geschiedenis* (Dordrecht: FORIS, 1985).

William H. Frederick

PE MAUNG TIN (1888–1973), Burmese literary scholar, epigrapher, and historian. For many years professor of Pali language and literature at Rangoon College (later University of Rangoon), Pe Maung Tin published a number of works on literature, among them *Myanma Sapei Thamaing* (1956?; A History of Burmese Literature). He also studied and published works on Buddhist thought, and in the late 1950s he was visiting professor of Buddhism at the University of Chicago. His connection with history lay in his acquaintance with the languages and vocabulary of early inscriptions and texts dealing with the Burmese past. He collaborated closely for several decades with Gordon H. Luce (1889–1979), the British scholar of Burmese antiquities whom his sister married, and with him he published annotated translations of some of the most important records of the Burmese past, particularly *The Chronicle of the City of Tagaung* (1921), *The Glass Palace Chronicles* (1923), *Selections from the Inscriptions of Pagan* (1928), and *Inscriptions of Burma* (5 vols., 1933–1956). The last work covers materials from the earliest pagan sources down to 1364, when a new dynasty was founded, and thus represents the largest part of known Burmese inscriptions. Pe Maung Tin also collaborated with two Burmese colleagues in editing a modern version of *Mahayazawindawgyi* (3 vols., 1960–1961; The Great Royal Chronicle) by U Kala and edited a modern version of Silavamsa's *Yazawingyaw* (n.d.). He was apparently opposed to the idea of a broad synthesis or extended analysis, and he never composed a general history of early Burma, even though his knowledge of the primary sources obviously equipped him for such a task better than many of his colleagues. His articles in the *Journal of the Burma Research Society* focused tightly on particular topics—women, Buddhism—as they were reflected in the inscriptions, and he contented himself with reporting what he saw as accurately as he could. Thus he did not participate in the creation of a nationalist historiography, but he did accomplish more than any Burmese of his generation in laying a good foundation for future historical researchers, Burmese as well as foreign. Not unlike famed literati in earlier centuries, he was both knowledgeable about the past and a skilled author and connoisseur of the written word.

Bibliography: Pe Maung Tin, "Buddhism in the Inscriptions of Pagan," *Burma Research Society 50th Anniversary Publication* 2 (Rangoon: *Journal of the Burma Research Society* 1960), pp. 423–441; Pe Maung Tin and Gordon H. Luce, "The Chronicle of the City of Tagaung," *Journal of the Burma Research Society* 9 (1921): 29–54; Gordon H. Luce and Pe Maung Tin, *Inscriptions of Burma*, 5 vols. (Rangoon: Rangoon University Press, 1933–1956).

William H. Frederick

PHAN BOI CHAU (Nghe-An, 1867–Hué, 1940), Vietnamese patriot, author, and historian. Born in Nghe-An Province, the only son of a scholar-gentry family of very modest means, Chau was a diligent student of the Confucian classics from an early age. Under different circumstances he would have become an ardent supporter of the monarchy, but in 1874 he witnessed an attack by the king's troops on anti-French scholar-gentry groups in Nghe-An and Ha-Tinh, and a decade later he watched his own efforts to mobilize resistance collapse owing to apathy and rumored opposition. Disillusioned and tied down by family obligations, he stayed at home and studied for the regional civil examinations. In 1900 he passed with highest honors, but shortly afterward his father died, freeing Chau to embark on a career as an anticolonial activist and patriot reformer. Until his capture by the French in Shanghai and his return to Vietnam for sentencing in 1925, Phan Boi Chau pursued schemes to bring independence and governmental reform to Vietnam, many of them involving hoped-for aid from Japan. Unlike some contemporaries with the same general goals, he advocated the use of violence to overthrow the colonial regime. All of his plans along these lines failed, and by the time of his capture his ideas had in a very real sense been made obsolete by those either more ideological or less radical than he. The French, rather than create a martyr by executing him, allowed him a circumscribed existence in Hué, where he spent the remainder of his days.

Phan Boi Chau, perhaps in large part because of his Confucian training, looked to history for lessons and a guide to the future, and his writings—including two autobiographies, one written in the early twentieth century and one a few years before his death—were frequently historical in nature. His *Luu Cuu Huyet Le Tan Thu* (1903?; Ryukyu's Bitter Tears) appeared merely to describe Ryuku's fall to Japanese expansion, but it was in fact—and was clearly understood as— a warning drawn from history and a discussion by analogy of Vietnam's own predicament with French rule. Chau's most famous historical work, *Viet Nam Vong Quoc Su* (1905; The History of the Loss of Vietnam) took up the theme more directly. Written in Japan, in Chinese and at the instigation of Chinese revolutionary thinker Liang Ch'i-ch'ao, this book was aimed primarily at Chinese readers, for whom Liang believed it would serve as a warning, but it was of course also directed at educated Vietnamese. *Viet Nam Vong Quoc Su* begins with a sweeping view of the Vietnamese past, critical especially of the Nguyen Dynasty for its reliance on the Chinese model in all matters and for its inability to play international politics to its own benefit, for example, by setting British and Germans against the French. This Vietnamese history was organized in terms of the country's unity and loss of independence, and has served as the prototype for most modern national histories since. Chau also paid much attention to the biographies of those whom he saw as defenders of the nation, and he discussed seventeen modern (late nineteenth-century) patriots of the Can Vuong movement; this was the first such treatment of modern heroes in Vietnam. The remainder of the work analyzed the cruelty and crippling effects of French colonial policy, and asked whether Vietnam indeed had any future left. Chau's response was that it did, if the Vietnamese so wished and were willing to struggle or even die in order to reach their goal. Although he never abandoned Confucianism entirely, in his historical treatment of Vietnam's past and future Chau identified the nation with popular will and proposed it, rather than the ideas of the educated elite, as the principal moral sanction for revolt. In doing so, and in altering the focus of his examination of Vietnam's past, he became the first modern Vietnamese historian.

Bibliography: Phan Boi Chau, *Phan Boi Chau Nien Bieu* (Year to Year Activities of Phan Boi Chau), (Hanoi: NXB Van Su Dia, 1957), French translation by Georges Boudarel, *France Asie/Asia*, 22, no. 3–4 (1968): 3–210; Phan Boi Chau, *Viet Nam Vong Quoc Su* (Chinese original and modern Vietnamese trans. by Ta Thuc Khai), *Dai Hoc Van Khoa* (Journal of the Faculty of Letters, University of Saigon), 1961; David G. Marr, *Vietnamese Anti-colonialism* (Berkeley: University of California Press, 1971); Alexander B. Woodside, *Community and Revolution in Modern Vietnam* (Boston: Houghton Mifflin, 1976).

William H. Frederick

PHAN THANH GIAN (1796–1867), Vietnamese civil servant and historical scholar. Reputedly the son of a well-to-do Chinese farmer who escaped the Manchus by fleeing to Vietnam and serving Nguyen Anh in his war against the Tay Son, Gian took his mandarinal degrees and acquired a reputation for filial piety and upright behavior. Early in his career he showed that he could be a severe and daring critic of existing institutions. Yet at the same time he was known for his scrupulous fairness and his unwillingness to judge people on the basis of their social status alone. He was courageous enough in 1852 to memorialize Tu Duc (reigned 1848–1883) in a harsh vein, saying that the emperor had surrounded himself with sycophants and incompetents, and was also guilty of extravagant, morally lax living. Perhaps in part because of his forthright, fearless manner, the court appointed him to deal with the French in the wake of the Treaty of Saigon (1862); he recommended a conciliatory position, but considered this approach to have been an utter failure when French forces seized further provinces in 1867. In that year he returned all his honors to the court and committed suicide, an event that may conveniently be taken to represent the beginning of the end for the traditional Confucian ethos in Vietnam.

Although he was by no means a specialist in historical studies, Gian's grasp of the traditional literature was firm, and his reputation for moral rectitude fitted him in the eyes of the court for the position of chief editor of the *Kham Dinh Viet Su Thong Gian Cuong Muc* (53 vols., 1856–1884; Text and Commentary of the Complete Mirror of Vietnamese History as Ordered by the Emperor). This work is the last of the comprehensive Vietnamese histories in the traditional manner. It covers Vietnam's past from origins (c. 2789 B.C.) to 1789, and it generally seeks to place the entire past in perspective from the point of view of the Nguyen Dynasty (1802–1945), which saw as its principal goal the creation of a stable, orthodox government and society. The Tay Son, for example, were portrayed as having failed to receive the favor of Heaven, and therefore they were rightly opposed by the Nguyen forces in the name of justice and tranquility. Quite different from histories such as those by Le Quy Don, however, the *Cuong Muc* expressed the view that the possibilities for change in history were in fact narrow, that Heaven determined everything, and that where crises of state and society were concerned, for example, there could be little in the way of freedom in arriving at a solution. While many modern scholars, Vietnamese and foreign alike, have interpreted this outlook as fatalistic, this may be somewhat misleading since the work does emphasize that rulers can and ought to take steps to invoke Fortune or cosmic influence. It is perhaps better to identify the view simply as conservative Confucian and therefore to some extent already obsolete in mid-nineteenth-century Vietnamese society. Thus, the work over which Gian presided was more a farewell to a fading past and an increasingly irrelevant historiography, rather than a guide for the future.

Bibliography: Philippe Langlet, *L'Ancienne historiographie d'Etat du Vietnam*, 2 vols. (Paris: Ecole Française d'Extrême-Orient, 1985); Philippe Langlet, "La Tradition Viet-namienne," *Bulletin des Etudes Indochinoises de Saigon*, new series 45, 2–3 (1970); Alexander Woodside, "Conceptions of Change and of Human Responsibility for Change in Late Traditional Vietnam," in David Wyatt and Alexander Woodside, eds., *Moral Order and the Question of Change: Essays on Southeast Asian Thought* (New Haven, Conn.: Yale University Southeast Asian Studies, 1982), pp. 104–150); modern Vietnam-ese translation of *Kham Dinh Viet Su Thong Gian Cuong Muc* (Saigon: Bo Van Hoa Giao-duc, 1960–1974); partial French translations: Abel des Michels, *Annales Impériales de l'Annam* (Paris: E. Leroux, 1889–1892).

William H. Frederick

RIZAL Mercado y Alonzo Realonda, José Protacio (Kalamba, 1861–Manila, 1896), Filipino doctor, patriot, writer, and historian. José Rizal is best known as the greatest national martyr of the Philippines, but he was also the first modern Filipino to write down historical views from a thoroughly indigenous perspective, and his work laid the foundation for a contemporary Filipino historiography. Rizal's family was among the wealthiest in the Kalamba, Laguna region of Luzon, though his father was tied to the Spanish colonial government's system of leasing land to the Filipino elite. His mother was one of the best educated Filipinas of her day, but both she and Rizal's brother, Paciano, ran afoul of suspicious colonial authorities and were jailed as common criminals, injustices that Rizal never forgot. The young Rizal was groomed as an intellectual and showed early promise. After tutoring at home, where he read in the family's library of over one thousand volumes, he was educated at the Ateneo de Manila and, after 1882, in Spain, France, and Germany. He went home in 1887, was again in Europe from 1888 to 1891, and then returned to the Philippines until his death. In 1896 he was shot by a Spanish firing squad because the colonial authorities came to believe that he was the soul of a political movement seeking independence.

Rizal's most frequently read works are his novels *Noli me Tangere* (1887; The Lost Eden) and *El Filibusterismo* (1891; The Subversive). Today these works are largely appreciated as literature, but Rizal made clear that they were intended as a history of the Philippines in the 1870s and 1880s, aimed directly at educated Filipino readers. He sought to discard myths and to get behind the half-truths which he believed his countrymen frequently accepted as truth. His goal was objectivity, which he understood largely in terms of rationalist and scientific ideas of late nineteenth-century Europe. Rizal also wanted to write what today would be called social and intellectual history; the form of the European novel merely gave him an opportunity to examine a wider range of possibilities than, say, an essay or a traditional history. To some degree it is true that the novels state the case for violent revolution against colonial rule, but they also contain eloquent arguments for a more peaceful evolution. Rizal's own outlook on the matter probably oscillated, but, ironically, toward the end of his life, his historical work seems to have convinced him that the peaceful stance was correct. Although nearly all of Rizal's extensive writings concern the historical process, several works are of particular importance to the development of Filipino historiography. He spent 1888–1889 studying the Spanish Jesuit Antonio de Morga's *Sucesos de las Islas Filipinas* (1609; Historical Events of the Philippine Islands), and a year later he published a new edition of this work, with his own notes. He considered Morga to be generally impartial, and on the basis of his own research he sought to correct factual errors and occasional slanders in order to present Filipinos with a comparatively unvarnished view of their past and "awaken them to reality." Between 1889 and 1890 Rizal also published "Filipinas Dentro de Cien Años" (The Philippines a Century Hence), "Sobre la Indolencia del Filipino" (On the Indolence of the Filipino), and, in Tagalog, "Letter to the Women of Malolos." In these works it became abundantly clear that Rizal had embraced a philosophy of history founded on a sense of national community, propelled in time and along a continuum of progress by the interaction of social and cultural forces. (He appears to have rejected the Marxist view of dialectics and social change, finding it oversimplified.) Rizal believed progress to be linear and upward-moving, and he looked forward to changes in the Filipino mentality. He was in fact rather hard on his own people, and his was not by any means a blindly nationalist historical perspective. At the opening of "Filipinas Dentro Cien Años" Rizal wrote, "In order to study the destiny of a people, it is necessary to open the book of its past." He favored doing so as honestly and critically—and as scientifically—as he knew how, letting the chips fall where they might.

Bibliography: José Rizal, "Filipinas Dentro de Cien Años," *La Solidaridad* (1889) I, pp. 96–99, and succeeding issues; José Rizal, *The Lost Eden*, trans. Léon Maria Guerrero (Bloomington: University of Indiana Press, 1961); *Epistolario Rizalino*, ed. Teodoro Kalaw (Manila: Bureau of Printing, 1930–1931); Eufronia M. Alip et al., "Rizal's Historical Commentaries," in *International Congress on Rizal* (Manila: José Rizal National Centennial Commission, 1961), pp. 100–118; Reynaldo C. Ileto, "Rizal and the Underside of Philippine History," in Alexander Woodside and David K. Wyatt, eds., *Moral Order and the Question of Change: Essays in Southeast Asian Thought* (New Haven, Conn.: Yale University Southeast Asian Studies, 1982), pp. 274–337; Ricard R. Pascal, "Rizal's Philosophy of History," in L. Y. Yabes, ed., *José Rizal on His Centenary* (Quezon City: University of the Philippines, 1963), pp. 74–96.

William H. Frederick

THIOUNN (Kampong Tralach, 1864–1941), Khmer (Cambodian) colonial civil servant and supervisor of chronicle compilation. Born into a Vietnamese-

Cambodian family outside royal and official circles, Thiounn was one of a comparatively small number of "new men" who rose to power under the French. At nineteen he was an official interpreter to the government, became prominent in the Council of Ministers, and in 1902 was appointed minister of the palace. He was also minister of fine arts, a position he held until his death. Portrayed by critics as corrupt and exploitative, Thiounn was seen by French officials as a progressive and loyal supporter; he was widely acknowledged to be intelligent and genuinely interested in the arts. Beginning in 1903 he headed a commission charged with composing a major official chronicle of the *bangsavatar* (literally, "lineage incarnation") type. He was particularly associated with a version produced early in the twentieth century and continued in 1934 (with later additions) under the title *Brah raj bansavatar maha ksatr khmaer* (Royal Chronicle of the Great Khmer Kings), sometimes known as the *Thiounn Chronicle*. This chronicle generally follows the conventions of the precolonial genre, but expresses dates according to the Western (Christian) calendar and makes adjustments to allow for the inclusion of such information as appointments of high-ranking French officials, holding of government (as opposed to royal) ceremonies, and the like. Thiounn's name is often used to identify this newer lineage of royal Khmer chronicles, separate from that associated with the nineteenth-century official known as Nong (q.v.). The exact nature of Thiounn's role in compiling the chronicle that bears his name—apparently written largely by the then chief of the palace chronicle section, Okna Prajnadhipati Yin—is unclear. Some internal evidence suggests, however, that he may have taken a greater than ordinary personal interest in the project, and may even have seen to it that the local history of his home region of Lovek, as known through oral tradition, was emphasized in certain portions.

Bibliogaphy: David Chandler, "Cambodian Palace Chronicles (*rajabangsavatar*) 1927–1949: Kingship and Historiography at the End of the Colonial Era," in Anthony Reid and David Marr, eds., *Perceptions of the Past in Southeast Asia* (Singapore: Heinemann, 1979), pp. 207–217; Khin Sok, "Les Chroniques Royales Khmeres," *Mon-Khmer Studies* 6 (1977): 177–215—French translation: Mak Phoeun, trans., *Chroniques royales du Cambodge* (Paris: Ecole Française d'Extrême-Orient, 1981); Michael Vickery, "Cambodia After Angkor, the Chronicular Evidence for the Fourteenth to Sixteenth Centuries," Ph.D. diss. (Yale University, 1977).

William H. Frederick

THIPAKORAWONG, Chaophraya (Kham Bunnag) (1813–1870), Thai statesman, philosopher, and historian. Son of Dit Bunnag, who was head of the Royal Pages Department and later Phra Khlang (minister of the treasury), Thipakorawong was a palace page as a youngster, for a number of years director of police, and then responsible for managing the visits of foreigners anxious to negotiate new trading agreements with the Thai government. In 1855, after the successful negotiation of the Bowring Treaty, he was appointed Phra Khlang, a position he held until a few years before his death. A devout Buddhist, Thipakorawong lived simply and delighted in discussing religious issues, especially with foreign guests. His earliest writings concerned religion and included a biography of Mohammed (*Prawat Ruang Phra Nabimahamad*) as well as a defense of Buddhism against Christianity, *Kitchanukat* (A Book Explaining Various Things), which in 1867 was the first letterpress publication produced entirely by Thai printers.

Thipakorawong is most frequently remembered as a historian, and except for the *Phongsawadan Yuan* (Vietnamese Chronicle) all his historical works were, remarkably enough, written during the last two years of his life. His masterpiece is clearly the *Phraratchaphongsawadan Krung Rattanakosin Ratchakan thi 1–4* (Royal Chronicle of the First, Second, Third, and Fourth Reigns of the Chakri Dynasty) (PRR), which he composed at the request of King Chulalongkorn (reigned 1868–1910). Thipakorawong possessed neither exceptional literary talent nor the inclination to give his historical writing a sacred tone; his work offered straightforward, chronologically arranged accounts of events in the course of which he infrequently offered his own view. The PRR was, after all, to be an official dynastic history, and Thipakorawong did not deviate from that purpose; using Prince Paramanuchitchinorot's sketchy history of the early Chakri reigns, he added new material from royal documents (many of them now lost) and subtracted inconvenient topics (the reign of Taksin, for example) to create a work unmistakably of the traditional *phongsawadan* type in which Buddhism and kingship are the key institutions. Yet Thipakorawong's is probably the last of the great traditional historical writings, for he did attempt a few changes that were taken up by more adventurous successors. He simplified the customary vocabulary of traditional histories, for example, especially that relating to royal matters, and he made it obvious that he did not view the king as so august as to be utterly beyond reproach. In his own way, for example, he was disapproving of Rama II. (His writings on religion showed that he could be exceptionally critical when the occasion demanded.) While he was not apparently directly interested in problems of causation and did not take what today would be called a critical attitude toward his historical sources, Thipakorawong did occasionally express his own evaluation of human activities and motivation, for the purpose of instructing future generations. And while he never seems to have contemplated writing a history of the Thai people or state as a whole, he did attempt to introduce new topics to the standard *phongsawadan* genre, especially those not customarily connected with kings and the court. In this fashion Thipakorawong's work was of critical importance to those who, like Prince Damrong Rajanubhab (q.v.), later undertook something more akin to a revolutionary step in Thai historiography.

Bibliography: Henry Alabaster, *The Modern Buddhist: Being the Views of a Siamese Minister of State on His Own and Other Religions* (London: Trubner and Co., 1870); *The Dynastic Chronicles, Bangkok Era, Fourth Reign*, trans. Chadi Flood (Kanjanavanit), 2 vols. (Tokyo: Centre for East Asia Cultural Studies, 1965–1966); Somjai Phirotthirarach, "The Historical Writings of Chaophraya Thipakorawong," Ph.D. diss. (Northern Illinois University, 1983).

William H. Frederick

TRAN TRONG KIM (1883–1953), Vietnamese civil servant, philosopher, and historian. One of the most important figures in creating the system and content of Franco-Vietnamese education during the colonial period, Tran Trong Kim graduated from the Hanoi Interpreters' School around the turn of the century and began teaching at the Hanoi Pedagogical Institute in 1911. In 1924 he headed the commission responsible for approving textbooks used in primary education; later he directed Hanoi's primary schools and acted as inspector of schools. He retired in 1942, spent a period of time in Singapore under Japanese protection, and in March 1945 was returned to Vietnam, where he somewhat reluctantly accepted Emperor Bao Dai's summons to form an "independent" government, and act as prime minister, in order to prevent direct Japanese rule. Kim's first scholarly attentions were paid to the question of ethics in primary schools. He was an adherent of Confucian ethics but wished to see them demystified in order that they might become more serviceable in modern society. Toward that end in 1913 he wrote an ethics primer for school use. This work emphasized the concept of "conscience" (certainly not a traditional Confucian idea) and spoke of the role of the individual in society. From 1917 to 1934 he wrote for the periodical *Nam Phong* (The Vietnamese Ethos), and in 1930 he completed the monumental *Nho Giao* (The Confucian Teaching), which attempted to treat Confucianism as a philosophy equivalent to Western philosophies (as distinct from an ethical system) and as an appropriate foundation for a sense of nationalism among modern Vietnamese intellectuals. In all of this, history figured importantly, and in the debates that erupted over the message of *Nho Giao*, questions of historical values and outlook—especially Chinese versus Vietnamese, for Kim had scarcely mentioned Vietnam in his book—were raised frequently. History, as Kim appreciated and wrote it, was the quintessential Confucian "science" concerned with the laws of nature, with research and classification.

Kim is most widely remembered for his *Viet Nam Su Luoc* (2 vols., 1928; A Brief History of Vietnam), used in public schools and reprinted many times down to the late 1950s. This work, which according to a poll taken in the early 1940s was one of the three most highly respected pieces of modern Vietnamese scholarship, was undoubtedly of enormous influence in shaping public thinking about history, and it clearly was the model for several generations of conservative history texts and other treatments of the Vietnamese past. The approach was linear and Confucian-nationalist. Kim went far out of his way to smooth out the rougher spots of Vietnamese political history in particular, so that a fully rationalized, comprehensible national history could be grasped. He handled the many troublesome problems of his own generation by largely avoiding discussion of the twentieth century, and he faced other difficult issues by attempting a synthesis of major opposing views. On the question of how to treat the Tay Son rulers and the Nguyen Dynasty which eventually defeated them in 1802 after years of bitter warfare, Kim acknowledged the legitimacy of the Tay Son emperor Quang Trung, since the Le court had sought Chinese aid. But he then argued that the Tay Son lost this legitimacy in the chaos following Quang Trung's death, when it appeared that only Gia Long was able to answer the people's need for leadership and was thus able to unite the nation. This construction, and the conservative outlook on which it rested, were inevitably caught up in the political contests of the postwar era, and it remains to be seen whether or in what form it will survive in post–1975 Vietnam.

Bibliography: Tran Trong Kim, *Nho Giao* (Saigon: Tan Viet, 1962); Tran Trong Kim, *Viet Nam Su Luoc* (Hanoi: Vinh and Thanh, 1928), most recent edition (Saigon: Tan Viet, 1964); David G. Marr, *Vietnamese Tradition on Trial, 1920–1945* (Berkeley: University of California Press, 1981); Alexander B. Woodside, *Community and Revolution in Modern Vietnam* (Boston: Houghton Mifflin, 1976).

William H. Frederick

WICHITWATHAKAN, Luang (1898–1962), Thai statesman and author of popular histories. Wichitwathakan, whose social origins were very modest, spent a number of years in the monkhood, where he was educated and studied independently. He left the *sangha* abruptly and joined the Ministry of Foreign Affairs, receiving assignments in Paris and Geneva. He returned home in the late 1920s and soon after became the spokesman for the promoters of the 1932 coup and their government. He served in government from 1934 to 1962 in many different capacities, among them director of the Department of Fine Arts and special adviser to the Phibun and Sarit Cabinets. Wichitwathakan's historical writings, of which there came to be a great number, were aimed at the general public and were frequently characterized by ultranationalistic purpose; they are in many respects typical of nationalist works produced elsewhere in Southeast Asia in the decade or two after World War II. His *Prawatsat Sakon* (World History) appeared in twelve volumes in 1931 and was reprinted as late as 1971. In subsequent years there flowed a stream of monographs, pamphlets, articles, plays, radio scripts, and more, all seeking to extol the Thai nation. His version of Thai political history excluded the monarchy as much as possible, thereby departing from the *phongsawadan* tradition and the efforts of his contemporary, Prince Damrong Rajanubhab (q.v.). That Wichitwathakan's writing was a useful weapon to the government of the day is especially clear in his *Thailand's Case* (1942), written in English to explain Thailand's side in its quarrel with France over territory in Indochina. This pamphlet appeared to many to support Thai expansionism; other materials offered pictures of the Thai and neighboring peoples which in tone and thrust bore an uncomfortable resemblance to Nazi portraits of the Germans and their neighbors. Wichitwathakan was criticized by historians and other intellectuals for his methodology and his extremism, but he reached a very broad audience that does not appear to have been equally concerned about these issues or about Wichitwathakan's use of history with ideological intent.

Bibliography: Luang Wichitwathakan, *Prawatsat Sakon* (Bangkok: Wiriyanuphap, 1930); Luang Wichitwathakan, *Thailand's Case* (Bangkok: Thanom Punnahitananda, 1941); Charnvit Kasetsiri, "Thai Historiography from Ancient Times to the Modern

Period,'' in Anthony Reid and David Marr, eds., *Perceptions of the Past in Southeast Asia* (Singapore: Heinemann, 1979), pp. 156–170.

William H. Frederick

WIRYOSUPARTO, Sucipto (Solo, Central Java, 1915–Canberra, Australia, 1971), Indonesian historian. Educated in Dutch-language schools in the prewar colonial government's system. Sucipto's university-level training was cut short by the Japanese occupation of the Netherlands East Indies. He graduated from the University of Indonesia in 1952, received his M.A. degree from India's Vishvabharati University two years later, and earned his doctorate from the University of Indonesia in 1960 with a dissertation on Old Javanese literature. He taught at his alma mater and served as dean of the Faculty of Arts (1961–1964); after 1967 he taught at the Australian National University, where he died in 1971 while giving a lecture.

Sucipto's historical writing unquestionably belongs to the nationalist stream in postwar Indonesia, some of his positions being more extreme in this regard than those espoused by his contemporary, Muhammad Yamin (q.v.). His ideas were more specifically tied to the politics of Sukarno's Guided Democracy and ideology of the Pancasila, or five principles, than those of any other historian of his day. He was first known for his high school text, *Dari Lima Zaman Pendjadjahan Menudju Zaman Kemerdekaan* (3 vols., 1955; From Five Colonial Periods to Independence). This work reflects its immediate postrevolutionary times by throwing the spotlight on ''350 years of colonial rule'' and a continuous, unitary ''general warfare'' by indigenes against it; Dutch versus Indonesian, colonial versus colonized, were the black-and-white categories into which all events and personages were divided. Sucipto also suggested to young readers that the revolution was still unfinished, though he did not offer a clear view of what the future might hold. His article, ''Prapantja Sebagai Penulis Sedjarah'' (1960; Prapanca as Historian), was typical of his efforts to right what he saw as the wrongs of Dutch colonial historians, and he claimed the fourteenth-century writer as fully acceptable into the fraternity of historians. This kind of approach to historiography was not always treated kindly by critics, and Sucipto's attempts to work out a Sukarno-ist, Pancasila-ist, national philosophy of history were subjected to derision in many quarters. His lecture, ''Pantjasila, Manipol, Usdek Sebagai Dasar Penafsiran Sedjarah Indonesia'' (1961; Pancasila and Manipol-Usdek as the Foundation of an Indonesian Interpretation of History), was especially controversial, and Sucipto was often seen as an apologist for the regime. His works are not frequently read today, but his influence, through his original text, in shaping the unitary national and nationalist history schoolchildren have continued to read, was considerable.

Bibliography: Sucipto Wiryosuparto, *Dair Lima Zaman Pendjadjahan Menudju Zaman Kemerdekaan* (Jakarta: Indira, 1967); Sucipto Wiryosuparto, *A Short Cultural History of Indonesia*, 2d ed. (Jakarta: Indira: 1964); H. A. J. Klooster, *Indonesiërs Schrijven Hun Geschiedenis* (Dordrecht: FORIS, 1985).

William H. Frederick

YAMIN, Muhammad (Sawahlunto, West Sumatra, 1903–Jakarta, 1962), Indonesian lawyer, political figure, writer, and historian. The son of Minangkabau local nobility, Yamin began his education in the traditional manner, but in 1914 moved to the first of a series of Dutch-Indonesian and Dutch schools, finally graduating in 1932 with the highest law degree available in colonial Indonesia. Drawing on his legal background, he worked in a variety of capacities, mostly of a political or governmental nature, and between 1951 and his death in 1962 he held many important posts, among them minister of education and minister of information. As a teenager he exhibited cultural and regional pride, writing poems in praise of his native Minangkabau and taking an active role in the group Jong Sumatranen Bond (The Young Sumatrans' League), which he headed from 1926 to 1928. But he spent most of his life on Java and early turned toward a broader nationalism that embraced the entire archipelago. In 1928 he helped formulate the famous Youth Oath, which laid down the principles of one people, one nation, and one language for Indonesia.

Yamin's historical writing, which runs to many volumes covering a broad array of topics, follows the nationalist, pan-Indonesian theme with great vigor, and though his harshest critics would find it distasteful to do so, we may with little exaggeration call Yamin the father of modern Indonesian history. Yamin's first historical work of note was *Gadjah Mada* (1948), on the life and times of the famed fourteenth-century minister of state. Gajah Mada, who is thought to have taken an oath not to rest until the vast archipelago had fallen under the sway of Majapahit, was portrayed by Yamin as an architect of Indonesian unity, certainly a theme in keeping with the national revolution then in progress. It is said that during a visit to the archaeological site of the old Majapahitan court, Yamin picked up a terra cotta head from among some shards and claimed it to be a portrait of Gajah Mada himself. The figure appeared on the book cover and has ever since been identified with Gajah Mada, though there is no real evidence for such a link. Yamin was fascinated with the problem of finding historical roots for an Indonesian nation. He returned to Majapahit for a much closer look in his *Tatanegara Majapahit* (7 vols. in 4, 1962; The Structure of the State of Majapahit), and pushed his theme much harder and further back in time in *Sang Merah Putih Enam Ribu Tahun* (1958; Six Thousand Years of the Red and White Flag), in which he attempted to argue, using philological, archaeological, anthropological, and other insights, that the Indonesian flag and national colors it displayed were deeply rooted in ancient symbolism. His *Naskah Persiapan Undang-Undang Dasar 1945* (3 vols., 1960; Documents on the Preparation of the 1945 Constitution) presented original documents and extensive commentary on the drafting of Indonesia's constitution, and despite the possibility that Yamin tampered with some of the evidence and the order in which it appeared, the work is a basic source for modern Indonesian history.

Like many postwar nationalist writers of history elsewhere in Southeast Asia, Yamin was criticized for his mishandling of methodology, his fascination with creating national heroes, his unrelenting and often overblown claims for the nation, and his romantic efforts to synthesize a "truly Indonesian" philosophy of history. The most cutting reproach, however, may have been that leveled at his reliance, when all was said and done, on Western historical thinking and research. Yamin's scheme of periodization for the Indonesian past, which he called the *pancawarsa*, or five eras, attracted criticism from all sides, and not only for its rather sophomoric symbolism, designed to coincide with the Pancasila (five principles), the state ideology. One fellow historian noted disparagingly that the scheme was just as objectionable and unusable as the Western model on which, in one way or another, it was based, and did not reflect Indonesian historical realities. Today most of Yamin's works are not much read, and his historiographical notions have not proven durable. Something of their spirit may still be found, however, in the general run of "official" and textbook histories, and his role in emphasizing the importance of history in the young Republic of Indonesia is widely acknowledged.

Bibliography: Mohammad Yamin, *Gadjah Mada Pahlawan Persatuan Nusantara*, 4th printing (Jakarta: Balai Pustaka, 1954); Mohammed Yamin, *Naskah Persiapan Undang-Undang Dasar 1945* (Jakarta: Jajasan Prapantja, 1959–1960); Mohammed Yamin, *6000 Ribu Tahun Sang Merah Putih* (Jakarta: Dhama, 1951); H. A. J. Klooster, *Indonesiërs Schrijven Hun Geschiedenis* (Dordrecht: FORIS, 1985); Deliar Noer, "Yamin and Hamka: Two Routes to an Indonesian Identity," in Anthony Reid and David Marr, eds., *Perceptions of the Past in Southeast Asia* (Singapore: Heinemann, 1979), pp. 249–262.

William H. Frederick

YI YI (192?–1983?), Burmese historian. Although her doctoral dissertation at the University of London concerned "English Traders in the South China Sea 1670–1715" (1958), Yi Yi established herself as a leading historian of the Konbaung period (1752–1885), about which she wrote extensively in Burmese and English. She was for many years a researcher with the Burmese Historical Commission. Her journal articles treat in detail such topics as archival sources for eighteenth- and nineteenth-century Burmese history, the administrative structure of the Burmese kingdom, and the ceremonies and rhythms of daily life at the court. Her concern with the fine points of historical research led her to write *Myanma Ingaleik Pyithkadein 1701–1820* (1965; Burmese-English Almanac for the Years 1701–1820) and *Thuteithana Abidanmya Hmatsu* (1974; Burmese Research Dictionary). Very cautious in matters of interpretation, in her historical work Yi Yi took a rather different tack from colleagues with an aggressively nationalist agenda. In her view the minutiae of even the comparatively recent Burmese past needed careful examination before conclusions could be drawn with any confidence. Perhaps this was so especially because she was painfully aware of both the distortions made by British colonial historians and those made by Burmese for the opposite reasons. She did not live to write a general history of Konbaung Burma, but she was able to complete a useful study of the prelude to that period, *Myanma Naingngan Acheianei* (1975; Burma in the First Half of the Eighteenth Century).

Bibliography: Yi Yi, "Additional Burmese Historical Sources, 1752–1778," *Southeast Asian Archives* 2 (1969): 119–138; Yi Yi, "Burmese Sources for the History of the Konbaung Period, 1752–1885," *Journal of Southeast Asian History* 6 (1965): 48–66; Yi Yi, "The Judicial System of King Mindon," *Journal of the Burma Research Society* 45 (1962): 7–27; Yi Yi, "Life at the Burmese Court Under the Kanbaung Kings," *Journal of the Burma Research Society*, 44 (1961): 85–129; Yi Yi, *Myanma Naingngan Acheianei* (Rangoon: Burma Historical Commission, 1973 [i.e., 1975]).

William H. Frederick

Great Historians: Spanish

ALTAMIRA Y CREVEA, Rafael (Alicante, 1866–Mexico City, 1951), Spanish historian. Altamira y Crevea was also a jurist, occupying a regular seat in the Permanent Court of the Hague; a pedagogue, general director of primary education, 1911; an essayist, literary critic, novelist, and author of short stories. Educated as a jurist and influenced by Gumersindo de Azcárate and Joaquín Costa Martínez (q.v.), Altamira devoted his first research, including his doctoral thesis, *Historia de la propiedad comunal* (1890; History of Communal Property), and *Historia del derecho español* (1903; History of Spanish Law), to the history of Spanish law. From Francisco Giner and from youthful collaboration with the Institución Libre de Enseñanza (the Free School), he attained a lifelong concern for pedagogy. Some of his early books, *La enseñanza de la historia* (1891; Teaching History) and *Ideario pedagógico* (Pedagogical Ideology) expressed this interest. Speaking to the Royal Academy of History, he chose the topic, "The Social Value of Historical Knowledge." Altamira belonged to the group of intellectuals and reformers known as *regeneracionistas*, "the Generation of 1898," who reacted against the Spanish decadence revealed in 1898 as the Spanish colonial rule in America and Southeast Asia collapsed. According to these intellectuals, history furnished a basis for national rebirth. Guided by this patriotic goal, Altamira wrote works of a general nature and syntheses, rather than scholarly monographs. He viewed himself as a historian, stripping away a mass of errors and legends that had hindered the achievement of true national consciousness. His most influential work was *Historia de España y de la civilización española* (4 vols., 1900–1911; History of Spain and Spanish Civilization). He wrote to bring back the Spanish people's faith in themselves, to persuade them that they were capable of overcoming difficulties, just as they had in former times, and to restore national self-confidence through reexamining the cultural achievements of the centuries of imperial greatness. Following the model of Karl Lamprecht's (q.v.) *kulturgeschichte*, he investigated not only politics and military history, but also geography, economic factors, ideas, religion, and law. He intended to write the "internal history" of his country. A one-volume summary of the *Historia* (1902) was translated into numerous other languages and remained in print up to the 1970s. For many readers in a global audience, this has been the basic history of Spain.

In 1909 Altamira was sent to Latin America on a cultural mission and afterward became chair of the Department of American Political Institutions in the University of Madrid. He published studies of Spanish legislation for the Indians and essays on the relationship that Spain should have with the Latin American republics. In the year of Altamira's retirement, 1936, the Spanish Civil War broke out, and, for his republican, liberal, and pacifist convictions, he was forced into exile.

Bibliography: John E. Fagg, "Rafael Altamira (1866–1951)," in S. William Halperin, ed., *Essays in Modern European Historiography* (Chicago and London, 1970), pp. 3–21; Luis García de Valdeavellano, "Don Rafael Altamira o la historia como educación," (Rafael Altamira or History as Education), in *Seis semblanzas de historiadores españoles* (Six Portraits of Spanish Historians), (Seville, 1978), pp. 75–108; *Homenaje de la ciudad de Alicante a Rafael Altamira en el centenario de su nacimiento* (Tribute to Rafael Altamira on the Centenary of His Birth, by the City of Alicante), (Alicante, 1973); Javier Malagón Barcelo, *Rafael Altamira y Crevea: el historiador y el hombre* (Rafael Altamira y Crevea: The Historian and the Man), (Mexico City, 1971).

Antonio Niño Rodríguez

BOSCH GIMPERA, Pedro (Barcelona, 1891–Mexico City, 1974), Spanish historian. Educated as a classical scholar, Bosch Gimpera left memorable translations of Homer. After completing studies at the University of Barcelona, he received a grant to study in Germany (1911–1914). There he studied classical archaeology and prehistory with A. Schulten and Gustaf Kossinna (q.v.). After 1914 Bosch Gimpera in Catalonia, H. Obermaier, head of a new national Committee for Paleontological and Prehistorical Research, and Granada's M. Gómez-Moreno began, in Spain, the scientific study of prehistory. In 1915 Bosch Gimpera became professor at the University of Barcelona and was active in the Institut d'Estudis Catalans, which produced many outstanding prehistorical researchers. With A. Schulten and L. Pericot, he published *Fontes Hispaniae Antiquae* (4 vols., 1922) and additional essays on the ethnological foundations of the Peninsula and Catalonia. During the Second Republic, he was head of the University of Barcelona and minister of justice in the government of Catalonia in 1937. After Francisco Franco's victory in the Civil War, he went into exile, finally settling in Mexico from 1942 until his death in 1974. There, he extended his activity to the Ibero-American area, although his primary fields continued to be Catalonian and European. His most important work, *Etnología de la Península Ibérica* (Ethnology of the Iberian Peninsula), modified—as V. Gordon

Childe (q.v.) had done—the way of thinking on prehistory. Bosch Gimpera regarded it in terms of culture and disregarded chronological obsessions.

Bosch Gimpera's interpretation of Peninsular prehistory has remained valid. In his view, the Iberian substratum was scarcely modified by the successive invasions (Celts, Carthaginians, Romans, Visigoths, Arabs), which had only involved political changes and not demographic changes. In a new edition of his work prepared in Mexico, *El poblamiento antiguo y la formación de los pueblos de España* (1945; The Ancient Population and the Formation of the Peoples of Spain), he stressed the prehistoric ethnic pluralism of the Peninsula, which defined the present reality,

Bibliography: Juan Comas, ed., *In Memoriam Pedro Bosch Gimpera, 1891–1974* (Mexico City, 1976); Fermín del Pino, ''Antropólogos en el exilio'' (Anthropologists in Exile), in J. L. Abellán, ed., *El exilio español de 1939* (The Spanish Exile of 1939), (Madrid, 1978), vol. 6, pp. 48–69.

Juan-Sisinio Pérez Garzón

CÁNOVAS DEL CASTILLO, Antonio (Malaga, 1828–Madrid, 1897), Spanish historian, politician, and journalist. Cánovas del Castillo's main characteristic was the indissoluble union between his political principles and his historical approach. Three main works highlight his evolution as an historian and as a politician: *Historia de la Decadencia de España desde el advenimiento de Felipe III al trono hasta la muerte de Carlos II* (1854; History of Spanish Decadence from the Advent of Philip III to the Throne until the Death of Carlos II), *Bosquejo Histórico de la Casa de Austria en España* (1869; Historical Outline of the House of Austria in Spain) and *Estudios del reinado de Felipe IV* (1888–1889; Studies on the Reign of Philip IV). His common subject was the history of Spain during the period of Austrian dynasty in the sixteenth and seventeenth centuries. The first of these works accurately reflects the prevailing historiography in the central decades of the last century, the main characteristics of which were usually the nationalism and pragmatism of moderate liberalism. The history of the Spanish national past was seen as the history of a monarchy, which was held responsible for the establishment of a centralist and constitutional state. In the *Bosquejo histórico*, Cánovas revised, as a consequence of his drifting to more conservative political positions, a great part of his previous interpretations. He grew more lenient toward the actions of the Austrian monarchs of Spain. Finally, in *Estudios del reinado de Felipe IV*, he reflected in his history his own experience as a statesman involved in the effort to govern Spain. Cánovas' importance rests with his wide scholarship and his brilliant use of language, but above all with his inclusion of Spanish history within the European environment and his offering of fundamental interpretations about the place Spain had occupied and was occupying among other nations.

Bibliography: J. L. Comellas, *Cánovas* (Madrid, 1965); Melchor Fernández Almagro, *Cánovas, su vida y su política* (Madrid, 1972); Esperanza Illán Calderón, *Cánovas del*

Castillo. Entre la historia y la política (Madrid, 1985); J. Pérez de Guzmán y Gallo, "Foreword," *Bosquejo histórico de la Casa de Austria* (Madrid, 1911).

María Teresa Elorriaga Planes

COLMEIRO Y PINEDO, Manuel (Santiago de Compostela, 1818–Madrid, 1894), Spanish historian. Member of the Royal Academy of History from 1857 and of the Academy of Political and Moral Sciences, as well as of many other national and foreign societies. Colmeiro y Pinedo was a prototype of the scholar-intellectual of his times. Within the scope of the rising socioprofessional structure of the bourgeoisie, he played the roles of politician, jurisconsult, and university professor. Of his many historical works, two are representative: *Las Cortes en los antiguos reinos de Leon y Castilla* (1861; The Legislative Assemblies in the Ancient Kingdoms of Leon and Castile), and *Historia de la economía política en España* (1863; History of Political Economy in Spain). In the first, he undertook to organize and analyze the acts produced by the medieval legislative assemblies of Leon and Castile, including the municipal statutes and the privileges for settlers' territories, as well as, finally, documents of the Kingdoms of Aragon and Navarre. He achieved several important goals: compilation and preservation of ancient legal documents, careful and critical evaluation of the authenticity of sources and of previous texts, hence an advance in methodology, and finally, in presentist terms, legitimation of a constitutional state in Spain through having found in the past a tradition of representative government. The *Historia de la economía política* fits within changes begun in Spanish historiography at the beginning of the nineteenth century as a consequence of the change in mentalities. As historiography developed in Spain, studies in political economy were also progressing, both aiming at a common goal: criticism of the institutions of the Ancient Regime. This is the political framework within which Colmeiro's history of Spain's political economy from the Phoenicians to the eighteenth century was written. He treated legal regulations, deliberations of the legislative assemblies, writings of economists, and the work of previous historians. The main virtue of this synthesis rests with the encouragement its appearance gave to the study of economic history in Spain. Colmeiro expressed his didactic purpose in the preface: to "set forth the part played by the Spanish nation in the progress of riches . . . to show the previous causes driving this monarchy to decadence in the 17th century, as well as the causes of its restoration, and finally, to offer examples of proper and wrong management of public affairs to the State's Administration, reminding of the axiom that history is the master of life."

As a liberal, Colmeiro lauded a strong central government as the proper agency to be responsible for fiscal matters, while he argued that the economy itself should be free from interventionist regulations and other state-supported hindrances to free enterprise. Of course, individual property as an undeniable right was a fundamental assumption. Colmeiro's work reflected many of the historical conceptions developed in Europe from the eighteenth century. He believed in the permanent progress of humanity and in the importance of legal institutions for the social lives of the people, that is, in a government of laws. He was, in short, a liberal romantic nationalist.

Bibliography: Paloma Cirujano, Teresa Elorriaga, and Juan S. Pérez-Garzón, *Historiografía y nacionalismo español. 1834–1868* (Madrid, 1985); Manuel Colmeiro, *Historia de la economía política en España*, with "Preliminary Note," by Gonzalo Anes (Madrid, reissued 1962).

María Teresa Elorriaga Planes

COSTA MARTÍNEZ, Joaquín (Monzon, 1846–Graus, 1911), Spanish historian, jurist, and political essayist. Born to a family of peasants, Costa Martínez did not achieve a university education until rather late in his life. After he did complete advanced studies at the University of Madrid, his political convictions, including religious agnosticism, made him persona non grata to the conservatives of the restored monarchy, who prevented him from achieving a university appointment. He cooperated with the Institución Libre de Enseñanza (the Free School), a free university founded by opponents of the regime, but he had to make his living as a public prosecutor and notary. Mostly self-taught, Costa acquired a wide philosophical, legal, and historical education. From reading Theodor Mommsen (q.v.) and Numa-Denis Fustel de Coulanges (q.v.), he became familiar with newer techniques of research and criticism. The number, variety, and uneven quality of his works testify both to his wide scholarship and to his lack of a fixed method. He preferred to play with generalizations and interpretations rather than to dwell on details or pursue thorough analysis. In his studies of legal history, Costa emphasized usage as the foundation, that is, he took a social view. In this respect his work, *Derecho consuetudinario del Alto Aragón* (1880; Customary Law of Upper Aragon) was of substantial importance. Costa emphasized the survivals of past usages in the law in two of his most important works, *Derecho consuetudinario y economía popular in España* (1902; Customary Law and Popular economy in Spain) and *Colectivismo agrario en España* (1898; Agrarian Collectivism in Spain). In the 1898 work, he drew a picture of Celtiberian social, political, and religious institutions, emphasizing the existence of an uninterrupted national collectivist tradition over many centuries.

Unfortunately, Costa often indulged his love for abstract ideas, his sense of construction, and an excessive urge to systemize. These trends were especially prominent in his early writings, when philosophy and dogmatics prevailed in his mind over historical culture. Yet, he was also devoted to the comparative method and was the first historian to apply this perspective to the history of Spanish law. His use of sources was innovative. In *Introducción a un tratado de política sacado textualmente de los refraneros, romanceros y gestas de la Península* (1881; Introduction to a Political Treatise Drawn from Peninsular Proverbs, Ballads, and Epics), he took advantage of the rich materials offered by medieval popular poetry for depicting ideas and institutions of the period.

He drew heavily on the treatises of sixteenth- and seventeenth-century Spanish theologians and jurisconsults for his studies in philosophy and dogmatics of law. Costa also entered politics and participated in the agonies of the "regeneracion-istas" as they beheld Spain's decadence at the end of the nineteenth century. Many of his activities were devoted to denouncing the dominant political regime, for example, his *Oligarquía y caciquismo como fórmula actual de gobierno en España. Urgencia y modo de cambiarla* (1902; Oligarchy and Caciquism as the Present Mode of Government in Spain. Crisis and a Way to Resolve It). Costa's wonderfully original personality and energy resulted in a truncation of his work and life due to the divorce between his vocation, scholar, and his profession, politician.

Bibliography: Rafael Altamira, "Joaquín Costa. Aspecto general de su obra y singularmente en lo histórico" (Joaquín Costa: An Overview of His Work, Focus on History), *Temas de historia de España* (Themes in the History of Spain) 2 (Madrid, 1929); George Cheyne, *Joaquín Costa, el gran desconocido* (Joaquín Costa, the Great Unknown), (Barcelona, 1972); Aparicio Ciges, *Joaquín Costa, el gran fracasado* (Joaquín Costa, the Great Failure), (Madrid, 1930); *Coloquio sobre el legado de Costa* (Colloquy on the Legacy of Costa), (Saragossa, 1984); Eduardo de Hinojosa, "Joaquín como historiador del derecho" (Joaquín Costa as an Historian of the Law), *Anuario de historia del derecho español* (Yearbook of Spanish Legal History) 2 (1952): 5–12.

Antonio Niño Rodríguez

HINOJOSA Y NAVEROS, Eduardo de (Alhama de Granada, 1852–Madrid, 1919), Spanish historian and jurisconsult. After studying law, philosophy, and arts at the University of Granada, Hinojosa y Naveros obtained doctorates in both fields in Madrid in 1876. As an archivist at the Archaeological Museum of Madrid, he wrote several outstanding monographs. A trip to Germany in 1878 put him in touch with German studies on legal history. As a consequence of his fine knowledge of European, mainly German, bibliography, his work, *Historia del derecho romano según las más recientes investigaciones* (2 vols., 1880, 1885; History of Roman Law According to Current Research) was the best on its subject. In 1882 he became chairman of the Department of Ancient and Medieval Historical Geography at the Higher of Diplomas, a post he left in 1884 to become chairman of the History of Medieval Spanish Institutions in the Central University of Madrid. His intended synthesis, *Historia general del derecho español* (1887; General History of Spanish Law) remained unfinished, with a single volume going up to the Visigothic period.

Hinojosa y Naveros understood the history of law as a specialized branch of historiography, which should be cultivated in accord with its own method, in the manner of Theodor Mommsen (q.v.). He wrote several books on medieval legal history: *El dominico Fray Francisco de Vitoria, gran maestro del derecho público en Europa* (1889; Francisco de Vitoria, Dominican, Master of European Public Law) and *Influencia que tuvieron en el derecho público de su patria y singularmente en el derecho penal los filósofos y teólogos españoles de los siglos XVI y XVII* (1890; The Influence of Philosophers and Theologians on Spanish

Public Law and Especially Criminal Law in the Sixteenth and Seventeenth Centuries).

After the 1890s, during his mature period, Hinojosa y Naveros became a medievalist and abandoned synthetic works for monographs. As an active member of the Conservative party, he was governor of Barcelona and took the opportunity to write several articles on specific laws in Catalonia and to complete his major work, *El régimen señorial y la cuestión agraria en Cataluña durante la Edad Media* (1905; The Feudal System and the Agrarian Issue in Catalonia During the Middle Ages), a monograph based on wide-ranging archival research and great familiarity with published sources. It was a unique study, for Hinojosa y Naveros scarcely mentioned political and military aspects of history, concentrating instead, through looking at diplomas, on how ancient laws were actually applied. He focused on institutions and social classes or estates and compared conditions as he understood them to have been in Spain with what had been published on Germany, France, and Italy. In this respect, he showed the influence of the French school (Numa Denis Fustel de Coulanges [q.v.]) and of the German (Georg Waitz [q.v.] et al.). Hinojosa y Naveros hoped to end the scientific isolation of Spain. Participating in the International Congress of History in Berlin in 1908, he lectured on "El elemento germánico en el derecho espanol" (The Germanic Element in Spanish Law), and he also introduced German historiographical scholarship to Spain and translated into Spanish a number of historical works. After 1910, he chaired the history section of the Center for Historical Research in Madrid, and there he gathered an excellent group of students. After Hinojosa, the history of law was born in Spain, and medieval studies were oriented to the economic and social aspects.

Bibliography: A. García Gallo, "Estudio preliminar" (Preliminary Study), in *Obras completas de Eduardo de Hinojoso* (Complete Works of Eduardo de Hinojosa), 3 vols. (Madrid, 1948–1974); Pérez de Guzmán, *Necrología de don Eduardo de Hinojosa y Naveros* (Obituary Notice), (Madrid, 1919); Teodoro Lascaris Comneno, *Eduardo de Hinojoso* (Madrid, 1959); R. Levene, "La concepción de Eduardo de Hinojosa sobre la historia de las ideas políticas y jurídicas en el derecho español y su proyección en el derecho indiano" (Eduardo de Hinojosa's View of History and of Political and Legal Ideas in Spanish Law and Their Application to the Study of Laws for Indians), *Anuario de historia del derecho español* (Yearbook of Spanish Legal History), 23 (1953): 259–287; C. Sánchez Albórnoz, "En el centenario de Hinojosa" (On the Centenary of Hinojosa), *Cuadernos de historia de España* (Spanish Historical Review), 17 (1952): 5–19.

Antonio Niño Rodriguez

LAFUENTE, Modesto (Rabanal de los Caballeros, 1806–Madrid, 1866), Spanish historian. Professor and director of the Diplomatic School (1856), and president of the Committee for Archives, Libraries, and Museums. Considered the utmost representative of Spanish nationalistic historiography of the nineteenth century. Lafuente's *Historia General de España* (30 vols., 1850–1859; General History of Spain) was the most important history published in Spain after Juan de Mariana's history of the seventeenth century. The *Historia* was the most widely read and used work for many decades, enormously disseminated. This fact reflects the achievement of one of Lafuente's purposes: to educate the public on theories of national progress, as well as to create patriotic consciousness. The *Historia* reached from prehistory to the nineteenth century and was built around two main axes: the origins and evolution of the Spanish nation, and the elements that had delayed or accelerated the process of national unification in the course of the centuries. In Lafuente's opinion, the elements defining the existence of a nation were territorial sovereignty, legislative and political unity, religious unity, and national identity. His evaluation of historical progress, therefore, was rooted in the periods (Catholic monarchs, war of independence against Napoleon) when the unifying tendencies were emphasized in national politics. He thereby defined an essential Hispanic character and revealed the existence of a national identity composed of traits, such as individualism, leadership, tendency to rebel, and religiosity. As he wrote the history of the Spanish people, laws, and institutions, these elements were progressively driving toward a culmination in the form of a national state in the nineteenth century. Thus, legal-institutional history assumed capital importance. Lafuente generalized as conceptual tools terms such as nation, freedom, justice, and national sovereignty, which he then used as standards for evaluating different periods of Spanish history. Notwithstanding the religious spirit that pervaded his work, Lafuente defended the splitting of church and state and criticized the intervention in civil life represented by the Inquisition. He did not restrict himself to reciting facts and, clearly influenced by Enlightenment theorizing and by Johann Gottfried von Herder's notion of unity in the historical process, he drew general laws defining the evolution of the nation. Although he claimed to be objective, he analyzed the past more or less explicitly in a manner so as to justify his own times. Lafuente took on himself the task of conferring on Spain a national history that it had lacked. His work established for many decades the guidelines for interpreting the Spanish past from a liberal and nationalistic viewpoint.

Bibliography: Paloma Cirujano, Teresa Elorriaga y Pérez Garzón, *Historiografía y Nacionalismo español* (Madrid, 1985).

Paloma Cirujano

MADOZ IBAÑEZ, Pascual (Pamplona, 1806–Genoa, 1870), Spanish historian. Madoz Ibañez's main activity was politics, which he practiced in the ranks of progressive liberalism, as minister of finance in the Progressive Bienium, 1854–1856. His reputation as an historian comes from a single work, *Diccionario geográfico-estadístico de España y sus posesiones en Ultramar* (16 vols., 1848–1850; Geographical and Statistical Dictionary of Spain and Its Overseas Possessions), one of the most ambitious books written in the nineteenth century. Madoz Ibañez undertook the project after the Academy of History had dropped it as too difficult a task. He received help from fifteen hundred collaborators, who collected facts from all the provinces and colonial territories of Spain in order to include them in the Dictionary after strict checking and criticism. The book offered "the situation of public education, of welfare, criminality, civil litigation, industry, trade, navigation, territorial surface, population, territorial riches and taxes" as well as the history and origins of many places. Madoz Ibañez's declared aim was "to make known what the depicted country is, what it can be in due course and what it was in other times." Thus, he introduced in Spain, by means of this and other projects, the application of statistics and their importance for the study of economy and sociology. Because of its scope, the *Diccionario* is a necessary work today for knowledge of Spanish society in the central years of the last century.

Bibliography: Francisco J. Paredes Alonso, *Pascual Madoz (1805–1870): Libertad y progreso en la monarquía isabelina* (Pamplona, 1982).

María Teresa Elorriaga Planes

MASDEU, Juan Francisco (Palermo, 1744–Valencia, 1817), Spanish historian. Masdeu was born to a Barceloner, treasurer of the Bourbon family's army, and was the brother of two Jesuits, José Antonio and Baltasar, outstanding proponents of Neo-Scholasticism. A Jesuit himself, educated in Bologna and Rome, he lived through the expulsion of his order from the lands of the Bourbons and ended his life, after several vicissitudes, as a teacher after 1815 in Valencia, upon the return of absolutism to Spain. Because of his acute and critical mind, Masdeu suffered expurgation by the Roman *Index*. (His work, *Iglesia española* [The Spanish Church], of a regalist nature and written in 1815, was not published until 1841.) He also felt the wrath of orthodox Catholics (Marcelino Menéndez Pelayo [q.v.] included him among the heterodoxes) and the ire of liberals because of his frequent writings against the new regime. Nonetheless, his major work, *Historia crítica de España y de la cultura española* (Critical History of Spain and Spanish Culture), was a model of enlightened and encyclopedical historiographic activity, because of its critical precision, its exhaustive documentary evidence, and its firm specialization. The first two volumes were published in Italian, and between 1783 and 1805 another twenty volumes appeared in Spanish covering the period up to the eleventh century. The feature distinguishing Masdeu's *Historia* was rationalist criticism of the past, demythifying whatever was accumulated by legend, interested parties, or religious motives—to such an extent that he denied the existence of the Cid. He is doubtless a bridge between traditional scholarship and the rationalism which, in the nineteenth century, would give way to the classification of historical knowledge as science. He envisaged history not only as political exposition but, above all, as the analysis of the internal life of a people: "population, government, religion, army, agriculture, factories, trade, fine arts, and finally, the progress of the mind, which must draw interest above all the other things, not only for the philosopher and the politician, but also for every rational man." The basis for his critical precision, the main reason leading him to write a work entitled *Historia crítica*, was the fabulous solidity of his documentary support. Abundant bibliography, support by contemporary sources, and constant quotations are only aspects of this working system, which in no case gave in to fabulation. For this reason also, his style is clear, setting aside that tradition which considered history as a narrative art. Many of his demythifications have been subsequently accepted, although in his time he suffered the diatribes of many unfriendly critics. His were interpretative innovations that have been recovered to a great extent and that nowadays attract attention because of their validity and the lack of response they found in their time.

Bibliography: Benito Sánchez Alonso, *Historia de la historiografía española* (History of Spanish Historiography), vol. 3 (Madrid, 1950), pp. 188–207.

Juan-Sisinio Pérez Garzón

MENÉNDEZ PELAYO, Marcelino (Santander, 1856–Santander, 1912), Spanish historian. Professor at the University of Madrid, 1878–1898, and director of the National Library, 1898. Until 1890, Ménendez Pelayo was influenced by his professor, Gumersindo Laverde. The polemical character of Menéndez's works defending the Spanish past was strongly conservative. Three themes in his writing, "Catholic, Spanish, and free," reflect the multiple influence of German romantic historiography, of Scottish syncretism, and of the eclecticism of Cousín Reid and the Spanish traditionalists, Donoso Cortés and Jaime Balmes. Defining himself as an eclecticist, which eclecticism—as Benedetto Croce (q.v.) pointed out—sometimes showed a degree of incertitude, from the doctrinal and theoretical points of view, he emerged as a traditionalist. He disagreed with the cultural atmosphere of his time and launched an enormous scholarly effort against liberal tendencies, which he considered alien to Spanish nature and to have caused national tradition (*volkgeist*) to be deserted. He aimed to criticize the present, to reconstruct the past, and to regenerate the future. He assumed the renovation of Spanish culture would be based on tradition—a basic component in the formation of national consciousness—stating that "a people may improvise everything except its own intellectual culture," and that scholarship, straightforward historical research, was the way to elaborate the concept of what was the "essentially Hispanic" ethos. The legend of Menéndez Pelayo in Spain began with his *Historia de los Heterodoxos Españoles* (History of the Spanish Heretics), a work that responded to Laverde's initiative and thought. It was a picture of Spanish religious life from its beginnings, a story evidencing deep knowledge of theology, philosophy, and national history. The Catholic dimension of his views was evident. This work made use of many previously unknown documents and attempted to reevaluate the great Spanish Catholic historians of the sixteenth to the nineteenth centuries. *Historia de la Ciencia Española* (1876, History of Spanish Science) presented an exhaustive picture of Spanish intellectual activity of modern times.

Modern readers note a certain lack of development of subjects and observe that Menéndez Pelayo sometimes proceeded to conclusions out of mere glimpses. *La Historia de las Ideas Estéticas en España* (1882; History of Aesthetic Ideas in Spain) was a solid scholarly work, participating in the theory of art for art's sake, analyzing the character of artistic creation in Christian peoples, and classifying the same into different doctrines. Up to 1890, he was methodologically more intuitive than reflective. Although inclined to synthesis, he restricted himself to gathering information, admitting that while "no judgment can be issued without facts to judge over," yet "barren and bare gathering of facts is not history, but a store of materials to proceed with it." At times it was simply the excessive ambition of his plans as an historian that prevented him from having an overview. In his second period of scholarship, after the death of his teacher in 1890, he focused on literary history, comparative literature, and literary criticism. His studies of Lope de Vega, the origins of the novel, and the Spanish poets belong to this period. Menéndez Pelayo has been considered the Spanish Louis de Bonald or Joseph de Maistre, with his defense of Church and monarchy creating a school and his writings becoming the matter for conservative movements. He was the man of the nineteenth century most lauded by the founders of twentieth-century Spanish totalitarianism. Where the polemic aspect in his work coexisted with the historical one, a school was created for the ideas rather than for the methodology.

Bibliography: E. Capestany, *Menéndez Pelayo and His Work* (Buenos Aires, 1981); E. Fernández, *Menéndez Pelayo* (Florida, 1967); P. Sainz, *Estudios sobre Menéndez Pelayo* (Madrid, 1984).

Paloma Cirujano

MILLARES CARLO, Agustín (Las Palmas of Great Canary, 1893–Majorca, 1978), Spanish historian, paleographer, philologist, and bibliographer. Professor of paleography in the universities of Granada (1921) and Madrid (1926). After the Spanish Civil War, he went into exile in Mexico, where he was a university professor, and also in Venezuela. A disciple of Menéndez Pidal, Millares was especially interested in books and documents, and in 1944 he started an exhaustive study of Hispanic-American archives. His *Album de paleografía hispanoamericana de los siglos XVI y XVII* (1955; Album of Sixteenth- and Seventeenth-Century Hispanic-American Paleography), done in collaboration with José Ignacio Mantecón, was an outstanding study of West Indian paleography, a work that opened new areas for research in the history of America, facilitating the use of documentation and its proper interpretation. Millares published many texts from the colonial period and carried out numerous historiographic and bibliographic studies, such as his works on Bartolomé de las Casas, José Domingo Rus, Father Anchieta, and others. His work as a biobibliographer, including his *Repertorio bibliográfico de los archivos mexicanos* (1959; Bibliographical Repertory of Mexican Archives), was structured around biographical notices, bibliographical studies, and lists of documents and works by the analyzed authors. Millares wrote over four hundred works and is one of the most important Spanish Americanists.

Bibliography: Javier Malagon, *Los historiadores y el exilio español*; Juan A. Ortega, *El exilio español en México* (Mexico City, 1982).

Paloma Cirujano

MURGUÍA, Manuel (Froxel, 1833–La Coruña, 1923), Spanish historian. Director of the Archive of Simancas and of the General archive of Galicia (1870), president of the Royal Academy of Galicia (1906). Murguía was involved with history, art criticism, literature, and political thought. His regionalism was a meditation on the reconstruction of the Galician personality as a national phenomenon, as well as a separate, local fact. The *Diccionario de escritores gallegos* (Dictionary of Galician Writers), which he never completed, appeared in 1862. In *Los Precursores* (1886; The Precursors), he analyzed the renascence of Galician literature. In *Galicia* (1888), he achieved an important study of Galician prehistory, as well as an anthropological and ethnological analysis of the Celts, their religion and customs, and of the history of several Galician towns. *Historia de Galicia* (1865–1913; History of Galicia), in which he only went up to the tenth century, was a basic work in Galician historiography. A follower of Augustin Thierry (q.v.) and devoted to the goal of producing an entertaining, aesthetic, vivid narrative, he offered hitherto unknown data and notes intended to recover Galicia's own sources. Using concepts of psychology and his knowledge of custom, he compared Galician characteristics to those of other groups in Spain and their analogy with some peoples of Central Europe (a theory that was thereafter to be confirmed by Margot Sponer). He tried to reconstruct national personality by means of ethnographic, ethnological, and folkloric studies, as well as to reveal the past from the perspectives of individual, family, and society. Because of a lack of data, he sometimes had to limit his description to battles of the nobility. Murguía's major contribution was his conscientious gathering of documents and his careful assessment and critical study of sources and archives. He has been considered the father of Galician historiography.

Paloma Cirujano

PIRALA Y CRIADO, Antonio (Madrid, 1824–Madrid, 1903), Spanish historian, politician, and journalist. Contemporary Spanish history was the subject of all his historiographic output. His progressive liberalism did not prevent his being objective; on the contrary, his historical accounts accurately depicted facts and were limited to the documents consulted abundantly and carefully by the author. In 1853 he published the *Historia de la guerra civil y de los partidos liberal y carlista* (5 vols., History of the Civil War and of the Liberal and Carlist Parties), a study which even today is of major importance for knowledge of Spain's political history in the first half of the nineteenth century. In 1895 Pirala published his *Anales desde 1843 hasta el fallecimiento de D. Alfonso XII* (Annals from 1843 to the Death of Alfonso XII), which completed and enlarged previous works; between 1895 and 1898, *Anales de la guerra de Cuba* (Annals of the Cuban War) appeared, and, after his death, three more volumes of contemporary history: *España y la Regencia. Anales de diez y seis años (1885–1902)* (Spain and the Regency. Annals of Sixteen Years). In 1892, he was appointed a member of the Academy of History. Seeing an intimate link between current policies and the study of history, he wrote, "He who rejects history rejects the future."

María Teresa Elorriaga Planes

SÁNCHEZ-ALBORNOZ Y MENDUIÑA, Claudio (Madrid, 1893–Avila, 1984), Spanish historian and politician. As a loyal Republican, Sánchez-Albornoz remained in exile from 1939 until 1983 and was president of the Republican government-in-exile, 1959–1970. Three aspects of his historiography stand out: research, molding of historians, and polemic intent. As a medievalist, his methodology involved extreme caution in the use of documents. His *Los orígenes de la nación española. El reino de Asturias* (1972–1975; Origins of the Spanish Nation. The Kingdom of Asturias) was based on a study of geography and on the establishment of a strict chronology. He saw history as almost a natural science, whose hypothesis could be proved or disproved by experimental probing of documentary evidence. As a disciple of Eduardo Hinojosa y Naveros (q.v.), he pursued the history of institutions in works such as *Ruina y extinción del municipio romano en España e instituciones que lo reemplazan* (1943; Collapse and Extinction of the Roman Municipality in Spain and Successor Institutions) or *Estudio sobre las instituciones medievales españolas* (1965; Studies in Medieval Spanish Institutions), among others. He was among the founders, in 1924, of the *Anuario de historia del derecho español* (Yearbook of Spanish Legal History), a journal devoted to a new methodology brilliantly developed in Spain during the early twentieth century, the exposition of legal change in history, and the relationship of the law to other social forces. His written accomplishment was enormous. Among other subjects, he devoted time to the study of Islamic culture in the Peninsula: *El Ajbar Maymu'a. Problemas historiográficos que suscita* (1944; The Historiographical Problems of Ajbar Maymu'a); *La España musulmana según los autores islamitas y cristianos medievales* (1946; Muslim Spain According to Medieval Islamic and Christian Authors). As a professor in the universities of Barcelona and Madrid, and an organizer of historical enterprise, he was also skilled, establishing in Spain the Institute of Medieval Studies of the Center of Historical Research and then, in Argentina, the Institute of Spanish History in Buenos Aires, where the *Cuadernos de historia de España* (Spanish Historical Review) has been published since 1944. As a polemicist, defending the "truth of history," he was frequently involved in important historiographical debates. In 1943 he published *En torno a los orígenes del feudalismo* (On the Origins of Feudalism) against the theories of the German medievalist, Heinrich Brunner; he also published *España, un enigma histórico* (1957; Spain, an Historical Enigma) and *Despoblación y repoblación del Valle del Duero* (1966; Depopulation and Repopulation of the Valley of the Duero), refuting the views of Menéndez Pidal. The Dei Lincei

Academy of Rome awarded him the Feltrinelli Prize in 1971, and, in 1984, his own country recognized him with the Prince of Asturias Prize.

Bibliography: Because Sánchez-Albornoz died so recently no comprehensive evaluations of his contribution to historiography have yet been published. The following are tributes published while he lived: *Homenaje de Asturias a Claudio Sánchez Albornoz* (Tribute by Asturias to Claudio Sánchez Albornoz), (Oviedo, 1980); *Homenaje al professor Claudio Sánchez Albornoz* (Tribute to Professor Claudio Sanchez Albornoz), (Buenos Aires, 1964).

María Teresa Elorriaga Planes

VICENS VIVES, Jaime (Gerona, 1910–Lyon, 1960), Spanish historian. Educated under Antonio de la Torre, an expert in the reign of the Catholic monarchs, and influenced by Catalan historiography of the 1930s, Vicens Vives' doctoral thesis included both aspects: *Ferran II i la ciutat de Barcelona*, 1479–1516 (3 vols., 1936–1937; Ferdinand II and the City of Barcelona, 1479–1516). Purged from the university at the end of the Civil War, he went ahead with his research on the social framework of Fernando the Catholic's reign, resulting in his *Historia de los remensas en el s. XV* (History of Fifteenth-Century Peasants Bound to the Soil). In 1946 he was appointed professor at the University of Saragossa and, in 1949, at Barcelona, where in a single decade before his death he carried out an amount of work that has made him a symbol of historiographical renewal in Spain. Participation in the Ninth International Congress of Historical Sciences in Paris, as well as contact with Lucien Febvre (q.v.) and the *Annales* school, marked the turning point of his methodological premises. After these encounters, he began new tasks—on the one hand dismantling and criticizing the prevailing academic inertia, characterized by an anodyne history often affected by Francista political views, and on the other hand promoting new approaches, opening new research, and creating a school that has supplied many of the best contemporary Spanish historians. In short, he opened the path of social and economic history in the style of the *Annales*. In 1952 his *Aproximación a la historia de España* (Introduction to Spanish History) indicated the new direction, and the next year he began publishing the *Indice histórico español* (Spanish Historical Index), as well as *Estudios de historia moderna* (Studies in Modern History). He also collaborated on a new interpretation of the history of Catalonia (*Biografies catalanes*—Catalan Biographies), carried out with J. Nadal the first synthesis of economic history—*Manual de historia económica de España* (1959; Manual of Spanish Economic History), and oversaw the first attempt to interpret Spanish history integrating economy, society, and culture in *Historia económica y social de España y América* (5 vols., 1961; Economic and Social History of Spain and America). In Vicens' work, it is difficult to classify a consistent theory of historical process. He was influenced by Braudelian analysis of space and time, situationalist interpretation of economic history, the concept of mentalities in historical explanation—all without abandoning his continual concern for positivist research, which, from the time of his earliest publications, kept him working in the archives.

Bibliography: "Jaime Vicens (1910–1960)," *L'Avenc*, no. 83 (Barcelona, June 1985); J. Mercader Riba, "Jaime Vicens i Vives: su obra histórica" (Jaime Vicens Vives: His Historical Work), *Arbor*, no. 255, pp. 265–284; M. and J. L. Peset, "Vicens Vives y la historiografía del derecho en España" (Vicens Vives and Historiography of Law in Spain), *Ius Commune*, no. 6 (V. K. Frankfurt am Main, 1977), pp. 177–262.

Juan-Sisinio Pérez Garzón

Great Historians: Spanish American

ALAMÁN, Lúcas (Guanajuato, Mexico, 1792–Mexico City, 1853), Mexican historian and political leader. Alamán belonged to a prominent family and studied at the Mexico City Royal Mining Seminary as well as in London and Paris. Mexican deputy to the Spanish Cortes (Parliament) in 1821, he was one of the leaders of Mexico's conservative political faction. Appointed secretary of foreign relations by Presidents Guadalupe Victoria (1823–1825) and Vicente Guerrero (1830–1832), he helped draft Antonio López de Santa Anna's dictatorial program of government in 1853 and that year, for the third time, became secretary of foreign relations. An active promoter of financial and industrial organizations and director of industry (1824–1846), he participated in the creation of the Agricultural Credit Bank (Banco de Avio) of the Industry Development Agency (Junta de Fomento de la Industria) and in the establishment of textile mills in Orizaba and Celaya. He also reorganized Mexico's National Archives and was the founder of the Mexico City National Museum of Antiquities, where, for the first time, the country's pre-Colombian archaeological treasures were displayed to the public. Closely associated with a tumultuous and chaotic period of Mexico's history, Alamán was often exposed to violent criticism from his political opponents.

In his later years, Alamán turned to the study of history and used his multiple talents and interests to write two fundamental works of Mexican historiography: the three-volume *Disertaciones sobre la historia de la República mexicana* (Dissertations on the History of the Mexican Republic), published between 1844 and 1849, which covered the conquest and colonial periods; and the five-volume *Historia de México desde los primeros movimientos que prepararon su independencia en el año de 1808 hasta la época presente* (History of Mexico from the First Movements that Prepared Its Independence in 1808 up to the Present

Times), published between 1849 and 1852, and which has been considered an essential source for an understanding of early nineteenth-century Mexico. He incorporated in both studies his extensive research of archival and printed material as well as his personal knowledge of many of the events he depicted. Though lacking objectivity, particularly as far as political matters were concerned, Alamán's *Disertaciones* and *Historia de México* were brilliantly written works. Consistent with his conservative viewpoint, Alamán argued that the Spanish colonial legacy had not been detrimental to Mexico's development. He presented Hernán Cortés as an epic hero, praised the work of the missionaries, and emphasized the prudence and ability of the Spanish viceroys. All this, he contended, had prepared Mexico well for its independent course and had provided the country with a cultural legacy which, in turn, enabled it to withstand the past and possible future encroachments by the United States. A confirmed nationalist, Alamán believed in the moral mission of history, the knowledge of which he viewed as a safeguard against the unrestrained rising force of political demagogy.

Bibliography: Lúcas Alamán, *Obras de d. Lúcas Alamán* (Mexico, 1899), 10 vols.; Moises González Navvarro, *El pensamiento político de Lúcas Alamán* (Mexico City, 1952).

Nikita Harwich Vallenilla

AMUNÁTEGUI, Miguel Luís (Santiago de Chile, 1828–Santiago de Chile, 1888), Chilean historian, journalist, and politician. Amunátegui studied the humanities at the Santiago National Institute, where he also taught literature courses (1847). He began working in the Chilean Statistical Office and was later commissioned by President Manuel Montt to write a defense of Chile's claim to several Patagonian islands disputed by Argentina (1853–1855). Appointed chief of instruction at the Ministry of Justice, Education, and Public Instruction (1853), he later became undersecretary of the interior (1862). A prominent member of Chile's liberal movement, he championed the separation of church and state and was an advocate of secondary school and university-level education for women. He served as editor in several liberal newspapers and founded *El independiente* (The Independent) to further his political views. President of the Chamber of Deputies in 1867 and again in 1871, he was appointed minister of the interior and foreign relations in 1868. Unsuccessful candidate for the presidency in the 1876 elections, he was again minister of foreign relations in José Manuel Balmaceda's government (1887). Amunátegui combined his distinguished public career with a lifelong interest in history, which he pursued, at an early stage, together with his brother, Gregorio. He worked extensively in Chilean private and public archives and focused his research on the independence and early nineteenth-century periods, which he studied from a liberal political viewpoint. Written in the classical tradition of nineteenth-century historiography, his histories and biographies featured a straight narration of events rather than conceptual analysis. However, his biography of Chile's independence hero Bernardo O'Higgins did examine the need for a strong centralized government so as to ensure the consolidation of the new Chilean state. Amunátegui has been acknowledged as one of the founders of modern Chilean historiography.

Bibliography: Miguel Luís Amunátegui, *La crónica de 1810* (Santiago, 1876–1899), 3 vols.; Miguel Luís Amunátegui, *Descubrimiento y conquista de Chile* (Santiago, 1862); Miguel Luís Amunátegui, *La dictatura de O'Higgins* (Santiago, 1852); Miguel Luís Amunátegui, *Vida de don Andrés Bello* (Santiago, 1882); Gertrude Matyoka Yeager, "Barros Araña, Vicuña Mackenna, Amunátegui: The Historian as National Educator," *Journal of Inter-American Studies and World Affairs*, 19, no. 2 (May 1977): 173–199.

Nikita Harwich Vallenilla

ARBOLEDA LLORENTE, José María (Popayán, 1886–Bogotá, 1969), Colombian prelate, journalist, and historian. Arboleda founded the Popayán newspaper *El Cometa* (The Comet) in 1911, and was the editor of *La Sanción* (Approval) in 1915 and *Patria* (Fatherland) in 1920. Appointed general director of public instruction in 1918, he became rector of the Cauca Central University in 1925. He was also president of the Cauca Historical Center and editor of its journal, *Popayán*, in 1926. He dedicated himself to the task of organizing the Cauca Central Archive, which he divided chronologically into three sections: Colonial (1540–1810); Independence (1810–1832); and Republican (from 1832 on). He also arranged its documentary holdings according to general subjects such as civil law, ecclesiastical history, judicial history, military history, and biographical material. Based on this material and that from other archives, Arboleda wrote his study *El indio en Colombia* (1948; The Indian in Colombia); *Historia de Colombia* (1951; History of Colombia) and what has been considered his major work, *Popayán a través del arte y de la historia* (1966; Popayán Through Art and History).

Bibliography: J. Leon Helguera, "José María Arboleda Llorente," in *Academias Colombiana y del Cauca de la Historia* (Popayán, 1969).

Nikita Harwich Vallenilla

ARCAYA, Pedro Manuel (Coro, 1874–Caracas, 1958), Venezuelan historian, sociologist, jurist, politician, and diplomat. Son of Camilo Arcaya and Ignacia Madriz, Arcaya belonged to one of Coro's leading patrician families. After completing his formal education in his native town, he obtained his law degree from Caracas Central University in 1895 and began practice in Coro. He was virtually self-taught in the social sciences. His private library, which numbered over seventy thousand volumes at his death and is now part of the Caracas National Library, is probably the best of its kind available in Venezuela. Though primarily a jurist and sociologist, Arcaya published a number of articles and pamphlets on Venezuelan historical topics between 1892 and 1918, which were collected in 1928 under the title *Estudios de Sociologia Venezolana* (Studies on Venezuelan Sociology) and confirmed their author as a prominent representative of the Venezuelan Positivist school. Member of the Supreme Federal Appeal Court (1909–1913), Arcaya became attorney general in 1913, minister of the interior (1914–1917 and 1925–1929), senator for his native state (1918–1922),

Venezuelan minister plenipotentiary (1922–1923), and ambassador (1930–1935) to the United States. One of his major achievements as minister of the interior was the preparation of a new Civil Code, which was approved in 1916 and remained in force for over half a century, and which introduced in Venezuelan legislation the principles of positive law adapted to the traditions, customs, and social development of the Venezuelan population. He also promoted the 1925 constitutional reform which prohibited the introduction and circulation in Venezuela of "communist ideas."

A staunch defender of the Juan Vicente Gómez regime, Arcaya was the only public figure, after Gómez's death in 1935, who decided to face in Court, personally and successfully, the political accusations leveled against him. A keen observer of Venezuela's past, Arcaya insisted on the need to analyze the psychological and ethnic roots that conditioned the social stratification of the colonial period and helped explain the country's evolution throughout the nineteenth century. For Arcaya, scientific thought, once applied to history, can help discover the laws that define a particular society's evolutionary process. The historical method can thus establish a link between past and present, can seek to explain both the past and the present, and, at the same time, must lead to the path toward the future.

Bibliography: Pedro Manuel Arcaya, *El Cabildo de Caracas* (Caracas, 1965); Pedro Manuel Arcaya, *Estudios de sociología venozolana* (Caracas: Editorial Cecilio Acosta, 1941); Pedro Manuel Arcaya, *Memorias* (Madrid: Talleres del Instituto Geográfico y Catastral, 1963); Pedro Manuel Arcaya, *Población de origen europeo de Coro en la época colonial* (Caracas: Academia Nacional de la Historia, 1972); Carlos Felice Cardot, *Pedro Manuel Arcaya* (Caracas: Italgráfica, 1972); Alicia de Nuño, *Ideas sociales del positivismo en venezuela* (Caracas: Universidad Central de Venezuela, 1969); Hector Parra Márquez, *El Doctor Pedro Manuel Arcaya* (Caracas: Empresa El Cojo, 1965); Arturo Sosa Abascal, *Ensayos sobre el Pensamiento Político Positivista Venezolano* (Caracas: Ediciones Centauro, 1985).

Nikita Harwich Vallenilla

ARGUEDAS, Alcides (La Paz, 1879–Chulumani, Bolivia, 1946), Bolivian writer, politician, historian, and diplomat. Born into a prominent patrician family, Arguedas completed his secondary education at the National College (1898) and at the University of La Paz where he obtained his law degree in 1903. He spent over twenty years of his life as a Bolivian diplomatic agent in several Latin American countries (including Colombia and Venezuela) and in Europe, particularly in France, where he attended lectures at the Paris Collège Libre des Sciences Sociales and in Spain, where he was strongly influenced by the disenchanted and pessimistic outlook of the Spanish literary "Generation of 1898." A member of the Bolivian Chamber of Deputies (1916) and Senate (1940), he headed his country's Liberal party and wrote for the La Paz newspapers *El Comercio* (Trade) and *Los Debates* (Debates), the latter of which he founded in 1916. Although primarily remembered as the author of the novel *Raza de bronce* (Race of Bronze) (1919), considered one of the masterpieces of contemporary

Latin American literature, Arguedas also produced three remarkable studies on Bolivia: the sociological essay *Pueblo enfermo* (1909; Diseased Folk); the *Historia general de Bolivia: el proceso de la nacionalidad, 1809–1921* (General History of Bolivia: The Process of Nationality, 1809–1921), which he prepared in 1922 for the France-Amérique Committee and which, in fact, came to be a shortened version of his monumental four-volume *Historia de Bolivia* (History of Bolivia), published between 1920 and 1926. Arguedas once defined history as "morals in action"; he therefore viewed his work with the eyes of a moralist whose prime task must be to pass judgment, however controversial. In *Pueblo enfermo*, he projected a negative, almost derogatory, image of the Bolivian people whom he denounced, among other things, as lazy, treacherous, and dishonest. These defects, however, were but the consequence of centuries of oppression borne by all segments of Bolivian society. This accusatory account made a strong impact on its readers, both in Bolivia and abroad, particularly in Spain, where the book was highly praised for its crude statement of facts.

Arguedas used a similar approach in his *Historia de Bolivia*. Even though it relied on well-documented research, the book made clear its author's intention to denounce and criticize, which he did in a direct, humorless style: Bolivia had remained a backward country because its history was merely the sequence of its barbarous caudillos' brutal passions. Arguedas was concerned with creating categorical definitions for given periods of Bolivia's history. Many of these periods are still referred to in Arguedas' terms: "the learned caudillos," 1828–1848; "the mob in action," 1848–1857, and so on. Despite its inflexible and pessimistic message, Arguedas believed in a possible future regeneration, providing the objective material conditions of Bolivian society were to be changed through improved education, self-discipline, and productivity.

Bibliography: Alcides Arguedas, *Obras Completas* (Mexico City, 1959–1960), 2 vols.; B. Charles Arnade, "The Historiography of Colonial and Modern Bolivia," *Hispanic American Historical Review* 42, no. 3 (August 1962): 333–384.

Nikita Harwich Vallenilla

BARALT, Rafael María (Maracaibo, 1810–Madrid, 1860), Venezuelan writer, philologist, historian, and diplomat. Baralt grew up during the tumultuous years of the independence wars. As a young child, he moved with his family to his mother's native island of Santo Domingo. He returned to Maracaibo in 1821 and served in the Venezuelan militia while completing his education, in his hometown and in Bogotá where he graduated in 1828. Appointed to the regimental staff of general Santiago Mariño, he participated in the western Venezuela military campaign of 1830, the documents of which he subsequently organized for publication. From 1830 until 1840 he lived in Caracas where he became active in political and intellectual circles and soon acquired a distinguished reputation as a poet and prose writer. On his own initiative, he began collecting information on Venezuelan history. He was then asked to join the team, under the direction of the geographer Agustin Codazzi, who had been commissioned by the Venezuelan government to write an outline of the country's history and geography, including an atlas. With the help of Ramón Díaz Martínez for the sections on the conquest and colonial period, Baralt prepared the manuscript for the historical part of the work and also helped write the geography outline. He then traveled to Paris at the end of 1840, to supervise both publications. The three-volume illustrated edition of the *Resumen de la Historia de Venezuela* (1841; Outline of the History of Venezuela) was an immediate success. Baralt returned to Venezuela for a few weeks in 1841 and was then sent on a diplomatic trip to London to discuss the boundary situation between Venezuela and British Guiana. After completing his mission, Baralt decided to settle in Spain where he spent the rest of his life, first in Seville (1841–1845) and then in Madrid (1845–1860). He soon became involved in the intellectual life of the peninsula; wrote a number of books on Spanish political issues, in which he expressed his liberal standpoint: freedom of the press, the Cortes (the Spanish Parliament); and achieved notoriety in his studies on the Spanish language, particularly with his *Diccionario de Galicismos* (Dictionary of Gallicisms) of 1855. In 1853 he was the first Latin American to be elected to the Spanish Royal Academy. He became director of the official newspaper *La Gaceta de Madrid* (The Madrid Gazette) and manager of the National Printing Office (1854). The Dominican Republic then appointed him minister plenipotentiary with the task of negotiating with Spain the treaty of recognition for the new republic. But political intrigues marred the negotiations; charges were brought against Baralt by the Spanish government who barred him from all public office (1857). Though cleared in the courts, Baralt was left with his health irretrievably impaired.

Baralt's *Resumen de la Historia de Venezuela* encompasses the time span from 1498 up to 1830, with a chronological appendix from 1831 to 1837, and has been considered the classical work of modern Venezuelan historiography, despite its shortcomings. Its most serious flaw is the unbalanced treatment it gives to the colonial period as opposed to the section on the wars of independence, a situation reproduced in virtually every Venezuelan history textbook up to the present. Often inappropriately referred to as a "romantic historian," Baralt was lucidly reserved in his judgments on events and individuals and insisted on the specific aspects of Venezuelan culture.

Bibliography: Rafael María Baralt, *Resumen de la Historia de Venezuela* (Maracaibo: Universidad del Zulia, 1960), 3 vols.; Pedro Grases, *Rafael María Baralt* (Caracas: Ministerio de Educación, 1973); Agustín Millares Carlo, *Rafael María Baralt (1810–1860). Estudio biográfico, crítico y bibliográfico* (Caracas: Universidad Central de Venezuela, 1969).

Nikita Harwich Vallenilla

BARROS ARAÑA, Diego (Santiago de Chile, 1830–Santiago de Chile, 1907), Chilean historian, journalist, politician, and diplomat. Barros Araña studied law at the Santiago National Institute and began teaching history at the University of Chile. He became involved in his country's liberal movement and earned considerable notoriety through his incisive articles, published between 1855 and 1858, particularly in the liberal newspapers *El país* (The Country) and *Actualidad* (Present Times). His political commitment forced him into exile, first in Argentina, Uruguay, and Brazil, and later in Europe. He took the opportunity to carry out extensive archival research, particularly in Spain where he located the manuscript of an important chronicle of the 1598 Araucan War, written in verse by Fernando Alvarez de Toledo, one of the Spanish soldiers who participated in the campaign, and entitled *Purem Indómito*, which he had subsequently published in Leipzig (1860). Upon his return to Chile, Barros Araña continued publishing many of the documents he had collected. Appointed rector of the Santiago National Institute (1863–1872), where he also held a chair in history until his death, he was sent to Argentina in 1876 on a diplomatic mission to negotiate a boundary dispute. He later became dean of the Faculty of Philosophy and Humanities (1892) and rector (1893–1897) of the University of Chile. Barros Araña's lifelong dedication to historical research, which began with the publication of his four-volume *Historia de la independencia de Chile* (History of Chile's Independence), between 1854 and 1858, culminated with his monumental sixteen-volume *Historia General de Chile* (General History of Chile), published between 1884 and 1902, which today remains a valuable research aid, particularly for the country's colonial and independence periods. A thorough scholar who paid meticulous attention to documentary accuracy and detailed factual account, Barros Araña was also capable of perceptive analysis as shown in his two-volume study on Chile's economic and political development during President Manuel Bulnes's administration, *Un decenio de la historia de Chile, 1841–1851* (A Decade in Chilean History, 1841–1851), published in 1905–1906. Following his death, his vast private library and archive were donated to the Chilean National Library where a special "Barros Araña Room" was created to house this material as a tribute to one of the country's most outstanding historians.

Bibliography: Ricardo Donoso, *Barros Araña, educador, historiador y hombre público* (Santiago de Chile, 1931); Carlos Orrego Barros, *Diego Barros Araña* (Santiago de Chile, 1952).

Nikita Harwich Vallenilla

BASADRE, Jorge (Tacna, Peru, 1903–Lima, 1980), Peruvian historian, legal scholar, and educator. Born in Chilean-occupied Tacna, following the 1879–1884 War of the Pacific, Basadre attended clandestine Peruvian schools before entering the Lima German College and, later, San Marcos University where he obtained his doctoral degrees in literature (1928) and law (1936) and embarked on a long and distinguished career as a faculty member. He held both the chairs of Peruvian history (1928–1954) and of Peruvian legal history (1938–1954). Basadre belonged to a generation strongly influenced by the Mexican and Russian revolutions, by World War I, and by university reform movements. He was a committed scholar, as well as a champion for academic and political freedom. Director of the San Marcos Library on two occasions (1930–1931 and 1935––

1942), he became director of the Peruvian National Library after a disastrous fire in 1943 had all but destroyed its book and manuscript collection. For five years (1943–1948), he successfully carried out the tremendous task of rebuilding the library's holdings, while also donating his own sizable library to the nation. Appointed minister of public education (1945 and 1956–1958), he served as director of cultural relations of the Pan American Union (1958–1960) and as president of the Peruvian Historical Institute (1956–1962). He was also visiting professor to various universities in Europe and the United States.

Basadre researched primarily the post independence and contemporary periods of Peruvian history and, together with political aspects, studied the economic, social, and regional development of Peru. His monumental *Historia de la República del Perú* (History of the Republic of Peru), considered a milestone in twentieth-century Latin American historiography, grew from a two-volume 1939 edition to the seventeen-volume sixth edition, published in 1968. In such an immense study, he was able to combine careful attention to detail with incisive analysis and a profound general assessment of Peru's historical process. His outlook on such a process was optimistic in that he saw in Peruvian and Latin American history, in general, a steady progress toward a wealthier, more stable society, a goal that united the elites as well as the masses. His other major works include the 1971 three-volume *Introduction a las bases documentales para la historia de la República del Perú con algunas reflexiones* (Introduction to Basic Documents for the History of the Peruvian Republic with Some Thoughts), a most comprehensive bibliographical tool, and his 1956 *Los fundamentos de la historia del derecho* (The Basic Elements of the History of Law), which provided a brilliant synthesis of the development of Western and Peruvian legal thought.

Bibliography: Thomas M. Davies, Jr., "Jorge Basadre (1903–1980)," *Hispanic American Historical Review* 61, no. 1 (February 1981): 84–86; Cesar Pacheco Velez, "Jorge Basadre," *Revista de Historia de America*, no. 92 (July-December 1982): 195–213.

Nikita Harwich Vallenilla

BRICEÑO IRAGORRY, Mario (Trujillo, 1895–Caracas, 1958), Venezuelan writer, historian, teacher, politician, and diplomat. After completing his secondary education in Valera, Briceño Iragorry studied law at the Andes University of Merida (Venezuela) where he obtained his first degree in 1920. He entered the Venezuelan Foreign Service in 1921, was consul in New Orleans (1923–1925), and, upon his return to Venezuela, received his doctoral degree in law from the Caracas Central University. He combined his diplomatic activities with teaching positions at the high school and university levels. In 1928 he was appointed secretary of Caracas Central University. He also held posts in the Trujillo Carabobo and Bolivar state legislatures and governments. Minister plenipotentiary to Central America, based in Costa Rica (1936–1941), he was Venezuelan ambassador to Colombia in 1949. Exiled in Madrid during the Marcos Pérez Jiménez dictatorship (1952–1958), he returned to Venezuela a few months before his death. From the early 1920s on, Briceño became interested in historical research, which he carried out together with archaeological, ethnological, and linguistic investigations. As a scholar, he wrote more than thirty books, as well as numerous pamphlets and articles. Though mainly a political historian who concentrated on the colonial period and the early nineteenth century, his work also touched on cultural and social aspects. His better known studies include *Casa León y su tiempo: aventura de un anti-héroe* (1946; Casa León and His Time: The Adventure of an Anti-hero); *El Regente Heredia; o la piedad heroica* (1947; The "Regente" Heredia; or Heroic Pity); *Los Riberas: Historias de Venezuela* (n.d.; The Ribera Family: Stories of Venezuela), and, above all, *Tapices de Historia Patria: esquema de una morfología de la cultura colonial* (1934; Tapestries of Fatherland History: An Outline of the Formation of Colonial Culture). Using the tools of interdisciplinary investigation, as well as his literary insights as a writer, Mario Briceño Iragorry considered historical study as a way of defining a nationalistic criterion, nationalism being, for him, "at the stage of a collective evaluation, the manifestation of a given community's personality."

Bibliography: Mario Briceño Iragorry, *Obras Selectas* (Caracas: Edime, 1954); Rafael Ramón Castellanos, *Bibliografía del Doctor Mario Briceño Iragorry* (Trujillo: Ejecutivo del estado Trujillo, 1981); Ramón Losada Aldana, *Una doctrina de la venezolanidad: Mario Briceño Iragorry* (Caracas: Editorial Pensamiento Vivo, 1958); Arturo Uslar Pietri y Mariano Picón Salas, *Homenaje a Mario Briceño Iragorry en el sexto aniversario de su muerte* (Caracas: Editorial Arte, 1964).

Nikita Harwich Vallenilla

BULNES, Francisco (Mexico City, 1847–Mexico City, 1924), Mexican historian and political thinker. An engineer by profession, Bulnes later taught at Mexico City's National Engineering School. A staunch supporter of the Porfirio Díaz regime, he served, for many years as deputy to the Mexican National Congress, where he worked particularly in the Budget and Finance Commissions. He was a prominent member of the technocratic body of advisers of the Díaz administration, usually referred to as the Científicos (Scientists). Yet, he also developed an interest in the social sciences, particularly history, which he interpreted in the light of positivism. His essays on various aspects of Mexico's historical evolution were brilliantly written critical and thought-provoking reappraisals. *Las grandes mentiras de nuestra historia* (Our History's Great Lies), published in 1901, paved the way for his two studies on Benito Juárez: the 1904 *El verdadero Juárez* (The Real Juárez) which started a polemic with Justo Sierra (q.v.) over Mexico's famous nineteenth-century political leader; and the 1909 *Juárez y las revoluciones* (Juárez and the Revolutions). *La guerra de independencia, Hidalgo-Iturbide* (The War of Independence. Hidalgo-Iturbide), published in 1910, sought to analyze the motivating social forces behind Mexico's independence movement. Wholly identified with the *porfiriato*, Bulnes was forced into a four-year exile at the outbreak of the Mexican Revolution (1911–1915). Upon his return, he set out to write both a defense of the Díaz regime and an assessment of the revolution as a social phenomenon. Inspired by Alexis de Tocqueville's (q.v.) *L'Ancien Régime et la Révolution*, *El verdadero Díaz y la revolución* (The Real Díaz and the Revolution), published in 1916, caused a powerful impact in its time and remains one of the classical analyses of the *porfiriato*. Finally, *Los grandes problemas de México* (Mexico's Major Problems), published in 1924, lucidly discussed the issues raised by the 1910 revolution in terms of Mexico's future economic, social, and cultural developments.

Bibliography: Francisco Bulnes, *El verdadero Díaz y la revolución*, 4th ed. (Mexico City: Imprenta Nacional, 1960); Francisco Bulnes, *El verdadero Juárez* (Mexico City, 1904); Francisco Bulnes, *La guerra de independencia. Hidalgo-Iturbide* (Mexico City, 1910); Francisco Bulnes, *Las grandes mentiras de nuestra historia* (Mexico City, 1901); Francisco Bulnes, *Los grandes problemas de Mexico*, 2d ed. (Mexico City: Centro de Estudios Históricos del Agrarismo en México, 1981).

Nikita Harwich Vallenilla

BUSTAMANTE, Carlos María de (Oaxaca, Mexico, 1774–Mexico City, 1848), Mexican historian, journalist, and politician. Graduated from secondary school with a major in arts and humanities, Bustamante studied jurisprudence in France and was awarded his title of lawyer in Guadalajara in 1801. He alternated his law practice with journalism, founded the newspaper *Diario de México* (Mexico's Daily), and published *El juguetillo* (The Small Toy), a revolutionary propaganda periodical. He served as an army officer in the Mexican independence war (1810–1816), later became Emperor Agustin de Iturbide's private secretary (1821–1823), and was a deputy in Mexico's National Congress for twenty-four years (1822–1846). He was directly involved in the major political events of Mexico's turbulent first half of the nineteenth century. An active spokesman of the liberal movement, a talented journalist, and a prolific writer, he focused his interest on the study of Mexico's history. Although his works on the colonial period are worthy of attention, his major contribution to Mexican historiography remains his six-volume *Cuadro histórico de la Revolución de la América Mexicana* (Historical Framework of Mexican America's Revolution), published between 1823 and 1832, a detailed account of the country's struggle for independence. Written from a liberal standpoint in contrast with Lúcas Alamán's (q.v.) conservative interpretation, the *Cuadro histórico* provides valuable first-hand material. Bustamante was himself an eyewitness to many of the events he narrated, but his own partisan views often biased his analytical capacity.

Bibliography: Carlos María de Bustamante, *Apuntes para la historia del gobierno del general don Antonio López de Santa Anna* (Mexico City, 1848); Carlos María de Bustamante, *Cuadro histórico de la revolución de la América mexicana* (Mexico City, 1823–1832), 6 vols.; Carlos María de Bustamante, *Los tres siglos de México durante el gobierno español hasta la entrada del ejército trigarante* (Mexico City, 1826–1838), 4 vols.; Carlos María de Bustamante, *México por dentro y por fuera bajo el gobierno de los Virreyes* (Mexico City, 1831); Victoriano Salado Alvarez, *La Vida azarosa y romántica de don Carlos María de Bustamante* (Madrid, 1933).

Nikita Harwich Vallenilla

CAILLET-BOIS, Ricardo R. (Buenos Aires, 1903–Buenos Aires, 1977), Argentine historian. Graduated from the Division of History of the Buenos Aires National Institute of Secondary Education, Caillet-Bois was one of the first prominent professional twentieth-century Argentine historians. He taught at the National University of Buenos Aires (from 1928 on), at the University of La Plata (1929), and at the Buenos Aires National College, where he was appointed rector in 1935. During the years of the Juan Domingo Perón regime, he had to give up his teaching positions, which he resumed after Perón's overthrow. In 1955 he became director of the National University of Buenos Aires' Institute of Historical Research and editor of its *Bulletin*. He served briefly as president of the National Education Council in 1957 and as Argentine ambassador to Unesco in 1959. He was particularly active as Argentine representative to the Pan American Institute of Geography and History and was president of Argentina's National Academy of History from 1970 until 1972. He was interested in a wide variety of historical topics, relating primarily to Argentine political and diplomatic history. He analyzed, for instance, the effects of the French Revolution on the Rio de la Plata provinces as well as the antecedents of the British invasions to Argentina in the early nineteenth century. His two books on the historical justification for Argentina's claim to the Falkland Islands, published in 1948 and 1953, strongly influenced his country's political circles and public opinion at large over the issue, which eventually led to the Argentine invasion of the islands and subsequent war with Great Britain in 1982. A prestigious prize for historical research, jointly sponsored by the Pan American Institute of Geography and History and the Argentine government, bears his name.

Bibliography: Ricardo R. Caillet-Bois, *Alejandro Duclos Guyot, emisario napoleónico antecedente de las invasiones inglesas de 1806–1807* (Buenos Aires, 1929); Ricardo R. Caillet-Bois, *Ensayo sobre el Río de la Plata y la revolución francesa* (Buenos Aires, 1929); Ricardo R. Caillet-Bois, *Las Islas Malvinas* (Buenos Aires, 1953); Ricardo R. Caillet-Bois, *Una tierra argentina: Las Islas Malvinas* (Buenos Aires, 1948); James R. Scobie, "Obituary: Ricardo R. Caillet-Bois (1903–1977)," *Hispanic American Historical Review* 59, no. 1 (February 1979): 120–121.

Nikita Harwich Vallenilla

CARDOZO, Efraím (Villarica, Paraguay, 1906–Villarica, Paraguay, 1973), Paraguayan historian, journalist, and politician. Cardozo studied at the Asunción National College and obtained his doctoral degree in law from the University of Asunción in 1932. Secretary to Paraguayan President José Guggiari (1928–1931), he was also secretary of his country's delegation to the League of Nations Commission on the Chaco question (1933–1934). Professor at the Asunción National College, he served as secretary of the National Boundary Commission, was director of the daily newspaper *El Liberal* (The Liberal) in 1934, and founder of the daily *El Guaireño* in 1971. A multitalented literary and political figure, Cardozo served as congressman and senator, minister of justice, and minister of public instruction and in 1971 was elected president of Paraguay's Liberal

Radical party. His opposition to General Alfredo Stroessner's dictatorial regime led him into exile on several occasions. As a historian, Cardozo was able to use his political and diplomatic experience in his work on contemporary Paraguayan history, particularly with reference to the country's boundary disputes with its neighbors. Less partisan in these studies, such as the 1932 *Aspectos de la cuestión del Chaco* (Aspects of the Chaco Question), than most of his colleagues, he applied scrupulous documentary research techniques in order to determine the correct boundary lines, as shown in his 1930 *El Chaco en el régimen de las intendencias. La creación de Bolivia* (The Chaco During the Intendency Regime. The Creation of Bolivia). His interest in the War of the Triple Alliance (1865–1870), in which Paraguay nearly disappeared as a nation, led to the publication of *Visperas de la Guerra del Paraguay* (On the Eve of the Paraguayan War) in 1956 and of *El Imperio del Brasil y el Rio de la Plata, antecedentes y estallido de la Guerra del Paraguay* (The Brazilian Empire and the River Plate: Antecedents and Outbreak of the Paraguayan War) which earned him the Alberdi-Sarmiento Prize in Buenos Aires in 1961. Cardozo was also a noted historian of Paraguay's colonial past in which he saw the roots of the country's national heritage and published valuable studies on Paraguayan historiography and cultural tradition as well as a useful general survey of Paraguay's history.

Bibliography: Efraím Cardozo, *Breve historia del Paraguay* (Asunción, 1965); Efraím Cardozo, *El Chaco en el régimen de las Intendencias. La creación de Bolivia* (Asunción, 1930); Efraim Cardozo, *El Imperio del Brasil y el Río de la Plata. Antecedentes y estallido de la Guerra del Paraguay* (Buenos Aires, 1961); Efraím Cardozo, *El Paraguay colonial: las raíces de la nacionalidad* (Asunción, 1959); Efraím Cardozo, *Historiografía paraguaya* (Asunción, 1959); Efraím Cardozo, *Vísperas de la Guerra del Paraguay* (Asunción, 1956); Dennis Joseph Vodarsik, "Efraím Cardozo (1906–1973)," *Hispanic American Historical Review*, 54, no. 1 (February 1974): 116.

Nikita Harwich Vallenilla

CARRERA STAMPA, Manuel (Portsmouth, England, 1917–Mexico City, 1978), Mexican economic historian and archivist. Carrera Stampa took his first degrees in law and history at the National University of Mexico, studied at the National School of Anthropology, and later attended the recently founded Center for Historical Studies of the Colegio de México (College of Mexico). His early interest focused on art history, a subject on which he continued to write throughout his lifetime. He also soon became involved in archival research. Until 1949, he was known primarily for his articles, but that same year he published three major reference works that brought him considerable notoriety: *Missiones mexicanas en archivos europeos* (Mexican Missions in European Archives); *Planos de la ciudad de México desde 1521 hasta nuestros días* (The Maps of Mexico City from 1521 to the Present); and *Guía del archivo del antiguo Ayuntamiento de la Ciudad de Mexico* (A Guide to the Archive of Mexico City's Old Townhall), which for the first time brought the contents of this important municipal archive to the attention of the scholarly world. Also in 1949 he published in the *Hispanic American Historical Review* an article, "The Evolution of Weights and Measures in New Spain,'' which has been acknowledged as the standard reference on the subject. Carrera Stampa's contribution to Latin American archivology was further enhanced by his promotion of the International Committee on Archives of the Panamerican Institute of Geography and History and by the publication, in 1952, of *Archivalia Mexicana*, a general guide to Mexican archival collections, which for many years, became the indispensable research tool for Mexicanist scholars. After having completed postgraduate work at Northwestern and Georgetown universities and obtained his doctoral degree in history from the Colegio de México in 1953, Carrera Stampa was appointed professor at the University of Mexico's Faculty of Accounting and Administration. In 1956 he became a member of the Mexican Academy of History, where he served for many years as secretary. From the early 1950s on, he turned his attention primarily to the economic and social history of the colonial period. His 1954 book, *Los gremios mexicanos* (The Mexican Craft Guilds), provided a valuable assessment of the role played by these professional organizations in Mexico's colonial society. Finally, in the late 1950s and 1960s he took up the subject of Indian history, together with sideline fields of study such as the history of Mexico's mail service, the urban development of Mexico City, or the history of Mexico's National Academy of History. A thorough scholar, Carrera Stampa was less an analyst than a compiler of data, which he provided for the subsequent use and evaluation of his scholarly readers.

Bibliography: Charles Gibson, ''Manuel Carrera Stampa (1917–1978),'' *Hispanic American Historical Review* 59, no. 3 (August 1979): 476–477.

Nikita Harwich Vallenilla

CHAMORRO, Pedro Joaquín (Managua, 1891–Managua, 1952), Nicaraguan historian, journalist, politician, and diplomat. A member of a distinguished family of the Nicaraguan oligarchy, Chamorro completed his secondary school education in Nicaragua and El Salvador and graduated in law from the Eastern and Central University of Granada, Nicaragua, in 1918. Secretary of the Nicaraguan legation in Italy and at the Holy See (1921), he was appointed secretary of the liberal government of President José Moncada. Owner and director of *La Prensa* (The Press), one of Managua's leading daily newspapers, he was secretary at the 1938 Conference on the boundaries between Nicaragua and Honduras, celebrated in San José, Costa Rica. Considered an important figure in Nicaragua's intellectual development in the first half of the twentieth century, Chamorro was a strong advocate for the liberal principles of free press and freedom of thought, which led him to withstand, on various occasions, vicious attacks from the Somoza regime authorities. As a historian, he is known primarily for his important studies on Central America's nineteenth-century political evolution, particularly his *Historia de la federación de la América Central, 1823–1840* (History of Central America's Federation, 1823–1840), published in 1951, which provided a valuable documentary appendix and has become the standard reference work for the study of the period. Also worthy of interest is his 1933 study on the invasion of Nicaragua by the North American adventurer William Walker in 1856, *El último filibustero* (The Last Filibuster). Written in the traditional narrative vein, nonetheless, Chamorro's works objectively attempted to analyze the role the Spanish Catholic heritage played in Central American culture.

Bibliography: Pedro Joaquín Chamorro, *El último filibustero* (Managua, 1933); Pedro Joaquín Chamorro, *Historia de la federación en América Central (1823–1840)* (Madrid, 1951); Ernesto Mejía Sánchez, "Pedro Joaquín Chamorro," *Revista de Historia de América*, no. 34 (December 1952): 545–548.

Nikita Harwich Vallenilla

COSÍO VILLEGAS, Daniel (Mexico City, 1898–Mexico City, 1976), Mexican historian, writer, teacher, diplomat, and promoter of cultural institutions. After completing his secondary studies at the National Preparatory School, Cosío Villegas studied engineering, philosophy, and literature, and obtained his first degree in law from Mexico's National School of Jurisprudence in 1925. He later studied economics at Harvard University and agricultural economics at the Universtiy of Wisconsin, and obtained his master of arts degree from Cornell University. He also attended postgraduate-level courses at the London School of Economics and at the Paris École Libre des Sciences Politiques. During his long and distinguished career as a professor, he taught at the National Preparatory School, the National School of Jurisprudence, and the Schools of Law and of Philosophy and Letters of Mexico's Autonomous National University. He was also visiting professor at the Central University of Madrid and at the Institute of Latin American Studies of the University of Texas in Austin. Appointed general secretary of Mexico's Autonomous National University, he was instrumental in founding the National School of Economics, of which he became director in 1933, as well as its quarterly journal, *El trimestre económico* (The Economic Trimester), which he edited from 1934 until 1948. In 1935 he founded the prestigious publishing house Fondo de Cultura Económica (Economic Culture Fund) and served as its director from 1935 until 1949. He was cofounder of the School of Economics of the University of Nuevo León in Monterrey, and was a key promoter for the creation, in Mexico City, of the Casa de España (Spain House), the initial gathering place for a distinguished group of exiled scholars who had left Spain during the Civil War (1936–1939), which eventually became the Colegio de México (The College of Mexico), one of Latin America's most prestigious institutions for research and advanced study in the social sciences. President of the Colegio (1958–1963) and founder of its Center for Historical Studies, Cosío Villegas also served as founding editor (1951–1961) of the center's renowned journal, *Historia Mexicana* (Mexican History) and of *Foro Internacional* (International Forum), a journal specializing in international issues. Economic and financial adviser to the Mexican secretary of finance, and to the Mexican Central Bank and National Bank for Mortgages and Public Works, he was Mexico's special ambassador to the United Nations Economic and Social Council (1957–1968), president of the United Nations Special Fund, and president of the United Nations Economic and Social Council Coordination Committee.

The impressive achievements of Cosío Villegas' public career paralleled his multitalented scholarly endeavors as a historian, economist, sociologist, or political scientist. His early works, such as the two-volume study *Sociologia Mexicana* (Mexican Sociology), published in 1924, focused on an analysis of Mexico's national identity. Later studies concentrated on economic history issues, like his 1939 book *El comercio del azúcar en el siglo XVI* (The Sugar Trade in the Sixteenth Century). However, it was as a critical appraiser of contemporary Mexico's political and social developments that Cosío Villegas reached his greatest notoriety. The monumental ten-volume *Historia Moderna de México: 1867–1911* (Modern History of Mexico: 1867–1911), edited under his supervision and to which he contributed various chapters, paved the way for a subsequent analysis of the revolutionary and postrevolutionary periods, together with the edition of basic bibliographical guides. A lucid appraiser of Mexico's historical evolution, Cosío Villegas, in his later years, evaluated, at times with critical irony, the structures of his country's political system.

Bibliography: Martin Needler, "Review Essay: Daniel Cosío Villegas and the Interpretation of Mexico's Political System," *Journal of Inter-American Studies and World Affairs*, 18, no. 2 (May 1976): 245–251; Stanley R. Ross, "Daniel Cosío Villegas (1898–1976)," *Hispanic American Historical Review* 57 (1977): 91–103.

Nikita Harwich Vallenilla

CUERVO, Luís Augusto (Cúcuta, 1893–Bogotá, 1954), Colombian historian, politician, and diplomat. Soon after obtaining his doctoral degree in law from the National University of Bogotá (1915), Cuervo was elected mayor of Colombia's capital (1919) and served on various occasions as representative to the Colombian Congress. Governor of Santander, he was also Colombian minister plenipotentiary to Bolivia. A driving force behind the Colombian National Academy of History, he distinguished himself as editor of the *Boletín de Historia y Antiguedades* (Bulletin of History and Antiques). Like many of his contemporaries, Cuervo combined his political and diplomatic career with the teaching and writing of history. His scholarly research centered on Colombia's political history of the independence and postindependence periods, as well as on linguistic and cultural studies. He focused his attention on the various conventions, congresses, and meetings that were held during the years of the Gran Colombia Republic and on the political process that led to that republic's breakup in 1830. Based on numerous archival and documentary collections, Cuervo's work has been considered of great significance for later historians working on this particular period.

Bibliography: Luís Augusto Cuervo, *Apuntes historiales* (Bogotá, 1925); Luís Augusto Cuervo, *Notas históricas* (Bogotá, 1929); Luís Augusto Cuervo, *Ensayos históricos* (Bogotá, 1947); Luís Augusto Cuervo, *La Monarquía en Colombia* (Bogotá, 1916).

Nikita Harwich Vallenilla

DÍAZ DÍAZ, Oswaldo (Gachetá, Colombia, 1910–Bogotá, 1967), Colombian historian and playwright. Díaz Díaz studied at La Salle College and received his law degree from the Bogotá National University in 1935. Professor of literature and history in various Bogotá secondary schools, he was vice-rector of San Bartolomé College. Although his works were primarily produced on radio broadcasts, he achieved wide notoriety as a playwright; his theatrical writings were collected later in a four-volume edition (1963–1966). Díaz Díaz was also an acknowledged historian who specialized in the independence period of Colombia's history. He participated in the multivolume edition of the *Historia Extensa de Colombia* (Extensive History of Colombia) and was appointed secretary of the Colombian National Academy of History in 1961. One of his better known books was his 1962 *Los Almeydas: episodios de la resistencia patriótica contra el Ejército Pacificador de Tierra Firme* (The Almeydas: Episodes of the Patriotic Resistance Against the Mainland Pacifying Army), which traced the independence activity of a landowning family that led a guerrilla movement in Colombia's northeastern highlands. In a subsequent study, *La reconquista española* (The Spanish Reconquest), of 1964–1967, he broadened his coverage of the period and, based on a wide array of first-hand documents, concluded that Colombia's independence brought about deep social changes, as a result of the guerrilla struggle against the reestablishment of Spanish rule.

Bibliography: Oswaldo Díaz Díaz, *La reconquista española* (Bogotá, 1964–1967); Oswaldo Díaz Díaz, *Los Almeydas: episodios de la resistencia patriota contra el Ejército Pacificador de Tierra Firme* (Bogotá, 1962); J. León Helguera, "Oswaldo Díaz Díaz, 1910–1967," *Hispanic American Historical Review* 48, no. 3 (August 1968): 440–441.

Nikita Harwich Vallenilla

FURLONG CARDIFF, Guillermo (Villa Constitución, Santa Fé, Argentina, 1889–Buenos Aires, 1975), Argentine Jesuit priest and historian. The son of the Irish immigrants James Furlong and Anna Cardiff, Furlong Cardiff grew up in the Irish community of Santa Fé Province and it was only when he began secondary school in 1902 that he started to learn Spanish. In 1903 he joined the Jesuit order as a novice in Cordoba, and, in 1905, he was sent to Spain and to the United States to complete his education. After obtaining his Ph.D. from Georgetown University (1914), he returned to Argentina where he took up teaching positions at the Buenos Aires Seminary (1914–1916) and Saviour College (1916–1922). He also began research in the Buenos Aires National Archives, as well as in various provincial and private archive collections. He became a close friend of the Argentinian historian Enrique Peña who stimulated and encouraged his interest in historical investigation. From 1922 to 1926 he traveled across Europe, collecting archival material concerning the Guaraní wars (1753–1756), the Inquisition, and, more generally, the work of the Jesuit order in colonial South America. He also consulted many of the original manuscripts written by Jesuit missionaries who had been expelled from the Indies after 1767. He had excerpts of this material published in the Buenos Aires *Revista Ecle-*

siástica del Arzobispado (Archbishopric Ecclesiastical Journal). Upon his return to Argentina, via Brazil, he continued with his teaching and research occupations. Transferred to the Montevideo Sacred Heart College (1930–1935), he went through the Uruguayan National Archives as well as through numerous private archive collections. He also visited the Chilean and Bolivian archives. From 1935 on, he resumed his teaching duties at Saviour College. A founding member since 1938 of the Argentine National Academy of History, he was director of the La Plata Literary Academy and editor of its review *Estudios*.

With a more than forty-year-long career devoted to historical investigation, Furlong's bibliographical production reaches nearly two thousand items, including books, pamphlets, and articles. He was interested in a wide range of subjects and disciplines such as bibliographical studies, music, architecture, mathematics, medicine, and natural history. He even did some innovative work on the role of women in colonial society. He participated in geographic explorations and conducted ethnological and linguistic studies. One of his major achievements was his three-volume study *Historia social y cultural del Río de la Plata: 1536–1810* (The Social and Cultural History of the Río de la Plata: 1536–1810), published in 1969, in which he discussed, among other items, the important role played by craft guilds in colonial society. His main interest, however, focused on the missionary activity of the Jesuits in the colonial Río de la Plata region, which he staunchly defended against earlier criticism in works such as *Los Jesuitas y la cultura rioplatense* (1933; The Jesuits and the Río de la Plata Culture); and *Misiones y sus pueblos guaraníes* (1962; Missions and Their Guaraní Towns). He was thorough and precise in his writing, attempting, in his own words, to seek the truth concerning the people and events of a historical era.

Bibliography: Abel Rodolfo Geoghegan, "Bibliografía de Guillermo Furlong, S. J. (1912–1974)," in Academia Nacional de la Historia, *Boletín* 5, no. 48 (Buenos Aires, 1975): 401–546; Magnus Morner, "Obituary: Guillermo Furlong Cardiff (1889–1974)," *Hispanic American Historical Review* 55, no. 1 (February 1975): 92–94.

Nikita Harwich Vallenilla

GARCÍA, Genaro (Fresnillo, Mexico, 1867–Mexico City, 1921), Mexican historian. The son of Trinidad García, a distinguished member of Porfirio Díaz's cabinet, García received his early education in San Luis Potosi and later studied law in Mexico City, where he was admitted to law practice in 1891. He pursued an administrative career in the academic world as director of the National Preparatory School, director of the National Museum, and professor at the National Conservatory of Music and at the School of Jurisprudence. He was primarily a scholar, however, whose dedication to historical research led to the publication of nearly one hundred bibliographical entries. Many of these were collections of documents on Mexican history, particularly his seven-volume compilation *Documentos históricos mexicanos* (Mexican Historical Documents), published between 1910 and 1911. But Genaro García was also the author of carefully researched monographs that focused on the colonial and independence periods of Mexican history. Particularly worth mentioning is his *Carácter de la conquista española en América y en México* (1901; The Character of the Spanish Conquest in America and in Mexico), which triggered a widespread polemic over the ethics and righteousness of the Spanish Conquest in the New World. A thorough scholar, García collected research material throughout his lifetime. His personal historical library was considered to be one of the richest in all of Mexico. An important bibliographical compilation on Mexico's independence, on which he was working when he fell ill, was published posthumously in 1937.

Bibliography: Herbert I. Priestley, "Death of Genaro García," *Hispanic American Historical Review* 4, no. 4 (November 1921): 772–773.

Nikita Harwich Vallenilla

GARCÍA CALDERÓN, Francisco (Valparaiso, 1883–Magdalena, Peru, 1953), Peruvian historian. Literary critic, political philosopher, and diplomat. Son of Francisco García Calderón and Carmen Rey Basadre. García Calderón's father, the president of the Provisional Peruvian government, had been deported by the Chilean occupation forces during the War of the Pacific between Peru and Chile (1879–1884). Upon his return to Peru in 1889, he was elected senator and appointed rector of the San Marcos University of Lima where young Francisco graduated in philosophy and literature in 1903. Strongly influenced by the French neo-idealism of Henri Bergson and Emile Boutroux, Francisco García Calderón (the younger) was soon acknowledged as one of the main disciples of the Uruguayan writer José Enrique Rodó, whose essay, *Ariel*, served as the cultural reference point for a new generation of Latin American intellectuals. Shortly after his father's death in 1905, García Calderón moved to Paris with the rest of his family. Apart from a short trip back to Peru in 1910, he remained in Europe nearly until the end of his life. Minister plenipotentiary of Peru in Belgium (1911–1918) and France (1918–1920), where he attended the 1919 Versailles Peace Conference, he was dismissed from the Peruvian Diplomatic Service after Augusto B. Leguía's 1919 coup d'etat. Reappointed minister plenipotentiary to France upon Leguía's downfall in 1930, he was arrested in Vichy by the German occupying forces, when Peru joined the Anti-Axis Río de Janeiro Agreement of January 1942. Confined to the Aud Godesberg Castle near Bonn, he was later transferred to Geneva. He had been suffering for some time from an acute mental illness and, upon his return to Peru in 1947, he spent his remaining years in an asylum near Lima.

A prolific writer, García Calderón was one of the towering Latin American intellectual figures of his time. His articles and books dealt with literary topics as well as with many contemporary philosophical and political issues, such as World War I and the Russian Revolution, as well as the future of Europe, of idealistic philosophy, or of the League of Nations. However, his main contributions to Latin American historiography are to be found in his 1907 study of Peruvian society, originally written in French, *Le Pérou contemporain* and, above all, in *Les démocraties latines de l'Amérique* (1912), translated into English in

1913 under the title *Latin America: Its Rise and Progress* and in *La creación de un continente* (1913; The Creation of a Continent). A brilliant counterpoise to Alexis de Tocqueville's (q.v.) celebrated treatise on democracy in the United States, *Les démocraties latines de l'Amérique*, which was only first translated into Spanish in 1979, analyzes the evolution of Latin American societies, from the sixteenth century on, in an attempt to define and explain the essence and originality of their political and cultural institutions. A leading role as to the future progress of this multiracial and seemingly anarchic community of republics falls on its elites who can then, through an enlightened form of popular autocracy and the promotion of continental unity (an idea further expanded in *La creación de un continente*), seek common solutions to common problems and withstand the menacing alien forces of economic and cultural imperialism.

Bibliography: Francisco García Calderón, *Ideologías* (Paris: Garnier Hermanos, 1917); Francisco García Calderón, *La creación de un continente* (Paris: Paul Ollendorf, 1913); Francisco García Calderón, *Le Pérou contemporain: étude sociale* (Paris: Dujarric and Cie., 1907); Francisco García Calderón, *Les démocraties latines de l'Amérique* (Paris: Flammarion, 1912); Jorge Basadre, *Peru: problema y posibilidad. Ensayo de una síntesis de la evolución histórica del Perú* (Lima: Librería Francesa Científica, 1931); Benjamín Carrión, *Los creadores de la nueva América: José Vasconcelos, Manuel Ugarte, F. García Calderón y Alcides Arguedas* (Madrid: Sociedad General Española de Librarias, 1928); Mario Vargas Llosa, "Francisco García Calderón," *Cultura Peruana*, nos. 97 and 98 (Lima: July-August 1956).

Nikita Harwich Vallenilla

GIL FORTOUL, José (Barquisimeto, 1861–Caracas, 1943), Venezuelan historian, philosopher, politician, and diplomat. Son of José Espíritusanto Gil García and Adelaida Fortoul. Gil Fortoul's father was a distinguished political figure and a spokesman for the progressive wing of the Conservative party. After completing his secondary education at La Concordia College of El Tocuyo, Gil Fortoul studied law at Caracas Central University where he graduated in 1885 and was an active member of intellectual clubs such as the Sociedad de Amigos del Saber (Society of the Friends of Knowledge) which promoted the teachings of the positivist and evolutionist schools of thought. Appointed Venezuelan consul in Bordeaux (1886–1890), he became familiar with the works of Emile Durkheim, Gabriel Tarde, and Léon Duguit, among others, and wrote two important works: *Filosofía Constitucional* (Constitutional Philosophy) and *Filosofía Penal* (Penal Philosophy) which were published in Caracas in 1890 and 1891. From 1891 to 1910, with occasional trips back to Venezuela, Gil Fortoul pursued his diplomatic career in Europe, while contributing with numerous articles to various Caracas newspapers and journals. His growing interest in historical topics motivated the publication in 1896 of *El Hombre y la Historia* (Man and History), where he championed the need for a renewed interpretation of historical phenomena in the light of social evolution; history would then truly become a science in its own right. In 1898 the Venezuelan government commissioned him to write a *History of Venezuela* which he completed in two volumes between 1907 and

1909, under the title of *Historia Constitucional de Venezuela* (Constitutional History of Venezuela). Upon his return to Venezuela in 1910, he embarked on a political career that led him to become minister of public instruction (1911–1912), president of the Senate (1913 and 1915), president of the Government Council (1913), and president of the Republic (1913–1914) during the delicate transition period that witnessed the consolidation of Juan Vicente Gómez's dictatorial regime. He also inaugurated the chair of constitutional law at Caracas University in 1916. Between 1917 and 1924 he returned to Europe on several diplomatic missions. Even though Gil Fortoul defined himself as a "liberal democrat," he supported the Gómez regime because it meant a truce with regard to the violent confrontations that had existed among Venezuelan political parties throughout the nineteenth century and that, for him, represented one of the main stumbling blocks toward achieving national progress. After serving as director of the semiofficial regime newspaper *El Nuevo Diario* (The New Daily) from 1932 until 1934, he retired to private life.

Like many of his contemporaries, Gil Fortoul was a prolific writer. His books covered a wide range of topics, from novels and poetry (of a rather mediocre quality) to a treatise on fencing. His *Historia Constitucional*, however, stands out as a major achievement in positivist historiography and carried an impact even beyond the boundaries of his native land. He was one of the first to view the historical development of Venezuela as a whole, taking into account the country's economic, social, and psychological idiosyncrasy. His own as well as his family's political experience gave him first-hand knowledge, completed through documentary research, of the events he discussed.

Bibliography: José Gil Fortoul, *Historia Constitucional de Venezuela* (Caracas: Parra León Hermanos Editores, 1930), 3 vols.; José Gil Fortoul, *Obras Completas* (Caracas: Ediciones del Ministerio de Educacion, 1957), 8 vols.; Antonio Mieres, *Ideas positivistas en Gil Fortoul y en su historia* (Caracas: Universidad Central de Venezuela, 1981); Juan Penzini Hernandez, *Vida y obra de José Gil Fortoul* (Caracas: Ediciones de Ministerio de Relaciones Exteriores, 1972); Elena Plaza, *José Gil Fortoul. Los nuevos caminos de la razón: la historia como ciencia* (Caracas: Ediciones del Congreso de la República, 1985); Tomás Polanco Alcantara, *Gil Fortoul: una luz en la sombra* (Caracas: Editorial Arte, 1979).

Nikita Harwich Vallenilla

GONZÁLEZ, Juan Vicente (Caracas, 1811–Caracas, 1866), Venezuelan writer, journalist, teacher, and historian. A foundling at birth, González took up the name of his adoptive family. After he graduated from Caracas Central University in 1830, he began a lifetime career in political journalism. Initially a spokesman for the Venezuelan Liberal party, he soon changed his views and became a staunch defender of conservatism and achieved wide notoriety through his brilliantly written polemics. A teacher of grammar and history in various secondary schools, including his own El Salvador del Mundo (Saviour of the World) College, he also served a term in the National Congress in 1848. His outspoken opposition to what he considered injustice and errors in government, together with his irascible personality, gained him a wide reputation as a major critic of Venezuela's political system and, eventually caused his imprisonment in 1863. While in jail, he wrote his *Manual de historia universal* (Universal History Handbook) which soon became a standard textbook for secondary school history classes in Venezuela, as well as in several other Latin American countries. González wrote the book entirely from memory, without any kind of source materials. Despite these obvious limitations, the *Manual de historia universal* showed the influence of European romantic historians, particularly Italy's Cesare Cantù (q.v.), and developed a providentialist philosophy of history in the line of orthodox Catholic belief. These biases, however, did not hinder the work's high literary quality and original point of view in terms of what González considered to be Latin America's role within a worldwide perspective. Also worth mentioning is his biography of José Felix Ribas, one of the heroes of Venezuela's independence, which conveyed an epic dimension to the events narrated.

Bibliography: Juan Vicente González, *Biografía de José Felix Ribas* (Caracas: Ministerio de Educacion 1946); Juan Vicente González, *Historia del poder civil en Colombia y Venezuela* (Caracas: Librería Cruz del Sur, 1951); Diego Carbonell, *Juicios históricos. Juan Vicente González* (Caracas: Editorial Elite, 1938); Hector Cuenca, *Juan Vicente González* (Caracas: Fundacion Eugenio Mendoza, 1953); Antonio Mieres, *La Historia de Juan Vicente González en sus Fuentes* (Caracas: Universidad Central de Venezuela, 1977).

Nikita Harwich Vallenilla

GONZÁLEZ SUÁREZ, Federico (Quito, 1844–Quito, 1917), Ecuadorean prelate and historian. Because of his poor health as a child, González Suárez received most of his early education at home. After studying in the School of Law and Humanities at the University in Quito and at San Luis Seminary, he joined the Jesuit order from 1862 until 1872. He then served as secular priest in Cuenca (1872–1883), was elected to the Ecuadorean Senate in 1894, and was appointed bishop of Ibarra the following year. In 1906 he became archbishop of Quito. Throughout his lifetime, he combined his clerical duties with his intellectual pursuits, particularly in the field of historical research. He carefully studied the works of his predecessors, particularly the earlier general histories of Ecuador written by Juan de Velasco and Pedro Fermín Cevallos. His initial intention was to update the multivolume Cevallos study, but the amount of errors and gaps it contained made him decide to write his own version of Ecuadorean history. He started out his research in the Quito archives but soon found it necessary to spend an extended period of time at the Archives of the Indies in Seville. The first volume of his monumental *Historia general de la república del Ecuador* (General History of the Republic of Ecuador) was published in 1890 and revealed its author's great interest in using archaeological, as well as documentary, evidence in order to trace the development of Ecuador's indigenous population. In the six volumes that followed, the last one being published in 1903, González carried out a rigorous and critical analysis of the documents he used, while upholding the tenets of scientific historiography, regardless of the consequences. In this respect, the fourth volume of González's *Historia general* caused a fierce polemic, because in it he had criticized the Church, particularly the Dominican order, for several notorious scandals that had occurred during the colonial period. González felt it necessary to support his contentions before the Vatican which apparently acknowledged the documentary evidence he provided. In an essay published after his death under the title *Defensa de mi criterio histórico* (A Defense of My Historical Criteria), he wrote that he sought the truth in history and would not lie for any reason, even if it should cost him his clerical position. Up to the present day, González's *Historia general* remains a landmark in Ecuadorean historiography, while its author has been consecrated as one of the country's most outstanding modern historians.

Bibliography: Federico González Suárez, *Defensa de mi criterio histórico* (Quito, 1937); George A. Brubaker, "Federico González Suárez, Historian of Ecuador," *Journal of Inter-American Studies* 5, no. 2 (April 1963): 235–248; Nicolas Jiménez, *Biografía del ilustrísimo Federico González Suárez* (Quito, 1936); Federico González Suárez, *Historia general de la república del Ecuador, escrita por Federico González Suárez, presbitero* (Quito, 1890–1903), 7 vols.; Federico González Suárez, *Prehistoria ecuatoriana* (Quito, 1904).

Nikita Harwich Vallenilla

GUERRA Y SANCHEZ, Ramiro (Batabanó, Cuba, 1881–Havana, 1970), Cuban historian, sociologist, teacher, and diplomat. Guerra graduated in pedagogy from the University of Havana in 1899 and combined his teaching career with his research interest in Cuban history. He was professor of Spanish colonial and Cuban history at the University of Havana (1927–1930), and he served briefly as secretary to Cuba's President Gerardo Machado. Cuban delegate at the 1944 Bretton Woods Monetary and Financial Conference, he headed his country's delegation at the 1945 San Francisco Conference that completed the Charter of the United Nations Organization. He was Cuban representative at the United Nations Economic and Social Council in 1946, and he was appointed editor of the influential Havana daily newspaper *El Diario de la Marina* (The Navy Daily). Considered one of Cuba's outstanding modern historians, Ramiro Guerra applied a rigorous and critical analysis to the sources he used. He also insisted in considering Cuban history from a worldwide perspective. His 1927 study on the Cuban sugar industry, *Azúcar y población en las Antillas*, an abridged version of which was translated into English in 1964 under the title *Sugar and Society in the Caribbean*, was one of the first ever written on the subject and took into account its social as well as its economic and political aspects. In his *Guerra de los diez años* (Ten Years' War) which retraced the events of the 1868–1878 rebellion against Spanish rule, he analyzed the international implications of this preindependence movement. Guerra believed that history changes as new material appears and new interpretations develop. Consequently, there should be many historical studies of each particular event, as each new generation makes its contribution to the history of a given nation, which may, in turn, lead to a general synthesis of a country's historical development. Bearing this in mind, Guerra gave special attention to his two volume general survey of Cuban history, *Historia de Cuba*, first published in 1921–1925 and updated as a single-volume high school manual in 1938. He and various collaborators promoted the edition of the monumental ten-volume *Historia de la Nación Cubana* (History of the Cuban Nation), published in 1950–1952, which to this date remains a landmark in Cuban historiography.

Bibliography: Ramiro Guerra, *Azúcar y población en las Antillas*, 5th ed. (Havana: Casa de las Américas, 1961); Ramiro Guerra, *Guerra de los 10 anos, 1868–1878*, 3d ed. (Havana, 1972), 2 vols.; Ramiro Guerra, *Historia de Cuba* (Havana, 1921–1925), 2 vols.; Ramiro Guerra, *Manual de historia de Cuba*, 2d ed. (Havana, 1964); Francisco Dominguez-Company, ''Dr. Ramiro Guerra y Sánchez,'' *Revista de Historia de América*, no. 70 (July-December 1970): 498–500.

Nikita Harwich Vallenilla

JAIMES FREYRE, Ricardo (Tacna, Peru, 1868–Buenos Aires, 1933), Bolivian historian, politician, diplomat, and poet. Son of the historian and diplomat Julio Lucas Jaimes, who was Bolivian consul in Tacna at the time of his birth. After completing his studies at the San Marcos University of Lima, Jaimes Freyre returned to Bolivia, where he served as private secretary to President Mariano Baptista and was later appointed secretary of the Bolivian legation in Buenos Aires, where he became a close friend of the poets Leopoldo Lugones and Rubén Darío. In 1894, together with Darío, he founded in Buenos Aires the *Revista de América* (America's Magazine), an important landmark of the *modernista* literary movement, in which he published many of the poems he later collected in the volume *Castalia bárbara* (1899; Barbarous Castalia). Political motives kept him away from his home country, and between 1900 and 1920 he settled in the Argentinian town of Tucumán where he was a professor at the local National College and founded the *Revista de Letras y Ciencias Sociales* (Journal of Literature and Social Sciences) in 1905. His training in the social sciences was essentially self-taught. He traveled throughout South America and Europe, where he worked in the Spanish and British archives.

Jaimes Freyre's research was primarily concerned with the regional history of the Province of Tucumán, a subject on which he has been acknowledged as a foremost authority, through his various books: *Tucumán en 1810* (1909; Tucumán in 1810); *Historia de la República de Tucumán* (1911; History of the Tucumán Republic); *El Tucumán Colonial* (1915; Colonial Tucumán), among others. Although he became a naturalized Argentine citizen (1916), took up a chair at the University of Tucumán, and became one of the town's municipal councilors (1917), he returned to Bolivia in 1920 upon being elected to its National Congress. In 1921 he was appointed minister of public instruction. Then he served as Bolivian delegate to the League of Nations in Geneva, became minister of foreign relations (1922), and was sent as minister plenipotentiary to

Washington (1923) and as commissioner of Bolivian trade to Brazil (1924). He ran unsuccessfully for the Bolivian presidency in 1925 and returned in 1927 to Buenos Aires, where he spent his remaining years. Although better known as a poet and prominent figure of Latin America's literary heritage, he was nonetheless an accomplished historian, whose interests encompassed medieval European as well as Latin American history, which was quite unusual at the time. He was also a passionate writer, was concerned about the form and rigorously documented the content of his work.

Bibliography: Ricardo Jaimes Freyre, *El Tucumán colonial (documentos y mapas del Archivo de Indias)* (Buenos Aires, 1915); Ricardo Jaimes Freyre, *Historia de la edad media y de los tiempos modernos* (Buenos Aires, 1895); Ricardo Jaimes Freyre, *Historia de la República de Tucumán* (Buenos Aires, 1911); Ricardo Jaimes Freyre, *Los conquistadores* (Buenos Aires, 1962); Ricardo Jaimes Freyre, *Tucumán en 1810* (Tucumán, 1909); Manuel Carrasco, *Estampas históricas* (Buenos Aires, 1963).

Nikita Harwich Vallenilla

JIJÓN Y CAAMAÑO, Jacinto (Quito, 1890–1950), Ecuadorean historian, archaeologist, political leader, and industrialist. A member of a prominent and wealthy old family of the Quito Conservative oligarchy, Jijón y Caamaño attended the Central University of Quito and studied history under Archbishop Federico González Suárez (q.v.). A prominent politician and leader of the Conservative party (1924–1939), he was elected senator for the Pichincha Province and ran unsuccessfully for the Ecuadorean presidency in 1940. Professor at the Central University of Quito, he was also the owner of several wool and cotton textile mills in Ecuador and Colombia. Considered González Suárez' most accomplished disciple, Jijón y Caamaño was a strong advocate of an interdisciplinary approach to the study of history and developed a strong interest in archaeology. A dedicated researcher, he worked in various European and American archives and helped gather documentary evidence to support the contents of the controversial fourth volume of González Suárez' *General History of the Republic of Ecuador*. His own works centered primarily on the pre-Hispanic and colonial history of Ecuador. He undertook a critical reading of Juan de Velasco's chronicle and, through archaeological evidence, was able to set the grounds for the scientific study of Ecuador's pre-Hispanic cultures. As such, he has been considered one of his country's most significant historians.

Bibliography: Jacinto Jijón y Caamaño, *Antropología prehispánica del Ecuador* (Quito, 1952); Jacinto Jijón y Caamaño, *El Ecuador interandino y occidental ante de la conquista castellana* (Quito, 1940); Isaac J. Barrera, *Historiografía del Ecuador* (Mexico City, 1956).

Nikita Harwich Vallenilla

LEVENE, Ricardo (Buenos Aires, 1885–Buenos Aires, 1959), Argentine historian and promoter of cultural institutions. Levene studied at the Buenos Aires National College and graduated in law from the University of Buenos Aires in 1906. After teaching history at the National College (1906), he was appointed professor of sociology (1911), professor of judicial and social sciences (1914) at the University of Buenos Aires, and professor of history at the University of La Plata (1919), where he founded the Faculty of Humanities and Education, the Library of Human Sciences, and its scholarly journal *Humanidades* (Humanities). A prominent figure in Argentine higher education, he became dean of the Faculty of Humanities and later, as president of the University of La Plata, he expanded the institution's program of studies to include medicine and journalism and enlarged the schools of astronomy, agronomy, and veterinary science. Outside of university circles, he promoted the creation of the National Commission on Museums and Historical Monuments, over which he presided and which enabled him to oversee the restoration and conservation of Argentina's archaeological and historical remains. He founded and directed the Institute of Legal History and in 1926 established the Historical Archives of the Province of Buenos Aires. In 1938, he was also instrumental in converting the Junta of American History and Numismatics into the Argentine National Academy of History, which he later headed.

A prolific writer, considered one of the outstanding historians of twentieth-century Argentina, Levene, in his early years, concentrated on the late colonial and independence periods of Argentine history. Unlike most of his fellow historians, he did not limit himself to political history. His two-volume *Investigaciones acerca de la historia económica del Virreinato* (Research on the Economic History of the La Plata Viceroyalty), published in 1927–1929, was a pioneering study in its field. Levene also produced a number of important monographs on the history of Argentine law and wrote a number of penetrating essays on the social and cultural history of Argentina. His major work was the monumental ten-volume *Historia de la nación argentina* (History of the Argentine Nation), edited under his supervision between 1936 and 1942, and to which he contributed several chapters. One of his more controversial studies, *Las Indias no eran colonias* (The Indies Were Not Colonies), published in 1951, argued that Spain's American possessions were "provinces," or "ultramarine kingdoms," in accordance with the institutional provisions of the Castillian crown, and not mere colonies or trading factories. The point raised by Levene is still a matter of heated debate in Latin American-related historiography.

Bibliography: José M. Mariluz Urquijo, "Ricardo Levene, 1888–1959," *Hispanic American Historical Review* 39, no. 4 (November 1959): 643–646.

Nikita Harwich Vallenilla

LEVILLIER, Roberto (Paris, 1886–Buenos Aires, 1969), Argentine historian, journalist, and diplomat. Levillier's parents emigrated from France to Argentina when he was four years old. He received his early education in Buenos Aires and in 1900 began working for the daily newspaper *El País* (The Country). He continued his studies in Europe (1906–1907) and upon his return was appointed private secretary to the intendent of Buenos Aires, Manuel Güiraldes. He attended the University of Buenos Aires Law School and returned to Europe (1910–1915), where he became involved in historical research. His first monograph, *Orígenes Argentinos* (Argentine Origins), published in Paris in 1912, was intended as a sociological study, suggesting that a discernible Argentine community had existed since the sixteenth century. Levillier's research in the Archives of the Indies in Seville led to the subsequent publication of several documentary compilations on Argentina's colonial history (1915–1916). He later promoted the edition, sponsored by the Argentine Congress Library, of a multivolume collection of sources on Argentine history, which reproduced thousands of documents from the Spanish archives. He entered the Argentine foreign service in 1918 and served in several European and Latin American countries until his retirement in 1942. He pursued his diplomatic career together with his historical studies and was able to utilize the archival material of the various countries where he lived. During his stay in Peru (1922–1926), he completed the research for one of his more important works, the three-volume *Nueva crónica de la conquista de Tucumán* (New Chronicle of the Conquest of Tucumán), published between 1926 and 1932. In 1934 he proposed that the League of Nations Assembly edit a comprehensive history of America's indigenous cultures, but the project, though initially accepted, was finally scrapped.

In his later works, Levillier turned to biographies of Spanish conquerors in South America; of particular merit is his three-volume study on Francisco de Toledo, published between 1935 and 1942. After his retirement, Levillier became fully involved with historical research. His cartographical studies led to the publication of his two-volume *América, la bien llamada* (1947–1948; The Well-Named America), in which he analyzed the Spanish and Portuguese navigation routes to the New World in the fifteenth and sixteenth centuries. He later devoted an important two-volume work on the life and activity of Amerigo Vespucci. A distinguished member of Argentina's National Academy of History (since 1956) and a columnist of the Buenos Aires leading daily newspaper *La Nación* (The Nation), in his works Levillier acknowledged the positive role of the Spanish heritage in shaping the culture and traditions of Latin America.

Bibliography: Ricardo R. Caillet-Bois, "Roberto Levillier (1886–1969)," *Revista de Historia de América*, no. 71 (January-July 1971): 156–160; Atilio Cornejo, *Roberto Levillier, historiador de América* (Salta, 1952).

Nikita Harwich Vallenilla

MARIÁTEGUI, José Carlos (Moquegua, Peru, 1895–Lima, 1930), Peruvian writer, journalist, and political thinker. Mariátegui came from a lower middle-class family, never had more than an elementary education, and began working, at the age of fourteen, as an assistant linotype-operator and proofreader in a Lima newspaper. His early writings, between 1914 and 1917, included poems, plays, and literary essays. He also became involved with the Peruvian labor movement and defended the workers' cause in the magazine *La Razón* (Reason). Exiled to Europe (1919–1923) at the beginning of Augusto B. Leguía's dictatorial regime, he completed his education, learned to speak both French and Italian, and came into contact with the French and Italian intellectual left, particularly through Henri Barbusse and Antonio Gramsci (q.v.). He clarified his commitment to Marxist ideology and, from there on, directed his intellectual efforts to social criticism. Upon his return to Peru, he was at first associated with Victor Raul Haya de la Torre in the APRA (Alianza Popular Revolucionaria Americana) reformist movement (1924–1926), but he soon turned to a more radical position. Although Mariátegui never held a university chair, he occasionally lectured at Lima's recently founded Popular University, and he achieved wide notoriety through his articles, which appeared in newspapers and magazines of all political persuasions, as well as through his union-organizing activities. His home in Lima's Washington Street also became an important meeting place for students, workers, artists, writers, or anyone else who wanted to discuss current events, books, painting, music, politics, or a recent issue of his influential journal, *Amauta*, which he founded in 1926 and edited until his death. Whether or not Mariátegui was a founder or *the* founder of the Peruvian Communist party in 1928, of which he became the first general secretary, is a matter of debate, but as an intellectual and political activist, he was unquestionably dedicated to socialism.

Mariátegui's most important work consisted in a collection of essays, entitled *Siete ensayos de interpretación de la realidad peruana* (Seven Interpretative Essays on Peruvian Reality). First published in 1928, to date it has gone through more than forty editions, including translations in numerous foreign languages. The paradoxes of Peruvian society, radically divided between a tiny European-oriented élite who controlled wealth, education, and power and a vast majority of non-Spanish-speaking native Americans and mestizos who lived in their own separate worlds, were seen by Mariátegui as stemming directly from the monopolization of the country's resources by the conquering Europeans from the sixteenth century on. He thus presented a powerful interpretative model of Peru's history: "The Spanish conquerors destroyed this impressive [Inca] productive machine without being able to replace it. The indigenous society and the Inca economy were wholly disrupted and annihilated by the shock of the conquest. Once the bonds that had united it were broken, the nation dissolved into scattered communities." In global terms, Mariátegui anticipated the economic historians of the "Dependency School": "From the standpoint of world history, South America's independence was determined by the needs of the development of Western or, more precisely, capitalist civilization. The rise of capitalism had a much more decisive and profound influence on the evolution of independence than the philosophy and literature of the Encyclopedists." Mariátegui sought to achieve an original application of Marxist thought to Latin America's indigenous reality.

Bibliography: José Carlos Mariátegui, *Obras Completas* (Lima: Biblioteca Amauta, 1957–1970), 20 vols.; Hernando Aguirre Gamio, *Mariátegui, destino polémico* (Lima: Instituto Nacional de Cultura, 1975); Armado Bazán, *Mariátegui y su tiempo* (Lima: Biblioteca Amauta, 1969); Jesus Chavarría, *José Carlos Mariátegui and the Rise of*

Modern Peru (Albuquerque: University of New Mexico Press, 1979); Yerko Moretic, *José Carlos Mariátegui: su vida e ideario, su concepción del realismo* (Santiago de Chile: Ediciones de la Universidad Técnica del Estado, 1970); Guillermo Rouillón, *Bio-bibliografía de José Carlos Mariátegui* (Lima: Universidad Nacional Mayor de San Marcos, 1963); Harry E. Vanden, *National Marxism in Latin America. José Carlos Mariátegui's Thought and Politics* (Boulder, Colo.: Lynne Rienner Publishers, 1986).

Nikita Harwich Vallenilla and
Eduardo Pérez Ochoa

MEDINA, José Toribio (Santiago de Chile, 1852–Santiago de Chile, 1930), Chilean historian, diplomat, and bibliographer. Medina studied humanities and law at the Chilean National Institute and obtained his law degree in 1873. Secretary of the Chilean legation in Lima (1874), he fought in the War of the Pacific (1879–1884) and was appointed auditor of war of the Reserve Army, based in Bolivia's occupied territories. In 1886 he established his own printing press to publish his books and traveled widely throughout Latin America and Europe in search of bibliographical and documentary materials. He was a mul-titalented scholar, his interests ranging from history, anthropology, and num-ismatics to linguistics and literature. Acknowledged as Chile's and possibly Latin America's greatest bibliographer, he worked during his lifetime in practically every important archive and library from Mexico to Buenos Aires, as well as in Europe, particularly in Spain, where he served as first secretary of the Chilean legation in Madrid, and the Vatican. He published well over one hundred vol-umes, primarily documentary and bibliographical compilations referring to the colonial period. Of particular note are his thirty-volume *Colección de documentos inéditos para la historia de Chile desde el viaje de Magallanes hasta la batalla de Maipó* (1518–1818) (Collection of Unpublished Documents for the History of Chile from Magellan's Trip up to the Battle of Maipó [1518–1818]), published between 1888 and 1902; his seven-volume *Biblioteca Hispanoamericana: 1493–1810* (Hispanic American Library: 1493–1810), published between 1898 and 1907; and his three-volume *Biblioteca Hispano-Chilena*) (Hispanic Chilean Li-brary), published between 1897 and 1899. He was thorough and methodical in his assessment of the documents, which he not only reproduced but often also carefully annotated.

Medina also collected documentary material for a history of the Araucanian Indians, as well as for the study of the colonial press in Chile and several other Latin American countries, particularly Mexico. He later became interested in the history of the Inquisition in America and used the material he had copied from the Archives of the Indies in Seville and from the Vatican Archives for the publication of various monographical studies on the activity of the Inquisition in Peru (1887), Chile (1890), New Granada (1899), the Provinces of the River Plate, and Mexico (1905), as well as for a general introductory work, *La Primitiva Inquisición americana* (1491–1569) (The Early American Inquisition [1491–1569]). He was critical of the role played by the Inquisition Courts and of the lingering influence he considered they had left on Latin America's collective mentality. A tireless worker and an astute collector of historical documents, José Toribio Medina gathered a considerable personal library and archive as well as a valuable collection of coins and medals, which he donated to Chile's National Library in 1923. His books are still considered prime reference material for the study of colonial Latin America.

Bibliography: Maury A. Bromsen, ed., *José Toribio Medina, Humanista de América* (Santiago, 1969); Armando Donoso, *José Toribio Medina (1852–1930)* (Santiago de Chile, 1952); Sarah Elizabeth Roberts, *José Toribio Medina. His Life and Works* (New York, 1941).

Nikita Harwich Vallenilla

MITRE, Bartolomé (Buenos Aires, 1821–Buenos Aires, 1906), Argentine historian, political leader, and statesman. Mitre belonged to a long-established Buenos Aires family. His father, Ambrosio Mitre, had been an active participant in the May 1810 independence movement. He spent his early childhood in the small provincial town of Carmen de Patagones, on the Río Negro, and, because of his family's opposition to Juan Manuel de Rosas' dictatorial regime, he emigrated to Montevideo, where he graduated from the Military Academy in 1839. He became embroiled in the violent political struggles of Uruguay, Bolivia, Peru, and Chile, alternating exile with appointments such as that of director of Bolivia's Military Academy (1849). In Chile, he worked as a journalist, both in Valparaiso and Santiago, and he became a close friend of his compatriot in exile Domingo Faustino Sarmiento (q.v.). In 1851 he returned to Uruguay, joined the forces of the Argentine leader Justo José de Urquiza, and participated in the decisive battle of Caseros (1852) which marked the downfall of the Rosas regime. His rising political career led him to be elected governor of the Buenos Aires Province in 1860, but he soon came to oppose Urquiza, an opposition that was finally solved in the battlefield with Mitre's victory at Pavón (1861). Elected president of a unified Argentine Republic (1862–1868), Mitre brought peace to the traditionally antagonistic provinces under his jurisdiction, encouraged economic development through the construction of roads and ports, and promoted public education with the creation of the Buenos Aires National College.

After his presidency, Mitre remained active in foreign affairs, while serving as senator for Buenos Aires. He was also the founder, in 1870, of one of Argentina's leading daily newspapers, the Buenos Aires based *La Nación* (The Nation). In 1874 he once again ran for the presidency but lost the election and afterward launched an unsuccessful rebellion against the new government. Captured and imprisoned, he was soon pardoned and remained a respected figure of Argentine politics until his death.

A multitalented personality, Mitre was a distinguished journalist and writer, as well as a knowledgeable bibliophile, and dedicated a lifelong interest to the study of Argentina's history. He dealt mainly with the political history of the independence period and is known primarily for two major biographical works:

Historia de Belgrano y de la independencia argentina (History of Belgrano and of Argentine Independence), originally published in 1859; and *Historia de San Martín y de la emancipación sudamericana* (History of San Martín and of South America's Emancipation), published in three volumes between 1887 and 1890. Mitre insisted that the historian should examine all available evidence, particularly primary documents. For his biography of San Martín, he personally visited all the battlefield sites and drew his own cartographical sketches when no precise maps were available. In his later years, he developed the outline for a *Historia del descubrimiento, conquista y población del Rio de la Plata* (History of the Discovery, Conquest, and Population of the River Plate), which remained unfinished. He founded the Institute of History and Geography, both in Montevideo and Buenos Aires, for the protection of archival materials and the sponsorship of historical research. He advocated a precise, detailed, and erudite form of historical writing, which some criticized as dull and unimaginative but which he believed was necessary as the initial stage for the proper clarification of the events of the past. In this respect, Mitre has been considered the founder and leader of modern Argentine historiography.

Bibliography: Bartolomé Mitre, *Obras Completas* (Buenos Aires, 1938–1942), 10 vols.; Ángel Acuña, *Mitre historiador* (Buenos Aires, 1936), 2 vols.; Ricardo R. Caillet-Bois, *El americanismo de Mitre y la crítica histórica* (Buenos Aires, 1971); William H. Jeffrey, *Mitre and Argentina* (New York, 1942); Ricardo Levene, *Las ideas históricas de Mitre* (Buenos Aires, 1940).

Hebe Carmen Pelosi and Isabel De Ruschi

MOLINARI, Diego Luis (Buenos Aires, 1889–Buenos Aires, 1965), Argentine historian, politician, and diplomat. Molinari graduated in law from the University of Buenos Aires, where he held the chairs of Argentine history in the Faculty of Philosophy and Literature (1933–1946) and economic history in the Faculty of Economics (1934–1946). Minister plenipotentiary to several Latin American countries (1917–1922), he was a Radical party congressman (1924–1928) and senator (1928–1930) and later became Peronist senator for Buenos Aires (1948–1952). Director of the Institute for Historical Research of the Faculty of Philosophy and Literature of the University of Buenos Aires, he was one of the leading scholars of the so-called Revisionist School in Argentine historiography. His first book, *La representación de los Hacendados, su ninguna influencia en la vida económica y en los sucesos de Mayo de 1810* (The Landholders' Representation, Its Total Lack of Influence on the Economic Life and on the Events of May 1810), originally published in 1914, proved wrong all the previous interpretations of the event that triggered Argentina's independence movement. He later wrote several important studies on the slave trade and Portuguese policies in the River Plate area during the sixteenth and seventeenth centuries, and further analyzed the background years of the May Revolution. However, his more renowned "revisionist" interpretations focused on Argentina's nineteenth-century caudillos. Particularly in *Prolegomenos de Caseros* (Prolegomena to Caseros), written in 1962, he reanalyzed the controversial figure of Juan Manuel de Rosas, who dominated Argentina's history between 1829 until his fall in 1852, and who had previously been consistently denigrated by the country's traditional historiography. Molinari saw the fall of Rosas as the first step toward a renewed form of "colonialism," embodied in the subservience to Europe which characterized all the subsequent liberal governments. Far from being merely a bloodthirsty barbarian, Rosas had also represented a social, economic, and cultural alternative in Argentina's historical development. Molinari's interpretation undoubtedly provided a scholarly breakthrough for the study of nineteenth-century Argentina. However, the obviously implied parallel between Rosas and Juan Domingo Perón carried the historical controversy well into the forefront of present-day Argentina's political debate.

Nikita Harwich Vallenilla

MORA, José María Luis (San Francisco de Chamacuero, Mexico, 1794–Paris, 1850), Mexican priest, political leader, journalist, diplomat, and historian. Mora obtained his doctoral degree in theology in 1819 from Mexico City's San Ildefonso College, where he later taught philosophy, history, and law and opened the first course in political economy. In the chaotic years of Mexico's postindependence, Mora emerged as one of the country's leading political thinkers. Although a priest, he laid the foundations for Mexican liberalism and supported a number of issues, such as secular control over education and nationalization of Church wealth, which became the rallying banners of the country's anticlerical movement. Mora's ideas not only influenced the reforms of the Benito Juárez regime, but also played a significant part in the ideological debates of the 1910 Mexican Revolution. As a historian, Mora is chiefly remembered as the author of the three-volume study *México y sus revoluciones* (Mexico and its Revolutions), published in Paris in 1836, which stands in Mexican historiography as a counterpoise to Lucas Alamán's (q.v.) *Historia de México* (History of Mexico). As an intellectual vitally involved in Mexico's political strife, Mora was not concerned by his writings' lack of objectivity. He viewed his country's historical development from a liberal perspective, in opposition to Alamán's conservative interpretation, and argued for the necessary renovation of Mexico's political and social system. Yet, at the same time, his unquestionable literary talent and deep knowledge of the events he depicted were combined to produce a valuable and penetrating analysis of Mexico's past heritage and contemporary socioeconomic conditions.

Bibliography: José María Luis Mora, *México y sus revoluciones* (Paris, 1836), 3 vols.; José María Luis Mora, *Obras sueltas*, 2d ed. (Mexico City, 1963); Arturo Arnaiz y Freg, *Estudio biográfico del doctor en teología y licenciado en derecho, don José María Luis Mora* (Mexico City, 1934); Charles A Hale, *Mexican Liberalism in the Age of Mora, 1821–1853* (New Haven, Conn.: Yale University Press, 1968); Joaquín Ramírez Cabañas, *El doctor Mora* (Mexico City, 1934).

Nikita Harwich Vallenilla

MORENO, Gabriel René (Santa Cruz de la Sierra, 1836–Valparaiso, 1908), Bolivian historian, bibliographer, and literary critic. Moreno began his studies in his native town and continued his education in Sucre, Bolivia, and in La Serena, Chile (1854). He studied humanities at the San Luis College and graduated in law from the Santiago National Institute (1858). Gabriel René-Moreno spent most of his life in Chile where he was appointed professor at the Santiago National Institute. From the early 1860s on he began to hyphenate his middle surname with his family name. He has been considered one of the major bibliographical and documentary historians of his age. His early works include a number of critical essays on Bolivian literature. His bibliographies, which were published between 1874 and 1905, deal essentially with Bolivian topics and are not just mere lists of books, pamphlets, newspaper references, or archival collections. Each volume carries a lengthy introduction, which constitutes a genuine historical study, and most entries carry a carefully annotated critical and interpretative analysis. Influenced by positivist historiography, Moreno emphasized the need for extensive research based on primary documentation. At the same time, in works such as the two-volume *Ultimos días coloniales en el Alto-Perú: Documentos inéditos, 1808* (1896–1901; The Last Colonial Days in Upper Peru: Unpublished Documents, 1808), Moreno focused on the social forces that come into play within a given society, as well as on their cultural and psychological motivations. Criticized because of his sometimes brash statements, particularly with regard to what he considered the negative effects of racial mixture in Latin America's social evolution, Gabriel René-Moreno left a permanent mark on Bolivian historiography. His lifelong dedication to research led him to collect an impressive personal library which at the end of his life he donated to the Bolivian government.

Bibliography: Valentín Abecía Baldivieso, "El historiador Gabriel René-Moreno," *Revista de Historia de America*, no. 88 (July-December 1979): 123–153; Ramiro Condarco Morales, *Grandeza y soledad de Moreno* (La Paz: Talleres Gráficos Bolivianos, 1971); Enrique Finot, *Elogio de Gabriel René-Moreno* (Washington, D.C., 1934); Juan Siles Guevara, *Contribución a la bibliografía de Gabriel René-Moreno* (La Paz: Universidad Mayor de San Andrés, 1967).

                                                                  Nikita Harwich Vallenilla

O'LEARY, Juan Emiliano (Asunción, 1880–Asunción, 1968), Paraguayan historian, educator, and diplomat. After graduating from the Asunción National College in 1899, O'Leary attended the National University of Paraguay. He held the chairs of geography, Spanish literature, and American history at the Asunción Teacher Training School and National College. Appointed director of the National College (1910–1917), he served as a conservative Colorado party congressman in the Paraguayan Chamber of Deputies. He later served as his country's diplomatic representative in Spain, Italy, and the Holy See and became director of Paraguay's National Archives, Museums, and Libraries in 1934. His archival work was particularly significant in that he helped rebuild the Paraguayan archives, which had been virtually destroyed during the War of the Triple Alliance (1865–1870). His research interest was focused mainly on Paraguayan nineteenth-century history, specifically on the origins and events of the disastrous War of the Triple Alliance. His *Historia de la Guerra del Paraguay contra la Triple Alianza* (History of Paraguay's War against the Triple Alliance), published in 1911, initiated a revisionist school of historiography on the subject, which culminated with his classical study on the life and career of Paraguay's controversial nineteenth-century leader, Francisco Solano López. *El mariscal Solano López* (Field-marshal Solano López), first published in 1926, more than a biographical narrative, was a reinterpretation, based on carefully researched documentary evidence, of Paraguay's historical process. Contrary to what had been previously written, O'Leary convincingly showed that López had actually been a champion of Paraguayan nationalism.

Bibliography: Juan Emiliano O'Leary, *El mariscal Solano López* (Asunción, 1926); Juan Emiliano O'Leary, *El Paraguay en la unificación argentina* (Asunción, 1924); Juan Emiliano O'Leary, *Historia de la Guerra del Paraguay contra la Triple Alianza* (Asunción, 1911); Diego Carbonell, *Escuelas de Historia en América* (Buenos Aires, 1943).

Nikita Harwich Vallenilla

OROZCO Y BERRA, Manuel (Mexico City, 1816–Mexico City, 1881), Mexican engineer, politician, geographer, and historian. Educated at the Octaviano Chausal Lancasterian College of Mexico City, Orozco graduated in topographical engineering in 1834 and received a law degree in 1847. He alternated his law practice with the teaching of mathematics, was secretary of the Puebla municipal government, and later, served briefly as director of the National Archives. Secretary of development in 1862, he supervised the building of the Mexico City fortifications to withstand the impending French invasion. Though he was a supporter of Benito Juárez, he was unable to leave the capital city when the French arrived. He accepted Maximilian's rule and served in the imperial government as undersecretary of development (1864), counselor of state (1865), and director of the National Museum (1866). After Maximilian's downfall in 1867, Orozco y Berra was imprisoned and fined for collaborating with the French, but his past liberal record and critical attitude during the occupation soon allowed him to regain his moral and political stature. His early works included poetry and literary essays, but he then concentrated his attention on geography, ethnography, and history. In 1856 he published a book on Mexico's indigenous population, probably the first modern ethnographic study written in the country. He also became involved in a multivolume project, the *Diccionario universal de historia* (Universal Historical Dictionary), published between 1853 and 1856, including three volumes of appendices. A major reference tool in its time, though now antiquated, the *Diccionario* enabled Orozco to broaden the scope of his own research which focused primarily on the pre-Hispanic and colonial periods. He was one of the first in Mexico to make extensive use of auxiliary sciences such as anthropology, paleontology, ethnography, and, particularly, geography, when studying a given historical topic. He was thus one of the first Mexican scholars to approach history from an interdisciplinary perspective and used a similar "global" approach in his various works on Mexico's historical geography.

Bibliography: Manuel Orozco y Berra, *Historia antigua y de la conquista de México* (Mexico City, 1880), 4 vols.; Manuel Orozco y Berra, *Historia de la dominación española en México* (Mexico City, 1938), 4 vols.; Manuel Orozco y Berra, *Historia de la geografía en México* (Mexico City, 1880).

Nikita Harwich Vallenilla

ORTIZ Y FERNANDEZ, Fernando (Havana, 1881–Havana, 1969), Cuban jurist, ethnologist, sociologist, and historian. The son of a Spanish father and a Cuban mother, Ortiz y Fernandez spent his early years in the Balearic island of Menorca where he completed his secondary education (1894). He took his first law degree at the University of Barcelona (1901) and obtained his doctoral degree from the University of Madrid the following year. He then entered the Cuban consular service and was appointed in Genoa (1902–1906), where he also began academic research under the guidance of the famous Italian criminologist Cesare Lombroso. His first articles, which dealt with crime and suicide among blacks in Cuba and with the superstitious beliefs of Cuba's criminal population, were published in Lombroso's journal *Archivio di Psichiatria, Neuropatologia, Antropologia criminale e Medicina legale* (Archive of Psychiatry, Neuropathology, Criminal Anthropology, and Legal Medicine). These early essays, strongly influenced by Lombroso's legal positivism, led to the publication of *Hampa afrocubana. Los negros brujos (Apuntes para un estudio de etnología criminal)* [1906; Afro-Cuban Underworld. The Black Wizards (Notes for a Study on Criminal Ethnology)], with a preface signed by Lombroso. That same year, he returned to Cuba, where he was appointed district attorney to the Havana Courts, and, in 1908, he became professor of the Havana University Law Faculty. He continued his sociological studies on criminology, publishing his *Hampa afrocubana. Los negros esclavos. Estudio sociológico y de derecho público* (1916; Afro-Cuban Underworld. The Black Slaves. A Study in Sociology and Public Law). In 1917, as a Liberal party candidate, he was elected to the Cuban Congress, where he was an outspoken advocate of political reform. At the same time, he continued publishing various innovative studies on Cuban folk traditions and became editor of the influential *Revista Bimensual Cubana* (Cuban Bi-Monthly Review).

Ortiz's opposition to Gerardo Machado's dictatorial regime forced him into exile to the United States (1930–1933). Upon his return, he resumed his various academic and cultural activities, and in 1937 he founded the Society for Afro-Cuban Studies. His major historical work, *Contrapunteo cubano del tabaco y del azúcar*, translated into English in 1947 under the title *Cuban Counterpoint: Tobacco and Sugar*, was first published in 1940, with an introduction by the illustrious anthropologist Bronislaw Malinowski. In this classical study, based on the historical significance of tobacco and sugar in Cuban society, Ortiz, through a skillful multidisciplinary approach, provided a masterly synthesis of Cuba's collective soul. His later works, which include the penetrating 1947 essay *El Huracán, su mitología y sus símbolos* (The Hurricane, Its Mythology and Symbols), focus on African influences in Cuba's popular culture. Ortiz remained in Cuba after the 1959 Revolution and was one of the founders of the Cuban Academy of Sciences. Undoubtedly one of contemporary Latin America's most distinguished scholars, Fernando Ortiz shares with Brazil's Gilberto Freyre the merit of having recovered the significance of the African tradition for the understanding of Latin America's collective identity.

Bibliography: *Bio-bibliografía de don Fernando Ortiz* (Havana: Biblioteca Nacional José Martí, 1970); *Orbita de Fernando Ortiz* (Havana: Unión de Escritores Artistas de Cuba, 1973).

Nikita Harwich Vallenilla

OSPINA VÁSQUEZ, Luis (Medellín 1905–Medellín, 1977), Colombian economic historian. Grandson of the former President Mariano Ospina Rodríguez, Ospina Vásquez belonged to a wealthy family of the Colombian liberal oligarchy. He obtained his degree in law from the Bogotá National University and served briefly in the Departmental Assembly of Antioquia and in the Colombian National Senate. He was also a professor at the University of Medellín and a member of the Colombian National Planning Council. He specialized as a historian in a branch generally neglected in Latin American historiography: economic history. His fame as one of Colombia's leading economic historians rests primarily on one major book, published in 1955, *Industria y protección en Colombia: 1810–1930* (Industry and Protection in Colombia, 1810–1930). It deals with Colombia's industrial development throughout the nineteenth century, particularly with regard to the important role played by Medellín as the pioneering center for manufactured production, and analyzes the relationship between industrial growth and government policy. The book also includes an important introductory chapter on the colonial period. Because he suffered from gradual blindness in his final years, Ospina was forced to abandon scholarly research and devoted himself to the foundation of an institute for the study of his native region of Antioquia, which came into being in 1976 and for which he provided the library and permanent financial support.

Bibliography: Luis Ospina Vásquez, *Industria y protección en Colombia, 1810–1930* (Medellín, 1955); Frank Safford, "Obituary: Luis Ospina Vásquez," *Hispanic American Historical Review* 58, no. 3 (August 1978): 466–467.

Nikita Harwich Vallenilla

PARRA PÉREZ, Caracciolo (Mérida, Venezuela, 1888–Paris, 1964), Venezuelan historian, diplomat, and politician. Son of Ramón Parra Picón and Juana Pérez. After receiving his law degree from the Andes University of Mérida (1910), Parra Pérez traveled to Paris where he completed postgraduate studies in law and political science. In 1913 he entered the Venezuelan diplomatic service, served in France (1913–1919), Switzerland (1919–1926; 1937–1938), Italy (1927–1936), Great Britain (1936), and Spain (1939–1941), and headed the Venezuelan delegation at the General Assemblies of the League of Nations in Geneva from 1923 until 1939. Appointed minister of foreign affairs (1941–1945) by President Isaias Medina Angarita, he represented Venezuela at the 1945 San Francisco Conference, where he headed one of the Preparatory Commissions for the future United Nations organization and was the official reporter for the Universal Declaration of Human Rights with regard to the International Court of Justice of The Hague. Upon the overthrow of the Medina Angarita government by a military coup d'etat in October 1945, Parra Pérez was forced into a short exile and settled in Paris where he decided to spend the rest of his life. From 1951 until 1958 he headed the Venezuelan permanent delegation at Unesco, and in 1962 he was elected member of the Institut de France.

Together with his diplomatic career, Parra Pérez developed a lifelong dedication to historical research. Although his 1932 study *El régimen español en Venezuela* (The Spanish Regime in Venezuela) has been considered one of the more thorough general presentations of the Venezuelan colonial period, his main interest centered on the years of independence and the early nineteenth century, as seen through the lives of Francisco de Miranda, the precursor of Venezuela's emancipation, and of Santiago Mariño, one of Simón Bolívar's lieutenants. His biography of Miranda, originally published in French under the title *Miranda et la Révolution Française* (1925), was followed by several monographs including the *Historia de la Primera República* (History of the First Republic) of 1927. It was through Parra Pérez that Miranda's personal archives, which had been lost for over a century, were located in London in 1926 and brought back to Venezuela. His work on Mariño, which remained unfinished, consisted of the five-volume *Mariño y la Independencia de Venezuela* (Mariño and Venezuela's Independence) and its three-volume sequence *Mariño y las guerras civiles* (Mariño and the Civil Wars), all published between 1954 and 1960. The Miranda and Mariño studies, however, went far beyond a mere biographical narrative, placing the events described within the broader context of national and world developments, and showed the author's conscious tendency to define an idealistic philosophy of history in terms of the interaction between the individual and his own "historical circumstances."

Bibliography: Caracciolo Parra Pérez, *El Régimen Español en Venezuela* (Madrid: Javier Morata, 1932); Caracciolo Parra Pérez, *Historia de la Primera República de Venezuela*, 2d ed. (Madrid: Ediciones Guadarrama, 1959), 2 vols.; Caracciolo Parra Pérez, *Marino y la Independencia de Venezuela* (Madrid: Ediciones Cultura Hispánica, 1954–1957), 5 vols.; Caracciolo Parra Pérez, *Marino y las Guerras Civiles* (Madrid: Ediciones Cultura Hispanica, 1958–1960), 3 vols.; Caracciolo Parra Pérez, *Miranda et la Révolution Française* (Paris: Librairie Pierre Roger, J. Dumoulin, 1925); German Carrera Damas, ed., *El concepto de la historia en Caracciolo Parra Pérez* (Caracas: Universidad Central de Venezuela, 1962); Tomás Polanco Alcantara, *Con la pluma y con el frac. Rasgos biográficos del Dr. Caracciolo Parra Pérez* (Caracas: Banco Central de Venezuela, 1982).

Nikita Harwich Vallenilla

PRADO Y UGARTECHE, Javier (Lima, 1871–Lima, 1936), Peruvian jurist, political philosopher, and historian. Educated at the Lima Jesuit College, Prado y Ugarteche received his doctoral degree in jurisprudence from the University of San Marcos, where he later became professor of the history of philosophy, dean of the School of Letters, and rector (1915). Appointed minister of war and minister of foreign affairs during President Augusto B. Leguía's first administration, he successfully carried out the boundary settlement negotiations with Brazil, Bolivia, and Chile. His diplomatic achievements won him considerable prominence and led to his nomination as a Civil party candidate for the 1912 presidential elections, but internal political divisions caused him to withdraw. Associate justice of the Peruvian Supreme Court, he was elected several times to the Peruvian Senate (1908–1913 and 1919). Prado y Ugarteche belonged to Latin America's positivist generation. His early writings centered on the history of ideas and the development of philosophy in Peru. At the same time, he applied the theories of social evolution to the study of his country's historical processes. His major work in this respect, *El estado social del Perú durante la dominación española* (The Social Conditions of Peru during the Spanish Domination), published in 1894, became a historiographical landmark. During his term as rector of San Marcos University, he delivered a number of thought-provoking lectures in which he urged the renovation of historical and literary studies in Peru. His twenty-thousand-volume private library and particularly his archaeological collection of pre-Colombian objects, gained worldwide fame.

Bibliography: Javier Prado y Ugarteche, *El estado social del Peru durante la dominación española* (Lima, 1894); Javier Prado y Ugarteche, *El método positivo* (Lima, 1890); Javier Prado y Ugarteche, *La evolución filosófica* (Lima, 1891); Javier Prado y Ugarteche, *La nueva época y los destinos históricos de los Estados Unidos* (Lima, 1919).

Nikita Harwich Vallenilla

RAMA, Carlos M. (Montevideo, 1921–Rome, 1982). Uruguayan social and cultural historian. Rama graduated in law and social sciences from the University of Montevideo, where he later became professor of sociology and history. He also taught at the universities of Santiago de Chile and San Juan in Puerto Rico and was invited, as visiting professor, to the universities of Bordeaux and Barcelona. His early books were general works on the history of ideas; among these are *La Historia y la Novela* (History and the Novel) and *Las ideas socialistas en el siglo XIX* (Socialist Ideas in the Nineteenth Century), both published in 1947. He later turned his attention to the study of contemporary Spanish problems. While doing postgraduate research at the Sorbonne University and at the Paris Institut Français d'Histoire Sociale, between 1952 and 1954, he prepared the material for three important books on Spain: *La crisis española del siglo XX*

(The Spanish Twentieth Century Crisis), published in 1958; *Ideología, regiones y clases sociales en la España contemporánea* (Ideology, Regions and Social Classes in Contemporary Spain), published in 1960; and *Itinerario español* (A Spanish Itinerary), published in 1961. However, it is mainly as a specialist of contemporary Uruguayan and Latin American social history that Carlos Rama has achieved recognition. His chronology and bibliography of socialist and workers' movements in Latin America, originally published in French in a series sponsored by the *Institut Français d'Histoire Sociale* in 1959, paved the way for the subsequent studies *Las clases sociales en el Uruguay* (Social Classes in Uruguay) of 1960, the *Historia del movimiento obrero y social Latino-Americano contemporáneo* (The History of the Contemporary Latin American Social and Working-Class Movement) of 1967, and *Sociología de América Latina* (Latin American Sociology) of 1970. In this respect, Rama was a strong advocate for the revision of the traditional criteria that still governed most of Latin America's historiography and called for the application of new interdisciplinary perspectives to historical phenomena.

Bibliography: Carlos Rama, *Garibaldi y el Uruguay* (Montevideo, 1968); Carlos Rama, *Historia del movemiento obrero y social Latino-Americano contemporaneo* (Montevideo, 1967); Carlos Rama, *Las Clases sociales en el Uruguay* (Montevideo, 1960); Carlos Rama, *Sociología de América Latina* (Montevideo, 1970).

Nikita Harwich Vallenilla

RAVIGNANI, Emilio (Buenos Aires, 1886–Buenos Aires, 1954), Argentine historian, sociologist, and politician. Ravignani attended Buenos Aires National College and graduated in law from Buenos Aires National University in 1910. Professor of Roman law (1913) and sociology (1914–1916) at the University of La Plata, he also taught at the National College and at the University of Buenos Aires, where he became director of the Historical Research Institute (1921–1951) and editor of its influential *Bulletin*. A prominent member of Argentina's Radical party (Unión Cívica Radical), he served in the Buenos Aires municipal government and was elected to the National Chamber of Deputies (1936–1942 and 1946–1947). Exiled in Uruguay during Juan Domingo Perón's dictatorship, he organized the University of Montevideo's Institute of Historical Research. Ravignani trained several generations of Argentine historians and strongly contributed to the establishment of high standards for twentieth-century Argentine historical writing. The *Manual de historia de la civilización argentina* (History of Argentine Civilization Textbook), published in 1917 to which he contributed together with others, represented a major historiographical breakthrough in that it combined both a historical and sociological approach to the study of the nation's past and emphasized the need to consider Argentina's historical processes from a regional perspective. Ravignani also promoted the application of geography and cartography to historical writings. Yet, his own major contribution was in the field of constitutional history, particularly with his six-volume study *Las Asambleas constituyentes argentinas* (Argentina's Constituent Assemblies), which for the first time provided the faithful transcription of many important documents, a critical assessment of their content, as well as a detailed analysis of the underlying political and social context of Argentina's parliamentary evolution.

Bibliography: Emilio Ravignani, *Asambleas constituyentes argentinas* (Buenos Aires, 1937–1940), 6 vols.; Emilio Ravignani, *Cartografía histórica americana: Un censo de la provincia de Buenos Aires en la época de Rosas, año 1836* (Buenos Aires, 1922); Emilio Ravignani, *El pacto de la Confederación Argentina* (Buenos Aires, 1938); Emilio Ravignani, *Historia del derecho argentino* (Buenos Aires, 1919); Emilio Ravignani, *Una comprobación histórica: el comercio de ingleses y la "Representación de Hacendados" de Moreno* (Buenos Aires, 1914); Romulo D. Carbía, *Historia crítica de la historiografía argentina* (La Plata, 1939); *Homenaje a E. Ravignani* (Buenos Aires: Academia Nacional de la Historia, 1941); "Obituaries: Emilio Ravignani," *Hispanic American Historical Review* 34, no. 3 (August 1954): 417.

Nikita Harwich Vallenilla

REAL DE AZÚA, Carlos (Montevideo, 1916–Montevideo, 1977), Uruguayan historian and politician. Real de Azúa attended the Montevideo University of the Republic. He initially followed his family's political tradition and became a member of the conservative Colorado party. His devoutly Catholic upbringing influenced his youthful admiration for José Antonio Primo de Rivera's Spanish Phalangist movement, which he publicized in his book *España de cerca y de lejos* (Spain at Close Range and from Afar), written in 1943 upon his return from a trip to the Iberian peninsula. He soon evolved toward a more detached view with regard to dogmatic ideologies and eventually left the Colorado party. His critical assessment of his country's political evolution, coupled with a militant anti-imperialistic stance, convinced him of the need to reevaluate, as rigorously as possible, the turbulent twentieth century of Uruguay's history. His major work, *El patriciado uruguayo* (1961; The Uruguayan Patriciate), considered by scholars as a classic in Latin American historiography, both explained and denounced what he saw as the failure of the country's oligarchy in devising a sound political and social system. In his later book, *El impulso y el freno* (The Curbed Impulse), Real de Azúa further illustrated his previous arguments through his analysis of the three-year government term of Uruguay's President Luis Batlle Berres (1947–1950). The Uruguayan welfare state, of which Batlle was a well-meant exponent, was, according to Real de Azúa, but an illusion that would eventually lead to economic, social, and political collapse.

Bibliography: Carlos Real de Azúa, *El impulso y su freno* (Montevideo, 1964); Tulio Halperín Donghi, "Obituary: Carlos Real de Azúa," *Hispanic American Historical Review* 58, no. 4 (November 1978): 697–699; Carlos Real de Azúa, *El patriciado uruguayo* (Montevideo, 1961); Carlos Real de Azúa, *España de cerca y de lejos* (Montevideo, 1943).

Nikita Harwich Vallenilla

RESTREPO, José Manuel (Emvigada, Colombia, 1781–Bogotá, 1863), Colombian historian and statesman. Restrepo studied at the San Bartolomé College of Bogotá and was received as a lawyer before the Bogotá Royal Audiencia in 1808. Secretary to the governor of the province of Antioquia, Dionisio Tejeda, he was elected, as representative for Antioquia, to the First Congress of the United Provinces of New Granada in 1811 and in 1814 he was part of the executive triumvirate of the independent republic of New Granada. During the course of the independence wars, he was forced to seek refuge in Jamaica and, later, in the United States. Political governor of Antioquia (1819), he was elected deputy to the 1821 Cúcuta Congress and helped draft the constitution of the republic that united the former territories of Ecuador, Venezuela, and Colombia. Minister of the interior (1821–1830) during the stormy years of Simon Bolívar's leadership, he was sent, after the dissolution of Gran Colombia, as minister plenipotentiary to Ecuador (1831) and was later appointed president of Colombia's Academy of Arts, Sciences, and Letters (1833) and director of public credit. An important eyewitness to South America's independence movement, Restrepo made a conscious effort, throughout his public career, to collect documents, pamphlets, newspapers, and other materials that would enable him to write about those events he had lived through. His ten-volume *Historia de la revolución de la república de Colombia* (History of the Colombian Republic Revolution) was first published in Paris in 1827; a revised second edition, which included the section on the history of the independence revolution in Venezuela, was published in Besançon in 1858. One of the first authoritative detailed chronicles of the wars of independence, the work also attempted to explain and analyze, as objectively as possible, the historical significance of these events. Restrepo, as such, has been rightfully considered one of the founding fathers of modern Colombian historiography. Also worth mentioning is the diary he wrote during his exile in the United States, *Diario de un emigrado* (An Emigré's Diary), because of the many interesting insights he gives on the society and customs of the Northern Republic. Several of his unpublished manuscripts, including his military diary, his autobiography, and his *Historia de la Nueva Granada* (History of New Granada), which dealt with the period between 1832 and 1859, were published a century later by his grandson, Monsignor José Restrepo Posada.

Bibliography: José Manuel Restrepo, *Historia de la Nueva Granada* (Bogotá: Editorial Cromos, 1952), 2 vols.; José Manuel Restrepo, *Historia de la revolución de la república de Colombia* (Medellín: Editorial Bedout, 1970), 6 vols.; Rafael M. Meza Ortíz, *Don José Manuel Restrepo* (Bogotá, 1948).

Nikita Harwich Vallenilla

ROJAS, Arístides (Caracas, 1826–Caracas, 1894), Venezuelan naturalist, historian, philologist, and bibliographer. Son of José María Rojas Ramos and Dolores Espaillat, who had emigrated to Venezuela from the island of Santo Domingo in 1822. Young Arístides attended the Independence College of Caracas, as well as the literary and political discussions that took place in his father's famed nearby bookstore and printing shop. He studied at Caracas Central University where he graduated in medicine in 1852. Following his father's death in 1855, he, together with his brother Marco Aurelio, took over the family business. From 1857 until 1864, he completed postgraduate studies in medicine and the natural sciences in Europe and the United States and settled, for a time, in Puerto Rico. Strongly influenced by the work of Alexander von Humboldt, he was a promoter of the new scientific theories on evolution, but, at the same time, he believed it necessary to combine the aesthetic quality of literary thought with the rigor of scientific endeavors. He wrote on multiple subjects such as geology, seismology, and statistics, published children's textbooks, explored various parts of Venezuela, and was the founder, in the early 1870s, of the American Bibliographic Society. From 1875 until the end of his life, he set aside his medical practice and devoted himself entirely to research and writing, surrounded by his extensive personal library and his various collections of coins, pre-Hispanic objects and botanical species. His *Estudios indígenas. Contribución a la historia antigua de Venezuela* (Indigenous Studies. A Contribution to the Ancient History of Venezuela), published in 1878, was one of the first major works to consider the scientific knowledge of its pre-Hispanic populations as a necessary prerequisite for the historical understanding of Venezuela's culture and nationality. In 1890 the Venezuelan government commissioned the publication of his numerous notes and studies on the country's history, but only the first volume of his *Estudios históricos. Orígenes venezolanos* (Historical Studies. The Venezuelan Origins) came out in his lifetime (1891). A multitalented Renaissance man, Arístides Rojas has been considered the founding father of scientific research applied to the study of Venezuela's history.

Bibliography: Pedro Grases, *Bibliografía de Don Arístides Rojas (1826–1894)* (Caracas: Fundación para el Rescate del Acervo Documental Venezolano, 1977); Enrique Bernardo Nuñez, *Arístides Rojas: anticuario del Nuevo Mundo* (Caracas: Ediciones de *El Universal*, 1944); Juan Saturno Canelón, *Arístides Rojas, mensajero de la tolerancia* (Caracas: Litografía del Comercio, 1944); Arturo Uslar Pietri, *Arístides Rojas (1826–1894)* (Caracas: Fundación Eugenio Mendoza, 1953).

Nikita Harwich Vallenilla

ROJAS, Ricardo (Tucumán, Argentina, 1882–Buenos Aires, 1957), Argentine historian, journalist, politician, and academic. Rojas attended secondary schools in Santiago del Estero and Buenos Aires and graduated from the University of Buenos Aires. He was a regular contributor for Argentine capital daily newspapers *El País* (The Country) and *La Nación* (The Nation). Professor of literature at the University of La Plata (1909–1920) and at the University of Buenos Aires (1913–1946), and he was dean of the Institute of Argentine Literature (1926–1930) and rector of the University of Buenos Aires (1926–1930). He also initiated the chair of Hispanic American Studies at the University of Madrid in 1928. A prominent leader of the Argentine Radical party, he was sent to prison and subsequently exiled to Tierra del Fuego in 1934 and ran for the Senate in 1946. A true and widely traveled man of letters, Rojas wrote on a variety of subjects, including poetry, drama, literary criticism, politics, philosophy, education, and folklore. In his historical works, he was particularly concerned with strengthening the Argentine national spirit. While acknowledging the heritage of Western culture, Rojas saw the need to convey to Argentina's massive population of immigrants a renewed sense of pride for their adopted country. He thus opposed Argentina's cultural regionalism and, toward this end set forth examples of national achievements in his widely publicized biographies of José San Martín, *El Santo de la Espada: Vida de San Martín* (The Saint of the Sword: The Life of Saint Martin) and of Domingo Faustino Sarmiento (q.v.), *El Profeta de la Pampa*: *Vida de Sarmiento* (The Prophet of the Pampa: The Life of Sarmiento). At the same time, while upholding the advantages of liberalism and political democracy, he praised Spain's role in the formation of Argentina's as well as Latin America's cultural heritage.

Bibliography: Ricardo Rojas, *El Profeta de la Pampa: Vida de Sarmiento* (Buenos Aires, 1945); Ricardo Rojas, *El Santo de la Espada: Vida de San Martín* (Buenos Aires, 1933); Ricardo Rojas, *Ensayo de crítica histórica sobre episodios de la vida internacional argentina* (Buenos Aires, 1951); Ricardo Rojas, *Eurindia: ensayo de estética fundado en la experiencia histórica de las culturas americanas* (Buenos Aires, 1924); Ricardo Rojas, *La restauración nacionalista* (Buenos Aires, 1909); Earl T. Glauert, "Ricardo Rojas and the Emergence of Argentine Cultural Nationalism," *Hispanic American Historical Review* 43, no. 1 (February 1963): 1–13.

Nikita Harwich Vallenilla

SALDÍAS, Adolfo (Buenos Aires, 1850–La Paz, 1914), Argentine historian and politician. Saldías studied at the Buenos Aires National College and obtained his law degree in 1874. He combined political involvement, as a member of the National Autonomist party, with an active career as a journalist and writer and a lifelong dedication to historical research and analysis. His first historical work was a monograph on Argentine freemasonry, to which he belonged. Elected to the Buenos Aires legislature in 1877, he published, the following year, his *Ensayo sobre la historia de la Constitución Argentina* (Essay on the History of the Argentine Constitution), where he argued that a genuine sense of national unity and constitutional government in Argentina had resulted from Bartolomé Mitre's (q.v.) victory at the battle of Pavón in 1861, which marked the end of a long period of civil strife. The regional caudillos had been defeated, and it was now possible for Mitre to impose the rule of law over the rule of men. However, because of his participation in the unsuccessful insurrection of Buenos Aires in 1880, Saldías was forced into a brief exile. Upon his return, he was appointed professor at the University of La Plata and was elected to the 1882 Constituent Assembly. Between 1881 and 1887, he published a multivolume *Historia de Rosas y de su época* (History of Rosas and His Time) which presented a critical interpretation of Juan Manuel de Rosas, Argentina's leading caudillo in the first half of the nineteenth century. Once again exiled to Uruguay for his intervention in the 1890 revolt against President Miguel Juárez Celman, Saldías began writing what has been considered his major historical work, the *Historia de la Confederación Argentina* (History of the Argentine Confederation), which became, for many years, the standard reference for the 1854–1862 period of Argentina's history. Director of the newspaper *El Argentino* (The Argentine) in 1893, Saldías became minister of public works in the Buenos Aires provincial government (1898) and later shared with Manuel Ugarte the Buenos Aires province governing ticket. A prominent member of the so-called Generation of 1880, Adolfo Saldías was strongly influenced by the positivist theories on social evolution and social organicism. These views, present throughout most of his work, were particularly reflected in his 1910 study, *Un siglo de instituciones* (A Century of Institutions), in which he argued that society went through a process of rhythmic evolution, similar to that of a living being. In this respect, Rosas represented an inevitable stage in a progression toward constitutional government under the rule of law. Saldías died in La Paz, while serving as Argentine minister plenipotentiary to Bolivia.

Bibliography: Julio Irazusta, *Adolfo Saldías* (Buenos Aires, 1964).

Nikita Harwich Vallenilla

SARMIENTO, Domingo Faustino (San Juan, Argentina, 1811–Asunción, Paraguay, 1888), Argentine writer, political leader, and statesman. Sarmiento's parents belonged to leading families of the San Juan Province. He attended elementary and secondary school in his native town; he was mainly self-taught, however. Sarmiento began working in 1827 as manager of an aunt's general store but soon became involved in the turbulent political life of the times. He fought unsuccessfully, together with his father, against the local rule of Juan Facundo Quiroga and was forced to emigrate to Chile (1831), where he worked as a schoolteacher, storekeeper, and mining foreman. He returned to San Juan in 1838 and became an active promoter of cultural activities. His opposition to Juan Manuel de Rosas' dictatorial regime once again sent him into exile to Chile. He began writing in the leading Santiago newspapers and acquired a growing reputation as a teacher and intellectual leader. Appointed director of the Santiago Teacher Training School, he held an important literary polemic with the Venezuelan scholar and poet Andrés Bello over the direction Chilean literature should take. Sarmiento, together with the youthful members of the so-called Chilean Generation of 1842, defended the values of romanticism in contrast to what they considered an outmoded form of classicism. In 1845 the Chilean government sent Sarmiento on a three-year mission to Europe and the United States for the purpose of studying their educational system. Upon Rosas' downfall in 1852, Sarmiento returned briefly to Argentina, but only in 1855 did he begin the political career that led him to occupy the positions of governor of San Juan Province (1862–1864), minister plenipotentiary to the United States (1864–1868), and president of the Republic (1868–1874).

A towering figure in his country's political and intellectual development, Sarmiento has been considered one of the founding fathers of the Argentine nation. As a historian, he is remembered primarily as the author of *Civilización y Barbarie, Vida de Juan Facundo Quiroga* (Civilization and Barbarity, The

Life of Juan Facundo Quiroga), written and published in Santiago in 1845. More than a biography of the early nineteenth-century caudillo, Sarmiento's *Facundo*, universally praised as a classic of Latin American literature and political thought, traced Argentina's historical background and included a sociological interpretation of dictatorship, viewed as the manifestation of a primeval barbarous force, which had to be fought and curbed in order to ensure social progress.

Bibliography: Enrique Anderson Imbert, "El historicismo de Sarmiento," *Cuadernos Americanos* 4, no. 5 (Mexico City, 1945); Allison Williams Bunkley, *The Life of Sarmiento* (Princeton, N.J., 1952); Frances W. Crowley, *Domingo Faustino Sarmiento* (New York, 1972); Raul Orgaz, *Sarmiento y el naturalismo histórico* (Córdoba, Argentina, 1940).

Nikita Harwich Vallenilla

SIERRA, Justo (Campeche, Mexico 1848–Madrid, 1912), Mexican historian, writer, and educational reformer. Son of Justo Sierra O'Reilly, an influential lawyer and journalist, and of Concepción Méndez Echazarreta, both of whom belonged to distinguished families of the Yucatán oligarchy. After attending the Scientific and Commercial State Secondary School of Mérida (Yucatán), young Justo moved to Mexico City, following his father's death in 1861 and completed his studies at Franco-Mexican High School and at San Ildefonso College, where he obtained his law degree in 1871. A regular contributor to various newspapers and literary periodicals, Justo Sierra was one of the founding members of the Society of Free Thinkers in 1870 and, together with several friends, founded in 1878 the newspaper *La Libertad* (Freedom), which followed Auguste Comte's (q.v.) positivist philosophy and Herbert Spencer's organic conception of society, and served as the ideological reference point for the Porfirio Díaz regime and its body of technical councillors, the Científicos (Scientists). Professor, after 1877, at the Escuela Nacional Preparatoria (National Preparatory School) where he taught history, sociology, and education, Sierra was a relentless advocate of educational reform, which he considered the indispensable tool for social progress. Elected to the Mexican Congress (1880), he proposed a constitutional amendment that would introduce compulsory elementary education (which was approved in 1881) and called for the creation of a Ministry of Public Instruction (1883). Appointed Supreme Court magistrate (1899), he became education undersecretary of the Ministry of Justice and Public Instruction (1901) and secretary of public instruction and fine arts (1905). His efforts at educational reform were crowned by success with the enactment of the 1908 Law on Public Education and with the inauguration, in September 1910, of the new National University of Mexico. Appointed by President Francisco I. Madero minister plenipotentiary to Spain (1912), he died while in office.

A major literary figure of his time, Justo Sierra, both personally and in his work, served as an inspiration for several generations of Mexican thinkers. His most important historical endeavor was the two-volume general history of Mexico entitled *Mexico: su evolución social* (1900–1902), translated into English in 1904 as *Mexico: Its Social Evolution*. In this collective work Sierra contributed two chapters, published separately in 1940 under the title *Evolución política del pueblo mexicano* (The Political Evolution of the Mexican People). Considered a "fundamental document for the understanding of Mexico's past," Sierra's book began a new trend in Mexican historiography by emphasizing the role the mestizos played in the nation's development, as opposed to the Indian or Spanish heritage. It stands out as a landmark of Latin American positivist thought. Sierra's other important historical work was *Juárez: su obra y su tiempo* (Juarez: His Life and Times), which he wrote in 1906 as a rebuttal to Francisco Bulnes' (q.v.) critical study on the great nineteenth-century Mexican reformer.

Bibliography: Justo Sierra, *Obras Completas* (Mexico City: Universidad Nacional Autónoma de México, 1948), 15 vols.; Luis Gonzalez Obregon, *Don Justo Sierra historiador* (Mexico City: Imprenta del Museo Nacional, 1907); Edmundo O'Gorman, *Justo Sierra y los orígenes de la Universidad de México, 1910* (Mexico City: Centro de Estudios Filosóficos, 1950); Silvio Zavala, "Tributo al historiador Justo Sierra," in *Memorias de la Academia Mexicana de la Historia* 5, no. 4 (Mexico City, 1946).

Nikita Harwich Vallenilla

SIERRA, Vicente D. (Buenos Aires, 1893–Buenos Aires, 1982), Argentine historian. Son of Vicente Sierra and Francisca Quintana. Although he attended courses at the National College of La Plata National University, Sierra was mainly self-taught in the social sciences. He was professor of Argentine history at the High College for Teacher Training (1944), of historiography at the National Institute for High School Teachers (1944–1945), director of the Institute of Historical Investigation of the Faculty of Philosophy and Literature at the University of Buenos Aires (1946–1947), and, from 1955 on, professor of Argentine history at both the Saviour College and the University of the Argentine capital. He also held municipal office (1946–1947) and was national director at the Public Transport Ministry (1948–1950). In 1960 he was president of the Argentine Commission on Ecclesiastical History and contributed to its journal, *Archivum*. His early field of interest was colonial history, and one of his first books *El sentido misional de la conquista de América* (The Sense of Mission in the Conquest of America), published in 1942, placed him with the pro-Hispanic historians of the revisionist school who sought to dispel the so-called dark legend of the Spanish conquest. This was also the theme of his *Así se hizo América (La expansión de la hispanidad en el siglo XVI)* [Thus Was America Made (The Expansion of the Spanish World in the Sixteenth Century)] which earned him the 1955 Reyes Católicos Prize in Spain. From 1956 until 1981, he worked on a monumental eight-volume *Historia de la Argentina* (History of Argentina), which is particularly useful to scholars because of its extensive bibliography. Sierra set out to achieve a sense of unity in his "Argentine history" so as to define the real content of Argentine national identity. According to him: "Man must reclaim his past in order to impose himself over what is perishable, and seek a remedy for his own insignificance through the creation of an historical reality in which, whether or not by choice, he is an active participant.'' The elusive question of national identity was—and still is—a particularly delicate question for a country that withstood, like Argentina, a massive influx of foreign immigration at the turn of the twentieth century. Sierra, therefore, considered it essential to ''assert the national soul'' and ''fortify a sense of nationality'' that might eventually form the rallying consensus for the country's deep political divisions.

Bibliography: Miguel Angel Scenna, *Los que escriben nuestra historia* (Buenos Aires, 1976).

Nikita Harwich Vallenilla

SILVA HERZOG, Jesús (San Luis Potosí, Mexico, 1892–Mexico City, 1985), Mexican economic historian and economic adviser. After completing his elementary education in his hometown, Silva Herzog studied at the Paine Uptown Business School in New York City (1912–1914) and later received his doctoral degree in economics from the Mexico National Autonomous University. Professor at the National School of Agriculture (1924–1940), he was the founder of the Mexican Institute of Economic Research in 1928. Director of the Library and Economic Archives of the Finance Secretariat (1928), he became Mexico's first ambassador to the Soviet Union (1929–1930). Undersecretary of public education (1933–1934), he was special economic adviser to the secretary of finance (1936–1941) and played a key role in the conflict that led to the nationalization of Mexico's oil industry in 1938. He was the first general manager of the new National Oil Company (1939–1940), before its name was changed to that of Petróleos Mexicanos (PEMEX). Founder and director of the Financial Studies Department of the Finance Secretariat (1942–1945), he was appointed subsecretary of finance (1945–1946). Member of the Board of Governors of Mexico's National University (1945–1962), he was the editor of the influential journal *Cuadernos Americanos* (American Notebooks) from 1948 until 1971. Apart from a long and distinguished public and academic career, Silva Herzog stands out as one of Mexico's leading economic historians. His early works were specialized monographs on topics such as the cost of living in Mexico or the salaries of railroad workers (1930). He later wrote a number of significant general studies on Mexico's agrarian problem (1934) and on the nationalization of the oil industry (1941). In various thought-provoking essays, he analyzed the economic and political consequences of the Mexican Revolution and also dedicated his attention to the documentary history of economic thought in Mexico. His most popular book, the two-volume *Historia de la Revolución Mexicana* (1967; History of the Mexican Revolution), has gone through various editions and has been translated into several foreign languages. It critically assesses many of the events in which he himself was an active participant. He concluded that the revolution lost its radical impetus from the mid–1940s on, but that by then Mexico had reached a new stage in its political, social, and economic development.

Bibliography: Jesús Silva Herzog, *Apuntes sobre la evolución económica de México* (Mexico City, 1927); Jesús Silva Herzog, *El pensamiento económico en México* (Mexico City, 1947); Jesús Silva Herzog, *El problema agrario en México y en algunas otras naciones* (Mexico City, 1934); Jesús Silva Herzog, *Historia de la Revolución Mexicana* (Mexico City, 1967); Jesús Silva Herzog, *La Revolución Mexicana en crisis* (Mexico City, 1943); Jesús Silva Herzog, *Una encuesta sobre el costo de la vida en México* (Mexico City, 1931).

Nikita Harwich Vallenilla

VALLENILLA LANZ, Laureano (Barcelona, Venezuela, 1870–Paris, 1936), Venezuelan historian, sociologist, politician, journalist, and diplomat. Son of José Vallenilla Cova and Josefa Maria Lanz Morales, both of distinguished Spanish ancestry. The Vallenilla family had been active in Venezuelan history since the time of the Spanish conquest. Vallenilla Lanz was essentially self-taught in the social sciences through his own reading. Taking advantage of a diplomatic appointment in Europe (1904–1910), he also attended lectures at the Sorbonne University and at the Collège de France in Paris. He was primarily influenced by such diverse authors as Hippolyte Taine (q.v.), Célestin Bouglé, Edouard Laboulaye, Ernest Renan (q.v.), and Gustave Le Bon in considering historical phenomena as social processes. At the same time, he acknowledged the teachings of Charles Langlois and Charles Seignobos (q.v.) in terms of the need for a rigorous and critical analysis of historical documents. Finally, he also partook of the interdisciplinary eclecticism promoted by René Worms through the Institut International de Sociologie and its journal, the *Revue Internationale de Sociologie*. While in Europe, Vallenilla started writing down notes on Venezuelan history of the colonial and independence periods, which were then published in various Caracas newspapers and journals. Originally, his idea was to prepare a book on the evolution of Venezuela's political and social institutions.

Upon his return to Venezuela, Vallenilla combined his historical research with an intense journalistic activity and political career. Director and organizer of the National Archive (1911–1915), he was appointed director of *El Nuevo Diario* (The New Daily, 1915–1931), the semiofficial newspaper of the Juan Vicente Gómez regime. President of the Venezuelan Senate on various occasions, director of the National Academy of History (1924–1927), and minister plenipotentiary to France (1931–1935), Vallenilla Lanz was recognized as a foremost figure of the so-called Venezuelan Positivist School. This recognition was mainly the result of three collections of previously written essays, published under the titles of *Cesarismo Democrático: estudios sobre la bases sociológicas de la constitución efectiva de Venezuela* (1919; Democratic Caesarism: Studies on the Sociological Base of the Effective Constitution of Venezuela); *Críticas de sinceridad y exactitud* (1921; Critique of Sincerity and Accuracy), and *Disgregación e Integración* (1930; Separation and Integration). Widely acclaimed throughout Latin America and translated into French and Italian, *Cesarismo* focused on the interpretation of Venezuela's and, by extension, of Latin America's social evolution throughout the nineteenth century, which led to the necessary rule of the popular caudillo as a means of consolidating national unity and ensuring the orderly progress of this heterogeneous society. Often misunderstood and violently criticized because of the political implications of its controversial theory, Vallenilla's book nonetheless contributed to a critical revision of Venezuela's history, a revision completed through his other two works, particularly *Disgregación e Integración*, which focused on the political organization and social structure of Venezuela's colonial period, with a special emphasis on the institution of the municipal councils (Cabildos).

Bibliography: Laureano Vallenilla Lanz, *Cesarismo Democrático: estudios sobre las bases sociológicas de la constitución efectiva de Venezuela* (Caracas: Tipografía Emp. El Cojo, 1919); Laureano Vallenilla Lanz, *Críticas de Sinceridad y Exactitud* (Caracas: Tipografía Universal, 1930); Federico Britto Figueroa, *La contribución de Laureano Vallenilla Lanz a la comprensión histórica de Venezuela* (Caracas: Universidad Santa Maria, 1983); German Carrera Damas, comp., *El Concepto de la Historia en Laureano Vallenilla Lanz* (Caracas: Universidad Central de Venezuela, 1966); Nikita Harwich Vallenilla, *"Arma y Coraza": Biografía Intelectual de Laureano Vallenilla Lanz* (Caracas: Universidad Santa Maria, 1983); José Ramón Luna, *El Positivismo en la Historia del Pensamiento Venezolano* (Caracas: Editorial Arte, 1971); Artuso Sosa Abascal, *La filosofía política des Gomecismo. Estudio del pensamiento de Laureano Vallenilla Lanz* (Barquisimeto: Centro Gumilla, 1974).

Nikita Harwich Vallenilla

VASCONCELOS, José (Oaxaca, Mexico, 1882–Mexico City, 1959), Mexican historian, philosopher, politician, and educator. Vasconcelos received his secondary education at the Campeche Institute and at the National Preparatory School in Mexico City, and received his law degree from the University of Mexico in 1905. Cofounder in 1909 of the influential Ateneo de la Juventud (Youth Atheneum), he joined the Mexican Revolution as a supporter of Francisco I. Madero. He showed little sympathy for popular leaders such as Pancho Villa and Emiliano Zapata; instead he furthered his efforts toward the more moderate elements whom he felt could carry on Madero's initial policies. In 1914 he became minister of public instruction in the short-lived government of Eulalio Rodríguez, a position to which he was again appointed by President Alvaro Obregón. During his three years in office (1921–1924), Vasconcelos carried out far-reaching reforms that left a permanent mark on Mexico's educational and cultural life. Schools were founded throughout the country, particularly in rural areas where special community development programs for adults and for the Indian population were promoted; masses of books were published and distributed to further popular education; active support was given to musicians and folk-singing groups. Vasconcelos invited foreign scholars, like the Chilean poetess Gabriela Mistral, to teach in Mexico and commissioned native artists to decorate the walls of public buildings and was thus the promoter of Mexico's famous school of mural painters. A growing opposition to some of his policies forced his resignation in 1924, and his defeat in the 1929 presidential elections forced him into exile. He traveled to Europe, the United States, Asia, and South America, and lived in Argentina where he was visiting professor at the School of Social Studies of the University of La Plata. He returned to Mexico in 1936.

A towering intellectual figure of his time, Vasconcelos was, altogether, a philosopher, sociologist, and historian. In a series of essays—*Pitágoras, una teoría del ritmo* (Pythagoras, a Theory of Rhythm) (1916), *La raza cósmica* (The Cosmic Race) (1925), *Indología* (Indology) (1929), and, particularly, *Ulises criollo* (American Ulysses) (1935)—he developed a theory of human and social evolution. Humankind, he believed, progressed through three different stages: materialistic, intellectual or rationalist, and aesthetic. At the same time, society was evolving toward a fusion of races, which would first be achieved in Latin America where the beginnings of a "cosmic race" were already apparent. Latin Americans should, therefore, transcend narrow nationalisms in order to hasten the advent of a new cultural era. A synthesizer and model builder of the past, rather than a traditional scholar, Vasconcelos shared the view that history must be understood in terms of a philosophical system. His own contribution to Mexican historiography included his *Breve historia de México* (Brief Outline of Mexico's History), first published in 1937, as well as his memoirs, a valuable, though highly biased, account of the events of the Mexican Revolution.

Bibliography: José Vasconcelos, *Obras Completas* (Mexico City: Libreros Mexicanos Unidos, 1957–1961), 4 vols.; Robert A. Potash, "Historiography of Mexico Since 1821," *Hispanic American Historical Review* 40, no. 3 (August 1960): 396–397.

Nikita Harwich Vallenilla

VICUÑA MACKENNA, Benjamin (Santiago, 1831–Santa Rosa de Colmo, Chile, 1886), Chilean historian and political leader. Educated at the Santiago National Institute (1846–1848), Vicuña Mackenna received his law degree from the University of Chile in 1857. He published his first articles at the age of seventeen and soon became committed to the cause of Chilean liberalism. In 1851 he and a group of young intellectuals participated in a failed rebellion against the conservative government of President Manuel Montt. Exiled to the United States (1853–1855), Vicuña Mackenna wrote a diary of his travels in which, like Alexis de Tocqueville (q.v.) twenty years before, he consigned many penetrating observations on the society and political customs of the Northern Republic. Upon his return to Chile in 1856, he served as editor of the newspaper *La Asamblea Constituyente* (The Constituent Assembly), was one of the founders of the Liberal Democratic party (1858), and in 1863 became editor of Santiago's influential daily *El mercurio* (The Mercury). That same year, he was elected deputy to the Chilean Congress. Special diplomatic envoy to the United States (1865) and Europe (1870), he ran unsuccessfully for the presidency in 1876. Unlike many of his contemporaries, Vicuña Mackenna pursued a thorough examination of the sources he used in his historical studies. He carefully researched his subjects and attempted a fair analysis of the data collected, which he combined with an imaginative and lively literary style. Considered one of nineteenth-century Chile's finest historians, though several of his contemporaries questioned his objectivity, he focused his work on the biographical study of the independence war leaders, particularly in his 1862 *Los jirondinos chilenos* (The Chilean Girondins) which renewed the interpretation of the country's independence movement. He also analyzed Manuel Montt's government in a six-volume study that incorporated his own life experiences.

Bibliography: Benjamín Vicuña Mackenna, *El ostracismo de los Carreras* (Santiago de Chile, 1857); Benjamín Vicuña Mackenna, *La Historia de los diez años de la administración de Montt* (Santiago de Chile, 1868), 6 vols.; Ricardo Donoso, *Don Benjamín Vicuña Mackenna: Su vida, sus escritos y su tiempo, 1831–1886* (Santiago de Chile, 1925); Guillermo Feliú Cruz, "Interpretación de Vicuña Mackenna: Un historiador del Siglo XIX," *Atenea* 95, nos. 291–292 (September-October 1949): 144–181; Eugenio Orrego Vicuña, *Vicuña Mackenna, vida y trabajos* (Santiago de Chile, 1932); Benjamín Vicuña Mackenna, *Los jirondinos chilenos* (Santiago, 1862); Benjamín Vicuña Mackenna, *Páginas de mi diario durante tres años de viaje, 1853–1854–1855* (Santiago, de Chile, 1856).

Nikita Harwich Vallenilla

ZAVALA, Lorenzo de (Tenoch, Mexico, 1788–San Jacinto, Texas, 1836), Mexican historian and politician and one of the founders of the Republic of Texas. Zavala studied at the Franciscan Seminary of San Ildefonso in Mérida (Yucatán). A liberal from his early youth, he fought against Spanish rule in Mexico, which led him to a three-year imprisonment in the island prison of San Juan de Ulua, where he spent part of his time studying medicine and English. Elected representative for Yucatán to the Spanish liberal Parliament of 1820, he later represented Yucatán at the Mexican National Congress, and as president of the Chamber of Deputies, he was the first to sign the federal constitution of 1824. Secretary of finance in the Vicente Guerrero government (1829–1833), he was appointed minister to France in 1833. Critical of Antonio López de Santa Anna and his conservative regime, he went into exile to Europe and the United States. Involved since 1830 in a land development business in Texas, he was a strong supporter of the Texan independence movement. In 1836 he became the first vice-president of the Republic of Texas. Long regarded as a traitor by his fellow Mexicans because of his involvement in the Texas war of independence, Zavala was nonetheless an important contributor to the historiography of his country of origin. His *Ensayo histórico de las revoluciones de la Nueva España* (Historical Essay on the Revolutions of New Spain), published in Paris in 1831–1832, as well as his *Albores de la República* (The Dawning of the Republic) and *Umbral de la Independencia* (The Threshold of Independence), both published for the first time in 1949, present a valuable interpretation of Mexico's historical processes. Zavala tried to draw political lessons from his observations of the country's society and political institutions. His intention was to show the value of liberalism over conservative ideology and, in a sense, to present what he believed to be the proper political system for Mexico's future development.

Bibliography: Lorenzo de Zavala, *Albores de la República* (Mexico City, 1949); Lorenzo de Zavala, *Ensayo histórico de las revoluciones de Nueva España* (Paris, 1831–1832); Lorenzo de Zavala, *Umbral de la Independencia* (Mexico City, 1949); Raymond Estep, "The Life of Lorenzo de Zavala," Ph.D. diss. (University of Texas, Austin, 1942); Louis Wiltz Kemp, *The Signers of the Texas Declaration of Independence* (Houston, 1944).

Nikita Harwich Vallenilla

ZUM FELDE, Alberto (Montevideo, 1888–Montevideo, 1951), Uruguayan historian, literary critic, journalist, and politician. A civil servant, assigned to the Uruguayan Ministry of Foreign Affairs, Zum Felde was also a professor in the National University of Montevideo's Faculty of Humanities. Director of Uruguay's National Library, he served as editor of two of Montevideo's leading newspapers, *El diario* (The Daily) and *El día* (The Day). Elected to the Uruguayan Chamber of Deputies, he proved himself a gifted orator. One of Uruguay's outstanding intellectual figures of the twentieth century, Zum Felde specialized in social and intellectual history. His 1911 study, *Uruguay ante el concepto sociológico* (Uruguay Faced with the Sociological Concept) and the later *Evolución histórica del Uruguay* (Uruguay's Historical Evolution), considered the country's historical processes in the renovating light of sociological positivism. The 1930 *Proceso intelectual del Uruguay y crítica de su literatura* (The Intellectual Process of Uruguay and a Critique of Its Literature) was widely distributed throughout Latin America and consolidated its author's already well-established international reputation. In this work, Zum Felde focused on the history of ideas and analyzed the evolution of Uruguayan culture throughout the nineteenth and early twentieth centuries in terms of its role in the consolidation of a genuine national identity. Less extreme in his conclusions than his illustrious countryman José Enrique Rodó, Zum Felde argued that exacerbated nationalism and exclusive reliance on European models as a means of opposing a perceived threat from Anglo-Saxon materialistic values were not desirable solutions for Latin America. Only a process of conscious introspection would help determine the truly original features of Latin American thought and lead to viable national projects.

Bibliography: Alberto Zum Felde, *El problema de la cultura americana* (Buenos Aires, 1943); Alberto Zum Felde, *El Uruguay ante el concepto sociológico* (Montevideo, 1911); Alberto Zum Felde, *Evolución histórica del Uruguay* (Montevideo, 1920); Alberto Zum Felde, *Proceso intelectual del Uruguay y crítica de su literatura* (Montevideo, 1930), 3 vols.; Joseph R. Baranger, "The Historiography of the Río de la Plata Area Since 1830," *Hispanic American Historical Review* 39, no. 4 (November 1959): 629.

Nikita Harwich Vallenilla

Great Historians: Swedish

ÅBERG, Niels (1888–1957), Swedish pre- and protohistorian. Professor at the University of Uppsala. Åberg's scientific work centered on many comprehensive problems from the Stone Age up to the Viking period. His entire work bears the stamp of three tendencies: (1) The Swedish school, dominated by men such as Oscar Montelius (q.v.), O. Almgren, and B. Salin, who initiated studies of stylistics and typology. Åberg thus published a series of papers on typology or based on the typological method of this school, for example, *Bronzezeitliche und früheisenzeitliche Chronologie*, I–V (1935–1939). His definition in *Reallexikon der Vorgeschichte* 13 (1929) developed the typological method and principles. (2) The ethnological school of culture circles, which applied systematically, as Åberg did also, the "culture circle" idea (*KulturKreise*) to all of European pre- and protohistory. See his *Vorgeschichtliche KulturKreise in Europa, Bilderatlas mit erlauterndem Text* (1936). (3) The school of Gustaf Kossinna's (q.v.) notion of the Indo-Europeans' Northern Country. Åberg made this zone the center out of which, in his view, a series of cultural trends diffused to the Southwest, the South, and the Southeast, a prominent idea in *Das nordische Kulturgebiet in Mitteleuropa während der jungeren Steinzeit* (1918). The same orientation accounts for the special interest he had in the German antiquities of the various stages of the history of the German tribes. His *Nordische Ornamentik in Vorgeschichtlicher Zeit* (1931) is one of a number of studies that may be considered models of the typologico-stylistic analysis applied to certain categories of objects, or models of classification or of determination of relative or absolute chronology. Åberg has been reproached for his tendency to neglect significant detail for the sake of a preconceived idea and also for his flagrant lack of attention to the regional cultural differences, especially in his work on Central European areas. Thus, his use of the "cultural province" concept for Hungary was bitterly criticized by Ion Andriesescu (q.v.) and Ion Nestor (q.v.).

Bibliography: J. Filip, *Encyklopädisches Handbuch der Ur- und Frühgeschichte Europas* I (Prague, 1966), p. 2.

Ligia Bârzu

AHNLUND, Nils (Uppsala, 1889–Stockholm, 1957), Swedish historian. Professor in Stockholm 1928–1955; member of the Swedish Academy beginning in 1941. Ahnlund viewed himself as a disciple of Harald Hjärne (q.v.) and his tradition. If so, this influence might be evidenced by his interest in diplomatic and political history, particularly that of the Great Power Era in Swedish history, by his concern with contemporary affairs, writing newspaper articles, and by his versatile interests, his erudition, and his prolific writings. Ahnlund graduated in 1918 with a dissertation called "Gustaf Adolf inför tyska kriget" (King Gustavus Adolphus Before the War in Germany). This is vintage diplomatic history, covering four years of deliberations. In several other books Ahnlund dealt with the king and the Thirty Years' War. He wrote one biography of the king, and another of his chancellor, in 1940, *Axel Oxenstierna intill Gustaf Adolfs död* (Chancellor Axel Oxenstierna until the Death of King Gustavus Adolphus). The Great Power Era is also covered in *Ståndsriksdagens utdaning 1592–1672* (The Shaping of the Parliament of the Estates 1592–1672), from 1933, which was Ahnlund's contribution to the quincentenary of the Riksdag (Swedish Parliament). He showed an interest in historiography, with some biographies of history-writers, as well as in cultural, local, and urban history, for example, with town monographs dealing with Sundsvall and Stockholm. In 1928 he became the first occupant of a chair of history instituted by the city of Stockholm. Ahnlund was a champion not only of meticulous research but also of historical writing. His preference for a narrative discourse made him shun not only daring "constructions"—placing himself in opposition to the Weibull (q.v.) brothers—but also methodological ventures as ends in themselves, particularly if they were conspicuously exhibited in the text. "The scaffoldings should not be left standing," as he put it.

Ragnar Björk

BOLIN, Sture (Höganäs, Skåne [Scania], 1900–Lund, 1962), Swedish historian. Professor at the University of Lund beginning in 1938. A disciple of Lauritz Weibull (q.v.), Bolin graduated in 1927 with a dissertation entitled "Fynden av romerska mynt i det fria Germanien" (The Findings of Roman Coins in Free Germania). The main thesis is that finds of coins do not necessarily indicate wealth; rather, they denote only periods of war and devastation, because it is in times of unrest and insecurity that people bury their treasures. Bolin's statistical treatment of the material also enabled him to detect the trade routes of the sixth and seventh centuries. Moving in the borderland between history, archaeology, and numismatics, Bolin devoted himself to problems of the Viking Era in Scandinavian history and of the early Middle Ages in European history. In his inaugural lecture as professor, succeeding Lauritz Weibull, in 1938, "Muhammed, Karl den store och Rurik" (Mohammed, Charlemagne, and Rurik), published in *Scandia* in 1939, he sketched a trading system of huge dimensions. The silver export from the Caliphate (from Afghanistan) was related to the fur and slave trade involving the Nordic countries and Russia, and to the development of the Carolingian Empire. This was to some extent a polemic against Henri Pirenne's (q.v.) thesis of the closed Mediterranean. In 1958 Bolin summed up many of his ideas in his major work, *State and Currency in the Roman Empire*. Here he claimed that the state power used an overvalued currency as a kind of taxation. Bolin also produced many astute, mathematically advanced, source-critical examinations. An exception to his main themes was his study in contemporary history, *Det ensidiga våldet* (The Unilateral Violence), from 1944, in which he tried to fathom the genesis of the outbreak of war in 1939.

Ragnar Björk

GEIJER, Erik Gustaf (Ransäter, Värmland 1783–Stockholm, 1847), Swedish historian and poet. Professor at the University of Uppsala beginning in 1817; member of the Estate of the Clergy of the Riksdag (Swedish Parliament), 1828– 1830, 1840–1841; member of the Swedish Academy in 1824; a predominant figure in nineteenth-century cultural life in Sweden. Geijer's prominence as an historian rests on a twofold foundation: an ability to adopt philosophical and historical thinking, and to transform it into a view of history distinctly of his own making, and clearly to be seen in his works of history; second, an apprehension of the evolving character of the society of his time, which when fused with his view of history, enabled him to be one of the first historians ever to write a history of society, or *Gesellschaftsgeschichte*. After graduating in 1806 with a dissertation, written in Latin, called "De ingenio politico medii aevi" (On the Spirit of Medieval Society), he hesitated between a career as an historian and as a clergyman. His steadfast Christian faith, encompassing a personal God, was both then and later to mold his philosophical thinking in characteristic ways. One of these ways was the personality principle, which emphasized that a person becomes a person only in society and that the right of the individual should be seen less as a laissez-faire free-for-all-ideal, and more as every person's equal right and, also, equal responsibility, not only individually but for everybody else, given a Christian moral code. Later he tied the idea of association, in the sense of that of Lorenz von Stein, to this notion. Raised with Enlightenment philosophical ideas, including a tolerant and optimistic view of human beings as well as a notable moral-didactic urge, Geijer in the 1810s encountered Romanticism, mainly as espoused by Schelling. He developed an aesthetic view of history—not unnatural for a poet of his eventual stature—and also a demand for what he called "the historical sense," meaning a relativistic and historicist quality in the understanding of periods and peoples.

An organic view of society was adopted simultaneously and can be found in his lectures and publications at the end of the decade, among them *Feodalism och republikanism* (1818–1821; Feudalism and Republicanism), from 1818–1819 (published in German in 1821). In these two models of governing and organizing society Geijer discerned two opposing considerations, which were to guide much of his later thinking: on the one hand, the widened "patriarchate," that is, the personal relationship of fidelity between the king and his followers (his subjects), of feudalism, and, on the other hand, the mutual obligations of free persons in an association, of republicanism. Geijer struggled to find a synthesis between what was nationally unifying, something thus far best represented by the kings, and the demand for freedom, justice, and protection in contemporary society. While acknowledging not only the rise of a middle class, but also the growth of "a mass without property," neither of whom had any say in political life, in the mid–1840s, Geijer found himself accused of resorting to "condemnation of the aristocracy" (presumed to be a theme in Swedish history writing), when he criticized the old Four Estate Riksdag (Parliament) for petrification and for only seeing to narrow group interests. Again, the idea of association was on Geijer's mind as a way to remedy this narrowness. Early fascinated by Nordic antiquity, Geijer now began work on two national histories in a national-romantic vein, the more elaborate of which, *Svenska folkets historia, I–III* (History of the Swedish People, vols. 1–3), was published during the years 1832–1836 and simultaneously in German. During the 1820s, Geijer had acknowledged an Hegelian dialectic view of history, wherein history was seen in the light of a process of renewal. However, a supra-individual, abstract, and amoral process, letting Reason evolve through necessity and without responsibility, was not in keeping with Geijer's gradually emerging view of history. There was an ethical judgment to be made of every event and action in history, and the kind of morality which Geijer favored was that of the responsibility of a person as an individual. Ludwig Feuerbach's emphasis on humans as the overall perspective and measure of history also became that of Geijer, and the "I" found in the "you" way of reasoning corresponded to Geijer's personality principle. But he disavowed Feuerbach's anthropological view of religion. Good and evil, just and unjust, really were there in the world, and evil could be identified as social injustice, lack of freedom, and lack of equality. His compassion and his insight into social problems are mirrored in the collection of articles from 1839, *Fattigvårdsfrågan* (The Problem of Poverty), which was published in English in 1840 as *The Poor Laws and Their Bearing on Society*. It is but one example of Geijer's reluctance to support laissez-faire liberalism, and it also forms the background to his interest in utopian socialism. During the 1830s, under the impact of the historical events of his day, such as the Revolution of July 1830, Geijer's political views radicalized. His much celebrated "Defection" in 1838 ("I have defected from myself," as he put it in a letter), from the "conservative" to the "liberal" camp, was followed by a corresponding reorientation in his historical views and works. In the fall of 1844 Geijer gave three lectures, which were later collected under the title *Om vår tids inre samhällsför-hållanden* (On the Internal Conditions of Society in Our Time). There he developed a theory of history, which evolved into a theory of society. In line with ideas expressed by Alexis de Tocqueville (q.v.) in his *De la Democratie en Amerique*, which Geijer read, a dynamic view of history was explicated. A general tendency toward societal equality might be discerned in history. This development has specific structural causes of a combined social, economic, and cultural character. The eternal problem of the relation between freedom (voluntarism) and necessity (determinism) was interpreted with categories taken from John Stuart Mill. Geijer's "doctrine of circumstances," or "the doctrine of cause and effect applied to human action" (our will, by influencing some of the circumstances, can modify our future habits or capabilities of willing), might be applied to a specific historical epoch and its peculiar circumstances. If one does not expect history to be teleologically determined in the manner of Georg Wilhelm F. Hegel (q.v.) or Karl Marx (q.v.), and if one expects every group and class in society to encompass a yearning for freedom, one may develop an emancipatory theory of history and society. This Geijer did.

Bibliography: Bengt Henningsson, *Geijer som historiker* (Geijer as an Historian), (Uppsala, 1961); Thorsten Nybom, "Historikern Erik Gustaf Geijer" (Erik Gustaf Geijer, the Historian), in *Geijer-jubileet i Uppsala 1983* (The Geijer Bicentennial in Uppsala 1983), (Uppsala, 1983).

Ragnar Björk

HECKSCHER, Eli F. (Stockholm, 1879–Stockholm, 1952), Swedish economic historian. Professor of economics and statistics at the Stockholm School of Economics, 1909–1929; holder of the first professorship in the discipline of economic history in Sweden, at the Stockholm School of Economics, 1929–1945. Heckscher might be termed the benefactor of economic history in Sweden, as both science and discipline. Although his specialization in economic history did not specifically correspond to the interests of his teacher, he considered himself a disciple of Harald Hjärne (q.v.) in important respects. The reason for this was Hjärne's emphasis on universalism and synthesis, ideals to which Heckscher showed much dedication. Their common outlook was also witnessed by the presence of contemporary affairs in their respective writings. Heckscher graduated in 1907 with a dissertation on the importance of the railroads for Sweden's economic development, and two years later he won a professorship at the newly founded Stockholm School of Economics. His responsibilities, economics and statistics, had few predecessors in Swedish historical research. An exception had been the late nineteenth-century historian Hans Forssell, who had tried to calculate the population and the economic conditions of Sweden in the sixteenth century. Eventually, Heckscher followed suit. During the last decades of his life he devoted himself to *Sveriges ekonomiska historia från Gustaf Vasa* (1935–1949; *An Economic History of Sweden*, 1954) which covered almost three centuries up to 1815. Heckscher's most renowned work internationally was his big, synthetic study from 1931, *Merkantilismen* (*Mercantilism*, 1935, and also translated into German [1932], Italian, Spanish, and other languages). In a kind of overture study, he had examined the effects of *Kontinentalsystemet* (1918; *The Continental System. An Economic Interpretation*, 1922). In *Mercantilism* the author tried to discern and formulate a body of mercantilist economic doctrines that served as prevalent and tenuous guides for mercantilist policies, such as creating favorable terms of trade and a stable and authoritative state power, as part of a nation-building process. Firmly based in a comparative study, including, above all, France and Britain, Heckscher attempted a sort of objective synthesis in relating Adam Smith's negative and Gustav Schmoller's positive assessments of mercantilist policies. Heckscher saw the ideas of mercantilism as reactions to the static and ethically circumscribing ideas of the Middle Ages. Thus, in a sense, even the cruder principles of mercantilism could be seen as progressive. While the economics of the medieval town was characterized by a "policy of provision," mercantilism's dominant trait was a "policy of protection." Heckscher's concern was primarily with problems of trade and monetary policies, as reflected both in his historical works and in his essays on purely economic questions. His was also a plea for theory in economic history, and he was a pioneer in co-ordinating theory with the treatment of statistical sources. Starting out as a conservative in politics, he gradually became more liberal in his outlook, and this was in line with his distinct liberalism in economic thinking, much in the classical vein of Alfred Marshall, and, in general, of John Stuart Mill.

Bibliography: A. W. Coats, "In Defence of Heckscher and the Idea of Mercantilism" *The Scandinavian Economic History Review* 5, no. 2 (1957): 173–187; D. C. Coleman, "Eli Heckscher and the Idea of Mercantilism," *The Scandinavian Economic History Review* 5 no.1 (1957): 3–25; Arthur Montgomery, "Eli Heckscher som vetenskapsman" (Eli Heckscher as Scientist), *Ekonomisk tidskrift*, 55 (1953): 149–185.

Ragnar Björk

HJÄRNE, Harald (Skövde, Västergötland, 1848–Uppsala, 1922), Swedish historian. Professor at the University of Uppsala, 1885–1913; member of the Riksdag (Swedish Parliament) 1902–1908 and 1912–1918; member of the Swedish Academy from 1903. Hjärne as a historian can best be characterized as a striver toward universalism. This means the versatile crossing of borders—geographic, disciplinary, linguistic, and, as it were, temporal. Hjärne graduated in 1872 with a dissertation on the so-called Council in Swedish Antiquity, a legal study. After some years as editor of a cultural-political magazine, giving him both a lifelong penchant for expressing himself within the space of an article, and a lust for journalism, witnessed by numerous newspaper articles through the years, Hjärne's career as a historian began to take shape and gather speed. Already well versed in the languages and history of classical antiquity and Western Europe, he now acquired Russian, Polish, and other Slavic languages, and, later on, also Japanese. His never-ceasing concern with Eastern European affairs— with a northern, Baltic gravitation—put him on solid ground when he stressed his universalist conviction that the history and fate of Sweden and the Nordic countries must be seen in a much wider context of a Baltic, a Central European, and, particularly during Sweden's Great Power Era in the seventeenth century, an all-European sphere.

Hjärne's universalist and synthetic approach to history took expression both synchronically and diachronically. He discussed the "European system of states" of the sixteenth, seventeenth, and eighteenth centuries in systemic terms, as having a delicate balance, and he viewed the different nations as actors having different combinations of resources at their disposal, giving his reasoning a slight geopolitical twist. Diachronically, he emphasized the perseverance of the classical heritage. Although historically adjusted in expression, the classical heritage was still preserved in character, and it was the mission of its heirs among the nations of Europe to uphold these values. A major instrument in managing this was the law, and law-making was a responsibility of the state power. This strategic, long-term mission of preserving cultural values, Hjärne meant, was perceived by the historical actors, and they combined this insight with a comprehension of tactical short-term efforts needed to ward off threats, and to uphold a military, political, and religious balance. During the centuries which Hjärne studied most intensely, this threat, he held, came from the East, and Sweden for several decades carried the ultimate responsibility to secure the culture of the rest of Europe as well as the balance of the state system, using a kind of containment policy. This kind of reasoning can be found in *Karl XII. Omstörtningen i Östeuropa 1697–1703* (1902; Charles XII. The Upheaval in Eastern Europe 1697–1703), as well as in several other books and articles dealing with Russia and Eastern Europe, and with King Gustavus Adolphus and the Thirty Years' War. These kinds of studies required that the historian have an unsentimental insight into the workings of *Realpolitik* as well as a fine-tuned sense of the more abstract and pervasive ideas that guide people in a longer perspective. Hjärne's closeness to everyday political life, his colossal erudition, and his attachment to classical culture as well as to Protestant religion, served him in this endeavor. In a tradition from Erik Gustaf Geijer (q.v.) Hjärne advocated the primacy of the state. This is so, he claimed, because history is the science of organized culture, and the state, in its law-giving, organizing capacity, is a necessary means to reach a developed stage. Culture was very important to Hjärne, but it could not be seen in isolation from the state and, hence, not from politics either. In the main, these views were shared by his older pupils, like Nils Edén, Sam Clason, and K. G. Westman, all of whom eventually became Cabinet ministers. Hjärne, though a universalist, never displayed much interest in social and economic history, in a strict sense, or in the theory of society proper. In this, one of his most prominent pupils, Eli Heckscher (q.v.), "the father of Swedish economic history," conspicuously differed.

At the turn of the century Hjärne launched a loose but potentially far-reaching research program centering around King Charles XII. Several of his younger disciples became involved in it, and they were to learn the languages needed and to travel to the relevant European archives bringing back material from diplomatic and other sources. Thus, together they would make a kind of interdisciplinary contribution to complete the picture. The Hjärne tradition is to strive toward a truthlike, that is, a congruent or verisimilar, depiction of society. This might be compared to the goal of conclusiveness espoused by Lauritz Weibull (q.v.) and his pupils. Hjärne, the revered teacher, combined extensive learning and a keen sense of sketching patterns and syntheses in a limited space, without lapsing into speculative philosophizing about history, with a highly skeptical, at times ironic, attitude. His critical skepticism took the form both of a methodical source-criticism, and of a constant questioning of earlier historical authorities. Hjärne excelled in this kind of scrutinizing in the historical seminars which he organized in the 1880s and which became efficient training grounds for his pupils.

Bibliography: Rolf Torstendahl, *Källkritik och vetenskapssyn i svensk historisk forskning 1820–1920* (Source-criticism and View of Science in Swedish Historical Research, 1820–1920), (Uppsala, 1964), pp. 249–296. (Other studies on Hjärne are forthcoming.)

Ragnar Björk

MONTELIUS, Oscar (Stockholm, 1843–Stockholm, 1921), Swedish prehistorian and warden of the Stockholm Museum. Montelius formed around himself a real school in which leading representatives of European prehistory were trained, for instance Arne Michel Tallgren (q.v.). He initiated three lines of research. First, he enlarged on the studies of several forerunners—Christian Jurgensen Thomsen, Johann Freidrich Danneil, G. Mortillet, and Hans Hildebrand—and proved scientifically the theoretical principles of the typological method (*Die Typologische Methode*, 1903). Then, on the basis of this typological criterion, he drew up the first system of relative chronology applied to the Metal Age in North Germany and Scandinavia (*Die Chronologie der ältesten Bronzezeit in Norddeutschland und Skandinavien*, 1900). Montelius proposed six stages and based on his proposal both on accurate archaeological observations originating in closed discoveries (cemeteries) and on a series of types established on the basis of stylistic criteria. The success of Montelius' system was ensured by its well-grounded construction and principles. It can be compared to the chronology of the Old Stone Age established by Gabriel de Mortillet (q.v.). Montelius' system was used not only in the specific space for which it had been designed, but also throughout Europe. It is still in use in several zones, for example, in Poland. Montelius was also the first to apply the method of "cultural synchronism," and he paid special attention to relations between Europe, the Aegean world, and the Orient. He devised a system of "absolute chronology" for the German-Scandinavian space. His preoccupation with better understanding the evolution of the Mediterranean world and its links with Europe north of the Alps resulted in a substantial book on prehistoric Italy, the first scientific presentation of this zone: *La civilisation en Italie depuis l'introduction des metaux* (2 vols., 1904). Even though correctives were made later in Montelius' typological method, and although the Scandinavian system of chronology was to be replaced, for Central Europe, with other solutions, Montelius' contribution to the progress of prehistoric science remains incontestable.

Bibliography: Jan Filip, *Encyklopädisches Handbuch der Ur- und Frühgeschichte Europas* 2 (Prague, 1967), p. 849; *Montelio Septuagenario dedicata* (On Montelius' Seventieth Anniversary), (Stockholm, 1913).

Ligia Bârzu

WEIBULL, Lauritz (Lund, 1873–Lund, 1960), Swedish historian. Professor at the University of Lund, 1919–1938. Weibull perceived himself as a militant historian. His adversaries were Swedish historians of an older, more traditional vein, several of whom were Harald Hjärne's (q.v.) pupils. According to Weibull, they were locked up in a nationalistic view of Swedish history, which made them unable to exercise the thorough criticism necessary to free history writing from both unreliable source material and idealistic prejudice concerning the greatness of putatively great men and eras in Swedish history. Weibull took to the area of source-criticism as his battlefield, and he came out a brilliant champion of his cause. He argued fiercely and, when he met with resistance, he fought unrelentingly, sometimes sarcastically. Weibull graduated in 1900 with a traditional dissertation, written in 1899, on diplomatic history, "De diplomatiska förbindelserna mellan Sverige och Frankrike 1629–1631" (Diplomatic Relations Between Sweden and France, 1629–1631). This work is considered to have been partly influenced by his father, Martin Weibull, a professor of history, in choice of subject and in style. Before Lauritz Weibull addressed himself wholly to history, he occasionally devoted himself to literary history and its comparative methods, and he wrote several essays on prominent Swedish men of letters. During the first decade of the twentieth century he worked in archives, making himself well acquainted with all kinds of source material. His publications concerned cultural history and local history, primarily dealing with Skåne (Scania), his home province, and he also began some huge editing works. Not until 1911 did he really manage to catch the eye of the research community. His study *Kritiska undersökningar i Nordens historia omkring år 1000* (Critical Investigations into the History of the Nordic Countries around the Year 1000) is pathbreaking in its radical elimination of tendential chronicles and mythical sagas as sources for the Viking Era in Nordic history. Sources were left totally out of consideration once they were judged unreliable in any sense at all. Weibull found himself in a polemic, and his uncompromising attitude is mirrored in his pamphlet *Historisk-kritisk metod och nordisk medeltidshistoria* (Historical-critical Method and Nordic Medieval Research) from 1913. Gradually he won adherents, but not until 1919, and after a fierce battle, did he win his professorship in Lund. From then on he assiduously reared disciples to adopt, carry out, and spread his principles. In this he succeeded well. In 1928 the first issue of a new magazine, *Scandia*, appeared, and it was to be the main forum for the evolving Weibullian school of history. The three founders were Lauritz Weibull, who stayed on as editor until 1957, his brother Curt (born 1886), and the prominent Danish historian Erik Arup (q.v.). These names are symptomatic of Lauritz Weibull's feeling of bonds. Most of his studies covered the period in history when the Province of Skåne (Scania) was Danish, and some of his closest personal and scientific contacts were across the strait, Öresund, with Denmark. This contributed greatly to his feelings of animosity toward the Swedish nationalist historians of Uppsala and Stockholm. Although Weibull and his disciples emphasized source-criticism as the great divide, the methodological practices of Hjärne and several of his pupils might not really warrant that. No doubt Weibull was radical and provocative in propagating his source-critical principles, but perhaps he displayed more audacity in the next step in the research process, that is, in reconstructing an argument for some historical circumstance with the help of the few reliable sources that remained. The objective was more to reach conclusiveness in the argumentation than to end up with a truthlike, or verisimilar, picture of society, which one may hold was characteristic of Hjärne and his disciples. The buildup of the argument should, as Weibull put it, "follow the strictest laws of a strict logic."

Weibull might be termed a positivist in his emphasis on substantiated, empirical evidence, but the "strict logic" allowed resourceful and daring calculations and deductions in the construction of new patterns of history. Weibull did not differ from his adversaries in Uppsala and Stockholm when it came to choice of subject area. He dealt with political history, often with a juridico-ideological character. His pupils shared and sometimes sharpened his minimum demands concerning source-criticism, and they adopted his inclination to reveal great historical figures as just power players, but they widened the approach when it came to norms for what constituted not only unobjectionable but also meaningful and desirable research. His successor in Lund, Sture Bolin (q.v.), used sophisticated numismatics to interpret society; Per Nyström, a sole Marxist, dealt with social issues; and Sven A. Nilsson and Erik Lönnroth—the latter Curt Weibull's pupil—adopted a more complete view of society, which went beyond pure politics into the realms of state finance, for example, as the basis of the exercise of power. The tide in Swedish historical writing was now beginning to run more in favor of "society" than of the "state."

Bibliography: Birgitta Odén, *Lauritz Weibull och forskarsamhället* (Lauritz Weibull and the Research Community), (Lund, 1975); Rolf Torstendahl, "Minimum Demands and Optimum Norms in Swedish Historical Research 1920–1960," *Scandinavian Journal of History* 6, no. 2 (1981): 117–141.

Ragnar Björk

Great Historians: Swiss

BURCKHARDT, Jacob (Basel, 1818–Basel, 1897), Swiss historian. Burckhardt is probably the only Swiss historian (and among his fellow historians one of the few) who has played a vital role in European culture, going beyond historiography. He not only wrote important historical works, but was also one of the few diagnosticians of his time. He came from an old Basel family and was the son of the leading clergyman of his native city who himself was an active historian. Having received a thorough classical education in the gymnasium in Basel, Jacob also attended university there and studied theology before going to Berlin to study history. There Leopold von Ranke (q.v.), Johann G. Droysen (q.v.) and August Boeckh, but also the art historian Franz Kugler, were his great teachers. From his youth on, he was accustomed to seeing works of art as witnesses of the historical past. A stay in Bonn and travels in Italy, the Netherlands, and France refined his feeling for art and cultural history. In 1844, a year after he completed his doctorate, he attained his habilitation at the University of Basel. At first he devoted himself to Swiss history; then he made a living as a journalist. Already at that time his concern with cultural values increasingly led him to a conservatism that viewed the nineteenth-century belief in political and economic progress with skepticism. Equally skeptically, he viewed the radical changes in Switzerland and its beginning as a confederation of states. The diminutive, limited state of Basel became his intellectual and political home. With the Revolution of 1848, his relations with his friends in Germany and to Germany itself began to cool off; the opposite took place with regard to Italy and its works of art which he experienced in several travels and which were basic to his work. After his professional hopes in Basel had come to naught, at least for the time being, he took up his first full-fledged teaching appointment at the Polytechnic Institute in Zürich. From there he returned as a

full professor to the University of Basel where he was active from then on, first
as a professor of history and later as chairman of art history. It was the time of
his great works.

In 1853 *The Age of Constantine the Great* appeared, a broadly designed
portrayal of the downfall of antiquity and its religion, a masterpiece of cultural
history which at the same time illustrated Burckhardt's unique sense for caesurae
in time. This becomes even clearer in what is probably the most famous of his
books, *The Civilization of the Renaissance in Italy* (1860), in which—a few
years after Jules Michelet (q.v.)—he dealt with the notion of epochs and at the
same time conceived of the state as a work of art, the development of the
individual, the reawakening of antiquity, the discovery of the world and of man.
All of this was gathered from a great wealth of source materials he had read.
At the same time Burckhardt was the first historian to grasp the uniqueness of
the Renaissance and what set it apart from the Middle Ages. He thereby created
one of the most outstanding works of nineteenth-century historiography. Between
the two books lies *Cicerone: An Introduction to the Enjoyment of the Works of
Art of Italy* (1855), a fruit of his travels and his self-education in seeing, as
Werner Kaegi put it, "basically not intended for orientation before monuments
but for quiet reading, for preparation and remembering." *The Art of the Renaissance in Italy* (1867) still followed as part of a handbook which, however,
limited itself to architecture. In his lifetime Burckhardt published no more books,
totally devoting himself instead to teaching and to lectures. He was professor
of history until 1886 and of art history until 1893. For him academic teaching
meant exclusively lectures. Although he himself had been in Ranke's seminars,
he conducted none himself and therefore had few doctoral students. Burckhardt's
fame has undergone some changes in this century. Until World War I it rested
mainly on his book on the Renaissance and the *Guide*, but the works published
from his estate soon came to be considered significant and timely, for example,
the *Greek Cultural History* (1898–1902) derived from lectures, with its impressive and pessimistic analysis of the polis as a carrier of culture and an institution
oppressive of the individual. Most significant, however, are *The Reflections on
World History* (1905), an introductory lecture on historiography. The original
version of it was not published as a critical edition until 1982. Today it is—next
to Georg Wilhelm Hegel (q.v.) and Karl Marx (q.v.)—probably the most read
work in the nineteenth-century philosophy of history. In it Burckhardt develops
and discusses the doctrine of the three forces—the state, religion, and culture—
the question of happiness and unhappiness (or luck and bad fortune), and the
nature of historical greatness. In the last analysis he sees the meaning of history
in the fact that it does not make one "clever for once" but "wise forever." The
Reflections on World History differ from the traditional philosophies of history
by their renunciation of a chronologically graspable process and by their extension
to the typical and the analogous. Thereby it anticipates twentieth-century models
(Max Weber [q.v.], Oswald Spengler) down to the structuralists. Burckhardt's
living influence on posterity has been increased further by his letters which often

reveal almost a visionary gift for seeing major changes in the world, of coming dictatorships and ideologies. Here he coined the famous phrase of the great *simplificateurs*. Thus, the letter writer contributed to keeping interest alive in the historian after World War II.

Bibliography: W. Kaegi, *Jacob Burckhardt. Eine Biographie*, 7 vols. (Basel, 1947–1982).

Peter Stadler

FUETER, Eduard (Basel, 1876–Basel, 1928), Swiss historian. Werner Kaegi considered Fueter the most original Swiss historian after Jacob Burckhardt (q.v.). His personality, work, and career were equally unconventional; therefore, his professional failure is at least in part caused by the narrowness and narrow-mindedness of conditions in Switzerland in his time. Fueter came from an artistically talented extended family, was himself an active musician, and later wrote musical critiques and musicological essays. He studied history in Basel and Berlin and received his doctorate at the age of twenty-three with a dissertation on "The Swiss Share in the Election of Charles V" (1899) and worked in Göttingen on the edition of the documents of the German Reichstag with a study, "Kirche und Staat in England im 15. Jahrhundert" (1903), which revealed more interest in social history than in theology. He completed his habilitation in Zurich and became editor of the *Neue Zürcher Zeitung*. The first great accomplishment of this time was the *Geschichte der neueren Historiographie* which appeared in 1911 (4th ed., 1984 with an introduction by Hans Conrad Peyer). This work of sophisticated breadth from the early Italian Renaissance to the turn of the twentieth century placed historians within the currents of intellectual history, presented them as exponents of these currents, and at the same time characterized them and assessed them critically. In contrast to the attitude dominant in Germany not everything pointed to historicism; Fueter's view was rather a West European one and he saw in Guicciardini, Voltaire, the English Enlightenment historians as well as in Alexis de Tocqueville (q.v.) and Hippolyte Taine (q.v.) climaxes of historiographic development comparable to Barthold Georg Niebuhr (q.v.), Leopold von Ranke (q.v.), and Heinrich von Treitschke (q.v.). He had a consciously sociological approach, which in the "Concluding Remarks" to the book sounded like the expression of a creed.

The reception of his work outside of the German-speaking countries was indeed friendlier than inside; it was translated into French as early as 1914. To it the author owed the friendship of Benedetto Croce (q.v.) which is documented in their correspondence. His next great work was his *Geschichte des europäischen Staatensystems 1492–1559* (1919) which he wrote for the very prestigious series edited by Bülow and Friedrich Meinecke (q.v.), *Handbuch der mittleren und neueren Geschichte*, for which he had also written his history of historiography. This book was likewise highly original, beginning with a structurally conceived analysis of the powers that were involved in the European controversy, their potentials, their administrative and military means, as well as the possibilities created by modern diplomacy. The history of events plays only a secondary role. Fueter's thesis, according to which the main issue in the dispute was Italy, had probably been suggested to him by Macchiavelli and Guicciardini, but also by the Venetian documents. Almost of its own accord it shifted its emphasis to the Western national states, especially France and Spain, while Germany shifted more to the background, passing the Reformation off as an episode. Thus, its effect was probably underestimated, as far as Western Europe was concerned. However, it was precisely this book that provided methodological stimuli which then could be utilized by the *Annales* School in its own way.

Between these two works, which can be considered the building blocks of European historiography, lies World War I. Fueter had taken over the department in charge of foreign policy of the *Neue Zürcher Zeitung*. Much attention was paid to his weekly reports; they were by no means friendly to the Allies, but they offended readers in the pro-German area of Zurich. Thus, he made himself enemies, and a private affair led to his downfall. In 1921 he lost his position with the newspaper and at the university; he moved to Basel and spent his last years as an employee of a bank. In the same year (1921) his *Weltgeschichte der letzten hundert Jahre (1815–1920)* appeared in which he fought against the eurocentric perspective. However, most noticed was his negative view of the Bismarckian and the post-Bismarckian period, the reactionary character of its social history. It also shows the outbreak of the war of 1914 as essentially caused by the structure of dominance. These criteria and impulses have been largely incorporated by recent scholarship, but at that time they were met with indignation. Thus, any hope of an academic career vanished completely, including one in America. In the year of his death, 1928, Fueter's last book appeared, *Die Schweiz seit 1848*, a work that is just as modern as it is brilliant. It has retained its value to this day. The impetuses which Fueter offered to social history were hardly noted by his generation, which was strongly tied to political history. Thus, his failure does not only involve a personal fate: It was also the result of the inflexible mentality of the scholars of his generation.

Bibliography: H. C. Peyer, *Der Historiker Eduard Fueter. Sein Leben und Werk* (Basel, 1982).

Peter Stadler

Great Historians: Turkish

ALTINAY, Ahmet Refik (Istanbul, 1880–Istanbul, 1937), Turkish historian. Officer in the Ottoman Army (teacher of history, French, geography), author (newspaper and magazine articles on historical subjects, poet), professor of history at Istanbul University (1918–1933). Ahmet Refik was one of the founders of modern Turkish historiography and its most effective popularizer in the early part of this century. His bibliography includes nearly 150 items (excluding newspaper articles), over half of them books; some of them are in print today, over eighty years since their first appearance. Although most of his works were on Ottoman history, he published a few biographies of European rulers whose careers affected the Ottomans, as well as some translations of French positivist historians whose work influenced his own. He wrote different sorts of work for different audiences. In one series of books he published transcriptions of Ottoman archival documents on numerous topics, and these educated many Turkish and European scholars to the vast Ottoman documentary resources on political, social, and economic history. Among these documentary collections were his *Osmanli Devrinde Türkiye Madenleri* (1931; The Mines of Turkey in the Ottoman Era), *Anadolu' da Türk Aşiretleri* (1930; The Anatolian Turkish Tribes), and *Hicri X., XI., XII., XIII. Asirda Istanbul Hayat 1* (4 vols., 1917–1932; *Istanbul Life in the Tenth-Thirteenth Muslim Centuries*). These volumes are still of use to Ottoman historians. Refik also edited texts for the Turkish Historical Society (which he once headed); among the most important of these were his editions of the last two volumes of Evliya Çelebi and his edition of the *Silahdar Tarihi* of Fındıklılı Mehmet Aga, published in 1928. Leaving aside some twenty-three schoolbooks which remained in use from 1912 up through the 1960s (and are thus his most subtly influential works), Refik's most widely read books were on special topics, mostly biographical, to remind his readers of the many facets of Ottoman society at its height. These works were popular in style, chronicling events rather than analyzing processes, and often without exact documentation. Among the more popular and lasting of these studies are *Lale Devri* (The Tulip Age), first published in 1908, *Kadınlar Saltanati* (The Sultanante of Women), a four-volume series on the harem's political role, published in 1916–1923, and others in a long series entitled *Geçmis Asırlarda Türk Hayatı* (Turkish Life in Past Centuries), published from 1915 through 1933. Ahmet Refik was very much a late Ottoman intellectual, a proud member of both the last generation educated in Ottoman schools and the first generation of a Europeanizing Turkey. His work displays three general historiographical themes. The first is a simple positivism, a concern for factual presentation in preference to analytical approaches. It is no surprise to find that he published collections of documents without discussing the principles behind his choices. Second, Refik was a romantic, and his biographical works illustrate this very clearly: he had a feel for the striking anecdote or tableau. Finally, a strain from which no member of his generation was free emerges in his work: Turkish nationalism permeates his writing and has helped keep it popular with subsequent generations. Devoted to the traditions that nurtured him, Refik did his utmost to inspire a new and different generation with the memories of what Turkish rulers of prior ages had accomplished. There is no other Turkish historian of his age whose work was read so widely and for so long.

Bibliography: Muzaffer Gökman, *Tarihi Sevdiren Adam, Ahmet Refik Altınay* (Istanbul, 1978); Resad Ekrem Koçu, *Ahmet Refik* (Istanbul, 1938), with selections; Otto Spies, *Die türkische Prosaliteratur der Gegenwart* (Leipzig, 1943).

Rudi Paul Lindner

ÂSIM Efendi, Mütercim Ahmet (Gaziantep, 1755? –Üsküdar, 1819), Turkish learned man (*âlim*), translator, philologist, and Ottoman court historiographer. Âsim began to study Arabic, Persian, Turkish, and the Islamic sciences at an early age and became known for his learning. After serving as secretary (*katip*) in provincial law courts, he went to Istanbul in 1790 and soon won the patronage of Sultan Selim III with his translation of a Persian dictionary. Âsim was appointed professor (*müderris*) in 1796, judge (*Kadi*) of Salonika in 1814, and court historiographer (*vakanüvis*) from 1807 to his death in 1819. As court historiographer, he compiled an Ottoman history from the Treaty of Sistova (1791) to the accession of Sultan Mahmud II (1808) which was published (date uncertain) in two volumes. *Tarih-i Âsim* (Âsim's History), written in an ornate style, is generally regarded as the most important *vakanüvis* history written between those of Mustafa Naima and Ahmet Cevdet Pasa (q.v.). Âsim relied heavily on the chronicles of previous court historiographers but added his own record and critical view of events. His account of Selim III's reform efforts and the opposition to them which culminated in Selim's deposition and Mahmud's accession is especially comprehensive. As a conservative, he criticized the Western-inspired reforms of the period without directly attacking his imperial patron. Âsim's translation of al-Jabarti's Arabic chronicle of Napoleon's invasion of Egypt in 1798 and the ensuing French occupation remains unpublished. He is best known as the translator (*mütercim*) of the Persian dictionary, *Burhan-ı Katı* (1799), and the Arabic dictionary, *al-Kamus al-Muhit* (3 vols., 1814–1817). These works have been cited among the earliest contributions to the simplification of the Turkish language, and Âsim is considered a pioneer in Turkish-language reform.

Bibliography: "Âsim Efendi (Mütercim Ayintabli Ahmed)," *İstanbul Ansiklopedisi*, vol. 2, pp. 1105–1107; Franz Babinger, "Âsim, Ahmad," *Encyclopaedia of Islam*, New Edition, vol. 1, p. 707; Franz Babinger, *Die Geschichtsschreiber der Osmanen und ihre Werke* (Leipzig, 1927), pp. 339ff; I. M. K. İnal, *Son Asir Türk Sairleri* (Turkish Poets of the Last Century), (Istanbul, 1930), vol. 1, pp. 66–72; M. Fuad Köprülü, "Âsim Efendi," *İslam Ansiklopedisi*, vol. 1, pp. 653–73.

Richard L. Chambers

ATÂULLAH Efendi, Şanizade (Istanbul, 1771–Tire, 1826), Turkish learned man (*âlim*), physician, and Ottoman court historiographer. Şanizade studied at the Süleymaniye Medical College (*Tip Medresesi*) and the Engineering School (*Mühendishane*) in Istanbul and became known for his vast erudition in medicine, mathematics, physics, astronomy, military science, law, history, literature, calligraphy, music, painting, and clock-making. He knew several Eastern and Western languages and was fluent in French. Şanizade entered the learned ranks (*ilmiye*) as a teacher (*müderris*) in 1793, became judge (*kadi*) of Eyup in 1814, succeeded Mutercim A. Âsim Efendi, (q.v.) as court historiographer (*vakanüvis*) in 1819, and two years later acquired the title of judge of Mecca. He was dismissed and replaced as court historiographer by Şeyhizade Esat in 1825. Following the destruction of the Janissaries in 1826, he was banished to Tire in Anatolia and died there in the same year. His alleged connection with the Bektaşi dervish order, his association with the Beşiktaş Society which was viewed with suspicion by the sultan, and the intrigues of the court physician, Mustafa Behçet, who envied Şanizade's medical knowledge, all contributed to his downfall. Şanizade first attracted Sultan Mahmud II's attention with his books on medicine, most of which were translated from French or Italian. They include works on anatomy, physiology, surgery, internal medicine, and vaccination and mark the beginning of modern medicine in Turkey. Şanizade was the first to translate modern medical vocabulary into Turkish. He also translated works on military science and wrote peotry under the pen-name, Atâ. His chronicle, *Şanizade Tarihi* (Şanizade's History), is a continuation of Âsim's Ottoman chronicle and covers the years 1808–1821. It was published in four volumes (1867–1875) many years after his death. Şanizade is the first Turkish historian known to have used French sources; his work, though traditional in style, is more moderate in tone than those of his predecessors. The introduction, a commentary on the science of history, was admired by Mahmud II and later by Ahmet Cevdet Pasa (q.v.), who wrote a somewhat similar introduction to his own history.

Bibliography: "Atâullah, [Şanizade]," *Inönö Ansiklopedisi*, vol. 4, pp. 124–125; "Ataullah Efendi, Şanizade," *Meydan Larousse*, vol. 1, pp. 814–815; Franz Babinger, *Die Geschichtsschreiber der Osmanen und ihre Werke* (Leipzig, 1927), pp. 346–347; I. M. K. İnal, *Son Asir Türk Şairleri* (Turkish Poets of the Last Century), (Istanbul, 1930), vol. 1, pp. 110–24; "Şanizade Ataullah Efendi," *Türkiye Ansiklopedisi*, vol. 5, pp. 204–205.

Richard L. Chambers

BARKAN, Ömer Lütfi (Edirne, 1905, 1902, or 1903–Istanbul, 1979), Turkish historian. One of the founders of Ottoman social and economic history and one of the most influential figures in modern Turkish historiography. Barkan's early publications, beginning in 1935, deal with the Ottoman system of landholding and its repercussions in the twentieth-century world, not only in Turkey itself but also in the Balkan countries which had once formed part of the Ottoman Empire. Barkan began his work from the premise that the principles of Islamic law are not in themselves sufficient to explain the shape taken by the Ottoman system of landholding. For this reason, in the late 1930s and early 1940s he was particularly concerned about the relationship between administrative practice as derived from the declared will of the sultan (*kanun*) to Islamic law as elaborated by pre-Ottoman and Ottoman jurists. In this early period, Barkan appears mainly as a legal historian, and his monumental edition of the tax regulations of different Ottoman provinces (*liva kanunnameleri*) is the culmination of his work during those years: *XV. ve XVI. Asırlarda Osmanlı Imparatorluğunda Zirai Ekonominin Hukuki ve Mali Esasları*, vol. 1 *Kanunlar* (Istanbul, 1943; The Legal and Financial Foundations of the Agricultural Economy in the Ottoman Empire). However, at the same time, Barkan began to study the issue of labor control in the Ottoman Empire during 1450–1600. He insisted that Ottoman peasants were free men and women, subject to the jurisdiction of ordinary courts. By corollary, the holders of public tax grants who joined the sultan's army (*sipahi*) and who might at first glance be equated with European knights, possessed no jurisdictional rights over the peasants in the villages assigned to them. At the same time Barkan studied in great detail various types of agricultural laborers who were more dependent on the will of the state or foundation administrators than ordinary peasants. In his eyes, these marginal categories of dependent agricultural laborers truly constituted a parallel to European serfs. But at the same time he emphasized that the Ottoman state in its "classical" sixteenth-century shape tended to merge all these different categories into one unified group of peasants working family-sized farms. This judgment seems to assume that initial variation and later convergence of peasant conditions did not also occur in European feudalism.

From the late 1940s and early 1950s onward, Barkan gradually shifted his research interests to a demographic history of the Ottoman Empire based on Ottoman sources, particularly the fifteenth- and sixteenth-century tax registers, which in principle were meant to record the entire Ottoman taxpaying population.

His map of early sixteenth-century Ottoman Rumelia, based on this documentation has proved the starting point for all further research in this matter (*Istanbul Üniversitesi İktisat Fakültesi Mecmuasi*, 1949–1950, explanations in vol. 15 1953–1954. The counterpart map concerning Anatolia has unfortunately not been published. Barkan's dialogue with Fernand Braudel (q.v.), beginning with the review of the first edition of Braudel's book on the Mediterranean, (French version in: *Istanbul Üniversitesi Iktisat Fakültesi Mecmuasi*, 1949–1950), proved fertile for both sides. In his later years Braudel continued to be sensitive to new research on the Ottoman Empire, while Barkan's concern with the practical conditions of work, as opposed to the purely legal framework, surely owes something to the impact of *Annales*. In the 1950s Barkan's concern with social and economic history found its mature expression in *Süleymaniye Cami ve Imareti Insaati, 1550–1551* (2 vols., 1972; The Construction of the Süleymaniye Mosque and Hospices). Here he dealt not only with the organization of a large construction site and the procurement of construction materials, but also with the recruitment, pay, and social background of the workers who built one of the major monuments of Ottoman architecture. During the last fifteen or twenty years of his career, Barkan's main scholarly endeavor was to make accessible Ottoman sources usable for a history of Ottoman prices between about 1450 and 1650. For that purpose he published a wide-ranging selection of documents, usually with long comments and tabulations. Among the materials published are lists of income and expenditure concerning the Ottoman central government, major pious foundations, and the Palace. In addition, two book-length publications deal with the estate inventories of personages associated with the Ottoman central administration, and the pious foundations of Istanbul, respectively: "Edirne Askeri Kassamı 'na ait Tereke Defterleri (1545–1659)," *Belgeler*, III, 5–6 (1966): (The Probate Inventory Registers of the Edirne Official in Charge of Dividing up Inheritances Left by Ottoman State Functionaries) and along with Ekrem H. Ayverdi, *Istanbul Vakıfları Tahrir Defteri (953/1546 tarihli)* (1970; The 1546 Register of Istanbul Pious Foundations).

Barkan's concern with prices was also expressed in the construction of the first long-term Ottoman price curve, based on the wholesale food prices paid by Istanbul and Edirne pious foundations. An English version of this article is available as "The Price Revolution of the Sixteenth Century: A Turning Point in the Economic History of the Near East," *International Journal of Middle East Studies* 6(1975): 3–28. Barkan's interpretation of this curve constitutes the beginning not only of all later discussion of Ottoman price history, but also of the problem as to when and how Ottoman state and society became incorporated into a world economy dominated by European capitalism. Barkan's peculiar quality as a historian was his ability to combine an immersion in the intricacies of Ottoman archival sources with an awareness of world historical trends, primarily the European history of the early modern period. Moreover, many of his basic hypotheses have formed the background for all later discussion of the classical Ottoman system. Throughout his lifetime, he remained very aware of these discussions, even though he scarcely approved of the uses to which a younger generation of scholars has sometimes put his work.

Bibliography: Anonymous on behalf of the publisher Gözlem Yayınları in: *Ömer Lütfi Barkan, Türkiyede Toprak Meselesi* (Istanbul, 1980), pp. 5–22, 905–913; Robert Mantran in: *Mémorial Ömer Lütfi Barkan*, Bibliothèque de l'Institut français d'Etudes Anatoliennes d'Istanbul 28 (Paris, 1980), pp. VII–XVII; Irène Mélikoff, *Turcica 13* (1981): 7–9; Halil Sahillioğlu, *Istanbul Üniversitesi Iktisat Fakültesi Mecmuasi* 41, 1–4 (1982–1983): 1–38; Mahmut Şakiroğlu, *Belleten* 44, 173 (1980): 153–177.

Suraiya Faroqhi

CEVDET Paşa, Ahmet (Lofça [Lovec, Bulgaria], 1822–Istanbul, 1895), Turkish learned man (*âlim*), statesman, and Ottoman court historiographer. After traditional studies in his birthplace, Cevdet went to Istanbul in 1839, attended classes in the religious colleges (*medreses*), and studied mathematics, astronomy, Persian, and other subjects privately with reputable scholars. Entering the learned ranks (*ilmiye*) in 1844, Cevdet's exceptional talents attracted attention and the patronage of the head of the learned hierarchy, Şeyhülislam Arif Hikmet. This patron recommended Cevdet as an adviser on Islamic law to Grand Vezir Mustafa Reşid Paşa. Through this contact with the leading figures of the Tanzimat reform movement, Cevdet's education and career took a new turn. He learned French, became a close friend of Faud Paşa, and was drawn into the world of administration and politics. Although he retained his official connection with the learned profession until 1866 and rose to the rank of chief judge (*kazasker*) of Anatolia, he functioned primarily as a bureaucrat, taking an active part in law, education, and language reforms and in provincial inspection and pacification. In 1850 he became the first director of the Teachers' College (*Darülmuallimin*) and chief secretary of the Education Council (*Meclis-i Maarif*). As a member of the Tanzimat Council, he figured prominently in the legal and judicial reforms of the late 1850s. Appointed court historiographer (*vakanüvis*) in 1855, he relinquished that post in 1866 when he was transferred to the bureaucratic ranks (*mülkiye*) and appointed governor (*vali*) of Aleppo with the rank of vezir. Cevdet returned to Istanbul in 1868 to assume the presidency of the Council of Judicial Ordinances (*Divan-ı Ahkâm-ı Adliye*) and soon thereafter was named minister of justice. Under his direction, the composition of a civil law code (*Mecelle*) based on the Hanafi school of Islamic law was begun. Five volumes were completed by 1870 when Cevdet was appointed governor of Bursa. Soon recalled, he continued, while holding various other high positions, to direct the composition of the *Mecelle* until the final volumes were published in 1877. Between 1868 and 1890, Cevdet was four times minister of justice, three times minister of education, once each minister of interior, minister of commerce, and minister of imperial endowments; and, for ten days in 1879, he served as president of the Council of Ministers. He also served brief terms as governor of Yanya and governor of Syria in the 1870s.

Out of office from 1882 to 1886 and again from 1890 until his death in 1895, Cevdet occupied himself with scholarly and literary pursuits. His famous *Tarih-i Cevdet* (Cevdet's History) ranks with Naima's chronicle as a masterpiece of Turkish historiography. This twelve-volume history of the Ottoman Empire from the Treaty of Küçük Kaynarce (1774) to the destruction of the Janissaries (1826) was written over a thirty-year period beginning in the 1850s. The traditional annalistic style of presentation is frequently interrupted by full, critical accounts of important developments; and a more modern, simple writing style is employed after Volume 5. In the last decade of his life, Cevdet revised and radically rearranged the work with volume 1 becoming an introduction reminiscent of Ibn Khaldun's *Muqaddimah* (Prolegomena). This final edition (*Tertib-i Cedid*) was published in 1891–1892. Cevdet has left two important sources for nineteenth-century Ottoman history. Begun while he was court historiographer, *Tezâkir-i Cevdet* (Cevdet's Memoranda) records contemporary events, presents problems and personalities known personally to him, and concludes with an extensive autobiography (*Tezkere # 40*). These memoranda have been edited by Cavit Baysun (1953–1967). Cevdet's *Mâruzat* (Petitions) was written at the request of Sultan Abdülhamit II and complements the *Tezâkir* with observations on the period 1839–1876. The first part is lost, but parts two through five have been edited by Yusuf Halaçoğlu (1980). Cevdet also wrote *Kırım ve Kavkaz Tarihçesi* (1889–1890; Short History of the Crimea and Caucasus), based largely on a work by Halim Giray, and he completed Pirizade Mehmet Sait's Turkish translation of Ibn Khaldun's (1860–1861) *Muqaddimah*. Cevdet's mastery of the simplified literary style that gained acceptance in the nineteenth century is best shown in his *Kısas-ı Enbiya ve Tavarih-i Hulefa* (The Prophets' Tales and the Caliphs' Stories) which he composed late in life. Immensely popular, it has had many printings including a two-volume edition in the modern Turkish alphabet (1952). Other products of his pen include works on Turkish grammar, eloquence, calendar reform, logic, and law.

Bibliography: H. Bowen, "Ahmad Djewdet Pasha," *Encyclopaedia of Islam*, New Edition, vol. 1, pp. 284–286; Istanbul University, Faculty of Letters, *Ahmed Cevdet Paşa Semineri, Bildiriler* (Ahmed Cevdet Paşa Seminar. Communications), (Istanbul, 1986); Ebül 'ula Mardin, *Medenî Hukuk Cephesinden Ahmet Cevdet Paşa* (Ahmet Cevdet Paşa from the Civil Law Front), (Istanbul, 1946); Ümid Meriç, *Cevdet Paşa'nin Cemiyet ve Devlet; Görüsü* (Cevdet Paşa's View of Society and State), (Istanbul, 1975); Ali Ölmezoğlu, "Cevdet Paşa," *İslam Ansiklopedisi*, vol. 3, pp. 114–123.

Richard L. Chambers

LÛTFI Paşa, Ahmet (Istanbul, 1816–Istanbul, 1907), Turkish learned man (*âlim*), bureaucrat, and Ottoman court historiographer. Lûtfi interrupted his traditional religious education with one year of study in the Military Engineering School (Hendesehane-i Berrî) and in 1831 entered the learned ranks (*ilmiye*) as a teacher (*müderris*). Ten years later he transferred to the scribal ranks (*mülkiye*) and worked in various offices of the Ottoman bureaucracy, among them the

Grand Vezir's Secretariat (Sadaret Mektubi Kalemi), Police Council (Zabtiye Meclisi), and Medical Council (Tıbbiye Meclisi), Education Council (Maarif Meclisi), and Official Records Office (Takvimhane). During these years his duties included collating official documents, translating from Persian and Arabic, teaching Turkish composition at the Medical School (Mekteb-i Tıbbiye), editing the official Ottoman gazette, *Takvim-i Vakayi* (Calendar of Events), and supervising government printing. In 1865 Lûtfi succeeded Ahmet Cevdet Pasa (q.v.) as court historiographer. From his death in 1907 to the appointment of Abdurrahman Şeref in 1909, that post remained vacant. Lûtfi returned to the learned hierarchy in 1876 with the rank of judge (*kadi*) of Istanbul, was promoted to chief judge (*kazasker*) of Anatolia in 1880, and became chief judge of Rumelia in 1881. He was a member of the Council of State (*Şura-yı Devlet*) in 1877 and again in 1887. *Tarih-i Lûtfi* (Lûtfi's History) is a continuation of Cevdet's Ottoman history but pales by comparison to it. Volumes 1–7 were published between 1873 and 1889; Volume 8 was edited and published in 1910 with supplementary notes and a biographical sketch of Lûtfi by his successor, the last Ottoman court historiographer, Abdurrahman Şeref; and Münir Aktepe's edition of volume 9 appeared in 1984. Volumes 10–15 are found in manuscript in the Turkish Historical Society Library in Ankara. Lûtfi's chronicle draws on information from the *Takvim-i Vakayi* and government documents and is written in a straightforward style. It covers the years 1825–1876 and points out the democratic elements in the reforms of that period. *Divançe-yi Lûtfi* (1885; Lûtfi's Small Divan) contains some of his poetry as well as historical materials in verse form. He also prepared a Turkish translation of a work attributed to al-Ghazali which he presented to Sultan Abdülmecid (c. 1840), and an alphabetically arranged dictionary, *Lugat-ı Kamus*, of over fifty thousand words from Mutereim A. Asim Efendi's (q.v.) Turkish translation of the Arabic dictionary *al-Kamus al-Muhit*. Only the first two parts of the Âsim dictionary were published (1865–1866 and 1869–1870), but the manuscript is in the Archaeological Museum Library in Istanbul.

Bibliography: Franz Babinger, *Die Geschichtsschreiber der Osmanen und ihre Werke.* (Leipzig, 1927), pp. 384–385; I. M. K. Inal, *Son Asır Türk Şairleri* (Turkish Poets of the Last Century), (Istanbul, 1930), vol. 1, pp. 890–896; Bursali Mehmet Tahir, *Osmanlı Müellifleri* (Ottoman Authors), (Istanbul, 1924), vol. 3, pp. 136–137; M. Münir Aktepe, "Lûtfi Efendi, Ahmad," *Encyclopaedia of Islam*, New Edition, vol. 5, pp. 836–837; *Tarih-i Lûtfi* (Lûtfi's History), (Istanbul, 1910), vol. 8, pp. 4–6.

Richard L. Chambers

Great Historians:
United States

ADAMS, Henry (Boston, 1838–Washington, D.C., 1918), essayist, novelist and historian of the United States. Professor at Harvard University (1870–1876). Although he was a successful teacher, Adams left the university to live the life of an independent gentleman scholar and intellectual. Today some of his chapters are still read as history, but Henry Adams better represents the historian as source. As the son of a great family of considerable wealth, that had produced two presidents, John Adams and John Quincy Adams, themselves of a philosophical bent, Adams had opportunities to develop and to use those qualities of mind—imagination, attention to and memory for detail, willingness to try out new analytical frameworks, and a restless seeking for spiritual peace—which make his writings an invaluable source, a record of the impressions made on a sensitive and active mind by, first, the quest for "laws" of social science, then by the romantic and relativistic pessimism of the fin de siècle, and finally, by the fear, then less common, that technology would defeat human efforts to control it. Adams' *The History of the United States During the Jefferson and Madison Administrations* (9 vols., 1889–1984) represented his effort to write history in the Rankean mode and to measure the linear progress of the American people from 1800 to 1817. The first six chapters of volume 1 and the last four chapters of volume 9 were an attempt, perhaps the first in the United States, to write coherent thematic social history, history of the people as "force," whose energy occasionally yielded "representative types" but not heroes in the manner of Francis Parkman (q.v.). God, who had served as cause in the work of George Bancroft (q.v.) and others, was also strikingly absent from the pages of Henry Adams. Adams' originality was in his effort to describe the lives of ordinary people by using the census, depicting the condition of roads and fields and analyzing diet as well as national character. Men did not command the course of history. While Thomas Jefferson was president, "Congress and the Executive appeared disposed to act as a machine for recording events, without guiding and controlling them." With characteristic irony, Adams chronicled the chasm between human intentions and the historical results. The scientific historian was not a lawyer: "The lawyer is required to give facts the mould of a theory; the historian need only state facts in their sequence." Writing to a friend in 1894, he noted that many "serious students of history" had felt while doing their work "that they stood on the brink of great generalization that would reduce all history under a law as clear as the laws which govern the material world." Yet, during the last years of the century, Adams came to doubt the possibility of social laws equivalent to the laws of physics. Articulating a new romantic and relativistic subjectivism, he began to argue that many "facts" were probably unreliable, that an historian's observations and conclusions were affected by his "education, his society and his age." There were, he decided, errors, "blunders which no precaution and no anxiety for truth" could prevent the historian from committing. Personal reasons and religious doubts may have led to this change in perspective, a new direction reflected in his books of cultural analysis and criticism, *Mont-Saint-Michel and Chartres* (1904), *The Education of Henry Adams* (1906), and in several famous essays, "The Rule of Phase Applied to History" (1909) and "Letter to American Teachers of History" (1910). These works, especially *The Education*, are written in a mood of gloom, pessimism, and failure.

Adams had read Karl Pearson and Henri Poincaré, who questioned the certainties of nineteenth-century science. He was aware of experiments with radiation and electricity which suggested unmeasurable forces. New ideas of human psychology suggested a fragmented self rather than a unity. Modern man, he wrote, "took at once the form of a bicycle rider, mechanically balancing himself by inhibiting all his inferior personalities, and sure to fall into the subconscious chaos below, if one of his inferior personalities got on top. The only absolute truth was the subconscious chaos below, which every one could feel when he sought it." He ended his life with a series of questions, such as "the effects of unlimited [technological] power on limited mind," which continue to resonate. He had, says T. Jackson Lears, "the courage of his contradictions."

Bibliography: Keith R. Burich, "Henry Adams, the Second Law of Thermodynamics, and the Course of History," *Journal of the History of Ideas* 48 (1987): 467–483; Keith R. Burich, " 'Our power is always running ahead of our mind': Henry Adams's Phases of History," *The New England Quarterly* 67 (1989): 163–187; Donald Hall, "Henry Adams's History," *The Sewanee Review* 95 (1987): 518–525; William Jordy, *Henry Adams: Scientific Historian* (New Haven, Conn., 1952); T. Jackson Lears, "In Defense of Henry Adams," *Wilson Quarterly* 7 (1983): 82–93; J. C. Levenson, *The Mind and Art of Henry Adams* (Boston, 1957); Ernest Samuels, *Henry Adams*, 3 vols. (Cambridge, Mass., 1948–1964); Edward N. Saveth, "Introduction," *The Education of Henry Adams and Other Selected Writings* (New York, 1963), pp. ix–xlvii; Elizabeth Stevenson, *Henry Adams* (New York, 1956).

Ellen Nore

ANDREWS, Charles M. (Wethersfield, Conn., 1863–East Dover, Conn., 1943), historian of the colonial era of the United States. Andrews was professor of History at Johns Hopkins University (1907–1910) and at Yale University (1910–1931). Emphasizing institutional history, he was a founder of the "imperial school" of colonial history, a viewpoint that saw the American Revolution in the international context of the worldwide British Empire. Andrews did important work in his doctoral dissertation, "The River Towns of Connecticut: A Study of Wethersfield, Hartford, and Windsor" (1889), in which he disputed the popular Teutonist theory of the origins of American institutions in tribal meetings in premedieval German woods. Much of the research for his major work, *The Colonial Period of American History* (4 vols., 1934–1938) was carried out in British archives, which he was the first to explore. He developed a theme that has endured in the writing of North American colonial history: the emergence of the colonial assemblies as centers of power which the British were unable to control. "Primarily," he wrote, "the American Revolution was a political and constitutional movement and only secondarily one that was either financial, commerical or social." History, he wrote in 1894, is "the telescope and microscope of social man." And he did not appear, in his lifetime, to question the attainability of "scientific" history. In 1898 he spoke thus of evidence: "To my mind it is not essential that we should know what subjects to study beforehand, but rather it is important that we should know what material is available and let that guide our thoughts." In 1924, delivering a presidential address to the American Historical Association, he reflected a devotion to the historical monograph written in straightforward, plain prose: "The monograph in history corresponds to the experiment in the laboratory." He did not like history told as a story of progress or the use of the metaphors of Darwinian evolution. He did not expect to find "laws'" of historical development. He saw his own writings as value-free reports on documentary research.

Bibliography: A. S. Eisenstadt, *Charles McLean Andrews: A Study in American Historical Writing* (New York, 1956); Jessica Kross, "Charles M. Andrews," in *Twentieth-Century American Historians*, vol. 17 of *Dictionary of Literary Biography* (Detroit, 1983), pp. 9–17.

Ellen Nore

BAINTON, Roland Herbert (Ilkeston, England, 1894–New Haven, Conn., 1984), American historian. Termed by fellow scholars "the Nestor of Reformation history in America," Bainton began the study of Latin at age twelve and the following year that of German. After receiving a B.A. from Whitman College (Walla Walla, Washington) in 1914, he went on to a B.D. from Yale Divinity School in 1917 and a Ph.D. in 1921. In 1927 he was ordained a Congregationalist minister after he had already embarked on an academic career. Holding a joint appointment at Yale University in the Divinity School and in the History Department, he rose from the rank of instructor of church history in 1920 to become Titus Street professor of ecclesiastical history in 1936, a chair held until his retirement in 1962. A significant feature of his celebrated Reformation history course was that social, economic, political, and intellectual matters were important, as they affected or were affected by the Reformation. In his classes he stressed the use of original sources, and this meant that students needed to read foreign languages. Realizing, however, that students would need sources in English too, he published his *Bibliography of Materials Available in English on the Continental Reformation* in 1935. Another service was rendered advanced students and scholars in 1948, when he joined two American and three German scholars to found an international journal, the *Archiv für Reformationsgeschichte*. Of his numerous books and articles, some were directed toward scholars, others were written for children, and still others were intended for both scholars and the reading public. His best-seller, *Here I Stand: A Life of Martin Luther* (1950), fell into the last-named category. Its clear, readable style, the absence of paginal footnotes, the dramatic descriptions of Luther and the events in which he figured, and the reproductions of German woodcuts all won the general reader. Scholars praised his unbiased treatment, his reliance on original sources (these were cited in the back of the book), and his inclusion of the social and political contexts of Luther's background. Another well-received book was *Erasmus of Christendom* (1969); instead of presenting the usual picture of a caustic-tongued iconoclast, it portrayed a pious product of the *Devotio Moderna* and a critic of war and all forms of violence. His three-volume *Women of the Reformation* (1971, 1973, 1977) was written not simply because women had been neglected by historians, but because they were sometimes the ones who initiated church reforms. Another set of studies, *The Travail of Religious Liberty: Nine Biograhical Studies* (1951) and *Hunted Heretic: The Life and Death of Michael Servetus, 1511–1553* (1953), dealt with toleration and persecution. His conclusion was that persecution "thwarts, warps, and crushes individuals," but he cautioned his readers to be wary of judging sixteenth-century persecutors, both Catholic (such as Torquemada) and Protestant (such as Calvin), for they had believed they were doing the right thing "for truth and . . . concern for the victim." "Seldom do we reflect," he added, "that we . . . do not hesitate for the preservation of our culture to reduce whole cities to cinders." His influence still lingers. *Here I Stand* remains one of the best biographies of Luther. His famous course at Yale on the Reformation prepared the way for the adoption of similar university courses elsewhere. By his example he helped to break the tendency of church historians to remain within the narrow perspectives of their own sectarian religious affiliations.

Bibliography: Miriam Usher Chrisman, "Humanitas Pietas: The Shoulders on Which We Stand," *The Sixteenth Century Journal* 14, no. 1 (1983): 3–9; Georgia Harkness, "Roland H. Bainton: A Biographical Appreciation," in Franklin H. Littell, ed., *Reformation Studies: Essays in Honor of Roland H. Bainton* (Richmond, Va., 1962); Steven H. Simpler, *Roland H. Bainton: An Examination of His Reformation Historiography* (Lewiston, N.Y., 1985).

Louise Salley Parker

BANCROFT, George (Worcester, Mass., 1800–Washington, D.C., 1891), historian of the United States. Democratic party politician, speechwriter for Presidents Andrew Jackson, James K. Polk, and Andrew Johnson, and diplomat, as minister to Berlin (1867–1874). The nineteenth century was a time of great optimism among literate white males in the United States, and Bancroft's *History of the United States from the Discovery of the American Continent to the Present Time*, 10 vols. (1834–1875), and its several revisions (1876, 1883–1885) were written for an audience that believed in American uniqueness and virtue, as opposed to decadent Europe, and in Divine Providence as the origin of an expanding empire. Bancroft epitomized romantic idealism, which he studied and experienced at the University of Göttingen, where he obtained a Ph.D. in 1820, and at the University of Berlin, where he attended lectures by Georg Wilhelm F. Hegel (q.v.). In Bancroft's view, the historian as a man of letters should select universal themes, should seek those elements that form the Zeitgeist of the nation, and should show the working of the national spirit throughout the nation's history. But it was the American context in which Bancroft lived, a time when he saw what appeared to him as the triumph of democracy, capitalism, national centralization, and antislavery, which made idealism seem the necessary explanatory device. The exceptionalism of what would become the United States existed from the beginning of colonial history: "The elements of our country, such as she exists today, were already there. Of the institutions of the Old World, monarchy had no motive to emigrate. . . . The feudal aristocracy had accomplished its mission in Europe; it could gain no new life. . . . Priestcraft did not emigrate . . . to the forests of America. . . . Nothing came from Europe but a free people. . . . Like Moses, they had escaped from Egyptian bondage to the wilderness, that God might there give them the pattern of the tabernacle" (vol. 2, 1837). His *History of the Formation of the Constitution of the United States of America*, 2 vols. (1882) also shows the hand of God and sees that document as a materialization of the spirit of freedom.

Bancroft used documents but with little regard for their context. He remains great as a source of intellectual history of the ruling groups of the nineteenth century. He saw the entrepreneurial exuberance, the proliferation of great corporations, the nationalism of the northern victory in the Civil War, the democracy of universal white male suffrage, as well as the cable, the steam engine, and the end of slavery as evidence that "the God who rules history is knowable." In 1882 he expressed a viewpoint, still popular among some groups in the United States, that "the ignorance and prejudices that come from isolation are worn away in the conflict of the forms of culture. We learn to think the thought, to hope the hope of mankind. Former times spoke of the dawn of civilization in some land; we live in the morning of the world." In the United States, he originated the cult of national innocence and progress.

Bibliography: Lilian Handlin, *George Bancroft: The Intellectual As Democrat* (New York, 1985); Mark A. DeWolfe Howe, *The Life and Letters of George Bancroft*, 2 vols. (New York, 1908); David Levin, *History As Romantic Art* (Stanford, Calif., 1959); Russell

B. Nye, *George Bancroft: Brahmin Rebel* (New York, 1944); Richard C. Vitzthum, *The American Compromise: Theme and Method in the Histories of Bancroft, Parkman, and Adams* (Norman, Okla., 1974).

Ellen Nore

BEARD, Charles A. (Knightstown, Ind., 1874–New Haven, Conn., 1948), historian of the United States. Lecturer in the Department of History, Columbia University (1904–1906), professor of politics and government in the Department of Public Law, Columbia University (1907–1917). Beard was president of both the American Political Science Association (1926) and the American Historical Association (1933). He was a far-ranging scholar and debator, who wrote monographs as well as synthetic works that changed the way people thought about the history of the United States. He also attempted in his writings on the philosophy of history to bring to the attention of the profession European thinking on the relativity of knowledge. Although he had written several books before *An Economic Interpretation of the Constitution of the United States* appeared in 1913, it was this work that brought him national attention. In writing about the origins of the Constitution, Beard rejected the notions of divine guidance offered by George Bancroft (q.v.), the emphasis of the Teutonists on the political genius of certain races, and the assertions of idealists who saw the Constitution as the fruit of philosophical speculation which represented, in a Hegelian sense, "the spirit of the people." Drawing on the ideas of European scholars, such as Rudolph von Jhering, whose phrase *Zweck im Recht* (concrete interest reflected in the law) Beard took as a theme of his interpretation, and employing the imaginative and novel technique of collective biography, Beard surveyed the economic interests of the members of the convention. Using as a source the Treasury Records of 1790, which no one had used before, Beard showed that a majority of the members of the constitutional convention probably held public securities in 1787. In his view, the Constitution represented a victory of certain economic interests, "financial, mercantile, and personal property interests generally," over other, more popular, agrarian interests "based on paper money." He concluded that "the mercantile and manufacturing interests wrote their *Zweck im Recht*; and they paid for their victory by large concessions to the slaveowning planters of the south." Thus, "The Constitution was not created by 'the whole people' as the jurists have said . . . it was the work of a consolidated group whose interests knew no state boundaries and were truly national in their scope." In *Economic Origins of Jeffersonian Democracy* (1915), Beard speculated that the divisions over the Constitution had extended into the 1790s and were the basis for the first political parties in the United States.

Beard's books on the Constitution were studded with suggestions for further research, unanswered questions, and guesses. Many of his specific hypotheses have been subjected to devastating criticisms, but his greatness lay in the fact that he reoriented scholarship on the origins of the Constitution and of American political parties. Beard never accepted the particular thesis of Frederick Jackson

Turner (q.v.) on the significance of the frontier in American history. Turner, Beard thought, had neglected the "semi-feudal plantation system" of the South, the urban dimension, and the importance of the working classes to the development of democracy. With his wife, Mary Ritter Beard, Beard published *The Rise of American Civilization* (1927), in which the unique material abundance of America, a fact dictated by geography, was the central theme—not ideology, institutions, or racial characteristics unique to Anglo-Saxons. At the end of his life, Beard's interest shifted to recent American foreign policy, and he published two books extremely critical of President Franklin Roosevelt's abuses of the democratic process in the pursuit of a foreign policy, intervention in World War II, that had not been honestly presented to the American public. *American Foreign Policy in the Making, 1932–1940* (1946) and *President Roosevelt and the Coming of the War, 1941: A Study in Appearances and Realities* (1948) were path-breaking books, which questioned the constitutionality of many of President Roosevelt's prewar actions and catalogued a number of occasions on which the president had lied to the public or their representatives in the government.

In "Written History as an Act of Faith," his presidential address to the American Historical Association in 1933, and in numerous other books and articles, Beard speculated on the nature of history. The relativity of human knowledge was a main current of Western thought by the time Beard wrote, and he was influenced by the popularizations of the New Physics, by Benedetto Croce's (q.v.) writings on the subjective nature of not only hypotheses but also of fact, and by Karl Mannheim's social theory of knowledge. Rejecting the absolute relativism of Croce, Beard adopted from Alfred North Whitehead the notion that facts do exist outside of the mind of the observer. "What I have tried to say so that it can be understood," Beard wrote in 1938, "is that no historian can describe the past *as it actually was* and that every historian's work— that is, his selection of facts, his emphasis, his omissions, his organizations, and his methods of presentation—bears a relation to his own personality and to the age and circumstances in which he lives. This is relativism as I understand it." In his writing, Beard consistently stressed the political nature of history. It was, he said, "a prism" in the hands of policymakers, and therefore, historians had an inevitable "public responsibility." It was not, as so many of his critics said, that history *should* be propaganda, but rather that it *could* be propaganda. The scientific method and the rejection of any absolutist interpretation of events, coupled with a recognition of one's own biases, could, he urged, only produce greater freedom of choice within democracy and an escape from the totalitarian shadow lurking in what Mannheim, referring to Sorel, had spoken of as the "intellectual twilight" of the twentieth century.

Bibliography: Howard K. Beale, ed., *Charles A. Beard: An Appraisal* (Lexington, Ky., 1954); Bernard C. Borning, *The Political and Social Thought of Charles A. Beard* (Seattle, 1962); John Braeman, "Charles A. Beard," in *Twentieth-Century American Historians*, vol. 17 of *Dictionary of Literary Biography*, edited by Clyde N. Wilson

(Detroit, 1983), pp. 191–197; John Patrick Diggins, "Power and Authority in American History: The Case of Charles A. Beard and His Critics," *American Historical Review* 86 (1981): 701–730; Eugene D. Genovese, "Beard's Economic Interpretation of History," in *Charles A. Beard: An Observance of the Centennial of His Birth* (Greencastle, Ind., 1976; Ellen Nore, *Charles A. Beard: An Intellectual Biography* (Carbondale, Ill., 1983).

                                                                                        Ellen Nore

BECKER, Carl Lotus (Black Hawk County, Iowa, 1873–Ithaca, N.Y., 1945), American historian. Educated in history by Frederick Jackson Turner (q.v.) and Charles Homer Haskins (q.v.) at the University of Wisconsin (B.A., 1897, Ph.D., 1907), and by James Harvey Robinson (q.v.) at Columbia University, Becker taught modern European history at the University of Kansas (1902–1916) and Cornell University (1917–1941) and published in both American and European history. He was interested less in the record of events, "of what men have done," and more in "the state of mind that had conditioned events." He had the gift of psychological insight, an intuitive and intellectual comprehension of the moods and ideas of an individual, a group, or an epoch. He evolved a style in which content and form, sense and sound, were fused to convey his nuanced perceptions of past impulses and thoughts. Among American historians he remains perhaps the finest stylist of the twentieth century. He applied his psychological and literary gifts to the writing of several major histories and to three issues that concerned his generation: epistemology, or the nature and validity of historical knowledge; the idea of progress; and the prospects of the United States as an experiment in democracy. On each issue he held suspended polar opposites between which his mind moved. For example, on epistemology, as a young historian he apparently believed that a research historian of integrity could attain an exact, objective statement of what had happened. But from 1910 to 1940, in four thoughtful essays, including "Everyman His Own Historian" (1931), he gave the most significant American exposition of historical relativism. Every historian, he held, is affected by present conditions and needs and *should* be so affected. Like James Harvey Robinson and other "New Historians," with whom he sympathized, he believed history should be useful. Yet he always wore his relativism with a difference: while meeting present needs, research historians were nevertheless honor bound to get their facts straight; nor should their service to their generation be narrowly practical. "The value of history is not scientific but moral: by liberating the mind, by deepening the sympathies, by fortifying the will, it enables us to control, not society, but ourselves."

In 1940 Becker returned to the faith that professional historians were building a core of objective historical knowledge beyond the play of the wind and weather of changing climates of opinion. His essays on epistemology were accompanied by major historical works. His solid doctoral dissertation, "The History of Political Parties in the Province of New York: 1760–1776" (1909), advanced the argument that the American Revolution was fought not simply over home rule (apart from Great Britain), but also over who should rule at home in each colony, a thesis that is still being debated. In his *Eve of the Revolution* (1918) he sought to convey less a record of what colonial Americans did than "a sense of how they thought and felt about what they did." *The Declaration of Independence* (1922) was an outstanding essay on the interplay of formal ideas, popular philosophy, and revolutionary psychology. His *Heavenly City of the Eighteenth Century Philosophes* (1932) brilliantly compared the climates of opinion of the thirteenth, eighteenth, and twentieth centuries, arriving at the paradoxical conclusion that the eighteenth, so intellectually arrogant, was closer to the thirteenth than to the twentieth. His brilliant and brilliantly successful high school textbook, *Modern History: The Rise of a Democratic, Scientific, and Industrialized Civilization* (1931), delighted and enlightened high school, college, and graduate students and their teachers. As the title suggests, it was "New History" in action, though Becker would have disclaimed the label.

Bibliography: Milton M. Klein, "Detachment and the Writing of American History: The Dilemma of Carl Becker," in Alden Vaughn and George Billias, eds., *Perspectives on Early American History* (New York, 1973); Charlotte Watkins Smith, *Carl Becker: On History and the Climate of Opinion* (Ithaca, N.Y., 1956); Cushing Strout, *The Pragmatric Revolt in American History: Carl Becker and Charles Beard* (New Haven, Conn., 1958); Burleigh T. Wilkins, *Carl Becker: A Biographical Study in American Intellectual History* (Cambridge, Mass., 1961).

Harold T. Parker

BEMIS, Samuel Flagg (Worcester, Mass., 1891–New Haven, Conn., 1973), historian of the foreign relations of the United States. Professor at Colorado College (1917–1920), Whitman College (1923–1925), George Washington University (1925–1935), and Yale University (1935–1961). Bemis founded the discipline of diplomatic history in the United States. He wrote a number of specialized monographs: *Jay's Treaty: A Study in Commerce and Diplomacy* (1923), *Pinckney's Treaty: A Study of America's Advantage from Europe's Distress, 1783–1800* (1926), *John Quincy Adams and the Foundations of American Foreign Policy* (1949), and *John Quincy Adams and the Union* (1956), all of which exemplify his contention that the study of diplomacy and foreign policy requires using the archives of all nations concerned in the event in order for the narrative to contain all points of view. His *A Diplomatic History of the United States* (1936) was used by thousands of college students in five editions. Bemis' essays were collected in *American Foreign Policy & The Blessings of Liberty & Other Essays* (1962). He had worked during World War II and afterward for the U.S. government, and he believed in and supported with his writings the activist foreign policy of the United States after World War II. The size, wealth, and economic strength of the United States, he argued, made it the only real champion of liberty in the world. While revisionists spoke of American imperialism in the Third World, he wrote of expanding the area of freedom. A firm anticommunist, he believed that risking nuclear war was a necessity for American diplomats. His influence as the founder of the study of diplomatic history continues.

Bibliography: Thomas A. Bailey, "The Friendly Rivals: Bemis and Bailey," Society for Historians of American Foreign Relations *Newsletter*, 10 (1979): 12–17; Russell H. Bostert and John A. DeNovo, "Samuel Flagg Bemis," *Proceedings of the Massachusetts Historical Society* 85 (1973): 117–129; Kendrick A. Clements, "Samuel Flagg Bemis," in *Twentieth Century American Historians*, vol. 17 of *Dictionary of Literary Biography*, edited by Clyde N. Wilson. (Detroit, 1983), pp. 64–70.

Ellen Nore

BREASTED, James Henry (Rockford, Ill., 1865–New York City, 1935), American historian and archaeologist. Breasted excelled in the study of ancient languages. After graduating from Northwestern College in Naperville, Illinois, he enrolled in the Congregational Institute (later the Chicago Theological Seminary) in 1887. Toward the end of the second year he won a prize for his mastery of Hebrew. Eventually, he learned, on his own, Latin, Greek, Aramaic, Syriac, Babylonian cuneiform, Arabic, ancient Egyptian, French, and German. He continued his study of Hebrew at Yale University under William Rainey Harper (1890–1891), who encouraged him to enroll in the seminar of the great German Egyptologist, Adolf Erman, at the University of Berlin. After earning a Ph.D. in Oriental Studies from Berlin in 1893, he accepted the invitation of the archaeologist Flinders Petrie to visit the Cairo Museum to study and translate the inscriptions there. The following year he accepted President Harper's invitation to become assistant director of the Haskell Oriental Institute at the newly founded University of Chicago. Thereafter, Chicago was the headquarters and base of Breasted's activities.

From the start Breasted's work developed along several main lines. Since his salary was so low ($66.66 per month), he turned in desperation to teaching extension classes and giving public addresses. In this way he stimulated interest in ancient history and in his research and was able to finance several trips abroad. Over the decades his research projects grew in magnitude: first, simply to copy, translate, and publish in four volumes the ancient Egyptian inscriptions found in the Cairo Museum and in the museums of Europe and the United States; then, in 1902 and 1905, supported by Rockefeller funds, to do the same for all the inscriptions found in the Nile Valley; and after World War I, to identify the remains of ancient civilizations along the Tigris-Euphrates river valleys. Surprising "finds" were uncovered: for example, by the Nile Expedition of 1905, a temple of Ikhnaton and a city founded by him in Nubia, where no temple or town was believed to exist so far south. By 1932 the Oriental Institute which Breasted had founded at the University of Chicago was excavating in northern Syria, central Turkey, Iraq, and Iran, while the Megiddo Expedition in Palestine was unearthing that city dating back to Solomon's time. To bring the new discoveries to the public's attention, Breasted wrote an outstanding secondary school textbook, *Ancient Times: A History of the Early World* (1916), and for mature readers two works, *A History of Egypt from the Earliest Times to the Persian Conquest* (1912) and *The Conquest of Civilization* (1926). They bore the message that history should present "the life of man in all its manifestations" and that "one age grows out of another, and each civilization profits by that which has preceded it." In his last masterwork, *The Dawn of Conscience* (1934), Breasted raised the following question: how and when did earliest man, an "unmoral savage," ever develop a sense of morality? From "ancient documents," he concluded that civilization and a moral consciousness appeared first in Egypt. "I had more disquieting experiences before me when . . . I found that the Egyptians had possessed a standard of morals far superior to that of the Decalogue over a thousand years before the Decalogue."

Bibliography: Herman Ausubel, *Historians and Their Craft: A Study of the Presidential Addresses of the American Historical Association, 1884–1945* (New York, 1950), pp. 83, 244–245, 344–347; Charles Breasted, *Pioneer to the Past: The Story of James Henry Breasted, Archaeologist* (New York, 1943); "James Henry Breasted," *The National Cyclopedia of American Biography*, vol. 29, pp. 257–258; Edith W. Ware, "James Henry Breasted," *Dictionary of American Biography*, vol. 21, Supplement 1, pp. 110–113.

Louise Salley Parker

BRINTON, Clarence Crane (Winsted, Conn., 1898–Cambridge, Mass., 1968), American historian. Formally educated at Harvard University (B.A., 1919) and Oxford University (Ph.D., 1923), Brinton taught at Harvard from 1923 until his retirement in 1968, apart from wartime duty (1942–1945) with the Research and Analysis branch of the Office of Strategic Services (OSS). Between 1926 and 1959 he published sixteen books. Perhaps their outstanding characteristic was their range. His subject areas were the French Revolution and intellectual history, but within each area he did many things and lived in "many mansions." In *The Jacobins* (1930), for instance, he wrote a detailed monographic history: He tabulated the membership lists of the Jacobin clubs in French departmental and municipal archives to reach the startling (and durable) conclusion that the bulk of the members were not riff-raff or maladjusted psychopaths but respectable middle-class men who were carried by the fervor and ideals of the revolutionary movement into actions they ordinarily would not have taken. By contrast, in his volume for the "Langer series," *A Decade of Revolution 1789–1799* (1934), he placed the French Revolution in its broad European context. He wrote idiographic biography in his brilliant *The Lives of Talleyrand* (1936), but he also published the nomothetic *Anatomy of Revolution* (1938), which sought uniformities, generalizations, and even some "laws" in the background and course of the English Puritan Revolution of the seventeenth century, the American and French revolutions of the eighteenth, and the Russian Revolution of the twentieth. Following Vilfredo Pareto in his use of biological analogies, he compared revolution to a disease which in its course passes from prodrome to fever and crisis before reaching convalescence.

In intellectual history Brinton recognized that the scholar could write the history of a special field (e.g., the history of philosophy), or establish the text and thought of a single thinker, or, like Arthur Oncken Lovejoy (q.v.), trace the career of a single idea. He himself usually preferred to do something else: "to try to find the relations between the ideas of the philosophers, the intellectuals, the thinkers, and the actual way of living of the millions who carry the tasks of civilization." Here too he wrote a monograph, *The Political Ideas of the English Romanticists* (1926); a biography, *Nietzsche* (1941); and three surveys, *English Political Thought in the Nineteenth Century* (1933), *Ideas and Men: The Story of Western Thought* (from Plato to the present) (1950), and *The History of Western Morals* (from the Ancient Near East to the Twentieth Century) (1959). In *From Many One: The Process of Political Integration, the Problem of World Government* (1948) he brought his vast historical knowledge to bear on a contemporary issue. His attitude throughout his career was that of an urbane, intelligent, enlightened gentleman who prized reason, moderation, and common sense and who as a scholar objectively tried to understand all sorts and conditions of men, even fanatics and fools. The great historiographical controversies of the past one hundred years—the question of ethical judgment, "scientific" history versus "New History," historical relativism versus the new realism—did not agitate him. With the working eclecticism of the American historians of his generation, he superbly applied to each historical problem the best of all schools and the approaches (critical scrutiny of evidence, narrative of unique events, comparative method, social science procedures) that seemed appropriate.

Bibliography: Elizabeth C. Altman, "C. Crane Brinton," *International Encyclopedia of the Social Sciences*, vol. 18 (Biographical Supplement), pp. 72–75; David D. Bien, "Crane Brinton," *French Historical Studies* (1969): 113–119; James Friguglietti, "Crane Brinton: An American Historian of France's Revolution," *Proceedings* (1986) *of the Sixteenth Consortium on Revolutionary Europe 1750–1850* (Athens, Ga., 1987), pp. 175–186; Barry O. Jones, "Crane Brinton and the French Revolution," *Melbourne Historical Journal* 9 (1970): 14–24.

Harold T. Parker

COMMONS, John R. (Hollansburg, Ohio, 1862–Raleigh, N.C., 1945), economist and historian of labor in the United States. Professor of political economy, University of Wisconsin at Madison (1904–1932). As a student, Commons rejected the theories of Marx and Engels in favor of the work of Gustav Schmoller and other members of the German "historical school." These men had advocated the social welfare programs with which Bismarck had hoped to reduce the militance of the Social Democrats. This view of political economy admitted class conflict and saw the solution to class tensions in protection of the weaker classes by the state and in mediation by public servants who represented no class interest. Economics was not a set of classical rules, Commons thought, following this line of historical reasoning. The study of economics must be tied to the cultural and institutional context of the nation. Thus, Commons was a non-Marxist admirer of corporate capitalism. He shared the racial prejudices and Protestant ethnocentrism of many contemporaries, an outlook reflected in *Race and Immigrants in American Life* (1911) and in the research he did on immigration for the federal government during the first decade of the twentieth century. Yet, he advocated the study of American labor history as a way of proving that the survival of capitalism depended on recognizing conservative, nonsocialist, racially and sexually exclusive organizations, such as the American Federation of Labor. As an "expert" on American labor, Commons' services as statistician, witness, drafter of social welfare legislation, and mediator were in demand. Because of his public visibility, his writings on labor history, though few in number, were mightily influential. He completed the editing of a ten-volume *Documentary History of American Industrial Society* (1910–1911), and he edited two of four volumes of essays, *The History of Labor in the United States* (1918–1935) by his students.

Commons' major writing in labor history is "American Shoemakers, 1648–1895," which prefaces the *Documentary History*. Here, he hypothesized that all changes in shoemaking had resulted from outside forces, namely, the extension of the market and credit systems. Shoemakers had changed in 250 years from independent artisans to workers on an assembly line, not because of changes in the mode of production, but because of an expanding market. "Instead of 'exploitation' growing out of the nature of production, our industrial evolution shows certain evils of competition imposed by an 'unfair' menace." Common ownership was too "idealistic" a remedy for the competitive menace. The "practical remedy" was "protective organization or protective legislation." Commons argued that the American labor movement was different from European labor movements first, because the easy availability of free land made American workers more like expectant capitalists and less hostile to private property; second, because universal manhood suffrage had not been an issue in the United States as it had been in Europe; third, because the federal system dispersed power and presented no single focus for workers' political energies; fourth, because employers were able to divide and conquer an ethnically diverse working class; and finally, because trade unions had been more unstable in the United States owing to a more unstable business cycle with higher peaks and lower depths than in Europe. The "Wisconsin School" of labor history, founded by Commons, continues to influence the writing of labor history.

Bibliography: Leon Fink, "John R. Commons, Herbert Gutman and the Burden of Labor History," *Labor History* 29 (1988): 313–323; Lafayette G. Harter, Jr., *John R. Commons : His Assault on Laissez-Faire* (Corvallis, Oreg., 1962); Maurice Isserman, " 'God Bless Our American Institutions': The Labor History of John R. Commons," *Labor History* 17 (1976): 309–328.

Ellen Nore

DEBO, Angie (Kansas, 1890–Enid, Okla., 1988), historian of Native Americans of the United States and of people and society in Oklahoma. As a young child, Debo accompanied her parents to Oklahoma Territory where she grew up on a farm. In 1913, she was a member of the first graduating class of Marshall (Oklahoma) High School; in 1918, she graduated from the University of Oklahoma, received a master's degree in history from the University of Chicago in 1924 and a doctorate from the University of Oklahoma in 1933—"all this time," she wrote, "alternating her own education with periods of rural school, high school and college teaching."

Active as a researcher and writer, Debo never held a university professorship. In 1947, she became curator of maps at the library of Oklahoma State University. In numerous temporary positions before 1947, she assisted other historians in collecting reminiscences of Indians and others who were important in Oklahoma history. This work reflected a life-long interest in preserving the sources for history of various groups of Native Americans. (See Debo, "Major Indian Record Collections in Oklahoma," in *Indian-White Relations: A Persistent Paradox*, 1976.) During the 1930s, she was state supervisor of the Federal Writers' Project, a federally funded organization, which produced the Oklahoma volume of the American Guide Series. Beginning with her master's thesis ("The Historical Background of The American Policy of Isolation," 1924), which she co-published with her mentor at the University of Chicago, J. Fred Rippy, Debo wrote nine books, co-authored another, edited three others and produced dozens of articles and reviews. Her best-known books, *The Rise and Fall of the Choctaw Republic* (1934; new ed., 1967), a revision of her doctoral thesis which won the John H. Dunning Prize of the American Historical Association, *And Still the Waters Run* (1940; new ed., 1972), *The Road to Disappearance : A History of the Creek Indians* (1941; new ed., 1967), and *The Five Civilized Tribes of Oklahoma* (1951), attempt histories of the Choctaw, Creek, Cherokee, Chickasaw and Seminole peoples after they had been induced or forced by white invaders to exchange ancestral lands in the eastern United States for lands further west in what became Oklahoma. In a time when many historians of the United States wrote mainly from the point of view of the powerful, and when the "Indian" of popular culture was stereotyped as a deceitful savage deserving the reprimand of the blue-uniformed U.S. cavalry, Debo argued that the history of Native American peoples had both a universal and a national significance: "The history of the Choctaw Indians," she wrote in 1934, "records the life of a separate people with a sharply defined citizenship, an autonomous government, and distinctive social customs and institutions. It reveals a political, social, and economic existence as active and intensive and as closely circumscribed as that of any of the famous small republics of the past. On the other hand the separate thread of Choctaw history is at all times closely interwoven with the larger fabric of American history as a whole." Ahead of her time among historians of the United States, she investigated the interaction between the customs and practices of the Choctaw and other native peoples forced to migrate to Oklahoma and the legal ways and institutions of "the more numerous race" which came to surround them in the later nineteenth century. Her last book, *Geronimo: The Man, His Time, His Place* (1976), an effort to view this much-mythologized Apache leader in his "native setting," resulted from twenty-five years of careful investigation. Her gifts as a storyteller were never more apparent than in this attempt to replace "the bloody stereotype of the savage Indian" with "the human individual behind the lurid representations."

Debo also broke new ground in the field of local history with *Prairie City: The Story of an American Community* (1944), which employed the chronology of her own home village, Marshall, Oklahoma, only fifty-four years old in 1944, and which used information from "county records, newspaper files, census statistics . . . headstones of remote country cemeteries," and interviews with "pioneers" to describe the history of "a typical, rather than an actual, community, a composite of numerous Oklahoma settlements, of which some are still in existence, and others have long been ghost towns." Her method was sound, she urged, because it was "not the actual little town that matters, but its universal significance." She began by citing a local Irish farmer: " 'Iv'rything that iver happened annywhere has happened at Mar-rshall, Oklahoma.' "

In all of her books and articles, she presented the riches of oral informants. She explored archives of photographs and indicated for later historians the value of this information. She made an analogy between the method of the historian and the methods of the cattle rancher: "I have learned to work thoughts, corralling, cutting, branding, putting each in its right 'bunch'." Just before she died, the American Historical Association presented her with a citation for her lifelong achievement in ethnohistory. When asked about the variety of sources, her use of ethnology and other non-traditional techniques, she replied, "Well, after all, Herodotus did it."

Bibliography: Barbara Abrash, Glenna Matthews, Anita R. May, "Angie Debo," *Organization of American Historians Newsletter* 17 (February, 1989): 3; *Angie Debo: A Biographical Sketch and a Bibliography of Her Published Works* (Stillwater, Okla., 1980); Glenna Matthews and Gloria Valencia-Weber, *Indians, Outlaws and Angie Debo* (Documentary film, 1988. PBS Video, 1320 Braddock Place, Alexandria, Va. 22314).

Ellen Nore

DRAPER, John William (St. Helen's near Liverpool, England, 1811–Hastings, N.Y., 1882), chemist, physiologist, inventor, and American historian. Educated in chemistry at the University of London, where he started his lifetime investigations of the chemical effects of light, Draper migrated with his family to Virginia at age twenty-one. Securing an M.D. from the University of Pennsylvania, he became, in 1840, a professor of chemistry and physiology, one of the founders of the medical school of the University of the City of New York, and in 1850 the medical school's president. In "pure" science he published a stream of articles and books on physics, chemistry, physiology, medicine, and photography. He also applied his incisive intellectual power to the writing of history and published two books of outstanding merit, *A History of the Intellectual Development of Europe* (2 vols., 1863), a pioneer intellectual history, and *A History of the American Civil War* (3 vols., 1867–1870), the first scholarly account of that conflict. He was writing in the optimistic heyday of evolutionary materialism, whose basic premises he accepted and in the first book applied. In his view, material particles, unchangeable in substance and subject to eternal and invariable law, move with respect to each other and give rise to galaxies, plants, and animals; the evolution of the nervous system of the animal series, from simple reflex automatisms to intelligent reasoning power, is recapitulated by each human individual from infancy to intelligent adulthood. Likewise, the history of each society, subject to the invariable laws of the desires and necessities of the corporeal organization of human beings, follows the same curve. The intellectual development of the Greeks from 640 B.C. (Thales) to A.D. 529 (closure of schools of philosophy in Athens) passed through the ages of Credulity, Inquiry, Faith, Intellect, and Decrepitude. The intellectual development of Western Europe had passed through the same stages and was now in the triumphant phase of intellect, including the ascendancy of free scientific discovery and its practical applications in the Industrial Revolution. This reasoning by analogy (animal series, human individual, society) seems naive, but the theme is developed with such knowledge and intellectual acuteness that the book still stimulates thought. A spinoff from *Intellectual Development* was *The History of the Conflict Between Science and Religion* (1874). A tract for the times (the Vatican Council of 1870 and the German *Kulturkampf*), it has less value. He came to the history of the Civil War with the impartiality of an English immigrant who had resided in both Virginia and New York. As a scientist he attributed the conflict to differing geographical conditions, including climate, which gave rise to differing economies and social institutions and values. Secretary of State William Seward supplied him with Union and captured Confederate documents, and General William Tecumseh Sherman not only gave him access to his papers but also corrected the entire manuscript for errors of detail. The resulting 1,882 pages were the first authoritative account of the Civil War.

Bibliography: Howard K. Beale, "What Historians Have Said About the Causes of the Civil War," in Donald Sheehan, ed., *The Making of American History*, vol. 1, 3d ed. (New York, 1963); Allan D. Charles, "John W. Draper," *Dictionary of Literary Biography*, vol. 30, pp. 63–68; Donald Fleming, *John William Draper and the Religion of Science* (Philadelphia, 1950).

Harold T. Parker

DU BOIS, W. E. B. (Great Barrington, Mass., 1868–Accra, Ghana, 1963), historian of African Americans in the United States. Professor of Latin, Greek, German, and English at Wilberforce University (1895–1897), of economics and history at Atlanta University (1897–1910), and of sociology at Atlanta University (1934–1944). Outside of academe, Du Bois had many other careers. His greatness was to remind Americans that many generalizations about American society have been based on the experiences of middle-class white males. For example, historians have often posited an American who is optimistic about the economic future and who has great hopes for social mobility. The writings of W. E. B.

Du Bois on the history of the black experience in the United States reveal the ethnocentrism of much of American history. "We who are dark," he wrote, "can see America in a way that white Americans cannot." Aside from his Harvard doctoral thesis, "The Suppression of the African Slave Trade to the United States of America, 1638–1870," published in 1896 as Volume 1 of the Harvard Historical Studies, Du Bois's most important purely historical work was *Black Reconstruction in America, 1860–1880* (1935) in which he pioneered in emphasizing themes that are now standard fare in histories of this period: the role of black legislators in the state governments, the more democratic constitutions written by conventions including members of both white and black constituencies, the provision by the Reconstruction governments for the beginning of free public education in the South, and the economic problems of rebuilding after the war's destruction. Du Bois wrote at a time when Reconstruction historiography was dominated by racists and white supremacists. He was a superb essayist, writing in 1897, in a piece that appeared as Chapter 1 of *The Souls of Black Folk: Essays and Sketches* (1903): "One feels his two-ness—an American, a Negro, two souls, two thoughts, two unreconciled strivings, two warring ideals in one dark body. . . . The history of the American Negro is the history of this strife,—this longing to attain self-conscious manhood, to merge his double self into a better and truer self. . . . He would not Africanize America for America has too much to teach the world and Africa. He would not bleach the Negro soul in a flood of white Americanism, for he knows that Negro blood has a message for the world. He simply wishes to make it possible for a man to be both a Negro and an American, without being cursed and spit upon."

Bibliography: Herbert Aptheker, "Du Bois as Historian," *Negro History Bulletin* 32 (1969); Francis L. Broderick, W. E. B. Du Bois: *Negro Leader in a Time of Crisis* (Stanford, Calif., 1959); Gerald Horne, *Black and Red: W. E. B. Du Bois and the Afro-American Response to the Cold War, 1944–1983* (New York, 1986); Rayford W. Logan, *W. E. B. Du Bois: A Profile* (New York, 1971); Manning Marable, *W. E. B. Du Bois: Black Radical Democrat* (Boston, 1986); Arnold Rampersad, *The Art and Imagination of W. E. B. Du Bois* (Cambridge, Mass., 1976).

Ellen Nore

FRANK, Tenney (near Clay Center, Kan., 1876–Oxford, England, 1939), American historian. Born into a Swedish pioneer family, Frank was reared on a farm until the age of fourteen, when his parents moved to Kansas City. There one of his high school teachers aroused his interest in classical studies. Following a program in classics at the University of Kansas, he received his B.A. in 1898 and his M.A. in 1899, thanks to the support of scholarships in Latin and geology. Another scholarship (1899–1901) as well as an opportunity to teach Latin (1901–1904) enabled him to further his classical education at the University of Chicago, where he earned his Ph.D. in 1903. From 1904 to 1919 he was professor of Latin at Bryn Mawr College. At first his articles were syntactical in nature before he turned to history with an article, "A Chapter in the Story of Roman Imperialism'' (1909), and with a book, *Roman Imperialism* (1914). His book departed from the rationale of Continental European historians that "territorial expansion is a matter of course." Drawing from his youthful experience in agrarian Kansas, Frank argued that during the Republic Romans were basically an agricultural people who clung "with a fair degree of fidelity to a rule which forbade wars of aggression." Until Julius Caesar "expansion was an accident rather than a necessity," and even Augustus showed "indifference to any program of aggrandizement." Frank's book received instant recognition, especially in Britain. In 1919 Frank accepted a professorship in Latin at Johns Hopkins University. Additional publications followed in rapid succession: *The Economic History of Rome to the End of the Republic* (1920, 1927); *Virgil: A Biography* (1922); *A History of Rome* (1923); *Roman Buildings of the Republic* (1924); *Catullus and Horace: Two Poets in Their Environment* (1928); *Life and Literature in the Roman Republic* (1930); and *Rome and Italy of the Empire* (1940). Of these his *Economic History*, a pioneer work, has been considered his best. While teaching in the American Academy at Rome (1916–1917), he was able to observe museum artifacts of early Latium and to apply his firsthand knowledge of farming methods and geology to an on-the-spot archaeological inspection of an elaborate network of underground channels and dams. He concluded that in the sixth century B.C. Latium was "cultivated with an intensity seldom equalled anywhere." The results were a rich soil, a strong core of small farmers in a densely populated land, and a sound foundation of economic wealth to sustain Rome's political and military strength. Trade, which came later in the fourth century, was generally the domain of Greeks and Orientals. His *History of Rome*, destined for the general public as well as for the college classroom, elaborated a thesis already advanced in his earlier books and treated in detail in an article in the *American Historical Review* of July 1916, that one of the causes of the decay of the Roman republic and empire was the adulteration of the original Italic stock by foreigners, especially those from Syria and Asia Minor. These newcomers lacked the stern family morality, and the sound political sense, moderation, and patriotism of the sturdy farmers of earlier days.

Bibliography: T. Robert S. Broughton, "Tenney Frank," *Dictionary of American Biography*, vol. 22, Supplement 2, pp. 203–205; Norman W. DeWitt, "Tenney Frank," *American Journal of Philology* 60 (1939): 273–287; Arthur Stanley Pease, "Tenney Frank (1876–1939)," *Proceedings of the American Academy of Arts and Sciences* 84 (1940): 123–124.

Louise Salley Parker

GIPSON, Lawrence Henry (Greeley, Colo., 1880–Pennsylvania, 1971), historian of the North American colonial period. Professor of history at the College of Idaho (1907–1910), Wabash College (1910–1924), and Lehigh University (1924–1952). Gipson was the greatest of the Imperial School of historians of the colonial era. "London," he wrote, speaking of his history, "is always the nerve center." The fifteen volumes of *The British Empire Before the American*

Revolution (1936–1970) may never be surpassed in detail and thoroughness of approach to the institutional history of the empire. Gipson focused on the economic, military, and political aspects of the story and did not venture to write either social or intellectual history. Although massively researched, his books are not fine examples of the use of English language and rhetoric. He sought the truth about the British Empire, and he was at the center of a famous school of thought, but he noted that, "no one historian or school of historians can be definitive. . . . each really serious effort to evoke the past usually contains valuable insights as well as blind spots."

Bibliography: Jackson Turner Main, "Lawrence Henry Gipson, Historian," *Pennsylvania History* 36 (1969): 22–48; Richard B. Morris, "The Spacious Empire of Lawrence Henry Gipson," *William and Mary Quarterly*, 3d Series, 24 (1967): 169–189; J. Barton Starr, "Lawrence Henry Gipson," in *Twentieth Century American Historians*, vol. 17 of *Dictionary of Literary Biography*, edited by Clyde N. Wilson (Detroit, 1983), pp. 187–190.

Ellen Nore

GOTTSCHALK, Louis Reichenthal (Brooklyn, N.Y., 1899–Chicago, 1975), American historian. Educated in history at Cornell University (B.A., 1919; Ph.D., 1921), Gottschalk taught briefly at the universities of Illinois and Louisville before joining the faculty of the University of Chicago in 1927, where he remained until retirement in 1964. Methodologically, he was a transition figure from the "Rankean" tradition (see Leopold von Ranke) of writing narrative history of the political elite from critically analyzed documents to the social scientific history of a moving synthesis of social forces. At Cornell he learned chiefly from Charles Hull, a professor of American history, the "scientific" historical method; that is, the intense, critical appraisal of primary evidence. From Carl Lotus Becker (q.v.) he caught an interest in ideas as they were held by historical characters, a concern for excellent writing that matched each word with the image in the historian's mind, and an absorption in questions of epistemology (historical relativism or, broadly, the nature and validity of historical knowledge). Gottschalk began his two studies of Jean Paul Marat and of the Marquis de Lafayette while he was still under the dominating influence of the Cornell experience. His one-volume biography, *Jean-Paul Marat: A Study in Radicalism* (1927), and his six-volume life of Lafayette to 1790 (1935–1973) were distinguished by their nonpartisan tone, the cool, competent appraisal of contradictory evidence, and lucid exposition. They were in essence a discriminating delineation of the interplay of temperament, events, and ideas in the evolving careers of two revolutionary leaders. While Gottschalk was working on the Marat and Lafayette biographies, he was having a series of maturing experiences that led him to become a leader in the comparative study of revolutions and, methodologically, a specialist on generalizations in history. Preparation of his textbook, *The Era of the French Revolution* (1929), yielded four articles on the causation of that event and four additional essays on the comparative study of major revolutions and the generalizations that might be derived therefrom. Out of teaching a "Laboratory Course in Historical Method" grew his manual for apprentice historians, *Understanding History* (1950). As a member of the Social Science Research Council's first Committee on Historiography he helped prepare its celebrated Bulletin 54, *Theory and Practice in Historical Study* (1946). He also participated in writing Bulletin 53 on *The Use of Personal Documents in History, Anthropology, and Sociology* (1945), and he edited a report on *Generalization in the Writing of History* (1963). As vice-president of Unesco's International Commission for a History of the Scientific and Cultural Development of Mankind, he edited and co-authored Volume 4 of its history. His volume, entitled *The Foundations of the Modern World* (1969), covered the years 1300 to 1775.

In the ongoing methodological discussion involved in these manuals, bulletins, and histories, Gottschalk played a mediating role and articulated the working eclecticism of the American research historian of the 1950s and 1960s. He agreed with the historical relativists that the historian is affected by present conditions, but he cautioned that every historian must make a conscious effort to exclude bias from his account. To those who, like John Lothrop Motley (q.v.), Lord Acton (q.v.), and Henry Charles Lea (q.v.), wished to judge historical personages, Gottschalk quietly observed that the historian was not equipped by his professional training to make value judgments. To historians of the social science persuasion he insisted that they incorporate into their approach what seemed most useful in the Rankean tradition: the intense scrutiny and validation by well-tested procedures of each source and statement. On the other hand, to the narrative-of-unique-events school, he personally crusaded in behalf of generalizations in historical study, generalizations which historians either formulate themselves or appropriate from the social sciences.

Bibliography: Stanley Idzerda, "When and Why Lafayette Became a Revolutionary," *Proceedings* (1977) *of the Seventh Consortium on Revolutionary Europe 1750–1850* (Athens, Ga., 1978), pp. 34–50; Harold T. Parker, "Louis Gottschalk," *International Encyclopedia of The Social Sciences*, vol. 18 (Biographical Supplement), pp. 253–257; Niels Steengaard, "Universal History For Our Times," *Journal of Modern History* 45 (1973): 72–82.

Harold T. Parker

GUTMAN, Herbert (New York City, 1928–Nyack, N.Y., 1985), historian of immigrants, workers, and slaves in the United States. Professor at Fairleigh Dickinson University, the State University of New York at Buffalo, Stanford University, the University of Rochester, and, from 1975 to 1985, professor of history at the Graduate Center of the City University of New York. Gutman employed the technology, computers, now available to social historians, but his quantitative findings were always incorporated into a rich context of literary sources. His own careful scholarship was always accompanied by generous acknowledgment of the work of colleagues, as he was committed to the notion of history as a communal enterprise. He wrote about the ordinary people who built the United States, "wage earners and . . . other dependent classes in this country such as slaves." He tried, he said, "to Americanize" the insights of E. P. Thompson on "the processes by which new subordinate classes are formed, how they develop . . . the ways in which who workers *had been* affected who they *became.*" The best history of all subordinate groups, he said, involved far more than examining "irregular outbursts of collective, democratic protest." There existed, he thought, an important "tension within all modern dependent groups between individualist (utilitarian) and collective (mutualist) ways of dealing with and sometimes overcoming historically specific patterns of dependence and inequality. That tension changes over time. It differs from group to group. It reveals itself in very diverse ways, reflecting regional, racial, ethnic, gender, and other differences." *Work, Culture, and Society in Industrializing America* (1976) contains essays which, in specific contexts, develop these theoretical propositions.

In *Slavery and the Numbers Game* (1975), a critique of Robert W. Fogel's and Stanley L. Engerman's *Time on the Cross*, a massive quantitative study of slavery as an economic and social system, Gutman discussed the role of quantitative data in the writing of social history. Fogel and Engerman had argued that their evidence showed planters working hard, and succeeding, in the task of making their captives into diligent laborers. This, they urged, partially explained the profitability of slavery as well as the behavior of the slaves, who, like free workers, responded to incentives within the system. Gutman not only found many errors in the basic information of Fogel and Engerman, but also he criticized their model for explaining slave beliefs and behavior. The question Fogel and Engerman were asking, Gutman noted, was the same question asked earlier by Ulrich B. Phillips (q.v.), though their answer was not based on racist assumptions, namely, what did enslavement do to Africans and their descendants? The answer to this question does not explain slave belief and behavior: "We need also to ask what Africans and their Afro-American descendants did as slaves. That is a very different question, and the answers to it are not the mirror-image of what owners did to slaves." Quantification, Gutman urged, is a useful method for the social historian, "especially the social historian concerned with dependent and exploited classes," as it aids in establishing "regularities, and regularities help the social historian to define different aspects of otherwise often obscure social experiences." But "assumptions about the real world which such regularities partially describe must be rigorously and critically examined. An adequate theory of human behavior is needed." *The Black Family in Slavery and Freedom, 1750–1925* (1976) was Gutman's effort to change the way slavery had been conceptualized by several generations of historians and social scientists. Historians of the 1950s and 1960s had often explained differences in slaves' behavior as a function of differences in treatment by the owners. External factors, such as, whether the captive lived on a plantation or a farm, was rural or urban, living in the upper South or the lower South, as well as the personality of the

owner, were traditional explanations of slave behavior. "The study of slaves
. . . became largely the study of their owners." In *The Black Family*, Gutman
studied class behavior, such as household arrangements, naming practices, marriage rules, and sexual practices among "groups of slaves who *experienced their
enslavement differently*. That is the essential point." Gutman saw himself participating in the writing of a "new labor history" to modify and/or replace the
story told by Old Leftists and John R. Commons (q.v.) and his students. The
new labor history "refuses to look at a period of history simply as a precursor
of the moment that we currently are living in. Freeing ourselves from the present
in that way brings to life movements, brings to life a politics of the past, that
were submerged by the crude presentism of the older labor history, whether of
the Left or the center." Asked if he were abandoning the notion of "historical
tasks" faced by workers, Gutman replied, "What does it mean to talk about
historical tasks that workers faced? We are letting in through the back door a
notion of fixed and predetermined historical development. We are measuring the
American worker (or the French worker or the Polish worker) against an ideal
type. That is the Whig fallacy of history once again." History's value, Gutman
said, is not as a set of "practical lessons for today." Studying history is "liberating for other reasons . . . it transforms historical givens into historical con-
tingencies. It enables us to see the structures in which we live and the inequality
people experience as only one among many other possible experiences. By doing
that, you free people for creative and critical (or radical) thought. . . . the essential
question for study," he said, echoing John-Paul Sartre, "is not what has been
done to men and women but what men and women do with what is done to
them."

   Bibliography: Andrew Gyory, "Published Works of Herbert G. Gutman: A Bibliography," *Labor History* 29 (1988): 400–406; (This issue of *Labor History*, entirely devoted
to Gutman, contains articles by friends and students: Nell Irvin Painter, Leon Fink, Alan
Dawley, Susan Levine, Bruno Cartosio, Sean Wiltz and Christine Stansell, Nathan Hug-
gins, David Brody and Daniel Leab, and David Montgomery.) Mike Merrill, "Herbert
Gutman,"[Interview and Bibliography] in Henry Abelove, Betsy Blackmar, Peter Dimock
and Jonathan Schneer, eds., *Visions of History* (New York, 1984), pp. 187–216; David
Montgomery, "Gutman's Nineteenth-Century America," *Labor History* 19 (1978): 416–
429.

Ellen Nore

HASKINS, Charles Homer (Meadville, Pa., 1870–Cambridge, Mass., 1937),
American historian. A precocious child and adolescent, Haskins began the study
of Latin and Greek before he was six, entered Allegheny College, where his
father taught Latin, before he was thirteen, transferred to Johns Hopkins University for his senior year, and there received his B.A. in 1887 and by 1890 his
Ph.D. in history under the direction of Herbert Baxter Adams. He supplemented
his graduate work with study at Berlin and at the Ecole des Chartes in Paris.
He opened his teaching career in history at Johns Hopkins (1889–1890); joined
the faculty of the University of Wisconsin in 1890; and became professor of

history (1902), Gurney professor (1912), and Henry Charles Lea professor of medieval history (1929) at Harvard, where he remained until his retirement in 1931. He was also for a time dean of the Harvard Graduate School. Always the innovator, he expanded History I to include both medieval and modern European history, restored courses in diplomatics and paleography for his graduate students in medieval history, and promoted interdisciplinary programs. As the outstanding medievalist of his generation, he was elected president of the American Historical Association in 1922. In his major works he combined the thorough research and critical method of the scientific school with the elegant and colorful style of the Romantics. Readers could both admire his erudition and enjoy his writings.

The earliest of Haskins' pioneer studies was *The Normans in European History* (1915). A unique aspect of the book was the breadth and sweep of its perspective. Ignoring the narrow limitations of national histories, he revealed how wherever the Normans happened to settle—England, Sicily, and southern Italy—they adapted readily to their new locales, masterfully founded and organized efficient, powerful states, and contributed to European culture. A detailed study filled with long Latin quotations, *Norman Institutions* (1918) was directed toward scholars of English constitutional history. Here he argued that when we examine Anglo-Saxon institutions on the eve of the Norman Conquest, institutions developed by the Normans in Normandy, and the emerging institutions in England after the Conquest, it is clear that a number of the post-Conquest institutions can be attributed to the Normans. The jury system, for example, was not of Anglo-Saxon origin as formerly supposed but, as he claimed, of Frankish derivation, brought over by the Normans. In his third major work, the *History of Mediaeval Science* (1924), his approach was different from that of Lynn Thorndike (q.v.), who stressed the importance of ''magic,'' and Pierre Duhem, who focused on cosmology. Haskins considered medieval science as one aspect of the totality of medieval culture. This angle of vision led to a series of scholarly discoveries, for example, that Greek and Arabic scientific knowledge entered Western Europe via Moslem Spain and Sicily much earlier than historians had realized and that this imported knowledge opened the way for medieval scholars to conduct their own experiments. In *The Renaissance of the Twelfth Century* (1927) he sought to shatter twin misconceptions: that the Middle Ages were a ''dark age'' extending from 476 to 1453, and that in this darkness the Italian Renaissance was a sudden, brilliant, skyrocketing burst of intellectual and artistic genius, unique and decisive in awakening the European spirit. To confute these views, which were a legacy of Jacob Burckhardt (q.v.) and John Addington Symonds, he described the striking cultural and intellectual advances of the Middle Ages, notably in the twelfth century. At the 1984 meeting of the American Historical Association's Centennial Session to honor him, it was announced: ''Haskins and his vision of the Twelfth-Century Renaissance are alive and well today. . . . The Haskins legacy is a living legacy, which continues to offer a guide and a mandate for present and future work in medieval intellectual history.''

Bibliography: R. P. Blake, G. R. Coffman, and E. K. Rand, ''Charles Homer Haskins,'' *Speculum* 14 (1939): 413–415; F. M. Powicke, ''Charles Homer Haskins,'' *En-*

glish Historical Review 52 (1937): 649–656; Joseph R. Strayer, "Charles Homer Haskins," *Dictionary of American Biography*, vol. 22 (Supplement 2), pp. 289–291; Sally N. Vaughn, "Charles Homer Haskins," *Dictionary of Literary Biography*, vol. 47, pp. 122–144.

Louise Salley Parker

HAYES, Carlton Joseph Huntley (near Afton, N.Y., 1882–Afton, N.Y., 1964), American historian. From age eighteen Hayes was identified with Columbia University, as undergraduate (B.A., 1904), as graduate student in history (Ph.D., 1909), and as member of its History Department from 1907 to his retirement in 1950. He came under the influence of his graduate director, James Harvey Robinson (q.v.), at a time when Robinson was still interested in a detailed analysis of primary evidence. Under his guidance Hayes prepared and in 1909 published *An Introduction to the Sources Relating to the Germanic Invasion*. He also followed his mentor when in 1912 Robinson proclaimed the "New History" of enlarged scope and contemporary relevance. However, while Robinson and others proclaimed the New History, Hayes wrote it. From 1912 to 1916 he prepared one of the great American textbooks on European history, the two-volume *Political and Social History of Modern Europe* (1916), which covered four centuries from the beginning of the sixteenth century. Unlike preceding textbooks in European history it emphasized the recent history of the past one hundred years and came down to the present—the outbreak and early campaigns of World War I. It stressed the themes in modern European history that explained the present situation. It also offered an enlarged synthesis of political, economic, and social history, and associated ideas. In a later version, *A Political and Cultural History of Modern Europe* (1932), he added to his synthesis science and philosophy, literature, and art. Clear, well organized, well proportioned, and relevant, his textbooks dominated the market for several decades. They were the way the New History came to hundreds of thousands of college students. Meanwhile, for more than forty years he was pursuing his own line of research into the history of nationalism. His interest had been stimulated by a current problem: Nationalism was a major cause of World War I, and obviously it needed the understanding that history alone could afford. His four books on the subject, *Essays on Nationalism* (1926), *France: A Nation of Patriots* (1930), *The Historical Evolution of Modern Nationalism* (1931), and *Nationalism: A Religion* (1960), recorded his maturing insights. He traced the successive types of nationalist philosophy from the humanitarian nationalism of the eighteenth-century Enlightenment (Bolingbroke, Rousseau, Herder) through the Jacobin nationalism of the French Revolution and the traditional nationalism of the conservative reaction (Burke, Bonald, Schlegel) to the liberal nationalism of the nineteenth century (Francois Guizot (q.v.), Giuseppi Mazzini) and its perversion in the integral nationalism of the twentieth century (Barrès, Maurras, the fascists). As an active layman in the Roman Catholic Church, he speculated on the relation of the Christian ideals of charity and justice and the universalism of his faith to the rival secular religion of nationalism.

Although Hayes undertook his investigations into nationalism too early to profit from later psychological and anthropological research, his books and his supervision of more than seventy doctoral dissertations rendered him one of the most eminent authorities in the field. His experience as an author of textbooks, his research, and his religious faith came together in his masterpiece, *The Generation of Materialism, 1871–1900* (1941), a volume in the William Leonard Langer (q.v.) series entitled The Rise of Modern Europe. Hayes' faith gave him a necessary distance and detachment from the selfish materialism and the mad nationalisms and imperialisms of the epoch; his long discipline as a textbook writer schooled him to perceive the essential substance and the illustrative incident; and his own researches provided much of the detailed knowledge.

Bibliography: Boyd Shafer, *Nationalism: Interpretations and Interpreters* (Washington, D.C., 1966); H. Vincent Moses, "Nationalism and the Kingdom of God According to Hans Kohn and Carlton J. H. Hayes," *Journal of Church and State* 17 (1975): 259–274.

Harold T. Parker

HILDRETH, Richard (Deerfield, Mass., 1807–Florence, Italy, 1865), historian of the United States. Although his *History of the United States of America* (vols. 1–3, 1849, vols. 4–6, 1851–1852) did not have a central theme and was organized on the basis of strict chronology, Hildreth's factual accuracy has rarely been at issue, and he presented many suggestions that later historians embroidered. Describing the history of the country from the precolonial voyages of exploration to 1821, Hildreth wrote history that, in many ways, was the opposite of the story told by George Bancroft (q.v.), whose tales of "our glorious ancestors,— and our glorious selves!" he despised. With a subtle appreciation of how differences in the economic foundations shaped social organization and institutions in the various regions of the country during the colonial period, Hildreth also attacked the myth of "a colonial golden age of fabulous purity and virtue" by criticizing the Englishmen's barbarous dealings with the Indians, the religious bigotry of the New England Puritans, and the excesses of the patriots in the Revolution. Although he agreed with fileopietistic historians that the Constitution was a necessary change as a final political settlement following the Revolution, he differed from them in stressing the economic motives of the men who wrote the Constitution. In his general use of self-interest as an explanation for behavior, he anticipated the work of important twentieth-century historians, such as, Charles A. Beard (q.v.), Carl Lotus Becker (q.v.), and Arthur M. Schlesinger, Sr. Hildreth had a definite philosophy of history drawn from the works of the Utilitarian Jeremy Bentham. He attempted a plain writing style in imitation of Bentham's ideal of "relating plain facts in plain English." He tried to avoid a priori assumptions, saying, "I am a mere experimental enquirer. . . . It is my object to investigate and expound human nature as it is, not as I or others may desire it to be." And he believed, with the Utilitarians, in progress, that is, that

"As a community grows more and more intelligent, the science of morals makes a constant progress, and diverges more and more from the rude and narrow maxims and notions of early times."

Bibliography: John Braeman, "Richard Hildreth," in *American Historians, 1607– 1865*, vol. 30 of *Dictionary of Literary Biography*, edited by Clyde N. Wilson, pp. 117– 133; Donald E. Emerson, *Richard Hildreth* (Baltimore, 1946); Alfred H. Kelly, "Richard Hildreth," in *The Marcus W. Jernegan Essays in American Historiography*, edited by William T. Hutchinson (Chicago, 1937), pp. 25–42; Arthur M. Schlesinger, Jr., "The Problem of Richard Hildreth," *New England Quarterly* 13 (1940): 223–245.

Ellen Nore

HOFSTADTER, Richard (Buffalo, N.Y., 1916–New York City, 1970), historian of the United States. Professor at the University of Maryland (1942–1946) and Columbia University (1946–1970). "It is not," he wrote in *The Progressive Historians: Turner, Beard, Parrington* (1968), "that the historian is under an obligation to be a muckraker or a moralist, or to venture upon some nagging one-sided quarrel with the behavior of ancestors and predecessors who were morally no frailer than himself." His point, Hofstadter declared, was "simply that the anguish of history, as well as its romance and charm, is there for the historian who responds to it." Coming from an urban background, with one parent a Protestant and the other Jewish, Hofstadter, as an intellectual and as an historian, wrote to present a complex portrait of certain aspects of the national experience. His work disparages the notion of "progress," defined culturally or morally. In the range of his themes, in the analysis of the irrational side of popular political expression, and in the constant probing of the role of intellectuals in a culture committed to egalitarianism, he created for himself a place as one of the most widely read and creative historians of the United States in the twentieth century. His first major book, *Social Darwinism in American Thought, 1860–1915* (1944), analyzed the transformation, in the American context, of Darwin's ideas into an ideology that could support either a rapacious corporate individualism or a communal concern with social improvement through modification of the social environment. "American society saw its own image in the tooth-and-claw version of natural selection . . . and its dominant groups were therefore able to dramatize this vision of competition as a thing good in itself." As the critics of Darwinian individualism grew stronger, the genetic metaphor was transformed into a rationalization for imperialism. "Fitter" nations subdued those countries unable to win the struggle. With a pessimism that would also appear in later works, Hofstadter concluded that, "so long as there is a strong element of predacity in society," social thought would continue to use the phrases of Social Darwinism, regardless of logic, since "changes in the structure of social ideas wait on general changes in economic and political life."

In *The American Political Tradition: And the Men Who Made It* (1948), Hofstadter used a series of twelve biographical essays treating, among others, such famous politicians as Thomas Jefferson, Andrew Jackson, Abraham Lincoln, and Herbert Hoover, to revise the emphasis of earlier progressive historians, such as Charles A. Beard (q.v.), on conflicts between special economic interests in the history of American politics. Hofstadter pointed instead to the areas of agreement, to the "central faith" in "sanctity of private property, the right of the individual to dispose of and invest it, the value of opportunity, and the natural evolution of self-interest . . . into a beneficent social order" which, he urged, had characterized American politics, a politics singularly devoid of "deep, persistent, and consistent class conflict." As Hofstadter wrote in 1967, this was the first statement of a controversial point of view known as "consensus history." His generation of historians, he noted, tended to reduce conflict in history to "a very *ad hoc* basis—that is, they postulate it as an affair of shifting groups and coalitions rather than as a continuing struggle based on enduring sets of fixed classes, such as agrarians and capitalists, or workingmen and industrialists." Unlike other historians who emphasized consensus, Hofstadter was a critic of the shared values. *The American Political Tradition* admitted that American traditions showed "a strong bias in favor of equalitarian democracy," but the essays supported the notion that "it has been a democracy in cupidity rather than a democracy of fraternity."

In writings during the 1950s, Hofstadter used many concepts, but not the methodology, from the social sciences—the idea of cultural patterns and lifestyles from anthropology and notions of mass "psychic crisis" and mass frustration and anxiety from social psychology. *The Age of Reform: From Bryan to F.D.R.* (1955) presented Hofstadter's use of these concepts to analyze Populism and Progressivism. Here he made his famous distinction between "status politics," behavior arising from personal motives, although these motives might be clothed in the rhetoric of conventional issues, and "interest politics," "the clash of material aims and needs among various groups and blocs." Populism and Progressivism derived their passion less from any clash over public policy than from the latent anxieties of farmers and certain groups of urban professionals worried about their declining prominence and replacement by new groups. Both of these reform movements were associated, in Hofstadter's version of history, with a regressive and rather sour nostalgia for a simpler past. Progressivism, he argued, "was to a very considerable extent led by men who suffered from the events of their time not through a shrinkage in their means but through the changed pattern in the distribution of deference and power." Particularly, in the case of the Populists, he emphasized a backward-looking politics of conspiracy which led, he thought, to the politics centered in fears of communist conspiracies in the decade after World War II. Trying to explain why so little reform, not to speak of revolution, had happened in the history of the United States, Hofstadter blamed the reformers themselves, rather than analyzing the power of conservative forces against change. In his work on American politicians, Hofstadter had written to discourage hero-worship and self-congratulation. In his descriptions of the mass movements, Populism and Progressivism, he hoped to remind intellectuals not to idealize "the people." "Intellectuals," he wrote in the beginning of *The Age of Reform*, ''periodically exaggerate the measure of agreement that exists between movements of popular reform and the considered principles of political liberalism. They remake the image of popular rebellion closer to their heart's desire. They choose to ignore not only the elements of illiberalism that frequently seem to be an indispensible part of popular movements but also the very complexity of the historical process itself.''

Hofstadter's ideal historian-intellectual was a detached, analytical mediator, one who creates not a simple, usable past pointing the way to a better future, but an ambivalent, complicated story that implicitly warns of the irrational undercurrents that might sweep the people in their wake. Writing at a time, the two decades after World War II, when politicized concern formulated as anti-communism threatened and constrained academic freedom and freedom of expression and action on the left, Hofstadter was determined to hypothesize about the obstacles to rational discourse in American politics. He took the elitist position that the irrational nature of American politics was a reflection of the irrationalism of the country. In *Anti-Intellectualism in American Life* (1963) and *The Paranoid Style in American Politics and Other Essays* (1965), he described a tension between the elite culture of the intellectuals and the democratic institutions and sentiments of the country. Writing of the intellectual in American political culture, Hofstadter concluded that his or her role had been mostly as ''either an outsider, a servant, or a scapegoat.'' Although many of his specific theses have been shaken by the sort of quantitative research he never undertook, Hofstadter focused his lens on important issues and wrote about them with style and grace. His rich and suggestive books are an important legacy and have already produced a prodigious literature in response.

Bibliography: Susan Stout Baker, *Radical Beginnings: Richard Hofstadter and the 1930s* (Westport, Conn., 1985); Paul Bourke, ''Politics and Ideas: The Work of Richard Hofstadter,'' *Historical Studies* (Melbourne), 17 (1976): 210–218; Robert M. Collins, ''The Originality Trap: Richard Hofstadter on Populism,'' *Journal of American History* 76 (1989): 150–168; Stanley Elkins and Eric McKitrick, eds., *The Hofstadter Aegis* (New York, 1974); Arthur M. Schlesinger, Jr., ''Richard Hofstadter,'' in Marcus Cunliffe and Robin Winks, eds., *Pastmasters* (New York, 1969), pp. 278–315; David Joseph Singal, ''Beyond Consensus: Richard Hofstadter and American Historiography,'' *American Historical Review* 89 (1984): 976–1004; S. Weiland, ''The Academic Attitude: Richard Hofstadter and The Anti-Intellectuals,'' *Antioch Review* 46 (1988): 462–472.

Ellen Nore

HOLBORN, Hajo (Berlin, Germany, 1902–Bonn, West Germany, 1969), American historian. Holborn received his professional training at the University of Berlin (Ph.D., 1924), where his most valued teachers were Friedrich Meinecke (q.v.) and Karl Holl, professor of theology. From 1926 to 1931 he served as *Privatdozent* at the University of Heidelberg. From 1931 to 1933 he held a joint appointment as lecturer at the University of Berlin and Carnegie professor of history and international relations at the School of Politics in Berlin. An active supporter of the Weimar Republic, he left Germany in 1933 for the United

States, where he became a naturalized citizen in 1940. From 1934 until his death he taught history at Yale University, holding a Sterling professorship from 1959. During World War II he served with the OSS, and from 1947 to 1949 he was consultant to the Department of State. In 1967 he was chosen president of the American Historical Association. He died in Bonn one day after receiving the first Inter Nations Award.

From the start of his scholarly career Holborn, like his mentor Meinecke, was interested in questions of political power, and his early articles were on Bismarckian diplomacy. But he was also philosophically concerned with the problems of internal German history. His first major book, which revealed the influence of Leopold von Ranke (q.v.) and Holl, was a biography, *Ulrich von Hutten* (1929), which in a revised and expanded edition was translated by Roland Herbert Bainton (q.v.) in 1937. Its theme was "humanism, nationalism, and Protestantism," and no better age, Holborn maintained, could have been selected, for never before or since had "the native German genius [been exhibited] in so untrammeled a fashion." Germany's greatest gift to Western civilization, Protestantism, originated then, while a rising tide of nationalism revealed the impact made on Germany by Western European intellectual, cultural, and political currents. To Holborn, no better sixteenth-century figure could be found to represent the "interrelations" of the three elements than Hutten, who attempted to "bring them into a living synthesis," for he was an ardent promoter of German humanism, represented the cause of nationalism by staunchly supporting the "grievances of the German nation" against papal exactions, and, finally, aware of the need of spiritual assistance for his cause, joined Luther's side. Thus was Hutten "intimately bound up with the rise of the Reformation." After Holborn's emigration to the United States his experiences during the 1930s and 1940s and his reflections thereon broadened his perspective. His monumental three-volume *The History of Modern Germany* (1959, 1963, 1969) was the answer to a personal quest: what in the story of Germany's past from the Reformation will help to explain the rise of Hitler's Germany? His answer, presented in a complex narrative, was animated by "the belief that we can hope to understand history only if we try to visualize the totality of historical life." This belief led him "to extend the scope of the history of Germany beyond the political and constitutional history to social and economic as well as to religious and intellectual history," and to place the German story within the matrix of European trends. Within the narrative a recurring but not obtrusive theme is when, where, and how did Germany diverge from Western Europe. Along the way he points to the destructive effects of the Thirty Years' War, the replacement of the cosmopolitan and natural law philosophy of Kant with the strident nationalism of the War of Liberation against Napoleon, and the "apotheosis of the state" in Georg Wilhelm F. Hegel's (q.v.) philosophy, Bismarck's unification of Germany by aggressive diplomacy and military force and his sham constitutionalism, the acceptance of the Bismarckian state by most German liberals, the continuing strength of conservative landowners, bureaucrats, jurists, and generals in the Weimar Republic, and the myth of "the stab in the back" and its exploitation by Hitler. The result of these and other divergencies was in the nineteenth and twentieth centuries a revolution, an aberration of the German spirit not only from Western Europe but from its truest self. Historical thinking had thus enabled Holborn to identify the essential reality of a contemporary situation.

Biliography: Felix Gilbert, "Hajo Holborn: A Memoir," *Central European History* (1970), vol. 3, pp. 3–16; Hans Kohn, "Hajo Holborn's *History of Modern Germany*," *Central European History* (1970), vol. 3, pp. 140–56; Leonard Krieger, "Hajo Holborn," *American Historical Review* 75 (1969): 333–336.

Louise Salley Parker and Harold T. Parker

IRVING, Washington (New York City, 1783–Sleepy Hollow, N.Y., 1859), U.S. author and diplomat. Irving was the first internationally acclaimed author from the United States. As historian, he often used history for his own purposes rather than writing it for its own sake. In his first history, *A History of New York* (1809), he uses the history of Dutch New York to mock and satirize his contemporary New Yorkers. He also mocks historians through the character of the supposed author, Diedrich Knickerbocker, and history itself. He has Knickerbocker confess to the reader that his Book 1 is, "like all introductions to American histories, very learned, sagacious, and nothing at all to the purpose." Later, in 1844, in writing of William H. Prescott's (q.v.) *Conquest of Mexico*, he repeats the same opinion: "I should not have had any preliminary dissertation on the history, civilization, &c., of the natives, as I find such dissertations hurried over, if not skipped entirely by a great class of readers, who are eager for narrative and action. I should have carried on the reader with the discoverers and conquerors, letting the newly explored countries break upon him as it did upon them." In 1826 Irving, having gained some fame as author of sketches and tales, found himself in Madrid, in the home of Obediah Rich, a collector of Columbian manuscripts, at a time shortly after the publication of Martin Fernandez de Navarette's *Colleccion de los viajes*, a gathering of manuscript transcriptions. Being so favorably situated, Irving decided to write a biography of the explorer: "I shall endeavor to make it the most complete and authentic account of Columbus & his voyages extant . . . to produce a work which shall bear examination as to candour & authenticity." Irving achieved his intention, satisfying the scholars as well as the public; his *Life and Voyages of Christopher Columbus* (1828) went through 175 editions in twelve languages in the nineteenth century. Despite Irving's statement about Columbus, "it is proper to show him in connexion with the age in which he lived, lest the errors of the times should be considered his individual abuses. It is not the intention of the author, however, to justify Columbus on a point where it is inexcusable to err," some have accused him of romanticizing Columbus. But Irving was never a romantic. He did, however, have great sympathy for this man who, like himself, sought to win fame in a foreign land.

While *Life and Voyages* was the first of Irving's works to bear his name, rather than a pseudonym, he published his next history, *A Chronicle of the Conquest of Granada* (1829), under the pseudonym of Fray Antonio Agapida. Although Agapida's history of Granada is more complete and exact than that of Knickerbocker's history of New York, Irving's purpose is the same—to use history to satirize contemporary people and events, this time the people and events of contemporary Spain. In 1831 Irving published, under his own name, *Voyages and Discoveries of the Companions of Columbus*, expeditions he considered "as springing immediately out of the voyages of Columbus, and fulfilling some of his grand designs." The tone of this book is more sprightly than the two previous ones, and it would not be far-fetched to suggest that Irving chose those companions whose characters were most like those of his contemporary authors. After a seventeen-year absence in Europe, Irving returned to the United States in 1832 and turned to American themes. Today *Astoria* (1836) and *The Adventures of Captain Bonneville* (1837) remain as major documents of the Western fur trade (partly because many of the manuscripts Irving worked from have disappeared). But both books have a quality of illusion about them—Irving presents the facts, but not all the facts that he knows. Both books are arguments for the westward expansion of the United States.

Of Irving's biographies of literary figures, "A Biographical Sketch of Thomas Campbell" (1815), *Biography of Margaret Miller Davidson* (1841), and *Oliver Goldsmith: A Biography* (1849), his life of Goldsmith is to be noted for Irving's attempt, not just to record Goldsmith's life and letters, common for most biographies of the day, but to understand the psychology of Goldsmith, the reasons and emotions that lay behind his works and actions. The same attempt to understand is shown in *Mahomet* (1849), a life of the prophet designed for the popular audience. A hurriedly composed companion volume, *Mahomet's Successors* (1850), is entirely different, a history of the rise of an empire, from 632 to 710: "in this period, which did not occupy fourscore and ten years, and passed within the lifetime of many an aged Arab, the Moslems extended their empire and their faith over the wide regions of Asia and Africa." Irving does not explicitly draw the parallel with the United States, which had, in less than ninety years, extended its empire from one ocean to another, but he clearly expects the reader to learn and profit from the story of the past. Irving again looked to the past to teach the present in his last great work, his *Life of Washington* (1855). Writing when the strains that were to produce the Civil War were evident, Irving wrote the story of the founding of the United States, focusing on the leader who favored neither North nor South, who "knew no divided fidelity, no separate obligation." When he was praised for the work's readability, Irving responded, "that is what I write it for. I want it so clear that anybody can understand it. I want the action to shine through the style." It is Irving's style that made him one of the great nineteenth-century literary historians.

Bibliography: Mary W. Bowden, *Washington Irving* (Boston, 1981); Henry Pochman, Herbert Kleinfield, and Richard Rust, eds., *The Complete Works of Washington Irving*

(Boston, 1969–1985); Stanley T. Williams, *The Life of Washington Irving* (New York, 1935).

JAMESON, J. Franklin (Somerville, Mass., 1859–Washington, D.C., 1937), historian of the American Revolution and organizer of the profession in the United States. Instructor of history, Johns Hopkins University (1882–1888), professor of history at Brown University (1888–1901) and at the University of Chicago (1901–1905), director, Department of Historical Research, Carnegie Institution of Washington (1905–1928), chief, Division of Manuscripts, Library of Congress, and holder of the Library's Chair of American History (1928–1937). Jameson, as a writer of history, published a monograph, *The American Revolution Considered as a Social Movement* (1926), which was an influential attempt to suggest that the Revolution involved social as well as institutional changes as stressed by historians of the "Imperial School." Yet, Jameson's greatness was rather as an organizer of the historical profession in the United States. He was a key founder and managing editor of the *American Historical Review* from 1895 to 1901 and again from 1905 to 1928. As the first editor of the *Review*, he established it as the major historical journal in the United States and as an acclaimed example of its type in the world. At the Carnegie Institution, he initiated projects, such as the twenty-five year campaign for a National Archives of the U.S. government, which was established by an Act of Congress in 1934, the bibliographical guide, *Writings on American History*, and a national historical publications commission. He was chairman of the Committee of Management of the *Dictionary of American Biography* from 1924 until the original edition was completed in 1936. He had a decided interest in black history and assisted Carter G. Woodson (q.v.) in securing funding of *The Journal of Negro History*. Although he was often criticized by contemporaries for his devotion to fact-finding at the expense of synthesis and for favoring, as editor of the *Review*, articles with national rather than regional or local themes, as well as institutional history, Jameson's energy shaped the standards and the activities of the profession during five decades.

Bibliography: Ruth Anna Fisher and William Lloyd Fox, eds., *J. Franklin Jameson: A Tribute* (Washington, D.C., 1965); August Meier and Elliott Rudwick, "J. Franklin Jameson, Carter G. Woodson, and the Foundations of Black Historiography," *American Historical Review* 89 (1984): 1005–1015; Morey D. Rothberg, " 'To Set a Standard of Workmanship and Compel Men to Conform to It': John Franklin Jameson as Editor of the *American Historical Review*," *American Historical Review* 89 (1984): 957–975; Richard A. Shrader, "J. Franklin Jameson," in *Twentieth-Century American Historians*, vol. 17 of *Dictionary of Literary Biography*, edited by Clyde N. Wilson (Detroit, 1983), pp. 230–235.

Ellen Nore

LANGER, William Leonard (Boston, 1896–Boston, 1977), American historian. Langer appropriately entitled his autobiography *In and Out of the Ivory*

Tower (1977). Not since Andrew Dickson White had an American historian combined to such an eminent degree careers in both scholarship and public service. Educated at Harvard University (B.A., 1915; Ph.D., 1923), Langer was won by his graduate supervisors, Robert Howard Lord and Archibald Cary Coolidge, to the history of international relations. After four years of teaching at Clark University (1923–27), he joined the Harvard Department of History and remained a member of the faculty until his retirement in 1964. His first three books, *The Franco-Russian Alliance 1890–1894* (1929), *European Alliances and Alignments 1871–1890* (1931), and *The Diplomacy of Imperialism 1890–1902*, (2 vols., 1935), had a common theme: the nature and operation of the international system of European states from 1870 to 1902, that is, from Bismarck's organization of national powers to assure Germany's predominance and European peace to the dissolution of his arrangements after his retirement in 1890. Langer's approach was basically Rankean: masterfully to narrate the complex continuing negotiations among European governments by shifting from capital to capital, from foreign ministry to foreign ministry, and seeing the situation with the eyes of the chief officials responsible for foreign policy and diplomatic intercourse. In the first book, *The Franco-Russian Alliance*, he was content to do just that. But he became aware that he who knows only European diplomatic history cannot understand it. There were deeper currents—economic developments, tides of national sentiment, events in Asia and Africa, an outburst of imperialism, profound psychological compulsions—that affected the international game and were affected by it. In *European Alignments* and *The Diplomacy of Imperialism* Langer pioneered in trying to incorporate these currents into the narrative of diplomatic intrigue.

With the advent of World War II Langer left the ivory tower of Harvard for the wartime confusions of Washington. There he organized and then administered from 1941 to 1946 the Research and Analysis branch of the Office of Strategic Services (OSS). Essentially, the scholarly experts that he assembled researched, analyzed, and evaluated the information which the nation's political, military, and diplomatic leaders needed. Residence in Washington brought him invitations and opportunities to write from the archives of the Department of State and other agencies the history of recent American foreign policy. He did this in another triad of narrative histories: *Our Vichy Gamble* (1947) and (with S. Everett Gleason) *The Challenge to Isolation 1937–1940* (1952) and *The Undeclared War 1940–1941* (1953). In these he again displayed a masterful grasp of huge amounts of documentary evidence. However, he was now writing from the national perspective of his own country and of its national interest, and it was not always possible for him to maintain the treasured role of impartial historian. Still, the three books served their purpose of providing the basis for informed discussion. Upon his return to teaching at Harvard in the 1950s, he resumed his European perspective. In 1931 he had launched a twenty-volume series entitled The Rise of Modern Europe from A.D. 1250 until the present. As contributors, he had enlisted leading historians and had insisted that for their periods of expertise they attempt "to see Europe as a cultural unit. . . . Each volume, while basically political history, should take account of philosophical currents, literature, art and science." Although a few volumes fell short of the ideal, the "Langer series" as a whole "remains," to quote Leonard Krieger, "the outstanding collaborative achievement by American historians in the general field of European history." Langer now had time to complete his own contribution to the series: *Political and Social Upheaval (1832–1852)* (1969). He also revised his *Encyclopedia of World History* (1940, 1972) and published essays on psychoanalysis and history, the social-psychological effects of epidemics, and the influence of diet on population. Until the end he was at the pioneering, innovative, cutting edge of historical research.

   Bibliography: Carl E. Schorske, "Introduction," pp. ix–xliv in William L. Langer, *Explorations in Crisis: Papers on International History* (Cambridge, Mass., 1969); Carl E. Schorske, "William L. Langer," *International Encyclopedia of the Social Sciences*, vol. 18 (Biographical Supplement), pp. 402–405.

Harold T. Parker

LEA, Henry Charles (Philadelphia, 1825–Philadelphia, 1909), American historian. Lea's career as a historian was remarkable and astounding. Hailed as "America's most prominent medievalist of the nineteenth century," he had scarcely any formal schooling, was not a teacher, and rarely traveled beyond his nation's borders. Yet, thanks to the efforts of a splendid tutor, he was grounded in classical studies, mathematics, literature and composition, and foreign languages. As an adolescent, he was first attracted to science and literature to the extent of publishing articles in each field. At eighteen, he entered his father's publishing house while continuing to write and publish during his spare time. Gradually, his interest shifted to medieval history and specifically to the history of the medieval Church. He was led in that direction, he explained, because he was impressed by the might of the Latin Church, "not only in spiritual but in temporal affairs," and wished to learn the secrets that enabled it to attain its position of absolute power. After two rather brief books, *Superstition and Force* (1866) and *Studies in Church History* (1869, 1883), he began the publication of multivolume works that won him accolades in Europe and America. These included his three-volume *History of Auricular Confession and Indulgences in the Latin Church* (1896), a two-volume edition of *History of Sacerdotal Celibacy in the Christian Church* (1907), and, most notably, his masterpiece, the three-volume *History of the Inquisition in the Middle Ages* (1888) and the four-volume *History of the Inquisition of Spain* (1906–1907). The two Inquisitions, Lea observed, were somewhat different in their origins and their effects. The first rose in a natural way as the Church, with the support of the orthodox, confronted in southern France a rapid rise of dangerous heresies, especially Albigensianism. When the use of "milder means seemed . . . to aggravate the evil," stronger methods were deemed necessary to destroy "the emissaries of Satan." Thus, the Inquisition provided the papacy "with a powerful weapon

. . . of political aggrandizement, tempted secular sovereigns to imitate the example, and prostituted the name of religion.'' Although the Inquisition in Spain was founded by Ferdinand and Isabella, Lea disagreed with Leopold von Ranke (q.v.) that the Inquisition was a "mere political agency.'' Spain's rulers, Lea observed, were devoutly motivated to establish religious unity, mainly at the expense of the Jewish *Conversos*, whose sincerity was in question. Other methods were utilized to strengthen royal authority. As for religious unity, that was eventually achieved but at a terrific price. Lea concluded, "the great lesson taught by the history of the Inquisition is that the attempt of man to control the conscience of his fellows reacts upon himself'': The Inquisition with its auto de fe was an "object of terror to the whole population,'' "the land was robbed of its most industrious classes,'' and "Spain [was left] the most uncultured land in Christendom.'' In his *Inquisition in the Spanish Dependencies* (1908) he concluded that in the colonial tribunals "we see the Inquisition at its worst,'' because distance from Spain had precluded a restraining hand. In the end, this state of affairs meant the loss of Spain's colonies and the retardation of their political and industrial development.

Lea's "scientific history,'' as it came to be labeled, rested on the following principles: go directly to the sources, approach the subject with an open mind, be so familiar with the period under study as to feel a part of it and view it from that standpoint, "avoid polemics'' and moralizing, and judge the past by its own standards. Because of his wealth, Lea, who could not leave his publishing house for long, was able to employ searchers and copyists to visit foreign archives to locate, borrow, or copy manuscripts. Although he believed ethical values were a part of history, he maintained that the facts would reveal them. This view was contrary to the earlier method of looking for lessons in history and demonstrating them to readers. His writings encountered some criticism from Catholic quarters, but the famous English Catholic historian Lord Acton (q.v.) wrote: "The work which has been awaited so long has come over at last, and will assuredly be accepted as the most important contribution of the new world to the religious history of the old.'' Later, Acton invited Lea to contribute a chapter, "The Eve of the Reformation,'' to the *Cambridge Modern History*, even though Lea's philosophy of ethical judgment by the standards of the historical epoch was contrary to Acton's own pronouncements of judgment by an unchangeable code of right and wrong. Honorary degrees from several universities, including Harvard and Princeton, as well as the presidency of the American Historical Association (1903), were bestowed on Lea, who had never received a college degree. Charles Homer Haskins (q.v.) described Lea's *Inquisition* as "the most extensive, the most thorough history of the Inquisition which we possess.''

Bibliography: Lord Acton, "Review: *History of the Inquisition of the Middle Ages. By Henry Charles Lea*,'' *English Historical Review* 3 (1888): 773–788; William M. Armstrong, "Henry C. Lea: Scientific Historian,'' *Pennsylvania Magazine of History and Biography* 80 (1956): 465–477; Edward Sculley Bradley, *Henry Charles Lea: A Biography* (Philadelphia, 1931); Charles Homer Haskins, "Two American Mediaevalists,'' *Studies in Mediaeval Culture* (Oxford, 1929), pp. 256–262; John M. O'Brian, "Henry Charles Lea: The Historian as Reformer,'' *American Quarterly* 19 (1967): 104–113.

Louise Salley Parker

LOVEJOY, Arthur Oncken (Berlin, Germany, 1873–Baltimore, Md., 1962), American philosopher and historian. Educated in philosophy by George Holmes Howison at the University of California at Berkeley (B.A., 1895) and then by Josiah Royce and William James at Harvard University, Lovejoy fruitfully interplayed his interests in philosophy and in history to become one of the leading intellectual historians of his generation. His major publication in philosophy was *The Revolt Against Dualism: An Inquiry Concerning the Existence of Ideas* (1930). In it he defended "epistemological and psychophysical dualism against a variety of monisms." His major intellectual history was *The Great Chain of Being* (1936). In it he applied his method of "unit-ideas" to the notion in Western thought of a hierarchic chain of being from a deity to the lowest creature. By analysis he decomposed the notion into three elemental unit-ideas of plenitude, continuity, and gradation. Starting with Plato and Aristotle, he then traced the ramifications and multi-combinations of these ideas in philosophy, theology, literature, science, and political theory for over two millennia until the close of the eighteenth century, when the idea of a static chain of being began to be replaced by ideas of development, evolution, and becoming. In the hands of a master such as Lovejoy, the methodology of unit-ideas proved to be richly illuminating and vivifying. But when applied by lesser scholars to such subjects as the idea of freedom, it has tended to deteriorate into sterile definition and dissection divorced from intellectual life. Perhaps for that reason his overall program for intellectual historians—to undertake the history of every major unit-idea in Western culture—has not been carried out. Nevertheless, as a historian he is remembered for the excellence of his own work, for the stimulus he gave to intellectual history, notably by the founding in 1940 of the *Journal of the History of Ideas*, and for his frontal attack on historical relativism in "Present Standpoints and Past History" (*Journal of Philosophy* 36: 477–489). Like the relativists, Lovejoy recognized that the historian lived in the present and was affected by present conditions. But whereas the relativist argued that this "presentist predicament" rendered objective historical knowledge impossible and that the historian should write history to meet present problems, Lovejoy maintained that through critical reading of the evidence in a process of "self-transcendence" the historian could write accounts that increasingly agreed with what actually happened. Furthermore, he said, "the first business" of the historian was to seek to establish the past on its own terms. History thus studied, written, and read was a "mind-enlarging, liberalizing, sympathizing discipline, an enrichment of present experience." In contrast, a history that focuses on present problems dangerously distorts the account and threatens its usefulness for the present. In brief, in historical inquiry it is not pragmatic to be pragmatic.

Bibliography: William F. Bynum, "The Great Chain of Being after Forty Years: An Appraisal," *Historical Sciences* 13 (1975): 1–38; Lewis S. Feuer, "Arthur O. Lovejoy," *International Encyclopedia of the Social Sciences*, vol. 18, pp. 464–469; Daniel J. Wilson, "Arthur O. Lovejoy and the Moral of The Great Chain of Being," *Journal of the History of Ideas* 41 (1941): 249–265; Daniel J. Wilson, *Arthur O. Lovejoy and the Quest for Intelligibility* (Chapel Hill, N.C., 1980).

Harold T. Parker

MAHAN, Alfred Thayer (West Point, N.Y., 1840–Washington, D.C., 1914), naval officer of the United States and historian of the influence of sea power on history from the middle of the seventeenth century to the end of the Napoleonic Wars. Mahan's greatness was related to more than his three major historical works, *The Influence of Sea Power upon History, 1660–1783* (1890), *The Influence of Sea Power upon the French Revolution and Empire, 1793–1812* (1892), and *Sea Power in Its Relations to the War of 1812* (1905), although, as narratives of battles and strategies, his writings remain authoritative and readable. Mahan's thesis, that command of the sea was essential for a nation to attain the greatest internal security and external power and influence, came at a time when naval rivalry between Western nations was intensifying and when the measure of external power was the possession of colonies. As an anonymous British reviewer said of Mahan's first book, it "was as oil to the flame of 'colonial expansion' everywhere leaping into life." In the United States, his work was known and praised by imperialists such as Theodore Roosevelt and Henry Cabot Lodge. He was invited to deliver hundreds of lectures and to write many articles and other books detailing the implications for public policy of his historical writings. Thus, he became, as Julius Pratt said, "through the medium of his interpretation of history, one of the leading propagandists of his generation."

Bibliography: Julius Pratt, "Alfred Thayer Mahan," in William Hutchinson, ed., *The Marcus W. Jernegan Essays in American Historiography* (New York, 1937), pp. 207–226; Richard S. West, *Admirals of American Empire: The Combined Story of George Dewey, Alfred Thayer Mahan, Winfield Scott Schley and William Thomas Sampson* (New York, 1948).

Ellen Nore

MALIN, James C. (Edgeley, N.D., 1893–Lawrence, Kan., 1979), historian of the United States. Professor of history at the University of Kansas (1921–1963). As an historian of the grasslands area of the United States, Malin was perhaps the first historian to write as an ecologist. He also spent much time and effort developing a philosophy of history. His work does not have a wide popular audience, but he is highly respected among historians in his specialization, as well as among historians with a purely theoretical bent. Malin's *The Grasslands of North America: Prolegomena to Its History* (1947) is central to understanding the evolution of ideas about grassland regionalism among scientists and ordinary members of the public and is also an important study of the adaptations that farmers made when they moved to the environment of the grasslands. Malin tested some of the propositions of Walter Prescott Webb's (q.v.) *The Great Plains* (1933), and by doing studies at the subregional level found that, in contrast to Webb's emphasis on climate and geography as the sole determinants of farming practices, "inadequate capital resulting in small badly equipped farms was almost as serious an obstacle to successful occupancy of the plains as the difficulties of adaptation [to the subhumid environment]." Allan G. Bogue, speaking of the multitude of community studies that Malin completed, remarked that Malin may have been "the first American historian to coin the admonition . . . that history needed 'to be written from the bottom up.' " Malin's studies of the lives of plain farming folk in the Midwest convinced him that all great inventions in human history had resulted from experiments and adaptations by common men over long periods of time. Philosophically, he was rather unusual in the twentieth century in believing that history could and should be written to present and analyze the past as it actually happened.

Many of Malin's writings did battle with those whom he called "subjective relativists," such as, Charles A. Beard (q.v.) and Carl Lotus Becker (q.v.). His philosophy of history depended on "recognition of objective reality as an absolute . . . . Truth itself," he maintained, "is not relative, it is absolute." Calling himself an "objective relativist," he admitted that, "the mind of man is finite, not infinite." But, given this limitation, in a world of facts existing outside the mind of the observer, the historian, he wrote, "may assemble his facts in sufficient quantity to approach the ideal of comprehension of the whole [unique] man and of the whole [unique] situation," no two of which are ever alike. Because the historian can be certain of facts, "he may divest his work of the limitations of his own self . . . and thus make himself virtually culture-loose, a substantially disembodied mind freed from the limitation of present time and space, and their ties upon his judgment." Malin accused the "subjective relativists" of converting history into a mere policymaking activity when they suggested that, by creating a frame of reference based on his or her unique circumstances, the historian "remade the past." His own position was that, although the past might condition the present, for himself it was a past developed in the past and not "created" in the present. The use of history was not to direct current and future affairs. History was an intellectual enterprise with no immediate pragmatic value. These and many other ideas are developed in a collection of his essays, *On the Nature of History* (1954).

Bibliography: Allan G. Bogue, "The Heirs of James C. Malin: A Grassland Historiography," *Great Plains Quarterly* 1 (1981): 105–131; Robert W. Johannsen, "James C. Malin: An Appreciation," *Kansas Historical Quarterly* 38 (1972):457–466; Robert S. LaForte, "James C. Malin, Optimist: The Basis of His Philosophy of History," *Kansas History* 6 (1983): 110–119; Thomas H. LeDuc, "An Ecological Interpretation of Grasslands History: The Work of James C. Malin as Historian and as Critic of Historians," *Nebraska History* 31 (1950): 226–233.

Ellen Nore

MATTINGLY, Garrett (Washington, D.C., 1900–Oxford, England, 1962), American historian. A leading scholar in Renaissance history, Mattingly received his professional training at Harvard University (B.A., 1923; M.A., 1926; Ph.D., 1935). Those who helped shape his career were Charles Homer Haskins, (q.v.), Charles Howard McIlwain (q.v.), and especially Roger B. Merriman, famous for his four volumes on *The Rise of the Spanish Empire*. Another influence was Bernard De Voto of Northwestern University, who assisted him in developing a narrative style for his histories. During 1922 and 1923 a Sheldon traveling fellowship and in 1937 the first of three Guggenheim fellowships enabled him to pursue research in major European archives. After teaching at Northwestern (1926–1928) and Long Island University (1928–1942), in 1947 he accepted a professorship at Columbia University, where he remained until his death.

Mattingly is known for three major books. The first, *Catherine of Aragon* (1941), was hailed by both scholars and the general reading public, who made it a best-seller. Written in a pictorial narrative style reminiscent of Francis Parkman (q.v.) at his best, the book read like a novel. The closely drawn picture of a tragic but courageous woman deserted by her husband, Henry VIII, and involved in a European power struggle, aroused sentiments of sympathy and excitement. For scholars, bibliographies and chapter-notes in the back of the book made up for the lack of paginal footnotes; it was obvious that the book rested on a solid foundation of archival sources. Moreover, a new picture of Catherine emerged, that of a woman of decision-making abilities, learned, resourceful, true to her marriage vows, loyal to her king and her faith. Although Mattingly did not indulge in the practice of overt moralizing, he let the facts speak for themselves. His next book, *Renaissance Diplomacy* (1955), was rated by scholars as his best. To his dismay, however, the book did not sell too well with the public. In this pioneer work, he had turned to the Italian communes of the fifteenth century to study their unique set of diplomatic institutions and practices, including the resident embassy and the development of the balance of power concept, which spread beyond Italy to become the "characteristic symptom of the new power relations of the nascent modern world." For those readers anticipating the application of "amoral" Machiavellian policies in Italy, Mattingly assured them that routine diplomacy was based on "patience, truthfulness, loyalty, and mutual confidence," and that Machiavelli himself in practice was no Machiavellian. In an article published in *The American Scholar* (1958) he maintained that *The Prince* was a satire; Machiavelli's "advice" could not have worked. In his third book, *The Armada* (1959), he returned to the narrative form. Based on an exhaustive examination of the primary sources, both printed and manuscript, and using certified details to fill in a pictorial narrative of tremendous verve that restored the excitement of the original events, the book fitted the struggle between Philip II's Spain and Elizabeth I's England into the "broader European context in which it had been brewed." Attempting to view the spectacle from the perspective of contemporaries, Mattingly described it as "the beginning of Armageddon . . . between the forces of light and the forces of darkness." But in his eyes the outcome of the defeat of the Armada was not decisive: "Nobody commanded the seas." This conclusion dismissed the claims of those who saw in the rout of the Armada the rise of the English Empire and the decline of the Spanish. However, he admitted that Jules Michelet (q.v.), James Anthony Froude (q.v.), John Lothrop Motley (q.v.), and Leopold von Ranke (q.v.) "had a case" when they agreed that the English victory meant a defeat throughout Europe for the Counter-Reformation. Nevertheless, he believed that even had Spain won, "the final picture of Europe" would not have changed greatly, for neither side, Catholic or Protestant, possessed the "unity" or the "necessary force."

Bibliography: J. H. Hexter, "Garrett Mattingly: Historian," in Charles Howard Carter, ed., *From the Renaissance to the Counter-Reformation: Essays in Honor of Garrett Mattingly* (New York, 1965), pp. 13–28; Donald R. Kelley, "Garrett Mattingly," *Dictionary of American Biography*, Supplement 7, pp. 517–518; Robert M. Kingdon, "Garrett Mattingly," *American Scholar*, 51, no.3 (1982): 396–402.

Louise Salley Parker

McILWAIN, Charles Howard (Saltsburg, Pa., 1871–Cambridge, Mass., 1968), American historian. McIlwain received his professional training at Princeton and Harvard universities—B.A. (1894) and M.A. (1898) from Princeton and a second M.A. (1903) and Ph.D. (1911) from Harvard, where his mentor was Charles Gross. After successive appointments at Miami University (Oxford, Ohio), Princeton University, and Bowdoin College, he joined the faculty of Harvard University in 1911. From 1926 until his retirement in 1946, he held the chair of Eaton professor of the science of government, thus combining in his person the study of history and political science. Other honors included a Pulitzer Prize for *The American Revolution* (1923), the Eastman visiting professorship at Oxford University, and the presidency of the American Historical Association (1936). The first of his major works was *The High Court of Parliament and Its Supremacy* (1910). Following the strategy of striving to ascertain what institutions were exactly by seeing them through the eyes of contemporaries, he opened this study with some general statements of what Parliament after 1066 was and what it was not. Because England was a "feudal state" and its "central assembly was a feudal assembly," it was possessed "with the general characteristics of feudal assemblies. One of these characteristics was the absence of law-*making*. The law was declared rather than made." He next explained that Parliament then "was more a court than a legislative, while . . . ordinary courts were legislative [and] . . . judicial." By the thirteenth or fourteenth century parliaments such as those in the reign of Edward I were still not true legislative assemblies. Even in the time of the Tudors, the central assembly was still the "High Court of Parliament." This thesis conflicted with that of William Stubbs (q.v.), famous for his three-volume *Constitutional History of England*, which held that the Model Parliament of 1295 was a true Parliament. Albert Frederick Pollard (q.v.) popularized McIlwain's thesis in his *Evolution of Parliament*, and McIlwain's interpretation became the standard view. In his *Growth of Political Thought in the West from the Greeks to the End of the Middle Ages* (1932),

McIlwain raised thought-provoking questions and conclusions. Applying his constant strategy of trying to view past institutions and concepts as contemporaries saw them, he arrived at historical meanings of constitutional monarchy, absolutism, and nation that surprise us. Thus, a thirteenth-century English king "under the law" was not a "constitutional ruler of the modern type." In the same period, a king's authority was " 'absolute' and practically irresponsible, but . . . not 'arbitrary.' " And the idea of nationality grew so slowly that "disaffected English barons in 1215 had few qualms . . . in proclaiming a Dauphin of France King of England." In his *Constitutionalism: Ancient and Modern* (1940), he examined the various brands of constitutionalism from the Greeks and Romans to the present, concluding, "never in recorded history . . . has the individual been in greater danger from the government than now . . . and never has there been such need that we should clearly see this danger and guard against it."

From his knowledge of constitutional history, McIlwain was aghast at the rise of totalitarianism and feared that the American people might lose their liberties if they and their government ever forgot that they too lived under the rule of fundamental law. Thus, his effort to avoid what he termed "retrogressive modernism" produced a new vision of the past that was yet relevant to understanding current institutions. His address as president of the American Historical Association was entitled "The Historian's Part in a Changing World" (1936). True to his conception of the historian's task, he frontally attacked historical relativism as propounded by former presidents of the American Historical Association, James Harvey Robinson (q.v.), Carl Lotus Becker (q.v.), and Charles A. Beard (q.v.). To be sure, he said, the historian is affected by present conditions and should meet present needs, but that historian best serves the present who first seeks to understand the past on its own terms.

Bibliography: Peter Bachrach, "Charles H. McIlwain," *International Encyclopedia of the Social Sciences*, vol., 9, pp. 511–512; Bryce Lyon, *The Middle Ages in Recent Historical Thought: Selected Topics* (Washington, D.C., 1959); S. E. Thorne, "Charles Howard McIlwain," *American Philosophical Society Yearbook* (1970), pp. 146–149.

Louise Salley Parker

MILLER, Perry (Chicago, 1905–Cambridge, Mass., 1963), American historian. Instructor, assistant professor, and professor of American literature, Harvard University, 1931–1963. Miller wrote and edited numerous major works on late eighteenth- and early-nineteenth century American literature and culture, among them "From Edwards to Emerson" (1940); *The Raven and the Whale: The War of Words and Wits in the Era of Poe and Melville* (1956); *The American Transcendentalists: Their Prose and Poetry* (1956); *Consciousness at Concord: The Texts of Thoreau's Hitherto 'Lost Journal' (1840–1841) Together with Notes and a Commentary* (1958); *The Golden Age of American Literature* (1959); *The Legal Mind in America: From Independence to the Civil War* (1962); and *Margaret Fuller: American Romantic* (1963). His most important and influential works, however, were his studies of American Puritan theology, literature and culture, works that set a new standard for American intellectual history, that legitimized and broadened the New England Puritans as a field of study, and that shaped a generation's understanding of the Puritans. Discouraged by his teachers from choosing the Puritans as a dissertation topic because of what they perceived as limitations of the field, and having come of age, as he wrote in the preface to the 1959 reprint of *Orthodoxy in Massachusetts*, "within an emotional universe dominated by H. L. Mencken," a universe in which "the word 'Puritan' served as a comprehensive smear against every tendency in American civilization which we held reprehensible," Miller nonetheless was determined to demonstrate "the majesty and coherence of Puritan thinking." An agnostic fascinated by the ironies, paradoxes, and intellectual vigor of New England Puritanism, Miller saw in it a microcosm of American society and "a sort of working model for American history."

Miller's first study of the Puritans, his doctoral dissertation published under the title, *Orthodoxy in Massachusetts, 1630–1650: A Genetic Study* (1933), attacked the conventional view, held by such historians as James Truslow Adams, that the Puritan intellect was grim, rigid, and narrow. He argued in this and his major work, *The New England Mind: The Seventeenth Century* (1953), that the Puritans were to be seen in relation not only to Calvin, but to other early reformers as well, and also as having incorporated the neo-Platonism of Ramus and thus strains of liberalism and humanism from the Renaissance. Although sometimes charged with overemphasizing Puritan intellect while neglecting the emotional life, Miller's achievement is based in part on his analysis of Puritan thought as an expression of psychology and emotion, the very source of much of its irony and paradox that so attracted him. For example, in his preface to *The Puritans* (1938), edited with Thomas H. Johnson, he wrote, "Puritanism would make every man an expert psychologist, to detect all the makeshift 'rationalizations,' to shatter without pity the sweet dreams of self-enhancement in which the ego takes refuge from reality." Consistently, his analyses of the Puritans emphasized the link between mind and heart, as in *Orthodoxy:* "to understand the operation of their minds, we must realize what they conceived was at stake, what tremendous urgencies drove them to such desperate shifts." Even his biography *Jonathan Edwards* (1949), which, in trying to demonstrate Edwards' debt to Locke, focused on the intellectual rather than the daily life of Edwards, developed the premise that "No writer ever emerged more directly out of his passions, the feuds, and the anxieties of his society; his peculiar kind of objectivity must, in fact, be interpreted, not as insensitivity to his surroundings, but as an effort to protect himself against their clutch." He was criticized—mostly posthumously— for diminishing the Calvinist background of the Puritan intellect, for ignoring the separatists and other New England sects, for treating concepts at the expense of individuals, and for directing literary scholars into the history of theology rather than the treatment of works, especially poetry. Yet many of Miller's ideas have become doctrine—the humanistic influence of the Renaissance on New

England thought, and the "Plain Style" of Puritan sermons, for example—and even the criticism of his work as well as subsequent studies of New England Puritanism have taken place on the very ground he established and first surveyed.

Bibliography: John C. Crowell, "Perry Miller as Historian: A Bibliography of Evaluations," *Bulletin of Bibliography and Magazine Notes*, no. 34 (1977): 77–85; David A. Hollinger, "Perry Miller and Philosophical History," *History and Theory*, no. 7 (1968): 25–59; Kenneth S. Lynn, "Perry Miller," *The American Scholar* 52, no. 2 (1983): 221–227; Richard Reinitz, *Irony and Consciousness: American Historiography and Reinhold Neibuhr's Vision* (Lewisburg, Pa., 1980).

Ronald E. Tranquilla

MOTLEY, John Lothrop (Dorchester, Mass., 1814–Kingston Russell near Dorchester, England, 1877), American historian and diplomat. Motley belonged to that galaxy of midnineteenth-century Americans—George Bancroft (q.v.), Henry Charles Lea (q.v.), Francis Parkman (q.v.), and William H. Prescott (q.v.)—who wrote multivolume narrative histories on a grand theme in the grand manner. His three major historical works, *The Rise of the Dutch Republic* (1856), *History of the United Netherlands* (1860, 1867), and *The Life and Death of John Of Barneveld* (1874), nine stout volumes in all, narrated the struggle of the northern provinces of the Netherlands against the imperial power of Spain until 1619. A graduate of Harvard University (1831) who had spent two years at the universities of Göttingen and Berlin without learning anything of critical historical method, he came to the composition of his first book as a storyteller whose two novels had failed. He had formed his concept of the Dutch struggle for liberty from the romantic account of Friedrich Schiller. He wrote as a partisan admirer of the valiant Dutch freedom fighters against an oppressive, cruel, and evil Spanish tyranny. He wrote as a moralist. He believed, like Lord Acton (q.v.), that the historian should judge by absolute standards of right and wrong. He hoped his narrative would edify, instruct statesmen and politicians, and inspire his readers to love freedom and hate despotism. And he wrote as a dramatist whose great scenes—the relief of Leyden, the assassination of William the Silent, the trial and execution of Barneveldt, for example—still enthrall. *The Rise of the Dutch Republic* became a best-seller in Great Britain and the United States, acclaimed by such scholars as François Guizot (q.v.), James Anthony Froude (q.v.), and Prescott as a history of outstanding merit. It won him appointment as ambassador of the United States to Austria (1861–1867) and to Great Britain (1869–1870). However, during the heyday of scientific, analytical history of the twentieth century, its reputation declined precipitously. Its lack of objectivity, its focus on the story (and the political one at that), and its factual errors all told against it.

Today the tendency is to view Motley as a maturing historian whose second book was better than the first, and whose last one was best of all. For his first book he had incorporated details from the archives of Dresden, Brussels, and The Hague only to add color and verisimilitude. But for his last two books his close association with the Dutch school of professional historians, then (after the German) the second in the world, introduced him to the critical method. His own multiarchival researches into the manuscript repositories of London, Paris, Madrid, Vienna, The Hague, and Brussels modified his view of the past. His zeal for freedom and his sense of drama remained undiminished, but his stark black-and-white judgments of human personality became grays, his adversarial narrative of two antagonists widened to a flow of European complexity, and his natural humanity and humor, so apparent in his family life and letters, emerged in his history. In his lifetime he thus accomplished the transition from a "literary" historian to a masterly professional investigator.

Bibliography: Owen Dudley Edwards, "John Lothrop Motley," *Dictionary of Literary Biography*, vol. 30, pp. 175–192; Oliver Wendell Holmes, *John Lothrop Motley: A Memoir* (London, 1878).

Harold T. Parker

NICHOLS, Roy F. (Newark, N.J., 1896–Philadelphia, 1973), historian of the United States. From 1925 until 1953, Nicholas was a professor at the University of Pennsylvania. He was the rare historian who combined very detailed narrative with theoretical concepts. In his essay "The Genealogy of Historical Generalizations" (1963), he affirmed that "if the writing of history is to have its greatest significance and be more than a mere narrative of events, it ought to attempt to communicate the meaning of what men have done." His chosen subject was political history, and he began to write political history at a time when that area seemed exhausted, when, he noted in his autobiography, *An Historian's Progress* (1968), "unselective descriptive chronicles were coming to have a minimum of meaning." American historians were abandoning "history as past politics" and "politics as present history" for the study of intellectual and social questions. Nichols' greatness comes from his largely successful effort to study political history as a branch of cultural history. In a society in which the public has a role in the political process, he argued, the political system will be a vivid display of that society's culture. As he wrote in "History in a Self-Governing Culture" (1967), "The distinguishing characteristic of the society known as the United States of America is the fact that it is a democratic culture dedicated to a self-government in which all are technically involved and in which this interest is demonstrably central to the self-identification of the people. It can be used as the hallmark of the culture."

Nichols' most famous book, *The Disruption of American Democracy* (1948) describes the failure of the Democratic party in the 1850s, its destruction and disintegration as a major institution that had embraced people in all parts of the nation, in the face of the explosive questions that resulted in the Civil War. The party could not "cope under stress," that is, it could not resolve sectional cultural antagonisms when they became politicized. Nichols did not like the strain in American historical writing which stressed American uniqueness instead of the commonality of human experience in the Western world. The American Civil

War was thus, in his view, not a unique conflict in anything but its particular causes. "At various times in the nineteenth and twentieth centuries," he urged, "there has been the common phenomenon of national unification, generally including a phase of social war, notably in Germany, Italy, and the Dual monarchy. Similar struggles on the field of battle or over the negotiation table have resulted in division as well as unification, in such instances as the separation of Belgium from Holland. . . . The American Civil War was perhaps only an example of this type of metanationalistic reaction." In *Blueprints for Leviathan: American Style* (1963) and in *Invention of the American Political Parties* (1967), he was particularly attentive to the English roots of American institutions. David M. Potter (q.v.) concluded of Nichols' scholarship that "perhaps its greatest importance is in its major contribution to the rehabilitation of American political history."

Bibliography: John A. Garraty, "Roy F. Nichols: The Causes of the Civil War," in Garraty, *Interpreting American History: Conversations With Historians* (New York, 1970); David M. Potter, "Roy F. Nichols and the Rehabilitation of American Political History," in Don E. Fehrenbacher, ed., *History and American Society: Essays of David M. Potter* (New York, 1973), pp. 192–217; Carol Reardon, "Roy F. Nichols," in *Twentieth-Century American Historians*, vol. 17 of *Dictionary of Literary Biography*, edited by Clyde N. Wilson (Detroit, 1983), pp. 328–332.

Ellen Nore

PARKMAN, Francis (Boston, 1823–Boston, 1893), historian of the United States. As a member of a wealthy and privileged family, Parkman pursued his chosen career in history as a literary artist of independent means. His narrative history, his epic tales of heroic deeds against the background of the untamed lands of North America in the eighteenth century, still command an audience in the twentieth century. In 1851 he published the first of his stories, *The History of the Conspiracy of Pontiac and the Indian War After the Conquest of Canada* (revised and enlarged 1868). Near the end of *Pontiac*, after the early victories of the Native Americans have been destroyed by a series of defeats at British hands, Parkman announces his artistic and moral goals as an historian, that is, to illustrate the relationship between natural beauty and the moral beauty of heroism: "There are few so imbruted by vice, so perverted by art and luxury, as to dwell in the closest presence of Nature, deaf to her voice of melody and power, untouched by the ennobling influences which mould and penetrate the heart that has not hardened itself against them." Thus, Parkman urges, in this and in all his histories, that "it is the grand and heroic in the hearts of men which finds its worthiest symbol and noblest inspiration amid these desert realms—in the mountains . . . in the radiance of the sinking sun; in the interminable forest." Indians, in Parkman's histories, could not be heroes, as they did not combine their undoubtable courage with moral sensitivity, a quality possessed only by white avatars of civilization. His major work in nine volumes, *France and England in North America* (1865–1892), continues these themes.

Although Frenchmen could, in Parkman's view, become heroes, as, for example, his LaSalle, the final victory of the British over the French in North America was presented by Parkman as an example of Anglo-Saxon superiority. New France could not endure because its people had been reduced "to subjection and dependence through centuries of feudal and monarchical despotism." As Catholics who lacked the "reflection, forecast, industry and self-reliance" of their Anglo-Saxon enemies, the French in Canada were like all Frenchmen—emotional, greedy, and unwilling to face unpleasant facts.

Reader, heroic subject, and narrator are merged in Parkman's writings. The intended audience consists of white, upper class, English-speaking males who, through these histories, will be able to meditate on their own heroic potential, a potential called forth and developed by the encounter with enemies in what these urban readers would know as a wild landscape. "The narrator," wrote Parkman, stating his intention, "must seek to imbue himself with the life and spirit of the time. He must study events in their bearings near and remote; in the character, habits, and manners of those who took part in them. He must himself be, as it were, a sharer or a spectator of the action he describes." If they are no longer "history", Parkman's writings remain great examples of English prose.

Bibliography: David Levin, *History as Romantic Art: Bancroft, Motley, Prescott, and Parkman* (Stanford, Calif., 1959); Otis Pease, *Parkman's History: The Historian as Literary Artist* (New Haven, Conn., 1953); Richard C. Vitzthum, *The American Compromise: Theme and Method in the Histories of Bancroft, Parkman, and Adams* (Norman, Okla., 1974).

Ellen Nore

PARRINGTON, Vernon Louis (Aurora, Ill., 1871–Winchcomb, Gloucester, England, 1929), American historian. University professor, instructor of English and French, College of Emporia (1893–1897); instructor of English and modern languages (1897–1898) and professor of English (1898–1908), University of Oklahoma; and assistant professor of English (1908–1912) and professor of English (1912–1929), University of Washington. Parrington's reputation as a historian rests entirely on his one major work in three volumes, *Main Currents of American Thought: An Interpretation of American Literature from the Beginnings to 1920*. Admittedly biased, unfinished, and today largely unread, once it was formidable; it is still important because it was the first attempted survey and synthesis of American intellectual history from its beginning through the early twentieth century. Writing in the waning years of the Populist era, and showing the influence, as did Charles A. Beard (q.v.), of J. Allen Smith's economic and class interpretation of the Constitution, Parrington explained his purpose in the "Introduction" to the first volume, *The Colonial Mind, 1620–1800* (1927), as being "liberal rather than conservative, Jeffersonian rather than Federalistic." Through biographical sketches of individual figures, this first volume cast the Puritans as an elitist, closed society that was impervious to the liberalism of the

Renaissance and that held sway until the eighteenth century asserted that "it is the right and duty of citizens to re-create social and political institutions to the end that they shall further social justice." Volume 2, *The Romantic Revolution in America, 1800–1860* (1927), charged that the forces of capitalism and imperialism had overwhelmed the humane impulses of the Jeffersonian and Jacksonian eras. Volume 3, *The Beginnings of Critical Realism* (1930), unfinished and published posthumously, despairs over the decline of Democratic liberalism in the face of scientific determinism and "the custodianship of America by the middle class," finding hope only in the writing of a few realists and muckrakers who used literature as an instrument of social action.

More thorough and careful historians who followed would find the development of America more complex and would reject Parrington's once influential book because of its melodrama, its overestimation of European influences on American thought, its doctrinaire rather than aesthetic judgments of writers, its neglect of metaphysics and theology, science, and social science. Richard Hofstadter's (q.v.) 1967 intellectual biography is a description of Parrington's "abrupt decline." Fifteen years earlier, John Higham had called *Main Currents* "a noble ruin on the landscape of our scholarship." Perhaps now it would be more in keeping with the often extravagant ocean and seaside metaphors of the book to say it is a scholarly Titanic.

Bibliography: Joseph B. Harrison, *Vernon Louis Parrington: American Scholar* (Seattle, 1929); John Higham, "The Rise of American Intellectual History," *American Historical Review* no. 56 (1952): 460–461; Richard Hofstadter, *The Progressive Historians: Turner, Beard, Parrington* (New York, 1968), pp. 349–439, 486–494; Wesley Morris, *Toward a New Historicism* (Princeton, N.J., 1972), pp. 35–51; Robert A. Skotheim and Kermit Vanderbilt, "Vernon Louis Parrington," *Pacific Northwest Quarterly* 53, no. 3 (1962): 100–113; Lionel Trilling, *The Liberal Imagination: Essays on Literature and Society* (New York, 1950), pp. 124–148.

Ronald E. Tranquilla

PHILLIPS, Ulrich B. (LaGrange, Ga., 1877–New Haven, Conn., 1934), historian of the Southern United States. Professor at Tulane, Wisconsin, Michigan, and Yale universities. Although his social outlook was that of a white supremacist and racist, Phillips' scholarly works were not written in behalf of that ideology. They assumed it. While lauding the values of the planter class, he regretted the economic, social, and political outcomes of slavery. His first important book, *A History of Transportation in the Eastern Cotton Belt to 1860* (1908), illustrates these themes. Dedicated to "the Dominant Class of the South, who in the piping ante-bellum time schooled multitudes, white and black, to the acceptance of higher standards," the volume yet documents Phillips' pessimistic conclusion that "building of railroads led to little else but the extension and the intensifying of the plantation system and the increase in the staple output. Specialization and commerce were extended, when just the opposite development, towards diversification of products and economic self-sufficiency, was the real need." *American Negro Slavery: A Survey of the Supply, Employment and Control of Negro*

Labor as Determined by the Plantation Regime (1918) and *Life and Labor in the Old South* (1929) analyzed and documented the capitalistic nature of the plantation system, argued that an ethic of paternalistic responsibility for "child-like" Negroes was an important aspect of plantation life, and maintained that the slave system tended to be unprofitable, had achieved its maximum expansion, and might gradually have yielded to a wage-labor system. Regarding blacks as an inferior race, Phillips regarded the plantation as a system of cultural education for them, and he noted that slavery was more than an economically desirable labor system to the planters; they saw it as an essential mechanism for social control of the black race.

Phillips developed the implications of slavery-as-social-control in his most famous essay, "The Central Theme of Southern History," (1928), reprinted in a collection of his shorter pieces, *The Course of the South to Succession*, published posthumously in 1939. The Civil War had resulted from the planters' determination to defend the essence of Southernism and Southern society, that is, the premise that the South was and should always be "a white man's country." Phillips did not defend slavery in his history. Yet, a moral point of his writing was to contrast what he saw as the humane paternalism of the slave-owning planters with the lack of connection between social power and social responsibility concealed by the cash nexus of a system of wage labor. The tone of Phillips' writing offends modern readers who cannot agree with his patronizing attitude toward the Negro. Despite this fallacy, he recognized that racism was perhaps the most powerful component of Southernism. Thus, his writings are a subtle and essential introduction to the history of the United States.

Bibliography: Merton L. Dillon, *Ulrich Bonnell Phillips: Historian of the Old South* (Baton Rouge, La. and London, 1985); Eugene D. Genovese, "Race and Class in Southern History: An Appraisal of the Work of Ulrich Bonnell Phillips," *Agricultural History* 41 (1967): 345–358; John Herbert Roper, *U. B. Phillips: A Southern Mind* (Macon, Ga., 1984); David Joseph Singal, "Ulrich B. Phillips: The Old South as the New," *Journal of American History* 63 (1977): 871–891; John David Smith, "The Historiographic Rise, Fall, and Resurrection of Ulrich Bonnell Phillips," *Georgia Historical Quarterly* 65 (1981): 138–153; W. K. Wood, "U. B. Phillips, Unscientific Historian: A Further Note on His Methodology and Use of Sources," *Southern Studies* 21 (1982): 146–162.

Ellen Nore

POTTER, David M. (Augusta, Ga., 1910–Palo Alto, Calif., 1971), historian of the United States. Educated at Emory and Yale universities, Potter taught at Mississippi and Rice (1936–1942), at Yale (1942–1961), and at Stanford (1961–1971). He was also the Harmsworth professor at Oxford (1947–1948) and president of both the Organization of American Historians (1971) and the American Historical Association (1971). For his rethinking of traditional questions, his venturing into new areas of inquiry, and his pithy and often witty prose, Potter, though not well known to the general public in the United States, was respected and admired by historians in many fields. His own work was concentrated in the areas of the Civil War, especially on the reasons for that bloody conflict, the history of the South, focusing on what gave that region its distinctive character, and the social history of the United States, with emphasis on the problems of describing the "American character" and, at the time of his death, alienation. Historical methodology and the social role of historians were lifelong concerns. Potter's doctoral dissertation, *Lincoln and His Party in the Secession Crisis* (1942), reissued with a new preface in 1962, exemplified his view that the most important task of the historian writing on public policy "is to see the past through the imperfect eyes of those who lived it and not with his own omniscient twenty-twenty vision." In asking why the Republicans in 1861 rejected both compromise on their principle of nonextension of slavery into the territories of the United States and the secession of the Southern states, Potter was certain that "no one chose the American Civil War, because it lay behind the veil of the future; it did not exist as a choice" when decisions were made.

In all of his work on the Civil War and the South, Potter warned against confusing historical understanding with efforts to justify past events. Writing about the distinctiveness of Southern regional culture, he disagreed with historians and intellectuals who emphasized agrarianism, nor did he fully accept any explanation based on caste and class in that region. In *The South and the Sectional Conflict* (1968), he argued that Southerness may be rooted in "the folk culture" of the area, where "the relation of people to one another imparted a distinctive texture as well as a distinctive tempo in their lives." In his posthumous book, *The Impending Crisis, 1848–1861* (1976), he suggested that Southern nationalism was not as important before the Civil War as the values shared with Northerners but that, after the Civil War, white Southerners had a sense of Southern separateness resulting "from the shared sacrifices, the shared efforts, and the shared defeat (which is often more unifying than victory) of the Civil War." The explanation of Southern secession in his last book is consistent with Potter's psychological emphasis in describing human motivation. Hence, in 1860, "the [white] people of the slaveholding states were not united in any commitment to southern nationalism. . . . But they *were* united by a sense of terrible danger" (Potter's italics). In the final analysis, Potter believed that historical generalizations were inevitably subjective. It was, he wrote, "perhaps more than conceivable that the process of historical interpretation is simply too intricate to be reduced to any kind of rules or formulas."

In his most famous book, *People of Plenty: Economic Abundance and the American Character* (1954) and in many of the essays collected by Don E. Fehrenbacher and published in *History and American Society* (1973), Potter exemplified his dictum that the historian must turn from a "traditional concern with questions of the means of attaining our social model [public policy] to questions about the basic soundness of our social ideals, and about the tenability of the model, even about the nature of society itself . . . the historical sources of anxiety, and of aggression, and of alienation." The optimism characteristic of people from the United States, he urged in *People of Plenty*, came not from the influence of the frontier on popular expectations, but rather, from the effect of economic abundance, which led people to expect security, first in the form of widely available land during the colonial and early national periods and later, in the nineteenth and twentieth centuries, in the form of jobs created by a vast and successful industrial base. With the expectation of economic security fostered by an abundant economic foundation went an expectation of, and belief in, the possibility of social mobility. Potter signaled that this faith in upward mobility and equalitarianism had psychological costs: The quest for equality was, after all, "an unattainable ideal" which, "while it could not fulfill its promise to create a classless society . . . has destroyed the one value which seemed inherent in the traditional class society—namely, that sense of the organic, recognized relationship between the individual and the community which was defined by the individual's status." It was this fundamental conservativism, epitomized by his suggestion that people who know and accept their place in a social hierarchy might be less anxiety-ridden than those in quest of social mobility and equality, that attracted Potter to the study of social history. Although Potter wrote eloquent and subtle history of public policy, there was a set of assumptions in this sort of endeavor that he did not like: "the study of policy always assumes that man can modify his circumstances, control his environment, shape his ends, and perhaps even become the captain of his own fate." On the other hand, social and cultural history, he wrote, "tends to emphasize underlying given factors and intractible components in the life of a people. . . . forces. . . . which lie beyond social control." Although he left no "school," Potter's writings are a well from which historians and other intellectuals will draw suggestions for years to come.

Bibliography: Sir Denis Brogan, "David M. Potter," in Marcus Cunliffe and Robin Winks, eds., *Pastmasters* (New York, 1969), pp. 316–344; Robert W. Johannsen, "David M. Potter, Historian and Social Critic," *Civil War History* 20 (1974): 35–44; Michael Kammen, "On Predicting the Past: Potter and Plumb," *Journal of Interdisciplinary History*, no. 1 (1974): 109–118.

Ellen Nore

PRESCOTT, William H. (Salem, Mass., 1796–Boston, 1839), historian of imperial Spain and Spanish America. Born to a family already wealthy, Prescott was not compelled to take up any career, but he became an historian out of the Protestant New Englander's sense that one has a duty to make use of one's talents. Because of his partial blindness and the constraints of other physical problems, Prescott never saw the Spain of his first history, *The Reign of Ferdinand and Isabella the Catholic* (1838) or his last, *History of the Reign of Philip the Second, King of Spain* (vols. 1 and 2, 1855, vol. 3, 1858), although he had spent some time with relatives in the Azores, which gave him a sympathy for Catholic Iberian culture unusual in antipapist New England. Prescott's most popular work, *History of the Conquest of Mexico* (1843), as well as his best-selling *History of the Conquest of Peru* (1847) and his other writings, embody no philosophy of history beyond a commitment to construct unified epic narratives based as completely as possible on documentary sources. His histories treat elite politics, war, and diplomacy. He excluded social and economic topics. Concentrating on letters and memoirs, he used no legal documents. His descriptions of the conquering of Mexico and Peru are told entirely from the Spanish imperial point of view. Prescott originated, in the United States, the practice of supplying bibliographic footnotes, and he was the first historian living in the United States to attempt serious scholarly study of Spanish and Spanish American history.

Bibliography: Donald Darnell, *William Hickling Prescott* (Boston, 1975); Guillermo Felix Cruz, *El imperio español y los historiadores norteamericanos*, 2 vols. (Santiago de Chile, 1960); C. Harvey Gardiner, *William Hinckling Prescott, A Biography* (Austin, Tex., 1969); David Levin, *History as Romantic Art: Bancroft, Prescott, Motley, and Parkman* (Stanford, Calif., 1959).

Ellen Nore

RHODES, James Ford (Cleveland, Ohio, 1848–Cleveland, Ohio, 1927), historian of the Civil War and Reconstruction in the United States. Rhodes was the son of a wealthy industrialist and retired at the age of thirty-five to become a gentleman scholar. His major work, *History of the United States from the Compromise of 1850*, appeared in seven volumes between 1893 and 1906. His story ended in 1877. In explaining the Civil War, his central theme was slavery: It explained, he wrote, "practically all the main currents of American national history down to the close of Reconstruction." The South, he argued, "went to war to extend slavery." Drawing on the works of George Bancroft and Richard Hildreth (q.v.), Rhodes' account of the coming of the Civil War was unusual in its very strong emphasis on slavery as the cause of that conflict but was very regular in its nationalism and Anglo-Saxonism. Rhodes' most durable contribution to historiography was his portrayal of Reconstruction as an irresponsible experiment of a vengeful North attempting to impose Africanization on the South. Rhodes, like those who followed him in this racist reading of national history, John Burgess and William A. Dunning, both of Columbia University, held the view common among educated white males of his class, a view based on the "science" of the late nineteenth century, that blacks suffered arrested mental development after the age of thirteen or fourteen. Therefore, he wrote a history of Reconstruction as "Black Terror"—"negro rule forced on the South at the point of the bayonet." Writing in an age when the American caste system was everywhere taking legal form in laws preventing blacks from voting and from sharing in many of the amenities available to white citizens, Rhodes' history had great and tragic consequences.

Bibliography: Robert Cruden, *James Ford Rhodes* (Cleveland, 1961); Mark A. DeWolfe Howe, *James Ford Rhodes, American Historian* (New York, 1969).

Ellen Nore

ROBINSON, James Harvey (Bloomington, Ill., 1863–New York City, 1936), American historian. Throughout his professional career Robinson was a crusader for enlightenment through the study of history. He participated in the first historiographical revolution in the United States—the professionalization of history-teaching and -writing along lines that were thought to be Rankean—and he was a leader in the second revolution that sought to expand the scope of professional history and to enlist the aid of the social sciences in its interpretation. These two revolutions were international, but under the battle cry "The New History" Robinson assembled a complex of interconnected ideas whose combination was unique and influential. His ideas came not all at once but one by one. After completing an undergraduate degree and a master's in history at Harvard University, he earned a Ph.D (1890) at the University of Freiburg under the supervision of Herman Eduoard von Holst. There he was thoroughly grounded in "scientific" historical method: the critical scrutiny of primary evidence for authenticity, interpretation of meaning, and reliability. When he returned to the United States to teach history at the University of Pennsylvania (1891–1895) and then at Barnard College and Columbia University (1895–1918), he insisted with the zeal of a convert that graduate and undergraduate students should critically examine the primary sources of the history they studied. The experience, he thought, lent reality and vividness to history, instilled in the students habits of skepticism and critical judgment, and established in their minds the history of each age on its own terms. With Edward P. Cheyney, his colleague at Pennsylvania, he initiated the publication of the Translations and Reprints Series of primary sources for classroom use, and on his own he issued a volume of extracts, *Petrarch* (1898), with a scholarly introduction. However, teaching and conversation with his colleagues broadened his conception of history.

As early as 1892, influenced perhaps by the economist Simon Patten, he urged that historians seek the aid of social scientists. By 1896 he thought that history should not be limited to a chronicle of political, constitutional, and military events but should record the manifold activities and permanent achievements of humanity in all fields. He began to say that Leopold von Ranke's (q.v.) celebrated dictum, "wie es eigentlich gewesen" (how it really happened), whose depth Robinson never appreciated, should be altered to "wie es eigentlich geworden" (how it came about). In 1902 he embodied these beliefs in the first great American textbook on European history, *An Introduction to the History of Western Europe*. Abreast of current scholarly publications and based often on his own reading of the primary sources, it was reliable, well written, and fun to read. At Columbia University in 1904 he started his celebrated course on intellectual history, "The History of the Intellectual Class of Europe." From his courses and seminars came many historians of distinction, including Carl Lotus Becker (q.v.), Carlton Joseph H. Hayes (q.v.), Preserved Smith (q.v.), and Lynn Thorndike (q.v.). In about 1904, for reasons that are obscure, he shifted to a presentist view of the historian's knowledge and function. To be sure, Robinson's goal was constant—to enlighten through the study of history. Nor did he ever abandon the critical scrutiny of primary evidence to ascertain what occurred. But he now believed the facts selected for presentation should be chosen not for the importance they had at the time or for furthering our comprehension of an epoch on its own terms, but for their usefulness for understanding present problems. Present needs, not past standpoints, should dictate the history that should be told. Recent history, it follows, should be emphasized, an expanded past should be applied to present concerns, and the insights of social science should be appropriated. History would then become an instrument for the achievement of rational social progress. In his manifesto *The New History* (1912) he proclaimed, "The present has hitherto been the willing victim of the past, the time has now come when it should turn on the past and exploit it in the interests of advance." In *The Mind in the Making* (1921) Robinson demonstrated by example how his approach illuminated a current problem. The core chapters on the history of humanity compare not unfavorably with Condorcet's sketch, the *Histoire de l'esprit humain*. In chapters on our animal heritage, the savage mind, and Western intellectual history since the Greeks, Robinson mobilized animal, child, and social psychology, anthropology, and history to show how impulses and ideas that had once been useful have prevented us from applying our intelligence creatively to the problems of a rapidly changing technological society. The remedy for the resultant cultural lag between technological and cultural change was to bring to bear upon society those creative modes of thinking that natural scientists had employed for centuries. Thus, knowledge of history both identified the problem and provided the answer.

Bibliography: Crane Brinton, "James Harvey Robinson," *Dictionary of American Biography*, vol. 22 (supplement 2), pp. 562–566; Luther V. Hendricks, *James Harvey Robinson: Teacher of History* (New York, 1946); Cushing Strout, "The Twentieth Century Enlightenment," *American Political Science Review* 49 (1955): 321–339.

Harold T. Parker

ROSTOVTZEFF, Michael Ivanovich (Zhitomir, Russia, 1870–New Haven, Conn., 1952), Russo-American historian. Son of the director and Latin teacher at the local gymnasium, Rostovtzeff specialized in historical-philological studies at the universities of Kiev and St. Petersburg (1892). His undergraduate thesis, "Pompeii in the Light of the New Excavations," foreshadowed his later historical work. After teaching Latin for three years at the gymnasium of Tsarkoe-Selo, he journeyed on a study/research fellowship to Turkey, North Africa, Spain, and Italy, worked in the Numismatic Collection of the British Museum and the Cabinet des Médailles at Paris, and settled down in the graduate seminars of Eugen Bormann and Otto Benndorf at the University of Vienna to study tax farming in the Roman Empire. As classic pioneer studies, both his master's thesis, "A History of the State Lease in the Roman Empire" (1898), and his doctoral dissertation, "The Roman Lead Tesserae" (1903), were later published. The dissertation was especially remarkable, for Rostovtzeff showed that one type of the commonplace multipurpose tokens (*tesserae*) labeled "anabolicum" had been used by the Romans as a tax on manufactured articles designated for the army. Rostovtzeff was now appointed professor of ancient history and of Latin at the St. Petersburg College for Women. Until the Bolshevik Revolution he was very interested in the archaeology of southern Russia, particularly in the art of the Asiatic peoples, the Scythians, and Sarmatians who settled on the southern steppes. Several important studies followed: *Ancient Decorative Painting of South Russia* (2 vols., 1914), *Scythia and the Bosporus* (1918), and *Iranians and Greeks in South Russia* (1922).

With the success of the Bolshevik Revolution, Rostovtzeff emigrated first to Great Britain, where he taught at Oxford University for two years, and then to the United States, where he was professor of ancient history successively at the University of Wisconsin (1920–1925) and Yale University (1925–1952). At Yale he served as director, organizer, and editor of its excavations at Dura-Europos on the Euphrates, where monuments were exposed dating from the third millennium through the later Roman Empire. Several of his publications relate to those findings: *Caravan Cities* (1932), *Dura and the Problem of Parthian Art* (1935), and *Dura-Europos and Its Art* (1938). However, his career was crowned by his massive trilogy: *The History of the Ancient World* (1926, 1927), *The Social and Economic History of the Roman Empire* (2 vols., 1926), and *Social and Economic History of the Hellenistic World* (3 vols., 1941). The emphasis on social and economic history, the skillful dovetailing of archaeological and literary evidence, the vivid descriptions of town and country in the Roman Empire, and the startling comparison of Thrace with southern Russia were outstanding features of his work. However, his volumes were vigorously criticized for anachronistic application of modern concepts—"capitalism," "socialism," "bourgeoisie," and "proletariat"—to classical society. Apparently affected by his traumatic experiences during the Bolshevik Revolution, Rostovtzeff attributed the decline and fall of Rome to the triumphal alliance of the military and the rural proletariat against the directing bourgeoisie.

Bibliography: G. W. Bowersock, "*The Social and Economic History of the Roman Empire* by Michael Ivanovich Rostovtzeff," *Daedalus* (Winter 1974): 15–23; J. F. Gilliam, "Michael Ivanovich Rostovtzeff," *Dictionary of American Biography*, Supplement 5, 1951–1955, pp. 594–596; A. H. M. Jones, "Michael Ivanovich Rostovtzeff, 1870–1952," pp. 347–361; Arnaldo Momigliano, *Studies in Historiography* (London, 1966), pp. 91–104; C. Bradford Welles, "Michael Rostovtzeff," *Architects and Craftsmen in History: Festschrift für Abbot Paysan Usher* (Tübingen, 1956), pp. 55–73.

Louise Salley Parker

SALOMONE, A. William (Guardiagrele, Italy, 1915–Philadelphia, 1989), Italian and modern European cultural historian. Salomone pioneered the study of Italian history in the United States in the postwar period and founded the Society for Italian Historical Studies. His bicultural education began at a classical Italian preparatory school and was followed by higher education in the United States. His 1943 doctoral dissertation, published in 1945, *Italian Democracy in the Making*, was a passionate and acute historical investigation of the ministry of Giovanni Giolitti (1904–1914). Salomone defined and named this period "the Giolittian era." As such, he characterized it as a time when the liberal ideals of the Risorgimento struggled to take shape against the complex social, cultural, and economic forces of early twentieth-century Europe. For Salomone, Giolitti's ministry planted the "seedlings" of democracy. Salomone's convincing and well-documented analysis enticed Gaetano Salvemini (q.v.), the outspoken antifascist in exile at Harvard, to reevaluate his negative anti-Giolittian position, which he did publicly in the Introduction to Salomone's work. The controversy sparked impassioned discussion on both sides of the Atlantic and culminated in parliamentary debate. Salomone's revision of the earlier work, *Italy in the Giolittian Era (1960; L'eta giolittiana)*, documents the famous debate between Salvemini and Palmiro Togliatti.

Salomone's craft as historian, with its subtle blend of skillful investigation and penetrating analysis of cultural currents, politics, and social changes has a compelling appeal to both the serious scholar and layperson; it is a complex tapestry that entices and involves but never preaches. Nowhere is this style more effective than in his 1971 study, *Italy from the Risorgimento to Fascism: An Inquiry into the Origins of the Totalitarian State*, which includes essays by foremost historians (Federico Chabod [q.v.], Benedetto Croce [q.v.], Salvemini) and the author's own analysis. Salomone also selected, translated, and introduced the writings of "young Italians who fought and died in the struggle against Fascism to reopen all the possibilities of the Risorgimento:" Pietro Gobetti, Nello Rosselli (q.v.), Antonio Gramsci (q.v.), Lauro De Bosis, and Giovanni Pintor. The study concludes with an "analytical chronological summary" of Italian history and historiography from 1814 to 1922, which provides an invaluable tool for future study of this period of "Italy's collective crisis of conscience and morality." In Salomone's 1979 article, "From the Crisis of the Renaissance to the Cultural Revolution of the Risorgimento," the author concisely details Italy's cultural development from 1494 to 1860. Machiavelli, Vico, Mazzini, and Carlo Cattaneo (q.v.) are discussed in this progression which allows the reader to see the maturation of the "idea" of the Risorgimento, "long before it became a national-political experiment at the creation of a unitary state." Salomone's writing of history ultimately draws from his careful investigation of sources, his attention to political and social change, and his intuitive sensitivity to the triumphs and tragedies of the human condition.

Bibliography: Frank J. Coppa, ed., *Studies in Modern Italian History* (in honor of A. W. Salomone) (New York, 1986); A. William Salomone, "Actualism," "Futurism," "Modernism," "Problemism," and "Vichianism," in *Handbook of World History* (New York, 1967); in Georg Iggers and Harold Parker, eds., A. William Salomone, "Contemporary Italian Historiography," *International Handbook of Historical Studies* (Westport, Conn., 1979), pp. 233–251; A. William Salomone, "From the Crisis of the Renaissance to the Cultural Revolution of the Risorgimento," *The Culture of Italy: Medieval to Modern* (Toronto, 1979), ed. Chandler, pp. 95–117; A. William Salomone, "Garibaldi and the Risorgimento," *Autobiography of Garibaldi* (New York, 1971), 3 vols., 1, 15–70; A. William Salomone, "Momenti di storia, frammenti di ricordi, con Salvemini tra Stati Uniti e Italia," *Archivio Trimestrale*, lug.-dic (1982): 795–821; A. William Salomone, "The Nineteenth-Century Discovery of Italy: An Essay in American

Cultural History,'' *American Historical Review* 73 (June 1968): 1389–1391; A. William Salomone, ''Nineteenth-Century Thought and Culture,'' *Perspectives on the European Past: Conversations with Historians*, ed. Norman F. Cantor (New York, 1971), II, 113–142.

Ilia Salomone-Smith

SARTON, George (Ghent, Belgium, 1884–Cambridge, Mass., 1956), historian of science. Sarton's father, who was a Mason, prized freedom, tolerance, and intellectual honesty above all things and these had a deep influence on him. Sarton showed early self-reliance and a precocious, vivid intellectual curiosity. He studied philosophy at the University of Ghent (1902) but soon abandoned it temporarily for sciences and graduated D.Sc. (Phys., Math.) in 1911 with a dissertation entitled ''Les principes de la mécanique de Newton.'' An active member of the Association of the Socialist Students of the University, he wrote many articles as well as two social and romantic novels: *Une vie de poète* (1905) and *La Chaîne d'or* (1909), under the pseudonym of Dominique de Bray. He founded the journal *Isis* in 1913, and it proved to be one of the first institutional tools he needed: He had decided to devote his life to the history of science. This feeling of a mission to perform probably explains his decision to emigrate after the German Army invaded Belgium. In April 1915 he fled from England to the United States, with books, a few dollars, a little English, and the steady decision to teach only the history of science. After temporary appointments and guest lectures at some American universities, he became a research associate at the Carnegie Institution (1918–1949). He also lectured at Harvard (1916–1951), at first without an appointment but with a room in the Widener Library, which was soon the well-known headquarters of the history of science. This situation continued throughout his professional life. Until 1951 he edited and directed *Isis*, the official record of the History of Science Society, founded in 1924. An occasional fellow-journal, *Osiris*, was created in 1936. Both, but particularly *Isis*'s Critical Bibliographies as *status quaestionis*, are inseparable from his masterpiece, *Introduction to the History of Science* (5 vols., 1927–1948), first conceived as a systematic survey of the history of science from Homer to the nineteenth-century—but in fact going only to the fourteenth century. It is the first complete account of medieval science, that is ''systematized positive knowledge, . . . the only human activity . . . truly cumulative and progressive.'' It is also the first to integrate Western and Eastern science into a single synthesis where he condemns neglect of Eastern civilizations as ''provincialism.'' Sarton did not recognize himself as a medievalist; he preferred the eighteenth and nineteenth centuries. However, he considered medieval science indispensable to an understanding of the continuity of human progress. The Middle Ages were falsely considered to be the ''Dark Ages,'' he said, because of the historians who, devoted exclusively to Western thought, showed only their darkest side.

For Sarton, the history of science was an encyclopedic discipline: He had contacts with Henri Berr (q.v.). In his work one finds very few references to political or economic history, or to the history of art, because "they throw light from the outside." The history of religion he considered quite different: Science and religion were inseparable and not understandable one without the other, and the history of medieval thought was dominated "by a continual and desperate endeavor to reconcile the facts of rational experience with some system of knowledge considered a priori as perfect and unimpeachable." Magic was essentially unprogressive and conservative. But alchemy and astrology had to be considered differently: They always tried to integrate new experimental facts, which were valuable in spite of wrong interpretation. The theory of music, as a part of mathematics, was considerable but not as much as philology, "the systematic organization of the language being one of the most important preliminary tasks required for the development and transmission of knowledge." As for historiography, historical research was for Sarton a scientific undertaking, historical writings being "products and symbols of their age, whatever their lack of objectivity." But "the historian can analyze to some extent the actions of people; he can not explain them." As regards the history of science, it enlightens not only the progress of each scientific discipline, but its relations to all the others, and becomes useful because of the tendency of scientific specialization. "Science is not a being but a becoming, . . . and love of science, simply the love of truth." He recognized himself as a positivist but "with a strain of mysticism," and he wanted to emerge into a new humanism, "a reconciliation of science and art, truth and beauty." His language is that of a visionary, trying to convince. He wanted to illustrate his main postulates—nature is one, science is one, humankind is one—in the whole of his work to help us to understand the real significance of human progress. Sarton wrote fifteen books and about three hundred articles and notes, besides editing *Isis* with its seventy-nine critical bibliographies. A complete list is to be found in the memorial issue published in *Isis* (1957). Among them are *Introduction to the History of Science* (3 vols. in five parts, 1927–1948); *The History of Science and the New Humanism* (1931); *The Study of the History of Science* (1936; 2d ed., 1956), with *The Study of the History of Mathematics; A History of Science* I. *Ancient Science through the Golden Age of Greece* (1952); II. *Hellenistic Science and Culture in the Last Three Centuries B.C.* (1959); and *Horus: A Guide to the History of Science*, 1952; *Six Wings: Men of Science in the Renaissance* (1957).

Bibliography: A. André-Félix and H. Elkhadem "George Sarton," *Biographie nationale* [de Belgique], 38 (1974): col. 713–733; H. Elkhadem, "L'historiographie des sciences du moyen âge islamique chez George Sarton," *Technologia* [Brussels], (1984): 73–87; "The George Sarton Memorial Issue," *Isis* (1957): 281–350; May Sarton, *I Knew a Phoenix* (1959); A. Thackray and R. K. Merton, "George Sarton," *Dictionary of Scientific Biography*, 12, (1975): 107–114; A. Thackray and R. K. Merton, "On Discipline Building: The Paradoxes of George Sarton," *Isis* (1972): 473–495.

SMITH, Preserved (Cincinnati, Ohio, 1880–Louisville, Ky., 1941), American historian. Smith received his B.A. from Amherst College (1901) and his M.A.

(1902) and his Ph.D. (1907) from Columbia University. After successive appointments at Williams College, Amherst, Harvard, and Wellesley, he joined the faculty of Cornell University in 1922. There he remained until his death. At Columbia he had studied under James Harvey Robinson (q.v.) while Robinson was still interested in the intense, critical scrutiny of primary evidence. Smith's dissertation, published in 1907, was thus a critical appraisal of Luther's *Table Talk* as it had been recorded by his students. He cautioned his readers to examine the students' notes "with discrimination" for "they show all degrees of accuracy." His next publication, *The Life and Letters of Martin Luther* (1911), was a surprising choice. Thomas Carlyle's (q.v.) "great man" theory was then considered passé in learned circles. Moreover, for Smith, traditional religion, morality, and politics were hindrances to progress. Why then did he write a biography of Luther when Smith himself recognized that "the deepest part of Luther's life was his religion"? Smith's answer was his admiration for a courageous man who successfully defied the authority of what Smith regarded as a monolithic, tyrannical, universal Church. In this view Luther was a hero of progress, and the Reformation was the greatest event of modern history. At that time Smith's biography was considered the best in English.

The biography of Luther was matched by Smith's solid, scholarly *Erasmus: A Study of His Life, Ideals and Place in History* (1923). New primary sources, especially Percy S. Allen's "masterly edition" of Erasmus' epistles, gave Smith the opportunity to offer a fresh treatment containing new factual data. The book is enjoyable perhaps because Smith found the subject congenial. To him Erasmus's "undogmatic Christianity" and his emphasis on "the ethical and the reasonable" appealed. From biography Smith moved into general synthesis. Published in 1920, his *Age of the Reformation* was a thorough summary of European and American research as it presented the sweep of Reformation history in its social, economic, intellectual, and political context. This book has been rated by some as his best work. In the closing decades of his life, he devoted his energies to what he hoped would be his magnum opus, a four-volume comprehensive *History of Modern Culture*. He lived long enough only to publish the first two volumes: *The Great Renewal 1543–1687* (1930) and *The Enlightenment 1687–1776* (1934). Dismissing the accomplishments between the time of the ancient Greeks and Romans and the midsixteenth century as unworthy of attention, he examined the culture of "North Atlantic People" in "modern times." Its dominant features, he thought, were the growth of wealth, democracy, popular education, a secular attitude, and science. Of these, science was the most significant, for the various aspects of modern culture were "to a great extent dependent on its progress." However, the two volumes not only discussed advances in science, but also treated such topics as morals and manners, music and drama, political theory, and art.

Bibliography: Wallace K. Ferguson, "Preserved Smith," *Dictionary of American Biography*, Supplement 3, pp. 725–726; John A. Garraty, "Preserved Smith, Ralph Volney Harlow, and Psychology," *Journal of the History of Ideas* 15 (1954): 456–465; William

Gilbert, "The Work of Preserved Smith (1880–1941)," *Journal of Modern History*, 23 (1951): 354–365.

Louise Salley Parker

STEPHENSON, Carl (Fayette, Ind., 1886–Ithaca, N.Y., 1954), American historian. Stephenson received his B.A. (1907) and M.A. (1908) from De Pauw University and his Ph.D. from Harvard (1914). After teaching medieval history at several universities, he became a full professor at the University of Wisconsin, where he remained for ten years (1920–1930) before moving to Cornell University, where he taught until his death. Among those whose advice and example had a profound effect on his research career were Charles Gross of Harvard, Gross' successor Charles Homer Haskins (q.v.), and Henri Pirenne (q.v.), under whom Stephenson studied for a year at the University of Ghent. Gross recommended a study of English medieval towns; Haskins advised a preparatory study of Continental municipal history, as English institutions could not have existed in a vacuum; and Pirenne's theory of the origins of Continental towns awakened Stephenson's resolve to apply that thesis to his study of English boroughs. The fruits of this research were published in his *Borough and Town* (1933), covering the period extending roughly from the Germanic invasions to 1200, in which he argued that it was not until the coming of the Normans that English boroughs developed into commercial centers or towns. This thesis was in conflict with that held by some British historians, especially James Tait, who insisted that Anglo-Saxon boroughs had become trading communities before 1066. Even so, Stephenson's emphasis on Continental-English connections and the importance of topographical study won adherents to his case. His *Mediaeval Institutions: Selective Essays*, published in 1954 but containing articles that had appeared as early as 1922, revealed again his awareness of the entire Western European institutional context, while focusing on one particular, local system. For example, in his essays on taxation he demonstrated that the French *taille* was similar to the German *bede*, which he saw developing during the post-Carolingian era, when "every lord took what he could from his dependents." What happened in German- and French-speaking lands occurred in England, where the *taille* (tallage) was introduced by the Normans. His chapters on feudalism and, to some degree, his brief study *Mediaeval Feudalism* (1942) likewise presented several novel interpretations. To be sure, on the origin of feudalism he agreed with Heinrich Brunner and Ferdinand Lot that the eighth-century union of vassalage and fief-holding spelled feudalism, and he concurred with George Burton Adams' belief that feudalism was nonexistent in pre-Norman England. But he could not accept Adams' reason for arriving at that conclusion: namely, because no instance of *patrocinium* could be located, feudalism must not have existed. The deciding factor, Stephenson countered, was not the absence of *patrocinium*, but the lack in Anglo-Saxon England of the *destrier*, the large war-horse capable of bearing warriors in coats of mail. These chargers were brought over from France by the Normans. He also argued against the prevailing view that feudalism was a disruptive, chaotic, and particularistic system that was responsible for the dissolution of the Carolingian Empire. That empire fell, he said, because its unwieldy size was ill-adapted to an agrarian economy. In states that were not too large, feudalism proved a constructive force enabling rulers in Flanders, Normandy, Anjou, the Ile-de-France, and England to create centralized states.

Bibliography: Malcolm Bean, "Carl Stephenson," *Dictionary of American Biography*, Supplement 5, pp. 655–656; Bryce D. Lyon, "Introduction," pp. vii–xii in Carl Stephenson, *Medieval Institutions: Selected Essays* (Ithaca, N.Y., 1954).

Louise Salley Parker

SUSMAN, Warren I. (1927–Minneapolis, 1985), historian of American culture. Professor of history at Reed College and at Rutgers University (1960–1985). Susman did not write monographs, and he did not devote his work as an historian to a single theme. His form was the essay, supplemented by the personal encounter. Many of his most significant writings are collected in *Culture As History: The Transformation of American Society in the Twentieth Century* (1984). Taking a bold approach, he sought always to provoke his audience, and he succeeded, as one cannot read a single paragraph of any essay he wrote, whether it be "The Nature of American Conservativism," a long rambling discussion illustrating the difficulties of finding *a* conservativism in America in the 1960s, or "Culture and Communications," a meditation on the relationship between "popular" culture and "high" culture, without asking a question, disagreeing, or thinking of another example, perhaps a counter-example. "There must be some relationship [between popular culture and high culture], if not in form, in content (issues, problems, themes), or if not in content perhaps in form ("advanced" literature's fascination for the "forms" of modern art, the film, etc., as literary devices)." In Susman's view, the cultural historian's task was "to discover the *forms* in which people have experienced the world—the patterns of life, the symbols by which they cope with the world." Looking at the 1930s, which is often characterized by other historians as a decade when many Americans looked to the left, Susman noted in his introduction to *Culture and Commitment, 1929–1945* (1973), a book of photographs and written documents from elite as well as popular sources, "that the period, while acknowledging in ways more significantly than ever before the existence of groups outside the dominant ones and even recognizing the radical response as important, is one in which American culture continues to be largely middle-class culture." The middle class responded to the depression, not with heroic leftist resistance and radicalism, but rather with "fear and shame," which, in turn, shaped the forms of popular culture that proved so attractive—radio comedies that depended on "a kind of ritual humiliation of the hero," Walt Disney's transformations of "our most grotesque nightmares into fairy tales and pleasant dreams," games such as Contract Bridge, Monopoly, and the "pinball machine," which combined "mere luck and chance" with "stern rules." Susman suggested that the oppressively nationalistic and in many ways conformist tendencies of the period after World War II had their roots in middle-class fear and shame of the 1930s, as the "age of culture and commitment" gave way to the longing for order and participation in power symbolized by the Pentagon, completed in 1945. In a profession filled with specialists, Susman was a grand and daring synthesizer. His essays are a marvelous and subtle introduction to patterns of meaning in the forms of American culture.

Bibliography: T. Jackson Lears, "In the American Grain," *The Nation* 240 (1985): 532–535.

Ellen Nore

THORNDIKE, Lynn (Lynn, Mass., 1882–New York City, 1965), American historian. Thorndike earned his B.A. from Wesleyan University (1902) and his M.A. (1903) and Ph.D. (1905) from Columbia University. His dissertation, "The Place of Magic in the Intellectual History of Europe," was directed by James Harvey Robinson (q.v.). From instructor of history at Northwestern University (1907–9) Thorndike moved to Western Reserve University (1909–24), where he attained a full professorship, and finally to Columbia University, where he remained until retirement in 1950. His first publication, *History of Medieval Europe* (1917), became a popular text in higher educational institutions. His *Short History of Civilization* (1926) was a seminal production, not only because it was a world history, but also because it covered far more than political history in chapters such as "Persian and Arabic Culture" and "Scientific Progress in Early Modern Europe." His magnum opus was his eight-volume *History of Magic and Experimental Science* (1923–1958), which grew out of his dissertation and covered the period extending from the Roman Empire to the close of the seventeenth century. Realizing that the title was ambiguous, he explained that a more accurate title would have read: "a history of the relations between magic and experimental science." As for "magic," he defined it as "the occult arts and sciences, superstitions, and folk lore." "Magicians," he added, "were perhaps the first to experiment." He wished "to make clearer . . . the Latin learning of the medieval period, whose leading personalities . . . are inaccurately known." His findings convinced him that the medieval centuries had been unjustly perceived by the modernist as "retrogressive" or "stagnant," for not only were ancient Greek and Arabic scientific texts preserved and studied, but medieval men "added questions . . . and . . . discoveries of their own." The spirit of curiosity abounded, and men were not averse to questioning ancient authorities. If superstitions existed, they also prevailed among the ancient Greeks and Romans; however, the Middle Ages was making progress in ridding itself of these and in taking strides forward in science, as in the "conception of gas . . . among . . . alchemists" and in "theories to explain the influence of the moon on tides or the suspension of our globe in mid-space." But during the period that he liked to term the "so-called Renaissance," Thorndike found "emphasis on style rather than science, and show rather than substance." Even Leonardo da

Vinci, Copernicus, and Vesalius lost some of their luster as Thorndike maintained that "the germs of [their] scientific discoveries" had appeared earlier.

Though Thorndike's impressive and ground-breaking production won international recognition and became a classic in its field, it was not immune from criticism. Especially censorious was George Sarton (q.v.), who carped about the misleading title and averred that Thorndike had not recorded a "cumulative" and "progressive activity," as a history of science should do. Furthermore, Sarton claimed, Thorndike did not understand true science. If he had, he would know that magic only leads to "anti-science." Thorndike responded to Sarton in his article "The True Place of Astrology in the History of Science" by quoting a passage from Sarton which recognized that Roger Bacon, "when pondering on the nature of force," had "thoughts [which] were partly astrological." In his brilliant and witty presidential address, "Whatever Was, *Was* Right," before the American Historical Association (1955), Thorndike denied that the past should be viewed with any standard of modern knowledge in mind or any sense of progression toward that standard. Like his predecessor as president, Charles Howard McIlwain (q.v.), he asserted that past events should be studied for themselves and in relation to other events of their time. In his textbooks and his pioneer works on the history of science, he had corrected many errors of fact and interpretation and had followed his mentor Robinson in greatly expanding the scope of the historian's attention, but he refused to follow Robinson and other "New Historians" when they urged that historical events be selected to meet a present standard or need.

Bibliography: Marshall Claggett, "Lynn Thorndike," *Isis* 57 (1966): 85–89; Dana B. Durand, "Magic and Experimental Science: The Achievement of Lynn Thorndike," *Isis* 33 (1942): 691–712.

Louise Salley Parker

TURNER, Frederick Jackson (Portage, Wis., 1861–Pasadena, Calif., 1931), historian of the United States. After receiving a bachelor of arts and a master's degree from the University of Wisconsin, Turner studied for his doctorate at the German-inspired graduate center at Johns Hopkins University. He held teaching posts at the University of Wisconsin (1889–1909) and at Harvard University (1910–1924). During his career of forty-five years, Turner published only two books, *Rise of the New West* (1906) and a collection of essays, *The Frontier in American History* (1920). After his death, two more volumes were brought out by students: *The Significance of Sections in American History* (1932) and *The United States, 1830–1850: The Nation and Its Sections.* (1935). What was the relationship in the history of the United States between "frontier," "free land," and "democracy" ? Turner posed the question and delivered his answers mostly in the form of analytical essays. Today, almost none of his specific generalizations is left as part of the story of the westward movement of white peoples on the North American continent, but, because he set the terms of the historical discussion for so many years, he has gained a position among the "great." Turner did not precisely define the term *frontier*. At times, he used geographical language: "the Western wilds from the Alleghenies to the Pacific"; occasionally, he wrote of "frontier" as a state of being, that is, as the presence at the edge of settlement of an area of unoccupied land; the frontier was also a process that conquered the white male settler, making him into a "savage," a stage from which he evolved into more and more "advanced" stages until the frontier moved on, leaving in its wake communities of shrewd, inquisitive, innovative, practical, restless, energetic, optimistic, and egalitarian people. In Turner's thinking, European influences on North American institutions were overshadowed by the local environment; it was this environmental situation, in successive stages, and not New England and the South, not slavery and racial politics, neither great men nor moral issues, that had shaped the past of the United States.

Students of Turner suggest that the ideas of the Italian economist, Achille Loria, who theorized that there was a significant relationship between political freedom in a nation and the availability of free land, had a decisive influence on Turner. Free land had been, Turner argued, the foundation of North American democracy. Free land had acted in history as a "safety valve" by drawing out of the settled areas those people who might have been discontented enough to promote revolution. These ideas emerged in the social context of the 1890s, when the United States was gripped by a strong economic depression, when the wage cuts instituted by employers to save profits caused many bitter strikes, and when the large corporation was emerging as a feature of life in the United States. The Census Bureau had announced the effective end of the geographical frontier, and Turner's agrarianism found an echo in numbers of educated white North Americans who longed for a simpler present. Later in his life, Turner added to his repertoire an explanation of conflict in North American history based on the idea of competing sections: north, south, and west. "The significance of the section in American history is that it is the faint image of a European nation and that we need to re-examine our history in the light of this fact. Our politics and our society have been shaped by sectional complexity and interplay not unlike what goes on between European nations." Turner's geographical determinism, his ethnocentrism, and his evolutionary habit of mind make him a classic late-nineteenth-century post-Darwinian intellectual nationalist. History was to be the fountain of national pride. The historian's role was not to criticize. Hence, he had no feeling for what Richard Hofstadter (q.v.) called "the shame" of North American history—ruthless speculation in public lands, vigilantism, environmental waste, racism, and genocidal responses to the Native Americans and other nonwhites. The significance of urban history escaped him. In dismantling his legacy, historians have perpetuated Turner's fame.

Bibliography: Ray Allen Billington, *Frederick Jackson Turner: Historian, Scholar, Teacher* (New York, 1973); Richard Hofstadter, *The Progressive Historians: Turner, Beard, Parrington* (New York, 1968); David M. Potter, *People of Plenty* (Chicago,

1954); Jackson C. Putnam, "The Turner Thesis and the Westward Movement: A Reappraisal," *Western Historical Quarterly*, no.4 (1976): 377–404; Michael C. Steiner, "The Significance of Turner's Sectional Thesis," *Western Historical Quarterly*, no.4 (1979): 347–366.

Ellen Nore

WEBB, Walter Prescott (East Texas, 1888–Austin, Tex., 1963), historian of the United States. Instructor and then professor at the University of Texas (1918–1958). Webb wrote large-scale dramatic syntheses at a time when the historical profession in the United States was producing more and more specialized monographs on small subjects. His works which are still remembered and read are *The Great Plains* (1931) and *The Great Frontier* (1952). In The *Great Plains*, he described a vision of "the compelling unity of the American West," a unity, he wrote, "exemplified in the geology, the geography, the climate, vegetation, animal life and Indian life, all background forces operating with telling effect on those people who in the nineteenth century crawled" over wagon trails into the subhumid environment of the Great American Desert beyond the ninety-eighth meridian, an environment not conquered until barbed wire was invented to take the place of wood in fencing, not populated by Easterners until the railroad existed to carry people with speed and comfort, not farmed until the windmill and irrigation arrived to soften dry soil, and not secured from its Native American inhabitants until the revolver reversed the advantage of bow and arrow over single-shot guns. Webb had absorbed the perspective of the Italian economist, sociologist, and philosopher Achille Loria (1857–1943) through reading and studying with the geographer and geographical determinist, Lindley Miller Keasbey. Loria had stressed the impossibility of despotism when the people had access to land, that is, to an independent economic base. Keasbey had emphasized environment as the primary determinant of social institutions. *The Great Frontier* combines these concepts on a world scale to tell of "a boom of gigantic proportions" which began in the Western world after Columbus' voyages and "accelerated until all the new lands had been appropriated. This boom," according to Webb, "accompanied the rise of modern civilization and attended the birth of a set of new institutions and ideas designed to service a booming society, chief among them modern democracy and capitalism and the idea of progress." With the end of the Great Frontier after 1900, "the efficacy of democracy and capitalism were questioned, put in strain." Without abundant land and resources, Webb suggested, the capitalist world made less sense. "These boom-born ideas and institutions have been," he wrote in 1958, "fighting a defensive action." Webb was not sufficiently interested in empirical research to substantiate his themes. He was a poet and storyteller, a painter of striking canvases. As his fellow Texan, J. Frank Dobie, said of him, "Walter Webb never lets facts stand in the way of truth." The greatest historians build grand syntheses and let others tear them down. Webb lived his life and presented his wonderful theories with unforgettable humor, delight, and hope.

Bibliography: Joe B. Frantz, et al., *Essays on Walter Prescott Webb* (Austin, Tex., 1976); Necah Stewart Furman, *Walter Prescott Webb: His Life and Impact* (Albuquerque, N. Mex., 1976); Gregory M. Tobin, *The Making of A History: Walter Prescott Webb and the Great Plains* (Austin, Tex., 1976).

Ellen Nore

WHITE, Andrew Dickson (Homer, N.Y., 1832–Ithaca, N.Y., 1918), American educator, historian, diplomat. White led an active and useful life as professor of history at the University of Michigan (1857–1864) and at Cornell University (1865–1885), where he served as its innovative and progressive co-founder, with Ezra Cornell, and its first president until 1885; as co-organizer of the American Historical Association and its first president (1884); as minister plenipotentiary and then ambassador to Germany (1879–1881, 1897–1903), as minister plenipotentiary to Russia (1892–1894), and as president of the American delegation to the Peace Conference of The Hague (1899). Throughout his career as teacher and author, he interrelated his interest in history with his interest in public questions. Introduced to history at Yale University (B.A., 1853; M.A., 1857) and by the finest lecturers at the Sorbonne, the Collège de France, and the University of Berlin, he came to his courses in medieval and modern European history at the University of Michigan resolved to contribute to the solution of contemporary questions by "raising up a new race of young men who should understand our own time and its problems in the light of history." He continued along that line as his audience enlarged to embrace the educated reading public of the United States and eventually of Europe. At first he proceeded at the level of immediate analogy and practical application. Rejected for service in the Union Army because of his frail constitution, he advised his students who were going off to fight in the Civil War to read *The Rise of the Dutch Republic* by John Lothrop Motley (q.v.) to learn "how free peoples have conducted long and desperate wars for the maintenance of their national existence and of liberty." Later, when "greenback" (paper money) inflation threatened the United States, he drew on his knowledge of the French Revolution to publish a warning essay, *Fiat Money Inflation in France* (1876), about the catastrophic effects such a policy had wrought.

While he was still at Michigan, White's reading of Henry Thomas Buckle (q.v.), Charles Darwin, Herbert Spencer, John William Draper (q.v.), and William E. Lecky (q.v.) enlarged his vision. History became for him "less and less a matter of annals [of events], and more and more a record of the unfolding of humanity." He retained his faith in a higher power that worked toward good, and he added a faith in the evolution of humanity to ever higher levels. In his presidential message to the American Historical Association he challenged his fellow historians to seek the general laws of that beneficent development. So, when he personally experienced illiberal persecution—his free, nonsectarian Cornell University, which placed the sciences on an equality with the humanities, was unfairly attacked by fundamentalist preachers for being a hotbed of "atheism," "infidelity," and "indifferentism"—he replied by placing the incident in the perspective of the evolution of humanity. In a speech that grew into his two-volume magnum opus, *A History of the Warfare of Science and Theology* (1896), he insisted that the quarrel had always been not between science and religion, but between science and the dogmatic theology that had linked religion to erroneous views of the universe. The great religions, he generalized, had emerged from myth and legend, and science was freeing them from the mistakes of ignorance and superstition. In the same spirit of studying the individuals and events that had contributed most to human progress, he wrote his second major work, *Seven European Statesmen* (1910). He presented Sarpi, Grotius, Thomasius, Turgot, Stein, Cavour, and Bismarck as statesmen who had served "the great interests of modern states and, indeed, of universal humanity."

Bibliography: Glenn C. Altschuler, *Andrew D. White: Educator, Historian, Diplomat* (Ithaca, N.Y., 1979); George Lincoln Burr, "Andrew Dickson White," *Dictionary of American Biography*, vol. 20, pp. 88–93; Andrew Dickson White, *Autobiography*, 2 vols. (New York, 1905).

Harold T. Parker

WOODSON, Carter G. (New Canton, Va., 1875–Washington, D.C., 1954), historian of the Negro people in the United States. While working on a doctorate in history at Harvard, Woodson was told by a well-known professor that blacks had no history. Woodson devoted a lifetime to disproving that notion. Although he did not hold a regular position with any American university, he founded many institutions vital to the study of Black American history: the Association for the Study of Negro Life and History (1915), the *Journal of Negro History* (1916), and the *Negro History Bulletin* (1937). He published more than twenty scholarly monographs and volumes of documents, many of them on his own press at a time when it was difficult for black intellectuals to get their work accepted for publication. Many of his works, such as *The Education of the Negro Prior to 1861* (1915) and *The Mis-Education of the Negro* (1933), contained his thesis that better educational opportunities for blacks would improve race relations in the United States. He was a pioneer in using data from the United States census in such books as *Free Negro Owners of Slaves in the United States in 1830* (1924), *Free Negro Heads of Families in the United States in 1830* (1925), and *The Rural Negro* (1930). He was a tireless collector of documents important to black history, documents that might have been lost but for his efforts in a society dominated by white supremacists. Many of his books are, in fact, little more than extracts from the documents he so assiduously collected, for example, *The Mind of the Negro as Reflected in Letters Written During The Crisis, 1800–1860* (1926). Yet, his work remains a starting point for many later writers using more sophisticated methodologies. Woodson wanted black Americans to know their own history as a way of promoting "individualism and self-respect" among them. Whereas modern historians have emphasized the problems of being a black individual in a society of racists, Woodson thought improvement would come through better educational opportunities for blacks, opportunities granting them their history.

Bibliography: John Hope Franklin, ''The New Negro History,'' *Journal of Negro History* 42 (1957): 89–97; Frank J. Klingberg, ''Carter G. Woodson, Historian, and His Contribution to American Historiography,'' *Journal of Negro History* 41 (1956): 66–68; Earl E. Thorpe, *Black Historians: A Critique* (New York, 1971).

Ellen Nore

Great Historians:
Yugoslavian

GAVRILOVIĆ, Mihailo (Aleksinac, 1868–London, 1924), Serbian historian and diplomat. After graduating in history at the *Velika Škola* (Great School) in Belgrade, Gavrilović obtained a government fellowship for the study of history in the École des hautes études in Paris. His dissertation *Étude sur le traité de Paris de 1259 entre Louis IX, roi de France et Henri III, roi d'Angleterre* (Paris, 1899), resulted from research made in French and British archives. Returning to Serbia, Gavrilović was appointed director of the newly established state archive in Belgrade in 1900. The archive was chaotic, with documents stored in cellars and inaccessible to researchers. Familiar with the organization of European archives, Gavrilović put the archival funds in order, acquired new ones, and during a decade (1900–1910) laid the groundwork for the development of modern Serbian archives. The dynamic epoch preceding the war required able diplomats. In 1911, on the eve of the Balkan wars, Gavrilović was appointed Serbian minister in Cetigne, the capital of Montenegro. From there he was asked to represent his country in the Vatican in 1914. In 1917, Gavrilović was not able to accept his newly assigned post in Petrograd because of the revolution in Russia. Instead, in 1918, he became deputy minister of foreign affairs and, the next year, ambassador of the newly formed Kingdom of Serbs, Croats, and Slovenes in London. His diplomatic career prevented Gavrilović from pursuing scholarly activity, although he collected a huge amount of documents in the Vatican archives during his stay in Rome.

During studies in Paris Gavrilović collected a large number of French documents concerning the 1804–1813 Serbian uprising. The collection was published in Beograd in 1904 on the occasion of the centenary of the uprising: *Ispisi iz pariskih arhiva-Gradja za istoriju Prvog srpskog ustanka* (Transcripts from Parisian Archives—Sources for the History of the First Serbian Uprising). Besides

Serbia, the collection included sources relative to the European parts of the Ottoman Empire, especially Bosnia. In touch with Serbian archives, from 1903 until 1911 Gavrilović published several studies dealing with the history of the first four decades of the nineteenth century. Among them were studies of the Serbo-Ottoman peace attempts in 1806–1807, Franco-Serbian (1804–1807) and Anglo-Serbian relations (in the 1830s), and the activity of the Serbian emigration at the Congress of Vienna (1814–1815) and of the Serbian delegation to Constantinople (1830). Most of these studies, first published in the *Srpski Književni Glasnik* (Serbian Literary Herald), were reprinted later in the book *Iz novije srpske istorije* (1926; The More Recent Serbian History). However, these studies were only offsets of his major magnum opus, the history of the reign of Prince Miloš Obrenović, published from 1908 until 1912 in three volumes: *Miloš Obrenovic*, I (1813–1820); II (1821–1826); and III (1827–1835). The manuscript of the fourth volume, covering the last period of Miloš' rule from 1835 to 1839, was lost forever during the retreat of the Serbian government from the country in 1915. The history of Miloš is a monumental work based on primary sources taken from domestic Serbian, French, Austrian, and Russian archives. It is an objective and impartial description of the personality, politics, and diplomacy of the founder of the modern Serbian state, which included the general political, economic, and social development of the country during his times. Serbian historians before Gavrilović dealt mainly with the Middle Ages and based their research on reappraising previous writings instead of plunging into archives. The role Gavrilović played in Serbian historiography is often compared with that of Leopold von Ranke (q.v.) in German historiography. Gavrilović was able to join together the research of primary sources with their critical evaluation and to connect Serbian development with that of Europe.

Bibliography: Slobodan Jovanović, "Mihailo Gavrilović," *Srpski književni glasnik* 13, no. 9 (Belgrade, 1924): 425–427; Olga Jelisavetov, "Rad Mihaila Gavrilovića u Državnoj arhivi," *Arhivski almanah* 2–3 (1960): 15–21; Slobodan Jovanović, Preface to *Iz novije srpske istorije-Studije Mih. Gavrilovića*, (Belgrade, 1926), pp. iii–xii; Gavrilo Kovijanic, "Skolovanje Mihaila Gavrilovića i osvrt na njegov rad," *Aphivski pregled* 1–2 (1968): 15–33; Radovan Samardžić, "Mihailo Gavrilović," *Pisci srpske istorije* (Belgrade, 1981), pp. 157–191.

Dimitrije Djordjevic

JOVANOVIĆ, Slobodan (Novi Sad, 1869–London, 1958), Serbian and Yugoslav historian, lawyer, and political scientist. Born into a family of intellectuals and the son of a prominent politician (Vladimir, 1833–1922), Jovanović studied law in Geneva. After a short career in the Ministry of Foreign Affairs, he taught constitutional law and political theory at the University of Belgrade (1897–1941). He was one of the founders of the *Srpski Književni Glasnik* (Serbian Literary Herald) and its director (1920–1922), as well as chancellor of Belgrade University, member and president of the Royal Serbian Academy of Sciences (1928–1931), member of the Polish Academy, and many other international scholarly societies, among them the Institut de France. As an expert in constitutional law, he was often consulted by various governments in Serbia and Yugoslavia. Jovanović participated in discussions concerning the 1917 Corfu Declaration, and was a member of the Yugoslav delegation at the 1919 Paris Peace Conference and of the committee to draft the 1921 Yugoslav Constitution. In 1937 he founded and became president of the Serbian Cultural Club in Belgrade, initiated by intellectuals and professionals to foster Serbian interests in the Yugoslav state. Involved somewhat involuntarily in politics, Jovanović became vice-president in the government following the anti-Nazi putsch in Belgrade on March 27, 1941, and was forced to leave the country after the German invasion of Yugoslavia. From January 1942 to June 1943 he was premier and vice-premier of royal Yugoslav governments in exile in London, which supported General D. Mihailovich in Yugoslavia. For this activity in 1946 a revolutionary Yugoslav court sentenced Jovanović in absentia to twenty years of prison. He spent the rest of his life in London where he presided over the emigré Yugoslav committee, published the journal *Poruka* (Message), and continued writing historical essays.

Jovanović's scholarship was interdisciplinary. He was a happy combination of jurist and historian. The bibliography of his works published prior to World War II includes twenty-two books (some in several volumes) and numerous articles dealing with constitutional law, political theory, history, and literature. Jovanović started as a literary critic but soon moved to legal and historical studies. In the field of constitutional law and political theory he studied parliamentarianism, bicameralism, sovereignty, and ministerial responsibility. His book *Ustavno pravo Kraljevine Srba, Hrvata i Slovenaca* (Beograd, 1924; The Constitutional Law of the Kingdom of Serbs, Croats, and Slovenes) is a profound analysis of the 1921 Constitution. Jovanović's favorite genres were biographies and literary essays on prominent European and Yugoslav individuals. Among them were studies of Plato, Machiavelli, Burke, Dumouriez, Mirabeau, Danton, Carlyle (q.v.), Gladstone, and Marx (q.v.). He portrayed a plethora of Serbian and Yugoslav personalities, among them the historian Franjo Rački (q.v.), Bishop Juraj Strossmayer, writers and critics. J. Skerlić and Lj. Nedić, and men of politics Sv. Marković, N. Pašić, P. Todorović, D. Dimitrijević-Apis as well as many others. However, Jovanović's main work represents the history of nineteenth-century Serbia. He explored in eight volumes Serbian political, constitutional, diplomatic, social, economic, and cultural developments during the period 1838 to 1903. This monumental series includes the rule of the ''Defenders of the Constitution'' (*Ustavobranitelji*) after the 1839 abdication of Prince Miloš, followed by the reign of Prince Mihailo, Prince (later King) Milan, and his son Aleksandar. The history is based on meticulously studied primary sources and memoirs coupled with personal reminiscences. It deploys the drama of human relations in the context of historical events. Portraits of rulers, politicians, and peasant tribunes, their rational and irrational reactions are colorfully depicted. Jovanović was a superb stylist, and his pages are a literary masterpiece.

Many biographers compare Jovanović with Thomas Babington Macaulay (q.v.) because like Macaulay he based his proof on evidence and suggested rather than drew conclusions. Even his political opponents, while rejecting his methods and approach, did not deny his knowledge and analytical mind. In fact, Jovanović was opposed to philosophical and historical materialism. As a scholar, he was a French-type positivist, a philosophical liberal, and a skeptical pragmatist. In politics he was a monarchist devoted to parliamentarianism and constitutionalism. A Serbian nationalist, he espoused Yugoslavism as an assessment of proper Serbian interests. His political stand was determined by sensibility, family heritage, and history.

Bibliography: Dimitrije Djordjevic, "Slobodan Jovanović," in Walter Laqueur, ed., *Historians in Politics* (London, 1974), pp. 253–272; Michael Boro Petrovich, "Slobodan Jovanović (1869–1958): The Career and Fate of a Serbian Historian," *Serbian Studies* 3, no. 1/2 (1984–1985): 3–25; Ilija Pržić, "Bibliografija radova Slobodana Jovanovica," *Sabrana dela Slobodana Jovanovica* (Belgrade, 1935), vol. 16, pp. 439–463. For the period 1941–1954, see Kosta St. Pavlović, *Poruka*, no. 25 (London, 1954): 9–10 and no. 53–54 (1959): 44–45, 52; Radovan Samardžić, "Slobodan Jovanović," *Pisci Srpske istorije* (Belgrade, 1986), vol. 3, pp. 185–200.

Dimitrije Djordjevic

KUKULJEVIĆ, Sakcinski Ivan (Varaždin, 1816–Castle Tuhakovec, Croatia, 1889), Croatian historian, writer, and politician. Descendant of a noble Croatian family related to the Venetian De Sacci family (from which he took his name Sakcinski). In 1833 Kukuljević joined the cadet school in Krems (Austria). After a brief military service in Milan, Italy he resigned (1842) and entered politics. Kukuljević ardently espoused the ideas of the Illyrian movement in Croatia which fostered the national renaissance and cultural unity of the Yugoslavs. He was the first to use the Croatian vernacular in the Diet in Zagreb in 1843 and was responsible for the Diet's decision, made in 1847, to replace Latin with the Croatian language in public affairs of Croatia. During the revolutionary days of 1848, Kukuljević was the leader of the popular movement in Croatia, to which he formulated the political program and became a member and president of the country's government (1848–1850). He supported ban (provincial chief) Josip Jelačić, opposed Hungary, and fought for the unification of Croatia, Slavonia, and Dalmatia into a Triune Kingdom. Kukuljević was the initiator of the idea to summon an all-Slavic congress and preached the federalization of the Habsburg monarchy into a free union of autonomous peoples. During the reaction following the collapse of the 1848 movement, Kukuljević withdrew temporarily from politics and turned toward scholarship. After the October Diploma (1860), he organized the Independent Popular party and published its journal *Domobran* (Country's Defender, 1864). After the 1867 dualistic reorganization of the Habsburg monarchy, having been removed from the high offices he held in Croatia, Kukuljević gave up politics and dedicated his activities to scholarship. From 1874 until 1889 he was the president of the *Matica Hrvatska*.

Kukuljević was among the most versatile writers and scholars in nineteenth century Croatia: He was a poet, a novelist, a dramatist, an historian, and an organizer of historical archives. His first poems and historical novels were written in German and translated into Croatian. His literary work, including historical dramas, novels, and poems (among the poems was the patriotic-political poem entitled *Slavjanke* —The Slavians), were published in the four-volume collection *Različita Djela* (1842–1848; Diverse Works). This literature was inspired by historical motives and was supplied with historical comments. Kukuljević extolled the struggle for national freedom and for the unity of the South Slavs, and opposed German and Hungarian pressures. The same motives inspired Kukuljević's research and writing in history to which he finally dedicated all his time and energy. Although not an historian by training, Kukuljević, became one of the founders of modern Croatian historiography. Appointed state archivist (1848–1860), he brought back to Croatia the archival material concerning his country stored in Budapest and organized domestic archives. During his travels to Venice, Dalmatia, Italy, and Bosnia, he was able to further collect relevant historical sources. In 1850 Kukuljević organized Društvo za povjest-nicu jugoslavensku (The Society for Yugoslav History) and started its journal *Arkiv za povjestnicu jugoslavensku* (The Archive for Yugoslav History) of which he became the editor. From 1858 to 1860 he published the first history of Yugoslav art (*Slovnik umjetnika jugoslavenskih*, 4 vols.). He offered support and assistance to Fran Miklosič in collecting sources for medieval Serbian, Bosnian, and Dubrovnik history. In 1859 he edited the *Monumenta Serbica* (VIII–XIV C) and prepared the *Codex diplomaticus regni Croatiae Slavoniae et Dalmatiae a Jaec. IV–XIV*, of which one volume (up to the year 1200) was published in 1874–1875. Further pioneering works included *Iura regni Croatiae Dalmatiae et Slavoniae* (I–III, 1861–1862), *Acta Croatica* (1863)—a unique collection of medieval Glagolitic charters—and the *Bibliografija hrvatska*, I *Tiskane knjige* (1860, 1863; Croatian Bibliography, Printed books). In 1886 Kukuljević published biographies of prominent Croatians in the country's political and cultural life (*Glasoviti Hrvati*). Studies about the Croatians during the War for Succession (1877), Bulgarian, Croatian, and Serbian rulers and their crowns (1881), as well as some others were published in *Rad* of the Yugoslav Academy in Zagreb. As a poet and novelist Kukuljević was a national romanticist, a disciple of the German school, and was influenced by Sir Walter Scott and Lord Byron. As an historian he was a dilettante-genius, with great talent and perseverance. He never published a comprehensive history of Croatia, and he dealt mainly with the political history of Croatia and the South Slavs, from Roman times until the nineteenth century. Besides his published pioneering works he left to later Yugoslav historians unpublished manuscripts, collections of documents, and a rich library that became fundamental for the development of the Academy of Sciences and the University in Zagreb.

Bibliography: A. Barac, *Hrvatska Književnost*, I, *Književnost ilirizma* (Zagreb, 1954), pp. 278–287; B. Kukuljević, *Mladost Ivana Kukuljevića Sakcinskoga* (Zagreb, 1907); V. Novak, "Nastanak i nestanak 'Monumenta Serbica'—Diplomatara I. Kukuljevića-Sakcinskoga," *Glas Srpske Akademije nauka* 234 (Belgrade, 1959): 1–49; T. Smičiklas,

"Život i djela Ivana Kukuljevića Sakcinskog," *Rad Jugoslavenske akademije* (Zagreb, 1892): 110; B. Šulek, "Ivan Kukuljević Sakcinski," (Vienna, 1889), pp. 489–490.

Dimitrije Djordjevic

NOVAKOVIĆ, Stojan (Šabac, Serbia, 1842–Niš, 1915), Serbian historian, politician, and diplomat. Studied law and philosophy in Belgrade. Novaković's activity developed in the field of scholarship, domestic politics, and diplomacy. As a scholar, he became a prestigious historian, a university professor (1875–1880), and a member and president of the Royal Serbian Academy of Sciences (1906–1915). During his services in the state administration he was three times minister of education in various governments (1873, 1875, 1880–1883), once minister of interior (1884), and was a member of the State Council (from 1883). He reorganized and modernized the educational system in Serbia, and the National Library and the Museum in Belgrade. The Law on Primary Education (1882) introduced compulsory education in the country and extended it to six years. Entering politics in 1880, Novaković founded the Progressive party (essentially conservative) and chaired it. Twice he became prime-minister (1895–1896 and 1909). Primarily an Austrophile, during his second Cabinet he switched to Russia. Novaković served for twelve years as representative of his country in Constantinople (1886–1891 and again in 1897–1899), Paris (1900), and St. Petersburg (1900–1905). He presided over the Serbian delegation at the 1912–1913 peace negotiations with the Ottomans.

Novaković dedicated the main part of his energies to scholarship. In 1858 at the age of sixteen, he published his first study. During the next fifty years of intense productivity, Novaković's bibliography totaled four hundred papers and articles, among which were some fifty books. He also left behind virtually thousands of letters and comments, addressed to colleagues and friends, related to scholarly and political issues. Novaković's scholarly activity was versatile. He started with philology and literature. In 1867 he published the first history of Serbian literature as well as grammars of the Serbian language (1869–1874). In 1869 he produced the first Serbian bibliography of works published from 1741 to 1867, and collected and published Serbian popular epic poetry. At the same time Novaković translated works of European historians, among them Leopold von Ranke (q.v.). However, his main achievements belong to historiography and its related disciplines. Novaković directed research and writing toward two epochs: (1) the Serbian people and the state during the Middle Ages and (2) the origins and development of modern statehood in the nineteenth century. He collected and commented on medieval charters, hagiographies, apocrypha, chronicles, travel records, and laws. Novaković's collection of *Monuments of Law in Serbian Medieval States* (1912) and his *Comments on the Emperor Dušan's Codex* are still indispensable for research. Novaković became the founder of the discipline of historical geography in Serbia with studies that described the territory of the state under Stephan Nemanja, the Serbian regions in the tenth and twelfth centuries, the administration during the reign of the Nemanjides, and so on. Novaković was especially attracted to the period of ascendance of the state and the period of its collapse under the Ottoman invasion. The best studies he produced were those related to the medieval village and the peasantry (*Selo*, 1891). The history of the Serbs and the Turks in the fourteenth and fifteenth centuries (1893) was somewhat hastily written, as well as studies of the last Serbian rulers (the Branković family). On the occasion of the 1904 centenary of the Serbian uprising against the Turks Novaković produced five books during four years (1903–1907). In them he discussed the situation created in the Ottoman Empire prior to the uprising, the rebellion against the *Dahies*, the peace negotiations of the insurgents with the Ottomans in 1806–1807, the formation of modern Serbian statehood, and laws and constitutions in Karageorge's Serbia. Several essays concerning a larger Balkan region were published in a separate volume (*Balkanska pitanja*, Balkan problems). As an active participant in the daily politics of his country, Novaković wrote about crises he witnessed. He wrote about the 1885 Serbo-Bulgarian war (1908) and the crisis resulting from the Austro-Hungarian annexation of Bosnia and Hercegovina in 1908. The semi-mcmoirs *Dvadeset godina ustavne politike u Srbiji 1883–1903* (1912; Twenty Years of Constitutional Policy in Serbia, 1883–1903) are an important testimony of Serbian politics at the end of the century. During the last years of his political activity Novaković espoused the ideology of Yugoslav unification and in 1911 published a visionary essay predicting the formation of Yugoslavia. Novaković approached many disciplines and historical epochs; it became an advantage and a disadvantage. He plunged into the virgin land of Serbian history. The wealth of material as well as his prolific production resulted in strip mining instead of deep digging. His style was dry and devoid of imagination. Novaković favored the critical method created by Ilarion Ruvarac (q.v.) but was less radical in its application. Novaković was the product of the nationalistic era of the 1860s and 1870s. Although his work was criticized by the younger generation of Serbian historians for hasty production, insufficient use of primary sources, and lack of synthesis, Novaković remains one of the greatest historians in Serbia because of the breadth of his work and the new fields for research which he opened.

Bibliography: Bibliography of Novaković's works: *Godišnjak Srpske Kraljevske Akademije nauka*, vol. 24 (Belgrade, 1911); Supplemented by R. Dimitrijević, "Prilozi biografiji Stojana Novakovića," *Prilozi za književnost, jezik, istoriju i folklor*, no. 1–2 (Belgrade, 1958): 201–218 and M. Živanovic, "Bibliografija posebnih iz danja radova Stojana Novakovića," in *Bibliotekar*, no. 5–6 (Belgrade, 1965): 283–297; Sima Ćirković, Preface to St. Novaković, *Srbi i Turci u XIV u XV veku* (Belgrade, 1980), pp. 5–13; Sima Ćirković, "Tradicije i istorska tradicija u delu Stojana Novakovića," Preface to Stojan Novaković, *Istorija i tradicija* (Belgrade, 1982), pp. vii–xx; Dimitrije Djordjevic, "Stojan Novaković-Historian, Politician, Diplomat," *Serbian Studies* 3, no. 3–4 (Chicago, 1985–1986): 39–57; P. Popovic, St. Stanojević, Sl. Jovanović, Lj. Protić, and J. Jovanović, *Spomenica Stojana Novakovica* (Belgrade, 1921).

Dimitrije Djordjevic

OSTROGORSKY, Georgije (St. Petersburg, 1902–Belgrade, 1976), Byzantinist and Yugoslav historian. Studied philosophy, sociology, and economics in

Heidelberg (1921–1924), and Byzantine history and art in Paris (under Charles Diehl and Gabriel Millet, 1924–1925). After obtaining a Ph.D. in Heidelberg, Ostrogorsky taught Byzantine history in Wroclav (1928–1933). In 1933 he moved to Belgrade where he stayed for the rest of his life and was appointed professor of Byzantine history at Belgrade University and director of the Institute of Byzantine Studies of the Serbian Academy of Sciences and Arts (an institute he founded in 1948). Elected to the Serbian Academy in 1948, Ostrogorsky became one of its most active members. His research and scholarly achievements brought him international recognition: memberships in the American Academy of Arts and Sciences, academies in Athens, Palermo, and Naples, corresponding memberships in the American Medieval Academy, the Académie des Inscriptions et Belles Lettres in Paris, the British, Belgian, Viennese and Göttingen academies, the Royal Society in London, and so on. Ostrogorsky was awarded a Ph.D. *honoris causa* by Oxford and Strasbourg universities. He started his research in the socioeconomic development of the Byzantine Empire. His dissertation "Die ländische Steuergemeinde des byzantinischen Reiches im X Jahrhundert" (1927) penetrated into the peasant world and proved that the peasant commune existed in Byzantium before the coming of the Slavs. Ostrogorsky continued to study the village and the changes it went through during the shocks that hit the empire from the seventh to the tenth centuries. He also studied the conflict between the central authorities and the aristocratic bureaucracy and its effects on peasantry. In one of his most important works, the *Pronija* (1951), Ostrogorsky analyzed this specific type of military landholding and stressed differences between Byzantine and Western Europe and feudalism. In *Quelques problèmes d'histoire de la paysannerie byzantine* (1956) he analyzed the struggle between the central authorities and feudal lords over the small peasant property. He further directed his research toward the development of the central and provincial administration (the *thema*) and the development of the cities (Byzantine Cities in the Early Middle Ages, 1959).

Ostrogorsky became attracted to cultural history, especially the conflict over iconoclasm and its impact on art, religion, and politics (*Studien zur Geschichte des byzantinischen Bilderstreits*, 1929; *Les débuts de la Querelle des Images*, 1930). He studied the character of the imperial authority, of the co-rulers as well as the ideology of imperial power. Byzantine studies brought Ostrogorsky to the history of the South Slavs which gradually became his favorite subject. The result of his research contributed to the chronology of Serbian rulers in the ninth and tenth centuries and the impact Byzantium had on the establishment and ideology of the medieval Serbian state. His latest research was crowned by a monograph on the Serej region after Dushan's death (*Serska oblast posle Dušanov smrti*, 1965). In general, Ostrogorsky's Byzantine studies had a large South Slav dimension in the background. As a young scholar, Ostrogorsky produced a general history of Byzantium. Entitled *Geschichte des byzantinischen Staates*, it was first published in 1940 in Munich; there were three German editions, three editions in Serbo-Croatian, and one in Slovenian languages, and, it was translated into French, English, Polish, and Italian, totaling sixteen editions. This history is generally considered the best survey of the Byzantine past in existence today. As teacher and organizer of Byzantine studies, Ostrogorsky formed a school of Byzantinists in the institute and at the university in Beograd. At the International Congress of Byzantine Studies in 1976 in Athens, Ostrogorsky's name was ranked among the greatest Byzantinists of our time.

Bibliography: J. Ferluga, "Georg Ostrogorsky (1902–1976)," *Jahruch für Geschichte Osteuropas*, n.s. 25 (1977), pp. 632–636; A. P. Každan, "Koncepcija istorii Vizantijskoj imperii u trudah G. A. Ostrogorskogo," *Vizantiiskii Vremennik* 39 (1978): 76–85; B. Krekić, B. Radojčić, and I. Djurić, "Bibliografija radova akademika Georgija Ostrogorskog," *Zbornik Filozofskog fakulteta*, vol. 12–1 (Spomenica Georgija Ostrogorskog), (Belgrade, 1974), pp. 1–14; *Sabrana dela Georgija Ostrogorskog*, vols. 1–6 (Belgrade, 1969–1970); *Zbornik radova Vizantološkog instituta SANU*, vol. 18 (In recordationem et memoriam Georgii Ostrogorsky), pp. 269–285.

Dimitrije Djordjevic

RAČKI, Franjo (Fužine, 1828–Zagreb, 1894), Croatian historian and politician. Rački started his education in his native country, in Rajeka, Varaždin, and Senj, and studied theology in Vienna. In 1852 he was ordained in Senj but returned to Vienna to obtain a Ph.D. in theology. There he met Bishop J. J. Strossmayer (1815–1905) and established a lifelong friendship and collaboration with the great promoter of the idea of Yugoslav unity. Influenced by the historian Sakcinski Ivan Kukuljević (q.v.), Rački moved to the College of Saint Hieronimi in Rome where he studied history, paleography, diplomatics, sphragistics, epigraphy, and heuristics. During adolescence Rački espoused the idea of South Slav unity, emphasized in the Illyrian movement in the 1830s and applied in the revolutionary days of 1848. Priest and canon, Rački belonged to the reformist movement in the Catholic Church, based on religious tolerance. Actively engaged in politics, he supported the federalization of the Habsburg monarchy in close collaboration with all the Yugoslavs. A member of the Croatian Diet (1861) and a representative of the Popular party, he fought side by side with Strossmayer in favor of Croatian state rights in regard to Hungary. Rački opposed the 1867 dualistic reorganization of the Habsburg Empire and requested the revision of the 1868 Croatian-Hungarian compromise. Disappointed with the issue, he temporarily withdrew from politics. In 1880 he organized the Independent Popular party and started the journal *Obzor* (Horizon), carrying on the idea of Yugoslav unity.

Rački ranks among the most prominent Croatian and Yugoslav historians of the second half of the nineteenth century. In 1859 he published his first book (in two parts) on the life and activity of St. Cyrill and Methodius (*Viek i djelovanje sv. Cyrilla i Methodia, slovjenskih apoštolov*). His further research included studies on the Croatian Dynasty and state rights (*Odlomci iz državnog prava hrvatskoga za narodne dinastije*, 1861) later enlarged in scope to incorporate the history of the Yugoslavs and sources concerning their development in the Middle Ages: *Ocjena starijih izvora za srbsku i hrvatsku provijeat srednjega vijeka, Pokret na slovenskom jugu koncem XIV i početkom XV stoljeća; Borba Južnih Slovena za državnu neodvisnost u XI vijeku* (The Evaluation of Older Sources for the Serbian and Croatian History of the Middle Ages; The Movement on the Slavic South at the End of the Fourteenth and the Beginning of the Fifteenth Centuries; The Struggle of the South Slavs for State Independence in the Eleventh Century). A methodical and critical commentator, Rački pointed to both unifying and disruptive elements that influenced the development of the South Slavs. The same accuracy is present in his studies of the Bogomils, the charters of the Croatian Court Chancellory, and the history of the renaissance in Dubrovnik, Dalmatia, and Croatia. Rački was awarded, for scholarly work, the presidency of the newly formed (1867) Yugoslav Academy of Sciences and Arts in Zagreb, a position he held for the following twenty years. He was remarkably active in the academy: twenty-six volumes of the series *Starine* (Antiquities) were published under his editorship. He published the collection *Documenta historiae croaticae periodum antiquum illustrantia* (1877), besides studies dealing with Latin and Glagolitic paleography and diplomatics. Rački was the founder of the *Journal Književnik* (The Literary Journal) for language and history of Croats and Serbs. Because of Rački's scholarly work and his strong views on the unity of the Yugoslavs in past and future times, V. Novak, one of his many biographers, named him "the greatest Yugoslav of the nineteenth century."

Bibliography: V. Novak, *Franjo Rački* (Belgrade, 1958); V. Novak, *Franjo Rački u govorima i raspravama 1828–1894* (Zagreb, 1925); K. Milutinović, "Franjo Rački i Mihailo Polit-Desančić," *Studije iz srtske i hrvatske istoriografije* (Novi Sad, 1986), pp. 80–123; T. Smičiklas, *Život i djela dr. Franje Račkoga* (Zagreb, 1895); Vladimir Zagorski, *François Rački et la renaissance scientifique et politique de la Croatie, 1828–1854* (Paris, 1909).

Dimitrije Djordjevic

RUVARAC, Ilarion (Gremska Mitrovica, 1832-Monastery Grgeteg, 1905), Serbian historian. Ruvarac received his first education in the high schools in Sremski Karlovci (Vojvodina) and Vienna. He continued the study of law in Vienna from 1852 to 1856. Returning home, Ruvarac graduated from the seminary in Karlovi in 1859. In 1861 he entered the monastic order, changed his lay name Jovan to Ilarion, and became professor and director of the Serbian seminary. In 1874 he was promoted archimandrite (abbot) of the monastery of Grgeteg, in the Fruš-kagora. He finally settled in 1882 in Grgeteg where he spent the rest of his life dedicated to historical research. Because of his scholarship he was elected member of the Royal Serbian Academy of Sciences and corresponding member of the Yugoslav Academy of Sciences and Arts in Zagreb. Ruvarac became attracted to history during his studies in Vienna, where he was able to profit from the city's libraries and become acquainted with the modern and critical approach to history. Under the German influence transmitted through Czech scholars to the South Slavs, humanistic sciences penetrated into the Indo-European community of languages and popular traditions. The Czech linguist P. J. Šafařik (q.v.) and the German historian Leopold von Ranke (q.v.) were among those scholars who influenced the young Ruvarac. The critical evaluation of sources enticed Ruvarac to reappraise the myths embodied in contemporary Serbian historiography. At the age of twenty-four he published the Review of Domestic Sources for the Old Serbian History (*Pregled domaćih izvora stare srpske povjestnice*, 1856) in which he rejected the uncritical acceptance of old chronicles, annals, and biographies (*žitija*) of medieval Serbian rulers, in an attempt to separate truth from legend. In his next study, Contribution to the Examination of Serbian Heroic Popular Poetry (*Prilog k ispitivanju srbskih junačkih pesama*, 1857–1858), Ruvarac opposed the irrational idolatry of the myth used as an historical source. In further studies he continued fighting dilettantism and romanticism in Serbian historiography. Until Ruvarac, historians stated that the Serbs moved to Hungary in 1690 after a previously reached agreement between the Patriarch and the Austrian emperor. Using available sources, Ruvarac found the statement incorrect and concluded that the Serbian migration was intruding into Hungary. He also opposed the story of Count Djordje Branković's descendance from the last *despots* and proved that the count invented his genealogy for political purposes (*Odlomci o grofu Djordju Branković u i Arseniju Čarnojeviću, patrijarhu*, republished by the Serbian Academy in 1896). Dealing with the reign of Prince Lazar (1887), Ruvarac showed that the alleged treason of Vuk Branković at the battle of Kosovo in 1389 was the product of popular poetry, and was not confirmed by historical sources. He denied that Prince Lazar (and not Tsar Lazar) was assassinated by King Vukašin, but that he died from natural causes. He also revealed that a good number of mythical heroes were later created by the people's imagination. In the study *Montenegrina, prilošci istoriji Crne Gore* (1897, 1898: Montenegrina, Contribution to the History of Montenegro) Ruvarac destroyed the belief of a lasting independence of Montenegro and proved that the country was under Ottoman rule throughout the sixteenth and seventeenth centuries. He also analyzed and critically approached sources concerning Serbian rulers and patriarchs during the Middle Ages.

Before Ruvarac Serbian historiography in the nineteenth century moved in a circle, starting from and ending with the history of Jovan Rajić. Ruvarac marked a fresh start by critically evaluating sources and popular traditions. His poignant revision of accepted "facts" and values provoked great indignation among the nationalistic public and traditionalist historians. His opponents Panta Srećković (1834–1903) and Miloš Milojević (1840–1907) called him "the annihilator of national ideals" and "traitor of the Serbian people." Ruvarac retaliated with a bitter polemic in which he ridiculed the ignorance of his adversaries. Ruvarac was not a history writer but a researcher in history. He never produced a comprehensive historical work, but rather collected sources and analyzed fragments necessary for a final review of the historical mosaic. Critical appraisal of sources usually requires more time and energy than history writing. His main ambition was to correct committed errors, and in his war for historical truth he cleared many misconceptions in Serbian history. His composition and style were flawed. For example, the composition of his treaties was interrupted by large excursions that proved his knowledge but diverted him away from the main topic. The style was dry. However, he generated a new Serbian critical historiography that immediately found followers among the new generation of historians. For that reason Ruvarac was named "the father of critical Serbian historiography."

Bibliography: Bibliography of works: B. Marinković, "Ruvarac i njegovo delo," *Istraživanja* (Novi Sad: Institut za izučavanje istorije Vojvodine 1973), II, pp. 453–505. About Ruvarac: Kosta Milutinović, "Ilarion Ruvarac and Jaša Tomić," *Studije iz srpske i hrvatske istoriografije* (Novi Sad, 1986), pp. 25–64; Jovan Radonić "Ilarion Ruvarac," *Slike iz istorije i književonsti* (Belgrade, 1938), pp. 469–499; *Spomenica Ilarionu Ruvarcu* (1832–1932), (Novi Sad, 1932); *Spomenica Ilarionu Ruvarcu* (Novi Sad, 1955).

Dimitrije Djordjevic

ŠIŠIĆ, Ferdo (Vinkovci, 1869–Zagreb, 1940), Croatian and Yugoslav historian. Šišić studied history in Vienna and Zagreb, where he wrote the dissertation "Zadar i Venecija od 1159 do 1247" (1900) in which he explored the Crusaders' capture of the city and the ethnographic changes of its population. After several years of teaching on the high school level, in 1906 Šišić was appointed professor of Croatian history at the University of Zagreb, where he taught for the following thirty-eight years. He was only briefly involved in daily politics as a member of the Yugoslav-oriented Croato-Serbian Coalition and deputy in the Croatian Diet (1908–1911). He participated, as an expert, in the Yugoslav delegation at the Paris Peace Conference. However, all of his energies and activities were dedicated to research and scholarship, which were rewarded by membership in the Yugoslav Academy of Sciences in Zagreb, and Serbian, Czechoslovakian, Polish, Rumanian, and Hungarian academies. Šišić followed in the footsteps of the school established by his predecessors Franjo Rački (q.v.), Tadija Smičiklas (q.v.), and Natko Nodilo (1834–1912). This school initiated the critical evaluation of historical sources and studied Croatian and Yugoslav history in the framework of European historical development. Šišić based his studies on research done through many years in numerous domestic and major European libraries and archives, especially those in Dalmatia, Italy, Austria, and Hungary. His productivity was versatile and rich. It can be classified under four categories: general Croatian history; monographs and articles on specific aspects and historical events in Croatian and Yugoslav history; publication of sources; and textbooks for university students. His studies covered several historical epochs, from the origins of Croatian statehood in the tenth century to the formation of Yugoslavia in 1918. Roman and Byzantine influences, the German and Magyar expansion, and the Ottoman invasion of the Balkans offered Šišić a rich ground for research. He wrote several general histories of Croatia, including the three-volume *Hrvatska povijest* (1906–1913), *Pregled provijesti hrvatskog naroda od najstarijih dana do godine 1873* (1916; Review of the History of the Croatian People from the Ancient Days until 1873), *Die Geschichte der Croaten* (I Teil,

1917), and one of his best studies, *Povijest Hrvata u vreme narodnik vladara* (1925; Croatian History During National Rulers). An enlarged version of the two last-named works was reissued in 1925. Šišić's ambition to carry Croatian history to 1918 was never accomplished. Instead, he published *Jugoslovenska misao. Istorija ideje jugoslovenskog narodnog ujedinjenja i oslobodjenja* (1927; The Yugoslav Idea. History of the Yugoslav Idea of National Unification and Liberation, 1927). Šišić was at his best in monographs and studies concerning the Croatian popular dynasty and major events that led to the turning point in Croatian history. Two of his studies dealt with decisive battles that changed the destiny of Serbs, Croats, and the South Slavs: the battle at Nikopolis in 1396 (published in 1896 and translated into German in 1899 as *Die Schlacht bei Nikopolis, 1396*) and the battle on the field of Krbava in 1493 (*Bitka na Krbavskom polju*, 1893). Šišić researched the beginnings of Croatian statehood on the Adriatic littoral, the death of King Zvonimir, the relations between the Hungarian King Koloman and the Croats in 1102, the genealogy of the Croatian national dynasty, and the history of the city of Lab. He refuted the false assumption of the Slavic origins of the Byzantine Emperor Justinian. Moving toward the late Middle Ages, Šsić produced two remarkable monographs on the Bosnian and Croatian *Ban Mladen Šubić*, offering great insights into the situation prevailing in Croatia during the first half of the fourteenth century and on the *Vojvoda Hrvoje Vukčić-Hrvatinić* (1350–1416), and the succession of the throne in Hungary. In several studies he wrote about two feudal lords, Zrinski and Frankopan, and their rebellion in 1670. Šišić also described in lively terms the personality and activity of the Slavonian adventurer Baron Trenk and his *pandurs*. Šišić was interested in the nineteenth and twentieth centuries and produced treatises dealing with Yugoslav lands during the Napoleonic era, the Illyrian movement, the Croatian opposition to centralism and absolutism, the effects of the dualistic reorganization of the Habsburg monarchy on the South Slavs and Bishop Strossmayer, and the activity of the political parties, including his own Croato-Serbian coalition. To this he added studies concerning nineteenth-century Serbian history. Finally, as a member of the Yugoslav delegation in Paris in 1919 he produced studies on the city of Rijeka (also in French) and on the Adriatic Question at the Paris Conference. A major part of Šišić's scholarship was dedicated to the publication of historical sources. Among those the most important were *Hrvatski Saborski spisi (Acta Comitalia regni Croatiae, Dalmatiae et Slavoniae)* for the period 1526–1630 in five volumes. He produced the best annotated edition of the *Ljetopis popa Dukljanina*, a chronicle that intrigued generations of Yugoslav historians. Two publications were of special importance for the history of the Yugoslav movement: the first, including fourteen hundred letters of correspondence between Bishop Strossmayer and Franjo Rački (1928–1931), and the second, documents concerning the formation of the Kingdom of Serbs, Croats, and Slovenes (1920). As an educator Šišić influenced generations of modern Croatian historians.

Bibliography: Biography and bibliography in F. Šišić, *Pregled provijesti hrvatskoga naroda*, Jaroslav Šidak, ed. (Zagreb, 1962, 3d. ed.), pp. 491–507; V. Novak, "Ferdo

Šišić,'' *Ljetopis Jugoslavenske akademije znanosti i umjetnosti*, no. 54 (Zagreb, 1949), pp. 362–430.

Dimitrije Djordjevic

SMIČIKLAS, Tadija (Reštovo, 1843–Žumberak, 1914), Croatian historian. Studied in Vienna, where he returned after graduation to prepare for the exam for the professorship, and worked as a member of the Institut für oesterreichische Geschichtsforschung. After teaching in several Croatian high schools, Smičiklas was appointed professor of Croatian history with special reference to Austrian and Hungarian history at the University of Zagreb in 1882. He taught until 1905 when he retired to dedicate his activities to the Yugoslav Academy of Sciences and Arts of which he became president (1896–1914). Smičiklas was also very active in the *Matica hrvatska* and was elected president of that organization in 1889. During his studies in Vienna Smičiklas joined the Yugoslav movement initiated by Bishop J. J. Strossmayer and the historian Franjo Rački (q.v.). He became a member of the Independent Popular party and was its representative in the Croatian Diet (1884–1887, 1897–1902). However, involvement in politics was of secondary importance to him: Smičiklas continued the struggle of his predecessors Sakcinski Ivan Kukuljević (q.v.) and Rački in favor of Croatian emancipation, but his primary vocation was scholarship.

Smičiklas' main contribution to Croatian historiography was the first synthesis of Croatian history from ancient times to 1848, *Poviest hrvatska* (2 vols., 1879, 1882; Croatian History) which distinguished him from his predecessors who approached it in a fragmentary fashion. It was based on literature and archival sources, especially in its second part, and it dealt not only with political but also social issues. Representative of the pragmatic historical school, Smičiklas was the promoter of the unification of Croatian lands divided in the Habsburg monarchy, which unification he supported by historical documentation. The goal of his writing was to stimulate the spirit of national emancipation of the Croatian people in regard to Hungary after the 1868 Croato-Hungarian compromise. In the chapter, ''O razdiobi povijesti hrvatske'' (About the Periodization of Croatian History, Vol. 1, pp. xxiii–xxxii), Smičiklas offered the first modern periodization of that history which was not based on the chronology of rulers and dynasties, but on the idea of resistance and the relations of Croats with the surrounding states, trying to prove the continuity of Croatian state rights until its personal union with Hungary. Based on the critical evaluation of archival sources and written with a brilliant and lively style, Smičiklas' history became the bible of Croatian national and political emancipation. For his generation Smičiklas did what František Palacky had done for Bohemia. He contributed to the national renaissance more than any politician of his time. Smičiklas offered a synthesis in the book about the bicentennial of the liberation of Slavonia (*Dvjestogodišnjica oslobodjenja Slavonije*, 1891, vol. 1) in which he described the rule of the Ottomans in Slavonija during the seventeenth and the beginning of the eighteenth centuries. Some generalizations were also present in Smičiklas' favorite genre of biographies, among which were the biographies of F. Rački, Ivan Kukuljević, Šime Ljubić, Ivan Crnčić, and R. Lopašić, which were important for the history of Croatian historiography. Among others, he wrote about prominent national leaders, members of the Illyrian movement and the politicians I. Draškovic, I. Mažuranić, and J. J. Strossmayer. Some of these sketches were included in *Spomen-knjiga Matice Hrvatske* (1892; Memorial-book of *Matica hrvatsko*). Smičiklas started the series *Codex Diplomaticus regni Croatiae, Dalmatiae et Slavoniae 1102–1373*, a codex of medieval Croatian charters and documents of which he was the editor from 1904 until 1914. He also edited and commented on the "Annuae" of B. A. Krčelić, an important source for Croatian history in the eighteenth century. As a distinguished scholar and a representative of national ideas and trends. Smičiklas enjoyed considerable esteem from the intellectual public of his generation.

Bibliography: F. Šišić, "Dr. Tadija Smičiklas," *Savremenik* (Zagreb, 1914), pp. 341–345; P. Karlić, *Dr. Tadija Smičiklas* (Zadar, 1914); M. Kostrenčić, *Predavanja održana u Jugoslavenskoj akademiji znanosti i unijetnosti*, no. 20 (Zagreb, 1962).

Dimitrije Djordjevic

STANOJEVIĆ, Stanoje (Novi Sad, 1874–Vienna, 1937), Serbian and Yugoslav historian. Born to a well-to-do family of Serbian intellectuals in Vojvodina, Stanojević studied the history of Balkan peoples and the Byzantine Empire in Vienna. His dissertation *Die Biographie Stefan Lazarević's von Konstantin dem Philosophen als Geschichtsquelle* (*Archiv für Slavische Philologie* 18) was published in 1896. Stanojević completed studies in Leipzig, Moscow, and St. Petersburg, and the Russian Archaeological Institute in Constantinople and Munich, working with the best historians of his day: K. Jiriček, K. Krumbacher (q.v.), and F. I. Uspensky (q.v.). In 1900 Stanojević began teaching at the University of Belgrade and in 1920 was elected a member of the Royal Serbian Academy of Sciences. As an officer of the Serbian Army he took part in the 1912–1913 and 1914 campaigns, and in 1915 he published *Štahoće Srbija?* (What Does Serbia Want?), a study of Serbian war aims. After the 1915 invasion of the country, he was sent to Russia where he taught in Petrograd; he continued teaching at the Sorbonne in Paris (1917). Stanojević was a member of the Yugoslav delegation at the Paris Peace Conference in 1919. Parallel to scholarly work, he took an active part in politics, was the founder of the daily newspaper *Politika*, and wrote essays, criticisms, and comments in political and literary journals. Stanojević organized the Historical Association in Novi Sad, and was the director of the Yugoslav Historical Journal (1935–1937), and of the institute to collect historical sources of the University in Belgrade.

As a young scholar Stanojević opposed the old romanticist trend in Serbian historiography and joined the critical revision of a history based on popular tradition, which was initiated by Ilarion Ruvarac (q.v.). His research and writing included the medieval and modern history of the Serbs and Yugoslavs, their relations with the Byzantine Empire, and the study of medieval charters and sources. In 1908 he published a history of the Serbian People (*Istorija srpskog naroda*) which was among the first to be written at the time. Later, Stanojević organized a twenty-volume collective work entitled *Srpski narod u devetnajestom veku* (The Serbian People During the Nineteenth Century), including the modern history of Serbs in Serbia, the Habsburg monarchy, and the Ottoman Empire. Among his works in medieval Serbian history are studies dealing with the sources of Nemanja's biographers (1895), the genealogy of Archbishop Danilo (1895), the Jakšić family (1901), and the Emperor Dušan (1921). The best among them is *Borba za samostalnost katoličke crkve u Nemanjićkoj državi* (1912; The Struggle for Independence of the Catholic Church in Nemanja's State). However, Stanojević never accomplished his ambitious plan to write a comprehensive history of medieval Serbia in nine volumes, of which he finished only the first one dealing with historical sources: *Istorija srpskog naroda u Srednjem veku: Izvori i istoriografija* (1937; History of the Serbian People in the Middle Ages: Sources and Historiography). Stanojević also planned to write a large general work on the relations between the Serbs and the Byzantine Empire, of which only two volumes appeared: *Vizantija i Srbi*, I: *Balkansko Poluostrvo do 7 veka*; II, *Kolonizacija Slovena na Balkanskom Poluostrvu* (vol.1, 1903; The Balkans Until the Seventh Century and Vol. 2, 1906; Colonization of the Balkans by the Slavs). His bibliography also includes the history of the South Slavs from the seventh to the eighth centuries, and the history of Bosnia and Hercegovina, written as a reaction to the Austro-Hungarian annexation of these two provinces in 1908. The book was placed on the black list in Austria-Hungary. During World War I Stanojević, in order to promote the unification of the Yugoslavs, wrote a series of books and articles to acquaint the European public with the Serbian and Yugoslav question (*Le problème yougoslave; La civilisation du peuple serbe au moyen-age; Le rôle des Serbes de Hongrie dans la vie nationale du peuple serbe; Historie nationale succincte des Serbes, Croates et Slovenes*). Stanojević studied medieval Serbian charters and diplomatics, and historical geography and produced an historical atlas of Serbian lands. Finally, he was the organizer and editor of the four-volume encyclopedia *Narodna enciklopedija srpsko-hrvatsko-slovenačka* (Zagreb, 1924–1929) to which many prominent Yugoslav scholars, politicians, and intellectuals contributed. Stanojević's model was the great historian Edward Gibbon. A prolific writer, an excellent organizer of scholarly studies, and a good narrator, Stanojević was at the same time a protagonist of Yugoslav unification.

Bibliography: "Bibliografija radova St. Stanojevića," *Glasnik istoriskog društva u Novom Sadu* (1938): 33–34; V. Corović, "Stanoje Stanojević," *Jugoslovenski istoriski časopis* (Belgrade, 1939), pp. 1–2; *Glasnik Istoriskog društva u Novom Sadu* (Novi Sad, 1938), pp. 3–4 (dedicated to St. Stanojević); K. Milutinović, *Studije iz srpske i hrvatske istoriografije* (Novi Sad, 1986), pp. 163–183; J. Radonić, "O Stanoju Stanojeviću," *Letopis Matice Srpske*, (Novi Sad), p. 348.

Dimitrije Djordjevic

INDEX OF HISTORIANS

SUBJECT INDEX

Bichurin, Nikita Yakovlevich, *532–33*
Biography: Brazilian, of Otávio Sousa,
91–92; English, of Albert F. Pollard,
209; as focus of Jan Romein, 185; as
genre of Washington Irving, 745; in
history of al-Jabartī, 15–16; Japanese,
of Tokutomi Sohô, 453–54
Bismarck, Otto von, Hans Rothfels on,
307–8
Blache, P. Vidal de la, influence on Lucien Febvre, 237
Blanch, Luigi, *380–81*
Bloch, Marc, 80, *221–23*, 466, 492; association with Henri Berr, 220–21;
comparison to Frederic Maitland, 205;
work of Lucien Febvre with, 237–38
Blok, Petrus Johannes, *172–73*, 179; criticism of, by Pieter Geyl, 176
Bobrzyński, Michał, *477–79*; contrasted
with Władysław Konopczyński, 483;
criticism of, by Stanisław Smolka, 497
Bogdan, Ioan, *513*; studies of continued
by Petre Panaitescu, 524–25
Bogomil heresy, Jordan Ivanov on, 99
Bohemia: Bertold Bretholz on, 145; his-
tory of, by Josef Šusta, 158; František
Palacký on, 152–54, 155–56
Bolin, Sture, *694–95*
Bolivia: Alcides Arguedas on, 645; Ga-
briel René Moreno as bibliographer of,
672
Bollandists, 73–74
Bonenfant, Paul, *67–68*
Bonwick, James, *36–37*
Bortolotti, Franca Pieroni, *381–83*
Bosch Gimpera, Pedro, *626–27*
Botev, Hristo: Mikhail Dimitrov on, 96;
Jacques Nathan on, 103; Dimiter
Strashimirov on, 106
Botta, Carlo, *383–84*
Boucher de Crèvecoeur de Perthes,
Jacques, *223*
Bourdeau, Louis, *224*, 232
Bourinot, John, *109–10*
Brabant, duchy of, and Paul Bonenfant
on, 68
Brah raj bansavatar maha ksatr khmaer

(Royal Chronicle of the Great Khmer
Kings), 617
Brătianu, Gheorghe I., *514–15*
Braudel, Fernand, *224–27*, 238; dialogue
with Ömer Barkan, 711. See also An-
nales School
Bray, Dominique de. See Sarton, George
Breasted, James Henry, *724–25*
Bréhier, Louis, *227–28*
Bretholz, Bertold, *145–46*; and Josef Pe-
kař, 155; and Josef Šusta, 158
Breuil, Abbé Henri-Edouard-Prosper,
228–29; influence on Annette Laming-
Emperaire, 244–45
Briceño Iragorry, Mario, *648–49*
Brinton, Clarence Crane, *725–26*
Bronze Age: concept of, 169; Danish,
Sophus Müller on, 167; Arne Tallgren
on, 62
Bruck, Moeller van den, 307
Brunner, Otto, *47–48*; criticism by Clau-
dio Sánchez-Albornoz, 637
Buarque de Holanda, Sérgio, 83–84
Bucher, Karl, influence on Johan Hui-
zinga, 179
Buckle, Henry Thomas, *187–88*, 232,
434; analysis by Alexandru Xenopol,
527; influence on Fukuzawa Yukichi,
438; influence on W. E. Lecky, 369
Buddhism: Burmese, Pe Maung Tin on,
612; Central Asian and Indian, Sergei
Oldenburg on, 565; in India and
China, Chen Yinque on, 123–24; Japa-
nese, Tsuji Zennosuke on, 455–56;
sources of, by Fyodor Shcherbatsky,
572
Buginese people, Raja Ali Haji on, 598–
99
Bulnes, Francisco, *649–50*; rebuttal by
Justo Sierra, 685
Bunyoro, 6; J. W. Nyakatura on, 7–8
Burckhardt, Jacob, 298, *703–5*; ideas
compared to Johan Huizinga, 180; in-
fluence on Federico Chabod, 391; and
Jules Michelet, 252
Burke, Edmund, politics of, 207
Burma: Maung Htin Aung on, 603–4; Pe

riography founder of, 643; Diego Barros Araña as general historian of, 646–47; José Toribio Medina as bibliographer of, 668–69; Benjamin Vicuña Mackenna as historian of, 689–90

China: Nikita Bichurin as Russian historian of, 532–33; cultures and religions of, Vassily Vassiliev on, 582–83; Naitô Konan as Japanese historian of, 444–45. *See also* Chinese historians *section*

Chinese historiography, Gu Jiegang as historian in, 128–29

Chmel, Joseph, *48–49*

Ch'oe Nam-sŏn, *461–62*

Chou Dynasty, inscriptions of, Guo Moruo on, 129

Christianity: Herbert Butterfield on, 190; central theme of Cesare Balbo, 377; Adolf Harnack as historian of, 281; Adolfo Omodeo as historian of, 417–19; Ernest Renan as historian of, 260–61; R. H. Tawney's connection of, with capitalism, 213. *See also* Protestantism; Roman Catholic Church

Chronicle, as style of Nīqūlā al-Turk, 27

Chronology: Joseph Déchelette as innovator in prehistoric, 233; historical, of Chen Yuan, 125; organizing principle of al-Jabartī, 15

Científicos (Scientists): Francisco Bulnes as member of, 649

Civilization: defined by François Guizot, 242; Fukuzawa Yukichi as historian of, 438–39; Arnold Toynbee on, 214. *See also* Universal history

Civil War (U.S.): John W. Draper as first scholar of, 730; James Ford Rhodes on, 765

Colegio de México, origins of, 654

Colenbrander, Herman Theodor, *173–74*

Colletta, Pietro, *392–93*

Collingwood, Robin George, *193–94*; and concepts of Wilhelm Dilthey, 272

Colmeiro y Pinedo, Manuel, *628–29*

Colombia: Oswaldo Díaz Díaz as historian of, 656; industrial development in Luis Ospina Vásquez on, 675; wars of

independence in, José Manuel Restrepo on, 680

Colonialism: British, Romesh Dutt on, 352–53; Italian, Alberto Aquarone on, 376; Sardar Panikkar on, 360. *See also* Imperialism

Commission Royale d'Histoire, organization of, 68

Commons, John R., *726–27*; ideas of, modified by Herbert Gutman, 736

Comparative history: of Lev V. Cherepnin, 534; of feudalisms, by Asakawa Kan'ichi, 437; of Otto Hintze, 284, 285; of Japanese Meji period, by Hattori Shisô, 441; legal, of Nakada Kaoru, 446; of social institutions in Australia and New Zealand, by William Reeves, 468. *See also* History; Universal history

Comte, Auguste, *231–32*, 549, 555; influence on Henry Thomas Buckle, 188; influence on Louis Bourdeau, 224; influence on Justo Sierra, 684. *See also* Positivism

Condliffe, John Bell, *466–67*

Confucian classics, Fan Wenlan on, 126

Confucianism, influence on Phan Thanh Gian, 614–15

Conze, Werner, *270*

Cook, Captain James, John Beaglehole on, 466

Cortesão, Jaime, *503–4*

Cosío Villegas, Daniel, *654–55*

Costa, Horacio de la, *599–600*

Costa Martínez, Joaquín, 625, *629–30*

Cracow school: break with, by Stanisław Kutrzeba, 486; contrasted to Władysław Smoleński, 495; of Polish historiography, 481; distance from, of Karol Potkański, 491; Stanisław Smolka as representative of, 496

Creighton, Donald Grant, *112–14*

Croatia: evaluation of historical sources in, 794; first historical synthesis of, 796; Sakcinski Ivan Kukuljević on, 786–87

Croatian language, use by Sakcinski Ivan Kukuljević, 786

Croatians, Marin Drinov on, 97

Croce, Benedetto, 194, *393–95*, 418, 435, 769; association with Guido de Ruggiero, 396; discussion with Luigi Einaudi, 398; encounter with Antonio Labriola, 410; friendship with Eduard Fueter, 705; historicism of, opposed by Giorgio Levi Della Vida, 411; influence on Charles A. Beard, 721; influence on José Bello, 85; translation of, by Hani Gorô, 440; and Nino Valeri, 432–33; Walter Maturi, as follower of, 413

Cromwell, Oliver, Thomas Carlyle on, 190

Cuba: African influence in, Fernando Ortiz y Fernandez on, 674–75; Ramiro Guerra y Sanchez as historian of, 662–63

Cucuteni, Hubert Schmidt on, 312

Cuervo, Luís Augusto, *655*

Cult of Personality, Hans Kruus as victim of, 60

Cultural history: Jacob Burckhardt as innovator in, 704–5; Johan Huizinga as theorist of, 179

Culture: concepts of center and periphery in study of, 167; diffusion of, in prehistory of V. Gordon Childe, 192; Leo Frobenius and method of "cultural morphology," 3

Cumont, Franz, *70–71*

Cuoco, Vincenzo, *395–96*

Czech language, Pavel Šafařík on, 157

Czechoslovakia: Kamil Krofta as historian of, 149–50; language and literature, Josef Dobrovský on, 146–47; musicology, Zdeněk Nejedlý on, 150–51; relationship to nation, Josef Pekař on, 154–56

Dacia, Constantin Daicoviciu on, 515

Daicoviciu, Constantin, *515*

Dai Nihon shi (History of Great Japan), 449

Dalberg, John Emerich Edward, 187

Damrong Rajanubhab, Prince, *600–602*, 618, 620

D'Annunzio, Gabriele, 433

Darwin, Charles, influence on Sin Ch'ae-ho, 462–63

Darwinism: influence on Karl Kautsky, 288; sympathy by Jurjī Zaydān, 28. *See also* Evolution; Evolutionism

Debo, Angie, *727–29*

Déchelette, Joseph, *232–33*

De la Costa, Horacio, 606

Delbrück, Hans, *270–71*

Delcourt, Marie, *71–72*

Delehaye, Hippolyte, *72–73*

De los Reyes y Florentino, Isabelo, *602–3*

Democracy: definition by Alexis de Tocqueville, 267; as seen by Ernst Sars, 473

Demography, historical, in work of Henri Pirenne, 80

De Ruggiero, Guido, *396–97*

Derzhavin, Nikolai Sevastyanovich, *534–35*

Dewey, John, 128

Díaz Díaz, Oswaldo, *656*

Diehl, Charles, *233–34*

Dike, Kenneth Onwuka, *1–2*

Dilthey, Wilhelm Christian Ludwig, *271–73*; and continuation of work by Johann Droysen, 275; influence on Władysław Konopczyński, 482; influence on Otávio Tarquínio de Sousa, 92

Dimitrov, Mikhail Dafinchkiev, *96*

Diplomatic history: Austrian, and Heinrich Friedjung, 50; break from by Pierre Renouvin, 261–62; European, and Sir Lewis Namier, 207; founding of, in United States, 723; in France, 254; Old Russian, and Vladimir Pashuto, 567–68

Djavakhishvili, Ivan Alexandrovich, *535–36*

Dobrovský, Josef, *146–47*, 152, 157

Documents: Ioan Bogdan as model editor of, 513; editing of medieval Hungarian, by László Fejérpataky, 340; editions of Ottoman, by Ahmet Altinay, 707; importance of literary texts as, 257; János Karácsonyi as editor of,

About the Editor-in-Chief

LUCIAN BOIA is Lecturer in Historiography at the University of Bucharest, Romania, and the editor of *Great Historians from Antiquity to 1800: An International Dictionary.*